WHERE ~~TO SKI~~
AND *SnoWboard* 2004

The 1,000 Best Winter Sports Resorts in Europe and North America

GET THE COST OF THIS BOOK REFUNDED WHEN YOU BOOK YOUR NEXT HOLIDAY!
If you book your next winter sports holiday through the specialist travel agency Ski Solutions, you can get the cost of this book knocked off the bill.

There's no catch. Ski Solutions sells the complete range of package holidays offered by UK bonded tour operators. And if that choice isn't enough, they can tailor-make a holiday just for you.

When you make your booking, fill in the two forms at the back of the book. Ski Solutions will knock £15.99 off your bill. That's all there is to it.

Ski Solutions are on 020 7471 7700.

GET THE NEXT EDITION FREE!
BY SENDING US RESORT REPORTS
We are keen to get feedback on the resorts our readers visit. The 100 best reports earn a free copy of the new edition, in advance of publication. What's more, regular book winners may be invited to become 'resort observers', getting free lift passes in exchange for specially detailed reports.

On page 10 there's guidance on what feedback we need. Send e-mails to:
reports@snow-zone.co.uk
or write to:
Where to Ski and Snowboard
FREEPOST SN815
The Old Forge
Norton St Philip
Bath BA2 7ZZ

WHERE *to* SKI AND *Snowboard* 2004

The 1,000 Best Winter Sports Resorts in Europe and North America

Edited by
Chris Gill
and
Dave Watts

NortonWood

Published in Great Britain by
NortonWood Publishing
The Old Forge
Norton St Philip
Bath BA2 7LW
United Kingdom

tel 01373 835208
e-mail mailbox@snow-zone.co.uk

Editors Chris Gill and Dave Watts
Assistant editors Mandy Crook,
Catherine Weakley, Emma Morris,
Leigh Thompson, Robin Campbell,
Henry Druce, Wendy-Jane King,
Sheila Reid
Australia/NZ editor Bronwen Gora
Contributors Chris Allan, Alan Coulson,
Nicky Holford, James Hooke,
Tim Perry, Adam Ruck,
Helena Wiesner, Ian Porter

Advertising manager Sam Palmer

Design by Fox Design Consultants
Production by Guide Editors
Contents photos generally
by Snowpix.com / Chris Gill
Production manager Ian Stratford
Production designer Leon White
Proof-reader Sally Vince
Printed and bound in the UK
by Warners (Midlands) plc

10 9 8 7 6 5 4 3 2 1

ISBN 0 9536371 5 8

A CIP catalogue entry for this book is
available from the British Library.

Book trade sales are handled by
Portfolio Books Ltd
Unit 5, Perivale Industrial Park
Horsenden Lane South
Greenford UB6 7RL

tel 020 8997 9000
fax 020 8997 9097
e-mail sales@portfoliobooks.com

Individual copies of the book can be
bought by credit card from:
chartmail.seekbooks.co.uk
or our own web site at:
www.snow-zone.co.uk
or by phoning:
01373 835208

This edition published 2003
Copyright (text and illustrations)
© Chris Gill and Dave Watts 2003

The right of Chris Gill and Dave Watts
to be identified as Authors of this
Work has been asserted by them in
accordance with the Copyright,
Design and Patents Act 1988.

Although every care has been taken in
compiling this publication, using the
most up-to-date information available
at the time of going to press, all details
are liable to change and cannot be
guaranteed. Neither NortonWood
Publishing nor the Editors accept any
liability whatsoever arising from errors
or omissions, however caused.

Contents

Resort chapters

6

7

About this book

It's simply the best

We believe that *Where to Ski and Snowboard* is the best guide to ski and snowboard resorts that you can buy. Here's why:

- By making the most of technology we were able to go to press later than ever this season (August as opposed to June a few editions ago) and get the late-breaking news to make the book **up to date for the 2003/04 season ahead**. To see what we mean, check out our What's new chapter, crammed with new resort developments, some announced only a few days before we went to press.

- We work hard to make our information **reader-friendly**, with clear cross-heads and verdicts for the main aspects of each resort.

- We don't hesitate to express **critical views**. We learned our craft at Consumers' Association, where Chris became editor of *Holiday Which?* magazine and Dave became editor of *Which?* itself – so a consumerist attitude comes naturally to us.

- Our resort chapters give an **unrivalled level of detail** – including scale plans showing the extent and layout of each major resort, as well as all the facts you need to have at your fingertips.

- We benefit enormously from the **reports that hundreds of readers send in on the resorts they visit**. The 100 best reports are rewarded by a free copy of the book, and many of our best regular reporters get a free week's lift pass. Prove your worth by sending us useful reports, and you could join the elite band who get to ski for free.

- We use **colour printing** fully – this year more than ever. We include not only piste maps for every major resort but also scores of photographs, chosen not just to add colour but to allow you to see for yourself what the resorts are like.

Our ability to keep on improving *Where to Ski and Snowboard* is largely due to the support of our advertisers – many of whom have been with us since the first edition in 1994. We are grateful for that support, and hope our readers will in turn support our advertisers.

We are uncompromising in our commitment to helping you, our readers, to make an informed choice; and we're confident that you'll find this edition the best yet. Do report on your holiday this winter, to make next year's book even better.

Enjoy your skiing and riding this season.

Chris Gill and Dave Watts
Norton St Philip, 6 August 2003

(As this page goes off to the printer, we are waiting to see whether today does or does not turn out to be the hottest on record. Roll on winter!)

GET YOUR MONEY BACK
when you book a holiday

You can reclaim the price of Where to Ski and Snowboard when you book a winter sports holiday for the 2003/04 or 2004/05 seasons. All you have to do is book the holiday through the specialist ski travel agency Ski Solutions.

Ski Solutions is Britain's original and leading ski travel agency. You can buy whatever kind of holiday you want through them.

Ski Solutions sells the package holidays offered by all the bonded tour operators in Britain (apart from the very few who are direct-sell only). And if that isn't enough choice, they can tailor-make a holiday, based on any form of travel and any kind of accommodation. No one is better placed to find you what you want than Ski Solutions.

Making a claim
Claiming your refund is easy. At the back of the book are two vouchers. When you make your definite booking, tell Ski Solutions that you want to take up this offer. Cut out the vouchers and send one to Ski Solutions and the other to Where to Ski and Snowboard (the addresses are on the vouchers).

Phone Ski Solutions on
020 7471 7700

Get next year's edition **free!**
by reporting on your holiday

There are too many resorts for us to visit them all every year, and too many hotels, bars and mountain restaurants for us to see. So we are very keen to encourage more readers to send in reports on their holiday experiences. As usual, we'll be giving 100 copies of the next edition to the writers of the best reports.

There are five main kinds of feedback we need:

- what you particularly **liked and disliked** about the resort
- what aspects of the resort came as a **surprise** to you
- your other suggestions for **changes to our evaluation** of the resort – changes we should make to the ratings, verdicts, descriptions etc
- your experience of **queues** and other weaknesses in the lift system, and the **ski school** and associated childcare arrangements
- your feedback on **individual facilities** in the resort – the hotels, bars, restaurants (including mountain restaurants), nightspots, equipment shops, sports facilities etc.

You can send your reports to us in three ways. In order of preference, they are:

- by e-mail to: reports@snow-zone.co.uk (don't forget to give us your postal address)
- word-processed and printed on paper
- handwritten on a form that we can provide.

Consistently helpful reporters are invited to become 'resort observers', which means that when possible we'll arrange free lift-passes in your holiday resorts, in exchange for detailed reports on those resorts.

Our postal address is:
Where to Ski and Snowboard, FREEPOST SN815,
The Old Forge, Norton St Philip, Bath BA2 7ZZ

Issues of the season

The editors have their say

WINTER SPORTS HOLIDAYS BOOMING

Over a million ski and snowboard holidays were taken last season by people living in the UK, according the annual Ski & Snowboard Industry report produced by the Thomson, Crystal and Simply Ski group of companies. This is 6% up from the year before, and more than double the number taken in 1990/01, 12 years back. A lot of the growth is accounted for by more people taking second holidays and short breaks, and partly fuelled by cheap flights. More people are now booking their holidays on the internet and through specialist travel agents, rather than through mainstream high-street travel agents. That's a good thing for most of the specialist operators advertising in this book, because high-street agents generally don't sell holidays offered by smaller operators. We hope you'll support the businesses – large and small – who choose to advertise in these pages; without their support, we could not afford the detailed research and expensive presentation that make this book special.

STEP FORWARD, ANDORRA

If you are one of the many readers who devour every edition of *Where to Ski and Snowboard*, keeping the current one by your bedside year-round, you may already have noticed a radical change this year. After two editorial visits in the last three years, we have decided that Andorra can no longer be treated as a second-division budget destination, and bundled together with Bulgaria at the back of the book. It can now stand on its merits alongside the four Alpine countries – and jumps by alphabetical accident to the very front.

More Brits now go to Andorra for winter holidays than visit Switzerland, Canada and the USA combined – and Andorra is neck-and-neck with Italy as the third most popular country. It is an excellent choice for beginners and early intermediates, so long as you don't mind its Spanish-package-holiday feel, with lots of young Brits looking for a good time fuelled by cheap alcohol.

And yet Andorra is still living in the Middle Ages. If the locals could agree on a joint lift pass, the adjacent areas of Soldeu and Pas de la Casa (which have been linked by lift and piste for years now) would rival some of the Alps' best-known names for extent and variety. But they can't – apparently the result of some ancient feud between the two communities. Insane. If you were to buy both passes, it would be the most expensive skiing in Europe.

SKI CLUB CENTENARY

Congratulations to the Ski Club of Great Britain, which is celebrating its centenary. On 6 May 1903, 14 young men sat down at a table in the Café Royal and formed a club to promote the sport of skiing.

As Sally Cartwight, chairman of the Ski Club, pointed out at the club's centenary ball, in those days there were no lifts or pistes, so everyone had to walk up and choose their own way down. Leather boots were tied on to planks of wood and clothing was good quality wool tweeds – heavy and not waterproof. Now we moan about slow chair-lifts and crowded pistes. But we've never had it so good. Let's hope that skiing will survive the next 100 years of global warming.

AFTER YOU. NO, AFTER YOU!

Is it a new thing, or is that we've only just woken up to it? Either way, we hate it: the business of being required to eat irritatingly early or unbearably late in Alpine restaurants. For restaurants, it's a way of cramming in the absolute maximum number of diners; for diners, it ruins the evening. Not only do you have to eat your hard-earned dinner at a time when no right-thinking person would dream of it – typically, 7.15 or 9pm – but also you have to accept that the time you spend over it is constrained. Dally over a cognac at the end of the early sitting, and you'll be made painfully aware of the group standing in the lobby waiting to occupy your space. Dally at the the end of the late sitting, and you're in for the chairs-on-tables-here-comes-the-hoover treatment.

This season we've encountered this silly system in otherwise excellent restaurants in Chamonix, Verbier and Les Menuires, to name but three. But we don't just accept it, we get around it. How? By booking for the late sitting, and turning up an hour early. Of course, this trick can work only if the first sitting is not full, but it never is. It worked well for us; let us know how it works for you.

FLIMSY EXCUSES

From last year's edition: "Flims now grades its slopes according to its own innovative Slope System™: yellow for 'backcountry' (or off-piste), red for 'freestyle', blue for 'beginner', green for 'allround', orange for 'dorfpiste' (home run). Difficult slopes are indicated by black diamonds – two for difficult and three for very difficult. So, for instance, one formerly black run is marked green with two black diamonds. We regard this system as confusing and dangerous."

From a subsequent announcement from the Flims lift company: "Due to the many confusions with our slope system we decided to cancel them. It means that our guests will await the well known red, blue, black coloured signals." So, you can now contemplate going to this under-rated, very extensive resort with confidence that you will have some idea how steep a given slope is.

We should note that the new Flims map shows flattish (and therefore tedious) linking runs in a distinct colour. They've picked orange, which is perhaps not ideal (and on our own tiny version of the map we've used green, to avoid confusion with red), but the idea is sound, especially of course for boarders and tiny persons on short skis, who are likely to find such runs hard work.

FINDING YOUR WAY AROUND VERBIER

While we're ranting about Swiss piste maps, we really can't avoid bringing up yet again the problem of Verbier. Last season, at long last, Téléverbier commissioned a new piste map – something we've been suggesting for years. They didn't commission a new set of piste signs, which are equally needed, but that's obviously a much greater investment, and we've learned to be patient.

The new map is an improvement: it shows most parts of the very complex mountain more clearly. But it still doesn't show some parts at all sensibly – notably La Chaux and Savoleyres – and it probably never will until it is broken into parts, with appropriate views for different parts of the mountain. This is a standard technique in North America, but it seems to meet a lot of resistance in the Alps. However, the really bad news about Verbier's new map is that – wait for it – the pistes are still unidentified. They are identified on the

mountain, by numbers; but the numbers don't appear on the map.

That Téléverbier should have gone to the lengths of having a new map created without seriously tackling these problems is insane. One reader reporting this year calls it 'laughable', and in a way it is. But from another point of view you might call it criminal.

QUEUE BLUES
It always seems faintly sad that one of the things visitors to North America are always thrilled by is the lift queues (or lines, to use the vernacular). Not the existence of them, but the organisation of them, and the way North Americans so politely and cheerfully submit to the discipline of (a) waiting their turn and (b) filling the available seats. You expect first-time visitors to be wowed by the snow, and the grooming, and the ungroomed-but-safe terrain – and what happens? They come back over the moon about the lift lines.

It would be nice to think that the differences between the civilised lines of North America and the unruly queues of Europe would decline over time, but we don't see much sign of it. Brits apart, not many Europeans (whether resort manager or resort customers) cross the pond and get to understand the benefits of controlled queueing. And if exposure to American-style lines chez Disney is having any effect on the youth of Europe, we haven't noticed it. On the contrary, several reporters this year have detected a deterioration in organisation of queues and of behaviour in them, notably in Austria.

We're pleased that some European resorts have noticed that the easy way to fill chair-lifts is to have a singles line, where people not picky about who they ride with can join a separate, fast-moving line and slide in to fill any vacant seats. Unfortunately, few lifties or native customers have much enthusiasm for this efficient use of lift capacity, and we have reports of singles being physically prevented from joining chairs by the occupants from the main queue.

Perhaps in resorts where British custom dominates we might succeed in getting attitudes to change. Certainly it was noticeable that in British-dominated Andorra, lifties on the gondolas from both Soldeu and Arinsal villages were keen to fill all places at peak times – and even loaded your skis for you to make sure they were.

BOARDERS SIGN UP HERE
We are boarders, of a kind. We both learned to board, some years back. But we don't do it habitually and, particularly, in the course of our research visits to resorts we don't do it much at all. We get around more quickly, safely and easily on skis. So it's not surprising that whenever we get a half-decent report on a resort from a boarder, we find it extremely helpful. It sheds light on the particular things that do and do not work for boarders, which it's otherwise hard to work out. So here's an appeal: if you're a boarder, please report back on your holiday this season, and help us make the next edition as helpful as possible to the boarding community.

REPORTS FROM SKIERS TOO, PLEASE
Of course, we still need reports from skiers, too. What's especially useful is the insights that readers give us into aspects of resorts that we find it difficult to judge for ourselves on fleeting visits: on ski schools, lift queues, bars, restaurants, hotels and so on. Some examples: 'The ski school was a delight, and class sizes averaged three!' said someone of Winter Park this year. New Generation in

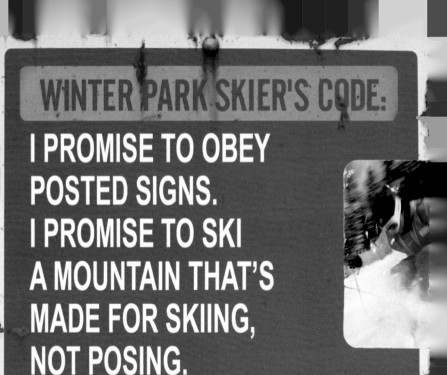

WINTER PARK SKIER'S CODE:

I PROMISE TO OBEY POSTED SIGNS.
I PROMISE TO SKI A MOUNTAIN THAT'S MADE FOR SKIING, NOT POSING.

The perfect skiing vacation is waiting for you deep in the Colorado Rockies. Once you arrive, you'll find Winter Park Resort is unlike the big, glitzy, presumptious, and most of all, pricey resorts. Here, you can find skiing like it used to be, along with prices like it used to be.

WINTER PARK RESORT®

colorado's favorite®

skiwinterpark.com

Find out more about Winter Park Resort:

Courchevel was reported to be 'really excellent', with 'outstanding lessons with a thoughtful instructor'. Another reporter said of the Tignes ESF: 'I can quite see how it could turn a child away from skiing permanently'. Reports that capture the essence of a place in vivid language are also very useful. For example, this year someone described Pas de la Casa in Andorra as 'ugly, characterless, with loads of restaurants with plastic-covered faded photos to show the discerning eater what a whopper cheeseburger and chips actually looks like.' Thanks to all those who sent in reports; as usual, the 100 best have earned free copies of this edition.

LIES, DAMN LIES AND RESORT STATISTICS

You would think that the new resort of Arc 1950 would be set at 1950m; but you'd be wrong. It is actually at just over 2000m. Why underplay its height? The problem is that it is just below Arc 2000, which is actually at around 2100m. Jean-Marc Silva, Director of Arc 1950, explains: 'The name Arc 2000 was conceived in the 1960s and the idea was to conjure up images of the future and the next millennium.' So now you know: altitude has nothing to do with it.

Keen readers of this book may recall our revelation four years ago that another part of Les Arcs was misrepresented in less surprising fashion: Arc 1800 is in fact spot-on 1700m. And the various parts of Courchevel are all well below their advertised heights.

So if heights aren't heights, what about lifts? Our proofreader nearly had a heart attack when she saw that the new Paradiski area combining Les Arcs and La Plagne was claiming only 144 lifts; we knew La Plagne had 108 and Les Arcs had 54 – and that the new cable-car linking the resorts was being counted as two lifts because there are two cabins working independently. So that added up to 164 lifts. On closer examination we saw that the Paradiski information said La Plagne had only 88 lifts. We emailed La Plagne and they confirmed 108. The Paradiski people will be changing their figures.

There's a lot of nonsense talked about piste quantities, too. The Trois Vallées has been claiming 600km of pistes and 200 lifts ever since the first edition of this book, nine years ago. It has since added lifts and pistes, so those figures can't still be correct – but they are nice round figures. Another nice round number is Courmayeur's 100km of pistes. This can't be right – you can ski all the pistes in half a day; Kitzbühel claims only 160km, but must be three times the size.

One day, we'll devise a method of quantifying the slopes of different resorts sensibly. Suggestions are welcome.

EXCHANGE RATE WORRIES

As we go to press in early August 2003 the £ has fallen against most ski country currencies in the past year. Against the euro (used by Andorra, Austria, France and Italy) you get around 1.35 euros for your tourist pound compared with over 1.5 a year ago – making local prices for things such as lift passes and drinks around 12% higher. The news is almost as bad in Canada where your pound will buy just C$2.20 compared with 2.40 a year ago. Switzerland however has become relatively better value: you get SFr2.10 as opposed to 2.20 a year back, meaning prices are only 5% or so higher in terms of pounds. The one ray of good news is the USA where the pound remained more or less constant at $1.55. US lift passes and lessons are always expensive compared with Europe, but at least they haven't got more so ... yet. Maybe this is the year to head for the US.

What's new?

ANDORRA

ARINSAL/PAL Work has started on the long-awaited gondola from La Massana to Pal, expected to open for the 2004/05 season. For 2003/04 a drag-lift in the Arinsal beginner area will be replaced by a quad chair. For 2002/03 a new FreeStyle area was built and the gondola from Arinsal had its capacity increased by 50%.

PAS DE LA CASA For 2002/03 more snowmaking was installed on the runs back to the resort and in the beginners' area. The half-pipe was moved from Grau Roig to near Pas de la Casa village.

SOLDEU For 2002/03 a new fast six-seater chair-lift was installed from Riba Escorxada to Tossal de la Llosada. Free guided tours of the pistes were introduced, and more snowmaking was installed.

AUSTRIA

ALPBACH Snowmaking capacity is to be increased to cover a total of 35km/22 miles for 2003/04. Last season a new quad chair replaced one of the Muldenlift drags behind Gmahkopf.

BAD GASTEIN More snowmaking is promised for the 2003/04 season. A fast quad has replaced the slow triple chair from the Angertal up to Stubnerkogel, speeding up the link from Schlossalm.

ELLMAU/SOLL For 2002/03 a new eight-seater gondola was built from Scheffau to Brandstadl. A T-bar was replaced by a six-pack, and another on Hartkaiser was replaced by a quad.

HINTERTUX/LANERSBACH For 2002/03 the slow double chair up to Horbergjoch in the Rastkogel area was replaced by a covered eight-seat chair, improving access to the new link with Mayrhofen's slopes.

INNSBRUCK For 2003/04 an eight-person gondola is planned for Stubaier Gletscher, running from the Eisgrat restaurant at 2900m/ 9,510ft to the highest slopes at the top of the Schaufelspitze.

ISCHGL For 2003/04 a fast six-seater chair is due to replace an old T-bar from above Bodenalp into the Höllenkar bowl. A new fast six-seater chair from Alp Trida will serve local blue slopes.

KITZBÜHEL 2002/03 brought three new fast chair-lifts at or near Pass Thurn. The Bichlalm area was given over entirely to off-piste slopes, with the top drag to Stuckkogel replaced by a snowcat. The Fleck blue run down to Kirchberg now has snowmaking all the way down.

LECH For 2003/04 two more fast covered chairs are planned – an eight-seater replacing the Steinmähder chair, and a six-pack replacing the Hasensprung chair. For 2002/03 a fast six-pack with covers replaced a slow triple chair-lift to the Kriegerhorn.

MAYRHOFEN For 2003/04 there are plans to replace two double chairs in the Horberg sector: the Tappenalm will become an eight-seater and the Knorren a six-pack.

MONTAFON For 2003/04 the Zamangbahn gondola is to be upgraded from four- to six-seat cabins. Increased snowmaking is due in the Silvretta Nova, Hochjoch, Golm and Schafberg areas.

OBERTAUERN The Zehnerkar cable-car is to be replaced by a gondola for 2003/04. A six-seat chair will replace the Seekarspitz drag-lift and a quad chair will replace the Achenrain double chair.

Saalbach-Hinterglemm For 2003/04 the Asitzmulden and Zehner T-bars are due to be replaced by six-seat chairs. For 2002/03 the Schattberg Ost cable-car was replaced by an eight-seat gondola.

Schladming For 2002/03 the Fastenberg T-bar on Planai was replaced by a covered six-seat chair going much higher up the mountain.

Sölden For 2003/04 an eight-person gondola is planned on the Rettenbach glacier, replacing an existing T-bar and going higher.

St Anton For 2003/04 two new fast six-person chair-lifts are planned: one to replace the Arlenmähder T-bar and allow access to the runs to Rauz; the other to be on Rendl, replacing the T-bar to Gampberg.

Westendorf For 2003/04 a new quad chair is planned to replace the Schneeberg drag-lifts on the nursery slopes near the centre.

Zell am See The Zeller Bergbahn, the main lift out of the village, is being upgraded for 2003/04.

FRANCE

Alpe d'Huez For 2003/04 the Lac Blanc chair-lift will be upgraded to a quad and capacity on the Alpe Auris chair-lift will be increased. Snowmaking is being increased in the Lievre Blanc area.

Les Arcs For 2003/04 the long-awaited cable-car link to La Plagne is due to open – forming one of the world's biggest lift-linked ski areas, called Paradiski (see separate chapter). Also new is the first phase of a new village called Arc 1950, below Arc 2000 and connected to it by a gondola. The Bois de l'Ours chair up to Arpette and the Marmottes double drag up to above Arc 2000 are to be replaced by six-packs.

Avoriaz For 2003/04 the Zorre chair, at the top of the gondola up from Morzine, is due to be replaced by a fast six-seater.

Châtel For 2003/04 two new drags are planned: the Contrebandiers will form another link between Châtel and Torgon; the Bossons drag will access the terrain-park and boarder-cross at Super-Châtel.

La Clusaz/Le Grand-Bornand For 2003/04 La Clusaz's Beauregard cable-car is to be replaced, tripling the capacity. Le Grand-Bornand is planning to replace the Maroly drag-lift with a fast six-person chair.

Courchevel For 2003/04 the Creux/Fruit drags are to be replaced by a quad to improve the link between 1650 and 1850.

Les Deux-Alpes The weekly Super Ski pass now covers La Grave.

Flaine/Samoens An eight-seat gondola linking the village of Samoëns to mid-mountain is finally to open for 2003/04. On the nursery slopes at Samoëns 1600, a quad chair will replace a drag-lift.

Maurienne Valley For 2003/04 there will be new fast six-packs in both Valloire and Val Cenis. The major development is the creation of a big new lift network linking Le Corbier, La Toussuire, St-Sorlin-d'Arves and other villages; we've given Les Sybelles a new chapter.

Know the best place for an argument?

The best skiing in the Alps. The best snow from open day in November until the closing day in May. The greatest variety in 440 km of pisted runs and snow left untouched just for you. The best ski guides to open the enormity of the Arlberg. Skischools and snowboard parks that mean fun for every age. Just 120 minutes from Zurich or Munich, you can practically commute. Lech - Zürs - Stuben am Arlberg - Austria at its best. Beyond argument.

ZÜRS   **Lech ZÜRS ARLBERG**   **Stuben**

MEGÈVE In 2002/03 a new gondola replaced the existing one in the Princesse area – more than doubling the capacity.

LES MENUIRES For 2003/04 the drag-lifts at La Becca and Les Combes are due to be replaced by a fast six-seater chair-lift.

MÉRIBEL For 2003/04 more snowmaking is planned. For 2002/03 the Plan des Mains chair was replaced by a fast six-seater.

MONTGENÈVRE For 2003/04 a chair is to replace the Tremplin drag. For 2002/03 a moving walkway linked the two sectors of slopes.

MORZINE/LES GETS For 2003/04 the Chavannes chair out of Les Gets and the Charniaz chair which links Morzine to Les Gets are to be replaced by six-packs. In 2002/03 a six-pack replaced the two Nauchets drag-lifts and a six-pack was built on the La Rosta slopes.

LA PLAGNE For 2003/04, the long-awaited cable-car link to Les Arcs is due to open – forming one of the world's biggest lift-linked ski areas, called Paradiski (see separate chapter). The capacity of the Roche de Mio gondola will be increased by 30 per cent. A new red piste will link the glacier area to the cable-car to Les Arcs.

SERRE CHEVALIER For 2003/04 the Bletonet chair-lift at the bottom of Chantemerle is due to be replaced by a fast six-pack, doubling capacity. A new big air terrain-park is due near the Echaillon piste.

STE-FOY-TARENTAISE For 2003/04 snowmaking is planned for a run down to the resort.

ST-MARTIN-DE-BELLEVILLE Improvements to the drag-lift from the church up to the gondola are finally scheduled for 2003/04. For 2002/03 a gondola replaced the chair out of the village.

LES SYBELLES The La Toussuire-Le Corbier Super Grand ski area is being linked to St-Sorlin-d'Arves and other nearby villages to form this major new lift/piste network, covered by its own chapter here.

LA TANIA For 2002/03 new snow-guns were installed to cover the blue Folyères piste from Praz-Juget down to the centre of the resort. More snowmaking is planned for 2003/04.

TIGNES For 2002/03 the slow Tommeuses chair-lifts were at last replaced by a fast eight-seater, cutting queues and journey time.

VAL-D'ISÈRE For 2003/4 a six-pack will replace the old two-person up-and-over Leissières chair. For 2002/03 the Bellevarde cable-car was replaced by the much more powerful 24-person Olympique gondola.

VALMOREL For 2003/04 the terrain-park will have a new drag-lift.

VAL-THORENS For 2003/04 the Plateau drags will be replaced by a chair. The resort's third Funitel gondola should be in place, replacing the Bouquetin chair towards Méribel.

ITALY

BORMIO For 2003/04 the cable-car from the main car park to Bormio 2000 is to be replaced by a gondola.

COURMAYEUR For 2003/04, a boarder-cross run is planned.

LIVIGNO For 2002/03 a new fast quad chair was installed for access to the Mottolino lifts from valley level.

MADONNA DI CAMPIGLIO For 2003/04 the old Genziana chair-lift is due to be replaced by a fast quad with covers.

MONTEROSA SKI A new cable-car linking Alagna's slopes with Gressoney's is due for 2003/04.

SAUZE D'OULX/SANSICARIO In Sansicario two new lifts have been built: a six-seat gondola from Cesana to the resort and a quad above it.

Selva/Sella Ronda For 2003/04 a new gondola will run from Siusi to Alpe di Siusi and a fast quad will replace a drag-lift on Alpe di Siusi. The Alta Badia area plans to add two new chair-lifts. Arabba is planning three replacement chairs.

Sestriere For 2003/04 the triple Trebials chair-lift is to be upgraded to a quad, and the Garnel drag-lift is to be replaced with a quad.

La Thuile For 2002/03 the Piccolo San Bernardo chair was replaced by a faster covered quad.

SWITZERLAND

Arosa A quad chair has replaced the Plattenhorn T-bar.

Crans-Montana For 2002/03 a new terrain-park was opened on La Tza at Aminona. The Nationale and Barmaz chairs were upgraded.

Davos The 70-year-old Parsennbahn railway was finally replaced for 2002/03. Snowmaking is to be increased for 2003/04.

Grindelwald For 2003/04 the Läger double chair-lift on Männlichen is to be replaced by a fast covered quad, doubling capacity. On First, the valley runs will have snowmaking. For 2002/03 a fast quad chair replaced the old Schilt T-bar at the top of First.

Saas-Fee There is a new children's fun-park by the sports area, with snow carpet, tubing and magic carpet.

St Moritz A bigger, faster cable-car from Corviglia to Piz Nair replaced the old queue-prone one for 2002/03. And a fast six-pack replaced the FIS and Pitschen T-bars on Corviglia.

Verbier For 2002/03 the capacity of the jumbo Funitel gondola from Les Ruinettes was increased by 25%. Verbier's first six-pack replaced the Saxon chair and Nord drag on the back of the Savoleyres ridge.

Wengen For 2003/04 the old Innerwengen chair is due to be replaced.

Zermatt Two new fast six-seater chair-lifts are planned for 2003/04, one from Trockener Steg to Furggsattel, replacing a queue-prone T-bar; and the other from Riffelberg to Gifthittli. More snowmaking is also planned. A new eight-seater gondola opened for 2002/03, replacing the old Zermatt-Furi-Schwarzsee gondola and cable-car.

UNITED STATES

CALIFORNIA

Heavenly A 120m/400ft-long super-pipe is planned for 2003/04.

Lake Tahoe/Squaw Valley Phase 2 of the new base village at Squaw Valley will open for 2003/04.

Mammoth Phase 1 of the Village development, including a gondola up to Canyon Lodge, is expected to open for 2003/04. The huge Super-Duper half-pipe, with 7m/23ft walls, was opened in 2002/03.

COLORADO

Aspen For 2003/04 the Ajax Express fast quad to the top of Aspen Mountain will be replaced with a new one. The steep terrain in Highland Bowl has been extended and a free snowcat service introduced. The terrain-park at Snowmass has doubled in size.

Beaver Creek For 2003/04 the Westfall double chair from Red Tail Camp to above Spruce Saddle will be replaced by a fast quad.

Breckenridge For 2002/03 a six-pack was built on Peak 7 serving new intermediate runs. A new fast quad now runs from above Beaver Run on Peak 9 to Peak 8. On Peak 8 a third terrain-park and half-pipe aimed at intermediates and novices has been created.

CRESTED BUTTE For 2003/04 a new quad will access the slopes from the Prospect ski-in/ski-out development, with four new blue trails.

KEYSTONE For 2002/03 Arapahoe Basin installed snowmaking covering eleven runs and 125 acres from top to bottom of the mountain.

TELLURIDE For 2002/03 the Sprite Air Garden terrain-park was trebled in size and revamped. A new steeper half-pipe was also built.

VAIL For 2003/04 there'll be a new moving carpet lift in the beginner area at Eagle's Nest. Rock and stump removal continues at Blue Sky Basin and there will be new machines for terrain-park preparation.

WINTER PARK In 2002/03 Winter Park redesigned and expanded its terrain-parks and half-pipe.

UTAH

ALTA/SNOWBIRD For 2003/04 snowmaking will be improved. For 2002/03 snowcat skiing/boarding was introduced in Grizzly Gulch.

DEER VALLEY 2003/04 will see new glade skiing for Empire Canyon. The Ruby chair-lift was replaced by a fast quad for 2002/03.

PARK CITY 2002/03 saw the opening of the Eagle Superpipe.

REST OF THE WEST

BIG SKY/MOONLIGHT BASIN The north face of Lone Mountain is to be developed for 2003/04. A long six-seat chair-lift will access two new bowls with 1,400 acres of terrain to form a separate new resort.

SUN VALLEY For 2003/04 a half-pipe on the lower Warm Springs run below the Challenger chair is planned.

CANADA

WESTERN CANADA

BANFF In Sunshine Village a fast quad chair is planned for 2003/04, replacing the existing slow chair up to Mount Standish. For 2002/03 the Wawa T-bar on Mount Standish was replaced by a quad chair.

BIG WHITE/SILVER STAR Big White has bought Silver Star; a shared lift pass and daily bus and helicopter shuttles allow day-trips there. Silver Star had a new fast quad and a six-pack for 2002/03.

KICKING HORSE In 2002/03, a new quad chair from Crystal Bowl to Blue Heaven opened up another 100 acres of terrain. The capacity of the Golden Eagle Express gondola was doubled.

LAKE LOUISE For 2002/03 the Top of the World chair at the top of the Front Side was upgraded from a fast quad to a six-pack.

PANORAMA For 2003/04 a fast quad will replace the slow, queue-prone, Horizon double chair and the Champagne T-bar above it; and the Summit T-bar to the top will be replaced by a fixed-grip quad.

SUN PEAKS The opening for 2002/03 of the new Mt Morrissey area, served by a fast quad, has taken the skiable terrain up to over 3,400 acres – the second biggest area in BC (Whistler is the biggest).

EASTERN CANADA

TREMBLANT For 2003/04 there will be two new runs – a blue and a black – and a second terrain-park.

SPAIN

BAQUEIRA-BERET For 2003/04 there are plans to expand the slopes beyond Port de la Bonaigua, with new access into the system via a new fast quad east of the pass. The existing Bonaigua double chair will be replaced by a fast quad. On Cap de Baqueira the Luis Arias drag is being replaced by a chair, with a new black piste beneath it.

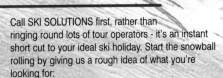

We are a ski travel agency as opposed to a ski tour operator.
When you call us you immediately place at your disposal a choice
of thousands of holidays offered by a wide variety of different
reputable, fully bonded tour operator, both large and small.

We sell you the holiday you want,
not the holiday we need to sell

Summer has its attractions, too
Sailing on a magnificent 48ft yacht

- **Discover Yachting days for novices**
- **2- or 3-day cruises for keen sailors**
- **Ocean racing for non-racers**
- **Weekend charters for groups**

If you're new to sailing, you'll find our Discover Yachting days in the Solent the perfect introduction. If you're not, our Book-a-Berth programme offers the chance to join a crew of like-minded people for some exciting passages – from relaxing south-coast cruises to overnight races across the Channel. Or you could get a group together, and take over a boat with skipper. Our fast, stable, spacious 48ft yachts, based in the Solent, take 8 guests in comfort.

Yacht Ventures

t 01373 835201
www.yachtventures.com
info@yachtventures.com

Paradiski

The new link between Les Arcs and La Plagne

by **Dave Watts**

December 2003 will see the opening of the world's largest cable-car – a double-decker that will hold 200 people. It will link the French resorts of Les Arcs and La Plagne to form a joint ski area that will be one of the biggest in the world, called Paradiski. With 420km/261 miles of pistes and 164 lifts only the Three Valleys and the Portes du Soleil will be significantly bigger. Add in a lot of off-piste terrain and you could argue the new area will be bigger than either.

The new cable-car called the Vanoise Express will span the 2km/1 mile wide valley between Plan-Peisey (in the Les Arcs area) and 300m/980ft above Montchavin (in La Plagne) in less than four minutes. There will be no pylons and the cable-cars will swing at least 300m/980ft above the valley floor giving spectacular views through the transparent walls. Two cars will operate independently, on separate cables, so you won't have to wait for one to fill before the other can set off; and if one is out of action the other can still operate. Each shifts 2,000 people an hour and is designed to be able to operate in bad weather and high winds, so you won't get stranded miles from home. The lower deck holds 120 people and the upper deck 80.

The Vanoise Express cost around 15 million euros to build (over £10 million) and before committing itself, the Compagnie des Alpes (the majority shareholder) commissioned research into its use. It

→ This is the valley the Vanoise Express will span, starting from the centre of the photo, 300m/980ft above Montchavin (in the foreground, with Les Coches above it)

MONTCHAVIN AND LES COCHES
TOURIST OFFICES

KEY FACTS

For Paradiski area

Slopes	1200-3250m
	3,940-10,660ft
Lifts	164
Pistes	420km
	261 miles
Green	5%
Blue	54%
Red	28%
Black	13%

LIFT PASSES

Paradiski
Covers lifts in Les Arcs area and La Plagne area.
6-day pass €220 (over 60 €187; under 14 €165). Also covers a day in the Three Valleys, Val d'Isère-Tignes, Les Saisies and Pralognan-en-Vanoise.

Paradiski Découverte
Covers Grand Domaine Les Arcs plus one day Paradiski extension. 6-day pass €190 (over 60 €162; under 14 €143). Extension is valid Sat-Tue only, unless bought through certain UK tour operators. Pass also covers a day in the Three Valleys, Val d'Isère-Tignes, Les Saisies, Pralognan.

found that 80% of visitors with lift passes for over five days said they would buy a pass that allowed them to use the new cable-car and visit the resort they were not staying in at least once during their holiday. When to visit would depend mainly upon the weather but most people envisaged making one or two trips around the middle of their holiday.

This led the company to devise an innovative pricing system whereby one-day extensions to a six-day La Plagne- or Les Arcs-only lift pass cost half as much at weekends (15 euros) as during the week (30 euros). And as well as offering a six-day pass covering the whole Paradiski region, they are offering one (Paradiski Découverte), which includes just one day's extension for the use of the Vanoise Express and the lifts in the other resort. When bought in the resort this extension is valid only Saturday to Tuesday; but when bought through certain tour operators that also arrange your accommodation, you can use the extension on any day of your stay.

They have also anticipated the problem of the cable-car getting oversubscribed at the end of the day taking people back to the resort they are staying in. So they tell us that on busy days they will hand out tickets for a return journey at a particular time when you make the outward journey in the morning. Sounds sensible but what happens when people miss their allocated slot remains to be seen.

The linking of these two major resorts is good news for the great British piste-basher who likes to cover as much ground as possible. In truth, both La Plagne and Les Arcs alone have enough pistes to keep anyone happy for a week. But a visit or two to the other resort during the week will add interest and variety. And if you set out to get from your home base to both far-flung outposts of Villaroger in Les Arcs and Champagny-en-Vanoise in La Plagne in a day you'll have done some travelling. The new link will also be good for off-piste skiers and boarders coming down from La Plagne's Bellecôte glacier. You'll now be able to slide all the way down to Nancroix and have lunch at our favourite L'Ancolie restaurant (see Les Arcs chapter) and catch the free bus or a taxi for the short ride back up to the Vanoise Express instead of having to get a costly taxi back to Montchavin if you are based in La Plagne.

The new link can be enjoyed not only by holidaymakers staying in Les Arcs and La Plagne. Six-day passes for the Three Valleys and for Val-d'Isère-Tignes will be valid for a day in Paradiski, so hopefully tour operators will lay on excursions to enable their guests in other

paradiski

Savoie – France

TWO WHITE OPEN SPACES BECOME ONE ...

THE SKI AREAS OF
LES ARCS[1] AND LA PLAGNE
HAVE SAID

YES

THE EVENT THIS CHRISTMAS[2]

Here, happiness knows no bounds :
420 kilometres of thrills, sensations, discoveries and escapes, from top to bottom, bottom to top, longways, widthways, crosswise, at every altitude, on every face, for all ages, for all the snowsports. Something you've always dreamed of ? From Christmas 2003 it's a reality.

In less than 4 minutes, Vanoise Express, the super-fast link between la Plagne and Les Arcs, will teleport you from one side of the Peisey-Nancroix valley to the other.

Erna Low

ersonalised holidays since 1932
e original ski specialist for unbeatable value and quality

el : 0870 750 6820
4 hrs: 020 7584 7820
info@ernalow.co.uk
ww.ernalow.co.uk

→ Opening at Christmas 2003 . In the meantime, check out

www.paradiski.com

resorts to be among the first to sample this new link. If you have your own transport the quickest way into the Paradiski slopes will be Champagny-en-Vanoise (La Plagne) from the Three Valleys (you can see Champagny's slopes from Courchevel) and it is just a short drive across the valley. From Val d'Isère or Tignes, the nearest link is from Villaroger (where a chair goes up from Le Pré to the Les Arcs slopes). This is a short drive down the access road (look for the turning to Villaroger when you reach the village – not the resort – of Ste-Foy).

If you want to make the most of the new link it makes sense to stay near one of the cable-car stations. Plan-Peisey and nearby Vallandry in Les Arcs are basically small modern developments but built in a low-rise and much more sympathetic style than the original purpose-built Les Arcs resorts. They don't have much more than a handful of bars, restaurants and shops at the moment and are quiet places to stay but a lot of UK tour operators are building chalets here. The old village of Peisey, 300m/980ft below, is still unspoiled by tourism, with two bars and two restaurants and linked by bucket lift to Plan-Peisey, right by the new cable-car.

Montchavin in La Plagne is a well-restored traditional old village with modern additions built in traditional style, as are the buildings in nearby newly developed Les Coches. Between them Montchavin and Les Coches have eight restaurants, six bars and a nightclub. To reach the new cable-car you need just one lift out of either village.

UK tour operators offering chalet packages to these resorts include: Erna Low (self-catering chalets with good views in Vallandry; they can arrange apartments too), Esprit Ski, Ski Beat, Ski Hiver, Ski Olympic and the Family Ski Company. Made to Measure can arrange apartments and hotels.

Heli-skiing

Getting high in the Bugaboos

by **Dave Watts**

If you like off-piste skiing, heli-skiing is the ultimate dream. Canada is the heli-skiing capital of the the world because of its miles of wilderness and regular snowfalls. If you can afford it (or even if you can't!) you should give Canadian heli-skiing a whirl. I have tried it several times by the day. But last winter I did a whole week in a remote mountain lodge in the Bugaboos, run by Canadian Mountain Holidays. It was an amazing experience, and one that I can't wait to repeat. Neither can most CMH guests (80% are repeat visitors and nearly all the 44 people on my trip intended to go again – some tried to book on the spot).

I arrived with trepidation. It had been one of the worst winters ever in western Canada for avalanches. But once there I was reassured. Not surprisingly, the safety precautions were impeccable. There were safety briefings on the bus from Banff and after our arrival (a 13-minute flight for us and our luggage from a dusty car park in the middle of nowhere until we landed in the middle of a snowy wilderness by the lodge that was to be home for the week).

Next morning we had a 90-minute training and practice session in small groups, using the latest Barryvox digital transceivers to locate and dig out supposed avalanche victims. Every morning the guides met to discuss the weather and avalanche forecast and decide which runs were safe and could be 'opened' and which were doubtful, so would remain 'closed'. A snow safety guide checked out any doubtful areas, dug snow-pits to examine the stability of snow layers and triggered avalanches using bombs if necessary. Every evening the guides met again to discuss the day and to exchange information about snow conditions and avalanche danger with all CMH's other eleven operations and the western Canada avalanche database.

None of the other guests saw any of this behind-the-scenes activity. They were free to enjoy the holiday in safety. On our first evening the head guide announced that the weather forecast for tomorrow was mixed and they had not been able to get up to the highest slopes with the best snow for days. But the next day dawned

CMH FACTS

CMH has twelve areas in Canada where it has heli-skiing operations. Six of these are based in remote lodges that you are flown into and out of by helicopter. It has been going for almost 40 years. Prices for six-and-a-half days guided heli-skiing in groups of eleven, seven nights full-board, special skis for the week and transfers from Calgary airport or Banff are from C$5,000 to C$8,000. That includes skiing a guaranteed minimum vertical of 30,500m/100,000ft. Additional runs cost $77 per 1000m/3,280ft. If you don't hit the guaranteed minimum you get a refund at $83 per 1000m/3,280ft. On our trip I did just 180m/590ft less than the guaranteed minimum. And it seemed like a lot of skiing. Most lodges take 44 people each week and they get booked up well in advance. When we went to press a few places were left for 2003/04. But you can book now for 2004/05.

31

SCOTT ROWED

The chopper takes off after dropping people at the top of yet another run with virgin powder ➔

↑ The scenery around the glaciers rivals that of the Alps and the Dolomites. That's our group on the left, heading off for the first run of our last day

DAVE WATTS; ALEC PYTLOWANY

clear and sunny. After a stretching class, breakfast and the transceiver and rescue training we were ready to leave, collecting the special Volkl Explosiv CMH special edition skis we had been fitted for the previous night, which make powder skiing much easier.

We flew right to the top runs on the Bugaboo glacier under the magnificent Matterhorn-shaped Bugaboo Spire, where we skied gentle powder runs to warm up. Three runs before lunch, with the helicopter waiting for us in the middle of nowhere to whisk us back up. Lunch was delivered to us on the mountain – soup, sandwiches and cookies, enjoyed among the fabulous scenery of gaping glacial crevasses. Then six more runs after lunch, gradually getting steeper and the last two offering 1000m vertical of perfect, virgin knee-deep powder. You would never get those conditions on an alpine run except in the first few hours after a snowfall – and after a long hike.

The next day dawned cloudy and warm. So we headed for the trees. The guide sets off through trees and disappears in two turns. You ski (or board) with a buddy to pick you out of the snow if you fall – ski where you like between the trees and try to head in the general direction of the guide's yelps and calls. The snow was surprisingly light and powdery and we managed 12 runs in the day. Tuesday and Wednesday the wind got up, which meant we had to stay low and could ski for only half a day each time. But no-one minded, because we were all so tired from days one and two.

Thursday was another epic: nine runs on distant glaciers. The first few in shin-deep powder, then on to firm wind-blown snow in high, spectacular scenery that reminded me of Val d'Isère off-piste runs. Friday was another curtailed day, with just four runs in the trees. Saturday was our final day. We woke to a brilliant blue sky with not a cloud in sight. We were flown as high as you can get, to over 3000m on the Vowell glacier, and landed amid spectacular scenery to rival anything in the Alps or Dolomites. Long runs of 1000m vertical in ankle-deep powder made turning easy – for the first time I counted 100 successive turns without stopping. We did just five runs before we had to fly to the lodge to head for home. But what a morning!

What else? Well the staff were great and so was the food (seared ahi tuna, rack of lamb and apple tart is typical). You sit at communal tables of twelve or so, as in a catered chalet. The bedrooms all had en-suite facilities and the lodge had a bar, a lounge with log fire, walls full of old skiing photos, a big hot tub, a sauna and two excellent masseurs.

It is the holiday of a lifetime: splendid isolation in a vast wilderness and run after run of virgin snow; skiing you could not get in any other way. To my mind, well worth the money.

UK Representative for CMH
Powder Skiing in North America
61 Doneraile Street
London SW6 6EW
t 020 7584 2841
f 020 7589 9531
info@psna.co.uk
www.cmhski.com

New gear for 2004

Skis give more fun, boots give more comfort

by **Dave Watts**

TOP FREERIDE SKIS:
Rossignol Bandit B2
Salomon Scream 10 Pilot Hot

↑ Rossi's Bandit B2 is wider than its predecessor the Bandit XX; Salomon's Scream 10 Pilot Hot uses its SpaceFrame technology

The speed of technical change in ski and snowboard equipment is faster than ever before. Each year major breakthroughs are made that make riding mountains easier and more fun. Over the last few years skis have got shorter, wider and more shaped. One of the benefits of the new technologies is that skis are becoming more versatile: a freeride ski that floats easily off-piste can now also carve on-piste and work well through the bumps too. Wider freeride skis now allow you to venture into off-piste powder and crud with much more confidence that you won't do a head plant. Shorter skiercross skis have made piste skiing much faster and more fun. And twin-tips have multiplied as more and more skiers head for the terrain-parks to outsmart the snowboarders with their new tricks. With boots the big trend is still towards custom fitting for comfort and control, and towards 'soft' boots rather than hard plastic shells for beginners and intermediates. And more and more gear is appearing to protect you from injury if you fall.

With skis the big story for 2004 is shape and torsional strength. Skis are continuing to get wider and shorter but still with big sidecuts to make turning easy. The challenge for manufacturers has been to make sure their skis still flex easily from tip to tail while remaining torsionally stiff, so that they don't twist underfoot when you put them on edge. New technological developments have enabled them to do that including, for example, Salomon's SpaceFrame, Head's Intellifibers, Atomic's Beta profile, Völkl's Double Grip, Dynastar's Autodrive and Rossignol's Oversize technology. All this may sound like marketing hype. But it does work – as I found out last March when I went on a week-long test of all the 2004 skis organised by the Snowsports Industries of Great Britain (a trade body of UK equipment distributors and retailers). There wasn't a poor ski on the test.

WIDER AND SHAPLIER FOR THE POWDER

Freeride skis are just getting fatter and fatter – and all the better for it. One of my favourite skis for the last few years has been the Rossignol Bandit XX. This year that has been replaced by the Bandit B2 which was perhaps my favourite ski of the whole test. The XX profile was (tip, waist, tail in mm) 110-74-100. The B2's are 113-76-103. The extra width underfoot makes a big difference. It floats well off-piste but feels incredibly smooth on-piste too. It has great edge hold and turning power but is also very forgiving if you get things wrong.

Many skis designed primarily for on-piste use are getting much wider too, which gives you much more stability underfoot and the confidence to take on steeper and tougher runs. Skiercross skis are all the rage again for 2004. The best of these are built just like the manufacturers' top race skis but with a much more radical sidecut

33

FEEL THE EDGE

than is allowed by the FIS (the international racing federation) rules. For example, Atomic's GS11 race ski has a profile of 99-64-89 at its 181cm length and a turning radius of 21 metres. Its top Skiercross ski, the SX11, uses the same construction but has a profile of 106-66-96 – a huge difference which gives it a turning radius of just 18 metres. The result is a ski that won the approval of all the expert skiers on the test, such as former British downhill stars Martin and Graham Bell. Mere mortals would only get the best out of them if they skied them very hard and very fast.

But there are many skiercross models that don't need such speed or skill. For example, the Salomon Crossmax 8 Pilot, Rossignol RPM 70 and Völkl Supersport 4 Star.

↑ Atomic's top Supercross SX11 is the expert skier's favourite skiercross ski. The Völkl Supersport 4 Star and Salomon Crossmax 8 Pilot are easier to handle

For those who don't know, I should explain that skiercross is the newest type of ski race – and much more exciting for spectators than regular downhill and slalom races. Instead of racing one at a time against the clock, in skiercross four or more skiers start at the same time. They then fly as fast as possible down a course that has bends, banks and jumps, and the only rule is that whoever crosses the finish line first wins. Collisions and falls are the norm and add to the fun. But you don't have to race to enjoy skiercross skis.

Skis sold as all-round on-piste skis have a much less race-oriented construction than most skiercross skis. They are built to require less power and speed to get the best out of them and to allow you to have more fun with less effort. They too are benefitting from having more shape and width. For example, my favourite on-piste ski on test was the Rossignol T-Power Cobra X. The 2004 model has a profile of 111-67-98. This compares with last season's Cobra X profile of 99-64-89. The extra width is part of Rossignol's Oversize concept.

INTEGRATED BINDINGS NOW THE NORM

It is only three years since Salomon introduced the first integrated binding system to skis. Its innovative Pilot system – where the binding is attached to the sides of the skis through specially drilled holes, rather than to the top – allowed the ski to flex naturally and gave better edge grip and transmission of power from boot to ski. Traditional bindings are mounted on to the surface of the ski and prevent the ski from flexing naturally – they create a 'flat spot' under your boot. For 2004 Salomon has modified the Pilot system to make it even more effective.

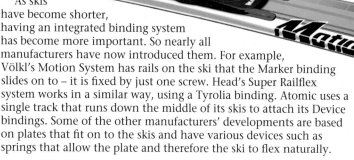

↑ The Völkl Motion and Salomon Pilot (smaller picture) are two of the integrated binding systems designed to allow skis to flex naturally

As skis have become shorter, having an integrated binding system has become more important. So nearly all manufacturers have now introduced them. For example, Völkl's Motion System has rails on the ski that the Marker binding slides on to – it is fixed by just one screw. Head's Super Railflex system works in a similar way, using a Tyrolia binding. Atomic uses a single track that runs down the middle of its skis to attach its Device bindings. Some of the other manufacturers' developments are based on plates that fit on to the skis and have various devices such as springs that allow the plate and therefore the ski to flex naturally.

BOOT UP FOR COMFORT AND PERFORMANCE

The big news on the boot front is that they are becoming more comfortable without sacrificing performance. Over the last few years nearly every manufacturer has introduced custom-fit inner boots across all or part of its range. In most cases, the inner boot is heated up and it then automatically moulds to the shape of your foot when you put it in. This has revolutionised boot comfort for every level of performance. Another major development has been the introduction of softer plastic parts to make getting boots on and off easier, integrated with more rigid plastic for support and power.

↑ Two soft boots for intermediates Rossignol Soft Light 1 Salomon Verse

Two seasons ago, the first soft boots appeared on the market, aimed primarily at first-time buyers and intermediate skiers looking for comfort and ease of use. The concept was to produce a boot which had the look and comfort of a soft snowboard boot but retained the support and power transmission needed for skiing. Now virtually every manufacturer has a 'soft' boot of some description. But some of these are not true 'soft' boots, more hard shells which are made to look soft in some way. One of the best true soft boots is the Soft Light 1 from Rossignol. This is an improvement on the first Soft boot, brought out in 2001. The Soft Light 1 uses a rigid plastic skeletal frame for support and transmission to the ski, combined with a two-buckle closure system and an integrated, laced inner boot for optimum comfort and ease of use.

Whenever you buy boots – hard or soft – make sure you use a shop with a good boot-fitter and always have a custom-built footbed made to the shape of your foot. This will support your foot and distribute pressure evenly under the whole foot, improving comfort and control and reducing muscle cramps and foot fatigue.

New gear

35

HOLD THE EDGE

↑ Tecnica Icon Alu
HotForm for experts

New gear

↑ More and more
people are wearing
helmets.
Top: Carrera Typhoon
Advance
Bottom: Leedom Limit
(a children's helmet)

PROTECTION RACKET

More and more people are now wearing helmets to prevent
potentially lethal head injuries. America led the way with this and
now Europe is catching up fast. Few people would dream of going
cycling without wearing a helmet but most people ski or snowboard
faster than they cycle, so if helmets make sense on a bike they should
do on snow, too. Children should certainly wear helmets. A wide
range of body protection clothing is available too. Back protection
and shorts to protect your coccyx, hips, buttocks and thighs are
probably the most important garments to consider (especially if you
intend to learn to snowboard which can be very painful!).

New on the UK market for this winter are Snowskins. These are
compression leggings developed in Australia to enhance blood
circulation and reduce muscle fatigue from lactic acid build-up. They
work in a similar way to compression stockings sold to help prevent
deep vein thrombosis on long-haul flights. They enable you to ski
longer and harder, reduce muscle pain and tiredness, reduce the risk
of injury, wick away perspiration and keep you warm. If worn after
skiing as well they will help your legs recover faster.

It is also worth getting fit and working on some specific muscle
groups to help you avoid injury on the slopes; ideally ask a sports
trainer or physio for a programme tailored to your own needs. Body
Factor (part of Snow+Rock and contactable on 01932 564364) is a
specialist in this field and has branches in London's Covent Garden
and in Chertsey, Surrey (just off junction 11 of the M25).

GET ON BOARD

Snowboarders are blessed with the luxury of riding in soft boots, so
whether you're racing down for the last chair of the day or hiking
into the backcountry for fresh powder turns your feet will be
comfortable and warm. Snowboard boots are stiffer and more
supportive than ever to offer greater precision and control, allowing
you to ride harder, faster and more safely. Boots are designed with an
inner liner and outer shell; this makes them easy to get on and off
and you can adjust each individually for optimum fit.

This season sees a host of new and proven performance-
enhancing features. The innovative Boa lacing system featured on
Vans boots, replaces traditional laces with a wire cable and
tensioning dial; twisting the dial tightens the cable to provide a
snug, effortless, pressure-free fit. Many boots, such as the Burton
Hail, now feature custom-fit liners that can be heated up and
moulded to the shape of your foot, giving you increased comfort and
a more precise fit. And, as with ski boots, it is worth paying extra to
have a customised footbed made to support your foot properly – see
earlier in this chapter. Salomon's F24 features their new 'Self' ankle
pads that have been engineered to match the texture and natural
shock absorption of human tissue; positioned around sensitive parts
of the ankle, they takes boot comfort to a new level.

Two-strap bindings are still by far the most popular design. They

↑ Left: Salomon F24 has ankle pads for extra comfort and shock absorption
Right: Vans Fargo Boa has an innovative lacing system with a wire cable and tensioning dial

offer plenty of adjustability, which is the basis of achieving the stance that you need. As you climb the price ladder you'll receive greater comfort, support and responsiveness.

The innovative Flow Binding system has firmly taken command of the market for step-in bindings, offering the speed and efficiency of a step-in system with the flexibility of almost any conventional snowboard boot. A single large strap goes over the front of the boot; the high back drops back for you to slide your foot in, then is raised and tensioned and you're ready to ride.

As the number of female snowboarders continues to rise so has the choice of women's boards, boots and bindings. All are specifically designed to complement the female form and provide performance, support and comfort.

As all snowboards have become very similar in both shape and profile it has become increasingly important to seek advice from a good retailer about which boards you should consider for your ability level and budget. Relative beginners should go for an all-mountain board, designed to work in any terrain and allow the rider to experiment and develop their technique and style. There is a wide selection of boards aimed at first-time buyers for £200 or less, many of which offer wide versions for riders with size 10 feet upwards.

Intermediate riders have a huge choice of boards often benefitting from hand-me-down technology from previous seasons' high-end models. The Option Redline is the perfect example of such a board, combining the forgiving, confidence-boosting ride of a medium flex with plenty of performance in reserve to satisfy advanced riders.

The Salomon ERA has the new SpaceFrame construction and is

SNOW + ROCK TIP

TOP BOARDS FOR INTERMEDIATES:
Nitro Punisher
Option Redline

↑ Option Redline
(top surface on left,
base on right)

New gear

38

another board that combines a forgiving tip-to-tail flex with a much stiffer torsional flex to give solid edge grip in even the hardest of snow conditions. It also features special 'pods' on which the bindings sit, to allow the board to flex smoothly and naturally beneath.

Advanced riders need look no further than the K2 Recon Riser for the ultimate precision-riding tool. Integrating a 6mm riser plate into the deck of the board gives you the rapid edge-to-edge performance of the narrow board combined with greater toe and heel clearance. The increased leverage lets you lay over powerful carves, no longer in fear of toe-drag or icy pistes. It's also the big-footed rider's dream.

WHY BUY IN THE UK?
There are lots of reasons. For a start, if anything goes wrong you can take the gear back to where you bought it to get it replaced or the problem sorted. And, in general, UK shops have a wider range of brands and sizes than shops in the mountains – which often tend to stock mainly local brands (eg French brands in France).

Prices in the UK are now as competitive as in Europe. Readers used to get annoyed when they bought gear in the UK and then found it on sale significantly cheaper in ski resorts. That has changed as a result of manufacturers pricing in euros and UK retailers being determined to match European prices. And if you buy in North America, remember that you'll have to pay duty and VAT when you bring your gear back to the UK.

Some retailers have price-match guarantees. Snow + Rock, for example, offers a price pledge that says it will refund the difference if you find you can buy something cheaper anywhere in Europe within 21 days of purchase. It also offers good packages of skis and bindings – this winter it has an intermediate package of Head boots, skis, bindings, poles and ski bag for only £259.

If you buy skis or a snowboard costing over £250 from any shop participating in a special Snowlife promotion between 15 September and 31 December 2003, you will receive a voucher for a free return flight to one of six destinations in Europe (including Geneva and Zurich) from four UK airports. You just have to pay the airport taxes and other charges. And you can take someone with you for just £85 plus taxes. Go to www.snowlife.org.uk for full details of the offer.

AND FINALLY
If you own your own skis or board, have them serviced before you go away. And try on your old boots to make sure they still fit and aren't in need of adjustment or repair. It also pays everyone to invest in some technical ski socks that wick away moisture, keep your feet warm and dry and provide you with a better fit in your boots; always wear a clean pair every day. And a good way of staying in contact with friends or family in the mountains is by buying a set of walkie-talkies; they work up to two miles apart and you incur no mobile phone charges.

↑ Left: K2 Recon
Riser
Right: Salomon ERA

Family holidays

Which ones work best?

by **Chris Gill**

It's some years now since the Gill family's annual ski holidays ceased to provide me with really useful material for these annual bulletins from the child-rearing front. These days, with our younger child approaching teenhood, we don't make much use of specialised childcare or other family-oriented facilities. Son Alex skis with Dad, or with anyone else he can find who might make his days more interesting by being less obsessed by safety. Daughter Laura 'skis' with Mum, which is family-speak for getting up late, lunching early and taking an unnatural interest in shopping. (Soon, of course, the kids will be going out clubbing all night, and it would be nice to think that as a result I might find myself becoming much better informed about nightlife – but of course the kids aren't going to want to communicate the results of their nocturnal forays to their dear old dad.)

But I do still take an interest in how ski resorts and ski companies deal with families. Well, someone involved in Where to Ski and Snowboard has to. We know a large proportion of our readers travel in family groups, and that there are lots of decisions to be made in the course of arranging a family trip. So some guidance follows.

But here's an idea for next year: if you take the kids skiing, send me an e-mail listing the five most valuable lessons it taught you, and for next year's family holiday bulletin I'll aim to produce a distillation. Address: cg@snow-zone.co.uk; subject: Family ski holidays. I look forward to hearing from you.

LESSON 0: YOU HAVE TO LEARN YOUR OWN LESSONS

Your children and mine are individuals, and what has worked for mine may not work for yours. So what follows may or may not be of help to you in figuring out how to go skiing as a family.

LESSON 1: LEAVING THEM BEHIND DOESN'T WORK

When Alex was a year old, Val and I went for a week in Norway, leaving him at home with his nanny. OK, Norway wasn't the ideal place, considering my preference for proper lunches and proper wine with dinner, but, even allowing for my increasingly disgruntled frame of mind, the trip wasn't a success.

By day four, we were missing the boy dreadfully, and counting down the hours to the flight back to Newcastle. It all seems difficult to believe, now that he is 15.

LESSON 2: IT PAYS TO DEVELOP HARD HEARTS

I am full of admiration for people who from an early age thrust their children into various socially challenging environments in which the resourceful brats prosper to everyone's very evident satisfaction – and, crucially, keep it up until the kids are grown up. We managed to do it when our kids were tiny, and their screams of protest at being left in the care of an unfamiliar someone didn't require a reasoned reply. We somehow lost the plot, though, once the kids learned how to manipulate our emotions fully.

We seem to have conceded long ago that (a) holidays are meant to be holidays for the kids as well as for the parents, and that sending them to ski school is inconsistent with having a holiday from school; (b) we don't see enough of the kids in the normal course of life and

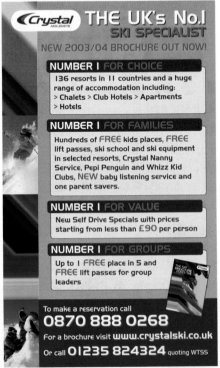

should take the opportunity that holidays present to spend more time with them. Curiously, this second argument is deployed only when the threat of ski school is present. On summer holidays, with no such threat, we are not required to spend any time at all with the kids. Strange.

LESSON 3: IT'S WORTH PLUGGING INTO UK TOUR OPERATORS

If your kids, like mine, are used to the mollycoddling that passes for child-rearing in Britain, it's enormously reassuring to know that if you travel with a suitably equipped tour operator the kids' mollies can be coddled endlessly by nannies who share our values.

These days there are countless companies providing services of this kind, including the major mainstream operators. But there are specialists, and the advertising in this chapter is as good a guide as you will find to their identities. It's perhaps particularly worth pointing out that Esprit Ski, after a brief flirtation with the idea of becoming a general operator, has gone back to its roots and is again specialising in family holidays. Mark Warner also deserves a mention: its chalet-hotels generally contain excellent childcare facilities.

LESSON 4: THERE IS NO RIGHT AGE TO START

Some people will tell you to start your kids on skis as soon as possible. My advice is to let the kids decide for themselves when to start. As it happens, both of our kids made a start, with different results, at age four. Following his distressing experience at the hands

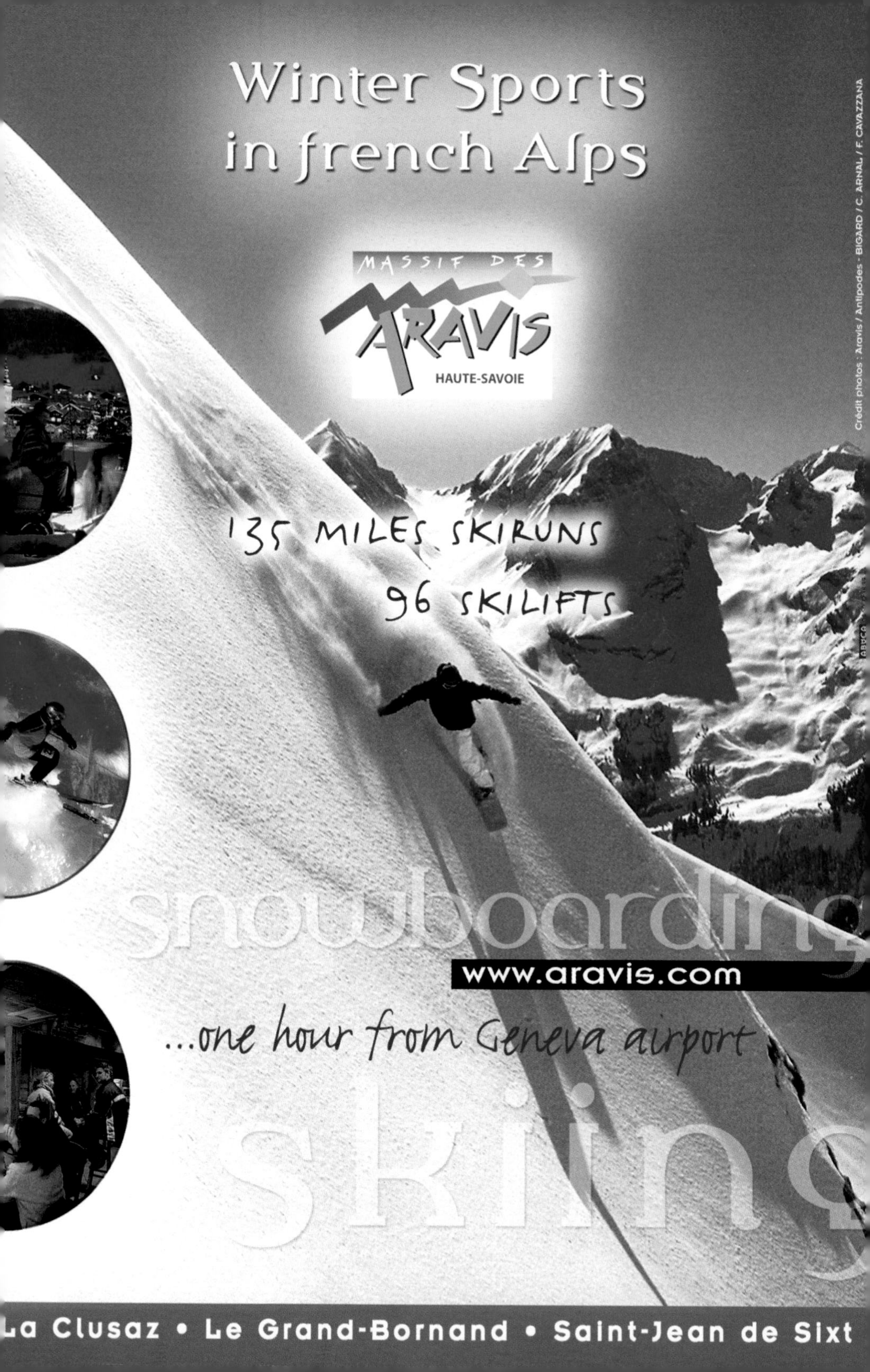
Winter Sports
in french Alps
MASSIF DES
ARAVIS
HAUTE-SAVOIE
135 MILES SKIRUNS
96 SKILIFTS
snowboarding
www.aravis.com
...one hour from Geneva airport
skiing
La Clusaz • Le Grand-Bornand • Saint-Jean de Sixt
Crédit photos : Aravis / Antipodes - BIGARD / C. ARNAL / F. CAVAZZANA

of the ESF (see Lesson 5), son Alex took a year off, basically got the hang of it under my guidance at age six, and then really learned how to do it in America at age seven (see Lesson 6). Laura also started at age four, but purely by coincidence: she was checked into the nursery in Killington, discovered they had no arrangements for playing out in the snow and decided skiing was a more attractive option than sitting indoors all day.

LESSON 5: THE ESF IS A DISGRACE, TO BE AVOIDED

I know that there are conscientious and competent instructors working in the Ecole du Ski Français, and that there are people whose children have consistently had enjoyable and profitable lessons with the school. I know that the grim experience of my son Alex, aged four, at the hands of a branch of the ESF tells us very little. I know that there simply are cultural differences between the French and the British in the child-rearing area which complicate the business of handing over our kids to their care. I acknowledge that I have had successful lessons in the ESF myself, occasionally.

But I also know that every year the ESF, uniquely, generates reports from readers that tell of scandalous disregard for the well-being and even the safety of the kids in its charge. I'm not suggesting a boycott, but I am suggesting that you improve the chances of successful lessons for your kids if you choose alternative schools where they exist.

Where there isn't a choice, there are other ways of improving those chances. The Family Ski Company, an expanding specialist in this market, has hit on the neat idea of sending a minder along to lessons with the youngest kids, to pick them up off the snow, blow

Get next year's edition free

There are too many hotels, nightspots and mountain restaurants for us to see them all every year – so we need reports on your holiday experiences. As usual, the 100 best reports will earn copies of next year's edition.

We want to know:
• what you particularly **liked and disliked** about the resort
• what aspects of the resort came as a **surprise** to you
• your suggestions for **changes to our evaluation** of the resort
• your experience of **lift queues** and of the **ski school** and associated childcare
• your feedback on other **individual facilities** – hotels, bars, restaurants etc.

e-mail: reports@snow-zone.co.uk
mail: our address is at the front of the book; we'll send a form if you like.

their noses and generally make them feel that they are at the centre of the universe, which of course is what they are used to and therefore expect. I went along to see this arrangement in operation last winter, and it seems to work.

LESSON 6: THOSE WHO CAN AFFORD IT SHOULD CONSIDER AMERICA
Childcare and child tuition in the US is marvellous – the people doing it are skilled, caring, jolly and English-speaking. I can still picture the lift attendant in Killington who first got Laura to ride a drag-lift by running up the slope beside her, holding her upright and shouting encouragement. What more could you ask? Well, you could ask for a low child-to-pro ratio, and in the States you get one. The downside is that the cost is huge – something like three or four times the cost of the equivalent classes in Austria, for example.

Is it worth it? If you plan to use the facilities all day, every day for a week, probably not, for most people. If on the other hand you are thinking of spending part of your week looking after the kids yourself and part of it child-free, paying over the odds for a better chance of a successful outcome is quite an appealing option.

LESSON 7: THE RIGHT RESORT CAN HELP A LOT
It's obvious, isn't it? If your children are mobile, and likely to want to leave the confines of your accommodation, you want them to step out into a traffic-free environment and to find gentle slopes for sledging and snowballing only yards away. If they are of skiing age, you want them to be able to ski to and from the door, so that you don't have to choose between carrying their kit to the lift and a major disciplinary hearing every morning in order to get them to do it for themselves

These ideal places exist, and with dedicated study of the hundreds of pages that follow can be identified. But don't forget it's your holiday, too. See next lesson.

LESSON 8: THE WRONG RESORT CAN WORK QUITE WELL
The main reason you are going skiing – well, the main reason I am going skiing, at least – is to have enjoyable days out on the mountain. I want extensive slopes, some challenges, good snow, decent restaurants, grand views.

Sometimes, the search for this combination has led to resorts that might not be top of the list for a family holiday – Val-d'Isère and Chamonix, for example. These holidays have worked out OK largely because we have travelled with tour operators – Mark Warner and Esprit, in these two cases – who relieved us of our parental responsibilities to such a degree that the drawbacks of the resort were painlessly overcome, ferrying the kids to ski school for example. Back to lesson 3, then.

LESSON 9: DON'T EXPECT APPRECIATION
I started skiing in my twenties, and have an abiding sense of what a privilege it is to be high in the mountains in February, when I could be in a grey, damp Britain. My kids, it seems, would just as soon be at home playing computer games. Of course, your kids are likely to be different. See Lesson 0.

All-inclusive holidays

Come home on-budget

by **Chris Gill**

For anyone who wants to keep control of their holiday spending, there's nothing to beat an all-inclusive holiday. If you're heading for the beaches of the Caribbean, it's not difficult to find places where everything you're going to need is included in the crystal-clear upfront cost, from flights down to snorkel kit and all-day cocktails. When heading for the slopes, it's not so easy. Work through enough brochures and you'll track down a few package deals based on full board. But wine with meals? Not widely done, except in catered chalets that are only half-board. Ski equipment, tuition and a lift pass? Nope: perhaps surprisingly, no one sells packages that include absolutely everything. But there are a couple of companies that do roll most of these components into their packages: Club Med and Equity Ski.

CLUB MED

Club Med is the big name in this game, and one it's difficult to escape, such is the scale of its operation. The brightly painted extension to Aime-la-Plagne? It's Club Med. The place with the swooping roofs in Arc 2000? The twin round tower blocks in Sestriere? The big old Palace hotel in Villars? Ditto Wengen? They're all Club Med 'villages'.

Some of these are grand hotels that had found their traditional markets disappearing, but some are purpose-built and some of the recently developed 'villages' – notably the trio of very smart chalet-style places they have in Méribel – are swanky, modern hotels that are impressive by any standard. The great majority of the ski properties are in France (it's a French company), but Club Med has taken over a handful of old hotels in Swiss resorts and also now has places in Italy (Sestriere and Cervinia), America (Crested Butte) and Japan (Sahoro).

The 'village' terminology is misleading to the beginner. It's presumably meant to strike a chord with Club Med's summer clientele. The company (which not long ago celebrated its 50th birthday) started out running all-inclusive summer holidays, and those holidays do take place in something like self-contained holiday villages. The ski villages are really hotels with ski shops in the basement (and nurseries in most).

Club Med holidays are available with or without flights and transfers. They all include insurance. But perhaps the defining characteristic of the Club Med package is that it includes all meals, including beer and wine – and, because this is a French operation, lunch is just as serious a meal as dinner. Usually, lunch is taken back at the village (most are in high resorts, where this is not a problem) but in Chamonix and a couple of Swiss resorts Club Med has taken over a mountain restaurant where you have your included lunch without descending to the village.

Clearly, the full-board formula has its attractions. Well, it has one attraction: that your lunch (and accompanying drinks) are paid for. You have to weigh against this the fact that most of the villages are in resorts with big lift networks where, in the normal course of events, you wouldn't be heading back to base for lunch every day – beginners apart, many people would be planning on having lunch

savouring the views on a remote mountaintop, or in some equally remote village in another valley.

Generally, Club Med prices include your lift pass and tuition (the Méribel villages are an exception). Some do only half-day tuition, but most do a full day. Skiing or boarding equipment costs extra, but is available on-site in all villages except Flaine – so at least you don't have to schlepp around the resort. They carry a range of kit, including performance skis.

Most villages have childcare facilities, and for many Club Med regulars these are at the heart of the formula – though how well they will work for English-speaking kids must be open to doubt. There is a mini club (included in the holiday cost) in most of the villages for ages 4 to 13; the deal includes dinner and evening entertainment until 9pm. A couple of villages have a petit club for ages 2 to 4, and a couple have a baby club for ages 4 months to 2 years; these facilities cost extra.

A handful of villages welcome children but make no special provision for them. Club Med recommends these for couples and singles. And two villages are 'Adults Only' – open only to those over 18, recommended for singles. It was to one of these – Val-Thorens (the other is in Alpe d'Huez) – that a pal and I went, a few seasons back, for a taste of the Club Med recipe. We went in early December, when Val-Thorens was only half-open, Courchevel was just waking up and Méribel was pretty much still asleep. First clue as to how Club Med makes money: the place was apparently full, even at that early stage of the season.

There was a pretty international crowd, although naturally French-dominated. There were very few Brits – there were only five of

SNOWPIX.COM / CHRIS GILL

Club Med in Arc 2000 – the blocks with the swooping roofs, in the middle, contain two 'villages', offering different blends of facilities. ↓

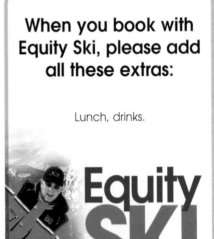

us on the transfer minibus from Geneva, and the village has 180 rooms – a lot of Israelis, quite a few Dutch, the occasional Russian. So it wasn't difficult to find dinner tables where English rather than French was the lingua franca. In what is apparently a standard Club Med arrangement, meals were taken at big round tables for eight people, and you just cruised around until you found a likely-looking bunch of companions. Bottles of house wine were freely distributed by waiters, and beer was on tap. All the food was served via buffets, the most popular bits of which generated queues at peak times. The food – with an exotic theme on some evenings – was pretty good, though not exactly a highlight of the day. We didn't hesitate to skip the lunch at base occasionally and splash out on a mountain restaurant meal, and when an invitation came our way late in the week to dine out in a smart restaurant elsewhere in the resort, the change of scene was welcome.

We joined the free ski classes most days, and wound up in a friendly French-speaking advanced group with a Gitane-smoking ESF instructor who spoke good English – when his failing respiratory system permitted him to speak at all. We had a lot of fun. He took us off-piste in what I later discovered to be dangerous circumstances, but that's ESF instructors for you.

Val-Thorens is a 'three-trident' village, the most common kind on the Club Med three-point rating scale. Two-trident places are simpler, and generally have only half-day ski school. Single tridents aren't used. Four-trident places offer 'comfort of the highest standard'; there are three in Méribel, and others in Tignes, Val-d'Isère, St Moritz and Crested Butte.

EQUITY SKI

The other major programme that can be described as all-inclusive is that of Equity Ski. This company's pricing is a lot simpler than Club Med's. All their holiday prices (leaving aside the company's recently added north American programme) include the cost of your lift pass, equipment hire and insurance. And they all include either tuition or guiding around the slopes (it depends on where you are staying – you don't have a choice). On the other hand, they don't include lunch, and they include drinks with dinner only in the case of catered chalet holidays – so for most people two serious budget variables are introduced into the equation. On the other hand, with this arrangement (unlike the Club Med deal) you do have complete freedom to have lunch where you please, without feeling that you are wasting money.

The Equity accommodation is less uniform than Club Med's. The programme falls roughly into two halves. They offer a moderate number of Austrian and French resorts, in which they generally run their own catered chalets or hotels, and sometimes offer other hotels too. Then, in a larger number of Italian resorts, they offer two or three standard hotels that may be shared with other companies' clients, in the conventional way.

Equity's resorts are a mix of established big names – Val-Thorens, Mayrhofen, Sauze d'Oulx – and smaller, less well-known places such as St Michael and Le Corbier (part of the large, newly created Les Sybelles area, covered for the first time in this edition). includes one or two useful 'back-door' resorts attached to major ski areas – St-Martin-de-Belleville for the Trois Vallées, Folgarida for Madonna di Campiglio, Canazei for the Sella Ronda.

Luxury chalets

The ultimate ski holiday?

by **Chris Gill**

In the beginning, the catered chalet business – explained in the box later in this chapter, for the benefit of those not familiar with the concept – didn't do luxury. It was only in the late 1980s that one or two companies realised that there might be a market for indulgent holidays without the fleets of bellboys and room-service waiters that hotels are obliged to lay on. All you had to do was provide comfortable and stylish accommodation, good food and wine, and a little bit of personal service – just enough to make the customer feel the staff are there to do something other than have a good time. The new formula worked, probably better than anyone would have expected.

The top end of the chalet market has been shaken up in a big way this past summer by the demise of The Ski Company Ltd, which owned or operated some of the very best chalets on the UK market.

You can find isolated luxury chalets in all sorts of places, from Austria to Aspen, but the breed in general is still not widespread: most are concentrated in the more upmarket French mega-resorts.

The greatest concentration is found in Méribel, particularly in the hands of long-time local specialist Meriski. This company, more than any other, illustrates the transformation of the chalet business. In the 1980s it was a run-of-the-mill chalet operation, but then it successfully repositioned itself upmarket, and now has a wide range of impressively comfortable chalets.

Following the demise of The Ski Company Ltd, Descent International now has an enviable portfolio of properties in the secluded Brames area of the resort. The famously luxurious chalet Brames is the grandest property I have visited in Méribel, with two-storey living room and some beautiful bedrooms, and a glorious view up the valley towards Mont Vallon. To this the company has now been able to add the equally desirable 10-bed chalets Aurore and Boréale, nearby, which share an outdoor heated pool. Up in the Belvédère area, Elegant Resorts' beautifully furnished chalet Génépi has multiple en suite whirlpool baths, as well as an outdoor hot-tub.

VIP has six impressive chalets including Indiana Lodge, right on the slopes with great views over town and an outdoor hot-tub, and Kublai Lodge, with Indonesian decor, steam room, gym and cinema. Belvedere Chalets has four properties. Scott Dunn Ski has three – in terms of luxury, towards the lower end of this company's increasingly impressive range of properties.

If you like the idea of luxury but want to keep the cost down, consider staying with Bonne Neige down in the old village of Les Allues, served by the gondola linking Brides-les-Bains to Méribel. Les Allodis is a converted barn that makes a real change from the modern properties that dominate in Méribel – all beams and antique furniture, but with mod cons including an outdoor hot-tub.

Courchevel, in the next of the Three Valleys, is well established as the smartest resort in France, and clearly doesn't lack smart chalets. Traditionally, relatively few of them have found their way on to the UK package market, but this seems to be changing.

FlexiSki has two beautiful, rustic 10-bed chalets off the Bellecôte piste – Anemone, one of Courchevel's originals, and the recently built Vizelle, with its splendid top-floor living/dining room. But these two are now rather eclipsed by the recently added pair of chalets Chinchilla and Hermine. Scott Dunn Ski has several properties in Courchevel, of which the undoubted gem is the recently refurbished Aurea, costing twice as much as some of the company's more modest offerings.

A favourite of mine – though far from the swankiest on the UK

market – is Lotus Supertravel's 10-bed chalet Founets, which has a lovely high-ceilinged sitting/dining room and a great position. The company's Plein Sud and Aiguille de Fruit look impressive, too.

Next-door to Courchevel, La Tania has developed quite a range of comfortable chalet properties in its decade of existence, including the best of the Ski Amis range, the 14-bed Balkiss. Snowline have several properties here, too.

Val-d'Isère is the other great chalet resort in France. Scott Dunn's already impressive portfolio here has really grown this last summer, with the acquisition of The Ski Company Ltd's grand enclave of four modern chalets right out at the southern extremity of the resort, with splendid views from their picture windows – Bergerie, Mistral, Lafitenia, all 10-bed, and the 18-bed Chardon. But even these properties are put in the shade by Scott Dunn's 12-bed Eagle's Nest – an extraordinary place, complete with an indoor jet-stream pool, and all four floors linked by lift.

YSE's Mountain Lodges are an old favourite, offering no picture windows but splendidly atmospheric and comfortable living rooms, with stone walls and ample leather sofas. VIP's now has 20 very smart places, 12 of which are spacious, stylish chalet-apartments in their newly-built Aspen Lodge on the main street, with a reception desk, lounge area with coffee bar, and open fireplace. The 200-year-old Farmhouse by the church has received rave reviews and the new Bel Sol (for six) is right by the slopes with designer furnishings. Lotus Supertravel has one luxury contender in the form of chalet Renard.

Chamonix isn't particularly known for luxury chalets, but locally based Collineige has secured an enviable range of highly individual properties, ranging from characterful old houses through rustic retreats to modern architect-designed chalets. Flexiski's brand-new

THE CHALET HOLIDAY IN ITS ORIGINAL FORM

The catered chalet holiday is a uniquely British idea. Tour operators install their own cooks and housekeepers in private chalets which they take over for the season. They package them with travel from the UK, normally offering half-board. Dinner is a no-choice affair at a communal table, including wine unlimited in quantity. You can either book a whole chalet (the smallest typically sleep around six or eight) or book space in a larger chalet that you share with whoever else turns up.

In the early days of the chalet, in the 1960s and 70s, taking a chalet holiday meant roughing it in creaky old buildings, putting up with spartan furniture and paper-thin walls, and with six or more people sharing a bathroom. And the chalet girl – always a girl, back then – was often straight out of college or finishing school, and more intent on having a fun season on the slopes than preparing gourmet meals. Happily, things have changed.

Luxury chalets

and fully equipped eight-bed chalet Bornian looks wonderful, and enjoys a prime location with great views of Mont Blanc.

Morzine too is known mainly for cheap-and-cheerful properties, but Snowline's new Nebraska and Dakota Lodges sound exceptional – and in the nearby backwater of Essert-Romand is the deeply comfortable Chalet Gueret, rebuilt with all mod cons a few years back after the all-wood original burned down. The new Gueret is spacious and welcoming, with sympathetic, locally made furniture.

In Switzerland, Verbier is the chalet capital. Chalet Goodwood is much the best I have visited here – fabulously comfortable and stylish, in a central position. It is now run by Descent International. The company's equally swanky Septième Ciel could scarcely be in a more different location – high on the Savoleyres side of Verbier, a drive from the Place Centrale. Ski Verbier's portfolio includes several glorious properties. At the top of the range is the recently built Attelas, but a double-height living room makes chalet Danny equally compelling. Flexiski's Bouvreuil is a tastefully furnished apartment, and its new 'smart and spacious' chalet Ker Praet sounds impressive.

In Zermatt, Scott Dunn has long been the main source, and has gone up a gear this year with the acquisition of two central, spacious and stylish 10-bed apartments that were briefly offered by the Ski Company, plus three brand-new smaller apartments near the Klein Matterhorn lift station. Total's range here includes the Génépy, stylishly created within a lovely old wooden building.

In Austria, luxury chalets are curiously rare, but in St Anton Lotus Supertravel has the Chiara and Flexiski the Amalien Haus. Simply Ski's stylish and fully equipped Katharina has an excellent position in the centre, with good views from its picture windows.

Weekend breaks

Why a quick fix of the white stuff is addictive

A weekend away with just one day off work can give you three great days on the slopes, leaving you with the feeling of having been away for ages and returning to work feeling really refreshed. And it does not need to cost you an arm and a leg.

Short break ski trips have become much more popular in the last few years, partly because of the growth of budget airlines. I was very sceptical of them before I tried it myself several years ago. But now I am addicted to them. A quick fix of the white stuff really does seem almost as good as a week. I have had successful weekends all over the place. My first was to the classic weekend destination of Chamonix, which has local areas suitable for all types of weather and snow conditions. Next came Zell am See in Austria with skiing on the glacier at Kaprun. Then a weekend in Val-d'Isère at the time of the Premier Neige race – great fun. Other great pre-Xmas weekends have been in Courchevel and Saas Fee. A January weekend in Courmayeur one year was followed by a two-centre break in Lech and Ischgl the next. Then there was a long weekend taking in Courmayeur, the Grands Montets and the Portes du Soleil circuit in three days.

And I've met many other weekend addicts, including people who rent apartments for the season and go out every other weekend and others who book up 12 or so weekend flights well in advance and decide where to go when they know where the best snow is.

ARRANGING THE WEEKEND

The key to making the most of your time is to catch late flights each way – so it helps if you live near a suitable airport. Swiss has well-timed flights for Geneva from Heathrow and Zürich from Heathrow and London City (but book early as the late flights are very popular). EasyJet has suitable flights from both Gatwick and Luton to Geneva and Zürich and from Luton to Nice and Liverpool to Geneva. Alitalia has good flights to Milan. Ryanair has decently timed flights from Stansted to Salzburg, Turin and Verona.

We don't recommend flying to Munich if you are travelling out on a Friday or back on a Sunday – the queues on the motorway can be horrendous, as the whole of Munich seems to go weekend skiing and the airport is on the far side of the city from the Alps. Similarly, allow plenty of time if you are driving back to Lyon airport on a Sunday evening – we encountered very heavy traffic after leaving Courchevel in what we had thought was good time.

Booking a rental car or taxi in advance is usually cheaper than arranging one after you arrive. Several tour operators can arrange the rental as part of a complete weekend package. Taxis can be ridiculously expensive compared with the cost of renting a car. For example, you would expect to pay over £200 each way between Geneva airport and Courchevel by taxi if you book locally – but renting a small car for the weekend would be much less than the one-way taxi price. In our experience train and bus times between airports and resorts are more suitable for week-long visitors than for weekenders looking for maximum time on the slopes.

Using a weekend specialist, such as one of those advertising in this chapter, makes sense if you don't want the hassle of making your

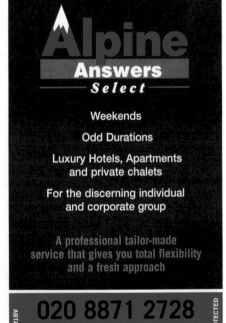

own arrangements. They know the best resorts to go to, can arrange transfers by their own staff or through local companies, and have special deals with hotels that do them good room rates or that might not otherwise take weekend bookings. Some arrange special weekend courses (eg with off-piste guides or even heli-skiing weekends) and can arrange groups of similar standard for you to ski with if you are travelling alone. And local tour operator representatives and contacts can save you valuable time arranging lift passes (beware of big weekend queues on Saturday and Sunday mornings) and equipment hire and advise on local restaurants and other facilities. Last season EasyJet teamed up with uptoyou.com to offer flexible breaks linked to their flights and web site.

CHOOSING A RESORT

As for choosing a resort, there are various considerations. Many people think they should go for a resort within a short drive of their arrival airport. But by definition, resorts close to major airports are close to large numbers of people poised to hit the slopes on fine weekends, which can mean queues for the lifts, crowds on the slopes and competition for hotel beds. These days most resorts are within striking distance of a major airport and an hour's extra transfer time is not really that much if it gets you to quieter slopes.

Resorts close to Geneva include Chamonix, St-Gervais, Megève and Les Contamines (all in the Mont Blanc area and sharing an area lift pass), Flaine and La Clusaz in France, and Villars and Les Diablerets in Switzerland. All these are within an hour or so of Geneva by car. Verbier and Crans-Montana in Switzerland are a bit further, as are the Three Valleys and other Tarentaise resorts – Val-

d'Isère can be reached in under three hours now – and Morzine and the Portes du Soleil resorts in France. EasyJet's Nice flight puts Isola 2000 within a 90km/55 mile drive.

Flying to Zürich opens up lots of other possibilities. Flims, Davos and Klosters are the nearest big resorts, and the less-well-known resorts of Engelberg and Andermatt are within easy reach. St Anton and Lech in Austria are within striking distance, as are the resorts of the Montafon valley. Ryanair's Salzburg flights make most of the eastern Austrian resorts a short drive away.

In Italy, Courmayeur is a popular weekend destination. Now that the Mont Blanc tunnel is open again, it is easily accessible from Geneva. Resorts such as Champoluc, Sauze d'Oulx and Sestriere are easily accessible from Milan or Turin. Ryanair's Verona flights put you very near the Sella Ronda resorts and Cortina d'Ampezzo.

Unless you are booking at short notice when you know the snow is good, we'd be tempted to avoid low resorts such as Megève and Villars – unless you have transport to get you to more snow-sure slopes. And because you don't want your whole weekend ruined by a white-out if it snows all the time, we'd also be tempted to avoid very high resorts where the skiing is entirely above the tree line – this rules out places such as Tignes and Val-Thorens in France, Obergurgl in Austria and Cervinia in Italy.

Another consideration is that hotels in big, popular winter resorts such as St Anton, Verbier and Val-d'Isère now often refuse to take weekend bookings except in very low season (eg early January or late March) because they can get more profitable week-long bookings. But many of the more summer-oriented resorts, which generally have accommodation spare in winter, are well worth considering – places such as Chamonix, Morzine, Engelberg, Villars and Mürren.

WHAT ABOUT PRICE?

The cost can vary enormously. The flight and transfer or car hire are the expensive fixed costs and obviously make a weekend proportionately more expensive than a full week. But as we said before, you do get three days' skiing (half a full week) for only one day off work, and the three days makes a substantial break. A four-night break is, of course, even better – it only costs two days off work and means you can travel out and back on Thursday and Monday evenings (quieter than Fridays and Sundays).

In general, through a good specialist tour operator, you can expect to pay from around £350 a head for flights, car hire and a double room in a 3-star hotel for three nights, assuming two people sharing. With lift passes and meals you could be looking at around £500. For a 4-star hotel add another £100 or so.

MIDWEEK BREAKS

If you can get away midweek there are many potential advantages. Flights (especially on the budget airlines) should be cheaper and accommodation may be too. And resorts that get busy at weekends such as Morzine, Verbier, Courmayeur and Champoluc can be very quiet mid-week in low season. Believe it or not but some people actually go skiing for one day. Airtours is running 2004 day trips to Chamonix from Manchester on 5 February and from Gatwick on 10 March. If all goes well you'll be on the slopes by 11.30am and have five hours before the lifts close, followed by a spot of après-ski and a flight which arrives home around 10.30pm.

by **Dave Watts**

Drive to the Alps

And ski where you please

by **Chris Allan**

More and more people from Britain are doing what the French, the Germans and the Dutch have done for years, and driving to their Alpine resorts. It has various advantages. For many people, it's just less hassle than checking in for a flight from Gatwick at dawn, and less tedious than sitting around waiting for a delayed charter plane that's stuck in Majorca. For families (especially those going self-catering), it simplifies the job of moving half the household to the Alps. If there are four or five people in your party, the cost can be lower than travelling by air. And for a few adventurous people, taking a car opens up the exciting possibility of touring around several resorts in one trip.

Cross-Channel ferries are faster and more pleasant than ever, with the possibility of a seriously good lunch on P&O's short crossings as an alternative to the quicker shuttle-trains through the tunnel. And the motorway networks in northern France and on the approaches to the Alps have improved immensely. You can now get to most resorts easily in a day, if you're based in south-east England.

For us, the freedom factor is the key. If the snow's bad in your resort, if the lift queues are horrendous or if the resort you've plumped for is a let-down, car drivers can try somewhere else.

Another plus-point is that you can extend the standard six-day holiday by two days by taking only one extra day off work – crossing the Channel early on a Friday morning and returning nine days later on the Sunday evening. On the outward journey, we often spend a day in a different resort before moving on to our final destination late on the Saturday. After a full day on the slopes on the final Saturday, driving for a few hours before stopping for the night means you won't find Sunday's journey too demanding, and you may even have time for a traditional French Sunday lunch.

AS YOU LIKE IT

If you fancy visiting several resorts, you can use one as a base and make day-trips to others when it suits you. This way, you can still take advantage of package holiday prices.

The key to turning this kind of holiday into a success is to go for a base that offers easy road access to other resorts. Our suggestions for France are in a separate chapter. A good choice in Austria is the Tirol: the resorts east of Innsbruck offer many options. Söll is a convenient base for exploring resorts such as Alpbach and Kitzbühel. Further

P&O Ferries has new twin super-ferries operating on its Dover–Calais route, setting new standards of comfort.

The two massive ships combine luxurious on-board facilities with a significant increase in capacity over the ships they replace, carrying 650 cars and 2,000 passengers. But for us the key feature is common to all seven P&O Dover–Calais ferries: the on-board branch of the famous West End restaurant, Langan's Brasserie. The seasonal menus – £15.50 for two courses, £19.25 for three – are excellent, as were the wines we tried. Recommended.

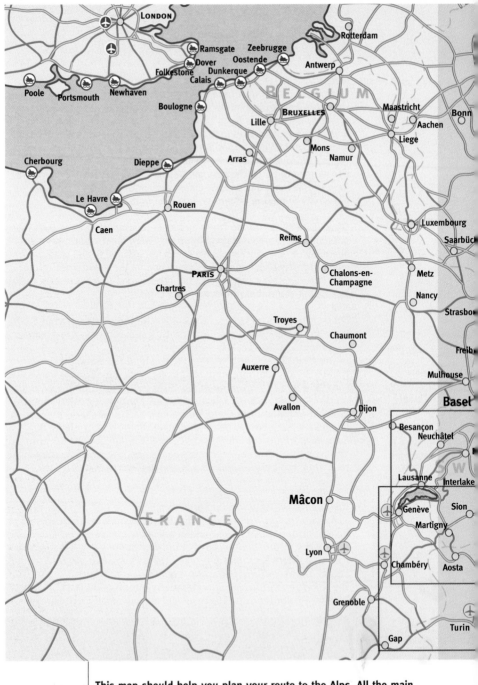

This map should help you plan your route to the Alps. All the main routes from the Channel and all the routes up into the mountains funnel through (or close to) three 'gateways', picked out on the map in larger type – Mâcon, Basel and Ulm. Decide which gateway suits your destination, and pick a route to it. Occasionally, using different Channel ports will lead you to use different gateways.

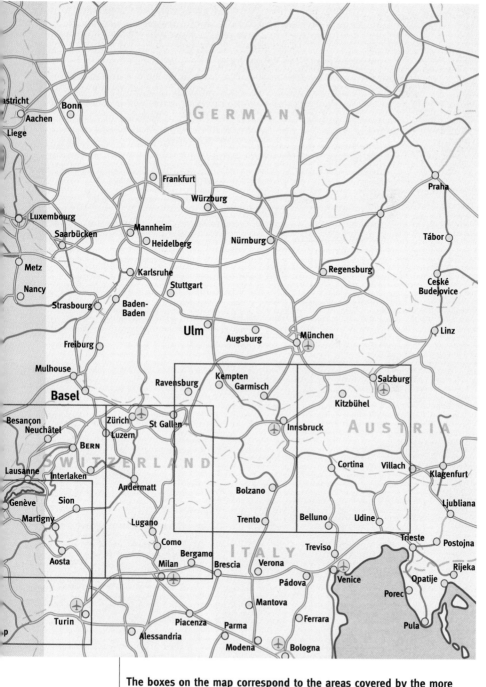

The boxes on the map correspond to the areas covered by the more detailed maps at the start of the main country sections of the book:
Austria page 110
France page 202
Italy page 376
Switzerland page 424

east, you can use Zell am See as a base to visit Bad Gastein and
Saalbach. Western Austria is not ideal for this sort of holiday, but
from St Anton you could make day-trips to Zürs, Ischgl and Serfaus.

AROUND THE ALPS IN SEVEN DAYS

If you want to see as much of the Alps as possible, consider making a
Grand Tour by car, moving every day or two to a different resort and
enjoying the complete freedom of going where you want, when you
want. Out of high season there's no need to book accommodation
before you go, so you can decide at the last minute which part of the
Alps and which countries to visit – where the snow is best, perhaps.

A touring holiday doesn't mean you'll be spending more time on
the road than on the piste – provided you plan your route carefully.
An hour's drive after the lifts have shut is all it need take.

Italy is far more suitable for tourers than day-trippers, provided
you're prepared to put up with some slow drives on winding passes.
You could start in Livigno, drive to Bormio and then to the
Dolomites, visiting Madonna di Campiglio and Selva, and finish
your Italian expedition in Cortina.

The major thing that you have to watch out for with a touring
holiday is the cost of accommodation. Checking into a resort hotel
as an independent traveller for a night or two doesn't come cheap.
You can save money by staying down the valley – and you don't
necessarily have to drive up to the slopes in the morning. For
example, you can take a funicular from Bourg-St-Maurice up to Les
Arcs; a gondola links Brides-les-Bains to Méribel.

Drive to the French Alps

To make the most of them

by **Chris Gill**

If you've read the preceding chapter, you'll have gathered that we are keen on driving to the Alps. But we're particularly keen on driving to the French Alps. The drive is a relatively short one, whereas many of the transfers to major French resorts from Geneva airport are relatively long. And the route from the Channel is through France rather than Germany, which for Francophiles like us means it's a pleasant prospect rather than a grim one.

TRAVEL TIME

The French Alps are the number-one destination for British car-borne skiers. The journey time is surprisingly short. From Calais, for example, you can comfortably cover the 900km/560 miles to Chamonix in about nine hours plus stops – with the exception of the final few miles, the whole journey is on motorways. And except on peak weekends the traffic is relatively light, especially if you steer clear of Paris. Look back at the map of Europe in the previous chapter to see what's involved.

With some southern exceptions, all the resorts of the French Alps are within a day's driving range, provided you cross the Channel early in the day (or overnight). Weekend traffic jams used to make the journey from Albertville to the Tarentaise resorts (from the Trois Vallées to Val-d'Isère) a nightmare for drivers and coach passengers alike; thanks to road improvements these are largely a thing of the past, but on peak-season Saturdays you can still encounter serious queues around Moutiers, where there is a traffic management scheme involving traffic lights placed well away from the town, to minimise pollution.

DAY-TRIP BASES

Most people driving to the French Alps do it simply because they find it a more relaxing way to get themselves, their kit and perhaps their kids to their chosen resort. But, as we have explained in the previous chapter, having a car opens up different kinds of holiday for the more adventurous. Day-tripping, for example.

In the southern French Alps, Serre-Chevalier and Montgenèvre are ideal bases for day-tripping. They are within easy reach of one another, and Montgenèvre is at one end of the Milky Way lift network, which includes Sauze d'Oulx and Sestriere in Italy – you can drive on to these resorts, or reach them by lift and piste. On the French side of the border, a few miles south, Puy-St-Vincent is an underrated resort that is well worth a visit for a day – as is Risoul, a little further south. The major resorts of Alpe-d'Huez and Les Deux-Alpes are also within range, as is the cult off-piste resort of La Grave. Getting to them involves crossing a high pass, but it's a major route linking Grenoble to Briançon and all points south, and is kept open pretty reliably.

The Chamonix valley is an ideal destination for day-trippers. The Mont-Blanc lift pass covers Chamonix, Les Contamines, Megève and others. Flaine and its satellites are fairly accessible – and so are Verbier in Switzerland, if the intervening passes are open, and Courmayeur in Italy, now that the Mont Blanc tunnel is open once

again. You could stay in a valley town such as Cluses, to escape resort prices altogether, or base yourself in a relatively cheap resort such as St-Gervais.

MOVING ON
A look at the map in this chapter shows that a different approach will pay dividends in the Tarentaise region of France. Practically all the resorts here – from Valmorel to Val-d'Isère – are found at the end of long winding roads up from the main valley. You could visit them all from a base such as Aime, but it would be hard work. If instead you stayed in a different resort each night, moving on from one to the next in the early evening, you could have the trip of a lifetime. Imagine a week in which you could explore the Three Valleys, La Plagne, Les Arcs and Val-d'Isère/Tignes.

GETTING THERE
The map in our Driving to the Alps chapter, ahead of this one, shows the main routes across France to the Alps. Whatever route you prefer across the Channel, the gateway to the French Alps is Mâcon – though if you're taking a short crossing to Calais, this may be only roughly true. Your route south is via Reims, Troyes and Dijon; but if you are heading for Geneva, to get to the northern French Alps, you no longer have to tangle with the busy A6 from Paris via Beaune to Mâcon and Lyon. The relatively new A39 autoroute south from Dijon means that you can head for Bourg-en-Bresse, staying well east of Mâcon. If you need an overnight stop north of Dijon, there are plenty of characterful towns to consider – Arras, St-Quentin, Laon, Troyes. Reims makes a particularly neat stopover – the autoroute passes close to the centre, with its impressive Gothic cathedral

From the more westerly Channel ports of Le Havre or Caen your route to Mâcon sounds dead simple: the A13 to Paris then the A6 south. But you have to get through or around Paris in the process.

The most direct way around the city is the notorious périphérique – a hectic, multi-lane urban motorway close to the centre, with exits every few hundred yards and traffic that is either worryingly fast-moving or jammed solid. If the périphérique is jammed it takes ages. The more reliable alternative is to take a series of motorways and dual carriageways through the south-west fringes of Greater Paris. One such route is signed fairly clearly, but with the aid of a detailed map (such as that in the Michelin road atlas) you can take a more direct route from Versailles to the A6 near Orly.

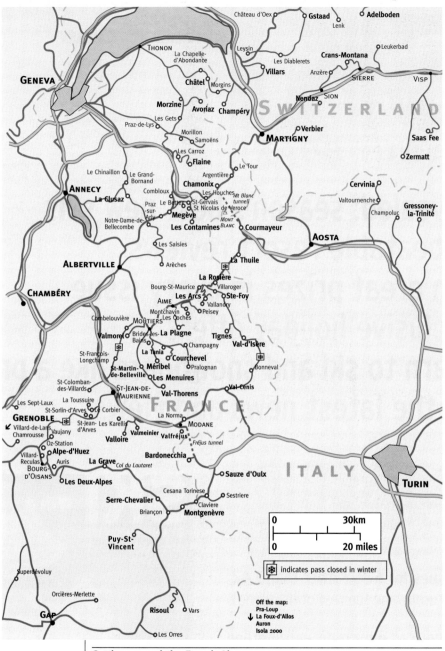

Getting around the French Alps

Pick the right gateway – Geneva, Chambéry or Grenoble – and you can hardly go wrong. The approach to Serre-Chevalier and Montgenèvre involves the 2058m/6,750ft Col du Lauteret; but the road is a major one and kept clear of snow or reopened quickly after a fall. Crossing the French-Swiss border between Chamonix and Verbier involves two closure-prone passes – the Montets and the Forclaz. When necessary, one-way traffic runs beside the tracks through the rail tunnel beneath the passes.

Flying to the Alps

Competition means good deals for consumers

by **Dave Watts**

EasyJet started the first cheap scheduled flights to the Alps by flying to Geneva six years ago. They have since taken over their rival Go and have by far the biggest range of flights to the key airports of Geneva and Zürich. They are also the only budget airline not to charge extra for carrying skis or snowboard (which can add up to £30 to the cost). The other cut-price airlines generally offer different airport options. And all this competition has made the bigger, established airlines smarten up their acts and offer some competitive deals. This is great news for independent skiers and riders, who can now get flights for under £100 return, rent a car for a week for under £200 (£50 each between four) and have affordable holidays they arrange themselves. Last year EasyJet started a service on their web site that allowed you to book accommodation and transfers too.

I have used budget flights a lot over the last few seasons. Nearly all flights have been pretty much on time, and their no-frills service and pay-as-you-eat food is all you need on a short flight of 90 minutes or less. They are particularly convenient for me because I live only 20 minutes from Stansted and 40 minutes from Luton, the airports they mainly operate from. From Heathrow, Swiss has well-timed flights for weekend or short-break trips and offers competitive fares. It can be cheaper than the 'cheap' airlines when flights start to get full.

All the cheap airlines are ticketless. None of them works through travel agents – you book direct with the airlines. They try to encourage bookings on the Internet rather than by telephone because it is cheaper for them, and there's usually a discount of a few pounds for booking on the web. You pay by credit card (for which there is often an extra charge) or debit card and all you need is a confirmation number. Prices vary according to demand, and in general the cheapest flights are for midweek early or late in the day, booked months in advance. As a flight fills up, the prices go up. But you may also get a bargain by booking at the last minute if the flight is not full. At their lowest, prices can be £40 return or less; at their peak they can be well over £200 return. I booked four March Saturday to Saturday flights to Geneva with EasyJet in July this year as soon as they released their winter flights for just £47 each return.

In general, flights have got more flexible. Although the budget airlines won't normally give you a refund if you decide not to travel, most will now allow you to change the flight time or route and the name of the passenger – but at a cost of perhaps £15 each way for each change (so £60 if you change both flights and passengers both ways). But check when you book because the rules change.

Policies on carrying skis and boards and on excess baggage vary. EasyJet has a 20kg baggage allowance plus 10kg of sports equipment such as skis. Ryanair has a measly baggage allowance of only 15kg and charges £15 each way for skis or board. Flybe and bmibaby both have 20kg baggage allowances and charge £10 each way for skis. Excess baggage is generally charged at £4/kg each way and can add up quickly. We have been told by some check-in staff that they have been instructed to enforce the baggage limits strictly as the airlines see this as a way of making money even if the fare is cheap.

AIRLINE CONTACT DETAILS

Phone numbers and web sites for the major airlines are listed on page 670.

Key airports for skiers include Geneva (for most French resorts and some Swiss and Italian), Zürich (for eastern Swiss and western Austrian resorts), Lyon (for many French resorts), Milan (for most Italian resorts except the Dolomites), Munich (for most Austrian resorts) and Barcelona (for Andorra and the Pyrenees), plus some smaller airports that we mention below.

EasyJet has several flights a day from Luton, Gatwick, East Midlands and Liverpool to Geneva, Barcelona and Nice (only 90km/55 miles from Isola 2000) and from Luton and Gatwick to Zürich and Milan. It flies from Stansted to Lyon and Munich and from Stansted and some other airports to Venice (for the Dolomites) and Malaga (for Sierra Nevada).

Ryanair flies from Stansted to Milan, Turin (nearer than Milan for western Italian resorts), Venice and Verona (for the Dolomites), Salzburg (very convenient for most Austrian resorts), Friedrichshafen (just over the German border but handy for western Austrian resorts), Klagenfurt (for the Carinthia region of Austria), Carcassonne and Perpignan (both for Andorra and the Pyrenees), Girona (for Andorra).

Flybe has flights from Southampton and Jersey and Guernsey to Geneva and from some regional airports to Milan and Toulouse. And bmibaby has daily flights from Manchester and weekly flights from Cardiff, Teesside and East Midlands to Geneva and some other relevant airports.

Swiss International Air Lines operates several direct flights a day from Heathrow, London City, Birmingham, Manchester and Dublin to Zürich and from Heathrow to Geneva. Late flights (8pm or so) to and from Heathrow and London City make short breaks particularly easy if you live in the south-east – but book well in advance as these late flights are very popular. There is also a useful Saturday flight between Heathrow and Sion, less than half an hour's transfer to, for example, Nendaz (for Verbier's slopes) and Crans-Montana, and a bit further to Saas-Fee, Zermatt and Verbier. Swiss carries skis or snowboard free on top of your 20kg baggage allowance. Check their web site for the lowest fares.

Alitalia has up to eight flights a day direct from Heathrow to Milan (five to Malpensa airport and three to Linate), which give access to many of the Italian resorts. From Milan, you can get connecting flights to Venice and Verona (both handy for the Dolomites). They allow 3kg extra baggage for skis or board.

British Airways goes to Geneva, Zürich, Munich, Milan, Venice and Verona.

Travel by train

For eight days on snow

by **Dave Watts**

Taking the train to the Alps can be a great way to get more time on the slopes without taking more time off work. You can leave on Friday night, arriving in your resort on Saturday morning, and return on the following Saturday night, arriving back home on the Sunday – eight days' skiing for five days out of the office. Even if you opt for a different service that doesn't deliver the eight-day week, travelling by train is one of the most restful ways to get to the Alps.

The most popular train destination, with several different direct and indirect services, is the Tarentaise valley in France. You can step off the train in Bourg-St-Maurice and on to a funicular straight up to Arc 1600, and there are quick bus transfers to the other famous mega-resorts of this region – Val-d'Isère, Tignes, La Plagne, Courchevel and Méribel, with slightly longer transfers to Les Menuires and Val-Thorens.

But you can travel by train, one way or another, to many other resorts. And many traditional resorts, especially in Switzerland, are on the rail network and therefore reachable without resorting to buses. How many times you'll have to change trains is another matter. You can also put your car on a motorail service (but no longer from Calais).

DIRECT TRAIN SERVICES TO THE FRENCH ALPS

Since 1997, Eurostar has offered a truly direct service to the Alps – you board the train at London Waterloo or Ashford in Kent and disembark at Moûtiers or Bourg-St-Maurice in the Tarentaise valley, without changing trains en route. The special winter services will run from 19 December through to mid-April. Standard return tickets cost from £179 (£269 for first class, which includes meals on board). Seats can also be booked as part of a package holiday. There's an overnight service which allows you two extra days' skiing or boarding – it leaves on Friday night, arriving early on Saturday morning, and returns late Saturday evening, arriving back in London on Sunday morning. The service uses standard Eurostar carriages with no special sleeping arrangements – you just doze (or not) in your seat. The daytime service gives you no more than the standard six days on the slopes: both outward and return services leave on Saturday morning, arriving late afternoon. The outbound service also stops at Ashford, in Kent, and Aime (between Moûtiers and Bourg-St-Maurice). The return service doesn't stop at Aime (due to passport control reasons).

All the other train services to the Alps involve a change somewhere along the line, but they can still be fairly convenient and also allow for extra time on the slopes. Unlike Eurostar, many of the other services are equipped with sleeping compartments.

The Snowtrain is another weekly overnight service to the Tarentaise giving an eight-day week on the slopes, but it starts from Calais. It runs from 26 December until 12 March, leaving Calais on Friday night and arriving in the Alps the following morning – first stop is Chambéry, then Albertville, Moûtiers, Aime, Landry and finally Bourg-St-Maurice. For the return journey you leave the Alps on Saturday evening, arriving in Calais early on Sunday morning. You cross the Channel by ferry from Dover (you can pay a supplement for a coach transfer from London or make your own arrangements and travel as a foot passenger). The train works on a charter basis and can be booked through UK tour operators – they have allocated spaces on each service. Overnight amenities include on-board couchettes (six drop-down berths to a compartment) and a disco/bar. Beware, it can get very noisy and crowded. It is possible to book a compartment for the exclusive use of four or five people on both legs of the journey. Booking independently costs £149 return for most of the season.

There is a similar Friday night sleeper service to the Tarentaise starting from Paris. It runs from 19 December until 2 April. You take the Eurostar to Paris from London Waterloo and change trains at Paris Gare du Nord for an overnight service to the Alps. The return journey leaves the Alps on Saturday evening, arriving in Paris early on Sunday morning. It costs £209 return including couchettes for most of the season. Some tour operators offer it as part of a package.

There are a number of indirect services available on the French railway throughout the week, but most mean crossing Paris from the Gare du Nord to the Gare de Lyon or Gare d'Austerlitz – the change of station is not difficult, though, with a direct metro, regular buses and plenty of taxis at your disposal. Indirect services to many Alpine destinations via Brussels or Lille also run every day of the week and involve only a change of platform. This can be easier than going via Paris, and the timing of the slower overnight services via Brussels may be more suitable for some holidaymakers; the services tend to be less frequent and are often more expensive, but are worth considering at peak dates.

Motorail (or autotrain) is another option, getting your car to the Alps without having to drive it. The French services have been cut back and the main option left is Paris to Lyon, going out overnight on Friday and back overnight on Saturday. An alternative is using a German DB AutoZug service from Dusseldorf, Hamburg or Cologne. Destinations include Salzburg, Innsbruck and Villach in Austria, Bolzano (in the Dolomites), Lörach (near the Swiss border at Basel), Narbonne (for Andorra and the Pyrenees) and Munich. Motorail will take some of the strain out the journey, save on hotel and petrol costs and mileage on your car, and allow you to visit several resorts.

For more details of French rail services contact Rail Europe on 08701 244 646 for overnight ski trains or 08705 848 848 for Eurostar trains. Or visit www.raileurope.co.uk.

Corporate ski trips

A great way to motivate your staff and clients

by **Dave Watts**

There are all kinds of reasons why companies find it valuable to get staff or clients together for a bit of a treat outside the usual business environment. Common ones include team building, rewarding performance, bonding with clients and holding conferences in exotic locations. And there are all kinds of places you can go and all kinds of activities you can lay on. But few can rival ski resorts and skiing for sheer impact. We do quite a bit of skiing, of course, but had never been involved in the corporate kind until last season's City Ski Championships. We were so impressed that this season we are one of its sponsors. If you are thinking of a corporate trip the easiest way to arrange it is through a specialist events organiser or tour operator who can take the hassle off your hands. As Chris Scudds of Alpine Events says, 'Our job is to make your job – before, during and after the event – as easy as possible and the event itself a resounding success.'

WHAT'S THE ATTRACTION?

The mountain/skiing/boarding environment is one that has lots of advantages for corporate events. The clear fresh air, sun and snowy, dramatic mountain scenery have a huge and immediate impact on people arriving from the European lowlands and their dreary winters. There is a great sense of fun and liberation and people are happy to cast inhibitions aside and let their hair down. And a winter sports break need not appeal just to skiers. Helena Kania went on a team building weekend to Morzine organised by her company Cable & Wireless and told us, 'I didn't set foot on skis or board but just loved the fresh air, sunshine, views and meeting up with the others in mountain restaurants. And we all got on much better when we got back to work after sharing a great experience.' The best resorts have a range of activities available, including ones that will fit naturally into the evening timetable. There are excellent and capacious hotels, many with conference facilities. The flights to the Alps from northern Europe are short. And the perceived status of ski resorts is high – whoever you invite will be in no doubt that they are being given a treat (as will their friends and business colleagues).

73

Caroline Odman of Singer & Friedlander on her way to winning the 2003 City Ski Championships; she beat all the men as well as the women
→

Corporate entertainment closer to home
Sailing in the Solent

- Entertain your most valued clients
- Reward your hard-working staff
- Weld your managers into a real team
- Get the attention of key journalists

Take them out for a day's sailing in the Solent on one (or more) of our imposing, powerful yachts, with lunch in a lively port or at anchor in a quiet creek. Your guests will find the day satisfying and memorable – quite unlike other, less involving forms of corporate entertainment. And you'll have an unrivalled opportunity to get to know them better.

Yacht Ventures

t 01373 835201
www.yachtventures.com
info@yachtventures.com

WHAT SORT OF CORPORATE EVENT WILL WORK?

More or less any event that is better done away from the office will work in the Alps. Examples of events that have been successfully held in ski resorts include those with these objectives:

• communication to middle managers of a new business strategy
• concentrated attempt to crack a crucial business problem
• staff morale boost after recent business difficulties
• new product launches to sales staff or key customers
• gathering together of staff from geographically spread sites
• team-building by giving groups shared objectives
• sales incentive 'prizes'
• client 'reward' to build business loyalty
• Christmas parties with a different feel to them.

HOW LONG A TRIP AND HOW BIG A GROUP?

Corporate trips of a few days are the norm – Thursday to Sunday, say. But you can have two full, action-packed days in the Alps by leaving on Friday after work and returning late on Sunday night – arriving back at work on Monday morning refreshed, invigorated and remotivated. Some companies take over a cluster of chalets for a week or two and have different groups moving in and out, staying for a variety of durations. Others hire helicopters for airport transfers and just go for one night. In principle, your group can be any size you like. A lot of groups are 30 to 50. But they can be much smaller. And much larger. When we were in Whistler last year the whole of the 550 room Fairmont Chateau Whistler had been taken over by a medical conference. With really small groups, be aware that the social success is going to depend on how the individuals mesh.

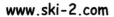

WHERE TO GO AND WHERE TO STAY?

How easy it is to settle on a resort for a corporate trip depends hugely on the nature of your project. If it's a dozen people travelling out together for a relaxed couple of days, you're really organising nothing more than a short holiday and a swanky chalet might be good. If you are getting a large group together from all corners of the globe and need serious conference facilities, you're playing a different ball game. Finding the right accommodation, meeting rooms and support services can be a real headache, and it's in dealing with this sort of challenge that the services of a tour operator or event management company will really pay off.

Because corporate trips tend to be short, you'll want to keep the travel time to the minimum, so that it doesn't dominate the proceedings. Transfer times from airports to resorts generally range from one to four hours, and you'll probably want to operate at the lower end of that range if you can.

You may want to have a particular range of activities available. Or you may want your choice of resort to carry a message to your 'delegates'. Choosing Courchevel or St Moritz is effectively saying 'No expense spared – nothing but the best for you.' Whatever you do, choose a resort with a good snow record and/or extensive snow-making. You don't want to invite people on a skiing break to find there's no snow. Avoid early season for the same reason. A March trip to a high resort will mean good snow and hopefully strong sunshine too. Don't get hung up on size – with only a couple of days to spend on the slopes, almost any resort has plenty of terrain, especially with good local guides to help you make the most of it.

ORGANISING THE SKIING

A typical corporate group will naturally contain a mixture of experienced skiers and non-skiers. You'll need to make sure everyone is equipped with suitable clothing, equipment and lift passes. You'll also want to organise tuition or guiding – preferably just for your group rather than stuffing your guests in ski school classes. Make sure you have enough instructors/guides so that you can form groups of equal ability.

Lunch in a mountain restaurant can be an opportunity to get your group together, but for a large and disparate group it can present some challenges. Another possibility, in good weather, is a swanky picnic, with plenty of champagne buried in the snow.

You might want to think about a race for delegates, though bear in mind that this won't appeal to the complete beginners in the group. Other forms of competition such as on-snow treasure hunts could be used to include non-skiers too.

WHAT OTHER ACTIVITIES?

Because it's likely that not everyone will want to go skiing or boarding, you'll need to be able to offer some other activities with a broad appeal. This may influence your choice of resort. Typical activities to consider would include dog-sledding, snowmobiling, skating, curling, tobogganing, ballooning, swimming, flights in planes or helicopters. Bear in mind that activities like these tend to occupy relatively short, defined periods of time. So you may need quite a range of activities to keep people busy all day. Then there are the evenings to consider. They are a time when all the group can be brought together, so it's important to think about how you're going

THE CORPORATE
SKI COMPANY

If you want to organise a winter sports event then you must call the specialist.

- With over 13 years of experience in planning and operating over 200 winter sports events, we have the knowledge and contacts required

- We work in Europe, Canada and the USA

- All programmes can combine skiing and non-skiing, meetings and presentations with social and fun activities

For more details contact:

Alex Jackson

The Corporate Ski Company

TEL: 020 7627 5500   Fax: 020 7622 6701

e-mail: alexj@vantagepoint.co.uk

www.thecorporateskicompany.co.uk

FULL MEMBER

ITMA
INCENTIVE TRAVEL &
MEETINGS ASSOCIATION

Corporate ski trips

flexiski corporate ski weekends

FlexiSki offers you tailor-made itineraries with expert advice and meticulous planning, staying in luxury chalets & first class hotels at...

St Anton, St Christoph, Lech, Chamonix, Courchevel 1850, Davos, Klosters, St Moritz and Verbier

for more information or a copy of our brochure please contact us...

tel   **0870 90 90 754**   email   reservations@flexiski.com
fax   0870 90 90 329   web   www.flexiski.com

to use those opportunities to best effect. You can organise activities with more of a team emphasis, and you can create social events that reinforce your message – perhaps taking over a whole bar or a mountain restaurant, for example. In the right resort, dinner in a mountain restaurant could be followed by dangerous descents on skis or toboggans.

MANAGEMENT ISSUES

Like any business project, a skiing trip brings its own administrative burdens. As well as making it all happen smoothly – which means managing the delegates as tightly as the suppliers of all the components making up the trip – someone has to control expenditure, and provide clear, always up-to-date information. This is a key area to sort out with your organising company.

SWISS INTERNATIONAL CITY SKI CHAMPIONSHIPS

The City Ski Championships have been organised by weekend skiing specialist Momentum Ski and held annually in Courmayeur in Italy's Aosta valley since 2000. Last season former Olympic gold medallist Tommy Moe of the USA and Britain's downhill star of the 1980s Konrad Bartelski got the event off to a flying start and not surprisingly Moe had the fastest overall time of the day. Around 200 skiers from 40 City firms raced and the overall City winner (much to some male chauvinists' dismay) was a woman: Caroline Odman of Singer & Friedlander who ripped down the course in just 54.62 seconds. The fastest man was Filippo Guerrini-Maraldi of Lloyds, who came in just 0.08 of a second behind. The team event winner was Accenture.

Tennis star Annabel Croft won the prize for unluckiest skier of the weekend – she fractured her wrist in the Fat Face training clinic the previous day. But she had a great time cheering on the others on the wonderful sunny day that we had for the race. And the race is only part of the attraction of the weekend. There was a welcome drinks party on the Friday evening, dinner at various restaurants, late night drinks in the Bar Roma, a race-side buffet on the piste, champagne reception courtesy of Veuve Clicquot, followed by gala presentation dinner in the evening and then ... clubbing at Poppie's till dawn followed by free Bloody Marys on the mountain next morning.

The 2004 event sponsored by Swiss International Airlines is from 5 to 8 February and promises to be even better with an additional dual slalom and ladies performance courses (including spa treatments!). Links of London is providing the trophies, Volvo the official cars, the London Capital Club is hosting the welcome drinks (and pre- and post- race parties in London) and the Ski Club of GB and Where to Ski and Snowboard are media partners. For more details contact Momentum Ski on 020 7371 9111 or see www.cityskichampionships.com.

Choosing your resort

Get it right first time

Most people get to go skiing or boarding only once or twice a year – and then only for a week at a time. So choosing the right resort is crucially important. This book is designed to help you get it right first time. Here is some advice on how to use our information to best effect – particularly for the benefit of readers with relatively narrow experience of different resorts. Chamonix, Châtel and Courchevel are all French resorts, but they are as similar as chalk and Camembert. Consider resorts in other countries – Alpbach in Austria, say, or Zermatt in Switzerland – and the differences become even more pronounced. And once you start to consider resorts in North America as well as those in Europe, the range of variation becomes extremely wide.

Lots of factors need to be taken into account. The weight you attach to each of them depends on your own personal preferences, and on the make-up of the group you are going on holiday with. On page 89 you'll find 20 shortlists of resorts which are outstanding in various key respects.

Each resort chapter is organised in the same way, to help you choose the right resort. This short introduction takes you through the structure and what you will find under each heading we use.

WHICH RESORT?

We start each chapter with a one-line verdict, in which we aim to sum up the resort in a few words. If you like the sound of it, you might want to go next to our What it costs rating, in the margin. These ratings, ranging from ①②③④⑤⑥ to ①②③④⑤⑥ , reflect the total cost of a week's holiday from Britain, including a typical package of flights plus half-board accommodation, a lift pass and meals and drinks on the spot. As you might expect with a six-point scale, three means on the low side of average, four means on the high side. Further on, in the margin text, we give the cost of lift passes in local currency; these are for the 2002/03 season. Below the What it costs rating, in the How it rates section, we rate each resort from 11 points of view – the more stars the better. (All these star ratings are brought together in one chart, which follows this chapter.) Still looking at the information in the margin, in most chapters we have a What's new section; this is likely to be of most use and interest in resorts you already know from past visits.

For major resorts, the next things to look at are our lists of the main good and bad points about the resort and its slopes, picked out with ➕ and ➖. These lists are followed by a summary in **bold type**, in which we've aimed to weigh up the pros and cons, coming off the fence and giving our view of who might like the resort. These sections should give you a good idea of whether the resort is likely to suit *you,* and whether you should read our detailed analysis of it.

You'll know by now whether this is, for example, a high, hideous, convenient, purpose-built resort with superb, snow-sure slopes for all standards of skier or boarder but absolutely no nightlife, or whether it's a pretty, traditional village with gentle wooded skiing, ideal for beginners if only there was some snow. We then look at each aspect in more detail.

THE RESORT

Resorts vary enormously in character and charm. At the extremes of the range are the handful of really hideous modern apartment-block resorts thrown up in France in the 1960s – step forward Les Menuires and Flaine – and the captivating old traffic-free mountain villages of which Switzerland has an unfair number. But it isn't simply a question of old versus new. Some purpose-built places (such as Valmorel) can have a much friendlier feel than some traditional resorts with big blocky buildings (eg Davos). And some places can be remarkably strung out (eg Vail) whereas others are surprisingly compact (eg Wengen).

The landscape can have an important impact – whether the resort is at the bottom of a narrow, shady valley (eg Ischgl) or on a sunny shelf with panoramic views (eg Crans-Montana). Some places are working towns as well as ski resorts (eg Bormio). Some are full of bars, discos and shops (eg St Anton). Others are peaceful backwaters (eg Arabba). Traffic may choke the streets (eg Sölden). Or the village may be traffic-free (eg Mürren).

In this first section of each chapter, we try to sort out the character of the place for you. Later, in the Staying there section, we tell you more about the hotels, restaurants, bars and so on.

THE MOUNTAINS

The slopes Some mountains and lift networks are vast and complex, while others are much smaller and lacking variation. The description here tells you how the area divides up into different sectors and how the links between them work.

Snow reliability This is a crucial factor for many people, and one that varies enormously. In some resorts you don't have to worry at all about a lack of snow, while others (including some very big names) are notorious for treating their paying guests to ice, mud and slush. Whether a resort is likely to have decent snow on its slopes normally depends on the height, the direction most of the slopes face (north good, south bad), its snow record and how much snowmaking it has. But bear in mind that in the Alps high resorts tend to have rocky terrain where the runs will need more snow than those on the pasture land of lower resorts. Many resorts have increased their snowmaking capacity in recent years and we list the latest amount they claim to have in the Key facts section and comment on it in the Snow reliability text. Bear in mind that snowmaking can operate only if temperatures are low enough (typically –2°C or less), so it's much more useful in midwinter than in spring.

Terrain-parks We summarise here the specially prepared fun parks and other terrain features most resorts now arrange for freestylers.

For experts, intermediates, beginners Most (though not all) resorts have something to offer beginners, but relatively few will keep an expert happy for a week's holiday. As for intermediates, whether a resort will suit you really depends on your standard and inclinations. Places such as Cervinia and Obergurgl are ideal for those who want easy cruising runs, but have little to offer intermediates looking for more challenge. Others, such as Sölden and Val-d'Isère, may intimidate the less confident intermediate who doesn't know the area well. Some, such as the Trois Vallées and Portes du Soleil, have vast amounts of terrain so that you can cover different ground each day. But some other well-known names, such as Alpbach and Courmayeur, and many North American resorts, have surprisingly small areas.

For cross-country We don't pretend that this is a guide for avid cross-country skiers. But if you or one of your group wants to try it, our summary here will help you gauge whether the resort is worth considering or whether it is a washout. It looks not just at the amount of cross-country available but also at its scenic beauty and whether or not the tracks are likely to have decent snow (many are at low altitude).

Queues Another key factor. Most resorts have improved their lift systems enormously in the last 10 years, and monster queues are largely a thing of the past. Crowding on the pistes is more of a worry in many resorts, and we mention problems of this kind here. On our piste maps, note that we mark with a chair symbol only fast chairs that shift large numbers of people per hour. Lifts not marked with a symbol are slow chairs or drag-lifts.

Mountain restaurants Here's a subject that divides people clearly into two opposing camps. To some, having a decent lunch in civilised surroundings – either in the sun, contemplating amazing scenery, or in a cosy hut, sheltered from the elements – makes or breaks their holiday. Others regard a prolonged midday stop as a waste of valuable skiing time, as well as valuable spending money. We are firmly in the former camp. We get very disheartened by places with miserable restaurants and miserable food (eg many resorts in America); and there are some resorts that we go to regularly partly because of the cosy huts and excellent cuisine (eg Zermatt).

Schools and guides This is an area where we rely heavily on readers' reports of their own or their friends' experiences. The only way to judge a ski school is by trying it. Reports on schools are always extremely valuable and frequently record disappointment.

Get next year's edition free

There are too many hotels, nightspots and mountain restaurants for us to see them all every year – so we need reports on your holiday experiences. As usual, the 100 best reports will earn free copies of next year's edition.

We want to know:
• what you particularly **liked and disliked** about the resort
• what aspects of the resort came as a **surprise** to you
• your suggestions for **changes to our evaluation** of the resort
• your experience of **lift queues** and of the **ski school** and associated childcare
• your feedback on other **individual facilities** – hotels, bars, restaurants etc.

e-mail: reports@snow-zone.co.uk
mail: our address is at the front of the book; we'll send a form if you like.

Facilities for children If you need nursery facilities, don't go to Italy. In other countries, facilities for looking after and teaching children can vary enormously between resorts. We say what is available in each resort, including what childcare arrangements are on offer from UK tour operators – often the most attractive option for Brits. But, again, to be of real help we need first-hand reports from people whose children have actually used the facilities.

SNOWBOARDING

The Mountains section applies to both skiers and snowboarders. But because certain things are important to snowboarding that aren't relevant (or aren't as relevant) to skiing, we also include a special assessment for snowboarders, picked out in a separate box. This covers issues such as whether the slopes present special attractions or problems (eg flat sections that snowboarders have to 'scoot' along), how much you can expect to have to use drag-lifts and whether you'll find specialist schools and shops in the resort.

STAYING THERE

How to go The basic choice is between catered chalets, hotels and self-catering accommodation. The catered chalet holiday remains a peculiarly British phenomenon. A tour operator takes over a chalet (or a hotel in some cases), staffs it with young Brits (or Antipodeans), fills it with British guests, provides half-board and free wine, and lets you drink your duty-free booze without hassle. You can take over a complete chalet, or share one with other groups. It is a relatively economical way of visiting the expensive top resorts.

Hotels, of course, can vary a lot but, especially in France and Switzerland, can work out very expensive. In North America, watch out for supplements: rooms are often capable of sleeping four, and UK tour operators are inclined to base their standard brochure prices on the assumption that you fill all available bed spaces.

Apartments can be very economical but most French ones, in particular, tend to be very small. It's not unusual for brochure prices to be based on four people sleeping in a one-room studio, for example – to be comfortable, pay extra for under-occupancy. But some recently built French apartments are more spacious and comfortable – where we know of these we name them.

We also look at what's available for independent travellers who want to fix their own hotels or self-catering accommodation. With hotels we've given each a price rating from ① to ①②③④⑤⑥ – the more coins, the more expensive the hotel.

Staying up the mountain/down the valley If there are interesting options for staying on the slopes above the resort village or in valley towns below it, we've picked them out. The former is often good for avoiding early-morning scrums for the lifts, the latter for cutting costs considerably.

Eating out The range of restaurants varies widely. Even some big resorts, such as Les Arcs, may have little choice because most of the clientele stay in their apartments or chalets. Others, such as Val-d'Isère, have a huge range available, including national and regional cuisine, pizzas, fondues and international fare. American resorts generally have an excellent range of restaurants – most people eat out. This is an area where we rely a lot on reporters recommending restaurants that were good last season – and we are often able to recommend some out-of-the-way restaurants that you might not otherwise find.

Après-ski Tastes and styles vary enormously. Most resorts have pleasant places in which to have an immediate post-skiing beer or hot chocolate. Some then go dead. Others have noisy bars and discos until the early hours. And, especially in Austrian resorts, there may be a lot of events such as tobogganing and bowling that are organised by British tour operator reps. For this section we are largely dependent on hearing from reporters who are keen après-skiers; sadly our readership doesn't seem to include many.

Off the slopes This is largely aimed at assessing how suitable a resort is for someone who doesn't intend to use the slopes – a non-skiing spouse or elderly relative or friend, for example. In some resorts, such as most French purpose-built places, there is really nothing to amuse them. In others, such as Seefeld in Austria, there are more people walking, skating and swimming than there are people skiing or boarding. Excursion possibilities vary widely. And there are great variations in the practicality of meeting skiers and boarders for lunch up the mountain.

ANDORRA / AUSTRIA

	ARINSAL	PAS DE LA CASA	SOLDEU	ALPBACH	BAD GASTEIN	ELLMAU	HINTERTUX	ISCHGL
Page	98	100	102	112	114	117	120	129
Snow	****	****	****	**	***	**	*****	****
Extent	*	***	**	*	****	****	**	****
Experts	*	*	*	*	***	*	***	***
Intermediates	**	***	***	**	****	****	***	****
Beginners	***	****	****	****	**	****	**	**
Convenience	***	****	***	**	**	***	**	***
Queues	***	***	***	***	***	****	***	****
Restaurants*	**	***	*	***	****	**	**	***
Scenery	***	***	***	***	***	***	***	***
Resort charm	*	*	*	*****	***	***	***	****
Off-slope	*	*	*	***	****	***	*	***

	KITZBÜHEL	LECH	MAYRHOFEN	OBERGURGL	OBERTAUERN	SAALBACH-HINTERGLEMM	SCHLADMING	SÖLDEN
Page	134	140	147	155	160	162	168	172
Snow	**	****	***	*****	****	***	****	*****
Extent	***	****	***	**	**	***	***	***
Experts	***	****	*	**	***	**	**	***
Intermediates	****	****	***	***	****	****	****	****
Beginners	**	****	**	****	****	***	****	**
Convenience	**	***	*	****	****	****	***	**
Queues	**	****	*	*****	****	***	****	***
Restaurants*	****	**	****	**	***	****	****	***
Scenery	***	***	***	***	***	***	***	***
Resort charm	****	****	***	****	**	****	****	**
Off-slope	*****	***	****	**	**	**	****	**

	SÖLL	ST ANTON	ST JOHANN IN TIROL	WESTENDORF	WILDSCHÖNAU	ZELL AM SEE	
Page	174	180	188	190	192	195	
Snow	**	****	**	**	**	**	
Extent	****	****	**	*	*	**	
Experts	*	*****	*	*	*	**	
Intermediates	****	***	***	**	**	***	
Beginners	***	*	****	****	****	***	
Convenience	**	***	***	***	***	**	
Queues	***	**	***	****	****	**	
Restaurants*	**	***	****	***	**	***	
Scenery	***	***	***	***	***	***	
Resort charm	***	****	***	****	***	***	
Off-slope	**	***	***	**	**	****	

* Refers to mountain restaurants only

Resort ratings at a glance

84

	ALPE-D'HUEZ	LES ARCS	AVORIAZ	CHAMONIX	CHÂTEL	LA CLUSAZ	LES CONTAMINES
Page	205	213	222	226	234	239	245
Snow	****	****	***	****	**	**	****
Extent	****	***	*****	***	*****	***	**
Experts	****	****	***	*****	***	***	**
Intermediates	****	****	****	**	****	****	***
Beginners	*****	****	****	*	**	****	***
Convenience	****	****	****	*	**	***	**
Queues	****	***	**	**	***	***	***
Restaurants*	****	**	****	**	***	****	****
Scenery	****	***	***	*****	***	***	****
Resort charm	*	*	**	****	***	****	****
Off-slope	***	*	*	*****	**	***	**

	COURCHEVEL	LES DEUX-ALPES	FLAINE	LA GRAVE	MEGÈVE	LES MENUIRES	MÉRIBEL
Page	247	257	262	269	274	280	282
Snow	****	****	****	***	**	****	***
Extent	*****	***	****	*	*****	*****	*****
Experts	****	****	****	*****	**	****	****
Intermediates	*****	**	*****	*	****	*****	*****
Beginners	****	***	*****	*	***	***	****
Convenience	****	***	*****	***	**	*****	***
Queues	****	**	****	****	****	****	****
Restaurants*	****	**	**	**	****	***	***
Scenery	***	****	****	****	****	***	***
Resort charm	**	**	*	***	****	*	***
Off-slope	***	**	*	*	****	*	***

	MONTGENÈVRE	MORZINE	LA PLAGNE	PUY-ST-VINCENT	RISOUL	LA ROSIÈRE	SERRE-CHEVALIER
Page	292	296	303	314	316	319	321
Snow	****	**	****	***	***	***	***
Extent	****	*****	****	**	***	***	****
Experts	**	***	***	***	**	**	***
Intermediates	****	****	*****	***	****	***	****
Beginners	*****	***	****	***	****	*****	****
Convenience	****	**	*****	*****	****	***	***
Queues	****	***	***	****	****	***	***
Restaurants*	**	***	***	***	***	*	***
Scenery	***	***	****	***	***	***	***
Resort charm	***	***	*	**	**	***	***
Off-slope	*	***	*	*	*	*	**

	STE-FOY	ST-MARTIN-DE-BELLEVILLE	LA TANIA	TIGNES	VAL-D'ISÈRE	VALMOREL	VAL-THORENS	
Page	329	332	340	343	352	364	366	
Snow	***	***	***	*****	*****	***	*****	
Extent	*	*****	*****	*****	*****	***	*****	
Experts	****	****	****	*****	*****	**	****	
Intermediates	***	*****	*****	*****	*****	****	*****	
Beginners	**	***	**	**	***	*****	****	
Convenience	***	***	****	****	***	*****	*****	
Queues	*****	****	****	****	****	****	***	
Restaurants*	**	****	****	***	**	**	****	
Scenery	***	***	***	***	***	***	***	
Resort charm	***	****	***	**	***	****	**	
Off-slope	*	*	*	*	**	**	**	

	BORMIO	CERVINIA	CORTINA D'AMPEZZO	COURMAYEUR	LIVIGNO	MADONNA DI CAMPIGLIO	MONTEROSA SKI	
Page	379	381	386	391	396	400	402	
Snow	***	*****	***	****	****	***	***	
Extent	**	***	***	**	**	***	****	
Experts	*	*	**	***	**	**	***	
Intermediates	***	****	***	****	***	****	****	
Beginners	**	*****	*****	**	****	****	**	
Convenience	***	***	*	*	**	**	****	
Queues	***	***	***	***	****	***	****	
Restaurants*	****	***	****	****	***	***	**	
Scenery	***	****	*****	****	***	****	****	
Resort charm	****	**	****	****	***	***	***	
Off-slope	****	*	*****	***	**	***	*	

	SAUZE D'OULX	SELVA	SESTRIERE	LA THUILE				
Page	405	410	418	420				
Snow	**	****	***	****				
Extent	****	*****	****	***				
Experts	**	***	***	**				
Intermediates	****	*****	****	****				
Beginners	**	****	***	****				
Convenience	**	***	****	***				
Queues	***	***	***	****				
Restaurants*	***	****	**	*				
Scenery	***	*****	***	***				
Resort charm	**	***	*	***				
Off-slope	*	***	*	**				

Resort ratings at a glance

85

* Refers to mountain restaurants only

Resort ratings at a glance

86

	ADELBODEN	ANDERMATT	AROSA	CHAMPÉRY	CRANS-MONTANA	DAVOS	FLIMS	GRIN'WALD
Page	427	429	431	433	435	440	447	449
Snow	**	****	***	**	**	****	***	**
Extent	***	*	**	*****	***	*****	****	***
Experts	**	****	*	***	**	****	***	**
Intermediates	***	**	***	****	****	*****	*****	****
Beginners	****	*	****	**	***	**	****	***
Convenience	***	***	***	*	**	**	***	**
Queues	***	**	****	****	***	**	***	**
Restaurants*	**	*	****	***	***	***	***	*****
Scenery	****	***	****	****	****	****	***	*****
Resort charm	****	****	**	****	**	**	***	****
Off-slope	****	**	****	***	****	*****	***	****

	GSTAAD	MÜRREN	SAAS-FEE	ST MORITZ	VERBIER	VILLARS	WENGEN	ZERMATT
Page	453	455	459	464	470	480	482	487
Snow	*	***	*****	****	***	**	**	****
Extent	****	*	**	*****	*****	***	***	****
Experts	**	***	***	****	*****	**	**	*****
Intermediates	***	***	****	****	***	***	****	****
Beginners	***	**	*****	**	**	****	***	*
Convenience	*	***	***	**	**	***	***	*
Queues	***	***	***	**	***	***	***	***
Restaurants*	***	**	***	****	***	***	****	*****
Scenery	***	*****	****	****	****	***	*****	*****
Resort charm	****	*****	*****	*	***	****	*****	*****
Off-slope	****	***	****	*****	***	****	****	****

	CALIFORNIA			COLORADO			COPPER MOUNTAIN	CRESTED BUTTE
	HEAVENLY	MAMMOTH		ASPEN	BEAVER CR'K	BRECK'RIDGE		
Page	501	510		516	523	525	530	532
Snow	****	****		*****	*****	*****	*****	****
Extent	***	***		****	**	**	**	*
Experts	***	****		*****	****	****	****	****
Intermediates	****	****		*****	****	****	****	***
Beginners	****	****		*****	*****	****	****	****
Convenience	*	**		**	****	***	****	***
Queues	****	****		****	*****	****	****	*****
Restaurants*	*	*		****	**	**	*	*
Scenery	****	***		***	***	***	***	***
Resort charm	*	**		****	***	***	**	****
Off-slope	**	*		****	***	***	*	**

	KEYSTONE	STEAMBOAT	TELLURIDE	VAIL	WINTER PARK		
Page	534	536	538	540	546		
Snow	*****	****	****	*****	*****		
Extent	**	***	**	****	***		
Experts	***	***	****	****	****		
Intermediates	****	****	***	*****	****		
Beginners	****	*****	*****	***	*****		
Convenience	**	***	****	***	***		
Queues	****	****	*****	**	****		
Restaurants*	***	***	*	**	***		
Scenery	***	***	****	***	***		
Resort charm	**	**	****	***	**		
Off-slope	**	**	**	***	*		

UTAH						
	ALTA	THE CANYONS	DEER VALLEY	PARK CITY	SNOWBASIN	SNOWBIRD
Page	553	555	557	559	564	566
Snow	*****	****	****	****	*****	*****
Extent	***	***	**	***	***	***
Experts	*****	***	***	****	****	*****
Intermediates	***	***	****	****	****	***
Beginners	***	***	****	****	**	**
Convenience	****	****	****	***	*	*****
Queues	***	****	****	****	*****	**
Restaurants*	**	***	****	**	**	*
Scenery	***	***	***	***	****	***
Resort charm	**	**	***	***	**	*
Off-slope	*	**	**	***	*	*

REST OF THE WEST				NEW ENGLAND			
	BIG SKY	JACKSON HOLE	SUN VALLEY		KILLINGTON	SMUGGLERS' NOTCH	STOWE	SUNDAY RIVER
Page	569	571	576		581	585	587	589
Snow	****	****	***		***	***	***	***
Extent	***	***	***		**	*	*	*
Experts	****	*****	***		***	***	***	**
Intermediates	****	**	****		***	***	****	****
Beginners	****	***	***		****	****	****	****
Convenience	****	***	**		*	*****	*	***
Queues	*****	***	****		****	****	****	****
Restaurants*	*	*	****		*	*	**	***
Scenery	***	***	***		***	***	***	***
Resort charm	**	***	***		*	**	****	**
Off-slope	**	***	***		*	*	*	*

* Refers to mountain restaurants only

Resort ratings at a glance

87

Resort ratings at a glance

	WESTERN CANADA BANFF	BIG WHITE	FERNIE	JASPER	KICKING HORSE	LAKE LOUISE	PANORAMA	WHISTLER
Page	598	604	606	611	613	615	620	624
Snow	****	*****	*****	***	*****	***	***	****
Extent	****	***	***	*	***	****	**	****
Experts	****	****	*****	**	****	****	****	*****
Intermediates	****	****	**	**	***	****	***	*****
Beginners	***	****	****	****	***	***	****	***
Convenience	*	****	****	*	*	*	****	****
Queues	****	*****	****	****	*****	****	****	***
Restaurants*	***	*	*	**	**	**	*	**
Scenery	****	***	***	***	***	*****	***	***
Resort charm	***	**	**	***	*	***	**	***
Off-slope	*****	**	**	***	*	****	*	**

	EASTERN CANADA TREMBLANT							
Page	634							
Snow	****							
Extent	*							
Experts	**							
Intermediates	***							
Beginners	****							
Convenience	****							
Queues	***							
Restaurants*	**							
Scenery	***							
Resort charm	****							
Off-slope	***							

	SPAIN BAQUEIRA		NORWAY HEMSEDAL		SWEDEN ÅRE		NEW ZEALAND QUEENST'WN	
Page	637		647		650		658	
Snow	***		****		***		**	
Extent	**		*		**		*	
Experts	***		**		**		***	
Intermediates	****		****		****		***	
Beginners	**		***		****		***	
Convenience	***		**		***		*	
Queues	***		****		****		***	
Restaurants*	**		*		***		*	
Scenery	***		**		***		****	
Resort charm	**		**		***		**	
Off-slope	*		*		***		*****	

* Refers to mountain restaurants only

Resort shortlists

To help you spot resorts that will suit you

To streamline the job of spotting the ideal resort for your own holiday, here are lists of the best ten or so resorts for 20 different categories. Some lists embrace European and North American resorts, but most we've confined to Europe, because America has too many qualifying resorts (eg for beginners) or because America does things differently, making comparisons invalid (eg for off-piste).

SOMETHING FOR EVERYONE
Resorts with everything from reassuring nursery slopes to real challenges for experts
Alpe-d'Huez, France p205
Les Arcs, France p213
Aspen-Snowmass, Colorado p516
Courchevel, France p247
Flaine, France p262
Mammoth, California p510
Vail, Colorado p540
Val-d'Isère, France p352
Whistler, Canada p624
Winter Park, Colorado p546

INTERNATIONAL OVERSIGHTS
Resorts that deserve as much attention as the ones we go back to every year, but don't seem to get it
Alta, Utah p553
Andermatt, Switzerland p429
Bad Gastein, Austria p114
Big Sky, Montana p569
Flims-Laax, Switzerland p447
Ischgl, Austria p129
Monterosa Ski, Italy p402
Risoul, France p316
Sun Valley, Idaho p576
Telluride, Colorado p538

RELIABLE SNOW IN THE ALPS
Alpine resorts with good snow records or lots of snowmaking, and high or north-facing slopes
Argentière, France p226
Cervinia, Italy p381
Courchevel, France p247
Hintertux, Austria p120
Lech/Zürs, Austria p140
Obergurgl, Austria p155
Saas-Fee, Switzerland p459
Val-d'Isère/Tignes, France pp352/343
Val-Thorens, France p366
Zermatt, Switzerland p487

OFF-PISTE WONDERS
Alpine resorts where, with the right guidance and equipment, you can have the time of your life
Alpe-d'Huez, France p205
Andermatt, Switzerland p429
Argentière/Chamonix, France p226
Davos/Klosters, Switzerland p440
La Grave, France p269
Lech/Zürs, Austria p140
Monterosa Ski, Italy p402
St Anton, Austria p180
Val-d'Isère/Tignes, France pp352/343
Verbier, Switzerland p470

SNOWPIX.COM / CHRIS GILL

Les Arcs doesn't get on the shortlist for village charm (this is Arc 2000, with Arc 1950 taking shape in the background) but it does get listed for convenience and one or two other things →

POWDER PARADISES
Resorts with the snow, the terrain and (ideally) the lack of crowds that make for powder perfection
Alta/Snowbird, Utah pp553/566
Andermatt, Switzerland p429
Aspen-Snowmass, Colorado p516
Big Sky, Montana p569
Fernie, Canada p606
Grand Targhee, Wyoming p571
La Grave, France p269
Jackson Hole, Wyoming p571
Kicking Horse, Canada p613
Monterosa Ski, Italy, p402
Red Mountain, Canada, p595
Snowbasin, Utah p564
Ste-Foy, France p329

BLACK RUNS
Resorts with steep, mogully, lift-served slopes within the safety of the piste network
Alta/Snowbird, Utah pp553/566
Andermatt, Switzerland p429
Argentière/Chamonix, France p226
Aspen-Snowmass, Colorado p516
Beaver Creek, Colorado p523
Courchevel, France p247
Jackson Hole, Wyoming p571
Whistler, Canada p624
Winter Park, Colorado p546
Zermatt, Switzerland p487

CHOPAHOLICS
Resorts where you can quit the conventional lift network and have a day riding helicopters or cats
Aspen-Snowmass, Colorado p516
Crested Butte, Colorado p532
Fernie, Canada p606
Grand Targhee, Wyoming p571
Lech/Zürs, Austria p140
Monterosa Ski, Italy p402
Panorama, Canada p620
Verbier, Switzerland p470
Whistler, Canada p624
Zermatt, Switzerland p487

HIGH-MILEAGE PISTE-BASHING
Extensive intermediate slopes with big lift networks
Alpe-d'Huez, France p205
Davos/Klosters, Switzerland p440
Flims/Laax, Switzerland p447
Milky Way: Sauze d'Oulx (Italy), Montgenèvre (France) pp405/292
La Plagne, France p303
Portes du Soleil, France/Switz p312
Selva/Sella Ronda, Italy p410
Trois Vallées, France p350
Val-d'Isère/Tignes, France pp352/343
Whistler, Canada p624

MOTORWAY CRUISING
Long, gentle, super-smooth pistes to bolster the frail confidence of those not long off the nursery slope
Les Arcs, France p213
Aspen-Snowmass, Colorado p516
Breckenridge, Colorado p525
Cervinia, Italy p381
Cortina, Italy p386
Courchevel, France p247
Megève, France p274
La Plagne, France p303
La Thuile, Italy p420
Vail, Colorado p540

RESORTS FOR BEGINNERS
European resorts with gentle, snow-sure nursery slopes and easy, longer runs to progress to
Alpe-d'Huez, France p205
Les Arcs, France p213
Cervinia, Italy p381
Courchevel, France p247
Flaine, France p262
Montgenèvre, France p292
Pamporovo, Bulgaria p639
La Plagne, France p303
Saas-Fee, Switzerland p459
Soldeu, Andorra p102

MODERN CONVENIENCE
Alpine resorts where there's plenty of slope-side accommodation to make life easy
Les Arcs, France p213
Avoriaz, France p222
Courchevel, France p247
Flaine, France p262
Les Menuires, France p280
Obertauern, Austria p160
La Plagne, France p303
Puy-St-Vincent, France, p314
Valmorel, France p364
Val-Thorens, France p366

WEATHERPROOF SLOPES
Alpine resorts with snow-sure slopes if the sun shines, and trees in case it doesn't
Les Arcs, France p213
Courchevel, France p247
Courmayeur, Italy p391
Flims, Switzerland p447
Montchavin/Les Coches, France p303
Schladming, Austria p168
Selva, Italy p410
Serre-Chevalier, France p321
Sestriere, Italy p418
La Thuile, Italy p420

BACK-DOOR RESORTS
Cute little Alpine villages linked to big, bold ski areas, giving you the best of two different worlds
Les Brévières (Tignes), France p343
Champagny (La Plagne), France p303
Leogang (Saalbach), Austria p162
Montchavin (La Plagne), France p303
Peisey (Les Arcs), France p213
Le Pré (Les Arcs), France p213
Samoëns (Flaine), France, p262
St-Martin (Three Valleys), France p332
Stuben (St Anton), Austria p180
Vaujany (Alpe-d'Huez), France p205

SNOW-SURE BUT SIMPATICO
Alpine resorts with high-rise slopes, but low-rise, traditional-style buildings
Andermatt, Switzerland p429
Arabba, Italy p410
Argentière, France p226
Les Contamines, France p245
Ischgl, Austria p129
Lech/Zürs, Austria p140
Monterosa Ski, Italy p402
Obergurgl, Austria p155
Saas-Fee, Switzerland p459
Zermatt, Switzerland p487

SPECIALLY FOR FAMILIES
Alpine resorts where you can easily find accommodation surrounded by snow, not by traffic and fumes
Les Arcs, France p213
Avoriaz, France p222
Flaine, France p262
Lech, Austria p140
Montchavin (La Plagne), France p303
Mürren, Switzerland p455
Risoul, France p316
Saas-Fee, Switzerland p459
Valmorel, France p364
Wengen, Switzerland p482

SPECIAL MOUNTAIN RESTAURANTS
Alpine resorts where the mountain restaurants can really add an extra dimension to your holiday
Alpe-d'Huez, France p205
La Clusaz, France p239
Courmayeur, Italy p391
Kitzbühel, Austria p134
Megève, France p274
St Johann in Tirol, Austria p188
St Moritz, Switzerland p464
Selva, Italy p410
Söll, Austria p174
Zermatt, Switzerland p487

DRAMATIC SCENERY
Resorts where the mountains are not just high and snowy, but spectacularly scenic too
Chamonix, France p226
Cortina, Italy p386
Courmayeur, Italy p391
Heavenly, California p501
Jungfrau resorts (Grindelwald, Mürren, Wengen), Switzerland pp449/455/482
Lake Louise, Canada p615
Saas-Fee, Switzerland p459
St Moritz, Switzerland p464
Selva, Italy p410
Zermatt, Switzerland p487

VILLAGE CHARM
Resorts with traditional character that enriches your holiday – from mountain villages to mining towns
Alpbach, Austria p112
Champéry, Switzerland p433
Courmayeur, Italy p391
Crested Butte, Colorado p532
Lech, Austria p140
Mürren, Switzerland p455
Saas-Fee, Switzerland p459
Telluride, Colorado p538
Wengen, Switzerland p482
Zermatt, Switzerland p487

LIVELY NIGHTLIFE
European resorts where you'll have no difficulty finding somewhere to boogy, and someone to do it with
Chamonix, France p226
Ischgl, Austria p129
Kitzbühel, Austria p134
Saalbach, Austria p162
St Anton, Austria p180
Sauze d'Oulx, Italy p405
Sölden, Austria p172
Pas de la Casa, Andorra p100
Val-d'Isère, France p352
Verbier, Switzerland p470

OTHER AMUSEMENTS
Alpine resorts where those not interested in skiing or boarding can still find plenty to do
Bad Gastein, Austria p114
Chamonix, France p226
Cortina, Italy p386
Davos, Switzerland p440
Gstaad, Switzerland p453
Innsbruck, Austria p125
Kitzbühel, Austria p134
Megève, France p274
St Moritz, Switzerland p464
Zell am See, Austria p195

Our resort chapters

How to get the best out of them

FINDING A RESORT

The bulk of the book consists of chapters devoted to individual major resorts, some also covering minor resorts that share the same lift system. These chapters are ordered alphabetically and grouped by country – first, the five major European destination countries in alphabetical order; then the US and Canada (where resorts are grouped by states or regions); then minor European countries; then Australasia. Note that Andorra, until now consigned to the minor category, has been promoted to the major group, and so is right at the front of the book.

There's a **chapter-by-chapter listing** on the facing page, as well as in the Contents section at the start of the book.

Short cuts to the resorts that might suit you are provided by a table of comparative **star ratings** and a series of **shortlists** of resorts with particular merits. To find these, just turn back a few pages towards the front of the book.

At the back of the book is an **index** to the resort chapters, combined with a **directory** giving basic information on hundreds of other minor resorts. Where the resort you are looking up is a minor resort covered in a chapter devoted mainly to a bigger resort, the page reference will take you to the start of that chapter, not to the exact page on which the minor resort is described.

There's further guidance on using our information in the chapter on Choosing your resort – designed to be helpful particularly to people with narrow experience of resorts, who may not appreciate how big the differences between one resort and another can be (ie like chalk and cheese).

READING A CHAPTER

The **cost** of visiting each resort is rated on a scale of one to six – ①②③④⑤⑥ to ①②③④⑤⑥ – reflecting the typical cost of a one-week trip based on a half-board package from the UK, plus a lift pass and an allowance for lunch in mountain restaurants. We assume two people sharing a room – even in the US, where package prices are often based on four people sharing.

Star ratings summarise our view of the resort in 11 respects, including how well it suits different standards of skier/boarder. The more stars, the better, on a five-point scale.

We give phone numbers and Internet addresses of the **tourist office** and phone numbers for recommended **hotels.**

The UK tour operators offering **package holidays** in each resort are listed in the index at the back of the book, not in the main chapters.

Our **mountain maps** show the resorts' own classification of runs – so those for the US and Canada show green, blue and black runs, and no red ones (unlike Europe). On some maps we also follow the North American convention of using black diamonds to indicate open expert terrain where the runs are not defined. We do not distinguish single-diamond terrain from the steeper double-diamond.

We show all the lifts on the mountain, including any definitely planned for construction for the coming season. We use the following symbols to identify **fast or high-capacity lifts**:

🚡 fast chair-lift

🚠 gondola

🚟 cable-car

🚞 funicular railway

THE WORLD'S BEST WINTER SPORTS RESORTS

To find a minor resort – or a major resort, if you don't know what country it's in – go to the index/directory at the back of the book

Resort chapters explained

93

Andorra

More Brits now go to Andorra for winter holidays than visit Switzerland, Canada and USA combined – and Andorra is neck and neck with Italy as the third most popular country to visit. Despite the building boom that this surge in popularity has triggered, it is still often difficult to find a bed, even in low season. It's also difficult to get away from fellow Brits. And from traffic and construction sites – Andorra has lots of both.

Andorra used to be seen primarily as a cheap and cheerful holiday aimed mainly at younger singles and couples looking for a good time in the duty-free bars and clubs as well as learning to ski or snowboard. And most of the resorts are still excellent for that market. Tour operator-organised pub crawls of 100+ guests are common. But there's more to it than that. The ski schools have always been excellent, with lots of native English-speaking instructors. In recent years, some more upmarket hotels have been built (though they often resemble Spanish summer package hotels and have self-service buffet meals). And lots of money has been pumped in to developing powerful lift systems and piste-grooming fleets that many well-known Alpine resorts would be proud of; this makes the slopes much more attractive to intermediates as well as beginners. Andorra beats the other so-called budget countries such as Romania and Bulgaria hands-down for both resort facilities and quality of slopes, though it's no longer quite as cheap.

But there are big differences in the characters of the resorts. Soldeu is the one that has tried hardest to move upmarket; chapters on Soldeu and the other two major resorts of Arinsal and Pas de la Casa follow.

This introduction includes some comments on the valley towns that are also marketed as ski resorts by some tour operators, and on the excellent out-of-the-way day skiing area of Arcalis.

Andorra has a relatively reliable snow record. Its situation close to both the Atlantic and the Mediterranean oceans, together with the high altitude of its resorts, means it usually gets substantial natural snowfalls. It has also invested heavily in snowmaking. This combination means you can book Andorra months in advance with some confidence. And an early reservation is necessary: late bookers can have difficulty finding an Andorra package.

Both package holiday prices and prices for drinks and extras such as instruction and equipment rental are generally lower than in the Alps. But some reporters have found duty-free luxury goods prices not the super-bargains they had expected.

Duty-free spirits prices and large, unmeasured helpings mean that nightlife can be very lively. If you want to spend your nights in the company of drunken young Brits, you will have no trouble finding places to do it. But in our recent experience you will equally have no trouble avoiding such scenes, and finding more civilised places in which to relax. As one of our 'more mature' reporters said this year: 'Great potential as a Geriatric Paradise ... with quality spirits at £3.50 a litre I was so impressed that I intend to organise a group in future years when most of my friends can travel in low season and can wax their zimmers and drink the duty-free booze until their hearts are content! Saga louts on tour – BEWARE!'

The sight of cranes is still common, as hotels and apartments are

PAS DE LA CASA – GRAU ROIG / JAVIER MONTES

← Andorra's slopes suit beginners and intermediates best: this is Grau Roig, the only wooded area of Pas de la Casa's slopes

↑ Arcalis is a remote ski area with no accommodation; locals drive here for the day, hence all the cars parked along the winding road in the distance

SNOWPIX.COM / CHRIS GILL

built to keep up with demand. It is no longer true to say that the resorts resemble giant construction sites, but they all have construction sites within them (or on the edge of them as they expand in sprawling fashion along the roadside). And don't be surprised if a 'new' hotel you visit still has building work going on within it to finish it off.

Adjacent resorts have linked their slopes together, meaning bigger ski areas and a bit more variety. Arinsal and Pal were linked by a new

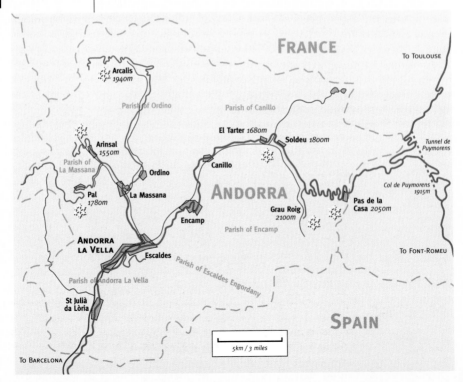

cable-car for the 2000/01 season – and have a joint lift pass. But the biggest nonsense in the ski world still exists in the Pas de la Casa-Soldeu area. The resorts' slopes have been physically linked by lift and piste for a few seasons and form an impressive area of 190km/118 miles, comparable with big-name resorts such as Kitzbühel and Les Deux-Alpes. But because of an ancient feud between the communities, there's no joint lift pass; to ski them both on the same day you have to fork out for two separate lift passes.

STAYING DOWN THE VALLEY
Several valley towns can be used as bases, either to use the slopes of one resort or to explore several resorts in the course of a week.

One obviously strong candidate here is **Encamp**, which has a powerful 18-seater gondola giving a quick way into the Pas de la Casa slopes. From the top of it you can actually ski into the Soldeu area as well, but you would need to have a day ticket for that area before you set off. Encamp seemed to us the least attractive of the valley towns (not least because of its situation on the traffic-choked main road), but we can't claim to have examined it closely.

La Massana is a more appealing town, and has the attraction of being quite well placed for access to Arcalis – an excellent but accommodation-free ski area directly to the north (see below). La Massana is more often used as a base for Pal and Arinsal, which are much closer. And we are assured that work has begun on the long-awaited gondola from La Massana to the Pal slopes and that it will be open for the 2004/05 season – which will make La Massana a good place to stay. **Ordino** is slightly nearer Arcalis, and pleasantly rustic.

The capital of **Andorra la Vella** is not far down the valley from Encamp (and the gondola into Pas de la Casa slopes) but is a more attractive (though still traffic-choked) base, especially for someone wanting a more rounded holiday. The duty-free shopping could fill a page, but probably the most interesting place is Caldea spa. The interior is laid out in a 'Hanging Gardens of Babylon' style, and the facilities are very impressive – indoor and outdoor pools, with fountains and waterfalls, saunas, hot-tubs, Turkish baths, hydrotherapy, sunbeds, massage ... even a grapefruit bath! There are plenty of high-quality, if relatively expensive, hotels. Andorra la Vella is not a big place, and most hotels are within easy walking distance of the centre. There is plenty of choice when it comes to dining out and plenty of bars and nightclubs that stay open until 4am. However, the clientele is generally a more sophisticated bunch, mainly Andorrans and Spaniards, and the 'drink-until-you-drop' attitude of the mountain resorts is rare.

SKIING AND BOARDING AWAY FROM THE MAIN RESORTS
Arcalis is the most remote area of slopes in Andorra, tucked away at the head of a long valley, and most British visitors to Andorra never hear about it. But it makes a very worthwhile day trip – the variety of the terrain is greater than in most of the main resorts, the slopes are usually deserted except at weekends (when locals pour in) and the snow is usually the best you will find. It provides excellent intermediate and beginner terrain, but of all Andorra's resorts it has the most to offer experts, including lots of off-piste between the marked runs. There is no accommodation at the mountain, just a day lodge and a lot of car parking, but buildings are now springing up along the Vall d'Ordino leading up to it.

LIFT PASSES

Ski Andorra
The Ski Andorra pass covers all four Andorran areas and allows skiing at any single one of them each day for five out of six consecutive days: €133
Under 12: €108

Phone numbers
From abroad use the prefix +376.

TOURIST OFFICE

t 864389
skiandorra@ski andorra.ad
www.skiandorra.ad

Arinsal

Much improved by the recent cable-car link with Pal

COSTS

①②③④⑤⑥

RATINGS

The slopes

Snow	★★★★
Extent	★
Expert	★
Intermediate	★★
Beginner	★★★
Convenience	★★★
Queues	★★★
Mountain restaurants	★★

The rest

Scenery	★★★
Resort charm	★
Off-slope	★

NEWS

Work has started on the long-awaited gondola from La Massana to Pal, expected to open for the 2004/05 season.

For 2003/04 a drag-lift in the beginner area will be replaced by a quad chair.

For 2002/03 a new FreeStyle area was built – claiming to be the most radical 40,000m² in Europe. It includes a huge half-pipe, Big Jump, terrain-park with spines, fun boxes, rails and quarter-pipes, boarder and ski cross run and a chill-out area.

Also in 2002/03 the gondola from Arinsal had its capacity increased by 50% by adding 14 cabins, a moving carpet was installed at the beginner area, more snow-guns were added and new activities such as dog-sledding, snowmobiling and snow-biking were introduced.

+ Lively bars

+ Ski school geared to British needs

+ Recent cable-car link with Pal is very good news for non-beginners

+ Pretty, tree-lined slopes in Pal

− Very confined and bleak local slopes

− Runs to village need good snow to be open, and don't lead to centre

− Long, linear and rather dour village, with no focus

− Obtrusive construction sites

Arinsal is the most British-dominated resort in Andorra, despite the fact that the village is the least attractive. This may be partly because the Spanish and French set their sights higher; but it is also because British tour operators offer packages here at tempting prices.

The resort attracts mainly first-time skiers and riders who come here for the cheap alcohol-fuelled nightlife as much as the experience on the slopes. But the village doesn't have many other attractions.

THE RESORT

Arinsal is a long, narrow village of grey, stone-clad buildings, near the head of a steep-sided valley north of Andorra la Vella. Development in recent years has been rapid.

There is some accommodation at Pal, but it is a bus-ride from the lift base. Staying in Arinsal (preferably close to the gondola station) and accessing the Pal slopes via the recent cable-car link makes better sense for most visitors. The gondola from the village centre is the main way to the slopes; for most guests, the alternative chair-lift 1km/0.5 miles out of town is irrelevant – though you can stay next to it and ski to the door in good conditions. Or you can drive to the top of the gondola.

There is attractive accommodation in the lower town of La Massana (see previous page). A gondola link from here to La Caubella on Pal's slopes is planned for 2004/05 and will make La Massana a good place to stay.

THE MOUNTAINS

The small local area above Arinsal's gondola is a narrow, east-facing bowl of open slopes. Pal's slopes, in contrast, are the most densely wooded of the Andorran resorts, calling to mind American resorts. They mainly face east; those down to the link with Arinsal face north.

Slopes Arinsal's slopes consist essentially of a single, long, narrow,

rather bleak bowl above the upper gondola station at Comallemple, with runs leading straight back towards that point served by a network of chairs and drags. Almost at the top is the cable-car link to and from Pal. Pal's slopes present a sharp contrast – the runs are prettily tree-lined and widely spread around the mountain, with four main lift bases, all reachable by road. The main one, La Caubella, is at the opposite extreme from the cable-car.

Terrain-parks Arinsal has a big new terrain-park, half-pipe and skier- and boarder-cross run – see News.

Snow reliability With most runs above 1950m/6,400ft, north-easterly orientation and an impressive 350 snow-guns, snow is relatively assured.

Experts These aren't great mountains for experts, but there are short, sharp black slopes at Arinsal, and quite long and challenging reds (and one black) at Pal. There are also special off-piste free-ride areas marked on the piste map in both Arinsal and Pal. We had a great time skiing fresh powder in the trees in the Pal free-ride area in 2003.

Intermediates Arinsal offers a reasonable range of difficulty, but any confident intermediate is going to want to explore the Pal slopes, which are much more interesting, varied and extensive. There are easy cruises, and a variety of challenges in the central and Seturia sections.

Beginners Around half the guests here are beginners. Arinsal and Pal both have gentle nursery slopes set apart from the main runs; they can get very

KEY FACTS	
Resort	1470m
	4,820ft
Slopes	1550-2560m
	5,090-8,400ft
Lifts	29
Pistes	63km
	39 miles
Green	10%
Blue	39%
Red	39%
Black	12%
Snowmaking	18km
	11 miles

Phone numbers
From abroad use the prefix +376.

TOURIST OFFICES
Arinsal
t 737020
pal@arinsal.ad
www.palarinsal.com
Pal
t 737000

crowded at peak times. There are long easy runs to progress to, as well.

Snowboarding It's a good place to learn. But over half the lifts are drags, including an awkward and unavoidable one on the way back from Pal. And there are some tedious flat sections in Pal too. One reporter said that crash helmets were compulsory in the terrain-park when he visited.

Cross-country There isn't any.

Queues Although there is only one lift out of the centre, queues are not a problem on weekdays. The cable-car link can close if the wind is high.

Mountain restaurants Mainly self-service, crowded, with snack food.

Schools and guides Arinsal's ski school is its pride and joy, and is geared to the British market – over half the instructors are native English-speakers. The reports we have are all positive. Class sizes can, however, be very large in peak season. English speaking is not so widespread in the Pal school.

Facilities for children There is a ski kindergarten for those aged 4 to 8 and a non-skiing nursery for children over one year old.

STAYING THERE

How to go There is a wide choice of hotel and self-catering packages.

Hotels Rooms in the hotel Arinsal (835640) are not large, but it is well run, ideally placed and has a pleasant bar. The Princesa Parc (736500) is a big glossy 4-star place close to the gondola, with a swanky spa. The Xalet Verdu (737140) is a smooth little 4-star. The St Gotthard (836005) is big but popular, except for its position a long way down the hill from the gondola. The Micolau (835052) is a characterful stone house, close to the centre, with simple rooms and a jolly, beamed restaurant. If there is snow to the valley, you can ski to the Crest (835866) at the old chair-lift station.

Self-catering There is a reasonable choice of places. Aparthotel Sant Andreu (836164) offers simple but comfortable apartments, with a relaxed bar-restaurant on site.

Eating out The Surf disco-pub does grills. Cisco's is a Tex-Mex place in a lovely wood and stone building. The Rocky Mountain is popular for steaks. The Micolau does good food. Borda Callisa does Indian.

Après-ski Arinsal has plenty of lively bars and discos such as Quo Vadis, El Cau, Surf, Cisco's and Rocky Mountain. El Derbi is heaving on karaoke night. If, like us, you prefer something quieter, head for Borda Callisa – out of the way and pleasantly relaxed – or the bar of the hotel Arinsal.

Off the slopes There are lots of activities (see News). Or go shopping in Andorra la Vella, half an hour away by infrequent bus or inexpensive taxi.

Arinsal

99

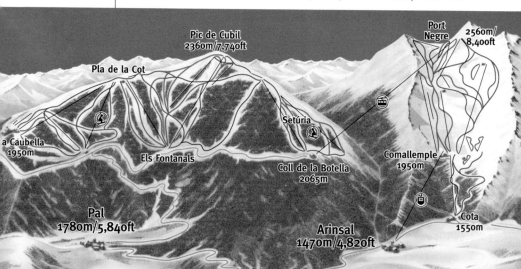

Pic de Cubil
236om/7,74oft

Pla de la Cot

Port Negre

2560m/8,400ft

Setúria

a Caubella
1950m

Els Fontanals

Coll de la Botella
2065m

Comallemple
1950m

Pal
178om/5,84oft

Arinsal
147om/4,82oft

Cota
1550m

Pas de la Casa

Andorra's biggest area and liveliest resort – shame about the lift pass

COSTS

① ② ③ ④ ⑤ ⑥

RATINGS

The slopes

Snow	****
Extent	***
Expert	*
Intermediate	***
Beginner	****
Convenience	****
Queues	***
Mountain restaurants	***

The rest

Scenery	***
Resort charm	*
Off-slope	*

NEWS

For 2002/03, more snowmaking was installed on the runs back to town and in the beginners' area.

The half-pipe was moved from Grau Roig to near Pas de la Casa village.

KEY FACTS

Resort	2100m
	6,890ft
Slopes	2050-2640m
	6,730-8,660ft
Lifts	31
Pistes	100km
	62 miles
Green	14%
Blue	20%
Red	42%
Black	24%
Snowmaking	29km
	18 miles

Phone numbers

From abroad use the prefix +376.

Central reservations phone number

For all resort accommodation call 801060.

TOURIST OFFICE

t 801060
info@pasgrau.com
www.pasgrau.com

+ Slopes to match many mid-sized resorts in the Alps

+ Andorra's liveliest nightlife

+ Choice of alternative bases to stay: Grau Roig (more attractive) and Encamp (cheaper)

+ Equally worthwhile Soldeu area is physically linked, but ...

- ... still no shared lift pass with Soldeu, although the lifts meet and the runs overlap

- Pas is an eyesore and the centre suffers from traffic (and fumes)

- Very few woodland slopes, and none directly above the village – unpleasant in bad weather

The tour op brochures (and the readers' reports we get) all say that Pas is Andorra's wildest party resort, and we don't doubt it. Having driven through it and skied down to it, we are quite happy to stay over the hill in Soldeu – or, for ideal access to the Pas slopes, secluded Grau Roig.

THE RESORT

Sited right on the border between Andorra and France, Pas de la Casa owes its development as much to duty-free sales to the French as to skiing. It is a sizeable collection of concrete-box-style apartment blocks and hotels, a product of the late 1960s and early 1970s. As one reporter put it: 'The resort reminded us of Playa de las Americas in Tenerife – ugly, characterless with loads of restaurants with plastic-covered faded photos to show the discerning eater what a whopper cheeseburger and chips actually looks like.' Most accommodation is conveniently placed near the lift base and slopes. The town centre boasts plenty of cheap shops and bars, as well as a sports centre. Reporters complain that that the heavy traffic generates fumes.

The resort attracts a lot of French visitors (so beware the February school holidays) and Spanish families, with only a smattering of Brits.

The lift system spreads from Pas over three adjacent valleys. The furthest from Pas has nothing but a lift station, but in the attractively wooded middle one is Grau Roig ('Rosh'). This is a mini-resort that acts as the access point for day visitors arriving by road, but it also makes a good base.

The road through from France goes on over the Port d'Envalira towards Soldeu and central Andorra but in 2003 a toll tunnel opened which avoids the pass and takes you to near Grau Roig. There is accommodation at the pass, which we suggest you avoid.

THE MOUNTAINS

Pas de la Casa has the most extensive slopes in Andorra; and Soldeu's slopes are right next door (but no shared lift pass – see left). With the exception of a couple of attractively wooded slopes in the central valley, the slopes are all open, and vulnerable to bad weather.

Slopes The treeless local slopes, facing north-east, descend from a high, north–south ridge; lifts go up to it at four points. Runs on the far side of the ridge converge on Grau Roig, where there is some wooded terrain at the head of the valley. And a single lift goes on further west to the bowl of Llac del Cubill, where the Pas area adjoins the Soldeu one. On the far side of this bowl is the arrival station of the 6km/4 mile gondola up from Encamp.

Terrain-parks There is a boarder-cross course and a half-pipe.

Snow reliability The combination of height and lots of snowmaking means good snow reliability and a season that often reaches late April. But on both our recent visits the snow has been better in Soldeu – maybe the grooming is better there.

Experts There are few challenges on-piste – the black runs are rarely of serious steepness, and moguls are rare. But there seem to be plenty of off-piste slopes inviting exploration.

Intermediates The slopes cater for confident intermediates far better, with plenty of top-to-bottom reds and blues on the main ridge, though they do rather lack variety.

Beginners There are beginner slopes in both Pas and Grau Roig. The Pas area

↑ Pas de la Casa looks better at night

PAS DE LA CASA – GRAU ROIG / JAVIER MONTES

LIFT PASS INSANITY

If they could agree on a joint lift pass the Soldeu-Pas de la Casa joint area would rival some of the Alps' best-known names for extent and variety. But they can't; so if you want to ski both in a day you need two passes – one for each area. This insanity is the result of an ancient feud between the communities which control the two areas. The result is that people stick to one area – paying for two passes makes it the most expensive skiing in Europe.

is a short but inconvenient bus-ride out of town. Progression to longer runs is easier in Grau Roig, too.

Snowboarding Boarding is popular with the young crowd the resort attracts. Drags are usually avoidable.

Cross-country There are loops totalling 12km/7 miles below Grau Roig.

Queues Queues are rarely serious, now that there are two fast chairs out of Pas, one a six-pack. But at weekends and French school holidays some can develop, especially at Grau Roig.

Mountain restaurants There are routine places at the ridge above Pas and the top of the gondola from Encamp. The Rifugi dels Llacs dels Pessons at the head of the Grau Roig bowl is by far the best place – a cosy, beamed table-service restaurant with excellent food.

Schools and guides The ski school has an excellent reputation, with good English spoken.

Facilities for children There are ski kindergartens at Pas and Grau Roig, and a non-ski one at the latter.

STAYING THERE

How to go There are lots of apartments and hotels and a few chalets.

Hotels Himalaia-Pas is close to the slopes, has a pool and is 'comfortable and recommendable', says a reporter. The Grau Roig hotel is in a league of its own for comfort and seclusion (note that some operators list it under Soldeu). Beware of hotels catering to the 18-30 crowd – one reader in the Camelot reported vibrations from the basement disco until 5.30am.

Eating out It's not a resort for gourmets – though one reporter had 'good charcuterie and paella at the restaurant next to the Burger King'.

Après-ski Après-ski is very lively. The Marseilles, Milwaukee and Safari bars are popular. The Billboard is 'by far the best club'.

Off the slopes Off-slope activity is limited to shopping, visiting the leisure centre or taking a trip to Andorra la Vella for more of the same.

Pas de la Casa

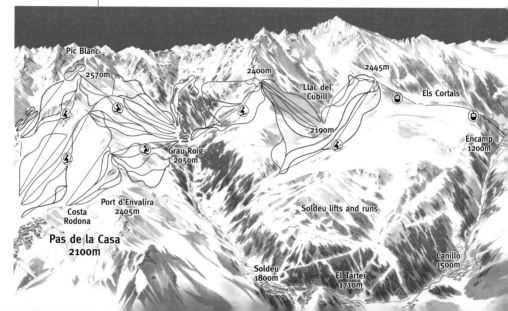

Pic Blanc
2570m
2400m
2445m
Llac del Cubill
Els Cortals
2190m
Grau Roig 2050m
Encamp 1200m
Port d'Envalira 2405m
Costa Rodona
Soldeu lifts and runs
Pas de la Casa 2100m
Canillo 1500m
Soldeu 1800m
El Tarter 1710m

Soldeu

Ideal for beginners and improvers, but check where you're staying

COSTS

①②③④⑤⑥

RATINGS

The slopes

Snow	****
Extent	**
Expert	*
Intermediate	***
Beginner	****
Convenience	***
Queues	***
Mountain restaurants	*

The rest

Scenery	***
Resort charm	*
Off-slope	*

NEWS

For 2002/03 a new high-speed six-seater chair-lift was installed from Riba Escorxada to Tossal de la Llosada. A four-person chair from Riba Escorxada was moved so that you can now reach Tossal de la Llosada from the bottom of the Solanelles area, too.

Free guided tours of the pistes were introduced, and more snow-making was installed. The Riba Escorxada ski school and children's snow garden areas were improved; and the terrain-park was expanded.

- ➕ Slopes to match many mid-sized resorts in the Alps
- ➕ Impressively efficient lift system
- ➕ Not as rowdy a resort as it once was
- ➕ Ski school has excellent British-run section for English-speaking visitors
- ➕ Equally worthwhile Pas de la Casa area is physically linked, but ...

- ➖ ... still no shared lift pass with Pas de la Casa, although the lifts meet and the runs overlap
- ➖ Slopes can get very crowded
- ➖ Village is on the main road through Andorra and suffers heavy traffic
- ➖ Some hotels are way out of town
- ➖ Not much to do off the slopes

If we were planning a holiday in Andorra, it would be in Soldeu (or the isolated hotel at Grau Roig, up the road – covered in the Pas de la Casa chapter). Despite the traffic, it is the least unattractive village, and its slopes are the most interestingly varied (though crowded). But we would want to explore the Pas de la Casa slopes, too, even if it meant spending more on lift passes. The alternative bases of El Tarter and Canillo, and accommodation being built along the busy main road that links them all, are often sold as Soldeu but are much quieter.

For many people the trickier question is whether to come here or to go somewhere completely different. Soldeu no longer competes on package holiday prices with the bargain basements of eastern Europe, so the alternatives are more likely to be in Austria or Italy. It's easy to find villages there that are a lot prettier than Soldeu, scenery that is more impressive, and off-slope diversions that are more, well, diverting. But you would often have to settle for less extensive and interesting slopes, less reliable snow, less carefully organised ski lessons and higher prices for lift passes, lessons and booze.

THE RESORT

The village is an ever-growing ribbon of modern buildings – not pretty, but mainly with traditional stone cladding – on a steep hillside, lining the busy road that runs through Andorra from France to Spain. Most are hotels, apartments or bars, with the occasional shop; for serious shopping – or any other off-slope diversions – you have to head down to Canillo (see end of this chapter) or Andorra la Vella.

The steep hillside leads down to the river, and the slopes are on the opposite side. A gondola takes you from the heart of Soldeu to the heart of the slopes at Espiolets, and a wide bridge across the river forms the end of the piste home, with elevators to take you up to the gondola.

El Tarter, a few miles by road and 200m/660ft vertical down the valley, and Canillo, another 200m/660ft lower, offer alternative lifts into the slopes. Between all three resorts, hotels and apartments are being built along the main road and sold under the Soldeu banner – so check carefully where your proposed accommodation is. If you are staying a bus-ride from Soldeu, you can leave skis, boards and boots (for a fee) at the bottom or top (cheaper says a reporter) of the gondola.

THE MOUNTAINS

The main local slopes are on open mountainsides above the woods, though there are runs in the woods back to all of the resort lift bases. At the eastern end, the slopes and lifts link with those of Pas de la Casa, but there's no joint lift pass. Keen skiers and riders will want to explore the Pas area, and will tailor their pass buying accordingly. There is easy access at Grau Roig, a few miles up the valley.

THE SLOPES
Pleasantly varied but crowded

The gondola rises over wooded, north-facing slopes to Espiolets, a broad shelf that is virtually a mini-resort – the ski school is based here, and there are extensive nursery slopes. A gentle run

Collada de
les Solanelles
2460m

Tossal de la
Llosada
2560m/8,400ft

Pic
d'Encampadana
2490m

Pic de la
Portella
2465m

Tosa dels
Espiolets
2350m

Espiolets
2250m

Riba Escorxada
2100m

El Forn
2000m

Soldeu
1800m/5,910ft

El Tarter
1710m/5,610ft

Canillo
1500m/4,920ft

KEY FACTS

Resort	1800m
	5,910ft
Slopes	1710-2560m
	5,610-8,400ft
Lifts	32
Pistes	92km
	57 miles
Green	24%
Blue	32%
Red	36%
Black	8%
Snowmaking	32km
	20 miles

LIFT PASS INSANITY

If they could agree on a joint lift pass the Soldeu-Pas de la Casa joint area would rival some of the Alps' best-known names for extent and variety. But they can't; so if you want to ski both in a day you need two passes – one for each area. This insanity is the result of an ancient feud between the communities which control the two areas. The result is that people stick to one area – paying for two passes makes it the most expensive skiing in Europe.

Soldeu has good early intermediate slopes, but they can get a lot more crowded than this →

to the east takes you to an area of long, easy runs served by one of Soldeu's four six-packs and a quad. And beyond that is an extensive area of more varied slopes, served by a quad and another six-pack, that overlaps with the Pas de la Casa area. Going west from Espiolets takes you to the open bowl of Riba Escorxada and the arrival point of the lift up from El Tarter. From here, a third six-pack serves sunny slopes on Tosa dels Espiolets and a fourth goes to the high-point of Tossal de la Llosada and the link with the slopes above Canillo. One problem is that, apart from the Canillo sector, many of the blue runs can get unpleasantly crowded.

TERRAIN-PARKS
A good one sponsored by Nike
The terrain-park above Riba Escorxada was expanded and redesigned for

2002/03. As well as jumps, rails and a half-pipe there's a boarder-cross run and a bumps area. Some lessons and free demonstrations are arranged for adults and children over 6.

SNOW RELIABILITY
Much better than people expect
Despite its name (Soldeu means Sun God) the slopes enjoy reliable snow. Most slopes are north-facing, with a good natural snow record and snowmaking on over a third of the pistes. The excellent grooming helps maintain good snow too.

FOR EXPERTS
Hope for good off-piste
It's a limited area for experts, at least on-piste. The Avet black run down to Soldeu deserves its grading, but most of the others would be no more than reds (or even blues) in many resorts.

Soldeu

103

LIFT PASSES

Soldeu/El Tarter
Covers all lifts in Soldeu, El Tarter, Canillo.

Main pass
1-day pass €29.50
6-day pass €138

Children
Under 12: 6-day pass €108
Under 6: free pass

Notes
Half-day pass available.

Alternative passes
The Ski Andorra pass covers all four Andorran areas and allows skiing at any single one of them each day for five out of six consecutive days for €133 (under 12: €108).

SCHOOLS

Soldeu
t 890591
El Tarter
t 890541
Canillo
t 890691

Classes
15hr: €88
Private lessons
€30 for 1hr for 1 or 2 people.

CHILDREN

The three nurseries – at Espiolets, Riba Escorxada and El Forn – take children from 3 to 10.

Children's classes at ski school cost €82 for 15 hours' tuition.

boarding

The excellent school and gentle beginner slopes make this a good place to learn. Intermediates may find the flattish areas of slopes irritating to scoot along but will welcome the many chair-lifts and few drags. Competent free-riders should enjoy the off-piste and weekend snowcat service when it's running (see Experts).

The blacks on Tosa dels Espiolets, for example, are indistinguishable from the neighbouring (and more direct) red and blue. But there is plenty of off-piste potential – notably in the bowl above Riba Escorxada, in the area where Soldeu meets Pas (we had a great time there in fresh powder on our 2003 visit), and above El Forn. And the off-piste remains untouched for days because most visitors are beginners and early intermediates. When conditions permit at weekends, a snowcat takes people up to Pic d'Encampadana whence a range of off-piste routes (dotted on our map) descend to Riba Escorxada.

FOR INTERMEDIATES
Pity there's still no joint pass
There is plenty to amuse all but the keenest intermediates. The area east of Espiolets is splendid for building confidence, while those who already have it will be able to explore the whole mountain. Riba Escorxada is a fine section for mixed ability groups. The relatively new Canillo/El Forn sector has an easy, little-used blue run along the ridge with excellent views all the way to Pal and Arinsal and an easy black in the valley. Many of the blues and reds have short steeper sections, preceded by a 'slow' sign and netting in the middle of the piste to slow you down. The great frustration for mileage-hungry intermediates is the lack of a joint Soldeu/Pas pass.

FOR BEGINNERS
One of the best
This is an excellent resort for beginners. It is relatively snow-sure, and there are numerous easy pistes to move on to (though the crowds can be off-putting). The Espiolets nursery area is huge, and served by moving carpet lifts. And the ski school is top-notch, with a special British section.

FOR CROSS-COUNTRY
Er, what cross-country?
There is no cross country in Soldeu. There is some not far away at Grau Roig (see Pas de la Casa chapter), but Andorra's serious cross-country resort

is La Rabassa, in the south-west corner of the country – 20km/12 miles of loops at an altitude of 2000m/6,600ft.

QUEUES
Crowds more of a problem
The lift system is on the whole impressively new and powerful – including four six-packs – and seems to be able to cope. But there are queues at the morning peak for both the gondola out of Soldeu and the chair from El Tarter; start early or late to avoid them. More of a problem can be crowds on the blue slopes (even in January when we were there) – the reds and blacks are much quieter.

MOUNTAIN RESTAURANTS
Not a highlight
The mountain restaurants are crowded and the food generally dull. There is a choice of places at Espiolets, including table-service at crowded refectory-style tables. The Roc de les Bruixes at El Forn claims to be 'gastronomic' but we lack reports on it. Reporters favour descending to El Tarter, particularly to the snack bar in the Hotel del Clos.

SCHOOLS AND GUIDES
One of the best for Brits
The ski school is effectively run as two units. One deals with English-speaking clients, is led by an Englishman and has mostly native-English-speaking instructors. 40% of the pupils are beginners, and the school has devised a special 'team teaching' scheme to cope with this number of beginners. The school has an excellent reputation for teaching and friendliness. And we have rarely seen such a high proportion of slope-users in ski school groups as we saw here. 2002/03 saw new Ski Workshop and Check-Up Clinics with small groups (maximum of eight and six respectively).

FACILITIES FOR CHILDREN
With altitude
Children are looked after at the mid-mountain stations. There are nurseries and snow playgrounds at Espiolets, Riba Escorxada and El Forn for children from two or three to ten years old.

↑ Newer buildings – both on and off the mountain – tend to be more attractive than those thrown up in Andorra's early days as a ski destination

SKI ANDORRA / SOLDEU TOURIST OFFICE

GETTING THERE

Air Toulouse 192km/119 miles (3½hr).

Rail L'Hospitalet-Près-L'Andorre (25km/16 miles); buses and taxis to Soldeu

ACTIVITIES

Indoor Ice skating, swimming, gym, squash, tennis

Outdoor Thermal spas, snowmobiling, dog sledding, snow-shoeing, tobogganing, helicopter rides

Phone numbers From abroad use the prefix +376.
Central reservations phone number Call 890501.

TOURIST OFFICE

t 890500
soldeu@soldeu.ad
www.soldeu.ad

STAYING THERE

HOW TO GO
Be careful where you stay
A wide range of UK tour operators offer packages here, mainly in hotels but with some apartments and chalets. Location is important – many places are an inconvenient bus-ride from town.

Hotels The best hotels are far removed from the standards of a decade ago.
(((④ **Sport Hotel Village** (870500) By far the best in town, with style and space in the public areas – comfortable chairs and sofas, high ceilings, beams and picture windows. Built over the gondola station by the family which sold the land to the lift company.
(((③ **Sport** (870600) Comfortable, good lounge areas, lively bar and a popular basement disco-bar. But dull buffet-style food. Not nearly as stylish as its sister hotel over the road. No ski room.
(((③ **Piolets** (871787) Pleasant enough, with a pool. Central.
((② **Himalaia** (878515) Recently refurbished, central.
Self-catering The Edelweiss apartments (870600) are spacious, pleasant and well placed opposite the Sport hotel.

EATING OUT
Some gourmand delights
We enjoyed excellent, satisfying meals at three cute rustic restaurants. Borda del Rector (Andorran run and authentic Andorran cuisine), nearer to El Tarter than Soldeu, was our favourite. The other two were both British-run: Snails and Quails, 3km/2 miles up the road in Bordes d'Envalira, and Fat Albert's in downtown Soldeu. L'Esquirol (Indian) and Pussycat have had good reports.

APRES-SKI
Lively
Après-ski is lively but mainly bars and rep-organised events (such as pub crawls with maybe 100 participants). The bar at Fat Albert's has videos shot on the mountain and often a live band. The Pussycat is a good late-night place, with changing party themes. The Piccadilly, under the Sport hotel, is popular. Aspen pub-restaurant and the nearby Avalanche are popular with the younger crowd. We liked the Villager under the Sport Village hotel. The Naudi has a quieter locals' bar. Expect noise from late-night revellers.

OFF THE SLOPES
Head downhill
There is little to amuse non-skiers in Soldeu itself. Down the valley in Canillo is the smart Palau de Gel (see below), and in Andorra la Vella the impressive Caldea spa, and some very serious shopping opportunities. Some of the bigger hotels have excellent sports facilities.

El Tarter 1710m/5,610ft

El Tarter has grown over recent years and is rather sprawling, with no real centre. Reporters recommend the hotel del Clos ('good food but up a steep hill') and del Tarter and the local ski school. But they complain that the resort is 'dull at night'. The Mosquit is a recommended pizzeria; a British-run bar, Peanuts, beneath it seems set to monopolise the British custom.

Canillo 1500m/4,920ft

If you like the idea of deserted local slopes and don't mind riding a gondola down at the end of the day, you could consider Canillo, which looked an acceptably pleasant spot as we repeatedly drove through it. It has the attraction of the impressive Palau de Gel – an Olympic ice-rink plus swimming pool, gym and other amenities.

Soldeu

Austria

Austria is a completely different holiday experience from the other Alpine countries. If you have never been there, you will notice a huge difference – many people who discover it fall in love with it and never want to go anywhere else. One essential ingredient is that the partying is as important as the skiing or riding in most Austrian resorts – après-ski starts early and finishes late. The other essential ingredient is the nature of the villages. There are no monstrous purpose-built block resorts as there are in France and few big resorts or places with steep, challenging slopes such as St Anton. Essentially, Austria is the land of cute little villages clustered around onion-domed churches; of friendly wooded mountains, reassuring to beginners and timid intermediates in a way that bleak snowfields and craggy peaks will never be; of friendly, welcoming people who don't find it demeaning to speak their guests' language; and of jolly, alcohol-fuelled après-ski action, starting in many resorts in mid-afternoon with dancing in on-mountain restaurants and going on as long as you have the legs for it. And Austrian resorts have made great strides in their attempt to catch up on the snowmaking front – most have radically increased their snowmaking capacity in recent years. In midwinter, especially, lack of snow generally goes hand in hand with low night-time temperatures, even at low altitudes, and snowmaking comes into its own. And the last couple of seasons have been bumper snow years for much of Austria. One thing to beware of, though, is Austria's strange aversion to credit cards. Reporter after reporter complains that many establishments do not accept cards – even quite upmarket hotels and restaurants as well as many ski lift companies. So check if they are accepted well in advance, and have access to plenty of cash in case you need it.

It's the après-ski that strikes most first-time visitors as being Austria's unique selling point. The few French resorts that have lively après-ski are dominated by British or Scandinavian holidaymakers (and resort workers); the French themselves are noticeable by their absence and you could be in London or Stockholm rather than France.

But Austrian après-ski remains very Austrian. Huge quantities of beer and schnapps are drunk, German is the predominant language and German drinking songs are common. So is incredibly loud Europop music. People pack into mountain restaurants at the end of the day and dance in their ski boots on the dance floor, on the tables, on the bar, on the roof beams, wherever there's room. There are open-air ice bars on the mountain, umbrella bars and countless transparent 'igloos' in which to shelter from bad weather. In many resorts the bands don't stop playing and the DJs don't stop working until darkness falls, when the happy punters slide off down the mountain in the dark to find another watering hole in town. After dinner the drinking and dancing starts again – for those who take time out for dinner, that is. Of course, not all Austrian resorts conform to this image. But lots of big-name ones with the best and most extensive slopes do. St Anton, Saalbach-Hinterglemm, Ischgl, Sölden and Zell am See, for example, fit this bill.

One thing that all Austrian resorts have in common is reliably comfortable accommodation – whether it's in 4-star hotels with

LECH TOURIST OFFICE

← Austria is full of cute little villages with onion-domed churches – this one is Lech

pools, saunas and spas, or in great-value family-run guest houses, of which Austria has thousands. The accommodation scene is very much dominated by hotels and guest houses; catered chalets and self-catered apartments are in general much less widely available (though there are one or two resorts, such as St Anton and Kitzbühel, where catered chalets are more easily come by).

Most Austrian resorts are real, friendly villages on valley floors, with skiing and boarding on the wooded slopes above them. They have expanded enormously since the war, but practically all the development has been in traditional chalet style, and the villages generally look good even without the snow that is the saving grace of many French and even some Swiss resorts. Unlike Courchevel and Verbier, many Tirolean resorts are as busy in August as in February.

Outside the big-name resorts the skiing is often quite limited. There are many Austrian resorts that a keen skier could explore fully in half a day. Those who start their skiing careers in such resorts may not be worried by this; those who have tried the bigger areas of France and developed a taste for them may find the list of acceptable Austrian resorts quite a short one.

Unfortunately, several of the resorts on that shortlist bring you up against another problem – low altitude, and therefore poor snow conditions. Kitzbühel is at 760m/2,500ft and Söll at 700m/2,300ft, for example. The top heights of Austrian resorts are relatively low, too – typically 1800m to 2000m (5,910ft to 6,560ft); as we have noted above, snowmaking is becoming more widespread, but it works only when the conditions are right. The resorts of the Arlberg, at the western end of the Tirol – St Anton, Lech and Zürs – stand apart from these concerns, with excellent snow records and extensive skiing. And there are other resorts where you can be fairly confident of good snow, such as Obergurgl, Obertauern and Ischgl, not to mention the year-round slopes on glaciers such as those at Hintertux, Neustift, Kaprun and Sölden. But for many other resorts our advice is to book late, when you know what the snow conditions are like.

There are some extensive areas of slopes that are little known in the UK and well worth considering. Bad Gastein, Schladming, Ischgl, Sölden and Lech spring to mind.

Snowboarders don't need big areas; and snowboarding in slushy snow is not as unpleasant as skiing in it. So it's not surprising that boarding in Austria is booming.

Nightlife is not limited to drinking and dancing. There are lots of floodlit toboggan runs and UK tour operator reps organise Tirolean, bowling, fondue, karaoke and other evenings. And not all resorts are raucous. Lech and Zürs, for example, are full of rich, cool, beautiful people enjoying the comfort of 4-star sophisticated hotels. And resorts such as Niederau in the Wildschönau and Westendorf and Alpbach in the Tirol are pretty, quiet, family resorts.

Austrian resorts are now easier to get to independently using cheap flights. EasyJet has flights from London Stansted to Munich and from Gatwick and Luton to Zürich (handy for resorts in western Austria). Ryanair has flights from Stansted to Salzburg, giving very short transfer times to lots of Austrian resorts. It also flies to Klagenfurt in Carinthia and to Friedrichshafen, just over the German border and handy for resorts in western Austria.

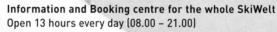

GETTING AROUND THE AUSTRIAN ALPS

The dominant feature of Austria for the ski driver is the thoroughfare of the Inn valley, which runs through the Tirol from Landeck via Innsbruck to Kufstein. The motorway along it extends, with one or two breaks, westwards to the Arlberg pass and on to Switzerland. This artery is relatively reliable except in exceptionally bad conditions – the altitude is low, and the road is a vital transport link.

The Arlberg – which divides Tirol from Vorarlberg, but which is also the watershed between Austria and Switzerland – is one of the few areas where driving plans are likely to be seriously affected by snow. The east–west Arlberg pass itself has a long tunnel underneath it; this isn't cheap, and you may want to take the high road when it's clear, through Stuben, St Christoph and St Anton. The Flexen pass

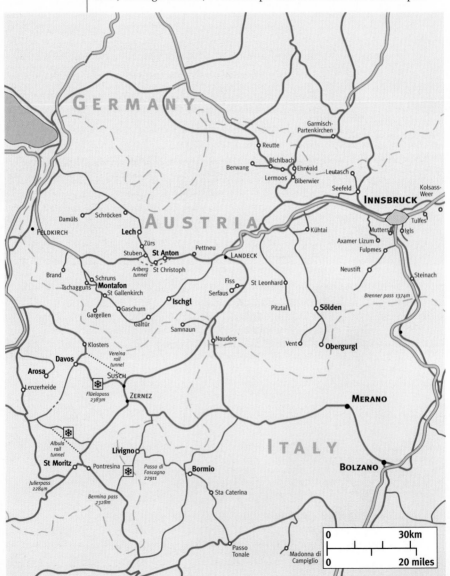

road to Zürs and Lech (which may be closed by avalanche risk even when the Arlberg pass is open) branches off just to the west of the Arlberg summit.

At the eastern end of the Tirol, the Gerlos pass road from Zell am Ziller over into Salzburg province can be closed. Resorts in Carinthia, such as Bad Kleinkirchheim, are usually reached by motorway, thanks to the Tauern and Katschberg tunnels. The alternative is to drive over the Radstädter Tauern pass through Obertauern, or use the car-carrying rail service from Böckstein to Mallnitz.

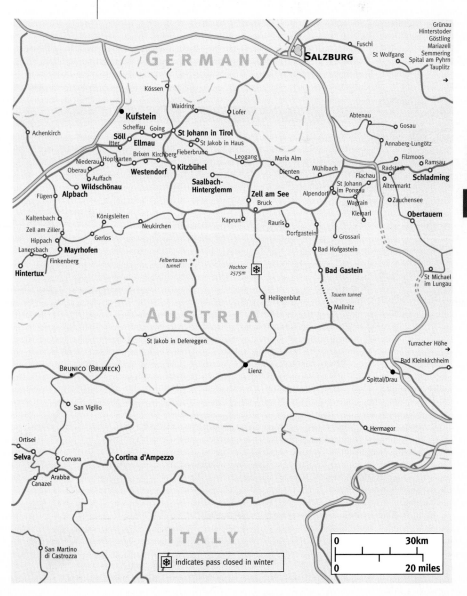

Alpbach

Traditional charm for those who like familiar slopes

NEWS

The snowmaking capacity, which has improved the main slopes down to the valley in recent years, is to be increased to cover a total of 35km/25 miles for 2003/04.

Last season a new quad chair replaced one of the Muldenlift drags behind Gmahkopf.

ALPBACH TOURIST OFFICE

A more reassuring place to take young children on holiday is difficult to imagine ↓

+ Charming traditional village with a relaxed atmosphere – great for young children

+ Good, varied, intermediate terrain, not without challenges for experts

+ Handy central nursery slopes

+ Several other worthwhile resorts within day-trip distance

– Limited slopes

– Main slopes are a shuttle-bus-ride away from the centre

– Few long easy runs for beginners to progress to

– Low altitude means lower slopes can suffer from poor snow – though a north-facing aspect and increased snowmaking have helped

Alpbach is an old British favourite – there is even a British club, the Alpbach Visitors. It is exceptionally pretty and friendly, and its small mountain is not without interest. It's the kind of place that inspires loyalty in its visitors – a regular reporter who has been going for 20 years claims only junior status.

THE RESORT

Alpbach is near the head of a valley, looking south across it towards the Wiedersbergerhorn, where most of the slopes are to be found. It's an exceptionally pretty, captivating place; traditional chalets crowd around the pretty church (the graves are lit by candles every night), and the nursery slopes are only a few steps away.

Alpbach is small, but not necessarily convenient. The main village is the place to stay for atmosphere and après-ski, but involves using a free shuttle-bus to and from Achenwirt, a mile away, where the main gondola goes up to Hornboden. The backwater hamlet of Inneralpbach is much more convenient for the slopes, with its own lifts up to the heart of the slopes.

The Inn valley is a few miles north, and trips east to Kitzbühel or west to Innsbruck are possible. The Hintertux and Stubaier glaciers are within reach.

THE MOUNTAIN

Alpbach's slopes, on two flanks of the Wiedersbergerhorn, are small and simple. Piste grooming is excellent.
Slopes Chair-lifts and drags serve the open, north-facing slopes above the tree line, with black runs following the lift lines and reds (and a single blue) taking less direct routes. The runs are mostly of 200m to 400m (650ft to 1,300ft) vertical, but you can get 500m/1,650ft down the second stage of the gondola, and 1000m/3,300ft when snow is good down to valley level. Behind Gmahkopf is a short west-facing slope where a new quad chair-lift replaced one of the Muldenlift drags last season. The small area at Reith (about 3km/2 miles down the valley from Achenwirt) is on the lift pass and is now accessed by an eight-seat gondola.
Terrain-parks There's a small terrain-park with half-pipe at the top of the main gondola.
Snow reliability Alpbach cannot claim great snow reliability, but at least most slopes face north. The village nursery slope and, increasingly, other runs (including the home run down to the gondola base station) have snowmaking.
Experts Alpbach isn't ideal, but the reds and the three blacks are not without challenge, and runs of 1000m/3,300ft vertical are not to be sniffed at. There are a number of off-piste routes to the valley, short tours are offered, and the schools apparently

KEY FACTS

Resort	1000m
	3,280ft
Slopes	670-2025m
	2,200-6,645ft
Lifts	20
Pistes	45km
	28 miles
Blue	15%
Red	70%
Black	15%
Snowmaking	25km
	16 miles

Phone numbers

From elsewhere in Austria add the prefix 05336.
From abroad use the prefix +43 5336.

TOURIST OFFICE

t 6000
info@alpbach.at
www.alpbach.at

take the top classes off-piste.
Intermediates There is fine intermediate terrain; the problem is that it's limited. This resort is for practising technique on familiar slopes, not high mileage.
Beginners Beginners love the sunny nursery slopes beside the village. But the main slopes are not ideal for confidence-building: most are classified red (there are only a couple of blues).
Snowboarding There's some good free-riding terrain, and the schools offer a range of options.
Cross-country 22km/14 miles of pretty cross-country trails rise up beyond Inneralpbach; the most challenging is about 8km/5 miles long and climbs 300m/1,000ft.
Queues Serious queues are rare, thanks to the efficient gondola and the recent chair-lift upgrades. At busy times, the Inneralpbach chair-lift is quieter than the Achenwirt gondola.
Mountain restaurants The area has squeezed in many mountain restaurants. Recommended are the Hornboden at the top of the gondola, the cosy Böglalm above Inneralpbach, the Kolberhof, and the Asthütte (Kafner Ast) for the sun. Achenwirt, at the lift base, doesn't really count as a mountain restaurant, but it is enthusiastically recommended.
Schools and guides Alpbach and Alpbach Aktiv are the two main ski schools. We have had excellent reports on both in the past, but the Alpbach school currently enjoys better support.
Facilities for children Reporters find the village very child-friendly, and babysitters can be arranged by the tourist office.

STAYING THERE

How to go Hotels and pensions dominate in UK packages.
Hotels Of the smart 4-star places, the Alpbacherhof (5237) and ancient Böglerhof (52270) get most votes. But simpler Haus Thomas (5944) – 'very clean ... you feel like part of the family' – Haus Angelika (5339) and Haus Theresia (5386) are recommended by visitors. The Alphof (5371) is 'excellent' – and its noisy disco has been replaced by additional health facilities. Pension Edelweiss is close to the nursery slopes and is reported to offer B&B and 'clean, spacious apartments and excellent value'.
Self-catering Quite a bit to choose from now, easily bookable through the tourist office web site.
Eating out The popular Post and Alphof both provide 'excellent food' according to a recent report, which also favoured the 'superb' Jakober and its non-smoking room. The Wiedersbergerhorn in Inneralpbach is worth a taxi-ride, not least for 'the absolutely delicious spit-roasted chicken'. The Rossmoos Inn is also recommended for its lively Tirolean evenings and 'superb' food.
Après-ski At peak times this is typically Tirolean, with lots of noisy tea-time beer-swilling in the bars of central hotels such as the Jakober and the Post. In the evening the Waschkuchl Bar is good for a drink. The Birdy Pub has late-night dancing.
Off the slopes There are pretty walks and trips to Innsbruck and Salzburg. There's also an indoor swimming pool and an outdoor ice rink.

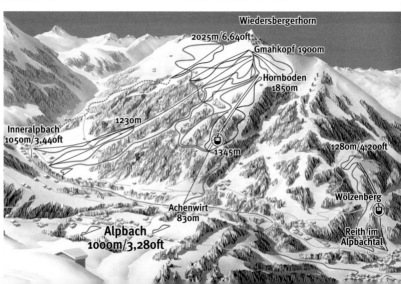

Bad Gastein

Spa-town resort with extensive slopes and few British visitors

COSTS

① ② ③ ④ ⑤ ⑥

RATINGS

The slopes

Snow	***
Extent	****
Expert	***
Intermediate	****
Beginner	**
Convenience	**
Queues	***
Mountain restaurants	****

The rest

Scenery	***
Resort charm	***
Off-slope	****

NEWS

More snowmaking is promised for the 2003/04 season. And the Bad Hofgastein spa is being revamped.

Night-skiing (on Wednesdays) was introduced last season on the 150m/490ft piste served by the Bucheben chair at the bottom of Stubnerkogel.

A new 'Kids Park' was opened in the Angertal. The ski school supervises the 'magic carpet, wave track and wolf's hole' and features a different theme – clowns one day, pirates the next – each week day.

A fast quad has replaced the slow triple chair from the Angertal up to Stubnerkogel, speeding up the link from Schlossalm.

+ Extensive, varied slopes above and below the tree line

+ Great for confident intermediates, and some under-used off-piste

+ More reliable snow than in most low-altitude Austrian resorts

+ Lots of good, atmospheric, traditional mountain restaurants

+ Plenty of off-slope facilities, notably thermal spas

+ Ski Alliance Amadé lift pass covers wide range of nearby resorts

– Slopes are split into five areas, only two of them linked

– Unless you have a car, you need to choose your location with care or budget for a lot of taxi rides

– Main resorts are spa towns, quite different from most Austrian resorts

– Bad Gastein itself has narrow, steep streets, congested with local traffic

– Timid intermediates must be wary of leaving the Schlossalm sector

The Gastein valley doesn't get the attention it deserves in Britain – though that may be changing, to judge by a minor flood of readers' reports received this year, all enthusiastic. With its grand hotels, trinket shops and cramped, steep setting, central Bad Gastein can come as a shock to those used to chalet-style Austrian villages – but there is always the alternative of rustic Dorfgastein or the spacious half-way house of Bad Hofgastein. With five spread-out mountains, the valley needs a top-notch public transport system, and it doesn't have one.

THE RESORT

Bad Gastein sits near the head of eastern Austria's Gastein valley. It is an old spa that has now spread widely, but still has a compact core. A bizarre combination of buildings is laid out in a cramped horseshoe, set in what is virtually a gorge. It mainly attracts a quite formal German/Austrian clientele. Up the hill, above the centre of the town, is a modern suburb with more of a ski-resort feel and easy access to the slopes of Stubnerkogel, which links with Bad Hofgastein's Schlossalm. Across town, the Graukogel area is a bus-ride from the centre. Sportgastein is a 25-minute bus-ride away at the head of the valley, with little in the way of resort development.

A confusing range of ski-bus routes (covered by the lift pass) connect the villages and lift stations. There are trains, too. The ski-bus service is not super-efficient, and a car is a distinct asset here. It also allows full exploitation of the Ski Alliance Amadé lift pass, which covers over 30 resorts ranging from here to Schladming and beyond. Also worth visiting but not included on the lift pass are snow-sure Obertauern and glacial Kaprun.

THE MOUNTAIN

Most of the runs are on the open slopes above the tree line. The terrain is generally quite challenging without being at all extreme – Bad Hofgastein's Schlossalm offers easier options.

Slopes Stubnerkogel, reached by gondola, has runs in all directions from the peak giving about 500m/1,600ft vertical on the open slopes above the tree line and rather more in the woods below it. The much smaller Graukogel, served by a two-stage double chair, is a steep, straightforward mountain. Its wooded runs are a great asset in bad weather, and quiet at other times. The higher, more exposed slopes of Sportgastein have the best snow in the area and are served by an eight-person two-stage gondola.

Terrain-parks See Dorfgastein.

Snow reliability Although of low altitude, the area has a relatively good snow record and there is snowmaking on crucial sections.

Experts There are few black runs but there are long, challenging reds. Graukogel has the World Cup slopes, and the other main sectors have plenty of opportunities to go off-piste. Sportgastein is also worth the trip.

KEY FACTS

Resort	1080m
	3,540ft

For the Gastein valley and Grossarl areas

Slopes	840-2685m
	2,760-8,810ft
Lifts	50
Pistes	200km
	124 miles
Blue	29%
Red	59%
Black	12%
Snowmaking	93km
	58 miles

For Bad Gastein and Bad Hofgastein only

Slopes	860-2685m
	2,820-8,810ft
Lifts	31
Pistes	131km
	81 miles

Intermediates Good intermediates will love all the areas, but the timid are better off on Schlossalm. The open north-facing slopes of Stubnerkogel down into Angertal are good, for both interest and snow-cover. The same is true of the Graukogel runs.

Beginners Nursery slopes are scattered and none combines convenience with reassuringly gentle gradients.

Snowboarding The valley hosts snowboard events, but doesn't seem to cater particularly well for holiday boarders. There's still a fairly high proportion of drag-lifts.

Cross-country There are an impressive 90km/56 miles of trails, but they are all along the valley floor.

Queues There are few problems outside the peak season.

Mountain restaurants Atmospheric, traditional huts abound. The Jungerstube, Bergstadl and Stubneralm have been recommended. Several huts that pander specially to children are marked on the piste map.

Schools and guides We lack recent reports.

Facilities for children There are facilities for all-day care and there's a 'Fun Centre' for kids at the top of the Stubnerkogel gondola. Also, new last winter, a snow adventure park run by the ski school at Angertal.

STAYING THERE

How to go Although apartments make up nearly 15% of the total beds available, British tour operators sell mainly hotel-based packages.

Hotels There are lots of smart 4-star and 3-star hotels with good spa facilities. A reporter recommends the rooms, food, spa and shuttle-bus of the refurbished, central Arcotel Elisabethpark (25510). The Wildbad (37610), nearer the main lift, was rated 'wonderful' by a reporter last year.

Eating out There is a fair range of restaurants, including surprisingly fine Chinese and seafood places.

Après-ski There are elegant tea rooms, sophisticated dances, numerous bars, discos and casinos, but the general ambience is rather subdued. The liveliest spots in town appear to be the Silver Bullet, with early evening live music, followed by Haegblooms where the 'atmosphere is fantastic', if 'jam-packed' is your style.

Off the slopes You can enjoy the naturally warm spas without testing the regenerative effect of radon (a radioactive, carcinogenic gas, inhalation of which is not encouraged in the UK). There are plenty of other things to do, including coach trips.

Bad Gastein

115

Phone numbers
Bad Gastein
From elsewhere in
Austria add the prefix
06434.
From abroad use the
prefix +43 6434.
Bad Hofgastein
From elsewhere in
Austria add the prefix
06432.
From abroad use the
prefix +43 6432.
Dorfgastein
From elsewhere in
Austria add the prefix
06433.
From abroad use the
prefix +43 6433.

TOURIST OFFICE

For all resorts in the
Gastein valley contact
the Bad Hofgastein
office
t 3393
info@gastein.com
www.gastein.com

Bad Hofgastein
860m/2,820ft
Bad Hofgastein is a sizeable, quiet, old
spa village set spaciously in a broad
section of the valley.

THE RESORT
Although sprawling, the village has a
pleasant pedestrianised centre. Queues
permitting, the slopes of Schlossalm
are reached by a funicular to Kitzstein
starting across the valley, a long walk
or short shuttle-bus-ride away; ski-
buses also go on to Angertal, where
there are efficient modern lifts not only
to Schlossalm but also to Bad
Gastein's slopes on Stubnerkogel.
There are also ski-buses to
Dorfgastein, making this a good base
for exploration of the whole valley.

THE MOUNTAINS
Schlossalm is a broad, open bowl, with
runs through patchy woods both to
Bad Hofgastein and Angertal.
The slopes Schlossalm is the valley's
gentlest area, with sunny open slopes
graded blue and red. But the top lifts
lead to some challenging terrain, and
the Kleine Scharte cable-car serves a
serious 750m/2,500ft vertical. A key
feature is the long red run from Hohe
Scharte behind the mountain, ending
at Kitzstein or the valley floor.
Terrain-parks See 'Snowboarding'.
Snow reliability Snowmaking is now
fairly extensive, but snow-cover down
to the bottom is unreliable, especially
on the sunny Angertal slopes.
Experts There are no real challenges
on the local pistes but there is ample
opportunity to go off-piste.
Intermediates All intermediates will
enjoy the Schlossalm slopes, and the
more confident can go further afield.
Beginners You have to catch a bus to
the limited nursery area at Angertal.
Snowboarding Pleasantly varied
terrain, but no special facilities except
at Grossarl (see Dorfgastein). Drag-lifts
are dotted around every sector.
Cross-country Bad Hofgastein makes a
fine base for cross-country when its
lengthy valley-floor trails have snow.
Queues Crowds are not generally a
problem, but the access funicular can
generate big queues at peak times.
Mountain restaurants Schlossalm's
huts are more than a match for
Stubnerkogel's. Kleine Scharte,
Aeroplanstadl, and Hamburger Skihütte
have been recommended.

Schools and guides We lack recent
reports.
Facilities for children The Angertal
school runs the village ski kindergarten
and the new snow adventure park.

STAYING THERE
How to go Bad Hofgastein is
essentially a hotel resort. Some are
within easy walking distance of the
funicular, a few provide courtesy
transport, and most of the rest are
close to bus stops.
Hotels A recent reporter found the
'impressive' facilities and half-board at
the 4-star St Georg (61000) to be
excellent value. The 3-star Rauscher
(64120) is handy for the shuttle-bus
and provides 'clean, spacious rooms
and good food'.
Self-catering Accommodation can be
organised through the tourist office.
Eating out There is a good range of
restaurants. Newly opened Piccola
Italiano, Osteria Divino and Noors are
'well worth a visit'. The Wintergarten is
an intimate restaurant, the Maier one
of the better informal places.
Après-ski It is quiet by Austrian
standards. At close of play the central
Piccolo ice bar is popular; there are
several good places for cakes, among
them Café Weitmoser, an historic little
castle. Later on, the Glocknerkeller and
the Rondo bar have live music in a
low-key ambience. We lack recent
reports on discos etc.
Off the slopes The ThermenTempel
houses a splendid thermal pool; it is
getting a major revamp. Other
amenities include ice skating, tennis,
squash, tobogganing and sleigh rides.

Dorfgastein 830m/2,720ft

Dorfgastein is a more rustic village
further down the valley. It has its own
extensive slopes, accessed by a two-
stage gondola or chair-lifts starting
well outside the village, linked with the
slopes of Grossarl in the next valley to
the east. Runs are varied and long –
from top to bottom, about 8km/5 miles
to either village – with a good mix of
open and wooded runs amid lovely
scenery. Unfortunately the low-altitude
nursery slopes can be cold and icy.
Over in Grossarl is a boarders-only
park with a half-pipe and two quarter-
pipes, jumps and other challenges. Bad
Hofgastein's funicular is 10-15 minutes
away by bus. There are a few shops
and après-ski places.

Ellmau

A quiet base from which to access the extensive Ski Welt area

117

COSTS

① ② ③ ④ ⑤ ⑥

RATINGS

The slopes

Snow	**
Extent	****
Expert	*
Intermediate	****
Beginner	****
Convenience	***
Queues	****
Mountain restaurants	**

The rest

Scenery	***
Resort charm	***
Off-slope	***

NEWS

Snowmaking now covers 135km/84 miles of pistes (over half the total).

In 2002/03 a new eight-seater gondola was built from Scheffau to the top of Brandstadl.

A T-bar on the upper mountain above Brixen was replaced by a fast six-pack, and another on Hartkaiser was replaced by a quad.

There are plans for a new chair-lift to replace a T-bar above Going.

KEY FACTS

Resort	800m
	2,620ft

For entire Ski Welt	
Slopes	620-1830m
	2,030-6,000ft
Lifts	93
Pistes	250km
	155 miles
Blue	43%
Red	48%
Black	9%
Snowmaking	135km
	84 miles

- ➕ Part of Ski Welt, Austria's largest linked ski and snowboard area
- ➕ Pretty, friendly slopes
- ➕ Excellent nursery slopes (but snow reliability can be a problem)
- ➕ Cheap by Austrian standards
- ➕ Quiet, charming family resort – more appealing than neighbouring Söll
- ➕ Massive recent investment in snowmaking has paid off, but ...

- ➖ Ski Welt is at low altitude, and has a poor natural snow record
- ➖ Main lift a bus-ride from village – though reachable via a drag-lift
- ➖ Upper-mountain runs are mostly short, and offer little for experts or adventurous intermediates
- ➖ Lack of nightlife other than rep-organised events
- ➖ Ski Welt slopes can get crowded at weekends and in high season

If you like the sound of the large, undemanding Ski Welt circuit, Ellmau has a lot to recommend it as your base – quieter than Söll, but with more amenities than other neighbours such as Scheffau (covered in the Söll chapter). And Austria's largest snowmaking system makes the area less risky than it was.

THE RESORT

Ellmau sits at the north-eastern corner of the Ski Welt. Although sizeable and becoming more commercialised each year, it remains quiet, with traditional chalet-style buildings, welcoming bars and shops, and a pretty church.

Ellmau has a compact centre, but its accommodation is scattered and the buses around the resort, necessary if you stay in the village, attract complaint for being infrequent. The position of your hotel is, therefore, quite important.

Make sure you get an Ellmau guest card entitling you to various discounts, including to the Kaiserbad leisure centre.

THE MOUNTAIN

The Ski Welt is the largest mountain circuit in Austria. It links Going, Scheffau, Söll, Itter, Hopfgarten and Brixen. The piste map covering this huge area is, not surprisingly, difficult to comprehend. Most runs are easy, and short – which means that getting around the area can take time, despite increasing numbers of fast lifts. Westendorf is covered by the Ski Welt pass, though its local slopes are not linked. Kitzbühel, Waidring,

SKI WELT

In an area dominated by big, unremarkable mountain restaurants, the Rübezahl hut is one of the most compelling ➔

Fieberbrunn and St Johann are in easy reach for day trips and are covered by the Kitzbüheler Alpenskipass.

Slopes Ellmau is close to the best slopes in the area, above Scheffau. The funicular railway on the edge of the village takes you up to Hartkaiser, from where a fine long red (a favourite with reporters) leads down to Blaiken (Scheffau's lift base station). A choice of gondolas (one new last season) take you up to Brandstadl.

Immediately beyond Brandstadl, the slopes become rather bitty; an array of short runs and lifts link Brandstadl to Zinsberg. From Zinsberg, excellent, long, south-facing pistes lead down to Brixen. Then it's a short bus-ride to Westendorf's pleasant separate area. Part-way down to Brixen you can head towards Söll, and if you head up Hohe Salve you get access to a long, west-facing run to Hopfgarten.

Ellmau and Going share a pleasant little area of slopes on Astberg, slightly apart from the rest of the area, and

LIFT PASSES

Ski Welt Wilder Kaiser-Brixental
Covers all lifts in the Wilder Kaiser-Brixental area from Going to Westendorf, and the ski-bus.

Beginners
Points tickets.

Main pass
1-day pass €30
6-day pass €148.50

Children
Under 16: 6-day pass €89
Under 6: free pass

Notes
Single ascent and part-day passes available.

Alternative passes
Kitzbüheler Alpen-skipass covers five large ski areas: Schneewinkel (St Johann), Ski Region Kitzbühel, Ski Welt Wilder Kaiser, Wildschönau and Alpbachtal.

well suited to the unadventurous and families. One piste leads to the funicular for access to the rest of Ski Welt. The main Astberg chair is rather inconveniently positioned, midway between Ellmau and Going.

Terrain-parks There is a terrain-park and quarter-pipe near Söll.

Snow reliability With a low average height, and important links that get a lot of sun, the snowmaking that the Ski Welt has installed is essential. And the Ellmau-Going sector now claims almost all its slopes are covered by snowmaking. This can, of course, only be used when it is cold enough and it cannot prevent slush and icy patches forming. This year reporters experienced slushy, spring-like conditions as early as late January. The north-facing Eiberg area above Scheffau holds its snow well.

Experts There's are steep plunges off the Hohe Salve summit, and a little mogul field between Brandstadl and Neualm, but the area isn't really suitable unless you seek out off-piste opportunities. The ski route from Brandstadl down to Scheffau is a highlight and you can go off-piste with a guide from Brandstadl to Söll.

Intermediates With good snow, the Ski Welt is a paradise for those who love easy cruising. There are lots of blue runs and many of the reds deserve a blue grading. It is a big area and you get a feeling of travelling around. The main challenge is when the snow isn't perfect – ice and slush can make even gentle lower slopes seem tricky. For timid intermediates the easy slopes of Astberg are on hand to Ellmau guests.

Beginners Ellmau has an array of good nursery slopes, now covered by snowmaking. The main ones are at the Going end, but there are some by the road to the funicular. The Astberg chair opens up a more snow-sure plateau at altitude. The Brandstadl-Hartkaiser area has a section of short, easy runs, and a nice long piste running the length of the funicular, which even near-beginners can manage.

Snowboarding Ellmau is a good place to try boarding as the local slopes are easy, but for decent boarders it is more limited.

Cross-country When there is snow, there are long, quite challenging trails, but trails at altitude are lacking.

Queues Continued introduction of new lifts has greatly improved this once queue-prone area.

Mountain restaurants The smaller places are fairly consistent in providing good-value food in pleasant surroundings. The Rübezahl above Ellmau is our favourite in the whole Ski Welt, but a reporter favours the Aualm, just below Brandstadl, especially for its cakes and glühwein. The hut at Neualm, halfway down to Scheffau, has also been recommended. The larger self-service restaurants are functional (the Jochstube at Eiberg is a pleasant exception) and suffer queues. Going is a good spot for a quiet lunch; the Liftstüberl's fish and schnitzels pleased a recent visitor.

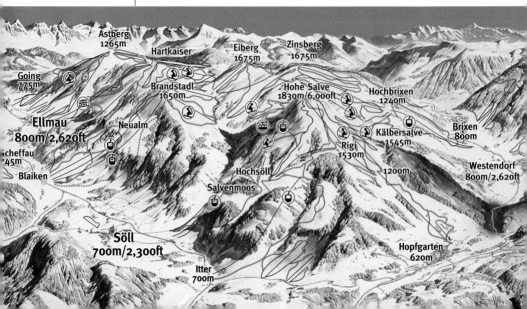

↑ Brandstadl above Scheffau gives a fine view of Söll's Hohe Salve.

SKI WELT

Schools and guides The three schools have good reputations – except that classes can be very large. As well as the main schools there are mountaineering schools that organise tours in the Wilder Kaiser and the Kitzbühel mountains.

Facilities for children Ellmau is an attractive resort for families, described by a regular visitor as 'so child friendly'. Kindergarten facilities seem to be satisfactory and include fun ideas such as a mini train to the lifts. We have had no recent reports, however.

STAYING THERE

How to go Ellmau is essentially a hotel and pension resort, though there are apartments that can be booked locally.
Hotels The Bär (2395) is an elegant, relaxed Relais & Châteaux chalet, but twice the price of any other hotel. 'Luxury without pretensions,' said a reporter who found the weekly gala dinner 'outstanding'. The Hochfilzer (2501) is central, well equipped (with outdoor hot-tub) and popular with reporters (as is the simpler Pension Claudia, which it owns – use of hotel facilities allowed).
Self-catering There is a wide variety. The Landhof apartments continue to impress – 'spacious, immaculately clean and well-equipped' – and offer

Phone numbers
From elsewhere in Austria add the prefix 05358.
From abroad use the prefix +43 5358.

TOURIST OFFICES

Ellmau
t 2301
info@ellmau.at
www.ellmau.at

Going
t 2438
info@going.at
www.going.at

pool, sauna and steam room. Our regular reporter on these matters rates the village supermarket 'excellent'.
Eating out The hotel Hochfilzer has a reputation for good food. A reader recommends the 'busy but spacious' Gasthof Lobewein for its 'substantial and always delicious' food. Café Bettina, midway between the funicular and the town, is good for coffee and cakes.
Après-ski The rep-organised events include bowling, sleigh rides, Tirolean folklore and inner-tubing, but there is little else. The Memory bar, although quiet, is a readers' favourite.
Off the slopes The Kaiserbad leisure centre is good. There are many excursions available, including Innsbruck, Salzburg and Vitipeno. Valley walks are spoiled by the busy main road.

Going 775m/2,540ft

Going is a tiny, attractively rustic village, well placed for the limited but quiet slopes of the Astberg and for the vast area of nursery slopes between here and Ellmau. Prices are low, but it's not an ideal place for covering the whole of the Ski Welt on the cheap.

Going is ideal for families looking for a quiet time, particularly if they have a car for transport to Scheffau when Astberg's runs have poor snow.

Hintertux/Tux valley

Powerful lifts, excellent snow, varied slopes and villages

COSTS

①②③④⑤⑥

HOW IT RATES

The slopes

Snow	*****
Extent	**
Expert	***
Intermediate	***
Beginner	**
Convenience	**
Queues	***
Mountain restaurants	**

The rest

Scenery	***
Resort charm	***
Off-slope	*

NEWS

In December 2002 the slow, old double chair up to Horbergjoch in the Rastkogel area was replaced by a fast, covered eight-seat chair, improving access to the new link with Mayrhofen's slopes.

Also last season a new panoramic terrace opened at the Gefrorene Wand station on the glacier. Down at the bottom of the Hintertux lifts, the Hohenhaus Tenne opened its five bars and is set to become an après-ski landmark.

➕ Hintertux has one of the best glaciers in the world, with some great runs for intermediates and experts on guaranteed good snow

➕ Massive investment in new lifts has linked Lanersbach to Mayrhofen and speeded up access to the glacier

➕ Some excellent off-piste opportunities

➕ A choice of quiet, unspoiled, traditional villages to stay in

➖ Lanersbach and Hintertux are a 15-minute bus-ride apart

➖ Not for those who want a huge choice of shops and throbbing nightlife on their doorstep

➖ Not ideal for beginners or timid intermediates, with few easy runs to valley level

➖ Glacier can be cold and bleak in midwinter, and there are lots of T-bars and slow chairs

The Tux valley has always had its attractions, chief among them the Hintertux glacier, which arguably has the most challenging and interesting runs of any lift-served Alpine glacier. For guaranteed good snow, Hintertux is simply one of the best places to go. But the valley now has much broader appeal. Since 2001 the friendlier, lower slopes of Lanersbach and its nearby twin, Vorderlanersbach, have been linked to those above Mayrhofen and Finkenberg, down in the Zillertal, to form a fair-sized circuit. With the glacier only 20 minutes away by bus, these quiet, traditional villages will now be more attractive bases for many people than either Hintertux or Mayrhofen (covered in its own chapter).

The Tux valley has a variety of small villages to stay in, linked by regular free ski-buses. A free night-bus also runs until 2am. Vorderlanersbach is the first village you come to as you enter the valley and Lanersbach is just beyond it. Both are small, traditional villages with attractive old buildings and small roads and paths, and their centres are bypassed by the main road so they remain peaceful and quiet. Both have gondola links into the local slopes; that from Vorderlanersbach leads to the links with the Penken-Horberg slopes above Mayrhofen – see separate chapter. Hintertux is at the head of the valley, a couple of minutes from the glacier lifts and 15 minutes by bus beyond Lanersbach. On the way up there you pass through two other villages, Juns and Madseit.

There are some good rustic restaurants and bars and a few places along the valley with discos or live music. But nightlife tends to be quieter than in many bigger Austrian resorts.

The Tux valley and Mayrhofen lifts now form what is called the Ski and Glacier World Zillertal 3000 (see Key Facts). Lift passes for four days or more also cover the countless resorts in the rest of the Ziller valley.

TVB TUX / JP FANKHAUSER

The Hintertux glacier has it all – not only guaranteed good snow and interesting slopes, but deck chairs and intense sunshine ➔

Hintertux 1500m/4,920ft

THE RESORT

Tiny Hintertux is bleakly set at the end of the Tux valley. It is little more than a small collection of hotels and guest houses; there is another, smaller group of hotels near the lifts, which lie a 15-minute walk away from the village, across a car park that fills with day-visitors' cars and coaches, especially when snow is poor in lower resorts.

THE MOUNTAINS

Hintertux's slopes are fairly extensive and, for a glacier, surprisingly challenging. The glacier is one of the best in the world, with varied terrain that attracts national ski teams for summer training. In winter it provides guaranteed good snow even when lower resorts are suffering badly.

Slopes A series of three speedy gondolas takes you up from the base to the top of the glacier (vertical rise 1750m/5,740ft) in under 20 minutes. The first stage is an eight-seater up to Sommerbergalm, while the second and third stages (linked by a short slope at Tuxer Ferner Haus) have 24-person cabins. On the two lower stages there is a parallel smaller gondola which is pressed into service to meet demand at peak times. From Sommerbergalm, a fast quad chair serves the slopes below Tuxer Joch; from the top of this sector, an excellent secluded off-piste run goes down to the base station. Between the top of the glacier and Tuxer Ferner Haus there are further chairs and drag-lifts to play on and links across to another 1000m/3,300ft-vertical chain of lifts below Grosser Kaserer on the west. Behind Gefrorene Wand is the area's one sunny piste, served by a triple chair. Descent to the valley involves a short ascent to Sommerbergalm on the way, now achieved by a six-seater chair-lift.

Terrain-parks There is Europe's highest World Cup half-pipe on the glacier (a popular hang-out throughout the summer), and a terrain-park.

Snow reliability Snow does not come more reliable than this. Even off the glacier, the other slopes are high and face north, making for very reliable snow-cover. The runs from Tuxer Ferner Haus down to Sommerbergalm have snowmaking as well.

Experts There is more to amuse experts here than on any other glacier, with a couple of serious black runs at glacier level and steep slopes and ungroomed ski routes beneath. A lot of the off-piste is little used and one

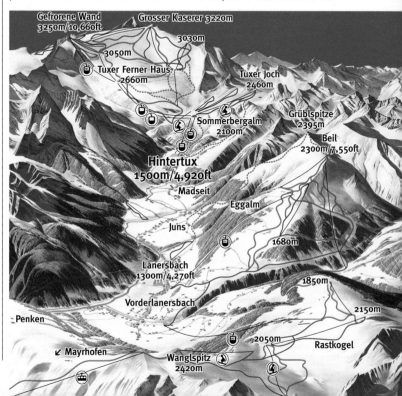

SCHOOLS

Hintertux/Madseit
t 87363
Happy Skiing Tux
t 87240
Luggi's
t 86808

Classes
(Luggi's prices)
6 days (2hr am and
pm) €116
Private lessons
1hr: €54; each
additional person €15

CHILDREN

All three ski schools
run children's classes
for children aged 4 to
14 where lunch is
provided. 6 full days
including lunch €147.

In Lanersbach, there
is also a kindergarten
for children aged 1 to
3 in the Tux Tourist
Association building.

GETTING THERE

Air Salzburg
200km/124 miles
(3½hr); Munich
176km/109 miles
(3hr); Innsbruck
88km/55 miles
(1½hr).

Rail Local line to
Mayrhofen; regular
buses from station.

reporter last year said, 'We found untracked snow not far from the lifts two weeks after the last snowfall.'

Intermediates The area particularly suits good or aggressive intermediates. The long runs down from Gefrorene Wand and Kaserer are fun. And there is a pleasant, tree-lined ski route to the valley from Sommerbergalm and another from Tuxer Joch. Moderate intermediates will love the glacier.

Beginners There is a nursery slope at valley level, but the glacier isn't the ideal place to progress to.

Snowboarding There are some great off-piste opportunities, but boarders complain about the number of T-bars.

Cross-country See the Lanersbach information that follows.

Queues There used to be huge queues at Hintertux when snow was poor elsewhere. Improved lifts have largely solved this problem. But the main runs can get crowded, and then it is best to head over to the quieter Kaserer lifts and runs.

Mountain restaurants The mountain restaurants tend to get very crowded and the big self-service places lack charm - 'rather soulless except for Tuxerjochhaus,' said a visitor this year. The 90-year-old Spannagelhaus is another exception, and there are great views from Gletscherhütte, at the top.

Schools and guides There are three schools, which serve all the resorts in Tux, but we lack reports on them.

Facilities for children All three ski schools run children's classes for children aged 4 to 14 and lunch is provided.

STAYING THERE

How to go Most hotels are large and comfortable and have spa facilities, but there are also more modest pensions.

Hotels Close to the lifts are the 4-star Vierjahreszeiten (8525) and Neuhintertux (8580). We have enjoyed staying in the 3-star Hintertuxerhof (85300) a short walk away; good food, sauna and steam room. Pensions Kössler (87490) and Willeiter (87492) are in the heart of the village.

Self-catering There are plenty of apartments.

Eating out Restaurants are mainly hotel-based. The Vierjahreszeiten is pleasant and informal.

Après-ski There can be a lively après-ski scene both at mid-mountain (Sommerbergalm) and at the bottom of the lifts as they shut; the new but woody Hohenhaus Tenne opened last season, with no fewer than five bars. The Rindererhof has a popular tea dance, and there are a couple of local bars. The free night-bus gets you to and from the other villages until 2am, but Hintertux is not the place for keen clubbers.

Off the slopes The spa facilities are excellent, including a thermal indoor pool, but there are many more options in Mayrhofen.

Lanersbach 1300m/4,270ft

Lanersbach and neighbouring Vorderlanersbach have long been attractive bases for anyone planning to explore the multiple resorts of the Zillertal and the higher Tuxertal. With the construction of direct links, via Rastkogel, with Mayrhofen's slopes their attractions are greatly reinforced.

THE RESORT

Lanersbach is an attractive, spacious, traditional village largely unspoiled by the busy road up to Hintertux that passes the main lift. Happily, the quiet centre near the pretty church is bypassed by the road, yet is within walking distance of the gondola up to Eggalm. The village is small and delightfully uncommercialised, but it has all you need in a resort. And prices are relatively low. Vorderlanersbach is even smaller, with a gondola up to the Rastkogel area.

THE MOUNTAINS

Slopes The slopes of Eggalm, accessed by the gondola from Lanersbach, offer a small network of pleasantly varied, intermediate pistes, including a blue back to the village. You can instead descend to Vorderlanersbach, where a gondola goes up to the higher, open Rastkogel slopes; here, two fast chairlifts - the latest a covered eight-seater - serve mixed red and blue runs and link with Mayrhofen's slopes. A 150-person cable-car brings you back. To get back from Rastkogel to Eggalm you have to take a red run shown on some local piste maps as a ski-route - a strange flaw in the system - or ride the gondola down to Vorderlanersbach.

Terrain-parks The Mayrhofen and Hintertux pipes and parks are easily accessed.

Snow reliability Snow conditions are usually good, at least in early season; by Austrian standards, these are high

im Zillertal
Tux
1300 - 3250 m

Winter as far as the eye can see!
235 km of ski runs: • 37 km • 135 km • 63 km
365 days of the year snowfun on the Hintertux Glacier
"The Glacier Tour" - a day's skiing of superlatives

Rooms, Brochures, Information
Tourismusverband Tux, A-6293 Tux, Lanersbach 472, Tel. ++43/(0)5287/8506, Fax 8508
e-mail: info@tux.at, www.tux.at with search for available rooms

www.tux.at

↑Lanersbach is a quiet village with good lift access to Eggalm and so to Rastkogel and Mayrhofen's Penken

TVB TUX / JP FANKHAUSER

ACTIVITIES

Indoor Bowling, swimming, tennis, squash, cave trekking, hotels with pools/ saunas/steam rooms/ solariums/fitness rooms open to public

Outdoor Ice rink, curling, 38km/24 miles of cleared paths, paragliding, tobogganing (2 runs of 5km/3 miles, 1 run of 3km/2 miles; all runs floodlit), snow-shoe tours, ice climbing, paragliding

Phone numbers
From elsewhere in Austria add the prefix 05287.
From abroad use the prefix +43 5287.

TOURIST OFFICE

Tux
t 8506
info@tux.at
www.tux.at

slopes and there is some snowmaking on Eggalm. But Rastkogel is basically south-facing, and the low links with Eggalm, in particular, are not reliable.
Experts There are no pistes to challenge experts, but there is a fine off-piste route starting a short walk from Beil and finishing at the village.
Intermediates The slopes suit intermediates best – especially now that they are linked in to Mayrhofen's Penken slopes.
Beginners Both areas have nursery slopes (as do Madseit and Juns) but there are few ideal progression slopes – most of the easy runs are on the higher lifts of the Rastkogel sector.
Snowboarding The area isn't great for novices – there are drag-lifts dotted around the mountains, some in key places.
Cross-country There are 14km/9 miles of cross-country trails, alongside the Tux creek, between Madseit and Vorderlanersbach, and a 6km/4 mile skating track in Juns/Madseit.
Queues We have no reports of any problems.
Mountain restaurants There's no shortage; Eggalm's modest area contains four, but this year's readers' favourite is Heidi's Skihütte, one of the two on Rastkogel.
Schools and guides There are three schools in the valley, but we lack recent reports on them.
Facilities for children The non-ski nursery takes children aged from one

to three, and the schools take children from four years upwards.

STAYING THERE
How to go Lanersbach and Vorderlanersbach are essentially hotel-based resorts.
Hotels The Lanersbacherof (87256) is a good 4-star with pool, sauna, steam and hot-tub close to the lifts, but it is also on the main road. The cheaper 3-star Pinzger (87541) and Alpengruss (87293) are similarly situated. In Vorderlanersbach the 3-star Kirchlerhof (8560) is 'really friendly, with comfortable rooms and excellent food', says a satisfied reporter who visits each season.
Self-catering Quite a lot of apartments are available.
Eating out Restaurants are mainly hotel-based, busy, and geared to serving dinner early.
Après-ski Nightlife is generally quiet by Austrian standards, which suits us. We enjoyed the jolly Hühnerstall in Lanersbach (an old wooden building with traditional Austrian music) and the ancient wine bar in Vorderlanersbach. There is a disco or two.
Off the slopes Off-slope facilities are fairly good considering the size of the resorts. Some hotels have pools, hot-tubs and fitness rooms open to non-residents. There is a tennis centre in Vorderlanersbach which also has squash and bowling. Innsbruck and Salzburg are possible excursions.

Innsbruck

A cultured city base for a range of little ski resorts – and a big glacier

125

COSTS

① ② ③ ④ ⑤ ⑥

KEY FACTS

Resort	575m
	1,890ft
Slopes	575-3210m
	1,890-10,530ft
Lifts	63
Pistes	130km
	81 miles
Blue	35%
Red	42%
Black	23%
Snowmaking	34km
	21 miles

NEWS

For 2003/04 a new eight-person gondola is planned for Stubaier Gletscher, running from the Eisgrat restaurant at 2900m/9,510ft to the highest slopes at the top of the Schaufelspitze.

It looks as if the Mutters ski area will stay closed for the 2003/04 season as new lifts planned for it have been delayed.

Innsbruck is not a ski resort in the usual sense. It is an historic university city of 130,000 inhabitants, with a vibrant cultural life, set at a major Alpine crossroads, and is a major tourist destination in summer. Its local slopes are of local interest. But the city has twice hosted the Olympic Winter Games, and it lies at the heart of a little group of resorts that share a lift pass and are accessible by efficient bus services. Among them is one of the three or four best glacier areas in the Alps – the Stubaier Gletscher.

The Inn valley is a broad, flat-bottomed trench hereabouts, but Innsbruck manages to fill it from side to side. It is a sizeable city, and as you would expect from its Olympic background it has an excellent range of winter sports facilities, as well as a captivating car-free medieval core. It has smart, modern, shopping areas, trendy bars and restaurants, museums (including, of course, one devoted to the Olympics), concert halls, theatres, a zoo and other attractions that you might seek out on a summer holiday, but normally wouldn't expect to find when going skiing.

Winter diversions off the slopes include over 300km/185 miles of cross-country trails, some at valley level but others appreciably above it; curling and skating at the Olympic centre; several toboggan runs totalling 55km/34 miles, the longest (above Birgitz) an impressive 10km/6 miles and 960m/3,150ft vertical; and rides on a four-man bob at Igls.

Not the least of the attractions of staying in such a place is that you don't pay ski resort prices for anything.

There are hotels, inns and B&Bs of every standard and style, with 3-star and 4-star hotels forming the nucleus. Among the more distinctive hotels are the grand 5-star Europa Tyrol (59310), the ancient 4-star Goldener Adler (571111) and the 3-star Weisses Kreuz (59479) in the central pedestrian zone, and the 4-star art nouveau Best Western Neue Post (59476).

As well as traditional Austrian restaurants there are several Italians, plus a smattering of more exotic alternatives from Mexican to Japanese.

There is an impressive 1400m/ 4,600ft vertical of slopes on the south-facing slopes of **Seegrube-Nordkette**. The focus of the slopes at Seegrube is reached by cable-car rising 1050m/ 3,450ft from Hungerburg on the outskirts of the city (with buses and a funicular up to the cable-car departure station). Although there are red runs to

LIFT PASSES

Innsbruck Gletscher Skipass
Covers Seegrube–Nordkette, Patscherkofel (Igls), Axamer Lizum, Glungezer (Tulfes), Schlick 2000 (Fulpmes), Mutters, Stubaier Gletscher. 6-day pass €145

Senior citizens
Over 60: 6-day pass €116

Children
Under 19: 6-day pass €116
Under 15: 6-day pass €87

Other passes
Super-Skipass covers all the above plus one day in the Arlberg (St Anton) and one day in Kitzbühel.

↑ Innsbruck has a captivating, car-free medieval centre

the valley, the snow is not reliable. You go up here expecting to ski the red runs of 370m/1,210ft vertical below Seegrube, served by a chair-lift. A further stage of the cable-car rises 350m/1,150ft vertical to access the Karinne ski route, which is said to be fearsomely steep (up to 70% gradient). You can ski it with a guide and collect a T-shirt and certificate to prove it.

But for visitors, if not for residents, skiing usually means heading for the opposite side of the Inn trench, to east or west of the side valley that runs southwards towards the Brenner pass and Italy. The Brenner road opens up the possibility of excursions to resorts in the Dolomites, such as Selva.

The standard Innsbruck lift pass covers the lifts in all the resorts dealt with here, except Seefeld. The extraordinarily wide-ranging Super-Skipass includes days in Kitzbühel to

Igls is a small, quiet resort linked by tram to Innsbruck, with limited local slopes, which hosted the men's downhill and bobsled events in the 1976 Olympics →

the east and St Anton to the west. Free ski-bus services run to and from all the lift-pass-covered areas, but only at the beginning and end of the day. A car makes life more convenient, especially if you are staying outside downtown Innsbruck.

There are terrain-parks at Seegrube, Axamer Lizum, Schlick 2000 and the Stubaier Gletscher.

TULFES 920m/3,020ft
Tulfes gets rather overshadowed by the Olympic resorts of Igls and Axamer Lizum, but it has some worthwhile runs.
The runs are on the north-facing slopes of Glungezer. A chair-lift from a car park above the village serves red and blue runs of 600m/1,970ft vertical. This leads to a drag up to the tree line serving a red run of 500m/1,640ft vertical. And this in turn leads to two drags serving open red runs from the top at 2305m/7,560ft – almost 1400m/4,600ft above the village. More snowmaking is planned for 2003/04.

Like Igls, the village sits on the shelf on the side of the Inn valley. There are a dozen hotels and gasthofs.

IGLS 900m/2,950ft
Igls seems almost a suburb of Innsbruck – the city trams run out to the village – but it is a small resort in its own right. Its famous downhill race course is an excellent piste.
The village of Igls is small and quiet, with not much in the way of diversions apart from the beautiful walks, the Olympic bob run and the tea shops. You can stay in Igls, and a couple of UK operators sell packages there. Most hotels are small and in the centre of the village, a bit of a walk from the cable-car station. An exception is the family-run 5-star Sporthotel (377241), which occupies the prime site, centrally placed between the tram and the cable-car stations: 'Excellent facilities, good food and nice bar,' says a reporter.

The skiing on Patscherkofel is very limited and revolves around the excellent, varied, long red run that formed the men's downhill course in 1976, when Franz Klammer took ski racing (and the Olympic gold medal) by storm. There is a blue-run variation on this run (with a five-minute hike to reach the start, says a 2003 reporter), but no other pistes. A cable-car rises 1050m/3,450ft from the village (and you can take it down if the lower runs are poor or shut). At the top, a chair

Phone numbers
Innsbruck & Igls
Calling long-distance
add the prefix 0512.
From abroad use the
prefix +43 512.
Tulfes
Calling long-distance
add the prefix 05223.
From abroad use the
prefix +43 5223.
Fulpmes
Calling long-distance
add the prefix 05225.
From abroad use the
prefix +43 5225.
Neustift
Calling long-distance
add the prefix 05226.
From abroad use the
prefix +43 5226.
Mutters
Calling long-distance
add the prefix 0512.
From abroad use the
prefix +43 512.
Axamer Lizum
Calling long-distance
add the prefix 05234.
From abroad use the
prefix +43 5234.

rises a further 275m/900ft to the summit offering wonderful views over Innsbruck and ski routes back down. A fast quad and a couple of drags serve slopes below the cable-car station. There is a short beginner lift at village level, and another a short bus-ride up the hill. We have received mixed reports on the grooming of the trails.

Après-ski is quiet. The resort suits families but our 2003 reporter would have preferred to stay in Innsbruck.

FULPMES 935m/3,070ft
Fulpmes is a sizeable village between Innsbruck and Neustift, on the way to the Stubaier Gletscher, with a fair-sized ski area of its own called Schlick 2000.
A two-stage gondola leads to a series of chair- and drag-lifts serving a few mainly short blue and red runs on the Sennjoch. There are also two ski-routes and a terrain-park.

STUBAIER GLETSCHER 1750m/5,740ft
The Stubaier Gletscher is one of the best glacier ski and snowboard areas in the world and you can visit here in summer as well as winter. The nearest place to stay is picturesque Neustift, 20km/12 miles away and served by regular buses.
The glacier is accessed by two alternative two-stage gondolas from the huge car park at Mutterberg. For 2003/04 another gondola right to the top of the slopes is planned – so you'll be able to get to the top by riding three successive gondolas.

On the glacier a variety of chair- and drag-lifts (including three six-person chairs) allow fabulous high altitude cruising on blue and red runs, which normally have excellent snow on slopes between 3200m and 2300m (10,500ft and 7,550ft). A lovely 10km/6 mile ungroomed ski-route down via a deserted bowl takes you down to the valley – or if you start at the top, a descent of about 14km/9 miles and 1450m/4,760ft vertical is possible. There is also good off-piste on the glacier to be explored with a guide.

There is a terrain-park and half-pipe, a fun area for kids at Gamsgarten and a 20m/66ft ice tower.

Continued improvements to the lifts have virtually eliminated what used to be enormous queues. Last season a reporter saw 'around 3,000 cars and coaches in the car park and although the glacier was busy, we never had to queue for more than two minutes'.

Neustift is an attractive Tirolean village halfway along the Stubai valley, with the main road bypassing the village centre. It has a small area of local slopes, but what you go for is the glacier. There are lots of 4- and 3-star hotels in the village – the Sonnhof (2224) and the Hoferwirt (2560) have been recommended by reporters. Most of the restaurants are hotel-based – reporters recommend Bellefonte's pizzas and the Hoferwirt.

MUTTERS 830m/2,720ft
Almost as close to Innsbruck as Igls, Mutters is a charming rustic village at the foot of long slopes of 900m/2,950ft vertical. Sadly, its slopes have been closed since the 2001/02 season and it is unlikely that they will re-open in time for 2003/04.
Four new lifts are planned here, including a new access gondola from just outside the village. They will serve a couple of long red runs and one long blue right back to the valley as well as shorter runs near the top. A lift and piste link with the slopes of Axamer Lizum is also planned. But, when we went to press, the project had been put on hold while various objections were dealt with. It was unlikely the slopes would be open for 2003/04.

The half-dozen hotels in the village divide equally into 3-star and 4-star categories. There is a lively après-ski scene and great off-slope facilities including tennis courts, saunas, skating rinks and 40 curling lanes.

AXAMER LIZUM 1580m/5,180ft
The mountain outpost of the Inn-side village of Axams is a simple ski station and nothing more, but it does have some good slopes and reliable snow conditions – and, as a reporter says, 'You feel as if you are in a wilderness.'
Axamer Lizum could scarcely offer a sharper contrast to Igls. It offers much more varied slopes and a network of lifts, with the base station at a much higher altitude. The slopes here hosted all the Olympic Alpine events in 1976 except the men's downhill, and this is the standard local venue for weekends – hence the huge car park, which is the most prominent feature of the 'resort'.

The main slopes on Hoadl and Pleisen are blues and reds, almost entirely above the trees but otherwise nicely varied, and there is scope to 'play in gullies and bumps, as well as true off-piste,' says our reporter. The

Innsbruck

vertical of the main east-facing slopes above the main lift station is 'only' 700m/2,300ft, but for good skiers at least there is the possibility (given good snow conditions) of a 1300m/4,250ft descent at the end of the day from Pleisen to the outskirts of Axams – an easy 6.5km/4 mile black. On the opposite side of the valley, a chair-lift serves a fairly easy black slope.

There are plans for increased snowmaking for 2003/04 bringing coverage to 75% of the slopes. A new restaurant is also planned on Hoadl.

There are two good nursery lifts, and two ski schools.

You can stay up here – there is a 4-star hotel at the lift base, the Lizumerhof (68244) – 'nice rooms and decent modern Austrian cuisine,' says a reporter – and there are a couple of 3-stars, too. But there's little in the way of après-ski apart from a couple of bars – the Alm bar is the most atmospheric – and you have to eat in your hotel or go to Axams.

There is also accommodation not far away at lower altitude in Axams – including four 3-star hotels – and in other nearby villages such as Götzens (one 4-star hotel, two 3-star gasthofs) and Birgitz (two 3-star hotels).

SEEFELD 1200m/3,940ft

Seefeld is a smart all-round winter holiday resort in a pretty setting, with highly recommended cross-country trails and off-slope activities, and a couple of small, separate areas of downhill slopes.

A classic postwar Tirolean tourist development, Seefeld is well designed in traditional Tirolean style, with a large, pedestrian-only centre. You can

get there by train, if you wish, since it's on a main railway line.

Seefeld's slopes are divided into two main sectors – Gschwandtkopf and Rosshütte. Both are on the outskirts and reached from most hotels by a regular free shuttle-bus.

Gschwandtkopf is a rounded hill with 300m/1,000ft of intermediate vertical down two main slopes, while Rosshütte is more extensive and has a terrain-park and half-pipe. The top of Rosshütte can be reached by a funicular – 'very efficient,' says a reader – and then a cable-car, and runs finish in adjacent Hermannstall. From Rosshütte two six-seater chairs go to the shoulder of Härmelekopf – an improvement on the old cable-car, allowing repeated runs as well as the long red run down.

Rosshütte has some seriously steep off-piste challenges for experts and will offer intermediates an interesting day out from Innsbruck – but the terrain is of no interest for a week's stay. The nursery slopes in the central village are broad and gentle, with snowmaking.

Seefeld's 200km/125 miles of excellent cross-country trails are some of the best in Europe and are one reason why Innsbruck has been able to hold the Winter Olympics twice and, more recently, the Nordic World Ski Championships.

Lots of people come here for the curling, skating and swimming rather than skiing. The upmarket nature of the resort is reflected in the hotels – there are six 5-stars and almost 30 4-stars. On our last visit we stayed at the 4-star Hiltpolt (2253), which was very comfortable with good food.

Phone numbers
Seefeld
Calling long-distance add the prefix 05212. From abroad use the prefix +43 5212.

TOURIST OFFICE

Seefeld
t 2313
info@seefeld.tirol.at
www.seefeld-tirol.com

INNSBRUCK TOURISMUS

Axamer Lizum is popular with locals at weekends, but has no real village at the foot of the slopes to stay in ➔

Ischgl

One of Austria's best – but a well-kept secret on the British market

129

COSTS

① ② ③ ④ ⑤ ⑥

RATINGS

The slopes

Snow	****
Extent	****
Expert	***
Intermediate	****
Beginner	**
Convenience	***
Queues	****
Mountain restaurants	***

The rest

Scenery	***
Resort charm	****
Off-slope	***

NEWS

On the Ischgl side, a new high-speed six-seater chair is planned for 2003/04 to replace an old T-bar bringing people back from above Bodenalp into the Höllenkar bowl. On the Samnaun side, another new high-speed six-seater chair from Alp Trida will serve some local blue slopes. And three ski routes are being newly laid out and improved. More snowmaking is being installed.

The 2002/03 season saw a new six-pack from below Idalp to Pardatschgrat, a new black run to Höllenkar from Greitspitz and more snowmaking. A new covered car park was built at the Silvretta gondola.

➕ Charming old Tirolean village, expanded in sympathetic fashion

➕ High slopes with reliable snow

➕ Lots of good intermediate runs

➕ Great modern lift system (including three gondolas, 17 high-speed chairs and a double-decker gondola)

➕ Wide range of accommodation from luxury hotels to simple B&Bs

➕ Very lively après-ski

➖ Not ideal for beginners or timid intermediates, for various reasons

➖ English less-widely spoken than is usual in Austria

➖ Few seriously steep runs

➖ Very little wooded terrain to give shelter in bad weather

➖ EuroTrash-style après-ski – e.g. table-dancing in plush 4-star hotels – and a lot of heavy drinking

Very few UK tour operators offer packages to Ischgl (which is dominated by German visitors) and the resort has a very low profile in Britain. But it deserves better; it receives rave reviews from almost every reader who goes there and in our view it should be on most people's Austrian short-list.

Samnaun is tour-op-free, and likely to remain so. But for independent travellers it has attractions – it's a charming, relaxed village, has good home runs and for a party including some novices makes a better base than Ischgl.

THE RESORT

Ischgl is a quite compact village tucked away in the long, narrow Paznaun valley, south of St Anton on the Swiss border (the skiing is shared with Swiss Samnaun). It's set where a stream (the Fimbabach) joins the river Trisanna, and part of the village is built on high ground between the converging rivers.

The narrow main street plus a couple of side streets are traffic-free – the village is bypassed by the valley road up to Galtür – and at the west end of the pedestrian zone is the main access lift, the 24-person Silvrettabahn, up to the main mid-mountain focus of Idalp. Two other gondolas – one to Idalp, the other to the higher point of Pardatschgrat – start close together on

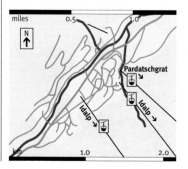

the eastern fringe of the village, beside the Fimbabach. Because of the high ground in between, getting to these lifts from the middle of the village used to be hard work; but now an underground moving carpet connects them to the heart of the village.

The buildings are practically all in traditional chalet style, and the place has a neat, prosperous air. The wooded flanks of the valley rise steeply from the village, which as a result gets almost no sun in early season. There's a selection of lively bars, an excellent sports centre and a fair number of shops to stroll round. But drunken early-evening revellers can be intrusive.

Choice of location is much less important since the construction of the underground walkway, but the best spot, all things considered, is on or near the main street. Beware of accommodation across the bypass road, a long way from the lifts.

There is no need for vehicular transport in the resort, but there are frequent buses up the valley to Galtür (covered by the regional ski pass), which is described at the end of this chapter, and a car makes trips to St Anton and Lech viable. It's a very long taxi-ride back from Samnaun, should you get stuck there.

KEY FACTS

Resort	1400m
	4,590ft
Slopes	1400-2870m
	4,590-9,420ft
Lifts	42
Pistes	200km
	124 miles
Blue	25%
Red	60%
Black	15%
Snowmaking	60km
	37 miles

THE MOUNTAINS

Ischgl is a fair-sized, relatively high, snow-sure area. Practically all the slopes are above the tree line, and bleak in bad weather, the main exception being the steep lower slopes above the village and a couple of short runs low down in the Fimbatal. The slopes are shared with duty-free Samnaun in Switzerland.

There are increasing numbers of ski routes on the piste map – some adding options, some (regrettably) replacing pistes. These routes are unpatrolled, and avalanche-controlled only 'in the immediate area of avalanche warning signs'.

THE SLOPES
Cross-border cruising

The sunny **Idalp** plateau, reached by two of the village gondolas, is the hub of the slopes. It can be very crowded, especially at ski school meeting time and the end of the day. Pardatschgrat, reached by the third gondola, is about 300m/1,000ft higher. From here it's an easy run down to Idalp – with the alternative of long, challenging runs towards Ischgl. Lifts radiate from Idalp, leading to a wide variety of mainly north-west- and west-facing runs.

A short piste brings you to the lifts serving the **Höllenkar** bowl, leading up to the area's south-western extremity and high-point at Palinkopf. There are further lifts beyond Höllenkar, on the west-facing flanks of the Fimbatal.

On the Swiss side the hub of activity is **Alp Trida**, surrounded by south- and east-facing runs with great views. From here a scenic red run goes down to Compatsch, from where there are buses to Ravaisch – for the cable-car back – and Samnaun-Dorf. From Palinkopf there is a beautiful long run down an unspoiled valley to Samnaun-Dorf. It is not difficult, but it is excessively sunny in parts and prone to closure because of avalanche risk. There is a long, flat stretch at the end.

TERRAIN-PARKS
One of Europe's best

Between Idjoch and Idalp is a championship half-pipe and an excellent terrain-park with jumps for beginners to professionals, a quarter-pipe, rails, a boarder-cross course and a GS course with timing. There's a separate kids' snowboard area with boarder-cross, snakes, waves and jump.

SNOW RELIABILITY
Very good

All the slopes, except the runs back to the resort, are above 2000m/6,560ft and many of those on the Ischgl side are north-west-facing. So snow conditions are generally reliable (which can lead to crowds when bus-loads of visitors arrive from lower resorts). There is snowmaking on various runs including several above Idalp, the two main descents to Ischgl and some key slopes on the Samnaun side.

FOR EXPERTS
Not much on-piste challenge

Ischgl can't compare with nearby St Anton for exciting slopes, and some of the runs marked black on the piste map would be red elsewhere. But there is plenty of beautiful off-piste to be found with a guide – and, because there are few experts around, it doesn't get tracked out quickly. The best areas to head for are Greitspitz and Palinkopf – the wooded lower slopes of the Fimbatal are delightful in a snowstorm. The best steep piste is 4, from Pardatschgrat towards Ischgl. You can do the top half of this repeatedly by catching the gondola at the mid-station. The variant 4a, into Velilltal, is now a ski-route.

FOR INTERMEDIATES
Something for everyone

Most of the slopes are wide, forgiving and ideal for intermediates.

At the tough end of the spectrum our favourite runs are those from Palinkopf down to Gampenalp and on

boarding

Ischgl was one of the first resorts to wholeheartedly welcome boarders. It has one of the best terrain-parks in Europe and is constantly improving it. The lifts are generally boarder-friendly; and although there are still lots of drag-lifts, where there is a drag, there's often a chair option. The area is well-suited to beginners and intermediates; experts will love Ischgl after fresh snow, even if the gradients are less impressive than in St Anton. Silvretta Sports and Intersport Mathoy are recommended snowboard shops.

LIFT PASSES

Two-Country VIP Skipass
Covers all lifts in Ischgl and Samnaun and local buses.

Main pass
1-day pass €37.50
6-day pass €163.50

Senior citizens
Over 60: 6-day pass €130.50

Children
Under 16: 6-day pass €98
Under 7: free pass

Notes
VIP Skipass is available to those staying in Ischgl, Samnaun or Mathon only on presentation of a guest card. Note that the lift pass office does not take credit cards.

Alternative passes
Regional ski pass covers Ischgl, Samnaun, Galtür, Kappl and See.

along the valley to the secluded restaurant at Bodenalp.

There are also interesting and challenging black runs down the Hollspitz chair, and from both the top and bottom of the drag-lift from Idjoch up to Greitspitz. The reds from Pardatschgrat and Velillscharte down the beautiful valley to Velilltal and the red from Greitspiz into Switzerland are great for quiet, high-speed cruising.

For easier motorway cruising, there is lots of choice, including the Swiss side, where the runs from the border down to Alp Trida should prove ideal. The red runs that take you back to Idalp on the return journey are not difficult. But there are frequent moans about the red runs down to Ischgl itself; neither is easy, conditions can be tricky, and beer-lubricated crowds don't help. Quite a few people ride the gondolas down instead.

FOR BEGINNERS
Not ideal
Beginners go up the mountain to Idalp, where there are good, sunny, snow-sure nursery slopes and a short beginners' drag-lift. The blue runs on the east side of the bowl offer pleasant progression for fast learners. But away from this area there are few runs that are ideal for the near-beginner.

FOR CROSS-COUNTRY
Plenty in the valley
There are 48km/30 miles of cross-country track in the Paznaun valley between Ischgl, Galtür and Wirl. This tends to be pretty sunless, especially in early season, which is away from the main slopes, which makes meeting downhillers for lunch inconvenient.

QUEUES
An amazing transformation
Ischgl used to be renowned for its queues, but visitors these days are mightily impressed by the number of fast chairs on the mountain – as well as the three gondolas out of Ischgl and the double-decker cable-car out of Samnaun. Queues can form both in the village (the Silvrettabahn is most queue-prone) and at various points up the mountain. Some may look serious, but most shift quickly.

MOUNTAIN RESTAURANTS
Much improved
Mountain restaurants tend to be very crowded but quite good quality, with over half now offering table-service. The Paznauner Taja, above Bodenalp, is an attractive, rustic chalet, but gets very crowded. There is table-service upstairs and often a band playing on the terrace, or throbbing disco music. Down in Fimbatal is the Bodenalpe, a quieter, rustic table-service restaurant.

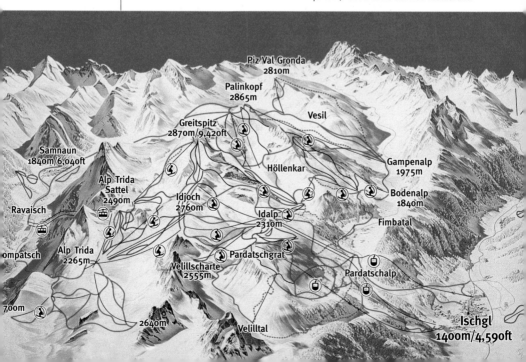

Ischgl
1400m/4,590ft

Idalp is the hub of Ischgl's slopes and the restaurant terraces there have good views →

CHILDREN

The childcare facilities are up the mountain at Idalp and available 6 days a week. There's a ski kindergarten for children aged 3 to 5 (€41 per day). From the age of 5 children can join the ski school (6 full days €148). There's also a non-skiing nursery that takes toilet-trained children. Lunch is available with all these options.

GETTING THERE

Air Innsbruck 100km/62 miles (1½hr); Zürich 210km/130 miles (3hr); Munich 300km/186 miles (3hr).

Rail Landeck (30km/19 miles); frequent buses from station.

SCHOOLS

Ischgl-Silvretta
t 5257/5404
schischule@ischgl.at

Classes
5 days (2hr am and pm) €148

Private lessons
€108 for 2hr; each additional person €15

At Idalp there is a big self-service cafeteria, and a good table-service alternative (splendid views from the terrace). There's also a smaller, crowded self-service nearby. The self-service up at Pardatschgrat tends to be quieter. The Schwarze Wand pizzeria at the top of Höllenkar is recommended by reporters. From Gampenalp you can be towed by snowmobile to the remote Heidelberghüttel.

The restaurants on the Swiss side at Alp Trida are pleasant. The Alp Bella (table- or self-service) has been recommended for a quiet time. Above the big Alp Trida self-service is the upmarket Marmotte, with table-service indoors and out (reservations needed).

Recommended by several reporters is the Schmuggler Alm in Samnaun – the first house you get to if you take the long red from Palinkopf: 'Table service, great food, good value – and they take euros.' But a recent visitor complains of 'rude DJs, brash barmen and Eurotrash music'.

SCHOOLS AND GUIDES
Good despite language problems
The school meets up at Idalp and starts very late (10.30 to 12.30 and 1.30 to 3.30) – perhaps to allow people to get over their hangovers. In the past we've had rave reports of both adult and children's classes, but recent reporters said class sizes were large at around 12 people and their instructor spoke limited English. As well as normal lessons the school organises off-piste tours – this area is one of the best in the Alps for touring.

FACILITIES FOR CHILDREN
High-altitude options
The childcare facilities are all up at Idalp, but we have no first-hand reports of the service they provide.

STAYING THERE

HOW TO GO
Few packages
Very few British tour operators offer Ischgl – they find it difficult to get firm allocations of affordable rooms.
Hotels There is a good selection from luxurious and expensive to basic B&Bs. Beware: some don't take credit cards.
(((((5) **Trofana Royal** (600) One of Austria's most luxurious hotels, with prices to match. A celebrity chef runs the kitchen. Sumptuous spa facilities.
(((((5) **Madlein** (5226) Convenient, 'hip', modern hotel. Pool, sauna, steam room. Nightclub and disco.
(((((5) **Elisabeth** (5411) Right by the Pardatsch gondola with lively après-ski. Pool, sauna and steam room.
(((((5) **Solaria** (5205) Near the Madlein and just as luxurious, but with a 'friendly family atmosphere'.
(((((5) **Piz Tasna** (5277) Up hill behind church: 'Quiet location, friendly, lovely views over village, excellent food.'
(((((4) **Sonne** (5302) Highly rated by reporters. In the centre of the village. Lively stube. Sauna, hot-tub, solarium.
(((((3) **Jägerhof** (5206) 'Jewel of a hotel,' said a reporter. Friendly, good food, large rooms. Sauna and steam.
(((((3) **Christine** (5346) Probably the best B&B in town. 'Huge rooms, nice views, good position near the lifts.'

ACTIVITIES

Indoor Silvretta Centre (bowling, billiards, swimming pool, sauna, steam baths, solarium), museum, library, gallery, tennis courts

Outdoor Curling, skating, sleigh rides, hiking tours, 7km/4 miles floodlit toboggan run

Phone numbers
Ischgl
From elsewhere in Austria add the prefix 05444.
From abroad use the prefix +43 5444.
Galtür
From elsewhere in Austria add the prefix 05443.
From abroad use the prefix +43 5443.
Samnaun
From elsewhere in Switzerland add the prefix 081.
From abroad use the prefix +41 81.

TOURIST OFFICES

Ischgl
t 52660
info@ischgl.com
www.ischgl.com
Galtür
t 8521
info@galtuer.com
www.galtuer.com
Samnaun
(Switzerland)
t 868 5858
info@samnaun.ch
www.samnaun.ch

② **Dorfschmeide** (5769) Small, central B&B recommended by a reporter.
Self-catering Some attractive apartments are available.

EATING OUT
Plenty of choice
Most of our reporters eat in their hotels. For a lighter meal such as pizza try the Nona, the Schatzi or the Trofana Alm, which is as much a bar as a restaurant, and for fondue the Kitzloch, with its galleries over the dance floor. The Allegra and Salz & Pfeffer have been recommended. The Grillalm and Salnerhof are popular.

APRES-SKI
Very lively
Ischgl is one of the liveliest resorts in the Alps, from early afternoon on. Lots of people are still in ski boots late in the evening. After your last run head for Trofana Alm near the Silvrettabahn or the Schatzi bar of the hotel Elisabeth by the Pardatschgratbahn – indoor and outdoor bars and scantily clad dancing girls. Niki's Stadl across the road is a great place to sing along to live Austrian hits. The Kitzloch is said to have lost out a bit to these two places. The Sunn-Alm at the hotel Sonne gets crowded and has live music. The Kuhstahl under the Sporthotel Silvretta and Fire & Ice over the road are both lively all evening. Guxa, 'a cigars and cocktails type of place', and Allegra liven up after dinner, and the Golden Eagle is 'good for live bands'. Two reporters recommend the Coyote Ugly at the hotel Madlein; another describes it as 'a lapdancing bar that just manages to avoid seediness'. There's now a branch of the famous Pacha nightclubs, also in Ibiza and London. The club under the hotel Post has an ancient Roman theme. The Post also has a casino.

OFF THE SLOPES
No sun but a nice pool
The village gets little sun in the middle of winter, and the resort is best suited to those keen to hit the slopes. But there's no shortage of off-slope activities. There are 24km/15 miles of marked walks, a 7km/4 mile floodlit toboggan run and a splendid sports centre. And you can browse upmarket shops, which sell Versace and Bogner.
   It's easy to get around the valley by bus, and there are restaurants that pedestrians can get to by gondolas.

STAYING DOWN THE VALLEY
Too far without a car
Ischgl is fairly isolated, but it is possible to stay in Landeck – an excellent base for visiting the surrounding resorts, including Serfaus, Nauders, Sölden and St Anton.

Galtür 1585m/5,200ft

Galtür hit the headlines when it was struck by a devastating avalanche in 1999, but the village centre has since been rebuilt and fortified.
   It is a charming, peaceful, traditional village clustered around a pretty little church, amid impressive mountain scenery. Quieter, sunnier and cheaper than Ischgl, it is a good base for a quiet family holiday. There are good 3- and 4-star hotels – the Almhof (8253), Flüchthorn (8202), 'quiet and friendly' Alpenrose (8201) and Ballunspitze (8214) have been recommended. There are a couple of jolly bars.
   Galtür's own slopes are not very challenging, but its black runs are ideal for intermediates and there are fine nursery slopes plus good 'graduation' pistes for improvers. The school has a high reputation. Galtür has 60km/37 miles of cross-country loops.
   Off-slope facilities are limited, but there's a natural ice rink and a sports centre with pool, tennis and squash. While the bus service to Ischgl is reasonably frequent during the day, it finishes early in the evening.

Samnaun 1840m/6,040ft

Samnaun is a small, quiet duty-free community in a corner of Switzerland more easily reached from Austria. A recent reporter did not see any other Brits there all week.
   There are four small components, roughly 1km/0.5 miles apart: Samnaun-Dorf, prettily set at the head of the valley is the main focus, with some swanky hotels and duty-free shops; Ravaisch, where the cable-car goes up; tiny Plan; and the hamlets of Laret and Compatsch, at the end of the main run down from the slopes. We've stayed happily on the edge of Dorf in the Waldpark B&B (8618310), and have eaten well at La Pasta. A reporter recommends the Hotel Post (8619200) and the Stammerspitze Café. There's a smart AlpenQuell spa-pool-fitness centre.
   The Schmuggler Alm (see Mountain restaurants) is a popular après-ski spot.

Kitzbühel

Wonderful old town and extensive slopes, but unreliable snow

134

COSTS

① ② ③ ④ ⑤ ⑥

RATINGS

The slopes

Snow	**
Extent	***
Expert	***
Intermediate	****
Beginner	**
Convenience	**
Queues	**
Mountain restaurants	****

The rest

Scenery	***
Resort charm	****
Off-slope	*****

NEWS

2002/03 brought three new fast chair-lifts, replacing drag-lifts at or near Pass Thurn – the Bärenbadkogel II six-pack, the Hartkaser eight-seater and the Resterkogel quad.

In a development that is unique in the Alps, the small Bichlalm area was given over entirely to off-piste slopes, with the top drag to Stuckkogel replaced by a snowcat.

The popular Fleck blue run (number 25) into the valley at Kirchberg now has snowmaking all the way down.

There are plans to upgrade the Gaisberg chair at Kirchberg to a quad, and to build a gondola in the Saukaser valley between Pengelstein and Jochberg, so that going to Jochberg will no longer involve a bus-ride home. This is most likely to be completed in 2005.

➕ Large, attractive, varied slopes offering a sensation of travel

➕ Beautiful medieval town centre

➕ Vibrant nightlife

➕ Plenty of off-slope amenities, both for the sporty and not-so-sporty

➕ A surprisingly large amount of cheap and cheerful accommodation

➕ Jolly mountain restaurants

➖ Often poor snow, especially on lower slopes (though an increasing amount of snowmaking)

➖ Surprisingly little challenging terrain – though plenty of off-piste

➖ Disjointed slopes, with quite a lot of bussing to get around them

➖ Disappointing nursery area

➖ Some crowded pistes

Kitzbühel is an impressive name to drop in the pub; its Hahnenkamm downhill course is the most spectacular on the World Cup circuit. And there is a lot to like about the resort and the mountains around it. But – and it's a big but– we have visited Kitz countless times, and (like most of our reporters) rarely found decent snow on the lower slopes. Serious money has been invested in snowmaking (not least to prevent cancellation of the famous race). But Kitzbühel's low altitude is at the root of the problem. Our advice is to wait until you know the conditions are good, and book at the last minute.

The resort has a beautiful, traffic-free, old centre complete with cobbled streets and lovely buildings, including expensive, elegant hotels. But this is no Gstaad: there is also a huge amount of inexpensive accommodation which attracts low-budget visitors, many of whom are young and like to party in its famous après-ski haunts.

THE RESORT

Set at a junction of broad, pretty valleys, Kitzbühel is a large, animated town, with separate areas of local slopes on each side. The beautiful walled medieval centre – with quaint church, cobbled streets and attractively painted buildings – is traffic-free and a compelling place to stay.

But the much-publicised old town is only a small part of Kitzbühel; the resort spreads widely, and busy roads surround the old town, reducing the charm factor somewhat. Visitors used to peaceful little Austrian villages are likely to be disappointed by its urban nature. But many visitors love the sophisticated, glitzy, towny ambience and swanky shops and cafes.

The bus service around town and to the outlying slopes is 'busy at the end of the day but reliable' says a recent visitor. But having a car is useful for visiting lots of other resorts covered by the Kitzbüheler Alpenskipass.

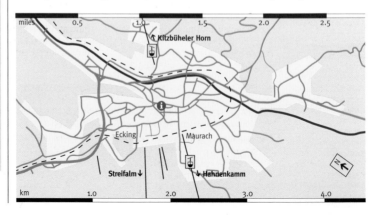

The Hahnenkamm downhill course looks intimidating, but beyond it are mainly gentle intermediate slopes ➔

KEY FACTS

Resort	760m
	2,500ft
Slopes	800-2000m
	2,620-6,560ft
Lifts	58
Pistes	160km
	100 miles
Blue	45%
Red	41%
Black	14%
Snowmaking	60km
	37 miles

LIFT PASSES

Kitzbühel
Covers all lifts in Kitzbühel, Kirchberg, Jochberg, Pass Thurn, Bichlalm and Aschau, linking buses, and 50% reduction for swimming pool.

Main pass
1-day pass €33
6-day pass €155

Senior citizens
Over 60:
6-day pass €140

Children
Under 19:
6-day pass €124
Under 17:
6-day pass €86
Under 6: free pass

Notes
Single ascent tickets for the major lifts. Beginners' Ski Pass and Area Day Cards. Graded prices for late start day passes.

Alternative passes
Selective Ski Pass for any 8 days during the season in Kitzbühel ski region. Kitzbüheler Alpen-skipass covers five large ski areas – Kitzbühel, Schneewinkel (St Johann), Wilder Kaiser, Alpbach and Wildschönau. Flexible pass also available for any 6 days during the season.

The size of Kitz makes choice of location important. The two main lift stations are both within walking distance of the old centre. But many visitors prefer to be close to the Hahnenkamm gondola, south-west of the centre. Beginners should bear in mind that the Hahnenkamm nursery slopes are often lacking in snow, and then novices are taken up the Horn.

THE MOUNTAINS

Kitzbühel's extensive slopes – shared with Kirchberg – offer a very attractive mixture of entirely open runs higher up and patchy forest lower down. Most face north-east or north-west.

THE SLOPES
Big but bitty

The slopes are divided into four areas. The two biggest are (almost) linked by piste, in one direction only – you get back by bus. A new gondola link is planned, probably for 2005.

The **Hahnenkamm-Pengelstein** sector is by far the largest. After the gondola or chair-lifts from the edge of the town, you descend into the bowl of Ehrenbachgraben, where several chair-lifts fan out. One goes up to Ehrenbachhöhe, the arrival point of lifts from Kirchberg. Another takes you to the gentle peak of Steinbergkogel, the high point of the sector. Beyond is the slightly lower peak of Pengelstein, whence several long runs lead down to the west; shuttle-buses serve their end-points at Aschau and Skirast.

Pengelstein is the start of the usual 'ski safari' route to the higher area of **Jochberg-Pass Thurn**. The route takes you to Trampelpfad, a short walk or taxi-ride from the Jochberg lifts. A more amusing alternative is the Giggling piste from Steinbergkogel to Hechenmoos, where you can get the shuttle-bus. Pass Thurn is well worth the excursion, for better snow and fewer crowds. Runs are short, but at last a few fast chairs are starting to

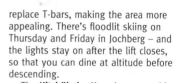

replace T-bars, making the area more appealing. There's floodlit skiing on Thursday and Friday in Jochberg – and the lights stay on after the lift closes, so that you can dine at altitude before descending.

The **Kitzbüheler Horn** is accessed by a gondola starting close to the railway station, some way from the centre. The second stage leads to the sunny Trattalm bowl, but the alternative cable-car takes you up to the summit of the Horn, from where a fine, solitary piste leads down into the Raintal on the east side. There are blue, red and black runs back towards town.

The small and sunny **Bichlalm** area has undergone a radical character change, from an undemanding backwater for sunbathers to an entirely off-piste sector – no grooming, no patrols – with the top half served by snowcat. When conditions are good, the top station (Stuckkogel) accesses an off-piste route to Fieberbrunn.

The piste map has been greatly

135

boarding

Kitzbühel was slow off the mark with boarding, keeping to its image of World Cup downhill venue/skier party town. However, things have changed, and now there is a boarder-cross course (as well as a half-pipe and terrain-park) on the Kitzbüheler Horn, an area with few drag-lifts. The Kasereck and Silberstuben runs on the Hahnenkamm are said to be a natural fun terrain. Many lifts in the main area are drags, but all major lifts are gondolas and chair-lifts – the area suits beginners and intermediates well.

improved by the addition of altitudes and mountain restaurants. And a reporter praised 'the people in bright jackets at the main lift stations, who offer advice on closures, directions etc'.

TERRAIN-PARKS
Take the Hornbahn
There is a half-pipe, with a music system, and a terrain-park on the Kitzbüheler Horn.

SNOW RELIABILITY
More snowmaking now
In a normal year, snow on the lower slopes can be thin or non-existent at times (though the snow at the top is often OK). The problem is that Kitzbühel's slopes have one of the lowest average heights in the Alps. To make matters worse, the Horn is also sunny – although many slopes are above the mid-station at 1270m/ 4,170ft. The expansion of snowmaking in recent years has improved matters when it's cold enough to make snow – major runs right down to Kitzbühel, Kirchberg, Klausen and Jochberg are covered. But many slopes still remain unprotected. If snow is poor, head for Pass Thurn. Otherwise, take a car for snow-searching excursions.

FOR EXPERTS
Plan to go off-piste
Steep slopes – pistes and off-piste terrain – are mostly concentrated around the bowl of Ehrenbachgraben. The most direct of these are challenging mogul fields. Nearby is the Streif red, the basis for the famous Hahnenkamm Downhill race – see the feature panel. When conditions allow, there is plenty of gentler off-piste potential elsewhere – some of it safely close to pistes, some requiring a guide. We're intrigued by the transformation of Bichlalm into an off-piste reserve, complete with snowcat service, and await reports.

FOR INTERMEDIATES
Lots of alternatives
The Hahnenkamm area is prime intermediate terrain. Good intermediates will want to do the World Cup downhill run, of course (see feature panel). And the long blue of 1000m/3,300ft vertical to Klausen from Ehrenbachhöhe is also satisfying. The east-facing Raintal run on the Horn is excellent for good intermediates to hone their skills on.

Most intermediates will want to head off on the safari route to Pass

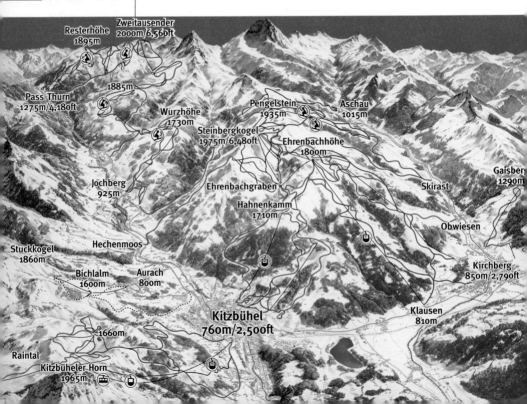

THE HAHNENKAMM DOWNHILL

Kitzbühel's Hahnenkamm Downhill race, held in mid-January each year, is the toughest as well as one of the most famous on the World Cup circuit. On the race weekend the town is packed and there is a real carnival atmosphere, with bands, people in traditional costumes and huge (and loud) cowbells everywhere.

The race itself starts with a steep icy section before you hit the famous Mausfalle and Steilhang, where even Franz Klammer used to get worried. The course (now thankfully served by snow-guns) starts near the top of the new gondola and drops 860m/2,820ft to finish amid the noise and celebrations right on the edge of town. Ordinary mortals can now try most of the course after the race weekend, whenever the snow is good enough – it's an unpisted red ski route mostly. We tried it in 2001 and found it steep and tricky in parts, even when going slowly – it must be terrifying at race speeds of 80mph or more. The course is normally closed from the start of the season until after the race.

ACTIVITIES

Indoor Aquarena Centre (2 pools, 2 slides, sauna, solarium, mud baths, aerated baths, underwater massage) – discounted entry with lift pass – indoor tennis hall, fitness centre, beauty centre, bridge, indoor riding school, local theatre, library, museum, jazz club, casino, 2-screen cinema

Outdoor Ice rink (curling and skating), horse-riding, sleigh rides, toboggan run, ballooning, ski-bobs, flying school, wildlife park, hang-gliding, paragliding, 40km/25 miles of cleared walking paths (free guided tours), copper mine tours

Thurn. The runs above Jochberg are particularly good for mixed abilities. Less adventurous types have some fine runs either side of Pengelstein, including the safari route and the Hieslegg piste above Aschau. The short, high runs at the top of the Pass Thurn area are ideal if you're more timid. There are also easy reds down to both Pass Thurn and Jochberg. Much of the Horn is good cruising.

FOR BEGINNERS
Not ideal
The Hahnenkamm nursery slopes are no more than adequate, and prone to poor snow conditions. The Horn has a high, sunny, nursery-like section, and precocious learners will soon be cruising home from there on the long Hagstein piste. There are some easy runs to progress to if the snow is OK. But there are many more conveniently arranged places to start.

FOR CROSS-COUNTRY
Plentiful but low
There are nearly 40km/25 miles of trails scattered around, but all are at valley level and therefore prone to lack of snow.

QUEUES
Still some problems
Replacing the old Hahnenkamm cable-car with a speedy six-person gondola has vastly reduced morning queues. However, once up the mountain there are some bottlenecks at slow old chairs and drags, particularly on Pengelstein. A reporter last winter found the Maierl chairs out of Kirchberg particularly tiresome – a right turn to the gondola at Klausen is the alternative. But we have had reports of queue-free weeks. Both the Horn and the Hahnenkamm can have overcrowded pistes. When lifts and pistes are busy here, head for Pass Thurn. We continue to receive complaints about the warning signs for avalanche danger and closed or icy pistes being in German only.

MOUNTAIN RESTAURANTS
A highlight
There are many restaurants, now thankfully marked on the piste map. 'One of the reasons we keep going back,' says one of our Kitz regulars. 'Excellent; made stopping for lunch a real pleasure,' says an Austria convert this year. On the Horn the Hornköpflhütte's good food and sunny

SCHOOLS

Rote Teufel (Red Devil)
t 62500
info@rote-teufel.at

Hahnenkamm Egger
t 63177

Kitzbüheler Horn
t 64454
sebastianzwicknagl@
utanet.at

Total
t 72011
hinterseer@skischule-total.at

Reith
t 65496
josef-dagn@
schischule-reith.at

Aurach
t 65804
skinoichl@tirol.com

Classes
(Rote Teufel prices)
6 days (2hr am and pm) €116.50

Private lessons
€160 for 1 day

CHILDREN

Most schools cater for small children, offering lunchtime supervision as well as lessons on the baby slopes – generally from the age of 3 or 4 (6 days approx €140). There is no non-ski nursery, but babysitters and nannies can be hired.

---

terraces still get praised despite a slight climb involved to reach it. Alpenhaus 'does excellent self-service meals for great prices', the Gipfelhaus is quieter with 'good views and food'. Gasthof Hagstein, an attractive farmhouse, serves up Austrian favourites. At Jochberg-Pass Thurn the Jägerwurzhütte and Trattenbachalm are recommended, and Panoramaalm has great views. Hanglalm is said to have 'the best Kaiserschmarrn'. In the Hahnenkamm sector the Seidlalm is 'well worth seeking out and very quiet'. Melkalm 'is also worth the effort of finding'. The Hochbrunn with its 'very friendly' staff is 'highly recommended for strudel'. The Kasereckhütte on the main run to Jochberg is 'brilliant'. The expensive Hochkitzbühel table-service restaurant at the top of the gondola has good food, but service has been criticised.

SCHOOLS AND GUIDES
Mixed reviews
There are now half-a-dozen competing schools. We get conflicting reports on the original school, Rudi Sailer's famous Red Devils. In contrast to the 200-strong Red Devils, the other schools emphasise their small scale and personal nature. The Total school is the best established of these and includes video analysis. A reporter said: 'Never seen so many British instructors. Very good.' But a couple said, 'Our child's instructor was so cautious that they had virtually no fun.'

FACILITIES FOR CHILDREN
Not an ideal choice
There is no non-ski nursery, but provided your children are able and willing to take classes, you can deposit them at any of the schools. The Total school has supervision until 5pm.

STAYING THERE

HOW TO GO
Mainly hotels and pensions
Kitz is essentially a hotel resort.
Chalets A few tour operators run chalet-hotels here.
Hotels There is an enormous choice, especially of 4-star and 3-star hotels.
((((5) **Tennerhof** (63181) Luxurious former farmhouse, with renowned restaurant. Beautiful panelled rooms.
((((5) **Schloss Lebenberg** (6901) Modernised 'castle' with smart pool, and free shuttle-bus to make up for

---

secluded but inconvenient location. Free nursery for kids aged 3-plus.
(((4) **Weisses Rössl** (625410) Smartly traditional exclusive 5-star aparthotel.
(((4) **Goldener Greif** (64311) Historic inn, elegantly renovated; vaulted lobby-sitting area, panelled bar, casino.
(((4) **Jägerwirt** (6981) Modern chalet with 'helpful staff and wonderful food'. Not ideally placed.
(((4) **Schwarzer Adler** (6911) Traditional hotel, near centre, highly praised by a reporter again this year. 'Great food and lovely leisure centre in basement.'
(((4) **Schweizerhof** (62735) Comfortable chalet right by Hahnenkamm gondola.
(((3) **Hahnenhof** (62582) Small and traditional, with rustic charm.
(((3) **Strasshofer** (62285) A favourite with a regular reporter – 'central, family-run, friendly, good food, good with children, quiet rooms at back'.
((2) **Mühlbergerhof** (62835) Small, friendly pension in good position.
Self-catering Many of the best (and best-positioned) are attached to hotels.

EATING OUT
Something for everyone
There is a wide range of restaurants to suit all pockets, including pizzerias and fast-food outlets (even McDonald's). Some 4-star hotels have excellent restaurants; Zur Tenne and Maria Theresia have been recommended by reporters. But the Unterberger Stuben ('Excellent but expensive,' says a reporter) vies with Schwedenkapelle for the 'best in town' award. Good, cheaper places include the Huberbräu-Stüberl and Zinnkrug. Goldene Gams has both a traditional Austrian dining room and one serving modern Italian and French food. On Fridays and Saturdays you can dine at the top of the Hahnenkamm gondola.

APRES-SKI
A main attraction
Nightlife is a great selling point of Kitz. There's something for all tastes, from throbbing bars full of teenagers to quiet little places, nice cafes and smart spots for fur-coat flaunting.
Immediately after the slopes close, the town is jolly without being much livelier than many other Tirolean resorts. To enjoy live music with a 'young and lively crowd' try the Sportbar Hölzl, also recommended for cheap drinks and TV sport. Cafes Praxmair, Kortschak, Langer and

↑ If only you could count on snow like this at valley level

GETTING THERE

Air Salzburg 80km/50 miles (1½hr); Munich 160km/99 miles (2hr); Innsbruck 95km/59 miles (1½hr).

Rail Mainline station in resort. Postbus every 15 min from station.

Phone numbers
Kitzbühel
From elsewhere in Austria add the prefix 05356.
From abroad use the prefix +43 5356.
Kirchberg
From elsewhere in Austria add the prefix 05357.
From abroad use the prefix +43 5357.

TOURIST OFFICES

Kitzbühel
t 621550
info@kitzbuehel.com
www.kitzbuehel.com
Kirchberg
t 2309
info@kirchberg.at
www.kirchberg.at

Rupprechter are among the most atmospheric tea time places for cakes and pastries. Stamperl is a very lively bar. Later the Big Ben and Fonda bars are popular with Brits. The American-style Highways bar and s'Lichtl (with thousands of lights hanging from the ceiling) get packed. Seppi's Pub is recommended for sport on TV, pizzas and the eccentric owner. Royal, Olympia and Take 5 are the main discos. The Londoner Pub is a famous drinking place, well summarised by a report this year: 'Very crowded, very noisy and great fun, but the bar staff were mostly rude and arrogant.'

OFF THE SLOPES
Plenty to do
The lift pass gives a 50% reduction for the pools in the impressive Aquarena leisure centre. There's a recently refurbished museum and concerts are organised. The railway makes excursions easy (eg to Salzburg and Innsbruck) and reps organise coach trips.

Kirchberg 850m/2,790ft

THE RESORT
Kirchberg is a large, spread out, lively village. There are two ways into the slopes shared with Kitzbühel, both a bus-ride from the village centre – a gondola at Klausen on the road to Kitzbühel, or the much slower Maierl chair-lifts in the opposite direction.

THE MOUNTAIN
Slopes Both main access lifts take you to Ehrenbachhöhe, at the heart of the Kitzbühel slopes. The separate small Gaisberg area is on the other side of the valley.
Snow reliability Only a few metres higher than neighbouring Kitzbühel, Kirchberg suffers from the same unreliable snow.
Experts Few challenging slopes.
Intermediates The main slopes back to Kirchberg are ideal for intermediates when snow is good.
Beginners There's a beginner lift and area at the foot of the Gaisberg slopes.
Snowboarding Kitzbühel has the edge, with the terrain-park on the Horn.
Cross-country There are plenty of trails – but at valley level so they can be affected by lack of snow. The area above Aschau is good and there is a night-time track on Lake Schwarz.
Queues As with Kitzbühel, poor snow conditions can cause overcrowding.
Mountain restaurants There are some good local huts.
Schools and guides There are three schools but we lack recent reports.
Facilities for children There are non-ski and ski kindergartens.

STAYING THERE
How to go There's a wide choice of chalet-style hotels and pensions.
Hotels The 4-star Klausen (2128) is close to the main gondola and has its own après-ski bar, the Sporthotel Tyrol (2787) is a bit out of the village centre with pool and spa facilities.
Self-catering There is some available.
Eating out Mostly in hotels or guest houses, but there's a pizzeria and a steak house too.
Après-ski There's a good toboggan run on Gaisberg. Nightlife is very lively both in bars and in discos. Good bars include the Boomerang, the Londoner (with frequent live music), and Fuchslokal.
Off the slopes Some hotels have swimming pools, saunas and so on.

Lech

Captivating blend of reliable snow, extensive slopes and village charm

COSTS

① ② ③ ④ ⑤ ⑥

RATINGS

The slopes

Snow	★★★★
Extent	★★★★
Expert	★★★★
Intermediate	★★★★
Beginner	★★★★
Convenience	★★★
Queues	★★★★
Mountain restaurants	★★

The rest

Scenery	★★★
Resort charm	★★★★
Off-slope	★★★

NEWS

For 2002/03 a high-speed, six-seater chair-lift with covers replaced a slow triple chair-lift to the Kriegerhorn. For 2003/04 two more high-speed covered chairs are planned – an eight-seater replacing the current Steinmähder chair towards Zuger Hochlicht, and a six-pack replacing the Hasensprung chair from the top of which a red run feeds the Steinmähder chair. There may also be a new T-bar at Rüfikopf to make access to the ski routes that start here easier. A small new mountain restaurant is also planned for Lech's slope.

➕ Picturesque Alpine village

➕ Sunny and usually uncrowded slopes with excellent snow record and extensive snowmaking

➕ Fair-sized, largely intermediate piste network plus good and extensive off-piste terrain

➕ Easy access to the tougher slopes of St Anton and other Arlberg resorts

➕ Lively après-ski scene

➕ Some very smart hotels

➖ Surprising shortages of compelling mountain restaurants and village shops for window-shopping

➖ Local traffic intrudes on main street of Lech (and spoils Zürs entirely)

➖ Very few tough pistes, so the adventurous must go off-piste

➖ Blue runs back to the village are rather steep for nervous novices

➖ Generally expensive

➖ Still quite a few slow, old lifts

Lech and its higher, linked neighbour Zürs are the most fashionable resorts in Austria, each able to point to a string of rich and vaguely royal visitors. But, like all such 'exclusive' resorts, they aren't actually exclusive in any real sense. A holiday here is unlikely to be cheap, but it doesn't have to cost any more than in countless other international resorts in the Alps. We don't feel out of place here, and neither would you. We often see Lech described as 'a very chic resort' – but it has none of the flash shops of St Moritz or Cortina, for example.

The real point about these resorts is that their combination of impressive snowfall, traditional Alpine atmosphere (in Lech, if not in Zürs) and excellent hotels offering a truly personal service from their family owners is a rare and attractive thing. One of the few other Austrian resorts to offer it is St Anton, over the hill, covered by the same lift pass, and easily visited by bus.

One group of people who are likely to find a holiday here costly is adventurous skiers who lack the 'alpine experience' needed to tackle the ski routes that Lech offers instead of black pistes: you'll need an instructor to hold your hand.

THE RESORT

Lech is an old farming village set in a high valley that spent long periods of winter cut off from the outside world until the Flexen Pass road through Zürs was constructed at the end of the 19th century. (Even now, the road can be closed for days on end after an exceptional snowfall; a road tunnel is planned, but is not imminent.)

The village is attractive, with its upmarket hotels built in traditional chalet style, its gurgling river plus bridges, its adequately impressive scenery and the high incidence of snow on the streets. But its appeal is dimmed slightly by traffic on the main street that forms its spine: although the pavements have been widened and parking is controlled, it can still get very busy, especially at weekends.

The clientele is largely German and Austrian, with very few Brits. The fur coat count is one of the highest in the Alps, but now countered by what one reporter called 'the Russian mafia, with ski wear left over from the 1980s'.

The heart of the village is a short stretch of the main street beside the river; most of the main hotels are clustered here. Right on this street is the base station of the Rüfikopf cable-car, departure point for exploration of the Zürs slopes. A short walk away, across the river, are the Schlegelkopf chair-lifts, leading up into Lech's main

Car-free Oberlech, 250m/820ft above Lech, is a popular place for lunch and a quiet and convenient place to stay →

KEY FACTS

Resort	1450m
	4,760ft

For Arlberg region	
Slopes	1305-2650m
	4,280-8,690ft
Lifts	83
Pistes	260km
	162 miles
Blue	35%
Red	42%
Black	23%
Snowmaking	65km
	40 miles

For Lech-Zürs only	
Slopes	1450-2450m
	4,760-8,040ft
Lifts	32
Pistes	110km
	68 miles

area of slopes. Chalets, apartments and pensions are dotted around the valley, and the village spreads along the main street for 2km/1.5 miles. Some of the cheaper accommodation is quite a walk from the lifts.

Not far from the centre is the cable-car up to Oberlech – a small, traffic-free collection of 4-star hotels and chalets set on the mountainside above Lech; the cable-car works until 1am, allowing access to Lech's much livelier nightlife and shopping. If you stay there, luggage is delivered to your hotel via underground tunnels, leaving you unburdened for the short, snowy walk from the cable-car.

Zug is a hamlet, 3km/2 miles from Lech, with a lift into the Lech-Oberlech area. The limited accommodation here is mostly bed and breakfast with one 4-star hotel. From Lech, Zug makes a good night out: you can take a horse-drawn sleigh to a fondue at the Rote Wand, Klösterle or Auerhahn, followed by a visit to the Rote Wand disco.

As well as Lech and Zürs, the Arlberg lift pass covers St Anton, St Christoph and Stuben, all reachable by car, by free but busy ski-bus, or by less crowded post-bus.

THE MOUNTAINS

Most of the slopes are treeless, the main exception being the lower runs below Oberlech.

The toughest runs here are classed as unpatrolled 'ski routes' (as at St Anton – read that chapter for more on this), or 'high-alpine touring runs', which are not protected against avalanche and should be skied only with a guide. We don't have much of a problem with the latter category – in

other resorts, these off-piste runs would simply not appear on the piste map at all. But the ski route concept is bad news, reducing the resort's responsibility for runs that are a key part of the area, and that should be patrolled pistes. The only ways down to Zug, for example, are ski routes. And of the eight identified runs from the Kriegerhorn, six are ski routes.

The piste map attempts to cover the whole of the Arlberg region in one view, and as a result is unclear in places – particularly around Oberlech.

THE SLOPES
One-way traffic
The main slopes centre on **Oberlech**, 250m/820ft above Lech (just below the tree line), and can be reached from the village by chair-lifts as well as the cable-car. The wide, open pistes above Oberlech are perfect for intermediates and there is also lots of off-piste. Zuger Hochlicht, the high point of this sector, gives stunning views.

The **Rüfikopf** cable-car takes Lech residents to the west-facing slopes of Zürs. This mountainside, with its high point at **Trittkopf**, is a mix of quite challenging intermediate slopes and flat/uphill bits. On the other side of the village the east-facing mountainside is of a more uniform gradient. Chairs go up to **Seekopf** with intermediate runs back down. There's a chair up to **Muggengrat** (the highest point of the Zürs area) from below Zürsersee. This has a good blue run back under it and accesses the Muggengrat Täli (aka Zürser Täli) – a lovely long red with lots of nearby off-piste options away from all the lifts back down to Zürs. The long, scenic ski route back to Lech is accessed via the Madloch chair –

LIFT PASSES

Arlberg Ski pass
Covers all St Anton,
St Christoph, Lech,
Zürs and Stuben lifts,
and linking bus
between Rauz and
Zürs.

Main pass
1-day pass €37.50
6-day pass €174

Senior citizens
Over 65 (60 for
women): 6-day pass
€149

Children
Under 15: 6-day pass
€104
Under 19: 6-day pass
€149

Notes
Single ascent, half-
day and afternoon
'taster' tickets
available. Pass also
covers Sonnenkopf
(10 lifts) at Klösterle,
7km/4 miles west of
Stuben (free bus link
from Stuben).

which is slow and vulnerable to closure
by wind. You can peel off part-way
down and head for Zug and the chair-
lift up to the Kriegerhorn above
Oberlech. There are no lifts back
towards Zürs, so the circuit is
clockwise-only.

TERRAIN-PARKS
In Lech only
There's a good terrain-park above Lech
at the Schlegelkopf, with jumps, a
boarder-cross and a half-pipe.

SNOW RELIABILITY
One of Austria's best
Lech and Zürs both get a lot of snow,
but Austrian weather station records
show a big difference between them
despite their proximity. Lech gets an
average of almost 8m/26ft of snow
between December and March, almost
twice as much as St Anton and three
times as much as Kitzbühel; but Zürs
gets 50% more than Lech. The altitude
is high by Austrian resort standards
and there is excellent snowmaking on
Lech's sunny lower slopes.

This combination, together with
excellent grooming, means that the
Lech-Zürs area normally has good

coverage from December until April.
And the snow is frequently better here
than on St Anton's predominantly
south-facing slopes.

FOR EXPERTS
Off-piste is main attraction
There are only two black pistes on the
map, and there is no denying that for
the competent skier who prefers to
stick to patrolled runs the area is very
limited. There are the two types of off-
piste route referred to above. The piste
map recommends that ski routes, of
which there are lots, should be used
only 'by skiers with alpine experience
or accompanied by a ski instructor' –
the vast majority of people don't
bother with an instructor. But experts
will get a lot more out of the area if
they do have a guide, as there is
plenty of excellent off-piste other than
the marked ski routes, much of it
accessed by long traverses. Especially
in fresh snow, it can be wonderful.

Many of the best runs start from the
top of the Steinmähder chair (a new
fast eight-seater from 2003/04), which
finishes just below Zuger Hochlicht.
Some routes involve a short climb to
access bowls of untracked powder.

boarding

Lech's upper-crust image has not stood in the way of its snowboarding development, and it continues to improve its facilities. Chairs and cable-cars, with hardly any drags, and perfectly manicured pistes make the area ideal for beginner and intermediate boarders although the west facing slopes at Zürs have many flat/uphill sections. Lessons are with the local ski school. More confident boarders should hire a guide and track some powder.

From the Kriegerhorn there are shorter off-piste runs down towards Lech and a very scenic long ski route down to Zug. Most runs, however, are south- or west-facing and can suffer from sun.

At the end of the season, when the snow is deep and settled, the off-piste off the shoulder of the Wöstertäli from the top of the Rüfikopf cable-car down to Lech can be superb. There are also good runs from the top of the Trittkopf cable-car in the Zürs sector, including a tricky one down to Stuben.

Experts will also enjoy cruising some of the steeper red runs and will want to visit St Anton during the week, where there are more challenging pistes as well as more off-piste.

Heli-lifts are available to a couple of remote spots, at least on weekdays.

FOR INTERMEDIATES
Flattering variety for all

The pistes in the Oberlech area are nearly all immaculately groomed blue runs, the upper ones above the trees, the lower ones in wide swathes cut through them. It is ideal territory for leisurely cruisers not wanting surprises. And even early intermediates will be able to take on the circuit to Zürs and back, the only significant red involved being the beautiful long (and not at all difficult) ski route back to Lech from the top of the Madloch chair in Zürs.

It's worth noting that the final blue-run descents to Lech (as opposed to Oberlech) are uncomfortably steep for nervous novices.

More adventurous intermediates should take the fast Steinmähder chair to just below Zuger Hochlicht and from there take the scenic red run all the way to Zug (the latter part on a ski route rather than a piste). And if you feel ready to have a stab at some off-piste, Lech is a good place to try it.

Zürs has many more interesting red runs, on both sides of the village. We particularly like the west-facing reds from Trittkopf and the usually quiet east-facing Muggengrat (aka Zürser) Täli, which starts in a steep bowl – you can take the plunge, or skirt it on a catwalk.

FOR BEGINNERS
Easy slopes in all areas

The main nursery slopes are in Oberlech, but there is also a nice isolated area in the village dedicated purely to beginners. There are good, easy runs to progress to, both above and below Oberlech.

FOR CROSS-COUNTRY
Picturesque valley trail

There are two cross-country trails in Lech. The longer one is 15km/9 miles; it begins in the centre of town and leads through the beautiful Zug valley, following the Lech river and ending up outside Zug. The other begins behind the church and goes to Stubenbach

SCHOOLS

Lech
t 2355
skischule-lech@aon.at
Oberlech
t 2007
Zürs
t 2611
ernst.haas@
skischule-zuers.at

Classes
(Lech prices)
6 days (2hr am and
2hr pm) €155
Private lessons
€188 for 1 day; each
additional person €15

CHILDREN

There are ski
kindergartens in Lech,
Zürs and Oberlech
taking children from
age 3, from 9am to
4pm.

Children's ski school
classes take children
from the age of 3½
up to 13 (6 days
€142).

GETTING THERE

Air Zürich 200km/124
miles (2½hr);
Innsbruck 110km/68
miles (1½hr).

Rail Langen (15km/9
miles); 9 buses daily
from station, buses
connect with
international trains.

ACTIVITIES

Indoor Tennis, hotel
swimming pools and
saunas, squash,
museum, art gallery,
hotel spas

Outdoor 30km/19
miles of cleared
walking paths,
toboggan run (from
Oberlech), artificial ice
rink (skating, curling),
sleigh rides,
helicopter rides

(another hamlet in the Lech area). In
Zürs there is a 3km/2 mile track
starting at Zürs and going to the
Flexen Pass. This starts at 1600m/
5,250ft and climbs to 1800m/5,910ft.

QUEUES
No recent complaints
The resort proudly boasts that it limits
numbers on the slopes to 14,000 for a
more enjoyable experience. There have
been significant lift improvements in
recent years, and recent reporters have
not complained of any problems. But
there are one or two bottlenecks – the
Schlegelkopf fast quad out of Lech
gets very busy at times – and there are
still lots of drag-lifts and slow chair-
lifts, which means you spend a lot of
time riding lifts. The crucial Madloch
double chair at the top of the Zürs
area must still generate peak-time
queues on the one-way circuit to Lech.

MOUNTAIN RESTAURANTS
Seriously disappointing
There are surprisingly few cosy
mountain huts in the area, and fewer
still with table service.

At Oberlech, there are several big
sunny terraces set prettily around the
piste – though a reporter who recently
spent a fortnight investigating the
options here found no food of any
merit. Quite often you'll find a live
band playing outside one of the
restaurants here. The Ilga Stube is
reported to have 'good food, rustic
atmosphere, friendly staff and
reasonable prices'. The Alter Goldener
Berg is a lovely old building, but the
food and service are not reliable. The
Mohnenfluh, at the top of the nursery
lift, is said to do 'excellent' food.

The self-service Seekopf restaurant
does decent food and has a good sun
terrace – but you may have to queue
to even get into the food serving area.
Also popular is the self-service
Palmenalpe above Zug, but it too gets
very crowded. The Schröfli Alm, just
above the bottom of the Seekopf lift,
is a pleasant chalet.

In view of the lack of options at
altitude, we'll allow ourselves a couple
of valley-level suggestions. Hûs Nr 8,
at the end of the route back from Zürs
to Lech, is 300 years old and has good
traditional food. In Zug, the hotel Rote
Wand is popular, and the gasthof
Auerhahn is roundly recommended by
a reporter, not least for its 'exquisite'
dumplings – yes, really.

SCHOOLS AND GUIDES
Excellent in parts
The ski schools of Lech, Oberlech and
Zürs all have good reputations and the
instructors speak good English. Group
lessons are divided into no fewer than
10 ability levels. One past visitor
enjoyed 'the best lessons I have ever
had'. In peak periods, however, you
should book both instructors and
guides well in advance, as many are
booked regularly every year by an
exclusive clientele.

FACILITIES FOR CHILDREN
Oberlech's fine, but expensive
Oberlech does make an excellent
choice for families who can afford it,
particularly as it's so convenient for
the slopes. The Sonnenburg and the
Goldener Berg have in-house
kindergartens. Reporters tell us the
Oberlech school is great for children,
with small classes, good English
spoken and lunch offered.

STAYING THERE

HOW TO GO
Surprising variety
There is quite a variety of
accommodation from luxury hotels
through to simple but spotless B&Bs.
Hotels There are three 5-star hotels,
over 30 4-star and countless more
modest places.
((((5) **Arlberg** (2134-0) Patronised by
royalty and celebrities (Princess Diana
used to stay here). Elegantly rustic
chalet, centrally placed. Pool.
((((5) **Post** (2206-0) Lovely old Relais
& Chateaux place on main street with
pool, sauna. 'Perfect,' says a reporter.
((((4) **Krone** (2551) One of the oldest
buildings in the village, in a prime spot
by the river.
((((4) **Tannbergerhof** (2202-0)
Splendidly atmospheric inn on main
street, with outdoor bar and popular
disco (tea-time as well as later). Pool.
((((4) **Haldenhof** (2444-0) Friendly and
well run, with antiques and a fine
collection of prints and paintings.
((((4) **Burg Vital** (Oberlech) (2291-930)
'Excellent – no criticism,' said a
reporter of this plush luxury hotel with
pool, sauna and squash.
((((4) **Burg** (2291-0) Sister hotel of Burg
Vital – same facilities and with famous
outdoor umbrella bar by the cable-car.
((((4) **Sonnenburg** (Oberlech) (2147)
Luxury on-piste chalet (popular for
lunch). Good children's facilities. Pool.

The gurgling river runs right next to Lech's busy main street ↗

Phone numbers

Lech and Zürs
From elsewhere in Austria add the prefix 05583.
From abroad use the prefix +43 5583.

Stuben
From elsewhere in Austria add the prefix 05582.
From abroad use the prefix +43 5582.

TOURIST OFFICES

Lech
t 21610
info@lech-zuers.at
www.lech-zuers.at

Zürs
t 2245
zuersinfo@lech-zuers.at
www.zuers.at

Stuben
t 3990
info@stuben.at
www.stuben.com

((((4) **Monzabon** (2104) Well placed and 'characterful, with friendly staff,' says a reporter – but 'meals too grand'. Pool.
(((3) **Pension Angerhof** (2418) Beautiful ancient pension, with wood panels and quaint little windows.
(((3) **Pension Fernsicht** (2432) Pension with spa facilities.
Self-catering There is lots available to independent bookers.
Chalets There are a couple run by British tour operators, including Total's chalet-hotel with pool and sauna.

EATING OUT
Mainly hotel-based
There are over 50 restaurants in Lech, nearly all of them in hotels. Reporter recommendations include the Krone, Ambrosius (above a shopping arcade), and the Post, which serves Austrian nouvelle-type food. The Madlochblick has a typically Austrian restaurant, very cosy with good solid food. Hûs Nr 8 is one of the best non-hotel restaurants (see Mountain restaurants) and does good fondue. Pizzeria Charly is popular for all kinds of Italian food. Bistro Casarole is a small casual place with a short menu of excellent, substantial grills. Last season S'Pfefferkörndl introduced a twice-weekly, 6-course Carpe Diem Lying Dinner where you lounge on cushions after having your feet washed on the way in. In Oberlech hotel Montana was highly recommended by a 2003 reporter and there is a good fondue at the Alte Goldener Berg, a tavern built in 1432. In Zug the Rote Wand is excellent for fondues, Kaiserschmarren (a delicious chopped pancake and fruit dessert) and a good night out. A reporter recommends Gasthaus Älpele near Zug – 3km/2 miles from the road, up the valley on the cross-country route – for its atmosphere and good food. Transport is provided in covered wagons attached to a snowcat.

APRES-SKI
Good but expensive
The umbrella bar of the Burg hotel at Oberlech is popular immediately after the slopes close, as is the champagne bar in Oberlech's Hotel Montana. Down in Lech itself the outdoor bars of hotels Krone, in a lovely setting by the river, and Tannbergerhof are popular. There's an afternoon disco inside the Tannbergerhof. Later on, discos in the hotels Kristberg, Arlberg, Almhof-Schneider and Krone liven up too. The latter's Side Step specialises in 60s and 70s music. S'Pfefferkörndl is a good place for a drink, and you can get a steak or pizza there until late. The smart, modern Fux bar and restaurant has live music, pop art in the toilets and a huge wine list.

For a change of scene, the Rote Wand in Zug has a disco.

Taxi James is a shared minibus taxi, which charges a flat fare for any journey in Lech/Zürs – you phone and it picks you up within half an hour.

OFF THE SLOPES
At ease
Many visitors to Lech don't indulge in sports and the main street often presents a parade of fur-clad strollers. The range of shopping is surprisingly limited, with Strolz's plush emporium right in the centre the main attraction.

Lech

It's easy for pedestrians to get to Oberlech or Zug to meet friends for lunch – or for slope users to get back to the resort. The village outdoor bars make ideal posing positions. There are various sporting activities and 30km/19 miles of walking paths – the one along the river to Zug is especially beautiful.

Zürs 1720m/5,640ft

Ten minutes' drive towards St Anton from Lech, Zürs is almost on the Flexen Pass, with good snow virtually guaranteed. Austria's first recognisable ski lift was built here in 1937.

The village is even more upmarket than Lech, with no hotels of less than 3-star standing, and a dozen 4-star and 5-star hotels around which life revolves. Last season we stayed at the 5-star Zürserhof (25130) for a couple of nights and found it excellent – great service, food and spa facilities. But apart from the excellent hotels, we find Zürs a difficult place to like. It has nothing resembling a centre (there are few shops) and the traffic doesn't so much intrude as ruin the place. Nightlife is quiet. There's a disco in the Edelweiss hotel (26620) and a piano bar in the Alpenhof (21910). Mathie's-Stüble and Kaminstüble are worth trying, as is Vernissage, at the Skiclub Alpenrose (22710), which is reported to be the best nightspot in town. Serious dining means the Zürserhof and the Lorünser (22540). All phone numbers given are for 4- or 5-star hotels.

Many of the local Zürs instructors are booked for the entire season by regular clients, and more than 80% of them are booked privately.

Stuben 1405m/4,610ft

Stuben is linked by lifts and pistes to St Anton, but is on the Vorarlberg side of the Arlberg pass (St Anton is over in the Tirol). There are infrequent but timetabled buses between the village and Lech and Zürs, and more frequent ones from Rauz, reachable on skis.

Dating back to the 13th century, Stuben is a small, unspoiled village where personal service and quiet friendliness are the order of the day. Modern developments are kept to a minimum. The only concessions to the new era are a few unobtrusive hotels, a school, two or three bars, a couple of banks and a few little shops. The old church and traditional buildings, usually snow-covered, make Stuben a really charming Alpine village.

The Albona mountain above Stuben has north-facing slopes that hold powder well and some wonderful, deserted off-piste descents including beautifully long runs down to Langen (where you can catch the train) and back to St Anton. These are, however, 'high-alpine touring runs' and should be taken seriously. The slow village chair can be a cold ride. A quicker and warmer way to get to St Anton in the morning, if you have a car, is to drive up the road to Rauz. Stuben has sunny nursery slopes separate from the main slopes, but lack of progression runs make it unsuitable for beginners.

Evenings are quiet, but several places have a pleasant atmosphere. The charming old Post (7610) is a very comfortable 4-star renowned for its fine restaurant.

LECH TOURIST OFFICE

Zürs is set high on the road that goes to Lech and is the launch point for a couple of good scenic runs away from all the lifts (you can see one arriving here from the left) ↓

Mayrhofen

Traditional British favourite with newly expanded area of slopes

147

COSTS

① ② ③ ④ ⑤ ⑥

RATINGS

The slopes

Snow	***
Extent	***
Experts	*
Intermediates	***
Beginners	**
Convenience	*
Queues	*
Mountain restaurants	****

The rest

Scenery	***
Resort charm	***
Off-slope	****

NEWS

In 2001/02 a 150-person cable-car linked the Penken slopes with those of Rastkogel above Vorderlanersbach, previously a bus-ride away. This area links to the Eggalm area above Lanersbach. The link back is by a fast six-pack. All this has meant a 40% increase in Mayrhofen's terrain to a total of 143km/90 miles.

Last season a fast, covered eight-seat chair replaced the old double up to Horbergjoch in the Rastkogel area.

For 2003/04 there are plans to replace two double chairs in the Horberg sector: the Tappenalm will become an eight-seater and the Knorren a six-pack.

+ New lifts for last season increased the local terrain by 40%

+ Snow-sure by Tirol standards, and you have the snow guarantee of the Hintertux glacier nearby

+ Various nearby areas on the same lift pass, and reached by free bus

+ Lively après-ski – though it's easily avoided if you prefer peace

+ Excellent children's amenities

+ Wide range of off-slope facilities

– No runs back to the village from Penken – the main area of slopes

– Smaller Ahorn area – the best bet for novices – is completely separate

– Main access lift is still inadequate – as well as being inconveniently sited for many visitors

– Slopes can be crowded

– Mainly short runs, though newly linked slopes are longer

– Few challenging pistes

Mayrhofen has long been a British favourite. Many visitors like it for its lively nightlife, but it's also an excellent family resort, with highly regarded ski schools and kindergartens and a fun pool with special children's area. The liveliest of the nightlife is confined to a few places, easily avoided by families. And there are quieter alternative bases, including Finkenberg (covered in this chapter) and Lanersbach (covered in the Hintertux chapter).

Mayrhofen's main Penken-Horberg slopes are unusual for Austria, being entirely above the tree line, with no pistes down to valley level. The upside is better-than-average snow, for the Tirol; the downside, shorter-than-average runs (typically around 350m/1,150ft vertical). The recently built link with Lanersbach opens up some welcome longer runs, as well as adding around 40% to the accessible slopes.

THE RESORT

Mayrhofen is a fairly large resort sitting in the flat-bottomed Zillertal. Most shops, bars and restaurants are on the one main, long, largely pedestrianised street, with hotels and pensions spread over a wider area. As the village has grown, architecture has been kept traditional.

Despite its reputation for lively après-ski, Mayrhofen is not dominated by lager louts. They exist, but tend to gather in a few easily avoided bars. The central hotels are mainly slightly upmarket, and overall the resort feels pleasantly civilised (though we have had a few complaints about traffic).

The main lift to Penken is set towards one end of the main street, while the cable-car to the much smaller and increasingly neglected Ahorn sector is out in the suburbs, about 1km/0.5 miles from the centre. The free bus service can be crowded and it finishes early (5pm), so location is important. The original centre, around the market, tourist office and

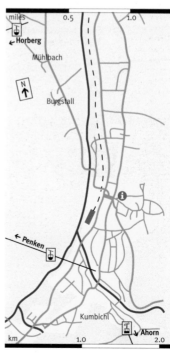

KEY FACTS

Resort	630m
	2,070ft

For Ski and Glacier
World Zillertal 3000

Slopes	630-3250m
	2,070-10,660ft
Lifts	67
Pistes	234km
	145 miles
Blue	28%
Red	57%
Black	15%
Snowmaking	86km
	54 miles

For Mayrhofen-
Lanersbach only (ie
excluding Hintertux
glacier)

Slopes	630-2500m
	2,070-8,200ft
Lifts	46
Pistes	145km
	90 miles

For Ziller valley

Slopes	630-3250m
	2,070-10,660ft
Lifts	166
Pistes	492km
	306 miles

bus/railway stations, is now on the edge of things. The most convenient area is on the main street, close to the Penken gondola station.

Free buses mean you can have an enjoyably varied week visiting different areas on the Ziller valley lift pass, including the extensive Arena slopes linking Zell to Königsleiten and the excellent glacier up at Hintertux. But if you plan to split your time between the Lanersbach-Mayrhofen slopes and the glacier, consider staying in Lanersbach (see Hintertux chapter).

The buses get packed at peak times, so it's worth planning your outings carefully ('Get the 8am bus and you'll be in Hintertux just as the lifts open,' recommends a reporter).

THE MOUNTAINS

Practically all Mayrhofen's slopes are above the tree line, and of moderate difficulty. When you buy a lift pass, make sure it covers the Hintertux glacier, unless you are absolutely confident that you won't want to try it. Signposting of the mountain is reportedly poor: 'Many made the same mistake as us (twice!) and ended up in Finkenberg as the lifts closed – with a huge queue for the hourly bus.'

THE SLOPES
Rather inconvenient

Lifts to the two main sectors are a longish walk or a bus-ride apart, and you normally have to take them down as well as up.

The larger area is **Penken-Horberg,** accessed by the main jumbo gondola from one end of town. It is also accessible via gondolas at Hippach and Finkenberg, both a bus-ride away. You cannot get back to Mayrhofen on snow – you either catch the main gondola down or, if cover is good, you can descend to either Finkenberg or Hippach on unpisted ski-routes. A jumbo cable-car now links the Penken area with **Rastkogel** slopes above Vorderlanersbach, which is in turn linked to **Eggalm** above Lanersbach – see the Hintertux chapter. These new links are a great step forward, but getting to Eggalm depends on good snow on a low, sunny run, and getting back from Rastkogel is reported to involve 'either a stiff climb to catch the cable-car down or a long and, in parts, difficult red run'.

The smaller, gentler **Ahorn** area seems to be going into decline. A reader who learned to ski there returned last season to find the place deserted at 4pm.

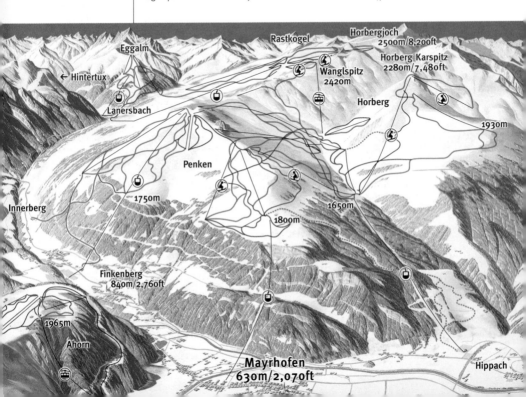

There are plenty of mountain restaurants with reasonable prices – but few that are notably cute →

SKI ZILLERTAL 3000 / JP FANKHAUSER

LIFT PASSES

Ski and Glacier World Zillertal
1-, 2- or 3-day passes cover Penken, Eggalm, Rastkogel and Hintertux glacier areas; 4-day and over passes include all Ziller valley lifts, ski-bus and railway.

Main pass
including glacier
1-day pass €34
6-day pass €161

Children
Under 19: 6-day pass €129
Under 15: 6-day pass €97
Under 6: free pass

Notes
Part-day passes available.

Alternative passes
Zillertaler ski pass also available without Hintertux glacier.

SCHOOLS

Die Roten Profis (Manfred Gager)
t 63800
m.gager@tirol.com

Total (Max Rahm)
t 63939
smt@aon.at

Mount Everest (Peter Habeler)
t 62829
peter@habeler.com

Classes
(Roten Profis prices)
6 half days (2½hr am or pm) €96

Private lessons
2½hr: €109 for 1 person.

TERRAIN-PARKS
Look good to us
There is a terrain-park and a half-pipe on Penken.

SNOW RELIABILITY
Good by Austrian standards
Although the lifts go no higher than 2500m/8,200ft, the area is reasonably good for snow-cover because practically all of Mayrhofen's slopes are above 1500m/4,900ft. Snowmaking covers nearly all the main slopes in the Penken-Horberg area. And there is one of the best glaciers in the Alps at Hintertux. As mentioned above, poor snow on the run linking to Eggalm can be a problem.

FOR EXPERTS
Head off-piste
Mayrhofen itself doesn't have much for experts. But there are worthwhile challenges to be found (including off-piste areas, such as from the top of the Horbergjoch at the top of Rastkogel down to the bottom of the big cable-car). And reporters staying here and visiting the other resorts on the valley lift pass have been more than happy. The long unpisted trail to Hippach is the only challenging local slope, and is rarely in good order – as a report from a repeat visitor testifies: 'Snow conditions were the best I've known, yet some parts were extremely tricky due to poor snow-cover.'

FOR INTERMEDIATES
On the tough side
Most of Mayrhofen's slopes are on the steep side of the usual intermediate range – great for confident or competent intermediates. And last season's expansion made the area much more interesting for avid piste-bashers. But most of the runs in the main Penken area are short. And (except on Ahorn) there are few really gentle blue runs, making the area less than ideal for nervous intermediates or near beginners. Overcrowding of many runs can add to the intimidation factor.

If you're willing to travel, each of the main mountains covered by the Ziller valley pass is large and varied enough for an interesting day out.

FOR BEGINNERS
Overrated: big drawbacks
Despite its reputation for teaching, Mayrhofen is not ideal for beginners. The Ahorn nursery slopes are excellent – high, extensive and sunny – but it's a rather tiresome journey to and from them and intermediate mates will want to be on Penken most of the time. The overcrowded slopes and restaurants add to the hassle. The Penken nursery area is less satisfactory and there are very few easy blues to progress to from the nursery slopes.

FOR CROSS-COUNTRY
Go to Lanersbach
There is a fine 20km/12 mile trail along the valley to Zell am Ziller, plus small loops close to the village. But snow here is not reliable. Vorderlanersbach has a much more snow-sure trail.

QUEUES
Still some problems
The Penken jumbo-gondola is very oversubscribed at peak times. A reporter this year experienced a

Mayrhofen

149

boarding

Mayrhofen is not ideal for learning to snowboard – the nursery slopes are inconvenient and the lifts are mainly drags. For intermediates, the Penken slopes are good and the lifts are mainly gondolas and chairs. The British Championships used to be held here and now there is a new annual event called the Brit Games. More advanced riders will enjoy the Hintertux glacier, further up the valley – see separate chapter.

AUSTRIA

150

ACTIVITIES

Indoor Bowling, adventure pool, 2 hotel pools open to the public, massage, sauna, squash, fitness centre, indoor tennis centre at Hotel Berghof (3 courts, coaching available), indoor riding-school, pool and billiards, cinema

Outdoor Ice-skating rink, curling, horse-riding, horse sleigh rides, 45km/28 miles of cleared paths, hang-gliding, paragliding, tobogganing (2 runs), snowrafting

CHILDREN

All three ski schools run children's classes for children aged 4 or 5 to 14 where lunch is provided (6 days including lunch €178). Two of them run ski kindergartens for younger children – hourly care also possible.

Wuppy's Kinderland non-skiing nursery at the fun pool complex takes children aged 3 months to 7 years, 9am to 5pm, Monday to Friday.

'chaotic' 45-minute queue and resorted to taking a bus to Finkenberg or Hippach to avoid the 'scrum'. And there are queues to get down at the end of the day, too. The slopes can also get very crowded, causing queues for some lifts.

MOUNTAIN RESTAURANTS
Plenty of them
Most of Penken's many mountain restaurants are attractive and serve good-value food but can get crowded – Vronis has been recommended, as has the Schneekar restaurant at the top of the Horberg section. Bergrast, at the top of Penken, with 'a huge sun terrace, great views and first-class toilet facilities' was found to be 'well run and clean' and have a 'good choice' of self-service food. Gschössalm is reportedly a convenient but crowded meeting place. Penkenjochaus is a bit more orderly with 'friendly staff'.

SCHOOLS AND GUIDES
Excellent reputation
Mayrhofen's popularity is founded on its three schools, and a high proportion of guests take lessons. We have received many positive reports over the years. But we have heard of a complete beginner in a class of 15 with an instructor who spoke no English – 'we got by on sign language'.

FACILITIES FOR CHILDREN
Good but inconvenient
Mayrhofen majors on childcare and the facilities are excellent. But you may prefer resorts where children don't have to be bussed around and ferried up and down the mountain. And we had a report last year of a five-year-old girl being abandoned when her ski lesson lesson ended 15 minutes before her father arrived, despite previous assurances of supervision.

STAYING THERE

HOW TO GO
Plenty of mainstream packages
There is a wide choice of hotel holidays available from UK tour operators, but few catered chalets.
Hotels Most of the hotels packaged by UK tour operators are centrally located, a walk from the Penken gondola.
(((((5) **Elisabeth** (6767) The resort's only 5-star hotel – an opulent chalet in a fair position near the post office.
((((4) **Manni's** (633010) Well-placed, smartly done out; pool.
((((4) **Kramerwirt** (6700) Lovely hotel simply oozing character. A visitor reports 'friendly and helpful staff, comfortable rooms, varied and interesting half-board menu'.
(((3) **Strass** (6705) Best-placed of the 4-stars, very close to the Penken gondola. Lively bars, disco, fitness centre, solarium, pool, but rooms lack style.
(((3) **Neuhaus** (6703) 'First class facilities,' says a recent visitor, but the rooms above the bar are not ideal.
(((3) **Rose** (62229) Well placed, near centre. Good food.
(((3) **Neue Post** (62131) Convenient family-run 4-star on the main street – 'good food and nice big rooms'.
(((3) **Waldheim** (62211) Smallish, cosy 3-star gasthof, near the gondola.

EATING OUT
Wide choice
Most visitors are on half-board, but there is a large choice of restaurants. Manni's is good for pizzas ('but expensive, especially for wine'). Wirthaus zum Griena is a 'wonderful old wooden building offering traditional farmhouse cuisine'. A favourite with tour op reps is the Mount Everest in the Andrea hotel. The 'lively' Rundum is recommended this year for its 'good service'.

APRES-SKI
Lively but not rowdy
Nightlife is a great selling point. Mayrhofen has all the standard Tirolean-style entertainments, such as folk dancing, bier kellers and tea dances, along with bowling, sleigh rides, tobogganing, but also some seriously lively bars and discos.

At close of play, the Happy End umbrella bar, at the top of the Penken gondola, is lively, and the Ice bar, in the hotel Strass, gets packed out but is reportedly 'basic'. Some of the other

GETTING THERE

Air Salzburg 170km/106 miles (3hr); Munich 190km/118 miles (2½hr); Innsbruck 65km/40 miles (1hr).

Rail Local line through to resort; regular buses from station.

Phone numbers From elsewhere in Austria add the prefix 05285. From abroad use the prefix +43 5285.

TOURIST OFFICES

Mayrhofen t 6760 mayrhofen@zillertal.tirol.at www.mayrhofen.com

Finkenberg t 62673 info@finkenberg.at www.finkenberg.at

SKI ZILLERTAL 3000 / JP FANKHAUSER

The cable-car link to Rastkogel is an impressive 150-person affair ↓

bars in the Strass are rocking places later on. However, the Sport's Arena disco is said to be 'for the kids', meaning people under 27! A visitor this year preferred the atmosphere in the Lobby bar of the Strass, which has live music and a disco, and Apropos – 'great music'. The bars at the base of the Horbergbahn were favoured by one group this year despite the need for a taxi back. Mo's American theme bar and Scotland Yard remain popular, but a recent visitor found the latter 'dated, dirty and smoky'. The Schlussel disco is reportedly 'still the best all-round late-night venue'. Try Am Kamin or the small casino (both in the hotel Elisabeth) if you're after more Manhattan than Mayrhofen. The Neue Post bar and the Passage are good for a quiet drink.

OFF THE SLOPES
Good for all
The village travel agency arranges trips to Italy, and Innsbruck is easily reached by train. There are also good walks and sports amenities, including the swimming pool complex – with saunas, solariums and lots of other fun features. Pedestrians have no trouble getting up the mountain to meet friends for lunch.

Finkenberg 840m/2,760ft

Finkenberg is a much smaller, quieter village than Mayrhofen.

THE RESORT
Finkenberg is no more than a collection of traditional-style hotels, bars, cafes and private homes spread along the busy, steep main road between Mayrhofen and Lanersbach. Most hotels are within walking distance of the gondola, and many of the more distant ones run minibuses to the lift station.

THE MOUNTAIN
Finkenberg shares Mayrhofen's main Penken slopes.
Slopes A gondola gives good direct access to the Penken slopes – and in good conditions you can ski back to the village on a ski-route.
Snow reliability The local slopes are not as well-endowed with snowmaking as those on Mayrhofen's side of the mountain.
Experts Not much challenge, though we did find a black run not marked on the piste map.
Intermediates The whole newly expanded area opens up from the top of the gondola.
Beginners There's a village nursery slope, but it's a sunless spot, and good conditions are far from certain.
Snowboarding No special facilities.
Cross-country Cross-country skiers have to get a bus up to Lanersbach.
Queues The gondola gives queue-free access to the Penken.
Mountain restaurants See the recommendations given for Mayrhofen.
Schools and guides There are two schools. The Finkenberg School has a particularly good reputation.
Facilities for children There's a non-ski nursery, and the ski nursery takes children from age four.

STAYING THERE
Hotels There are quite a few. Sporthotel Stock (6775) has great spa facilities and is owned by the family of former downhill champion Leonard Stock.
Eating out The restaurants are mostly hotel-based.
Après-ski The main après-ski spots are the Laterndl Pub and Finkennest, and there are rep-organised events such as tobogganing and bowling.
Off the slopes Curling, ice-skating, swimming and good local walks.

Montafon

Extensive slopes, well off the beaten package path

COSTS

① ② ③ ④ ⑤ ⑥

NEWS

For 2003/04 the
Zamangbahn gondola
is to be upgraded
from four to six-seat
cabins, making this
clearly the most
efficient way into the
Hochjoch slopes.

2003/04 should also
bring increased
snowmaking in the
Silvretta Nova,
Hochjoch, Golm and
Schafberg ski areas.

2001/02 saw the
installation of a six-
pack and a fast quad
on Silvretta Nova.
The new lifts access
several new runs.
Improvements on
Hochjoch include an
eight-person chair-lift
and some extra
pistes at Seebliga.
And there's a six-
pack in place of the
old T-bar up to the
top of Grüneck at
Golm.

152

The 40km/25 mile-long Montafon valley contains no less than eleven resorts and five main lift systems. Packages from the UK are few (accommodation on a serious scale is not easy to find), but for the independent traveller the valley is well worth a look – especially the Silvretta Nova area (linking Gaschurn and St Gallenkirch) and high, tiny, isolated Gargellen.

The Montafon is neglected by the UK travel trade. Its location in Vorarlberg, west of the Arlberg pass, makes it a bit remote from the standard Austrian charter airport of Salzburg – and the valley lacks the large hotels that big operators apparently need.

The valley runs south-east from the medieval city of Bludenz – parallel with the nearby Swiss border. The first sizeable community you come to is Vandans, linked to its Golm ski area by gondola. Next are Schruns, at the foot of Hochjoch, and Tschagguns, across the valley at the foot of Grabs. Further on are St Gallenkirch and Gaschurn, at opposite ends of the biggest area, Silvretta Nova. Up a side valley to the south of St Gallenkirch is Gargellen, close to the Swiss border – a tiny village, but not unknown in Britain.

The valley road goes on up to Partenen, where it climbs steeply to Bielerhöhe and the Silvrettasee dam, at the foot of glaciers and Piz Buin (of sunscreen fame) – the highest peak in the Vorarlberg. In summer you can drive over the pass to Galtür and Ischgl. In winter Bielerhöhe is a great

launch pad for ski-tours, and there are high, snow-sure cross-country trails totalling 26km/16 miles on and around the frozen lake. You get there by taking a cable-car from Partenen to Trominier, and then a mini-bus – free with the area lift pass.

There are more ordinary cross-country trails along the valley, and an 11km/7 mile woodland trail at Kristberg, above Silbertal – up a side valley to the east of Schruns. Trails total 100km/62 miles.

The shared valley lift pass covers the respectable post-bus service and the Bludenz-Schruns trains, as well as the 65 lifts – so exploration of the valley does not require a car.

The top heights hereabouts are no match for the nearby Arlberg resorts; but there is plenty of skiing above the mid-mountain lift stations at around 1500m/5,000ft, and most of the slopes are not excessively sunny, so snow reliability (aided by snowmaking on quite a big scale) is reasonable. Practically all the pistes are accurately classified blue or red, but there are plentiful off-piste opportunities

KEY FACTS

Resorts	650-1425m
	2,130-4,675ft
Slopes	680-2395m
	2,230-7,855ft
Lifts	65
Pistes	209km
	130 miles
Blue	54%
Red	32%
Black	14%
Snowmaking	81km
	50 miles

ARCHIV MONTAFON TOURISMUS

Most of the skiing is on wide, open slopes above mid-mountain
→

On the map:
Piz Buin 3310m
Bielerhöhe
2010m
1720m
2100m
2275m/7,46oft
Schafberg
2150m
Grüneck 2085m
tenen 1480m
Silvretta Nova
1850m
Gargellen 1425m/4,68oft
Hochegga 1600m
1520m
Golm
1000m
Gaschurn ooom/3,28oft
Gortipohl
St Gallenkirch 900m/2,95oft
Kreuzjoch 2395m/7,86oft
2300m
Grabs
Tschagguns
Vandans
1850m
Hochjoch
1335m
Schruns 700m/2,300ft
Silbertal
Kristberg

TOURIST OFFICE

Montafon
t 722530
info@montafon.at
www.montafon.at

The tourist office is in Schruns, so from elsewhere in Austria add the prefix 05556, from abroad use the prefix +43 5556.

(including 37km/23 miles of 'ski routes'). There are snowboard terrain-parks in most sectors, and a half-pipe at Silvretta Nova.

There are 10 ski schools in the valley, operating in each of the different ski areas. And eight ski kindergartens take kids from age three.

Tobogganing is popular, and there are several runs on the different mountains – the Silvretta Nova's 6km/4 mile floodlit run down to St Gallenkirch being the most impressive.

GARGELLEN 1425m/4,68oft

Gargellen is a real backwater – a tiny village tucked up a side valley, with a small but varied piste network on Schafberg that is blissfully quiet.

The eight-person gondola from the village up to the Schafberg slopes seems rather out of place in this tiny collection of hotels and guest houses, huddled in a steep-sided, narrow valley. The runs it takes you to are gentle, with not much to choose between the blues and reds; but there is lots of off-piste terrain. There are four unpatrolled ski-routes. A special feature is the day-tour around the Madrisa – a small-scale off-piste adventure taking you over to Klosters in Switzerland. It involves a 300m/1,000ft climb, but is otherwise easy.

The altitude of the village (the highest in the Montafon) and north-east facing slopes make for reasonable snow reliability. And there is now snowmaking on one of the several pistes to the valley, which include a couple of excellent away-from-the-lifts runs at the extremities of the area. With care you can ski to the door of the hotel Madrisa (6331) among others. Behind the hotel is a rather steep nursery slope. There are three pleasant mountain restaurants, including two rustic huts at the tree line – the Obwaldhütte and the Kessl-Hütte. The former holds a weekly après-ski party after the lifts close, followed by a torchlit descent. (Slide shows and bridge are more typical evening entertainments.)

SCHRUNS 700m/2,300ft

Schruns is the most rounded resort in the valley – a towny little place, with the shops in its car-free centre catering for locals and for summer tourists.

A cable-car and gondola (which is about to get a performance boost) go up from points outside the village into the Hochjoch slopes. Above the trees is a fair-sized area of easy blue runs, with the occasional red alternative, served by slow chairs and drags and the fast eight-seat Seebliga chair. There are restaurants at strategic points – the Wormser Hütte is a climbing refuge with 'stunning' views. Parents can leave their kids under

Phone numbers
Gargellen
From elsewhere in Austria add the prefix 05557.
From abroad use the prefix +43 5557.

supervision at the huge NTC
Dreamland children's facility at the top
of the cable-car, by the skier services
building. The blue run from Kreuzjoch
back to Schruns is exceptional: about
12km/7.5 miles long and over
1600m/5,250ft vertical. Snow-guns
cover the lower half of this, plus the
Seebliga area.

Easily accessible across the valley
are the limited slopes of Grabs, above
the rather formless village of
Tschagguns, and the more extensive
area of Golm, where a gondola goes
from Vandans up to a handful of chairs
and drags serving easy slopes above
the trees, and offering a vertical
descent of over 1400m/4,590ft. A six-
pack now goes to the top of the area.
Snow-guns cover two major upper
slopes, and the red run to the valley.

As you are reminded at every
opportunity, Ernest Hemingway
ensconced himself in Schruns in
1925/26, and his favourite drinking
table in the hotel Taube (72384) is still
there to be admired. The Löwen (7141)
and the Alpenhof Messmer (726640)
are elegant, well-equipped 4-stars with
big pools, the former a hub of the
après-ski scene.

GASCHURN / ST GALLENKIRCH
1000m/3,280ft / 900m/2,950ft
**Silvretta Nova is the biggest lift and
piste network in the valley. As a result,
German cars fill to overflowing the
huge car parks at the valley lift
stations. Gaschurn is an attractive
place to stay.**
The two main resorts here are quite
different. Whereas St Gallenkirch is
strung along the main road and

spoiled by traffic, Gaschurn is a
pleasant village, bypassed by the
valley traffic, with the wood-shingled
Posthotel Rössle (83330) in the centre.

The lift network covers two parallel
ridges running north-south, with most
of the runs on their east- and west-
facing flanks. The slopes are accessed
from three points along the valley. A
gondola from Gaschurn takes you up
to the east ridge, while another
gondola from St Gallenkirch goes up to
Valisera on the west ridge. A chair-lift
to Garfrescha gives access to the
central valley from Gortipohl – on the
road between the two resorts.

This is the most challenging area in
the valley, with as many red as blue
runs, and some nominal blacks. Most
of the slopes are above the tree line,
typically offering a modest 300m/
1,000ft vertical. The Rinderhütte six-
pack has opened up extra red pistes
from the top of the area. There is lots
of off-piste potential, including steep
(and quite dangerous) slopes down
into the central valley. The map shows
four 'ski routes'; outrageously, their
status is not explained.

There are lots of mountain
restaurants, many impressive in
different ways. At the top of the east
ridge is the state-of-the-art Nova
Stoba, with seats for over 1,500 people
in various rooms catering for different
markets, including splendid panelled
rooms with table-service. The big
terrace bar gets seriously boisterous.
At the top of the other ridge is the
splendidly woody Valisera Hüsli.

There is snowmaking on one-third
of the slopes, with cover down to two
of the valley stations.

Obergurgl

Chalet-style hotels on high, snow-sure slopes attract a loyal clientele

155

COSTS

① ② ③ ④ ⑤ ⑥

RATINGS

The slopes

Snow	*****
Extent	**
Expert	**
Intermediate	***
Beginner	****
Convenience	****
Queues	*****
Mountain restaurants	**

The rest

Scenery	***
Resort charm	****
Off-slope	**

NEWS

No new lifts are planned for 2003/04, but a couple of years ago there was substantial investment in the resort. This included a new eight-seater gondola from Untergurgl to Hochgurgl to a point high on the Wurmkogl slopes, a four-seater chair-lift to replace the Übungs drag-lift in the Gaisberg sector and a new six-pack, which replaced the Steinmann and Sattel drag-lifts.

＋ Glaciers apart, one of the Alps' most reliable resorts for snow – especially good for a late-season holiday

＋ Excellent area for beginners, timid intermediates and families

＋ Mainly queue- and crowd-free

＋ Traditional-style village with very little traffic

＋ Jolly tea-time après-ski

＋ Obergurgl and Hochgurgl slopes are now linked by gondola

－ Limited area of slopes, with no tough pistes and now no terrain-park or half-pipe

－ Exposed setting, with few sheltered slopes for bad weather

－ Few off-slope leisure amenities except in hotels

－ Disappointing mountain restaurants

－ Village is spread-out and disjointed

－ For a small Austrian resort, rather expensive

A loyal band of visitors go back every year to Obergurgl or higher Hochgurgl, booking a year in advance in recognition of the limited supply of beds. They love the high, snow-sure, easy intermediate slopes, the end-of-the-valley seclusion and the civilised atmosphere in the reassuringly expensive hotels.

We're unconvinced. If we're going to a bleak, high, snow-sure resort where there is not much to do but ski or board, we'd rather go somewhere with rather more skiing or boarding to do. But, of course, most such places aren't in Austria – important to some – and their hotels might be less reassuringly expensive.

THE RESORT

Obergurgl is based on a traditional old village, set in a remote spot, the dead end of a long road up past Sölden. It is the highest parish in Austria and is usually under a blanket of snow from November until May. The surrounding slopes are bleak, with an array of avalanche barriers giving them a forbidding appearance.

Obergurgl has no through traffic and few day visitors. The village centre is mainly traffic-free, and entirely so at night. Village atmosphere is relaxed during the day, jolly immediately after the slopes close, but rather subdued later at night; there are some nightspots, but most people stay in their hotels. The resort is popular with British families and well-heeled groups looking for a relaxing winter break.

Despite its small size, this is a village of parts. At the northern entrance to the resort is a cluster of hotels near the main Festkogl gondola, which takes you to all the local slopes. This area is good for getting to the slopes and for ease of access by car, but it's a long walk or a shuttle-bus from the village centre and the nursery slopes. The road then passes another

group of hotels set on a little hill to the east, around the ice rink (beware steep, sometimes treacherous walks here). The village proper starts with an attractive little square with church, fountain, and the original village hotel (the Edelweiss und Gurgl). Just above are the Rosskar and Gaisberg chair-lifts to the local slopes. There is an underground car park in the centre of the village.

Hochgurgl, a bus-ride (or gondola-ride) away, is little more than a handful of hotels at the foot of its own slopes. It looks like it might be a convenience resort dedicated to skiing from the door, but it isn't: from nearly

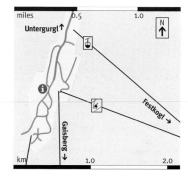

KEY FACTS

Resort	1930m
	6,330ft
Slopes	1795-3080m
	5,890-10,100ft
Lifts	23
Pistes	110km
	68 miles
Blue	32%
Red	50%
Black	18%
Snowmaking	22km
	14 miles

LIFT PASSES

Obergurgl ski pass
Covers lifts in
Obergurgl and
Hochgurgl, and local
ski-bus.

Main pass
1-day pass €36
6-day pass €175

Senior citizens
Over 60: 6-day pass
€131

Children
Under 16: 6-day pass
€107
Under 8: free pass

Notes
Half-day passes
available.

all the hotels you have to negotiate roads and/or stairs to get to or from the snow. Hochgurgl is even quieter than Obergurgl at night.

In the valley below Hochgurgl (and linked by gondola) is Untergurgl, also linked to Obergurgl by regular ski-buses. For a budget base, it is worth considering. For a day out, it's a short bus or car trip to Sölden (see separate chapter), and a long car trip to Kühtai (a worthwhile high area near Innsbruck). Much closer is the tiny touring launch-pad of Vent.

THE MOUNTAINS

The slopes of Obergurgl and Hochgurgl are about 4km/2 miles apart but are now directly linked by gondola, as well as by road. Even so, the slopes are still surprisingly limited, and lacking interest or challenge for adventurous intermediates or experts. You don't get the sense of travel, as you do in bigger Alpine resorts. Most of the slopes are very exposed – there are few woodland runs to head to in poor conditions. Wind and white-outs can shut the lifts and, especially in early season, severe cold can curtail enthusiasm.

The lift pass is quite expensive for the relatively small area.

THE SLOPES
Limited cruising

Obergurgl is the smaller of the two linked areas. It is in two sections, well linked by piste in one direction, more loosely in the other. The gondola and the Rosskar fast quad chair from the village go to the higher Festkogl area.

This is served by two drags and a chair up to 3035m/9,96oft (you can join the Rosskar lift at its mid-station too). From here you can head back to the gondola base or over to Gaisberg, with its high point at Hohe Mut, reached by a long, slow chair. On the lightly wooded lower part of this area, two new fast chair-lifts have replaced three drag-lifts. A double chair up from Obergurgl's village square provides the other link on to the Gaisberg slopes. There are two 'ski routes', one of them the only run from Hohe Mut. The piste map used to explain that these are unpatrolled, but no longer does so.

The Top Express gondola is the obvious way to travel to **Hochgurgl** during the day. But there is still the alternative of a regular and reliable free shuttle-bus to Untergurgl, for the gondola up to Hochgurgl.

The slopes of Hochgurgl consist of two high, gentle bowls, either side of the Schermerspitze, served by the continuing gondola and chair-lifts, and open mountainsides either side of the 'village' served by drag-lifts. From Wurmkogl there are spectacular views of the Dolomites. A single run leads down through the woods from Hochgurgl to Untergurgl.

TERRAIN-PARKS
They have shut them down

You can tell the type of clientele Obergurgl attracts by the fact that they scrapped the terrain-park, half-pipe and quarter-pipe they used to maintain. It's not a resort for young party-loving jibbers.

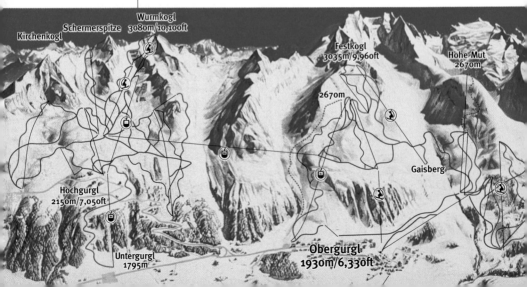

Kirchenkogl · Schermerspitze · Wurmkogl 3080m/10,100ft · Festkogl 3035m/9,96oft · Hohe Mut 2670m · 2670m · Gaisberg · Hochgurgl 2150m/7,05oft · Untergurgl 1795m · Obergurgl 1930m/6,330ft

Obergurgl is remotely set amid high, bleak scenery at the end of the long road up through the Oetz valley →

OBERGURGL TOURIST OFFICE

SNOW RELIABILITY
Excellent
Obergurgl has high slopes and is arguably the most snow-sure of Europe's non-glacier resorts – even without its snowmaking, which is now impressively extensive. It has a longer season than most Austrian resorts.

FOR EXPERTS
Not generally recommendable
There are few challenges on-piste – most of the blacks could easily be red, and where they deserve the grading it's only for short stretches (for example, at the very top of Wurmkogl). But the Hohe Mut ski route can have big moguls, and there is a fair amount of enjoyable off-piste to be found with a guide – and the top school groups often go off-piste when conditions are right. This is a well-known area for ski touring, and we have reports of very challenging expeditions on the glaciers at the head of the valley.

FOR INTERMEDIATES
Good but limited
There is some perfect intermediate terrain here, made even better by the normally flattering snow conditions. The problem is, there's not much of it. Keen piste-bashers will quickly tire of travelling the same runs and be itching

to catch the bus to Sölden, down the valley – unfortunately, there is no pass-sharing arrangement.

Hochgurgl has the bigger area of easy runs, and these make good cruising. For more challenging intermediate runs, head to the Vorderer Wurmkogllift, on the right as you look at the mountain. Less confident intermediates may find the woodland piste down from Hochgurgl to the bus stop at Untergurgl tricky.

The Obergurgl area has more red than blue runs but most offer no great challenge to a confident intermediate. There is some easy cruising around mid-mountain on the Festkogl. The blue run from the top of the Festkogl gondola down to the village, via the Gaisberg sector, is one of the longest cruises in the area. And there's another long enjoyable run down the length of the gondola, with a scenic off-piste variant in the adjoining valley.

In the Gaisberg area, there are very easy runs in front of the Nederhütte and back towards the village.

FOR BEGINNERS
Fine for first-timers or improvers
The inconveniently situated Mahdstuhl nursery slope above Obergurgl is adequate for complete beginners. And the gentle Gaisberg run – under the

boarding

Obergurgl is a traditional ski destination, attracting an affluent and (dare we say it?) 'older' clientele. It doesn't attract many young snowboarders – as is evidenced by it closing down its terrain-park a couple of seasons ago. But the resort is actually pretty good for snowboarding. Beginners will be pleased to find that most of the slopes can be reached without having to ride drag-lifts. And there's some good off-piste potential for more advanced riders.

↑ Good snow, easy pistes and comfortable chalet-style hotels is what Obergurgl is all about
OBERGURGL TOURIST OFFICE

SCHOOLS

Obergurgl
t 6305
Hochgurgl
t 626599

Classes
(Hochgurgl prices)
6 days (2hr am and pm) €150
Private lessons
€55 for 1hr for 1 or 2 people; each additional person €15

CHILDREN

Both ski schools take children over the age of 5 (6 full days including lunch €150). Children can join the ski kindergarten from the age of 3.

The village kindergarten in Obergurgl also takes children from the age of 3.

The Alpina, Austria and Hochfirst hotels (among others) have in-house kindergartens.

---

chair out of the village – is ideal to move on to as soon as a modicum of control has been achieved. The easy slopes served by the Bruggenboden chair are also suitable.

The Hochgurgl nursery slopes are an awkward walk from the hotels, but otherwise satisfactory. And there are good blue slopes to move on to.

The quality of the snow makes learning here easier than in most lower Austrian resorts.

CROSS-COUNTRY
Limited but snow-sure
Three small loops, one each at Obergurgl, Untergurgl and Hochgurgl, give just 12km/7 miles of trail. All are relatively snow-sure and pleasantly situated. Lessons are available.

QUEUES
Few problems
Major lift queues are rare. You can expect high-season queues for the village lifts at the start of ski school, but these tend to clear quickly. The resort is remote and has not attracted many day-trippers in the past, even when lower villages have been short of snow. But a regular visitor reported 'many more day visitors this year, due to quicker access from Untergurgl via the gondola and increased coach/car parking'. So crowds may become more of a problem.

MOUNTAIN RESTAURANTS
Little choice
Compared with most Austrian resorts, mountain huts are neither numerous nor very special. At Gaisberg the Nederhütte is jolly, and David's Skihütte is friendly, cheerful and good value. The 'traditional and welcoming'

Schönwieshütte, a 10-minute walk from the piste, has excellent views, as does the small hut at Hohe Mut. At Hochgurgl, Wurmkogelhütte is the only place for a proper meal – a big, but pleasantly woody and spacious, self-service. The tiny hut above it at Wurmkoglgipfel is in an exceptional position and does limited food. Many people return to one village or the other for lunch – one recent reporter 'much preferred' their hotel's sun terrace to 'shaded mountain huts'.

SCHOOLS AND GUIDES
Mainly good news
We've had nothing but good reports of the Obergurgl school in the last few years, with good English spoken and excellent lessons and organisation: 'highly efficient, very thorough testing of pupils before being put into a class', 'big effort to make school fun'. Class sizes are normally between four and nine though we have received reports telling of 15 to a class at busy times.

FACILITIES FOR CHILDREN
Check out your hotel
Children's ski classes start at five years and children from age three can join Bobo's ski-kindergarten. There is also a non-skiing kindergarten, the Pingu Club, for kids aged three and up. There's lunchtime supervision for ski school and kindergarten children alike. Many hotels offer childcare of one sort or another, and the Alpina has been particularly recommended.

STAYING THERE

HOW TO GO
Plenty of good hotels
Most package accommodation is in hotels and pensions. Demand for rooms in Obergurgl exceeds supply, and for once it is true that you should book early to avoid disappointment.
Hotels Accommodation is of high quality: most hotels are 4-stars, and none is less than a 3-star. Couples have been surprised to be asked to share tables even at 4-star hotels.

A cheaper option is to stay down the valley in Untergurgl, where the 4-star Jadghof (6431) is recommended. Some hotels don't accept credit cards.
(((4 **Edelweiss und Gurgl** (6223) The focal hotel – biggest, oldest, one of the most appealing; on the central square, near the main lifts. Pool.
(((4 **Alpina de Luxe** (600) Big, smart

GETTING THERE

Air Innsbruck 99km/62 miles (2hr); Salzburg 288km/179 miles (3hr); Munich 204km/127 miles (4hr).

Rail Train to Ötz; regular buses from station, transfer 1½hr.

ACTIVITIES

Indoor Saunas, whirlpools, steam baths, massage, bowling, pool and billiards, squash, table tennis

Outdoor Natural skating rink (open in the evenings), snow-shoe outings

Phone numbers
From elsewhere in Austria add the prefix 05256.
From abroad use the prefix +43 5256.

TOURIST OFFICE

t 6466
info@obergurgl.com
www.obergurgl.com

chalet with excellent children's facilities. Pool.
((((**Hochfirst** (63250) Recommended by a recent reporter. Good spa facilities, comfortable, four or five minutes from gondola. Casino.
((((**Berggasthof Gamper** (6545) 'Excellent,' says a recent reporter – 'Good food, friendly staff.' Far end of town, past the square.
((((**Crystal** (6454) If you don't mind the ocean-liner appearance, it's one of the best near the Festkogl lift.
((((**Gotthard-Zeit** (6292) Spacious, comfortable, good food. Spa facilities. Small pool. Sun terrace. Recommended.
(((**Wiesental** (6263) Comfortable, well situated, good value.
(((**Granat-Schlössl** (6363) Amusing pseudo-castle, surprisingly affordable.
((**Alpenblume** (6278) Good B&B hotel, well-placed for Festkogl lift.
((**Haus Gurgl** (6533) B&B near Festkogl lift; friendly, pizzeria, same owners as Edelweiss und Gurgl.
Hochgurgl has equally good hotels.
((((**Hochgurgl** (6265) The only 5-star in the area. Luxurious, with pool.
((((**Angerer Alm** (6241) 'Excellent facilities and most welcoming staff,' says a recent reporter. Pool.
(((**Sporthotel Ideal** (6290) Well situated for access to the slopes. Pool.
(((**Laurin** (6227) Well equipped, traditional rooms, excellent food.
Self-catering The Lohmann is a high-standard large modern apartment block, well placed for the slopes, less so for the village centre below. The 3-star Pirchhütt has apartments close to the Festkogl gondola, and the Wiesental hotel has more central ones.

EATING OUT
Wide choice, limited range
Hotel dining rooms and à la carte restaurants dominate. This a year a reporter recommends the independent and rustic Krumpn's Stadl (where staff dress in traditional clothing) and the Jenewein. The Romantika at the hotel Madeleine and the Belmonte are popular pizzerias. Hotel Alpina has a particularly good reputation for its food – though a recent report says the Gotthard-Zeit and Hochfirst are 'just as good'. The restaurant at the Gamper is pleasantly cosy. The two restaurants in the Edelweiss und Gurgl are reportedly 'superb', and food at the Josl 'excellent'. Nederhütte (which has a fondue evening with live music, which 'rocks', says a 2003 reporter) and

David's Skihütte up the mountain are both open in the evenings. Remember, credit cards are not widely accepted.

APRES-SKI
Lively early, quiet later
Obergurgl is more animated in the evening than you might expect. The Nederhütte mountain restaurant has lively tea dancing – you have to ski home afterwards though (or ride down on a snowmobile, says a reporter). All the bars at the base of the Rosskar and Gaisberg lifts are popular at close of play – the Umbrella Bar outside the Edelweiss hotel is particularly busy in good weather. The Hexenkuchl at the Jenewein is also popular.
    Later on, the crowded Krumpn's Stadl barn is the liveliest place in town with live music on alternate nights. The Josl, Jenewein and Edelweiss und Gurgl hotels have atmospheric bars. The Bajazzo is a more sophisticated late-night haunt. The Edelweissbar and Austriakeller are discos (the latter appealing, when we visited, to an extraordinary age range – 6 to 60). There's a casino at the Hochfirst.
    Hochgurgl is very quiet at night except for Toni's Almhütte bar in the Olymp Sporthotel – one of three places with live music. There's also the African Bar disco.

OFF THE SLOPES
Very limited
There isn't much to do during the day, with few shops and limited public facilities. Innsbruck is over two hours away by post-bus. Sölden (20 minutes away) has a leisure centre and shopping facilities. Pedestrians can walk to restaurants in the Gaisberg area to meet friends for lunch and there are 11km/7 miles of hiking paths. The health suite at the Hochfirst has been recommended as being open to non-residents.

Obergurgl

159

Obertauern

Small, varied area, with great snow record and lively après-ski scene

COSTS

① ② ③ ④ ⑤ ⑥

HOW IT RATES

The slopes

Snow	****
Extent	**
Expert	***
Intermediate	****
Beginner	****
Convenience	****
Queues	****
Mountain restaurants	***

The rest

Scenery	***
Resort charm	**
Off-slope	**

NEWS

The Zehnerkar cable-car is to be replaced by a gondola for 2003/04. A six-seat chair will replace the Seekarspitz drag-lift and a quad chair will replace the Achenrain double.

Last season a fast quad chair-lift, the Zentralbahn, replaced the old drag-lift.

- + Excellent snow record
- + Well-linked, user-friendly circuit
- + Slopes for all abilities
- + Good modern lift system
- + Good mountain restaurants
- + Lively but not intrusive après-ski
- + Compact resort centre – family-friendly if you pick your spot

- – Village lacks traditional charm
- – Slopes are of limited vertical
- – Lifts and snow can suffer from exposure to high winds

If you like the après-ski jollity of Austria but have a hankering for the good snow of high French resorts, Obertauern could be just what you're looking for. The terrain is a bit limited by French standards, and the village is no Alpbach. But it's a lot prettier than Flaine – and if you've grown up on slush and ice in lower Austrian resorts, moving up in the world by 1000m/3,300ft or so will be something of a revelation.

THE RESORT

In the land of postcard resorts grown out of rustic villages, Obertauern is different – a mainly modern development at the top of the Tauern pass road. Built in (high-rise) chalet style, it's not unattractive – but it lacks a central focus of shops and bars. Although the core is compact, there is accommodation spread widely along the road, and beginners in particular need to make sure their choice of accommodation, ski school and nursery slope will work together.

THE MOUNTAIN

The slopes and lifts form a ring around the village. The Tauern pass road divides them into two unequal parts; that apart, the slopes are well linked to make a user-friendly circuit that can be travelled clockwise or anticlockwise in a couple of hours. Visitors used to big areas will soon start to feel they have seen it all. Vertical range is limited, and runs are short – most major lifts are in the 200m to 400m (650ft to 1,300ft) vertical range. There's now a clearer piste map but

Seekarspitze 2210m
Hundskogel 2135m
Seekareck 2160m
Plattenspitze 2050m
Gamskarspitz 2030m
Hochalm 1945m
1980m
Kringsalm
1915m
Grünwaldkopf 1970m
1790m
Obertauern 1740m/5,710ft
1700m
Schaidber 1630m/5,35
1630m/ 5,350ft
1665m
1850m
Gamsleitenspitze 2315m/7,600ft
1985m
Zehnerkarspitze 2190m

The core of the village is compact, but beginners must take care that they are not based miles from the nursery slope their ski school will be using →

KEY FACTS

Resort	1740m
	5,710ft
Slopes	1630-2315m
	5,350-7,600ft
Lifts	29
Pistes	120km
	75 miles
Blue	50%
Red	35%
Black	15%
Snowmaking	85km
	53 miles

Phone numbers
From elsewhere in Austria add the prefix 06456.
From abroad use the prefix +43 6456.

TOURIST OFFICE

t 7252
info@ski-obertauern.com
www.obertauern.com

reporters complain that while pistes are numbered on the mountain, they are not on the map.

Slopes Most pistes are on the sunny slopes to the north of the road and village: a wide, many-faceted basin of mostly gentle runs, some combining steepish pitches with long schusses. The slopes on the other side of the road – on Gamsleitenspitze, to the south-west – are generally quieter and have some of Obertauern's most difficult runs. There is floodlit skiing from one chair-lift twice a week.

Terrain-parks There is a terrain-park at Hochalm.

Snow reliability The resort has exceptional snow reliability because of its altitude. But lifts can be closed by wind (which may blow snow away too).

Experts There are genuinely steep black pistes from the Gamsleiten chair, but it is prone to closure. There is good off-piste throughout the area and reporters recommend joining an off-piste guided group.

Intermediates Most of Obertauern's circuit is of intermediate difficulty. Stay low for easier pistes, or try the tougher runs higher up. In the Hochalm area, the Seekareck and Panorama chairs take you to challenging runs. The chair to Hundskogel leads to a red and a black. And over at the Plattenkar quad there are splendid black/red runs.

Beginners Obertauern has very good nursery slopes, but they are spread around and beginners must beware long walks. The Schaidberg chair leads to a drag-lift serving a high-altitude beginners' slope and there is an easy run to get you back to the village.

Snowboarding Drag-lifts are optional.

Cross-country There are 17km/11 miles of trails in the heart of the resort.

Queues When nearby resorts have poor snow, non-residents arrive by the bus-load. However, the modern lift system is impressively efficient. The occasional queues for the Zehnerkar should now be a thing of the past, with a gondola replacing the cable-car this season. The Sonnenlift double chair from the bottom end of the resort is a bottleneck at ski school start time.

Mountain restaurants Mountain restaurants are plentiful and good, but crowded. The Edelweisshütte 'has to be savoured at least once' for the afternoon sing-songs. The old Lürzer Alm at village level remains popular.

Schools and guides There are six schools. 'Bondi Bill', a previously commended instructor, is still with Skischule Krallinger. We have had a favourable report this year of Frau Holle school. A visitor's four children thrived on the 'caring attitude' and 'excellent English'.

Facilities for children Most of the schools take children.

STAYING THERE

How to go Two major British tour operators offer packages here.

Hotels Practically all accommodation is in hotels (mostly 3-star and 4-star) and guest houses. The following have been recommended: Steiner (7306) – 'lavish spa facilities, magnificent food'; Enzian (72070) – 'very good facilities'; Schütz (72040); Edelweiss (72450); Gamsleiten (72860) – 'definitely upmarket'; Alpina (73360).

Eating out The choices are mostly hotels and the busy après-ski bars at the foot of the north-side lifts. The Hochalm restaurant at the top of the Grünwaldkopf quad sometimes serves early-evening meals.

Après-ski Obertauern has a lively and varied après-ski scene. The Latsch'n Alm, with terrace and dancing, is good at tea time. Later, try the Lürzer Alm, with farmyard-style decor and a disco. The Taverne has various bars, a pizzeria, and a disco. The Römerbar, Bar Havana and the Rossenhimmel nightclub are worth a look.

Off the slopes There's an excellent, large sports centre – fitness room, tennis, squash and badminton, sauna and steam bath, no pool – but there's little else to do in bad weather. However, Salzburg is an easy trip.

For lunch with friends, non-skiers can ride the Zehnerkar gondola or Grünwaldkopf chair or work up an appetite walking to the Kringsalm hut.

Saalbach-Hinterglemm

Attractive villages, lively nightlife and good intermediate circuit

COSTS

①②③④⑤⑥

RATINGS

The slopes

Snow	★★★
Extent	★★★
Expert	★★
Intermediate	★★★★
Beginner	★★★
Convenience	★★★★
Queues	★★★
Mountain restaurants	★★★★

The rest

Scenery	★★★
Resort charm	★★★★
Off-slope	★★

KEY FACTS

Resort	1000m
	3,280ft
Slopes	930-2095m
	3,050ft-6,870ft
Lifts	56
Pistes	200km
	124 miles
Blue	45%
Red	49%
Black	7%
Snowmaking	70km
	43 miles

+ Large, well-linked, intermediate circuit with impressive lift system

+ Saalbach is a big but pleasant, affluent village, lively at night

+ Village main streets largely traffic-free

+ Atmospheric mountain restaurants dotted around the slopes

+ Sunny slopes

+ Large snowmaking installation and excellent piste maintenance

– Large number of low, south-facing slopes that suffer from the sun

– Limited steep terrain

– Nursery slopes in Saalbach are not ideal – sunny, and crowded in parts

– Saalbach spreads along the valley – some lodgings are far from central

– Hinterglemm sprawls along a long street with no clearly defined centre

– Saalbach can get rowdy at night

Saalbach-Hinterglemm is one of Austria's major resorts, with a claimed 200km/ 124 miles of pistes. Compared with other big names nearby, it emerges well: it has better expert terrain and better mountain restaurants than the Ski Welt (Söll, Ellmau etc), more impressive lifts and snowmaking than Kitzbühel, and has the edge on both in terms of village altitude and skiing convenience.

If you cast the net wider, though, you become more aware of what a weakness it is to have most slopes facing south, especially when those slopes are mainly below the 1900m/6,23oft mark. There is a limit to what snowmaking can achieve, especially in February and March.

THE RESORT

Saalbach and Hinterglemm are separate villages, their centres 4km/2 miles apart, which have expanded along the floor of their dead-end valley. They haven't quite merged, but a few years ago they adopted a single shared identity. This doesn't mean they offer a single kind of holiday.

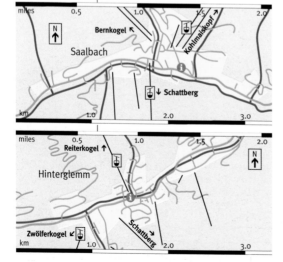

Saalbach is an attractive, typically Austrian village, with traditional-style (although mostly modern) buildings huddled together around a classic onion-domed church. But it is more convenient than most Austrian villages, with pistes coming right down to the traffic-free village centre; the result is close to an ideal blend of Austrian charm with French convenience.

Saalbach has a justified reputation as a party town – but those doing the partying seem to be a strangely mixed bunch. Big-spending BMW and Mercedes drivers, staying in the smart, expensive hotels that line the main street, share the bars with teenagers (including British school kids) spending more on alcohol than on their cheap and cheerful pensions out along the road to Hinterglemm. It can get very rowdy, with drunken revellers still in their ski boots long after dark.

Hinterglemm also has lifts and runs close to the centre, and offers quick access to some of the most interesting slopes. It is a more diffuse collection of hotels and holiday homes, where prices are lower and less cash is flashed. The main street, lined with bars and hotels, has been relieved of through traffic, which is not quite the

For the 2003/04 season there are plans to replace the Asitzmulden and Zehner T-bars with six-seat chairs, covered in the case of the Zehner. This will bring the number of fast chairs up to 10; in combination with seven gondolas this amounts to an impressive system.

2003/04 should also bring more snow-making capability.

For 2002/03 the old queue-prone cable-car from Saalbach to Schattberg Ost was replaced by a new eight-seat gondola complete with mid-station.

same as being traffic-free. It is lively without being rowdy, and for many people is the more attractive option.

In both villages, the amount of walking depends heavily on where you stay. There is an excellent valley bus service, but it isn't perfect: it finishes early, gets very busy at peak times and doesn't get you back to hotels in central Hinterglemm, or to hotels set away from the main road. Taxis are plentiful and not expensive.

Several resorts in Salzburg province are reachable by road – including Bad Hofgastein, Kaprun and Zell am See, the last a short bus-ride away.

THE MOUNTAINS

The slopes form a 'circus' almost entirely composed of intermediate, lightly wooded slopes.

THE SLOPES
User-friendly circuit

Travelling anticlockwise, you can make a complete circuit of the valley on skis, crossing from one side to the other at Vorderglemm and Lengau. You have to tackle a red run from Schattberg West, but otherwise can stick to blues. Going

clockwise, you have to truncate the circuit because there is no lift on the south side at Vorderglemm – and there is more red-run skiing to do (and a black if you want to do the full circuit). Crossing the valley at the two villages is not nearly so convenient, involving walks of a minute or two.

On the south-facing side, five sectors can be identified – from west to east, **Hochalm**, **Reiterkogel**, **Bernkogel**, **Kohlmaiskopf** and **Wildenkarkogel**. The last connects via Seidl-Alm to Leogang – a small, high, open area, leading to a long, narrow, north-facing slope down to Leogang village, broadening towards the bottom. An eight-person gondola brings you most of the way back.

The links across these south-facing slopes work well: when traversing the whole hillside you need to descend to the valley floor only once – at Saalbach, where (irritatingly) the main street separates Bernkogel from the slopes of Kohlmaiskopf.

The north-facing slopes are different in character – two distinct mountains, with long runs from each to the valley. An eight-seat gondola has replaced the old, queue-prone cable-car from

← Schattberg, on the shady side of the valley: challenging red runs and a genuine black

SNOW RELIABILITY
A tale of two sides

The south-facing slopes are in the majority, and can suffer when the sun comes out. Most are above 1400m/ 4,600ft, which helps. The north-facing slopes keep their snow better but can get icy. The long north-facing run down to Leogang often has the best snow in the area. Piste maintenance is good, and snowmaking covers many top-to-bottom runs – but the low altitude is a problem that won't go away.

FOR EXPERTS
Little steep stuff

There are few challenging slopes. Off-piste guides are available, but snow conditions and forest tend to limit the potential. The main attractions are the north-facing slopes. The long (4km/2.5 mile) Nordabfahrt run beneath the Schattberg gondola is a genuine black – a fine fast bash first thing in the morning if it has been groomed. The Zwölferkogel Nordabfahrt at Hinterglemm is less consistent, but its grading is justified by a few short, steeper pitches. The World Cup downhill run from Zwölferkogel is interesting, as is the 5km/3 mile Schattberg West-Hinterglemm red (and its scenic 'ski route' variant).

FOR INTERMEDIATES
Paradise

This area is ideal for both the mileage-hungry piste-basher and the more leisurely cruiser. For those looking for more of a challenge, the most direct routes down from Hochalm, Reiterkogel, Kohlmaiskopf and Hochwartalm are good fun. Only the delightful blue from Bernkogel into Saalbach – 'the ultimate cruiser', to quote a recent visitor – gets really crowded at times. The alternative long ski route is very pleasant, taking you through forest and meadows.

The north-facing area has some more challenging runs, with excellent relentless reds from both Schattberg

---

LIFT PASSES

Skicircus Saalbach Hinterglemm Leogang
Covers Saalbach, Hinterglemm and Leogang lifts, and the ski-bus.

Main pass
1-day pass €33.50
6-day pass €159

Children
Under 19: 6-day pass €143
Under 16: 6-day pass €79.50
Under 6: free pass

Notes
Supplement for use of pool in Hinterglemm. Sun ticket available for pedestrians, points cards for beginners.

Alternative pass
Salzburg Super Ski Card covers all lifts and pistes in Salzburgerland including Zell am See, Kaprun, Schladming and Bad Gastein.

Saalbach to **Schattberg**. The high, open, sunny slopes behind the peak are served by a fast quad.

From Schattberg, long runs go down to Saalbach, Vorderglemm and Hinterglemm. From the last, lifts go not only to Schattberg but also to the other north-facing hill, **Zwölferkogel**, served by a two-stage eight-seater gondola. Drags serve open slopes on the sunny side of the peak, and a gondola provides a link from Lengau and the south-facing Hochalm.

The Hinterglemm nursery slopes are floodlit every evening, and well used.

TERRAIN-PARKS
Excellent

There's a large half-pipe on Bernkogel above Saalbach, another below Seidl-Alm and terrain-parks on the north-facing slopes just above Hinterglemm (floodlit) and below Kl. Asitz on the way to Leogang. (The Asitzmulden T-bar serving this one is to be replaced by a six-pack for the coming winter – a much more attractive arrangement.) There are also dedicated 'carving' zones on the pistes.

boarding

Saalbach is great for boarding. Slopes are extensive, lifts are mainly chairs and gondolas (though there are some connecting drags), and there are pistes to appeal to beginners, intermediates and experts alike – with few flats to negotiate. For experienced boarders, there's off-piste terrain between the lifts.

SCHOOLS

Saalbach

Fürstauer
t 8444 e fuerstauer@
skischule-saalbach.at

Aamadall (Snow Academy)
t 6246 e aamadall@
aamadall.com

Hinterholzer
t 7607
e schischule.saalbach
@holiday.at

Wolfgang Zink
t 0664 1623655
e zink@aon.at

Snowboard
t 20047
e school@board.at

Hinterglemm

Snow and Fun
t 63460
e gensbichler@
skischule.com

Activ
t 0676 5171325
e info@skischule-
activ.at

Heugenhauser
t 8300 e skischule@
heugenhauser.at

Classes
(Fürstauer prices)
6 days (4hr) €162

Private lessons
€90 for 2hr, for 1 or
2 people; extra
person €10

CHILDREN

Some ski schools
take children in
miniclubs from about
age 3 and can
provide lunchtime
care. From about 4½
children join ski
school (€137 for 6
days – Fürstauer
prices).

Several hotels have
nurseries.

West and Zwölferkogel, and a section
of relatively high, open slopes around
Zwölferkogel. None of the black runs is
beyond an adventurous intermediate.
The long, pretty cruise to Vorderglemm
gets you right away from lifts.

Our favourite intermediate run is the
long cruise on north-facing snow down
to Leogang. But getting to it via the
little bowls on Asitz takes time.

FOR BEGINNERS
Best for improvers
Saalbach's two nursery slopes are right
next to the village centre. But they are
south-facing, and the upper one gets a
lot of through-traffic, and the lower
one is very small; the lift is free.

Alternatives are trips to the short,
easy runs at Bernkogel and Schattberg.
Hinterglemm's spacious nursery area
is separate from the main slopes. It is
north-facing, so lacks sun in midwinter,
but is more reliable for snow later on.

There are lots of easy blue runs to
move on to, especially on the south-
facing side of the valley.

FOR CROSS-COUNTRY
Go to Zell am See
Trails run beside the road along the
valley floor from Saalbach to
Vorderglemm and between
Hinterglemm and the valley end at
Lindlingalm. In mid-winter these trails
get very little sun, and are not very
exciting. The countryside beyond
nearby Zell am See offers more scope.

QUEUES
Main bottleneck eliminated
Queues are a problem only in high
season, when the lifts from Saalbach
up the south-facing slopes can entail
waits of up to 15 minutes at peak
times, which include the end as well as
the start of the day. Replacement of
the Schattberg cable-car by a gondola
has eliminated the other regular queue,
but it has increased pressure on the
double chair to Schattberg West that
you need to get to Hinterglemm. High-
season queues can also arise for the
chair to Hasenauer Köpfl and the drag
to Bründlkopf. And the double chairs
towards Schattberg from Hinterglemm
get crowded at the end of the day.

MOUNTAIN RESTAURANTS
Excellent quality and quantity
The area is liberally scattered with
around 40 attractive huts that serve
good food. Many have pleasant rustic

interiors and a lively ambience.

On the south-facing slopes, the
Panorama on the Kohlmaiskopf slope,
Thurner Alm close to Bründlkopf and
Walleggalm on Hochalm serve
particularly good food. Across in the
Hinterglemm direction, the
'enterprising' Rosswaldhütte is
recommended, not least for its
'excellent rösti'. The little
Bernkogelhütte, overlooking Saalbach,
has a great atmosphere. Reporters
recommend the Bärnalm near the top
of the Bernkogel chair – 'good food,
good value'.

The Wildenkarkogel Hütte has a big
terrace and possibly the loudest
mountain-top music we've heard, with
resident DJ from mid-morning. The Alte
Schmiede at the top of the Leogang
gondola, with rustic decor including
water wheels, is recommended for its
'good food' including 'the best pizza in
the area', although you may have to
wait for it.

The Simalalm at the base of the
Limbergalm quad chair is 'great for the
sun and the views'. On the north-facing
slopes, the Bergstadl halfway down the
red run from Schattberg West has
stunning views and good food.
Ellmualm, at the bottom of the Zehner
lift was commended again this year,
the toilets being an 'outstanding'
feature. The 12er-Treff umbrella bar at
the top of the Zwölferkogel gondola is
good for lounging in the sun.

SCHOOLS AND GUIDES
An excess of choice
We're all in favour of competition but
visitors to Saalbach-Hinterglemm may
feel that they are faced with rather too
much of this particular good thing,
with no less than eight schools to
choose from. We have had conflicting
reports of the Fürstauer school. One
visitor this year says it was 'terrific'
and the instructors 'took great care of
our children', who made excellent
progress. But an adult beginner had
some complaints. A Hinterglemm
boarder had 'worthwhile' lessons with
Snow and Fun.

FACILITIES FOR CHILDREN
Hinterglemm tries harder
Saalbach doesn't go out of its way to
sell itself to families, although it does
have a ski kindergarten. Hinterglemm
has some good hotel-based nursery
facilities – the one at the Theresia is
reportedly excellent.

AUSTRIA

GETTING THERE

Air Salzburg, transfer 2hr. Munich, transfer 3½hr.

Rail Zell am See; hourly buses, transfer 40 min.

166

ACTIVITIES

Indoor Swimming pools, sauna, massage, solarium, bowling, billiards, tennis (Hinterglemm), squash

Outdoor Floodlit tobogganing, snow tubing, snowmobiling, sleigh rides, skating, ice hockey, ice climbing, curling, 40km/25 miles of cleared paths, paragliding

Phone numbers
Saalbach
From elsewhere in Austria add the prefix 06541.
From abroad use the prefix +43 6541.

Leogang
From elsewhere in Austria add the prefix 06583.
From abroad use the prefix +43 6583.

STAYING THERE

HOW TO GO
Cheerful doesn't mean cheap
Chalets We are aware of a few 'club hotels' but Saalbach isn't really a chalet resort.

Hotels There are a large number of hotels in both villages, mainly 3-star and above. Be aware that some central hotels are affected by disco noise.

Saalbach

((((4)) **Alpenhotel** (6666) Luxurious, with open-fire lounge, disco, small pool.

((((4)) **Berger's Sporthotel** (6577) Liveliest of the top hotels, with a daily tea dance, and disco. Good pool.

((((4)) **Kendler** (62250) Position second to none, right next to the Bernkogel chair. Classy, expensive, good food.

((((4)) **Saalbacher Hof** (71110) Retains a friendly feel despite its large size.

(((3)) **Haider** (6228) Best-positioned of the 3-stars, right next to the main lifts.

(((3)) **Kristiana** (6253) Near enough to lifts but away from night-time noise. 'Excellent food.' Sauna, steam bath.

(((3)) **König** (6384) Cheaper 3-star and more basic rooms.

Hinterglemm

((((4)) **Theresia** (71140) Hinterglemm's top hotel, and one of the best for families. Out towards Saalbach, but nursery slopes nearby. Pool.

((((4)) **Egger** (63220) 'I'll stay here next time, on the slopes,' says a reader.

(((3)) **Wolf** (63460) Small but well-equipped 4-star in the the nursery-sharing scheme. 'Especially good' food, excellent position. Pool.

(((3)) **Sonnblick** (64080) Convenient 3-star in a 'quiet location' with 'friendly service' and 'the comfiest holiday beds I have slept in', says a recent guest.

((2)) **Haus Ameshofer** (8119) Beside piste at Reiterkogel lift. 'Great value ski-in, ski-out B&B,' says a reporter.

Self-catering There's a big choice of apartments for independent travellers.

EATING OUT
Wide choice of hotel restaurants
Saalbach-Hinterglemm is essentially a half-board resort, with relatively few non-hotel restaurants. Peter's restaurant, at the top of Saalbach's main street, is atmospheric and serves excellent meat dishes cooked on hot stones. A recent visitor enjoyed the excellent food, with 'an emphasis on the meatier, richer dishes', at the Hotel Neuhaus. The Wallner Pizzeria on the main street is good value. The Auwirt hotel on the outskirts of Saalbach has a good à la carte restaurant.

APRES-SKI
It rocks from early on
Après-ski is very lively from mid-afternoon until the early hours and can get positively wild. In Saalbach the rustic Hinterhagalm at the top of the main nursery slope is packed by 3.30. When it closes around 6pm, the crowds slide down to Bauer's Skialm and try to get into the already heaving old cow shed to continue drinking and dancing. The tiny Zum Turn (next door to the church and cemetery) is a medieval jail that also gets packed from 4pm until late.

Castello's 'at the bottom of the main street' is the place to be, according to a visitor this year. The Neuhaus Taverne has live music and attracts a mature clientele. Bobby's Bar is cheap, often full of British school kids, has bowling and serves Guinness. Bar No 8 attracts a young clientele and dancing on tables and chairs. King's Disco livens up after midnight. Classic Bar is recommended for its 'smart lap-dancing room'. Arena disco has go-go dancers and is very popular, as are Heli's and Bergers. A reader recommends the Burgeralm: '3km up the toboggan track, marvellous atmosphere and reindeer steaks before a 1am descent.'

↑ An excellent, long, north-facing run takes you down to the quiet village of Leogang
SAALFELDEN LEOGANG TOURISTIK GMBH

Leogang 800m/2,620ft

A much less expensive alternative to Saalbach-Hinterglemm.

THE RESORT
Leogang is an attractive, although rather scattered, quiet, farming community-cum-mountain resort. It's best to stay at Hütten, near the lift.

THE MOUNTAIN
The village is linked to the eastern end of the Saalbach-Hinterglemm circuit.
Slopes A gondola from Hütten takes you into the ski area. The local slopes tend to be delightfully quiet.
Snow reliability The local slopes have some of the best snow in the region, being north- and east-facing, with snowmaking on the run home.
Experts Not much challenge locally.
Intermediates Great long red run cruise home from the top of the gondola. Plus the circuit to explore.
Beginners Good nursery slopes by the village, and short runs to progress to.
Snowboarding The whole area is great for boarding and there's a half-pipe.
Cross-country The best in the area. There are 20km/12 miles of trails, plus a panoramic high-altitude trail.
Queues No local problems.
Mountain restaurants A couple of good local huts.
Schools and guides Leogang Altenberger school has a high reputation – 'excellent service and lessons; highly recommended'.
Facilities for children There is a non-ski nursery, and children can start school at four years old.

STAYING THERE
Hotels The luxury Krallerhof (82460) has its own nursery lift, which can be used to get across to the main lift station. The 4-star Salzburgerhof (73100) is one of the best-placed hotels, within a two-minute walk of the gondola; sauna and steam.
Self-catering There are quiet apartments available.
Eating out Restaurants are hotel-based. The upscale Krallerhof has the excellent food you would expect. The much cheaper Gasthof Hüttwirt has a high reputation for home cooking.
Après-ski The rustic old chalet Kraller Alm is very much the focal tea-time and evening rendezvous.
Off the slopes Excursions to Salzburg are possible.

In Hinterglemm there are a number of ice bars, which are crowded immediately after the lifts close, including the Gute Stube of Hotel Dorfschmiede in the centre of town with loud music blasting out and people spilling into the street. A wider age group enjoys the live music later on at the smart, friendly Tanzhimmel – an open, glass-fronted bar with a dance floor. The Hexenhäusl gets packed and has an animated model of a witch revealing her undergarments. A similar fascination with moving models is demonstrated at the rustic Goasstall by the piste down from Sportalm, where a model goat is equally revealing (and where real goats graze behind glass near the men's toilet). Bla Bla is small, modern and smart, with reasonable prices. The Almbar has good music and some dancing.

Tour operator reps organise tobogganing, sleigh rides and bowling.

OFF THE SLOPES
Surprisingly little to do
Saalbach is not very entertaining if you're not into winter sports. There are few shops other than supermarkets and ski shops. Walks tend to be restricted to the paths alongside the cold cross-country trails or along the Saalbach toboggan run to Spielberghs. But there are excursions to Kitzbühel and Salzburg.

TOURIST OFFICES

Saalbach
t 680068
contact@saalbach.com
www.saalbach.com

Leogang
t 8234
office@sale-touristik.at
www.leogang-saalfelden.at

Schladming

Old and pretty town with extensive intermediate slopes

COSTS

① ② ③ ④ ⑤ ⑥

RATINGS

The slopes

Snow	★★★★
Extent	★★★
Expert	★★
Intermediate	★★★★
Beginner	★★★★
Convenience	★★★
Queues	★★★★
Mountain restaurants	★★★★

The rest

Scenery	★★★
Resort charm	★★★★
Off-slope	★★★★

NEWS

Continuing the major investment in the area over the last five years, the ancient Fastenberg T-bar on Planai was replaced last season by a covered six-seat chair going much higher up the mountain. This is part of a plan to 'steer' people eastwards towards Hauser Kaibling and so relieve the pressure on Planai and Hochwurzen at peak times.

➕ Extensive slopes on four interlinked mountains

➕ Excellent slopes for intermediates

➕ Extensive snowmaking operation and good piste maintenance

➕ Very sheltered slopes, among trees

➕ Lots of good mountain restaurants

➕ Charming town with friendly people and a life independent of tourism

➕ Ski Alliance Amadé lift pass covers wide range of nearby resorts

➖ Slopes lack variety – one mountain is much like the others

➖ Very little to entertain experts, on- or off-piste

➖ Most runs are north-facing, so can be shady and cold in early season

➖ Nursery slopes (at Rohrmoos) are inconvenient unless you stay beside them – and beginners are expected to pay for a full lift pass

Since its four previously separate mountains were linked by lifts and pistes, Schladming has been able to compete with major resorts that are better known internationally. A keen intermediate who wants to make the most of the links can get a real sense of travelling around on the snow. And as the list of plus-points suggests, we see many attractions in the place.

If you like your slopes to be reassuringly consistent, Schladming has a strong claim on your attention. If on the other hand you like the spice of variety and the thrill of a serious challenge, you might find it all rather tame.

The resort does not offer one of Austria's wildest après-ski scenes, but that doesn't seem to bother most of our reporters, who enjoy its established, valley-town ambience.

THE RESORT

The old town of Schladming has a long skiing tradition and has hosted World Cup races for many years. It sits at the foot of Planai, one of four mountains that are now linked by lifts and pistes to offer 115km/71 miles of runs. A gondola starting close to the centre goes most of the way up this home mountain. To the east is the small, rustic village of Haus, where a cable-car and gondola go up to the highest of the four linked mountains, Hauser

Kaibling. From the western suburbs of Schladming there are chair-lifts back towards Planai and on towards the next mountain to the west, Hochwurzen. The latter chain of lifts passes through Rohrmoos, a quiet, scattered village set on what is effectively a giant nursery slope.

The town (it is definitely not a village) has a charming, traffic-free main square, prettily lit at night, around which you'll find most of the shops, restaurants and bars (and some appealing hotels). The busy main road

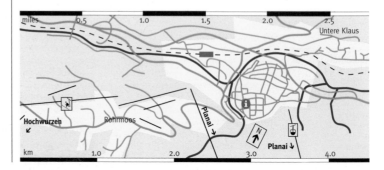

KEY FACTS

Resort	745m
	2,440ft

For the Sportregion
Schladming-Ramsau/
Dachstein area

Slopes	745-2015m
	2,440-6,610ft
Lifts	88
Pistes	167km
	104 miles
Blue	29%
Red	61%
Black	10%
Snowmaking	100%

For Schladming only

Slopes	745m-2015m
	2,440ft-6,610ft
Lifts	52
Pistes	115km
	71 miles

bypasses the town and is separated from it by a river. Much of the accommodation is close to the centre – just a few minutes' walk from the Planai gondola – but it can be noisy in the early hours because of nearby bars. The modern sports centre and tennis halls are five minutes' walk from the centre. Rohrmoos makes an excellent base for beginners who aren't looking for lively nightlife. Haus is preferable for those looking for more of a village atmosphere.

It can be quicker to get to a particular hill by car, taxi or bus rather than on skis or board – though we've had mixed reports about the efficiency of the bus services. Reporters have been impressed with the free Internet access at the top of the Planai gondola: 'We sent emails instead of postcards,' said one.

Apart from the main slopes we describe here, there are five or six other separate mountains. To the east, beyond Haus, is Galsterbergalm, above Pruggern. Fageralm is above Forstau, up a side valley to the west. North of the main valley, Ramsau has its own low slopes and access to the Dachstein glacier. And near Gröbming is the small area of Stoderzinken. The Ski Alliance Amadé lift pass also covers many other resorts in this part of Austria. Trips to Bad Gastein are feasible by rail but include at least one change. Drivers can also visit Wagrain/Flachau, Kleinarl and Maria Alm. Tour operators organise day trips to other resorts, too. Snow-sure Obertauern is not far away but is not included on the lift pass.

THE MOUNTAINS

Most pistes are on the wooded north-facing slopes above the main valley, with some going into the side valleys higher up, and there are some open slopes above the trees. Complaints about the piste map and on-mountain signing have dried up, though we don't see much change in the map.

THE SLOPES
Four linked sectors – and more
Each of the linked sectors is quite a serious mountain with a variety of lifts and runs to play on. **Planai** and **Hauser Kaibling** are linked at altitude via the high, wooded bowl between them. In contrast, the links with **Hochwurzen** (where you can try night skiing or boarding; though it is not included on the lift pass) and the fourth linked mountain, **Reiteralm,** are at valley level. So although the links offer the ability to travel around, getting around the whole area can take time – and involves some uninteresting linking runs. Although from Schladming it's perfectly possible to get to Hauser Kaibling or Hochwurzen on skis, if you want to spend time on Reiteralm it's more practical to get the bus, or a taxi, to the lift base at Pichl or Gleiming. The link between Planai and Hochwurzen involves riding a lift through a tunnel, whichever way you are travelling.

All the mountains have fairly similar terrain and views, with mainly red runs of much the same pitch down through heavily wooded north-facing slopes.

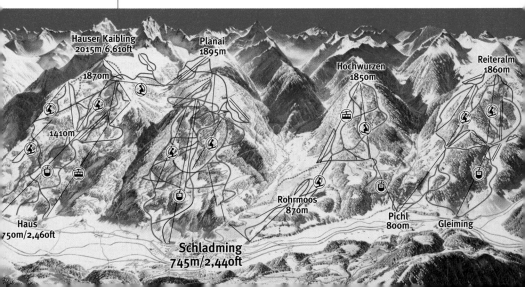

Hauser Kaibling
2015m/6,610ft

1870m

1410m

Planai
1895m

Hochwurzen
1850m

Reiteralm
1860m

Rohrmoos
870m

Pichl
800m

Gleiming

Haus
750m/2,460ft

Schladming
745m/2,440ft

LIFT PASSES

Ski Alliance Amadé Ski Pass
The lift pass covers over 270 lifts in more than 30 ski resorts in this part of Austria: the Gastein valley and Grossarl; Salzburger Sportwelt; Hochkönigs Winterreich. Buses, trains and road tolls between the resorts are covered.

Main pass
1-day pass €32.50
6-day pass €156

Children
Under 19: 6-day pass €144
Under 16: 6-day pass €78
Under 6: free pass

Notes
Part-day tickets are available.

Alternative pass
Salzburg Super Ski Card covers all lifts and pistes in Salzburgerland including Zell am See, Kaprun and Saalbach-Hinterglemm.

SCHOOLS

Tritscher
t 22647
office@tritscher.at

Blue Tomato (snowboarding)
t 24223
info@blue-tomato.at

Hopl
t 61268
info@hopl.at

Classes
(Tritscher prices)
5 days (2½hr am and 2hr pm) €120

Private lessons
Half day €80; each additional person €15.

CHILDREN

At Rohrmoos the nursery takes children from 18 months.

Children can join ski school from age 4 – €160 for 5 days (Tritscher prices).

TERRAIN-PARKS
Three to try
There are two terrain-parks and half-pipes on the main linked area, with another park on the Galsterbergalm.

SNOW RELIABILITY
Excellent in cold weather
Schladming's impressive snowmaking operation makes it a particularly good choice for early holidays; and the northerly orientation of the slopes and good maintenance help keep the slopes in better shape than in some neighbouring resorts. Schladming claims 100% snowmaking, and certainly the main runs to the valley have full cover. Be wary of the steep bottom part of the World Cup downhill run back to town – it can get extremely icy. The best natural snow is usually found on Reiteralm and Hochwurzen.

FOR EXPERTS
Strictly intermediate stuff
Schladming's status as a World Cup downhill venue doesn't make it macho. The steep black finish to the Men's Downhill course and the moderate mogul runs at the top of Planai and Hauser Kaibling are the only really challenging slopes. Hauser Kaibling's off-piste is good, although limited.

FOR INTERMEDIATES
Red runs rule
The area is ideal for intermediate cruising. The majority of runs are red but it's often difficult to distinguish them from many of the blues.

The open sections at the top of Planai and Hauser Kaibling have some more challenging slopes. And the two World Cup pistes, and the red that runs parallel to the Haus downhill course, are ideal for fast intermediates.

Hauser Kaibling has a lovely meandering blue running from top to bottom for the less confident intermediates, and Reiteralm has some gentle blues with good snow. Runs are well groomed, so intermediates will find the slopes generally flattering.

FOR BEGINNERS
Good slopes but poorly sited
Complete beginners generally start on the extensive but low-altitude Rohrmoos nursery area – fine if you are based there, a bus-ride away if you are not. Another novice area near the top of Planai is more convenient for most people and has better snow, but the runs are less gentle.

FOR CROSS-COUNTRY
Extensive network of trails
Given sufficient snow-cover, there are 300km/186 miles of trails in the region, and the World Championships have been held at nearby Ramsau. There are local loops along the main valley floor and in the valleys between Planai and Hochwurzen.

QUEUES
Avoid peak periods
The area (especially the Planai gondola first thing) can have queues at peak-season and weekends. The upgraded gondola at Haus has relieved pressure there, but the Reiteralm gondola is slow. The new six-pack on the eastern side of Planai seems likely to put pressure on the Burgstallalm chair above it. Reporters recommend avoiding peak February dates and going to Fageralm on busy days.

MOUNTAIN RESTAURANTS
Plenty of nice places
There are plenty of attractive rustic restaurants in all sectors, though Planai probably has the edge. A visitor last season, returning to Austria after a decade skiing elsewhere, said, 'It was an absolute delight to be reminded of what I had been missing!' Onkel Willi's is popular for its live music, open fire, indoor nooks and crannies and large terrace, Mitterhausalm is good, and the Schladminger Hütte at the top of the Planai gondola has 'great food'. The Knapplhof at Hauser Kaibling is full of ski racing mementos and the Waldfriedalm at Hochwurzen is 'great value for huge pizzas'.

boarding

Schladming is popular with boarders. Most lifts on the spread-out mountains are gondolas or chairs, with some short drags around. The area is ideal for beginners and intermediates, except when the lower slopes are icy, though there are few exciting challenges for expert boarders bar the off-piste tree runs. The Blue Tomato snowboard shop – reportedly 'well organised' – runs the specialist snowboard school.

↑ The resort has a long racing history

GETTING THERE

Air Salzburg 90km/56 miles (1½hr).

Rail Mainline station in resort.

ACTIVITIES

Indoor Swimming, sauna, bowling, indoor tennis court, squash, museum

Outdoor Ice skating, curling, night skiing, floodlit toboggan run (8km/5 miles), sleigh rides, 50km/31 miles of cleared paths in the Schladming and surrounding area, paragliding

Phone numbers
Schladming
From elsewhere in Austria add the prefix 03687.
From abroad use the prefix +43 3687.
Haus
From elsewhere in Austria add the prefix 03686.
From abroad use the prefix +43 3686.

TOURIST OFFICES

Schladming
t 222680
touristoffice@
schladming.com
www.schladming.com
Haus
t 22340
haus-ennstal@aon.at
www.haus.at

SCHOOLS AND GUIDES
Generally okay reports
We have generally had good reports in the past, but we lack recent ones.

FACILITIES FOR CHILDREN
Rohrmoos is the place
The extensive gentle slopes of Rohrmoos are ideal for building up youngsters' confidence. The nursery here takes children from 18 months.

STAYING THERE

HOW TO GO
Packages mean hotels
Packaged accommodation is in hotels and pensions, but there are plenty of apartments for independent travellers.
Hotels Most of the accommodation is in modestly priced pensions but there are also a few more upmarket hotels.
((((4) **Sporthotel Royer** (200) Big, smart and comfortable, a few minutes' walk from the main Planai lift. Pool.
(((3) **Alte Post** (22571) Characterful old inn with great position on the main square. Good food, but some rooms small and a reporter complains of her bed being an uncomfortable sofa-bed.
(((3) **Zum Stadttor** (245250) Similarly priced, although less charming and well placed. 'Comfortable with excellent food,' says a reporter.
(((3) **Kirchenwirt** (22435) Just off the main square. 'Traditional atmosphere, wonderful food,' says a recent visitor.
(((3) **Neue Post** (22105) Large rooms, friendly, good food, central.
(((3) **Schladmingerhof** (23525) Bright, modern 'fairly basic' chalet in peaceful position, out in Untere Klaus.
Self-catering Haus Girik (22663) is close to the gondola.

EATING OUT
Some good places
We had a great meal at Fritzi's gasthaus (which has a good reputation). Other recommendations include the Kirchenwirt hotel ('excellent home cooking'), Giovanni's (for pizza), Gasthof Brunner ('good value') and Talbachschenke ('good grills and atmosphere'). Hotels Neue and Alte Post are 'good but expensive'.

APRES-SKI
Explore the side streets
Some of the mountain restaurants are lively at the end of the afternoon, but reporters agree that down in the town there's a disappointing lack of tea time animation. Charly's Treff (with umbrella bar) opposite the Planai gondola is the main exception (and has great photos of local hero Arnold Schwarzenegger). The Siglu also rocks from 3pm.

There is, however, no lack of options later on – many of the central bars open later and stay open until dawn. The local Schladminger beer is worth a try. Popular spots include the local brewpub Schwalbenbräu. The Beisl is a smart, beautiful bar attracting a varied age group. Hanglbar has wooden decor and middle-of-the-road music and occasional karaoke. Maria's Mexican is 'relaxing' with chilled music and margueritas. The Porta gets very crowded and has live music. The Sonderbar is a disco with three bars.

OFF THE SLOPES
Good for all but walkers
Non-skiers are fairly well catered for. Some mountain restaurants are easily reached on foot. The town shops and museum are worth a look. Train trips to Salzburg are easy (and recommended as worth a day off the slopes by several readers). Buses run to the old walled town of Radstadt. There's a public pool and ice rink.

Haus 750m/2,460ft

Haus is a real village with a life of its own and its own ski schools and kindergartens. The user-friendly nursery slopes are between the village and the gondola. There's a railway station, so excursions are easy, but off-slope activities and nightlife are very limited. Hotel prices are generally lower than in Schladming. Hotel Gürtl (2383) has been recommended for 'good food and ambience'.

Sölden

Extensive, snow-sure, intermediate slopes plus throbbing nightlife

COSTS

① ② ③ ④ ⑤ ⑥

RATINGS

The slopes

Snow	★★★★★
Extent	★★★
Expert	★★★
Intermediate	★★★★
Beginner	★★
Convenience	★★
Queues	★★★
Mountain restaurants	★★★

The rest

Scenery	★★★
Resort charm	★★
Off-slope	★★

KEY FACTS

Resort	1380m
	4,530ft
Slopes	1380-3250m
	4,530-10,660ft
Lifts	34
Pistes	141km
	88 miles
Blue	32%
Red	52%
Black	16%
Snowmaking	27km
	17 miles

SÖLDEN TOURIST OFFICE

The runs above Giggijoch are some of Sölden's easiest – the resort suits adventurous intermediates best ↓

+ Excellent snow reliability, with access to two glaciers

+ Fairly extensive network of slopes suited to adventurous intermediates

+ Impressive lift system, now linking with glacier slopes

+ Very lively après-ski/nightlife

– Busy road through sprawling village

– Some central hotels are distant from the two main lifts

– Inconvenient beginners' slopes

– Drink-fuelled nightlife too rowdy for many visitors

– Limited off-slope activities

Sölden is virtually unknown on the UK package market. But it deserves a serious look from all keen intermediates. It has recently invested massively in new lifts to link its home slopes with snow-sure runs on the Rettenbach and Tiefenbach glaciers. There are some seriously long runs as well as some seriously rowdy and alcoholic après-ski (which can be avoided by staying off the main street).

THE RESORT

Despite its traditional Tirolean-style buildings and tree-filled valley, Sölden is no beauty: it is a large, traffic-filled place that sprawls along both sides of a river and busy main road. The resort attracts a young, lively crowd – mostly Dutch and German – bent on partying.

Gondolas from opposite ends of town go up to Sölden's home slopes – the peak of Gaislachkogl and the lift junction of Giggijoch, above the satellite resort of Hochsölden. A free shuttle-bus serves both lift stations.

THE MOUNTAIN

The two similar-sized home sectors are linked by chair-lifts out of the Rettenbachtal that separates them. The Rettenbach and Tiefenbach glaciers – 15km/9 miles away by road, and until quite recently closed in winter – are now connected by a series of fast lifts from Rotkogl. The piste from the

Rettenbach glacier to the Tiefenbach glacier goes through a tunnel. The return trip is by chair-lift.

Slopes The Gaislachkogl runs are almost entirely red or black, but there are several blue runs around Giggijoch. Both main sectors have red runs through trees to the village. The glacier slopes are blues and easy reds, with a new red ski route that brings you back to the heart of the home slopes.

Terrain-parks There are two in winter above Giggijoch: the BASE boarder park has a half-pipe, kickers and rails; the BASE Easycross area has a boarder-cross run with waves and jumps. In the summer there's a park on the Rettenbach glacier.

Snow reliability Most of the area is over 2100m/6,890ft – a good height for Austria – and north-east-facing, so the slopes are generally reliable for snow – and there is snowmaking, too. With access to glaciers as well, Sölden is now one of the best Alpine bets.

Experts None of the black pistes dotted around Sölden's map is particularly serious, but there are quite a few non-trivial reds. And there are extensive off-piste possibilities – particularly from Gaislachkogl to the mid-station. At the top of the valley is one of the Alps' premier touring areas.

Intermediates Most of Sölden's main slopes are red runs ideal for keen intermediates, and there are some serious verticals to be racked up; from the top of the new gondola to the village will be a drop of over 1800m/5,910ft. There are several easy blacks, and the long, quiet piste down to

For 2003/04, a new eight-person gondola is planned on the Rettenbach glacier, replacing an existing T-bar and going higher.

For 2002/03, a new red ski route was opened from the Rettenbach glacier to the heart of the home slopes – allowing you to take chairs up to the main area or to carry on back to town.

Phone numbers
From elsewhere in Austria add the prefix 05254.
From abroad use the prefix +43 5254.

TOURIST OFFICE

t 5100
info@soelden.com
www.soelden.com

Gaislachalm is ideal for high-speed cruising. Giggijoch offers gentler gradients, but gets extremely crowded.
Beginners The beginners' slopes are situated inconveniently – just above the village at Innerwald – and are prone to poor snow. Near-beginners can use the blues at Giggijoch.
Snowboarding Sölden is not ideal for beginners but there's great free-riding for experienced boarders. And all drag-lifts can be avoided.
Cross-country There are a couple of uninspiring loops by the river, plus small areas at Zwieselstein and Vent.
Queues Recent upgrades have done away with most of the queues.
Mountain restaurants The self-service places around Giggijoch get very crowded – try Schwarzkogel on run 24 instead, says a regular visitor. She also recommends Gampealm, towards the end of piste 11, an atmospheric old hut with 'good value food and substantial soups'. To escape the crowds try the cluster of places around Gaislachalm (Silbertal has 'good variety, large portions and 1 litre beers') – or head down the excellent red piste 7 to the calm, rustic s'Pfandl at Ausserwald.
Schools and guides The three schools all restrict class sizes to seven or eight.
Facilities for children Children of three and up can join the ski kindergarten. There are special family lift pass deals.

STAYING THERE

How to go There are few UK packages.
Hotels Sölden has some good hotels. The 5-star Central (22600) is the best and one of the biggest in town. The 4-star Regina (2301), by the Gaislachkogl lift is heartily recommended by a reporter. The Haus Karl Grüner B&B (2477) above town on run 7 is highly praised by a regular visitor (with restaurants for dinner '2 to 10 minutes' walk'). Self-catering apartments at the Posthäusl (31380) are of good quality.
Eating out Reporter recommendations include the Tavola in the hotel Rosengarten, Cafe Hubertus, Nudeltopf and Corso for pizza; and s'Pfandl at Ausserwald for Tirolean stuff.
Après-ski Sölden's après-ski is famous. It starts up the mountain, notably at Giggijoch, and progresses via bars in the main street – notably the greenhouse-style Dominic Bla-Bla – to countless places with live bands and throbbing discos, and table dancing and striptease at Andy's Rodelhütte. Somewhat tamer are the nightly toboggan evenings, with drinking and dancing before an exciting 6km/4 mile floodlit run back to town from the Gaislachalm mountain restaurant.
Off the slopes There's a sports centre, swimming pool and an ice rink. Trips to Innsbruck are possible.

Sölden

173

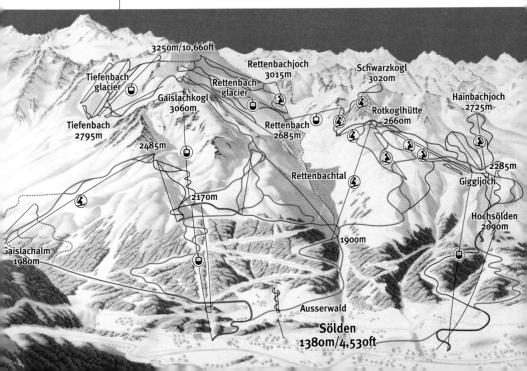

Tiefenbach glacier
3250m/10,66oft
Rettenbachjoch
3015m
Schwarzkogl
3020m
Tiefenbach 2795m
Gaislachkogl 3060m
Rettenbach glacier
Hainbachjoch 2725m
Rotkoglhütte 2660m
Rettenbach 2685m
2485m
2170m
Rettenbachtal
2285m
Giggijoch
Hochsölden 2090m
1900m
Gaislachalm 1980m
Ausserwald
Sölden
1380m/4,53oft

Söll

Lively village with extensive Ski Welt slopes and lots of snowmaking

COSTS

①②③④⑤⑥

RATINGS

The slopes

Snow	**
Extent	****
Expert	*
Intermediate	****
Beginner	***
Convenience	**
Queues	***
Mountain restaurants	**

The rest

Scenery	***
Resort charm	***
Off-slope	**

NEWS

In 2002/03 a new eight-seat gondola – from Scheffau to Brandstadl was a welcome addition.

A T-bar running from Brixen's mid-station to the top station was replaced by a six-pack and the one up to Hartkaiser was replaced by a quad.

There are plans to replace the chairs from Hopfgarten up to Rigi with a gondola but this may take a couple of years to materialise.

+ Part of Ski Welt, Austria's largest linked ski and snowboard area

+ Local slopes are the highest in the Ski Welt and north-facing, so they keep their snow relatively well

+ Massive recent investment in snowmaking has paid off

+ Plenty of cheap and cheerful pensions for those on a budget

+ Pretty village with lively après-ski

– Poor natural snow record

– Long walk or infrequent buses from the village to the lifts

– Little to amuse experts or good intermediates

– Ski Welt slopes can get crowded at weekends and in high season – and slopes above Söll are the most crowded of all

– Mostly short runs in local sector

Söll has long been popular with groups of British beginners and intermediates, attracting a mixture of young singles looking for a fun time and families looking for a quiet time. In the 1980s it gained notoriety as prime lager-lout territory; it still has some loud bars but has calmed down a lot. Many visitors find the village surprisingly small and are disappointed by the distance between it and the slopes (and by the bus service).

Its main drawback has always been snow – or lack of it. Because of its low altitude and sunny slopes, pistes have often been slushy or bare, not just in Söll but also throughout the extensive Ski Welt circuit. But this problem has been tackled by a massive investment in snowmaking, and over half of the Ski Welt's 250km/155 miles of piste are now covered by snowmaking – more than in any other Austrian ski area. This ensures the region's main pistes and links stay open, though it can't prevent slush and ice developing.

When the snow is good Söll can be a great place for a holiday, cruising the attractive and undemanding pistes of Austria's largest linked area.

THE RESORT

Söll is a small, pretty, friendly village – much smaller than you might expect from its reputation; you can explore it in a few minutes and there aren't many shops. New buildings are traditional in design and there's a huge church near the centre which, according to a reporter, is well worth a visit at dusk as the graveyard is lit with candles. The pretty scenery adds to Söll's charm, and it benefits from being off the main road through the Tirol.

The slopes are a bus- or taxi-ride or a 15-minute walk from the centre, the other side of a busy road with a pedestrian tunnel underneath. You can leave your equipment at the bottom of the gondola for a small charge. The bus service has been criticised by most reporters as being too infrequent.

There is some accommodation out near the lifts but most is in or around the village centre – a free ski-bus-ride from the slopes. Being on the edge of town nearest the lifts is best for those who are prepared to walk to the slopes. The other side of town has the advantage that you can board the bus there before it gets too crowded. Be aware that some guest houses are literally miles from the centre and lifts, and that the ski-bus does not serve every nook and cranny of this sprawling community.

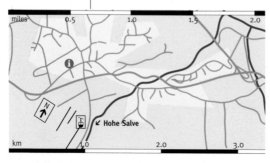

Söll

KEY FACTS

Resort	700m
	2,300ft

For entire Ski Welt	
Slopes	620-1830m
	2,030-6,000ft
Lifts	93
Pistes	250km
	155 miles
Blue	43%
Red	48%
Black	9%
Snowmaking	135km
	84 miles

SCHOOLS

Söll-Hochsöll
t 5454

ProSöll
t 0664 256 0184

Austria
t 20250

Classes
(Söll-Hochsöll prices)
5 4-hr days: €115

Private lessons
€43 for 1hr; each
additional person €15

THE MOUNTAINS

The Ski Welt covers Hopfgarten, Brixen, Scheffau and Ellmau. It is the largest linked area in Austria, and will easily keep an early or average intermediate amused for a week. But that doesn't make it a Trois Vallées. It is basically a typically small, low, pastoral Austrian hill multiplied several times. One section is much like another, and most slopes best suit early to average intermediates. Runs are short and scenery attractive rather than stunning – although the panoramic views from the Hohe Salve are impressive.

Westendorf is separate, but covered by the area pass. The Kitzbüheler Alpenskipass also covers many other resorts easily reached by car including Kitzbühel – an impressive total of 260 lifts and 680km/423 miles of pistes.

THE SLOPES
Short run network
A gondola takes all but complete beginners up to the shelf of Hochsöll, where there are a couple of short lifts and connections in several directions.

These include an eight-person gondola to the high point of Hohe Salve. From here there are stunning views and runs down to Kälbersalve, Rigi and Hopfgarten. Rigi can also be reached by chairs and runs without going to Hohe Salve – to which it is itself linked by chairs. Rigi is also the start of runs down to Itter. From Kälbersalve you can head down south-facing runs to Brixen or up to Zinsberg and Eiberg and towards Ellmau.

A quicker way to Ellmau without taking as many south-facing slopes is by using a cable-car from Hochsöll.

We continue to receive criticism of the piste map, which is hopelessly over-ambitious in trying to show the whole area in one view.

TERRAIN-PARKS
Not a major feature
There is a terrain-park and a quarter-pipe near Hochsöll.

SNOW RELIABILITY
Artificial help saves the day
With a very low average height, and important links that get a lot of sun, the snowmaking that the Ski Welt has installed in recent seasons is essential. At 135km/84 miles and covering over half the area's pistes, it is Austria's biggest snowmaking installation. We were there one January before any major snowfalls, and snowmaking was keeping the links open well. It did not, however, stop slush and ice forming.

FOR EXPERTS
Not a lot
The two black runs from Hohe Salve towards Hochsöll and Kälbersalve and the black run alongside the Brixen gondola are the only challenging pistes. There are further blacks in Scheffau and Ellmau, but the main challenges are off-piste – from Brandstadl down to Söll, for example.

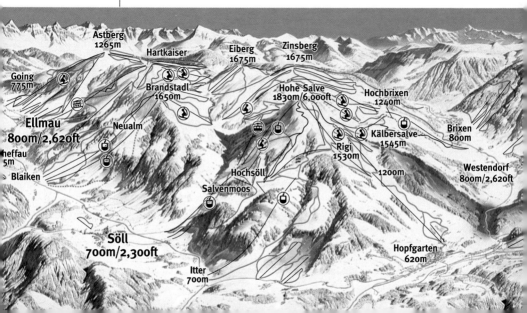

↑ There are plenty of jolly restaurants dotted around the slopes
SKI WELT

LIFT PASSES

Ski Welt Wilder Kaiser-Brixental
Covers all lifts in the Ski Welt area from Going to Westendorf, and the ski-bus.

Beginners
Points tickets.

Main pass
1-day pass €30
6-day pass €148.50

Children
Under 16: 6-day pass €89
Under 6: free pass

Notes
Single ascent and part-day passes available.

Alternative passes
Söll pass covers 12 lifts, 34km/21 miles of piste. Kitzbüheler Alpenskipass covers four other large areas: St Johann, Kitzbühel, Wildschönau and Alpbach.

FOR INTERMEDIATES
Mainly easy runs
When blessed with good snow – not something to bank on – the Ski Welt is a paradise for early intermediates and those who love easy cruising. There are lots of blue runs and many of the reds in truth deserve a blue grading. It is a big area and you really get a feeling of travelling around – we skied it for two days on our last visit and felt we only scratched the surface. The main challenge you may find is when the snow isn't perfect – ice and slush can make even gentle slopes seem tricky. In general the most difficult slopes are those from the mid-stations to the valleys: the most direct of the runs between Brandstadl and Blaiken, the pistes down to Brixen and the red run from Hochsöll back to Söll, for example. Higher up, the red from Hohe Salve to Rigi is a good cruise.

FOR BEGINNERS
Excellent when snow is good
The big area of nursery slopes between the main road and the gondola station is ideal when snow is abundant – gentle, spacious, uncrowded and free from good skiers whizzing past. But it can get icy or slushy. In poor snow the Hochsöll area is used. Near-beginners and fast learners can get home to the bottom station when the narrow blue from Hochsöll is not too icy.

FOR CROSS-COUNTRY
Neighbouring villages are better
Söll has 30km/19 miles of local trails but they are less interesting than those between Hopfgarten and Kelchsau or the ones around and beyond Ellmau. Lack of snow-cover is a big problem.

QUEUES
Much improved
Continued introduction of new lifts has greatly improved this once queue-prone area. The new gondola at Scheffau-Blaiken should have cut the weekend queues there. When snow is poor, the linking lifts to and from Zinsberg and Eiberg get crowded.

MOUNTAIN RESTAURANTS
Good, but crowded
There are quite a few jolly little chalets scattered about, but we have had a few complaints of insufficient seating and long queues. The atmospheric Stöckalm (a converted cow shed), Kraftalm and Gründlalm are all near Hochsöll. Further afield, the Neualm, halfway down to Blaiken, is one of the best huts in the Ski Welt. The nearby Brandstadl 'offers a great selection of Tirolean fare at good prices'. The Jochstube at Eiberg is self-service but has a good atmosphere and excellent Tiroler Gröstl. Above Brixen the Filzalm is a good place for a quick drink on the way back from the circuit or you could indulge in the 'excellent Kaiserschmarren' at the Almfried. Check out our Ellmau chapter for more.

SCHOOLS AND GUIDES
Two to choose from
The Söll-Hochsöll school has a fairly good reputation. But we have a report of an 'instructor with little patience'.

FACILITIES FOR CHILDREN
Fast becoming a family resort
Söll has fairly wide-ranging facilities – the Söll-Hochsöll ski kindergarten, a Mini Club, which looks after children aged three to five who don't want to spend all day on the slopes, and a special kids-only drag and slope on the opposite side of the village to the main lifts. Reports welcome.

boarding

Söll is a good place to try out boarding: slopes are gentle and there are plenty of gondolas and chairs. For competent boarders it's more limited – the slopes of the Ski Welt are tame.

CHILDREN

The ski schools take children from age 5 in special snow-gardens on the nursery slopes from 9.45 to 4pm (5 days €115 – Söll-Hochsöll prices). Once they progress to Hochsöll, care has to be arranged with the instructor.

Next to the main ski kindergarten, the Söll-Hochsöll school operates a Mini Club for children aged 3 to 5 from 9.45 to 4pm.

ACTIVITIES

Indoor Swimming, sauna, solarium, massage, bowling, squash

Outdoor Natural ice rink (skating, curling), sleigh rides, 3km/2 miles of floodlit ski and toboggan runs, snow-shoeing, winter walking, paragliding, hang-gliding

Phone numbers
Söll
From elsewhere in Austria add the prefix 05333.
From abroad use the prefix +43 5333.

Hopfgarten
From elsewhere in Austria add the prefix 05335.
From abroad use the prefix +43 5335.

STAYING THERE

HOW TO GO
Mostly cheap, cheerful gasthofs
The major mainstream tour operators offer packages here.
Hotels There is a wide choice of simple gasthofs, pensions and B&Bs, and an adequate amount of better-quality hotel accommodation – mainly 3-star.
⟨⟨3⟩ **Greil** (5289) One of only two 4-star options – attractive, but out of the centre far from the lifts and pool.
⟨⟨3⟩ **Postwirt** (5081) Attractive, central, traditional 4-star with built-in stube.
⟨⟨3⟩ **Bergland** (5454) Small 3-star, well placed between the village and lifts.
⟨⟨3⟩ **Panorama** (5309) 3-star far from lifts but with own bus stop; wonderful views; pleasant rooms; good cakes.
⟨⟨3⟩ **Tulpe** (5223) Next to the lifts.
⟨2⟩ **Feldwebel** (5224) Recently renovated, central 3-star.
⟨2⟩ **Schirast** (5544) Next to the lifts.
⟨2⟩ **Gasthof Tenne** (5282) B&B gasthof between centre and main road.
Chalets There are few catered chalets but a couple of big 'club hotels' run by British tour operators.
Self-catering The central Aparthotel Schindlhaus has nice accommodation, though the best apartments in town are attached to the Bergland hotel.

EATING OUT
A fair choice
Some of the best restaurants are in hotels. The Greil and Postwirt are good, but the Schindlhaus is said to be the best. Giovanni does excellent pizzas, while other places worth a visit include the Dorfstub'n and the Venezia.

APRES-SKI
Still some very loud bars
Söll is not as raucous as it used to be, but it's still very lively and a lot of places have live music. The Salvenstadl (Cow Shed) bar was recommended as 'the best with live music' by a reporter last year. Pub 15 is a bit sleazy but lively. The Whisky Mühle is a large disco that can get a little rowdy, especially after other bars close. There's a floodlit piste and separate toboggan run – both from top to bottom of the gondola. At the bottom you could try the two new bars, the Talstation and the Hexenkessel – reports welcome. For a romantic evening you can hire the Gerhard Berger VIP gondola, complete with leather upholstery, curtains and champagne.

OFF THE SLOPES
Not bad for a small village
You could spend a happy day in the wonderfully equipped Panoramabad: taking a sauna, swimming, lounging about. The large baroque church would be the pride of many tourist towns. There are numerous coach excursions, including trips to Salzburg, Innsbruck and even Vipiteno over in Italy.

Hopfgarten 620m/2,030ft

Hopfgarten is an unspoiled, friendly and traditional resort tucked away from the busy Wörgl road.

THE RESORT
The village is a good size: small enough to be intimate, large enough to have plenty of off-slope amenities. Most hotels are within five minutes' walk of the chair-lift to Rigi (due for replacement by a gondola in the next few years).

THE MOUNTAIN
Hopfgarten offers queue-free access to Rigi and Hohe Salve – the high point of the Ski Welt.
Slopes When snow is good, the runs down to Hopfgarten and the nearby villages of Brixen and Itter are some of

Söll

177

GETTING THERE

Air Salzburg 94km/58 miles (2hr); Innsbruck 73km/45 miles (1½hr).

Rail Wörgl (13km/8 miles) or Kufstein (15km/9 miles); bus to resort.

Phone numbers

Brixen
From elsewhere in Austria add the prefix 05334.
From abroad use the prefix +43 5334.

Scheffau
From elsewhere in Austria add the prefix 05358.
From abroad use the prefix +43 5358.

Itter
From elsewhere in Austria add the prefix 05335.
From abroad use the prefix +43 5335.

---

the best in the Ski Welt. But the fine, and relatively snow-sure, runs above Scheffau are irksomely distant.

For a change of scene, and perhaps less crowded pistes, take a bus to Westendorf (see separate chapter) or Kelchsau, both on the Ski Welt pass.

Snow reliability The resort's great weakness is the poor snow quality on the south-west-facing home slope.

Experts Experts should venture off-piste for excitement.

Intermediates The whole Ski Welt is great for intermediates.

Beginners There is a convenient beginners' slope in the village, but it is sunny as well as low, so lack of snow-cover is likely to mean paying for a lift pass to go up to the higher blue runs.

Snowboarding A terrain-park near Hochsöll can be accessed from the Hohe Salve above Hopfgarten.

Cross-country Hopfgarten is one of the best cross-country bases in the area. There are fine trails to Kelchsau (11km/7 miles) and Niederau (15km/9 miles), and the Itter-Bocking loop (15km/9 miles) starts nearby. Westendorf's trails are close.

Queues There's only a two-person chair out of the village, so queues can be a problem in the morning.

Mountain restaurants See Söll.

Schools and guides Partly because Hopfgarten seems to attract large numbers of Australians, English is widely spoken in the two schools.

Facilities for children Hopfgarten is a family resort, with a nursery and ski kindergarten.

STAYING THERE

How to go Cheap and cheerful gasthofs, pensions and little private B&Bs are the norm here.

Hotels The exceptions to the rule are the comfortable 4-star hotels Hopfgarten (3920) with pool, and Sporthotel Fuchs (2420), both well placed for the main lift.

Eating out Most of the restaurants are hotel-based, but there are exceptions, including a Chinese and a pizzeria.

Après-ski Après-ski is generally quiet, though a lively holiday can usually be ensured if you go with Aussie-dominated Contiki Travel.

Off the slopes Off-slope amenities include swimming, riding, bowling, skating, tobogganing and paragliding. The railway makes trips to Salzburg, Innsbruck and Kitzbühel relatively easy to achieve.

Brixen 800m/2,620ft

It may not be pretty, but Brixen has a queue-free, high-capacity gondola up to the main Ski Welt slopes.

THE RESORT

Brixen im Thale is a very scattered roadside village at the south-east edge of the Ski Welt, close to Westendorf. The main hotels are near the railway station, a bus-ride from the lifts.

THE MOUNTAIN

When snow is good, Brixen has some of the best slopes in the Ski Welt.

Slopes All three runs under the gondola are fine things – an unpisted route and black and red pistes. There's a small area of north-facing runs, including nursery slopes, on the other side of the village at Kandleralm.

Snow reliability A chain of snow-guns on the main south-facing piste helps to preserve the snow as long as possible.

Experts The black run alongside the Brixen gondola is one of the few challenging pistes in the area.

Intermediates Some challenging local slopes for intermediates to tackle.

Beginners The nursery slopes are secluded and shady, but meeting up with friends for lunch is a hassle – the area is a bus-ride from the village.

Snowboarding See Söll.

Cross-country Snow permitting, Brixen is one of the best cross-country bases in the Ski Welt: a 5km/3 mile loop up the mountain at Hochbrixen provides fine views and fairly reliable snow.

Queues New lifts have improved the once queue-prone area.

Mountain restaurants The Filzalm above Brixen has been recommended.

Schools and guides The ski school runs the usual group classes, and mini-groups for five to seven people.

Facilities for children Brixen is not as suitable as other Ski Welt resorts, but it has an all-day ski kindergarten.

STAYING THERE

How to go There are plenty of hotels and pensions.

Hotels The hotel Alpenhof (88320) and the Sporthotel (8191) are both 4-star hotels with pools.

Eating out Mainly hotel-based.

Après-ski Après-ski is quiet, but livelier Westendorf is a short taxi-ride.

Off the slopes Activities include tennis, hotel-based spa facilities and days out to Salzburg, Innsbruck and Kitzbühel.

↑ Eiberg offers some north-facing snow – but the hill's vertical is a mere 140m/460ft

SKI WELT

Scheffau 745m/2,440ft

This is one of the most attractive of the Ski Welt villages.

THE RESORT
Scheffau is a rustic little place complete with pretty white church. It is spacious yet not sprawling and has a definite centre, a kilometre off the busy main road, which increases its charm at the cost of convenience – you can ski to the Ski Welt lifts at Blaiken (where there are several hotels) but need a bus to get back.

THE MOUNTAIN
Scheffau is well placed for the Ski Welt's best (and most central and snow-sure) section of pistes.
Slopes Two gondolas (including an eight-seater new last season) give rapid access directly to Brandstadl.
Snow reliability Nearby Eiberg is the place to go when snow is poor.
Experts The pistes above Blaiken are some of the longest and steepest in the Ski Welt.
Intermediates This is as good a base as any in the area.
Beginners The nursery slope is in the village, making Scheffau a poor choice for mixed-ability parties.
Cross-country See Söll and Ellmau.
Queues The new gondola should eliminate weekend queues at Blaiken.
Mountain restaurants See Söll, Ellmau.
Schools and guides The school is well regarded, but groups can be large.
Facilities for children Both the ski kindergarten and non-ski nursery have good reputations.

STAYING THERE
How to go Major operators offer packages here.
Hotels The best hotels – both with pool, sauna and steam room – are the 4-star Kaiser (8000) and 3-star Alpin (85560) – 'excellent food, lots of choice, spacious rooms'. The Wilden Kaiser (8118), Blaiken (8126) and Waldhof (8122) are good value gasthofs near the gondolas.
Eating out There aren't many village restaurants, and those staying in B&B places are advised to book tables.
Après-ski 'Non-existent,' says a happy reporter. The usual rep-organised events such as bowling and tobogganing are available.
Off the slopes Walking apart, there is little to do. Tour operators organise trips to Innsbruck and Salzburg.

Itter 700m/2,300ft

Itter is a tiny village halfway around the mountain between Söll and Hopfgarten, with nursery slopes close to hand and a gondola just outside the village into the Ski Welt, via Hochsöll.

There's a hotel and half a dozen gasthofs and B&Bs. The school has a rental shop, and when conditions are good this is a good beginners' resort.

TOURIST OFFICES

Söll
t 5216
info@soell.com
www.soell.at

Hopfgarten
t 2322
info@hopfgarten.tirol.at
www.hopfgarten.com

Brixen
t 8433
brixen@skiwelt.at
www.brixenimthale.at

Scheffau
t 7373
scheffau@skiwelt.at
www.scheffau.com

Itter
t 2670
itter@skiwelt.at
www.itter.at

St Anton

Non-stop on- and off-slope action and pretty village base

NEWS

For 2003/04 two new high-speed, six-person chair-lifts with covers are planned. One will replace the Arlenmähder T-bar which runs from just above the Arlberg pass; the new top station will be higher, allowing access to the Ulmer Hütte restaurant and the runs to Rauz. The other chair will be on Rendl, replacing the T-bar to Gampberg. The resort tells us that runs served by both these new lifts will be remodelled to create more intermediate pistes.

For 2002/03 two rope tows with a moving carpet in-between were installed to take you from the roundabout on the edge of town near the Galzig cable-car to the Rendl gondola. So you no longer need to take the bus or walk – but you still need to on the way back as the new system works only one way.

➕ Extensive, varied slopes for experts and adventurous intermediates, with more to explore in Lech-Zürs a bus-ride away

➕ Heavy snowfalls, backed up by a fair amount of snowmaking

➕ Very lively après-ski, from mid-afternoon onward

➕ Despite expansion, the resort retains some traditional charm – and the animated village centre is now train-free as well as (mainly) car-free

➕ Improved lift system has made Nasserein a viable base and reduced queuing problems, but ...

➖ Still some serious lift queues, at resort level and at mid-mountain

➖ Slopes far from ideal for beginners or timid intermediates

➖ Most of the tough stuff is off-piste – and the distinction between piste and off-piste is unhelpfully blurred

➖ Pistes can get very crowded – some of them dangerously so

➖ Main slopes get a lot of sun, quickly affecting the snow conditions

➖ Resort spreads widely, with some long treks to key lifts and bars

➖ Can get rowdy, with noisy drunks in the central streets in the early hours

St Anton is undeniably a big-league resort. For competent skiers and riders with an appetite for non-stop action and the stamina to keep up with it, we'd rate it even higher: it is one of the great resorts, with an après-ski scene that can be as taxing as the splendid bowls below the Valluga. The combination draws ski bums from around the world, as well as lots of regular holiday visitors.

But it won't suit everyone, as our ➖ points make clear. Many people who might be thinking of trying an Austrian change from Val-d'Isère, or of taking a step up from Kitzbühel, are liable be put off by this list, and rightly so. The St Anton formula works brilliantly for some people, but very badly for others.

The 2001 Alpine World Ski Championships have left a legacy that is worthwhile, but not quite the transformation that is advertised. The new leisure/conference centre looks as dreary as its name – Arlberg-well.com – sounds silly. Removal of the divisive railway line to the far side of the river has certainly simplified access to the lifts, but where the railway was there is now just a kind of gap. The improved lifts from village level to Gampen have eased the queues and given the suburb of Nasserein a huge boost. Further investment in lifts and pistes is planned for next season (see News) but the improvement that is most needed is a new piste or two back to the village from Galzig, to relieve pressure on the spectacularly overcrowded Steissbachtal. There are off-piste routes that could be developed, given the will. If they can move the railway ...

THE RESORT

St Anton is at the foot of the road up to the Arlberg pass, at the eastern end of a lift network that spreads across to St Christoph and across the pass to Stuben. The resort is a long, sprawling mixture of traditional and modern buildings crammed into a narrow valley. It used to be sandwiched between a busy road and the mainline railway – but the railway was moved before the start of the 2000/01 season, and where once there were tracks now there is a little area of parkland.

Although it is crowded and commercialised, St Anton is full of character, its traffic-free main street lined by traditional-style buildings. It is an attractively bustling place, day and night. More than one reporter has observed that it has better-than-usual everyday shopping.

The main hub of the resort is around the base stations of the two-stage cable-car up via Galzig to Valluga Grat and the fast quad chair up to Gampen. The attractive, lively main

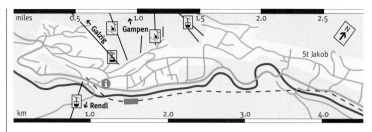

KEY FACTS

Resort	1305m
	4,280ft

For Arlberg region	
Slopes	1305-2650m
	4,280-8,690ft
Lifts	83
Pistes	260km
	162 miles
Blue	25%
Red	50%
Black	25%
Snowmaking	65km
	40 miles

For St Anton, St Christoph and Stuben only	
Slopes	1305-2650m
	4,280-8,690ft
Lifts	41
Pistes	120km
	75 miles

ST ANTON TOURIST OFFICE

Rendl, in the distance, generally offers St Anton's quietest intermediate slopes ↘

street and its hotels are only a short walk from these lifts, and for most purposes a location on or close to this main street is ideal.

The resort spreads down the valley, thinning out before broadening again to form the suburb of Nasserein. This backwater now has an eight-person gondola up to Gampen, and makes a quite appealing base for a quiet time. The nightlife action is a short bus-ride or 15-minute walk away. Staying between St Anton centre and Nasserein is also a more attractive idea since the Fang chair-lift, which gives access to the Nasserein gondola, was built.

On the other side of the main road a gondola goes up to the Rendl area. This is now linked one-way by rope tows and a moving carpet from the

end of St Anton's main street (see News) – but the return journey still involves a bus-ride or short walk.

St Anton spreads up the hill to the west of the centre, towards the Arlberg pass – first to Oberdorf, then Gastig, 10 minutes' walk from the centre. Further up the hill are the suburbs of Dengert and Moos – a long way out, but quite close to the slopes.

Regular buses go to Stuben, Zürs and Lech (all described in the Lech chapter) and the much less well-known but worthwhile Sonnenkopf area above Klösterle. These buses can get crowded early and late in the day. Minibus-style taxis can be economic if widely shared.

Serfaus, Nauders, Ischgl and Sölden are also feasible outings by car.

St Anton

181

THE MOUNTAINS

The main slopes are essentially open: only the run from Rendl to the valley offers much shelter from bad weather.

St Anton vies with Val-d'Isère for the title of 'resort with most underclassified slopes'. There are plenty of red pistes that would be black in many other resorts, and plenty of blues that would be red.

Many of the most popular steep runs marked on the piste map are classified as 'ski routes'. These have widely spaced markers, they may be groomed occasionally in part, but they are not patrolled and are protected from avalanches only 'in the immediate vicinity of the markers'.

Clearly you should not ski such runs alone, and the piste map recommends them only for people with 'alpine experience or with a ski instructor'. In theory this puts these routes out of bounds for many holidaymakers, but in practice many tackle them without the services of an instructor. One reader sums up the problem with admirable clarity: 'It is entirely unreasonable to expect everyone to take guides on these routes, and it seems irresponsible to ignore the fact that people will go on them. On some of the ski routes there were snow-guns. This doesn't fit with the idea that you're on your own.' Another reader points out that the routes vary from 'an easy red to a double-black-diamond nightmare'. On Rendl there is a drag-lift serving no pistes but only a single ski route. The situation is, to quote another reader, 'absurd'.

Until 1999, the piste map also showed several 'high-alpine touring runs' not marked on the ground at all, and not protected against avalanche. These no longer appear on the map, though runs of that kind are still shown over in Lech and Stuben. Read the Lech chapter for more on these.

The Arlberg region piste map is poor, attempting to fit too many different mountain aspects into a single view. It's at its worst over in Lech, but it's also unsatisfactory on Galzig. Fortunately the on-mountain maps and signs are clearer. Reporters have complained of poor and limited piste grooming. One said this year, 'Many runs are left unpisted for days at a time.' The local cable TV, showing the state of some of the pistes and queues, can be very useful.

THE SLOPES
Large linked area
St Anton's slopes fall into three main sectors, two of them linked.

The major sector is that beneath the local high-spot, the **Valluga**, accessed by cable-car via **Galzig**. The tiny top stage of the cable-car to the Valluga itself is mainly for sightseeing – you can take skis or a board up only if you have a guide to lead you down the tricky off-piste run to Zürs. The slightly lower station of Valluga Grat gives access to St Anton's famous high, sunny bowls, and to the long, beautiful red/blue run to Rauz, at the western

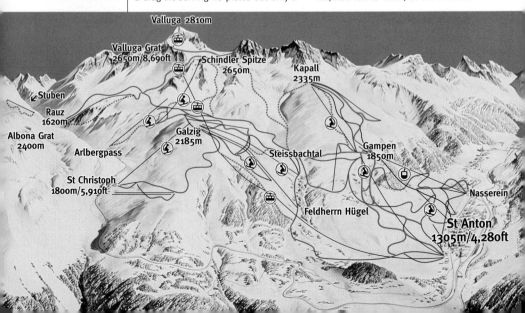

LIFT PASSES

Arlberg Ski Pass
Covers all St Anton, St Christoph, Lech, Zürs and Stuben lifts, and linking bus between Rauz and Zürs.

Beginners
Limited pass covering beginners' lifts.

Main pass
1-day pass €37.50
6-day pass €174

Senior citizens
Over 65 for men and 60 for women: 6-day pass €149

Children
Under 15: 6-day pass 104
Under 19: 6-day pass €149

Notes
Single ascent, half-day and afternoon 'taster' tickets available. Pass also covers Sonnenkopf (10 lifts) at Klösterle, 7km/4 miles west of Stuben (free bus link from Stuben).

THE VALLUGA RUNS

The off-piste runs in the huge bowl beneath the summit of the Valluga, reached by either the Schindlergrat chair or the Valluga I cable-car, are justifiably world-famous. In good snow, this whole area is an off-piste delight for experts.

Except immediately after a fresh snowfall, you can see tracks going all over the mountain. There are two main ski routes marked on the piste map – both long, steep descents that quickly get mogulled. The Schindlerkar is the first you come to and it divides into two – the Schindlerkar gully being the steeper option. For the second, wider and somewhat easier, Mattun run, you traverse further at the top. Both these feed down into the Steissbachtal gully where there are lifts back up to Galzig and Gampen. The Schweinströge – a high-alpine route no longer shown on the map – starts off in the same direction as the red run to Rauz, but you traverse the shoulder of the Schindler Spitze and down a narrow gully.

end of St Anton's own slopes. From here you can go on to explore the rather neglected slopes of Stuben.

All of these high runs can also be accessed by riding the Schindlergrat triple chair. Other runs from Galzig go south-west to St Christoph and east into the Steissbachtal. Most of the runs in this whole sector funnel into this 'Happy Valley', producing incredible congestion, especially late in the day.

Beyond this valley, with lift and piste links in both directions, is the **Gampen-Kapall** sector, reachable by chair-lift from central St Anton or gondola from Nasserein. From Gampen at mid-mountain, pistes lead back to St Anton and Nasserein. Or you can ride a six-pack on up to Kapall to ski the treeless upper mountain.

A handful of lifts serve the west-facing runs at the top of **Rendl**, with a single north-facing piste returning to the gondola bottom station.

TERRAIN-PARKS
Head for Rendl
On Rendl, just below the top of the gondola, is St Anton's only terrain-park. This includes a half-pipe, quarter pipe, jumps, rail slides and a washboard (several humps in a row).

SNOW RELIABILITY
Generally very good cover
If the weather is coming from the west or north-west (as it often is), the Arlberg gets it first, and as a result St Anton and its neighbours get heavy falls of snow. They often have much better conditions than other resorts of a similar height, and we've had great fresh powder here as late as mid-April. But many of the slopes face south or south-east, causing icy or heavy conditions at times. It's vital to time descents of the steeper runs off the Valluga to get decent conditions.

The lower runs are now well equipped with snowmaking, which generally ensures the home runs remain open (though possibly too hard or too slushy to be enjoyable).

FOR EXPERTS
One of the world's great areas
St Anton vies with Chamonix, Val-d'Isère and a handful of other resorts for the affections of experts. There are countless opportunities for going off-piste and guidance is very desirable. It has some of the most consistently challenging and extensive slopes in the world. The jewel in the crown is the off-piste terrain in the bowls beneath the Valluga – see feature panel. The ultimate challenge, perhaps, is to go with a guide off the back of the Valluga. The initial pitch is very, very steep (a fall can be fatal) but after that the run down to Zürs is very beautiful and usually deserted. Reporters who

Riffelscharte
2650m/8,690ft
Gampberg
2405m/7,890ft
Rendl
St Anton
305m/4,280ft
Moostal

have tried it have loved it.

Lower down, there are challenging runs in many directions from both Galzig and Gampen-Kapall. These lower runs can be doubly tricky if the snow has been hit by the sun.

The Rendl area across the road has plenty of open space beneath the top lifts and there is some delightful fun to be had off the back of this ridge.

One of our reporters particularly liked the Sonnenkopf area down-valley from Stuben for its excellent off-piste route to Langen. See also the Stuben section at the end of the Lech chapter.

The few black pistes offer genuine challenges. These include the World Championship race courses – Kandahar from Kapall down to Gampen and the previously red Fang run from there down to the village.

On top of all this, bear in mind that many of the red runs on the piste map are long and challenging, too.

FOR INTERMEDIATES
Some real challenges

St Anton is well suited to good, adventurous intermediates. They will be able to try the Mattun run and the easier version of the Schindlerkar run from Valluga Grat (see feature panel). The run from Schindler Spitze to Rauz is very long (over 1000m/3,300ft vertical), varied and ideal for good (and fit) intermediates. Alternatively, turn off from this part way down and take the Steissbachtal to the lifts back

to Galzig. The Kapall-Gampen section is also interesting, with sporty bumps among trees on the lower half. Good intermediates may enjoy the men's downhill run from the top to town.

Less adventurous intermediates will find St Anton less to their taste. There are few easy cruising pistes. The most obvious are the short blues on Galzig and the Steissbachtal (aka 'Happy Valley'). These are reasonably gentle but get uncomfortably crowded. The blue to St Christoph is generally quieter. The narrowish blues between Kapall and Gampen can have some challenging bumps. For the best easy cruising, take the bus to Lech.

In the Rendl area a variety of trails suitable for good and moderate intermediates criss-cross, including a lovely long tree-lined run (over 1000m/3,300ft vertical from the top) back to the valley gondola station. This is the best run in the whole area when visibility is poor, though it has some quite awkward sections.

FOR BEGINNERS
Far from ideal

St Anton has better nursery slopes now, near the Fang lift. But there are no easy, uncrowded runs for beginners to progress to. A mixed party of experts, intermediates and novices would be better off staying in Lech or Zürs; those who want to explore St Anton can get on the bus to Rauz.

boarding

Though steeped in skiing tradition, St Anton is moving with the times and improving facilities for boarders. Although we don't really recommend it to beginners, for good boarders it is one of the best free-ride areas in the world, with lots of steep terrain and natural hits. There are still a few T-bars around but fast chair-lifts are now the main ways around the mountains. Two further T bars are due to be replaced next season by chairs (see News). The Arlberg ski school has a special Snowboard Academy section.

SCHOOLS

Arlberg
t 3411
skischool.arlberg@
st-anton.at
St Anton
t 3563
office@skistanton.com
Piste to Powder
t 0664 174 6282,
UK 01661 824318
Various levels of off-piste tuition and/or guiding around the Arlberg region.

Classes
(Arlberg prices)
6 days (2½hr am and 2hr pm) €190
Private lessons
€202 for full day; each additional person €17

FOR CROSS-COUNTRY
Limited interest
St Anton is not a great cross-country resort, but trails total around 35km/22 miles and snow conditions are usually good. There are a couple of uninspiring trails near town, another at St Jakob 3km/2 miles away, and a pretty trail through trees along the Ferwalltal to the foot of the Albona area. There is also a tiny loop at St Christoph.

QUEUES
Improved, but still a problem
Queues are not the problem they once were, since the replacement of several lifts by fast chairs. But they can still be tiresome in peak season and at weekends. Recent reporters found long queues for the cable-car to Galzig and one hit 'massive' queues for the chair to Gampen, which attracts crowds when higher lifts are closed. At mid-mountain, both the cable-car to Valluga Grat and the alternative Schindlergrat chair can have serious queues, as can the Zammermoos chair out of the Steissbachtal. There are US-style 'singles lines' at some lifts; but, despite taped exhortations in several languages, the chairs are rarely filled.

Perhaps more of a worry than the lift queues are the crowded trails. Clearly the worst is the Steissbachtal which can be uncomfortably crowded even in January and a nightmare on a March weekend. Run 1 home at the end of the day is also crowded. Several reporters recommend going Rendl or Stuben on busy days or heading down to Rauz or St Christoph and getting a bus back to town rather than tangling with the Steissbachtal. This long-standing problem is not going to go away until the resort creates an alternative easy piste from Galzig to the village.

MOUNTAIN RESTAURANTS
Plenty of choice
We often end up lunching in St Christoph at the atmospheric Hospiz Alm. But some readers have met poor service, and it isn't cheap. The cosy Arlberg Taja St Christoph just above it, and Traxl's ice bar at the Maiensee Hotel, have been recommended by readers. Other recommendations include the self-service restaurant at Galzig for 'superb views and tasty food', Sennhütte on the Galzig home run and Rodelalm on Gampen: 'A real hut with good food at low prices and a lovely fire.' Slightly lower still on Galzig, the Mooserwirt serves typical Austrian food at what seem high prices, but 'the portions are absolutely massive'; the Krazy Kanguruh does burgers, pizzas and snacks; the Taps Bar next door 'good goulash soup'.

Over on Rendl, the self-service Rendl restaurant is said to offer 'excellent food and value', with zero queuing even when busy. Bifangalm, near the end of the run to the valley, is 'friendly and atmospheric'.

The restaurant at Kapall received a bad review from one of our reporters this year: 'A very limited menu and the atmosphere of a transport cafe.'

SCHOOLS AND GUIDES
Mixed reports
The relatively new St Anton school has brought much-needed competition to the Arlberg school, which still generates conflicting reports. 'Complete beginner group much too big despite our complaints and we learned more from our friends,' said one reporter. Another complained of old fashioned technique: 'They need to turn the clock forward.' But some reporters were very happy: 'Children and parents were delighted ... kids

GETTING THERE

Air Innsbruck
100km/62 miles
(1½hr); Zürich
200km/124 miles
(3hr).

Rail Mainline station
in resort.

CHILDREN

The kindergarten at
the Kinderwelt (2526)
takes toilet-trained
children aged 30
months to 14 years,
from 10am to 4.30.
Ski tuition with the
Arlberg ski school in
a special snow-garden
is available for
children aged 4. Both
schools take children
aged 4 to 14 (6 days
including lunch €190
at Arlberg school).

ACTIVITIES

Indoor Swimming
pool (also hotel pools
open to the public,
with sauna and
massage), tennis,
squash, bowling,
museum, cinema in
Vallugasaal

Outdoor Swimming
pool, 15km/9 miles of
cleared walks, natural
skating rink (skating,
curling), sleigh rides,
tobogganing,
paragliding

Phone numbers
From elsewhere in
Austria add the prefix
05446.
From abroad use the
prefix +43 5446.

were taught well'; 'Our guide was
excellent.' We have skied with
excellent off-piste guides, and
reporters who have hired a guide to
tackle the runs from the top of the
Valluga have had a great day. We have
also heard good reports of Piste to
Powder, a guiding outfit run by British
guide Graham Austick.

FACILITIES FOR CHILDREN
Getting better
St Anton might not seem an obvious
resort for family holidays, but the
resort works hard to accommodate
families' needs: the youth centre
attached to the Arlberg school is
excellent, and the special slopes both
for toddlers (at the bottom) and bigger
children (up at Gampen) are well done.
At Nasserein there is a moving carpet
lift on the baby slope, and a reporter
rates this an 'absolutely ideal' place to
stay with young kids.

STAYING THERE

HOW TO GO
Austria's main chalet resort
There's a wide range of places to stay,
from quality hotels to cheap and
cheerful pensions and apartments.
Chalets In the land of the pension, St
Anton also has many catered chalets
offered by UK tour operators. Many are
in the suburbs – with the new gondola
Nasserein now makes a convenient
chalet base.
Hotels There is one 5-star hotel and
lots of 4- and 3-stars and B&Bs.
((((5)) **Raffl's St Antoner Hof** (2910)
Best in town, but its position on the
bypass is less than ideal. Pool.
(((4)) **Schwarzer Adler** (22440)
Centuries-old inn on main street.
Widely varying bedrooms.
(((4)) **Alte Post** (2553) Atmospheric
place on main street with lively après-
ski bar. Endorsed by a reporter.

(((4)) **Post** (2213) Comfortable if
uninspiring 4-star at the centre of
affairs, close to both lifts and nightlife.
(((4)) **Sporthotel** (3111) Central position,
varied bedrooms, good food. Pool.
(((3)) **Grischuna** (2304) Welcoming
family-run place in peaceful position up
the hill west of the town; close to the
slopes, five minutes to the cable-car.
(((3)) **Goldenes Kreuz** (22110)
A comfortable B&B hotel halfway to
Nasserein, ideal for cruising home.
Self-catering There are plenty of
apartments available but package
deals are few and far between. The
Bachmann apartments (2334) near the
Nasserein gondola have been highly
recommended by a 2003 reporter.

EATING OUT
Mostly informal
Plain, filling fare is the norm, with
numerous places such as the
Trödlerstube and Reselehof serving big
portions of traditional Austrian food.
The Fuhrmannstube is singled out for
'great value, with an excellent menu
and cheery owner'. At the Museum, as
well as learning about the history of
the resort, you can enjoy upmarket
food and wine in elegant panelled
rooms. Similarly ambitious in culinary
terms but quite different in style is
Ben.venuto, in the Arlberg-well.com
building: stark decor, eclectic menu
and excellent cooking. Bobo's serves
good, although expensive, Mexican. A
reporter recommends Dixies for pizza,
pasta, steaks and fish, though others
prefer Scotty's or Pomodoro for pizza.
In Nasserein, the Tenne is noted for
game dishes, while Alt St Anton is a
cosy chalet doing a good range of
excellent traditional dishes. The
toboggan run above Nasserein is
floodlit a couple of nights a week, and
you can stop off at the Rodelalm for
traditional food, beer and schnapps –
booking is essential.

TOURIST OFFICE

t 22690
st.anton@netway.at
www.stantonamarlberg.com
www.tiscover.com/st.christoph

ST ANTON TOURIST OFFICE

The fine run from the Valluga (in the distance) is the link with Stuben, where there is exciting off-piste, some reached by hiking ↘

APRES-SKI
Throbbing till late

St Anton's bars rock from mid-afternoon until the early hours. Après-ski starts in a collection of bars on the slopes above the village. The Krazy Kanguruh is probably the most famous, but the Mooserwirt is now the 'in' place, filling up with revellers as soon as the lunch trade finishes – reputedly dispensing more beer than any other bar in Austria. By 4pm tables inside and out are being danced on. The Griabli opposite has live bands and is almost as popular. All this is followed by a slide down the piste in the dark. The bars in town are in full swing by 4pm, too. Most are lively, with loud music; sophisticates looking for a quieter more relaxed time are less well provided for. The Underground bar has a great atmosphere and live music, but gets packed. Equally popular are the Hazienda, Piccadilly and, for late-night dancing, Stanton. Recent reporters have recommended Scotty's (in Mark Warner's chalet-hotel Rosanna, with extended happy hour), Jacksy's, Pub 37, Bobo's, Alibi and Funky Chicken. In Nasserein, Tom Dooley's is 'relaxed and welcoming'.

OFF THE SLOPES
Some improvement

St Anton is a resort for keen skiers and riders. But the new fitness, swimming and skating facilities of Arlberg-well.com are impressive. The village is lively during the day, with a fair selection of shops. Getting by bus to the other Arlberg resorts is easy, as is visiting Innsbruck by train. Many of the best mountain huts are not readily accessible by lift for pedestrians.

STAYING DOWN THE VALLEY
Nice and quiet

Beyond Nasserein is St Jakob. It can be reached on snow, but is dependent on the free shuttle-bus in the morning. Pettneu is a quiet village further down the valley, with slopes that most suit beginners. It's best for drivers.

St Christoph 1800m/5,910ft

A small, exclusive collection of pricey hotels, restaurants and bars right by the Arlberg Pass, with drag-lifts for local slopes and a fast quad chair-lift to the heart of St Anton's slopes. It's quiet at night. The best hotel of all is the huge 5-star Arlberg-Hospiz (2611).

St Anton

187

St Johann in Tirol

Relax on easy runs with plenty of pit stops and friendly locals

NEWS

2002/03 saw the introduction of floodlit skiing on Monday, Wednesday and Friday evenings from 7.00 to 9.30.

For 2001/02 a new eight-seater gondola replaced the old single-person chair from Oberndorf, greatly improving access for day-trippers and taking pressure off the main village gondola.

In recent years a lot more snowmaking has been installed and it now covers almost half the slopes.

- ➕ Charming traffic-free centre
- ➕ Lots of mountain restaurants
- ➕ Plenty of off-slope activities
- ➕ Easy to visit neighbouring resorts
- ➕ Few Brits by Tirol standards
- ➕ Ideal for beginners and intermediates
- ➕ Relatively good snow record

- ➖ Very small area, with little to interest experts or keen piste-bashing intermediates
- ➖ Weekend crowds from Germany
- ➖ Can be especially crowded when nearby resorts with less reliable snow are suffering

This charming and friendly resort is an attractive place for beginners and leisurely part-timers who like to spend as much time having drinks and lunch as they do actually cruising the slopes. Keener and more proficient skiers and boarders will soon get bored unless they are prepared to visit surrounding resorts covered by the local pass or the Kitzbüheler Alpenskipass.

THE RESORT

St Johann is a sizeable valley town where life doesn't revolve entirely around skiing. Reporters emphasise the friendliness of the locals. The attractive traffic-free centre, where most of the hotels are found, is wedged between a railway track, main roads and rivers, and the five-minute walk to the main lift includes a level crossing and walking beside a busy road. But there is the alternative of staying in hotels near the lift base. There is also accommodation in the hamlet of Eichenhof to the east, with drag-lifts into the slopes.

The local pass covers several other resorts to the north and east; Fieberbrunn and Waidring's Steinplatte are particularly worth a visit. The Kitzbüheler Alpenskipass covers the whole region, and Kitzbühel itself is only 10 minutes by car or train.

THE MOUNTAINS

St Johann's local slopes are on the north-facing side of the Kitzbüheler Horn – the 'back' side of Kitzbühel's 'second' and smaller mountain.

Slopes The main access lift from the village is a gondola to Harschbichl with a mid-station at Angereralm. From the top, a choice of north-facing pistes lead back through the trees towards town – mainly reds on the upper mountain, blues lower down. A sunnier sector of west-facing pistes lead down to the new gondola at Oberndorf.

Terrain-parks St Johann has a terrain-park, a half-pipe and a carving course.

Snow reliability St Johann gets more snow than neighbouring Kitzbühel and the Ski Welt, and this, together with its largely north-facing slopes, means that it often has better conditions. It also has substantial snowmaking.

Experts There is nothing here to

Kitzbüheler Horn 2000m

Harschbichl 1700m/5,58oft

Bergstation Penzing 1465m

Jodlalm 1500m

Eichenhof

St Johann in Tirol 650m/2,13oft

Oberndorf

KEY FACTS

Resort	650m
	2,130ft
Slopes	670-1700m
	2,200-5,580ft
Lifts	17
Pistes	60km
	37 miles
Blue	41%
Red	47%
Black	12%
Snowmaking	28km
	17 miles

Phone numbers
From elsewhere in Austria add the prefix 05352.
From abroad use the prefix +43 5352.

challenge an expert. The long black run on the piste map is really a moderate red – and the snow suffers from the strong afternoon sun.

Intermediates The slopes are varied. But keen piste-bashers will ski them all in a day and are likely to want to go on to explore nearby resorts. Decent intermediates have a fairly direct-running piste between Harschbichl and town and the black mentioned above. There are some easier red runs on the top part of the mountain, but the best (3a and 4b) are served by long drags or a slow, old chair. The Penzing piste is served by a high-speed quad chair. The less adventurous are better off getting off the village gondola at the mid-station and taking gentle pistes down from there.

Beginners The main nursery slopes are excellent. The slopes served by the first stage of the village gondola make good runs to progress to – though the last part just above the village is a bit steep for some. 'Superb. I could not have picked a better place to learn to ski,' said one past reporter.

Snowboarding It's drag-lifts or nothing on the nursery slopes.

Cross-country Given good snow, St Johann is one of the best cross-country resorts in Austria. The wide variety of trails totals 75km/47 miles.

Queues Rare except at peak times.

Mountain restaurants With 14 restaurants spread over just 60km/37 miles of piste, St Johann must have the densest array of huts of any sizeable resort in Europe. All those tried by a recent visitor were found to be 'very clean', providing 'excellent food, especially the Hochfeld', near the upper Hochfeld chair. The Harschbichlhütte is recommended for 'excellent food'. Our favourite is the Angerer Alm, just above the gondola mid-station. It serves excellent local food and has the most amazing wine cellar. The Besgeigeralm is a lovely rustic restaurant on the Oberndorf side.

Schools and guides The St Johann and Eichenhof schools have a good reputation. This was confirmed by a recent visitor who said that 'nothing was too much trouble' and that the 'excellent' instructor spoke good English.

Facilities for children The village nursery, geared to the needs of workers rather than visitors, offers exceptionally long hours. We have no recent reports of how this works in practice.

STAYING THERE

How to go British tour operators concentrate on hotels, but there are numerous apartments available.

Hotels All hotels are 3- or 4-star. The 4-stars are best placed for the slopes. There are dozens of B&B pensions. The 4-star Sporthotel Austria (62507) is near the lift, with pool, sauna and steam. The Post (62230) is a 13th-century inn on the main street – 'By far the nicest,' says a resort regular. Fischer (62332) is central, 'very comfortable' with 'friendly staff and good food'.

Self-catering There are plenty of apartments to rent.

Eating out The restaurants stick mostly to good old-fashioned Austrian cooking. The Huber-Bräu is a working brewery, which serves good food but closes early. The Bären specialises in Tirolean dishes. For a special meal, locals recommend the Ambiente. The Rialto does good pizza and the Villa Masianco Mexican and pizza.

Après-ski Ice bars and tea dancing greet you as you come off the slopes – Max's Pub, at the bottom of the main piste, is a focal point. Jagglbäck, on the main street, is popular day and night. Cafe Rainer hosts ski school presentations, Bunny's is lively and the Almbar is 'very small, with great music and hosts, flowing schnapps and discarded underwear hanging from the ceiling'. What more could you want? Platzl is a comfortable late-night bar with excellent service. The Scala is the main disco. Tour reps organise sleigh rides, and tobogganing and the resort itself puts on an event most evenings.

Off the slopes A public pool with sauna, steam-room and solarium, indoor tennis, artificial ice rink, curling and 40km/25 miles of cleared walks. The railway makes for easy outings to Salzburg or Innsbruck.

St Johann in Tirol

Westendorf

Lively, friendly resort with own area as well as access to the Ski Welt

190

COSTS

① ② ③ ④ ⑤ ⑥

HOW IT RATES

The slopes

Snow	**
Extent	*
Expert	*
Intermediate	**
Beginner	****
Convenience	***
Queues	****
Mountain restaurants	***

The rest

Scenery	***
Resort charm	****
Off-slope	**

NEWS

In 2003/04 beginners should benefit from a new quad chair, which is planned to replace the Schneeberg drag and T-bar lifts on the nursery slopes near the centre.

+ Charming traditional village

+ Access to the extensive Ski Welt circuit via nearby Brixen

+ Good local beginners' slopes

+ Jolly if rather limited après-ski scene

− Limited local slopes

− Lack of challenges for experts

− Poor natural snow record, though half the pistes now benefit from snowmaking

Westendorf is on the Ski Welt lift pass (Austria's biggest lift-linked ski and snowboard area – see chapters on Söll and Ellmau). The main circuit is a short bus-ride away, but the resort has its own beginner and intermediate slopes and its prettiness and friendliness win many repeat visitors.

THE RESORT

Westendorf is a small Tirolean village with a charming main street and attractive onion-domed church (it was declared 'Europe's most beautiful village' in the European Floral Competition a few years ago).

The centre is close to the village nursery slopes and a five-minute walk from the main gondola on the edge of the village.

THE MOUNTAIN

The local slopes are small, but you can get into the Ski Welt circuit easily via a bus to Brixen and then a gondola.

Slopes A two-stage gondola takes you to Talkaser, from where one main north-west-facing red run goes back to the resort (with blue options on the lower half). Short west- and east-facing pistes at the top run below the peaks of Choralpe, Fleiding and Gampen. A couple of red runs from Fleiding go down past the lifts to hamlets served by buses.

Terrain-parks There's a good terrain-park with a half-pipe.

Snow reliability Westendorf's snow reliability is a bit better than some other Ski Welt resorts and half its pistes now have snowmaking.

Experts There are no real challenges and no black slopes.

Intermediates Nearly all the local terrain is intermediate and there is the whole of the Ski Welt to explore, which has mile after mile of great intermediate runs.

Beginners Extensive village nursery slopes are Westendorf's pride and joy. And there are a couple of easy blues

higher up that you can progress to.

Snowboarding The planned new chair on the nursery slopes will make life easier for beginners.

Cross-country There are 30km/19 miles of local cross-country trails along the valley but snow-cover is erratic.

Queues Given good conditions, queues are rare, and far less of a problem than in the main Ski Welt area. If poor weather closes the upper lifts, queues can become long.

Mountain restaurants Alpenrosenhütte is woody and warm, with good food; a recent visitor enjoyed the quiet Brechhornhaus; Gassnerhof is good but you have to catch a bus back to town.

Schools and guides The three ski schools have quite good reputations, though classes can be over-large. One reporter tells of her teenage son's 'excellent' private lesson with the Top school: 'He's been skiing since he was three, but this was a revelation.' Another praises the Westendorf school:

Fleiding is the hub and high-point of Westendorf's slopes
→

That north-facing slope on the left needs a few trails cut through the woods, if you ask us →

KEY FACTS

Resort	800m
	2,620ft

For Westendorf only

Slopes	800-1890m
	2,620-6,200ft
Lifts	13
Pistes	45km
	28 miles
Blue	38%
Red	62%
Black	0%
Snowmaking	23km
	14 miles

For Ski Welt

Slopes	620-1830m
	2,030-6,000ft
Lifts	93
Pistes	250km
	155 miles
Blue	43%
Red	48%
Black	9%
Snowmaking	135km
	84 miles

Phone numbers
From elsewhere in Austria add the prefix 05334.
From abroad use the prefix +43 5334.

TOURIST OFFICE

t 6230
westendorf@skiwelt.at
www.westendorf.com

'Teachers very good, good value, great prize-giving in town hall.'
Facilities for children Westendorf sells itself as a family resort. Both the nursery and the ski kindergarten are open all day.

STAYING THERE

How to go A couple of mainstream operators offer packages here.
Hotels There are central 4-star hotels – the Jakobwirt (6245) and the 'excellent' Schermer (6268) – and a dozen 3-star ones. The 3-star Post (6202) is 'good value, right in the centre, few facilities except rooms, dining room and bar'. Many reporters stay in more modest guest houses. Haus Wetti (6348) is popular and away from the church bells. Pension Ingeborg (6577) has been highly recommended and is next to the gondola.
Self-catering The Schermerhof

apartments are of good quality.
Eating out Most of the best restaurants are in hotels – the Schermer, Mesnerwirt, Post and Jakobwirt are good. The Wastlhof and Klingler have also been recommended. Booking ahead is advisable. Get a taxi to Berggasthof Stimlach for a good evening out.
Après-ski Nightlife is lively but it's a small place with limited options. The One for the Road Bar and Liftstüberl, at the bottom of the gondola, are packed at the end of the day. The Moskito Bar has live music and theme nights but is said by a (42-year-old) reporter to be 'a bit of a dive'. The Village Pub, next to the hotel Post, is very popular and sells draught Guinness.
Off the slopes There are excursions by rail or bus to Innsbruck, Salzburg and Kitzbühel. Walks and sleigh rides are very pretty.

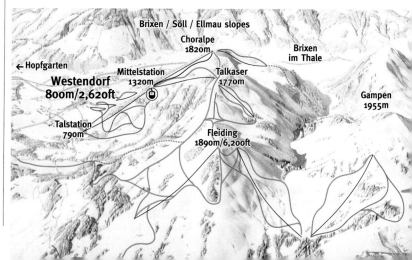

Wildschönau

Niederau and neighbours – family resorts with friendly slopes

TVB WILDSCHONAU

COSTS

① ② ③ ④ ⑤ ⑥

RATINGS

The slopes

Snow	**
Extent	*
Expert	*
Intermediate	**
Beginner	****
Convenience	***
Queues	****
Mountain restaurants	**

The rest

Scenery	***
Resort charm	***
Off-slope	**

NEWS

The last major new lift was a six-pack replacing two drag-lifts on Schatzberg.

New snowmaking for 2003/04 will bring coverage up to nearly 30% of pistes.

Plans for a lift link between Schatzberg and Alpbach are still on the drawing board – the proposed link would greatly improve the appeal of both areas.

In the past two seasons cross-country trails have increased by 20km.

Alpine Ski World Championships for the Disabled 2004
These will be held in the resort from 27 January to 7 February 2004. Events include Downhill, Super G, GS and Slalom. Competitors from 30 nations including Great Britain are expected.

Sleigh rides are one of the traditional attractions of the area →

+ Attractive, traditional, family-friendly villages

+ Good nursery slopes at Niederau and Oberau

+ Jolly après-ski scene

− Shuttle-buses or a drive between three separate ski areas

− Limited slopes in separate areas

− Poor snow reliability (but snowmaking is increasing)

Wildschönau is the dramatic-sounding name adopted by a group of attractive small resorts in the Tirol – Niederau, Oberau and Auffach. The slopes may be limited, but the resorts suit families looking for a friendly, civilised atmosphere.

THE RESORT

Niederau is the main resort; it's a spread-out little place, with a cluster of restaurants and shops around the gondola station forming the nearest thing to a focal point – but few hotels are more than five minutes' walk from a main lift. Auffach, 7km/4 miles away, is a smaller village but has the area's highest and most extensive slopes. On a low col between the two is Oberau – almost as big as Niederau and the valley's administrative and cultural centre. The villages are unspoiled, with traditional chalet-style buildings; roads are quiet, except on Saturdays; and the valley setting is lovely.

THE MOUNTAINS

Niederau's slopes are spread over a wooded mountainside that rises no higher than 1600m/5,250ft. The slopes at Auffach continue above the tree line.

Slopes The main lift from Niederau is an eight-person gondola to Markbachjoch. A few minutes' walk away is the alternative chair-lift, and above it is a steep drag to the high point of Lanerköpfl. Beginner runs at the bottom of the mountain are served by several short drag-lifts.

A reliable half-hourly (free) bus goes to Auffach. Its sunny, east-facing area, consisting almost entirely of red runs, goes up to Schatzberg, with a vertical of 1000m/3,300ft. The main lift up is a two-stage gondola. Drags and a six-pack serve the top runs.

The Kitzbüheler Alpen ski pass covers resorts in the Schneewinkel, Kitzbühel ski region, Ski Welt, and Alpbachtal as well.

Terrain-parks There's a 90m/300ft half-pipe and terrain-park with a quarter-pipe, jumps, snake and wave on Schatzberg.

Snow reliability The low altitude means that snow reliability is relatively poor – and if you can't use all the runs back to Niederau, the piste area there is tiny. Auffach is a better bet, with most of its runs above mid-mountain. Snowmaking has been increased in recent years and is now quite extensive. Grooming is good.

Experts The several black pistes are short and not severe, so are unlikely to hold your interest for long. There are

exciting relaxing

WILDSCHÖNAU
Tirol

Wildschönau Tirol

The 51km of piste give skiers everything they are looking for, steep slopes and gentle family runs. The Wildschönau offers its guests a lift capacity that sets it aside from other resorts. With two gondolas, two chair lifts and 22 drag lifts there is no time lost by queuing and there are no overcrowded lifts.

The gentle Wildschönau hills are particularly suitable for families but there are also plenty of opportunities for experienced skiers, e.g. the FIS runs for the giant slalom and Super G and some magnificent deep-snow slopes. There is also a measured section where skiers can test their top speed. Carvers and snowboarders are welcome on all pistes and the Schatzberg mountain offers an enormous fun park with a half pipe, high jump, fun-box, snake, quarter pipe and wave ride both for fun and competition.

The Wildschönau is the host of the 6th Alpine Ski World Championships for the disabled. 27.01. – 07.02.2004

For more information contact:
Tourismusverband Wildschönau
A-6311 Wildschönau / Austria
Phone +43 5339 8255-0
Fax +43 5339 2433
E-Mail: info@wildschoenau.com
www.wildschoenau.com

KEY FACTS

Resort	830m
	2,720ft
Slopes	830-1905m
	2,720-6,250ft
Lifts	26
Pistes	51km
	32 miles
Blue	34%
Red	50%
Black	16%
Snowmaking	15km
	9 miles

Phone numbers

From elsewhere in Austria add the prefix 05339.
From abroad use the prefix +43 5339.

TOURIST OFFICE

t 8255
info@wildschoenau.
tirol.at
www.wildschoenau.
com

off-piste routes to be found, though – the Gern route, from the top of Schatzberg down a deserted valley to the road a little way from Auffach, is marked on the piste map.

Intermediates Niederau's ungroomed gully black runs are too awkward for most intermediates. The red runs generally merit their status, but don't add up to a lot. Auffach has more intermediate terrain, and the long main piste, from the top of Schatzberg to the village, is attractive.

Beginners There are excellent nursery slopes at the top and bottom of Niederau's main slopes, but the low ones don't get much sun in midwinter. Auffach has a slope just above the village. Oberau has its own nursery slopes, with a short black run above them. A real problem is the lack of really easy longer runs to progress to.

Cross-country There are 50km/31 miles of trails along the valley, which are good when snow is abundant.

Queues There are few queues in either of the main areas.

Mountain restaurants These are scarce but good, causing lunchtime queues as ski schools take a break. Many people lunch in the villages.

Schools and guides The ski schools have good reputations – a recent reporter raved about his beginner lessons. But classes can be large.

Facilities for children The kindergarten and nursery take kids from age two.

STAYING THERE

How to go There are a number of attractive hotels and guest houses in the three main villages – many with pools. Several major operators run packages to Niederau and Oberau.

Hotels In Niederau the 4-star Sonnschein (8353) is reportedly the best hotel. The Austria (8188) is another central recommendation. Last year a reporter gave the hotel Vicky, run by Thomson, a rave review – 'friendly staff, excellent food, brilliant crèche'. In Oberau is the oldest hotel in the valley – the 3-star Kellerwirt (8116), dating from 1200.

Eating out The restaurants at the hotels Alpenland and Wastl-Hof in Niederau have been recommended.

Après-ski Niederau has a nice balance of après-ski, neither too noisy for families nor too quiet for the young and lively. The Heustadl umbrella bar is popular at tea time. The Almbar and the Cave bar are popular later on. The Drift-Inn bar at Thomson's hotel Vicky is also recommended.

The other villages are quieter, once the tea-time jollity is over for the night.

Off the slopes There are excellent sleigh rides, horse-riding, organised walks and the Slow Train Wildschönau – on wheels not rails. Several hotel pools are open to the public and there's an outdoor ice rink. The best toboggan run is at Auffach. Shopping excursions to Innsbruck are possible.

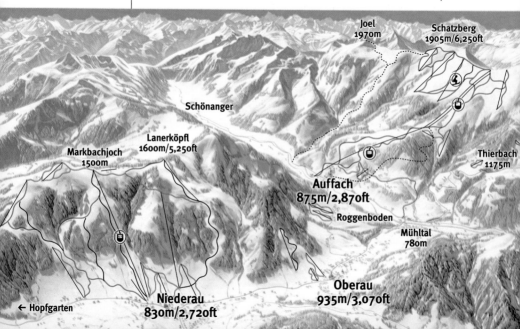

Zell am See

Charming lakeside town, varied slopes and glacier option at Kaprun

NEWS

In Zell am See the Zeller Bergbahn, the main lift out of the village, is being upgraded for 2003/04 to improve its performance.

In Kaprun, a 15-person gondola has now replaced the funicular that suffered a tragic fire in autumn 2000. The first stage of the Gletscherjet opened for the 2001/02 season and the upper section opened last winter.

+ Pretty, tree-lined slopes with great views down to the lake

+ Lively, but not rowdy, nightlife

+ Charming old town centre with beautiful lakeside setting

+ Lots to do off the slopes

+ Huge range of cross-country trails

+ Kaprun glacier nearby

+ Varied terrain including a couple of steep black runs

− Sunny, low slopes often have poor conditions despite snowmaking, which makes the area more limited

− Trek to lifts from much of the accommodation, and sometimes crowded buses

− Less suitable for beginners than most small Austrian resorts

− The Kaprun glacier gets lengthy queues when it is most needed

Zell am See is not a rustic village like most of its Austrian rivals, but a lakeside summer resort town with a charming old centre. For a small area, Zell's slopes have a lot of variety and challenging terrain, but not enough to keep a keen intermediate or expert happy for long – only 75km/47 miles of piste, if you ignore Kaprun's Kitzsteinhorn glacier. Zell is close to Kaprun, but if snow is in short supply Zell visitors have no special claim: you have to queue for access along with visitors bussed in from Saalbach, Kitzbühel and other low resorts.

THE RESORT

Zell am See is a long-established, year-round resort town set between a large lake and a mountain. Its charming, traffic-free medieval centre is on a flat promontory, and the resort has grown up around this attractive core. A gondola at the edge of town (served by ski-buses) goes up one arm of the horseshoe-shaped mountain, and there are hotels around here, too. 2km/1 mile away in the Schmittental, in the centre of the horseshoe, are two cable-cars; there is some accommodation, too.

A more radical alternative is to stay in Schüttdorf, 3km/2 miles away, where there is another gondola. But it is a characterless dormitory with little else going for it. Though closer to Kaprun, this is, perversely, a drawback unless you have a car. Trying to get on a glacier bus is tough, as they tend to be full when they leave Zell. Cross-country skiers and families wishing to use the Areitalm nursery stand to gain most from staying in Schüttdorf.

Kaprun's snow-sure glacier slopes are only a few minutes by bus; Saalbach is easily reached by bus and Bad Hofgastein by train. At a push, Wagrain, Schladming and Obertauern are car trips.

THE MOUNTAINS

Zell's mountain is horseshoe-shaped. The easiest runs are along the open ridges, with steeper pistes descending through woods to the Schmittental.

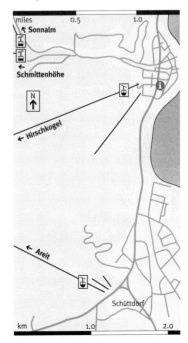

KEY FACTS

| Resort | 755m |
| | 2,480ft |

For Zell and Kaprun

Slopes	755-3030m
	2,480-9,940ft
Lifts	57
Pistes	130km
	81 miles
Blue	43%
Red	38%
Black	19%
Snowmaking	63km
	39 miles

For Zell only

Slopes	755-2000m
	2,480-6,560ft
Lifts	28
Pistes	75km
	47 miles
Snowmaking	50km
	31 miles

For Kaprun only

Slopes	785-3030m
	2,580-9,940ft
Lifts	29
Pistes	55km
	34 miles
Snowmaking	13km
	8 miles

THE SLOPES
Varied but limited

The town gondola (Zeller Bergbahn) takes you to Mittelstation. From there it's either an easy or a steep run to the cable-car station in the Schmittental. Or you can take a chair up to Hirschkogel to meet the gondola up from Schüttdorf – you can ride this up further or take an alternative chair to Schmittenhöhe. This is also where the main Schmittental cable-car brings you. A gentle cruise and a single short drag-lift moves you to Sonnkogel. Here several routes lead down to Sonnalm mid-station – where another cable-car from the Schmittental arrives. A black piste runs from here to the valley floor. At the end of the day you can take a gentle piste back to town or ride one of the lifts down.

TERRAIN-PARKS
Man-made and 'natural'

There's a half-pipe on Schmittenhöhe and a terrain-park on the Kitzsteinhorn glacier. A boarder last winter also enjoyed 'half-pipes' that had evolved on the glacier slopes.

SNOW RELIABILITY
Good snowmaking, but lots of sun

Zell am See's slopes get so much sun the snow can suffer as a result. Lots of slopes are now well covered by snow-guns, including the sunny home run to Schüttdorf and 70% of the lower slopes. But though reporters have seen 'lots of snowmaking in evidence', slush, ice and closed runs have still marred their holidays. The Kaprun glacier is snow-sure, but expect long queues there (and for buses to get there) when snow is short elsewhere.

FOR EXPERTS
Several blacks, but still limited

Zell has more steep slopes than most resorts this size, but can't entertain an expert for a week. When we were last there it was fabulous speeding down the immaculately groomed black runs 13 and 14 – they were deserted first thing in the morning. However, as a reporter points out, 'they are more like French reds'. Off-piste opportunities are limited.

FOR INTERMEDIATES
Bits and pieces for most grades

Good intermediates have a choice of fine, long runs, but this is not a place for mileage. All blacks are usually well groomed and within a brave intermediate's capability, and there's a lovely cruising run between Areit and Schüttdorf when conditions are good. Some Sonnkogel pistes are also suitable. The timid can cruise the ridge all day on quiet, attractive runs, or

Kitzsteinhorn
3030m/9,940ft

Alpincenter
2450m/8,040ft

Maiskogel

Schmittenhöhe
2000m/6,560ft

Berghotel

Hirschkogel
1720m

Breiteck

Sonnkogel
1850m

Glocknerhaus

Areit
1410m

Mittelstation
1320m

Sonnalm
1400m

Kaprun
785m/2,580ft

Schüttdorf

Schmittental

Zell am See
755m/2,480ft

LIFT PASSES

Europa–Sportregion Kaprun–Zell am See
Covers all lifts in Zell and Kaprun, and buses between them.

Beginners
Points card or limited pass.

Main pass
1-day pass €34.50
6-day pass €164

Children
Under 15: 6 days: €82
Under 6: free pass

Notes
1-day pass price is for Schmittenhöhe (Zell) only. Kitzsteinhorn-only and Maiskogel-only day passes also available.

Alternative passes
Salzburg Super Ski Card covers huge area round Salzburg province from Abtenau to Zell and is available for 3 days or more.

SCHOOLS

Zell am See
t 72324
skischule@zellamsee.at

Sport Alpin
t 0664 453 1417
info@sport-alpin.at

Classes
(Zell prices)
5 days (2hr am and pm) €135

Private lessons
€50 for 1 hr

head past Mittelstation to Zell's cable-cars on an easy blue.

Kaprun's high, snow-sure glacier runs are also ideal for intermediates not looking for too great a challenge.

FOR BEGINNERS
Two low nursery areas
There are small nursery slopes at the cable-car area and at Schüttdorf, both covered by snow-guns. Near-beginners and fast learners have plenty of short, easy runs at Schmittenhöhe, Breiteck and Areit. Some are used by complete beginners when snow conditions are poor lower down, but it means buying a lift pass.

FOR CROSS-COUNTRY
Excellent if snow allows
The valley floor has extensive trails, including a superb area on the Kaprun golf course. At altitude there are just two short loops, one at the top of the Kaprun glacier, and the other at the top of the Zell gondola.

QUEUES
Not normally a problem
Zell am See doesn't have many problems except at peak times, when the cable-cars are generally the worst hit. One reporter recommends getting to Schmittenhöhe via the Sonnalm cable-car as a quieter route.

When snow is poor there are few daytime queues at Zell – many people are away queueing at Kaprun – but getting down by lift at the end of the day can involve delays.

MOUNTAIN RESTAURANTS
Plenty of little refuges
There are plenty of cosy, atmospheric huts dotted around the Zell slopes, helpfully named on the piste map. Among the best are Glocknerhaus, Kettingalm, Areitalm ('superb, freshly made strudel') and Breiteckalm. Pinzgauer Hütte, in the woods at the back of Schmittenhöhe, is also recommended by reporters. The Berghotel at Schmittenhöhe is good, but expensive. Its bar with loud music is lively in the afternoons (see Après-ski). The Panorama-Pfiff gets crowded, but 'has wonderful views and quite good food'.

SCHOOLS AND GUIDES
A wide choice
There is a choice of schools in both Zell am See and Kaprun. We lack recent reports, but a reporter last year found boarding lessons from the main Zell school to be 'well organised', though classes were a bit large and English not always spoken fluently. There are also specialist cross-country centres at Schüttdorf and at Kaprun.

FACILITIES FOR CHILDREN
Schüttdorf's the place
We have no recent reports on the childcare provisions, but staying in Schüttdorf has the advantage of direct gondola access to the Areitalm snow-kindergarten, and the Ursula Zink nursery is at Zeller-Moos, just outside Schüttdorf. There's a children's adventure park on the mountain.

Zell am See

boarding

Zell is well suited to boarders. There's a high proportion of chairs, gondolas and cable-cars. You'll also find plenty of life in the evenings. The Kaprun glacier has powder in its wide, open bowl. But it also has a high proportion of drag-lifts – a day of this and the 'small walk' to enter the terrain-park exhausted some late-season visitors last winter who said 'a chair-lift would be most welcome'.

CHILDREN

The schools take children from age 4 and offer lunch-time care (5 days including lunch: €187.50). The Areitalm snow kindergarten runs from 9am to 4.30 for children from age 3.

The village nursery is Ursula Zink (56343), which takes children from age 3, from 9.30 to 3.30.

GETTING THERE

Air Salzburg 87km/54 miles (2hr); Munich 180km/112 miles (3hr).

Rail Station in resort.

TVB ZELL AM SEE

Zell's lakeside setting is very unusual ↓

STAYING THERE

HOW TO GO
Choose charm or convenience
Lots of hotels, pensions and apartments.
Hotels A broad range of hotels (more 4- than 3-stars) and guest houses.
((((4) **Salzburgerhof** (7650) Best in town – the only 5-star. It is nearer the lake than the gondola, but has courtesy bus and pool.
((((4) **Tirolerhof** (7720) Excellent 4-star in old town. 'Greatly improved' pool, hot-tub and steam room, 'very comfortable, very friendly and efficient staff,' says a reporter this year.
((((4) **Eichenhof** (47201) On outskirts of town, but popular and with a minibus service, great food and lake views.
((((4) **Alpin** (7690) Modern 4-star chalet next to the Zell gondola.
((((4) **Zum Hirschen** (7740) Comfortable 4-star, easy walk to gondola. Sauna, steam, splash pool, popular bar.
((((4) **Schwebebahn** (724610) Attractive 4-star in secluded setting in the Schmittental, by the cable-cars.
((((4) **Metzgerwirt** (72520) 4-star close lake and centre. 'Very good, really wild decor, friendly,' says a visitor.
((2) **Margarete** (72724) B&B in the Schmittental, by the cable-cars.
Self-catering Lots of options. Apartment Hofer (72430) is mid-range and close to the Ebenberg lift (linking to the gondola); no boarders. More comfortable are the 3-star Diana (72436) and Seilergasse (68787), both in the centre, and the Mirabell (72665), close to the Zell gondola.

STAYING UP THE MOUNTAIN
Three options
As well as the Berghotel (72489) at the top of the Schmittenhöhe cable-car, the Breiteckalm (73419) and Sonnalm (73262) restaurants have rooms.

EATING OUT
Plenty of choice
Zell has more non-hotel places than is usual in a small Austrian resort. The Ampere is quiet and sophisticated; Giuseppe's is a popular Italian with excellent food; and Kupferkessel and Traubenstüberl both do wholesome regional dishes. There are Chinese restaurants in Zell and Schüttdorf. Car drivers can try the excellent Erlhof.

APRES-SKI
Plenty for all tastes
Après-ski is lively and varied, with tea dances and high-calorie cafes, plus bars and discos aplenty. 'Even as a 55-year-old I had a great time pubbing,' says a reporter. When it's sunny, Schnapps Hans ice bar outside the Berghotel, up the mountain at Schmittenhöhe, really buzzes, with 'great music, a crazy DJ and dancing on tables and on the bar. All ages loved it'. The Diele disco bar rocks; Crazy Daisy on the main road has two crowded bars and 'the group loved it' says one reporter. Classics (which used to be Evergreen) has a live band and 60s and 70s music. The Viva disco allows no under 18s; one reader proclaimed it 'excellent'. Or try the smart Hirschenkeller, the cave-like Lebzelter Keller and the Sportstüberl, with nostalgic ski photos adorning the walls.

OFF THE SLOPES
Lots of choices
There is plenty to do in this year-round resort. The train trip to Salzburg is a must, Kitzbühel is also well worth a visit and Innsbruck is within reach.

You can often walk across the frozen lake to Thumersbach, plus there are good sports facilities, a motor museum, sleigh rides and flights.

ACTIVITIES

Indoor Swimming, sauna, solarium, fitness centre, spa, tennis, squash, bowling, museum, art gallery, cinema, library, massage, ice skating

Outdoor Riding, skating, curling, floodlit toboggan runs, plane flights, sleigh rides, shooting range, swimming (Kaprun), ice-sailing, ice-surfing, tubing

Phone numbers
Zell am See
From elsewhere in Austria add the prefix 06542.
From abroad use the prefix +43 6542.

Kaprun
From elsewhere in Austria add the prefix 06547.
From abroad use the prefix +43 6547.

TOURIST OFFICES

Zell am See
t 770
zell@gold.at
www.zellamsee.com

Kaprun
t 808021
kaprun@kaprun.net
www.europa-sport-region.co

Kaprun 785m/2,580ft

THE RESORT
Kaprun is a spacious, charming and quite lively village. The main road to the glacier bypasses it, leaving the centre pleasantly quiet.

THE MOUNTAIN
There is a small area of slopes on the outskirts of the village at Maiskogel, served by a cable-car and drag-lifts and best suited to early intermediates, and there is also a separate nursery area. But most people will want to spend most of their time on the slopes of the nearby Kitzsteinhorn glacier or on Zell am See's slopes. Both are an often crowded bus-ride away. The lift pass covers only one ascent of the Kitzsteinhorn access gondola per day.

Slopes A 15-person, two-stage gondola has now replaced the funicular, which suffered a tragic fire in autumn 2000. The first-stage runs parallel with the existing eight-person gondola, ending in the same mid-mountain area. The second stage, up to the Alpincenter and main slopes, runs parallel to a fast quad chair. The main slopes are in a big bowl above the Alpincenter served by a cable-car, lots of T-bars and three chairs. The area above the top of the Alpincenter is open in summer and is particularly good for an early pre-Christmas or late post-Easter break.

Snow reliability Snow is nearly always good because of the glacier. And more snowmaking was added for 2002/03.

Queues The new gondola has a 50% higher capacity than the funicular it replaced, so queues at the bottom should be much relieved. But queues up on the mountain have always been bad at times when crowds are bussed in because snow is poor elsewhere.

Mountain restaurants There are three decent mountain restaurants – the Gletschermühle and Krefelderhütte near the Alpincenter, and the Häusalm near the new gondola mid-station. All these get busy. Bella Vista at the top of the mountain has good views.

Experts There's little to challenge experts except for some good off-piste; the one slightly tough piste starts at the very top.

Intermediates Pistes are mainly gentle blues and reds and make for great easy cruising on usually good snow. From Alpincenter there is an entertaining red run down to the new gondola mid-station. This is our favourite run on the mountain, though it does get crowded. There's also a good unpisted ski route.

Beginners There are a couple of nursery slopes in the village and there are gentle blues on the glacier to progress to.

Snowboarding There's a terrain-park on the glacier and some excellent natural half-pipes.

Cross-country The Kaprun golf course is superb, but at altitude there is just one short loop – at the top of the glacier.

Schools and guides There are several ski schools all offering the usual classes.

Facilities for children All of the schools offer children's classes and there's a kindergarten in the village.

STAYING THERE
How to go There are some catered chalets and chalet-hotels.

Hotels The Orgler (8205), 'spacious' Mitteregger (8207) and Tauernhof (8235) are among the best hotels.

Après-ski Nightlife is quiet, but the Baum bar is lively.

Eating out Good restaurants include the Dorfstadl, Hilberger's Beisl and Schlemmerstube.

Off the slopes Off-slope activities are good, and include a fine sports centre with outdoor rapids.

France

France overtook Austria as the most popular destination for British skiers and snowboarders some years ago, and it is by far the most popular country with our readers. It's not difficult to see why. France has the biggest lift-and-piste networks in the world; for those who like to cover as many miles in a day as possible, these are unrivalled. Most of these big areas are also at high altitude, ensuring high-quality snow for a long season. And French mountains offer a mixture of some of the toughest, wildest slopes in the Alps, and some of the longest, gentlest and most convenient beginner runs.

French resort villages can't be quite so uniformly recommended; but, equally, they don't all conform to the standard image of soulless, purpose-built service stations, thrown up without concern for appearance during the boom of the 1960s and 70s.

The French resorts we flock to are big names, where prices are never going to seem low; but when the pound was down near 7 francs they seemed criminally high. Since the advent of the euro, they haven't been that bad, but as we go to press in July 2003, a pound buys less than 1.4 euros, down from 1.5 a year ago – and at that level things are going to seem pretty pricey this coming winter.

Towards the front of the book there is a special chapter on driving to the French Alps – increasingly popular, especially with people going self-catering. The northern French Alps are easy to get to by car, and comfortable apartments are becoming more common as the French continue their retreat from the short-sighted ways of the 1960s.

ANY STYLE OF RESORT YOU LIKE

The main drawback to France, hinted at in our introduction, is the monstrous architecture of some of the purpose-built resorts. But not all French resorts are hideous. Certainly, France has its fair share of Alpine eyesores, chief among them central Les Menuires, central La Plagne, Flaine, Tignes, Isola 2000 and Les Arcs. The redeeming features of places like these are the splendid quality of the slopes they serve, the reliability and quality of the snow, and the amazing slope-side convenience of most of the accommodation.

But the French have learnt the lesson that new development doesn't have to be tasteless to be convenient – look at Valmorel, Belle-Plagne and Les Coches, for example, and the newer parts of Isola 2000, Flaine or Les Menuires. Val-Thorens, always one of the more acceptable new resorts, is being extended sensitively, too.

If you prefer, there are genuinely old mountain villages to stay in, linked directly to the big lift networks. These are not usually as convenient for the slopes, but they give you a feel of being in France rather than in a winter-holiday factory. Examples include Montchavin or Champagny for La Plagne, Vaujany for Alpe-d'Huez, St-Martin-de-Belleville for the Trois Vallées and Les Carroz, Morillon or Samoëns (now with a gondola to the slopes) for Flaine. There are also old villages with their own slopes that have developed as resorts while retaining some or all of their rustic ambience – such as Serre-

SNOWPIX.COM / CHRIS GILL

← Courchevel 1850 is the most fashionable and one of the best high-altitude French resorts

Getting around the French Alps

Pick the right gateway – Geneva, Chambéry or Grenoble – and you can hardly go wrong. The approach to Serre-Chevalier and Montgenèvre involves the 2058m/6,750ft Col du Lauteret; but the road is a major one and kept clear of snow or reopened quickly after a fall. Crossing the French-Swiss border between Chamonix and Verbier involves two closure-prone passes – the Montets and the Forclaz. When necessary, one-way traffic runs beside the tracks through the rail tunnel beneath the passes.

Chevalier and La Clusaz. Megève deserves a special mention – an exceptionally charming little town combining rustic style with luxury and sophistication; shame about the traffic.

And France has Alpine centres with a long mountaineering and skiing history. Chief among these is Chamonix, which sits in the shadow of Mont Blanc, Europe's highest peak, and is the centre of the most radical off-piste terrain in the Alps. Chamonix is a big, bustling town, where skiing and boarding go on alongside tourism in general. At the opposite end of the vacation spectrum is tiny La Grave, at the foot of mountains that are almost as impressive – the highest within France – but with only a few simple hotels.

One of the most welcome developments on the French resort scene in recent years has been the availability of genuinely comfortable and stylish apartments, in contrast to the cramped and frankly primitive places that have dominated the market since the 1960s. Central to this shift has been a company called MGM, which has developed apartments (and some chalets) in 10 resorts, mostly with their own pool and spa, as well as rooms of normal size.

This trend is reinforced by the involvement in French resorts of North American money and expertise, in the form of investment by the Canadian company Intrawest. In the last few years the company has become active in land development in Les Arcs, Les Menuires, La Plagne and Flaine.

It is Intrawest, developers of Whistler and other pace-setting resorts in North America, that has driven a revolutionary development in (or rather just below) Les Arcs 2000. This new development – Arc 1950 – offers accommodation of a quality and style rarely seen on a large scale in French resorts. Intrawest seems to

Introduction

203

have got it right so far – the first phases of Arc 1950 sold out within
hours of being put on the market, in advance of construction. The
first apartments should be on the rental market for the 2003/04
season.

Intrawest has also played a part in the plans of the increasingly
powerful Compagnie des Alpes. This enterprise now has a serious
stake (in some cases a majority stake, and in one or two cases 100%)
in the lift companies of Chamonix, Tignes, La Plagne, Les Arcs, Les
Menuires, Méribel and Flaine – as well as Courmayeur in Italy and
Saas-Fee and Verbier in Switzerland. Major developments such as the
cable-car link between La Plagne and Les Arcs, due to open for the
coming 2003/04 season, start to make sense in this context.

France has advantages over most rival destinations in the
gastronomic stakes. While many of its mountain restaurants serve
fast food, most also do at least a *plat du jour* that is in a different
league from what you'll find in Austria or the US. It is generally
possible to find somewhere to get a half-decent lunch and to have it
served at your table, rather than queuing repeatedly for every
element of your meal. In the evening, most resorts have restaurants
serving good, traditional, French food as well as regional specialities.
And the wine is decent and affordable.

Many French resorts (though not all) have suffered from a lack of
nightlife, but things have changed in recent years. In resorts
dominated by apartments with few international visitors, there may
still be very little going on after dinner, but places like Méribel are
now distinctly lively in the evening. (It should also be said that
nightlife isn't important to many British holidaymakers. Most of our
reporting readers say they can't recommend nightspots because all
they want to do after dinner is to fall into bed.)

France is unusual among European countries in using four grades
of piste instead of the usual three – a system of which we heartily
approve. The very easiest runs are classified green; except in Val-
d'Isère, they are reliably gentle. Since it's relative novices who care
most about choosing just the right sort of terrain to build
confidence, this is a genuinely helpful system, and one that ought to
be adopted internationally.

AVOID THE CROWDS
French school holidays mean crowded slopes, so they are worth
avoiding if possible. The country is divided into three zones, with
three fortnight holidays staggered over a four-week period – this
season, 7 Feb to 8 Mar; from 14 Feb to 1 Mar the Paris/Bordeaux
holidays overlap with the other zones – Lyon/Grenoble in the first
week, Marseille/most of northern France in the second week.

Alpe-d'Huez

An impressive and improving all-rounder; a pity it's so sunny

COSTS

① ② ③ ④ ⑤ ⑥

RATINGS

The slopes

Snow	****
Extent	****
Expert	****
Intermediate	****
Beginner	*****
Convenience	****
Queues	****
Mountain restaurants	****

The rest

Scenery	****
Resort charm	*
Off-slope	***

NEWS

For 2003/04 the Lac Blanc chair-lift will be upgraded to a quad and chairs will be added to the Alpe Auris chair-lift to increase capacity.

There is a new chalet development above Les Bergers.

Snowmaking is being increased in the Lievre Blanc area.

For 2004/05 a Funitel jumbo gondola will be built from the top of the existing Marmotte gondola to the Sarenne glacier, creating a second route to the glacier. This is part of a plan to make fuller use of the glacier; following the new Glacier chair in 2001, the lower Herpie chair was added in 2002, opening up some new runs.

Some buildings are in traditional style, but most are not →

➕ Extensive, high, sunny slopes, split interestingly into various sectors

➕ Huge snowmaking installation to keep runs open despite the sun

➕ Vast, gentle, sunny nursery slopes right next to the resort

➕ Efficient, modern lift system, with few long waits

➕ Grand views of the peaks in the Ecrins national park

➕ Some good, surprisingly rustic mountain restaurants

➕ Short walks to and from the slopes

➕ More animated than most purpose-built resorts

➕ Pleasant alternative bases in outlying villages and satellites

➖ In late season the many south-facing runs can be icy early in the day and slushy in the afternoon

➖ Some main intermediate runs get badly overcrowded in high season

➖ Many of the tough runs are very high, and inaccessible or very tricky in bad weather

➖ Practically no woodland runs to retreat to in bad weather

➖ Run gradings tend to understate difficulty

➖ Messy, sprawling resort with a hotchpotch of architectural styles, no central focus and very little charm

There are few places to rival Alpe-d'Huez for extent and variety of terrain – in good conditions, it's one of our favourites. But, in late season at least, despite an ever-expanding snowmaking network, the 'island in the sun' suffers from the very thing it advertises: strong sun means that ice can make mornings miserably hard work, however alluring the prospect of slushy moguls in the afternoons.

The village has few fans, but if you don't like the sound of it you always have the alternative of staying in rustic Villard-Reculas, Vaujany (with its mighty cable-car), or in the more ski-stations of Oz-en-Oisans or Auris.

THE RESORT

Alpe-d'Huez is a large village spread across an open mountainside, high above the Romanche valley, east of Grenoble. It was one of the venues for the 1968 Grenoble Winter Olympics, and then grew quickly in a seemingly unplanned way. Its buildings come in all shapes, sizes and designs (including a futuristic church which hosts weekly organ concerts). Many look scruffy and in need of renovation, although some wood cladding and general smartening-up can now be seen. It is a large, amorphous resort; the nearest thing to a central focus is the main Avenue des Jeux in the middle, where you'll find the swimming pool, ice skating and some of the shops, bars and restaurants. The rest of the resort spreads out in a triangle, with lift stations at two of the apexes.

The bus service around the resort is free with the lift pass, and there's a

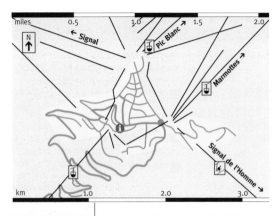

KEY FACTS

Resort	1860m
	6,100ft
Slopes	1120-3320m
	3,670-10,890ft
Lifts	87
Pistes	230km
	143 miles
Green	35%
Blue	27%
Red	25%
Black	13%
Snowmaking	53km
	33 miles

handy, but slow, bucket-lift (with a piste beneath it) running through the resort to the main lifts at the top. It doesn't operate in the evenings.

A short distance from the main body of the resort (and linked by chair-lift) are the 'hamlets' – apartment blocks, mainly – of Les Bergers and L'Eclose.

Les Bergers, at the eastern entrance to the resort, is convenient for the slopes (with its own nursery area), but it's a trek from most of the other resort facilities. There are a couple of bar/restaurants and several shops near the slopes. This quarter is now being expanded uphill by construction of a chalet suburb, convenient for skiing but remote from the village centre.

L'Eclose, to the south of the main village, is the least convenient location and has even less to offer.

There is accommodation down the hill in the old village of Huez, linked by lift to the resort.

Outings by road are feasible to other resorts covered on a week's lift pass, including Serre-Chevalier and Les Deux-Alpes. The day trip to Les Deux-Alpes by helicopter for a surprisingly modest fee of around £40 return is 'highly recommended'.

THE MOUNTAINS

Alpe-d'Huez is a big-league resort, ranking alongside giants like Val-d'Isère or La Plagne for the extent and variety of its slopes. Practically all the slopes are above the tree line, and there may be precious little to do when a storm socks in; the runs around Oz are your best bet (if you can get to them).

The piste grading is unreliable; it occasionally overstates difficulty, but more often does the opposite.

THE SLOPES
Several well-linked areas

The slopes can be divided into four main sectors, with good connections between them.

The biggest sector is directly above the village, on the slopes of **Pic Blanc**. There is sport here for everyone, from excellent tough pitches at the top to vast, gentle beginner slopes at the bottom. The huge Grandes Rousses gondola, otherwise known as the DMC (a reference to its clever technology), goes up in two stages from the top of the village. Above it, a cable-car goes up to 3320m/10,890ft on Pic Blanc itself – the top of the Sarenne glacier – where the runs are genuinely black. A lower area of challenging runs at Clocher de Macle, previously accessed by a slow chair, is much more attractive now that it is served by the recently extended Marmottes gondola.

The Sarenne gorge separates the main resort area from **Signal de l'Homme**. A spectacular down-and-up fast chair-lift accesses this area from the Bergers part of the village. From the top you can take excellent north-facing slopes back down towards the gorge, or head south to Auris or west to the old hamlet of Chatelard. The return from here is now by a double chair-lift, instead of the famously tricky drag-lift of old.

On the other side of town from Signal de l'Homme is the small **Signal** sector, reached by drag-lifts next to the main gondola or by a couple of chairs lower down. Runs go down the other side of the hill to the old village of Villard-Reculas. The Signal blue run back to Alpe-d'Huez is now floodlit three nights a week.

The **Vaujany-Oz** sector consists largely of north-west-facing slopes, accessible from Alpe-d'Huez via good red runs from either the mid-station or the top of the big gondola. At the heart of this sector is Alpette, the mid-station of the two-stage cable-car from Vaujany. From here a disastrously sunny red goes down to Oz, and a much more reliable blue goes north to the Vaujany home slopes around Montfrais. The links back to Alpe-d'Huez are made by the top cable-car from Alpette, or a gondola from Oz.

Since the black Fare piste was created from below Alpette to Enversin, just below Vaujany, an on-piste descent of 2200m/7,220ft has been possible – not the biggest

Alpe-d'Huez

LIFT PASSES

Visalp
Covers all lifts in Alpe-d'Huez, Auris, Oz, Vaujany and Villard-Reculas.

Beginners
One-day beginner pass €10.50

Main pass
1-day pass €33
6-day pass €171.50

Senior citizens
Over 60: 6-day pass €121.50
Over 70: free pass

Children
Under 16: 6-day pass €121.50
Under 5: free pass

Notes
Pass for 6 days or more allows one day's skiing at each of Les Deux Alpes, Serre-Chevalier, Puy-St-Vincent and the Milky Way in Italy. The pass also covers the Alpe d'Huez sports centre (skating and swimming) and the pool in Vaujany.

Alternative passes
Passes for Auris only, Oz-Vaujany only, Villard-Reculas only.

---

vertical in the Alps, but not far short. The area does offer the longest piste in the Alps – the 16km/10 mile Sarenne on the back of the Pic Blanc (see the special feature box).

TERRAIN-PARKS
A choice
There's a good terrain-park and a half-pipe near the main lift base as well as in Auris.

SNOW RELIABILITY
Affected by the sun
Alpe-d'Huez is unique among major purpose-built resorts in the Alps in having mainly south- or south-west-facing slopes. The strong southern sun means that late-season conditions may alternate between slush and ice on most of the area, with some of the lower runs being closed altogether. There are shady slopes above Vaujany and at Signal de l'Homme – and there is a glacier area on the Pic Blanc, open in summer. This area is being enlarged, but will still be too small to pin all your hopes on in the winter; it is no Grande Motte. The orientation of the slopes is a real drawback of the area as a whole.

In more wintry circumstances the runs are relatively snow-sure, the natural stuff being backed up by extensive snowmaking, covering the main runs above Alpe-d'Huez, Vaujany and Oz, though there is none on the back of Signal down to Villard-Reculas.

FOR EXPERTS
Plenty of blacks and off-piste
This is an excellent resort for experts, with long and challenging black runs (and reds that ought to be black) as well as serious off-piste options.

The slope beneath the Pic Blanc cable-car, usually an impressive mogul-field, is reached by a 300m/1,000ft tunnel from the back side of the mountain. The tunnel exit was altered a few years ago, supposedly creating a less awkward start to the actual slope; but it is still tricky. The slope itself is of ordinary black steepness, but can be very hard in the mornings because it gets a lot of sun. The run splits up part-way down – a couple of variants take you to the Lac Blanc chair back up to the Pic Blanc cable-car.

The terrain opened up by the new glacier lift includes some excellent off-piste. The long Sarenne run on the back of the Pic Blanc is described in a special feature box. There are several off-piste variants. There are also other very long off-piste descents over the bigger glaciers to the north and east, with verticals of 1900m to 2200m (6,000ft to 7,220ft), for which guidance is essential. Some end up in Vaujany, others in Clavans (where you need a taxi back), others in more remote spots where you need a helicopter back.

There is good off-piste in several other sectors, too – notably from Signal towards Villard-Reculas and Huez – and from Signal de l'Homme in

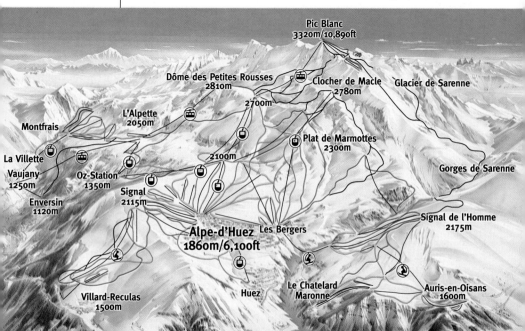

various directions; the slopes above Auris are a particular favourite of locals. And there's abundant off-piste on the lower half of the mountain that is excellent in good snow conditions, including lovely runs through scattered trees at the extreme northern edge of the area above Vaujany. We've never found the black Fare piste to Vaujany open, but a reporter rates it 'great – cold and shady'.

Some of the upper red pistes are tough enough to give experts a challenge. These include the Canyon and Balme runs accessed by the Lièvre Blanc chair-lift from the gondola mid-station – runs which are unprepared and south-facing (late in the day, perhaps best tackled on a board), and steep enough to be classified black in many resorts. Above this, the Marmottes II gondola serves another series of steep black runs from Clocher de Macle including the beautiful, long, lonely Combe Charbonniere.

FOR INTERMEDIATES
Fine selection of runs
Good intermediates have a fine selection of runs all over the area. In good snow conditions the variety of runs is difficult to beat. Every section has some challenging red runs to test the adventurous intermediate. The most challenging are the Canyon and Balme runs, mentioned previously. There are lovely long runs down to Oz and to Vaujany. The off-piste among the trees above Vaujany, mentioned earlier, is a good place to start your off-piste career in good snow. The

Villard-Reculas and Signal de l'Homme sectors also have long challenging reds. The Chamois red from the top of the gondola down to the mid-station is beautiful but quite narrow, and miserable when busy and icy. Fearless intermediates should enjoy most of the super-long black runs from Pic Blanc.

For less ambitious intermediates, there are usually blue alternatives. The main Couloir blue from the top of the big gondola is a lovely run, well served by snowmaking, but it does get scarily crowded at times.

There are some great cruising runs above Vaujany; but the red runs between Vaujany and Alpe-d'Huez can be too much for early intermediates. Unless you are prepared to travel via Oz on gondolas, you are effectively confined to one sector or the other.

Early intermediates will also enjoy the gentle slopes leading back to Alpe-d'Huez from the main mountain, and the Signal sector.

FOR BEGINNERS
Good facilities
The large network of green runs immediately above the village is as good a nursery area as you will find anywhere. Sadly, it carries a lot of fast through-traffic. A large area embracing half a dozen runs has been declared a low-speed zone protégée, but the restriction is not policed and so achieves very little. Add to the quality of the slopes the convenience, availability of good lessons, a special lift pass covering 11 lifts, and Alpe-d'Huez is difficult to beat.

THE LONGEST PISTE IN THE ALPS – AND IT'S BLACK?

It's no surprise that most ski runs that are seriously steep are also seriously short. The really long runs in the Alps tend to be classified blue, or red at the most. The Parsenn runs above Klosters, for example – typically 12km to 15km (7 miles to 9 miles) long – are manageable in your first week on skis. Even Chamonix's famous Vallée Blanche off-piste run doesn't include steepness in its attractions.

So you could be forgiven for being sceptical about the 'black' Sarenne run from the top of the Pic Blanc to the Sarenne gorge that separates the resort from the Signal de l'Homme sector. Even though the vertical is an impressive 2000m/6,500ft, a run 16km/10 miles in length means an average gradient of only 11% – typical of a blue run. Macho-hype on the part of the lift company, presumably?

Not quite. The Sarenne is a run of two halves. The bottom half is virtually flat (boarders beware) but the top half is a genuine black if you take the direct route – a demanding and highly satisfying run (with stunning views) that any keen, competent skier will enjoy. The steep mogul-field near the top can now be avoided by taking a newly created easier option; and the whole run can now be tackled by an adventurous intermediate. The run gets a lot of sun, so pick your time with care – there's nothing worse than a sunny run with no sun.

↑ There is a huge area of gentle slopes immediately above the village – this is only one part, above Les Bergers

AGENCE NUTS / OT ALPE-D'HUEZ

the old trouble spots was eliminated.

The small Pic Blanc cable-car is still queue-prone and is often closed by bad weather; both problems should be relieved by the planned Marmottes III gondola, due in 2004. Two of the black runs down the face of Pic Blanc require use of the Lac Blanc chair-lift to get back up to the cable-car; the inadequate double chair is being replaced by a quad. Although they may not cause queues, there are lots of old drag-lifts scattered around.

A greater problem than lift queues, over much of the area, is that the main pistes can be unbearably crowded. We and our reporters rate the Chamois and Couloir runs from the top of the DMC worst we have ever seen.

FOR CROSS-COUNTRY
High-level and convenient
There are 50km/31 miles of trails, with three loops of varying degrees of difficulty, all at around 2000m/6,560ft and consequently relatively snow-sure. You need a cross-country pass to use the trails.

QUEUES
Generally few problems
Even in French holiday periods, the modern lift system ensures there are few long hold-ups. Queues can build up for the gondolas out of the village, but the DMC shifts its queue impressively quickly. The Marmottes I gondola was given extra cabins for 2001/02, shortening waiting times. With the recently installed Lièvre Blanc quad and Marmottes II gondola, one of

MOUNTAIN RESTAURANTS
Some excellent rustic huts
Mountain restaurants are generally good – even self-service places are welcoming, and there are many more rustic places with table-service than you'd expect to find in French purpose-built resorts. One of our favourites is the cosy little Chalet du Lac Besson, on one of the cross-country loops north of the big gondola mid-station – the route to it now has piste status (the Boulevard des Lacs blue), but is no easier to follow in practice.

The pretty Forêt de Maronne hotel at Chatelard, below Signal de l'Homme, is delightful and has a good choice of traditional French cuisine. The Combe Haute, at the foot of the Chalvet chair in the gorge towards the end of the Sarenne run, is welcoming but gets very busy. The Hermine, at the base of the Fontfroide lift, is recommended for basic but good-value food. The terrace of the Perce-Neige, just below the Oz-Poutran gondola mid-station, attracts crowds. The Plage des Neiges at the top of the nursery slopes is one of the best places available to beginners. The Bergerie at Villard-Reculas has good views and is highly recommended by reporters. The Alpette and Super Signal places are also worth a visit.

boarding
The resort suits experienced boarders well – the extent and variety of the mountains mean that there's a lot of good free-riding to be had. And, if there's good snow, the off-piste is vast and varied and well worth checking out with a guide. Unfortunately for beginners, the main nursery slopes are almost all accessed by drag-lifts, but these can be avoided once a modicum of control has been achieved. Planète Surf is the main snowboard shop.

SCHOOLS

ESF
t 0476 803169

International
t 0476 804277
mgm.international@
wanadoo.fr

Classes (ESF prices)
6 days (3hr am and
2½hr pm) €149

Private lessons
€31 for 1hr, for 1 or
2 people.

CHILDREN

The main schools run
ski kindergartens.

At Les Bergers the
ESF Club des Oursons
(0476 803169) takes
children from age 4
during ski school
hours (6 days €135).

The Eterlous day care
centre (0476 806785),
in Les Bergers, has a
private slope area
and takes children
aged 2 to 11 all day.

Les Crapouilloux day-
care centre (0476
113923), next to the
tourist information
office, takes kids from
2 to 11.

The International
school (0476 804277)
runs the Baby-Club
for children aged 3 to
4, and the Club des
Marmottes for those
aged 4 to 12.

The Club Med nursery
takes children from 4,
with or without
lessons.

Chantebise 2100, at the DMC mid-
station, offers slick and cheerful table
service. The Cabane du Poutat, halfway
down from Plat de Marmottes, is
recommended for good food and
service. Back in the village, lunch on
the terrace at the hotel Christina – by
the top of the bucket-lifts – is a
pleasant option.

The restaurants in the Oz and
Vaujany sectors tend to be cheaper. At
Montfrais, the Airelles is a rustic hut,
built into the rock, with a roaring log
fire, atmospheric music and excellent,
good-value food. The Auberge de
l'Alpette gets two enthusiastic
recommendations this year, both
emphasising 'really good value'.

SCHOOLS AND GUIDES
Contrasting views of the schools
We have a couple of reasonable
reports on the ESF, which has
apparently improved its act recently –
'Good spoken English and good level
of instruction.' However, class sizes are
seemingly on the big side. One recent
reporter counted 14 in a class.

A reporter this year endorses
favourable past reports of Masterclass,
an independent school run by private
British instructor Stuart Adamson: 'We
cannot praise him too highly.' Class
sizes are limited to eight. Advance
booking during high season is advised.
The Bureau des Guides also has a
good reputation.

FACILITIES FOR CHILDREN
Mixed reports
We've had rave reviews in the past of
the International school's classes for
children. Reports on the ESF, on the
other hand, have been mixed. Les
Crapouilloux day-care centre is 'very
well organised' and has been
recommended, as has tour operator
Crystal's child care operation by a
reporter last season.

HOW TO GO
Something of everything
Chalets UK tour operators run quite a
few chalet-hotels, and some are
offering smaller chalets in the new
development above Les Bergers.
Hotels There are more hotels than is
usual in a high French resort, and
there's a clear downmarket bias, with
more 1-stars than 2- or 3-stars, and
only two 4-stars. There is a huge Club
Med at Les Bergers.
((((4) **Royal Ours Blanc** (0476 803550)
Central. Luxurious, with good food.
Superb fitness centre. Free (but often
oversubscribed) minibus to the lifts.
(((3) **Au Chamois d'Or** (0476 803132)
Good facilities, modern rooms, one of
the best restaurants in town and well
placed for main gondola.
(((3) **Cimes** (0476 803431) South-facing
rooms, excellent food; close to cross-
resort lift and pistes.
(((3) **Grandes Rousses** (0476 803311)
Recommended for 'superb food' and
views down valley; close to lifts.
((2) **Mariandre** (0476 806603)
Comfortable hotel with good food,
recommended by readers. Some small
rooms. Next to the bucket-lift.
((2) **Gentianes** (0476 803576) Close to
the Sarenne gondola in Les Bergers; a
range of rooms, the best comfortable.
Self-catering There is an enormous
choice of apartments available. The
Pierre et Vacances residence near the
Marmottes gondola in Les Bergers
offers a high standard of
accommodation with good facilities.
The Maison de l'Alpe close to the DMC
has been recommended for its ideal
location and good facilities.

EATING OUT
Good value
Alpe-d'Huez has dozens of restaurants,
some of high quality; many offer good
value by French resort standards. The
Crémaillère, at the bottom end of
town, is highly recommended by a
frequent visitor. Au P'tit Creux gets a
similarly positive review for excellent
food and ambience, though a reporter
this year thought it 'getting expensive'.
The 'outstanding' Génépi is a friendly
old place with good cuisine. The
Pomme de Pin is also very popular.
The Fromagerie and Rabelais are
others worth a try. And the Origan,
Remise and Pinocchio pizzerias serve
good, wholesome Italian fare.

GETTING THERE

Air Lyon 150km/93 miles (3hr); Geneva 220km/137 miles (4hr); Grenoble, 63km/39 miles (1½hr).

Rail Grenoble (63km/39 miles); daily buses from station.

ACTIVITIES

Indoor Sports centre (tennis, gym, squash, aerobics, climbing wall), library, cinema, swimming pool, billiards, bridge

Outdoor Artificial skating rink (skating and curling), 30km/19 miles of cleared paths, outdoor swimming pool, hang-gliding, paragliding, all-terrain carts, quad-bikes

Phone numbers From abroad use the prefix +33 and omit the initial '0' of the phone number.

TOURIST OFFICE

Alpe-d'Huez t 0476 114444 info@alpedhuez.com www.alpedhuez.com

APRES-SKI
Getting better all the time

The resort gets more animated each year and there's now a wide range of bars on offer, some of which get fairly lively later on. One complaint is that they are widely dispersed, making pub crawls fairly time-consuming.

Of the British-run bars, the Roadhouse in Crystal's hotel Vallée Blanche and the Underground in Neilson's hotel Chamois are established favourites. O'Sharkey's and the Pacific (sister bar to the one in Val d'Isère) are also popular. Smithy's does good Tex-Mex food and can get pretty rowdy late on.

The little Avalanche bar is popular with locals and visitors alike, and often has live music. The P'tit Bar de l'Alpe takes some beating for atmosphere, and also has live music. The Sporting is a large but friendly French rendezvous with a live band. The Etalon and Free Ride cafes are also popular. And the Dutch-run Melting Pot does good tapas and is great for a relaxed drink, as is the Zoo.

The Stage One and Igloo discos liven up whenever the French are in town en masse.

OFF THE SLOPES
Good by purpose-built standards

There is a wide range of facilities, including an indoor pool, an open-air pool (boxer-style cozzies not allowed), Olympic-size ice rink and splendid sports centre – all of this covered by the lift pass. There's also an ice-driving school. Shops are numerous, but limited in range. The helicopter excursion to Les Deux-Alpes is amusing. It's a pity that the better mountain restaurants aren't easily accessible to pedestrians.

Villard-Reculas
1500m/4,920ft

Villard-Reculas is a secluded village, just over the hill (Signal) from Alpe-d'Huez, complete with an old church, set on a small shelf wedged between

Alpe-d'Huez

211

Selected chalets in Villard-Reculas

Phone numbers
From abroad use the prefix +33 and omit the initial '0' of the phone number.

an expanse of open snowfields above and tree-filled hillsides below. Following the installation of a fast quad chair up to Signal a few years back, the village is becoming more popular as an access point and it is now beginning to find its feet as a 'resort'. Its visitor beds are mainly in self-catering apartments and chalets, booked either through the tourist office or La Source – an English-run outfit which also runs a comfortable catered chalet in a carefully converted stone barn. There is one 2-star hotel, the Beaux Monts (0476 803032). There is a store 'almost like a trading post' and a couple of bars and restaurants.

The local slopes have something for everyone – including a nursery slope at village level – and there is a branch of the Ecole du Ski Français.

Oz-en-Oisans
1350m/4,430ft
The purpose-built ski station above the attractive old village of Oz-en-Oisans apparently now takes its parent's name. The village is now reasonably developed – with a ski school, three sports shops, nursery slopes, bars, four restaurants, a supermarket and a skating rink. There's also a large underground car park. Attractive new chalets and apartment blocks have been built in a sympathetic style, with much use of wood and stone and there is a hotel, the Hors piste (0476 798662). Two gondolas whisk you out of the resort – one goes to Alpette above Vaujany and the other in two stages to the mid-station of the DMC above Alpe d'Huez. To quote recent visitors, Oz is now 'taking off' and is 'relatively lively'. But another complains that there is still no nightlife. The main run home is liberally endowed with snow-guns, but it needs to be. One clear advantage of staying here is that the slopes above Oz are about the best in the area when heavy snow is falling – and those based elsewhere may not be able to reach them.

Auris 1600m/5,250ft
Auris is a series of wood-clad, chalet-style apartment blocks with a few shops, bars and restaurants, pleasantly set close to the thickest woodland in the area. It's a fine family resort, with everything close to hand, including a nursery and a ski kindergarten. There's also a ski school. Beneath it is the original old village, complete with attractive, traditional buildings, a church and all but one of the resort's hotels. Staying here with a car you can drive up to the local lifts or make excursions to neighbouring resorts such as Serre-Chevalier.

Unsurprisingly, evenings are quiet, with a handful of bar-restaurants to choose from. **The Beau Site (0476 800639), which looks like an apartment block, is the only hotel in the upper village. A couple of miles down the hill, the traditional Auberge de la Forêt (0476 800601) gives you a feel of 'real' rural France.**

Access to the slopes of Alpe-d'Huez is no problem, but there are plenty of local slopes to explore, for which there is a special lift pass. Most of the runs are intermediate, though Auris is also the best of the local hamlets for beginners.

Vaujany 1250m/4,100ft
Vaujany is a quiet, small (though growing) village perched on the hillside opposite its own sector of the domain. Hydro-electric riches have financed huge continuing investment. There's a giant 160-person cable-car that whisks you into the heart of the Alpe-d'Huez lift system, a two-stage gondola which takes you to Vaujany's local slopes, a superb new sports centre with a 'fantastic' pool and a new village centre by the lifts (with smart ski shop, cafe, deli and underground car park). Vaujany has a handful of simple hotels – a reporter heartily recommends the Rissiou, run by British operator Ski Peak – and some tasteful new self-catering developments up the mountainside. There are some lively bars, and a couple of discos. British, Dutch and Belgian visitors dominate.

A mile or two up the valley (at the mid-station of the gondola) is the even smaller and more rustic hamlet of La Villette (just one tiny bar-restaurant).

There are no village slopes, so even complete beginners have to ride the gondola to Montfrais, which has a mid-station at La Villette. There's a blue run back to La Villette, but it can be tricky enough to reduce early intermediates to tears. You normally have to ride from La Villette down to Vaujany. The local branch of the ESF gets very good reports from readers.

Les Arcs

Purpose-built convenience, with exciting developments this season

COSTS

① ② ③ ④ ⑤ ⑥

RATINGS

The slopes

Snow	****
Extent	***
Expert	****
Intermediate	****
Beginner	****
Convenience	****
Queues	***
Mountain restaurants	**

The rest

Scenery	***
Resort charm	*
Off-slope	*

➕ A wide range of runs to suit intermediates and experts

➕ New link with La Plagne means there's a vast area to explore

➕ Few serious queues

➕ Excellent woodland runs

➕ Easy access to the slopes from most (but not all) of the apartments

➕ Option of staying in quiet, more traditional, lower villages

➕ Very easy rail access from UK

➕ Splendid views of Mont Blanc massif

➖ Main village centres lack charm

➖ Few off-slope diversions

➖ Not the best resort for confidence-building green runs – but lots of annoying flats for boarders

➖ Still lot of slow old chairs and drags

➖ Very quiet in the evenings, and limited choice of bars/restaurants

➖ Some apartments are quite a walk from the nearest lifts

➖ Accommodation in high villages is nearly all apartments – few hotels; and chalets mainly in lower villages

We've always liked Les Arcs' slopes: they offer impressive variety, including some of the longest descents in the Alps, plenty of steep stuff, good cruising and a very attractive area of woodland runs at one end of the area. From this season they will be linked to those of La Plagne, giving an impressive 420km/ 261 miles of runs, putting it in the same league as the Three Valleys and Val-d'Isère/Tignes. For a keen mixed-ability group, it should be on your shortlist.

The main Les Arcs villages are classic, purpose-built French resorts, with all the usual advantages (altitude and ski convenience) and drawbacks (little or no village charm or animation). But for this season the new Arc 1950 village will be open – purpose-built convenience with a lot more style. And there are more traditional (still quiet) options at either end of the resort.

Arc 2000 with the fledgling Arc 1950 in its early stages of construction below it ↓

For 2003/04, the long-awaited cable-car link to La Plagne is due to open – forming one of the world's biggest lift-linked ski areas, called Paradiski. For more details see separate chapter near the start of the book.

Also new for 2003/04 is the first phase of a new village called Arc 1950 – the first venture into the Alps by Canadian company Intrawest. More details are given in a separate margin box.

Below the new village, the old Bois de l'Ours chair up to Arpette and the Marmottes double-drag up to above Arc 2000 are due to be replaced for 2003/04 by fast six-packs. A new Cabriolet (gondola) lift connecting Arc 1950 with Arc 2000 is also planned, and it will work in the evening as well as the day. The two Plan Vert drag-lifts up to Col de la Chal are to be removed.

FRANCE

214

THE RESORT

Les Arcs is made up of four modern resort units, linked by road, high above the railway terminus town of Bourg-St-Maurice. The four villages are all purpose-built and apartment-dominated, and offer doorstep access to the snow with no traffic hazards, but the original three lack Alpine charm, off-slope activities and much evening animation (we wait to see what charm 1950 offers when it opens for its first winter). However, reporters repeatedly comment on the friendliness of the locals.

Arc 1600 was the original Arc (it opened in December 1968). It has the advantage of a funicular railway up from Bourg-St-Maurice, giving easy access from Paris and the UK by train. Previous reporters have found it a bit of a struggle to get from the train to the funicular with lots of luggage, but there is now a free mini-train to shuttle you the short distance. Above the village, a trio of chair-lifts fans out over the lower half of the slopes, leading to links to the other Arcs. 1600 is set in the trees and has a friendly, small-scale atmosphere; and it enjoys good views along the valley and towards Mont Blanc. The central area is particularly good for families: uncrowded, compact, and set on even ground. But things are even quieter here at night than during the day.

Much the largest of the 'villages' is Arc 1800. It has three sections, though the boundaries are indistinct. Charvet

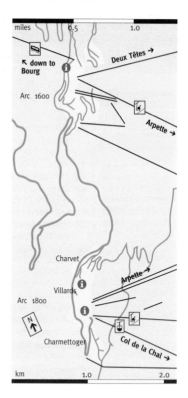

and Villards are small shopping centres, mostly open-air but still managing to seem as claustrophobic as the indoor arcades of neighbouring La Plagne. Both are dominated by apartment blocks the size of ocean liners (getting to the shops or the lifts may involve a much longer walk inside

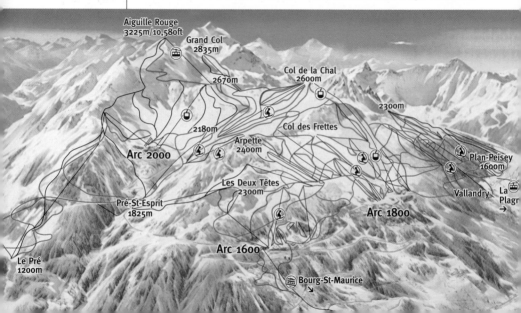

KEY FACTS

Resort	1600-2000m
	5,250-6,560ft
Slopes	1200-3225m
	3,940-10,580ft
Lifts	56
Pistes	200km
	124 miles
Green	1%
Blue	51%
Red	30%
Black	18%
Snowmaking	12km
	7 miles

For Paradiski area

Slopes	1200-3250m
	3,940-10,660ft
Lifts	164
Pistes	420km
	261 miles
Green	5%
Blue	54%
Red	28%
Black	13%

ARC 1950

We stayed in Arc 1950 in summer 2003 just after the first phase opened. It is attractively built in curving shapes in wood and stone, with great views of the mountains, and it is well furnished. But the bedrooms are disappointingly small (nothing like as big as those in North American condos), and the tiny kitchens are built into the living rooms. The outdoor hot-tub and small pool are attractions, however, as are the welcoming and efficient reception and the 'animations' every evening, such as fireworks, live music and wine tastings – when we stayed, there was a hurdy-gurdy player.

your apartment building than outside it). More pleasant on the eye is Charmettoger, with smaller, wood-clad buildings nestling among trees. Arc 1800 is now also spreading up the hillside, with relatively spacious apartments in Le Chantel. The lifts depart from the Villards area – chair-lifts to mid-mountain, and the big Transarc gondola to Col de la Chal at the head of the Arc 2000 valley.

Arc 2000 is just a few hotels, apartment blocks and the Club Med, huddled together in a bleak spot, with little to commend it but immediate access to the highest, toughest skiing. Although some new more upmarket apartments have been built over the last couple of years, there is only a handful of restaurants and shops – and it's a serious bus-ride to Arc 1600.

Just below Arc 2000, the new 'village' of Arc 1950 is being built. It promises to be by far the most attractive of the Les Arcs villages and is being built by the Canadian company Intrawest – who have developed several very attractive resorts in North America. A margin box gives more information on Arc 1950.

There are lifts all around Arc 1950 and 2000, including the Varet gondola up towards the Aiguille Rouge.

At the southern end of the area, linked by pistes but reachable by road only by descending to the valley, is Peisey-Vallandry. The key components of this composite resort are Vallandry and Plan-Peisey – recently developed lift-base resorts above the old village of Peisey, which has a bucket-lift up to Plan-Peisey. The whole area is known as Peisey-Nancroix. Vallandry is a bit more lively than Plan-Peisey. Chair-lifts go up from both bases to mid-mountain. The long-awaited cable-car link with La Plagne is set to open here for 2003/04.

There are a couple of alternative places to stay down in the valley at

the other, northern end of the ski area – see the end of this chapter.

Day trips by car to Val-d'Isère-Tignes or the Three Valleys are possible – both covered for a day with a six-day Paradiski or Paradiski Découverte pass. You can also get a reduced-price day pass for La Rosière/La Thuile with a Les Arcs pass.

THE MOUNTAINS

Les Arcs' terrain is notably varied; it has plenty of runs for experts and intermediates and a good mixture of high, snow-sure slopes and low-level woodland runs ideal for bad weather.

THE SLOPES
Well planned and varied

The slopes are very well laid out, and moving around is quick and easy – though direction-finding can be a problem at times. Arc 1600 and Arc 1800 share a west-facing mountainside laced with runs leading down to one or other village. At the southern end is an area of woodland runs – unusually extensive for a high French area – down to Plan-Peisey and Vallandry.

From various points on the ridge above 1600 and 1800 you can head down into the Arc 2000 bowl. On the opposite side of this bowl, lifts take you to the highest runs of the area, from the Aiguille Rouge and the Grand Col. As well as a variety of steep north-west-facing runs back to Arc 2000, the Aiguille Rouge is the start of a lovely long run (over 2000m/6,500ft vertical and 7km/4 miles long) right down to the hamlet of Le Pré near Villaroger. Arc 2000 has runs descending below village level, to the lift-base, restaurant and car park at Pré-St-Esprit, about 200m/650ft lower. You can reach Le Pré from here, via a short drag-lift (often closed, say reporters), and also via the Lanchettes chair at Arc 2000.

boarding

Les Arcs calls itself 'the home of the snowboard'. Local boy Regis Rolland played a big part in popularising the sport (not least with his 'Apocalypse Snow' movies), and the resort is constantly developing its boarding facilities – the terrain-park was moved and rebuilt for last season and is excellently maintained. Boarders are attracted by the great mix of terrain served mainly by boarder-friendly lifts. However, getting around can involve some long traverses on near-flat cat-tracks and some of the blues at Arc 2000 are too flat for comfort. 'I wouldn't stay in Arc 2000 because it's too much of a pain to get to,' says one intermediate reporter. Vallandry has great smooth runs for beginners and carvers. There are a couple of specialist board schools and shops.

TERRAIN-PARKS
State of the art
The terrain-park – Snowp'Arcs, just down from Arpette – was moved and rebuilt for last season. It's served by the Clair Blanc chair and you can buy a pass just to use the park, from 1800 or 1600 (22 euros a day last season). Features change throughout the season, says the resort, and there are two areas. The Games zone has two boarder-cross runs as well as jumps. The more advanced Display zone has a big hip jump and rails, and is by the Altiport restaurant. There is a half-pipe at Arc 2000 (floodlit at night), where you'll also find the Flying Kilometre – a speed skiing run on which you can try your luck travelling at 100kph/63mph or more!

SNOW RELIABILITY
Good – plenty of high runs
A high percentage of the runs are above 2000m/6,500ft and when necessary you can stay high by using lifts that start around that altitude. Most of the slopes face roughly west, which is not ideal. Those from the Col de la Chal and the long runs down to Le Pré are north-facing. There is limited snowmaking on some runs back to 1600, 1800 and Peisey-Vallandry. Reporters are still finding that grooming can be 'economical'.

FOR EXPERTS
Challenges on- and off-piste
Les Arcs has a lot to offer experts – at least when the high lifts are open (the Aiguille Rouge cable-car, in particular, is often shut in bad weather).

There are a number of truly black pistes above Arc 2000, and a couple in other areas. After a narrow shelf near the top (which can be awkward), the Aiguille Rouge-Le Pré run is superb, with remarkably varying terrain throughout its vertical drop of over 2000m/6,500ft. There is also a great deal of off-piste potential. There are steep pitches on the front face of the Aiguille Rouge, and secluded runs on the back side, towards Villaroger – the Combe de l'Anchette, for example. A short climb to the Grand Col from the chair-lift of the same name gives access to several routes, including a quite serious couloir and an easier option. The wooded slopes above 1600 are another attractive possibility – and there are open slopes all over the place.

FOR INTERMEDIATES
Plenty for all abilities
One strength of the area is that most main routes have easy and more difficult alternatives, making it good for mixed-ability groups. There are plenty of challenges, yet less confident intermediates are able to move around without getting too many nasty surprises. An exception is the solitary Comborcière black from Les Deux Têtes down to Pré-St-Esprit. This long mogul-field justifies its rating and can be great fun for strong intermediates. A recent reporter also found the Malgovert red, which starts from the same place, to be 'tricky, narrow and doesn't get pisted'.

The woodland runs at either end of the domain, above Vallandry and Le Pré, and the bumpy Cachette red down to 1600, are also good for better intermediates. Those who enjoy speed will like the Vallandry area: its well groomed runs have been remarkably uncrowded much of the time (though this may change as people head down to the new cable-car link to La Plagne). Good intermediates can enjoy the Aiguille Rouge-Le Pré run (with red and blue detours available to avoid the toughest bits of the black piste).

The lower half of the mountainside is good for mixed-ability groups, with a choice of routes through the trees. The red runs down from Arpette and Col des Frettes towards 1800 are quite steep but usually well groomed.

Cautious intermediates have plenty of blue cruising terrain. Many of the runs around 2000 are rather bland and prone to overcrowding. The blues above 1800 are attractive but also crowded. A favourite blue of ours is Renard, high above Vallandry, usually with excellent snow.

And of course, from 2003/04 there will be the whole of La Plagne's slopes to explore if you get bored locally.

FOR BEGINNERS
1800 best for complete novices

There are nursery slopes conveniently situated just above all three villages. The ones at Arc 1600 are rather steep, while those at 2000 get crowded with intermediate through-traffic at times. The sunny, spacious slopes at 1800 are best. There is a lack of attractive, long, green runs to move on to (there is now only one green run marked on the piste map). But Mont Blanc, above 1600, is a beautiful, gentle blue, and you can take the gondola up to Col de la Chal and enjoy good snow on easy blues towards 2000.

FOR CROSS-COUNTRY
Very boring locally

Short trails, mostly on roads, is all you can expect unless you travel down to the Nancroix valley's 40km/25 miles of pleasant trails.

QUEUES
Few problems now

Reporters have few complaints about queues except in one or two places. In sunny weather, Arc 2000 attracts the crowds and readers comment on non-trivial queues for both the gondola and the chair to Col de la Chal. In bad weather, it's the lifts serving the woodland slopes above Vallandry that cause the problem. There are sometimes lengthy waits for the Aiguille Rouge cable-car. 'Beware, a large proportion of the queue is hidden inside the cable-car building itself,' warns one reporter. A bigger problem than queues is the time taken riding slow old chair-lifts, some of them very long. At peak periods overcrowded pistes can be a problem, too. How well the new cable-car link to La Plagne copes with the crowds remains to be seen.

Chalets de l'Arc, above Arc 2000, one of the best mountain restaurants on the main slopes →

SCHOOLS

ESF
esf-arcs-1600@
wanadoo.fr

Arc 1600
t 0479 074309

Arc 1800
t 0479 074031

Arc 2000
t 0479 074752

Arc Aventures (ESI)
t 0479 074128
arc.aventures@
wanadoo.fr

Virages (ESI)
t 0479 077882
viragesmt@aol.com

New Generation
t 0479 010318
(UK: 01483 205402)
info@skinewgen.com

Initial-snow.com (in
Bourg-St-Maurice)
t 0612 457291
infos@
initial-snow.com

Club des Sports
t 0479 078205
info@sports-lesarcs.
com

Classes (ESF prices)
6 days (3hr am or
pm) €115

Private lessons
Half-day €115 for 1
or 2 people.

MOUNTAIN RESTAURANTS
An adequate choice

Lunch isn't generally a highlight of the day unless you head for the hamlets at the extremes of the area. At the south end, a five-minute taxi-ride from Vallandry will bring you to L'Ancolie, a delightful traditional auberge with superb food with set menus at 23 and 30 euros last season when we had superb wild boar terrine and magret de canard cooked in cider (there are only 20 covers, so call 0479 079320 to book). At the north end, the 500-year-old Belliou la Fumée at Pré-St-Esprit is charmingly rustic. The Ferme and Aiguille Rouge down at Le Pré are both friendly, with good food.

The restaurants scattered here and there on the main slopes are mainly unremarkable. An exception is the three-year-old Chalets de l'Arc, above Arc 2000 towards Col de la Chal – built in traditional wood and stone and serving good French food. The little Blanche Murée, just down from the Transarc mid-station, is consistently recommended – 'friendly service, fantastic food, reasonable prices'. The restaurant at Col de la Chal has fabulous views. The chain of Oxygene 3000 piste-side bars has been recommended for cheap and quick food – as has Pizza 2000 at Arc 2000.

SCHOOL AND GUIDES
New Brit school for 2003/04

The ESF here is renowned for being the first in Europe to teach ski évolutif, where you start by learning parallel turns on short skis, gradually moving on to longer skis. We have had reports of several beginners who astonished their experienced friends. One was 'doing perfect parallel turns on steep reds by the end of the week'. But we have reports of a couple being left behind at chair-lifts and limited English

CHILDREN

The ESF branches in all three stations take children from 3 (6 half-days 3hr am or pm €115). The International school's Club Poussin in 1800 starts at age 4.

At Arc 1600 the Garderie at the Hotel de la Cachette (0479 077050) runs three clubs for children from 4 months to 11 years, from 8.30 to 6pm, with ski lessons available.

At Arc 1800 various schemes running from 8.45 to 5.45 are offered by the Pommes de Pin (0479 041530). The Nurserie takes children aged 1 to 3, the Garderie those aged 3 to 6, and children aged 3 to 9 can have lessons through the two clubs based at the Garderie.

At Arc 2000 Les Marmottons (0479 076425) takes children aged 2 to 6 from 8.30 to 5.45, with lessons for those aged 3 to 6.

The Club Med (2000) has full childcare facilities – this is one of their 'family villages'.

GETTING THERE

Air Geneva 156km/97 miles (3½hr); Lyon 200km/125 miles (3½hr); Chambéry 127km/79 miles (2½hr).

Rail Bourg-St-Maurice; frequent buses and direct funicular to resort.

being spoken by some instructors. Private boarding lessons with the ESF have been 'very highly recommended'. The International school (Arc Aventures) has impressed reporters over the years: 'Good instruction with English well spoken.' We have had glowing reports of the Optimum ski courses, using British instructors, based in a catered chalet in Le Pré. But the big news this season is that the British ski school New Generation (made up of highly qualified young British instructors), which has operated in Courchevel for several seasons and Méribel for two, is expanding into Les Arcs for 2003/04 – see the Courchevel and Méribel chapters for more.

FACILITIES FOR CHILDREN
Good reports

We have received good reports on the Pommes de Pin facilities in Arc 1800 – 'great care and attention', 'patient approach to teaching'. Comments on children's ski classes are favourable, too – 'nearly all instructors spoke English', 'classes went smoothly'. A new children's area was built at 1800 for last season, complete with moving carpet lifts, a sledging track and a climbing wall. There are also a couple of Mauve discovery pistes, at 1800 and 1600, for children to find out about flora and fauna of the Alps.

STAYING THERE

HOW TO GO
New chalets and apartments

Most resort beds are in apartments. There is a Club Med at Arc 2000.
Chalets There are now several catered chalets in the Peisey-Vallandry area (see the end of the chapter), and Le Pré has a couple, but there are hardly any in the high Les Arcs 'villages'.
Hotels The choice of hotels in Les Arcs is gradually widening, particularly at the upper end of the market.
(((④ **Mercure Coralia** (1800) (0479 076500) Newish, and locally judged to be worth four stars rather than its actual three.
(((③ **Golf** (1800) (0479 414343) An expensive but good 3-star, with sauna, gym, kindergarten, covered parking.
(((③ **Cachette** (1600) (0479 077050) Renovated in the mid-1990s, with something of the style of an American hotel. But it can be 'dominated by kids' says one reporter – not surprising as 1600's childcare facilities are here.

(② **Aiguille Rouge** (2000) (0479 075707) Daily free ski guiding.
Self-catering The original apartments are mostly tight on space, so paying extra for under-occupancy is a sound investment. The recently built MGM Alpages de Chantel apartments above 1800 and the new Arc 1950 apartments (both bookable through Erna Low), are attractive and comfortable by French standards, with pools, saunas and gyms. They are both very convenient for skiing but the MGM ones not for much else. The Ruitor apartments, set among trees between Villards and Charmettoger, are reported to be 'excellent in all respects'. L'Aiguille Grive has been recommended for spacious apartments and excellent slope access. In Arc 2000 the Chalet des Neiges and Chalet Altitude have new 'luxury' apartments, with pool and fitness facilities.

EATING OUT
Reasonable choice in Arc 1800

In Arc 1600 and 2000 there are very few restaurants, none of them discussed here. 1800 has a choice of about 15 restaurants; an ad-based (so not comprehensive) guide is given away locally. The Petit Zinc restaurant in the Golf hotel has haute cuisine and high prices; it has a Friday evening seafood buffet. The Gargantus is a good, informal place, although very cramped and one reporter found poor service. Readers have been satisfied by 'enormous portions' at Equipage and 'good food and great service' at the Triangle Noir. Casa Mia is an excellent all-rounder with exceptionally friendly service. The Mountain Café does much more than the Tex-Mex it advertises, and copes well with big family parties. The Chalet de Milou has gourmet cuisine, 'including excellent fish'. A popular outing is to drive halfway down the mountain to the welcoming

and woody Bois de Lune at Montvenix, which has perhaps the best food in the area (booking advised – 0479 071792).

APRES-SKI
Arc 1800 is the place to be
1800 is the liveliest centre, though even so one reporter calls it 'very, very quiet'. The J.O. bar is open until the early hours and has a friendly atmosphere with live music. The friendly Red Hot Saloon has bar games and 'surprisingly good' live music. 'I danced until I couldn't stand anymore,' claimed one recent reporter, who also enjoyed the cocktails, atmosphere and live music at the Jungle Café. The

Fairway disco keeps rocking until 4am most mornings and the Apokalypse 'isn't terrible'. The cinemas at 2000, 1800 and 1600 have English-language films once or twice a week. In 1600 the bar opposite (and belonging to) the hotel Cachette has games machines, pool and live bands, and can be quite lively even in low season, and a recent reporter recommended the Beguin, at the top of the village, for a rare truly French experience. The Red Rock in 2000 is 'good for youngsters but too crowded for grown-ups'. The Whistler Dream, in the Chalet des Neiges could be worth a try. There is bowling at 1800 and skating at 1800 and 2000.

SNOWPIX.COM / CHRIS GILL

There are plenty of good cruising runs; this pic shows one going down to Arc 1800 ↓

Indoor Squash (3 courts 1800), saunas (1600, 1800), solaria, multi-gym (1800), cinemas, amusement arcades, music, concert halls, fencing (2000), bowling (1800)

Outdoor Natural skating rinks (1800 and 2000), floodlit skiing, speed skiing (2000), ski-jump, climbing wall (1800), organised snow-shoe outings, 10km/6 miles cleared paths (1800 and 1600), hang-gliding, horse-riding, sleigh rides, helicopter rides to Italy, ice grotto

Phone numbers
From abroad use the prefix +33 and omit the initial '0' of the phone number.

UK Representative
Erna Low Consultants
9 Reece Mews
London SW7 3HE
t 020 7584 2841
f 020 7589 9531
info@ernalow.co.uk
www.ernalow.co.uk

Les Arcs
t 0479 071257
lesarcs@lesarcs.com
www.lesarcs.com

Bourg-St-Maurice
t 0479 070492

Peisey-Vallandry
t 0479 079428
info@peisey-vallandry.com
www.peisey-vallandry.com

OFF THE SLOPES
Very poor
Les Arcs is not the place for an off-the-slopes holiday. There is very little to do; the only pubic pool is at Bourg-St-Maurice, though several of the newer apartment blocks have one. You can visit the Beaufort dairy and go shopping in Bourg-St-Maurice (cheaper for buying ski equipment), preferably on Saturday for the market, and there are a few walks – nice ones up the Nancroix valley. There's also an ice grotto at the top of the Transarc, which pedestrians can reach.

Bourg-St-Maurice
850m/2,790ft
Bourg-St-Maurice is a real French town, with cheaper hotels and restaurants and easy access to other resorts for day trips. The funicular goes straight to Arc 1600 in seven minutes – but beware, the last one down is currently at 7.30pm, though the resort may make it later this year. Hostellerie du Pt-St-Bernard (0479 070432) has been reported to be a reasonable 2-star hotel – 'looks tatty but friendly with super food'. Another reporter enjoyed the hospitality and comfort of the cheap and cheerful Savoyard (0479 070403) despite the noise: 'take earplugs to sell to other guests'.

Le Pré 1200m/3,940ft
Le Pré is a charming, quiet, rustic little hamlet with three successive chair-lifts (the first two quite slow) up to above Arc 2000. It has a couple of small bar-restaurants and a couple of British-run chalets, including a rustic one that owners Martin and Deirdre Rowe renovated and run themselves under the Optimum brand. We can personally vouch for their good food, free-flowing wine, jolly bar and basic but adequate bedrooms; and the ski courses they run (Martin used to run the school in Andorra) have received rave reviews from reporters. But Le Pré is not at all suitable for beginners.

Peisey-Vallandry
1600m/5,250ft
Plan-Peisey and Vallandry are the two slope-side resorts out of a cluster of five small villages known collectively as Peisey-Nancroix.
The cable-car leaves from Plan-

Peisey, which has one hotel, a few shops, bars and restaurants but no real focus other than the lift station. A high-speed six-seater chair takes you into the slopes. Ski Beat has eight recently-built chalets here (and one down in Peisey – see below). Family specialist Esprit Ski has five chalets (plus another which houses its comprehensive childcare facilities). The hotel Vanoise (0479 079219) has been recommended by readers for its position, food and 'extremely friendly and helpful staff'. Chez Félix restaurant has 'superb views down the valley'.
Vallandry is a few hundred metres away and linked by shuttle-bus. More new development has gone on here, with lots of new chalets and a small pedestrian-only square at the foot of the slopes with a small supermarket, a ski shop and a couple of bars and restaurants. A fast quad takes you into the slopes. Ski Olympic has a chalet-hotel towards the top of Vallandry with the Forêt, a Beatles-themed bar-restaurant, next to it. Erna Low has self-catered chalets just below the square, with great views.
Both Vallandry and Plan-Peisey are modern, low-rise developments, still small and quiet, but more development is planned, including a Club Med and some MGM apartments. Vallandry attracts a lot of Dutch guests.
The old village of Peisey is linked by day-time bucket-lift to Plan-Peisey. Peisey dates back 1,000 years, and has a fine baroque church. The other, mostly old, buildings house locals, a few tourists, a few shops and a couple of bars and restaurants. Ski Hiver has five chalets here and Ski Beat one.
Nancroix is a roadside hamlet notable only for the excellent L'Ancolie restaurant (a great place for dinner – see Mountain restaurants). Landry is an old village 6km/4 miles down the valley from Peisey.

Avoriaz

The best base on the Portes du Soleil circuit for snow

COSTS

① ② ③ ④ ⑤ ⑥

RATINGS

The slopes

Snow	★★★
Extent	★★★★★
Expert	★★★
Intermediate	★★★★
Beginner	★★★★
Convenience	★★★★
Queues	★★
Mountain restaurants	★★★★

The rest

Scenery	★★★
Resort charm	★★
Off-slope	★

NEWS

Investment in high-speed chairs, such as the much needed six-seater which replaced the double drag from Les Lindarets up to Avoriaz for 2001/02, have greatly reduced lift queue problems.

For 2003/04, the Zorre chair, which goes from the top of the gondola up from Morzine towards Avoriaz, is due to be replaced by a fast six-seater, which will reduce congestion and cut queues here.

Avoriaz has also been investing in runs with a difference lately. 'Snowcross' areas were introduced a couple of years ago – fun, ungroomed free-ride runs, which are avalanche controlled. And last year a third terrain-park was built and the half-pipe was made bigger. There is also now a special competition slope that ski schools use for children.

222

- ✚ Good position on the main Portes du Soleil circuit, giving access to very extensive, quite varied runs for all grades from novices to experts
- ✚ Generally has the best snow in the Portes du Soleil
- ✚ Accommodation right on the slopes
- ✚ Resort-level snow and ski-through, car-free village give Alpine ambience
- ✚ Good children's facilities

- ▬ Much of Portes du Soleil is low for a major French area, with the risk of poor snow or bare slopes low down
- ▬ Local pistes and lifts can get very crowded
- ▬ Non-traditional architecture, which some find ugly
- ▬ Little to do off the slopes
- ▬ Few hotels or chalets

For access to the impressive Portes du Soleil piste network, Avoriaz has clear attractions. In a low-altitude area where snow is not reliable, it has the best snow around – on relatively high, north-facing slopes of varying difficulty.

The purpose-built village may not suit everyone's architectural taste but we thought it had a pleasant, friendly feel to it when we stayed for a couple of nights in 2003. Strolling along the snow-covered main drag makes a very welcome change from the traffic fumes of many resort centres.

But there are drawbacks. It can get very crowded (especially at weekends), it is more expensive than lower-lying Châtel and Morzine and accommodation is mainly in fairly basic apartments (though there is a hip hotel there too).

THE RESORT

Avoriaz is a purpose-built, traffic-free resort perched above a dramatic, sheer rock face. From the edge of town horse-drawn sleighs or snow-cats transport people and luggage from car parks to the accommodation – or you can borrow a sledge for a small deposit and transport your own. The problem of horse mess has been cut since they now wear 'nappies' and staff on snowmobiles scoop up what escapes! Cars are left in pay-for outdoor or underground parking – a reporter advises the latter to avoid a chaotic departure if it snows (it took him three hours). You can book space.

The village is set on quite a slope, but chair-lifts and elevators in buildings mean moving around is no problem except when paths are icy. Pistes, lifts and off-slope activities are close to virtually all accommodation.

The village is all angular, dark, wood-clad, high-rise buildings, mostly apartments. But it is compact and snow-covered and has a friendly Alpine feel despite the architecture.

The evenings are not especially lively, but reporters have enjoyed 'a good ambience, both day and night',

and a 'brilliant parade in half-term week, with a fire-eating display'. Family-friendly events are laid on all season. A floodlit cliff behind the resort adds to its nocturnal charm.

The main consideration when choosing accommodation in this steep village is whether you want to go out at night. By day you can get around by using chair-lifts, but at night it's a walk uphill – or nip in and out of apartment blocks using internal lifts.

Avoriaz is above the valley resort of Morzine, to which it is linked by gondola (but not by piste). It also has good links to Châtel in one direction and Champéry in the other. Car trips are possible to Flaine and Chamonix.

KEY FACTS

Resort	1800m
	5,900ft

Portes du Soleil

Slopes	975-2275m
	3,200-7,460ft
Lifts	206
Pistes	650km
	400 miles
Green	13%
Blue	38%
Red	39%
Black	10%
Snowmaking	
	252 acres

Avoriaz only

Slopes	1100-2275m
	3,610-7,460ft
Lifts	38
Pistes	150km
	93 miles

THE MOUNTAINS

The slopes closest to Avoriaz are bleak and treeless, but snow-sure. They suit all grades from novice to expert and give quick access to the toughest runs in the Portes du Soleil. The whole circuit is easily done by intermediates of all abilities – and the booklet-style piste map makes for easy navigation. Reporters have praised the system of Discovery Routes around the Portes du Soleil – choose an animal that suits your ability and follow the signs displaying it. The circuit breaks down at Châtel, where you need the frequent shuttle-bus. The slopes of Morzine and Les Gets, accessed from the far side of Morzine, are part of the Portes du Soleil but not on the core circuit.

THE SLOPES
Short runs and plenty of them

The village has lifts and pistes fanning out in all directions. Staying in Avoriaz assures the comfort of riding mostly chairs – some other parts of the Portes du Soleil (especially on the Swiss side) have a lot of drags. A few new six-seat chairs have recently been installed in the Morzine/Les Gets area, but planned improvements in Switzerland are unlikely to happen in time for 2003/04.

Facing the village are the slopes of **Arare-Hauts Forts** and, when snow conditions allow, there are long, steep runs down to Les Prodains.

The lifts off to the left go to the **Chavanette** sector on the Swiss border – a broad, undulating bowl. Beyond the border is the infamous Swiss Wall – a long, impressive mogul slope with a tricky start, but not the terror it is cracked up to be unless it's icy (it gets a lot of sun). Lots of people doing the circuit (or returning to Champéry) ride the chair down. At the bottom of the Wall is the open terrain of Planachaux, above Champéry, with links to the still bigger open area around Les Crosets and Champoussin. There are several ways to return, but the most amusing is the chair up the Wall, with a great view of people struggling down it.

Taking a lift up from Avoriaz (or traversing from some of the highest accommodation) to the ridge behind the village is the way to the **Lindarets-Brocheaux** valley, from where lifts and runs in the excellent Linga sector lead to Châtel. Getting back is a matter of retracing your steps, although there are several options from Lindarets.

Morgins is the resort opposite Avoriaz on the circuit, and the state of the snow may encourage you to travel anticlockwise rather than clockwise, so as to avoid the low, south-facing slopes down from Bec de Corbeau.

TERRAIN-PARKS
Still leading the way

In 1993 Avoriaz became the first French resort to have a terrain-park, and now it boasts three. The Bleue du Lac up in the Arare area is aimed at experts, with advanced jumps such as tabletops, spines and hips, and a variety of rails. Last season, another park, the Chapelle, which is more suitable for novices, was created in the resort centre. It has boarder-cross features, as well as jumps. There's also a snowskate park here, and a centrally positioned big air jump, where there's a competition at 7pm on Wednesdays. At the foot of the main slopes is the excellent half-pipe, served by its own lift, and recently recreated to fit with Olympic norms – 120m/390ft long with 4.5m/15ft walls. There is a special snowboard pass (skiers can buy it too!) for those whose only interest is using the parks and the pipe. This gets you up in the cable-car from Prodains and includes the lifts serving the pipe and parks.

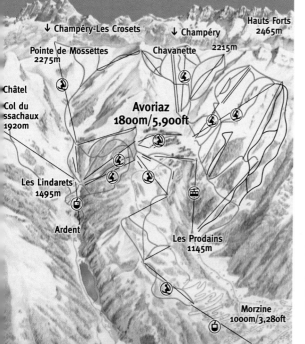

↓ Champéry-Les Crosets   ↓ Champéry

Hauts Forts 2465m

Pointe de Mossettes 2275m

Chavanette   2215m

Châtel

Col du ssachaux 1920m

Avoriaz 1800m/5,900ft

Les Lindarets 1495m

Ardent

Les Prodains 1145m

Morzine 1000m/3,280ft

LIFT PASSES

Portes du Soleil
Covers all lifts in all 12 resorts, and shuttle-buses.

Main pass
1-day pass €34
6-day pass €164

Senior citizens
Over 60: 6-day pass €131

Children
Under 16: 6-day pass €110
Under 5: free pass

Alternative passes
Avoriaz-only pass available. Beginner and snowboarder passes available for limited areas.

SCHOOLS

ESF
t 0450 740565
info@esf-avoriaz.com

International (L'Ecole de Glisse)
t 0450 740218
info@ecoledeglisse.com

Emery (snowboard)
t 0450 741264
ecoledesnowboard
emery@wanadoo.fr

BASS
t 0450 747691
info@britishskischool.co.uk

Classes
(ESF prices)
6 days (2½hr am and pm) €137

Private lessons
€30 for 1hr, for 1 or 2 people

GETTING THERE

Air Geneva 80km/50 miles (2hr); Lyon 200km/124 miles (3½hr).

Rail Cluses (42km/26 miles) or Thonon (45km/28 miles); bus and cable-car to resort.

Phone numbers
From abroad use the prefix +33 and omit the initial '0' of the phone number.

SNOW RELIABILITY
High resort, low slopes

Although Avoriaz town is high, its slopes don't go much higher – and some parts of the Portes du Soleil circuit are much lower. Considering their altitude, the north-facing slopes below Hauts Forts hold snow well. In general, the snow in Avoriaz is usually much better than over the border on the south-facing Swiss slopes.

Reporters generally say that grooming is good. And snow fences near exposed slopes have been erected to conserve snow. More snow-guns have been installed, mostly in the Lindarets area, where we have had complaints of lack of snow in the past.

FOR EXPERTS
Several challenging runs

Tough terrain is scattered about. The challenging runs down from Hauts Forts to Prodains (including a World Cup downhill) are excellent. There is a tough red, and several long, truly black runs, one of which cuts through trees – useful in poor weather. Two chair-lifts serve the lower runs, which snow-guns help to keep open. The Swiss Wall at Chavanette will naturally be on your agenda, and Châtel is well worth a trip. The black runs off the Swiss side of Mossettes and Pointe de l'Au are worth trying. Four 'snowcross' runs – ungroomed but avalanche controlled and patrolled – were introduced a couple of seasons ago, in the Hauts Forts, Lindarets, Chavanette and Mossettes areas. They are marked on the piste map, closed when dangerous and an excellent idea.

FOR INTERMEDIATES
Virtually the whole area

Although some sections lack variety, the Portes du Soleil is excellent for all grades of intermediates when snow is in good supply. Timid types not worried about pretty surroundings need not leave the Avoriaz sector; Arare and Chavanette are gentle, spacious and above the tree-line bowls. The Lindarets area is also easy, with pretty runs through the trees. Champoussin has a lot of easy runs, reached without too much difficulty via Les Crosets and Pointe de l'Au. Better intermediate have virtually the whole area at their disposal. The runs down to Pré-la-Joux and L'Essert on the way to Châtel, and those either side of Morgins, are particularly attractive – as are the long runs down to Grand-Paradis near Champéry when snow conditions allow. Brave intermediates may want to take on the Wall, but the chair to Pointe de Mossettes from Les Brocheaux is an easier route to Switzerland.

FOR BEGINNERS
Convenient and good for snow

The nursery slopes seem small in relation to the size of the resort, but are adequate because so many visitors are intermediates. The slopes are sunny, yet good for snow, and link well to longer, easy runs. The main problem can be the crowded pistes.

FOR CROSS-COUNTRY
Varied, with some blacks

There are 45km/28 miles of trails, a third classified as black, mainly between Avoriaz and Super-Morzine, with other fine trails down to Lindarets and around Montriond. The only drawback is that several trails are not loops, but 'out and back' routes.

QUEUES
Main problems now gone

Most of the bad queues have been eliminated by new high-speed lifts. But there can still be long queues to get out of Les Lindarets towards Châtel on the slow Chaux Fleurie chair-lift to Bassachaux. At weekends crowds on the pistes (especially around the village) can be worse than queues for

boarding

Avoriaz has always encouraged snowboarding, opening France's first terrain-park in 1993 – there are now three parks including a monster half-pipe (see Terrain-parks). The snowboard pass (28 euros for six days) is excellent value if you're interested only in the parks. There's a specialist snowboard school (Emery) and a snowboard village for children aged 6 to 16. Chalet Snowboard, the first chalet company to target snowboarders rather than skiers, has a couple of chalets at Les Prodains. Only a few (mainly avoidable) drags are left, and the six-pack chairs make for a comfortable ride. The new Snowcross free-ride areas (see the For Experts section) are a great innovation for riders who enjoy off-piste.

↑ Purpose-built Avoriaz is perched dramatically on top of a sheer cliff

SNOWPIX.COM / CHRIS GILL

CHILDREN

The ski schools take children between the ages of 4 and 12 (6 days €120).

Les P'tits Loups (0450 740038) takes children aged 3 months to 5, from 9am to 6pm; indoor and outdoor games. Book in advance.

Annie Famose's children's village (0450 740446) takes children aged 3 to 16, from 9am to 5.30.

The Club Med in Avoriaz is one of their 'family villages', with comprehensive childcare facilities.

ACTIVITIES

Indoor Health centre 'Altiform' (sauna, gym, hot-tub), squash, Turkish baths, cinema, bowling

Outdoor Paragliding, hang-gliding, snow-shoe excursions, ice driving, floodlit tobogganing, dog-sleigh rides, walking paths, sleigh rides, skating, snow-scooter excursions, helicopter flights

TOURIST OFFICE

t 0450 740211
info@avoriaz.com
www.avoriaz.com

the lifts, with care having to be taken to avoid collisions.

MOUNTAIN RESTAURANTS
Good choice over the hill

The charming, rustic chalets in the hamlet of Les Lindarets are one of the great concentrations of mountain restaurants in the Alps. A particular Lindarets favourite of ours is the Crémaillière which has wonderful chanterelle mushrooms and great atmosphere. The Pomme de Pin is recommended for its warm welcome and friendly service. The rustic Grenouille du Marais near the top of the gondola up from Morzine has good food, views and atmosphere. The Abricotine, with table service, at Les Brocheaux, Pas de Chavanette at the top of the Swiss Wall, and Yéti, at the top of town, have been recommended.

SCHOOLS AND GUIDES
Try BASS

The ESF has a good reputation, but classes can be large. The British Alpine Ski School (BASS) has British instructors and has been highly recommended, especially for 'quite excellent children's lessons'. Emery is a specialist snowboard school. A reporter had a 'very good' time with an English-speaking ESF guide, who 'took us to areas away from the usual crowd'.

FACILITIES FOR CHILDREN
'Annie Famose delivers'

The Village des Enfants, run by ex-downhill champ Annie Famose, is a key part of the family appeal of Avoriaz. Its facilities are excellent – a chalet full of activities and special slopes complete with Disney characters for children aged 3 to 16. There's a snowboard village too. Car-free Avoriaz must be one of the safest villages in the Alps, but there are still sleighs, skiers, and snowcats to watch out for.

STAYING THERE

HOW TO GO
Self-catering dominates

Alternatives to apartments are few.
Chalets There are several available – comfortable and attractive but mainly designed for small family groups.
Hotels There is one good hotel and a Club Med 'village'.
《《③ **Dromonts** (0450 740811) The original Avoriaz construction in the resort centre, recently taken over and renovated by a celebrity French chef and now in the *Hip Hotels* guidebook. It has special events such as wine tastings and cookery courses. We stayed there in 2003 and liked it.
Self-catering Some of the best apartments are in the Falaise area by the resort entrance. Past reporters have said that some apartments needed refurbishing. But the Falaise apart-hotel, Douchka, Sepia and Datcha residences have all been recommended.

EATING OUT
Good; booking essential

There are more than 30 restaurants. The hotel Dromonts has a Gastronomic restaurant with an excellent set-price six-course meal and a simpler Table du Marché restaurant. The Bistro and Cabane have been recommended for 'good food and value', as have the Petit Vatel ('excellent fish'), Fontaines Blanches and Douchka for Savoyard food, Intrets for 'pizza and pasta', and Au Briska, for a cosy night out. You can buy in advance meal vouchers for seven evening meals in a range of five restaurants, when you book Pierre & Vacances apartments. 'Restricted menu but excellent value,' says a reporter.

APRES-SKI
Lively, but not much choice

A few bars have a good atmosphere, particularly in happy hour. The Yeti is busy at 4pm. The Tavaillon attracts Brits and has Sky TV, and the Fantastique is worth a visit. For late-night dancing the Choucas and The Place have bands.

OFF THE SLOPES
Not much at the resort

Those not interested in the slopes are better off in Morzine, which has more shops and sports facilities – though Avoriaz does have the Altiform Fitness Centre, with saunas and hot-tubs. Pedestrians are not allowed to ride the chair-lifts, which is a shame.

Chamonix

Views to die for and slopes that can kill: hire a guide to go off-piste

RATINGS

The slopes

Snow	****
Extent	***
Expert	*****
Intermediate	**
Beginner	*
Convenience	*
Queues	**
Mountain restaurants	**

The rest

Scenery	*****
Resort charm	****
Off-slope	*****

NEWS

For 2002/03 snowmaking was increased at Le Tour. At Le Brévent there is a new Les Sources chair-lift.

Now that the Mont Blanc tunnel has reopened after the tragic fire of 1999, day trips to Courmayeur in Italy (covered by the Mont Blanc lift pass) are quick and easy once again.

226

➕ A lot of very tough terrain, especially off-piste

➕ Amazing cable-car to the Aiguille du Midi, for the famous Vallée Blanche (or just the views – it's on the pass)

➕ Stunning views of peaks and glaciers

➕ Lots of different resorts and areas covered on Mont Blanc lift pass

➕ Town steeped in Alpine traditions, with lots to do off the slopes

➕ Easy access by road, rail and air

➕ Excellent weekend destination

➖ Several separate mountains: mixed ability groups are likely to have to split up, and the bus service is far from perfect – we always take a car

➖ Pistes in each individual area are quite limited

➖ The few runs to the valley are often closed – and can be dangerous when open

➖ Crowds, queues, lots of road traffic

➖ Bad weather can shut the best runs

Chamonix could not be more different from the archetypal high-altitude, purpose-built French resort. Unless you are based next to one mountain and stick to it, you have to drive or take a bus each day. There is all sorts of terrain, but it offers more to interest the expert than anyone else, and to make the most of the area you need a mountain guide rather than a piste map. Chamonix is neither convenient nor conventional.

But it is special. The Chamonix valley cuts deeply through Europe's highest mountains and glaciers. The views are stunning and the runs are everything really tough runs should be – not only steep, but high and long. If you like your snow and scenery on the wild side, give Chamonix a try. But be warned: there are those who try it and never go home – including lots of Brits.

THE RESORT

Chamonix is a long-established tourist town that over the years has spread for miles along its valley in the shadow of Mont Blanc – the scale map below is one of the biggest in these pages.

On either side of the centre, just within walking distance of it, are lifts to two of the dozen slope areas in the valley – the famous cable-car to the Aiguille du Midi, and a gondola to Le Brévent. Also on the fringe of the

centre is the nursery slope of Les Planards. All the other lift bases involve drives or bus-rides – the nearest being the cable-car to La Flégère at the village of Les Praz.

Chamonix is a bustling town with scores of hotels and restaurants, visitors all year round and a lively Saturday market. The car-free centre of town is full of atmosphere, with cobbled streets and squares, beautiful old buildings and a fast-running river. Not everything is rosy: unsightly

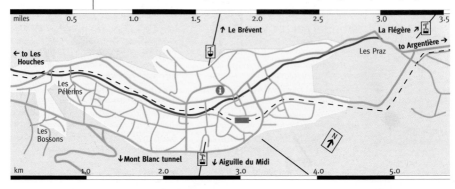

It's a lively,
interesting town by
day and by night →

OT CHAMONIX-MONT BLANC

KEY FACTS

Resort	1035m
	3,400ft
Slopes	1035-3840m
	3,400-12,600ft
Lifts	49
Pistes	152km
	94 miles
Green	21%
Blue	31%
Red	35%
Black	13%
Snowmaking	9km
	6 miles

modern buildings have been built on to the periphery (especially near the Aiguille du Midi cable-car station), some of the lovely old buildings have been allowed to fall into disrepair, and at busy times traffic clogs the streets around the pedestrianised centre. Most of the day the town squares and pavement cafes are crowded with shoppers and sightseers sipping drinks and staring at the glaciers above. It all makes for a very agreeable ambience, though the resort is in danger of being swamped by Brits (and Yanks): 'In many bars and restaurants I did not hear any French being spoken,' a recent visitor remarks.

Chamonix's shops deal in everything from high-tech equipment to tacky souvenirs. But reporters often comment on the number and excellence of the former, and Chamonix remains essentially a town for mountain people rather than for poseurs.

Strung out for 20km/12 miles along the Chamonix valley are several separate lift systems, some with attached villages, from Les Houches at one end to Le Tour at the other. Regular buses link the lift stations and villages (there's an evening service too) but can get very crowded and aren't always reliable – that to Les Houches is reportedly especially poor. Like many reporters, we rate a car as essential. A car also means you can get easily to other resorts covered by the Mont Blanc pass, such as Megève and Les Contamines, and Courmayeur in Italy.

The obvious place to stay is in downtown Chamonix – it has all the amenities you could want and some of the slopes are close at hand. For those who intend to spend most of their time in one particular area such as Argentière, Le Tour or Les Houches, staying nearby obviously makes sense. Whatever the choice, no location is convenient for everything.

THE MOUNTAINS

Once you get over the fact that the place is hopelessly disconnected, you come to appreciate the upside – that Chamonix has a good variety of slopes, and that each of the different areas is worth exploring. Practically all the slopes are above the tree line.

THE SLOPES
Very fragmented
The areas within the Chamonix valley – there are 11 in total – are either small, low, beginners' areas or are much higher up, above the wooded slopes that plunge to the valley floor, reached by cable-car or gondola.

The modern six-seater gondola for **Le Brévent** departs a short, steep walk from the centre of town, and the cable-car above takes you to the summit. At **La Flégère**, like Le Brévent, the runs are mainly between 1900m and 2450m (6,200ft and 8,040ft), and the stunning views of Mont Blanc are worth the price of the lift pass. The cable-car linking La Flégère and Le Brévent now makes this side of the valley more user-friendly – though reporters have found it's often closed by high winds.

A cable-car or chair-lift take you up to **Les Grands Montets** above Argentière. Much of the best terrain is still accessed by a further cable-car of relatively low capacity. This costs extra – 5 euros a trip in 2002/03 – though two free rides are included in a six-day pass. But it still attracts queues.

Le Tour has an area of mainly easy pistes which do extend down to the village. It is also the starting point for good off-piste runs, some of which end up over the border in Switzerland.

There is a valley piste map and an informative little Cham'Ski handbook, which includes all the local area piste maps with brief descriptions of each run and assessments of suitability for different abilities. But for navigation purposes the individual piste maps available at each area are best.

Most of our reporters have been more impressed than they expected with the piste grooming, but not with the signposting of the runs ('virtually non-existent' said a reporter last year).

TERRAIN-PARKS
Competitive

Head for Argentière and the Grands Montets for the hairiest action – the terrain-park and half-pipe host regular competitions. There's also a natural half-pipe/gully at Le Tour.

SNOW RELIABILITY
Good high up; poor low down

The top runs on the north-facing Grands Montets slopes above Argentière are almost guaranteed to have good snow, and the season normally lasts well into May. The risk of finding the top lift shut because of bad weather is more of a worry (and is the excuse for not including unlimited use of the lift on the main pass). There's snowmaking on the busy Bochard piste and the run to the valley, which can now be kept open late in the season. Le Tour has a snowy location and a good late-season record. The largely south-facing slopes of Brévent and Flégère suffer in warm

weather, and the steep runs to the resort are often closed. Don't be tempted to try these unless you know they are in good condition – they can be lethal. Some of the low beginners' areas have snowmaking.

FOR EXPERTS
One of the great resorts

The Grands Montets is justifiably renowned for its extensive steep terrain. To get the best out of the area you really need to have a local guide. Without one you either stick to the relatively small number of pistes or you put your life at risk. There is also lots of excellent off-piste reachable only by hiking up with touring equipment.

The Grands Montets cable-car takes you up to 3235m/10,610ft; if you've got the legs and lungs, climb the 121 steep metal steps to the observation platform and take in the stunning views. (But beware: it's 200 more steps down from the cable-car before you hit the snow.)

The ungroomed black pistes from here – Point de Vue and Pylones – are long and exhilarating. The Point de Vue sails right by some dramatic sections of glacier, with marvellous views of the crevasses. The off-piste routes from the top are numerous and

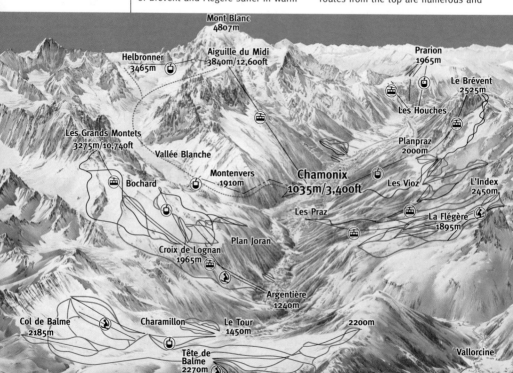

LIFT PASSES

Cham'Ski pass
Covers all areas in the Chamonix Valley and the bus services between them, except Grands-Montets cable-car and Les Houches area.

Beginners
Cham'Start 6-day pass covers all valley floor lifts.

Main pass
1-day pass €40
6-day pass €175.20

Senior citizens
Over 60: 6-day pass €148.90

Children
Under 15:
6-day pass €148.90
Under 11: 6-day pass €122.60
Under 4: free pass

Notes
6-day passes include two ascents on the Grands Montets cable-car and a day in Courmayeur.

Alternative passes
Ski-pass Mont Blanc covers lifts in the 13 resorts of the Mont Blanc area and Courmayeur in Italy.

often dangerous; the Pas de Chèvre route is serious stuff, eventually joining the Vallée Blanche run. There are many routes down the Argentière glacier.

The Bochard gondola serves a challenging red and a moderate black. Alternatively, head directly down the Combe de la Pendant bowl for 1000m/ 3,300ft vertical of wild, unpisted mountainside. The continuation down the valley side to Le Lavancher is equally challenging; it suffers frequently from lack of snow.

At Le Brévent there's more to test experts than the piste map suggests – there are a number of variations on the runs down from the summit. 'Superb when open,' said one visitor. Some are steep and prone to ice, and the couloir routes are very steep and very narrow. The runs in the sunny Col de La Charlanon are uncrowded and include one marked red run and lots of excellent off-piste if the snow is good.

At La Flégère there are several good off-piste routes – in the Combe Lachenal, crossed by the linking cable-car, for example – and a pretty tough run back to the village when snow-cover permits. Le Tour boasts little tough terrain on-piste but there are good off-piste routes from the high points to the village and over the back towards Vallorcine or into Switzerland.

FOR INTERMEDIATES
It's worth trying it all
For less confident intermediates, the Col de Balme area above Le Tour is

good for cruising and usually free from crowds. There are excellent shady runs on the north side of Tête de Balme.

More adventurous intermediates will also want to try the other three main areas, though they may find the Grands Montets tough going (and crowded). The bulk of the terrain at Le Brévent and La Flégère provides a sensible mix of blue and red runs; at Le Brévent the slopes have been redesigned to achieve this.

If the snow and weather are good, book a guide and do the Vallée Blanche (see feature panel).

A day trip to Courmayeur makes an interesting change of scene, especially when the weather's bad (it can be sunny there when Chamonix's high lifts are closed by blizzards or high winds).

FOR BEGINNERS
Best to learn elsewhere
If there is snow low down, the nursery lifts at La Vormaine, Les Chosalets, Les Planards and Le Savoy are fine for first-timers, who will not be bothered by speed-merchants there. But the separation of beginners' slopes from the rest inhibits the transition to real runs, and makes lunchtime meetings of mixed groups difficult. The slopes on the south side of the valley – Les Planards, in particular – can be dark and cold in winter. Le Savoy is sunny, but devoid of restaurants. Better to learn elsewhere, and come to Chamonix when you can appreciate the tough terrain.

boarding

Chamonix is a place of pilgrimage for advanced boarders, but not the best place to learn. Most of the areas are equipped mainly with cable-cars, gondolas and chairs, though there are quite a few difficult drags at Le Tour, which reporters say cause boarders problems. If you do the Vallée Blanche, be warned: the usual route is flat in places. If you're ready to tackle tougher off-piste, check out former British Champ Neil McNab's excellent Extreme Backcountry Camps (www.mcnab.co.uk).

THE VALLÉE BLANCHE

This is a trip you do for the stunning scenery. The views of the ice, the crevasses and seracs – and the spectacular rock spires beyond – are simply mind-blowing. The run, although exceptionally long, is not steep – mostly effortless gliding down gentle slopes with only the occasional steeper, choppy section to deal with. In the right conditions, it is well within the capability of a confident intermediate. But if snow is sparse the run can turn tricky – there can be patches of sheet ice, exposed stones and rocks and narrow snow bridges over gaping crevasses. And if fresh snow is abundant, different challenges may arise. Go in a guided group – dangerous crevasses lurk to swallow those not in the know. The trip is popular – on a busy day, 2,500 people do it; book in advance at the Maison de la Montagne or other ski school offices. Go early on a weekday to miss most of the crowds.

The amazing Aiguille du Midi cable-car takes you to 3840m/12,600ft. Across the bridge from the arrival station on the Piton Nord is the Piton Central; the view of Mont Blanc from the cafe a stair-climb higher should not be missed – and gives you the opportunity to adjust to the dizzying altitude. A tunnel delivers you to the infamous ridge-walk down to the start of the run. Be prepared for extreme cold up here. There is (usually) a fixed guide-rope for you to hang on to, and many parties rope up to their guides. You may still feel envious of those nonchalantly strolling down in crampons; you may wish you'd stayed in bed.

After that, the run seems a doddle. There are variants on the classic route, of varying difficulty and danger. Lack of snow often rules out the full 24km/15 mile run down to Chamonix; a short stairway and gondola link the glacier to the station at Montenvers, for the half-hour mountain railway ride down to the town.

FOR CROSS-COUNTRY
A decent network of trails

Most of the 42km/26 miles of prepared trails lie along the valley between Chamonix and Argentière. There are green, blue, red and black loops. All these trails are fairly low; they're cold and shady in midwinter, and they fade fast in the spring sun.

QUEUES
Morning and afternoon problems

The main lifts from the valley at Chamonix and Argentière produce queues at peak times – and getting down when the home runs are closed can be as bad as getting up the mountain in the morning. At Flégère a booking system comes into operation at the end of the day.

In poor weather Les Houches gets crowded and the queues for the Bellevue cable-car can then be bad.

There are still long queues for the top cable-car on Les Grands Montets – often all day long. When they reach 30 minutes a booking system operates, so you can go skiing until it's your turn to ride. Elsewhere on the Grands Montets, queues can be a problem even in January – and reporters are equally concerned about the low speed and worryingly frail nature of chair-lifts such as the Herse.

SNOWPIX.COM / CHRIS GILL

The Petit Rognon and its big brother Gros separate the various Vallée Blanche routes down the high ice-fields to the Séracs du Géant, visible on the left →

CHILDREN

The ESF runs classes for children aged 6 to 12 (6 days including supervised lunch €225). For children aged 4 to 6 there are lessons in a snow-garden. And children in either category can be looked after all day from 8.30 to 5pm.

The day-care centre at the Maison pour Tous (0450 533668) takes children aged 18 months to 6 years from 7.45 to noon and 2pm to 5.30.

The Panda Club (0450 550888, panda. bertrand@wanadoo.fr) takes children aged 10 months to 12 years.

The club at Argentière (0450 540476) has its own slopes, open to children aged 3 or more.

SCHOOLS

ESF
t 0450 532257)
infoski@esf-chamonix.com

Classes
6 half days: 142

Private lessons
32 for 1hr, for 1 or 2 people

MOUNTAIN RESTAURANTS
Surprisingly dull

The Bergerie at Planpraz on Le Brévent is the most attractive option – built in wood and stone, with self- and table-service; but it gets very busy. The dull little Panoramic at the top enjoys amazing views over to Mont Blanc and the food's fine. Altitude 2000 provides table-service at rip-off prices. There's a self-service place at La Flégère with a large terrace and excellent views.

On the Grands Montets the Plan Joran serves good food and does table-and self-service. The restaurant at Lognan has been smartly renovated. The rustic Chalet-Refuge du Lognan, off the Variante Hôtel run to the valley, and overlooking the Argentière glacier, has marvellous food and is very popular – book in advance.

At the top of the Le Tour gondola, the Chalet de Charamillon is an adequate self-service. The Refuge du Col de Balme – a short hike from the lifts – is charming, but has 'appalling' service.

SCHOOLS AND GUIDES
The place to try something new

The schools here are particularly strong in specialist fields – off-piste, glacier and couloir skiing, ski touring, snowboarding and cross-country. English-speaking instructors and mountain guides are plentiful, and specialist Chamonix tour operators can arrange them in advance for guests. At the Maison de la Montagne is the main ESF office and the HQ of the Compagnie des Guides, which has taken visitors to the mountains for 150 years. Both now offer ready-made week-long 'tours' taking clients to a different mountain or resort each day. A reporting couple this year rate the ESF Ski Fun Tour as 'fantastic – we cannot speak highly enough of the guides'. Competition is provided by a number of smaller, independent guiding and teaching outfits.

FACILITIES FOR CHILDREN
Better than they were

The Panda Club is used by quite a few British visitors and reports have been enthusiastic. The Argentière base can be inconvenient for meeting up with children for the afternoons. The Club Med nursery seems to go down well too. UK tour operator Esprit Ski has chalets here, with a nursery in the Sapinière chalet-hotel.

Beware the tendency to keep children on the valley nursery slopes for the convenience of the school when they really should be getting some miles under their skis.

STAYING THERE

HOW TO GO
Any way you like

There is all sorts of accommodation, and lots of it.

Chalets Many are run by small operators that cater for this specialist market. Quality tends to be high and value for money good. Collineige has a large selection – all very comfortable. We've good reports of Bigfoot's chalets and 'Mercedes mini-vans to run you to and from the slopes'. Flexiski's luxurious Chalet Bornian, new this season, sounds fabulous. HuSki and big tour operators have cheaper places.

Hotels A wide choice, many modestly priced, and the vast majority with fewer than 30 rooms. Bookings for a day or two are no problem – the peak season is summer. There's a Club Med 'village'. (((4 **Albert 1er** (0450 530509) Smart, traditional chalet-style hotel with 'truly excellent food' (Michelin stars). Visitors love the new indoor-outdoor pool. (((4 **Auberge du Bois Prin** (0450 533351) A small modern chalet with a big reputation; great views; bit of a hike into town; closer to Le Brévent. (((4 **Mont-Blanc** (0450 530564) Central, luxurious.

Chamonix

TOURIST OFFICES

Chamonix
t 0450 530024
info@chamonix.com
www.chamonix.com

Argentière
t 0450 540214
accueil@argentiere.
com

Les Houches
t 0450 555062
info@leshouches.com
www.leshouches.com

FRANCE

232

GETTING THERE

Air Geneva 85km/53 miles (1½hr). Lyon 220km/137 miles (3hr).

Rail Station in resort, on the St Gervais-Le Fayet/Vallorcine line.

Direct TGV link from Paris on Friday evenings and weekends.

ACTIVITIES

Indoor Sports complex (sports hall, gym, table tennis), indoor and outdoor skating and curling rinks, ice hockey, swimming pool with giant water slide, sauna, steam room, six indoor tennis courts, two squash courts, fitness centre, Alpine museum, casino, three cinemas, library, 10-pin bowling, climbing wall

Outdoor Ski-jumping, snow-shoe outings, mountain biking, hang-gliding, paragliding, flying excursions, heli-skiing, ice skating

((((④ **Jeu de Paume** (Lavancher) (0450 540376) Alpine satellite of a chic Parisian hotel: a beautifully furnished modern chalet half-way to Argentière: 'Tasteful, friendly staff ... lovely.'

(((③ **Alpina** (0450 534777) Much the biggest in town: modernist-functional place just north of centre.

(((③ **Gourmets & Italy** (0450 530138) Spot-on central mid-price B&B hotel.

(((③ **Labrador** (Les Praz) (0450 559009) Scandinavian-style chalet close to the Flégère lift. Good restaurant.

(((③ **Prieuré** (0450 532072) Mega chalet on northern ring-road – handy for drivers, quite close to centre.

(((③ **Vallée Blanche** (0450 530450) Smart, low-priced 3-star B&B hotel, handy for centre and Aiguille du Midi.

((② **Richemond** (0450 530885) Traditional, comfortable, with good public areas. 'Excellent, very good value, superb food,' says a reporter.

((② **Arve** (0450 530231) Central, by the river; small newly decorated rooms. 'Good value and superb service from Chamonix-born owners.'

((② **Pointe Isabelle** (0450 531287) Not pretty, but central; friendly staff, good plain food and well-equipped bedrooms.

① **Faucigny** (0450 530117) Cottage-style; in centre.

Self-catering Many properties in UK package brochures are in convenient but cramped blocks in Chamonix Sud. The Balcons du Savoy (0450 553232) are a cut above; great view, spacious rooms, use of a pool, a steam room and a solarium. The Splendid & Golf apartments in Les Praz (0450 559601) are charming and close to the Flégère cable-car. Erna Low has some luxury places available.

EATING OUT
Plenty of quality places

The top hotels all have excellent restaurants and there are many other good places to eat. The Sarpé is a lovely 'mountain' restaurant and The Impossible is rustic but smart and features good regional dishes. We always enjoy the Atmosphere, by the river, despite its two-sitting system. The Panier des Quatre Saisons is another favourite – much better than its shopping gallery setting would suggest.

Reader recommendations include the Crochon ('Good Savoyard fare, plus some varied and innovative dishes'), the Cabane next to the Labrador hotel

in Les Praz ('Excellent, go before the prices go up'), the Caleche ('Good food, atmosphere and service') and the Bumblebee ('Tiny, excellent, especially for veggies'). The Monchu is good for Savoyard specialities. The Casa Valerio offers 'good Italian at good prices'. The Spiga d'Oro is another recommended Italian, over a 'lovely' deli. There are a number of ethnic restaurants – Mexican, Spanish, Japanese, Chinese, Indian etc – and lots of brasseries and cafes.

APRES-SKI
Lots of bars and music

Many of the bars around the pedestrianised centre of Chamonix get crowded for a couple of hours at sundown – none more so than the Choucas video bar. During the evening, The Pub, Wild Wallaby's, the Mill Street bar and the Bar du Moulin are busy. The Chambre Neuf at the Gustavia hotel remains so until late. The Queen Vic is 'nice and dark and dingy with a snug, pool table, good music and Beamish on tap'. For a quiet drink, try the Brit-run Dérapage, with happy hours early and mid-evening. There's a lively variety of nightclubs and discos. The Choucas (again), and Dick's Tea bar are popular. The Cantina sometimes has live music and is open late. There are plenty of bars and brasseries for a quieter drink, too.

OFF THE SLOPES
An excellent choice

There's more off-slope activity here than in many resorts, though one reader complains that toddlers are not well catered for. Excursion possibilities include Annecy, Geneva, Courmayeur and Turin. The Alpine Museum is 'very interesting', the library has a good selection of English language books and there's a good sports centre and swimming pool.

Phone numbers
From abroad use the prefix +33 and omit the initial '0' of the phone number.

Argentière 1240m/4,070ft

The old village is in a lovely setting towards the head of the valley – the Glacier d'Argentière pokes down towards it and the Aiguille du Midi and Mont Blanc still dominate the scene down the valley. There's a fair bit of modern development but it still has a rustic appeal. A number of the hotels are simple, inexpensive and handy for the village centre – less so for the slopes – but the Grands-Montets (0450 540666) is a large chalet-style building, right next to the piste and the Panda Club for children. The family-run Montana (0450 541499) provides 'lovely rooms, excellent food'. Restaurants and bars are informal and inexpensive. The Office is always packed with Brits and Scandinavians. The Savoie bar is another traditional favourite – 'lively, friendly, well priced'.

Les Houches 1010m/3,310ft

Les Houches, 6km/4 miles from Chamonix, is not on the valley pass, but is covered by the regional Mont Blanc pass. It's a pleasant village, sitting in the shade of the looming Mont Blanc massif. There is an old core with a pretty church, but modern developments in chalet style have spread along the road up to Chamonix.

The area above Les Houches is served by a cable-car to Bellevue and a gondola to Prarion. Runs on the back of the mountain towards St-Gervais, and runs of 900m/3,000ft vertical down to Les Houches, make this the biggest single area of pistes in the Chamonix valley – mostly gentle blues and reds, good for building confidence. The largely wooded slopes are popular when bad weather closes other areas.

In good weather the slopes are quiet, and the views superb from the several attractive mountain restaurants, which are noticeably cheaper than others in the valley. Snow-cover on the lower slopes is not reliable, but there is a fair amount of snowmaking.

The village is quiet at night, but there are some pleasant bars and good restaurants including Vieilles Luges and the Terrain. Reporters enjoyed staying in the hotel Bois (0450 545035), with its 'helpful staff and excellent restaurant' and 'a good local band in the bar on Saturday'. Buses run in and out of Chamonix all evening.

Châtel

A distinctively French base for touring the Portes du Soleil

NEWS

For 2002/03 the triple Chaux des Rosées chair from Plaine Dranse was replaced by a high-speed six-pack, cutting queues here. Two new drag-lifts were also installed in Super Châtel's beginners' area, at the top of the gondola.

For 2003/04, two more new drags are planned. The Contrebandiers will form an additional link between Châtel and Torgon, and the Bossons drag will access the terrain-park and boarder-cross at Super-Châtel.

Yet more snowmaking is planned for next season, especially in Super-Châtel, and there will be improvements to some pistes in Linga.

234

- Very extensive, pretty, intermediate terrain – the Portes du Soleil
- Wide range of cheap and cheerful, good-value accommodation
- Easily reached – close to Geneva, and one of the shortest drives from the Channel
- Pleasant, lively, French-dominated old village, still quite rustic in parts
- Local slopes relatively queue-free
- Good views

- Both the resort and the highest skiing are low for a French resort, with the resulting risk of poor snow – though extended snowmaking has helped
- Bus or gondola ride to most snow-sure nursery slopes
- Queues can be a problem in parts of the Portes du Soleil circuit, particularly at weekends
- Village traffic can be congested at weekends and in peak season

Like neighbouring Morzine, Châtel offers a blend of attractions that is uncommon in France – an old village with plenty of facilities, cheap accommodation by French standards, and a large ski area on the doorstep. Châtel's original rustic charm has been largely eroded by expansion in recent years, but some of it remains, and the resort has one obvious advantage over smoother Morzine: it is part of the main Portes du Soleil circuit.

The circuit actually breaks down at Châtel, but this works in the village's favour. Whereas those doing the circuit from other resorts have to catch a bus mid-circuit, Châtel residents have the advantage of being able to time their bus-rides to avoid waits and queues. Those mainly interested in the local slopes should also consider Châtel. For confident intermediates, Châtel's Linga has few equals in the Portes du Soleil, while the nearby Torgon section has arguably the best views. The Chapelle d'Abondance slopes are pleasantly uncrowded at weekends. Châtel has become more beginner-friendly with nursery slopes at Super-Châtel and Pré-la-Joux, though these are a lift or bus-ride away.

THE RESORT

Châtel lies near the head of the wooded Dranse valley, at the north-eastern limit of the French-Swiss Portes du Soleil ski circuit.

It is a much expanded and now quite large but nonetheless attractive old village. New unpretentious chalet-style hotels and apartments rub shoulders with old farmhouses where cattle still live in winter.

Although there is a definite centre, the village sprawls along the road in from lake Geneva and the diverging roads out – up the hillside towards Morgins and along the valley towards the Linga and Pré-la-Joux lifts.

Lots of visitors take cars and the centre can get clogged with traffic – especially at weekends. Street parking is difficult but there is underground (pay-for) parking and day car parks at Linga and Pré-la-Joux (where the parking can

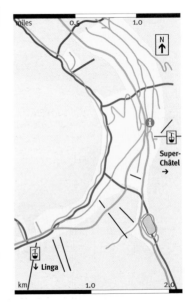

The Châtel area, like the whole of the Portes du Soleil, offers great intermediate terrain →

OT CHATEL / JEAN-FRANCOIS VUARAND

KEY FACTS

Resort	1200m
	3,940ft

for Portes du Soleil

Slopes	975-2275m
	3,200-7,460ft
Lifts	206
Pistes	650km
	400 miles
Green	13%
Blue	38%
Red	39%
Black	10%
Snowmaking	
	252 acres

For Châtel only

Slopes	1100-2205m
	3,610-7,230ft
Lifts	41
Pistes	83km
	52 miles

LIFT PASSES

Portes du Soleil
Covers all lifts in all 12 resorts, and shuttle-buses.

Main pass
1-day pass €34
6-day pass €164

Senior citizens
Over 60: 6-day pass €131

Children
Under 16: 6-day pass €110
Under 5: free pass

Alternative passes
Châtel pass covers Super-Châtel, Barbossine, Le Linga-Pré-La-Joux, Torgon and the link to Morgins.

get very full in peak season). Other main French Portes du Soleil resorts are easy to reach by piste, but not by road.

A central position gives you the advantage of getting on the ski-bus to the outlying lifts before it gets very crowded and simplifies après-ski outings. But there is accommodation near the Linga lift if that's the priority.

A few kilometres down the valley is the rustic village of La Chapelle-d'Abondance (see end of chapter).

THE MOUNTAINS

The Portes du Soleil is classic intermediate terrain, and Châtel's local slopes are very much in character. Confident intermediates, in particular, will find lots to enjoy in the Linga and Plaine Dranse sectors. If you travel the Portes du Soleil circuit, the booklet-style piste map makes for easy navigation. Reporters have also commented favourably on the system of Discovery Routes guiding you around the Portes du Soleil – choose an animal that suits your ability and follow the signs displaying it.

THE SLOPES
The circuit breaks down here
Châtel sits between two sectors of the Portes du Soleil circuit – linked together by an 'excellent, practically

continuous', free bus service. **Super-Châtel** is directly above the village – an area of easy, open and lightly wooded beginner slopes, accessed by a choice of gondola or two-stage chair. From here you can cross the Swiss border, either to quiet Torgon or clockwise around the Portes du Soleil to Morgins, Champoussin and Champéry, before going back into France above Avoriaz. You can also start from Petit Châtel – successive chairs take you to the link with Torgon. A reader recommended this route, but as the bus doesn't go here you need to be staying locally or have a car.

Linga is a bus-ride away. For intermediates and better, the area has some of the most interesting runs in the Portes du Soleil. The fastest way to Avoriaz is to stay on the bus at Linga and go to Pré-la-Joux. From here a high-speed quad goes to Plaine Dranse; then it's one more lift and run to Les Lindarets and the lifts to Avoriaz.

TERRAIN-PARKS
Head for Super Châtel
There's a terrain-park, with 15 features of varying difficulty at Super Châtel, plus a 120m/390ft long half-pipe and an 800m/half-mile long boarder-cross course. Music blasts out to help motivate you for the tricks. There's a big air jump on the Stade de Slalom in

boarding

Avoriaz is the hardcore destination in the Portes du Soleil, opening the first French terrain-park there in 1993, and now boasting three. But Châtel is not a bad place to learn or to go to as a budget option or as part of a mixed group of skiers and boarders, and the terrain-park here might seem less intimidating than the ones in Avoriaz if you're no expert. Most local lifts are gondolas or chairs. The Linga area also has good, varied slopes and off-piste possibilities, and the Stade de Slalom run there is floodlit every Thursday, is wired for sound and has a big air jump.

the Linga sector, and La Chapelle d'Abondance also has a 360m/1,180ft long park with half-pipe.

SNOW RELIABILITY
The main drawback

The main drawback of the Portes du Soleil is that it is low, so snow quality can suffer when it's warm. Châtel is at only 1200m/3,940ft and some runs home can be tricky or shut, especially from Super-Châtel. But a lot of snowmaking has been installed at Super-Châtel and on runs down to resort level. Linga and Pré-la-Joux are mainly north-facing and generally have the best local snow – a regular visitor tells us there is often good snow at Pré-la-Joux till May. But another told us of pistes to Morgins and Lindarets being closed in March.

FOR EXPERTS
Some challenges

The best steep runs – on and off-piste – are in the Linga and Pré-la-Joux area. Beneath the Linga gondola and chair, there's a pleasant mix of open and wooded ground which follows the fall line fairly directly. And there's a mogul field between Cornebois and Plaine Dranse which has been described as 'steeper and narrower than the infamous Swiss Wall in Avoriaz'. There are two blacks from the top of the Morclan chair at Super-Châtel, including a long run down to Barbossine which is quite narrow and tricky at the top. There's also a great off-piste route from Tête du Linga down the valley of La Leiche – hire a guide. Two pistes from the Rochassons ridge are steep and kept

well groomed. And the Hauts Forts sector beyond Avoriaz is challenging.

FOR INTERMEDIATES
Some of the best runs in the area

When conditions are right the Portes du Soleil is an intermediate's paradise. Good intermediates need not go far from Châtel; Linga and Plaine Dranse have some of the best red runs on the circuit. The moderately skilled can do the circuit without problem, and will particularly enjoy runs around Les Lindarets and Morgins. Even timid types can do the circuit, provided they take one or two short-cuts and ride chairs down trickier bits. The chair from Les Lindarets to Pointe de Mossettes leads to a red run into the Swiss area, which is a lot easier than the 'Swiss Wall' from Chavanette and also speeds up a journey round the circuit.

Leaving aside attempts to complete the circuit in both directions, there are rewarding out-and-back expeditions to be made clockwise to the wide open snowfields above Champoussin, beyond Morgins, and anticlockwise to the Hauts-Forts runs above Avoriaz.

FOR BEGINNERS
Three possible options

There are good beginners' areas at Pré-la-Joux (a bus-ride away) and at Super-Châtel (a gondola ride). And there are nursery slopes at village level if there is snow there. A recent reporter praised the Super-Châtel slopes and lifts which 'allow the beginner to progress' but criticised their access: 'Maybe a bus, then an uphill walk to the crowded gondola.' The Pré-la-Joux

SCHOOLS

ESF
t 0450 732264
info@est-chatel.com

International
t 0450 733192
ski.surf@freesbee.fr

Stages Henri Gonon
t 0450 732304
ecoleski@hotel-
arcenciel.fr

Francis Sports
t 0450 813251
francis-sports
@valdabondance.com

Snow Ride (Ecole de Glisse)
t 0608 337651)

Classes
(ESF prices)
6 half-days (2½hr am
or pm) €100

Private lessons
€30 for 1hr, for 1 or
2 people

CHILDREN

The ESF takes
children aged 5 to 13
(6 half-days €89
outside French school
holidays). The Ski and
Surf International
School and Snow
Ride take children
from 8.

Henri Gonon takes
children over 6.
Francis Sports caters
for 3 to 5 year olds at
the Pitchounes.

Le Village des
Marmottons (0450
733379, contact@
lesmarmottons.com)
takes children from 3
to 8, from 8.30 to
5.30, with ski lessons
for those aged 3 up.

In 2002/03 a nursery,
the Mouflets (0450
813819), for children
aged three months to
six years opened. For
next season it will be
larger and move to
near the lift-pass
office.

GETTING THERE

Air Geneva 75km/47
miles (1½hr).

Rail Thonon les Bains
(42km/26 miles).

slopes are easier to reach but 'have less
variety of slopes and quite a steep
drag-lift'.

FOR CROSS-COUNTRY
Pretty, if low, trails
There are plenty of pretty trails along
the river and through the woods on
the lower slopes of Linga, but
snow-cover can be a problem.

QUEUES
Bottlenecks being eased
Queues to get to Avoriaz have been
eased by the high-speed quad at Pré-
la-Joux installed a few seasons ago.
But there are still a couple of
bottlenecks, which tend to be worse at
weekends (although we do have
reports of little queuing even during
half-term and New Year). The worst is
at Les Lindarets, where there is often a
lengthy wait for the Chaux Fleurie
chair-lift to the Col du Bassachaux on
the way back to Châtel. But the queue
the other way up to Avoriaz has been
eased by the new six-pack introduced
for 2001/02. You can face queues to
get down from Super-Châtel if the
slope back is shut by poor snow.
Reporters have also found lengthy
queues at the Tour de Don and
Chermeu drag-lifts at certain times of
day, causing difficulties for skiers
rushing back to Super-Châtel to pick
up children from ski school.

MOUNTAIN RESTAURANTS
Some quite good local huts
Atmospheric chalets can be found,
notably at Plaine Dranse (the Bois Prin,
Chez Crépy, Tân o Marmottes and Chez
Denis have been recommended). In the
Linga area the Ferme des Pistes gets
the thumbs up. The Perdrix Blanche at
Pré-la-Joux scarcely counts as a
mountain restaurant, but is an attractive
(if expensive) spot for lunch. It does
get crowded as there's nowhere else.
At Super Châtel the Portes du Soleil at
the foot of the Coqs drags is much
better than the big place at the top of
the gondola. The Escale Blanche is
worth a visit. And in town the Vieux
Four (see Eating Out below) is handy
for the bus and Super-Châtel gondola
and popular for lunch.

SCHOOLS AND GUIDES
Plenty of choice
There are now six ski and snowboard
schools in Châtel. The International
school has been recommended by a

reporter and the ESF came in for
praise with comments such as 'very
helpful and customer-focused
instructors', and 'skiing progressed by
leaps and bounds'.

FACILITIES FOR CHILDREN
Increasingly sympathic
The Marmottons nursery (now with its
own snowmaking machine) has good
facilities, including toboggans,
painting, music and videos, and
children are reportedly happy there.
Francis Sports ski school has its own
nursery area with a drag lift and chalet
at Linga: 'Very organised, convenient
and reasonably priced.' The ESF had a
rave report last year: 'I was very
impressed. Our five-year-old grandson
had four instructors who all spoke
sufficient English and his skiing
progressed by leaps and bounds. They
also seemed very caring for the kids in
their charge.'

STAYING THERE

HOW TO GO
A wide choice, including chalets
Although this is emphatically a French
resort, packages from Britain are no
problem to track down.
Chalets A fair number of UK operators
have places here, including some
Châtel specialists.
Hotels Practically all the hotels are 2-
stars, mostly friendly chalets, wooden
or at least partly wood-clad. None of
the 3-stars is particularly well placed.
Cornettes in La Chapelle (see end of
chapter) is an interesting alternative.
⟨⟨⟨3 **Macchi** (0450 732412) Modern
chalet, most central of the 3-stars.
⟨⟨⟨3 **Fleur de Neige** (0450 732010)
Welcoming chalet on edge of centre;
Grive Gourmande restaurant does
about the best food in town.
⟨⟨⟨3 **Lion d'Or** (0450 813440) In centre,
'basic rooms, good atmosphere'.
⟨⟨2 **Belalp** (0450 732439) Very
comfortable, with excellent food.
⟨1 **Kandahar** (0450 733060) One for
peace-lovers, a Logis by the river, a
walkable distance from the centre.
⟨1 **Rhododendrons** (0450 732404)
'Great service, friendly, comfortable,
clean.'
Self-catering Many of the better places
are available through Châtel and self-
drive specialists. The Gelinotte (out of
town but near the Linga lifts and
children's village) and the Erines
(500m/1,640ft from the centre) look

ACTIVITIES

Indoor Swimming pool, bowling, cinema, library

Outdoor Skating rink, horse-drawn carriage rides, helicopter rides, dog-sledding, snow-shoe excursions, farm visits, toboggan run, floodlit skiing at Linga

Phone numbers
From abroad use the prefix +33 and omit the initial '0' of the phone number.

TOURIST OFFICES

Châtel
t 0450 732244
touristoffice@
chatel.com
www.chatel.com

La Chapelle-d'Abondance
t 0450 735141
ot@lachapelle
dabondance.com
www.lachapelle
dabondance.com

OT CHATEL /
JEAN-FRANCOIS VUARAND

The village is quite large but attractive and very close to the Swiss border (that's Switzerland in the background) ↓

good. The Flèche d'Or apartments are not well positioned for lifts or shops. The Avenières is right by the Linga gondola. A couple of reporters have mentioned that Châtel's supermarkets are small and over-crowded – it may be worth shopping on the way if you're driving. There is also a large supermarket if you drive out in the direction of Chapelle d'Abondance.

EATING OUT
Fair selection

There is an adequate number and range of restaurants. The Cornettes in La Chapelle-d'Abondance is one of our favourites – amazingly good-value menus with excellent food (but 'disappointing' desserts, comments one reporter). The Vieux Four (Old Oven), is beautifully rustic with lots of wooden beams, alcoves and ornaments and does great steaks and Savoyard specialities. The Fiacre serves similar food and is also popular. The Fleur de Neige hotel has a gastronomic restaurant (La Grive Gourmand) which does foie gras, truffles and the like. The Pierreir serves Savoyard specialities. The Ripaille, almost opposite the Linga gondola, was highly recommended by a past reporter, especially for its fish.

APRES-SKI
All down to bars

Châtel is getting livelier, especially at the weekends. The Tunnel bar is very popular with the British and has a DJ or live music every night. The Avalanche is a very popular English-style pub. The Godille – close to the Super-Châtel gondola and crowded at tea-time – has a more French feel. The bar in the hotel Soldanelles has been recommended. The bowling

alley, The Vieille Grange, also has a good bar.

OFF THE SLOPES
Better to stay in Morzine

Those with a car have some entertaining excursions available: Geneva, Thonon and Evian. Otherwise there is little to do but take some pleasant walks along the river, or visit the cheese factory and the two cinemas.

The tourist office organises daily events for non-slope-users. But those not using the slopes would find more to do in Morzine. The Portes du Soleil as a whole is less than ideal for those not using the slopes who like to meet their more active friends for lunch: skiers and boarders are likely to be above at some distant resort at lunchtime.

La Chapelle-d'Abondance
1010m/3,310ft

This unspoiled, rustic farming community, complete with old church and friendly locals, is 5km/3 miles along a beautiful valley from Châtel. 'A car and a bit of French is virtually essential,' says a reporter. It's had its own quiet little north-facing area of easy wooded runs for some years, but has more recently been put on the Portes du Soleil map by a gondola and three chair-lifts that now link it to Torgon in Switzerland and, from there, Super-Châtel. This section is only a spur of the Portes du Soleil circuit. But, taken together with Chapelle's own little area, it is worth exploring – good at weekends when Châtel gets crowded and 'excellent for beginners'.

Nightlife is virtually non-existent – just a few quiet bars, a cinema and torchlit descents.

The hotel Cornettes (0450 735024) is an amazing 2-star with 2-star rooms but 4-star facilities, including an indoor pool, sauna, steam room, hot-tubs, excellent restaurant (see Eating out) and atmospheric bar. Look out for showcases with puppets and dolls and eccentric touches, such as ancient doors that unexpectedly open automatically. It has been run by the Trincaz family since 1894. The Alpage and the Chabi are other hotel options. The Airelles apartments have received a favourable report.

La Clusaz – Le Gd-Bornand

Very attractive, distinctly French all-rounders; all they lack is altitude

COSTS

①②③④⑤⑥

RATINGS

The slopes

Snow	**
Extent	***
Expert	***
Intermediate	****
Beginner	****
Convenience	***
Queues	***
Mountain restaurants	****

The rest

Scenery	***
Resort charm	****
Off-slope	***

NEWS

For 2003/04 La Clusaz's Beauregard cable-car is to be replaced, tripling the capacity to 1,500 people an hour. And Le Grand-Bornand is planning to replace the Maroly drag-lift with a new high-speed six-person chair. Snowmaking capacity is to be increased in both resorts.

In Le Grand Bornand, for 2002/03 a new red piste was created from the top of Lachat, around the back of the mountain and down to the Maroly area. The Nordic Park – an area to learn and practice cross-country skiing – also opened, as did Espace Grand-Bo (a new resort centre incorporating cinema, conference hall and day nursery).

+ Mountain villages in a scenic setting, retaining traditional character

+ Extensive, interesting slopes – pistes best for beginners and intermediates

+ Very French atmosphere

+ Very short transfer from Geneva, and easy to reach by car from UK

+ Attractive mountain restaurants

+ Good cross-country trails

+ Slopes at La Clusaz and Le Grand-Bornand linked by shuttle-bus

– Snow conditions unreliable because of low altitude (by French standards)

– Not many challenging pistes for experts – though there are good off-piste runs

– Crowded at weekends

Few other major French resorts are based around what are still, essentially, genuine mountain villages that exude rustic charm and Gallic atmosphere. Combine that with over 200km/125 miles of largely intermediate slopes, above and below the tree line, spread over five linked sectors in La Clusaz and the separate Le Grand-Bornand area, and there's a good basis for an enjoyable, relaxed week.

The area's one big problem is its height, or lack of it. Snowmaking has been installed in recent years and is continually increased, but it's still on a modest scale, and of course makes no difference in mild weather. So pre-booking a holiday here remains, as in other low resorts, a slightly risky business.

THE RESORT

La Clusaz was once frequented almost entirely by the French. But it has developed into a major international resort – for both summer and winter seasons. And there is a substantial year-round presence of British residents in the area. As one of the most accessible resorts from Geneva and Annecy, it's good for short transfers, but it does get crowded, and there can be weekend traffic jams.

The village is built beside a fast-flowing stream at the junction of a number of narrow wooded valleys, and has had to grow in a rather rambling and sprawling way, with roads running in a confusing mixture of directions. But, unlike so many French resorts, La Clusaz has retained the charm of a genuine mountain village. (It's the kind of place that is as attractive in summer as under a blanket of snow in winter.) In the centre is a large old church, and other original old stone and wood buildings; and, for the most part, the new buildings have been built in chalet style and blend in well. Les Etages is a much smaller centre of accommodation

above the main town, where two of the mountain sectors meet.

La Clusaz has a friendly feel to it. The villagers welcome visitors every Monday evening in the main square with vin chaud and a variety of local

cheeses. There's a weekly market, tempting food shops and a wide choice of typically French bars.

For much of the season La Clusaz is a quiet and peaceful place for a holiday. But in peak season and at weekends the place gets packed out with French and Swiss families.

Le Grand-Bornand, also covered by the Aravis lift pass, is an even more charming village, with even more sense that it remains a mountain community. This is partly because most of the development as a winter sports resort has gone on up the road at the satellite village of Le Chinaillon, which has been developed in chalet style. Le Grand-Bornand has quite extensive slopes and is well worth exploring for a day or two, or considering as an alternative, quieter base.

Le Grand-Bornand and La Clusaz are linked by a free buses doing the 10-minute journey every 30 minutes during the day – these become more erratic in peak-time traffic.

If you are taking a car, you might also consider basing yourself at **St-Jean-de-Sixt** – a small hamlet midway between La Clusaz and Le Grand-Bornand, with a small slope nearby, mainly used for sledging.

THE MOUNTAINS

Like the village, the slopes at **La Clusaz** are rather spread out – which makes them all the more interesting (and scenic). There are five main areas, each connecting with at least one other. At **Le Grand-Bornand** the slopes spread out along the mountainside and can be accessed from either the village or Le Chinaillon up the road.

The Aravis pass, covering the lifts of both resorts, costs very little more than the La Clusaz pass.

THE SLOPES
Pretty and varied
Several points in **La Clusaz** have lifts giving access to the predominantly west- and north-west facing slopes of **L'Aiguille**. Links between this sector and the slightly higher and shadier slopes of **La Balme** area have improved massively in recent years: a long red and a black piste have replaced the off-piste route from L'Aiguille towards La Balme, and a gondola now returns you to Cote 2000 on L'Aiguille – cutting out the need to take a long, flat run back to La Clusaz. La Balme is a splendid, varied area with good lifts (a high-capacity

KEY FACTS

La Clusaz	
Resort	1100m
	3,610ft
Slopes	1100-2500m
	3,610-8,200ft
Lifts	55
Pistes	132km
	82 miles
Green	29%
Blue	32%
Red	29%
Black	10%
Snowmaking	
	50 acres

Le Grand-Bornand	
Resort	950m
	3,120ft
Slopes	1000-2100m
	3,280-6,890ft
Lifts	39
Pistes	82km
	51 miles
Green	33%
Blue	30%
Red	30%
Black	7%
Snowmaking	
	114 acres

La Tête des Annes
1870m

Col des Annes

Le Maroly

Le Lachat
2100m/6,890ft

Lac des Confins

Les Chenons
1275m

Le Bouchet

Le Chinaillon
1300m

La Clusaz
1100m/3,610ft

Le Grand-Bornand
950m/3,120ft

St-Jean-de-Sixt
960m/3,150ft

Aravis pass
Covers La Clusaz, Le Grand-Bornand, Saint-Jean-de-Sixt and Manigod, and shuttle service between resorts.

Main pass
6 days €142

Senior citizens
Over 60: 6 days €117.50
Over 75: free pass

Children
Under 15: 6 days €107
Under 5: free pass

La Clusaz pass
Covers all lifts in La Clusaz.

Main pass
6-day pass €131

Senior citizens
Over 60: 6 days €107
Over 75: free pass

Children
Under 15: 6 days €96
Under 5: free pass

Le Grand-Bornand pass
Covers all lifts in Le Grand-Bornand.

Main pass
6-day pass €111.50

Senior citizens
Over 60: 6 days €105.50
Over 75: free pass

Children
Under 15: 6 days €92.50
Under 9: 6 days: €68.50
Under 5: free pass

Snowboarding is popular in La Clusaz, and although there are still a lot of drag-lifts, most are avoidable. There are some good nursery slopes, served by chair-lifts, and great cruising runs to progress to. La Balme is a great natural playground for good free-riders. And both La Clusaz and Le Grand Bornand have decent terrain-parks to hang out in.

gondola from the bottom linking to a quad chair up to the top); from the top there are wonderful views towards Mont Blanc.

Going the other way from L'Aiguille leads you to **L'Etale** via another choice of easy runs and the Transval cable-car, which shuttles people between the two areas. From the bottom of L'Etale, you can head back along another path to the village and the cable-car (due to be enlarged for 2003/04) up to the fourth sector of **Beauregard** which, as the name implies, has splendid views and catches a lot of sunshine.

From the top of Beauregard you can link via another easy piste and a two-way chair-lift with the fifth area of **Manigod**. From here you can move on to L'Etale.

The main village at **Le Grand-Bornand** has two gondolas on the outskirts up to a gentle open area of easy runs (including nursery slopes)

lying between 1400m and 1500m (4,600ft and 4,900ft). Chairs fan out above this point, one going up to the high point of **Le Lachat**, where there are serious red and black runs. Other lifts and runs go across the mountainside to the slopes above **Le Chinaillon**. Here there is a broad, open mountainside with a row of chairs and drags serving blue and red slopes, and links to the rest of the domain – a wide area of blue and red runs.

TERRAIN-PARKS
Twin parks – double the fun
Both resorts have terrain-parks, although boarders tend to prefer La Clusaz, which is more lively – particularly at weekends. La Clusaz's park is on the Aiguille, while Le Grand-Bornand's area is at Maroly. Both have quarter- and half-pipes, tables, rails and boarder-cross runs.

La Clusaz

241

SNOW RELIABILITY
Variable because of low altitude

Most of the runs are west- or north-west facing and tend to keep their snow fairly well, even though most of the area is below 2000m/6,500ft. The best snow is usually on the north-west-facing slopes at La Balme, where a lift takes you up to 2500m/8,200ft. La Clusaz itself is at only 1100m/3,610ft and, in late season, the home runs can be dependent on snowmaking – of which there is now virtually blanket coverage. However, the long paths linking La Balme and l'Etale to the village are devoid of snow-guns and can suffer from lack of snow. The main lifts to Beauregard and Crêt du Merle will carry people down as well as up. You can also ride the gondolas down to Le Grand-Bornand and the runs above Chinaillon have extensive snowmaking facilities.

FOR EXPERTS
Plenty to do, especially off-piste

The La Clusaz piste map doesn't seem to have a lot to offer experts, but most of the sectors present off-piste variants to the pistes, and there are more serious adventures to undertake – all the more attractive for being ignored by most visitors.

The best terrain is at La Balme, where there are several fairly challenging pistes above mid-mountain. The black Vraille run, which leads to the speed skiing slope, is seriously steep. On the opposite side of the sector, the entirely off-piste Combe de Bellachat can be reached.

The Noire run down the face of Beauregard can be tricky in poor snow and is often closed. The Tetras on L'Etale and the Mur Edgar bumps run below Crêt du Loup on L'Aiguille have been reclassified as blacks, and rightly so. L'Aiguille has a good off-piste run down the neglected Combe de Borderan and the long Lapiaz black piste runs down the Combe de Fernuy – a continuation of the awkward black down from Cote 2000 to the parallel running Fernuy red.

In Le Grand-Bornand the steepest runs, including the black Noire du Lachat, go from the top of Le Lachat.

FOR INTERMEDIATES
Good if snow is good

Most intermediates will love La Clusaz if the snow conditions are good. Early intermediates will delight in the gentle slopes at the top of Beauregard and over on La Croix-Fry at Manigod, where there's a network of gentle tree-lined runs. And they'll be able to travel all over the area on the gentle, green linking pistes, where poling or walking is more likely to be a problem than any fears about steepness.

L'Etale and L'Aiguille have more challenging but wide blue runs.

More adventurous intermediates will prefer the steeper red slopes and good snow of La Balme and the long red down Combe du Fernuy from L'Aiguille.

Le Grand-Bornand is full of good cruising blue and red intermediate runs stretching in both directions above Le Chinaillon – well worth a visit for a day or two if you are staying in La Clusaz.

FOR BEGINNERS
Splendid beginner slopes

There is a nursery slope at village level at La Clusaz, and a couple of others just above it, but the best nursery slopes are up the mountain at the top of the Beauregard cable-car and at Crêt du Merle. The Beauregard area has lovely gentle blue runs to progress to, including one long run around the mountain right back to the village. There are also some good beginner slopes at Le Grand-Bornand and St-Jean-de-Sixt.

FOR CROSS-COUNTRY
Excellent

The region has much better cross-country facilities than many resorts, with around 70km/43 miles of loops of varying difficulty. In La Clusaz, one good area is near the Lac des Confins, reached by bus. There's also a lovely sunny area at the top of the Beauregard cable-car. At Le Grand-Bornand there are extensive trails in the Vallée du Bouchet and towards Le Chinaillon. Last season a new circuit called the Nordic Park – complete with bumps, gradients and bends – was built for cross-country skiers to learn and practice. And there are further trails at St-Jean-de-Sixt.

QUEUES
Not usually a problem

Lift queues aren't a problem, except on peak weekends or if the lower slopes are shut because of snow shortage. The chair-lifts up the front face of L'Aiguille are the main weekend black spots; they are avoidable. One recent reporter complained of racers being

SCHOOLS

La Clusaz
ESF
t 0450 024083
info@esf-laclusaz.com

Sno Academie
t 0450 326605
snoacademie@aol.com

Le Grand-Bornand
ESF
t 0450 027910
contact@esf-grand-bo.com

Starski
t 0450 270469
esi_starski@yahoo.fr

Classes
(ESF prices)
6 days (2hr am and 2hr pm): €134

Private lessons
€31 for 1hr for 1 to 3 people

↑ There aren't many places in the Alps where you can relax in a huge outdoor pool at the end of the day
ARAVIS / PASCAL LEBEAU

CHILDREN

The ESF runs lessons for children aged 5 to 11 (6 days €121).

The two all-day kindergartens in La Clusaz operate 8.30 to 6pm. The Club des Mouflets (0450 326957) takes non-skiing children from 8 months to 4½ years. The Champions' Club (0450 326950) takes children 3½ to 6.

Le Grand-Bornand kindergarten Les P'tits Maringouins (0450 027905) takes children from 3 months.

GETTING THERE

Air Geneva 50km/31 miles (1½hr); Lyon 160km/99 miles (2½hr).

given too much attention – with huge queues at one lift and several pistes closed throughout her stay.

MOUNTAIN RESTAURANTS
High standard

Mountain restaurants are one of the area's strong points. There are lots of them and, for the most part, they are rustic and charming, and serve good, reasonably priced – often Savoyard – food. We have had excellent reports on the Télémark above the chair lift to L'Etale and the Chenons at the bottom of La Balme. There are several other good restaurants higher up in the Aiguille sector, of which the Bercail is said to be the best. Chez Arthur at Crêt du Merle has a calm little table-service restaurant tucked away behind the crowded self-service. The restaurant at Beauregard by the cross-country trail is sunny and peaceful, with good views. The Relais de L'Aiguille at Crêt du Loup is also popular. In Le Grand Bornand, the Névé at Le Rosay and the Terres Rouges are recommended. The Vieille Ferme at Merdassier (see Eating out) is also open at lunchtime.

SCHOOLS AND GUIDES
Mixed reports

There are tales of large classes and poor instruction in ESF group lessons, but we've heard from some satisfied customers too – especially those who took private lessons. According to reports, the smaller Sno Academie – with smaller class sizes – is much more reliable.

FACILITIES FOR CHILDREN
Good – in theory

We have had mixed reports about the kindergarten in La Clusaz and none about those in Le Grand-Bornand. Generally, however, the resorts are places where families can feel at home.

STAYING THERE

HOW TO GO
Decreasing choice of packages

There's a fair choice of packages to La Clusaz, mostly from smaller operators, some of whom go to Le Grand-Bornand too. The drive from the Channel and the transfer from Geneva airport are both among the shortest you'll find.
Chalets There are some small chalets, including some charmingly rustic ones.
Hotels Small, friendly 2-star family hotels are the mainstay of the area; luxury is not an option here.
((3 **Carlina** (0450 024348) A reporter says it's the best; central with pool and grounds.
((3 **Beauregard** (0450 326800) Comfortable; on the fringe of the village. Pool. 'Fantastic for families, excellent food,' says a reporter.
((3 **Alp'Hôtel** (0450 024006) Comfortable modern chalet close to the centre, with good restaurant. Pool.
((3 **Alpen Roc** (0450 025896) Big but stylish, central and comfortable, although one reporter said his room was 'very cramped'. Pool.
((3 **Saytels** (0450 022016) Only 3-star in Le Grand-Bornand. Close to church.
((3 **Cimes** (0450 270038) 3-star in Le Chinaillon.
((2 **Aravis** (0450 026031) Traditional

ACTIVITIES

Indoor Various hotels have saunas, massage, hot-tub, weights rooms, aerobics, sun beds and swimming pools

Outdoor Ice skating, paragliding, micro-light flights, snow-shoe excursions, ice carts, winter walks, horse-drawn carriage rides, quad-bikes, swimming pool

Phone numbers

From abroad use the prefix +33 and omit the initial '0' of the phone number.

TOURIST OFFICES

La Clusaz
t 0450 326500
infos@laclusaz.com
www.laclusaz.com

Le Grand-Bornand
t 0450 027800
infos@legrandbornand.
com
www.legrandbornand.
com

St-Jean-de-Sixt
t 0450 022412
infos@saintjeandesixt.
com
www.saintjeandesixt.
com

Vallées des Aravis
t 0450 027874
infos@aravis.com
www.aravis.com

↑ Given good snow, the village level nursery slopes at La Clusaz make a great place to learn

ARAVIS / MP ROUGE-PULLON

place with 'dated' rooms but 'great' food, in la Clusaz centre, close to lifts. ⓒ **Alpage de Tante Pauline** (0450 026328) Dinky chalet at foot of L'Etale slopes (bus stop outside).

Self-catering There's quite a good choice, including self-catering chalets as well as apartments. Some are out of town and best for those with a car.

EATING OUT
Good choice

There's a wide choice of restaurants, some a short drive away, including the Vieux Chalet, which is one of our favourites – good food and service in a splendid, creaky old chalet. The St Joseph at the Alp'Hotel is regarded as the best restaurant in La Clusaz. Ecuelle is the place to go for Savoyard specialities. The Cordée and the Outa are simple places giving great value for money. At the other end of the price scale is the more formal Symphonie restaurant in the hotel Beauregard – highly recommended by a reporter.

We're told some of the best food in the area is at the Ferme du Lormay in La Vallée du Bouchet, about 5km/3 miles on from Le Grand-Bornand. But another reporter rates the Vieille Ferme at Merdassier his favourite place in the Alps – an old farm building with 'serious food, classy staff, perfect atmosphere'. The Foly, overlooking the Lac des Confins, is a firm favourite with both tourists and locals alike.

APRES-SKI
La Clusaz getting livelier

These resorts have always seemed to us typically quiet French family places, with the difference that La Clusaz is definitely the place to stay for a livelier time – especially at the weekend. The Caves du Paccaly, in the centre of La Clusaz, has woody decor and live music. The Pressoir is a focal bar, popular for sports videos. Pub le Salto is run by a British couple and has Sky TV and draught Guinness. The Bali bar is a more French central recommendation. The Ecluse disco has apparently made its dance floor opaque (it used to be glass with a floodlit river running beneath it – but we were told too many inebriated revellers decided to bathe in the river). Club 18 rocks, often with live bands.

OFF THE SLOPES
Some diversions

The villages are pleasant. It's easy for pedestrians to get around the valley by bus and to several good mountain restaurants for lunch. There are good walks along the valleys, and a day trip to the beautiful lakeside town of Annecy is possible. And La Clusaz has an excellent aquatic centre with indoor and outdoor pools, jacuzzi, sauna and steam rooms.

STAYING UP THE MOUNTAIN
Cheap and panoramic

There are three places to stay at the top of Beauregard.

Les Contamines

A hidden gem: a charming, unspoiled French village with reliable snow

COSTS

① ② ③ ④ ⑤ ⑥

RATINGS

The slopes
Snow ********
Extent ******
Expert ******
Intermediate *******
Beginner *******
Convenience ******
Queues *******
Mountain
restaurants ********

The rest
Scenery ********
Resort charm ********
Off-slope ******

NEWS

A 16-person gondola
on the back side of
the mountain, from
Belleville to La
Ruelle, replaced the
old chair-lift a few
seasons ago.

The long-rumoured
plan to link the
slopes with those of
Megève seems no
nearer to becoming
reality.

KEY FACTS

Resort 1160m
3,810ft

For Contamines
Montjoie / Hauteluce
Slopes 1160-2485m
3,810-8,150ft
Lifts 26
Pistes 120km
75 miles
Green 16%
Blue 23%
Red 40%
Black 21%
Snowmaking 3km
2 miles

+ Traditional, unspoiled French village
+ Fair-sized intermediate area
+ Good snow record for its height
+ Lift pass covers several nearby
resorts, easily reachable by road

– Limited scope for experts, and not
ideal for beginners
– Quiet nightlife
– Lifts a bus-ride from main village
– Can be some lengthy queues

Only a few miles from the fur coats of Megève and the ice-axes of Chamonix,
Les Contamines is a charming contrast to both, with pretty wooden chalets,
impressive old churches, a weekly market in the village square and prices more
typical of rural France than of international resorts. Its position at the shoulder
of Mont Blanc gives it an enviable snow record. What more could you want?

THE RESORT

The core of the village is compact, but
the resort as a whole spreads widely,
with chalets scattered here and there
over a 3km/2 mile stretch of the valley,
and the main access lift is 1km/half a
mile from the centre. You can stay by
the lift at Le Lay or in the charming
village centre, a shuttle-bus-ride from
the lifts. A car is useful, but the main
Mont Blanc lift pass option covers the
local buses, as well as the lifts of
Chamonix and Megève (among others).

THE MOUNTAINS

Most of the slopes are above the tree
line and there are some magnificent
views, though the runs down from
Signal are bordered by trees (as is the
run from La Ruelle down to Belleville).
They amount to a respectable 120km/
75 miles of pistes.

Slopes From Le Lay a two-stage
gondola climbs up to the slopes at
Signal. Another gondola leads to the
Etape mid-station from a car park a
little further up the valley. Above
these, a sizeable network of open,
largely north-east-facing pistes fans
out, with lifts approaching 2500m/
8,200ft in two places. You can drop
over the ridge at Col du Joly to south-
west-facing runs down to La Ruelle,
with a single red run going on down to
Belleville. From Belleville, a 16-person
gondola runs back up to La Ruelle. A
fast chair takes you the rest of the way
back up to Col du Joly.
Terrain-parks There is a boarder-cross
and a half-pipe on the Tierces slope,
accessed by the fast Tierces chair-lift.
Snow reliability Many of the shady
runs on the Contamines side are above
1700m/5,575ft, and the resort has a
justifiable reputation for good snow
conditions late into the season, said to

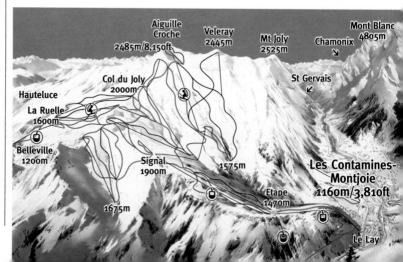

↑ Grand views of the Mont-Blanc massif

OT LES CONTAMINES / AGENCE NUTS

Queues There can be peak-period queues in the morning, especially if people are bussed in from other resorts with less snow. And the system has bottlenecks – where the two access gondolas meet for the second stage up to Signal, for example. But we've had a report of minimal queues even at weekends.

Mountain restaurants There are quite a few lovely rustic mountain restaurants – not all of which are marked on the piste map. The Ferme de la Ruelle is a jolly barn – though a reporter this year was unimpressed by the tartiflette – and Col du Joly has great views. Best of all are two cosy chalets – Roselette and Bûche Croisée.

Schools and guides We have had mixed reports in the past on the ESF – some parents thought their children's classes too strict and overcrowded. However, our most recent reports are positive. 'The best tuition I've ever experienced,' said one reporter last year. Excursions are offered, including a guided trip to the famous Vallée Blanche. The new International school opened a few seasons ago, and there are also two guiding companies.

Facilities for children The all-day village nursery, next to the central Loyers nursery slopes, takes children from one to seven years. Children can join ski school from age three.

be the result of proximity to Mont Blanc. There's snowmaking on the home runs from Signal down to the gondola bases.

Experts The steep western section has black runs, which are enjoyable but not terribly challenging for experts. The main attraction is the substantial and varied off-piste terrain – taking a guide is advisable. You can also visit the other resorts on the Mont Blanc lift pass – notably Chamonix.

Intermediates Virtually all the runs are ideal for intermediates, with a good blend of blues and reds. Some of the best run from the gondola's top station to its mid-station and others are served by the Roselette and Buche Croisee lifts. Given good snow, the south-facing runs down to La Ruelle are a delight. And the black runs are enjoyable for good intermediates.

Beginners In good snow, the village nursery area is adequate for beginners. There are other areas at the mid-station and the top of the gondola. The piste map shows no long greens to progress to but a reporter tells of a 'very gentle run from Col du Joly back to Le Signal' that is not on the map.

Snowboarding There is excellent off-piste boarding on offer. A guide is advisable.

Cross-country There are trails of varying difficulty totalling 29km/18 miles. One loop is floodlit twice a week.

STAYING THERE

How to go There are some catered chalets and a dozen modest hotels.

Hotels The 3-star Chemenaz (0450 470244) at Le Lay is praised by two reporters this year: 'Comfortable, and best food in the village.'

Eating out There are restaurants and crêperies in town for eating out. Recommendations include the Husky, Auberge du Barattet and the Op Traken – and the Savoisien and the Auberge du Chalezan for Savoie specialities.

Après-ski Après-ski is quiet, but there are several bars, some with live jazz on later. The Saxo near the gondola has been recommended. There's also a disco for late-night entertainment. Weekly events are organised, such as music and free vin chaud by the village fountain for a 6pm welcome on Saturdays and torchlit descents.

Off the slopes There are good walks, a toboggan run and a natural ice rink, but St-Gervais, Megève and Chamonix have more to offer.

Phone numbers
From abroad use the prefix +33 and omit the initial '0' of the phone number.

TOURIST OFFICE

t 0450 470158
info@lescontamines.com
www.lescontamines.com

Courchevel

Gourmet skiing and boarding – and it doesn't have to cost a fortune

RATINGS

The slopes

Snow	****
Extent	*****
Expert	****
Intermediate	*****
Beginner	****
Convenience	****
Queues	****
Mountain restaurants	****

The rest

Scenery	***
Resort charm	**
Off-slope	***

NEWS

For 2003/04 the difficult Creux and Fruit drag-lifts are to be replaced by a quad to improve the link between 1650 and 1850.

For 2002/03 an access ramp was built to provide easier access for children to the Jardin Alpin gondola, more of the Pralong area was separated off for beginners and snowmaking capacity was increased. A discounted lift pass for families was also introduced. The slalom course has been enlarged and improved.

➕ Extensive, varied local terrain to suit everyone from beginners to experts – plus the rest of the Three Valleys

➕ Great easy runs for near-beginners

➕ Lots of slope-side accommodation

➕ Impressive, continuously updated lift system, particularly above 1850

➕ Excellent piste maintenance, and widespread use of snowmaking

➕ Wooded setting is pretty, and useful in bad weather

➕ Choice of four very different villages – only 1850 is notably expensive

➕ Some great restaurants, and good après-ski by French standards

➖ Some pistes get unpleasantly crowded (but they can be avoided)

➖ Rather soulless villages with intrusive traffic in places – central 1850, especially, is surprisingly drab

➖ 1850 has some of the most expensive hotels, bars and mountain restaurants in the Alps

➖ Losing a little of its French feel as more and more British visitors discover its attractions

➖ Little to do away from the slopes, especially during the day – no public swimming pool, in particular

Courchevel 1850 – the highest of the four components of this big resort – is the favourite Alpine hangout of the Paris jet set, who fly directly in to the mini-airport in the middle of the slopes. Its top hotels and restaurants are among the best in the Alps, and the most expensive. But don't be put off: a holiday here doesn't have to cost a fortune (especially in the lower villages), the atmosphere is not particularly exclusive, and the slopes are excellent. Courchevel is the most extensive and varied sector of the whole Three Valleys, with everything from long gentle greens to steep couloirs. Many visitors never leave the Courchevel sector; but there is good access to the rest of the Three Valleys, too. Le Praz is an overgrown, but still pleasant village, 1550 is quieter and good for families, 1650 has more of a village atmosphere than it seems from the road through, and the posh bits of 1850 are stylishly woody. But overall the resort is no beauty. Well, nothing's perfect. Courchevel's long list of merits is enough to attract more and more Brits, but it remains much more French than Méribel, over the hill, as well as having better snow.

247

The Courcheneige hotel has a brilliant position on one of the home runs ➔

SKI
arrangements
.com

08700 110565
Crich Matlock, DE4 5DE

KEY FACTS

| Resort | 1260-1850m |
| | 4,130-6,070ft |

For the Three Valleys	
Slopes	1260-3230m
	4,130-10,600ft
Lifts	200
Pistes	600km
	370 miles
Green	17%
Blue	34%
Red	37%
Black	12%
Snowmaking	90km
	56 miles

For Courchevel/ La Tania only	
Slopes	1260-2740m
	4,130-8,990ft
Lifts	67
Pistes	150km
	93 miles

ALTITUDES

The component parts of Courchevel appear to be named by their altitudes. But they are examples of height hype. In fact:

1300 The lake and village centre are at 1260m

1550 The village centre is at 1480m

1650 The lift bases are below 1600m

1850 The skating rink, below the lift bases, is bang on the 1740m contour.

We revealed these facts in 1999, but our suggestion that new names be adopted – Courchevel ‹1850, for example – has fallen on deaf ears.

THE RESORT

Courchevel is made up of four varied villages, generally known by numbers supposed to represent their altitudes (but see Altitudes panel in margin). A road winds up the hill, running from Le Praz (1300) past 1550 and through 1650 to 1850. From the skiing point of view, things work a bit differently: runs go down from 1850 to 1550 and 1300, but the slopes of 1650 form a distinct sector.

1850 is the largest village, and the focal point of the area, with most of the smart nightlife and shops. Two gondolas go over its lower slopes towards the links with Méribel and the rest of the Three Valleys. It's conspicuously upmarket, with some very smooth hotels on the slopes just above the village centre, and among the trees of the Jardin Alpin a suburb is served by its own gondola. There's also a spreading area of smart private chalets. But the centre of the village is a bit of a messy sprawl, and the approach by road is, frankly, shabby.

While some readers 'couldn't afford a second week', others say it's 'not as upmarket as it's made out to be'. You can pay through the nose to eat, drink and stay, but more affordable places are not impossible to find.

1650 is 'calm and uncrowded, a world away from 1850', as a reader puts it. The main road up to 1850 cuts through 1650 but there's also an attractive old village centre, lively bars and quietly situated chalets. Its local slopes (whose main access is an escalator-served gondola) are also relatively peaceful. 1650 isn't the most convenient base for exploration of the Three Valleys, but a day trip to Val-Thorens is well within reach.

1550 is a quiet dormitory, a gondola ride below 1850. It has the advantage of having essentially the same position as 1850, with cheaper accommodation and restaurants. But it's a long trip to 1850 by road if you want to go there in the evening. Some accommodation is a fair distance from the gondola.

Le Praz (or 1300) is an old village set amid woodland. It's no Tirolean picture-postcard but remains a pleasant spot despite expansion and 'improvements' triggered by the 1992 Olympics – the Olympic ski jump is a conspicuous relic. It is 'excellent for children', with gondolas going up over the forest to 1850 and towards Col de

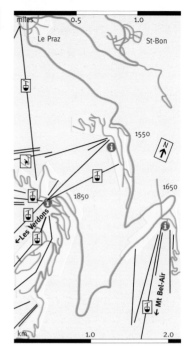

la Loze, for Méribel. Near-beginners face rides down as well as up: the pistes back to the village are red and black, and at this altitude snow conditions are often poor.

Free buses run between the villages, and within them a car is of no great value. Champagny is an easy road outing, for access to the extensive slopes of La Plagne.

THE MOUNTAINS

Although there are plenty of trees around the villages, most of the slopes are essentially open, with the conspicuous exception of the runs down to 1550 and to Le Praz, and the valley between 1850 and 1650. These are great areas for experts when the weather closes in. Piste maintenance is superb, and daily maps are available, showing which runs have been groomed overnight (normal in America but very rare in Europe). Snowmaking is abundant but the runs to Le Praz are still prone to closure in warm weather. Some slopes above 1850 get very busy, but you don't have to spend much time on them. Many reporters recommend buying only a Courchevel pass ('I was still finding new runs after two weeks') and buying extensions for the Three Valleys as necessary.

THE SLOPES
Huge variety to suit everyone

A network of lifts and pistes spreads out from **1850**, which is very much the focal point of the area. The main axis is the Verdons gondola, leading to a second gondola to **La Vizelle** and a nearly parallel cable-car up to **La Saulire**. Both the high points give access to a wide range of intermediate and advanced terrain (including a number of couloirs), Méribel and all points to Val-Thorens. You can also get over to 1650 from here.

To the right looking up from 1850 the **Chenus** gondola goes towards a second departure point for Méribel, the Col de la Loze. Easy and intermediate runs go back to 1850, with more difficult runs in the woods above **La Tania** (covered in a separate chapter) and **Le Praz**.

To the left of the Verdons gondola is the Jardin Alpin gondola, which leads to some great beginner terrain, and serves the higher hotels and runs until 8pm. It also gives access to 1650 via the valley of Prameruel.

1650 offers a good mix of beginner and intermediate slopes away from the crowds, and is an ideal area for confidence-building. A visitor reminds us that there are 'still too many drag-lifts' in this sector, and he has a point. At least the Creux and Fruit drags on the way to 1850 are being replaced by a chair this year. Getting to and from Méribel and the rest of the Three Valleys involves slightly more effort than from the rest of Courchevel, because of the intervening valley, but if you run late on the way back you can always catch the bus from 1850.

Courchevel

249

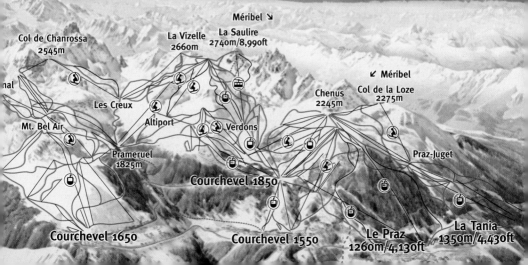

TERRAIN-PARKS
Something for everyone
The Plantrey terrain-park – just below
1850 and accessed via the Epicea and
Ecureuil lifts – is described by the
tourist office as for 'experienced
boarders'. It has a half-pipe, a baby
pipe and other features. The Verdons
terrain-park, just above 1850, has
rolling terrain of dunes and canyons
suitable for all levels of ability to enjoy
– as has the smaller Biollay area,
which offers 'roller coasters' and 'big
moguls to chew up, attack at your own
speed, in your own style'.

SNOW RELIABILITY
Very good
The combination of Courchevel's
orientation (its slopes are north- or
north-east-facing), its height, an
abundance of snowmaking and
generally excellent piste maintenance
usually guarantees good snow down to
at least the 1850 and 1650 villages. A
reporter comments: 'On a week when
snow was relatively scarce in the Alps,
we were pleasantly surprised by the
quality and quantity of the snow.' On
countless visits we have found that the

snow is usually much better than in
neighbouring Méribel, where the slopes
get the afternoon sun.

FOR EXPERTS
Some black gems
There is plenty to interest experts, even
without the rest of the Three Valleys.

The most obvious expert runs are
the couloirs you can see on the right
near the top of the Saulire cable-car.
The three main ways down were once
designated black pistes (some of the
steepest in Europe), but now only the
Grand Couloir remains a piste – it's the
widest and easiest of the three, but
you have to pick your way along the
narrow, bumpy, precipitous access
ridge to reach it.

There is a lot of steep terrain, on-
and off-piste, on the shady slopes of
La Vizelle, both towards Verdons and
towards the link with 1650. Some of
the reds on La Vizelle verge on black
and the black M piste is surprisingly
little used. If you love moguls, don't
miss the top of the black Suisses.
Chanrossa, which comes towards 1850
from the top of 1650, is quite difficult –
the off-piste just next to it is tougher.

OT COURCHEVEL

La Saulire has it all: a
link with Méribel, a
decent restaurant,
and seriously steep
descents on- and off-
piste ↓

LIFT PASSES

Three Valleys
Covers all lifts in Courchevel, La Tania, Méribel, Val-Thorens, Les Menuires and St-Martin-de-Belleville.

Beginners
8 free lifts in the Courchevel valley.

Main pass
1-day pass €39
6-day pass €193

Senior citizens
Over 60: 6-day pass €154
Over 72: free pass

Children
Under 13: 6-day pass €145
Under 5: free pass

Notes
Half-day, family and pedestrian passes available. 6-day pass valid for one day in either Tignes-Val-d'Isère, La Plagne-Les Arcs, Pralognan or Les Saisies.

Alternative passes
Courchevel pass covers Courchevel and La Tania only.

For a change of scene and a test of stamina, a couple of long (700m/2,300ft vertical), genuinely steep blacks cut through the trees to Le Praz.

There is plenty of off-piste terrain to try with a guide and a bit of climbing – high, north-facing slopes right at the top of the 1650 sector, for example (the Vallée des Avals is a great run). Also ask about the mysterious Hidden Valley in 1650, and the huge bowl accessed from the Creux Noir chair.

FOR INTERMEDIATES
Paradise for all levels

The Three Valleys is the greatest intermediate playground in the world, but all grades of intermediates will love Courchevel's local slopes too.

Above 1650 novices have the wonderful long runs of Pyramides and Grandes Bosses. Gentle blues such as Biollay in 1850 are fine, gentle slopes, leading to the two easy home runs.

Those of average ability can handle most red runs without difficulty. Our favourite is the long, sweeping Combe de la Saulire from top to bottom of the cable-car – but you have to time it right. Very pleasant first thing, when it's well groomed and free of crowds, it's a different story when it's icy or at the end of the day – cut up snow and very crowded. Creux, behind La Vizelle, is another splendid, long red that gets bumpy and unpleasantly crowded. Marmottes from the top of Vizelle is quieter and more challenging.

The Chenus sector has excellent blues and reds down towards 1850 and 1550, and through the trees towards La Tania – long, rolling cruises 'guaranteed to put a smile on your face'. Over at 1650, the reds on Mt Bel Air and Signal are excellent, if short, and usually quiet (or at least they were before the construction of the six-pack to the top of Signal).

boarding

For an upmarket resort, Courchevel goes out of its way to attract boarders. Except above 1650, it's easy to get around the Three Valleys using chairs and gondolas. The big snowboard hangout is 'Prends ta luge et tire toi', a combined shop/bar/Internet cafe in the centre of 1850.

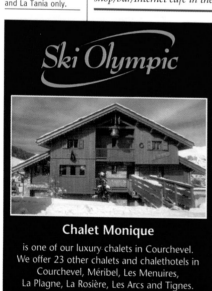

SCHOOLS

ESF in 1850
t 0479 080772
ski@esfcourchevel.com

ESF in 1650
t 0479 082608
ski@esf-courchevel1650.com

ESF in 1550
t 0479 082107
contact@esf-courchevel.com

Centre Pralong
t 0479 0111581

Ski Academy
t 0479 081199
courchevel@ski-academy.com

Supreme
t 0479 082787
(UK: 01479 810800)
info@supremeski.com

New Generation
t 0479 010318
(UK: 01483 205402)
info@skinewgen.com

Magic in Motion
t 0479 010181
magiccourchevel@aol.com

Oxygène
t 0479 419958
courchevel@oxygene-ski.com

Classes
(ESF 1850 prices)
6 days (2½hr am and pm): €210

Private lessons
€58 for 1½hr.

GUIDES

Mountain guides
t 0479 010366
guides.courch@wanadoo.com

FOR BEGINNERS
Great graduation runs

There are excellent nursery slopes above both 1650 and 1850. At the former, lessons are likely to begin on the short drags close to the village, but quick learners will soon be able to go up the gondola. The best nursery area is at 1850 in Pralong, above the village, near the airstrip. A reporter points out that getting to it from the village isn't easy, unless you go by road. A green path links this area with chairs to 1650, so adventurous novices can soon move further afield. The Bellecôte green run down into 1850 is an excellent, long, gentle slope – but like other runs into 1850 it is used by skiers returning to the village and does get unpleasantly crowded. It is served by the Jardin Alpin gondola, and a drag which is one of 11 free beginner lifts in Courchevel. 1550 and Le Praz have small nursery areas, but most people go up to 1850 for its more reliable snow.

FOR CROSS-COUNTRY
Long wooded trails

Courchevel has a total of 66km/41 miles of trails, the most in the Three Valleys. Le Praz is the most suitable village, with trails through the woods towards 1550, 1850 and Méribel. Given enough snow, there are also loops around the village.

QUEUES
There are always alternatives

Even at New Year and Easter, when 1850 in particular positively teems with people, queues are minimal, thanks to the excellence of the lift system (a New Year reporter this year comments on the absence of queues at 1650 'at pretty well any time'). The Chenus, Verdons and Jardin Alpin gondolas out of 1850 have all had their capacity increased over the past few years, improving

these old bottlenecks. However, as one reader points out, 'there can be a build-up at 1850 for the gondolas'. At such times 'it's best to avoid skiing back to 1850'. For example, try using the Plantrey chair, below 1850, or the Coqs chair, above it, to get over to the Col de la Loze, Le Praz and La Tania. The Biollay chair is very popular with the ski school (which gets priority) and can also be worth avoiding. Queues for the huge Saulire cable-car have been all but eliminated by the upgrading of the parallel Vizelle gondola. Many lifts now have American-style singles lines, but a reporter was unhappy that neither lift attendants nor French visitors appeared to be receptive to the idea.

MOUNTAIN RESTAURANTS
Good but can be very expensive

Mountain restaurants are plentiful and pleasant, but it is sensible to check the prices; for table-service restaurants reservations may be needed.

There are three expensive places on the fringes of Courchevel 1850 that just about count as mountain restaurants (you can ski away from them after your indulgent lunch). Most expensive is the big upmarket Chalet de Pierres, on the Verdons piste – a comfortable, smooth place in traditional style, doing excellent food (including a wonderful array of desserts) and accessible for pedestrians. Only a little way behind this for price comes the Cap Horn, near the airstrip – but last year's report of insanitary loos has been confirmed again this year. The Bergerie on the Bellecôte piste seems to attract a particularly fashionable crowd.

For a good-value lunch above 1850 try the busy Altibar, with a fine terrace, good food and both self-service and table-service sections. The Verdons is well placed for piste-watching and La Soucoupe is an atmospheric self-service place, now with table-service

CHILDREN

The ski schools all offer lessons for children, usually from the age of 3 or 4. Lessons for children aged 4 to 12 with ESF 1850 cost €219 for 6 days.

The two kindergartens in 1850 (0479 080847) and 1650 (0479 083369) take children from the age of 18 months, from 9am to 5pm.

Childminders are available for the under 2s.

OT COURCHEVEL

The steep wooded slopes above Le Praz are great for experts in falling snow ↓

upstairs too. The Panoramic at the top of Saulire is recommended for 'friendly service' and a 'nice fire'. Behind the main lift station at 1850 the Telemark terrace is a great suntrap, with good pizzas.

If we're paying the bill, our favourite Courchevel restaurant is the Bel Air, at the top of the gondola above 1650 – good food, friendly and efficient table-service, and a splendid tiered terrace. A reporter comments on the 'omelettes to die for' and another was impressed by the free brandy and a hot meal in 'ten minutes flat' during a blizzard last season. The Casserole ('nice sun terrace'), at the bottom of the Signal chair, was found to be 'expensive, but highly efficient'.

SCHOOLS AND GUIDES
Size is everything

Courchevel's branches of the ESF add up to the largest ski school in Europe, with a total of almost 500 instructors. We continue to receive reports critical of the standards of teaching and the 'indifference' of the ESF. One reporter reports a ripped calf muscle as being due to the inappropriate tuition he received and the ESF at 1650 was 'initially a disaster' for one reporter, but it 'perked up'.

Ski Academy is an independent group of French instructors – 'one brilliant, another OK', 'excellent and attentive', were the verdicts this year. Magic in Motion was rated 'good, but not outstanding like the one in La Tania'. Supreme in 1850 (owned and staffed by British instructors) was considered 'much better than ESF' by one reporter but earned a particularly negative report from another because of an instructor who was 'inattentive, insensitive and confidence-sapping'.

New Generation is a school that started as Le Ski School in 1650, linked to the tour operator of the same name – but has now branched out into 1850 and Méribel too. It consists of highly qualified young British instructors committed to giving clients enjoyment as well as technique. We are still receiving rave reviews about them, for adults and children alike: 'really excellent', 'outstanding private lessons with thoughtful instructor', 'young and highly motivated; adapt teaching to the clients' needs, not ski school dogma', 'we learned more in the week than we had over many years previously', 'we cannot praise the instructor enough'. Their shop is praised too: 'staff very helpful and knowledgeable'.

This coming season sees the arrival of another welcome competitor – Oxygène, well established in La Plagne and generally approved of by readers reporting from there.

The Bureau des Guides runs all-day off-piste excursions.

FACILITIES FOR CHILDREN
Lots of chalet-based options

A reporter last year found the ski kindergarten at 1850 over-stretched, with 19 children in a class of five to seven year olds. The ESF at 1850 has started to offer VIC (Very Important Children) lessons for English-speaking children between 6 and 12 years with a maximum of six children per group and an English-speaking ski instructor.

Several tour operators run their own nurseries using British nannies – an alternative that many families have found attractive.

GETTING THERE

Air Geneva 149km/93 miles (3½hr); Lyon 187km/116 miles (3½hr); Chambéry 110km/68 miles (2½hr). Direct flights to Courchevel altiport from London on request only (contact tourist office for details). Also scheduled flights from Geneva to Courchevel.

Rail Moûtiers (24km/ 15 miles); transfer by bus or taxi.

Phone numbers
From abroad use the prefix +33 and omit the initial '0' of the phone number.

FRANCE

254

STAYING THERE

HOW TO GO
Value chalets and apartments
Huge numbers of British tour operators go to Courchevel, with a wide choice of accommodation.

Chalets There are plenty of chalets available from dozens of UK tour operators. As usual in a French resort with a stock of ageing hotel buildings, there are also some chalet-hotels run by UK tour operators.

In 1850 there are several operators offering notably comfortable chalets, and a few that are genuinely luxurious. FlexiSki has two cosily woody chalets off the Bellecôte piste and have added two more luxurious chalets to their portfolio for 2003/04. Scott Dunn has several upscale places and has three new chalets on offer for 2003/04. Chalet Airea is their new premier chalet, with pool, jacuzzi, glass-floored steam room and terrace. Lotus Supertravel has a number of luxurious 'superchalets' – we have greatly enjoyed staying in the splendid Chalet Founets – and have two new places virtually beside the piste this year.

Mark Warner has two chalet-hotels in 1850; the Dahu is convenient and is reported to serve 'excellent food'.

In 1650 Le Ski is long-established as the leading UK operator, and now has 11 good-value chalets; its flagship chalet Rikiki is all en suite and set on the piste. Ski Olympic has two chalets and a central chalet-hotel, Les Avals, recommended as 'just brilliant – large rooms, high standard of catering, no

praise is enough for the staff'.

Esprit Ski and Simply Ski have a major childcare operation built around their several chalets down in Le Praz.

The big-league operators are in Courchevel, too. Neilson has a couple of chalets. Thomson's flagship St Louis chalet-hotel is in a great position just across from the Bellecôte piste. Crystal has a chalet-hotel with pool (New Solarium) in the pretty Jardin Alpin. Inghams has a wide range of chalets.

Hotels There are nearly 50 hotels in Courchevel, mostly at 1850 – including more 4-stars than anywhere else in France except Paris.

(((((5) **Bellecôte** (1850) (0479 081019) Our favourite among the more swanky places – it offers some Alpine atmosphere as well as sheer luxury.

(((((5) **Mélézin** (1850) (0479 080133) Superbly stylish and luxurious – and in an ideal position beside the bottom of the Bellecôte home slope.

(((((5) **Carlina** (1850) (0479 080030) Luxury piste-side pad, next to Mélézin.

(((((5) **Byblos des Neiges** (1850) (0479 009800) Next to first stop on Jardin Alpin gondola; spacious public rooms, good pool, sauna, steam complex.

((((4) **Alpira les Grandes Alpes** (1850) (0479 080335) 3-star on piste by main lifts. Readers enthuse: 'Helpful, personal service. Excellent, luxurious rooms.' 'Superb food, perfect location. Cannot be recommended too highly.'

((((4) **Rond Point** (1850) (0479 080433) Family atmosphere, central position.

(((3) **Croisette** (1850) (0479 080900) Next to main lifts; recently refurbished. It contains the popular Le Jump bar.

Selected chalets in Courchevel

Courcheneige (1850) (0479 080259) Pleasantly informal chalet in a quiet position on the Bellecôte piste, with a popular lunchtime terrace. 'A real find: fantastic location, lovely staff, good food,' says a reporter this year.

Ducs de Savoie (1850) (0479 080300) Pleasant, wood-built; well placed for skiing to the door, but only ten minutes' walk from centre.

Sivolière (1850) (0479 080833) No beauty, but comfortable (though small lounge), pleasantly set among pines.

Golf (1650) (0479 009292) Rather impersonal 3-star, in a superb position on the piste next to the gondola.

Ancolies (1550) (0479 082766) 'A real find,' said a US visitor impressed by the friendly staff and excellent food.

Edelweiss (1650) (0479 082658) 'Slightly run down', but good value and position we're told.

Peupliers (1300) (0479 084147) Well placed and cheap by local standards.

Self-catering There's a large selection of apartments, though high-season dates can sell out early. Some UK tour operators have places in the smart and central Forum complex in 1850 (some of these are offered as catered chalets,

too). As with all French apartments, check room dimensions and book a place advertised for more people than there are in your party. A reporter comments on the Maeva apartments at 1850: 'Typical French ski apartments – small; but ideally situated, and clean and well maintained.'

EATING OUT
Pick your price

There are a lot of good, very expensive French restaurants in Courchevel.

In 1850, among the best, and priciest, are the Chabichou (though a reporter calls it 'overrated') and the Bateau Ivre – both still with two Michelin stars. Recommendations for Savoyard food include the cosy Saulire (booking essential), the 'friendly' Fromagerie ('efficient service and decent food in good portions') and the Arbé ('decent steakhouse-type restaurant'). A reporter also recommends the Nuits de Bacchus (formerly the Plancher des Vaches) as 'a superb restaurant with a chef who really knows what he's doing'. The Chapelle grilled a 'fabulous and filling meal of lamb' on an open fire for one reader's party. A reporter praises the

Courchevel

255

FRANCE

ACTIVITIES

Indoor Artificial skating rink, climbing wall, gymnasium, bowling, exhibitions, (galleries in 1850 and 1650), cinemas, games rooms, billiards, language courses, computer courses, cookery courses, library. In hotels: health and fitness centres (swimming pools, saunas, steam-room, hot-tub, water therapy, weight-training, massage), squash (in the Caravelle), bridge (in the Chabichou))

Outdoor Hang-gliding, paragliding, flying lessons, parachuting (in spring), floodlit skiing, ski jumping, snow-shoe excursions, ice-driving, ice climbing, dog-sledding, snowmobile rides, horse-drawn sleigh rides, 17km/11 miles cleared paths, tobogganing, flight excursion, helicopter rides, hot-air ballooning.

TOURIST OFFICE

t 0479 080029
pro@courchevel.com
www.courchevel.com

pizzas but not the soup at the Via Ferrata and was concerned to watch the staff smoking in the kitchen. If you crave a burger late at night (it opens at 11pm) one reader recommends the Vache Qui Ski. Also mentioned by readers are the Cloche ('good atmosphere'), the Tremplin ('delicious crêpes', 'helpful and quick' at lunchtime, but 'snooty and old-style French' in the evening), the Smalto ('excellent Italian food) and the Cendrée ('a wonderful Italian'). Still in 1850, the Potinière does good, cheap pizzas, steaks and pasta. The Locomotive has an American feel, with railway-theme decor and a varied menu, though a reader reckons service is 'a bit surly', and the hotel Tovets is reported to have 'reasonable prices and delicious food'.

In 1550, the Oeil du Boeuf is good for grills. The Cortona does good-value pizza. In 1650 the Eterlou, Montagne and the Petit Savoyard ('divine fillet steak and pâté de foie gras dish') do good traditional Savoyard food and cheaper pizza and pasta. In Le Praz, Bistrot du Praz is expensive but excellent. The Ya-ca is small and 'very French'.

APRES-SKI
1850 has most variety

If you want lots of nightlife, it's got to be 1850. But it doesn't have the same loud Brit-oriented scene as Méribel, observes one reporter. There are some exclusive nightclubs, such as the Caves, with top Paris cabaret acts and sky-high prices. The popular Kalico has DJs and cocktails, and gets packed. The Bergerie does themed evenings – food, music, entertainment – but prices there are high.

The Jump at the foot of the main slope is the place to be as the lifts close, with the natural result that it does get impossibly packed. One reader

comments that there is 'no real large meeting place for après-ski'. The Saulire (aka Jacques) and the cheap and cheerful Potinière are also popular. Piggys is described as 'fur coats, pampered dogs and half a lager at £6'.

Cinemas in 1850 and 1650 show English-speaking films.

'Don't choose 1650 if it's nightlife you're after,' says a reporter this year. However, there are a few bars to socialise in. The Bubble is the hub, has satellite TV and Internet access. With cheap bar prices, happy hour, strong Mutzig beer and frequent live music, it has a largely British clientele. The Signal hotel, on the main street, is another favourite après-ski venue. Rocky's Bar (in Ski Olympic's chalet-hotel Avals) is popular – and a reporter enjoyed the 'interesting specialities, including flavoured vodkas'. Au Plouc is a tiny French bar. The Space pub has pool, games and live music.

In 1550 the Chanrossa bar is British-dominated, with occasional live music, the Taverne also has English owners. The tourist office tells us there is a new bar in 1550, the Barouf.

OFF THE SLOPES
1850 isn't bad

The Forum sports centre in 1850 includes a climbing wall in the shopping centre – good for spectating too. There are a fair number of shops in 1850 and excellent markets at most levels. There's a fun ice-driving circuit and an ice-climbing structure. A pedestrian lift pass for the gondolas and buses in Courchevel and Méribel makes it easy for non-slope users to get around the area and meet companions for lunch on the slopes. And you can take joyrides from the altiport and try to spot friends on the slopes below. A non-skier's guide to Courchevel, Méribel and La Tania is distributed free by the tourist office.

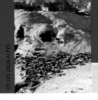

Les Deux-Alpes

It's a long way up to the glacier and a narrow way down

COSTS

① ② ③ ④ ⑤ ⑥

RATINGS

The slopes

Snow	****
Extent	***
Expert	****
Intermediate	**
Beginner	***
Convenience	***
Queues	**
Mountain restaurants	**

The rest

Scenery	****
Resort charm	**
Off-slope	**

NEWS

The weekly Super Ski pass now covers the off-piste Mecca of La Grave, reached by snowcat from the top of the glacier.

The resort has taken the terrain-park concept a step further, extending its existing impressive fun-park next to the Toura run and branding it as a SLIDE freestyle activity site, along with a 'cross' site (boardercross, drop offs, canyons) and a free-ride area with ledges and gullies.

- ➕ High, snow-sure slopes, including an extensive glacier area
- ➕ Varied high-mountain terrain, from motorways to steep off-piste slopes
- ➕ Efficient, modern lift system
- ➕ Excellent, sunny nursery slopes
- ➕ Stunning views of the Ecrins peaks
- ➕ Lively resort with varied nightlife
- ➕ Wide choice of hotels

- ➖ Piste network modest by mega-resort standards – we're sceptical about the claimed 200km/124 miles – and it's badly congested in places
- ➖ Only one easy run back to the resort; others are red or black, with snow often ruined by sun
- ➖ Virtually no woodland runs
- ➖ Spread-out, traffic-choked resort
- ➖ Few appealing mountain restaurants

We have a love–hate relationship with Les Deux-Alpes. We quite like the buzz of the village – arriving here is a bit like driving into Las Vegas from the Nevada desert – and we understand the appeal of its vibrant nightlife. We love the high-Alpine feel of its main mountain, and the good snow to be found on the north-facing runs in the middle of the mountain. But we're very unimpressed by the extent of those slopes, and we hate the piste congestion that results when most of the town's 35,000 visitors are crammed on to them. Crowding apart, keen intermediates spoiled by high-mileage French mega-resorts (and not up to the excellent off-piste) will simply find the usable area of slopes rather small.

THE RESORT

Les Deux-Alpes is a narrow village sitting on a high, remote col. Access is from the Grenoble-Briançon road to the north or by gondola from Venosc. The village is a long, sprawling collection of hotels, apartments, bars and shops, most lining the busy main street and the parallel street that completes the one-way traffic system. Although there is no centre as such, lifts are spread fairly evenly along the village and a couple of focal points are evident. And the resort has a lively ambience.

The village has grown haphazardly over the years, and there is a wide range of building styles, from old chalets through 1960s blocks to more sympathetic recent developments. It looks better as you leave than as you arrive, because all the balconies face the southern end of the resort.

Alpe de Venosc, at the southern end of town, has many of the nightspots and hotels, the most character, the fewest cars, the best shops and the Diable gondola up to the tough terrain around Tête Moute. More generally useful is the Jandri Express, now with an improved second stage, from the middle of the resort, where there is a popular outdoor ice rink and some

good restaurants and bars. The village straggles north from here, becoming less convenient the further you go.

The free shuttle-bus service saves on some very long walks from one end of town to the other.

The six-day pass covers a day in several nearby resorts including Alpe-d'Huez and Serre-Chevalier. Helicopter trips to Alpe-d'Huez are good value at £40 return – a 'must', says a reporter. More economical is the shuttle-bus service on Wednesdays.

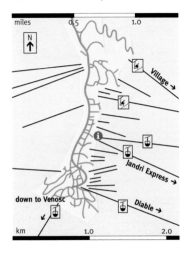

KEY FACTS

Resort	1650m
	5,410ft
Slopes	1300-3570m
	4,270-11,710ft
Lifts	58
Pistes	200km
	124 miles
Green	24%
Blue	39%
Red	24%
Black	13%
Snowmaking	
	59 acres

THE MOUNTAINS

For a big resort, Les Deux-Alpes has a disappointingly small piste area, despite recent improvements. Although extremely long and tall (it rises almost 2000m/6,560ft), the main sector is also very narrow, with just a few runs on the upper part of the mountain, served by a few long, efficient lifts. The piste-grading is rather inconsistent and some runs are graded differently on the map and on the mountain.

THE SLOPES
Long, narrow and fragmented

The western **Pied Moutet** side of Les Deux-Alpes is relatively little-used, although recent improvements in the lift and snowmaking systems have made the area more popular. It is served by lifts from various parts of town but reaches only 2100m/6,890ft. As well as the short runs back to town which get the morning sun, there's an attractive, longer north-facing red run down through the trees to the small village of Bons. The only other tree-lined run in Les Deux-Alpes goes down to another low village, Mont-de-Lans.

On the eastern side of the resort, the broad, steep slope immediately above it offers a series of relatively short, challenging runs, down to the

nursery slopes ranged at the bottom. Most of these runs are classified as black, and rightly so: they aren't groomed and are usually mogulled, and often icy when not softened by the afternoon sun. As a result, many visitors are forced to take the gondolas or the long winding green back down.

The ridge of **Les Crêtes** above the village has lifts and gentle runs along it, and behind it lies the deep, steep Combe de Thuit. Lifts span the combe to the main mid-mountain station at 2600m/8,530ft, at the foot of the slopes on **La Toura**. The middle section of the mountain, above and below this point, is made up primarily of blue cruising runs and is very narrow. At one point, there is essentially just a single run down the mountain. There is also the alternative of taking the roundabout (ie partly flat) blue Gours run to the bottom of the combe, where a chair-lift takes you up to Les Crêtes. This pleasant run passes the base of the Fée chair, serving an isolated (and neglected) black run.

The top **Glacier du Mont de Lans** section, served by drag-lifts and the warmer underground funicular, has some fine, very easy runs which afford great views and are ideal for beginners and the less adventurous. You can go from the top here all the way down to

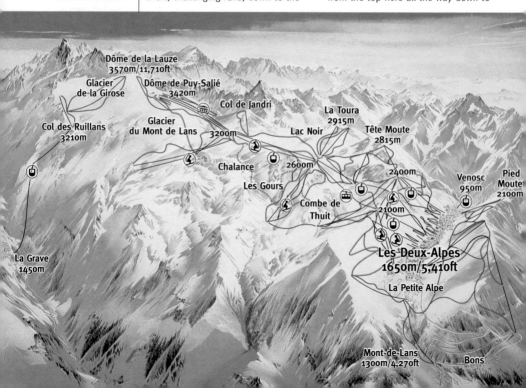

LIFT PASSES

Super ski pass
Covers all lifts in Les
Deux-Alpes, access to
La Grave, entry to
swimming pool and
skating rink.

Beginners
4 free lifts

Main pass
1-day pass €32
6-day pass €153

Senior citizens
Over 61: 6-day pass
€114.70
Over 75: free pass

Children
Under 14: 6-day pass
€114.70
Under 5: free pass

Notes
Half-day passes
available. 6-day pass
includes one day's
skiing in Alpe-d'Huez,
Serre-Chevalier, Puy-
St-Vincent and the
Milky Way.

Alternative passes
2 limited area passes:
'Ski sympa' covers 21
lifts, 'Grand ski'
covers 32 lifts.
La Grave: a
supplement for this
with a two-day or
longer pass.

SCHOOLS

ESF
t 0476 792121
esf.les2alpes@
wanadoo.fr

**International St-
Christophe**
t 0476 790421
ecole.ski.internationale
@wanadoo.fr

European Ski School
t 0476 797455
europeanskischool@
worldonline.fr

**Primitive School
Snowboard**
t 0476 790932

Classes
(ESF prices)
6 half days (2¼hr am
or pm) €120

Private lessons
€30 for 1hr, for 1 to
3 people

boarding

Les Deux-Alpes has been catering for snowboarders for years, and has built up an excellent reputation. There's a specialist Primitive school and lots of boarder-friendly facilities. Most of the lifts on the higher slopes are chairs. The terrain-park is relocated up to the glacier in the summer (access is by T-bar or funicular), which is where the Mondial du Snowboard competition is hosted each year. The ESF offers freestyle classes, using trampolines and a huge air-bag to practise on. But for beginner and timid intermediate boarders the narrow, flat crowded areas in mid-mountain and the routes down to the village are intimidating. There's some great off-piste in the local area for free-riders and the link to La Grave offers some of the best off-piste terrain in the world for advanced riders – hire a guide.

Mont-de-Lans – a descent of 2268m/7,440ft vertical which, as far as we know, is the world's biggest on-piste vertical. A walk (or snowcat tow) in the opposite direction takes you over to the splendid La Grave area for advanced skiers with a guide (lifts now covered by the Deux-Alpes pass).

TERRAIN-PARKS
Newly improved
There's a terrain-park with a boarder-cross, a half-pipe, music and a barbecue higher up the mountain in the Toura sector. This is relocated up to the glacier in the summer. There's even a kids' park.

SNOW RELIABILITY
Excellent on higher slopes
The snow on the higher slopes is normally very good, even in a poor winter – one of the main reasons for Les Deux-Alpes' popularity. Above 2200m/7,220ft most of the runs are north-facing, and the top glacier section guarantees good snow. You should worry more about bad weather shutting the lifts, or extremely low temperatures at the top, than about snow shortage. But the runs just above the village face west, so they get a lot of afternoon sun and can be icy at the beginning and end of the day. Snowmaking on some of the lower slopes helps keep them usable.

FOR EXPERTS
Off-piste is the main attraction
With good snow and weather conditions, the area offers wonderful off-piste sport. There are several good off-piste runs within the lift network, including a number of variations from underneath the top stage of the Jandri Express down to the Thuit chair-lift. The best-known ones are marked on the piste map. The Fée chair built a few years ago opened up new off-piste

possibilities into the Combe de Thuit. There are also more serious routes that end well outside the lift network, with verticals of over 2000m/6,560ft. One reporter recommends the renowned descent to St-Christophe (hire a guide, who will arrange transport back).

A Free Respect festival is held each year with free advice on off-piste safety and free-ride competitions.

The Super Diable chair-lift, from the top of the Diable gondola, serves the steepest black run around. The brave can also try off-piste variations here.

If the conditions are right, an outing across the glacier to the largely off-piste slopes of La Grave is a must.

FOR INTERMEDIATES
Limited cruising
Les Deux-Alpes can disappoint keen intermediates. A lot of the runs are either rather tough – some of the blues could be reds – or boringly bland. The steep runs just above the resort put off many. As one of our reporters (who classes himself as an 'advanced' skier) said, 'I myself fell from top to bottom. I was lucky. A girl in a different group broke her back. You cannot afford to be complacent here.'

The runs higher up generally have good snow, and there is some great fast cruising, especially on the mainly north-facing pistes served by the chair-lifts off to the sides. You can often pick gentle or steeper terrain in these bowls as you wish, but avid piste-bashers will explore all there is to offer in a couple of days. Many visitors take the opportunity of excursions to Alpe-d'Huez and Serre-Chevalier.

Less confident intermediates will love the quality of the snow and the gentleness of most of the runs on the upper mountain. Their problem might lie in finding the pistes too crowded, especially if snow is poor in other resorts and people are bussed in. At

CHILDREN

The ESF (0476 792121) and International St-Christophe (0476 790421) run kindergartens on more-or-less identical terms – taking children aged 3 to 6 until 5pm.

The Crèche du Village offers an excellent service for babies from 6 months to 2 years, from 8.30 to 5.30.

The Garderie du Bonhomme de Neige is for children aged 2 to 6 years from 9am to 5.30.

A list of babysitters is available from the tourist office.

The ski schools run classes for children aged 6 to 12 (6 mornings €100 with ESF).

The resort is going for the freestyle market in a big way with its new 'SLIDE activity sites' ↓

the end of the day, you can ride the Jandri Express down or take the long winding green back to town.

FOR BEGINNERS
Good slopes
The nursery slopes beside the village are spacious and gentle. The run along the ridge above them is excellent, too. The glacier also has a fine array of very easy slopes – but bear in mind that bad weather can close the lifts.

FOR CROSS-COUNTRY
Needs very low-altitude snow
There are three small, widely dispersed areas. La Petite Alpe, near the entrance to the village, has a couple of snow-sure but very short trails. Given good snow, Venosc, reached by a gondola down, has the only worthwhile picturesque ones. Total trail distance is 20km/12 miles. You can ski the Mont de Lans glacier with a qualified guide.

QUEUES
Can be a problem
Les Deux-Alpes has a great deal of hardware to keep queues minimal. But the village is large, and queues at the mid-morning peak can be 'diabolically' long for the Jandri Express and Diable gondolas. The Jandri queue moves quickly and the new eight-seater chair from the mid-station to the glacier has reduced the bottleneck for the second stage. Problems can also occur when people are bussed in when snow is in short supply elsewhere. The top lifts are prone to closure if it's windy, putting pressure on the lower lifts.

High winds caused one visitor to get stuck on a chair-lift for 10 minutes. 'Others in our chalet reported being stuck on a stationary lift for 45 minutes.' Another visitor reported queues for the gondolas back to the village when large numbers of people declined to tackle the tricky blacks or the crowded green run back down. The narrow mid-section of the mountain, particularly the Grand Nord blue run, is a real bottleneck late in the day.

MOUNTAIN RESTAURANTS
Still limited
There are mountain restaurants at all the major lift junctions, but they are generally pretty poor. For years the Pastorale, at the top of the Diable gondola, was the only recommendable place – then along came the splendid Chalet de la Toura, in the middle of the domain at about 2600m/8,530ft, with a big terrace, a welcoming woody interior and efficient table-service inside and outside. The pizzas are highly rated by one reporter. The Panoramic has been recommended.

SCHOOLS AND GUIDES
One of the better ESFs
The ski schools have a fairly good reputation for their teaching and English, although class sizes can be large. There are several specialist courses available, as well as off-piste tours and trips to other resorts. We had very good reports last year of the Primitive snowboard school – for both advanced (off-piste and in the half-pipe) and intermediate riders.

FACILITIES FOR CHILDREN
Fine for babies
Babies from six months to two years old can safely be entrusted to the village nursery. The kindergarten takes kids from two to six years, and there are chalet-based alternatives run by UK tour operators. There are also four free T-bars for children at the village level.

STAYING THERE
HOW TO GO
Wide range of packages
Les Deux-Alpes has something for most tastes, including that rarity in high-altitude French resorts, reasonably priced hotels.

Chalets There are a number of catered chalet packages available from UK tour operators, but some use apartments.
Hotels There are over 30 hotels, of which the majority are 2-star or below. There's a Club Med 'village' here, too.
(((3) **Bérangère** (0476 792411) Smartest in town (but dreary exterior) with an excellent restaurant and pool; on-piste, at less convenient north end of resort.
((2) **Mariande** (0476 805060) Highly recommended, especially for its 'excellent' five-course dinners. At Venosc end of resort.
((2) **Chalet Mounier** (0476 805690) Smartly modernised. Good reputation for its food, and well placed for the Diable bubble and nightlife.
((2) **Souleil'or** (0476 792469) Looks like a lift station, but pleasant and comfortable, and well placed for the Jandri Express gondola. The rooms and food are reportedly 'fantastic'.
((2) **Brunerie** (0476 792223) 'Basic and cheerful', large 2-star with plenty of parking and quite well positioned.
Self-catering Many of the apartments are stuck out at the north end of the resort – well worth avoiding.

EATING OUT
Plenty of choice
The hotel Bérangère has an excellent restaurant and the Chalet Mounier has a high reputation. The Petite Marmite has good food and atmosphere at reasonable prices. Bel'Auberge does classic French and is 'quite superb' – booking is advised. The Patate, the Dahu and Crêpes à Gogo are also recommended. Visitors on a budget can get a relatively cheap meal at either the Vetrata or the Spaghetteria and a moderately priced English breakfast at Smokey Joe's Tex-Mex.

APRES-SKI
Unsophisticated fun
Les Deux-Alpes is one of the liveliest of the French resorts, with plenty of bars, several of which stay open until the early hours. The Rodéo has a mechanical bucking bronco which attracts great numbers of rowdy après-skiers. The Windsor bar is another noisy British enclave. Corrigans, Smokey Joe's, the Secret Bar and the Baron are recommended. Bar Brésilien has 'great music and tremendous atmosphere'. The Avalanche is the most popular of the discos and the Opera is recommended by locals. There are quieter places too – the 'cosy' Bleuets is recommended.

The resort has contrived a couple of ways of dining at altitude – you can snowmobile to the glacier and back, eating on the way, or at full moon you can ski or board back to town after dinner (accompanied by ski patrollers).

OFF THE SLOPES
Not recommended
Les Deux-Alpes is not a particularly good choice for people not hitting the slopes. The pretty valley village of Venosc is worth a visit by gondola, and you can take a scenic helicopter flight to Alpe-d'Huez. There is a good pool and lots of scenic walks. Several mountain restaurants are accessible to pedestrians. Snowcat tours across the glacier provide wonderful views.

STAYING DOWN THE VALLEY
Worth considering
Close to the foot of the final ascent to Les Deux-Alpes are two near-ideal places for anyone thinking of travelling around to Alpe-d'Huez, La Grave and Serre-Chevalier, both Logis de France – the cheerful Cassini (0476 800410) at Le Freney, and the even more appealing Panoramique (0476 800625), at Mizoën.

Flaine

Extensive slopes, with traditional villages but bleak main resort

COSTS

① ② ③ ④ ⑤ ⑥

RATINGS

The slopes
Snow	****
Extent	****
Expert	****
Intermediate	*****
Beginner	*****
Convenience	*****
Queues	****
Mountain restaurants	**

The rest
Scenery	****
Resort charm	*
Off-slope	*

NEWS

We are assured that a new eight-seat gondola linking the village of Samoëns directly to Samoëns 1600 at mid-mountain in only eight minutes will at last be built for 2003/04 (it was originally planned for the 2001/02 season).

On the nursery slopes at Samoëns 1600, a new quad chair replacing the Damoiseaux drag-lift is also planned.

The first stage of the introduction of a hands-free lift pass system throughout the Grand Massif will happen for 2003/04.

In 2002/03 a new bowling alley with bar area and restaurant opened in Flaine.

There are long-term plans to expand Flaine's bed base and perhaps to build a funicular link from Magland, down in the valley, to bring in day visitors.

➕ Big, varied area, with off-piste challenges for experts as well as extensive intermediate terrain

➕ Huge recent investment in new lifts

➕ Reliable snow in the main bowl

➕ Compact, convenient, mainly car-free village, right on the slopes

➕ Excellent facilities for children

➕ Alternative of staying in traditional villages elsewhere in ski area

➕ Scenic setting, and glorious views

➕ Very close to Geneva airport

➖ Bleak 1960s Bauhaus buildings are not to everyone's taste, although architecturally 'listed'

➖ Main Flaine bowl has only a few short runs below the tree line, so bad weather can be a problem

➖ Links to outer sectors of the area are prone to closure by high winds

➖ No proper hotels in Flaine itself – only club hotels and apartments

➖ Not much nightlife

➖ Little to do off the slopes

So long as you don't care about the uncompromising architecture or narrow range of nightlife, Flaine has a lot going for it. It has slopes that intermediates will love, and lots of them – the area deservedly calls itself the Grand Massif. It also caters well for beginners, with free access to nursery slope lifts. There is challenging terrain for experts too – particularly for those prepared to take guidance and go off-piste. Many visitors, especially those with children, love it. It can get very busy at weekends because it is very close to Geneva.

The hotels have now all become club hotels run by tour operators such as Club Med and Crystal. The only alternative is to rent an apartment. But we increasingly receive reports from satisfied guests who choose to stay in the more traditional outlying villages such as Samoëns, Morillon and Les Carroz. The only problems are that these lower villages may suffer poor snow conditions and that links with the high Flaine bowl may be cut off in bad weather.

THE RESORT

We have to say we fall in the group that does not find Flaine's Bauhaus architecture attractive. The concrete massifs that form the core of the resort were conceived in the sixties as 'an example of the application of the principle of shadow and light'. They look particularly shocking from the approach road – a mass of blocks nestling at the bottom of the impressive snowy bowl. From the slopes they are less obtrusive, blending into the rocky grey hillside. One optimistic reporter even says, 'Strangely they do look great in black and white photos!'. For us, the outdoor sculptures by Picasso, Vasarely and Dubuffet do little to improve Flaine's austere ambience.

In common with other French Alpine purpose-built resorts, Flaine has improved its looks in recent years. The relatively new development of

Hameau-de-Flaine is built in a much more attractive chalet style – but is inconveniently situated 1km/0.5 miles from the slopes and main village.

In Flaine proper, everything is close by: supermarket, sports rental shops, ski schools, main lifts out etc. The resort itself is also easy to get to – only 70km/43 miles from Geneva, and about 90 minutes from the airport.

There are two parts to the main resort. The club hotels, and some apartments, are set in the lower part, Forum. The focus of this area is a

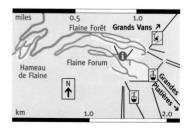

KEY FACTS

Resort	1600m
	5,250ft

Covers Grand Massif ski area	
Slopes	700-2480m
	2,300-8,140ft
Lifts	75
Pistes	265km
	165 miles
Green	12%
Blue	41%
Red	38%
Black	9%
Snowmaking	25%

For Flaine only	
Slopes	1600-2500m
	5,250-8,200ft
Lifts	28
Pistes	140km
	87 miles

Flaine has good facilities for children (and excellent slopes for adults, too) ↓

snow-covered square with buildings on three sides, the open fourth side blending with the slopes. Flaine Forêt, up the hillside and linked by lift, has its own bars and shops and most of the apartment accommodation.

There are children all over the place; they are catered for with play areas, and the resort is supposed to be traffic-free. This has become rather lax, in fact, and there is a fair amount of traffic; but the central Forum itself, leading to the pistes, is pretty safe. A regular bus service linking Hameau to the main village is said to be 'excellent'. A car is of no value in the resort, but does give you the option of visiting Chamonix (and Courmayeur via the Mont Blanc tunnel).

THE MOUNTAINS

With its 265km/165 miles of pistes, the Grand Massif is an impressive area, with plenty of scope for any level of skier or boarder, provided you can get to all of it – the greater part of the domain lies outside the main Flaine bowl and there are some fairly low altitude slopes. A 2003 reporter warns that only limited lifts/pistes were open before Christmas, despite good snow.

THE SLOPES
A big white playground
The day begins for most people at the **Grandes Platières** jumbo gondola, which speeds you in a single stage up

the north face of the Flaine bowl to the high-point of the Grand Massif, and a magnificent view of Mont Blanc.

Most of the runs are reds (though there are some blues curling away to the right as you look down the mountain, and one direct black). There are essentially four or five main ways down the barren, treeless, rolling terrain back to Flaine, or to chairs in the middle of the wilderness going back to the summit.

On the far right, the easy 14km/9 mile, picturesque Cascades blue run (one of the longest in the Alps) leads away from the lift system behind the Tête Pelouse and down to the outskirts of Sixt at 770m/2,530ft (giving a vertical drop of over 1700m/5,580ft). There is no lift back but there is a regular shuttle-bus service to the lifts at Samoëns or Morillon – there may be a lot of people waiting to get on the bus, though. Sixt has its own little west-facing area offering red and black slopes of 700m/2,300ft vertical – and is reachable from the bottom of Cascades run by drag-lift.

On the other side of the Tête Pelouse, a broad cat-walk leads to the experts-only **Gers** bowl. At the bottom, a flat trail links with the Cascades run or there's a drag back to the ridge.

Back at Platières, an alternative is to head left down the long red Méphisto (many of the runs in this area have diabolic names – Lucifer, Belzébuth etc) to the **Aujon** area. This opens up another sector of the bowl, again mostly red runs but with some blues further down. The lower slopes here are used as slalom courses. This sector is also reachable by gondola or drag-lifts from below the resort.

The eight-seater Grands Vans chair, reached from Forum by means of a slow bucket-lift (aka télébenne), gives access to the extensive slopes of Samoëns, Morillon and Les Carroz. You come first to the wide Vernant bowl equipped with three fast chair-lifts, one starting from a car park on the road up to Flaine. Beyond here the lie of the land is complicated, and the piste map does not represent it clearly. In good snow there is a choice of blues and reds winding down to **Les Carroz** or **Morillon**, the latter with a halfway point at 1100m/3,610ft. While there is a choice of blue, red and black runs on the top section above **Samoëns 1600**, the runs below here to Vercland are

boarding

Flaine suits boarders quite well – there's lots of varied terrain and plenty of off-piste with interesting nooks and crannies, including woods outside the main bowl. The key lifts are all now chairs or gondolas – with few unavoidable drag-lifts (beware of the vicious Aujon drag-lift though, which served the terrain-park last season!). There are two other terrain-park options, including one for kids. Black Side is the local specialist shop, in the central Forum.

LIFT PASSES

Grand Massif
Covers all the lifts in Flaine, Les Carroz, Morillon, Samoëns and Sixt.

Beginners
Four free lifts. Ski pass for beginners covers three more lifts.

Main pass
1-day pass €31
6-day pass €154

Senior citizens
Over 60: 6-day pass €130
Over 75: free pass

Children
Under 16: 6-day pass €122
Under 12: 6-day pass €112
Under 5: free pass

Alternative passes
Flaine area only – half and day passes available.

---

challenging blacks and reds (without snowmaking, so often closed).

Arrival back in Flaine can cause a problem: some reporters have said that it's difficult to get between the top of the resort and Forum. The trick is to loop round away from the buildings and approach from under the gondola – or catch the bucket down.

We have had past reports of lifts breaking down too often and being too easily closed because of high winds, cutting off links with the lower villages. Piste signing and grooming have, however, been praised. And the piste map has useful lists of the main connecting lifts and pistes between the different resorts.

TERRAIN-PARKS
Cater for kids to experts
There's a big terrain-park (called the JamPark Pro – standing for Jib and Air Maniacs) in the Aujon area of Flaine. Watch out for the vicious Aujon drag-lift, though, which is, according to a couple of reporters, as much of a challenge as the park! There's also an intermediates' park under the Charionde 2 chair on the Samoëns side, with green, red and black options and a variety of rails. And there's a kids' park, JamPark Kids, with a boarder-cross run under the Esserts quad on the Morillon side.

SNOW RELIABILITY
Usually keeps its whiteness
The main part of Flaine's slopes lie on the wide north- and north-west-facing flank of the Grandes Platières. Its direction, along with a decent height, means that it keeps the snow it receives. There is snowmaking on the greater part of the Aujon sector and on the nursery slopes. The runs towards Samoëns 1600 and Morillon 1100 are north-facing too, and some lower parts have snowmaking, but below here can be tricky or closed. The Les Carroz runs are west-facing and can suffer from strong afternoon sun, but a couple of runs have snowmaking.

FOR EXPERTS
Great fun with guidance
Flaine's family-friendly reputation tends to obscure the fact that it has some seriously challenging terrain. But much of it is off-piste and, although some of it looks like it can safely be explored without guidance, this impression is mistaken. The Flaine bowl is riddled with rock crevasses and potholes, and should be treated with the same caution that you would use on a glacier. There have been some tragic cases of off-piste skiers coming across nasty surprises, including a British skier falling to his death only yards from the piste.

All the black pistes on the map deserve their grading. The Diamant Noir, down the line of the main gondola, is a challenging 850m/2,790ft descent, tricky because of moguls, narrowness and other people rather than great steepness; the first pitch is the steepest, with spectators applauding from the overhead chair-lift.

To the left of the Diamant Noir as you look down are several short but steep off-piste routes through the crags of the Grandes Platières.

The Lindars Nord chair serves a shorter slope that often has the best snow in the area, and some seriously steep gradients if you look for them.

The Gers drag-lift, outside the main bowl beyond Tête Pelouse, serves great expert-only terrain. The piste going down the right of the drag is a proper black, but by departing from it you can find slopes of up to 45°. To the left of the drag is the impressive main Gers bowl – a great horseshoe of about 550m/1,800ft vertical, powder or moguls top to bottom, all off-piste. You can choose your gradient, from steep to very steep. As you look down the bowl, you see more adventurous ways into the bowl from the Grands Vans and Tête de Véret lifts.

There are further serious pistes on the top lifts above Samoëns 1600. Touring is a possibility behind the

Grandes Platières, and there are some scenic off-piste routes from which you can be retrieved by helicopter – such as the Combe des Foges, next to Gers.

FOR INTERMEDIATES
Something for everyone

Flaine is ideal for confident intermediates, with a great variety of pistes (and usually the bonus of good snow conditions, at least above Flaine itself). As a reporter puts it, 'There may not be many challenging runs, but there are very few dull ones.' The diabolically named reds that dominate the Flaine bowl are not really as hellish as their names imply – they tend to gain their status from short steep sections rather than overall difficulty, and they're great for improving technique. There are gentler cruises from the top of the mountain – Cristal, taking you to the Perdrix chair, or Serpentine, all the way home. The blues at Aujon are excellent for confidence-building, but the drag serving them is not.

The connections with the slopes outside the main bowl are classified blue but several blue-run reporters have found them tricky because of narrowness, crowds or poor snow. Once the connection has been made, however, all intermediates will enjoy the long tree-lined runs down to Les Carroz, as long as the snow is good. The Morillon slopes are also excellent intermediate terrain – the long green Marvel run to Morillon 1100 is an easy cruise with excellent signs along the way explaining (in English as well as French) about the local wildlife.

FOR BEGINNERS
Fairly good

There are excellent nursery slopes right by the village, served by free lifts which make a pass unnecessary until you are ready to go higher up the mountain. But a reporter warns that it is also used as a short cut back to the village for other skiers. There are no long green runs to progress to in the Flaine bowl – there is one above Morillon, though, and there are one or two gentle local blues (see 'For intermediates' above).

CROSS-COUNTRY
Very fragmented

The Grand Massif claims 64km/40 miles of cross-country tracks but only about 10km/6 miles of that is around Flaine itself. The majority is on the valley floor and dependent on low snow. There are extensive tracks between

ESF
t 0450 908100

International
t 0450 908441
ski.ecole.inter@
wanadoo.fr

Flaine Super Ski
Advanced skiers only
0450 908288

**Independent
instructors**
t 0450 478454
guy.pezet@
wanadoo.fr

Classes (ESF prices)
6 days (3hr per day)
€105

Private lessons
€26 for 1hr, for 1 or
2 people

CHILDREN

Both schools operate
ski kindergartens,
taking children aged
3 to 12 until 5pm.
Club Med Flaine
(0450 908166) has a
nursery for babies
aged from 4 months.
There is also an
independent nursery,
the Petits Loups
(0450 908782), for
children aged from 6
months to 4 years.

Ski classes for
children aged 5 to 12
cost €80 for 6 days
(ESF prices).

Morillon and Les Carroz, with some
tough uphill sections. Samoëns 1600
has its own tracks and makes the best
base for cross-country enthusiasts.

QUEUES
A few problems
The massive recent investment in new
lifts has eliminated some trouble
spots. But several reporters complain
of 20- to 30-minute queues for the
Vernant chair to get back to the Flaine
bowl in the afternoon (one suggests
coming back early, another going down
the Arolle piste and getting a bus back
from Car Park 4).

When the resort is full, the Grandes
Platières gondola is prone to queues
at the start of the day, but they move
quickly. The other main lift into the
Flaine bowl, the old Aup de Veran
gondola, also gets busy.

Queues elsewhere can build up at
weekends (it is very close to Geneva)
and when the lifts out of the Flaine
bowl are shut due to high winds or
when the weather is warm and the
lower resorts have poor snow (the
queues to go down can be worse than
those to go up when this happens).

Crowded pistes can also be a
problem, especially the Dolomie blue
(the only piste from Flaine towards
Samoëns, Morillon and Les Carroz).
And one reader saw two bad collisions
on crowded pistes during their one-
week stay.

MOUNTAIN RESTAURANTS
Back to base, or quit the bowl
In the Flaine bowl, there are few
restaurants above the resort's upper
outskirts. The Blanchot, at the bottom
of the Serpentine run, is popular and
rustic, with quite good, simple food,
but it can get crowded.

At Forum level, across the piste
from the gondola, is a pair of chalets
containing the welcoming Michet
('definitely worth a visit'), with very
good Savoyard food and table service,
and the self-service Eloge – friendly
but with a very limited menu. Up at
Forêt level, Chalet Bissac has a good
atmosphere, traditional decor and
excellent plain food. The nearby
Cascade is self-service, with a good
terrace. Epicéa near the end of the
Faust piste has a rustic atmosphere,
terrace and rave reviews.

Outside the Flaine bowl, we loved
the remote Chalet du Lac de Gers
(book in advance and ring for a

snowcat to tow you up from part way
down the Cascades run) – simple food
but splendid isolation and views of the
frozen lake. We also had an excellent
plat du jour at the rustic Igloo above
Morillon. The Chalet les Molliets near
the bottom of the Molliets chair is
charming and rustic. Reporters have
also recommended the Oreade at the
top of the gondola from Les Carroz.

SCHOOLS AND GUIDES
Getting better
The few reports we've had recently on
the ESF have been mixed and include
one report of a 'rude' instructor this
year. But recent reporters have praised
the International school ('excellent –
taking me off piste for the first time
and finding untracked powder' and 'big
into carving' said two 2003 reporters)
and the small specialist Super Ski
school ('small class sizes, good
instruction'). The ESF children's private
lessons in Samoëns were described as
'excellent'. One reporter criticised
Nouvelle Dimension in Les Carroz:
'Nobody spoke English and the teacher
had no patience with the English
beginner.'

FACILITIES FOR CHILDREN
Parents' paradise?
Flaine prides itself on being a family
resort, and the number of English-
speaking children around is a bonus.

Club Med Flaine has good childcare
facilities open to residents only. The
Petits Loups nursery takes children
from six months to four years. Some
other accommodation units have kids'
clubs of their own.

Hôtel
Le Bois de la Char

Your stay right on the pistes

Les Carroz-d'Arâches
40 minutes from Geneva Airport
10 minutes from highway A40

Tel: 00 33 (0) 4 50 90 06 18
E-mail: contact@hotel-boisdelachar.com
Website: www.hotel-boisdelachar.com

Photo credit: PHOTOTEM – Claude Monvoisin

GETTING THERE

Air Geneva 90km/56 miles (1½hr).

Rail Cluses (30km/19 miles); regular bus service.

Phone numbers
From abroad use the prefix +33 and omit the initial '0' of the phone number.

ACTIVITIES

Indoor Top Form centre (swimming pool complex with sauna, solarium, gymnasium, massage), bowling, arts and crafts gallery, cinema, auditorium, concerts, indoor climbing wall, cultural centre with library (some books in English)

Outdoor Natural ice rink, snow-shoe excursions, hang-gliding, paragliding para-skiing, helicopter rides, snow scooters, high mountain outings, ice-driving car circuit

STAYING THERE

HOW TO GO
Plenty of apartments
Accommodation is overwhelmingly in self-catering apartments.
Chalets There are few catered chalet options, but they include a couple of attractively traditional Scandinavian-style huts in Hameau. Crystal now run the Hotel Totem as a club-hotel and it had a couple of glowing 2003 reports.
Hotels All the hotels are now club-hotels, including a Club Med, run by tour operators of various nationalities. For a conventional hotel you have to go for one of the lower villages.
Self-catering The best apartments are out at Hameau. In Flaine Forêt, the Forêt and Grand Massif apartment buildings are attractively woody inside and there are hotel facilities such as a restaurant, bar and kindergarten.

EATING OUT
Not many stars
The Perdrix Noire in Forêt is a good bet – smart, busy but friendly. Its bar is also popular. The Michet (see 'Mountain restaurants') is open in the evening and is described as 'fantastic – great for fondue.' Try Chez la Jeanne, the Pizzeria in the shopping mall in Forum or La Grange for pizza. Chez Daniel offers a good range of Savoyard specialities, is good with kids, and has also been recommended for lunchtime crêpes and galettes. The Cîmes Rock is 'excellent but slow service' and 'it's best to go early because it gets very crowded' (see below).

APRES-SKI
Signs of life
Recent reports suggest that the après-ski scene is picking up. The resort is no longer limited to family groups, and some bars show signs of life.
The White Grouse pub has a big screen TV, rock music and punters trying to get pints in before the end of happy hour. The Flying Dutchman is 'cosy with lively music'. The bar at the bowling alley has a happy hour.
Later, the more French Cîmes Rock is liveliest, with bands or karaoke. The 'seedy', 'lively' Diamant Noir pool hall is open late. 'Avoid the Ski Fun unless you're dying for a late drink as it's 10 euros to get in and no great shakes,' says a reporter.

OFF THE SLOPES
Curse of the purpose-built
As with most purpose-built resorts, there are few walks, and no town to explore. Not recommended for people who don't want to hit the slopes. But there is a great ice-driving circuit where you can take a spin (literally) in your own car or, more sensibly, have a lesson in theirs (as we did). Snowmobile tours and the weekly torchlight descent are popular, and there's a cinema, gymnasium and swimming pool.

Les Carroz 1140m/3,740ft

This is a spacious, sunny, traditional, family resort where life revolves around the village square with its pavement cafes, restaurants and interesting little shops. It has a lived-in

feel of a real French village, with more animation than Flaine – 'a delight' says a recent visitor, who recommends the 3-star hotel Arbaron (0450 900267) for food, service and views. Even more highly recommended is the 2-star Bois de la Char (0450 900618): 'It is perfectly situated beside the piste. The food was good, the staff friendly and it was excellent value for money.' The Marlow pub 'seems to be the place to go' when you come off the slopes.

The gondola and chair-lift go straight into the Grand Massif area, but there's a steep 300m/1,000ft walk up from the centre – the nursery drag is a help or you can catch the free ski-bus (every 20 minutes).

Apartments make up a high percentage of the beds available, including new MGM apartments with indoor pool, sauna and spa facilities.

The ski school's torchlit descent is apparently 'not to be missed' – it starts off with fireworks and ends with vin chaud and live jazz in the square. The resort is hoping to build a terrain-park for the 2003/04 season.

Samoëns 720m/2,360ft

This is the only resort in France to be listed as a 'Monument Historique'. It was once a thriving centre for stone-masons and evidence of their work is clear in the centre. The central traffic-free area has a pretty square, medieval fountain, rustic old buildings, an ancient church, bars, restaurants and local shops – although one reporter felt that it didn't add up to a more charming village than Les Contamines, say. Despite the village's recent growth

on the outskirts, it still retains the feel of 'real' rural France.

A reporter recommends the Pizzeria Louisiana for its wood oven pizzas and 'highly alcoholic' ice creams. Another praises Chalet Fleurie (0450 901011) and Chardon Bleu (0450 907466), both a car-ride away in Verchaix.

A new 8-person gondola straight from the village to the slopes at Samoëns 1600 – originally planned to be built for 2001/02 – should finally open for Christmas 2003. This will cut out the need to take a bus to and from the lift at Vercland and greatly increase the attraction of basing yourself in Samoëns. It will take just eight minutes to get up to the heart of the local slopes at 1600m. The long-awaited lift was held up so long due to protests by environmentalists and other local objections. There is a good beginners' area at Samoëns 1600 and blue runs above it. Catching the gondola down at the end of the day is no hardship, as the lower runs to Vercland are often tricky or closed. There local hotels are mainly 2-star.

Morillon 700m/2,300ft

Not quite in the Samoëns league, but still a pretty rustic village, Morillon makes a good base, with an efficient gondola from the upper fringes of the village to the mid-mountain mini-resort of Morillon 1100 (Les Esserts) – also reachable by road. Up here there is a large and 'delightful' ski kindergarten plus good slopes for adult beginners and new apartments right on the piste – it's 'dead as a dodo in the evenings', though, says a reporter.

La Grave

A superb mountain for good skiers and free-riders

COSTS

① ② ③ ④ ⑤ ⑥

RATINGS

The slopes

Snow	***
Extent	*
Expert	*****
Intermediate	*
Beginner	*
Convenience	***
Queues	****
Mountain restaurants	**

The rest

Scenery	****
Resort charm	***
Off-slope	*

NEWS

La Grave does not change much, and that is half the charm of the place.

+ Legendary off-piste mountain

+ Usually crowd-free

+ Usually good snow conditions, with powder higher up

+ Link to Les Deux-Alpes

+ Easy access by car to other nearby resorts

– Rather drab, charmless village

– Poor weather spells regular lift closures – on average, two days per week

– Suitable for experts only, despite some easy slopes at altitude

– Nothing to do off the slopes

La Grave enjoys legendary status among experts. It's a quiet old village with around 500 visitor beds and just one serious lift – a small stop-start gondola serving a high, wild and predominantly off-piste mountainside. The result: an exciting, usually crowd-free area. Strictly, you ought to have a guide, but in good weather many people go it alone. It's great for a day trip if you are staying in a nearby resort such as Alpe-d'Huez, Les Deux-Alpes or Serre-Chevalier.

THE RESORT

La Grave is an unspoilt mountaineering village set on a steep hillside facing the impressive glaciers of majestic La Meije. It's rather drab, and the busy road to Briançon doesn't help. But it still has a rustic feel, and prices are low by resort standards. The village is small and the single lift is across the road. Storms close the slopes on average two days a week – so a car is useful for access to nearby resorts.

THE MOUNTAIN

A slow two-stage 'pulse' gondola (with an extra station at a pylon halfway up the lower stage) ascends into the slopes and finishes at 3200m/10,500ft. Above that, a short walk and a drag-lift give access to a second drag serving twin blue runs on a glacier slope of about 350m/1,150ft vertical – from here you can ski to Les Deux-Alpes. But the reason that people come here is to explore the legendary slopes back towards La Grave. These slopes offer no defined, patrolled, avalanche-protected pistes – but there are two marked itinéraires (with several variations now indicated on the 'piste' map) of 1400m/4,590ft vertical down to the pylon lift station at 1800m/5,910ft, or all the way down to the valley – a vertical of 2150m/7,050ft.

Slopes The Chancel route is mostly of red-run gradient; the Vallons de la Meije is more challenging but not too steep. People do take these routes without a guide or avalanche protection equipment, but we couldn't possibly recommend it.

There are many more demanding runs away from the itinéraires, including couloirs that range from the straightforward to the seriously hazardous, and long descents from the glacier to the valley road below the village, with return by taxi, bus, or strategically parked car. The dangers are considerable (people die here every year), and good guidance is essential. You can also descend

The best place for lunch is the Chancel refuge, with fabulous views back down to La Grave →

SNOWPIX.COM / CHRIS GILL

FRANCE

270

KEY FACTS

Resort	1450m
	4,760ft
Slopes	1450-3550m
	4,760-11,650ft
Lifts	4
Pistes	5km
	3 miles
Green/Blue	100%

The 'difficulty' figure relates to on-piste; practically all the skiing – at least 90% – is off-piste

Snowmaking	None

Phone numbers
From abroad use the prefix +33 and omit the initial '0' of the phone number.

TOURIST OFFICE

t 0476 799005
ot@lagrave-lameije.com
www.lagrave-lameije.
com

southwards to St-Christophe, returning by bus and the lifts of Les Deux-Alpes.

Terrain-parks There aren't any.

Snow reliability The chances of powder snow on the high, north-facing slopes are good, but there are essentially no pistes to fall back on if conditions are tricky. The biggest worry is poor weather keeping the mountain closed for several days at a time.

Experts La Grave's uncrowded off-piste slopes have earned it cult status among hard-core skiers. Only experts should contemplate a stay here – and then only if prepared to deal with bad weather by sitting tight or struggling over the Col du Lautaret to the woods of Serre-Chevalier.

Intermediates The itinéraires get tracked into a piste-like state, and adventurous intermediates could tackle the Chancel. But the three blue runs at the top of the gondola won't keep anyone occupied for long. The valley stations of Villar d'Arène and Lautaret, around 3km/2 miles and 8km/5 miles to the east respectively, and Chazelet, 3km/2 miles to the north-west, offer very limited slopes with a handful of intermediate and beginner runs.

Beginners Novices tricked into coming here can go up the valley to the beginner slopes at Le Chazelet, which has two cannons for snowmaking.

Snowboarding There are no special facilities for boarders, but advanced free-riders will be in their element on the open off-piste powder.

Cross-country There is a total of 30km/19 miles of loops in the area.

Queues Normally, there are short queues only at weekends – at the bottom station first thing, and at the mid-station later. If snow conditions back to the valley are poor, queues can build up for the gondola down from the mid and lower stations.

Mountain restaurants Surprisingly, there are three decent mountain restaurants; the best is the refuge on the Chancel itinéraire.

Schools and guides There are a dozen or so guides in the village, offering a wide range of services through their bureau. See also Hotels below.

Facilities for children Babysitting can be arranged through the tourist office.

STAYING THERE

How to go There are several simple hotels.

Hotels The Edelweiss (0476 799093) is a friendly 2-star with a cosy bar and restaurant. La Chaumine Skiers Lodge (www.skierslodge.com) is set 3km/ 2 miles above La Grave, owned by a Swede, and runs all-inclusive week-long packages, including guiding.

Self-catering Self-catering accommodation is bookable through the tourist office.

Eating out Most people eat in their hotels, though there are alternatives.

Après-ski The standard tea-time après-ski gathering place is the central Glaciers bar, known to habitués as chez Marcel. The Vieux Guide gets crowded later. The Candy bar is now called the Vallons. O'Neill's has shut but Bois des Fées has opened.

Off the slopes Anyone not using the slopes will find La Grave much too small and quiet.

Maurienne valley

A wide range of resorts, with prices below the French norm

COSTS

① ② ③ ④ ⑤ ⑥

NEWS

Valloire
For 2003/04 there will be a new fast six-pack and extra snowmaking.

For 2002/03 there were two new lifts: a quad chair from 2188m/7,180ft to the top of the slopes; and the new Arnouvaz triple chair. Snowmaking was increased.

Val Cenis
A new fast six-pack from Lanslebourg is planned for 2003/04.

Les Sybelles
This major development in the Maurienne region, involving lift links between several resorts – Le Corbier and La Toussuire among them – is covered in a new, separate chapter.

Go to the southern extremity of the Val-Thorens pistes or set off ski-touring northwards from La Grave, and you come to the same place: the Maurienne valley – a great curving trench cut by a river appropriately called the Arc. This backwater has over 20 winter resorts, ranging from pleasant old valley villages to convenience resorts purpose-built in the 1960s. What they have in common are prices that are low by French resort standards – and participation in a special five-day pass deal that allows you to visit a different resort each day.

For the coming 2003/04 season, some of these resorts are being linked by lift and piste to form an impressively large area called Les Sybelles, and we have given these resorts their own new chapter. The three resorts covered below are not linked, though some of them could be – indeed, in the 1970s grand plans were formulated to link Valfréjus with Valmeinier and Valloire to the west, and with Bardonecchia in Italy. But the linking lifts were never built.

A visit to the Maurienne can also take in Europe's highest resort, its biggest lift network and some of its best snow: Orelle, in the valley bottom, has a gondola up to the slopes of Val-Thorens, at the southern end of the Three Valleys.

VALLOIRE 1430m/4,690ft
Valloire is the best known of the Maurienne resorts internationally, and it offers the most extensive slopes, shared with the twin stations of Valmeinier 1500 and 1800. The village has a rustic French feel to it and retains a life as a farming community.

THE RESORT
The resort is quite a drive up from the valley. Despite considerable development, it has retained a feeling of 'real' France, complete with impressive old church, crêperies, fromageries, reasonable prices, villagey atmosphere – including a street market – and friendly locals.

THE MOUNTAIN
The 150km/93 miles of piste are spread over three similar-sized sectors, two above Valloire and the third above the separate resort of Valmeinier.
Slopes The sectors accessible from Valloire are Sétaz – shady slopes, part open and part wooded, served by gondola to Thimel at mid-mountain – and Crey du Quart – broad, open, west-facing slopes reachable from the village by chair-lift or gondola, or from Sétaz by chair-lift. Black, blue and green runs from Crey du Quart provide links to the two parts of Valmeinier (1500 and 1800) and so to the open west-facing slopes beyond. Each of these sectors has top heights in the

range 2400m to 2600m (7,870ft to 8,530ft) and verticals of around 1000m/3,280ft. The slopes are almost entirely of intermediate difficulty; Les Karellis (a 45-minute drive) is better for more taxing runs (and for better snow and scenery). One reporter complains about piste map inaccuracies.
Terrain-parks There's a terrain-park with a half-pipe and a boarder-cross course on the Valloire slopes.
Snow reliability Reliable snow-cover is not a strong point. Despite snow-guns on many of the lower slopes, ensuring that most of the area is reliably accessible, some important links – notably the runs down to Valmeinier 1500 from Crey du Quart – can suffer terribly from poor snow. One reporter found these closed in mid-February. The largely north-facing tree runs in the Sétaz area hold their snow well. Grooming is reportedly good.
Experts Sétaz has several black runs, but they don't represent a challenge for experts – the mogul field down to Valmeinier 1500 is steeper.
Intermediates There are plenty of intermediate options in all three sectors. The Crey du Quart section is particularly good for an easy day.
Beginners There are limited village nursery areas but better slopes up the mountain on Sétaz and Crey du Quart.
Snowboarding The extent of the terrain means that there is a fair bit of good free-riding to do. Novices beware: the

↑ Valloire is an unspoiled, traditional village in a pretty setting, high above the Maurienne valley itself

BERNARD GRANGE / OT DE VALLOIRE

return from Valmeinier includes some drag-lifts.

Cross-country There are 25km/16 miles of cross-country trails.

Queues There are few bottlenecks given good snow, but they do occur when lower slopes become patchy.

Mountain restaurants They are few but of good quality. The Mérégers's terrace is recommended. If descending to the village for lunch, the Maître Kanter is recommended.

Schools and guides The two schools are the ESF and the International.

Facilities for children The Aiglons nursery takes children from six months to six years.

STAYING THERE

How to go There's a fair choice of hotel and apartment accommodation.

Hotels The 3-star Grand (0479 590095) and 2-star Christiania (0479 590057) are recommended, both well placed.

Eating out Most of the restaurants are pizza and fondue joints. The Gastilleur has the best French cuisine in town.

Après-ski Après-ski is fairly quiet but picks up at the weekend. The Irish pub gets 'packed, with great atmosphere'.

Off the slopes There's an ice rink, a cinema, some walking paths and paragliding.

VALFREJUS 1550m/5,090ft

Valfréjus is a small and unusual modern resort – built in the woods, with most of the slopes higher up above the tree line.

THE RESORT

The resort is a compact and quite pleasant affair, built on a narrow, shady shelf, with woods all around. There are several apartment blocks grouped around the main lift station, and chalets scattered here and there on the hillside.

THE MOUNTAIN

There are runs of all grades back through the trees towards the village, but the focus of the slopes is Plateau d'Arrondaz, at 2200m/7,215ft, reached by gondola or chair-lift.

Slopes Above Plateau d'Arrondaz are steep, open slopes – genuine bumpy blacks, with excellent snow – on Punta Bagna (2735m/8,975ft), served by the second stage of the gondola, and gentler blue runs from Col d'Arrondaz. From both the top and the col there are also sunny intermediate runs to Le Pas du Roc on the back side of the hill, with chair-lifts back to both high points, or the option of the glorious, long, away-from-the-lifts blue Jeu run (with off-piste variations and some narrow paths along the way) to the village – all in all almost 1200m/3,400ft vertical.

Terrain-parks There's a natural terrain-park.

Snow reliability Snow-cover in the main open area is pretty reliable, but snowmaking on the lower runs to the village is urgently required.

Experts There is good off-piste sport above the main plateau and heli-skiing over the border in Italy is available.

Intermediates Within the small area, there is something for everyone. Near-beginners might welcome more easy blues, but it would be a good place for a confident intermediate to get in some serious practice on good snow.

Beginners There are nursery slopes at mid-mountain and village levels.

Snowboarding There's some good off-piste potential. Beginners can get around without having to negotiate any drags.

Cross-country Just a small 2km/1 mile loop up at Plateau d'Arondaz.

Queues A recent visitor reported no real problems, though the Pas du Roc chairs are very slow.

KEY FACTS

Valloire/Valmeinier

Slopes	1430-2595m
	4,690-8,510ft
Lifts	33
Pistes	150km
	93 miles
Green	25%
Blue	27%
Red	37%
Black	11%
Snowmaking	10km
	6 miles

Valfréjus

Slopes	1550-2735m
	5,090-8,970ft
Lifts	12
Pistes	52km
	32 miles
Green	20%
Blue	50%
Red	10%
Black	20%
Snowmaking	1 km
	0.5 miles

Val-Cenis

Slopes	1400-2800m
	4,590-9,190ft
Lifts	22
Pistes	80km
	50 miles
Green	21%
Blue	23%
Red	42%
Black	14%
Snowmaking	10km
	6 miles

Phone numbers

From abroad use the prefix +33 and omit the initial '0' of the phone number.

TOURIST OFFICES

Valloire
t 0479 590396
infos@valloire.net
www.valloire.net

Valmeinier
t 0479 595369
info@valmeinier.com
www.valmeinier.com

Valfréjus
t 0479 053383
info@valfrejus.com
www.valfrejus.com

Val-Cenis
t 0479 052366
info@valcenis.com
www.valcenis.com

Mountain restaurants The 'basic' Punta Bagna, at the top of the gondola, has superb views, and the Bergerie at the mid-station has table-service inside and out.

Schools and guides Lessons are offered by the ESF and the International school.

Facilities for children One nursery takes babies aged from three months to three years. Two nurseries take children aged three to six years.

STAYING THERE

How to go There are two hotels and 10 tourist residences in the resort.

Hotels The 3-star Valfréjus (0492 126212) is central and has a pleasant restaurant. The 2-star Grand Vallon (0479 050807) has superb views.

Eating out Restaurants in the village include a pizzeria and a crêperie.

Après-ski Après-ski is limited – the Snow Club, the Bois Brûlé and the Javana are the liveliest bars.

Off the slopes Activities are limited. There are marked walks and a natural skating rink and paragliding facilities.

VAL-CENIS 1400m/4,595ft

Val-Cenis is a marketing concept rather than a place. It comprises two pleasant villages in the Haute Maurienne, the high and remote part of the valley.

THE RESORT

Lanslebourg is a long, linear place, spreading along the Route Nationale 6 (a dead end in winter, when the road over the Col du Mont-Cenis becomes a piste). It's pleasant enough, but no great beauty. A bus-ride up the valley, Lanslevillard is more captivating – off the road, randomly arranged, rustic, and split into three.

THE MOUNTAIN

There are lifts up into the north-facing slopes from a number of base stations along the valley, including Lanslebourg and three points in Lanslevillard. The main one, a gondola, starts between the two villages, on the fringes of Lanslevillard.

Slopes Above mid-mountain is a good range of open runs to suit every ability, served by chairs and drags. Below mid-mountain all the runs are prettily wooded – there is usually an easy blue or green alternative to the various red runs back down as well.

Terrain-parks There is a terrain-park.

Snow reliability Most of the runs are north-facing and there is snowmaking on the protected tree runs back to each of the base stations.

Experts There is ample off-piste but little else to challenge experts. From the top station there is a good, mogulled black down the shady front face and a sunny isolated black over the back to the Col.

Intermediates There are intermediate runs all over the mountain allowing for some top-to-bottom cruises of up to 1400m/4,595ft vertical. A visit to Termignon's mainly easy slopes is highly recommended by 'impressed' reporters, but beware 'savage drags'.

Beginners There are easy runs by the base stations and winding through the forest – including a splendid green following the hairpin road from the Col.

Snowboarding Beginners should stay in Lanslevillard to avoid some long access drags.

Cross-country There are 6km/4 miles of free trails locally and a further 80km/50 miles of trails higher up at Bessans, further up the valley.

Queues Recent reporters confirm that queues are rare – 'mainly at the gondola in the afternoon' – and tend to move quite quickly.

Mountain restaurants A reporter recommends both the rustic Fema at mid-mountain and Mélèzes (table-service) at the gondola base.

Schools and guides A recent reporter comments that the instructors spoke very little English, but that the class sizes were small.

Facilities for children The two village nurseries take kids from six months. The tour operator Snowcoach has its own facilities for looking after non-skiing children.

STAYING THERE

How to go There are modest hotels in both villages.

Hotels The best is the 3-star Alpazur (0479 059369). The food and the outside hot-tub are also recommended.

Eating out There is a reasonable range of modest eating-out alternatives with a dozen restaurants in each village.

Après-ski Après-ski is quiet but there are a couple of discos open till late. The Napoleon and the Blue Ice bars received recommendations this year.

Off the slopes There is not a lot for non-skiers. There's a leisure centre in Lanslevillard, with a pool, and an artificial ice rink. And there are various walking paths to explore.

Megève

One of the traditional old winter holiday towns

COSTS

①②③④⑤⑥

RATINGS

The slopes

Snow	**
Extent	*****
Expert	**
Intermediate	****
Beginner	***
Convenience	**
Queues	****
Mountain restaurants	****

The rest

Scenery	****
Resort charm	****
Off-slope	****

NEWS

In 2002/03 a new gondola replaced the existing one in the Princesse area – more than doubling the capacity from 1,100 to 2,800 people per hour.

A new entertainment complex in the centre of town opened – it includes a piano bar, a disco and a restaurant.

Plans for a major extension of the slopes of Le Jaillet – linking them via Christomet to La Giettaz, west of Megève on the road to La Clusaz – seem to have been delayed. When we went to press no date had been set for this to happen.

➕ Extensive slopes, with miles of easy pistes, ideal for intermediates

➕ Scenic setting, with splendid views

➕ Charming old village centre, with very swanky shopping

➕ Some lovely luxury hotels

➕ Both gourmet and simple mountain lunches in attractive surroundings

➕ Excellent cross-country trails

➕ Different lift pass options cover other worthwhile resorts nearby

➕ Great for weekends – co-operative hotels, short drive from Geneva

➕ If it snows, deserted mountains

➕ Plenty to do off the slopes

➖ With most of the slopes below 2000m/6,560ft there's a risk of poor snow, especially on runs to the village – although the grassy terrain does not need a thick covering and snowmaking has improved a lot

➖ Three separate mountains, two linked by lift but not by piste, and the third not linked at all

➖ Not many challenging pistes – the few blacks are not extreme – but good off-piste potential

➖ Traffic jams and fumes at weekends and peak season

Megève is the essence of rustic chic. It has a medieval heart, but it was, in a way, the original purpose-built French ski resort – conceived in the 1920s as a French alternative to Switzerland's St Moritz. And although Courchevel took over as France's most fashionable winter sports resort ages ago, Megève's sumptuous hotels and chalets still attract plenty of 'beautiful people' with fur coats and fat wallets. Happily, you don't need either to enjoy it.

The risk of poor snow still makes us nervous about booking way ahead; but it is certainly true that a few inches of snow is enough to give skiable cover on the grassy slopes. And on our 2003 visit we had knee-deep powder and a fabulous time. What's more, the list of plus points above is as long as they come.

THE RESORT

Megève is in a lovely sunny setting and has a beautifully preserved traditional medieval centre, which is pedestrianised and comes complete with open-air ice rink, horse-drawn sleighs, cobbled streets and a fine church. Lots of smart clothing, jewellery, antique, gift and food shops add to the chic atmosphere.

The main Albertville-Chamonix road bypasses the centre, and there are expensive underground car parks. But the resort's clientele arrives mainly by car and the resulting traffic jams and fumes are a major problem, though a regular visitor detects improvement. It's worst at weekends, but can be serious every afternoon in high season.

The clientele are mainly well-heeled French couples and families, who come here as much for an all-round winter holiday and for the people-watching potential as for the slopes themselves.

The nightlife is, as you'd expect, smart rather than lively.

A gondola within walking distance of central Megève gives direct access to one of the three mountains, Rochebrune. This sector can also be reached directly by a cable-car from the southern edge of town. The main lifts for the bigger Mont d'Arbois sector start from an elevated suburb of the resort – though there is also a cable-car link from Rochebrune. The third sector, Le Jaillet, starts some way out on the north-west fringes of the town.

Staying close to one of the main lifts makes a lot of sense. Some accommodation is a long walk from the lifts, and the free bus services are not super-convenient.

There is a variety of different lift passes available, the widest-ranging covering Les Contamines, Les Houches and Chamonix. A car is handy for visiting other resorts included on the various passes.

THE MOUNTAINS

The three different mountains provide predominantly easy intermediate cruising, much of it prettily set in the woods and with some spectacular views. But there are tough runs to be found and large areas of off-piste that are neglected by most visitors. The wooded slopes make it a great resort to head for in poor weather. Some reporters complain that the piste grading is inconsistent.

THE SLOPES
Pretty but low

Two of the three areas are linked by a cross-valley cable-car, though not by piste. The third is separate.

The biggest, highest and most varied sector is **Mont d'Arbois**, accessible not only from the town but also by a gondola from La Princesse, way out to the north-east of town. It offers some wooded slopes but is mainly open, especially higher up.

Most of the slopes face more-or-less west, but there are north-east-facing slopes to Le Bettex and on down to St-Gervais. A two-stage gondola returns you to the top. You can work your way over to Mont Joux and up to the small Mont Joly area – Megève's highest slopes. And from there you can descend to the backwater village of St-Nicolas-de-Véroce (there's a splendid red run along the ridge with

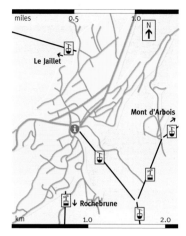

spectacular views of Mont Blanc in front and mile after mile of rolling peaks on both sides); tediously slow chair-lifts bring you back to Mont Joux. Directly behind Mont Joly, further up the same valley as St-Nicolas-de-Véroce, is the substantial resort of Les Contamines.

From the Mont d'Arbois lift base, the Rocharbois cable-car goes across the valley to **Rochebrune**. Alpette is the starting point for Megève's historic downhill course. A network of gentle, wooded, north-east-facing slopes, served by drags and chair-lifts, lead across to the high-point of Cote 2000.

The third area, and much the quietest, is **Le Jaillet**, accessed by

Megève

LIFT PASSES

Evasion Mont Blanc
Covers all lifts on Rochebrune, Mont d'Arbois, St-Gervais, Le Bettex, St-Nicolas, Le Jaillet, Combloux, Les Contamines.

Beginners
Pay by the ride.

Main pass
1-day pass €31
6-day pass €148

Senior citizens
Over 60: 6-day pass €133
Over 80: free pass

Children
Under 15: 6-day pass €118
Under 5: free pass

Notes
Half-day pass available in the afternoon.

Alternative passes
Mont Blanc pass covers all lifts in the resorts of the Mont Blanc area plus Courmayeur in Italy. Megève pass valid for Rochebrune, Mont d'Arbois, St-Gervais, St-Nicolas, Le Jaillet and Combloux. Jaco pass valid for Le Jaillet, Christomet and Combloux.

gondola from just outside the north-west edge of town and served mainly by slow, old lifts. From the top of the gondola are predominantly easy, east-facing pistes. The high point is Christomet. In the other direction, a series of long, tree-lined runs and lifts serves the area above Combloux.

TERRAIN-PARKS
Music to motivate
There is a 320m/1,050ft slope on Mont Joux with a half-pipe, quarter-pipe, pyramid and a section of challenging moguls. A sound system at the bottom helps to motivate the faint-hearted.

SNOW RELIABILITY
The area's main weakness
The problem is that the slopes are low, with very few runs above 2000m/6,560ft, and partly sunny – the Megève side of Mont d'Arbois gets the afternoon sun. So in a poor snow year, or in a warm spell, snow-cover and quality on the lower slopes can suffer badly – in which case you may need to ride the lifts back down.

Fortunately, the grassy slopes don't need much depth of snow, and the resort has expanded its snowmaking network to 252 snow-guns at the last count. Some runs are now entirely covered, including the long red Olympique run at Rochebrune. There is also a high standard of piste grooming.

FOR EXPERTS
Off-piste is the main attraction
One of Megève's great advantages for expert skiers is that it does not attract many of them, who are instead lured by Chamonix's steeper descents 45 minutes away. As a result you can often make first tracks on challenging slopes many days after a fresh dump.

The Mont Joly and Mont Joux sections offer the steepest slopes. The top chair here serves a genuinely black run, and the slightly lower Epaule chair has some steep runs back down and also accesses some good off-piste, as well as pistes, down to St-Nicolas.

The steep area beneath the second stage of the Princesse gondola can be a play area of powder runs among the trees. Cote 2000 has a small section of steep runs, including good off-piste.

The black run under the Christomet chair is no longer on the map and, given decent snow, could be a good spot to practise off-piste technique.

FOR INTERMEDIATES
Superb if the snow is good
Good intermediates will enjoy the Mont d'Arbois area most. The black runs below the Princesse gondola are perfectly manageable. The runs served by the Grand Vorasset drag and the most direct route between Mont d'Arbois and Le Bettex are also interesting. Similarly challenging are the steepest of the Jaillet sector pistes.

It's a great area for the less confident. A number of comfortable runs lead down to Le Bettex and La Princesse from Mont d'Arbois, while nearby Mont Joux accesses long, problem-free runs to St-Nicolas. Alpette and Cote 2000 are also suitable.

Even the timid can get a great deal of mileage in. All main valley-level lifts have easy routes down to them (although the Milloz piste to the Princesse mid-station is a little steep). There are some particularly good, long, gentle cruises between Mont Joux and Megève via Mont d'Arbois. But in all sectors, you'll find easy, blue runs.

FOR BEGINNERS
Good choice of nursery areas
There are beginner slopes at valley level, and more snow-sure ones at altitude on each of the main mountains. There are also plenty of very easy longer green runs to progress to.

FOR CROSS-COUNTRY
An excellent area
There are 75km/47 miles of varied trails spread throughout the area. Some are at altitude (1300m–1550m/4,270ft–5,090ft), making lunchtime meetings with Alpine skiers simple.

boarding

Boarding doesn't really fit with Megève's traditional, rather staid, upmarket image. But free-riders will find lots of untracked off-piste powder for days after new snowfalls. It's a good place to try boarding for the first time, with plenty of fairly wide, gentle runs and a lot of chair-lifts and gondolas; though there are a fair number of drag-lifts, they are generally avoidable. There are no specialist snowboard schools, but all the ski schools offer boarding lessons.

chalets offering great charm and good food and views at modest prices.

At the base of the Mont Joux lift, Chez Marie du Rosay is recommended, as is the Alpage on the back side of the hill, at Les Communailles.

At the foot of the Cote 2000 slopes is the popular Auberge de la Cote 2000, a former farm; Radaz, up the slope a little, enjoys better views.

Alpette, atop the Rochebrune ridge, offers excellent all-round views outside, a comfortable lounge inside.

At Combloux both restaurants adjacent to the to the top car park 'serve excellent food at acceptable prices', says a reporter.

SCHOOLS AND GUIDES
Adventurous

The two well-established schools offer expeditions to the Vallée Blanche and heli-skiing (in Italy), as well as normal teaching. The International school appears to be more popular with readers than its rival, the ESF. White Sensations is a new school with eight BASI-trained instructors. Off-piste guides are available. We had a great morning powder skiing in the trees with Alex Périnet (06 8542 8339).

FACILITIES FOR CHILDREN
Language problems

The kindergartens offer a wide range of activities. But lack of English-speaking staff (and companions) could be a drawback.

STAYING THERE

HOW TO GO
Few packages

Relatively few British tour operators go to Megève, but there is an impressive range of accommodation.

Chalets A few UK tour operators offer catered chalets. For a cheap and very cheerful base, you won't do better than Stanford's Sylvana – a creaky, unpretentious old hotel, reachable on skis, run along chalet lines. Stanford also offers another similar property, the Rond Point, in the centre. Simon Butler Skiing offers tuition-based holidays and chalet accommodation. We've received very positive feedback about the quality of instruction.

Hotels Megève offers a range of exceptionally stylish and welcoming hotels. There are simpler places, too. ((((4) **Mont Blanc** (0450 212002) Megève's traditional leading hotel –

SCHOOLS

ESF
t 0450 210097
International
t 0450 587888
Freeride
t 0450 930352
White Sensations
t 0450 210151

Classes
(ESF prices)
5 mornings (2½hr)
€110
Private lessons
€33 for 1hr, for 1 or 2 people

GUIDES

Compagnie des Guides
t 0450 215511

QUEUES
Few weekday problems

Megève is relatively queue-free during the week, except at peak holiday time. But school holidays and sunny Sunday crowds can mean some delays. The Lanchettes drag between Cote 2000 and the rest of the Rochebrune slopes gets busy – as does the cable-car linking the two mountains. Crowded pistes at Mont Joux and Mont d'Arbois can also be a problem.

MOUNTAIN RESTAURANTS
Something for all budgets

Megève has some chic, expensive, gourmet mountain huts but plenty of cheaper options too. Booking ahead is advisable for table-service places.

The Mont d'Arbois area is very well endowed with restaurants. There are two suave places popular with poseurs with small dogs and fur coats – the Club House and the Idéal Sports. The Ravière, tucked away in the woods near La Croix drag, is a tiny rustic hut which does a set meal and where booking is essential. The Igloo, with wonderful views of Mont Blanc, has both self- and table-service sections.

Above St-Nicolas are several little

CHILDREN

There are three kindergartens dotted around the sprawling resort, all offering skiing. Age limits and hours vary. Club des Piou-Piou (0450 589765) at the top of the Chamois lift takes 3 to 4 year olds. Meg'Loisirs (0450 587784) is a comprehensive nursery for ages 12 months to 6 years. La Princesse (0450 930086), at the Princesse gondola, takes ages 2½ to 6.

The ski schools run classes for 3 to 4 year olds (5 mornings €83) and 5 to 12 year olds (5 mornings €101).

GETTING THERE

Air Geneva 70km/43 miles (1hr); Lyon 180km/112 miles (2½hr).

Rail Sallanches (13km/8 miles); regular buses from station.

Phone numbers
From abroad use the prefix +33 and omit the initial '0' of the phone number.

---

elegant and fashionable. Right in the centre, and close to the main gondola. ((((4) **Chalet du Mont d'Arbois** (0450 212503) Prettily decorated, former Rothschild family home, now a Relais & Châteaux hotel in a secluded position above town, near the Mont d'Arbois gondola.
((((4) **Fer à Cheval** (0450 213039) Rustic-chic at its best, with a warmly welcoming wood-and-stone interior and excellent food. Close to the centre.
(((3) **Coin du Feu** (0450 210494) 'Very well managed' chalet midway between Rochebrune and Chamois lifts.
(((3) **Grange d'Arly** (0450 587788) Wrong side of the road, but still quite close to the centre; a beautifully furnished chalet.
(((3) **Ferme Hôtel Duvillard** (0450 211462) Smartly restored farmhouse, perfectly positioned for the slopes, at the foot of the Mont d'Arbois gondola.
((2) **Gai Soleil** (0450 210070) Comfortable family-run place – five minutes' walk from the centre of town and the main gondola.
((2) **Mourets** (0450 210476) Entirely inconvenient location but repeatedly recommended by readers: 'basic but spacious with good food and views'; 'very friendly'; 'excellent hosts'.
((2) **Sévigné** (0450 212309) Ten minutes from the centre, but 'really delightful – very quaint, excellent food'.
Self-catering There are some very comfortable and well positioned apartments – not cheap. You can reduce the cost by renting outside town. The tourist office in Combloux is a good starting point.

EATING OUT
Very French
Megève has lots of high-quality, expensive restaurants – many of which are recommended in the top restaurant guides. The Ferme de mon Père, for example, has three Michelin rosettes. This and the restaurants in all the best hotels are excellent but extremely expensive. The Cintra, also expensive and fashionable, is 'great for fresh seafood'. Michel Gaudin is one of the best in town – with good value menus.

Some reporters wish for more variety of cuisine. The Phnom-Penh is one of the few possibilities. Mama Mia is a popular Italian restaurant, though recent reports are mixed. The Pallas is recommended for pizzas

For a contrast to Megève's glitzy restaurants, one reporter recommends a trip to Le Pinocchio, a small pizzeria in Combloux. 'It is simple, very cheap and, provided you like pizza or pasta, very good indeed.' We eat at the Hostellerie between Megève centre and the Rochbrune cable-car; good value honest French food and wine.

APRES-SKI
Strolling and jazz
Megève is a great place to stroll around after the lifts close. But we found few atmospheric bars for a beer. And those looking for loud disco-bars will also be disappointed. Our favourite place was the Club de Jazz (aka the 5 Rues) – a very popular, if rather expensive, jazz club-cum-cocktail bar, that gets some big-name musicians and opens from tea-time to late. The

---

Sleigh rides are a popular pastime with Megève's affluent clientele →

MEGEVE TOURIST OFFICE / NUTS.FR

Cocoon, Aperitif and Roses are popular with Brits. The Puck has been entirely refurbished and re-opened last season. The casino, opened a few seasons ago, has more slot machines than blackjack tables. A new piano bar and a disco opened last season.

OFF THE SLOPES
Lots to do

There is something for most tastes, with an excellent sports centre, an outdoor ice rink, plenty of outdoor activities, two cinemas and a weekly market. Trips to Annecy and Chamonix are possible. And St-Gervais is worth visiting for a spa treatment. Walks are excellent, with 50km/30 miles of marked paths, many at altitude. There is a special map of the paths, classified for difficulty. Meeting friends on the slopes for lunch is easy.

STAYING UP THE MOUNTAIN
Several possibilities

As well as mid-mountain Le Bettex (see St-Gervais), there are hotels further up on the slopes, near the summit of Mont d'Arbois. One is the 3-star Igloo (0450 930584), another the 2-star Chez la Tante (0450 213130).

St-Gervais 850m/2,790ft

St-Gervais is a handsome 19th-century spa town set in a narrow river gorge, halfway between Megève and Chamonix, at the entrance to the side-valley leading up to St-Nicolas and Les Contamines. It has direct access to the Mont d'Arbois slopes via a 20-person gondola from just outside the town.

It's a pleasant place to explore, with interesting food shops and cosy bars, thermal baths and an Olympic skating rink. Prices are noticeably lower than in Megève. Two hotels convenient for the gondola are the Hostellerie du Nerey (0450 934521), a pleasantly traditional 2-star, and the 3-star Carlina (0450 934110), the best in town.

At the gondola mid-station is Le Bettex, a small collection of hotels, private chalets and new apartments, conveniently situated for the runs but with little evening animation.

You can go up, on the opposite side of St-Gervais, on a rack-and-pinion railway which in 1904 was intended to go all the way to the top of Mont Blanc but didn't quite make it that far – it actually takes you to the slopes of Les Houches (see Chamonix chapter).

Given enough snow, you can descend to St-Gervais off-piste.

Its position makes St-Gervais a good base for touring the resorts covered by the Mont Blanc regional lift pass, especially if you have a car.

Other resorts

Praz-sur-Arly and Notre-Dame-de-Bellecombe are much cheaper options for independent car travellers – they are not part of the Megève lift network (yet). Praz (1035m/3,400ft) is a small, quiet place, but has hotels, restaurants, bars, sports club, ski school and ski kindergarten. It has fair-sized slopes of its own, with short, mainly easy runs served by a rather slow old lift system. Most runs face roughly north, and a reporter found good snow here when many runs in Megève were closed. It links with the slopes of Notre-Dame (1130m/3,710ft) further along the road. Notre-Dame is a pleasant village with mainly apartment accommodation, simple hotels, and several bars and restaurants.

St-Nicolas-de-Véroce is part of the Megève lift network, and has a handful of simple small hotels.

One reporter spent a very rewarding few days based at the hotel Terminus (0450 936800) in Le Fayet, below St-Gervais, travelling to a different resort each day by coach.

Les Menuires

The bargain base for the Trois Vallées – but pick your spot with care

COSTS

① ② ③ ④ ⑤ ⑥

RATINGS

The slopes
Snow	****
Extent	*****
Expert	****
Intermediate	*****
Beginner	***
Convenience	*****
Queues	****
Mountain restaurants	***

The rest
Scenery	***
Resort charm	*
Off-slope	*

NEWS

For 2002/03 the Tortollet chair, from the valley bottom to the resort centre, was upgraded; the top of Mont de la Chambre gained snowmaking.

Extension of the resort continued with another phase of the chalet-style Hameau des Marmottes.

For 2003/04 the drag-lifts at La Becca and Les Combes are due to be replaced by a high-speed six-seater chair-lift. More new lifts for this area are in the pipeline.

OT LES MENUIRES / P JACQUES / FOC

Beyond the very resistible blocks of La Croisette, the alluring slopes of La Masse ↓

- ➕ The cheapest base for the 3V
- ➕ Great local slopes on La Masse, and quick links with Val-Thorens
- ➕ Extensive snowmaking
- ➕ Lots of slope-side accommodation
- ➕ New, outlying parts of the resort are much more attractive than core
- ➕ Good specialist food shops, although they are found in ...

- ➖ Gloomy indoor shopping malls
- ➖ Resort core is dominated by big, dreary apartment blocks
- ➖ Main intermediate and beginner slopes get a lot of sun
- ➖ No woodland slopes
- ➖ Some of the lower slopes get dangerously crowded as well as overexposed to the sun

Les Menuires is developing in the right way, adding traditional-style satellites where you can ignore the brutal architecture at the core of the resort. And the Belleville valley has a lot of terrain, including the excellent, challenging slopes on La Masse, rarely used by visitors from the other valleys.

THE RESORT

The original buildings that surround the main lift base, La Croisette, are among the worst examples of the thoughtless building of the 1960s/70s. The main centre has a particularly dire indoor shopping gallery. But the resort is trying hard to lose its reputation as one of the ugliest in the Alps. In outposts such as Reberty and Hameau des Marmottes, the latest additions are in stone-and-wood chalet style – and there are some luxury developments. These outposts have their own shops and bars – Les Bruyères is now a more-or-less self-contained resort.

THE MOUNTAINS

Les Menuires is set at about the tree line, with almost entirely open slopes.
Slopes The major part of the network spreads across the broad, west-facing mountainside between Les Menuires and St-Martin, with links to the Méribel valley at four points (mostly red runs, but there is one blue) as well as a link up the valley to Val-Thorens. Two fast

chairs and a gondola go up from La Croisette. Lifts to La Masse, a more challenging mountain, start below the village – a gondola and a chair-lift.
Terrain-parks There's a terrain-park with a half-pipe just above the village.
Snow reliability La Masse's height and orientation ensure good snow for a long season. The west-facing slopes are supplied with abundant artificial snow, but the snow lower down is often icy or slushy.
Experts The upper slopes of La Masse are virtually all of stiff red/soft black steepness. Dame Blanche is a particularly fine black, on the front of the hill – we'd love to catch it when groomed, or after fresh snow. There is also huge amounts of off-piste. Vallon du Lou is a broad, sweeping route towards Val-Thorens. Others go in the opposite direction to various villages. Don't ignore the other slopes: a reader recommends the descent from Roc de Fer to the village of Béranger.
Intermediates With good snow, you may be content with the local slopes, which are virtually all blue and red. In poor snow you can head up to Val-

KEY FACTS

Resort	1800m
	5,900ft

for the Three Valleys	
Slopes	1260-3230m
	4,130-10,600ft
Lifts	200
Pistes	600km
	370 miles
Green	17%
Blue	34%
Red	37%
Black	12%
Snowmaking	90km
	56 miles

For Les Menuires / St-Martin only	
Slopes	1450-2850m
	4,760-9,350ft
Lifts	42
Pistes	160km
	99 miles

Phone numbers
From abroad use the prefix +33 and omit the initial '0' of the phone number.

TOURIST OFFICE

t 0479 007300
lesmenuires@
lesmenuires.com
www.lesmenuires.com

Thorens, and there's blue as well as red-run access. Don't miss La Masse – the blacks are not super-steep – but beware the steep Masse drag-lift.

Beginners There are wide and gentle slopes and a special lift pass for beginners, but the snow quality on the nursery slopes is a worry. The blue slopes you progress to can get extremely crowded.

Snowboarding The number of drags is low and dwindling further year by year; but there are some flattish sections of piste in places. There is huge amounts of terrain to suit free-riders.

Cross-country There are 28km/17 miles of prepared trails along the valley floor between St-Martin and Val-Thorens.

Queues The fast six-packs up from La Croisette seem to have largely solved the problem of queues there, but have perhaps contributed to the worsening problem of acute overcrowding on the slopes down to the resort centre.

Mountain restaurants There are few remarkable places in this sector of the 3V. Just above Les Menuires is the very pleasant but quite pricey Etoile. At higher altitude there is 'excellent food and below average prices' at the Alpage, on the 4 Vents piste. Many people head down to the villages for lunch; you retain some sense of being on the mountain at the 'good value' Ferme, beside the piste at Reberty.

Schools and guides The ESF has the monopoly here; we lack recent reports.

Facilities for children This is very much a family resort, but a visitor reports that no English was spoken at the 'generally grubby' resort nursery and that her children were not allowed to stay together. Family Ski Company has its own nursery in Reberty – and sends a minder with kids going to ski-school, to make up for ESF 'brutality'.

STAYING THERE

How to go Some big UK tour operators offer holidays here, and some chalet operators have a presence in Reberty. There is a Club Med above Reberty, praised by a reporter this year.

Chalets Reberty Village has been virtually taken over by UK chalet operators. Family Ski Company has several attractive properties; Cabaniols has a splendid living room.

Hotels None of the hotels is above 3-star grading. Ours Blanc (0479 006166) is the best – a chalet-style 3-star on the slopes above Reberty 1850. Latitudes (0479 007510) is set on the lower fringe of Les Bruyères.

Self-catering The newer apartments are more attractive. The Montagnettes and Alpages, both in Reberty, are among the best, the latter being an MGM development with a pool. Residence les Cotes d'Or is reportedly 'very spacious for a French resort'.

Eating out Though some restaurants lack atmosphere, there's no shortage of good food, including Savoyard specialities. Alternatives include Italian and Tex-Mex. The Trattoria, with its 'rustic French' ambience, is highly recommended. The set menus at the Snow are 'reasonably priced' and the tartiflette is 'particularly good'. The Géant de Marmite is getting a name for its 'excellent food, good prices and pleasant atmosphere'. Chalet-boy night off is no problem in Reberty: La Ferme is one of the best places in the resort.

Après-ski There is no shortage of bars in La Croisette, but many are within the dreadful shopping gallery. The Taverne bar in Les Bruyères is 'lively and welcoming'. There are discos.

Off the slopes This is a resort for keen skiers and boarders.

Cime de Caron
3195m/10,480ft

Méribel

Mont de
la Chambre
2850m

Roc des
3 Marches
2700m

Mont de
la Challe
2575m

Tougnète
2435m

Val-Thorens
2300m

Point de
la Masse
2805m

Reberty

La Masse

Les Menuires
1800m/5,900ft

Saint-Martin-de-
Belleville ↓

Méribel

The best-looking base for the wonderful Three Valleys

COSTS

① ② ③ ④ ⑤ ⑥

RATINGS

The slopes

Snow	★★★
Extent	★★★★★
Expert	★★★★
Intermediate	★★★★★
Beginner	★★★★
Convenience	★★★
Queues	★★★★
Mountain restaurants	★★★

The rest

Scenery	★★★
Resort charm	★★★
Off-slope	★★★

NEWS

For 2002/03 the Plan des Mains chair was replaced by a fast six-seat chair, several pistes were widened, more snow-guns were installed, particularly at Altiport and down to Méribel-Village, and a discounted lift pass for families was introduced.

For 2003, more improvements to the resort's snowmaking facilities are planned, with a new installation next to the Combes lift and a new reservoir.

➕ In the centre of the biggest linked lift network in the world – ideal for intermediates, great for experts, too

➕ Modern, constantly improved lift system means little queueing and rapid access to all slopes

➕ Good piste grooming and snowmaking

➕ Pleasant chalet-style architecture

➖ Not the best snow in the Three Valleys, and pistes can get crowded

➖ Main village spreads over a wide area, with lots of accommodation well away from the slopes

➖ Expensive

➖ Méribel-Mottaret and Méribel Village satellites are rather lifeless

➖ Full of Brits

For keen piste-bashers who dislike tacky purpose-built resorts, Méribel is difficult to beat. The Three Valleys can keep anyone amused for a fortnight – and Méribel-Mottaret, in particular, has quick access to every part. And, unlike other purpose-built resorts, Méribel has always insisted on chalet-style architecture. What more could you ask?

Well, our ➖ points are mostly non-trivial. And other Three Valleys resorts have the edge in some respects. For better snow opt for Courchevel, and for the best snow Val-Thorens. For less crowded runs, Courchevel 1650. For lower prices, Les Menuires and perhaps St-Martin. But these other resorts have their drawbacks, of course. Regular visitors love Méribel, and regret their occasional expeditions elsewhere. And we still have a soft spot for it (one of us learned to ski here).

THE RESORT

Méribel occupies the central valley of the Three Valleys system and consists of two main resort villages.

The original resort of Méribel-les-Allues (now simply known as Méribel) is built on a single steepish west-facing hillside with the home piste running down beside it to the main lift stations at the valley bottom. All the buildings are wood-clad, low-rise and chalet style, making this one of the most tastefully designed of French purpose-built resorts. A road winds up from the village centre to the Rond Point des Pistes, and goes on through woods to the outpost of the Altiport (an airstrip with snow-covered runway for little planes with skis).

The resort was founded by a Brit, Peter Lindsay, in 1938, and has retained a strong British presence ever since – 'more like Kensington than France', commented one visitor this year. It has grown enormously over recent years, and although some accommodation is right on the piste, much of the newer building is more than a walk away – check your location carefully if you don't like having to rely on buses (or tour operator minibuses).

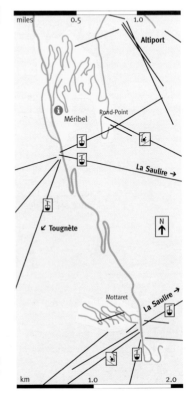

Not all parts of Méribel are quite as cute as this, but the founding father's original decision to build in chalet style has paid off →

KEY FACTS

| Resort | 1400-1700m |
| | 4,590-5,580ft |

For the Three Valleys	
Slopes	1260-3230m
	4,130-10,600ft
Lifts	200
Pistes	600km
	370 miles
Green	17%
Blue	34%
Red	37%
Black	12%
Snowmaking	90km
	56 miles

For Méribel only	
Slopes	1400-2950m
	4,590-9,680ft
Lifts	59
Pistes	150km
	94 miles

One clear exception is Belvédère, an upmarket enclave built on the opposite side of the home piste (there's a tunnel for road access). There are collections of shops and restaurants at a couple of points on the road through the resort – Altitude 1600 and Plateau de Morel. The hotels and apartments of Altiport enjoy splendid isolation in the woods, and are convenient for some of the slopes.

The satellite village of Méribel-Mottaret was developed in the early 1970s. The original development was beside the piste on the east-facing slope, but in recent years the resort has spread up the opposite hillside and further up the valley. Both sides are served by lifts for pedestrians – but the gondola up to the original village stops at 7.30 and it's a long, tiring walk up. Mottaret looks modern, despite wood-cladding on its apartment blocks. Even so, it's more attractive than many other resorts built for slope-side convenience. It has many fewer shops and bars and much less après-ski than Méribel. Some reporters have found it 'lacking in atmosphere' but others have found it makes a pleasant change. Yet another comments that for a full exploration of the whole Three Valleys, 'it's the best base'.

In recent years the hamlet of Méribel-Village, on the road from Méribel to La Tania and Courchevel, has acquired a chair-lift up to Altiport with a blue run back and has developed into a mini-resort. There are some luxury chalets and apartments here but little else apart from a fitness centre, one bar, a pizzeria and two restaurants, but if nightlife is not a priority it's a pleasant place to stay.

There are some alternative bases lower down the mountain (and the price scale), described at the end of this chapter.

Local buses are free (though some readers complain they are not frequent enough, and overcrowded at peak times), and many UK tour operators run their own minibus services to and from the lifts. A car is mainly of use for outings to other resorts. Lift passes for six days or more give you a day in Val-d'Isère-Tignes (an hour and a half away by car), La Plagne or Les Arcs (an hour or so away). But these expeditions involve long drives down to the valley and back up to the other resort. Why bother?

THE MOUNTAINS

Most of the slopes are above the tree-line, but there are some sheltered runs for bad-weather days. The lift system is well planned to cut out walks and climbs. Piste grading is not always reliable – there are some testing blues – and in an area where some slopes get the afternoon sun, snow conditions have a huge impact on difficulty.

The slopes of Courchevel, Les Menuires and Val-Thorens are covered in separate chapters. The last covers the 'fourth valley' – the Maurienne slopes, above Orelle. The links between resorts are not very well signed, and you have to plan your return carefully, taking account of likely queues and the weather. Taxi rides from Courchevel are affordable; the trip from Les Menuires is much longer.

THE SLOPES
Highly efficient lift system
The Méribel valley runs north-south. On the eastern side, gondolas leave both Méribel and Mottaret for **La**

Saulire. From here you can head back down towards either village or down the other side of the ridge towards Courchevel.

From Méribel a gondola rises to **Tougnète**, on the western side of the valley, from where you can get down to Les Menuires or St-Martin-de-Belleville. You can also head for Mottaret from here. From there, a fast chair then a drag take you to another entry point for the Les Menuires runs.

The Mottaret area has seen rapid mechanisation over the last decade. The **Plattières** gondola rises up the valley to the south, ending at yet another entry point to the Les Menuires area. To the east of this is the big stand-up gondola to the top of **Mont du Vallon**. There are wonderful views from the top. A fast quad from near this area goes south up to **Mont de la Chambre**, giving direct access to Val-Thorens.

TERRAIN-PARKS
There's a choice
The Plattières terrain-park – accessed from the second stage of the Plattières gondola – is for boarders only; it has two half-pipes (one for experts, one for novices), two quarter-pipes, three tables, a spine and a 650m boarder-cross. The Moon Park, near the Arpasson drag above the Tougnète gondola mid-station, has two half-pipes and a boarder-cross with various toys to play on.

SNOW RELIABILITY
Not the best in the Three Valleys
Méribel's slopes aren't the highest in the Three Valleys, and they mainly face east or west; the latter get the full force of the afternoon sun. So snow conditions are often better elsewhere. And grooming seems to be rather better in neighbouring Courchevel.

The lower runs now have

The home slopes are attractively wooded – but don't count on this kind of fluffy snow, or this lack of crowds ↗

OT MÉRIBEL / JEAN-MAURICE GOUEDARD

LIFT PASSES

Three Valleys
Covers all lifts in Courchevel, La Tania, Méribel, Val-Thorens, Les Menuires and St-Martin-de-Belleville.

Beginners
Two free lifts in Mottaret and two in Méribel; reduced price lift pass with lessons.

Main pass
1-day pass €39
6-day pass €193

Senior citizen
Over 60: 6-day pass €154
Over 72: free pass

Children
Under 13: 6-day pass €145
Under 5: free pass

Notes
Half-day and pedestrian passes available. 6-day pass and over valid for one day in Espace Killy (Tignes-Val-d'Isère), La Plagne-Les Arcs, Pralognan or Les Saisies.

Alternative passes
Méribel pass covers Méribel and Méribel-Mottaret only.

substantial snowmaking and lack of snow is rarely a problem, but ice or slush at the end of the day can be. The north-west-facing slopes above Altiport generally have decent snow.

At the southern end of the valley, towards Les Menuires and Val-Thorens, a lot of runs are north-facing and keep their snow well, as do the runs on Mont du Vallon.

FOR EXPERTS
Exciting choices

The size of the Three Valleys means experts are well catered for. In the Méribel valley, head for Mont du Vallon – voted 'the best skiing in the whole of the Trois Vallées' by one reporter's group this year. The long, steep Combe du Vallon run here is classified red; it's a wonderful, long, fast cruise when groomed, but presents plenty of challenge when mogulled. And there's a beautiful itinéraire (not marked on the piste map) in the next valley to the main pistes, leading back to the bottom of the gondola.

The slopes down from the top of the Val-Thorens sector were all off-piste when we old hands first visited Méribel. Since the new lifts were installed up here, there are two pistes back from Val-Thorens, but still plenty of opportunity for getting off-piste in the wide open bowls.

A good mogul run is down the side of the double Roc de Tougne drag-lift which leads up to Mont de la Challe. And there is a steep black run all the way down the Tougnète gondola back to Méribel. Apart from a shallow section near the mid-station, it's unrelenting most of the way.

At the north end of the valley the Face run was built for the women's downhill in the 1992 Olympics. Served by a fast quad, it's a splendid cruise when freshly groomed, and you can

terrify yourself just by imagining what it must be like to go straight down.

Nothing on the Saulire side is as steep or as demanding as on the other side of the valley. The Mauduit red run is quite challenging, though – it used to be black.

Throughout the area there are good off-piste opportunities. The ESF runs excellent-value guided groups.

FOR INTERMEDIATES
Paradise found

Méribel and the rest of the Three Valleys is a paradise for intermediates; there are few other resorts where a keen piste-basher can cover so many miles so easily. Virtually every slope in the region has a good intermediate run down it, and to describe them would take a book in itself.

For less adventurous intermediates, the run from the second station of the Plattières gondola back to Mottaret is ideal, and used a lot by the ski school. It is a gentle, north-facing, cruising run and is generally in good condition.

Even early intermediates should find the runs over into the other valleys well within their capabilities, opening up further vast amounts of intermediate runs. Go to Courchevel or Val-Thorens for the better snow.

Virtually all the pistes on both sides of the Méribel valley will suit more advanced intermediates. Most of the reds are on the difficult side.

FOR BEGINNERS
Strengths and weaknesses

Méribel has an excellent slope for beginners, but it's out of the resort at Altiport, which is a bit of a nuisance. There is a small nursery slope at Rond-Point, at the top of the village, mainly used by the children's ski school.

The Altiport area is accessible from the village by the Morel chair-lift, or by free bus. Once you have found your

SCHOOLS

ESF Méribel
t 0479 086031
esfmeribel@wanadoo.fr

ESF Méribel-Mottaret
t 0479 004949
esfmeribel@wanadoo.fr

Magic in Motion
t 0479 085336
magicmeribel@aol.com

New Generation
t 0479 010318
(UK: 01483 205402)
info@skinewgen.com

Classes
(ESF prices)
6 half-days (2½hr per day): €130

Private lessons
€89 for 2hr for 1 or 2 people

GUIDES

Mountain guide office
t 0479 003038

feet, a free drag-lift takes you half-way up one of the best and most attractively situated green pistes we know, the Blanchot – long, gentle, wide and tree-lined, with little through-traffic. Next, a longer drag takes you to the top of the Blanchot, then a chair a bit higher, then another chair higher still, on to an excellent blue usually blessed with good snow.

FOR CROSS-COUNTRY
Scenic routes
There are about 33km/20 miles in total. The main area is in the pine forest near Altiport, a pleasant introduction to those who want to try cross-country for the first time. There's also a loop around Lake Tuéda, in the nature reserve at Mottaret, and for the more experienced an itinéraire from Altiport to Courchevel.

QUEUES
3V traffic a persistent problem
Huge lift investment over the years has paid off in making the area virtually queue-free most of the time, despite the huge numbers of people. Generally, if you do find a queue, there is an alternative quieter route you can take. The real problems result from the tidal flows of people between the three valleys, in the morning (when the tide coincides with the start of ski school) and especially the late afternoon. Black spots to avoid at these times are: the Tougnète gondola at Méribel towards Les Menuires; the Plattières gondola at Mottaret towards Les Menuires; the

Côte Brune chair to Mont de la Chambre; the Plan des Mains chair (used by everyone returning from Val-Thorens), despite its recent upgrade to a six-pack.

MOUNTAIN RESTAURANTS
Less than wonderful
There are lots of places on the piste map, but few that are worth singling out – and not enough to meet the demand, so many get very crowded (you might want to take lunch early or late). The Chardonnet, at the mid-station of the Mottaret-Saulire gondola, has table-service and excellent food, but is expensive. The large terrace at the Rhododendrons, at the top of the Altiport drag, remains a popular spot – its varied menu encouraged one reader to eat there several times during his holiday. The Rond Point, just below the mid-point of the Rhodos gondola, offers tasty paninis as well as delicious rösti in the restaurant. The cosy Crêtes, below the top of the Tougnète gondola, continues to provide 'good food and service'. Lower down, at the bottom of the Roc de Tougne drags, the Tougniat is reportedly 'good inside and out'. The pricey Altiport hotel scarcely counts as a mountain restaurant, but has a great outdoor buffet in good weather and the 'best tarts in town'. Two self-service places notable for their views (but little else) are the Pierres Plates, at the top of Saulire, and the Sittelle, above the first section of the Plattières gondola. The Blanchot, next to the road to the

boarding

Méribel is increasingly boarder-oriented. The terrain locally and further afield has lots to offer and you rarely have to take a drag-lift – but there are quite a lot of flat sections on some of the main ways to/from Val Thorens. The resort hosts a number of big-air and boarder-cross competitions. Specialist shops include Board Brains (in Méribel), and Quiksilver Gotcha Surf (in Mottaret).

CHILDREN

The ESF runs the resort's facilities.

The Saturnins (0479 086690) in the Parc Olympique takes children aged 18 months to 3 years, offering indoor and outdoor activities.

The P'tits Loups kindergartens (two in Méribel, one in Mottaret) take children aged 3 to 5. Open 9am to 5pm.

A childminder list is available from the tourist office.

The ESF runs ski classes for English-speaking children: 6 half-days (2½hr) €110.

OT MERIBEL / JEAN-MAURICE GOUEDARD

Mottaret is the most convenient base for exploration of the whole of the Three Valleys area →

altiport, is recommended as 'a good place to meet non-skiers'.

SCHOOLS AND GUIDES
No shortage of instructors

The main schools all have English-speaking instructors.

The ESF is by far the biggest, with over 300 instructors. It has a special international section with instructors speaking good English. Recent reports have been mixed, but we've heard tales of instructors adopting the 'follow me' approach and classes covering an excessive range of abilities. The ESF offers useful alternatives to standard classes, such as off-piste groups, heli-skiing on the Italian border and 'Ski Discovery' tours of the Three Valleys.

Magic in Motion, the second largest school, also offers heli-skiing, couloir and extreme sessions in addition to skiing and boarding lessons. It keeps classes small, no more than seven, and has generally got good reports, though a visitor this year was not convinced it was any better than ESF.

New Generation, a new British school, seems set to extend the good reputation it has built up in Courchevel. One reader says, 'I cannot recommend them highly enough, they were patient and kept groups small.'

We've had mixed reports in the past of Snow Systems, which operates out of Mottaret; but this year a family was 'really impressed' by the small classes, the 'good English' spoken and the 'entertaining philosopher/instructor'.

FACILITIES FOR CHILDREN
Tour operators rule

We guess readers needing childcare plug into the facilities of chalet operators who run their own nurseries – we rarely get reports on the resort facilities. We have heard, though, that the Saturnins in the Olympic Centre caters well for toddlers.

STAYING THERE

HOW TO GO
Huge choice but few bargains

Package holidays are easy to find, both with big UK tour operators and smaller Méribel specialists. There are three Club Med 'villages', all in CM's top comfort category, none with the usual children's club facilities; two occupy very attractive hotel buildings in the Belvédère area.

Chalets Méribel has more chalets dedicated to the British market than any other resort, and over 50 operators offering them. What really distinguishes Méribel is the range of recently built luxury chalets. Some are perfectly positioned for the slopes, but many have minibuses on hand to compensate for their inconvenient

Méribel

287

GETTING THERE

Air Geneva 135km/84 miles (3½hr); Lyon 185km/115 miles (3½hr); Chambéry 95km/59 miles (2½hr).

Rail Moûtiers (18km/11 miles); regular buses to Méribel.

Phone numbers
From abroad use the prefix +33 and omit the initial '0' of the phone number.

locations. Méribel specialist Meriski has an extensive portfolio, including some of our own favourites. Lotus Supertravel's smaller range includes a couple of luxy places. Scott Dunn Ski has three thoroughly comfortable chalets, of which the 8-bed Petite Pia is probably the pick (at least if you get the master bedroom). At the top of Snowline's range is the beautifully decorated Indiana Lodge. Ski Activity and Ski Cuisine both have a good range of chalets including several that are all en suite. Belvedere Chalets – a relatively new operation – has three or four smart-looking places priced by the property, not the bed. If money is no object, try one of Descent International's luxury chalets, which include some former Ski Company ones as well as chalet Brames.

Of the few chalet-hotels, Mark Warner's Tarentaise has a great position, right on the piste at Mottaret.
Hotels Méribel has some excellent hotels, but they're not cheap.
((((Grand Coeur (0479 086003) Our favourite almost-affordable hotel in Méribel. Just above the village centre. Welcoming, mature building with plush lounge. Magnificent food. Huge hot-tub, sauna, etc.
((((Altiport (0479 005232) Modern and luxurious hotel, isolated at the foot of the Altiport lifts. Convenient for Courchevel, not for Val-Thorens.

((((**Mont-Vallon** (0479 004400) The best hotel at Mottaret; good food, and excellently situated for the Three Valleys' pistes. Pool, sauna, hot-tub, squash, fitness room, etc.
(((**Adray Télébar** (0479 086026) Welcoming piste-side chalet with pretty, rustic rooms, good food and popular sun terrace.
((**Roc** (0479 086416) A good-value B&B hotel, in the centre, with a bar-restaurant and crêperie below.
Self-catering There is a huge number of apartments and chalets to let in both Méribel and Mottaret. Make sure that the place you book is conveniently situated and has enough space. A reader recommends the Merilys apartments in Méribel: 'a fine place with very helpful staff'.

EATING OUT
Fair choice
There is a reasonable selection of restaurants, from ambitious French cuisine to relatively cheap pizza and pasta. For the best food in town, in plush surroundings, there are top hotels – Grand Coeur ('so pleased, we ate there several times'), Allodis and Kouisena in the Eterlou. Other readers' recommendations include: Chez Kiki – 'the best steaks we have tasted in a long time and an apple tart to die for'; the Taverne – 'nice relaxed atmosphere'; the Tremplin – 'good for

families, friendly service, reasonably priced'; and the Cactus Café – 'always busy and friendly, mainly British staff,' 'cheap meals, quieter in the evenings'.

Alternatives include the Galette, the Fromagerie, the Cava, the Plantin (on the road out towards La Tania) and Cro-Magnon up the hill in Morel – all popular for raclette and fondue. The Marée Blanche specialises in seafood and the Blanchot, just below Altiport, offers the choice of two dining areas, one dedicated to dishes of the region. Another reader recommends the Crocodile in the Hameau at Mottaret. Scott's does good American-style food.

At Les Allues, the Tsaretta will provide a free taxi service to transport you to enjoy the imaginative creations of the Australian chef. The Chaumière offers 'good value inclusive menus in pleasant, rustic surroundings'. The Chemina is another recommendation.

APRES-SKI
Méribel rocks – loudly
Méribel's après-ski revolves around British-run places. Dick's Tea Bar is now well established but is remote from the slopes. At close of play it's the piste-side Rond Point that's packed

– happy hour starts around 4pm – and has live music and toffee vodka. The sun terrace of Jack's, near the main lift stations, remains very popular.

The ring of bars around the main square do good business at tea time. The Taverne (run by the same company that owns Dick's Tea Bar) gets packed. Just across the square is the Pub, with videos, pool and sometimes a band. There are a couple of alternatives to the loud pubs complained about in the past. The Poste 'serves the best vin chaud'. The Dawido is comfortable and has a pool table.

There is late dancing at Scott's (next to the Pub) and, of course, there's Dick's Tea Bar (no longer free entry, we're told). One reader was put off by the queues at the Pub, another liked its 'busy atmosphere'. El Poncho's serves Mexican dishes and Desperados (beer mixed with tequila) but a reporter this year thought it was rather expensive.

In Mottaret the bars at the foot of the pistes get packed at tea time – Rastro ('As good as ever,' comments a regular visitor) and Down Town are the most popular, though reporters say that Zig-Zag has lower prices. Later on

ACTIVITIES

Indoor Parc Olympique (skating rink, swimming pool, climbing wall), fitness centres in hotels, bowling, billiards, library, bridge, two cinemas, concert hall, language and computer courses

Outdoor Flying lessons and excursions, snow-mobiles, snow-shoe excursions, ice climbing, ice driving, paragliding, 20km/12 miles of cleared paths, dog-sledding, hot air balloon

TOURIST OFFICE

t 0479 086001
info@meribel.net
www.meribel.net

the Rastro disco gets going. Both villages have a cinema.

OFF THE SLOPES
Flight of fancy
Méribel is not really a resort for people who want to languish in the village, but it is not unattractive. There's a good public swimming pool and an Olympic ice rink. You can also take joyrides in the little planes that operate from the altiport.

The pedestrian's lift pass covers all the gondolas, cable-cars and buses in the Méribel and Courchevel valleys, and makes it very easy for pedestrians to meet friends for lunch. There are pleasant, marked walks in the Altiport area and a signposted trail through some of the hamlets down to Les Allues (return from there or Le Raffort in the Olympic gondola).

A non-skier's guide to Courchevel, Méribel and La Tania is distributed free by the tourist office.

STAYING DOWN THE VALLEY
Quieter, cheaper choices
For the 1992 Olympics the competitors were accommodated in **Brides-les-Bains** (600m/1,970ft), an old spa town

way down in the valley, and a gondola was built linking it to Méribel. It is much cheaper than the higher resorts. It has some simple hotels, adequate shops and 'plenty of good-value restaurants and friendly bars used by locals', says a reporter. Ski Weekends runs its own chalet-hotel here, the Verseau. There is a casino, but evenings are distinctly quiet. The long gondola ride to and from Méribel (about 25 minutes) is tedious and can be cold, but in good conditions you can ski off-piste to one or other of the mid-stations at the end of the day. Given a car, Brides makes a good base for visiting other resorts.

Some UK tour operators have places in the old village of **Les Allues**, down the road from the resort and close to a mid-station on the gondola up from Brides-les-Bains. The pick of the chalets is probably Bonne Neige's Les Allodis – a carefully converted barn. But Ski Blanc have some good-looking places too. Next-door to one of them is an independent British-run playgroup. There are a couple of bars – and a good-value, well renovated hotel, the Croix Jean-Claude (0479 086105); rooms are small, though.

Méribel

291

Montgenèvre

The snowiest part of the Franco-Italian Milky Way circuit

COSTS

① ② ③ ④ ⑤ ⑥

RATINGS

The slopes

Snow	****
Extent	****
Expert	**
Intermediate	****
Beginner	*****
Convenience	****
Queues	****
Mountain restaurants	**

The rest

Scenery	***
Resort charm	***
Off-slope	*

NEWS

For 2002/03 a travelator – a moving walkway – was installed to link the Chalvet sector and the main area of slopes, and another 3km/1.5 miles of snowmaking was installed.

For 2003/04 a chair is to replace the Tremplin drag.

292

+ Good snow record, and local slopes largely north-facing – often the best snow in the Milky Way area

+ Plenty of intermediate cruising and good, convenient nursery slopes

+ Few queues on weekdays, unless people are being bussed in from other resorts with poor snow

+ A lot of accommodation close to the slopes, and some right on them

+ Great potential for car drivers to explore other nearby resorts

− Poor base for exploring the Italian Milky Way resorts unless you have a car

− Slow lifts and short runs can be irritating

− Busy road lined by tatty bars reduces village charm and family appeal – crossing can be tricky unless you use the new travelator

− Little to challenge experts on-piste

Montgenèvre is set at one end of the big Milky Way network, reaching over into Italy. It's a time-consuming trek from here to Sestriere and Sauze d'Oulx at the far end (you may have to ride some slow lifts down as well as up). But you can get to these worthwhile resorts much more quickly by car, which also facilitates day trips to other excellent French resorts such as Serre-Chevalier. And you may want to stay on the local slopes shared with Claviere (in Italy, but only a mile down the road), which will probably have the best snow in the region.

The village is quite pleasant once you get away from the main road. Sadly, you can't avoid the road altogether if you want to make use of the bigger area of slopes on the south side of the pass. But most visitors seem to come to terms with it, and don't find that it spoils their enjoyment. When moving between the two slope areas, at least, you can now hop on a travelator.

THE RESORT

Montgenèvre is a narrow roadside village set on a high pass only a mile from the Italian border – this is an area where the euro has really simplified things. At first glance the resort appears a rather inhospitable place – a collection of tatty-looking bars and restaurants lining the side of the sometimes windswept and often busy main road over the col. But the cheap and cheerful cafes and bars add an animated atmosphere sometimes missing from French resorts. And tucked away off the main road is a quite pleasant old village, complete with quaint church and friendly natives. The place gets a lot of snow, which adds to the charm factor.

The slopes are convenient, despite the road; most of the accommodation is less than five minutes from a lift. The main ones are gondolas from opposite ends of the village. On the village side of the road are the south-facing slopes of Le Chalvet. The more

OT MONTGENEVRE / A BENE

Sadly, the north-facing slopes in the background are separated from the village by a busy through-road →

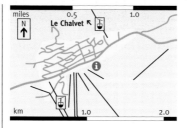

extensive north-facing slopes of Les
Anges and Le Querelay are across the
main road, with nursery slopes at the
bottom. Both sectors have piste links
with Claviere, gateway to the other
Italian resorts of the Milky Way –
Sansicario, Sestriere and Sauze d'Oulx.

Location is becoming more
important as the village expands –
some of the newer accommodation is
uphill, away from the slopes – though
there is a free shuttle-bus.

The best way to get to other resorts
is to travel by car. Serre-Chevalier and
Puy-St-Vincent, with lift pass sharing
arrangements, are easily reached, and
well worth an outing each. Different lift
pass options cater for most needs.

THE MOUNTAINS

Montgenèvre's local slopes are best
suited to leisurely intermediates, with
lots of easy cruising on blues and
greens, both above and in the woods.

Run gradings on the local area and
Milky Way piste maps have differed in
the past, which can be confusing –
however, none of the blacks are much
more than a tough red.

THE SLOPES
Nicely varied
The major north-facing Les Anges
sector offers easy intermediate slopes
above the mid-mountain gondola
station, with more of a mix of runs
lower down. It has a high-altitude link
via Collet Vert (reached by a quad
chair) to the slopes above Claviere, in
Italy (covered on the Monts de la Lune
lift pass). The main complaint about
the Claviere area is the number of
long, steep and awkward drag-lifts (we
have reports of kids 'dropping like
flies'). But this whole area around the
border is attractively broken up by
rocky outcrops and woods and the
scenery is quite spectacular. The runs
of the sunny Chalvet sector are mainly
on open slopes above its mid-
mountain gondola station. When

conditions permit, a 'charming' long
blue run from this sector goes down to
Claviere, for access to Italy.

TERRAIN-PARKS
High and remote
There's a terrain-park – with quarter-
pipe, jump and rope tow – and a
boarder cross near the Gondrans chair-
lift at the top of the Les Anges sector.

SNOW RELIABILITY
Excellent locally
Montgenèvre has a generally excellent
snow record, receiving dumps from
westerly storms funnelling up the
valley. The high north-facing slopes
naturally keep their snow better than
the south-facing area but both have
snowmaking on the main home pistes.

FOR EXPERTS
Limited, except for off-piste
There are very few challenging pistes
in the Montgenèvre-Claviere-Cesana
sectors. Many of the runs are
overclassified on the map. There is,
however, ample opportunity for off-
piste excursions, and heli-skiing on the
Italian side when conditions are right.

The remote north-east-facing bowl
beyond the Col de l'Alpet on the
Chalvet side is superb in good snow
and has black and red pistes, too. The
open section between La Montanina
and Sagnalonga on the Italian side is
another good powder area. Those with
a car should visit Sestriere for the
most challenging runs.

FOR INTERMEDIATES
Plenty of cruising terrain
The overclassified blacks are just right
for adventurous intermediates, though
none holds the interest for very long.
The pleasantly narrow tree-lined runs
to Claviere from Pian del Sole, the
steepest of the routes down in the
Chalvet sector and the runs off the
back of Col de l'Alpet are all fine in
small doses.

Average intermediates will enjoy the
red runs, though most are short. On
the major sector, both the runs from
Collet Vert – one into Italy and one
back into France – can be great fun.

Getting to Cesana via the lovely
sweeping run starting at the top of the
Serra Granet double-drag, and heading
home from Pian del Sole, is easier
than the gradings suggest, and can be
tackled by less adventurous
intermediates, who also have a wealth

LIFT PASSES

Montgenèvre-Monts de la Lune
Covers Montgenèvre and Claviere lifts.

Main pass
1-day pass €24
6-day pass €115

Senior citizens
Over 60: 6-day pass €93
Over 75: free pass

Children
Under 12: 6-day pass €93
Under 6: free pass

Notes
6-day and over Avantage Galaxie pass allows free day at each of Alpe-d'Huez, Les Deux-Alpes, Puy-St-Vincent and Serre-Chevalier, and discounted rate at La Grave.

Alternative passes
Montgenèvre only pass available.

boarding

There's plenty to attract boarders to Montgenèvre. There are good local beginner slopes and long runs on varied terrain for intermediates. The only real drawback is that many of the lifts in the area are drags, and you will have to use them to get around – getting over to Sestriere and back involves lots (and some flat sections to skate along as well). There are some excellent off-piste areas for more advanced boarders. Snow Box is the local specialist shop.

of cruising terrain high up at the top of the Les Anges sector. These are served by several upper lifts, but you have the option of continuing right down to town. These long, gentle runs are wonderfully flattering cruises.

Further afield, the run down to Claviere from the top of the Gimont drags, on the Italian side, is a beautifully gentle cruise.

FOR BEGINNERS
Good for novices and improvers
There is a fine selection of convenient nursery slopes with reliable snow at the foot of the north-facing area. Progression to longer runs could not be easier, with a very easy blue starting at Les Anges, leading on to a green and finishing at the roadside 600m/1,970ft below.

FOR CROSS-COUNTRY
Having a car widens horizons
Montgenèvre is the best of the Milky Way resorts for cross-country enthusiasts, but it's useful to have a car. The two local trails, totalling 25km/16 miles, offer quite a bit of

variety, but a further 75km/47 miles of track starts in Les Alberts, 8km/5 miles away in the Clarée valley.

QUEUES
No problems most of the time
The slopes are wonderfully uncrowded during weekdays, provided surrounding resorts have snow. Some lifts become crowded at weekends and when nearby Bardonecchia is lacking snow. And queues for the two gondolas out of the village can occur first thing. Links with Italy have improved but some walking can be involved and many of the lifts are still old and slow.

MOUNTAIN RESTAURANTS
Head for Italy
The few mountain restaurants in the Montgenèvre sector are of the large self-service canteen variety – but in the Claviere sector there is a choice of atmospheric little mountain huts, such as the 'cosy' and 'friendly' Montanina Restaurant at the top of the chair lift from Sagnalonga. Alternatively there are plenty of places to eat all along the main road back in the village.

CHILDREN

The village kindergarten (0492 215250) takes children aged 6 months up to 6 years, from 9am to 5pm. Meals you provide can be administered.

The ESF's kindergarten takes children aged 3 to 5, and children up to age 12 can join classes (6 half days €87).

SCHOOLS

ESF
t 0492 219046
esf.montgenevre@wanadoo.fr

A-Peak
t 0492 218330
info@a-peak.com

Classes (ESF prices) 6 half days €87
Private lessons €30 for 1hr

GETTING THERE

Air Turin 98km/61 miles (2hr); Grenoble 145km/90 miles (3hr); Lyon 253km/157 miles (4½hr).

Rail Briançon (15km/9 miles) or Oulx (20km/12 miles); buses available from both 5 times a day.

ACTIVITIES

Indoor Library, sauna, cinema

Outdoor Natural ice rink, paragliding, snow-shoeing, tobogganing, walking, horse riding

Phone numbers From abroad use the prefix +33 and omit the initial '0' of the phone number.

TOURIST OFFICE

t 0492 215252
office.tourisme.montgenevre@wanadoo.fr
www.montgenevre.com

SCHOOLS AND GUIDES
Encouraging reports
Our latest reports on the ESF are good ('great instructor, good with kids').

FACILITIES FOR CHILDREN
Pity about the traffic
The intrusive main road apart, Montgenèvre would seem a fine family resort. Reports on the school's children's classes have been complimentary of both class size and spoken English.

STAYING THERE

HOW TO GO
Limited choice
UK tour operators concentrate on cheap and cheerful catered chalets, though some apartments are also available and a few operators also package hotels.

Hotels There are a handful of simple places offering good value.
② **Valérie** (0492 219002) Central rustic old 3-star.
② **Napoléon** (0492 219204) 3-star on the roadside.
① **Alpet** (0492 219006) Basic 2-star near the centre.
① **Chalet des Sports** (0492 219017) Among the cheapest rooms in the Alps.
Self-catering Résidences La Ferme d'Augustin (0492 030457) are simple, ski-to-the-door apartments on the fringes of the main north-facing slopes, five minutes' walk (across the piste) from town.

EATING OUT
Cheap and cheerful
There are a dozen places to choose from. The Ca del Sol and the Cesar have been recommended by reporters. The Estable and Transalpin serve good-value traditional fare. Chez Pierrot and the Jamy have an authentic French feel. The 3-star Napoléon is the only hotel with a restaurant open to non-residents – a pizzeria. A trip to Claviere is worthwhile – reporters have testified to the excellence of the restaurants.

APRES-SKI
Mainly bars, but fun
The range is limited. The Graal is a friendly, unsophisticated place; the Ca del Sol bar is a cosy place with open fire. Pub Chaberton is recommended. The Blue Light disco is popular. The Refuge, the Crepouse and the Jamy are the focal cafe-bars at tea-time.

OFF THE SLOPES
Very limited
There is a weekly market and you can walk the cross-country routes, but the main diversion is a bus-trip to the beautiful old town of Briançon.

STAYING UP THE MOUNTAIN
Easily arranged, recommended
The Sport Hotel at Sagnalonga, halfway down the piste to Cesana (on the Italian side of the border) and reached by chair-lift or snowmobile, is offered by First Choice and recommended by two reporters this year – 'good-value self-service meals', but 'it's in need of re-decoration'. Even at half-term you get the immaculately groomed local slopes to yourself until skiers based elsewhere arrive, mid-morning. It's quiet in the evenings, but livens up considerably when Italian weekenders arrive to party.

Claviere 1760m/5,770ft

Claviere is a small, traditional village, barely a mile to the east of Montgenèvre and just over the border in Italy. It's no great beauty, and the main road to Montgenèvre and Briançon that divides it in two has an obvious impact, but visitors seem to like its quiet, relaxed ambience, and are ready to go again.

The slopes of Montgenèvre are as easily reached as those on the Italian side of the border. Stupidly, there is no shared pass sold here; you have to buy day extensions for the French slopes, or go up the road to Montgenèvre, where a shared pass is available.

Claviere's nursery slope is small and steep but usually uncrowded and snow-reliable. We have had mixed reports of its ski school – from 'lovely instructors, brilliant with the kids' to 'only average' and 'big classes'.

Morzine

A lively, year-round resort linked by lift to the Portes du Soleil

COSTS

① ② ③ ④ ⑤ ⑥

RATINGS

The slopes

Snow	**
Extent	*****
Expert	***
Intermediate	****
Beginner	***
Convenience	**
Queues	***
Mountain restaurants	***

The rest

Scenery	***
Resort charm	***
Off-slope	***

KEY FACTS

Resort	1000m
	3,280ft

for Portes du Soleil

Slopes	975-2275m
	3,200-7,460ft
Lifts	206
Pistes	650km
	400 miles
Green	13%
Blue	38%
Red	39%
Black	10%
Snowmaking	
	252 acres

For Morzine-Les Gets only

Slopes	1000-2020m
	3,280-6,630ft
Lifts	67
Pistes	140km
	87 miles

296

+ Part of the vast Portes du Soleil

+ Larger local piste area than other Portes du Soleil resorts

+ Good nightlife by French standards

+ Quite attractive old town – a sharp contrast to purpose-built Avoriaz

+ Nearby Les Gets very attractive

+ One of the easiest drives from the Channel (a car is very useful here)

+ Few queues locally

− Takes a while to get to Avoriaz and the main Portes du Soleil circuit

− Bus-ride or long walk to lifts from much of the accommodation

− Low altitude means there is an enduring risk of poor snow, though increased snowmaking has helped

− Low altitude or inconvenient nursery slopes

− Not a great resort for experts

− Weekend crowds

Morzine is a long-established French resort, popular for its easy road access, traditional atmosphere and gentle tree-filled slopes, where children do not get lost and bad weather rarely causes problems. For keen piste-bashers wanting to travel the Portes du Soleil circuit, the main drawback to staying in central Morzine is having to take a bus and cable-car or several lifts to get to Avoriaz and the main circuit. Morzine's local slopes can suffer from poor snow.

Such problems can be avoided by taking a car or using a tour operator who will drive you around. The little-used Ardent gondola, a short drive from Morzine, gives access to a clockwise circuit via Châtel, missing out often crowded Avoriaz. If local snow is poor, you can visit nearby Flaine by car, which is better than Avoriaz at coping with crowds looking for snow.

THE RESORT

Morzine is a traditional mountain town sprawling amorphously on both sides of a river gorge. In winter, under a blanket of snow, its chalet-style buildings look charming, and in spring the village quickly takes on a spruce appearance.

The old centre is next to the river, and shops, restaurants and bars line the road up to the Le Pléney lifts. Accommodation is widely scattered, and a good multi-route bus service links all parts of the town to outlying lifts, including those for Avoriaz.

As the extensive network of bus routes implies, Morzine is a town where getting from A to B can be tricky. It is well worth making sure that your accommodation is near the lifts that you expect to be using, which for most visitors means the gondola and cable-car to Le Pléney, the gondola to Super-Morzine or the cable-car to Avoriaz.

Morzine is a family resort, and village ambience tends to be fairly subdued. Our view that the resort suits

car drivers is widely shared. Roads are busy, but parking problems have been somewhat relieved by new car parks built quite recently near Le Pléney.

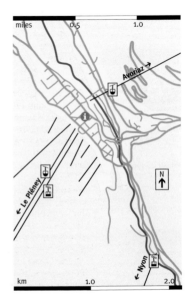

↑ The local Morzine-Les Gets slopes are the most extensive in the Portes du Soleil
OT LES GETS

NEWS

Morzine and the linked Les Gets area have benefited from a lot of new high-speed lifts recently, and more are planned. In 2002/03 a six-pack replaced the two Nauchets drag-lifts in the Les Chavannes-Le Ranfolly sector of Les Gets and a new six-pack was built on the La Rosta slopes. The Mont Chéry gondola was renovated and new six-seater bubbles installed.

For 2003/04 a new car park is planned at Les Perrières on the outskirts of Les Gets, with a drive-in lift pass office and new six-pack to take day visitors to the slopes. Also, the Chavannes chair is due to be replaced by a six-pack: good news, since it is the main way out of Les Gets towards Morzine (the gondola does not go as high).

The slow Charniaz chair in Morzine, up from Le Grand Pré to the Ranfolly sector, is also set to become a six-pack. And Morzine will have two electric buses next season – the first stage in a plan to reduce pollution and traffic.

THE MOUNTAINS

The local slopes suit intermediates well, with excellent areas for beginners and near-beginners too: 'More variety than expected,' said one reporter. Others have praised the system of Discovery Routes around the Portes du Soleil – choose an animal that suits your ability and follow the signs displaying it around the circuit.

THE SLOPES
No need to go far afield

Morzine is not an ideal base for the Portes du Soleil circuit (described in the Avoriaz, Châtel and Champéry chapters). But it has an extensive local area shared with Les Gets.

A cable-car and parallel gondola rise from the edge of central Morzine to **Le Pléney**, where numerous routes return to the valley, including a run down to Les Fys – a quiet junction of chairs which access **Nyon** and, in the opposite direction, the ridge separating Morzine from the **Les Gets** slopes. Nyon can also be accessed by cable-car, situated a bus-ride from Morzine, and is connected to the slopes of Les Gets higher up the valley that separates the two, with a lift up from Le Grand Pré to Le Ranfolly. The Nyon sector has two peaks – Pointe de Nyon and Chamossière – accessible from Nyon and Le Grand Pré respectively.

From Le Ranfolly you can descend directly to Morzine without using a lift. To get to Morzine from the slopes above Les Gets you go first to the mid-mountain lift junction of Les Chavannes, then to the Folliets chair which takes you up to Le Pléney.

Beyond Les Gets is another small but worthwhile sector, on Mont Chéry. The short walk or 'petit train' shuttle through the village from the base of Chavannes takes about five minutes.

One means of access to the main Portes du Soleil circuit (on the opposite side of the valley from Le Pléney) is via a gondola from near the centre of town – another handy 'petit train' shuttle service runs between this and the Le Pléney lifts. The gondola takes you up to **Super-Morzine**, and a series of pistes and lifts leads to Avoriaz. In the past, reporters have found this route 'not worth the trouble', but for 2003/04 the Zorre chair, which goes from the top of the Super-Morzine gondola, should be replaced by a fast six-seater chair, which will cut queues here. These alternatives are a bus-ride or short drive to either Les Prodains (from where you can get a cable-car to Avoriaz or a chair-lift into the **Hauts Forts** slopes above it) or to Ardent, where a gondola accesses Les Lindarets for lifts towards Châtel, Avoriaz or Champéry. The tree-lined slopes in Les Lindarets are good in poor visibility and the area at the top of the gondola is a good one for mixed ability groups to meet up. Car trips to Flaine and Chamonix are feasible.

TERRAIN-PARKS
Mont Chéry, or head for Avoriaz

There's a park at Mont Chéry called the 'Freestyle District', with five kickers, hip jumps, a gap jump and a couple of quarter-pipes. There are also boarder-cross and slalom courses here. There's another boarder-cross, aimed at children, in the Zone Enfant at the top of Les Chavannes. Avoriaz has much more to offer (see Avoriaz chapter).

SNOW RELIABILITY
Poor

Morzine has a very low average height, and it can rain here when it is snowing higher up. It had no snow last Christmas and New Year, for example, and it rained when we were there in January. There is some snowmaking, most noticeably on runs linking Nyon and Le Pléney, and on the runs back to town. Les Gets has increased its snowmaking – but more is needed.

LIFT PASSES

Portes du Soleil
Covers all lifts in all 12 resorts, and shuttle-buses.

Main pass
1-day pass €34
6-day pass €164

Senior citizens
Over 60: 6-day pass €131

Children
Under 16: 6-day pass €110
Under 5: free pass

Notes
Half-day passes available.

Alternative passes
Morzine-Les Gets pass and Morzine-Avoriaz pass available, also special snowboard pass for Mont Chéry area.

FOR EXPERTS
A few possibilities

The runs down from Pointe de Nyon and Chamossière are quite challenging, as are the black runs down the back of Mont Chéry. But for piste challenges the cable-car at Les Prodains is the place to head for, taking you up to Avoriaz. The Hauts Forts black runs, including the World Cup downhill course, are excellent. The above-the-tree-line slopes of Chamossière offer some of the best local off-piste possibilities, and Mont Chéry is also worth exploring. We've had reports of great off-piste off the back of Col du Fornet down towards the Vallée de la Manche (but you'd need a guide).

FOR INTERMEDIATES
Something for everyone

Good intermediates will enjoy the challenging reds and blacks down from the Chamossière and Pointe de Nyon high points. Mont Chéry has some fine steepish runs which are usually very quiet as everyone heads up from Les Gets towards Morzine ('The deserted red runs are a dream,' said a reporter).

Those of average ability have a great choice, though most runs are rather short. Le Ranfolly accesses a series of good cruisers on the Les Gets side of the ridge, and a nice piste back to Le Grand Pré. Le Pléney has a compact network of pistes that are ideal for groups with mixed abilities: mainly moderate intermediate runs, but with some easier alternatives for the more timid, and a single challenging route for the aggressive.

Less experienced intermediates have lots of options on Le Pléney, including a great away-from-it-all, snow-gun-covered blue cruise from the top to the valley lift station. Heading from Le Ranfolly to Le Grand Pré on the blue is a nice cruise. And the slopes down to Les Gets from Le Pléney are easy when conditions allow (they face south).

The new high-speed chairs built for 2002/03 make the Ranfolly and Rosta sectors more attractive.

And, of course, there is the whole of the Portes du Soleil circuit to explore by going up the opposite side of the valley to Avoriaz or Les Lindarets.

FOR BEGINNERS
Good for novices and improvers

The wide village nursery slopes are convenient, and benefit from snow-guns. Some of the best progression runs are over at Nyon. Adventurous novices also have the option of easy pistes around Le Pléney. Near-beginners can get over to Les Gets via Le Pléney, and return via Le Ranfolly.

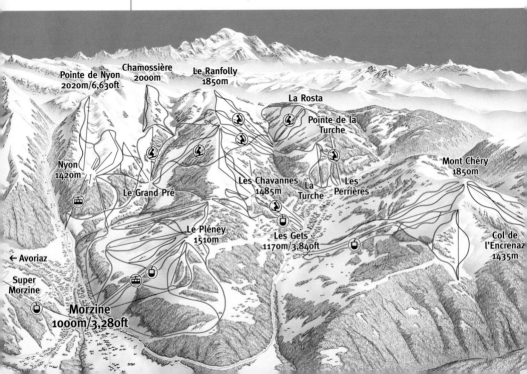

boarding

Avoriaz is the hard-core boarding HQ of the Portes du Soleil. But there's a boarding presence in Morzine too – Chalet Snowboard, who were the first chalet company to target snowboarders rather than skiers, has Morzine chalets, and former British Champ Becci Malthouse teaches with the British Alpine Ski & Snowboard school. With interesting, tree-lined runs and few drags, the local Morzine slopes are good for beginners and intermediates. And there's a terrain-park that might seem less intimidating than the big one in Avoriaz, over in Mont Chéry. There's a special snowboarders' pass if you just want to ride that area – 14.50 euros a day last season – and there's a snowpark map. The specialist shop Misty Fly runs big air comps every Monday – and broadcasts them on the Internet.

FOR CROSS-COUNTRY
Good variety
There is a wide variety of cross-country trails, not all at valley level. The best section is in the pretty Vallée de la Manche beside the Nyon mountain up to the Lac de Mines d'Or, where there is a good restaurant. The Pléney-Chavannes loop is pleasant and relatively snow-reliable.

QUEUES
Few problems when snow is good
Queues are not usually a problem in the local area but we had a report of 'horrendous queues and frequent lift breakdown in the Les Gets area' last

year – doubtless why the resort is building so many fast new lifts. The Nyon cable-car and Belvédère chair-lift (Le Pléney) are weekend bottlenecks. Queues to and from Avoriaz are much improved in recent times, but are still bad when snow is in short supply.

MOUNTAIN RESTAURANTS
Within reach of some good huts
The nice little place at the foot of the d'Atray chair is perhaps the best local hut. A recent reporter loved the tiny Lhottys hut, where he ate amazing fresh seafood. We had an enjoyable Savoyard lunch at the rustic Chez Nannon near the top of the Troncs chair between Nyon and Chamossière. The restaurant at the top of the Folliets chair has had several recommendations and the self-service on Mont Chéry was called 'one of the better I've been to in my time' by a reporter. The Crêtes de Zore above Super-Morzine is good.

SCHOOLS AND GUIDES
British ski school here
The British Alpine Ski & Snowboard School (BASS), featuring BASI-qualified instructors gets good reports: 'some of our group did the Techniques and Tactics course, another the Parallel Improvers; groups were generally about four in size; very happy with the service,' said a 2003 reporter. Reports on the ESF are generally good, except for some complaints about class sizes. One reporter told of '22 people in my son's class' in half-term week.

FACILITIES FOR CHILDREN
Lots of possibilities
The facilities of the Outa nursery are quite impressive, but we've received reports of poor English and low staff ratios. Jack Frosts is run by a qualified children's nurse from Northern Ireland. There is a big children's area, the Zone Enfant, in the Les Chavannes

CHILDREN

The Halte Garderie l'Outa (0450 792600) takes children aged 3 months up to 6 years. From age 3 they can have one-hour introductory lessons. The Piou-Piou (0450 791313) takes children aged 3 to 12, with ESF instruction and lunch provided (6 days €300). Jack Frost's (UK: 07721 912455; www.jackfrosts.com) takes babies upwards.

GETTING THERE

Air Geneva 75km/47 miles (1½hr). Lyon 195km/121 miles (3½hr).

Rail Cluses or Thonon (30km/19 miles); regular bus connections to resort.

Phone numbers From abroad use the prefix +33 and omit the initial '0' of the phone number.

ACTIVITIES

Indoor Skating, bowling, cinemas, massage, table tennis, fitness track

Outdoor Horse-riding, sleigh rides, snow-shoe classes, artificial climbing wall, tennis, paragliding

area. An ESF childcare centre, Club des Piou-Piou looks after children between the ages of 3 and 16 after skiing. The Dérêches Farm offers days learning about animals, snow-shoeing and tobogganing. The tour operator Esprit Ski has good facilities. Ski Famille and Ski Hillwood are other family specialists, based in Les Gets.

STAYING THERE

HOW TO GO
Good-value hotels and chalets

The tour operator market concentrates on hotels and chalets.

Chalets There's a wide choice, but position varies enormously. Chalet Gueret is an independently run luxury chalet (see Luxury chalets chapter).

Hotels The handful of 3-star hotels includes some quite smooth ones; and there are dozens of 2-stars and 1-stars. **(((4 Dahu** (0450 759292) 3-star linked to centre by footbridge over river; good restaurant; pool. Private shuttle to lifts. **(((4 Airelles** (0450 747121) Central 3-star close to Pléney lifts and Prodains and Nyon bus routes. Good pool. **(((4 Champs Fleuris** (0450 791444) Comfy 3-star next to Pléney lifts. Pool. **(((3 Tremplin** (0450 791231) Also next to the lifts; 'friendly staff, good food'. **(((3 Bergerie** (0450 791369) Rustic chalet, in centre. Friendly staff. Pool. **((2 Côtes** (0450 790996) Simple 2-star on the edge of town. Pool. **((2 Equipe** (0450 791143) One of the best 2-stars; next to the Pléney lift.

Self-catering The Télémark apartments, close to the Super-Morzine gondola, and the Udrezants, by the Prodains cable-car, have ben recommended.

EATING OUT
A fine choice

The best restaurant in town is probably the Taverne in hotel Samoyede – we had a great meal there including

lobster ravioli, truffle risotto and scallops. The Chamade looks the part (elegant table settings) but we have no reports of the food. The Airelles has a fine restaurant and the Dahu also has good food. The Grange does 'excellent food, but at a price'. Locals rate the Taverne and Chalet Philibert highly. The Etale is an atmospheric pizza place, also serving local specialities. Café Chaud is popular for fondue.

APRES-SKI
One of the livelier French resorts

On Tuesday evenings there's a 'ski retrospective' on the Le Pléney slopes, and on Thursdays there's a torchlight descent, followed by floodlit skiing. There are two cinemas.

Nightlife is good by French standards. The Dixie has sport on TV, MTV, a cellar bar and some live music. At the Crépuscule, near the Le Pléney lifts, dancing on the tables in ski boots to deafening music seems compulsory at après time. Just below, and all in the same building are: the Caverne which is popular with resort staff; the Bowling for, err … 10-pin bowling; the Boudha Café, with Asian decor, for a quieter drink. L'Opera was advertising 'nuits torrides' (striptease and lap dancing) last season. The tiny Sherpa, on the outskirts of town, is also worth a try. L'Opéra and The Paradis du Laury's are late night haunts.

OFF THE SLOPES
Quite good; excursions possible

There is an excellent ice rink, which stages ice hockey matches and skating galas. Some hotels have pools, which non-residents can pay to use. Buses run to Thonon for shopping, and car owners can drive to Geneva, Annecy or Montreux. There are lots of very pretty walks, and other activities include horse-drawn sleigh rides, horse-riding, paragliding and a cheese factory visit.

Les Gets 1170m/3,840ft

Les Gets is much smaller than Morzine and has a friendly feel and very French ambience. Several reporters said that it feels tucked away and rather secret. Its fine nursery slopes and reasonable prices make Les Gets a good choice for families and many others. But it's a major trek to get to and from the main Portes du Soleil circuit on snow – reporters say a car is a big advantage.

THE RESORT

Les Gets is a little old village of mainly traditional chalet buildings, 6km/4 miles from Morzine. The main road to Morzine bypasses the village centre, which is partly car-free and has plenty of attractive food and other shops and restaurants lining the main street. There's also a popular outdoor ice rink, which adds to the charm.

Although the village has a scattered appearance, most facilities are conveniently close to the main lift station – and the free 'petit train' shuttle is a 'quirky but useful' way of travelling around. It is fairly quiet in the evenings except at weekends when the atmosphere becomes more chic.

The local pass covers all Les Gets, Nyon and Le Pléney lifts, saves a fair bit on a Portes du Soleil pass, and is worth considering by less experienced skiers and riders if the snow is good.

THE MOUNTAINS

Les Gets is not an ideal base for the Portes du Soleil, but its local slopes are extensive.

Slopes As well as the local slopes that are linked to Morzine (see earlier in chapter), Les Gets has runs on Mont Chéry, accessed by a recently modernised gondola and parallel chair. The front slopes face south-east – bad news at this altitude; but the other two flanks are shadier.

Snow reliability Despite having a slightly higher elevation than Morzine, snow conditions can again be erratic. A lot more snow-guns, installed in recent years, have improved runs to the resort.

Terrain-parks The only one in the Morzine-Les Gets area is on Mont Chéry – see earlier in chapter.

Experts Black runs from the Chéry Nord chair are steep and challenging in parts.

A recent expert reporter was pleasantly surprised by the 'challenging terrain available with good snow, and beautiful tree-level skiing'.

Intermediates High-mileage piste-bashers will enjoy cruising the Portes du Soleil circuit, and the local slopes are not bad for the less adventurous.

Beginners The village nursery slopes are convenient, but there are better, more snow-sure ones up at Chavannes. Progression is simple, with an easy run between Chavannes and the resort and a pleasant green from La Rosta.

Snowboarding The local Les Gets and Morzine slopes are good for beginners and intermediates. Experts will enjoy the excellent terrain-park in Avoriaz.

Cross-country Morzine is better, with excellent trails. But Les Gets has 46km/29 miles of good, varied loops on Mont Chéry and Les Chavannes.

Queues Provided there's good snow, not much of a problem, though weekend crowds are a drawback, and a couple of reporters have complained about bad queue management.

Mountain restaurants See Morzine.

Schools and guides We've had mixed reports of the ESF, with tales of 'instructors shouting at our four-year-olds in French' but also of children enjoying 'a great instructor'. Hugh Monney, the founder of the British Alpine Ski & Snowboard School, runs the branch based here.

Facilities for children There is a non-ski nursery for children aged three months to four years, and two ski kindergartens, the Fripouilles and the Ile des Enfants, which is reputedly the better of the two. The ESF's Club Fantaski, for three-to five-year-old skiers, has been criticised for inattentive supervision in the past. The ESF also runs the P'tits Montagnys club, for four-to 12-year-olds. Tour operators Ski Famille and Ski Hillwood have been recommended.

STAYING THERE

How to go Several tour operators have catered chalets, including Ski Activity and Total Ski (which we've heard good reports of).

Hotels All the hotels are 3-star and below, mostly cheap and cheerful old 2-stars. The 3-star Crychar (0450 758050), 100m/330ft from central Les Gets at the foot of the slopes, is one of the best. The 2-star Alpen Sports (0450 758055) is a friendly, family run hotel – 'excellent food and good value for money' says a reporter. We've also had good reports of the the Nagano (0450 797146) and the Marmotte (0450 758033) – both 3-star.

Self-catering The tourist office has a list of apartments. A 2003 reporter was happy with his Lion D'Or apartment.

Eating out Most hotels have good restaurants. The Tyrol and the Schuss are good for pizza; the rustic Vieux Chêne for Savoyard specialities. The Flambeau, Tanière and Tourbillon have been recommended. The Boomerang brings an Australian flavour.

Après-ski Après-ski is quiet, especially on weekdays. The Pub Irlandaise (with 'an unusual Savoie version of porter') and the Bar Canadie above it were recommended by two reporters this year. Bar les Copeaux and the Bar Bush (English owned) have been recommended too. The Igloo is a popular disco.

Off the slopes There's a well-equipped fitness centre with a pool, and an artificial ice rink. The Mechanical Music Museum is strongly recommended by a reporter (barrel organs and music boxes, for example, with guided tours in English). Outings to Geneva, Lausanne and Montreux are possible.

Phone numbers
From abroad use the prefix +33 and omit the initial '0' of the phone number.

TOURIST OFFICES

Morzine
t 0450 747272
touristoffice@morzine-avoriaz.com
www.morzine.com

Les Gets
t 0450 758080
lesgets@lesgets.com
www.lesgets.com

SNOWPIX.COM / CHRIS GILL

La Plagne

A huge variety of villages spread across a vast playground

COSTS

① ② ③ ④ ⑤ ⑥

RATINGS

The slopes
Snow	****
Extent	****
Expert	***
Intermediate	*****
Beginner	****
Convenience	*****
Queues	***
Mountain restaurants	***

The rest
Scenery	****
Resort charm	*
Off-slope	*

NEWS

For 2003/04, the long-awaited Vanoise Express cable-car link to Les Arcs is due to open – forming one of the world's biggest lift-linked ski areas, called Paradiski. For more details see separate chapter near the start of the book.

Also for 2003/04, the Roche de Mio gondola will be renovated, increasing its capacity by 30% to 1,440 people an hour.

There are also to be improvements on the glacier. A fixed-grip quad chair will replace the top two drags (the area is mainly for summer skiing and rarely open in the winter). And a red piste will be built to link the glacier to the runs to the new Vanoise Express (more snowmaking will be installed too).

The Leitchoums drag above Belle Plagne will be replaced by a quicker one.

➕ Extensive intermediate slopes, plus plentiful, excellent off-piste terrain

➕ New link with Les Arcs means there's even more to explore

➕ Good nursery slopes

➕ High and fairly snow-sure – and with some wonderful views

➕ Purpose-built resort units are convenient for the slopes

➕ Attractive, traditional-style villages lower down share the slopes

➕ Wooded runs of lower resorts are useful in poor weather

➖ Pistes in the main bowl don't have much to offer experts

➖ Pistes can get very crowded in places

➖ Lower villages can suffer from poor snow – runs back to Champagny especially

➖ Unattractive architecture in some of the higher resort units

➖ Not many green runs for nervous beginners to go on to – though some blues are very easy

➖ Nightlife very limited

With 220km/137 miles of its own slopes and 86% of these being blue or red, the La Plagne area is an intermediate's paradise. And with much-needed lift improvements over the last few years, plus the new link with Les Arcs for 2003/04, the resort is going up in our estimation. It has a reputation for plug-ugly, soulless, purpose-built villages and some of them justify that view. But there are ten different villages to choose from – and as well as delightful old mountain villages at the foot of the slopes, there are some quite attractive purpose-built centres, too. While the slopes aren't steep enough for on-piste expert fun, those who are prepared to hire a guide can have a splendid time off-piste with some long descents which are often deserted and untracked compared with the classic off-piste runs of more macho resorts like Val-d'Isère.

THE RESORT

La Plagne consists of no fewer than ten separate 'villages'; six are purpose-built at altitude in the main bowl, on or above the tree line and linked by road, lifts and pistes; the other four are scattered around outside the bowl.

Each is self-contained with its own shops, bars, restaurants, schools and lift pass offices. Even the core resorts vary a lot in character. The first to be built, in the 1960s, was Plagne-Centre

– still the focal point for shops and après-ski. Typical of its time, it has ugly blocks and dreary indoor 'malls' that house a reasonable selection of shops, bars and restaurants. Some new developments just above Plagne-Centre are more pleasing to the eye.

Lifts radiate from Centre to all sides of the bowl, the major one being the big twin-cable gondola to Grande Rochette. A cable-car goes to the even more obtrusive 'village' of Aime-la-Plagne – a group of monolithic blocks.

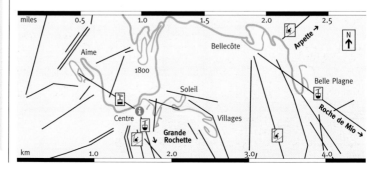

KEY FACTS

Resort	1800-2100m
	5,900-6,890ft

For La Plagne only

Slopes	1250-3250m
	4,100-10,660ft
Lifts	108
Pistes	220km
	137 miles
Green	9%
Blue	56%
Red	26%
Black	9%
Snowmaking	
	50 acres

For Paradiski area

Slopes	1200-3250m
	3,940-10,660ft
Lifts	164
Pistes	420km
	261 miles
Green	5%
Blue	54%
Red	28%
Black	13%

Below these two, and a bit of a backwater, is Plagne 1800, where the buildings are small-scale and chalet style, and many are indeed chalets on the UK package market. Access to the main bowl from here is by lifts to Aime-la-Plagne and reporters comment on a drag-lift, the Lovatière, which links with no other lifts.

A little way above Plagne-Centre is the newest development, Plagne-Soleil, still small as yet, but with attractive new chalets. This area is officially attached to Plagne-Villages, which is a rather strung-out but attractive collection of small-scale apartments and chalets in traditional style, handy for the slopes but for nothing else.

The two other core resort units are a bus-ride away, on the other side of a low hill. The large apartment buildings of Plagne-Bellecôte form a wall at the foot of the slopes down to it. Some way above it is Belle-Plagne – as its name suggests, easy on the eye, with a neo-Savoyard look, and entirely underground parking. Reporters have complained of exhaustion when moving between the different levels in Belle-Plagne (the bars and other facilities are mainly in the lower part), but have also praised the architecture.

Two high-speed chairs built for 2002/03 mean Bellecôte now has a quick alternative route to the gondola to Roche de Mio and the snow-sure glacier area. They also provide links to two of the lower resorts in the valleys outside the bowl – the old village of Montchavin and its recently developed neighbour Les Coches (above which is the new cable-car to Les Arcs), at the northern extremity of the area, and Champagny at the southern extremity. The update of the Roche de Mio gondola for 2003/04 should also improve the links. But last season reporters found the piste at the top of Roche di Mio crowded and dangerous. This may get worse with more people arriving up there – though the new piste from the glacier towards Montchavin may help.

At the western extremity is the modern Montalbert development. For a description of these lower villages, see the end of this chapter.

A free bus system between the core villages within the bowl runs until after midnight. But you may need to change in Plagne Centre. Lifts from Belle-Plagne to Plagne-Bellecôte, Aime-la-Plagne to Plagne-Centre, and Plagne-Centre to Plagne-Villages all run until 1am.

Trips by car to Val-d'Isère-Tignes or the Three Valleys are possible – and each is covered for a day with a 6-day Paradiski or Paradiski Découverte pass.

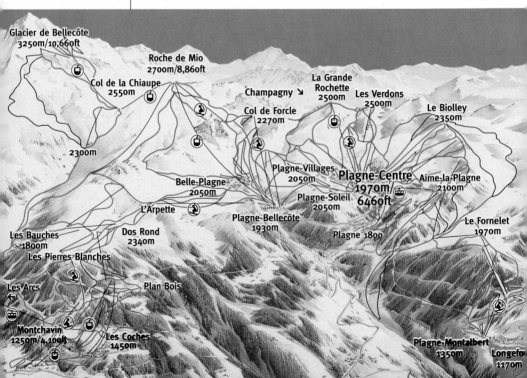

Map labels:
- ↓ Plagne-Centre
- La Grande Rochette 2500m
- Les Verdons 2500m
- Col de Forcle 2270m
- Belle-Plagne
- Plagne-Bellecôte ↓
- Les Borseliers
- Roche de Mio 2700m
- Col de la-Chiaupe 2550m
- Bellecôte 3417m
- Champagny-le-Haut
- Le Planay
- Champagny-en-Vanoise 1250m

THE MOUNTAINS

The majority of the slopes in the main bowl are above the tree line, though there are trees scattered around most of the resort centres. The slopes outside the bowl are open at the top but descend into woodland. The gondola up to the exposed glacier slopes on Bellecôte, to the west of the main bowl, is prone to closure by high winds or poor weather, and the top drags are normally shut in winter (as the new chair is likely to be). At Salomon Station in Plagne Centre you can test any Salomon equipment under the guidance of hosts/instructors (60 euros a day last season).

THE SLOPES
Multi-centred; can be confusing
La Plagne boasts 220km/137 miles of pistes over a wide area that can be broken down into seven distinct but interlinked sectors. From Plagne-Centre you can take a lift up to **Le Biolley**, from where you can head back to Centre, to Aime-la-Plagne or down gentle runs to **Montalbert**, from where you ride several successive lifts back up. But the main lift out of Plagne-Centre leads up to **La Grande Rochette**. From here there are good sweeping runs back down and an easier one over to Plagne-Bellecôte, or you can drop over the back into the predominantly south-facing **Champagny** sector (from which a lift

arrives back up at Les Verdons and another brings you out much further east near Col de Forcle). From the Champagny sector there are great views over to Courchevel.

From Plagne-Bellecôte and Belle-Plagne, you can head up to **Roche de Mio**, and have the choice of the newly refurbished gondola, or the two fast chairs installed for 2002/03 (the first of which also links with the Champagny sector). From Roche de Mio, runs spread out in all directions – towards La Plagne, Champagny or **Montchavin/Les Coches** and the new link with Les Arcs. Montchavin/Les Coches can also be reached by taking a chair from Plagne-Bellecôte to Arpette.

From Roche de Mio you can also take a gondola down then up to the **Bellecôte glacier**. The drag-lifts at the top are set to be replaced by a chair for this season. It will mostly serve summer skiing that is often shut in winter – but if open it offers excellent snow and stunning views. For 2003/04 a new red piste is planned from the bottom of the Chalet de Bellecôte lift at 2300m/7,550ft below the glacier to Les Bauches and the Montchavin slopes. Previously you could only do this off piste. So you can now descend 2000m/656oft vertical on piste from the top of the glacier to Montchavin.

Several reporters have indicated that run grading is inconsistent; some runs are more difficult than their grading suggests, others are easier.

The La Plagne bowl –
Belle-Plagne on the
left, Plagne-Villages in
the centre →
SNOWPIX.COM / CHRIS GILL

TERRAIN-PARKS
Spoilt for choice

There are terrain-parks at Belle-Plagne,
Montchavin-Les Coches, and last
season a new park was built in
Champagny. The biggest is at Belle-
Plagne, with big air, loads of kickers
and rails – plus deckchairs to chill in
and shovels to build your own kickers
if you want. The other two have a
selection of jumps. Plagne-Bellecôte
has a 100m/328ft half-pipe and a ski-
and boarder-cross run.

SNOW RELIABILITY
Generally good except low down

Most of La Plagne's runs are snow-
sure, being at altitudes between
2000m and 2700m (6,560ft and
8,860ft) on the largely north-facing
open slopes above the purpose-built
centres. But during the exceptionally
poor conditions of early 2002 several
reporters commented on poor piste
grooming, rocks and bare patches and
the need for more snowmaking on the
runs into the villages – especially the
busy runs into Plagne-Bellecôte. 40km/
25 miles of extra snowmaking is
planned over the next few seasons.

Runs down to the valley resorts can
cause more problems, and you may
have to take the lifts at times. This is
particularly true of Champagny, where
the two home runs are both south-
facing. The runs down to Les Coches
and Montchavin are north-facing and
have snowmaking – these, and a few
runs around Montalbert and Plagne-
Bellecôte, are the main ones with
snowmaking at the moment. But
reporters from last season found that
snow below 1800 was often patchy,
despite the snow-guns.

FOR EXPERTS
A few good blacks and off-piste

There are two great black runs from
Bellecôte to the chair-lift up to the
gondola mid-station at Col de la
Chiaupe – both beautiful long runs
with a vertical of some 1000m/3,280ft
that take you away from the lift
system. But these are often closed
because of too much or too little snow.

The Les Charmettes black at the end
of the long Emile Allais red down from
above Aime-la-Plagne is little used,
north-facing and very enjoyable in
good snow. A couple of drag-lifts take

boarding

*La Plagne offers terrain for all levels of rider – there's a good mix of long, easy
runs and high, open slopes with some fantastic off-piste options that should be
done with a guide. The broad, gentle pistes are ideal for beginners and carvers
(crowds permitting). There are also lots of areas to play in between the pistes, as
well as three terrain-parks, a boarder-cross and a half-pipe. Whether on- or off-
piste, be prepared for some flat areas, including the tunnel in the middle of the
Inversens run. And while most lifts are gondolas or chairs, there are still some
difficult drag-lifts. 'The flat bits are definitely a drawback,' said one reporter, 'but
you can get around without using the drags.' More difficult drag-lifts are
conveniently marked on the map – it's not a good idea to go all the way down
Emile Allais, for example, unless you're very experienced at riding them. Some
reporters faced a long walk back to 1800!*

Oxygène is a ski and snowboard school that operates in Val d'Isère, La Plagne and – new for 2003/04 – Courchevel. As well as on-piste group and private lessons, they offer off-piste tuition and guiding.

La Plagne contact details:
t 00 33 479 090399
laplagne@oxygene-ski.com
www.oxygene-ski.com

Most La Plagne visitors are beginners or intermediates. But the resort has some fabulous off-piste which remains delightfully deserted. This means you stand a chance of getting fresh tracks long after the last snowfall if you know where to go.

For adventurous intermediates looking to try off-piste for the first time there is a lot of easy off-piste in underused powder easily accessible between the pistes, for example under the new Carella chair-lift to Roche de Mio. And in fresh snow, you can find great powder in the woods above Montchavin and Montalbert.

More serious off-piste still within the capabilities of adventurous intermediates are numerous runs down from the Bellecôte glacier to Les Bauches (a drop of over 1400m/4,590ft) and in good snow down from L'Arpette to Macot at only 800m/2,620ft near Aime (you can return by bus or taxi). There are also great runs in the Biolley sector at the other end of the ski domain, right out beyond the furthest black run.

For more experienced off-piste skiers, the north face of Bellecôte presents a splendid challenge with usually excellent snow at the top. You can descend from here right down to Peisey-Nancroix (a drop of 2000m/over 6,500ft), have lunch at L'Ancolie (see the Les Arcs chapter) and then catch a taxi or the free bus for the short ride to the new Vanoise Express cable-car for the trip back to La Plagne. Another beautiful and out-of-the-way off-piste run from Bellecôte is over the Cul du Nant glacier to Champagny-le-Haut through the Vanoise National Park. This run starts with a long climb to the top of the glacier if the top lift isn't working (it rarely does in winter). You catch a shuttle-bus from the end of the run to Champagny and the gondola back up.

But don't dream of doing any off-piste runs without a fully qualified guide or instructor. Route finding is difficult, avalanche danger can be high and hidden hazards such as cliffs and crevasses lurk. Oxygène instructors know the area well and can find you the best powder stashes.

La Plagne

307

you back up. The Coqs and Morbleu runs also in the Aime-la-Plagne sector are seriously steep.

The long, sweeping Mont de la Guerre red, with a 1250m/4,100ft vertical from Les Verdons to Champagny, is also a beautiful run in good snow (a rare event).

There are other good long reds to cruise around on. But experts will get the best out of La Plagne if they hire a guide and explore the vast off-piste potential – which takes longer to get tracked out than in more 'macho' resorts. See the feature box.

FOR INTERMEDIATES
Great variety
Virtually the whole of La Plagne's area is a paradise for intermediates, with blue and red runs wherever you look. Your main choice will be whether to settle for one area for the day and explore it thoroughly, or just cruise around the pistes that form the main arteries of the network, or now, of course, take a trip to explore Les Arcs.

For early intermediates there are plenty of gentle blue motorway pistes in the main La Plagne bowl, and a long, interesting run from Roche de Mio back to Belle Plagne, Les Inversens (involving a tunnel). The blue runs either side of Arpette, on the Montchavin side of the main bowl, are glorious cruises. In poor weather the best place to be is in the trees on the gentle runs leading down to Montalbert. The easiest way over to Champagny is from the Roche de Mio area rather than from Grande Rochette.

Better intermediates have lots of delightful long red runs to try. Roche de Mio to Les Bauches is a drop of 900m/2,950ft – the first half, Le Clapet, is a fabulous varied run with lots of off-piste diversions possible; the second half, Les Crozats, was marked as a black but we hear is being changed to red for 2003/04. There are challenging red mogul pitches down from the glacier (you'll be able to carry on all the way down to Montchavin now using the new red piste to Les Bauches, then a blue – a vertical drop of 2000m/6,560ft). And the main La Plagne bowl has many enjoyable reds.

The Champagny sector has a couple of tough reds – Kamikaze and Hara-Kiri – leading from Grande Rochette. And

CHILDREN

There are ESF ski kindergartens in all the high resort units, generally taking children from age 3. The ESF also runs all-day nurseries in most of the villages, mostly taking children aged 2 to 6 (18 months to 3 years in Belle Plagne). In Centre, independent nursery Marie Christine does much the same. In Montchavin and Les Coches very young skiers go to the Nursery Club, the ESF taking over at age 4. Children's classes are available up to 13 or 16 depending on the village. 6 full days cost €166 (€225 during French February school holidays).

the long blue cruise Bozelet has one surprisingly steep section. The Mont de la Guerre red run, all the way down to Champagny (1250m/4,100ft vertical), is a satisfying run for adventurous intermediates (but is often closed).

FOR BEGINNERS
Excellent facilities for the novice
La Plagne is a good place to learn, with generally good snow and above average facilities for beginners, especially children. Each of the main centres has nursery slopes on its doorstep. There's a free drag-lift in each resort as well. There are no long green runs to progress to, but no shortage of easy blues. A reporter, while surprised there were not more greens to practise on at base level, particularly recommends Les Bouclets at Aime as 'wide and confidence building'. The Plan Bois area above Les Coches has good gentle slopes. Several reporters have commented that the blue runs back into Plagne 1800 are difficult for novices.

CROSS-COUNTRY
Open and wooded trails
There are 90km/56 miles of prepared cross-country trails scattered around. The most beautiful of these are the 30km/19 miles of winding track set out in the sunny valley around Champagny-le-Haut. The north-facing areas have more wooded trails that link the various centres. It's best to have a car if you want to make the most of it all.

QUEUES
Main problems being sorted
La Plagne used to have some big bottlenecks. Recent lift improvements have eased some of the worst problems, and hopefully the renovation of the Roche de Mio gondola will reduce the queues for that. But reporters still complain about long

waits for the Arpette chair from Plagne-Bellecôte towards Montchavin (partly caused by chairs being allowed to travel up half empty). And there are still several lifts that can generate queues that you can't avoid, once you've descended to them – at Les Bauches for example. The gondola to the glacier is queue-prone when snow is poor lower down.

Crowds on the pistes are now as much of a problem as lift queues, particularly above Bellecôte in the afternoon, and at Roche de Mio (and this is likely to get worse as more lifts are improved).

MOUNTAIN RESTAURANTS
An enormous choice
Mountain restaurants are numerous, varied and crowded only in peak periods, as many people prefer to descend to one of the resorts – particularly Champagny or Montchavin/Les Coches – at the end of the morning. Recommendations by readers include the Bergerie above Plagne-Villages, Chaudron at Plagne-Centre, Crystal des Neiges, Carroley, Plan Bois and Plein Soleil on the Montchavin/Les Coches slopes. Two great rustic restaurants in which to hole up in poor weather for a long lunch of Savoyard dishes are the Chez Pat du Sauget, above Montchavin, and Au Bon Vieux Temps, just below Aime-la-Plagne. Reservations may be required at either. Chalet des Colosses above Plagne Bellecôte and Chalets des Inversens at Roche de Mio ('fabulous views, good food') have been highly recommended. We love Roc des Blanchets at the top of the Champagny gondola – friendly staff, both table- and self-service, beautiful views over to Courchevel from the terrace and good basic cooking. The little Breton cafe at the bottom of the Quillis lift has been recommended. The Forperet, an old farm above Montalbert, is also popular and does good tartiflette.

SCHOOLS AND GUIDES
Better alternatives to ESF
Each centre has its own ESF school, offering classes for all abilities. But groups can be much too large (a visitor reports seeing classes of up to 20 students) and instructors speak English of varying standard. But reports about private lessons are generally positive, and the school in Les Coches came in for praise this year. However, the

ESF
Schools in all centres.
t 0479 900668 (Belle Plagne)

Oxygène
In Plagne-Centre
t 0479 090399

EL Pro
In Belle-Plagne
t 0479 091162

Reflex
In Plagne 1800
t 0613 808056

Evolution 2
In Montchavin
t 0479 078185

Classes (Belle-Plagne's ESF prices)
6 days €185 (€275 during French February school holidays)

Private lessons
€31 for 1hr

SNOWPIX.COM / CHRIS GILL

Plagne-Bellecôte; not a pretty sight but there are worse bits of La Plagne ↓

consensus seems to be that the alternatives are preferable. The Oxygène school in Plagne-Centre has impressed reporters, 'worked very hard with us, and was very patient'. And we have had glowing reports on the El Pro school in Belle-Plagne ('good English, asked us what we wanted to do, strong focus on technique and safety'). We have also had good reports on Evolution 2 (based in Montchavin) – 'Wonderful,' says the parent of one junior pupil. A new school, Reflex, started up last season (based in 1800), and a reporter noted that group classes are small. Antenne Handicap offers private lessons for skiers with any kind of disability.

FACILITIES FOR CHILDREN
Good choice
Children are well catered for with facilities in each of the villages. The nursery at Belle-Plagne is 'excellent, with good English spoken'. However, one reporter complained that her daughter was the only English speaker in her ESF class. A Club Med at Aime-la-Plagne is one of their 'family' villages. Several UK chalet operators run childcare services.

HOW TO GO
Plenty of packages
For a resort that is very apartment-dominated, there is a surprising number of attractive chalets available through British tour operators. There are few hotels, but there are some attractive, simple 2-stars in the lower villages. There are two Club Meds. Accommodation in the lower resorts is described at the end of the chapter.
Chalets There's a large number available – the majority are fairly simple, small, and located in 1800.
Hotels There are very few, all of 2-star or 3-star grading.
(2 **Balcons** (0479 557676) 3-star at Belle-Plagne. Pool.
(2 **Eldorador** (0479 091209) Adequate hotel in Belle-Plagne – 'Single rooms tiny, food good but service chaotic.'
(2 **Terra Nova** (0479 557900) Big, 120-room 3-star in Plagne-Centre.
Self-catering La Plagne is the ultimate apartment resort, but some are fairly grotty. The best we have seen are the Montagnettes in Belle-Plagne (spacious and attractive with good views) and the MGM apartments in Aime-la-Plagne.

La Plagne

GETTING THERE

Air Geneva 149km/93 miles (3½hr); Lyon 196km/122 miles (3½hr); Chambéry 92km/57 miles (2½hr).

Rail Aime (18km/11 miles) and Bourg-St-Maurice (35km/22 miles) (Eurostar service to Bourg-St-Maurice and Aime available); frequent buses from station.

Phone numbers
From abroad use the prefix +33 and omit the initial '0' of the phone number.

EATING OUT
A surprising amount of choice
Throughout the resort there is a good range of casual restaurants including pizzerias and traditional Savoyard places serving raclettes and fondue.

Reader recommendations in Plagne-Centre include the Métairie ('the most enjoyable we've encountered in the Alps') and the Refuge ('great meal in charming, rustic atmosphere') which is the oldest restaurant in La Plagne (dating from 1961) and decorated with bobsleigh memorabilia.

In Plagne-Villages, the Chevrette is good for pizzas and steaks, the Grizzli for Savoyard food. In Plagne 1800, the Loup Garrou, the Petit Chaperon Rouge and the Mama Mia pizzeria have been praised. At Aime-la-Plagne, Au Bon Vieux Temps (see Mountain restaurants) is open in the evening and the Soupe au Schuss, a secret buried deep in the main block, has 'exceptional' food.

In Plagne-Bellecôte, the Ferme and Chalet des Colosses have been recommended. In Belle-Plagne, so have Pappagone pizzeria, the Taverne de

Maître Kanter and, new last year, the Face Nord ('very friendly, lovely rabbit').

APRES-SKI
Bars, bars, bars
Though fairly quiet during low season, La Plagne has a wide range of après-ski, catering particularly for the younger crowd. In Belle-Plagne, Mat's (an English 'pub') and the Cheyenne are the main bars. The Maître Kanter has been recommended. The King Café (with a massive TV and occasional live music) is the liveliest bar in Plagne-Centre. Plagne-Centre will also have night skiing for 2003/04, thanks to new floodlights on the Stade de Slalom. Plagne 1800 is fairly quiet at night – the Mine (complete with old train and mining artifacts) is very popular with Brits, and a reader also recommends upstairs at the Loup Garrou. The Lincoln Pub in Plagne-Soleil is recommended. Plagne-Bellecôte is very limited at night, with only one real bar – Showtime, which is popular for Karaoke. But one reporter's group enjoyed the bowling, another the

UK Representative
Erna Low Consultants
9 Reece Mews
London SW7 3HE
t 020 7584 2841
f 020 7589 9531
info@ernalow.co.uk
www.ernalow.co.uk

TOURIST OFFICE

t 0479 097979
bienvenue@
la-plagne.com
www.la-plagne.com

tubing. Aime-la-Plagne is also quiet. Neal's and the Luna (Plagne-Centre), the Jet 73 (Plagne-Bellecôte) and the Saloon (Belle-Plagne) are the main discos. There are cinemas at Aime, Bellecôte and Plagne-Centre.

OFF THE SLOPES
OK for the active
As well as the sports and fitness facilities, winter walks along marked trails are pleasant. It's also easy to get up the mountain on the gondolas, which both have restaurants at the top. The Olympic bob-sleigh run is a popular evening activity (see feature box). Excursions are limited.

STAYING IN THE LOWER RESORTS
A good plan
Montchavin (1250m/4,100ft) is based on an old farming hamlet and has an attractive traffic-free centre. The new cable-car link with Les Arcs will go from 300m/980ft above the village, reached by a fast chair and a short slide down. There are adequate shops, a kinder-garten and a ski school. Reaching the La Plagne slopes involves a series of lifts; but the local slopes have quite a bit to offer – pretty, sheltered runs, well endowed with snowmaking, with nursery slopes at village level and up at Plan Bois. Those who venture further can return from Roche de Mio or the Bellecote glacier in one lovely long swoop. The more usual way home involves some of the trickiest blue runs we have encountered. Après-ski is quiet, but the village doesn't lack atmosphere and has a couple of nice little bars, a nightclub, cinema and night skiing. The Bellecôte hotel (0479 078330) is convenient for the slopes.

Les Coches (1450m/4,760ft) is 2km/1 mile away and shares the same slopes. It is a sympathetically designed modern mini-resort that reporters have liked for its 'small, quiet and friendly' feel and its traffic-free centre. It has its own school and kindergarten. The Last One pub is good for après-ski, with a big screen TV and live bands. Poze (for pizza) and Taverne du Monchu are recommended for eating out. There's a shuttle to the cinema in Montchavin.

Montalbert (1350m/4,430ft) is a traditional but much expanded village with quicker access into the main area – though it's a long way from here across to the Bellecôte glacier and the Les Arcs link. The local slopes are easy and wooded – a useful insurance against bad visibility. The Aigle Rouge (0479 555105) is a simple hotel.

Champagny-en-Vanoise (1250m/4,100ft) is a charming village in a pretty, wooded setting, with its modern expansion done sensitively. It is at the opposite end of the slopes from the new link to Les Arcs but well placed for an outing by taxi or car to Courchevel (or the beautiful Vanoise national park with its 500km/310 miles of marked walking paths). Given good snow, there are lovely runs home but their southerly orientation means you may have to take the gondola down instead. There are several hotels, of which the two best are both Logis de France. The Glières (0479 550552) is a rustic old hotel with varied rooms, a friendly welcome and good food. The Ancolie (0479 550500) is smarter, with modern facilities. The village is quiet in the evenings. A new artificial ice-climbing site in Champagny-le-Haut is planned for the coming season.

TRY THE OLYMPIC BOB-SLEIGH RUN – YOU CAN NOW DO IT SOLO

If the thrills of a day on the slopes aren't enough, you can round it off by having a go on the 1992 Winter Olympics bob-sleigh run (open certain nights of the week only). The floodlit 1.5km/1 mile run drops 125m/410ft and has 19 bends. You can go in a proper four-man 'taxi-bob' (80 euros in 2002/03), a special padded driverless bob-raft (33 euros), or, new last season, a mono-bob, 95 euros.

We tried the mono-bob and hurtled down solo at 100kph/62mph (in excess of the advertised speed!) lying almost horizontally – a great thrill, even if we did close our eyes on a couple of the sharper bends (the pressure in turns can be as high as 3g). Whether it is worth £70 to scare yourself silly is your shout! With the taxi-bob, you are one of three passengers wedged in behind the driver. You reach a maximum advertised speed of 110kph/68mph. Most people find the bob raft's 80kph/50mph quite thrilling enough. Be sure your physical state is up to the ride. It's a good idea to book ahead – and there are minimum age limits. Additional insurance is available (yours may not be valid).

Portes du Soleil

Low altitude cross-border cruising

peak retreats

Beat the crowds
Traditional resorts

0870 770 0407
www.peakretreats.co.uk
ABTA W5537

The Portes du Soleil vies with the Trois Vallées for the title of World's Largest Ski Area, but its slopes are very different from those of Méribel, Courchevel, Val-Thorens and neighbours. The Portes du Soleil's slopes are spread out over a large area, and most of them are part of an extensive circuit straddling the French-Swiss border; you can travel the circuit in either direction, with a short bus-ride needed at Châtel only. There are smaller areas to explore slightly off the main circuit. The runs are great for keen intermediates who like to travel long distances and through different resorts. There are few of the tightly packed networks of runs that encourage you to stay put in one area – though there are exceptions in one or two places. The area also has some nice rustic mountain restaurants, serving good food in pleasant, sunny settings.

The lifts throughout the area have been improved in recent years, with several new high-speed chair-lifts eliminating some bad bottlenecks. But the slopes are low by French standards, with top heights in the range 2000m to 2300m (6,560ft to 7,550ft) and good snow is far from assured (though snowmaking has been expanded in recent years). When the snow is good you can have a great time racing all over the circuit (as we have been able to do on our last few visits). But the slopes can get very crowded, especially at weekends and in the Avoriaz area.

Purpose-built Avoriaz has the most snow-sure slopes and is especially

OT CHATEL /
JEAN-FRANCOIS VUARAND

The Portes du Soleil has miles of easy cruising runs and an increasing number of high-speed chairs ↓

good for families, with a big snow-garden right in the heart of the car-free village. And it is good for snowboarders and freestylers, with three terrain-parks. But its local slopes do get crowded, especially at weekends when crowds pour in from nearby Geneva.

The other French resort on the main circuit is Châtel. Given good snow, it has some of the best runs in the area. It is an old and quite characterful village, but it's a busy, traffic-jammed place. It has some good beginner areas – at resort level and up the mountain.

Morzine is close to Avoriaz. It is linked by lift but there's no piste all the way back to town. It's a summer as well as a winter resort – a pleasant, bustling little town with good shops and restaurants, busy traffic and long walks to the lifts from much of the accommodation. The local slopes are extensive, and linked to those of the

slightly higher, quieter, traditional village of Les Gets. But they are low, and good snow is certainly not assured. You can use Morzine as a base to ski the main Portes du Soleil circuit, but it's not ideal. Les Gets is even further off the main circuit.

On the Swiss side, Champéry is a classic, charming, attractive Swiss village – but again just off the main circuit. You have to take a cable-car down from the main slopes as well as up to them or, if there is enough snow, a bus from a piste that ends out of town. Champéry used to be very popular with British tour operators, but few go there now.

Champoussin and Les Crosets are purpose-built mini-resorts set on the very extensive open slopes between Champéry and Morgins, with fairly direct links over to Avoriaz. Morgins, in contrast to Champéry, has excellent village slopes – but they are low and very sunny, and although its more serious local runs are enjoyable and prettily wooded, they are also limited in extent.

On a spur off the main circuit are the resorts of La Chapelle d'Abondance in France (which has one of our favourite hotel-restaurants) and Torgon in Switzerland (which has splendid views over Lake Geneva). This area can be reached from above the Super-Châtel area and is usually quiet even when the rest of the circuit is packed.

Portes du Soleil

313

Puy-St-Vincent

Underrated small modern resort with some serious slopes

314

COSTS

①②③④⑤⑥

RATINGS

The slopes

Snow	***
Extent	**
Expert	***
Intermediate	***
Beginner	***
Convenience	*****
Queues	****
Mountain restaurants	***

The rest

Scenery	***
Resort charm	**
Off-slope	*

NEWS

For 2003/04 there is to be a new family après-ski centre at 1800m.

For 2002/03 snowmaking was extended.

➕ Mostly convenient, purpose-built resort that isn't too hideous

➕ Good variety of slopes with challenges for all abilities

➕ Reasonable snow reliability

➕ Low prices by resort standards

➕ Friendly locals

➕ Some great cross-country routes

➖ Slopes very limited in extent by Alpine standards

➖ Some accommodation is inconveniently located

➖ Upper village has only apartment-based accommodation

➖ Limited après-ski

➖ Not a lot to do off the slopes

Puy-St-Vincent's ski area may be limited, but we like it a lot – more, to be honest, than we expected before we went. It offers a decent vertical and a lot of variety, including a bit of steep stuff. Provided you pick your spot with care, it makes an attractive choice for a family not hungry for piste miles.

THE RESORT

Puy-St-Vincent proper is an old mountain village, not far south-west of Briançon. The modern resort of PSV is a two-part affair – the minor part, Station 1400, is just along the mountainside from PSV proper at 1400m/4,590ft; the major part, Station 1600, is a few hairpins (or a chair-lift ride) further up (yes, at 1600m/5,250ft), and there are buildings in various styles scattered around the mountainside. Compact it may be, but 1600 is not perfectly laid out; depending on where you stay, beware walks to the lifts. We and our reporters have found PSV friendly ('even the lift operators') and well run.

THE MOUNTAINS

Within its small area, PSV packs in a lot of variety, with runs from green to black that justify their gradings.
Slopes There are gentle slopes between the two villages, but most of the runs are above 1600. A fast quad goes up to the tree line at around 2000m/6,560ft. Entertaining red runs go back down, and a green takes a less direct route. The main higher lift is a long chair to 2700m/8,860ft, serving excellent open slopes of red and genuine black steepness. The shorter Rocher Noir drag serves another steep slope, but also accesses splendid cruising runs that curl around the eastern edge of the area. These runs

KEY FACTS

Resort	1400-1600m	
	4,590-5,250ft	
Slopes	1250-2700m	
	4,100-8,860ft	
Lifts		16
Pistes		67km
		42 miles
Green		16%
Blue		37%
Red		41%
Black		6%
Snowmaking		10km
		6 miles

Phone numbers
From abroad use the prefix +33 and omit the initial '0' of the phone number.

are also accessed by a fast quad chair from just below 1600. The six-day Galaxie pass covers a series of major resorts beyond Briançon. More to the point for most visitors, it also covers a day's skiing above the valley hamlet of Pelvoux, 10 minutes' drive away. This area has blue, red and black runs, often used for race training, and a vertical of over 1000m/3,280ft served by a chair and a drag.

Terrain-parks There is a floodlit terrain-park with half-pipe at 1600.

Snow reliability The slopes face north-east and are reasonably reliable for snow. Snowmaking has increased and now covers one run down to 1400 and several above 1600.

Experts The black runs are short but genuinely black, and there are off-piste routes to be tackled with guidance. There are itinéraires outside the piste network, including one to the valley.

Intermediates Size apart, it's a good area for those who like a challenge – but there aren't many very easy runs.

Beginners Beginners should be happy on either of the nursery slopes, and on the long green from 2000m/6,560ft.

Snowboarding Boarders are not allowed on the Rocher Noir drag-lift.

Cross-country There are 40km/25 miles of cross-country trails, including some splendid routes between 1400m and 1700m (4,590ft and 5,575ft), ranging from green to black difficulty.

Queues Queues are rare – a recent reporter was surprised to find none on Easter Monday.

Mountain restaurants There is a modern but pleasantly woody restaurant at mid-mountain, but in good weather the sunny terraces down at 1600 are the natural choice.

Schools and guides You have a choice of French and International ski schools,

and a British tour operator, Snowbizz, has its own school, which a recent reader found 'excellent'; it provides free guiding in the afternoons, as well as 'good instruction' in 'great English' and in small groups.

Facilities for children There are nurseries taking children from 18 months in both villages, and both schools run ski kindergartens.

STAYING THERE

How to go A number of UK operators now offer accommodation here.

Hotels There are four cheap hotels in 1400, but none in 1600.

Self-catering 1600 consists entirely of apartments, and there are more in 1400. The cheaper apartments may be rather cramped.

Eating out The bar-restaurants in each village are the main dining options.

Après-ski Après-ski amounts to a few bar-restaurants in each village.

Off the slopes There are 25km/16 miles of walking and snow-shoe trails. Paragliding, dog-sled rides, floodlit tobogganing and outdoor ice skating (weather permitting) are available. And there is a cinema showing English-speaking films.

TOURIST OFFICE

t 0492 233580
courrier@puysaint vincent.net
www.puysaintvincent. com

SNOWPIX.COM / CHRIS GILL

The lone mountain restaurant at mid-mountain does a decent job, but the sunny terraces at resort level get most of the lunch-time business ➔

Risoul

Villagey modern resort in an attractive setting – and a big shared area

COSTS

① ② ③ ④ ⑤ ⑥

RATINGS

The slopes

Snow	★★★
Extent	★★★
Expert	★★
Intermediate	★★★★
Beginner	★★★★
Convenience	★★★★
Queues	★★★★
Mountain restaurants	★★★

The rest

Scenery	★★★
Resort charm	★★
Off-slope	★

NEWS

For 2003/04 there will be more snowmaking – on the Olympique Supérieure and Heureux pistes. This should ensure that the link between Vars and Risoul will be open from the start of the season.

➕ One of the more attractive and convenient purpose-built resorts

➕ Scenic slopes linked with Vars add up to a fair-sized area

➕ High resort with reasonable snow reliability

➕ Good resort for beginners, early intermediates and families

➕ Plenty of good-value places to eat

➖ Not many modern lifts – lots of long drag-lifts

➖ Not too much to challenge expert skiers and boarders

➖ Limited après-ski

➖ Little to do off the slopes

Slowly but surely the international market is waking up to the merits of the southern French Alps. Were they nearer Geneva, Risoul and its linked neighbour Vars would be as well known as Les Arcs and Flaine. The village of Risoul is a lot more attractive than either.

THE RESORT

Risoul, purpose-built in the late 1970s, is a quiet, apartment-based resort, popular with families. Set among the trees, with excellent views over the Ecrins national park, it is made up of wood-clad buildings – mostly bulky, but with some concessions to traditional style. It has a busy little main street that, surprisingly, is very far from traffic-free. But the village meets the mountain in classic style with an array of sunny restaurant terraces facing the slopes. Reporters have commented on the friendliness of the natives. The village does not offer many resort amenities. Airport transfers (usually from Turin) are not short.

THE MOUNTAINS

Together with neighbouring Vars, the area amounts to one of the biggest domains in the southern French Alps – the combined area is marketed as the Forêt Blanche.

Slopes The slopes, mainly north-facing, spread over several minor peaks and bowls, and connect with the sunnier slopes of neighbouring Vars via the Pointe de Razis and the lower Col des Saluces. Plans to install a new fast quad from Valbelle up to the Pic de Chabrières above Vars, the area's highest point – providing a third access link between the two – have been put on hold. The upper slopes are open, but those leading back into

KEY FACTS

Resort	1850m
	6,070ft

For the entire Forêt Blanche ski area

Slopes	1660-2750m
	5,450-9,020ft
Lifts	57
Pistes	180km
	112 miles
Green	18%
Blue	37%
Red	35%
Black	10%
Snowmaking	29km
	18 miles

Risoul are attractively wooded, and good for bad-weather days. Recent improvements in the lift system, including the introduction of some fast chairs, mean that the link can now be made in both directions without having to ride any drag-lifts. Nevertheless, reporters still complain that the system as a whole has too many 'long and steep' drag-lifts. Piste grooming is reportedly poor.

Terrain-parks There is a good terrain-park with a half-pipe, a boarder-cross and a big air near the village base.

Snow reliability Risoul's slopes are all above 1850m/6,070ft and mostly north-facing, so despite its southerly position snow reliability is reasonably good. Snowmaking is fairly extensive and is being extended. Visitors recommend going over to the east-facing Vars slopes for the morning sun, and returning to Risoul in the afternoon.

Experts The pistes in general do not offer much to interest experts. However, Risoul's main top stations access a couple of steepish descents. And there are some good off-piste opportunities if you take a guide.

Intermediates The whole area is best suited to intermediates, with some good reds and blues in both sectors. Almost all Risoul's runs return to the village, making it difficult to get lost in even the worst conditions. So intermediate children can be let off the leash without much worry.

Beginners Risoul's local area boasts some good, convenient, nursery slopes with a free lift, and a lot of easy longer pistes to move on to.

Snowboarding There is a lot of good free-riding to be done throughout the whole area, although beginners might find the large proportion of drag-lifts a problem, and there are weekly competitions.

Cross-country There are 45km/28 miles of cross-country trails in the whole domain, of which 20km/12 miles are in Risoul itself. A trail through the Peyrol forest links the two resorts together.

Queues Outside French school holidays, Risoul has impressively quiet slopes. Queues to get out of the village in the morning should be eased by the new eight-seat chair.

Mountain restaurants The mountain restaurants have increased in quantity and quality – the newish Tetras is a stylish chalet and the Refuge de Valbel is recommended, but most people return to the village terraces.

Schools and guides We have had mainly positive reports on the ESF and Internationale schools, but our most recent reporter describes his private ESF instruction as 'most indifferent'.

Facilities for children Risoul is very much a family resort. It provides an all-day nursery for children over six months. Both ski schools operate ski kindergartens, slightly above the village, reached by a child-friendly lift. One parent reckons many other drags have a dangerous 'whiplash' effect.

STAYING THERE

How to go Most visitors stay in self-catering apartments, but there are a few hotels and more chalets are becoming available from UK operators.

Hotels The Chardon Bleu (0492 460727) is handy for the slopes. You can also stay overnight at the Tetras mountain refuge (0492 460983) at 2000m/6,560ft.

Self-catering The Constellation Forêt Blanche apartments are adequate but cramped; the Bételgeuse and Pégase are new.

Eating out There's plenty of choice for eating out, from pizza to good French food, and it's mostly good value – the Ecureuil and the Snowboard cafe, at the foot of the slopes, have been highly recommended by reporters. More expensive is the Assiette Gourmande.

Après-ski Après-ski is limited to a cinema and a few fairly quiet bars. The best are the Licorne, the Cimbro, the Chérine and the Ecureuil. The Yeti is the liveliest and full of Scandinavians.

Off the slopes There is little to do; excursions to Briançon are possible.

Vars 1850m/6,070ft

THE RESORT

Vars includes several small, old villages on or near the road running southwards towards the 2110m/6,920ft Col de Vars. But for winter visitors it mainly consists of purpose-built Vars-les-Claux, higher up the road. The resort has convenience and reasonable prices in common with Risoul, but is bigger and has far more in the way of amenities. There are a lot of block-like apartments, but Les Claux is not a complete eyesore, thanks mainly to surrounding woodland. There are two centres: the original, geographical one – where the main gondola starts and which has most of the accommodation

↑ Risoul has a classic piste-resort interface, with countless sunny restaurant terraces

SNOWPIX.COM / CHRIS GILL

Phone numbers
From abroad use the prefix +33 and omit the initial '0' of the phone number.

TOURIST OFFICES

Risoul
t 0492 460260
otrisoul@tiscali.fr
www.risoul.com

Vars
t 0492 465131
vars.ot@pacwan.fr
www.vars-ski.com

and shopping – and Point Show, a collection of bars, restaurants and shops, 10 minutes' walk away at another main lift station.

THE MOUNTAINS
There are slopes on both sides of the village, linked by pistes and by chair-lift at the lower end of Les Claux. Lifts also run up from both sides of Ste-Marie, lower down the mountain.
Slopes The wooded, west-facing Peynier area is the smaller sector, and reaches only 2275m/7,465ft – though there are good long descents down to Les Claux and Ste-Marie. The main slopes are in an east-facing bowl beneath the Pic de Chabrières, with direct links to the Risoul slopes at the top and at the Col des Saluces. There's a speed-skiing course at the top (you can have a go on it, via the ski school). Beneath it are easy runs, open at the top but descending into trees, with red runs either side.
Terrain-parks There's a terrain-park just above Les Claux.
Snow reliability The main slopes get the morning sun, and are centred at around 2000m/6,560ft, so snow

reliability is not as good as in Risoul, but snowmaking is widespread.
Experts There is little of challenge for experts, though the Crête de Chabrières top section accesses some off-piste, an unpisted route and a tricky couloir at Col de Crevoux. The Olympic red run from the top of La Mayt down to Ste-Marie is a respectable 920m/3,020ft vertical.
Intermediates Most of the area is fine for intermediates, with a good mixture of comfortable reds and easy blues, particularly in the main bowl.
Beginners There is a nursery area close to central Vars, with lots of 'graduation' runs throughout the area. Quick learners will be able to get over to Risoul by the end of the week.
Snowboarding There is good free-riding to be done throughout the area, although beginners might find the large proportion of drag-lifts a problem.
Cross-country There are 25km/16 miles of trails in Vars itself. Some start at the edge of town, but those above Ste-Marie are more extensive.
Queues Queues are rare outside the French holidays, and even then Vars is not overrun as some family resorts are.
Mountain restaurants There are several in both sectors, but a lot of people head back to the villages for lunch.
Schools and guides Lack of English-speaking has been a problem.
Facilities for children The ski school runs a nursery for children from two years old. There is also a ski kindergarten. A list of babysitters can be obtained from the tourist office.

STAYING THERE
How to go There are a few small hotels, but Les Claux is dominated by apartment accommodation.
Hotels The Caribou (0492 465043) is the smartest of the hotels and has a pool. The Ecureuil (0492 465072) is an attractive, modern chalet (no restaurant). There are more hotels in the lower villages, including Ste-Marie.
Eating out The range of restaurants is impressive, with good-value pizzerias, crêperies and fondue places. Chez Plumot does proper French cuisine.
Après-ski Après-ski is animated at tea-time, less so after dinner – except at weekends when the discos warm up.
Off the slopes The amenities are rather disappointing, given the size of Vars – there are 35km/22 miles of walking paths and an ice rink, but that's it.

La Rosière

Pop over to Italy from the sunniest slopes in the Tarentaise

COSTS

① ② ③ ④ ⑤ ⑥

RATINGS

The slopes
Snow	★★★
Extent	★★★
Expert	★★
Intermediate	★★★
Beginner	★★★★★
Convenience	★★★
Queues	★★★
Mountain restaurants	★

The rest
Scenery	★★★
Resort charm	★★★
Off-slope	★

NEWS

For 2002/03 the terrain-park was improved, and new snowmaking at the foot of the slopes added. The Piccolo San Bernardo chair on the Italian side has been upgraded to a fast quad.

OT LA ROSIERE / ROGER GAIDE

Most of the buildings are fairly recent, small in scale and traditional in style ↓

- ➕ Attractive purpose-built resort
- ➕ Fair-sized area of slopes linked with La Thuile in Italy
- ➕ Sunny home slopes
- ➕ Heli-skiing over the border in Italy
- ➕ Good nursery slope
- ➕ Gets big dumps of snow when storms are funnelled up the Isère valley from the south-west, but ...

- ➖ Winds can be vicious, closing lift links with Italy
- ➖ Snow affected by sun in late season
- ➖ Lots of slow old lifts
- ➖ Few on-piste challenges for experts
- ➖ One run is much like another – though La Thuile is more varied
- ➖ Limited après-ski
- ➖ Few off-slope diversions

Like Montgenèvre, a long way to the south, La Rosière enjoys a position on the watershed with Italy that brings the twin attractions of big dumps of snow and access to cheap vino rosso. The former is crucial: given the sunny orientation of the slopes – very unusual in a modern French resort – average snowfalls wouldn't do the trick. The Chianti is less significant, because there are few attractive restaurants in which to consume it (see La Thuile chapter).

THE RESORT

La Rosière has been built in attractive, traditional chalet style beside the road that zigzags its way up from Bourg-St-Maurice to the Petit-St-Bernard pass to Italy (closed in winter). It's a quiet place with a few shops and friendly locals; but don't expect lively nightlife. The most convenient accommodation is in the main village near the lifts, or just below, in Le Gollet or Vieux Village. There is also accommodation by the other main lift, in Les Eucherts.

THE MOUNTAINS

The link with Italy means La Rosière has a big area of slopes. Its sunny home slopes are south-facing and offer great views over the valley to Les Arcs and La Plagne.

Slopes The chair and drag out of the

village take you into the heart of the slopes, from where a series of drags and chairs, spread across the mountain, takes you up to Col de la Traversette. From there, you can get over the ridge and to the lifts, which link with Italy at Belvedere.

Terrain-parks There is a terrain-park and a half-pipe.

Snow reliability Surprisingly good, despite its south-facing direction (you may find it has much more snow than the Italian side). Most of the area's snowmaking is in Italy. The link with Italy's slopes is prone to closure because of high winds or heavy snow.

Experts Other than excellent heli-skiing from just over the Italian border (including a very long run which ends up near Ste-Foy) and guided off-piste, there is little excitement for experts. The steepest terrain is on the lowest slopes, down the Marcassin run to Le Vaz and down the Ecudets and Eterlou runs to Les Ecudets.

Intermediates La Rosière would be nothing special on its own, but there's a fair amount to explore if you take into account La Thuile. Apart from the runs mentioned above, the bottom half of La Rosière's slopes are mainly gentle, open, blue and green runs, ideal for early intermediates to brush up their technique. The top half of the mountain, however, below Le Roc Noir and Col de la Traversette, boasts steeper and more interesting red runs.

KEY FACTS

Resort	1850m
	6,070ft

For combined La Rosière and La Thuile

Slopes	1175-2610m
	3,850-8,560ft
Lifts	36
Pistes	146km
	91 miles
Green	12%
Blue	36%
Red	35%
Black	17%
Snowmaking	22km
	14 miles

For La Rosière only

Slopes	1175-2385m
	3,850-7,820ft
Lifts	20
Pistes	47km
	29 miles

Phone numbers
From abroad use the prefix +33 and omit the initial '0' of the phone number.

TOURIST OFFICE

t 0479 068051
info@larosiere.net
www.larosiere.net

The red over the ridge from Col de la Traversette has good snow and views, but is narrow along its top section. Weaker intermediates can avoid it by taking a chair down.

Beginners There are good nursery slopes and short lifts near the village and near Les Eucherts.

Snowboarding The long drag-lift to Italy means the resort is best-suited to beginners content to stay on the La Rosière side.

Cross-country There are 12km/7 miles of trails near the altiport.

Queues Queues are not usually a problem – apart from early in the day on the chair out of the village – but it is much busier here than over in Italy.

Mountain restaurants A reporter recommends the self-service Plan du Repos for its 'friendly staff, huge pasta portions and lovely salads', but found the waiters at the Traversette were 'unable to cope with lunch-time crowds'. There are a couple of bars near the top, which are fine for picnics. The San Bernardo on the border is recommmended. Many people descend to the village; reporters recommend the Relais du Petit St Bernard – 'Good value, wide menu choice' – and the P'tit Relais – 'Lots of choice.'

Schools and guides There are two schools. Past reporters have praised the Evolution 2 school for its 'good teaching, sympathetic instructors and small groups', but reports of the ESF school have been less favourable: 'large groups' and 'insufficient supervision of small children'.

Facilities for children The Village des Enfants has a snow garden, and British tour operator Esprit runs a nursery.

STAYING THERE

How to go A number of British tour operators now offer packages here.

Hotels There are a few 2-star hotels in the village, and more in the valley.

Chalets Of the chalets available we have had reports of Chalethotel Roc Noir ('well placed', 'good food') and of Ferme d'Elisa ('lovely accommodation but a 150m/500ft hike up to the lifts').

Self-catering You can book through the resort's central booking service.

Eating out The Chalet, the Terrasse du Yéti and the Ancolie have all been recommended.

Après-ski Après-ski is limited to a couple of bars in the village.

Off the slopes There are scenic flights and walks and a cinema. The ski schools offer paragliding and organise various non-skiing expeditions on foot.

Staying up the mountain The Hotel San Bernardo, on the border and reachable only on skis, provided a memorable two-night stay for an adventurous reporter last season. 'Simple, comfortable and peaceful', with a 'spectacular collection of grappas'.

Chaz Dura 2580m
Col de Fourclaz
Col du Petit Saint Bernard 2190m
Belvedere 2610m/8,560ft
Le Roc Noir 2400m
Col de la Traversette 2385m
Cerellaz
Les Suches 2200m
Le Gollet
1175m
Les Eucherts
La Rosière 1850m/6,070ft
Le Vaz 1500m
La Thuile 1440m/4,720f
3485m   Glacier du Ruitor

Serre-Chevalier

One of a kind, with a growing band of enthusiastic visitors

COSTS

① ② ③ ④ ⑤ ⑥

RATINGS

The slopes
Snow	***
Extent	****
Expert	***
Intermediate	****
Beginner	****
Convenience	***
Queues	***
Mountain restaurants	***

The rest
Scenery	***
Resort charm	***
Off-slope	**

NEWS

For 2003/04 the Bletonet chair-lift at the bottom of Chantemerle is due to be replaced by a fast six-pack, doubling capacity.

A new big air terrain-park is due near the Echaillon piste.

A new casino is due to open in Briançon in 2004.

For 2002/03 the Myrtilles piste from Prorel was improved and reclassified as a blue run.

- ✚ Big, varied mountain, with something for everyone
- ✚ Interesting mixture of wooded runs (ideal for blizzards) and open bowls (with acres of off-piste)
- ✚ One of the few big French areas based on old villages with character
- ✚ Good-value and atmospheric old hotels, restaurants and chalets
- ✚ Lift pass covers days elsewhere
- ✚ Spectacular drive from Grenoble
- ✚ Generally quiet slopes, but ...

- ▬ Serious crowds in French holidays
- ▬ Slow, old lifts on upper mountain – including many drags, some vicious – make progress slow and generate queues in high season
- ▬ Busy road runs through the resort villages, with traffic jams at times
- ▬ A lot of indiscriminate new buildings – awful from the lower slopes
- ▬ Limited nightlife, especially in Le Monêtier and smaller hamlets
- ▬ Few off-slope diversions

Serre-Chevalier is a big-league resort, but isn't as well known internationally as many of its rivals to the north and west. Maybe that's because it doesn't lend itself to marketing hype – the slopes are not super-high, the lifts are not super-efficient, the hotels are far from super-smooth. But we like it a lot: it's one of the few French resorts where you can find the ambience you might look for on a summer holiday – a sort of Provence in the snow, with lots of small, family-run hotels and restaurants housed in old stone buildings.

The slopes are likeable, too. They are split into different segments, so you get a real sensation of travel. What really sets the area apart from the French norm are the woodland runs, making Serre-Chevalier one of the best places to be when snow is falling – though there are plenty of open runs, too.

The lift system, on the other hand, is far from likeable. The resort managers seem keen to invest in lift capacity at resort level, when a glance at our piste map or the at the high-season queues at mid-mountain shows that the upper mountain badly needs an injection of six-packs.

THE RESORT

The resort is made up of a string of 13 villages set on a valley floor running roughly north-west to south-east, below the north-east-facing slopes of the mountain range that gives the resort its name. From the north-west – coming over the Col du Lautaret from Grenoble – the three main villages are Le Monêtier (or Serre-Che 1500),

Villeneuve (1400) and Chantemerle (1350), spread over a distance of 8km/5 miles. Finally, at the extreme south-eastern end of the mountain, is Briançon (1200) – not a village but a town – the highest in France. Nine smaller villages can be identified, and some give their names to the communes: Villeneuve is in the commune of La Salle les Alpes, for example. Confusing.

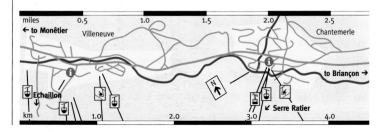

↑ The bottom of the Olympique black run to Chantemerle can be mayhem at the end of the day, especially if it's icy

OT SERRE-CHEVALIER / AGENCE ZOOM

Serre-Chevalier is not a smart resort, in any sense. Although each of its parts is based on a simple old village, there is a lot of modern development, which ranges from brash to brutal, and even the older parts are roughly rustic rather than chocolate-box pretty. (A ban on corrugated iron roofs would help.) Because the resort is so spread out, the impact of cars and buses is difficult to escape, even if you're able to manage without them yourself. But when blanketed by snow the older villages and hamlets do have an unpretentious charm, and we find the place as a whole easy to like.

There are no luxury hotels or notably swanky restaurants; on the other hand, there are more hotels in the modestly priced Logis de France 'club' here than in any other ski resort. This is a family resort, which fills up (even more than most others) with French children in the February high season. You have been warned.

The heart of the resort is **Villeneuve**, which has two gondolas and a fast quad chair going up to widely separated points at mid-mountain. The central area of new development near the lifts is brutal and charmless. But not far away is the peaceful and traditional hamlet of

Le Bez, which has a third gondola, and across the main road and river is the old stone village of Villeneuve, with its quiet main street lined by cosy bars, hotels and restaurants.

Not far down the valley, **Chantemerle** gives access to opposite ends of the mid-mountain plateau of Serre Ratier via a gondola and a cable-car, both with second stages above. Chantemerle has some tasteless modern buildings in the centre and along the main road. The old sector is a couple of minutes' walk from the lifts, with a lovely church and most of the small hotels, restaurants, bars and nightlife.

At the top of the valley, **Le Monêtier** has one main access lift – a fast quad chair to mid-mountain, reached from the village by bus or a steepish 10-minute walk, tricky when ice is around (though you can leave your boots at the lift base). Le Monêtier is the smallest, quietest and most unspoiled of the main villages (or 'deadly dull', to put it another way), with a bit of a Provençal feel to its narrow streets and little squares, and new building which is mostly in sympathetic style. Sadly, the through-road to Grenoble, which skirts the other villages, bisects Le Monêtier; pedestrians stroll about bravely,

KEY FACTS

Resort	1350-1500m
	4,430-4,920ft
Slopes	1350-2735m
	4,430-8,970ft
Lifts	77
Pistes	250km
	155 miles
Green	19%
Blue	19%
Red	49%
Black	13%
Snowmaking	40km
	25 miles

hoping the cars will avoid them.

Briançon has a gondola from right in the town to mid-mountain and on almost to the top. The area around the lift station has a wide selection of modern shops, bars, hotels and restaurants, but no character. In contrast, the lovely 17th-century upper quarter is a delight, complete with impressive fortifications, narrow cobbled streets and traditional restaurants, auberges and patisseries. Great views from the top, too.

Regular and reliable ski-buses (covered on the free guest card) circulate around each village and link all the villages and lift bases along the valley – but they finish quite early, and taxis aren't cheap.

A six-day area pass (or rather your receipt) covers a day in each of Les Deux-Alpes, Alpe-d'Huez, Puy-St-Vincent and the Milky Way (several reporters have enjoyed a day out to Montgenèvre, at the French end of that area). All of these outings are possible by public transport, but are much more attractive to those with a car. If driving, you are likely to approach over the high Col du Lautaret, which is very occasionally closed because of avalanche danger.

Turin airport is closer, but there are more cheap flights to Lyon airport.

THE MOUNTAINS

Trees cover almost two-thirds of the mountain, providing some of France's best bad-weather terrain. The Serre-Chevalier massif is not particularly dramatic, but from the peaks and some other points there are fine views of the Ecrins massif, the highest within France (ie not shared with Italy).

The trail map is supposed to have been improved, but it remains infuriatingly unclear and imprecise in places. Readers have found navigation is made even more challenging by 'particularly poor' signposting and the tendency of runs to 'change colour halfway down'. On our last visit, we found that the signposting at altitude is not up to the job when a storm socks in; take great care.

Piste classification is unreliable – many reds, in particular, could be classified blue, but there are occasional stiff blues, too.

THE SLOPES
Interestingly varied and pretty

Serre-Chevalier's 250km/155 miles of pistes are spread across four main sectors above the four main villages. The sector above **Villeneuve** is the most extensive, reaching back a good way into the mountains and spreading over four or five identifiable bowls. The main mid-station is Fréjus. This sector is reliably linked to the slightly smaller **Chantemerle** sector well below the tree line. The link from Chantemerle to **Briançon** is over a high, exposed col and is via a newish six-pack. The link between Villeneuve and **Le Monêtier** is liable to closure by high winds or avalanche danger. Travelling from here towards Villeneuve involves tackling a red run, so timid intermediates have to use the bus.

TERRAIN-PARKS
Fully featured

There's a big air in Briançon, a boarder-cross in Villeneuve and Chantemerle and a half-pipe in Villeneuve (though it's not always open), all with sound systems.

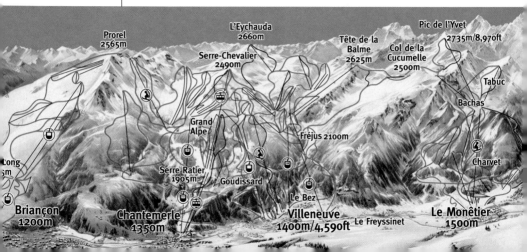

LIFT PASSES

Grand Serre-Chevalier
Covers all lifts in
Briançon,
Chantemerle,
Villeneuve and Le
Monêtier.

Beginners pass
Available

Main pass
1-day pass €30.50
6-day pass €152.50

Senior citizens
Over 65: 6-day pass
€108.50
Over 75: free pass

Children
Under 12: 6-day pass
€108.50
Under 6: free pass

Notes
Passes of 6 days or
more give one day in
each of Les Deux-
Alpes, Alpe-d'Huez,
Puy-St-Vincent and
Voie Lactée (Milky
Way). Reductions for
families.

Alternative passes
Passes covering
individual areas of
Serre-Chevalier
available.

SNOW RELIABILITY
Good – especially upper slopes

Most slopes face north or north-east
and so hold snow well, especially high
up (there are lots of lifts starting above
2000m/6,600ft). The weather pattern is
different from that of the northern Alps
and even that of Les Deux-Alpes or
Alpe-d'Huez, only a few miles to the
west. Serre-Che can get good snow
when there is a shortage elsewhere,
and vice versa. A reporter this year
reckons Le Monêtier tends to have the
best snow. There is snowmaking on
long runs down to each village, which
was further improved for 2002/03.
Piste grooming is generally excellent.

FOR EXPERTS
Deep, not notably steep

There is plenty to amuse experts –
except those wanting extreme steeps.

The broad black runs down to
Villeneuve and Chantemerle are only
just black in steepness, but they are
fine runs with their gradient sustained
over an impressive vertical of around
800m/2,620ft. One or the other may be
closed for days on end for racing or
training. The rather neglected Tabuc
run, sweeping around the mountain
away from the lifts to Le Monêtier, has
a couple of genuinely steep pitches but
is mainly a cruise; it makes a fine end
to the day. For moguls, look higher up
the mountain to the steeper slopes
served by the two top lifts above Le
Monêtier and the three above
Villeneuve. The runs beside these lifts
– on and off-piste – form a great
playground in good snow. The more
roundabout Isolée black is a readers'
favourite – 'scenic and challenging'
after a rather scary ridge start.

There is huge amounts of off-piste
terrain throughout the area. There are
also plenty of more serious off-piste
expeditions to be done. Highlights
include: Tête de Grand Pré to

Villeneuve (a climb from Cucumelle);
off the back of L'Eychauda to Puy-St-
André (isolated, beautiful, taxi-ride
home); L'Yret to Le Monêtier via Vallon
de la Montagnolle; Tabuc (steep at the
start, very beautiful). And the experts'
Mecca of La Grave is nearby.

FOR INTERMEDIATES
Ski wherever you like

Serre-Chevalier's slopes ideally suit
intermediates, who can buzz around
without worrying about nasty surprises
on the way. On the trail map red runs
far outnumber blues – but most reds
are at the easy end of the scale and
the grooming is usually good, so even
nervous intermediates shouldn't have
problems with them.

There's plenty for more adventurous
intermediates, though. Many runs are
wide enough for a fast pace. Cucumelle
on the edge of the Villeneuve sector is
a favourite – a beautiful long red, away
from the lifts, with a challenging initial
section. The red runs off the little-used
Aiguillette chair in the Chantemerle
sector are worth seeking out – quiet,
enjoyable fast cruises. Aya and Clos
Galliard at Le Monêtier are other
favourites.

If the reds are starting to seem a bit
tame, there is plenty more to progress
to. Unless ice towards the bottom is a
problem, the (often well-groomed)
blacks on the lower mountain should
be first on the agenda, and the
bumpier ones higher up can be tackled
if snow is good.

FOR BEGINNERS
All three areas OK

All three main villages have nursery
areas (at Chantemerle it's small, and
you generally go up to Serre Ratier or
Grand Alpe – both rated as good by a
recent beginner reporter) and there are
some easy high runs to progress to.
Villeneuve has excellent green runs

boarding

*Serre-Che is a snowboarding hot-spot, popular with advanced boarders because of
the off-piste, but it is not without problems for others. For beginners, local slopes
are limited and drag-lifts must soon be faced; progression from the nursery slope
up at Fréjus, for example, is tricky. The diverse pistes with open and tree-lined
runs also suit intermediates, though there are some annoying flat sections –
notably on the way to Le Monêtier – and descents to the valley can involve a
choice between winding paths and unpleasantly steep runs. In some areas there
are a lot of difficult-to-avoid and violent drag-lifts – one reporter's group stayed
mostly in the Chantemerle sector, simply because they could cover a lot of ground
using three major chair-lifts.*

above Fréjus. Both sectors have green paths down from mid mountain. But they are narrow, and not enjoyable when the runs become rutted and others are speeding along. Le Monêtier's easy runs are at resort level, next to excellent nursery slopes, and beginners have recommended it for 'better snow and fewer people'. But progression to long runs here isn't so easy, and the link to Villeneuve involves the red Cucumelle run.

FOR CROSS-COUNTRY
Excellent if the snow is good
There are 45km/28 miles of tracks along the valley floor, mainly following the gurgling river between Le Monêtier and Villeneuve and going on up towards the Col du Lautaret.

QUEUES
Investment needed high-up
A range of big lifts means there are few problems getting out of the valley. But the many old, slow lifts still cause queues at altitude, as well as slowing down the whole process of exploration. The main bottlenecks are the slow and unreliable Balme chair on the way to Le Monêtier, the Fréjus chair above the

Pontillas gondola, and the Grande Serre chair to the peak of Serre-Chevalier.

Of course, all these problems are worse in high season. More than most resorts, Serre-Chevalier seems to fill up with French families in the February holidays, producing serious queues all over the place.

The lower slopes above Chantemerle, in particular, can get hideously crowded, particularly when snow conditions are poor and progress therefore slow.

MOUNTAIN RESTAURANTS
Improving, except at Le Monêtier
Mountain restaurants are quite well distributed, and there are some good new places. But lunch is an important part of your day, you still need to plan it carefully.

For a serious lunch, we head for Pi Maï in the hamlet of Fréjus, a little way below the Fréjus lift station. Its table-service meals are not cheap, but the food is good and the spacious, rustic restaurant with log fire is a fine place to retreat to on a bad day. But we also like the sound of the newly opened Bivouac at the top of the Casse du Boeuf quad from Villeneuve – an

OT SERRE-CHEVALIER / AGENCE ZOOM

Le Monêtier is a nice quiet old village or 'deadly dull', depending on your point of view ↓

GETTING THERE

Air Turin 108km/67 miles (2½hr); Grenoble 92km/57 miles (2½hr); Lyon 200km/124 miles (3½hr).

Rail Briançon (6km/4 miles); regular buses from station.

SCHOOLS

ESF In all centres
t 0492 92241741
Génération Snow
t 0492 242151
generation-snow@
freesbee.fr
Buissonnière
t 0492 247866
infos@ecolebuisse.
com
Evasion
t 0492 240241
EurekaSKI
0689 316656
01326 375710 (in UK)

Classes (ESF prices)
6 days (3hr am and
2hr pm) €170
Private lessons
€29 for 1hr

GUIDES

Montagne Adventure
Off-piste, ski-touring
t 0492 240551
montagne@aol.com
**Compagnie des
Guides de l'Oisans**
Off-piste, ski tours, ice-climbing, snow-shoes
t 0492 247590
Montagne à la carte
Off-piste, ski-touring,
heli-skiing, climbing,
snow-shoes
t 0492 247320
montagnealacarte@
free.fr

'attractive chalet' with both self and 'first-class' table service (inside and out), both doing 'excellent' food. Just down the hill, but not easy to find, is the Echaillon, a lofty building with good food and table-service.

In the Chantemerle sector, recommendations are limited to the 'drab-looking' self-service Soleil, for its 'excellent fresh-cooked food'.

In the Briançon sector, the Pra Long chalet opened at the gondola mid-station a couple of seasons ago. Its huge sun deck has great views, food in both table- and self-service sections is 'excellent', and self-service prices are 'very reasonable'. The little chalet just down from the top of Prorel has great views and is reasonably priced.

Above Le Monêtier the choice is between the unremarkable self-service Bachas at mid-mountain and the cosy Peyra Juana much lower down, where we and readers alike have enjoyed excellent service, food and value. Both get packed on bad-weather days.

SCHOOLS AND GUIDES
Nearly all good
We have received a number of reports on the Ecole de Ski Buissonnière over the years – most of them full of praise. But this year a couple of early-intermediate boarders report being put together with a couple of experts, with predictably distressing results.

EurekaSKI is British-run by BASI instructors. Classes with a maximum size of six range from beginner to free-ride masterclass. There's a satisfaction guarantee: if you feel you don't benefit from your first session your money will be refunded. Our reporters had no need. One who took two private lessons 'learned more than I have previously in a week'. Another reports 'excellent instruction', but notes that parents with kids in the school found 2-hour lessons too short.

We lack recent reports on the ESF. But last year a near beginner reported 'appalling treatment' in a group with eight French: 'By Wednesday I was reduced to tears and we left our class halfway down a blue run.' What a marvellous institution, the ESF.

FACILITIES FOR CHILDREN
Facilities at each village
We have had no very recent reports, but the Ecole de Ski Buissonnière (see above) has been praised in the past, as has Les Schtroumpfs in Villeneuve.

STAYING THERE

HOW TO GO
A good choice of packages
There's a wide choice of packages from UK tour operators, offering all kinds of accommodation.

Chalets Several operators offer chalets in the different parts of the resort. Skiworld's chalet Pyrene and Handmade's chalet hotel Rif Blanc have both been approved by readers (and you can book into the latter for a couple of nights locally if there's room).

Hotels One of the features of this string of little villages is the range of attractive family-run hotels – many of them part of the Logis de France. There's also a Club Med in Villeneuve.
In Monêtier:
⟨⟨⟨3 **Choucas** (0492 244273) Smart, wood-clad rooms, and 'excellent, seven-course dinners in stone-vaulted restaurant – but mediocre breakfast and erratic service'.
⟨2 **Europe** (0492 244003) Simple but well run Logis in heart of old village, with pleasant bar and 'good food'. Parking tricky.
⟨2 **Alliey** (0492 244002) Our favourite place to eat (see Eating out).
In Villeneuve:
⟨2 **Christiania** (0492 247633) Civilised, family-run hotel on main road, crammed with ornaments.
⟨2 **Vieille Ferme** (0492 247644) Stylish conversion on the edge of the village.
⟨2 **Cimotel** (0492 247822) Modern and charmless, with good-sized rooms and 'excellent' food.
⟨1 **Chatelas** (0492 247474) Prettily decorated simple chalet by river.
In Chantemerle:
⟨2 **Plein Sud** (0492 241701) Modern; pool and sauna.
⟨2 **Boule de Neige** (0492 240016) Comfortable, friendly, in the old centre.
⟨1 **Ricelle** (0492 240019) Charming, but across the valley from the slopes in Villard-Laté. Good food.
Self-catering There are plenty of modern apartment blocks in Villeneuve, Briançon and Chantemerle. Few have charm.

EATING OUT
Unpretentious and traditional
In Le Monêtier, there are several good hotel-based options. Our favourite is the panelled restaurant of the Alliey, which offers excellent food at astoundingly moderate prices and an impressive wine list. The Auberge du

CHILDREN

Each of the main villages has its own non-ski nursery. At Villeneuve, Les Schtroumpfs (0492 247095) takes kids from age 6 months; meals not provided. At Chantemerle, Les Poussins (0492 244003) takes them from age 8 months; meals provided. At Le Monêtier, Les Eterlous (0492 244575) takes them from age 18 months (6 months out of school holiday times); meals not provided. Children from 3 years old can have a first try at skiing in the ski schools' snow gardens and from age 7 they can join ski school classes (ESF 6 days €166).

ACTIVITIES

Indoor Swimming pool, sauna, fitness centres, cinemas, bridge

Outdoor At Chantemerle: skating rink, paragliding, cleared paths, snow-shoe walks, snowmobiling. At Villeneuve: ice-driving circuit, skating rink, horse-riding, sleigh rides, cleared paths, paragliding, snow-shoe walks, snowmobiling. At Le Monêtier: skating rink, cleared paths, hang-gliding, hot springs, snow-shoe walks, ski-joring

Phone numbers From abroad use the prefix +33 and omit the initial '0' of the phone number.

TOURIST OFFICE

t 0492 249898
contact@ot-serrechevalier.fr
www.serre-chevalier.com

Choucas considers itself the best in town and is certainly the most expensive. The Europe has reliable French cooking at reasonable prices. There are a handful of non-hotel options; one reader this year reckons the Mangeoire is the best, despite its cow-based decor, so we will forgive the dire meal we had there a couple of years back. There are several competitors in the regional specialities market; the Boîte à Fromages does a 'magnificent' fondue.

In Villeneuve the Swedish run Vieille Ferme is a 'great, stylish eating place'. In the old part of Villeneuve, we have had mixed reports of the food at the Pastorale, a crowded vault with an open-fire grill. The Marotte, a tiny stone building with classic French cuisine, has been highly praised. The Noctambule and the Refuge specialise in fondue and raclette. And there are good crêperies – try the Petit Duc, or the Manouille. Over in Le Bez, the Bidule is said to have 'first-class food and service, at good value', while the Siyou in La Salle is good for 'local specialities at very reasonable prices'.

In Chantemerle, the Couch'où is good value for fondue and raclette, and has a pizzeria upstairs. Le Glacier is an 'excellent, cheap restaurant'. The candlelit Crystal is the smartest, most expensive place in town. The Kandahar is a charming pizzeria and the rustic Ricelle offers amazing value.

APRES-SKI
Quiet streets and few bars

Nightlife seems to revolve around bars, scattered through the various villages.

In Le Monêtier the Alpen has a happy hour, free nibbles and welcoming staff. The British-run Rif Blanc bar is popular and the new Que Tel warms up later on. If you want to forget you're in a ski resort (and see French smoking laws at their least

effective), hit the Cibouit.

In Villeneuve, Loco Loco in the old village is 'the place to go, with funky music and a French atmosphere'; it has a 'comfy sofa area in the loft'. The Frog has 'good atmosphere' and 'good dark local beer'. In Chantemerle the Yeti ('chock-full of Brits') and the Underground beneath it are focal. The Kitzbühel has a good atmosphere, particularly when sporting events are shown, and is 'not too full of fellow Brits'. After everything else has closed, a karaoke bar with 'an erratic door policy' may still let you in.

OFF THE SLOPES
Try the hot baths

Serre-Chevalier doesn't hold many attractions for non-slope-users, and it's certainly not for avid shoppers, but the old town of Briançon is well worth a visit. Here there is a new leisure complex with pools, sauna, hot-tub and steam room. Visitors have enjoyed walking in the valley on 'well-prepared trails', and the indoor-outdoor thermal bath in Le Monêtier makes a great place to watch the sun go down – but you need to book ahead. The swimming pool in the hotel Sporting in Villeneuve is open to non-residents. And each of the main villages has its own cinema.

STAYING UP THE MOUNTAIN
Worth considering

A seductive possibility is to stay at Pi Maï (0492 248363) in Fréjus, above Villeneuve (see Mountain restaurants).

Get next year's edition **free!**
by reporting on your holiday

There are too many resorts for us to visit them all every year, and too many hotels, bars and mountain restaurants for us to see. So we are very keen to encourage more readers to send in reports on their holiday experiences. As usual, we'll be giving 100 copies of the next edition to the writers of the best reports.

There are five main kinds of feedback we need:
- what you particularly **liked and disliked** about the resort
- what aspects of the resort came as a **surprise** to you
- your other suggestions for **changes to our evaluation** of the resort – changes we should make to the ratings, verdicts, descriptions etc
- your experience of **queues** and other weaknesses in the lift system, and the **ski school** and associated childcare arrangements
- your feedback on **individual facilities** in the resort – the hotels, bars, restaurants (including mountain restaurants), nightspots, equipment shops, sports facilities etc.

You can send your reports to us in three ways. In order of preference, they are:
- by e-mail to: reports@snow-zone.co.uk (don't forget to give us your postal address)
- word-processed and printed on paper
- handwritten on a form that we can provide.

Consistently helpful reporters are invited to become 'resort observers', which means that when possible we'll arrange free lift-passes in your holiday resorts, in exchange for detailed reports on those resorts.

Our postal address is:
Where to Ski and Snowboard, FREEPOST SN815, The Old Forge, Norton St Philip, Bath BA2 7ZZ

Ste-Foy-Tarentaise

Secret off-piste haven for those in the know

COSTS

① ② ③ ④ ⑤ ⑥

RATINGS

The slopes

Snow	***
Extent	*
Expert	****
Intermediate	***
Beginner	**
Convenience	***
Queues	*****
Mountain restaurants	**

The rest

Scenery	***
Resort charm	***
Off-slope	*

NEWS

Lots of new chalets and apartments have been built recently at the ski station, in traditional stone and wood style, and there are more to come. This means there's now more accommodation available at the slopes, both B&B and to rent. More shops are likely too – perhaps even a second ski shop. Last season the tourist office started a central reservations system, and some piste improvements were made.

For 2003/04 snowmaking is planned for a run down to the resort. The tourist office tells us that more lifts are on the cards for 2004/05. It's rumoured the Val d'Isère lift company will buy the Ste-Foy lift company.

- ➕ No crowds
- ➕ Lots of excellent off-piste and untracked powder
- ➕ Cheap lift pass and good value lodging
- ➕ Tarentaise mega-resorts nearby for a change of scene

- ➖ Tiny mountain hamlet offers few off-slope diversions
- ➖ Very limited piste network for high-mileage piste-bashers
- ➖ To get there easily, and to make the most of other resorts, you need a car
- ➖ Limited après-ski

This small area in the Tarentaise has been developed only since 1990. The millions who flock to the nearby mega-resorts of Val-d'Isère, Tignes and Les Arcs never give it a thought. But those in the know are well rewarded. It's an uncrowded gem with some wonderful off-piste slopes for experts and intermediates. Lots of ski instructors from the big resorts come here on their days off. And some bring their off-piste groups here for the day to escape the crowds back home.

THE RESORT

It is only now developing. Until a couple of seasons ago there was hardly any accommodation at the ski station. Now there is just a small development of MGM chalets and apartments. The ski station, also known as Bonconseil, is set 4km/2.5 miles off the main road between Val-d'Isère and Bourg-St-Maurice: turn off at La Thuile, just after the village of Ste-Foy. A complex at the foot of the lifts houses the tourist and ticket office, a cafe/bar, a small supermarket and a ski shop (Zigzags, which gets wildly differing reports, from 'horrible staff' and 'rudest ski shop in the world' to 'very helpful and well-equipped with everything for off-piste').

If you don't have a car it's most convenient to stay at the ski station, as free buses to and from Ste-Foy village run only every hour or so (the trip takes 20 minutes). Buses now visit nearby villages too, such as La Masure.

To make the most of the scattered restaurant scene and nearby resorts, however, it's a good idea to have a car. Parking can be rather challenging, though, because the old car park has been covered with apartments, and the only decent-sized one is now further down the road up to the ski station.

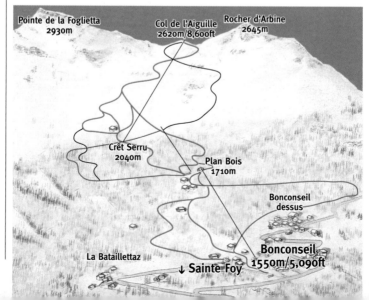

Pointe de la Foglietta
2930m

Col de l'Aiguille
2620m/8,600ft

Rocher d'Arbine
2645m

Crêt Serru
2040m

Plan Bois
1710m

Bonconseil
dessus

La Bataillettaz

↓ Sainte Foy

Bonconseil
1550m/5,090ft

↑ This is what Ste-Foy is all about: mile after mile of deserted off-piste

OT STE-FOY / MARK JUNAC

KEY FACTS

Resort	1550m
	5,090ft
Slopes	1550-2620m
	5,090-8,600ft
Lifts	5
Pistes	25km
	16 miles
Green	8%
Blue	15%
Red	54%
Black	23%
Snowmaking	Minimal

THE MOUNTAIN

Off-piste guides from Val regularly impress clients by bringing them to Ste-Foy's deserted slopes, accessed by three quad chairs, rising one above the other to the Col de l'Aiguille. Impressive as the off-piste can be, you may want to spread your wings from the tiny resort during a week's stay, particularly if the snow is unkind. Luckily Val d'Isère, Tignes, Les Arcs (via Villaroger) and La Rosière are all within easy reach (with a car). You're entitled to a free day in La Rosière, and almost half-price tariffs in all the rest, on presentation of a current Ste-Foy six-day pass – which at 93 euros last season was around half the price of neighbouring Val d'Isère. A day pass was a bargain 17 euros. 'Probably the best-value day's skiing I have ever had,' said a reporter this year.

Slopes The top lift accesses almost 600m/1,970ft of vertical above the tree line and superb, long off-piste routes on the back of the mountain. The two lower chairs serve a few pleasant green, blue and red runs through trees and back to the base station. Most reporters are amazed by the amount of terrain the few lifts access: 'Most of my ski career I've been in Verbier, Zermatt and Vail. Skiing in Ste-Foy is better.' But don't come here for miles of groomed pistes or modern lifts.

Terrain-parks There's a 2,500m² terrain-park near Crêt-Serru, with various jumps – hips, spines, table-tops – and rails.

Snow reliability The slopes face north or west. Snow reliability is good on the former but can suffer on the latter, especially as there is little snowmaking, except on the run down to the resort.

Experts Experts can pass happy times on and off the sides of Ste-Foy's black and red runs, exploring lots of easily accessible off-piste and trees in the huge bowl (the long black run marked on the piste map is pretty much an off-piste run). If there's been fresh snow, Ste-Foy can't be beaten for snaring first tracks. The top lift may take a while to open, but when it does, it is, as one reporter said, 'Awesome. People came from Val d'Isère, and you could see others ahead of you on the lift. That's a busy day in Ste-Foy.' The lack of crowds means you can still make fresh tracks days after a storm. There's more serious off-piste on offer too, for which you need a guide. There are wonderful runs from the top of the lifts down through deserted old villages to the road between Ste-Foy and Val-d'Isère and a splendid route which starts with a hike up to the Pointe de la Foglietta, and takes you through trees and over a stream down to the tiny village of Le Crot. The ESF

08700 110565
Crich Matlock, DE4 5DE

runs group off-piste trips, and arranges transport back to the station.

Intermediates Intermediates can enjoy 1000m/3,28oft vertical of uncrowded reds – ideal for confidence building and sharpening technique. The higher slopes are the more difficult – the red L'Aiguille is a superb test for confident intermediates, who would also be up to the off-piste routes. Anyone who doesn't fancy experimenting with off-piste will tire of the limited runs in a day or two and be champing at the bit to get to Val d'Isère or Les Arcs.

Beginners Not the best place, but there is a small nursery drag at the base. After that you can progress to a green run off the first chair and a gentle blue off the second.

Snowboarding Great free-riding terrain, with lots of trees and easily accessed powder between the pistes to play in. 'Loved it,' said a reporter this year.

Cross-country No prepared trails, but ask the tourist office about marked itinerary routes such as Planay dessus.

Queues You have more chance of winning the lottery than finding a lift queue at Ste-Foy.

Mountain restaurants There are two rustic restaurants at the top of the first chair. A reporter recommends Chez Léon as 'a winner'; you need to book (0479 069083). The Brevettes does good omelettes (but we've had reports of poor service and atmosphere). The Maison à Colonnes, at the base of the first lift, gets consistently good write-ups. For snacks there's also the Pitchouli bar in the main base building.

Schools and guides We've had good reports of ski school, especially for children (from age four). There's a good chance classes will not be large.

Facilities for children There is a nursery, Les P'tits Trappeurs, which takes children from age three to eight.

STAYING THERE

How to go Various small tour operators can organise chalets and hotels here – see the list in the resort directory. Ste-Foy is about 20 minutes from the Eurostar terminal at Bourg-St-Maurice.

Hotels We have had several glowing reports of Auberge sur la Montagne (0479 069583), just above the turn-off at La Thuile, which has excellent food and atmosphere and is run by an English couple. Recently refurbished, it has a sauna and hot-tub. Yellow Stone Chalet (0479 069606) is a Gîte de France at the ski station, run by an American and has been highly recommended, though some recent visitors found it rather expensive. Hotel Monal (0479 069007), in Ste-Foy village, is a basic 2-star, with a games room, bar and two restaurants.

Chalets Premiere Neige started last season and now has four catered chalets and four self-catered apartments. Peak Leisure has one chalet a couple of minutes down the road. Both will transport you around to different ski areas. Chalet Number One, in the village of La Masure, is run by British snowboarder Lloyd Rogers, serving good food in comfortable, rustic surroundings.

Self-catering There are quite a few apartments and chalets to rent in the area – the tourist office has a brochure and runs a central reservation system. And one of our assistant editors has one of the new MGM Fermes de Ste Foy chalets to rent, 100m/33oft from the lift (see www.ste-foy-chalet.co.uk).

Eating out Book the excellent Chez Mérie (0479 069016), in the village of Le Miroir, well in advance (for lunch, too). In La Thuile, book the Auberge sur la Montagne. In Ste-Foy village, the Grange at the Monal does 'good food'. Chez Léon opens by arrangement in the evenings. At the station the Ruelle has become the Bec de l'Ane pizzeria, which does take-away as well as eat-in.

Après-ski Pretty quiet. The Pitchouli at the ski station is the place to go for a drink later on, though its liveliness is unpredictable. It has table football and sometimes live music (which one reporter rated 'awful'!). The bar of the Monal can get busy, too, and may have live music.

Off the slopes There's not a lot to do off the slopes, but paragliding, dog-sledding and snow-shoeing are available.

Phone numbers
From abroad use the prefix +33 and omit the initial '0' of the phone number.

TOURIST OFFICE

t 0479 069519
stefoy@wanadoo.fr
www.saintefoy.net

OT STE-FOY / MARK JUNAC

Ste-Foy now has a few buildings at the lift base, but is still tiny ↓

Ste-Foy-Tarentaise

331

St-Martin-de-Belleville

Explore the Three Valleys from a traditional old village

COSTS

① ② ③ ④ ⑤ ⑥

RATINGS

The slopes

Snow	★★★
Extent	★★★★★
Expert	★★★★
Intermediate	★★★★★
Beginner	★★★
Convenience	★★★
Queues	★★★★
Mountain restaurants	★★★★

The rest

Scenery	★★★
Resort charm	★★★★
Off-slope	★

NEWS

For the 2002/03 season a gondola replaced the chair out of the village, the Blooley piste back to the village was widened and further snowmaking was installed to improve conditions at village level. A discounted Three Valleys lift pass for families was introduced.

The long-promised improvements to the drag-lift from the church up to the gondola are now scheduled for the 2003/04 season.

➕ Attractively developed traditional village with pretty church

➕ Easy access to the whole of the extensive Three Valleys network

➕ Long easy intermediate runs on rolling local slopes

➕ Extensive snowmaking keeps local runs open in poor conditions, but ...

➖ Snow at resort level suffers from altitude, and sun in the afternoon

➖ No green runs for beginners to progress to

➖ The climb up from the lower part of the village can be taxing

➖ Limited après-ski

➖ Few off-slope diversions

St-Martin is a lived-in, unspoiled village, with an old church (prettily lit at night), small square and buildings of wood and stone, a few miles down the valley from Les Menuires. As a quiet, inexpensive, attractive base for exploration of the Three Valleys as a whole, it's unbeatable. But note that it is not a particularly good base for the slopes of Val-Thorens, up the valley; it's a long trip, and most quickly done via Méribel, in the next valley – which of course means you need a Three Valleys lift pass.

THE RESORT

In 1950 St-Martin didn't even have running water or electricity. Later, while new resorts were developed nearby, St-Martin was a bit of a backwater, though it remained the administrative centre for the Belleville valley (which includes the resorts of Val-Thorens and Les Menuires). But in the 1980s chair-lifts were built, linking it to the slopes of Méribel and Les Menuires. The old village has been developed, of course, but the architecture of the new buildings fits in well with the old, and it remains a small place – you can walk around it in a few minutes. The main feature of the centre remains the lovely old 16th-century church – prettily floodlit at night. There are some good local shops and few 'touristy' ones. A regular visitor was pleased to report how 'unobtrusive' the new gondola station is.

OT ST-MARTIN-DE-BELLEVILLE / P JACQUES / FOC

Despite expansion, St-Martin remains a small village in traditional style ➜

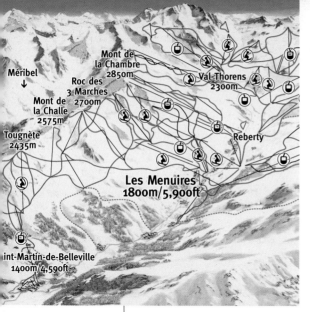

Méribel
↓
Mont de la Chambre 2850m
Roc des 3 Marches 2700m
Mont de la Challe 2575m
Val Thorens 2300m
Tougnète 2435m
Reberty
Les Menuires 1800m/5,900ft
int-Martin-de-Belleville 1400m/4,590ft

THE MOUNTAINS

The whole of the Three Valleys can be easily explored from here.

Slopes A new gondola – pronounced a 'vast improvement' by a visitor this year – followed by a fast quad take you to a ridge from which you can access Méribel on one side and Les Menuires on the other.

Terrain-parks There isn't a terrain-park in the St-Martin sector, but you can get to the one above Les Menuires or the one above Méribel relatively easily.

Snow reliability Natural snow reliability is not the best in the Three Valleys – the local slopes face west and get the full force of the afternoon sun, and the village is relatively low. But there is now snowmaking from top to bottom of the main run to the village, and reporters agree that it is impressively effective at keeping the run open.

Experts Locally there are large areas of gentle and often deserted off-piste. And access to La Masse for steep north-facing slopes is just one run – one very tedious traverse, sadly – away from the top of the local lifts.

Intermediates The local slopes are pleasant blues and reds, mainly of interest to intermediates – including one of our favourite runs in the Three Valleys: the long, rolling, wide Jerusalem red. The Verdet blue from the top of the Méribel lifts is a wonderful easy cruise with great views and is usually very quiet. The whole of

the Three Valleys is, of course, an intermediate's paradise.

Beginners St-Martin is not ideal – there's a nursery slope but no easy green runs to progress to.

Snowboarding There is some great local off-piste free-riding available.

Cross-country There are 28km/17 miles of trails in the Belleville valley.

Queues Queues are not usually much of a problem – 'We didn't queue all week,' comments one visitor, and reporters are unanimous in praising the new gondola, which takes skiers from the village to mid-mountain in six minutes, as 'greatly improving access'. The gondola will eventually be extended to Roc de Fer, as an alternative to the existing fast chair to Tougnète.

Mountain restaurants There are three atmospheric old mountain restaurants on the main run down to the village. The Chardon Bleu and the Corbeleys near the mid-mountain lift junction are good for lunch (though a reader complains that the waitress service in the Corbeleys is 'incredibly slow'), and the Loë, lower down, is popular as the lifts close. Lunch in the village is popular with people from other resorts in the Three Valleys. Brewski's terrace is popular for pies and burgers. For a real blow-out, the Bouitte in St-Marcel is one of the best restaurants in the Three Valleys and now has a Michelin star – it's a traditional, welcoming, rustic auberge with linen on the tables and with charming service. It's not cheap. You can get to it on skis off-piste, and the owners will ferry you to a lift.

Schools and guides The ski school is said to have instructors with good English, but not all past reporters have encountered them. We lack recent reports.

Facilities for children The Piou Piou club and ESF take children from two and a half years old from 9am to 5pm every day of the week.

STAYING THERE

How to go For such a small village there's a good variety of accommodation.

Hotels The Alp Hôtel (0479 089282), at the foot of the slope by the main lift and close to the nursery, is deservedly popular, and we are assured that it has not been sold to a German tour operator as previously reported. The

KEY FACTS

KEY FACTS	
Resort	1400m
	4,590ft

For the Three Valleys	
Slopes	1260-3230m
	4,130-10,600ft
Lifts	200
Pistes	600km
	370 miles
Green	17%
Blue	34%
Red	37%
Black	12%
Snowmaking	90km
	56 miles

For Les Menuires / St-Martin only	
Slopes	1450-2850m
	4,760-9,350ft
Lifts	42
Pistes	160km
	99 miles

Saint Martin (0479 008800) is right on the slope, and the Edelweiss (0479 089667) is in the village itself. All are 3-stars. There's simply furnished B&B accommodation slope-side at Brewski's – next to the bar of the same name but now marketed and managed by uptoyou.com. Rooms vary widely in size, but all are en suite and most have balconies with views.

Chalets The number of chalet beds in the resort is on the increase, with major UK operators starting to take an interest. Chalets de St Martin has traditionally been the main British chalet operator in town – it has operated here ever since the first lift was built. Ski Total now runs some of its chalets, but it still operates chalet Rousette, with cooking by professional chefs and a variety of quality wines to match the food (the owner is a wine merchant).

Self-catering Chalets de St Martin has a variety of self-catered chalets and apartments to rent, and plenty of others are available.

Eating out For such a small village there is a good variety of restaurants on hand. One reader found the Montagnard's rustic decor 'slightly contrived' but says the service was 'friendly' and the 'good helpings' of Savoyard food 'reasonably priced'. The Voûte is good value too and is recommended for its salads and pizzas. Brewski's evening menu has a more French emphasis. The Grenier, in the hotel St Martin, has impressed – 'Smart but not cheap.' The Etoile de Neige is a smart, traditionally French restaurant but a recent reporter thought that it was a bit over-priced when compared to the Bouitte, just up the road in St-Marcel, which is recognised as the best restaurant in the Belleville valley – see Mountain restaurants. A bit further up the valley, at Les Granges, is the rustic Chez Bidou – popular with locals and 'highly recommended for a Savoyard evening'.

Après-ski Après-ski centres around two bars. The Pourquoi Pas? piano bar is delightfully cosy, with a roaring log fire and comfortable easy chairs and sofas. Brewski's is a more animated bar with live bands most nights.

Off the slopes If you don't use the slopes, there are better places to base yourself. There are pleasant walks and a sports hall, and classical concerts that take place in the church.

Phone numbers
From abroad use the prefix +33 and omit the initial '0' of the phone number.

Les Sybelles

Much more than the sum of its parts

①②③④⑤⑥

Les Sybelles? No, we hadn't heard of it, either, until word began to get around that a group of little-known ski resorts in the Maurienne massif in the French Alps were linking to form an impressively large network. 310km/193 miles of pistes puts this new circus straight into the big league, alongside such giants as Val-d'Isère/Tignes, Davos/Klosters and the Sella Ronda. So: a chapter is born.

The links – which we are assured will be completed for 2003/04 – possess what you might call synergy. La Toussuire and Le Corbier, functional modern resorts already sharing a quite extensive but unremarkable area of slopes, gain an association with attractive villages and access to more interesting, steeper pistes. The cute villages of St-Sorlin-d'Arves and St-Jean-d'Arves add much-needed mileage to their nicely varied but limited slopes, while St-Colomban-des-Villards gets to be a serious ski resort.

La Toussuire and Le Corbier are the major resorts, selling on price and convenience, particularly for families. But in the run-up to completion of the links, St-Sorlin and St-Jean have attracted more of the major UK tour operators. Right now, none of the resorts is geared up for British visitors yet: information in English is hard to come by – but this should improve.

The creation of the new linked area involves construction of over a dozen lifts, linking Le Corbier, La Toussuire, St-Sorlin and St-Colomban to the hill that will be at the hub, L'Ouillon. It could have been done more simply, but only by making pistes on a steep, south-facing slope from Le Corbier down to St-Sorlin. The planned links are high – mostly between 2000m and 2600m (6,560ft and 8,530ft) – and of intermediate gradient, so they are relatively snow-sure, safe and easily negotiated by intermediates. The drawback is that getting from one resort to another is going to take time. The new linking lifts should access a lot of underused off-piste terrain.

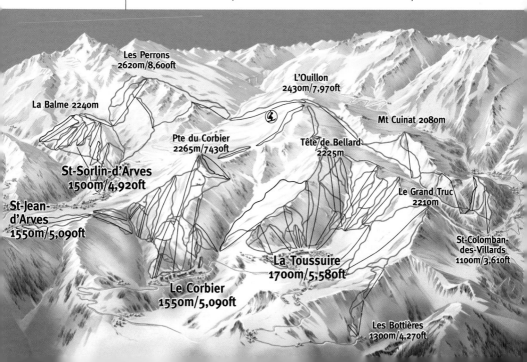

Slopes	1300-2620m
	4,270-8,600ft
Lifts	73
Pistes	310km
	193 miles
Green	18%
Blue	40%
Red	36%
Black	6%

% relate to number of runs not length of pistes

Snowmaking	
	193 guns

LE CORBIER 1550m/5,090ft

Le Corbier is the most widely known of the Sybelles resorts on the UK market. Its position gives it the slight advantage of direct links to St-Jean-d'Arves in one direction and La Toussuire in the other, in addition to its new link to St-Sorlin-d'Arves via L'Ouillon.

THE RESORT

Designed in the 1960s, Le Corbier is a no-compromise functional resort. Most of its accommodation is in eight inner-city-style tower blocks, one as high as 19 storeys, with subterranean shops beneath. To our eye, it looks like a mistake. But it does accommodate its 9,000 visitors efficiently in the minimum space, and in functional terms it is hard to criticise – it's a compact, family-friendly, traffic-free resort with all ski-in/ski-out accommodation. The apartment blocks line the foot of the slopes, creating a safe environment for children, and in the other direction the resort's balcony setting gives good views of the valley. And the resort assures us that all new building will be in traditional style.

THE MOUNTAIN

Le Corbier's contribution to the ski area measures 90km/60 miles of piste and is the gentlest of the sections. Although the altitudes are modest (top height 2265m/7,430ft, resort 1550m/5,090ft), it is all mountain pasture – there are hardly any trees.

Slopes A new chair whisks skiers up over 700m/2,300ft vertical to Pte du Corbier from where you use new pistes and lifts along the ridge to Pte de L'Ouillon and the links to St-Sorlin-d'Arves or La Toussuire. Runs spread across a wide, gentle, north-east-facing mountainside return to the resort – served by countless drags and slow chairs – and there are links at the extremities of this area to La Toussuire and St-Jean-d'Arves. There is a small area of floodlit skiing.

Snow reliability The mix of reasonable altitude and lack of crowds cutting up the pistes means the snow tends to stay in reasonable condition. The slopes get the morning sun. but there is snowmaking on all the main pistes back to the resort. The sunny, low connection from La Toussuire is the one problem spot, but there is now the option of the higher link.

Experts The area is more or less without challenge – the one black piste scarcely deserves a red grading. The off-piste options in the valley between Le Corbier and La Toussuire will be extended by the new linking lifts.

Intermediates Le Corbier's gentle slopes are ideal cruising terrain, though the runs aren't very long and they rather lack variety.

Beginners There is an extensive nursery area right in front of the resort, with gentle progression runs directly above. A new top-of-mountain nursery area has just been developed, too.

Snowboarding The wide, open terrain is ideal for riders, so long as they don't want anything too challenging.

Cross-country There are narrow loops across the mountainside either side of the resort, one of which leads to La Toussuire and back. It's all a bit bleak.

Queues The area is renowned for its uncrowded slopes, and the system is free of bottlenecks.

Mountain restaurants The piste map marks four in this sector, which seems adequate. Le Chalet 2000 is the highest – and it has a sunny terrace.

Schools Our one recent reporter judged the ESF 'disdainful, uncaring, very disorganised; bad tuition'.

Facilities for children The Baby Club accepts children from six months to three years and the ski kindergarten from three to six years. The ski kindergarten was liked by a reporter – 'nice, well equipped children's ski park and good instructors'. Its location up on the pistes can involve a bit of a hike.

STAYING THERE

How to go There are several UK operators selling packages here. Budget airlines serve several airports between two and three hours away.

Chalets Equity Ski runs its own chalet-hotel, described by one reporter as 'clean, comfortable and very good value' and approved by others, too.

Self-catering There's nothing larger than cramped two-bedroomed units on offer from central reservations.

Eating out Very limited indeed. This place was built for self-caterers.

Après ski Forget it. The torchlit descent is the highlight of the week. There is a nightclub, but outside French school holidays it does very little business.

Off the slopes Limited. There's a nice natural ice rink, and snowmobiles.

LA TOUSSUIRE 1700m/5,580ft

La Toussuire, along with Le Corbier, is one of the central resorts of the new network – the two have been linked at low altitude since 1986.

THE RESORT

La Toussuire has grown up over many years but is predominantly modern, with a central row of dreary-looking hotels and apartments at the foot of the slopes, dating from the 1960s and 1970s. The resort has now spread widely from here, with recently built wooden chalets as well as older hotels and small apartment blocks scattered across the mountainside.

THE MOUNTAIN

The local slopes amount to 45km/ 28 miles of piste all in one large, treeless bowl, which is generally slightly steeper than the Le Corbier slopes.

Slopes The resort sits in the pit of a wide bowl. From the aforementioned central row of buildings, drags and chair-lifts access the existing links to Le Corbier and serve short slopes facing north-east beneath Grande Verdette, which will be the start of the new linking lift towards L'Ouillon. Further around the bowl, chairs and drags go up to the high-point of Tête de Bellard (only 500m/1,640ft vertical above the village) and three other minor peaks, with runs back to the village and over the lip of the bowl to Les Bottières.

Snow reliability With every run above 1800m/5,910ft snow-cover is fairly assured, but some of the slopes are rather exposed to the sun – particularly the existing low-level connection to Le Corbier.

Experts There are few challenges here, and not much space left between the pistes. The main interest is the ungroomed black Vallée Perdue run, which descends the valley separating La Toussuire from Le Corbier, away from the lifts. The new lifts towards L'Ouillon will open up new off-piste routes down this valley.

Intermediates This is ideal terrain for cruisers who don't mind short runs – and there are a couple of longer, steeper reds on offer below Le Grand Truc and Tête de Bellard, too. The runs that go down to Les Bottières are some of the most appealing in the whole area.

Beginners There are nice, gentle

nursery slopes immediately above the centre of the village, and good, easy progression slopes. The Gorges blue from Le Marolay is the longest cruise, at 300m/980ft vertical.

Snowboarding There are quite a few drag-lifts in the area, and some parts of the mountain are served by nothing else.

Cross-country A narrow loop goes to Le Corbier and back, but it's never far from the road and the surroundings are quite bleak.

Queues These have not been a problem up to now.

Mountain restaurants There isn't much choice. A reporter recommends the Foehn at Le Marolay for its 'friendly service', the good views and an interesting interior of old photos, carvings etc. Les Carlines has been renovated and has a bigger terrace than before.

Schools A lack of English-speaking tuition can be a problem, though we understand that English classes are often laid on for Dutch visitors. The school guarantees classes will be no larger than 10.

Facilities for children The nursery accepts kids from three to six years old. English-speaking staff and English-speaking children to play with are unlikely.

STAYING THERE

How to go A few UK tour operators serve the resort.

Hotels There are several small 3-star and 2-star places. The 3-star Soldanelles (0479 567529) and Ruade (0479 830179) both have an indoor pool and sauna.

Self-catering The Ecrins chalets are large 3-star apartments (slightly above average). Most others are cheap and not-so-cheerful.

Eating out Mostly inexpensive pizzerias and bar-restaurants. The Savoyard specialities in the Envol and the Chamois are perfectly adequate.

Après ski Very quiet. The Alpen 'pub' is the main gathering spot but it's not exactly throbbing. The Tonneau and the Caltha are other bars for a quiet drink. The Fillimore nightclub rarely gets animated.

Off the slopes Not much. Snow-shoeing, snowmobiles, dog-sleigh rides, ice skating, hang-gliding, cinema.

ST-SORLIN D'ARVES 1500m/4,920ft
St-Sorlin's only link to the other resorts up to now has been a shuttle-bus to St-Jean, where a chair-lift goes up for access to Le Corbier.

THE RESORT

St-Sorlin-d'Arves is a real medium-sized village with a year-round life outside of skiing. It's a picturesque collection of well preserved traditional farmhouses, with a baroque church and long established shops – fromagerie, boulangerie, crafts and so on – alongside more modern resort development. Its setting on a narrow shelf gives fine views of the Aiguilles d'Arves but doesn't allow much room for expansion, so the village has grown in a ribbon-like fashion along its main street.

THE MOUNTAIN

St-Sorlin's local slopes form the biggest single sector of the new network, with 120km/75 miles of piste. Although still very much an intermediate mountain, it does offer more variety, including some steeper options, than the rest of the area. And the new lifts will add to the local slopes here in a way that they won't in Le Corbier and La Toussuire.

Slopes There are two distinct sections. The lower, gentler left side on La Balme is crammed with lots of short, easy runs while, in contrast, the higher, steeper right side on Les Perrons has long, sweeping, spaciously laid-out pistes. The new link lifts on Petit Perron will improve this area a lot, even for skiers who have no intention of setting off towards another resort.

Snow reliability Not bad. The Les Perrons slopes are the highest in the area and the important linking piste between Les Perrons and La Balme is covered by snowmakers. The other main run to the village is also covered.

Experts There isn't much, but Les Perrons had the best off-piste in the whole pre-existing area.

Intermediates The long top-to-bottom reds on Les Perrons are the best pistes in the whole area. There are only a couple of them but they have the whole mountain to themselves, giving a great away-from-it-all feel. La Balme is similar to Le Corbier and La Toussuire – short, leisurely runs.

Beginners The nursery slope is right by the village, and there are plenty of slopes to progress to on La Balme.

Snowboarding Most of St-Sorlin's existing lifts are drags.

Cross-country There's a narrow 16km/10 mile loop along a side valley past the foot of La Balme's Alpine area, with good views of the Aiguilles d'Arves.

Queues There are none to speak of, and it's difficult to imagine any of the new lifts being particularly oversubscribed.

Mountain restaurants There are two on La Balme and a further one at the main link to Les Perrons. We await reports.

Schools A lack of English-speaking tuition is a likely problem here.

Facilities for children The Petits Diables crèche accepts children from three months to six years. The ski kindergarten accepts kids from three and a half years old. A lack of both English-speaking staff and English-speaking kids to play with is a likely problem.

STAYING THERE

How to go Some major UK tour operators are planning to offer holidays here.

Hotels There are three small 2-star places – all attractive-looking chalets. The Beausoleil (0479 597140) looks the best bet.

Self-catering There are scores of small properties offered locally.

Eating out It's mostly cheap and cheerful pizzerias and raclette/fondue places. The Table de Marie and the Beausejour are the best bets.

Après-ski St-Sorlin-d'Arves is even quieter than the other resorts. Le Choucas and the Avalanche Café are bars with music. That's about it.

Off the slopes There is not much to do. The dog-sleigh rides are pleasant, and snow-shoeing is an option, but it's fairly tame territory.

ST-JEAN-D'ARVES 1550m/5,090ft

St-Jean-d'Arves is a traditional old village with the usual ancient church. It's a charming, friendly place of panoramic views and old, pitched-roof buildings.

It is not directly affected by the new lifts; as in the past, it remains linked to Le Corbier over the hill by lifts and runs, and by shuttle-bus to St-Sorlin-d'Arves along the valley. Although small, St-Jean-d'Arves is quite a scattered community, with at least two identifiable concentrations of chalets. Ski down to it from the link from Le Corbier, and you arrive at the mid-mountain hamlet of La Chal. St-Jean proper is across the valley at the foot of a north-facing ridge equipped with two drag-lifts.

Off-slope diversions are few – dog-sleigh rides, cheese farm visits, snow-shoeing. Après-ski is basic, with seven restaurants and bars and an Irish pub; resort entertainment includes night-sledging with music. The high-quality La Grange Eurogroup apartments offer the attractive Chalets Les Marmottes and La Fontaine du Roi apartments – by far the best self-catering option in the whole area.

ST-COLOMBAN-DES-VILLARDS 1100m/3,610ft

St-Colomban-des-Villards is a tiny old village in the next valley to La Toussuire, only a few miles up from the Maurienne valley.

In recent years it has developed a chain of drags and chair-lifts on north- and east-facing slopes to the south of the village, with a high point at Mt Cuinat, and for the 2003/04 season it will be linked to L'Ouillon, at the hub of Les Sybelles. A battery of snowmakers keeps the home slope down to the village open for most of the season.

LES BOTTIÈRES 1300m/4,270ft

Down the mountain, a little way from La Toussuire, this hamlet offers a more rustic base but extremely indirect access to the main network – it's three lifts just to get over to La Toussuire, before setting off for L'Ouillon.

Phone numbers
From abroad use the prefix +33 and omit the initial '0' of the phone number.

TOURIST OFFICES

La Toussuire
t 0479 830606
info@la-toussuire.com
www.la-toussuire.com

Le Corbier
t 0479 830404
info@le-corbier.com
www.le-corbier.com

St-Sorlin-d'Arves
t 0479 597177
info@saintsorlin
darves.com
www.saintsorlindarves
.com

St-Jean-d'Arves
t 0479 597330
info@saintjeandarves.
com
www.saintjeandarves.
com

St-Colomban-des-Villards
t 0479 593048
villards@wanadoo.fr
www.saintcolomban.
com

Les Bottières
t 0479 832709
bottieresaccueil@
worldonline.fr
www.savoie-
maurienne.com/
lesbottieres

La Tania

Small, family-friendly base for exploring the Three Valleys

COSTS

① ② ③ ④ ⑤ ⑥

RATINGS

The slopes

Snow	★★★
Extent	★★★★★
Expert	★★★★
Intermediate	★★★★★
Beginner	★★
Convenience	★★★★
Queues	★★★★
Mountain restaurants	★★★★

The rest

Scenery	★★★
Resort charm	★★★
Off-slope	★

+ Part of the Three Valleys – the world's biggest linked ski area

+ Quick access to the slopes of Courchevel and Méribel

+ Long, rolling, intermediate runs through woods back to the village

+ Greatly improved snowmaking

+ Attractively developed, small, traffic-free village

− Small development without much choice of après-ski – and no pharmacy or cashpoint

− Main nursery slope is part of the blue run to the village, and gets a lot of through-traffic

− Runs home are too steep for those progressing from the nursery slopes

− Some accommodation is a long walk from the centre and the main lifts

La Tania does not try to compete with its more upmarket neighbours, Courchevel and Méribel. It has carved out its own niche as a good-value, small, quiet, family-friendly base from which to hit the snow-sure slopes of Courchevel and to explore the whole of the Three Valleys. It is prettily set in the trees, and the wood-clad buildings make it one of the more attractive French purpose-built resorts (development started in the early 1990s, by which time lessons had been learned from the resorts that were developed in the 1960s and 70s, with their tiny apartments and uncompromisingly functional architecture). As a budget base for the Three Valleys, it has a lot to be said for it.

THE RESORT

La Tania is set just off the minor road linking Le Praz (Courchevel 1300) to Méribel. It has grown into a quiet, attractive, car-free collection of mainly ski-in, ski-out chalets and apartments set among the trees, most with good views. There are few shops other than food and sports shops and not much choice of bars and restaurants. You can walk around the place in a couple of minutes.

A gondola leads up into the slopes, and there are two wonderful sweeping intermediate runs down. The nursery slope is on your doorstep, and visitors say that La Tania is 'very child friendly'. The steepness of the runs back to the village is its key weakness.

Free buses go to Courchevel in the daytime, but a reporter warns that the service is erratic in the evenings. For those with a car Méribel is probably a bigger draw – 1850, Courchevel's main shopping and nightlife focus, is appreciably further.

← Provided you can handle the challenging blue run home, La Tania makes an excellent base – with woodland runs for bad-weather days but quick access to higher slopes when the sun comes out

NEWS

For 2002/03 38 new snow-guns were installed to cover the blue Folyères piste from Praz-Juget down to the centre of the resort. Still more snowmaking is planned for 2003/04.

A discounted lift pass for families is now available.

KEY FACTS

Resort	1350m
	4,430ft

For the Three Valleys		
Slopes	1260-3230m
	4,130-10,600ft
Lifts	200
Pistes	600km
	370 miles
Green	17%
Blue	34%
Red	37%
Black	12%
Snowmaking	90km
	56 miles

For Courchevel / La Tania only	
Slopes	1260-2740m
	4,130-8,990ft
Lifts	67
Pistes	150km
	93 miles

PISTE MAP

La Tania is covered on the Courchevel map earlier in the France section.

THE MOUNTAINS

As well as good, though limited, local slopes, the whole of the Three Valleys can be explored easily from here, with just two lifts needed to get to either the Courchevel or the Méribel slopes.

Slopes The gondola out of the village goes to Praz-Juget. From here a drag-lift takes you to Chenus and the slopes above Courchevel 1850 and a fast quad goes to the link with Méribel via Col de la Loze. An alternative way to the slopes above 1850 is to take two successive drag-lifts from the village to Loze. From all these points, varied, interesting intermediate runs take you back into the La Tania sector.

Terrain-parks There is no local terrain-park or half-pipe, but you can get to Courchevel's easily.

Snow reliability Good snow-cover down to Praz-Juget is usual all season. Below that the snow is less assured. Snowmaking now covers the whole of the blue run back to the village; some reporters found this satisfactory, but others found the slopes in bad condition and had to ride the gondola at times.

Experts There are no particular challenges directly above La Tania, but the Jean Blanc and Jockeys blacks from Loze to Le Praz are genuine challenges and there is good off-piste terrain close by in the Courchevel sector.

Intermediates There are two lovely, long, undulating intermediate runs back to La Tania – though on the higher slopes you have a choice of three or four pistes. Both Lanches and Dou des Lanches are excellent challenging reds. The blue way down is not the easiest of blues – an important flaw in the resort for many. The quick access to the rest of the Three Valleys' 600km/370 miles of well-groomed pistes makes the area an adventurous intermediate's paradise.

Beginners There is a good beginner area and lift right in the village and beginner children, in particular, are well catered for. But there are no very easy, long, local slopes to progress to; the intermediate runs back to the village are quite challenging. Think about Courchevel 1650 instead.

Snowboarding It's easy to get around on gondolas and chairs and avoid the drags.

Cross-country There are trails at altitude with links through the woods to Méribel and Courchevel. To our non-specialist eye, this looks a good base.

Queues A queue can build up for the village gondola but it is quick-moving, and one of the attractions of La Tania in general is the lack of crowds. Elsewhere in the Three Valleys there are a few remaining bottlenecks.

Mountain restaurants The Bouc Blanc, near the top of the gondola out of La Tania, has friendly table-service, good food and a big terrace, though this year a reporter pronounces it 'very uninspiring, having been one of our favourites last year'. Roc Tania, higher up at Col de la Loze is tiny, but very pretty inside – good for a scenic coffee stop; one reader found the food good at lunch time, another was disappointed with food and service. Check out the Courchevel and Méribel places, too.

Schools and guides Magic in Motion was 'highly thought of' by a reporter this year. We have no recent reports of the other schools that operate out of La Tania – ESF, Snow Ball and Arthur MacLean.

Facilities for children We have had excellent reports of tour operator Le Ski's nursery here. The local kindergarten takes non-skiing children from the age of three; the Jardin des Neiges takes skiing children from the age of four. A list of babysitters is available from the tourist office.

La Tania

Phone numbers
From abroad use the prefix +33 and omit the initial '0' of the phone number.

TOURIST OFFICE

t 0479 084040
info@latania.com
www.latania.com

STAYING THERE

How to go Around 30 British tour operators go here.

Hotels The Montana (0479 088008) is a slope-side 3-star next to the gondola with a sauna and fitness club. It was said by a reporter to be 'very good value, with friendly, English-speaking staff and excellent food'. The Mountain Centre (www.themountaincentre.com or 01273 897525 in the UK) has 'cheap backpacker-style accommodation' from £19 a night B&B with dinner costing 13 euros. Just our kind of place.

Chalets Several tour operators have splendid newish ski-in, ski-out chalets with fine views, though reporters have complained of 'poor soundproofing' in some. The choice gets wider every year.

Self-catering There are lots of apartments – and most are more spacious and better equipped than usual in France. The Saboia and the Christiania have been recommended. There is a deli and a bakery, as well as a small supermarket.

Eating out The Ferme de la Tania gets generally good reviews for its Savoyard fare – 'good service, good food' – but the Farçon was considered 'outrageously expensive and not all that good' by a reporter this year. Pub Le Ski Lodge has 'damn good chilli burgers'. The Chanterelles is 'highly recommended' for crêpes and pizzas ('excellent value for money') and the Taïga does 'very good pizzas and is friendly and quite cheap'.

Après-ski Pub Le Ski Lodge is the focal après-ski place. The hotel Montana bar and the Taïga (a bar-pizzeria) are quieter. But if you want a lively varied nightlife, you need to go elsewhere – La Tania is too small.

Off the slopes Unless you have a car, La Tania is not the best place for someone not intending to hit the slopes. However, snowmobile trips, snowshoeing, paragliding and husky dog sledding are possibilities, and the hotel Montana has a fitness club with a swimming pool. A non-skier's guide to Courchevel, Méribel and La Tania is distributed free by the tourist office.

Selected chalets in La Tania

Tignes

Good snow, great varied terrain and a resort that's ... er ... improving

COSTS

① ② ③ ④ ⑤ ⑥

RATINGS

The slopes

Snow	*****
Extent	*****
Expert	*****
Intermediate	*****
Beginner	**
Convenience	****
Queues	****
Mountain restaurants	***

The rest

Scenery	***
Resort charm	**
Off-slope	*

NEWS

For 2002/03 the slow Tommeuses chair-lifts – a major bottleneck on the way back from Val d'Isère – were at last replaced, by a high-speed eight-seater, cutting the journey time dramatically as well as the queues.

The resort embarked on a major redevelopment and refurbishment programme in the 1990s, which seems to have paid off in reporter satisfaction.

New hotels continue to be built. The four-star Village Montana suites opened last year in Les Almes and two new three-star hotels are planned for 2003/04.

OT TIGNES / DANIEL ROUSSELOT

The nursery slopes at Tignes-le-Lac are good and the big Aeroski gondola gets you quickly to Tovière and the link with Val d'Isère →

- ✚ Good snow guaranteed for a long season – about the best Alpine bet
- ✚ One of the best areas in the world for lift-served off-piste runs
- ✚ Huge amount of terrain for all abilities, with swift access to Val-d'Isère
- ✚ Lots of accommodation close to the slopes (though there is also quite a bit that involves some walking)
- ✚ Attempts to make the resort villages more welcoming are paying off

- ▬ Resort architecture not to everyone's taste (including ours)
- ▬ Bleak, treeless setting – hardly any woodland runs, and many slopes liable to closure during and after storms
- ▬ Still lots of long, slow chair-lifts
- ▬ Near-beginners looking for long green runs have to buy an area pass and go to the Val-d'Isère slopes
- ▬ Limited après-ski

The appeal of Tignes is simple: good snow, spread over a wide area of varied terrain, shared with Val-d'Isère. Together the two resorts form the enormous Espace Killy – a Mecca for experts, and ideal for adventurous intermediates.

We prefer to stay in Val, which is a more human place. But in many ways Tignes makes the better base: appreciably higher, more convenient, surrounded by intermediate terrain, with quick access to the Grande Motte glacier. And the case for Tignes gets stronger as results flow from the resort's campaign to reinvent itself in a more cuddly form. Cars have been largely pushed underground, new buildings are being designed in traditional styles and some old ones are getting a facelift. It all helps to combat the impression that you've landed on the Moon.

Tignes built some impressive lifts in the 1990s, but enjoyment of the expansive western side of the Tignes bowl – and some other areas of the Espace Killy, too – is limited by the time you spend riding slow chair-lifts. Upgrades are overdue.

But you keep coming back to the snow. On several occasions we have been mighty glad to be heading for Tignes rather than some lower resort with a cosier village and slicker lift system.

343

KEY FACTS

Resort	2100m
	6,890ft

For entire Espace Killy area	
Slopes	1550-3455m
	5,090-11,340ft
Lifts	97
Pistes	300km
	186 miles
Green	15%
Blue	46%
Red	28%
Black	11%
Snowmaking	24km
	15 miles

For Tignes only	
Slopes	1550-3455m
	5,090-11,340ft
Lifts	48
Pistes	150km
	93 miles

THE RESORT

Tignes was created before the French discovered the benefits of making purpose-built resorts look acceptable. But they are doing what they can to improve things. Traffic is now discouraged (and in places routed underground), and the villages are certainly more pleasant as a result, even if their 'traffic-free' status is pretty nominal.

The original and main village – Tignes-le-Lac – is still the hub of the resort. Some of the smaller buildings in the central part, Le Rosset, are being successfully revamped in chalet style. But the place as a whole is dreary, and the blocks overlooking the lake from the quarter called Le Bec-Rouge will be monstrous until the day they are demolished. It's at the point where these two sub-resorts meet that the lifts are concentrated – two slow old chair-lifts up the western slopes and a powerful gondola towards Tovière and Val-d'Isère. Some attractive new buildings are being added on the fringes, in a suburb known as Les Almes. A nursery slope separates Le Rosset from the slightly more inviting suburb of Le Lavachet, below which there are now good fast lifts up both sides of the valley.

Val-Claret (2km/1 mile up the valley, beyond the lake) was mainly developed after Le Rosset, and is a bit more stylish. The main part of the village, Centre, is an uncompromisingly modern-style development on a shelf above the valley floor; a couple of lifts go up the eastern slopes from here. Down on the valley floor there are major lifts up to the Grande Motte glacier, as well as lifts accessing the sides of the bowl and the slopes of Val-d'Isère. Beside the road along the valley to the lifts is a ribbon of more recent development in traditional style. The two levels of Val-Claret are linked by a couple of indoor elevators and stairs as well as by hazardous paths.

Below the high valley of the main resort villages are two smaller settlements. Tignes-les-Boisses, quietly set in the trees beside the road up to the main Tignes villages, consists of a barracks and a couple of simple hotels. Lower Tignes-les-Brévières is a renovated old village at the lowest point of the slopes – a favourite lunch spot, and a friendly place to stay.

Location isn't crucial, as a regular

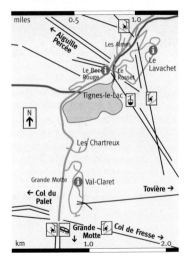

and very efficient free bus service connects all the villages until midnight – though in the daytime the route runs along the bottom of Val-Claret, leaving residents of Val-Claret Centre with some hiking.

A six-day pass covers a day in some other resorts, including the newly-linked Les Arcs and La Plagne (Paradiski) area and the Three Valleys, most easily reached with the aid of a car. Preserve your pass and you'll get a loyalty discount off next year's.

THE MOUNTAINS

The area's great weakness is that it can become unusable in bad weather. There are no woodland runs except immediately above Tignes-les-Boisses and Tignes-les-Brévières, heavy snow produces widespread avalanche risk and wind closes the higher chairs.

THE SLOPES
High, snow-sure and varied
Tignes' biggest asset is the **Grande Motte** – and the runs from, as well as on, the glacier. The underground funicular from Val-Claret whizzes you up to over 3000m/9,850ft in seven minutes. There are blue, red and black runs to play on up here, as well as beautiful long runs back to the resort.

The main lifts towards Val-d'Isère are efficient: a high-capacity gondola from Le Lac to **Tovière**, and a fast chair with covers from Val-Claret to **Col de Fresse**. You can head back to Tignes from either: the return from Tovière to Tignes-le-Lac is via a steep black run (not so difficult now the moguls are

regularly smoothed out), but there is an easier run to Val-Claret.

Going up the opposite side of the valley takes you to a quieter area where a strangely antiquated series of drags and slow chair-lifts (only one high-speed chair) serve predominantly east-facing slopes split into two main sectors, linked in both directions – **Col du Palet** and **L'Aiguille Percée**. From the latter, you can descend to Tignes-les-Brévières, on blue, red or black runs. (We're pleased to note that our campaign to get the Chardons run classified as red rather than blue has at last been successful.) There's an efficient gondola back.

The Col des Ves chair-lift, at the south end of the Col du Palet sector, is not normally opened until high season and reporters say that some lifts start later in the day than advertised.

TERRAIN-PARKS
Impressive facilities
Tignes has an impressive 2.4km/1.5mile Snow Park with jumps, bumps, ski- and boarder-cross course and a special area for children and beginners above

Tignes-le-Lac and accessed by the Palafour chair-lift. There is also a quarter-pipe and half-pipe, served by its own lift. Specific passes are available for just the park and pipes. For the summer season, Tignes builds a big terrain-park on the Grande Motte.

SNOW RELIABILITY
Difficult to beat
Tignes has all-year-round runs (barring brief closures in spring or autumn) on its Grande Motte glacier. And the resort height of 2100m/6,89oft generally means good snow-cover right back to base for most of the long winter season – November to May. The west-facing runs down from Col de Fresse and Tovière to Val-Claret suffer from the afternoon sun, although they now have serious snowmaking. Some of the lower east-facing and south-east facing slopes on the other side of the valley can suffer late in the season too.

FOR EXPERTS
An excellent choice
It is the off-piste possibilities that make Tignes such a draw for experts.

Tignes

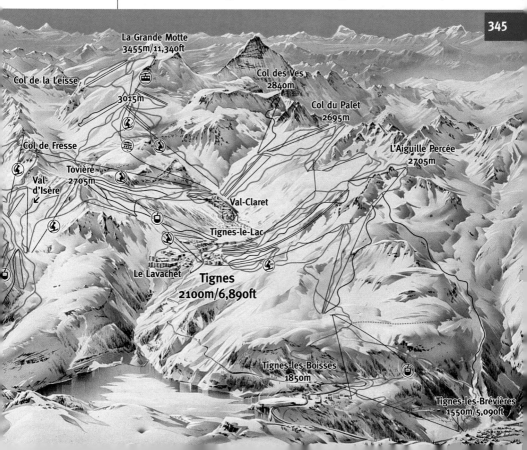

La Grande Motte
3455m/11,340ft

Col de la Leisse

3015m

Col des Ves
2840m

Col du Palet
2695m

Col de Fresse

L'Aiguille Percée
2705m

Tovière
2705m

Val-
d'Isère

Val-Claret

Tignes-le-Lac

Le Lavachet

Tignes
2100m/6,89oft

Tignes-les-Boisses
1850m

Tignes-les-Brévières
1550m/5,09oft

LIFT PASSES

L'Espace Killy
Covers all lifts in Tignes and Val-d'Isère.

Beginners
Free lifts on all main nursery slopes; special beginners' half-day pass.

Main pass
1-day pass €36.50
6-day pass €172.50

Senior citizens
Over 60: 6-day pass €147
Over 70: 6-day pass €86.50
Over 75: free pass

Children
Under 13: 6-day pass €129.50
Under 5: free pass

Notes
Half-day passes available. Discount on presentation of lift pass from any of previous three seasons. 6-day passes and over are valid for one day in the Three Valleys, one day in Valmorel and one day in La Plagne-Les Arcs, and half-price pass in Ste-Foy.

Alternative passes
Tignes-only pass available.

Go with one of the off-piste groups that the schools organise, and in good snow you'll have a great time.

One of the big adventures is to head for Champagny (linked to the La Plagne area) or Peisey-Nancroix (linked to the Les Arcs area) – very beautiful runs, and not too difficult. Your guide will organise return transport.

Another favourite of ours is the Tour de Pramecou, from the Grande Motte glacier. After some walking and beautiful isolated runs, you end up on a steep, smooth north-facing slope that takes you back to Val-Claret. There are other descents across the glacier to the Leisse chair-lift.

The whole western side of the bowl has lots of off-piste possibilities. The terrain served by the Col des Ves chair is often excellent. To the left (looking up) there are wonderfully secluded, scenic and challenging descents. On the right, lower down, is a less heavily used and gentler area, ideal for off-piste initiation. To the north, there are excellent variants on the Sache run to Les Brévières (see below).

Schools and guides offer the bizarre French form of heli-skiing: mountaintop drops are forbidden, but from Tovière you can ski down towards the Lac du Chevril to be retrieved by chopper.

The only serious challenge within the piste network is the long black run from Tovière to Tignes-le-Lac, with steep, usually heavily mogulled

sections. Parts of this run get a lot of afternoon sun. Our favourite black run is the Sache, from Aiguille Percée down a secluded valley to Tignes-les-Brévières, which can become very heavily mogulled at the bottom. A reporter recommends the black Silene piste in the same area: 'Big moguls – very challenging and enjoyable.'

FOR INTERMEDIATES
One of the best
For the keen intermediate piste-basher the Espace Killy is one of the top three or four areas in France, or the world.

Tignes' local slopes are ideal intermediate terrain. The red and blue runs on the Grande Motte glacier nearly always have superb snow. The glacier run from the top of the cable-car has been regraded from blue to red but is wide and mostly easy on usually fabulous snow. The Leisse run down to the chair-lift is now classified black and can get very mogulled but has good snow. The long red run all the way back to town is a delightful long cruise – though often crowded. The roundabout blue alternative (Génépy) is much gentler and quieter.

From Tovière, the blue 'H' run to Val-Claret is an enjoyable cruise and generally well groomed. But again, it can get very crowded.

There is lots to do on the other side of the valley. We particularly like the uncrowded Ves run reached by the low-capacity Col des Ves chair – the highest point of Tignes' non-glacier runs at 2840m/9,320ft. After an initial mogul field (sometimes quite challenging, which we presume is why the run has been reclassified from red to black) it becomes an interesting undulating and curvy cruise, usually with good snow and a few moguls. The runs down from Aiguille Percée to Tignes-les-Boisses and Tignes-les-Brévières are also scenic and fun. There are red and blue options as well as the beautiful Sache black run –

boarding

This is a big area, with a big boarder reputation, and it's a cheaper place to stay than Val d'Isère. There are some flat areas to avoid but the lift system relies more on chairs and gondolas than drags. There are long, wide pistes to blast down, with acres of powder between them to play in. And there's a good Snow Park (see Terrain-parks). There are three specialist snowboard schools (Kebra, Snocool and Surf Feeling). One reporter was impressed with the Evolution 2 boarding instructors: 'clear instruction and smaller class sizes than the ESF'. Hiring a guide and exploring the off-piste is recommended for good free-riders.

SCHOOLS

ESF
t 0479 063028
info@esf-tignes.com

Evolution 2
t 0479 064378
tignes@evolution2.
com

Snow Fun
t 0479 063615
tignes.ski-school
@voila.fr

Snocool
t 0615 345463
snocool@chez.com

Kebra
t 0479 064337
kebra.surfing@free.fr

333
t 0479 062088
contact@333school.
com

Classes (ESF prices)
5 half days: €107
Private lessons
€30.50 for 1hr

GUIDES

Bureau des Guides
t 0479 064276
bureau@
guidesdetignes.com
Tetra
t 0479 419707
tetrahp@wanadoo.fr

adventurous intermediates shouldn't miss it. The runs down from Aiguille Percée to Le Lac are gentle, wide blues.

FOR BEGINNERS
Good nursery slopes, but ...
The nursery slopes of Tignes-le-Lac and Le Lavachet (which meet at the top) are excellent – convenient, snow-sure, gentle, free of through-traffic and served by a slow chair and a drag. The ones at Val-Claret are less appealing: an unpleasantly steep slope within the village served by a drag, and a less convenient slope served by the fast Bollin chair. All of these lifts are free.

There are no easy longer runs in Tignes – for long green runs you have to go over to the Val-d'Isère sector. You need an Espace Killy pass to use them, and to get back to Tignes you have a choice between the blue run from Col de Fresse (which has a tricky start) or riding the gondola down from Tovière. And in poor weather, the high Tignes valley is an intimidatingly bleak place – enough to make any wavering beginner retreat to a bar with a book.

FOR CROSS-COUNTRY
Interesting variety
The Espace Killy has 40km/25 miles of cross-country trails. There are tracks on the frozen Lac de Tignes, along the valley between Val-Claret and Tignes-le-Lac, at Les Boisses and Les Brévières and up on the Grande Motte.

QUEUES
Very few
The queues here depend on snow conditions. If snow low down is poor, the Grande Motte funicular generates queues; the fast chairs in parallel with it are often quicker, despite the longer ride time. These lifts jointly shift a lot of people, with the result that the run down to Val-Claret can be unpleasantly crowded. The worst queues now are

for the cable-car on the glacier – half-hour waits are common.

Of course, if higher lifts are closed by heavy snow or high winds, the lifts on the lower slopes have big queues.

The famous afternoon queues for the slow Tommeuses chairs bringing Tignes residents back from the Val slopes to Tovière are now a fond memory, thanks to the fast eight-seat replacement. As one reporter said: 'It is an absolute godsend in what was a certain bottleneck.' It has cut queues at the Borsat quad to Col de Fresse, the easiest way back to Val-Claret.

Another reporter bemoans the lack of a hands-free lift pass system in Tignes saying: 'It's time the resort dragged itself into the 21st century.'

MOUNTAIN RESTAURANTS
An improvement at last
The restaurants built two seasons ago at the top of the Chaudannes chair – the Alpage for self-service and Lo Soli for table-service – are a huge improvement on the western side of the bowl. Their adjacent terraces share a superb view of the Grande Motte, and Lo Soli provides 'superb service'.

The opposite side of the bowl has the atmospheric chalet at the top of Tovière ('fairly basic' but 'very good portions') and the modern but pleasantly woody Chalet du Bollin – just a few metres above Val-Claret. Both offer table- and self-service.

The big Panoramic self-service restaurant at the top of the Grande Motte funicular has great views from its huge terrace, but it is traversed every few minutes by the next funicular-full of people. There's an excellent table-service 'cuisine gourmande' restaurant here too.

There are lots of easily accessible places for lunch in the resorts. One ski-to-the-door favourite of ours in le Lac is the ground-floor restaurant of the

Tignes

347

New building is in a much more attractive style than Tignes' original stark blocks. This is the Village Montana hotel in the new Les Almes area of Tignes-le-Lac →

OT TIGNES / DANIEL ROUSSELOT

GETTING THERE

Air Geneva 165km/103 miles (3½hr); Lyon 240km/ 149 miles (3½hr); Chambéry 136km/85 miles (2½hr).

Rail Bourg-St-Maurice (30km/19 miles); regular buses or taxi from station.

CHILDREN

The main schools run classes for children aged 4 to 12 (eg ESF 6 half days €118).

The hotel Diva in Val-Claret (0479 067000) has a nursery taking children from age 18 months.

The Marmottons kindergarten in Le Lac (0479 065167) takes children from 3 to 8.

hotel Montana, on the left as you descend from the Aiguille Percée. The Place is reported to be 'a genuine delight with good food and real family hospitality'. In Val-Claret the Fish Tank is described as 'very good value', and the Carline self-service restaurant as having 'cheerful staff and hearty portions'. In le Lac, l'Arbina serves 'absolutely first-class food'. In Les Brévières, a short walk round the corner into the village brings you to places much cheaper than the two by the piste. Sachette, for example, is crowded with artefacts from mountain life and offers 'lots of good, hearty cheese dishes'.

SCHOOLS AND GUIDES
Enormous choice
There are over half a dozen schools, including three specialist snowboard schools, plus various independent instructors. Reporters advise that pre-booking is 'essential' at busy times like Easter. The ESF and Evolution 2 are the main schools, with sections in each resort centre. Evolution 2 has received good reports, with class sizes of eight and standards of English good – the chaos on registration days is also mentioned. The ESF receives generally poor reports with large class sizes – up to 14 – and a 'follow me attitude' prevailing. One reporter said of his child's experience, 'I can quite see how it could turn a child away from skiing permanently.'

FACILITIES FOR CHILDREN
Mixed reports
In the past, we have had good reports on the Marmottons kindergartens, and on the 'experienced minders' of the Evolution 2 school in Le Lac. A reporter on the ESF considered the classes for five-year-olds too large.

STAYING THERE

HOW TO GO
Unremarkable range of options
All three main styles of accommodation are available through tour operators, mainly basic but some options are beginning to appear for those who like more creature comfort.

Chalets The choice of catered chalets is increasing. Total Ski have five chalets here for the first time in 2003/04. And child specialist Esprit Ski has a new chalet-hotel here. Ski Olympic's Chalet Rosset has been recommended by reporters: 'Superb, with a lovely lounge with views.' Neilson has a handful of places. Crystal's hotel-style Curling, plumb in the centre of Val-Claret, has neat public areas and spacious bedrooms.

Hotels The few hotels are small and concentrated in Le Lac. There are Club Meds at Val-Claret and Les Brévières.

((3) **Campanules** (0479 063436) Smartly rustic chalet in upper Le Lac, with good restaurant. One reporter was impressed enough this year to suggest that it deserved a 4-star rating.

((3) **Village Montana** (0479 400144) Stylishly woody 3-star complex on the east-facing slopes above Le Lac, with new 4-star suites section. Outdoor pool. Reporters praise it for 'spacious and comfortable' rooms, 'excellent 5-course dinners'. 'Lots of children in evidence too,' they say.

(2 **Arbina** (0479 063478) Well-run place close to the lifts in Le Lac, with lunchtime terrace, crowded après-ski bar and one of the best restaurants.

(2 **Marais** (0479 064006) Prettily furnished, simple little hotel in Tignes-les-Boisses.

Self-catering MGM's wood-clad L'Ecrin des Neiges apartments in lower Val-Claret are probably the best, with a pool. In upper Val-Claret, close to the Tovière chair, the Maeva 'Residence Le

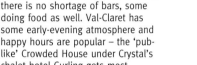
ACTIVITIES

Indoor 'Vitatignes' in Le Lac (balneotherapy centre with spa baths, sauna etc), 'Espace Forme' in Le Lac, 'Les Bains du Montana' in Le Lac, Fitness Club in Val-Claret (body-building, aerobics, squash, golf practice and simulation, sauna, hammam, Californian baths, hot-tub, swimming pool, massage), cinemas, covered tennis court, bowling, climbing wall

Outdoor Natural skating-rink, hang-gliding, paragliding, helicopter rides, snow-mobiles, husky dog-sleigh rides, diving beneath ice on lake, heli-skiing, 'La Banquise' for children (ice skating, snow sliding, solarium, snow activities, climbing activities, ski-joring)

Phone numbers
From abroad use the prefix +33 and omit the initial '0' of the phone number.

TOURIST OFFICE

t 0479 400440
information@tignes.net
www.tignes.net

Borsat' apartments are not too cramped, reasonably well equipped and with a communal lounge. The Chalet Club in Val-Claret is a collection of simple studios, but has the benefit of free indoor pool, sauna and in-house restaurant and bar. The supermarket at Le Lac is reported to be 'comprehensive but very expensive'.

EATING OUT
Good places scattered about
Each of the main centres has a range of restaurants, although the options in Le Lavachet are rather limited. Reservations are recommended for many restaurants. Finding anywhere with some atmosphere is difficult in Le Lac, though the food in some of the better hotels is good. We and readers have been impressed by the hotels Arbina and Campanules – 'Dinner is a class act from the waiting staff to the quality and presentation of the food,' said a reporter this year of the Campanules. Reporters recommend enthusiastically the small, friendly, atmospheric Clin d'Oeil – 'genuinely wholesome food made with the finest local ingredients'.

In Val-Claret the Cavern is recommended: 'Superb, and there's entertainment – have to book.' Pizza 2000 is recommended for 'reasonable prices, helpful staff, especially with large parties'. There is some debate over whether the pizzas are better here or at the Pignatta. The Ski d'Or is a swanky Relais & Châteaux hotel and according to one reporter, 'Its long established reputation is fully justified for its food and service as well as the host's hospitality.' Terrasses du Claret is recommended for large groups.

The Cordée in Les Boisses is said to offer unpretentious surroundings, great traditional French food, modest prices.

APRES-SKI
Early to bed
Tignes is rather quiet at night, though there is no shortage of bars, some doing food as well. Val-Claret has some early-evening atmosphere and happy hours are popular – the 'pub-like' Crowded House under Crystal's chalet hotel Curling gets most mentions. Other recommendations include the Fish Tank, a bar above the ski school meeting area – 'excellent audio visual system and satellite TV'.

Le Lac is a natural focus for immediate après-ski drinks, but don't expect anything too riotous. The bar of the hotel Arbina is our kind of spot – adequately cosy, spacious enough to absorb some groups, friendly service. It's a great place to sit outside and people watch. The Alpaka Lodge is recommended as 'relaxed with a staggering array of cocktails'.

The most animated bar in Le Lavachet is Harri's – 'as lively as ever', according to a 2003 reporter. The satellite TV here is popular.

Caves du Lac, Café de la Poste and Jack's are popular late haunts.

OFF THE SLOPES
Forget it
Despite the range of alternative activities, Tignes is a resort for those who want to use the slopes, where anyone who doesn't is liable to feel like a fish out of water. Some activities do get booked up quickly as well – a reporter said it was impossible to find a free dog-sleigh slot last April.

STAYING DOWN THE VALLEY
Only for visiting other resorts
See the Val-d'Isère chapter; the same considerations apply broadly here. But bear in mind that there are rooms to be had in simple hotels in Tignes-les-Boisses and Tignes-les-Brévières.

Tignes

Les Trois Vallées

The biggest lift-linked ski area in the world

Despite competing claims, notably from the Portes du Soleil, in practical terms the Trois Vallées cannot be beaten for sheer quantity of lift-served terrain. There is nowhere like it for a keen skier or boarder who wants to cover as much mileage as possible while rarely taking the same run repeatedly. It has a lot to offer everyone, from beginner to expert. And its resorts offer a wide range of alternatives – not only the quite widely known attractions of the big-name mega-resorts but also the increasingly appreciated low-key appeal of the smaller villages that have grown up more recently.

The runs of the Trois Vallées and their resorts are dealt with in six chapters. The four major resorts are Courchevel, Méribel, Les Menuires and Val-Thorens, but we also give chapters to St-Martin-de-Belleville, a small village down the valley from Les Menuires, and La Tania, a relatively new development between Courchevel and Méribel.

None of the resorts is cheap. **Les Menuires** is the cheapest but it is also the ugliest (though new developments around the original one are now being built in a much more acceptable style). The slopes around the village get too much sun for comfort, but across the valley are some of the best (and quietest) challenging pistes in the Trois Vallées on its north-facing La Masse. Down the valley from Les Menuires is **St-Martin-de-Belleville**, a charming traditional village which has been expanded in a sympathetic style. It has good-value accommodation and

improving lift links into the slopes of
Les Menuires and Méribel.

Up rather than down the Belleville
valley from Les Menuires, at 2300m/
7,550ft, **Val-Thorens** is the highest
resort in the Alps, and at 3230m/
10,560ft the top of its slopes is the
high point of the Trois Vallées. The
snow in this area is almost always
good, and it includes two glaciers
where good snow is guaranteed. But
the setting is bleak and the lifts are
vulnerable to closure in bad weather.
The purpose-built resort is very

convenient. Visually it is not
comparable to Les Menuires, thanks to
the smaller-scale design and more
thorough use of wood cladding, but it
still isn't to everyone's taste.

Méribel is a two-part resort. The
higher component, **Méribel-Mottaret**, is
the best placed of all the resorts for
getting to any part of the Trois Vallées
system in the shortest possible time.
It's now quite a spread-out place, with
some of the accommodation a long
way up the hillsides – great for access
to the slopes, less so for access to
nightlife. **Méribel** itself is 200m/660ft
lower and has long been a British
favourite, especially for chalet holidays.
It is the most attractive of the main
Trois Vallées resorts, built in chalet
style beside a long winding road up
the hillside. Parts of the resort are very
convenient for the slopes and the
village centre; parts are very far from
either. The growing hamlet of **Méribel-
Village** has its own chair-lift into the
system but is very isolated and quiet.

Courchevel has four parts. 1850 is
the most fashionable resort in France,
and can be the most expensive resort
in the Alps (though it doesn't have to
cost a fortune to stay there). The less
expensive parts – Le Praz (aka 1300),
1550 and 1650 – don't have the same
choice of nightlife and restaurants.
Many people rate the slopes around
Courchevel the best in the Trois
Vallées, with runs to suit all standards.
The snow tends to be better than in
neighbouring Méribel.

La Tania was built for the 1992
Olympics, just off the small road
linking Le Praz to Méribel. It has now
grown into a quiet, attractive, car-free
collection of chalets and chalet-style
apartments set among the trees, and is
popular with families. It has a good
nursery slope and lovely long
intermediate runs, but there are no
very easy runs back to it.

Les Trois Vallées

351

Val-d'Isère

On- and off-piste playground, with smart new lifts and reliable snow

COSTS

① ② ③ ④ ⑤ ⑥

RATINGS

The slopes

Snow	★★★★★
Extent	★★★★★
Expert	★★★★★
Intermediate	★★★★★
Beginner	★★★
Convenience	★★★
Queues	★★★★
Mountain restaurants	★★

The rest

Scenery	★★★
Resort charm	★★★
Off-slope	★★

KEY FACTS

Resort	1850m
	6,070ft

For entire Espace Killy area

Slopes	1550-3455m	
	5,090-11,340ft	
Lifts		97
Pistes		300km
		185 miles
Green		15%
Blue		46%
Red		28%
Black		11%
Snowmaking		24km
		15 miles

352

- ➕ Huge area linked with Tignes, with lots of runs for all abilities
- ➕ Big recent investment in new lifts
- ➕ One of the great resorts for lift-served off-piste runs
- ➕ High altitude of most slopes means snow is more or less guaranteed
- ➕ Wide choice of schools, especially for off-piste lessons and guiding
- ➕ For a high resort, the town is attractive, very lively at night, and offers a good range of restaurants
- ➕ Wide range of package holidays and accommodation
- ➕ Piste grooming and staff attitudes have improved noticeably

- ➖ Piste grading understates the difficulty of many runs – though moguls on greens now uncommon
- ➖ You're quite likely to need the bus at the start or end of the day
- ➖ Most lifts and slopes are liable to close when the weather is bad
- ➖ Runs to valley level often tricky
- ➖ Nursery slopes not ideal
- ➖ High-season crowds on some runs
- ➖ Still some lifts in need of upgrading
- ➖ Main off-piste slopes get tracked out very quickly
- ➖ Seems at times more British than French – especially in low season
- ➖ Few good mountain restaurants

Val-d'Isère is one of the world's best resorts for experts – attracted by the extent of lift-served off-piste – and for confident, mileage-hungry intermediates. But you don't have to be particularly adventurous to enjoy the resort, and the village ambience has improved greatly in recent years.

The list of drawbacks above looks long, but they are mainly petty complaints, whereas the plus-points are mainly things that weigh heavily in the balance, both for us and for the many enthusiastic reporters we hear from. The last of the plus-points – the clear recent improvements in piste grooming and lift staff attitudes – is as welcome as it is surprising. If the lift company would make a serious attempt to grade its runs sensibly, Val would make more friends than it does at present among nervous intermediates who panic on mogul fields.

Despite the lack of compelling mountain restaurants – normally a key requirement of your editors – this is, in the end, simply one of our favourite resorts in the world.

THE RESORT

Val-d'Isère spreads along a remote valley, which is a dead end in winter. The road in from Bourg-St-Maurice brings you dramatically through a rocky defile to the satellite mini-resort of La Daille – a convenient but hideous slope-side apartment complex and the base of lifts into the major Bellevarde sector of the slopes. The outskirts of Val proper are dreary, but as you approach the centre the legacy of the 1992 Olympics becomes more evident: new wood- and stone-cladding, culminating in the tasteful pedestrian-only Val Village complex. The few remnants of the original old village are tucked away behind this.

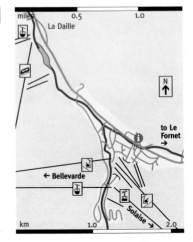

The centre of town with the nursery slopes behind the church. Lifts go up to the left to Solaise and to the right to Bellevarde →

OT VAL D'ISERE / CHRISTOPHE GUIBBAUD

NEWS

Two excellent new lifts opened for the 2002/03 season. The Bellevarde cable car was replaced by a plush new 24-seater (plus six standing if need be) gondola, the Olympique, which whisks 2,600 people an hour from the resort centre to the top in just five minutes.

And the slow Tommeuses chairs up to Tovière and a link with Tignes were replaced by a fast eight-seat chair, which has cut the journey time there dramatically

For the 2003/04 season a new high-speed six-seat chair-lift will replace the old two-person up-and-over Leissierès chair which forms a two-way link between the Solaise and Col de l'Iseran areas.

And a four-star luxury hotel is due to open in December 2003. Situated at the foot of the Bellevarde mountain, Les Barmes de l'Ours will feature luxury rooms, suites, apartments, restaurants, fitness and beauty centre and a swimming pool.

Many first-time visitors find the resort much 'prettier' than they expect a big-name high resort to be, and returning visitors generally find things improving.

Turn right at the centre and you drive under the nursery slopes and Val's big lifts up to Bellevarde and Solaise to a lot of new development beyond. Continue up the main valley instead, and you come to Le Fornet – an old village and the third major lift station.

There is a lot of traffic around, but the resort is working to get cars under control and make the centre more pedestrian-friendly.

The location of your accommodation isn't crucial. Free shuttle-buses run along the main street linking the main lift stations. It is one of the most efficient bus services we've come across; even in peak periods you never have to wait more than a few minutes. But in the evening frequency plummets and dedicated après-skiers will want to be within walking distance of the centre. The development up the side valley beyond the main lift station is

mainly attractive; some places are a pleasant stroll from the centre, but the farthest-flung are a long slog – unless you're happy to pay for taxis, you need a car or a tour operator that provides transport. La Daille and Le Fornet have their (quite different) attractions for those less concerned about nightlife.

A car is of no great value around the resort, but simplifies outings to other resorts. A six-day lift pass gives a day in the new Paradiski area (Les Arcs and La Plagne combined), plus the Trois Vallées. Other resorts nearby are Ste-Foy and La Rosière.

THE MOUNTAINS

Although there are wooded slopes above the village on all sectors, in practice most of the runs here are on open slopes above the tree line.

This year's reporters agreed that piste grooming continues to improve and is now generally described as 'good' (it was pretty awful a few years ago). We continue to get complaints about the poor signing though,

particularly at piste junctions – and, especially, of the piste grading. 'As erratic as ever' and 'inconsistent' said two reporters this year. Another wrote, 'This resort is a prime example of how colour blind the French are. We took some timid intermediates and they had to get the lift down every night.'

The local radio carries weather reports in English as well as French. Precision Ski is a highly-regarded British-run ski shop, which has a Snowtec centre at La Daille where you can test all the latest skis for 25 euros a day (refunded if you buy).

THE SLOPES
Vast and varied

Val-d'Isère's slopes divide into three main sectors. **Bellevarde** is the mountain that is home to Val-d'Isère's famous downhill course – the OK piste, which opens each season's World Cup Alpine circus in December (in 2003 it will be on the weekend of 13/14 December). You can reach Bellevarde by funicular from La Daille. Up to last season, this was the favoured route. But last season a powerful new gondola replaced the old cable-car from near the centre of town (see News). It has met with universal approval from our reporters. 'A revelation' says one, 'swallows crowds and is the smoothest ride ever,' says another. From the top you can get back down to the main lifts, play on a variety of drags and chairs at altitude or take a choice of lifts to the Tignes slopes, including the new fast Tommeuses chair-lift, which is a vast improvement on the slow chairs it replaced and provides quick access to the off-piste and pisted runs below it.

Solaise is the other mountain accessible directly from Val-d'Isère. The Solaise Express fast quad chair-lift takes you a few metres higher than the parallel cable-car. Once up, a short drag takes you over a plateau and down to a variety of chairs that serve this very sunny area of predominantly gentle pistes.

From near the top of this area you can catch a chair (which will be a new six-pack next season) over to the third main area, above and below the **Col de l'Iseran**. The area can also be reached

boarding

Val-d'Isère is good for boarders, though Tignes is a more popular boarder destination. Most of the main lifts are cable-cars, chair-lifts and gondolas, with very few drag-lifts. But there are a few flat areas where you'll need to scoot or walk. Experts will revel in the off-piste. There are several specialist snowboard shops and schools including Misty Fly. The village nursery area is ideal for trying boarding out and Le Fornet is good to progress to. The terrain-park is great.

3300m/10,83oft
Glacier de Pissaillas
Col Pers
2950m
Col de l'Iseran
2765m
2900m
Col de la Leisse
Col de Fresse
2770m
Tignes ⌄
Tour Charvet
Le Manchet
1940m
Tovière
2705m
2325m
Bellevarde
2705m
Solaise
2560m
Le Châtelard
Le Fornet
1930m
Le Laisinant
Val d'Isère
185om/6,070ft
La Daille
1785m

OT VAL D'ISERE / MARIO COLONEL

Pretty much the whole of Val d'Isère is in view here. The pic is taken from Le Fornet and La Daille is at the far end with the funicular going up to Bellevarde ↓

by cable-car from Le Fornet in the valley. The chair-lift ride is spectacular or scary, depending on your head for heights: it climbs over a steep ridge and then drops suddenly down the other side. The alternative way over, through a tunnel reached by a short, steep drag-lift, is now apparently closed because the tunnel collapsed.

The runs at Col de l'Iseran are predominantly easy, with spectacular views and access to the region's most beautiful off-piste terrain.

TERRAIN-PARKS
Beginners and experts welcome
There's a very good terrain-park above the top of the La Daille gondola. It is served by two drag-lifts and a rope-tow. As well as a half-pipe, quarter-pipes and boarder-cross courses there are assorted bumps, jumps and railslides catering to park-beginners and park-experts alike. 'Enough to keep you entertained for many hours,' said one reporter. Four snow-guns are used to ensure good snow-cover.

SNOW RELIABILITY
Difficult to beat
In years when lower resorts have suffered, Val-d'Isère has rarely been short of snow. Its height means you can almost always get back to the village, especially because of the snowmaking facilities on the lower slopes of all the main routes home. But even more important is that in each sector there are lots of lifts and runs above mid-mountain, between about 2300m and 2900m (7,550ft and 9,510ft). Many of the slopes face roughly north. And there is access to glaciers at Pissaillas or over in Tignes, although both take a while to get to.

FOR EXPERTS
One of the world's best
Val-d'Isère is one of the top resorts in the world for experts. The main attraction is the huge range of beautiful off-piste possibilities – see feature panel.

There may be better resorts for really steep pistes – there are certainly lots in North America – but there is plenty on-piste to amuse the expert here, despite the small number of

Oxygène is a ski and snowboard school that operates in Val d'Isère, La Plagne and – new for 2003/04 – Courchevel. As well as on-piste group and private lessons, they offer off-piste tuition and guiding

Val d'Isère contact details:
t 00 33 479 419958
valdisere@oxygene-ski.com
www.oxygene-ski.com

THE BEST LIFT-SERVED OFF-PISTE IN THE WORLD?

Few resorts can rival the extent of lift-served off-piste skiing in Val-d'Isère and Tignes; there are countless classic runs waiting to be discovered. With the help of Oxygène we have put together this brief glimpse of a few of them.

Some runs are ideal for adventurous intermediates looking to try off-piste for the first time. The Tour du Charvet starts from the top of the Grand Pre chair-lift on the back of Bellevarde. For most of the way it is very gentle, with only a few steeper pitches amid glorious scenery. It ends up at the bottom of the Manchet chair up to the Solaise area. The Pays Désert is on the Pissaillas glacier, high above Le Fornet and is reached by traversing away from the pistes at the top of the lift system, above cliffs. The terrain is generally very easy and the views superb. You end up at the Pays Désert T-bar.

For more experienced off-piste skiers, Col Pers is one of our favourite runs. Again, it starts a traverse away from the Pissaillas glacier. You go over a pass into a big, wide, fairly gentle bowl with glorious views and endless ways down. If the snow is good, you can drop down into the Gorges de Malpasset, and ski over the frozen Isère river back to the Le Fornet cable-car. Or you can take a higher route if there's not enough snow.

Over in Tignes, the Tour de Pramecou is another of our favourites. It starts from the Grande Motte area and after a long, flat section and a couple of short walks, you end up at the top of a long, steep, wide, north-facing slope where the snow is usually excellent. You swoop down this and end up on the Carline piste which takes you back to the bottom of the Motte.

There are endless other off-piste options such as Cugnai and Danaides on Solaise, Banane and the Couloir des Pisteurs on Bellevarde, the Vallon de la Sache and the North Face of the Grande Motte in Tignes. Plus many more.

But don't dream of doing any off-piste runs without a fully qualified guide or instructor, such as one from Oxygène. Route finding is difficult, avalanche danger can be high and hidden hazards such as cliffs and crevasses lurk.

Val-d'Isère

357

blacks on the piste map. Many of the red and blue runs are steep enough to get mogulled.

On Bellevarde the famous Face run is the main attraction – often mogulled from top to bottom, but not worryingly steep. Epaule is the sector's other black run – where the moguls are hit by long exposure to sun and can be slushy or rock-hard too often for our liking (it is prone to closure for these reasons too). There are several challenging ways down from Solaise to the village: all steep, though none fearsomely so. This has traditionally been classic bumps territory, but the resort's new enthusiasm for grooming has extended to these slopes. Says one reporter, 'Despite my moaning about the removal of virtually every mogul on the piste, it's a real pleasure to blast down Solaise as a first run in the morning. It's beautifully groomed and absolutely deserted, as everyone else continues up to Tête de Solaise.'

Wayne Watson of off-piste school Alpine Expérience puts a daily diary of off-piste snow conditions and runs on the web at www.alpineexperience.com.

FOR INTERMEDIATES
Quantity and quality

Val-d'Isère has even more to offer intermediates than experts. There's enough here to keep you interested for several visits – though there are complaints about crowded high-season pistes, and the less experienced should be aware that many runs are under-classified. This remains a regular reporter complaint.

In the Solaise sector is a network of gentle blue runs, ideal for building confidence. And there are a couple of beautiful runs from here through the woods to Le Laisinant, from where you catch the bus – these are ideal for bad weather, though prone to closure in times of avalanche danger.

Most of the runs in the Col de l'Iseran sector are even easier – ideal for early and hesitant intermediates. Those marked blue at the top of the glacier could really be classified green.

Bellevarde has a huge variety of runs ideally suited to intermediates of all levels. From Bellevarde itself there is a choice of green, blue and red runs of varying pitch. And the wide runs from Tovière normally give you the

Ski Club Rep Resort

skiclub.co.uk
0845 45 807 80
100 Years 1903-2003

choice of groomed piste or moguls.

A snag for early intermediates is that runs back to the valley can be challenging. The easiest way is to head down to La Daille, where there is a green run – but it should be classified blue (in some resorts it would be red). It gets very crowded and mogulled at the end of the day. None of the runs from Bellevarde and Solaise back to Val itself is really easy. The blue Santons run from Bellevarde takes you through a long, narrow gun barrel, which often has people standing around plucking up courage, making things even trickier. On Solaise there isn't much to choose between the blue and red ways down – and they're both narrow in places. At the top, there's no option other than the red run in full view of the lifts. Many early intermediates sensibly choose to ride the lifts down – take the chair for a spectacular view.

FOR BEGINNERS
OK if you know where to go
The nursery slope right by the centre of town is 95 per cent perfect; it's just a pity that the top is unpleasantly steep. The lifts serving it are free.

Once off the nursery slopes, you have to know where to find easy runs; many of the greens should be blue, or even red. One local instructor admits: 'We have to have green runs on the map, even if we don't have so many green slopes – otherwise beginners wouldn't come to Val-d'Isère.'

A good place for your first real runs off the nursery slopes is the Madeleine green run on Solaise – now served by a fast six-pack. The Col de l'Iseran runs are also gentle and wide, and not overcrowded. There is good progression terrain on Bellevarde, too, but no genuinely easy way back to the valley.

FOR CROSS-COUNTRY
Limited
There are a couple of loops towards La Daille and another out past Le Laisinant. More picturesque is the one going from Le Châtelard (on the road past the main cable-car station) to the Manchet chair. But keen cross-country enthusiasts should go elsewhere.

QUEUES
Few problems
Queues to get out of the resort have been kept in check by new lifts – first

the funicular at La Daille, then fast chair-lifts as alternatives to the two main cable-cars, and now the replacement of the Bellevarde cable-car by a big new gondola. For some years the quickest way to Tignes has been to take the fast quad to Col de Fresse, but replacing the slow and crowded Tommeuses chairs with a high-speed eight-person chair has made travel via Tovière a realistic proposition once again. Coming back from Val-Claret at the end of the day is now much quicker, thanks to a fast, dual-loading, six-person chair-lift direct to Col de Fresse, with a run down to La Daille. Make sure you get into the correct queue (on the left): half the chairs stop part-way up the hill, serving runs back into Val-Claret.

The number of slow chair-lifts scattered about the area, particularly in Tignes, is still a common complaint though. Crowded pistes is another.

The slow Lac chair that links the bottom of the Madeleine up to the Tête Solaise can generate queues. But the wait at the end of the day for the chair back from Col de l'Iseran to

Solaise should be eliminated by the new six-pack planned for 2003/04.

If you plan a return visit, keep your lift pass – those with a week's pass bought in the last three years are entitled to a 'loyal customer' reduction.

MOUNTAIN RESTAURANTS
Getting better – slowly

The mountain restaurants mainly consist of big self-service places with vast terraces at the top of major lifts.

The Fruitière at the top of La Daille gondola, a table-service place kitted out with stuff rescued from a dairy in the valley, continues to get good reports: 'Excellent, the best we have been to,' says one. The Folie Douce is a functional but popular self-service place at the same spot. Last season it was very lively on the terrace on warm afternoons, with people being entertained by a DJ and live musicians. Other recommendations: the Trifollet, about halfway down the OK run – 'fast service, good pizzas and an entertaining view of the slopes' – 'very good for egg and chips' – 'soak up the sun on the balcony or curl up in front

Val-d'Isère

359

SCHOOLS

Alpine Expérience
t 0479 062881 e info
@alpineexperience.com

ESF
t 0479 060234 e esf.
valdisere@wanadoo.fr

Evolution 2
t 0479 411672 e val
disere@evolution2.com

Misty Fly Snowboard
t 0479 400874

Mountain Masters
t 0479 060514

Ogier Ski School
t 0479 061893

Oxygène
t 0479 419958

Ski Concept
t 0688 672563

Snow Fun
t 0479 061979
info@snowfun.fr

Stages Val Gliss
t 0479 060072

Tétra Hors-Piste
t 0479 419707

Development Centre
t 0615 553156

Top Ski
t 0479 061480
e top.ski.val.isere@
wanadoo.fr

Classes (ESF prices)
6 days (3hr am, 2½hr
pm) €187
Private lessons
€33 for 1hr

GUIDES

Mountain guide office
t 0479 060567

of the log fire'; Marmottes, in the middle of the Bellevarde bowl – big sunny terrace, basic self-service (vending machines for coffee and hot chocolate); the Signal at the top of the Le Fornet cable-car – 'excellent service and value, huge portions' says one reporter, but 'mediocre food at the self-service section', says another; the 'small and friendly' Bar de L'Ouillette, at the base of the Madeleine chair-lift – 'good food at reasonable prices'; the Datcha, at the bottom of the Cugnai lift – 'excellent salads, if expensive'; and the Tanière, set between the two chairs going up Face de Bellevarde – 'food well priced and service friendly, popular with lifties and pisteurs'.

There are restaurants on the lower slopes at La Daille that are reachable on snow and by pedestrians. Tufs is 'a busy, friendly place that does rather a good pizza' and has a 'good-value buffet on the first floor', and the Toit du Monde just above it offers 'excellent service' and a mix of European and Asian cuisine (and is owned by violinist Vanessa Mae's mum).

Of course there are lots of places actually in the resort villages. When at Col de l'Iseran, one possible plan for lunch on a wintry day is to descend to the rustic Arolay at Le Fornet – 'The savoyard salad was excellent as was the omelette,' says one reporter, although another complained that 'the service was a bit haphazard'.

SCHOOLS AND GUIDES
A very wide choice
There is a huge choice of schools, guides and private instructors. But they all get busy and at peak periods it's best to book in advance. Practically all of the schools run off-piste groups at various levels of competence, as well as on-piste lessons. The Oxygène school helped us put together our run down on Val d'Isère's off-piste possibilities and have operated in the resort for seven seasons now. The ESF has received bad press in recent years but one 2003 reporter described a private lesson with them as 'one of the best ever'. Outside the ESF, practically all the instructors and guides speak good English, and many are native English-speakers.

We've heard from lots of satisfied Snow Fun pupils: 'excellent' is the general verdict among reporters. A regular reporter sent in a glowing report of an off-piste week led by Snow Fun founder Tchenko this year. There is also praise for Evolution 2: 'really good, with very encouraging instructors', 'extremely worthwhile'.

Last year the big news in the schools business was the launch of a new school, The Development Centre, based in a big new Precision Ski shop in the heart of the village. This group of British instructors offers intensive clinics for all levels of skier and has been highly praised: 'Two morning classes helped transform my skiing,' says one reporter. Mountain Masters is a group of highly-qualified British and French instructors and guides. Misty Fly is a specialist snowboard school.

There are two schools which specialise in guided off-piste groups – an excellent way to get off-piste safely without the cost of hiring a guide as an individual. We have had excellent mornings out with Alpine Expérience

CHILDREN

The ski schools offer children's classes from age 4 (ESF €182 for 6 days). Le Village des Enfants (0479 400981) takes children from 3 to 8, from 9 to 5.30 Sun-Thu, Fri 9am to 2pm. Le Petit Poucet (0479 061397) takes children from age 3, from 9am to 5.30. Snowfun's Teddy Bear Club and Superteddy classes takes children aged 3 to 6 for lessons of 1½hr and 2½hr per day respectively. Older children can be left in classes all day. The tourist office has a list of babysitters.

(Canadian, French, Italian, British guides) who also do 'excellent off-piste lessons' in the afternoons. Recent reports say Top Ski (mostly French guides) is 'highly recommended' and 'efficient' too.

Heli-trips can be arranged from over the border in Italy because heli-drops are banned in France.

FACILITIES FOR CHILDREN
Good tour op possibilities

Many people prefer to use the facilities of UK tour operators such as Mark Warner or Ski Beat. But there's a 'children's village' for 3- to 8-year-olds, with supervised indoor and outdoor activities on the village nursery slopes. A past reporter was 'very pleased' with the childcare there: 'The staff speak English, and are very organised, in particular about the children's safety.'

We have personal experience of the indifference of the ESF's handling of children, reinforced by a more recent report from the father of two children who were placed in classes of French pupils and subsequently 'abandoned in mid-class' by their instructors. Another

reporter complained that Evolution 2 constrained their son to the nursery slopes all week despite being capable of skiing greens and blues.

STAYING THERE

HOW TO GO
Lots of choice

More British tour operators go to Val-d'Isère than to any other resort. The choice of chalets and chalet-hotels is vast. There is a Club Med 'village'.
Chalets There is everything from budget chalets – some away from the centre, at Le Châtelard, Le Laisinant and Le Fornet – to the most luxurious you could demand, such as Eagle's Nest (run by Scott Dunn Ski) in the newly developed Les Carats district, and The Farmhouse (run by VIP) next to the church. Both Scott Dunn and VIP offer other luxury places, too, as do Finlays, Lotus Supertravel and Descent International. For 2003/04 Scott Dunn has taken over four of The Ski Company's group of chalets on the edge of the village. YSE is a Val d'Isère specialist with 27 chalets, including

OT VAL-D'ISERE / AGENCE NUTS

The area around the old core of the village is traditional in style although mainly modern ➜

GETTING THERE

Air Geneva 180km/112 miles (4hr); Lyon 220km/140 miles (4hr); Chambéry 130km/80 miles (3hr).

Rail Bourg-St-Maurice (31km/19 miles); regular buses from station.

Phone numbers
From abroad use the prefix +33 and omit the initial '0' of the phone number.

ACTIVITIES

Indoor Swimming pool, sports hall (basketball, volleyball, table tennis, badminton, trampoline and gymnastics), library, bridge, health centres in the hotels Christiania, Brussels and Le Val d'Isère (sauna, hammam, hot-tub, body building, massages, solarium etc), cinema

Outdoor Natural skating rink, hang-gliding, quad-bikes, all-terrain karts, ice driving, snow-mobiles, paragliding, snow-shoe outings, heli-skiing, microlight trips, ice-climbing, dog-sledding, walking

some luxury ones. Le Ski has six splendid all-en-suite chalets grouped together just behind the main street. Ski Beat has a smart five-unit chalet at La Daille.

There are several chalet hotels. Mark Warner has four, including the family-friendly Cygnaski, the nightlife hot spot Moris and the Val d'Isère in the centre, which enjoys free use of an outdoor swimming pool.

Hotels There are about 40 to choose from, mostly 2- and 3-star, but for such a big international resort surprisingly few are notably attractive. We look forward to inspecting the new Barmes de l'Ours when it opens (see News).

((((4) **Christiania** (0479 060825) Big chalet, probably best in town. Chic, with friendly staff. Sauna.

((((4) **Blizzard** (0479 060207) Comfortable. Convenient. Indoor-outdoor pool. Good food.

((((4) **Latitudes** (0479 061888) Modern, stylish. Piano bar, nightclub. Leisure centre: sauna, steam room, whirlpool.

(((3) **Grand Paradis** (0479 061173) Excellent position. Good food.

(((3) **Savoyarde** (0479 060155) Rustic decor. Leisure centre. Good food. Rooms a bit small.

(((3) **Kandahar** (0479 060239) Smart, newish building above Taverne d'Alsace on main street.

(((3) **Mercure** (0479 061293) Highly recommended by one of our most reliable reporters: 'It doesn't look much from the outside, but the food and the wine list are excellent.'

(((3) **Sorbiers** (0479 062377) Modern but cosy B&B hotel, not far out. 'Clean, comfortable, good-sized rooms.'

(((3) **Samovar** (0479 061351) In La Daille. Traditional, with good food. 'Very friendly and helpful staff.'

Self-catering There are thousands of properties to choose from. UK operators offer lots of them, but they tend to get booked up early. The MGM

Chalets du Laisinant apartments, out of town on the road to Le Fornet, look good. Local agency Val-d'Isère Agence has a large selection of places and a good brochure. The local supermarkets are well stocked.

EATING OUT
Plenty of good, affordable places

Restaurant standards are generally high. The 70-odd restaurants include Italian, Alsatian, Tex-Mex, even Japanese ones, but most offer good French dishes. A very helpful Guide des Tables is freely distributed. High-season visitors have found that it is essential to book ahead – especially on Wednesday when most UK chalet staff get the night off.

There are plenty of pleasant mid-priced places. The 'bustling and busy' Perdrix Blanche is popular, offering 'brilliant' fish dishes in particular. Or head for the Taverne d'Alsace, another old favourite – 'big and busy, but good fare'. Tufs and Toit du Monde nearby (formerly the Crêch'ouna) are open in the evenings (see Mountain Restaurants). Family-run Chez Paolo, next to the bus stop for Le Fornet, is praised for its 'excellent pizzas and pastas'.

But our favourite – and that of many reporters – for a special night out is the Chalet du Crêt, off the road on the northern edge of downtown Val. Set in a 300-year-old stone farmhouse, beautifully renovated by the Franco-British couple who run it, this place serves a fixed-price menu starting with a magnificent hors-d'oeuvres spread. Not cheap, but highly satisfying. One reporter who ate there last season says, 'It was an excellent meal as ever, superb food and our table of 10 racked up a wine bill to be proud of.' A rival for a top-of-the-range meal is the Grande Ourse by the nursery slope.

Those on tight budgets should try

Chez Nano (next to Dick's Tea Bar) – 'fantastic pizza and profiteroles'. The Melting Pot also gets good reviews for its unusual menu, which includes Thai dishes and 'a good selection of veggie options'. The Corniche is recommended for being 'traditional French, very enjoyable'; the Pub for being 'very French and well worth seeking out'; Casa Scara for 'good food, though the service was slow' and Grand Cocors for 'excellent food and choice'.

APRES-SKI
Very lively

Nightlife is surprisingly energetic, given that most people have spent a hard day on the slopes. There are lots of bars, many with happy hours followed by music and dancing later on.

The Folie Douce, at the top of the La Daille gondola, has become an Austrian-style tea-time rave, with music and dancing; normally you can ride the gondola down, but it can be closed by the weather, so be prepared to ski down. At La Daille the bar at the Samovar hotel is 'a good spot for a beer after skiing'. In downtown Val, Café Face (very lively, excellent) and the Moris pub (in the Mark Warner chalet) fill up as the slopes close, and Bar Jacques and the Perdrix Blanche bar are popular with locals. Bananas is a good place to soak up the last rays of the sun and has a cosy wooden interior. Victor's bar is popular before it turns into a restaurant later on –

black-and-white decor and stainless steel toilets. The basement Taverne d'Alsace is quiet and relaxing.

Later on, the famous Dick's Tea Bar is the main disco and gets packed, but it receives mixed reports, with one reporter complaining about flooded toilets and extortionate prices after 11pm and another saying 'so good we were boring and went there all the time'. The nearby Petit Danois is a good alternative and somewhat less frenetic than Dick's. Beware of the Red Erik beer – very tasty and strong. Café Face blasts out loud music.

For those who like a quieter time, there are hotel bars, piano bars and cocktail lounges.

OFF THE SLOPES
Not much

Val is primarily a resort for those keen to get on to the slopes – though one non-skiing reporter was 'very satisfied' with the facilities. The swimming pool has been renovated, but the other sports facilities are not particularly impressive. Reporters have commented on the range of shops, which is better than in most high French resorts. Lunchtime meetings present problems: the easily accessible mountain restaurants are few, and your friends may prefer lunching miles away in places like Les Brévières. One reporter suggests that it's worth watching out for firework displays and torchlit descents, described as 'spectacular'.

TOURIST OFFICE

t 0479 060660
info@valdisere.com
www.valdisere.com

OT VAL D'ISERE / PIERRE HUCHETTE
Some of the gentle runs on Solaise. The chair going up in the shadow over the ridge on the left is the link to the Col de l'Iseran area and will be a new six-pack for 2003/04 ↓

Val-d'Isère

363

Valmorel

Pretty, purpose-built resort with fair-sized area of slopes

COSTS

①②③④⑤⑥

RATINGS

The slopes
Snow	★★★
Extent	★★★
Expert	★★
Intermediate	★★★★
Beginner	★★★★★
Convenience	★★★★★
Queues	★★★★
Mountain restaurants	★★

The rest
Scenery	★★★
Resort charm	★★★★
Off-slope	★★

NEWS

For 2003/04 the terrain-park will be served by a new drag-lift.

For 2002/03 snowmaking was expanded and 10 new, quieter snow-guns replaced older ones (a good thing because some reporters have complained of noisy snow-guns keeping them awake at night).

364

+ Fairly extensive slopes provide something for everyone

+ The most sympathetically designed French purpose-built resort

+ Largely slope-side accommodation

+ Beginners and children particularly well catered for

− Few challenging pistes

− Fairly low in altitude, so good snow not guaranteed

− Little variety in accommodation or in restaurants and bars

− Still a lot of slow lifts

Built from scratch in the mid-1970s, Valmorel was intended to look and feel like a mountain village: a traffic-free main street with low-rise hamlets grouped around it. The end result is an attractive, friendly sort of place. The slopes are extensive by most standards and with good snow conditions there's enough here to keep everyone except real experts happy. Unashamedly aimed at the middle ground (intermediates, families and mixed-ability groups), Valmorel has considerable appeal because it has been so well put together.

THE RESORT

Valmorel is the main resort in 'Le Grand Domaine' – a ski area that links the Tarentaise with the Maurienne, by way of the Col de la Madeleine. Bourg-Morel is the heart of the resort – a traffic-free street where you'll find most of the shops and restaurants. It's pleasant and usually lively, with a distinctly family feel – but a 2003 reporter says the main street can get very crowded. Scattered here and there on the hillside are the six 'hameaux' with most of the accommodation. Hameau-du-Mottet is convenient – it is at the top of the Télébourg (the cross-village lift) with good access to the main lifts and from the return runs. All the mega-ski areas of the Tarentaise

are within driving distance – and an off-piste tour of some starts from the Col du Mottet above Valmorel.

THE MOUNTAINS

Beginners and intermediates will take to Valmorel. Those looking for more of a challenge will find it limited. Variety is provided by sectors of distinctive character, and the extent is enough to provide interesting day-trips. There are still a few long, awkward drag-lifts, but most can be avoided.

Slopes The pistes are spread out in an interesting arrangement over a number of minor valleys and ridges either side of the Col de la Madeleine. The most heavily used route out of the village is via the high-speed Altispace quad chair

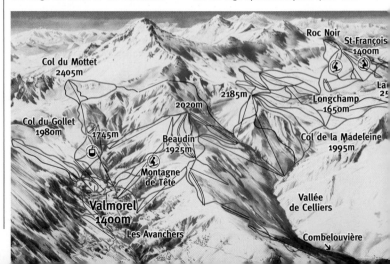

KEY FACTS

Resort	1400m
	4,595ft

For Grande Domaine	
Slopes	1250-2550m
	4,100-8,370 ft
Lifts	56
Pistes	153km
	95 miles
Green	33%
Blue	39%
Red	19%
Black	9%
Snowmaking	9km
	6 miles

For Domaine de Valmorel only	
Slopes	1250-2185m
	4,100-7,170ft
Lifts	38
Pistes	95km
	59 miles

Phone numbers
From abroad use the prefix +33 and omit the initial '0' of the phone number.

TOURIST OFFICE

t 0479 098555
info@valmorel.com
www.valmorel.com

with covers, which takes you over the main pistes down to the resort. From the top, a network of lifts and pistes takes you to the Col de la Madeleine and beyond that to Lauzière or the slopes of St-François and Longchamp at the far western end of the area. The Mottet sector and the Gollet area have their own runs back towards the village, or you can work your way to the Beaudin and Madeleine sectors.

Terrain-parks There's a terrain-park under the Crève Coeur chair, with a boarder-cross course and half-pipe. A special terrain-park-only pass is available (15 euros a day).

Snow reliability With many runs below 2000m/6,560ft, good snow is not guaranteed. Mottet is north-facing and usually has the best snow. There's snowmaking on the nursery slopes and the main runs back to the village.

Experts There are a few challenging pistes, but it is the off-piste that is attractive. Because the resort does not attract experts, off-piste powder can lie untracked for days after a snowfall. Gollet is usually a good place for moguls – plenty of them, but not too big and not too hard. There are steep black runs below the top section of the Mottet chair and some interesting off-piste variants. The Lauzière chair can seem a trek, but it's underused and a lot of fun, provided it hasn't suffered too much sun. You can also explore a lovely deserted north-facing off-piste run here if you hire a guide. Touring is a popular activity in the region.

Intermediates The whole area except the steepest black runs is ideal. The slopes down to St-François-Longchamp are within easy striking distance, and Valmorel is also a fine place for intermediates to get their first taste of off-piste on the gentle, open fields beside pistes. The red stretch of the main thoroughfare back to the village – from Beaudin along the line of the

snow-guns – can be quite daunting at the end of the day.

Beginners There are dedicated learning areas ('still the best we've seen, 10/10' according to one reporter) right by the village for both adults and children. Progress from novice to beginner usually sees the children heading for the top of the Pierrafort gondola and adults for the Beaudin sector.

Snowboarding There are decent intermediate runs – but new boarders will find some of the drag-lifts tricky.

Cross-country Trails adding up to 23km/14 miles can be reached by bus.

Queues There can be 10-minute waits for the Altispace chair out of town. The Frêne drags can't cope when everyone is returning to Valmorel. And there are a lot of slow, old chairs and drag-lifts.

Mountain restaurants There are half a dozen or so mountain restaurants in the area, none of them appalling or wonderful. Banquise 2000 has a great location at Col de la Madeleine; Prariond has been recommended.

Schools and guides We've had some good reports about the school over the years. Teaching for first-timers is a speciality of the resort.

Facilities for children Saperlipopette is a comprehensive childcare facility, and children taking ski lessons can have lunch there, too. Advance booking is essential except for very quiet times.

STAYING THERE

How to go Self-catering packages are the norm but there are some catered chalets, mainly aimed at families. One annual visitor prefers staying in Combelouvière below Valmorel – 'sunnier and quieter'.

Hotels There are only three hotels: the Planchamp (0479 099700) is the best, with a good French restaurant.

Self-catering The Athamante et Valeriane apartments have been praised by resort regulars.

Eating out You can check out most of Valmorel's restaurants in 15 minutes of wandering along the main street. The Grange and Ski Roc were recommended by a 2003 reporter.

Après-ski Immediate après-ski is centred on the lively outdoor cafes. After-dark activities are concentrated around the main street.

Off the slopes It's a very pretty but not a great place to hang around if you're not using the slopes – unless you are happy spending time in cafes.

Val-Thorens

Europe's highest resort, with guaranteed good snow

RATINGS

The slopes

Snow	★★★★★
Extent	★★★★★
Expert	★★★★
Intermediate	★★★★★
Beginner	★★★★
Convenience	★★★★★
Queues	★★★
Mountain restaurants	★★★★

The rest

Scenery	★★★
Resort charm	★★
Off-slope	★★

NEWS

For 2002/03, a new blue run was created from the top of the Grand Fond Funitel. This year, the nearby Plateau drags will be replaced by a chair.

A new 'hamlet' of 4-star luxury chalet-hotels was created, called L'Oxalys.

The resort's third Funitel gondola, promised but not delivered for last season, should be in place for 2003/04, replacing the Bouquetin chair towards Méribel (and guarantee the link even in quite bad weather).

More snowmaking is to be installed. In the resort, renovation work on the sports centre is to include a new swimming pool and a health centre.

- ⊞ Extensive local slopes to suit all abilities, and good access to the rest of the vast Three Valleys
- ⊞ The highest resort in the Alps and one of the most snow-sure, with north-facing slopes guaranteeing good snow for a long season
- ⊞ Convenient, gentle nursery slopes
- ⊞ Not as much of an eyesore as most high, purpose-built resorts
- ⊞ Compact village with direct slope access from most accommodation

- ⊟ Can be bleak in bad weather – not a tree in sight
- ⊟ Parts of the village are much less attractive to walk through in the evening than to ski past in the day
- ⊟ Not much to do off the slopes
- ⊟ Some very crowded pistes and dangerous intersections
- ⊟ Still some queues – especially for the Cîme de Caron cable-car

For the enthusiast looking for the best snow in the Alps, it's difficult to beat Val-Thorens. That wonderful snow lies on some pretty wonderful slopes, and the village – always one of the better-designed high-altitude stations – gets more attractive as it continues to develop.

But we still prefer a cosier base elsewhere in the Three Valleys. That way, if a storm socks in, we can play in the woods around Méribel or Courchevel; if the sun is scorching, we have the option of setting off for Val-Thorens. The formula simply doesn't work the other way round.

THE RESORT

Val-Thorens is built high above the tree line on a sunny, west-facing mountainside at the head of the Belleville valley, surrounded by peaks, slopes and lifts. The village streets are supposedly traffic-free. Practically all visitors' cars are banished to car parks, except on Saturday. But workers' cars still generate a fair amount of traffic, and weekends can be mayhem with people entering and leaving the resort. Many parts of the resort are designed with their 'fronts' facing the slopes, and their relatively dreary backs (described as 'tired' by one reporter) facing the streets. There are quite extensive shopping arcades, a fair choice of bars and restaurants, and a good (and improving) sports centre.

It is a classic purpose-built resort, with lots of convenient slope-side accommodation. It's quite a complex little village; but since it's very compact – our scale plan is one of the smallest in these pages – it doesn't matter much where you stay. At its heart is the snowy Place de Caron, where pedestrians mix with skiers and boarders. Many of the shops and restaurants are clustered here, along with the best hotels, and the sports centre is nearby. The village is basically divided in two by a little slope (with a drag-lift) that leads down from here to the broad main nursery slope running the length of the village. The upper half of the village is centred on the Place de Péclet. A road runs across the hillside from here to the new chalet-style Balcons development. The lower half of the village is more diffuse, with the Rue du Soleil winding down from the dreary bus station to the big Temples du Soleil apartments.

Seen from the slopes, the resort is not as hideous as many of its rivals. The buildings are mainly medium-rise and wood-clad; and some are distinctly stylish.

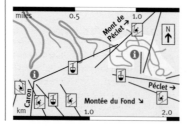

KEY FACTS

Resort	2300m
	7,550ft

For the Three Valleys	
Slopes	1260-3230m
	4,130-10,600ft
Lifts	200
Pistes	600km
	370 miles
Green	17%
Blue	34%
Red	37%
Black	12%
Snowmaking	90km
	56 miles

For Val-Thorens only	
Slopes	1800-3230m
	5,900-10,600ft
Lifts	56
Pistes	140km
	87 miles
Green	12%
Blue	32%
Red	45%
Black	11%

LIFT PASSES

Three Valleys
Covers all lifts in Courchevel, La Tania, Méribel, Val-Thorens, Les Menuires and St-Martin-de-Belleville.

Beginners
5 free lifts in Val-Thorens.

Main pass
1-day pass €39
6-day pass €193

Senior citizens
Over 60: 6-day pass €154
Over 72: free pass

Children
Under 13: 6-day pass €145
Under 5: free pass

Notes
Reductions for families. Half-day and pedestrian passes available. 6-day pass gives a day in Tignes-Val-d'Isère, La Plagne-Les Arcs, Pralognan or Les Saisies.

Alternative passes
Valley pass covers Val-Thorens and Les Menuires. Pass for Val-Thorens only also available.

THE MOUNTAINS

Take account of the height, the extent of its local slopes and the easy access to the rest of the Three Valleys, and the attraction of Val-Thorens becomes clear. The main disadvantage is the lack of trees. Heavy snowfalls or high wind can shut practically all the lifts and slopes, and even if they don't close, poor visibility can be a problem.

THE SLOPES
High and snow-sure
The resort has a wide piste going right down the front of it, leading down to a number of different lifts. The big **Péclet** gondola, with 25-person cabins, rises 700m/2,300ft to the Péclet glacier, with three red runs down. One links across to a wide area of intermediate runs served by lifts to cols either side of the **Pointe de Thorens**. You can take red or blue runs into the 'fourth valley', the Maurienne, from one of these – the **Col de la Montée du Fond,** now served by the Grand Fond jumbo gondola.

In the Maurienne valley two chairs go up to 3230m/10,600ft on the virgin flanks of **Pointe du Bouchet** – now the highest lift-served point in the Three Valleys. The black piste leading away from the lifts here has been abolished, apparently because the steepness of the start was causing serious falls. Coming back from the Maurienne involves tackling the red Falaise run, which a reporter calls 'horrendous'.

The cable-car to **Cîme de Caron** is one of the great lifts of the Alps, rising 900m/2,950ft in no time at all. It can be reached by skiing across from mid-mountain, or by coming up on the gondola which starts below the village. From the top there is the choice of red and black pistes down the front, or a black into the Maurienne.

The relatively low **Boismint** sector is overlooked by many visitors, but is actually a very respectable hill, with a total vertical of 860m/2,820ft.

Chair-lifts heading north from the resort serve sunny slopes above the village and also lead to the Méribel

↑ Europe's highest resort, with Europe's highest peak in the background and one of Europe's most effective lifts in the foreground – the Cîme de Caron cable-car, taking you up 900m/2,950ft

OT VAL-THORENS / BASILE / C PIRONON

valley. Les Menuires can also be reached via these lifts; the alternative Boulevard Cumin along the valley floor is nearly flat, and can be hard work, especially for kids – as the editorial offspring can confirm.

TERRAIN-PARKS
Adequate
The terrain-park towards the bottom of the Caron sector, served by a fast chair, has a half-pipe and a sound system.

SNOW RELIABILITY
Difficult to beat
Few resorts can rival Val-Thorens for reliably good snow-cover, thanks to its altitude and generally north-facing slopes. Snowmaking already covers

boarding

The best resort-level snow in Europe appeals to boarders as well as skiers – and pulls in considerable numbers. There are pistes to suit all abilities, and the good snow is great for beginners and carvers. There's plenty of off-piste choice for free-riders, though if you want trees you'll have to travel. The lifts are now mainly chairs and gondolas, though one or two drags remain.

20% of the pistes, including the crowded south- and west-facing runs on the way back from the Méribel valley, and it is due to be extended for 2003/04. Again there are reports that grooming is good but not frequent enough.

FOR EXPERTS
Lots to do off-piste

Val-Thorens' local pistes are primarily intermediate terrain. The fast Cascades chair serves a short but steep run – now restored to the piste map as a black – that quickly gets mogulled. The pistes down from the Cîme de Caron cable-car are challenging, but not seriously steep. The sunny Marielle run is one of the easiest blacks we've come across.

But there is huge amounts of off-piste to explore with a guide; it is rocky terrain, with serious hazards. The north-facing slopes reached from the Col, Grand Fond, Deux Lacs and Boismint lifts are all worth exploring, and there are long runs to be done from Cîme de Caron – notably the Lac du Lou run around the back of Boismint; this used to be a marked itinéraire, but the concept seems to have gone out of fashion here.

Over in the Maurienne valley there are further expanses – and the long black Pierre Lory piste (930m/3,050ft vertical) that existed briefly has reverted to off-piste status. We haven't skied it in either form, but a reader

describes it as a 'truly magnificent' run, mellowing into a schuss after the steep start that was its undoing as a piste.

You can also climb up from the top of the Péclet lifts and take a long off-piste run towards Méribel – a reasonable level of fitness needed.

FOR INTERMEDIATES
Unbeatable quality and quantity

The scope for intermediates throughout the Three Valleys is enormous. It will take a keen intermediate only 90 minutes or so to get to Courchevel at the far end, if not distracted by the endless runs on the way.

The local slopes in Val-Thorens are some of the best intermediate terrain in the region. Most of the pistes are easy reds and blues, made even more enjoyable by the excellent snow.

The snow on the red Col run is always some of the best around. The blue Moraine below it is gentle – 'fine cruising', reports a visitor this year – and popular with the schools. The runs on the top half of the mountain are steeper than those back into the resort. The Grand Fond gondola serves a good variety of red runs. The Pluviometre from the Trois Vallées chair is a glorious varied run, away from the lifts, though we're not sure its recent regrading as a blue was sensible. Adventurous intermediates shouldn't miss the Cîme de Caron runs. The black run is not intimidating – it's very wide and usually has good snow.

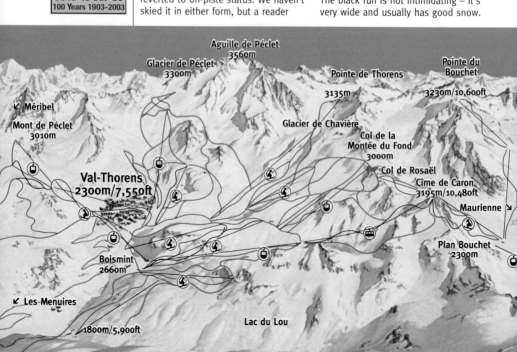

SCHOOLS

ESF
t 0479 000286
info@esf-valthorens.
com
Ski-Cool
t 0479 000492
info@ski-cool.com
Prosneige
t 0479 010700
info@prosneige.fr
International
t 0479 000196
esi@intl-skischool.
com

Classes (ESF prices)
6 half-days (3hr am)
€123
Private lessons
€30.50 for 1hr

CHILDREN

The ESF offers classes
for children aged 4 to
12 (6 mornings
€110). It can also
provide all-day care
and runs two Mini
Club nurseries, at the
top and bottom of
the resort, taking
children from age 3
months to 4 years.
The Pros Neige school
also offers classes for
children.

FOR BEGINNERS
Good late-season choice
The slopes at the foot of the resort are
very gentle and provide convenient,
snow-sure nursery slopes, now with
moving walkway lifts. There are no
long green runs to progress to, but the
blues immediately above the village
are easy. The resort's height and
bleakness make it cold in midwinter,
and intimidating in bad weather.

FOR CROSS-COUNTRY
Try elsewhere
Val-Thorens is a poor base for cross-
country, with only 4km/2.5 miles of
local trails.

QUEUES
Persistent at the Cîme de Caron
Recent reports suggest that the longest
queues are for the largest and most
rewarding lifts, notably the Cîme de
Caron cable-car, and the two Funitels.
The queues move fairly quickly, but
reporters warn that visits to the Cîme
de Caron really need to be timed to
miss the crowds.
    The Plein Sud six-pack chair-lift
does a good job of getting the crowds
out of the village towards Méribel and
Courchevel in the afternoon, and
should now deliver you to Val-Thorens'
third jumbo gondola, replacing the
Bouquetin chair. Check the Méribel
chapter for bottlenecks there.
    When snow is in short supply
elsewhere the pressure on the Val-
Thorens lifts can increase markedly.

MOUNTAIN RESTAURANTS
Lots of choice
For a high, modern resort, the choice
of restaurants is good. We've enjoyed
the Chalet de Genépi, on the run down
from the Moraine chair – great views
and an open fire – but a disappointed
visitor last season found the food
'appalling'. The Bar de la Marine, on

the Dalles piste, does excellent food,
but service can be stretched. The
Moutière, near the top of the chair of
the same name, is one of the more
reasonably priced huts. The Plan
Bouchet refuge in the Maurienne valley
is very popular and welcoming, but bar
service can be slow. You can stay the
night there, too. The Chalet Plein Sud,
below the chair of the same name, has
excellent views but a 'rather limited
menu'. The big Chalet de Thorens has
been praised for its food and
reasonable prices, but is in need of
refurbishment, according to one
reporter. The Chalets des 2 Lacs is
popular for friendly, efficient service.

SCHOOLS AND GUIDES
A mixed bag
Like so many branches of the ESF, this
one is incompetently run (to judge by
past reports – we lack new ones this
year). The ESF has a Trois Vallées
group for those who want to cover a
lot of ground while receiving lessons –
available by the day or the week, and
can include off-piste. In contrast,
reporters recommend the Prosneige
classes: 'really excellent – my wife's
skiing changed dramatically'; 'good
with children'. Ski Cool class sizes are
guaranteed not to exceed 10. They also
have off-piste courses. There are
several specialist guiding outfits.

FACILITIES FOR CHILDREN
Coolly efficient
Previous reports of the ESF nursery
were conflicting but a reader found the
facilities convenient and the service
efficient. In spite of the fact that the
staff were 'not particularly warm or
friendly', by the end of the week all
the children were 'comfortable' on skis.
The Prosneige takes children from the
age of five. New for 2002/03 was an
enclosed junior section at the base of
the Deux Lacs piste.

Val-Thorens

369

↑ The cable-car isn't so easy to spot in this shot of the great shady slopes of Cîme de Caron

OT VAL-THORENS / BASILE / MARK BUSCAIL

GETTING THERE

Air Geneva 159km/99 miles (3½hr), Lyon 193km/120 miles (3½hr), Chambéry 112km/70 miles (2½hr).

Rail Moûtiers (37km/23 miles); regular buses from station.

ACTIVITIES

Indoor Sports centre (tennis, squash, climbing wall, roller skating, golf simulator, swimming pool, saunas, massage, hot-tub, volleyball, weight training, table tennis, fitness, badminton, football), games rooms, music recitals, cinema, beauty centre

Outdoor Paragliding, sightseeing flights, snowmobiles, snow-shoe excursions, walks, toboggan run

Phone numbers
From abroad use the prefix +33 and omit the initial '0' of the phone number.

TOURIST OFFICE

t 0479 000808
valtho@valthorens.com
www.valthorens.com

STAYING THERE

HOW TO GO
Surprisingly high level of comfort
Accommodation is of a higher standard than in many purpose-built resorts.
Chalets These are catered apartments, and many are quite comfortable.
Hotels There are plenty of hotels, and there's a Club Med, too.
(((((5) **Fitz Roy** (0479 000478) The sole 4-star is a swanky but charming Relais & Châteaux place with lovely rooms. Pool. Well placed.
((((4) **Val Thorens** (0479 000433) Welcoming and comfortable; next door to Fitz Roy. 'Consistently good service.'
(((3) **Sherpa** (0479 000070) Highly recommended for atmosphere and food. Less-than-ideal position at the top of the resort.
(((3) **Val Chaviere** (0479 000033) Friendly, convenient, 'good food and plenty of it'.
(((3) **Bel Horizon** (0479 000477) Friendly, family-run 3-star, popular with reporters – 'cuisine wonderful'.
Self-catering The options include apartments of a higher standard than usual in France. The Résidences Village Montana is said to be 'outstanding'.

EATING OUT
Surprisingly wide range
Val-Thorens has something for most tastes and pockets. The Fitz Roy and the Val Thorens hotels do classic French food. For something more regional, the best bets are the 'excellent' Vieux Chalet and the Chaumière. The Scapin is cosily done out in wood and stone, with 'good' food. Other readers' recommendations include the Cabane ('excellent Savoyard fare'), the Ferme de Rosalie ('good but limited menu'), the Montana ('good food and service'), El Gringo's ('great for Tex-Mex food' and 'very

popular so get there early'), Auberge des Balcons ('wonderful raclette') and the Joyeuse Fondue. The Galoubet has been recommended for local specialities, including pierrades. The Blanchot is an unusually stylish wine bar with a simple but varied carte and of course an excellent range of wines. Several pizzerias are recommended, including the Grange, in the Temples du Soleil.

APRES-SKI
Livelier than you'd imagine
Val-Thorens is more lively at night than most high-altitude ski-stations. The Red Fox up at Balcons is crowded at close of play, with karaoke. At the opposite extreme the Sherlock in the Temples du Soleil is 'always lively'. The Frog and Roastbeef at the top of the village is a cheerful British ghetto with a live band at tea-time and half-price beer while it plays. It claims to be the highest pub in Europe. The Friends and the Viking pub are all lively bars on the same block. The Underground nightclub in Place de Péclet has an extended happy hour but 'descends into europop' when its disco gets going. The Malaysia cellar bar is recommended for good live bands, and gets very crowded after 11pm. Quieter bars include the 'very pleasant' O'Connells, the cosy Rhum Box (aka Mitch's) and the St Pierre.

OFF THE SLOPES
Forget it
There's a good sports centre, and the inadequate pool is being replaced at last. You can get to some mountain restaurants by lift, and the 360° panorama from the top of the Cîme de Caron cable-car is not to be missed. But it is not a good bet for a holiday off the slopes.

The French Pyrenees

Decent skiing and boarding at half the price of the Alps

It took us a long time to get round to visiting the resorts of the French Pyrenees – mainly because we had the idea that they were second-rate compared with the Alps. Well, it is certainly true that they can't compete in terms of size of ski area with the mega-resorts of the Trois Vallées and Paradiski. But don't dismiss them: they have considerable attractions, including price – hotels cost half as much as in the Alps, and meals and drinks are cheap.

The Pyrenees are serious mountains, with dramatic picturesque scenery. They are also attractively French. Unlike the big plastic mega resorts, many Pyrenean bases have a rustic, rural Gallic charm.

The biggest ski area is shared by **Barèges** and **La Mongie**. Between them they have 100km/62 miles of runs (70 pistes) and 45 lifts. Most lifts are drags and slow chairs but they have started a programme of installing high-speed chairs and have two so far with another planned for 2003/04.

The runs are best suited to intermediates, with good tree-lined runs above Barèges and open bowl skiing above La Mongie. The best bet for an expert is to try off-piste with a guide – one beautiful run away from all the lifts starts with a scramble through a hole in the rocks. There are two terrain-parks. Rustic mountain huts are scattered around the slopes.

Barèges is a spa village set in a narrow, steep-sided valley, which gets little sun in midwinter. It's also the second oldest ski resort in France and the pioneer of skiing in the Pyrenees. Accommodation is mainly in basic 1-star and 2-star hotels. One reporter stayed in nearby Luz in the Chimes hotel, describing the food as 'divine'. The rather drab buildings and one main street of Barèges grow on you, though there's little to do in the evenings other than visit the thermal spa and a restaurant. La Mongie, on the other hand, is a modern, purpose-built resort reminiscent of the Alps.

Cauterets is another spa town but a complete contrast to Barèges. It is much bigger and set in a wide, sunny valley. It is a popular summer destination, and even in March we were able to sit at a pavement cafe with a drink after dinner. It wasn't until 1964 that skiing started here, when the cable-car to the slopes 850m/2,790ft

above the town was built – you have to ride down as well as up. There are only 35km/22 miles of slopes (mainly intermediate), and a terrain-park, set in a bowl that can be cold and windy.

But Cauterets' jewel is its cross-country, a long drive or bus-ride from town at Pont d'Espagne and served by a gondola. It is the start of the Pyrenees National Park and the old smugglers' route over the mountains between France and Spain. The 36km/22 miles of snow-sure cross-country tracks run up this beautiful deserted valley, beside a rushing stream and a stunning waterfall.

Font-Romeu has 52km/32 miles of pistes and 29 lifts, serving mainly easy and intermediate pistes (15 of its 40 pistes are green) and is popular with families. The slopes get a lot of sun but it has 460 snow-guns – the biggest snowmaking set-up in the Pyrenees – and so cover is assured so long as it is cold enough at night to make snow. Weekend crowds arrive from nearby Perpignan and over the border from Spain and both lifts and pistes can get crowded. It has 90km/56 miles of cross-country skiing. The village is a bus-ride from the slopes and hotels are mainly 2- and 3-star.

The other major Pyrenean resort is **St-Lary-Soulan**, a traditional village with houses built of stone, with a cable-car at the edge going up to the slopes, of which there are 80km/50 miles, mainly suiting intermediates. It has a terrain-park and half-pipe. There's a satellite called **St-Lary-Espiaube**, which is purpose-built and right at the heart of the slopes.

One 2003 reporter also visited other small resorts such as Formiguères, Eyne and Les Angles and suggests staying down in a small valley town and taking an 'ancient, scenic, electric train called Le Petit Train Jaune' and taxis to resorts for a 'different' holiday.

Phone numbers
From abroad use the prefix +33 and omit the initial '0' of the phone number.

TOURIST OFFICES

www.pyrenees-online.fr
Barèges
t 0562 921600
www.tourmalet.fr
www.bareges.com
La Mongie
t 0562 919415
www.tourmalet.fr
www.bagneresdebigorre
-lamongie.com
Cauterets
t 0562 925027
www.cauterets.com
Font-Romeu
t 0468 306830
www.font-romeu.fr
St-Lary-Soulan
t 0562 395081
www.saintlary.com

Italy

Italy's recent popularity as a winter sports destination owed a lot to prices appreciably lower than in other Alpine countries. It is no longer quite such a bargain, so it now has to compete in terms of the quality of the holidays offered. And it is trying hard to do so. It has some enduring attractions such as its food and wine, the jolly atmosphere and the splendid scenery – especially in the Dolomites. And many resorts now have powerful, modern lift systems and huge snowmaking systems.

Italian resorts vary as widely in their characteristics as they do in location – and they are spread along the full length of the Italian border, from Sauze d'Oulx to the Dolomites. There are high, snow-sure ski stations and charming valley villages, and mountains that range from one-run wonders to some of the most extensive lift networks in the world.

A lot of Italian runs, particularly in the north-west, seem flatteringly easy. This is partly because grooming is immaculate, and partly because piste classification seems to overstate difficulty. Nowhere is this clearer than in the linked area of La Rosière in France and La Thuile – in Italy, despite the French-sounding name. Venturing from the Italian motorways to the French moguls is like moving from the shelter of harbour to the open sea.

THE AMAZING DOLOMITI SUPERSKI LIFT PASS

The Dolomiti Superski lift pass is one of the wonders of the world, covering 45 resorts and 460 lifts. We describe the most important resorts in our chapters on Cortina d'Ampezzo and Selva, but there are countless others worth a visit and we can only touch on a few here.

The Superski region, which straddles the provinces of Veneto, Trentino and Alto Adige/Südtirol (predominantly German-speaking, hence the alternative names), is broken down into 12 areas, each embracing a number of resorts.

One of the most interesting areas is in the north-east corner of the region, the Val Pusteria/Pustertal, which leads off eastwards towards the Slovenian border from the Brenner motorway. The main town is Brunico/Bruneck; we have fond memories of one of our first weeks on skis, spent near here on Plan de Corones/Kronplatz – an extraordinary dome-shaped mountain with easy, open slopes around its bare summit, and more testing stuff lower down. Brunico now has lift access to the mountain by gondola from an outlying suburb, and what looks like an exciting black run through the woods to the base.

Just to the east is the area know as the Alta Val Pusteria/Hochpustertal. There are three small towns dotted along the valley. Westernmost is Villabassa/Niederdorf, chiefly of interest to cross-country skiers. At the watershed of the gently sloping valley, where it starts to descend towards Slovenia, is Dobbiaco/Toblach, with some short slopes on its fringes and very scenic cross-country trails. And further east is San Candido/Innichen, with a long chair-lift serving intermediate slopes.

Up an elevated side valley from here (again with scenic cross-country trails) is the main resort of this area, the village of Sesto/Sexten. This has nursery slopes all around it, and two major lifts. From close to the village a cable-car gives access to a variety of open intermediate slopes on Gallo Cedrone/Hahnspiel, with a long red of 1100m/3,610ft vertical to the base of a gondola up from the Val Pusteria.

APT VAL DI FASSA / STEFANO ZARDINI

← The scenery in many Italian resorts is impressive; in the Dolomites it's simply fabulous. This is Sasso Lungo from Sasso Pordoi – Selva is around the corner to the right

WINTER SUN

The enjoyment hotline: **0039/0471/999 999** The enjoyment click:

... standing at the top of the world. Before you, the thrilling descent. In spectacular scenery with fantastic Alpine views ... and you're off ... down the mountain like a shot ... you arrive, your breath taken away. Now you feel it: crystal clear air, azure blue sky, and the snow gleaming and sparkling in the winter sun. Yet another gorgeous day – one of more than 300 days of pure sunshine.

After the excitement, it's time for some peace and quiet: relax in your alpine chalet. Spoil yourself with South Tyrolean delicacies such as world-famous Speck. In the evening, lose yourself in relaxation or revel in après-ski ...

"Südtirol"/South Tyrol greets families with children with open arms: you simply won't be able to drag the kids away from the friendly children's ski crèches ... and older children can play around safely on the piste.

Tomorrow the dream continues. Each day new, even more wonderful holiday experiences ... under the dazzling winter sun – in full sight of the magnificent Dolomites.

www.suedtirol.**info**

SÜDTIROL

ITALIA
THE MAGIC OF DIVERSITY

Many Italians based in the northern cities ski mainly at weekends, and it's very noticeable that many resorts become busy only at weekends. It's a great advantage for those of us who are there for the whole week. This pattern is especially noticeable at the chic resorts such as Cortina, Courmayeur and Madonna, and resorts which have not yet found international fame such as the Monterosa region; it's much less pronounced in parts of the Dolomites favoured by German visitors who, like Brits, tend to go for a week.

In general, Italians don't take their skiing or boarding too seriously. A late start, long lunch and early finish is the norm – leaving the slopes delightfully quiet for the rest of us. Almost everywhere mountain restaurants are welcoming places, encouraging leisurely lunching. Pasta – even in the most modest establishment – is delicious. And eating and drinking on the mountain is still cheaper than in other Alpine resorts, whatever the euro is doing to harmonise prices.

One thing that Italian resorts do have to contend with is erratic snowfalls. While the snow in the northern Alps tends to come from the west, Italy's tends to come from storms arriving from the south. So it can have great conditions when other countries are suffering; or vice versa. Italian resorts have extensive snowmaking and our observation is that they tend to use it more effectively than other Alpine countries. We have skied in Courmayeur and in the Dolomites when little natural snow had fallen, and in each case there was excellent cruising on man-made snow.

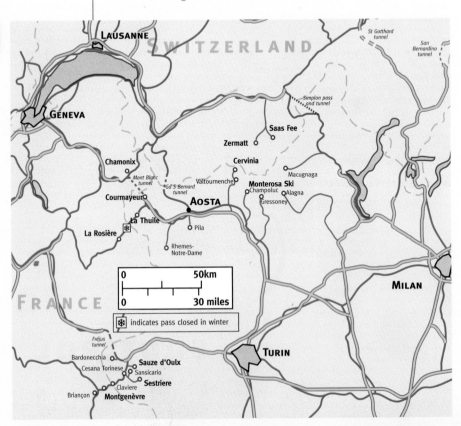

DRIVING IN THE ITALIAN ALPS

There are four main geographical groupings of Italian resorts, widely separated. Getting to some of these resorts is a very long haul, and moving from one area to another can involve very long drives (though the extensive motorway network is a great help).

The handful of resorts to the west of Turin – Bardonecchia, Sauze d'Oulx, Sestriere and neighbours in the Milky Way region – are easily reached from France via the Fréjus tunnel from Modane, or via the good road over the pass that the resort of Montgenèvre sits on.

Further north, and about equidistant from Milan and Turin, are the resorts of the Aosta valley – Courmayeur, Cervinia, La Thuile and the Monterosa area are the best known among them. Now that the Mont Blanc road tunnel from Chamonix in France has reopened,

Introduction

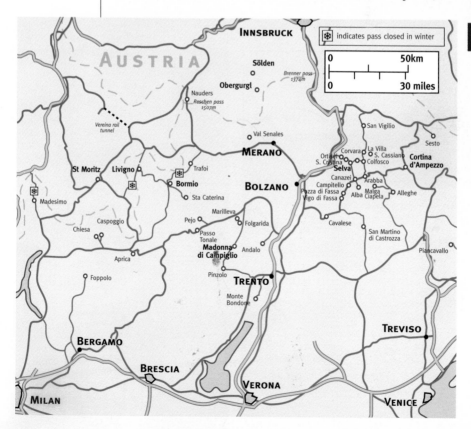

Courmayeur is again the easiest of all Italian resorts to reach from Britain. The Aosta valley can also be reached from Switzerland via the Grand St Bernard tunnel. The approach is high and may require chains. The road down the Aosta valley is a major thoroughfare, but the roads up to some of the other resorts are quite long, winding and (in the case of Cervinia) high.

To the east is a string of scattered resorts, most close to the Swiss border, many in isolated and remote valleys involving long drives up from the nearest Italian cities, or high-altitude drives from Switzerland. The links between Switzerland and Italy are more clearly shown on our larger-scale Switzerland map at the beginning of that section than on the map of the Italian Alps included here. The major routes are the St Gotthard tunnel between Göschenen (near Andermatt) and Airolo – the main route between Basel and Milan – and the San Bernardino tunnel reached via Chur.

Finally, further east still are the resorts of the Dolomites. Getting there from Austria is easy, over the Brenner motorway pass from Innsbruck. But getting there from Britain is a very long drive indeed – allow at least a day and a half. We wouldn't lightly drive there and back for a week's skiing, though we routinely do as part of a longer tour including some Austrian resorts. It's also worth bearing in mind that once you arrive in the Dolomites, getting around the intricate network of valleys linked by narrow, winding roads can be a slow business – it's often quicker to get from village to village on skis. Impatient Italian driving can make it a bit stressful, too.

CORTINA TO / D G BANDON
The scenery around Cortina is possibly even more spectacular than that around Selva ⬎

Bormio

A tall, narrow mountain above a very unusual, historic resort town

COSTS

① ② ③ ④ ⑤ ⑥

RATINGS

The slopes

Snow	★★★
Extent	★★
Expert	★
Intermediate	★★★
Beginner	★★
Convenience	★★★
Queues	★★★
Mountain restaurants	★★★★

The rest

Scenery	★★★
Resort charm	★★★★
Off-slope	★★★★

NEWS

For 2003/04 the cable-car from the main car park to Bormio 2000 is to be replaced by a gondola, which should eliminate queues morning and afternoon.

Bormio has been chosen to host the Alpine World Ski Championships in 2005, 20 years after it first staged them.

➕ Good mix of high, open pistes and woodland runs adding up to some good long runs

➕ Worthwhile neighbouring resorts

➕ Attractive medieval town centre – quite unlike any other winter resort

➕ Good mountain restaurants

➖ Slopes all of medium steepness

➖ Rather confined main mountain, with second area some way distant

➖ Still many slow old lifts

➖ Long airport transfers

➖ Crowds and queues on Sundays

➖ Central hotels inconvenient

If you like ancient Italian towns and don't mind a lack of Alpine resort atmosphere, you'll find the centre of Bormio very appealing – though you're unlikely to be staying right in the centre. Given the limited slopes of Bormio's own mountain, plan on taking the free bus out to the Valdidentro area and perhaps make longer outings, to Santa Caterina at least.

THE RESORT

Bormio, a spa since Roman times, has a splendid 17th-century town centre, with narrow cobbled streets and grand stone facades – very colourful during the evening promenade. It is in a remote spot, close to the Swiss border – though road improvements have cut the airport transfer to three hours.

The town centre is a 15-minute walk from the gondola station across the river to the south. There are reliable free shuttle-buses, but many people walk. Closer to the lifts is a suburban sprawl of hotels for skiers. Several major hotels are on Via Milano, leading out of town, which is neither convenient nor atmospheric.

THE MOUNTAINS

There's a nice mix of high, snow-sure pistes and lower wooded slopes. The main slopes are tall (vertical drop 1800m/5,900ft) and narrow. Most pistes face north-west and head to town.

Both the piste map and the piste marking need substantial improvement. Reporters have complained about the abundance of slow old lifts, and the resort policy of opening certain lift links only at weekends and busy times.

The Valdidentro area, a short bus-ride out of Bormio, shouldn't be overlooked. The open and woodland runs are very pleasant and usually empty (and have great views). Day trips to Santa Caterina (20 minutes by bus) and Livigno (90 minutes) are covered by the Alta Valtellina lift pass. **A six-day pass entitles you to a discount rate on a one-day pass in** St Moritz (3 hours away).

Slopes The two-stage Cima Bianca cable-car goes from bottom to top of the slopes via the mid-mountain mini-resort of Bormio 2000. An alternative gondola goes to Ciuk.

Terrain-parks There aren't any.

Snow reliability Runs above Bormio 2000 are usually snow-sure, and there is snowmaking on the lower slopes, though these were bare when we visited in late March. The Valdidentro area is more reliable, and the high, shaded, north-facing slopes of Santa Caterina usually have good snow.

Experts There are a couple of short

Cima Bianca
10m/9,88oft

2550m

2200m

Valdidentro

Val di Sotto

Oga
1535m

Le Motte
1430m

Bormio 2000

Ciuk
1620m

**Bormio
1225m/4,02oft**

KEY FACTS

Resort	1225m
	4,020ft

For Bormio and Valdidentro	
Slopes	1225-3010m
	4,020-9,880ft
Lifts	28
Pistes	75km
	47 miles
Blue	36%
Red	48%
Black	16%
Snowmaking	30km
	19 miles

For Bormio only	
Slopes	1225-3010m
	4,020-9,880ft
Lifts	17
Pistes	50km
	31 miles

ITALY

380

TOURIST OFFICE

black runs in the main area, but the main interest lies in off-piste routes from Cima Bianca to both east and west of the piste area.

Intermediates The men's downhill course starts with a steep plunge, but otherwise is just a tough red, ideal for strong intermediates. Stella Alpina, down to 2000, is also fairly steep. Many runs are less tough – ideal for most intermediates. The longest is a superb top-to-bottom cruise. The outlying mountains are also suitable for early intermediates.

Beginners The nursery slopes at Bormio 2000 offer good snow, but there are no very flattering longer pistes to move on to. Novices are better off at nearby Santa Caterina.

Snowboarding The slopes are too steep for novices, and there's little to attract experienced boarders either.

Cross-country There are some trails either side of Bormio, towards Piatta and beneath Le Motte and Valdidentro, but cross-country skiers are better off at snow-sure Santa Caterina.

Queues Both sections of the cable-car suffer delays in the morning peak period and on Sundays, but the fast quad from Bormio 2000 now relieves the pressure on the top half, and the new gondola to replace the cable-car from the main car park to Bormio 2000 in 2003/04 should reduce the problems with the bottom half. When the lower slopes are incomplete, queues form to ride down. Otherwise there are few problems outside carnival week.

Mountain restaurants The mountain restaurants are generally good. Even the efficient service at Cafe Bormio 2000 has a good choice of dishes. At the Rocca, above Ciuk, there is a welcoming chalet and a smart, modern place with table- or self-service. Cedrone, at Bormio 2000, has a good terrace and a play area for children. Several reporters recommend the very welcoming Baita de Mario, at Ciuk, as a great place for a long lunch.

Schools and guides The only recent report we have is of the Nazionale school, which offered 'satisfactory lessons in English'.

Facilities for children The ski school takes children from the age of three, from 10am to 4pm. The Bormio 2000 branch of the school has a roped-off snow garden at mid-mountain with a moving carpet lift.

STAYING THERE

How to go There are plenty of apartments, but hotels dominate the package market.

Hotels Most of Bormio's 40-plus hotels are 2- and 3-star places. The 4-star Palace (0342 903131) is the most luxurious in town. The Posta (0342 904753) is in the centre of the old town – rooms range from adequate to very good. The Baita dei Pinti (0342 904346) is the best placed of the top hotels – on the river, between the lifts and centre. The Ambassador (0342 904625) is close to the gondola.

Self-catering The modern Cristallo apartments have been recommended.

Eating out There's a wide selection of restaurants. The atmospheric Taulà at Valfurva does excellent modern food with great service. The Kuerc and the Vecchia Combo are also popular. The Rododendri (at Valfurva) is recommended and there are excellent pizzerias, including the Jap.

Après-ski The après-ski starts on the mountain at the Rocca, and there are popular bars around the bottom lift stations. The Clem Pub, Gordy's, Cafe Mozart and the Aurora are popular. Shangri-La is a friendly bar. The King's Club is said to be the best disco.

Off the slopes Diversions include thermal baths – apparently now including reopened Roman baths – riding and walks in the Stelvio National Park. There is also an excellent sports centre, ice rink and 'superb' swimming pool. St Moritz and duty-free Livigno are popular excursions.

Staying up the mountain The modern Girasole 2000 (0342 904652), at Bormio 2000, is simple but well run by an Anglo-Italian couple; lots of events for evening entertainment.

Cervinia

Mile after mile of high-altitude, snow-sure cruising

COSTS

① ② ③ ④ ⑤ ⑥

RATINGS

The slopes

Snow	★★★★★
Extent	★★★
Expert	★
Intermediate	★★★★
Beginner	★★★★★
Convenience	★★★
Queues	★★★
Mountain restaurants	★★★

The rest

Scenery	★★★★
Resort charm	★★
Off-slope	★

NEWS

For 2003/04 a planned tunnel under the road should make it possible to ski right down to the gondola station in Valtournenche (if there's enough snow for the run to be open).

KEY FACTS

Resort	2050m
	6,730ft

For Cervinia/ Valtournenche

Slopes	1525-3480m
	5,000ft-11,420ft
Lifts	30
Pistes	200km
	125 miles
Blue	28%
Red	60%
Black	12%
Snowmaking	17km
	11 miles

For Cervinia/ Valtournenche/ Zermatt combined

Slopes	1525-3820m
	5,000-12,530ft
Lifts	101
Pistes	450km
	280 miles
Snowmaking	60km
	38 miles

+ Extensive mountain with miles of long, consistently gentle runs – ideal for early intermediates and anyone wary of steep slopes or bumps

+ High, sunny and snow-sure slopes amid impressive scenery

+ Link with Zermatt in Switzerland provides even more spectacular views and good lunches

− Very little to interest good or aggressive intermediates and above

− Almost entirely treeless, with little to do in bad weather

− Lifts prone to closure by wind, particularly early in the season

− Link with Zermatt isn't quite as valuable as you might expect

− Mountain toilet facilities dire

− Steep uphill walk to main lifts, followed by lots of steps in station

− Few off-slope amenities

If there is a better resort for those who like gentle, late-season cruising on mile after mile of easy, snow-sure, well-groomed, sunny slopes we have yet to find it. And all this at the foot of the southern side of the Matterhorn (Monte Cervino), with the easiest of Zermatt's slopes just over the Swiss border and linked by lift and piste. But Breuil Cervinia (as the resort now styles itself) will not suit everyone. It can be cold and bleak in early season and the top lifts and link with Switzerland can close. The more adventurous will get bored by the easy slopes and find that Zermatt's most interesting challenges are out of range for a relaxing day trip. And the resort itself is a bit of an eyesore. Oh ... and the hole-in-the ground mountain loos tend to go down very badly with our readers.

THE RESORT

Cervinia is at the head of a long valley leading off the Aosta valley on the Italian side of the Matterhorn. The old climbing village developed into a winter resort in a rather haphazard way, and it has no consistent style of architecture. It's an uncomfortable hotchpotch, neither pleasing to the eye nor as offensive as the worst of the French purpose-built resorts. The centre is pleasant, compact and traffic-free. But ugly surrounding apartment blocks and hotels make the whole place feel less friendly and welcoming.

A lot of people stay near the village centre, at the foot of the nursery slopes. You can take a series of drags from here to the slopes. But the main gondola and cable-car to Plan Maison at mid-mountain start an awkward uphill walk away, above the village. To avoid the walk to these lifts, choose a hotel with its own shuttle-bus. But you

SNOWPIX.COM / CHRIS GILL

The upper, more modern part of Cervinia, as seen from the long Ventina run →

LIFT PASSES

Breuil-Cervinia
Covers all lifts on the Italian side of the border including Valtournenche.

Beginners
'First bends' passes available.

Main pass
1-day pass €30
6-day pass €155

Senior citizens
Over 65: 6-day pass €117

Children
Under 12: 6-day pass €117
Under 8: free pass with paying adult

Notes
Half-day pass available. Single and return tickets on some lifts. Daily extension for Zermatt lifts at Klein Matterhorn and Schwarzsee or for all areas.

Alternative passes
International Matterhorn pass includes Zermatt's Klein Matterhorn and Schwarzsee lifts. International Zermatt pass covers all of Zermatt. Limited area passes for Carosello/Cretaz (seven lifts).

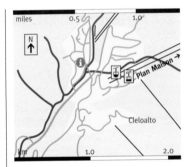

miles 0.5 1.0
Plan Maison →
Cieloalto
km 1.0 2.0

can't avoid the steps (120, counted one reporter) up to where you load the gondola. There is more accommodation further out at the Cieloalto complex and on the road up to it – but some of these buildings are among the worst eyesores.

As well as the usual souvenir shops there are some smart clothes shops and jewellers. At peak periods, the resort fills up with day trippers and weekenders from Milan and Turin who bring cars and mobile phones, making parts of the village traffic- and fume-ridden at times, and the hills alive with the sound of ringing tones.

There are surprisingly few off-slope amenities, such as kindergartens, marked walks and spa facilities.

The slopes link to Valtournenche further down the valley (covered by the lift pass) and Zermatt over in Switzerland (covered by a daily supplement, or a more expensive weekly pass). More about this later in the chapter.

Day trips by car are possible to Courmayeur, La Thuile and the Monterosa Ski resorts of Champoluc and Gressoney (all covered by the Aosta valley lift pass).

THE MOUNTAINS

Cervinia's main slopes are on a high, large, open and sunny west-facing bowl. It has Italy's highest pistes and some of its longest (13km from Plateau Rosa to Valtournenche – with only a short drag-lift part-way). Nearly all the runs are accessible to intermediates. The weather is more of a problem than steepness. If it's bad, the top lifts often close because of high winds. And even the lower slopes may be unusable because of poor visibility. There are few woodland pistes.

THE SLOPES
Very easy

Cervinia has the biggest, highest, most snow-sure area of easy, well groomed pistes we've come across – though we're very sceptical of the recent hike in the claimed total to 200km. The high proportion of red runs on the piste map is misleading: most of them would be classified blue elsewhere. The slopes just above the village are floodlit some evenings.

The main lifts take you to the mid-mountain base of **Plan Maison**. From there a further gondola, then a giant cable-car, go up to **Plateau Rosa** and a link with Zermatt (confusingly Plateau Rosa is called Testa Grigia on the Zermatt piste map, though we welcome the new handy piste map that has both Cervinia and Zermatt's slopes on it). Three successive fast quads (all with covers) from Plan Maison go up to a slightly lower point on the border, and another link with Zermatt.

From both links you can ski back on some of Cervinia's easiest slopes (from the top of the chairs) to Plan Maison or down to the village. If instead you turn right at Plateau Rosa you take the splendid wide Ventina run. You can use the cable-car to do the top part repeatedly, or go all the way down to Cervinia (8km/5 miles and over 1400m/4,600ft vertical). Or you can branch off left down towards **Valtournenche**. The slopes here are served by a number of slow old lifts above the initial modern gondola from Valtournenche to Salette. You can't get back to Plan Maison from this sector except by riding down the gondola.

There is also the small, little-used **Cieloalto** area, served by three lifts to the south of the cable-car at the bottom of the Ventina run. This has some of Cervinia's steeper pistes and can be very useful in bad weather as it has the only trees in the area.

Several reporters have criticised the 'inadequate' piste map.

TERRAIN-PARKS
Winter and summer
The terrain-park at Plan Maison, has jumps, boarder-cross course and a half-pipe, and the resort claims it is designed for everyone from beginners to experts. Reports on it would be welcome. In summer there's an even better one over the Swiss border on Zermatt's Klein Matterhorn glacier slopes.

boarding

Cervinia has great slopes for learning to snowboard – gentle, wide and usually with good snow. And the main lifts around the area are chairs, gondolas and cable-cars, but there are a lot of drag-lifts and some long flat bits as well. There's not much to interest better boarders – just as there's not much to interest better skiers.

SNOW RELIABILITY
Superb

The mountain is one of the highest in Europe and, despite getting a lot of afternoon sun, can usually be relied on to have good snow conditions. Lift closures due to wind are a bigger worry. Several reporters have complained about this and about the biting winds.

The village nursery slopes, the bottom half of the Ventina run and the runs under the top chair-lifts down to Plan Maison have snowmaking. But the run below the top of the gondola to lower-lying Valtournenche doesn't – and so is prone to closure.

FOR EXPERTS
Forget it

This is not a resort for experts (though heli-drops with guides can be arranged). There are several black runs scattered here and there, but most of them would be classified red elsewhere. Many reporters head over to Zermatt for more challenging slopes but don't necessarily find them – see 'The Zermatt Connection'.

FOR INTERMEDIATES
Miles of long, flattering runs

Virtually the whole area can be covered comfortably by average intermediates. And if you like wide, easy, motorway pistes, you'll love Cervinia: it has more long, flattering runs than any other resort. The easiest slopes are on the left as you look at the mountain. From top to bottom here there are gentle blue runs and almost equally gentle reds in the beautiful scenery at the foot of the south face of the Matterhorn.

The area on the right as you look at the mountain is best for adventurous intermediates. The Ventina run is a particularly good fast cruise. The long run down to Valtournenche is easy for most of its length, though the snow conditions on the lower part can be challenging. Good intermediates will be capable of the black runs.

One reporter warns that the start of the run from Plan Maison has now been regraded from red to blue on some maps – but is 'very tricky in parts and I saw children in trouble'.

Cervinia

383

THE ZERMATT CONNECTION

If the weather is good, you're bound to be tempted to go over to Zermatt. And quite right – the restaurants are simply the best, and it's only from the Swiss side that you get the classic view of the Matterhorn. But there are snags.

For a start, the two lift companies can't even convey clearly where you can cross over. Testa Grigia on one side of the joint map becomes Plateau Rosa on the other; Theodulpass becomes nameless. Pathetic.

Then there are the runs. You come first of all to even gentler glacier motorways than on the Cervinia side. There are more challenging pistes once you get down to Schwarzsee. But there is no way to get to Zermatt's classic terrain on Stockhorn and Rothorn without making the long descent to the village, and bussing, walking or taking a taxi the length of the village to other lifts.

You could do this, but you couldn't do it enjoyably – partly because you have to set off back early on account of the lift links back to the border. There can be long afternoon queues for the Trockener Steg-Klein Matterhorn cable-car, which may be eased by the new fast chair to Furggsattel for 2003/04. But this new chair may generate big queues for the slow and very exposed T-bar you need after that.

You can get a taste of Zermatt from Cervinia, but you're unlikely to get your fill.

FOR BEGINNERS
Pretty much ideal
Complete beginners will start on the good village nursery slope, and should graduate quickly to the fine flat area around Plan Maison and its gentle blue runs. Fast learners will be going all the way from the top to the bottom of the mountain by the end of the week.

FOR CROSS-COUNTRY
Hardly any
There are a couple of short trails, but this is not a cross-country resort.

QUEUES
Can still be problems
Although much improved recently, there are still some antiquated lifts, and the system still has drawbacks. The two main access lifts to Plan Maison can get crowded (twenty minute queues at peak times) and the alternative series of drags and chairs need upgrading. The series of slow lifts back up from Valtournenche are another source of complaint. There can also be queues for many lower lifts when upper lifts are shut due to wind.

MOUNTAIN RESTAURANTS
OK if you know where to go
The mountain restaurants are not as appealing as you might expect in an Italian resort (and the toilet facilities are generally primitive hole-in-the-ground affairs), so some reporters head over to Zermatt for lunch.

However, the Châlet Etoile, beneath the Rocce Nere chair-lift at Plan Maison, is highly praised by reporters: 'The best mountain restaurant I've been to,' says one, and 'Top quality cuisine in an authentic Italian style,' says another this year. So is the more

SNOWPIX.COM / CHRIS GILL

Monte Cervino (aka the Matterhorn) seen from the Italian side – the pistes aren't always this deserted →

basic table-service section of Rifugio Teodulo near the link with Zermatt reached by chair-lifts – excellent pasta. Booking is recommended at both.

Other reporter recommendations include the British-run Igloo, near the top of the Bardoney chair just off the Ventina piste, which serves huge burgers and has 'a UK-style toilet'. Baita Cretaz, near the bottom of the Cretaz pistes, is good value. The Bontadini at the top of the Fornet chair has been praised again this year ('good value and superb view').

The restaurants are cheaper and less crowded on the Valtournenche side. The Motta, at the top of the drag-lift of the same name, does excellent food, including goulaschsuppe that is 'out of this world'.

SCHOOLS AND GUIDES
Getting better
Cervinia has three main schools, Cervino, Breuil and Nuova Cielo Alto. Reports are fairly positive but one reporter this year complains of asking for an English instructor but getting an Italian. She also recommends pre-booking as demand was high – even in mid-March. In earlier years, we have had good reports on the private lessons: 'Excellent value and level of tuition very good with good standard of English and pleasant instructors.'

CHILDREN

The ski school runs a snow garden with mini-lift at the foot of the Cretaz slopes and one mini-lift in Plan Maison. Care arrangements 10am to 1pm.

GETTING THERE

Air Turin 118km/73 miles (2½hr). Geneva 220km/138 miles (2½hr).

Rail Châtillon (27km/17 miles); regular buses from station.

ACTIVITIES

Indoor Hotels with swimming pools and saunas, fitness centre, bowling

Outdoor Natural skating rink (until March), paragliding, hang-gliding, mountaineering, skidoos, heli-skiing

Phone numbers
From abroad use the prefix +39 (and do **not** omit the initial '0' of the phone number).

TOURIST OFFICE

t 0166 949136
breuil-cervinia@
montecervino.it
www.montecervino.it
www.cervinia.it

FACILITIES FOR CHILDREN
Could be better

The Cervino ski school runs a ski kindergarten. And there's a babysitting and kindergarten area at Plan Maison. The slopes, with their long gentle runs, should suit families.

STAYING THERE

HOW TO GO
Plenty of hotel packages

Most of the big tour operators come here, providing between them a wide selection of hotels, though other types of accommodation are rather thin on the ground. A Club Med opened two seasons ago.

Hotels There are almost 50 hotels, mostly 2- or 3-stars, but there are a few 4-stars.

((((4) **Hermitage** (0166 948998) Small, luxurious Relais et Château just out of the village on the road up to Cieloalto. Great views, pool, free bus to lifts.

(((3) **Excelsior Planet** (0166 949426) Recommended by two 2003 reporters; spa facilities and mini-bus to lift (both cost extra). In centre near Cretaz lifts.

(((3) **Sporthotel Sertorelli** (0166 949797) Excellent food, sauna and hot-tub. Ten minutes from lifts.

(((3) **Europa** (0166 948660) Friendly and family run; near Cretaz lifts. Pool.

((2) **Astoria** (0166 949062) Right by main lift station. Family run and simple. 'Comfortable but that's all,' says a reporter.

((2) **Marmore** (0166 949057) Friendly, family run, with 'quite good food'; on main street – an easy walk to the lifts.

Self-catering There are many apartments in the resort, but few are available through British tour ops.

EATING OUT
Plenty to choose from

Cervinia's 50 or so restaurants allow plenty of choice. The Chamois and Matterhorn are excellent, but quite expensive. The Grotta belies its name with good food ('best kids' pizza,' says a reader). Casse Croute also serves good pizzas. The Copa Pan has a lively atmosphere and is again recommended by several reporters. The Bricole and the Nicchia have also been praised, and the Maison de Saussure does 'very good local specialities'. An evening out at the Baita Cretaz mountain hut makes a change.

APRES-SKI
Disappoints many Brits

Plenty of Brits come here looking for action but find there isn't much to do except tour the mostly fairly ordinary bars. The Copa Pan (see Eating out) is lively, good value and serves generous measures. The Dragon Bar is popular with Brits and Scandinavians and has satellite TV and videos ('it's great if you're homesick,' says a recent reporter). Lino's (by the ice rink) ('excellent food and music'), the Yeti, Labatt and Café des Guides (with mementos of the owner's Himalayan mountaineering trips) are all recommended by reporters. The discos liven up at weekends. There are tour-rep-organised events such as snow-mobiling on the old bob-sled run, quiz nights, bowling and fondue nights.

OFF THE SLOPES
Little attraction

There is little to do for those who don't plan to hit the slopes. The pleasant town of Aosta is a four-hour round trip. Village amenities include hotel pools, a fitness centre and a natural ice rink. The walks are disappointing. The mountain restaurants that are reachable by gondola or cable-car are not special.

STAYING UP THE MOUNTAIN
To beat the queues

Up at Plan Maison, the major lift junction 500m/1,640ft vertical above the resort, Lo Stambecco (0166 949053) is a 50-room 3-star hotel ideally placed for early nights and early starts. Less radically, the Cime Bianche (0166 949046) is a rustic 3-star chalet on the upper fringes of the resort (in the area known as La Vieille).

STAYING DOWN THE VALLEY
Great home run

Valtournenche, 9km/5.5 miles down the road, is cheaper than Cervinia, has a genuine Italian atmosphere and a fair selection of simple hotels, of which the 3-star Bijou (0166 92109) is the best.

A newish gondola speeds you out of town. But the slow lifts above it mean it takes quite a time to reach the top. The exceptionally long run back down is a nice way to end the day – when it is all open (the bottom section is often closed due to lack of snow). The main street through the village is very busy with cars going to and from Cervinia.

Cortina d'Ampezzo

The scenery will take your breath away even if the slopes don't

COSTS

① ② ③ ④ ⑤ ⑥

RATINGS

The slopes

Snow	★★★
Extent	★★★
Expert	★★
Intermediate	★★★
Beginner	★★★★★
Convenience	★
Queues	★★★
Mountain restaurants	★★★★

The rest

Scenery	★★★★★
Resort charm	★★★★
Off-slope	★★★★★

NEWS

For 2002/03 a new 5-star hotel, Cristallo, with health spa and beauty centre opened. So did a new miniclub, Gulliver Park, for children aged three months to 12 years.

For 2003/04, Cortina is introducing charges on the buses around town and between lifts – each trip will cost about one euro, or you can buy a book card for the week.

➕ Magnificent Dolomite scenery – perhaps the most dramatic anywhere

➕ Marvellous nursery slopes and good long cruising runs

➕ Access to the vast area covered by the Dolomiti Superski pass

➕ Attractive, although rather towny, resort, with lots of upmarket shops

➕ Good off-slope facilities

➕ Remarkably uncrowded slopes

➖ Several separate areas spread around all sides of the resort and linked by buses

➖ Erratic snow record

➖ Expensive by Italian standards

➖ Gets very crowded in town and in restaurants during Italian holidays

➖ Very little to entertain experts

➖ Mobile phones and fur coats may drive you nuts

Nowhere is more picturesque than chic Cortina, the most upmarket of Italian resorts. Dramatic pink-tinged cliffs and peaks rise vertically from the top of the slopes, giving picture-postcard views from wherever you are.

Cortina's slopes are fine for its regular upmarket visitors from Rome and Milan, many of whom have second homes here and enjoy the strolling, shopping, people-watching and lunching as much as the odd leisurely excursion onto the slopes. For beginners and leisurely intermediates, the splendid nursery slopes and long, easy, well-groomed runs are ideal. For keen piste-bashers, Cortina's fragmented areas can be frustrating, especially if snow is scarce and the area is fragmented even more; but the access to the Sella Ronda and other Dolomiti Superski resorts, though time-consuming, is some compensation – having a car is best for exploring. For experts, there are few tough runs, and the best of those are prone to poor snow conditions and closure because they face south.

THE RESORT

In winter, more people come to Cortina for the clear mountain air, the stunning views, the shopping, the cafes and to pose and be seen than for the winter sports – 70 per cent of all Italian visitors don't bother taking to the slopes. Cortina attracts the rich and famous from the big Italian cities. Fur coats and glitzy jewellery are the norm.

The resort itself is a widely spread town rather than a village, with exclusive chalets scattered around the outskirts. The centre is the traffic-free, Corso Italia, full of chic designer clothes, jewellery and antique shops, art galleries and furriers – finding a ski shop can seem tricky. The cobbles and picturesque church bell tower add to the atmosphere. In early evening, the street is packed with people parading up and down in their finery and using their mobile phones. Seeing anyone dressed for the slopes at 5pm is rare.

Unlike the rest of the Dolomites, Cortina is pure Italy. It has none of the Germanic traditions of the Sud Tirol.

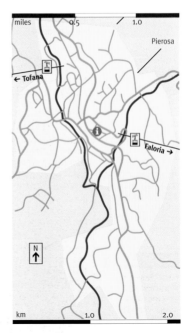

Surrounding the centre is a horrendous one-way system, often traffic-clogged and a nasty contrast to the stunning scenery everywhere else you look. The lifts to the two main areas of slopes are a fair way from the centre, and at opposite sides of town. Other lifts are bus-rides away. There's a wide range of hotels in the centre and scattered in the outskirts. Staying centrally is best. The local bus service is good, but no longer free – each trip costs about a euro. A car can be useful, especially for getting to the outlying areas and to make the most of other areas on the Dolomiti Superski pass. San Cassiano is not far to the west, with links from there to Corvara and the other Sella Ronda resorts.

THE MOUNTAINS

Cortina first leapt to fame as host of the 1956 Winter Olympics. At the time, it was very modern; now its facilities feel dated. There is a good mixture of slopes above and below the tree line.

THE SLOPES
Inconveniently fragmented
All Cortina's smallish separate areas are a fair trek from the town centre. The largest is **Socrepes**, accessed by chair- and drag-lifts a bus-ride away. You can reach it by piste from **Tofana**, Cortina's highest area, accessed by cable-car from near the Olympic ice rink. On the opposite side of the valley is the tiny **Mietres** area. Another two-

stage cable-car from the east side of town leads to the **Faloria** area, from where you can head down to chairs that lead up into the limited but dramatic runs beneath **Cristallo**.

Other areas are reachable by road. The cable-car from Passo Falzarego up to Lagazuoi accesses a beautiful red run to Armenterola, which takes you away from all signs of civilisation through the stunning scenery of the Hidden Valley. On the way to Passo Falzarego is the tiny but spectacular Cinque Torri area. Its excellent, north-facing slopes are accessed by a high-speed quad, followed by a one-person chair and a rope tow. It's worth taking them for the long red run down the back to Passo Giau. Another excellent red run down from Lagazuoi takes you back to the cable-car, or to the tiny Col Gallina area, from where you can take a pleasant green to Cinque Torri.

Reporters consistently praise the excellent grooming and quiet slopes but complain about the piste map not showing some runs, the way runs are named on the mountain but numbered on the map, poor piste marking, World Cup races disrupting January skiing, and having to take some cable-cars down as well as up if snow is poor or you want to avoid poling. A 2003 reporter commented on the number of very fast skiers tearing down the slopes – perhaps because the grooming is so good.

One way to tour the area is to use special ski itineraries, maps for which

Cortina d'Ampezzo

387

KEY FACTS

Resort	1225m
	4,020ft
Slopes	1225-2930m
	4,020-9,610ft
Lifts	51
Pistes	140km
	87 miles
Blue	33%
Red	62%
Black	5%
Snowmaking	133km
	83 miles

CORTINA TURISMO /
PAOLA DANDREA

There are lots of good, mountain restaurants with stunning views all around Cortina's slopes →

ITALY

boarding

Despite its upmarket chic, Cortina is a good resort for learning to board. The Socrepes nursery slopes are wide, gentle and served by a fast chair-lift. And progress on to other easy slopes is simple because you can get around in all areas using just chairs and cable-cars – though there are drags, they can be avoided. A specialist snowboard shop, Boarderline, organises instruction as well as equipment hire. There's little off-piste to interest experienced boarders, but the best is to be found off the back of Cinque Torri, and the tiny Col Gallina area. There are some nice trees and natural undulations under the one-person chair at Cinque Torri.

are available at the tourist and ski pass offices. 'Skitour Olympia' takes you on the 1956 Olympic downhill, GS and slalom courses and the Bobsled run. 'Skitour Romantic Views' covers the Lagazuoi-Cinque Torri area.

TERRAIN-PARKS
Not bad for first-timers
There is a terrain-park at Faloria which has some decent kickers and rails, and a half-pipe. We're told it's open to all, although there was a sign up saying 'snowboarders only' when we visited.

SNOW RELIABILITY
Lots of artificial help
The snowfall record is erratic – it can be good here when it's poor on the north side of the Alps (and vice versa). But over 90 per cent of the pistes are now covered by snowmaking, so cover should be good if it is cold enough to make snow. When we visited a few years ago, the link from Tofana to Socrepes was closed because of lack of snow on a key south-facing slope – which made the areas even more fragmented. In 2003 however, though natural snow was scarce it was very cold, and the pistes had ample cover.

FOR EXPERTS
Limited
The run down from the second stage of the Tofana cable-car at Ra Valles is deservedly graded black; it goes through a gap in the rocks, and a steep, narrow, south-facing section gives wonderful views of Cortina. It can be tricky in poor snow conditions.

Cortina's other steep run goes from the top of the Cristallo area at Forcella Staunies. A chair-lift takes you to a south-facing couloir which is often shut due to avalanche danger or poor snow.

Other than these two runs there are few challenges. There are some great, long red runs though, and if it snows there may not be much off-piste, but you'll also have very little competition for first tracks. Heli-skiing is available.

FOR INTERMEDIATES
Fragmented and not extensive
To get the most out of Cortina you must like cruising in beautiful scenery and not mind repeating runs.

The runs at the top of Tofana are short but normally have the best snow. The highest are at over 2800m/9,190ft and mainly face north. But be warned: the only way back down is by the

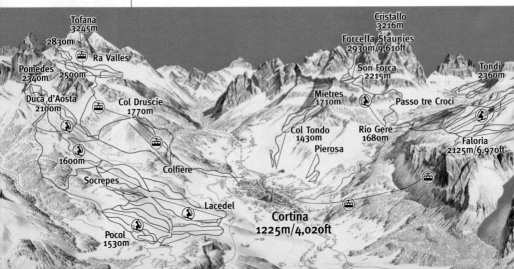

SCHOOLS

Cortina
t 0436 2911
info@scuolascicortina.
it

Azzurra Cortina
t 0436 2694
azzurracortina@libero.
it

Classes
(Cortina prices)
6 days (2½hr per day)
€178

Private lessons
€37 for 1hr; each
additional person €12

CHILDREN

There is non-skiing
childcare, and schools
offer all-day classes
for children.

Gulliver Park (0340
0558399) at Pocol
has a playground and
daily mini-disco and
takes children from 3
months to 12 years
from 9.30am to
4.30pm.

CORTINA TURISMO /
PAOLA DANDREA

The top chair serving
the south-facing black
run at Forcella
Staunies is
spectacularly set but
rarely open →

---

tricky black run described above or by
cable-car. The reds from the linked
Pomedes area offer good cruising.

Faloria has a string of fairly short
north-facing runs – we loved the Vitelli
red run, round the back away from the
lifts. And the Cristallo area has a long
blue run served by a fast quad.

It is well worth making the trip to
Cinque Torri for wonderful, deserted
fast cruising on usually excellent north-
facing snow. The Hidden Valley run
from Lagazuoi at the top of the Passo
Falzarego cable-car to Armenterola is a
must – a very easy red and one of the
most beautiful runs we've come across.
It offers isolation amid sheer pink-
tinged Dolomite peaks and frozen
waterfalls. Make time to stop at the
atmospheric Scotoni rifugio near the
end, then it's a long pole, skate or
walk to the welcome sight of a horse-
drawn sled (with ropes attached) which
tows the weary to Armenterola. Shared
taxis take you back to Passo Falzarego
(if you've time, try the slopes of Alta
Badia, accessed from Armenterola).

FOR BEGINNERS
Wonderful nursery slopes
The Socrepes area has some of the
biggest nursery slopes and best
progression runs we have seen. Some
of the blue forest paths can be icy and
intimidating. But you'll find ideal
gentle terrain on the main pistes.

FOR CROSS-COUNTRY
One of the best
Cortina has around 75km/47 miles of
trails suitable for all standards, mainly in
the Fiames area, where there is a cross-
country centre and school. Trails include
a 30km itinerary following an old railway
from Fiames to Cortina, and there is a
special beginner area equipped with
snowmaking.

QUEUES
No problem
Most Cortina holidaymakers rise late,
lunch lengthily and leave the slopes
early – if they get on them at all. That
means few lift queues and generally
uncrowded pistes – a different world to
the crowded Sella Ronda circuit. 'Lack
of queues was one of the highlights of
our holiday,' said one reporter.
Another recent visitor was delighted to
find the slopes got emptier in the
afternoons, as the Italians left the
slopes, but that lifts stayed open as
late as 5pm.

MOUNTAIN RESTAURANTS
Good, but get in early
Lunch is a major event for many
Cortina visitors. At weekends you often
need to book or turn up very early to
be sure of a table. Many restaurants
can be reached by road or lift, and
pedestrians arrive as early as 10am to
sunbathe, admire the views and idle
the time away on their mobile phones.

Although prices are high in the
swishest establishments, we've found
plenty of reasonably priced places,
serving generally excellent food. In the
Socrepes area, the Rifugio Col Taron is
highly recommended and the Pié de
Tofana, Rifugio Pomedes and El Faral
are also good.

At Cristallo the Rio Gere at the base
of the quad chair and Rifugio Son
Forca, with fabulous views at the top
of it (and owned by Alberto Tomba's
former trainer), are both worth a visit.

The restaurants at Cinque Torri, the
Scoiattoli ('magnificent home-made
pastas') and the Rifugio Averau, offer
fantastic views as well as good food,
and are non-smoking. The Rifugio
Fedare, over the back of Cinque Torri,
is also recommended and non-
smoking. Rifugio Lagazuoi, a short hike
up from the top of the Passo Falzarego
cable-car, also has great views and is
no smoking. Smoking always used to
be de rigeur in all restaurants here, but
non-smoking is now quite common.

Cortina d'Ampezzo

389

GETTING THERE

Air Venice 160km/100 miles (2hr). Treviso 132km/82 miles (1¾hr). Saturday transfers available for hotel guests (and Sunday, for Venice only); advance booking required.

Rail Calalzo (35km/22 miles) or Dobbiaco (32km/20 miles); frequent buses from station.

ACTIVITIES

Indoor Swimming pool, saunas, health spa, museums, art gallery, cinema, indoor tennis court, public library

Outdoor Rides on Olympic bob run, snowrafting down Olympic ski jump, crazy sledge for moonlit excursions, snow-shoe tours, all at Adrenalin centre; Olympic ice-stadium (2 rinks), curling, ice hockey, sleigh rides, horse-riding school, 6km/4 miles of walking paths, toboggan run, heli-skiing

Phone numbers From abroad use the prefix +39 (and do **not** omit the initial '0' of the phone number).

TOURIST OFFICE

t 0436 866252
cortina@dolomiti.org
www.cortina.dolomiti.org

SCHOOLS AND GUIDES
Mixed reports
Of the three ski schools, we've had mixed reports of the Cortina school over the years – though we lack recent reports. The Gruppo Guide Alpine offers off-piste and touring.

FACILITIES FOR CHILDREN
Better than average
By Italian standards childcare facilities are outstanding, with a choice of all-day care arrangements for children of practically any age. However, given the small number of British visitors, you can't count on good spoken English. And the fragmented area can make travelling around with children difficult.

STAYING THERE

HOW TO GO
Now with more packages
Hotels dominate the market but there are some catered chalets.

Hotels There's a big choice, from 5-star luxury to 1-star and 2-star pensions.
((((5) **Miramonti** (0436 4201) Spectacularly grand hotel, 2km/1 mile south of town. Pool.
((((5) **Cristallo** (0436 881111) New last year, with a spa-health clinic. A hike from the lifts and town centre, but there's a shuttle bus.
((((4) **Poste** (0436 4271) Reliable 4-star, at the heart of the town.
((((4) **Ancora** (0436 3261) Elegant public rooms. On the traffic-free Corso Italia.
((((4) **Parc Victoria** (0436 3246) Rustic 4-star with small rooms but good food, at the Faloria end of the town centre.
((((4) **Corona** (0436 3251) Family run 4-star, very friendly with good food and lots of original art. Near Tofana lift.
((((4) **Park Faloria** (0436 2959) Newish, near ski jump, splendid pool, good food.
(((3) **Olimpia** (0436 3256) Comfortable B&B hotel in centre, near Faloria lift.
(((3) **Menardi** (0436 2400) Welcoming roadside inn, a long walk from centre and lifts.
(((3) **Villa Resy** (0436 3303) Small and welcoming, just outside centre, with British owner.
(((3) **Montana** (0436 862126) 'Excellent B&B. Amazing value and central location,' says a 2002 reporter.
Self-catering There are some chalets and apartments – usually out of town – available for independent travellers.

EATING OUT
Huge choice
There's an enormous selection, both in town and a little way out, doing mainly Italian food. The very smart and expensive El Toulà is in a beautiful old barn, just on the edge of town. Many of the best restaurants are further out – such as the Michelin-starred Tivoli, Meloncino, Leone e Anna, Rio Gere and Baita Fraina. Reasonably priced central restaurants include the Cinque Torri and the Passetto for pizza and pasta. You can also arrange a night-time jaunt for a meal at a rifugio, travelling by snowmobile and sledge.

APRES-SKI
Lively in high season
Cortina is a lively social whirl in high season, with lots of well-heeled Italians staying up very late.

The Lovat is one of several high-calorie tea-time spots. There are many good wine bars: Enoteca has 700 wines and good cheese and meats; Osteria has good wines and local ham; and Villa Sandi, Brio di Vino and Febar have been recommended. The liveliest bar is the Clipper, with a bob-sleigh by the door. Discos liven up after 11pm.

OFF THE SLOPES
A classic resort
Cortina attracts lots of people who don't use the slopes. The setting is stunning, the town attractive, the shopping extensive and many mountain restaurants are accessible by road (a car is handy). And there's plenty more to do, such as swimming, ice skating and dog-sledding. There is an observatory at Col Drusciè which has star-gazing tours (call 0436 3146 to book). You can have a run (with driver!) down the Olympic bob-sleigh run. There's horse jumping and polo on the snow occasionally. Trips to Venice are easily organised.

Courmayeur

Seductive village, stunning scenery, limited slopes

<table>
<tr><td colspan="2">

COSTS

① ② ③ ④ ⑤ ⑥
</td></tr>
</table>

RATINGS

The slopes

Snow	****
Extent	**
Expert	***
Intermediate	****
Beginners	**
Convenience	*
Queues	***
Mountain restaurants	****

The rest

Scenery	****
Resort charm	****
Off-slope	***

NEWS

For 2003/04, a boarder-cross run is planned: the first special facility for boarders or freestylers. The snowmaking capacity will be increased by 10 per cent.

The Swiss International City Ski Championships in association with Momentum Ski are run here annually. This season's dates are 5 to 8 February 2004. For more details see 'Corporate ski trips' chapter.

The Mont Blanc tunnel reopened in March 2002 after the tragic fire of 1999. This makes day trips to Chamonix and access from Geneva airport quick and easy once again.

+ Charming old village, with car-free centre and stylish shops and bars

+ Stunning views of Mont Blanc massif

+ Pleasant range of intermediate runs

+ Day trips to Chamonix (including doing the Vallée Blanche run) possible

+ Good base for heli-skiing

+ Comprehensive snowmaking

+ Good mountain restaurants

– Lack of nursery slopes and easy runs for beginners to progress to

– No tough pistes

– Relatively small area, with mainly short runs; high-mileage piste-bashers will get bored in a week

– Slopes very crowded on Sundays

– Tiresome walk and cable-car journey between village and slopes

Courmayeur is very popular, especially at weekends, with the smart Italian set from Milan and Turin. It's easy to see why: it's very easy to get to and certainly the most captivating of the Val d'Aosta resorts.

The scenery, the charm of the village, the stylish bars and restaurants and the nightlife are big draws. The main slopes are fine but nothing special given their limited range of difficulty, inconvenient location across the valley from the village and their limited size; a keen piste-basher will cover Courmayeur in a day. But a day trip to Chamonix is easy, via the Mont Blanc tunnel.

The resort could make a jolly week for those who want to party as much as hit the slopes. It also appeals to those with quite different ambitions, who want to explore the spectacular Mont Blanc massif with the aid of a guide and other local peaks with the aid of a helicopter.

THE RESORT

Courmayeur is a traditional old Italian mountaineering village that, despite the nearby Mont Blanc tunnel road and modern hotels, has retained much of its old-world feel.

The village has a charming traffic-free centre of attractive shops, cobbled streets and well-preserved buildings. An Alpine museum and a statue of a long-dead mountain rescue hero add to the historical feel.

The centre has a great atmosphere, focused around the Via Roma. As the lifts close, people pile into the many bars, some of which are very civilised. Others wander in and out of the many small shops, which include a salami specialist and a good bookshop. At weekends people-watching is part of the evening scene, when the fur coats of the Milanese and Torinese take over.

The village is quite large and its huge cable-car is right on the southern edge of town, a fair distance from much of the accommodation. There is no shuttle-bus alternative to walking, but you can leave skis, boards and boots in lockers at the top – highly

recommended by reporters. There is another short walk from the top to the other lifts before you can get going.

Having accommodation close to the

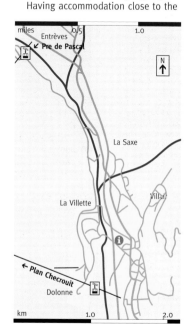

KEY FACTS

Resort	1225m	
	4,020ft	
Slopes	1210-2755m	
	3,970-9,040ft	
Lifts	23	
Pistes	100km	
	62 miles	
Blue	20%	
Red	70%	
Black	10%	
Snowmaking	18km	
	11 miles	

LIFT PASSES

Courmayeur Mont Blanc
Covers all lifts in Val Veny and Checrouit, and the lifts on Mont Blanc up to Punta Helbronner.

Beginners
Two free nursery lifts.

Main pass
1-day pass €32.50
6-day pass €169

Children
Under 12: 6-day pass €126.75
Under 8: €42.25 with accompanying adult

Notes
Single ascent on some lifts and half-day pass available. Passes for four or more consecutive days are valid for 1 day in Chamonix.

village cable-car is handy. Parking at the cable-car is very limited, but drivers can go to Entrèves, a few kilometres away, where there is a large car park at the Val Veny cable-car. Buses, infrequent but timetabled, link Courmayeur with La Palud, just beyond Entrèves, for the Punta Helbronner-Vallée Blanche cable-car.

THE MOUNTAINS

The pistes suit intermediates, but are surprisingly limited for such a well-known, large resort. They are varied in character, if not gradient. Piste marking could be improved.

THE SLOPES
Small but interestingly varied
The slopes are separate from the village: you have to ride a cable-car to them and either take it down or take a bus from Dolonne at the end of the day. The cable-car arrives at the bottom of the slopes at Plan Checrouit (where you can store your equipment).

There are two distinct sections, both almost entirely intermediate. The north-east-facing **Checrouit** area accessed by the Checrouit gondola catches morning

sun, and has open, above-the-tree-line pistes. The 25-person, infrequently running Youla cable-car goes to the top of Courmayeur's pistes. There is a further tiny cable-car to Cresta d'Arp. This serves only long off-piste runs but it is no longer compulsory to have a guide with you to go up it.

Most people follow the sun over to the north-west-facing slopes towards **Val Veny** in the afternoon. These are interesting, varied and tree lined, with great views of Mont Blanc and its glaciers. Connections between the Checrouit and Val Veny areas are good, with many alternative routes. The Val Veny slopes are also accessible by cable-car from Entrèves, a few miles outside Courmayeur.

A little way beyond Entrèves is La Palud, where a cable-car goes up in three stages to Punta Helbronner, at the shoulder of **Mont Blanc**. There are no pistes from the top, but you can do the famous Vallée Blanche run to Chamonix from here without the horrific ridge walk on the Chamonix side – you catch a bus or a taxi back from Chamonix through the Mont Blanc tunnel. Or you can tackle the tougher off-piste runs on the Italian side of

boarding

Courmayeur's pistes suit intermediates, and most areas are easily accessible by novices as the main lifts are cable-cars, chairs and gondolas – but it's all a bit steep for absolute beginners. The biggest draws for the more experienced are the off-piste routes to be done with a guide.

Mont Blanc. None of these glacier runs should be done without a guide.

La Thuile and Pila are an easy drive to the south, and Cervinia is reachable.

TERRAIN-PARKS
Little to offer
Like a lot of Italian resorts, Courmayeur has no terrain-park or half-pipe. However, the resort is planning to create a 500m boarder-cross run for 2003/04. This will be near the top high-speed chair (Plan de la Grabba).

SNOW RELIABILITY
Good for most of the season
Courmayeur's slopes are not high – mostly between 1700m and 2250m (5,600ft and 7,400ft). Those above Val Veny face north or north-west, so keep their snow well, but the Plan Checrouit side is rather too sunny for comfort in late season. There is snowmaking on most main runs, so good coverage in early- and mid-season is virtually assured – we were there in the January 2002 snow drought and enjoyed decent skiing entirely on man-made snow.

FOR EXPERTS
Off-piste is the only challenge
Courmayeur has few challenging pistes. The only black – the Competizione, on the Val Veny side – is not hard, and few moguls form elsewhere. But if you're lucky enough to find fresh powder – as we have been several times – you can have fantastic fun among the trees.

Classic off-piste runs go from Cresta d'Arp, at the top of the lift network, in three directions – a clockwise loop via Arp Vieille to Val Veny, with close-up views of the Miage glacier; east down a deserted valley to Dolonne or Pré St Didier; or south through the Youla gorge to La Thuile.

On Mont Blanc, the Vallée Blanche is not a challenge (though there are more difficult variations), but the Toula glacier route on the Italian side from Punta Helbronner to Pavillon most certainly is, often to the point of being dangerous. There are also heli-drops available, including a wonderful 20km/12 mile run from the Ruitor

glacier down into France – you catch the lifts back up from La Rosière and ski or board down to La Thuile (a taxi-ride from Courmayeur). And you can do a day trip to Chamonix through the Mont Blanc tunnel.

FOR INTERMEDIATES
Ideal gradient but limited extent
The whole area is suitable for most intermediates, but it is small. The avid piste-basher will find it very limited for a week's holiday.

The open Checrouit section is pretty much go-anywhere territory, where you can choose your own route and make it as easy or difficult as you like. The blue runs here are about Courmayeur's gentlest. In Val Veny, the reds running the length of the Bertolini chair are more challenging and very enjoyable. They link in with the pretty, wooded slopes heading down to Zerotta.

The Zerotta chair dominates Val Veny, with lots of alternatives from the top – good for mixed abilities since runs of varying difficulty meet up at several places on the way down.

The Vallée Blanche, although off-piste, is easy enough for adventurous, fit intermediates to try. So is the local heli-skiing (from £70 a drop including a guide); you are picked up on the piste so there's no wasted time.

FOR BEGINNERS
Consistently too steep
Courmayeur is not well suited to beginners. There are several nursery slopes, none ideal. The area at Plan Checrouit gets crowded, and there are few easy runs for the near-beginner to progress to. The small area served by the short Tzaly drag, just above the Entrèves cable-car top station, is the most suitable beginner terrain, and it tends to have good snow.

FOR CROSS-COUNTRY
Beautiful trails
There are 35km/22 miles of trails scattered around Courmayeur. The best are the four covering 20km/12 miles at Val Ferret, served by bus. Dolonne has a couple of short trails.

Courmayeur

393

SCHOOLS

Monte Bianco
t 0165 842477
montebianco@maestri
disci.com

Classes
5 days (3hr per day)
€137

Private lessons
€28 to €40 for 1hr
for 1 person; each
additional person
€5.50

CHILDREN

The Kinderheim at
Plan Checrouit (0165
842477) takes
children from the age
of 6 months, 9.30 to
4pm. Children taking
lessons can be
deposited at the ski
school in Courmayeur
at 9am, and they will
be looked after for
the whole day (lesson
am, play pm). (Ages:
from 4. 6 full days
including lunch and
childcare €180.)
There is a 'fun park'
for children at
Dolonne. The
Kinderheim at the
Sports Centre takes
children from the age
of 6 months.

QUEUES
Sunday crowds pour in

The Checrouit and Val Veny cable-cars
suffer queues only on Sundays, and
even these can be beaten with an early
start. There can be queues to go down
as well as up. Patience is needed when
waiting for the infrequent Youla cable-
car – 'Not sure it's worth waiting more
than 15 minutes for the one steep red,'
said a reporter. Overcrowded slopes on
Sundays, particularly down to Zerotta,
can also be a problem.

MOUNTAIN RESTAURANTS
Lots – some of them good

The area is lavishly endowed with 27
establishments ranging from rustic
little huts to larger self-service places.
Most huts do table-service of delicious
pizza and pasta and it is best to book.
But there are also snack bars selling
more basic fare and relying on views
and sun to fill their terraces.

Several restaurants are excellent.
Maison Vieille, at the top of the chair
of the same name and run by the
charming mountain man Giacomo, is
our favourite – a welcoming rustic
place with superb home-made pastas.
Chiecco, next to the drag-lift with the
same name at Plan Checrouit, has
good food and friendly service. The
pick of the Plan Checrouit places is the
Christiania – book a table downstairs.

On the other side of the mountain
in Val Veny is another clutch of places
worth noting – the Zerotta, at the foot
of the eponymous chair has a sunny
terrace and good food; the nearby
Petit Mont Blanc and the jolly Grolla

are also recommended. One of the
better snack bars is Courba Dzeleuna,
with incredible views and delicious
home-made myrtle grappa (beware of
the alcohol-soaked berries left in the
bottom of your glass if you want to hit
the slopes again), just below the top
of Dzeleuna chair.

SCHOOLS AND GUIDES
Good reports

'We had the best instructor for ages –
possibly ever,' said a reporter about
the Monte Bianco ski school. There is a
thriving guides' association ready to
help you explore the area's off-piste; it
has produced a helpful booklet
showing the main possibilities.

FACILITIES FOR CHILDREN
Good care by Italian standards

Childcare facilities are well ahead of
the Italian norm, but Courmayeur is far
from an ideal resort for a young family.

STAYING THERE

HOW TO GO
Plenty of hotels

Courmayeur's long-standing popularity
ensures a wide range of packages
(including some excellent weekend
deals), mainly in hotels. Tour op
Interski has cheap hotels out of town,
and buses people in. One or two UK
operators have catered chalets.
Hotels There are nearly 50 hotels,
spanning the star ratings.
((((4) **Grand Hotel Courmaison** (0165
831400) Luxury new hotel 2km/1mile
from town, with 'excellent food'. Pool.

GETTING THERE

Air Geneva 105km/65 miles (2hr). Turin 150km/93 miles (2hr).

Rail Pré-St-Didier (5km/3 miles); regular buses from station.

ACTIVITIES

Indoor Swimming pool and sauna at Pré-St-Didier (5km/3 miles), Alpine museum, cinema, library. Sports centre with climbing, skating rink, curling, fitness centre, indoor golf, squash, tennis, basketball, volley ball, sauna and Turkish bath

Outdoor Walking paths in Val Ferret, paragliding, snow-biking, dog-sledding

Phone numbers
From abroad use the prefix +39 (and do **not** omit the initial '0' of the phone number).

TOURIST OFFICE

t 0165 842060
apt.montebianco@psw.it
www.courmayeur.net

SNOWPIX.COM / CHRIS GILL

← They're all over the slopes: mountain restaurants, and stunning views of Mont Blanc

(((((4) **Gallia Gran Baita** (0165 844040) Luxury place with antique furnishings, panoramic views and 'superb food'. Pool. Shuttle-bus to cable-car.

(((((4) **Pavillon** (0165 846120) Comfortable 4-star near cable-car, with a pool. Friendly staff.

((((3) **Auberge de la Maison** (0165 869811) Small atmospheric 3-star in Entrèves under same ownership as Maison de Filippo (see Eating Out).

((((3) **Bouton d'Or** (0165 846729) Small, friendly B&B near main square.

((((3) **Berthod** (0165 842835) Friendly, family-run hotel near centre.

((((3) **Grange** (0165 869733) Rustic, stone-and-wood farmhouse in Entrèves.

((((3) **Triolet** (0165 846822) 'Excellent location 100m/300ft from lift. Comfy, well furnished.'

(((2) **Edelweiss** (0165 841590) Friendly, cosy, good-value; close to the centre.

(((2) **Lo Scoiattolo** (0165 846721) Good rooms, good food, shame it's at the opposite end of town to the cable-car.

Self-catering There is quite a lot available to independent bookers.

EATING OUT
Jolly Italian evenings

There is a great choice, both in downtown Courmayeur and within taxi-range; there's a handy promotional booklet describing many of them (in English as well as Italian). The touristy but very jolly Maison de Filippo in Entrèves is famous for its fixed-price, 36-dish feast. We've been impressed by the traditional Italian cuisine of both Pierre Alexis and Cadran Solaire. The Terrazza ('excellent pasta and very friendly, jolly service') is a rising star and has just been renovated. The Tunnel pizzeria and Mont-Frety ('good value', 'its antipasti is a must') and La Padella ('great pizza, raclette and fondue') have been recommended by reporters. Restaurants tend to be busy, so book well in advance.

APRES-SKI
Stylish bar-hopping

Courmayeur has a lively evening scene, centred on stylish bars with comfy sofas or armchairs to collapse in. Our favourites are the Roma (reporters have been very taken with the free canapés), the back room of the Caffè della Posta and the Bar delle Guide. The Cadran Solaire is where the big money from Milan and Turin hangs out. The American Bar has good music and an excellent selection of wines. The Red Lion is worth a visit if you're missing English pubs. Ziggy's is an Internet cafe popular with local teenagers. Poppys has been recommended for dancing. There are two good night clubs in Entrèves – Jimmys and the Maquis.

OFF THE SLOPES
Lots on for non-slope users

If you're not interested in hitting the snow you'll find the village pleasant – parading up and down is a favourite pastime for the many non-slope users the resort attracts (especially at weekends). You can go by cable-car up to Punta Helbronner, by bus to Aosta, or up the main cable-car to Plan Checrouit to meet friends for lunch. The huge sports centre is good (indoor tennis, climbing wall, ice skating, squash, golf practice, gym, sauna, steam, but no pool).

STAYING UP THE MOUNTAIN
Why would you want to?

Visiting Courmayeur and not staying in the charming village seems perverse – if you're that keen to get on the slopes in the morning, this is probably the wrong resort. But at Plan Checrouit, the 1-star Christiania (0165 843572 – see Mountain restaurants) has simple rooms and the 3-star Baita (0165 843570) is smarter; you need to book way in advance.

Livigno

Lowish prices and highish altitude – a tempting combination

COSTS

① ② ③ ④ ⑤ ⑥

RATINGS

The slopes
Snow	****
Extent	**
Experts	**
Intermediates	***
Beginners	****
Convenience	**
Queues	****
Mountain restaurants	***

The rest
Scenery	***
Resort charm	***
Off-slope	**

NEWS

For 2002/03 a new fast quad chair was installed for access to the Mottolino lifts from valley level, as an alternative to the existing gondola.

KEY FACTS

Resort	1815m
	5,950ft
Slopes	1815-2800m
	5,950-9,190ft
Lifts	33
Pistes	115km
	71 miles
Blue	35%
Red	48%
Black	17%
Snowmaking	70km
	43 miles

➕ High altitude plus snowmaking ensures a long season and a good chance of snow to resort level

➕ Large choice of beginners' slopes

➕ Modern and improving lift system

➕ Cheap by the standards of high resorts, with the bonus of duty-free shopping – a great place to treat yourself to new equipment

➕ Cosmopolitan, friendly village with some Alpine atmosphere

➕ Long, snow-sure cross-country trails

➖ No difficult pistes

➖ Long airport transfer – around 5hr

➖ Slopes split into two quite widely separated areas

➖ Village is very long and straggling, and a bit rough round the edges

➖ Few off-slope amenities

➖ Bleak, windy setting – often resulting in upper lifts being shut

➖ Not many really comfortable hotels bookable through UK tour operators

➖ Nightlife can disappoint

Livigno offers the unusual combination of a fair-sized mountain, high altitude and fairly low prices. Despite its vaunted duty-free status, hotels, bars and restaurants are not much cheaper than in other Italian resorts, but shopping is – there are countless camera and clothes shops. As a relatively snow-sure alternative to the Pyrenees or to the smallest, cheapest resorts in Austria, Livigno seems attractive. But don't overlook the long list of drawbacks.

THE RESORT

Livigno is an amalgam of three villages in a wide, remote valley near the Swiss border – basically a string of hotels, bars, specialist shops and supermarkets lining a single long street. The buildings are small in scale and mainly traditional in style, giving the village a pleasant atmosphere. The original hamlet of San Antonio is the nearest thing Livigno has to a centre, and the best all-round location. Here, the main street and those at right angles linking it to the busy bypass road are nominally traffic-free. The road that skirts the 'traffic-free' area is constantly busy, and becomes intrusive in the hamlets of Santa Maria, 1km/0.5 miles to the north, and San Rocco, a bit further away to the south (and uphill).

Lifts along the length of the village access the western slopes of the valley. The main lift to the eastern slopes is directly across the flat valley floor from the centre.

The bus services, on three colour-coded routes, are free and fairly frequent, but can get overcrowded at peak times and stop early in the evening. Minibus taxis are an affordable alternative for groups.

The lift pass covers Bormio and Santa Caterina, an easy drive or free bus-ride if the high pass **is open, and a six-day pass entitles you to a discount rate on a one-day pass** in St Moritz, reached via a road tunnel – a 'fantastic' day out, says a reader.

The airport transfer from Bergamo is long – five hours with a snack stop.

(map)

miles 0.5 1.0

← Costaccia

Sta. Maria

S. Antonio

Mottolino →

S. Rocco

Carosello

km 1.0 2.0

Livigno

LIFT PASSES

Alta Valtellina
Covers all lifts in Livigno, Bormio, Valdidentro and Santa Caterina

Main pass
1-day pass €29.50
6-day pass €148

Senior citizens
Over 60: 6-day pass €103

Children
Under 13: 6-day pass €103
Under 8: free pass

Notes
6-day pass entitles you to a discount on a 1-day pass for St Moritz.

Alternative passes
Half-day passes for Livigno only are available. Natura skipass classic covers lift pass, tuition, ski hire and a full day's pass for St Moritz.

boarding

Livigno attracts a fair number of boarders. There are some good, long, high runs for free-riders and carvers, as well as ample off-piste opportunities for intermediate riders. Most of the resort can be accessed by cable-cars and chairs; however, the excellent beginner slopes are mainly served by drags.

THE MOUNTAINS

The mainly open slopes, on either side of the valley, are more extensive than in many other budget destinations.

THE SLOPES
Improved links

There are three sectors, all of them suitable for moderate and leisurely intermediates, and two of them are reasonably well linked.

A two-seater chair from the nursery slopes at the north end of the village take you up to **Costaccia**, where a long fast quad chair-lift goes along the ridge towards the **Carosello** sector. The blue linking run back from Carosello to the top of Costaccia is flat in places and may involve energetic poling if the snow conditions and the wind are against you. Carosello is more usually accessed by the optimistically named Carosello 3000 gondola at San Rocco, which goes up, in two stages, to 2750m/9,020ft. Most runs return towards the village, but there are a couple on the back of the mountain, on the west-facing slopes of Val

Federia – served by a double drag-lift.

The ridge of **Mottolino** is reached by an efficient gondola from Teola, a tiresome walk or a short bus-ride across the valley from San Antonio. From the top, you can descend to fast quads on either side of the ridge or, if you must, take a slow antique chair up the ridge to Monte della Neve. There is now the alternative of a fast quad starting a little way along the valley, and linking with a six-pack to Monte della Neve.

Signposting is patchy and the piste map isn't always entirely accurate.

TERRAIN-PARKS
There, but empty

There's a half-pipe and a good, if underused, terrain-park/boarder-cross in the Mottolino area.

SNOW RELIABILITY
Very good, despite no glacier

Livigno's slopes are high (you can spend most of your time around 2500m/8,000ft), and with snow-guns on the lower slopes of Mottolino and Costaccia, the season is long.

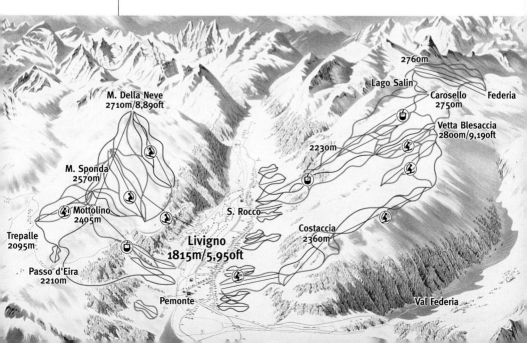

ITALY

FOR EXPERTS
Not recommended

The piste map shows a few black runs but these are not particularly steep. Even the all-black terrain served by the six-pack on Monte della Neve is really no more than stiff red in gradient. There is off-piste to be done, but guidance would be needed.

FOR INTERMEDIATES
Flattering slopes

Good intermediates will be able to tackle all of the blacks without worry. The woodland black run down from Carosello past Tea da Borch is narrow in places and can get mogulled and icy at the end of the day. The runs on the back of Carosello down to Federia are challenging, and bumpy. Moderate intermediates have virtually the whole area at their disposal. The long run beneath the Mottolino gondola is one of the best – and there is also a long under-used blue going less directly to the valley from the top. Leisurely types have several long cruises available in all sectors. The run beneath the Valandrea-Vetta fast chair, at the top of the Costaccia sector, is a splendid slope for confidence-building – 1.5km/1 mile long, dropping only 260m/850ft.

FOR BEGINNERS
Excellent but scattered slopes

A vast array of nursery slopes along the sunny lower flanks of Costaccia, and other slopes around the valley, make Livigno excellent for novices – although some of the slopes at the northern end are steep enough to cause difficulties. There are lots of longer runs suitable for fast learners and near-beginners.

CROSS-COUNTRY
Good snow, bleak setting

Long snow-sure trails (40km/25 miles in total) follow the valley floor, making Livigno a good choice, provided you don't mind the bleak scenery. There is a specialist cross-country school, and the resort organises major cross-country races.

QUEUES
Few problems these days

Despite reports of queues for the Costaccia chair at midday and short delays for the Carosello gondola in peak season, lift queues are not generally a problem. Investment in fast new chairs at Carosello and Mottolino has rid the area of long queues. A bigger problem is that strong winds often close the upper lifts, causing overcrowding lower down. The red run under the Mottolino gondola is prone to congestion.

MOUNTAIN RESTAURANTS
More than adequate

On Mottolino, the refuge at the top of the gondola is impressive, with smart self- and table-service sections, a solarium and a nursery, but 'immense' lunch-time queues. The rustic restaurants at Passo d'Eira and Trepalle are a good option for a quiet stop. And there are some more charming restaurants lower down. The welcoming Tea del Vidal is at the base of the same sector. Costaccia's Tea del Plan is pleasantly rustic and sunny, with good food and a great atmosphere. The self-service place at the top of Carosello is acceptable and Tea da Borch, in the trees lower down, serves great food in a Tirolean-style atmosphere, though the run down can be tricky. Lunch in the valley at the hotel Sporting (near the Carosello gondola station) is popular. The terrace at the hotel Möta, at the base of the Costaccia lifts, is also recommended.

CHILDREN

Alì Babà (Livigno Inverno / Estate) 0342 978050 (aged 3 years and over: 6 2hr lessons and 2hr nursery €160; lunch €26); Miniclub (Top Club Mottolino) 0342 997408; Peribimbi 0342 970711 (for 18-36 months).

GETTING THERE

Air Bergamo 200km/124 miles (5hr).

Rail Tirano (48km/30 miles), Zernez (Switzerland, 28km/17 miles); regular buses from station, weekends only.

ACTIVITIES

Indoor Saunas, fitness centre, games room, bowling, cinema

Outdoor Cleared paths, ice rink, snow-shoeing, horse-riding, ice climbing, paragliding, mountaineering

Phone numbers
From abroad use the prefix +39 (and do **not** omit the initial '0' of the phone number).

TOURIST OFFICE

t 0342 996379
info@aptlivigno.it
www.aptlivigno.it

SCHOOLS AND GUIDES
Watch out for short classes
There are several schools. English is widely spoken, and recent reports are complimentary. A common complaint is that most of the classes are short (two-hours). Another is that beginners spend too long on the nursery slopes before progressing up the mountain. It also seems to be the case that the schools on the Costaccia-Carosello side avoid the Mottolino sector altogether.

FACILITIES FOR CHILDREN
Not bad for Italy
The schools run children's classes. The Livigno Inverno/Estate school's Alì-Babà nursery offers all-day care and the staff speak English.

STAYING THERE

HOW TO GO
Lots of hotels, some apartments
Livigno has an enormous range of hotels and a number of apartments. There are some attractively priced catered chalets from UK operators.
Hotels Most of the hotels are small 2- and 3-star places, with a couple of 4-stars out of the centre.
Intermonti (0342 972100) Modern 4-star with all mod cons (including a pool); some way from the centre, on the Mottolino side of the valley.
Bivio (0342 996137) The only hotel in central Livigno with a pool.
Steinbock (0342 970520) Nice little place, far from major lifts but a short walk from some nursery slopes.
Loredana (0342 996330) Modern chalet on the Mottolino side. 'Pleasant food, good rooms'.
Larice (0342 996184) Stylish little 3-star B&B well placed for Costaccia lifts and slopes.
Montanina (0342 996060) Good central 3-star.
Camana Veglia (0342 996310) Charming old wooden chalet. Popular restaurant, well placed in Santa Maria.
Silvestri (0342 996255) 2-star in the San Rocco area: 'Great staff, comfortable rooms, filling meals'.
Self-catering All the big tour operators that come here have apartment options. Most are cheap and cheerful.

EATING OUT
Value for money
Livigno has lots of traditional, unpretentious restaurants, many hotel-based. Hotel Concordia has some of the best cooking in town. Mario's has one of the largest menus, serving seafood, fondue and steaks in addition to the ubiquitous pizza and pasta. Bait dal Ghet and the Bivio restaurant are popular with the locals, and the Rusticana does wholesome, cheap food. Pesce d'Oro is good for seafood and Italian cuisine. The Bellavista, Ambassador, Mirage, Grolla and the Garden are also recommended.

APRES-SKI
Lively, but disappoints some
It's not that there isn't action in Livigno, but simply that the scene is quieter than some people expect in a duty-free resort. Also, the best places are scattered about, so the village lacks evening buzz. At tea time many people return to their hotels for a quiet drink. But Tea del Vidal, at the bottom of Mottolino, gets lively, as does the Stalet bar at the base of the Carosello gondola. The Caffè della Posta umbrella bar, near the centre, is also popular. We hear Europe's highest brewery is in production at the Echo. Nightlife gets going only after 10pm. Galli's pub, in San Antonio, is 'a full-on party pub', popular with Brits. The Kuhstall under the Bivio hotel is an excellent cellar bar with live music, as is the Helvetia, over the road. The San Rocco end is quietest, but Daphne's and Marco's are popular. The stylish Art Cafe is also recommended. Kokodi and the Cielo are the main discos.

OFF THE SLOPES
Look lively, or go shopping
Livigno offers a small range of outdoor alternatives to skiing and boarding – horse-riding among them. Walks are uninspiring and there is no sports centre or public swimming pool. However, the duty-free shopping more than makes up for this. Trips to Bormio and St Moritz are popular.

Madonna di Campiglio

Extensive, easy slopes amid stunning scenery

COSTS

① ② ③ ④ ⑤ ⑥

RATINGS

The slopes

Snow	✱✱✱
Extent	✱✱✱
Expert	✱✱
Intermediate	✱✱✱✱
Beginner	✱✱✱✱
Convenience	✱✱
Queues	✱✱✱
Mountain restaurants	✱✱✱

The rest

Scenery	✱✱✱✱
Resort charm	✱✱✱
Off-slope	✱✱✱

NEWS

In 2002/03 the old terrain-park at Grostè was replaced with a bigger park and boarder-cross run called Ursus. Snowmaking was also increased.

For 2003/04, the old Genziana chair-lift on the way back from Monte Vigo and Marilleva is due to be replaced by a new high-speed quad with covers.

- ✚ Pleasant town with car-free centre
- ✚ Fairly extensive network of slopes, best for beginners and intermediates
- ✚ Excellent mountain restaurants
- ▬ Spread-out resort and infrequent shuttle-bus service
- ▬ Quiet après-ski

Like Cortina, Madonna is a pleasant Dolomite town with an affluent, almost exclusively Italian, clientele – though the scenery isn't in quite the same league. Folgarida and Marilleva, with which Madonna shares its slopes, are quite different, attracting some British groups, including schools.

THE RESORT

Madonna is a spread-out, modern, but traditional-style town with a pedestrian-only centre, set in a prettily wooded valley beneath the impressive Brenta Dolomites. There is more development 1km/0.5 miles south, and a frozen lake between the two.

Madonna attracts an affluent, young, Italian clientele. It has almost as many 4-star hotels as 3-stars, and lots of smart shops. Many visitors stay around the village in the day, and promenading is an early evening ritual.

There are several mountain access lifts, and they are quite widely spread; it's worth staying near one of them. The main nursery slopes are some way out at Campo Carlo Magno. The free ski-bus runs to a timetable, but is not frequent. Some hotels run minibuses.

THE MOUNTAINS

There are three areas of linked slopes around Madonna: Pancugolo to the west, Pradalago to the north, and Passo Grostè (the highest area) to the east. Pradalago is also linked by lift

Passo Grostè 2505m/8,220ft

Monte Spinale 2110m

Doss del Sabion 2100m

Val d'Agola

1540m

Pinzolo 770m

800m

Malga Grual

Pancugolo 2150m

Madonna di Campiglio 1520m/4,990ft

Pradalago 2145m

Doss del Pesa 2230m

Monte Vigo 2180m

Campo Carlo Magno 1860m

Monte Spolverino 2090m

Orti

1880m

1860m

Folgarida 1400m

Marilleva 1400m

1300m

↑ The town spreads along a prettily wooded valley, with slopes on both sides

MADONNA TOURIST OFFICE

KEY FACTS

Resort	1520m
	4,990ft
Slopes	1550-2505m
	5,085-8,220ft
Lifts	50
Pistes	150km
	93 miles
Blue	44%
Red	40%
Black	16%
Snowmaking	77km
	48 miles

Phone numbers
From abroad use the prefix +39 (and do **not** omit the initial '0' of the phone number).

TOURIST OFFICE

t 0465 442000
info@campiglio.net
www.campiglio.net

and piste to Monte Vigo, where the slopes of Folgarida and Marilleva also meet. There are long-term plans for a link between Pancugolo and the separate little resort of Pinzolo.

Slopes The terrain is mainly intermediate, both above and below the tree line. This year's reporters were very impressed with the grooming. Some recommend skiing the Marilleva and Folgarida slopes in the afternoon to avoid crowded ski school classes.

Terrain-parks A new terrain-park, called Ursus, complete with boarder-cross run, half- and quarter-pipes and big air jumps, was built last season at Grostè.

Snow reliability Although many of the runs are sunny, they are at a fair altitude, and there has been hefty investment in snowmaking. As a result, snow reliability is reasonable.

Experts Experts should plan on heading off-piste. But the 3-Tre race course and the Spinale Direttissima are steep. Pista Nera, above Folgarida, can be a challenging mogul field. And a 2003 reporter enjoyed the Orti/Marilleva black at Marilleva.

Intermediates Pancugolo, Madonna's racing mountain, is ideal: early or timid intermediates will love the area and have no difficulty exploring most of the network, though the connection to Folgarida is a bit trickier. Grostè and Pradalago have long, easy runs, though the former can get crowded.

Beginners It's a good resort for beginners, if you don't mind using the bus service out to the excellent nursery slopes at Campo Carlo Magno.

Snowboarding The resort is popular with boarders and some major events have been held here.

Cross-country There are 30km/19 miles of pretty trails through the woods.

Queues The links with Marilleva are the main bottleneck – queues are worst for those returning there from Madonna in the afternoon. A 2003 reporter tells of

a 35-minute wait for the Cinque Laghi cable-car to Pancugolo. The moving carpet link from Grostè to Pradalago is a bottleneck at midday. One reporter tells of pushy queues for the Pradalago chair at the start of ski school classes and another of afternoon queues for the Boch chair to Monte Spinale.

Mountain restaurants The Malga Montagnoli in the lower part of Grostè is a 'charming old refuge with a decent self-service'. The restaurant at Pancugolo has 'stunning views'. The Rifugio Graffer is recommended for its 'freshly cooked burgers'. The hotel Alaska, beside run 2 at Folgarida, was described as 'fantastic, great value'.

Schools and guides There are several ski schools, but some instructors don't speak English. A reporter had several complaints about the Nazionale.

Facilities for children Very limited.

STAYING THERE

How to go There is a wide choice of hotels and some self-catering.

Hotels The 4-star Spinale (0465 441116) is convenient. The central 3-star Milano (0465 441210) is also recommended. At Campo Carlo Magno the Zeledria (0465 441010) is 'a good 4-star with friendly staff'.

Eating out There are around 20 restaurants to choose from. Belvedere, the Roi and Stube Diana have all been recommended. Locanda degli Artisti is 'worth the expense for a special night out,' says a reporter this year. Some of the mountain huts are also open in the evening and will help with transport.

Après-ski Après-ski is quiet. Franz-Joseph Stube, Bar Suisse and Cantina del Suisse are recommended – and the Alpes is perhaps the smartest club. Enoteca Bacchus is a new wine bar.

Off the slopes Window-shopping, skating on the lake and walking are popular. There's also paragliding.

Monterosa Ski

Europe's best kept secret – an undiscovered gem

COSTS

①②③④⑤⑥

RATINGS

The slopes
Snow	✱✱✱
Extent	✱✱✱✱
Expert	✱✱✱
Intermediate	✱✱✱✱
Beginner	✱✱
Convenience	✱✱✱✱
Queues	✱✱✱✱
Mountain restaurants	✱✱

The rest
Scenery	✱✱✱✱
Resort charm	✱✱✱
Off-slope	✱

NEWS

A new cable-car linking the Alagna slopes with Gressoney's should be ready for 2003/04. Each car will hold 100 people and it will link Pianalunga and Passo dei Salati. It will run on double cables to enable it to operate even in strong winds. The run down from Passo dei Salati towards Alagna will, however remain off-piste – plans to make it an official piste have apparently been shelved for safety reasons.

There are plans to build another cable-car in a couple of years' time from Passo dei Salati to Cresta Rosa at 3500m, above Punta Indren. This will open up some stunning off-piste and remove the need to use the tiny, ancient cable-car to Punta Indren.

- ➕ Fairly extensive network of pistes
- ➕ Fabulous intermediate and advanced off-piste, including heli-skiing
- ➕ Beautiful scenery
- ➕ Good snow reliability and grooming
- ➕ Quiet, pretty, unspoiled villages

- ➖ Few steep pistes – mainly easy cruising
- ➖ Links to and from Alagna are off-piste only
- ➖ Few off-slope diversions
- ➖ Limited après-ski

Monterosa Ski is Italy's little-known and less extensive answer to France's Trois Vallées and has a good lift system which is set for further big development over the next few seasons. Yet it is hardly heard of on the international market. It is popular with Italians at weekends, when they drive up for the day from Milan and Turin. But during the week it is deserted. The pistes are mostly intermediate and set amid impressive scenery. And the off-piste is fabulous (and usually deserted). It is the only major ski area we have come across in Europe where there is no real well-developed resort to stay in. The villages that access the slopes have avoided commercialisation and still retain a friendly, small-scale, local ambience. Our advice is to get there soon before all this changes.

THE RESORT

The main resorts are Champoluc in the western valley, Gressoney, in the central valley, and Alagna to the east.

Champoluc is towards the end of a long, winding road up from the Aosta valley motorway. It is strung out along the road for quite a distance but retains a certain quiet charm and very Italian feel. The first part you come to is the attractive old village centre with the church and a fast-running river.

Small shops and hotels line the road between here and the gondola, several minutes' walk away. You can store boots and skis/board there overnight. More accommodation is on the road to Frachey, where there is a chair-lift into the slopes.

Gressoney La Trinité is a quiet, neat little village, with cobbled streets, wooden buildings and an old church. It is about 800m/0.5 miles from the chair-lift into the slopes, where there are a few convenient hotels. It is a bus-ride from the outpost of Stafal at the head of the valley, which is the link between the Gressoney and Champoluc slopes and has a few rather soulless blocks. Gressoney St Jean, a bigger village, is 5km/3 miles down the valley and has its own separate slopes. Local buses are covered by the lift pass.

The main resort in the east valley is Alagna, a strange place with some large, deserted and dilapidated

buildings as well as smaller charming wooden buildings and church.

Trips to Cervinia, La Thuile and Courmayeur (covered by the Aosta Valley pass) are possible by car.

THE MOUNTAINS

The slopes of Monterosa Ski are relatively extensive, and very scenic. The pistes are almost all intermediate (and well groomed), and the lifts are mainly chairs and gondolas, with few drag-lifts. The terrain is undulating and runs are long, but many lifts serve only one or two pistes. The piste map is poor: 'Woefully inadequate,' said a reporter. And a couple of reporters say the top lifts and the connection between Champoluc and Gressoney closed due to high winds during their stays, restricting the available terrain.

Slopes A gondola from Champoluc followed by two slow chairs takes you up to the steep, narrow, bumpy link with the rest of the slopes (which a lot of timid intermediates find very difficult). Taking the bus to the Frachey chair is a quicker way into the main cruising runs and the link via Colle Bettaforca with Stafal in the Gressoney valley, and avoids the tricky top run.

At Stafal a cable-car followed by a high-speed chair take you back to the Champoluc slopes and two successive gondolas opposite take you up to Passo dei Salati. From there runs lead

SKI arrangements
.com

08700 110565
Crich Matlock, DE4 5DE

KEY FACTS

Resort	1640m
	5,380ft
Slopes	1200-3550m
	3,940-11,650ft
Lifts	38
Pistes	180km
	125 miles
Blue	29%
Red	63%
Black	8%
Snowmaking	70km
	44 miles

back down to Stafal and to Gressoney La Trinité and Orsia, both served by chair-lifts. Or you can head towards Alagna on a popular off-piste run.

From Alagna a modern gondola goes to Pianalunga at mid-mountain. For 2003/04 a new cable-car from here will take you to Passo dei Salati. Before this was built the only way further up was by a two-person chair-lift up to a tiny, ancient cable-car, which accesses the high slopes around Punta Indren. The only ways back to Gressoney from here are off-piste. On the Alagna side there is lots of off-piste and an ungroomed black run that leads to an ancient bucket lift that you jump into while it is moving (it goes back to the bottom of the cable-car).

Gressoney St Jean and Antagnod, near Champoluc, have their own small areas of slopes.

Terrain-parks There were big air jumps last season near the top of the Champoluc gondola.

Snow reliability Generally good, thanks to snowmaking, altitude and grooming.

Experts The attraction is the off-piste, with great runs from the high-points of the lift system in all three valleys and some excellent heli-drops. A mountain guide is essential for getting the best out of the area. We had two fabulous days last season – one exploring the runs from Punta Indren and the other a heli-drop on Monte Rosa, skiing down to Zermatt and returning off-piste from the top of the Cervinia area. The bowls above Gressoney are little used and snow can lie untracked for days. Alagna

is a cult area for expert off-piste. There are a few black pistes but none of them really deserve their grading.

Intermediates For those who like to travel on easy, undemanding pistes, the area is great, with long cruising runs from the ridges down into the valleys. There isn't much on-piste challenge for more demanding intermediates, but those willing to take a guide and explore some of the gentler off-piste will have a great time. If you stick to the pistes, a weekend or mid-week break rather than a full week might be worth trying: 'It's great for a short break,' said a reporter.

Beginners The high nursery slopes at the top of the gondola at Champoluc are better than the lower ones at Gressoney. But Gressoney has better easy runs to progress to than Champoluc (where it is best to go to the Frachey chair or to Antagnod).

Snowboarding There is great off-piste free-riding.

Cross-country There are long trails around St Jean, and shorter ones up the valley; Brusson, in the Champoluc valley, has the best trails in the area.

Queues Only at weekends, when the hordes from Turin and Milan arrive, are there any queues. The worst bottleneck is the tiny top cable-car on the Alagna side, where waits of over an hour are possible. The double chair to Belvedere on the way back from Frachey/Bettaforca to Champoluc can have long queues at the end of the day. Pistes can get crowded at weekends, too, but the off-piste is still delightfully quiet.

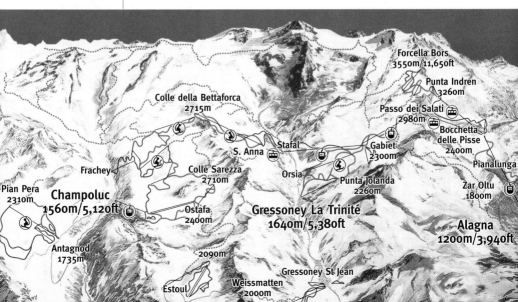

ITALY

404

There is fabulous, deserted off-piste amid great scenery ↗

MONTEROSA TOURIST OFFICE / SCUOLA DI ALPINISMO DEL MONTE ROSA

Phone numbers From abroad use the prefix +39 (and do **not** omit the initial '0' of the phone number).

TOURIST OFFICE

t 0125 303111
kikesly@monterosa-ski.com
www.monterosa-ski.com

Mountain restaurants The mountain restaurants are basic. The Chamois at Punta Jolanda, Bedemie on the way to Gressoney from Gabiet, Del Ponte above Gabiet, Vieux Crest and Belvedere, above Champoluc, and the Guglielmina, Lys and Gabiet refuges are recommended.

Schools and guides We have had good reports on the ski schools ('one of the best instructors I have had') and on the Monterosa mountain guides. Tour operator Ski2 runs its own ski school.

Facilities for children There is a special kids' ski school and snow park at Antagnod near Champoluc and a mini-club at Gressoney St Jean.

STAYING THERE

How to go More tour operators are discovering the area. We've had good reports of Monterosa specialists Ski 2.

Hotels At Champoluc the Castor (0125 307117) in the old centre is 'an absolute gem' with 'good food and magnificent puddings' and is managed by a British guy who married into the family that has owned it for generations. At the hotel California (0125 307977 – the owners speak no English) every room is dedicated to a pop star or group (eg the Byrds, Bob Dylan, Joan Baez, the Doors) and their music plays whenever you turn on the light. It's quite a way out of the centre. The Breithorn (0125 08734), two minutes from the gondola, is an excellent luxury 4-star, converted from a 100-year-old building with wonderful beamed bedrooms. The owner also has the luxury renovated Mascognaz chalet in a deserted village reached only by snowmobile – you can stay or have dinner up there for a supplement.

At Gressoney La Trinité several reporters recommend the Jolanda Sport (0125 366140), with gym and sauna, and right by the lift; Dufour (0125 366139) has also been mentioned. In Alagna, try the Monterosa (0163 923209) or Cristallo (0163 91285).

Eating out Both Gressoney and Champoluc have a few stand-alone restaurants, but most are in hotels.

Après-ski Après-ski is quiet. In Champoluc, the bar of the hotel Castor is cosy, the Golosono is a small atmospheric, authentic Italian wine bar, the Galion opposite the gondola is busy as the lifts close, the West Road in the California has karaoke some nights. At weekends, the disco beneath hotel California gets going.

Off the slopes There is little to amuse those who don't head for the slopes.

Sauze d'Oulx

'Suzy does it' still, but with more dignity than in the past

405

COSTS

① ② ③ ④ ⑤ ⑥

RATINGS

The slopes

Snow	**
Extent	****
Expert	**
Intermediate	****
Beginner	**
Convenience	**
Queues	***
Mountain restaurants	***

The rest

Scenery	***
Resort charm	**
Off-slope	*

NEWS

The Tuassieres drag-lift was rebuilt for 2002/03.

For 2003/04 there will be a new kindergarten, La Cinciarella.

In Sansicario two new lifts have been built: a 6-seat gondola from Cesana to the resort and a quad above it.

Turin has been chosen to host the 2006 Olympic Winter Games; most of the Alpine events will be held at Sansicario and Sestriere, and freestyle competitions at Sauze d'Oulx.

➕ Extensive and uncrowded slopes, great intermediate cruising

➕ Linked into Milky Way network

➕ Mix of open and tree-lined runs is good for all weather conditions

➕ Entertaining nightlife

➕ Some scope for off-piste adventures

➕ One of the cheapest major resorts there is – and more attractive than its reputation suggests

➖ Still lots of ancient lifts, making progress around the slopes slow

➖ Erratic snow record – and still far from comprehensive snowmaking

➖ Crowds at weekends

➖ Brashness and Britishness of resort will not suit everyone

➖ Very few challenging pistes – and hardly a mogul to be seen

➖ Mornings-only classes, and the best nursery slopes are at mid-mountain

➖ Steep walks around the village, and an inadequate shuttle-bus service

If you're looking for a cheap holiday in a resort with extensive slopes, put Sauze on your shortlist. In the 1980s it became known as prime lager-lout territory; but it always was a resort of two halves – young Brits on a budget alongside mature second-home owners from Turin – and these days the two halves seem to be much more in balance, especially at weekends. It still has lively bars and shops festooned in English signs, but sober Brits like you and us need not stay away. When we visit, we like it more than we expect to – as do many reporters.

We are slightly haunted, though, by the memory of the bare slopes of our first visit, in the mid-1980s. Thin cover three seasons ago brought it all back: Sauze is a resort that needs comprehensive snowmaking, and doesn't yet have it.

THE RESORT

Sauze d'Oulx sits on a sloping mountain shelf facing north-west across the Valle di Susa, with impressive views of the towering mountains forming the border with France. Most of the resort is modern and undistinguished, made up of block-like hotels relieved by the occasional chalet, spreading down the steep hillside from the foot of the slopes. Despite the shift in clientele described above, the centre is still lively at night; the late-closing bars are usually quite full, and the handful of discos do brisk business – at the weekend, at least.

Sauze also has an attractive old core, with narrow, twisting streets and houses roofed with huge stone slabs. There is a central car-free zone, but traffic roams freely through most of the village, which can be congested morning and evening. The roads can become icy and treacherous at night – with few pavements.

Out of the bustle of the centre,

where most of the bars and nightclubs are located, there are quiet, wooded residential areas full of secluded apartment blocks, and a number of good restaurants are also tucked out of the way of the front line. Chair-lifts go from the top of the village and from two points on its fringes. There's also a chair from nearby Jouvenceaux.

Most of the hotels are reasonably central, but the Clotes lift is at the top of the village, up a short but steep hill, and the Sportinia chair is an irritatingly long walk beyond that. Buses (not covered by the lift pass) are infrequent and can't cope with high-season crowds. The service around lunch-time is particularly poor.

KEY FACTS

Resort	1510m
	4,950ft

For Milky Way

Slopes	1390-2825m
	4,560-9,270ft
Lifts	92
Pistes	400km
	250 miles
Blue	12%
Red	67%
Black	21%
Snowmaking	80km
	50 miles

For Sauze d'Oulx-Sestriere-Sansicario only

Slopes	1390-2825m
	4,560-9,270ft
Lifts	53
Pistes	300km
	186 miles
Snowmaking	65km
	40 miles

ITALY

406

THE MOUNTAINS

Sauze's mountains provide excellent intermediate terrain. The piste grading fluctuates from year to year, if you believe the resort's map – and we're never sure we've caught up with the latest changes from blue to red and red to blue. But most reporters agree that many runs graded red or even black should really be graded blue; challenges are few and far between. (The same might be said of the whole extensive Milky Way area, of which Sauze is one extreme.)

THE SLOPES
Big and varied enough for most

Sauze's local slopes are spread across a broad wooded bowl above the resort, ranging from west- to north-facing. The main lifts are chairs, from the top of the village up to **Clotes** and from the western fringes to **Sportinia** – a sunny mid-mountain clearing in the woods, with a ring of restaurants and hotels (see Staying up the mountain) and a small nursery area.

The high point of the system is **Monte Fraiteve**. From here you can travel west on splendid broad, long runs to **Sansicario** – and on to chair-lifts near **Cesana Torinese** that link with **Claviere** and then **Montgenèvre**, in France, the far end of the Milky Way (both are reached more quickly by car).

You normally get to **Sestriere** from the lower point of Col Basset, on the shoulder of M Fraiteve. The alternative of descending the sunny slope from M Fraiteve itself has been reinstated after a few years of closure; but snow here is not reliable, which we're told is why the old lift from Sestriere up this slope was removed some years ago. You can make the link via the gondola but this is prone to closure in bad weather.

As in so many Italian resorts, piste marking, direction signing and piste map design are not taken particularly seriously.

The slopes of Montgenèvre and Sestriere are dealt with in separate chapters. If you have a car, you can go beyond Montgenèvre to Briançon, Serre-Chevalier and Bardonecchia.

TERRAIN-PARKS
Not in Sauze

There's no park or pipe here. The nearest is in the Sises sector of Sestriere.

SNOW RELIABILITY
Can be poor, affecting the links

The area is notorious for erratic snowfalls, occasionally suffering acute droughts. Another problem is that many of the slopes get a lot of afternoon sun. At these modest altitudes, late-season conditions are far from reliable. Reporters have found icy,

LIFT PASSES

La Via Lattea
Covers all lifts in Sauze d'Oulx, Sestriere, Sansicario, Cesana and Claviere.

Main pass
1-day pass €27
6-day pass €149

Senior citizens
Over 60: 6-day pass €137

Children
Under 12: 6-day pass €137
Under 8: free pass

Notes
One-day extension for Montgenèvre available.

boarding

Sauze has good snowboarding slopes – it's got local tree-lined slopes (with space in the trees, too), high, undulating, open terrain, and links to other resorts in the Milky Way. But although it has a fair number of chair-lifts, there are also lots of drags – a serious drawback for novice riders.

bare slopes at vital link points earlier in the season, too – particularly from M Fraiteve. There's snowmaking on a couple of slopes, notably the key home run from P Rocca via Clotes to the village.

FOR EXPERTS
Head off-piste

Very few of the pistes are challenging. The best slopes are at virtually opposite ends of Sauze's local area – a high, north-facing run from the shoulder of M Fraiteve, and the sunny slopes below M Moncrons.

The main interest is in going off-piste. There are plenty of minor opportunities within the piste network, but the highlights are long, top-to-bottom descents of up to 1300m/4,270ft vertical from M Fraiteve, ending (snow permitting) at villages dotted along the valleys. The best known of these runs (which used to be marked on the piste map but is no longer) is the Rio Nero, down to the road near Oulx. When snow low down is poor, some of these runs can be cut short at Jouvenceaux or Sansicario.

FOR INTERMEDIATES
Splendid cruising terrain

The whole area is ideal for confident intermediates who want to clock up the kilometres. For the less confident, the piste map doesn't help because it picks out only the very easiest runs in blue – there are many others they could manage. The Belvedere and Moncrons sectors at the east of the area are served only by drags but offer some wonderful, uncrowded high

cruising, some of it above the tree line.

The long runs down to Sansicario and down to Jouvenceaux are splendid, confidence-boosting intermediate terrain. Getting back to Sauze involves tackling some of the steepest terrain in the area – the black run from M Fraiteve to the Col Basset lifts at Malafosse. This presents a problem for many intermediates and is a serious shortcoming in the circuit. The run down to Sestriere gets a lot of sun but is worth it for the somewhat more challenging intermediate terrain on the opposite side of the valley. If conditions are too poor, you can always ride the gondola down.

At the higher levels, where the slopes are above the tree line, the terrain often allows a choice of route. Lower down are pretty runs through the woods, where the main complication can be route-finding. The mountainside is broken up by gullies, and pistes that appear to be quite close together but may in fact have no easy connections between them.

FOR BEGINNERS
There are better choices

Sauze is not ideal for beginners: its village-level slopes are a bit on the steep side and the main nursery area is up the mountain, at Sportinia. Equally importantly, the mornings-only classes don't suit everyone.

FOR CROSS-COUNTRY
Severely limited, even with snow

There is very little cross-country skiing, and it isn't reliable for snow.

Inefficient lifts mean that the slopes are not too crowded →

QUEUES
Slow lifts the biggest problem

There can be irritating waits at Sportinia when school classes are setting off, or immediately after lunch; otherwise the system has few bottlenecks. But, despite the recent introduction of three fast quads, most of the lifts are ancient and terribly slow. The chair-lift from the village to Clotes is an extreme case: a museum-piece which requires you to carry your skis in your lap and hit the ground running at the top. This lift is simply inadequate. Breakdowns of elderly lifts may also be a nuisance. And a February visitor reports that several lifts were opened only at weekends, when the Italian crowds arrive.

MOUNTAIN RESTAURANTS
Some pleasant possibilities

Restaurants are numerous and generally pleasant, though few are particularly special. One place that's certainly worth picking out is the hotel Capricorno, at Clotes – one of the most civilised and appealing lunch spots in the Alps. It is not cheap, though. There are several more modest mid-mountain restaurants, with the main concentration at Sportinia; a recent visitor reports friendly service but 'rubber pizzas' in those he tried. The Ciao Pais, at the top of the Clotes chair-lift, the Chalet Pian della Rocca and the Chalet Clot Bourget have also pleased visitors. The Marmotta on Triplex is one reader's tip for 'drinks and service with a smile'. The Soleil Boeuf in the Sansicario area is 'good value, with a nice sun terrace'.

SCHOOLS AND GUIDES
Lessons variable, large classes

Our only recent reporter pronounces his companions' lessons satisfactory, but past reports have been mixed. A visitor tells us that there is a guide who can be contacted through the tourist office.

FACILITIES FOR CHILDREN
Tour operator alternatives

The new village kindergarten, La Cinciarella, can be booked for evenings so long as there are at least three children using the facility. You might also want to look at the nursery facilities offered by some of the major UK tour operators in the chalets and chalet-hotels that they run here – Crystal and Neilson, for example.

STAYING THERE

HOW TO GO
Packaged hotels dominate

All the major mainstream operators offer hotel packages here, but there are also a few chalets.
Hotels Simple 2-star and 3-star hotels form the core of the holiday accommodation, with a couple of 4-stars and some more basic places. **Torre** (0122 850020) Cylindrical 4-star landmark 200m/650ft below the centre. Excellent rooms, 'good food', 'plenty of choice'; mini-buses to lifts. **Hermitage** (0122 850385) Neat chalet-style hotel beside the home piste from Clotes. **Gran Baita** (0122 850183) Comfortable place in quiet, central backstreet, with excellent food and good rooms, some with sunset views. **Biancaneve** (0122 850021) Pleasant, with smallish rooms. Near the centre. **Amis** (0122 858488) Down in Jouvenceaux, but near bus stop; simple hotel run by Anglo-Italian couple.
Self-catering Apartments and chalets available, some through UK operators.

EATING OUT
Caters for all tastes and pockets

Typical Italian banquets of five or six courses can be had in the upmarket Godfather and Cantun restaurants. The Falco does a particularly good three-course 'skiers' menu'. In the old town, the Borgo and the Griglia are popular pizzerias. The Lampione is the place to go for 'pub grub' – good-value Chinese, Mexican and Indian food. Sugo's spaghetteria provides delicious, filling and economic fare. The Pecore Nere also gets good reviews. Reservations are generally recommended.

APRES-SKI
Suzy does it with more dignity

Once favoured almost solely by large groups of youngsters, some of whom were very rowdy, the number and atmosphere of Sauze's bars now impress reporters young and old.

The Assietta terrace is popular for catching the last rays of the sun at the end of the day. The excellent New Scotch bar is also recommended, as is the Lampione, in the old town.

After dinner, more places warm up. One of the best is the smart, atmospheric cocktail bar Moncrons, which holds regular quiz nights.

GETTING THERE

Air Turin 84km/52 miles (1½hr).

Rail Oulx (5km/3 miles); frequent buses.

ACTIVITIES

Indoor Bowling, cinema, sauna, massage

Outdoor Artificial skating rink, torchlit descents, heli-skiing, ice-climbing, snow-shoeing

Phone numbers
From abroad use the prefix +39 (and do **not** omit the initial '0' of the phone number).

TOURIST OFFICES

Sauze d'Oulx
t 0122 858009
sauze@montagnedoc.it
www.montagnedoc.it
Cesana Torinese (Sansicario)
t 0122 89202

VIA LATTEA / SAUZE D'OULX
TOURIST OFFICES

Not the most flattering picture but it does show the rustic side of Sauze d'Oulx ➔

Reporters also like the Village Café (first beer free with freely available vouchers); you can eat here too ('good pizzas'). The Cotton Club provides good service, directors' chairs, video screen and draught cider. Miravallino is a 'very Italian' cafe bar. Paddy McGinty's offers 'a good variety of meals including Mexican and steaks'. The 'very cosy' Derby is nice for a quiet drink in a relaxed setting, and reporters this year tell us of a new bar, the Grotta, which offers free sandwiches with your drinks. Of the discos, the Bandito is a walk away, and popular with Italians. Schuss runs theme nights and drink promotions – entrance is normally free.

Tour operators' resort reps organise the usual range of activities, including torchlit descents, bowling and 'broomball' on the ice rink.

OFF THE SLOPES
Go elsewhere
Sauze is not a particularly rewarding place in which to while away the days if you don't want to hit the slopes. Shopping is limited, there are no gondolas or cable-cars for pedestrians and there are few off-slope activities. Turin or Briançon are worth a visit.

STAYING UP THE MOUNTAIN
'You pays your money ... '
In most resorts, staying up the mountain is an amusing thing to do and is often economical – but usually you pay the price of accepting simple accommodation. Here, the reverse applies. The 4-star Capricorno (0122 850273), up at Clotes, is one of the most comfortable hotels in Sauze, certainly the most attractive and by a wide margin the most expensive. It's a charming little chalet beside the piste, with a smart restaurant and terrace (a very popular spot for a good lunch) and only eight bedrooms.

Not quite in the same league are the places up at Sportinia. Thomson runs a couple of them now – one as a chalet-hotel. Reporters who stayed here enjoyed the isolation and easy access to the slopes – but access to the village depends on expensive skidoo taxis.

Sansicario 1700m/5,580ft

If any resort is ideally placed for exploration of the whole Milky Way, it is Sansicario. It is a modern, purpose-built, self-contained but rather soulless little resort, mainly consisting of apartments linked by monorail to the small shopping precinct. The 45-room Rio Envers (0122 811333) is a reasonably comfortable, expensive hotel. Visitors recommend lunch at the Soleil Boeuf – 'good value and nice sun terrace' and the Enoteca in the evening for fondue and grappa. The place will doubtless get a boost from the 2006 Olympics – the downhill and super-G races will be held here.

Selva/Sella Ronda

Endless intermediate slopes amid spectacular Dolomite scenery

410

COSTS

① ② ③ ④ ⑤ ⑥

RATINGS

The slopes
Snow	★★★★
Extent	★★★★★
Expert	★★★
Intermediate	★★★★★
Beginner	★★★★
Convenience	★★★
Queues	★★★
Mountain restaurants	★★★★

The rest
Scenery	★★★★★
Resort charm	★★★
Off-slope	★★★

KEY FACTS

Resort	1565m
	5,130ft

For the linked lift network of Val Gardena, Alta Badia, Arabba, and the Canazei and Campitello slopes of Val di Fassa

Slopes	1235-2520m
	4,050-8,270ft
Lifts	186
Pistes	395km
	245 miles
Blue	38%
Red	53%
Black	9%
Snowmaking	276km
	171 miles

For Val Gardena-Alpe di Siusi only

Slopes	1005-2520m
	3,300-8,270ft
Lifts	81
Pistes	175km
	109 miles
Blue	30%
Red	60%
Black	10%
Snowmaking	90km
	56 miles

+ Vast network of connected slopes – suits intermediates particularly well

+ Stunning, unique Dolomite scenery

+ Superb snowmaking and grooming

+ Jolly mountain huts with good food

+ Many new lifts have cut out all but a few bad bottlenecks on Sella Ronda

+ Good nursery slopes

+ Excellent value

− Small proportion of tough runs

− Lifts and slopes can be crowded, especially on Sella Ronda circuit

− High proportion of short runs, not so many long ones

− Selva is not a particularly attractive village, nor especially convenient

− Erratic snow record; slopes vulnerable to warm weather

This is an area unlike any other. The Sella Ronda is an amazing circular network of lifts and pistes taking you around the spectacular Gruppo Sella – a mighty limestone massif with villages scattered around it, the biggest of them being Selva (aka Wolkenstein) in Val Gardena (aka Gröden). As well as this impressive main circuit, there are major lift systems leading off it at four main points. In overall scale, the network rivals the famed Trois Vallées in France. And the Dolomiti Superski lift pass covers dozens of other resorts reachable by road.

The scenery is fabulous. But the Dolomite landscape that provides the visual drama also dictates the nature of the slopes. Sheer limestone cliffs rise out of gentle pasture land; you spend your time on the latter, gazing at the former. There is scarcely a black run to be seen, and runs of more than 500m/1,600ft vertical are rare, whereas runs of under 300m/1,000ft vertical are not.

Although we hinge this chapter on Selva, you certainly shouldn't overlook the several alternative bases around the circuit. For experts, in particular, Arabba has clear attractions. It's here that the classic Dolomite landscape gives way to a more familiar kind of terrain, with longer, steeper slopes. For nervous intermediates, on the other hand, the obvious alternative to Selva is Corvara.

THE RESORT

Selva is a long roadside village, almost merged with the next village of Santa Cristina. It suffers from traffic but has traditional-style architecture and an attractive church. The area is famed for wood carvings – you'll see them all over.

The village enjoys a lovely setting under the impressive pink-tinged walls of Sassolungo and the Gruppo Sella – a fortress-like massif about 6km/ 4 miles across that lies at the hub of the Sella Ronda circuit (see the feature box later in the chapter). Despite its World Cup fame (as Val Gardena, the name of the valley) and animated atmosphere, Selva is neither upmarket nor brash. It's a good-value, civilised family resort – and is undoubtedly the biggest and liveliest of the places to stay right on the Sella Ronda circuit.

For many years the area was under Austrian rule, and reporters admire the Tirolean charm of the resort. German is the main language, not Italian, and most visitors are German, too. Selva is also known as Wolkenstein and the Gardena valley as Gröden. The local dialect is Ladino, which has resisted being absorbed into German or Italian.

Ortisei is the administrative centre of Val Gardena but it is not so convenient for the Sella Ronda slopes. For a brief description of it and the other villages on or near the circuit, see the end of this chapter.

From Selva, gondolas rise in two directions. One goes east towards Colfosco and Corvara and the clock-wise Sella Ronda route. The other takes you south from the village to Ciampinoi and the anti-clockwise route. The most convenient position is near one of these gondolas. There are regular buses until early evening – free to ski pass holders – but reporters say they can get very oversubscribed and

LIFT PASSES

Dolomiti Superski
Covers 450 lifts and
1200km/745 miles of
piste in the
Dolomites, including
all Sella Ronda
resorts.

Main pass
1-day pass €35
6-day pass €175

Senior citizens
Over 60: 6-day pass
€149

Children
Under 16: 6-day pass
€123

Alternative pass
Val Gardena pass
covers all lifts in
Selva Gardena, S
Cristina, Ortisei and
Alpe di Siusi.

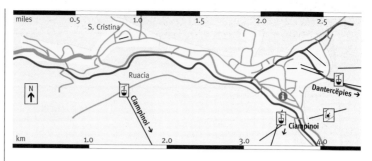

one complained about the lack of
buses to Corvara and Plan de Gralba.
Some prefer to share taxis. Others
suggest a beer or two before heading
home, to avoid the rush.

 The Dolomiti Superski pass covers
not only the Sella Ronda resorts but
dozens of others. It's an easy road trip
to Cortina – worth it for the fabulous
scenery alone. But many other drives
in this area are very tortuous and slow
– it's often quicker on skis.

THE MOUNTAIN

The slopes cover a vast area, all amid
stunning scenery and practically all
ideally suited to intermediates. There
are different piste maps for different
areas, and nearly every reporter
complains that they are inadequate
and confusing. Most recommend
buying the special Ordnance Survey-
type map with contour lines for the
whole Sella Ronda region. Piste
marking and signing also come in for
criticism, though the Sella Ronda route
itself is well signposted. Having to put
your pass in the machine at every lift
causes complaints, too.

THE SLOPES
High mileage piste excursions
A gondola and parallel-running chair
go up from Selva to **Ciampinoi**, from
where several pistes, including the
famous World Cup Downhill run,
spread out across the mountain and
lead back down to Selva, **Santa
Cristina** and **Plan de Gralba**. From Plan
de Gralba, you can head off towards
Passo Sella, **Canazei** and the rest of
the anti-clockwise Sella Ronda.

 Across the valley from the Ciampinoi
gondola (and now linked by a bridge,
eliminating the walk across the busy
road) is a chair that links with the
Dantercëpies gondola. This accesses
the clockwise Sella Ronda or you can
return to Selva on the Ladies Downhill
course. From the top you head down
to **Colfosco**, then lifts link with **Corvara**,
and you go on to **Arabba** and beyond.

 At Passo Pordoi, between Canazei
and Arabba, is the one breach in the
defences of the Gruppo Sella: a cable-
car goes up to Sass Pordoi at
2950m/9,680ft, giving access to off-
piste routes – and spectacular views.

 There are several linked areas that
are not directly on the Sella Ronda

STEFANO ZARDINI /
APT VAL DI FASSA

This is it, folks! The
Gruppo Sella massif
that the Sella Ronda
goes round. The
photo is taken from
Sass Pordoi. Canazei
is down to the left,
Arabba to the right
and Selva behind the
big rock in the
foreground. Pretty
spectacular scenery,
huh? →

ITALY

412

NEWS

Lots of new gondolas and fast chairs are transforming the slopes. Here we highlight the main recent or planned ones only. For 2003/04, a new 15-person gondola will run from Siusi to Alpe di Siusi and a fast quad will replace a drag-lift on Alpe di Siusi. The Alta Badia area plans to add two new chair-lifts. The old Biok will become a fast quad and the old Vallon chair above Corvara, which serves a good black run, will be replaced by a new fast two-seater chair. For 2002/03, Alta Badia added three new gondolas – a 15-person one replaced the cable-car out of La Villa and two 8-person ones replaced four long drags from Colfosco towards Dantercëpies.

Arabba is planning three replacement chairs for 2003/04; the most important one for the Sella Ronda circuit is the Burz chair out of the resort going anti-clockwise. Subject to final approval, this will become a fast quad, cutting lengthy queues. There are longer-term plans to cut the need to cross the busy main road here when doing the Sella Ronda.

The Cavazes-Grohmann chair on the clockwise Sella Ronda circuit above Passo Sella was upgraded to a quad for 2002/03.

For 2004/05 an underground funicular is planned at Santa Cristina linking the gondola towards Ciampinoi with that to Col Raiser.

circuit that are worth exploring. The biggest is the **Alta Badia** area to the west of Corvara, from which you can get down to **San Cassiano** and **La Villa**.

Local to Selva is the **Seceda** area, accessed by a gondola, a bus-ride from town and on the outskirts of Santa Cristina. You can head back down to the bottom or go on to **Ortisei**. And from Ortisei a cable-car goes up the other side of the valley to **Alpe di Siusi** – a gentle elevated area of quiet, easy runs, cross-country tracks and walks.

The Marmolada glacier near Arabba is open most of the winter and is now included on the main lift pass. One reader recommends it 'for the spectacular views rather than for the typically boring glacier slopes'.

TERRAIN-PARKS
A few widely-spread options
Near Selva, there are boarder-cross runs at Passo Sella by the Grohmann-Cavazes chair and at Piz Sella by the Comici chair, and there's a natural half-pipe near the Sotsaslong lift at Piz Sella. At Alpe di Siusi, there's a half-pipe by the Laurin chair and a kids' terrain-park by the Euro chair. Alta Badia has a terrain-park near the Brancia restaurant and the Dolomites Fun Park at Piz la Villa. There's a half-pipe at Belvedere above Canazei.

SNOW RELIABILITY
Excellent when it's cold
The slopes are not high – there are few above 2200m/7,220ft and most are between 1500m and 2000m (5,000ft and 6,500ft). And natural snowfalls are erratic. But we have experienced excellent pistes here in times of severe natural snow shortage – the area has has one of the largest snowmaking capacities in Europe. Most areas have snow-guns on the main runs to the resorts, and almost all Selva's local pistes are well endowed. World-class piste grooming adds to the effect. Typical reporter comments on the snowmaking are 'a revelation – quite superb', 'wonderful' and 'stunning'.

Problems arise only in poor snow years if it is too warm to make snow.

FOR EXPERTS
A few good runs
In general, experts may find the region too tame, especially if they're looking for lots of steep challenges or moguls.

Arabba has the best steep slopes (and snow). North-facing blacks and reds from Porta Vescovo back to Arabba are served by an efficient high-capacity gondola and are great fun. The black run down to La Villa is worth a visit, too. The Val Gardena World Cup piste, the 'Saslonch', is one of several steepish runs between Ciampinoi and both Selva and Santa Cristina. Unlike many World Cup pistes it is kept in racing condition for Italian team practices, but it is open to the public much of the time. It's especially good in January, when it's not too crowded. The unpisted trail down to Santa Cristina, accessed from the Florian chair on Alpe di Siusi, is not difficult, but pleasantly lonely.

Off-piste is limited because of the sheer-drop nature of the mountain tops in the Dolomites, but for the daring – and with a guide – there is excitement to be found. The itinerary from Sass Pordoi back to the cable-car station is not too difficult; the much longer route to Colfosco ends in a spectacular narrow descent through the Val de Mesdi.

FOR INTERMEDIATES
A huge network of ideal runs
The Sella Ronda region is famed for easy slopes. For early or timid intermediates, the runs from Dantercëpies to Colfosco and Corvara, and over the valley from there in the Alta Badia, are superb for cruising and confidence-boosting. They're easy to reach from Selva, but returning from Dantercëpies may be a little daunting. Riding the gondola down is an option.

Nearer to Selva, the runs in the Plan de Gralba area are gentle. The Alpe di Siusi runs above Ortisei are ideal for confidence-building – very gentle, quiet, amid superb scenery. On the rather neglected Seceda sector there is a splendid easy blue back to S Cristina.

Average intermediates have a very large network of suitable pistes, though there are few long runs. One notable one is the beautiful red swoop down the far side of the Seceda massif from Cucasattel to Ortisei. The Plan de Gralba area, the runs on either side of the Florian chair on Alpe di Siusi and the main pistes to San Cassiano and La Villa in the Alta Badia area are other recommended cruises. Don't neglect the Edelweiss valley, off the Sella Ronda circuit at Colfosco – 'nice, gentle slopes' and 'uncrowded and peaceful' said two 2003 reporters.

Several reporters also enjoyed the area above Canazei, below the Belvedere: 'Efficient lifts and good snow. The red to Lupo Bianco is a beautiful run through the trees.'

The runs back down to the valley direct from Ciampinoi are a bit more challenging, as are the descents from Dantercëpies to Selva. And, of course, most intermediates will want to do the Sella Ronda circuit at least once during a week – see feature panel. The spectacular Hidden Valley is also worth a visit. It's reached via a cable-car at

Lagazuoi, which you get to via a bus or shared taxi from Armentarola. See the Cortina chapter for details.

FOR BEGINNERS
Great slopes, but ...
Near-beginners have numerous runs, and the village nursery slopes are excellent – spacious, convenient, and kept in good condition. There are splendid gentle runs to progress to. Visiting beginners have thoroughly recommended the area in the past. However, we have varying reports about the school – see later.

FOR CROSS-COUNTRY
Beautiful trails
There are over 90km/56 miles of trails, all enjoying wonderful scenery. The 12km/7 mile trail up the Vallunga-Langental valley is particularly attractive, with neck-craning views all around. Almost half the trails have the advantage of being at altitude, running between Monte Pana and Seiseralm, and across Alpe di Siusi.

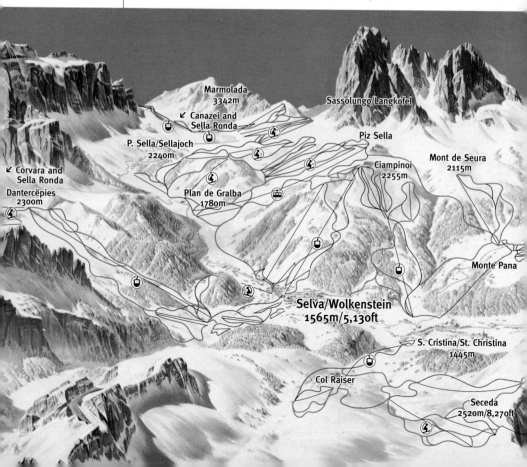

QUEUES
Still a few problems

New lifts have vastly improved the area, and there are now fewer bottlenecks. But we still get complaints about parts of the Sella Ronda circuit. The chair-lifts from Arabba in both directions have been a problem (but the anti-clockwise one is hopefully being replaced for 2003/04 – see News). A 2003 reporter complained bitterly about these and the drag-lifts back from Marmolada ('queues of over an hour'). The character of the queues can be an extra problem – 'Lots of pushing and shoving at Selva and even worse at Corvara,' says one reporter.

You may find the crowds on the Sella Ronda pistes worse than the queues for lifts.

MOUNTAIN RESTAURANTS
One of the area's highlights

There are lots of huts all over the area, and virtually all of them are lively, with helpful staff, good food, plenty of character and modest prices.

In Val Gardena the Panorama is a small, cosy, rustic suntrap at the foot of the Dantercëpies drag. On the way down to Plan de Gralba from Ciampinoi, the Vallongia Rolandhütte is tucked away on a corner of the piste. In the Plan de Gralba area the top station of the cable-car does excellent pizza; the Comici is atmospheric, with a big terrace. Piz Seteur is recommended late in the day (see Après-ski).

The trio of little huts in the Colfosco area – Forcelles, Edelweiss and Pradat – are all very pleasant.

THE SELLA RONDA

The Sella Ronda is one of the world's classic intermediate circuits. The journey around the Sella massif is easily managed in a day by even an early intermediate. The slopes you descend are almost all easy, and take you through Selva, Colfosco, Corvara, Arabba and Canazei. You can do the circuit in either direction by following very clear coloured signs. We prefer the clockwise route; it is slightly quicker and offers more interesting slopes; although the tedious series of drag-lifts above Colfosco on the anti-clockwise route has now been replaced by a gondola, it still takes a long time to get from Corvara to the top, not much of which is spent skiing. There are two free maps of the circuit available; for map-literate people, the better bet is the proper topographical one with contour lines.

The runs total around 23km/14 miles and the lifts around 14km/9 miles. The lifts take a total of about two hours (plus any queuing). We've done it in just three and a half hours plus some diversions and hut stops; five or six hours is a realistic time during busy periods, when there are crowds both on the pistes and on the lifts. If possible, choose low season or a Saturday, and set out early.

Not everyone likes it. 'It's a bit of a slog,' said one reporter. Others have found the circuit 'boring', and 'a bit of a rat race' but agree that 'it is a good way to get to other areas'. If you set out early, you can make more of the day by taking some diversions from the circuit. Among the most entertaining segments are the long runs down from Ciampinoi to Santa Cristina and Selva, from Dantercëpies to Selva, from the top of the Boe gondola back down to Corvara and from the top of the Arabba gondola. Take in all those in a day doing the circuit and you'll have had a good day.

Intermediates could take time out to explore the off-the-circuit Alta Badia area from Corvara. Groups of different abilities can do the circuit and arrange to meet along the way at some of the many welcoming rifugios.

ALTA BADIA

Ladinia Corvara
t 0471 836126
corvara@altabadiaski.
com

Colfosco
t 0471 836218
colfosco@altabadiaski.
com

La Villa
t 0471 847258
lavilla@altabadiaski.
com

S Cassiano
t 0471 849491
sancassiano@alta
badiaski.com

Pedraces
t 0471 839648
info@skiland.it

Dolomites
t 0471 844018
info@dolomiteski.it

ARABBA
scuolasci.arabba@
libero.it

VAL DI FASSA

Canazei Marmolada
t 0462 601211
info@scuolascicanazei.
com

Campitello
t 0462 750350
scuolascicampitello@
tin.it

Vajolet (Pozza di Fassa)
t 0462 763309
sci.vajolet@rolmail.net

Vigo di Fassa
t 0462 763125
scuoladisci.vigo@tin.it

Moena Dolomiti
t 0462 573770
scuolascimoena@tin.it

CHILDREN

The ski schools run a kindergarten for children aged 1 to 4, with skiing available for the older children. Those attending proper ski school classes can be looked after all day (6 days (24 hours) €143 at Selva school).

Phone numbers
From abroad use the prefix +39 (and do **not** omit the initial '0' of the phone number).

At Alta Badia the Piz Sorega above San Cassiano gets very crowded. La Brancia does 'wonderful polenta and delicious blackberry grappa'. Cherz above Passo di Campolongo has great views of Marmolada.

Around Arabba, Bec de Roces and Col de Burz are both suntraps (with 'amazing Bombardinos' at the latter). The rifugio at the top of the Porta Vescovo lifts has been recommended for 'excellent food' and 'stunning panoramic views'. Capanna Bill, on the long run down to Malga Ciapela, has wonderful views of Marmolada.

In the Seceda sector there are countless options. The cosy Sangon 'has bags of atmosphere', though a recent reporter pronounces Baita Gamsblut her favourite – 'super rustic hut with a good menu and a warm, friendly atmosphere'. The Seceda does 'wonderful food, served by waitresses in miniskirts or leather shorts', which brightened our reporter's day.

On Alpe di Siusi the rustic Sanon refuge gets a good review, particularly since 'the barman came out to serenade us with his accordion'. And the Williams hut at the top of the Florian chair has 'superb views'.

Above Canazei there are at least six huts scattered around the Belvedere bowl. Baita Belvedere is 'a good place for lunch, with excellent service' and a 'superb view'. Lower down, Lupo Bianco is a notable rendezvous point and suntrap. As well as restaurants, there are lots of little snow bars for a quick grappa.

SCHOOLS AND GUIDES
Mixed views

The Selva school is capable of good instruction, provided you get into a suitable group. One reporter found that the level of tuition was good 'but groups tended to alter on a daily basis, dependent on numbers'. The emphasis seemed to be on economic grouping rather than learners' needs. Another visitor calls the ski school at Pecol, above Canazei, 'excellent'.

FACILITIES FOR CHILDREN
Good by Italian standards

There are comprehensive childcare arrangements, but German and Italian are the main languages here and English is not routinely spoken. That said, in the past we have had reports of very enjoyable lessons and of children longing to return.

STAYING THERE

HOW TO GO
A reasonable choice

Selva and its neighbours now feature in quite a few tour operator brochures. More reporters stayed in Arabba than Selva this year.

Chalets There is a fair choice of catered chalets, including some good ones with en suite bathrooms.

Hotels There are a dozen 4-stars, over 30 3-stars and numerous lesser hotels. Few of the best are well positioned.

(((3 **Gran Baita** (0471 795210) Large, luxurious sporthotel, with lots of mod cons including indoor pool. A few minutes' walk from centre and lifts.

(((3 **Aaritz** (0471 795011) Best-placed 4-star, opposite the Ciampinoi gondola, and with an open fire.

((2 **Astor** (0471 795207) Family-run chalet in centre. Good value.

((2 **Continental** (0471 795411) 3-star situated right on the nursery slopes.

((2 **Linder** (0471 795242) 'Friendly, family-run with good food'.

((2 **Olympia** (0471 795145) Well positioned 3-star.

((2 **Pralong** (0471 795370) An uphill walk from the centre, but 'one of the best hotels we've visited', says a recent reporter.

((2 **Solaia** (0471 795104) 3-star chalet, superbly positioned for lifts and slopes.

Self-catering There are plenty of apartments to choose from. We have had excellent reports of the Villa Gardena (0471 794602) and Isabell (0471 794562) apartments.

EATING OUT
Plenty of good-value choices

Selva offers both Austrian and Italian food at prices to suit all pockets. The higher-quality restaurants are mainly hotel-based. The Bellavista is good for pasta and Costabella for Tirolean specialities and 'large measures of spirits'. Rino's has 'excellent pizza'.

APRES-SKI
Above average for a family resort

Nightlife is lively and informal, though the village is so scattered there is little on-street atmosphere. La Stua is an après-ski bar on the Sella Ronda route, with live music on some nights. For an early drink we are told that the Piz Seteur bar, above Plan de Gralba, is worth a little detour from the route – 'fun, loud and a bit raunchy' (pick the right day and you'll find scantily clad

GETTING THERE

Air Verona 190km/118 miles (3hr); Bolzano 40km/25 miles (45min); Treviso 130km/80 miles (2½hr).

Rail Chiusa (27km/17 miles), Bressanone (35km/22 miles), Bolzano (40km/25 miles); frequent buses from station.

TOURIST OFFICES

VAL GARDENA

Selva
t 0471 795122
selva@valgardena.it
www.valgardena.it

Ortisei
t 0471 796328
ortisei@valgardena.it
www.valgardena.it

ALTA BADIA
www.altabadia.org

Corvara
t 0471 836176
altabadia@dolomiti
superski.com
www.dolomitisuperski.
com/altabadia

Colfosco
t 0471 836145
altabadia@dolomiti
superski.com
www.dolomitisuperski.
com/altabadia

San Cassiano
t 0471 849422
altabadia@dolomiti
superski.com
www.dolomitisuperski.
com/altabadia

La Villa
t 0471 847037
altabadia@dolomiti
superski.com
www.dolomitisuperski.
com/altabadia

girls dancing on the bar). For a civilised early drink try the good value ski-school bar at the base of the Dantercëpies piste. Or the Costabella – cosy, serving good gluhwein. Café Mozart on the main street is 'a great place for coffee and cakes'.

Ardent après-skiers should visit the Posta Zirm in Corvara. 'The ski-boot tea dance was excellent,' recommends one reporter. But another visited three times and found 'we were usually the only people dancing'. Tour operators often organise transport back to other resorts.

For thigh-slapping in Selva later on, the Laurinkeller has good atmosphere though it's 'quite expensive', while the popular Luislkeller has loud music and barmaids in Tirolean garb.

The Bula has 'a DJ and great music'. The hotel Stella disco next door has a 'good crowd and is well used by Brits'.

OFF THE SLOPES
Good variety

There's a sports centre, snow-shoeing, lovely walks and sleigh rides on Alpe di Siusi. There is a bus to Ortisei, which is well worth a visit for its large hot-spring swimming pool, shops, restaurants and lovely old buildings.

Pedestrians can reach numerous good restaurants by gondola or cable-car. Car drivers have Bolzano and Innsbruck within reach and tour operators do trips to Cortina.

Ortisei 1235m/4,050ft

Ortisei is a market town with a life of its own, and its local slopes aren't on the main Sella Ronda circuit. It's full of lovely buildings, pretty churches and pleasant shops. The lift to the south-facing slopes is very central, and the north-facing Alpe di Siusi lifts are only slightly further out. The nursery area, school and kindergarten are at the foot of these slopes, but there's a fair range

of family accommodation on the piste side of the road. The fine public indoor pool and ice rink are also here.

There are hotels and self-catering to suit all tastes and pockets and many good restaurants, mainly specialising in local dishes. Après-ski is quite jolly, and many bars keep going till late.

Corvara 1570m/5,150ft

Corvara is the most animated village east of Selva, with plenty of hotels, restaurants, bars and sports facilities.

It's well positioned, with village lifts heading off to reasonably equidistant Selva, Arabba and San Cassiano. The main shops and some hotels cluster around a small piazza, but the rest of the place sprawls along the valley floor. The tea dance in the Posta Zirm has a widespread reputation (see Selva après-ski above). There's a covered ice rink, indoor tennis courts and an outdoor artificial climbing wall. The hotel Table is recommended by reporters for its piano bar and good cakes.

Colfosco 1645m/5,400ft

Colfosco is a smaller, quieter version of Corvara, 2km/1 mile away. It has a fairly compact centre with a sprawl of large hotels along the road towards Selva. It's connected to Corvara by a horizontal-running chair-lift. In the opposite direction, a new gondola heads off to Passo Gardena, from where you can then head on to Selva.

San Cassiano 1530m/5,020ft

San Cassiano is a pretty little village, set in an attractive, tree-filled valley. It's a quiet, slightly upmarket resort, full of well-heeled Italian families and comfortable hotels. The local slopes, the Alta Badia, though sizeable and

ACTIVITIES

Indoor Swimming, sauna, solarium, bowling alley, squash, artificial skating rink, ice hockey, museum, concerts, cinema, billiards, tennis, climbing wall, fitness centre

Outdoor Sleigh rides, torch-light descents, snow-shoeing, toboggan runs, paragliding, horse-riding, extensive cleared paths around Selva Gardena and above S Cristina and Ortisei

Phone numbers
From abroad use the prefix +39 (and do **not** omit the initial '0' of the phone number).

TOURIST OFFICES

VAL DI FASSA

Canazei
t 0462 601113
infocanazei@fassa.com
www.fassa.com

Campitello
t 0462 750500
infocampitello@fassa.com
www.fassa.com

Arabba
t 0436 780019
arabba@rolmail.net
www.arabba.org

fully linked, are something of a spur of the main Sella Ronda. Adventurers who want to do the circuit regularly will find it a tiresome business.

The best hotel in town is the 4-star Rosa Alpina (0471 849500). Nightlife is very limited: the Rosa Alpina has dancing and there's a bowling alley. Walking in the pretty scenery is the main off-slope activity; swimming is the other.

La Villa 1435m/4,710ft

La Villa is similar to neighbouring San Cassiano in most respects – small, quiet, pretty, unspoiled – but it is slightly closer to Corvara, making it rather better placed for the main Sella Ronda circuit. There is a home piste that features on the World Cup circuit, and village amenities include a pool and skating on a frozen lake.

Canazei 1440m/4,720ft

Canazei is a sizeable, bustling, pretty, roadside village of narrow streets, rustic old buildings, traditional style hotels and nice little shops, set in the Sella Ronda's most heavily wooded section of mountains. There's plenty going on generally – and it has been recommended by many reporters.

A 12-person gondola is the only mountain access point, but it shifts the queues (which can be long) quickly.

A single piste back to the village is linked to runs returning from both Selva and Arabba, but it is often closed. The local Belvedere slopes are easy, with mountain restaurants scattered here and there. The village nursery slope is good but inconvenient and so unlikely to be used after day one. The Bellavista at the top of the gondola has a lovely sun terrace and is recommended for 'excellent food'.

Lack of spoken English in the school can be a problem. Children have an all-day nursery and ski kindergarten. But again lack of English could be a problem.

There are no really luxurious hotels, but the grand 3-star Dolomiti (0462 601106) in the middle of town is one of the original resort hotels. The chalet-style Diana (0462 601477) is charming and five minutes from the village centre. The 4-star Astoria (0462 601302) has a pool and minibus transfers to and from the gondola.

There are numerous restaurants. The Stala, Melester and Te Cevana are all worth a try. And après-ski is really

animated. La Stua dei Ladins serves good local wines. The Husky and Roxy bars are worth a visit.

Off-slope entertainment consists of beautiful walks and shopping. There's also a pool, sauna, Turkish baths and skating in neighbouring Alba.

Campitello 1445m/4,740ft

Campitello is a pleasant, unremarkable village, smaller and quieter than next-door Canazei and still unspoiled.

It's quiet during the day, having no slopes to the village. A cable-car takes you up into the Sella Ronda circuit. If you don't wish to return by lift, take the piste to Canazei and catch a bus.

A recent reporter recommends the 4-star hotel Soroghes (0462 750060): 'Superb food and accommodation, helpful staff, excellent facilities.' Campitello is quite lively – we've had trouble getting near the bar of the throbbing Da Giulio in the early evening, and a recent reporter suggests that it's even busier later on. There's an ice rink. But there appear to be no children's facilities.

Arabba 1600m/5,250ft

Arabba is a small, traditional, still uncommercialised village. But the lifts into the Sella Ronda in both directions make it very convenient. The high, north-facing slopes have the best natural snow and steepest pistes in the Dolomites. It is not a good place for beginners though. For accommodation reporters recommend the large, 3-star Portavescovo (0436 79139): 'An excellent hotel, wonderful food, nicely furnished rooms and a well-equipped fitness centre.' It has the only pool in town. Chalets and self-catering accommodation are available.

Venues for eating out are limited. 7 Sass and Ru De Mont are cheap and cheerful pizzerias. The après-ski is also limited – but it is cheap. The atmospheric Rifugio Plan Boe has 'loud oom pah pah music' and is good for a last drink on the pistes before heading back to the village, says a reporter. The 'friendly' Bar Peter and hotel bars are the focal points. The lively Stube bar attracts tour op reps and young teenagers, say 2003 reporters. The Delmonego family's bar-caravan, at the bottom of the piste, is the tea-time rendezvous. The Hotel Portavescovo's happy hour is very good value.

Sestriere

Modern resort with access to the Milky Way

COSTS

①②③④⑤⑥

RATINGS

The slopes

Snow	✱✱✱
Extent	✱✱✱✱
Expert	✱✱✱
Intermediate	✱✱✱✱
Beginner	✱✱✱
Convenience	✱✱✱✱
Queues	✱✱✱
Mountain restaurants	✱✱

The rest

Scenery	✱✱✱
Resort charm	✱
Off-slope	✱

NEWS

For 2003/04 the 3-seat Trebials chair-lift is to be upgraded to a quad, and the Garnel drag-lift is to be replaced with a quad.

Turin has been chosen to host the 2006 Olympic Winter Games; Sestriere will host many of the Alpine events.

KEY FACTS

Resort	2000m
	6,560ft

For Milky Way area

Slopes	1390-2825m
	4,560-9,270ft
Lifts	92
Pistes	400km
	250 miles
Blue	12%
Red	67%
Black	21%
Snowmaking	80km
	50 miles

For Sestriere-Sauze d'Oulx-Sansicario only

Slopes	1390-2825m
	4,560-9,270ft
Lifts	53
Pistes	300km
	186 miles
Snowmaking	65km
	40 miles

➕ Part of the extensive Franco-Italian Milky Way area

➕ Snow reliability is usually good, with extensive snowmaking back-up

➕ Local slopes suitable for most levels, with some tougher runs than most neighbouring resorts

➕ Much of the purpose-built village is scruffy, though likely to improve for the 2006 Winter Olympics

➕ Situated at one extreme of the Milky Way area – so inconvenient for exploration of the whole network

➕ Weekend and peak-period queues

➕ Little après-ski during the week

Sestriere was built for snow – high, with north-west-facing slopes – and it has very extensive snowmaking, too. So even if you are let down by the notoriously erratic snowfalls in this corner of Italy, you should be fairly safe here – certainly safer than in Sauze d'Oulx, over the hill.

THE RESORT

Sestriere was the Alps' first purpose-built resort, developed by Giovanni Agnelli in the 1930s. It sits on a broad, sunny and windy col, and neither the site nor the village, with its large apartment blocks, looks very hospitable, though the buildings have benefited from recent investment. New building work, including a large residential building close to the Cit Roc chair, is already in evidence in preparation for the 2006 Olympics. There are some interesting buildings, but much of the village still seems rather scruffy. This is not the most convenient of purpose-built resorts, but location is not crucial. The satellite of Borgata, 200m lower, is less convenient for nightlife and shops.

THE MOUNTAINS

Sestriere is at one extreme of the big Franco-Italian Milky Way area. The local slopes have two main sectors: Sises, directly in front of the village, and more varied Motta, above Borgata – to the north-east and 225m/740ft higher.

Slopes There are mainly drag- and chair-lifts on the local north-west-facing slopes. Access to Sansicario and the rest of the Milky Way is via gondola from Borgata to Col Basset, at the top of the Sauze d'Oulx area, and a drag-lift back up to Monte Fraiteve. Snow permitting, the return to Sestriere is via the red run down from Monte Fraiteve to the northern side of the village or via a long red from the top of the gondola at Col Basset (though a reporter this year was assured that the

PISTE MAP

Sestriere is covered on the Sauze d'Oulx map a few pages back.

Phone numbers

From abroad use the prefix +39 (and do **not** omit the initial '0' of the phone number).

TOURIST OFFICE

t 0122 755444
sestriere@montagne doc.it
www.sestriere.it
www.vialattea.it

VIA LATTEA / SESTRIERE
TOURIST OFFICES

← There's floodlit skiing twice a week

VIA LATTEA / SESTRIERE
TOURIST OFFICES

Like all Italian resorts, Sestriere has a serious sunbathing contingent →

bottom half never opens), and usually you have to ride the gondola down. Signposting and the piste map are poor. There's night skiing on Wednesdays and Saturdays.

Terrain-parks The terrain-park next to the Cit Roc chair on Sises was rebuilt and enlarged for the 2002/03 season.

Snow reliability With most of the local slopes facing north-west and ranging from 1840m to 2825m (6,040ft to 9,270ft), and an extensive snowmaking network covering most of the Sises sector and half of Motta, snow-cover is usually reliable for most of the season. The notoriously erratic snowfalls in the Milky Way often leave the rest of the area seriously short of snow while the extensive snowmaking in Sestriere provides fairly reliable cover. The sunny runs down from Sauze suffer from poor snow and do not benefit from any artificial back-up.

Experts There is a fair amount to amuse experts – steep pistes served by the drags at the top of both sectors, and off-piste slopes in several directions from here and Monte Fraiteve.

Intermediates Both sectors also offer plenty for confident intermediates, who can explore practically all of the Milky Way areas, conditions permitting.

Beginners The terrain is good for beginners, with several nursery areas and the gentlest of easy runs down to Borgata. However, one reporter points out that there is a lack of easy intermediate runs to progress to.

Snowboarding Sestriere has a reasonable number of chairs, but there are also lots of drag-lifts.

Cross-country There are two loops covering a total of 10km/6 miles.

Queues The lifts are mainly modern though there are still some inadequate old ones. But queues for the main lifts occur at the weekends and holidays. The lifts from Borgata to Sestriere can be a bottleneck at the end of the day. Queues occur when poor weather closes the gondola link to Sauze. Reporters here, as in Sauze, complain that some lifts may be kept closed during the week, either to save money or conserve snow for the weekends.

Mountain restaurants A reporter this year recommends the Tana della Volpe at the top of the Banchetta chair, but on the whole the local mountain restaurants are only fair. There are better ones further afield.

Schools and guides Lack of spoken English can be a problem.

Facilities for children There are no special facilities for children.

STAYING THERE

How to go Most accommodation is in apartments.

Hotels There are a dozen hotels, mostly 3-star or 4-star. The Savoy Edelweiss (0122 77040) and the Du Col (0122 76990) are central, and just out of the village is the luxurious Principi di Piemonte (0122 7941). The distinctive towers in the centre are the Club Med quarters.

Eating out There are plenty of options. Try Lu Peirol for home-made ravioli and atmosphere. Tre Rubinetti has been highly recommended for 'outstanding Italian cooking' and an enormous wine list. Last Tango and the Baita are also well regarded.

Après-ski Après-ski is quiet during the week but becomes lively at weekends: the Prestige and Palace are two of the many little bars that liven up. The Pinky is one of the best of the bars that double as eateries, with lots of low sofas in the classic Italian casual-chic style.

Off the slopes There are some smart shops and there's a fitness centre, an ice rink and a sports centre. A swimming pool was built in 2003.

La Thuile

Little-known resort with extensive, easy slopes and link with France

420

COSTS

① ② ③ ④ ⑤ ⑥

RATINGS

The slopes

Snow	****
Extent	***
Expert	**
Intermediate	****
Beginner	****
Convenience	***
Queues	****
Mountain restaurants	*

The rest

Scenery	***
Resort charm	***
Off-slope	**

NEWS

For 2002/03 the Piccolo San Bernardo chair was replaced by a much faster covered quad. The old lift was refurbished and re-opened in the Cerellaz area as the 'new' Arnouvaz three-seater chair, with moving carpet.

+ Fair-sized area with good lift system linked to La Rosière in France

+ Free of crowds and queues

+ Excellent beginner and easy intermediate slopes

+ Some very handy accommodation

− Most of the seriously tough pistes are low down, and most of the low, woodland runs are tough

− Mountain restaurants are generally disappointing

− Not the place for lively après-ski

La Thuile deserves to be better known internationally. The slopes best suit beginners and intermediates not seeking challenges, but are not devoid of interest for experts, particularly if the snow conditions are good.

When you venture over the border to La Rosière, you'll notice that Italian grooming is better than French, and Italian piste classification often overstates difficulty. Moving from gentle red runs to bumpy blues may be a shock.

THE RESORT

La Thuile is a resort of parts. At the foot of the lifts is the modern Planibel complex, with places to stay, a leisure centre, bars, shops and restaurants – like a French purpose-built resort, but with a distinctly Italian atmosphere. But many people find this rather soulless and prefer to stay in the old town across the river (served by a regular free bus service). Much of the old town has been restored and new buildings (and an underground car park) tastefully added. There are reasonable restaurants and bars.

The slopes link with La Rosière, over the border in France. Courmayeur is easily reached by car, and Cervinia is about an hour away.

THE MOUNTAINS

La Thuile has quite extensive slopes, with the great attraction that they are normally very uncrowded. Many runs are marked red, but deserve no more than a blue rating. The lift system is excellent in general: a fast chair or gondola takes you up the mountain, and there are high-speed chairs to the top. There may be some queues at the Les Suches gondola first thing The new Petit St Bernard quad has speeded up getting to the Belvedere area and over into France.

Slopes The lifts out of the village take you to Les Suches, with shady black runs going back down directly to the village through the trees, and reds taking a more roundabout route. From

Chaz Dura 2580m
Col de Fourclaz
Belvedere 2610m/8,560ft
Col de la Traversette 2385m
↙ La Rosière
Cerellaz
Les Suches 2200m
La Thuile 1440m/4,720ft

Phone numbers
From abroad use the prefix +39 (and do **not** omit the initial '0' of the phone number).

TOURIST OFFICE

t 0165 884179
lathuile@lathuile.net
www.lathuile.net

CONSORZIO OPERATORI TURISTICA
LA THUILE

← Lots of broad, easy, well groomed slopes at altitude

here chairs and drags take you to Chaz Dura for access to a variety of gentle bowls facing east. You can go off westwards from here to the Petit St Bernard road. From both sides there are lifts back to the ridge, the high-point of Belvedere being the launch pad for excursions via the Col de la Traversette to La Rosière in France. The French slopes are largely south-facing and tend to be steeper.
Terrain-parks There are no specific facilities.
Snow reliability Most of La Thuile's slopes are north- or east-facing and above 2000m/6,560ft, so the snow generally keeps well. There's also a decent amount of snowmaking.
Experts The only steep pistes are those down through the trees from Les Suches: the steepest – the Diretta and Tre – are serious stuff. The area above the Petit St Bernard road has some genuinely black terrain and plenty of off-piste – the new quad will mean you can do quick circuits in this area.
    Heli-lifts are available. One of the best, to the Ruitor glacier, has a 20km/12 mile run into France ending near Ste-Foy, a short taxi ride from La Rosière and the lifts back to La Thuile.
Intermediates La Thuile has some good intermediate runs, and its link with La Rosière adds adventure; but the start of the route back from La Rosière is a fairly tricky red, and most of La Rosière is quite challenging. The bowls above Les Suches have many gentle blue and red runs, ideal for cruising and practising. There are also long reds through the trees back to the resort. The red runs on the other side of the top ridge, down towards the Petit St Bernard road, offer a greater challenge.
Beginners There are nursery slopes at village level and up at Les Suches. There's a good gentle green run above there, and easy blues. Promenade is 'a very easy blue and good for beginners', but is served by drag-lifts. You ride the gondola back down.
Snowboarding These are great slopes for learning. You need ride only chair-lifts and the gondola, and most of the slopes are easy. For the more experienced there are great tree runs, and the link with France offers off-piste possibilities. There is good free-riding, and some good carving runs.
Cross-country La Thuile has four loops of varying difficulty on the valley floor, adding up to 20km/12 miles of track.
Queues The resort has a very effective

lift system for the number of visitors, and all our reporters comment that they never had to queue.
Mountain restaurants There are few notable places – disappointing, for Italy. In the Riondet (on Chaz Dura) a reporter found 'genuinely good food and hospitality'. The place at the foot of the Chalets chair lift does 'tasty, reasonably priced food' and has a 'good atmosphere'.
Schools and guides Reporters say the ski school has reasonably sized classes and fair instruction in good English. Interski clients were overheard as being 'happy'.
Facilities for children There's an 'excellent' nursery, a Miniclub, and children over the age of five can join adult ski classes.

STAYING THERE

How to go The number of tour operators going there is increasing.
Hotels The choice is between the characterless 4-star Planibel, a few 3-stars and some simpler places.
Self-catering The Planibel apartments are spacious, right by the lifts and great value. Some 'have been refurbished and are quite smart', but others are 'tired and urgently need refurbishing'.
Eating out Reader recommendations include the Bricole 'expensive but well worth it', the Fordze (French/Italian local dishes) and the Rascard (pizza).
Après-ski Nightlife is 'not vibrant'. The Cage aux Folles is popular from 4pm till late. The Lord Whymper pub is quiet but recommended. The Bricole is the busiest and liveliest bar. The Fantasia disco at the Planibel warms up well after midnight.
Off the slopes The Planibel complex has a good pool, but there are few attractive walks or shops. Pedestrians can ride up the gondola for lunch.

Switzerland is home to some of our favourite resorts. For sheer charm and spectacular scenery, the essentially traffic-free villages of Wengen, Mürren, Saas-Fee and Zermatt take some beating. Many resorts have impressive slopes too – including some of the biggest, highest and toughest runs in the Alps, as well as a lot of reassuring intermediate terrain. For fast, efficient, queue-free lift networks, Swiss resorts rarely match French standards – but the real bottlenecks are gradually disappearing. And there are compensations – the world's best mountain restaurants, for example.

People always seem to associate Switzerland with high prices. In the recent past, we haven't found most Swiss resorts appreciably more expensive than most French ones – though some Swiss resorts such as Zermatt, Verbier and St Moritz do tend to be pricey. What is clear is that what you get for your money in Switzerland is generally first-class.

While France is the home of the purpose-built resort, Switzerland is the home of the mountain village that has transformed itself from traditional farming community into year-round holiday resort. Many of Switzerland's most famous mountain resorts are as popular in the summer as in the winter, or more so. This creates places with a much more lived-in feel to them, and a much more stable local community. Many villages are still dominated by a handful of

SNOWPIX.COM / CHRIS GILL

← Not all Swiss resorts have scenery to rival that of Zermatt, but some do – Wengen and Grindelwald, at least

423

families who were lucky or shrewd enough to get involved in the early development of the area.

This has its downside as well as advantages. The ruling families are able to stifle competition and prevent newcomers from taking a slice of their action. Alternative ski schools, competing with the traditional school and pushing up standards, are much less common than in other Alpine countries, for example.

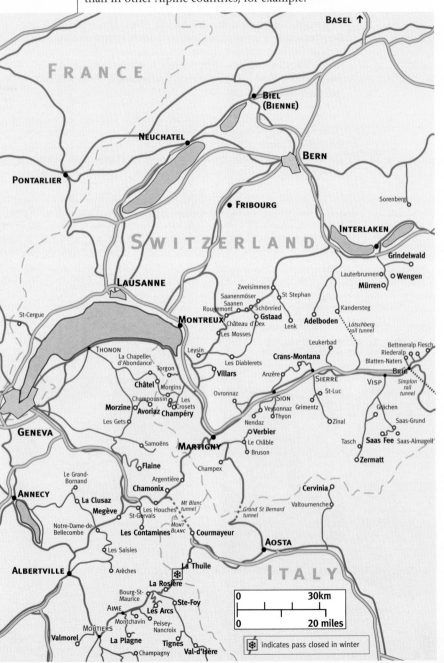

Switzerland means high living as well as high prices, and the swanky grand hotels of St Moritz, Gstaad, Zermatt and Davos are beyond the dreams of most ordinary holidaymakers. Even in more modest places, the quality of the service is generally high. The trains run like clockwork to the advertised timetable (and often they run to the top of the mountain, doubling as ski-lifts). The food is almost universally of good quality and much less stodgy than in

indicates pass closed in winter

neighbouring Austria. In Switzerland you get what you pay for: even the cheapest wine, for example, is not cheap; but it is reliable – duff bottles are very rare.

GETTING AROUND THE SWISS ALPS

Access to practically all Swiss resorts is fairly straightforward when approaching from the north – just pick your motorway. Many of the high passes that are perfectly sensible ways to get around the country in summer are closed in winter, which can be inconvenient if you are moving around from one area to another. There are car-carrying trains linking the Valais (Crans-Montana, Zermatt etc) to Andermatt via the Furka tunnel and Andermatt to the Grisons (Flims, Davos etc) via the Oberalp pass – closed to road traffic in winter but open to trains except after very heavy snowfalls.

St Moritz is more awkward to get to than other resorts, as well as being further away. The main road route is over the Julier pass. This is normally kept open, but at 2285m/7,500ft it is naturally prone to heavy snowfalls that can shut it for a time. The fallback is the car-carrying rail tunnel under the Albula pass. A major new rail tunnel opened in November 1999, offering an alternative route. The Vereina tunnel runs for 19km/12 miles from Klosters to a point near Susch and Zernez, down the Inn valley from St Moritz.

These car-carrying rail services are painless unless you travel at peak times, when there may be long queues – particularly for the Furka tunnel from Andermatt, which offers residents of Zürich the shortest route to Zermatt and the other Valais resorts. Another rail tunnel that's very handy is the Lötschberg, linking Kandersteg in the Bernese Oberland with Brig in the Valais. Apart from helicopters, there's no quicker way from Wengen to Zermatt.

There is a car-carrying rail tunnel linking Switzerland with Italy – the Simplon. But most of the routes to Italy are kept open by means of road tunnels. See the Italy introduction.

To use Swiss motorways (and it's difficult to avoid doing so if you're driving serious distances) you have to buy a permit to stick on your windscreen (costing SF40 in 2002/03). They are sold at the border, and are for all practical purposes compulsory.

Adelboden

Chocolate-box village with fragmented but extensive slopes

COSTS

① ② ③ ④ ⑤ ⑥

RATINGS

The slopes

Snow	**
Extent	***
Experts	**
Intermediates	***
Beginners	****
Convenience	***
Queues	***
Mountain restaurants	**

The rest

Scenery	****
Resort charm	****
Off-slope	****

KEY FACTS

Resort	1355m
	4,450ft
Slopes	1070-2355m
	3,510-7,730ft
Lifts	56
Pistes	170km
	106 miles
Blue	40%
Red	50%
Black	10%
Snowmaking	20km
	12 miles

There are short downhill slopes and snow-sure langlauf loops at Engstligenalp at the far end of the valley ↓

➕ Traditional chocolate-box-pretty mountain village

➕ Extensive slopes to suit all abilities, linked to Lenk

➕ Several other worthwhile resorts within day-trip range

➕ Good off-slope facilities

➖ Fragmented slopes – two sectors are a bus-ride away

➖ Low top heights mean unreliable snow-cover

➖ Few challenges unless you look off-piste

Adelboden is unjustly neglected by the international market: for intermediates who find relaxing, pretty surroundings more important than convenience for the slopes, it has a lot of appeal. The slopes are extensive, and investment in lifts over recent years has meant great improvements.

THE RESORT

Adelboden fits the traditional image of a Swiss mountain village: old chalets with overhanging roofs line the quiet main street (cars are discouraged), and 3000m/9,840ft peaks make an impressive backdrop. Adelboden is in the Bernese Oberland, to the west of the much better-known Jungfrau resorts (Wengen etc). These resorts are within day-trip range, as is Gstaad to the west.

The village is compact, and there are efficient buses to the outlying areas (covered on the lift pass); the ideal location for most people is close to the main street.

THE MOUNTAINS

Adelboden's slopes are split into five sectors (no longer six) – two of them unlinked and a bus-ride from the village. The rest of the sectors are linked, by piste if not by lift, and the ski area stretches across to the village of Lenk, with its own local slopes a bus-ride across the valley from the main body of slopes shared with Adelboden. The Swiss ski school has started running American-style free mountain tours on Sundays.

Slopes Lifts near the main street access three of the sectors. Schwandfeldspitz (aka Tschenten), just above the village, is reached by a cable-car/gondola hybrid. The main gondola to nearby Höchsthorn and then on to more remote Geils-Sillerenbühl starts down below the village at Oey (where there is a car park), but a connecting mini-gondola starts from close to the main street. This is much the biggest sector, with long, gentle runs (and some short, sharp ones) from 2200m down to 1350m (7,215ft down to 4,430ft) – back to the village and over to Lenk.

Engstligenalp, a flat-bottomed high-altitude bowl, is reached by a cable-car 4km/2.5 miles south of the resort; Elsigenalp is more remote, but more extensive.

Terrain-parks There's a good terrain-park and a half-pipe at Hahnenmoos, and a natural playground at Engstligenalp.

Snow reliability Most pistes are below 2000m/6,56oft and snowmaking is limited – so snow reliability is not a strong point, despite mostly north-facing slopes above 1500m/4,920ft.

Experts There are some genuine black pistes at Geils, and a less genuine one on Höchsthorn. Off-piste possibilities are good and remain untracked for

Labels on the map: 2355m/7,730ft · Engstligenalp · Luegli 2140m · Metschstand 2105m · Leiterl 2000m · 2290m Elsigenalp · Höchsthorn 1905m · Fleckli · Unter Birg · Geils 1710m · Hahnenmoos 1960m · Stoss 1645m · Elsigbach 1250m · Boden · Sillerenbühl 1975m · Adelboden 1355m/4,450ft · Oey · Stand 2020m · Laveygrat 2200m · Lenk 1070m/3,510ft · 1135m · Tschenten 1950m · 1540m · 1645m

NEWS

For 2002/03 there was a new winter hiking path and a new restaurant, both on Tschenten.

Phone numbers
From elsewhere in Switzerland add the prefix 033.
From abroad use the prefix +41 33.

TOURIST OFFICE

t 673 8080
info@adelboden.ch
www.adelboden.ch

ADELBODEN TOURIST OFFICE

The village is well up to chocolate-box standards ↓

much longer than in other, more macho resorts: the Laveygrat and Chummi chairs in the Geils bowl access routes down to both Adelboden and Lenk (though there are protected forest areas to avoid). Engstligenalp has off-piste potential too – and is a launching point for tours around the Wildstrubel.
Intermediates All five areas deserve exploration by intermediates. At Geils there is a lot of ground to be covered – and trips across to Lenk's gentle Betelberg area (covered by the lift pass) are possible.
Beginners There are good nursery slopes in the village and at the foot of nearby sectors. At Geils there are glorious long, easy runs to progress to.
Snowboarding Two specialist schools offer lessons. Beginners may find the high proportion of drag-lifts off-putting.
Cross-country There are extensive trails along the valley towards Engstligenalp with its high altitude, snow-sure circuit. There's also a short loop at Geils.
Queues The main gondola isn't entirely free of queues. And the old Hahnenmoos gondola is a bottleneck, overdue for replacement. If snow low

down is poor, the Engstligenalp cable-car becomes oversubscribed.
Mountain restaurants There are pleasant mountain restaurants with terraces in the Geils sector. Aebi is particularly charming. A past reporter recommended the Metschstand: 'Sunny, small, simple, but good.'
Schools and guides Past reports on the Adelboden ski school have been mixed – 'caring, good English', but 'mix of abilities within group'.
Facilities for children The kindergarten takes children from three to six years and there's a playroom and child-minding service up at Hahnenmoos. Several hotels have childcare facilities.

STAYING THERE

How to go The choice of how to go is wide. Several UK operators go there, and there are locally bookable chalets and apartments and some 30 pensions and hotels (mainly 3- and 4-star).
Hotels The 4-star Park Hotel Bellevue (673 8000) is expensive, but we have received good reports of its food and spa facilities. The central 3-star Adler Sporthotel (673 4141) is pretty and recommended. The little Bären (673 2151) is a simple but captivating wooden chalet.
Eating out Possibilities are varied, and include a couple of mountain restaurants. Guests on a half-board arrangement can 'dine around' at affiliated hotels twice a week.
Après-ski The après-ski is traditional, based on bars and tea rooms – the Time Out Pub is recommended.
Off the slopes There is a fair bit to do. There are hotel pools open to the public, indoor and outdoor curling and skating rinks, several toboggan runs, and hiking paths. Some mountain restaurants are easily reached on foot.

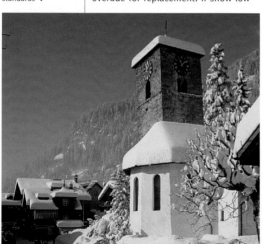

Andermatt

An old-fashioned resort with some great off-piste (and snow)

429

COSTS

① ② ③ ④ ⑤ ⑥

RATINGS

The slopes

Snow	****
Extent	*
Expert	****
Intermediate	**
Beginner	*
Convenience	***
Queues	**
Mountain restaurants	*

The rest

Scenery	***
Resort charm	****
Off-slope	**

NEWS

For 2003/04 there is to be a new shuttle-bus between Gemsstock and Winterhorn.

A new snow-shoeing trail was developed for 2002/03.

A new mountain restaurant is due to open at Gurschen during 2004.

+ Attractive, traditional village

+ Excellent snow record

+ Some excellent steep pistes, and great off-piste terrain

− Three separate areas of slopes are all fairly limited if you stay on-piste

− Unsuitable for beginners

− Limited off-slope diversions and après-ski

− Cable-car queues at weekends

Little old Andermatt was rather left behind in the mega-resort boom of the 1960s and 70s. But its attractions have not faded for those who like their mountains tall, steep and covered in deep powder. At first sight, quick access from Zürich makes it a tempting destination for a weekend break. But its attractions are not lost on the residents of Zürich, who arrive by the coachload and trainload.

THE RESORT

Andermatt is quite busy in summer and gets weekend winter business, but at other times seems deserted apart from groups of soldiers – there are barracks here. The town is quietly attractive, with wooden houses lining the dog-leg main street that runs between railway and cable-car stations, and some imposing churches. The railway is the only link in winter with the Grisons to the east and the Valais to the west – trains carry cars. Most people arrive by train, and links are easy from Zürich. The town is fairly small and location is not much of an issue – though there are no buses.

THE MOUNTAINS

Andermatt's skiing is split over three unlinked mountains. The slopes are almost entirely above the trees, and the individual areas are all limited in extent. You buy a pass covering the three mountains and trains between them. The Gotthard-Oberalp lift pass also covers the nearby resorts of Sedrun and Disentis – reached by train over the Oberalp pass.

Slopes A two-stage cable-car from the edge of the village serves magnificent, varied slopes on the open, steep and usually empty slopes of Gemsstock. Across town is the gentler Nätschen/Gütsch area. And a bus- or train-ride

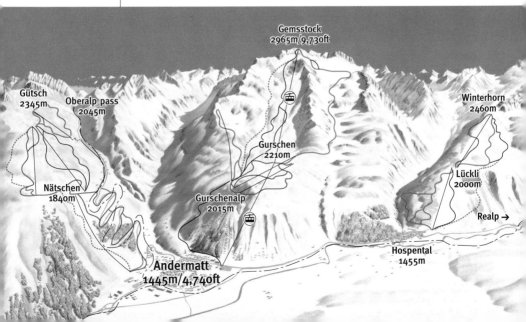

↑ The table-service terrace at mid-mountain is mainly notable for the views – but a new restaurant is under construction

SNOWPIX.COM / CHRIS GILL

KEY FACTS

Resort	1445m
	4,740ft
Slopes	1445-2965m
	4,740-9,725ft
Lifts	13
Pistes	56km
	35 miles
Blue	29%
Red	42%
Black	29%
Snowmaking	None

Phone numbers

From elsewhere in Switzerland add the prefix 041.

From abroad use the prefix +41 41.

TOURIST OFFICE

t 887 1454
info@andermatt.ch
www.andermatt.ch

along the valley is Winterhorn (above Hospental). There is also an isolated nursery slope further along at Realp.

Terrain-parks There are facilities (park and pipe) on Nätschen and Gemsstock.

Snow reliability The area has a justified reputation for reliable snow. Piste grooming is generally good.

Experts It is most definitely a resort for experts. The north-facing bowl beneath the top Gemsstock cable-car is a glorious, long, steep slope (about 800m/2,625ft vertical), usually with excellent snow, down which there are countless off-piste routes and one marked run, which branches into two. Outside the bowl, the Sonnenpiste is a fine open red run curling around the back of the mountain to the Gurschen mid-station, also flanked by off-piste opportunities. From Gurschen to the village there is a black run, not too steep but heavily mogulled. There are guides for off-piste adventure, and a trip off the back of Gemsstock is recommended, either back to the village, or down to Hospental. Nätschen and Winterhorn both have black pistes and off-piste opportunities.

Intermediates Intermediates needn't be put off Gemsstock: the Sonnenpiste can be tackled (especially as there are immaculately groomed sections of the piste 'created especially for carvers'),

and there is a pleasant red run and some short blues at mid-mountain. Winterhorn's modest lift system offers pistes to suit all abilities down the 1000m/3,280ft vertical, while Nätschen's south and west-facing mountain is perfect for confidence-building.

Beginners The lower half of Nätschen has a good, long, easy run. But this is not a good resort for beginners.

Snowboarding The cable-car accesses some great free-ride terrain.

Cross-country There is a 20km/12 mile loop along the valley towards Realp.

Queues The Gemsstock cable-car can generate morning queues in the village and at mid-mountain when conditions are attractive, especially at weekends. Things take a while to get going after heavy snow.

Mountain restaurants All sectors have them. A new restaurant at Gurschen is to open this year, and not before time.

Schools and guides The good work of the Swiss ski school is overshadowed by the excellent Alpine Adventures Mountain Reality, an off-piste guiding outfit run by Alex Clapasson.

Facilities for children There are no special facilities; but there are slopes they can handle at Nätschen and the Swiss school takes children's classes.

STAYING THERE

How to go Andermatt's accommodation is in cosy 2- and 3-star hotels.

Hotels Gasthaus Sternen (887 1130), in the centre, is an attractive old chalet with a cosy restaurant and bar. The 3-star Sonne (887 1226), between the centre and the lift, is welcoming and comfortable. The neighbouring 2-star Bergidyll (887 1455) is a British favourite. Alpenhotel Schlüssel (888 7088) is newish, with spacious rooms.

Eating out A recent reporter recommends the Schwarzen Bären for 'good traditional food' and the Kronen hotel's 'quite formal' Tre Passi restaurant for 'good game'.

Après-ski Après-ski revolves around cosy bars. The Spycher is about the liveliest. Later on, try the Piccadilly pub and the bars at the hotel Monopol ('great cocktails, stays open late'). At weekends the Gotthard disco is said to be 'lively'.

Off the slopes There's a toboggan run at Nätschen. The churches and the museum of local history, housed in an old wooden building, are worth a visit.

Arosa

Classic all-round winter resort – walkers are as welcome as skiers

431

COSTS

① ② ③ ④ ⑤ ⑥

RATINGS

The slopes
Snow	★★★
Extent	★★
Expert	★
Intermediate	★★★
Beginner	★★★★
Convenience	★★★
Queues	★★★★
Mountain restaurants	★★★★

The rest
Scenery	★★★
Resort charm	★★
Off-slope	★★★★

NEWS

A quad chair has replaced the Plattenhorn T-bar.

Plans for lifts to link Arosa to Lenzerheide-Valbella hold out the prospect of hugely increased mileage from 2006. The top of Arosa's Hörnli lifts is only about 2km/1 mile from the top of the Valbella lifts. The combined area will offer around 250km/155 miles of pistes, propelling Arosa into the big league.

KEY FACTS

Resort	1800m
	5,910ft
Slopes	1800-2655m
	5,910-8,710ft
Lifts	14
Pistes	70km
	43 miles
Blue	38%
Red	57%
Black	5%
Snowmaking	9km
	6 miles

➕ Classic winter sports resort ambience, with lots going on other than skiing/boarding

➕ Some of the best cross-country loops in the Alps

➕ Few queues

➕ Relatively good snow reliability

➕ Prettily wooded setting, but ...

➖ Some very block-like buildings in main village

➖ Spread-out village lacks a heart, and means some accommodation is inconveniently situated

➖ Slopes too limited for mileage-hungry intermediates

➖ Few challenging pistes for experts – though there is good off-piste

The classic image of a winter sports resort is perhaps an isolated, snow-covered Swiss village, surrounded by big, beautiful mountains, with skating on a frozen lake, horse-drawn sleighs jingling along snowy streets and people in fur coats strolling on mountain paths. Arosa is exactly that. It's just a pity that many of its comfortable hotels date from a time when pitched roofs were out of fashion.

THE RESORT

High and remote, Arosa is in a sheltered basin at the head of a beautiful wooded valley, in contrast to the open slopes above it. It's a long, winding drive or splendid rail journey from Chur (both take under an hour). The main resort development is around Obersee – a pretty spot, spoilt by the surrounding block-like buildings. Lifts go up from here into the Weisshorn sector of the slopes. The rest of Arosa is scattered, much of it spreading up the hill separating Obersee from the older, prettier Inner-Arosa, where lifts from opposite extremities go up into both sectors of the slopes. Arosa is quiet; its relaxed ambience attracts an unpretentiously well-heeled clientele of families and older people. Very few of them British, and much of the resort literature is printed only in German.

Some accommodation is a long walk from the lifts, but there is an excellent free shuttle-bus. Outings to other resorts are rather hard work.

THE MOUNTAINS

Arosa's slopes are situated in a wide open bowl, facing north-east to south-east, with all the runs returning eventually to the village at the bottom. All the slopes are above the tree line, except the home runs to Obersee.

Phone numbers
From elsewhere in Switzerland add the prefix 081.
From abroad use the prefix +41 81.

TOURIST OFFICE

t 378 7020
arosa@arosa.ch
www.arosa.ch

Slopes The slopes are spread widely over two main sectors. Although the very poor piste map doesn't show it, the major lift junction in the Weisshorn sector is Tschuggen, 500m/1,640ft away from the Mittelstation of the Weisshorn cable-car, and reachable from both Obersee and Inner-Arosa. From Mittelstation, you can take a chair to the lower peak of Brüggerhorn. A slow gondola from below Inner-Arosa is the main access to the Hörnli sector. Well used walking paths wind across the mountainsides, and great care is needed where they cross the pistes.
Terrain-parks There is a park and a half-pipe.
Snow reliability Arosa has relatively good snow reliability. The sunnier slopes are quite high, and the shadier Hörnli slopes hold their snow well. Grooming is good, and snowmaking on the home runs is often put into use.
Experts Arosa isn't the resort for a keen expert. The two black runs barely deserve their grading, but you can ski off-piste to and from Lenzerheide – with a guide. And there are several ungroomed 'free-ride' routes.
Intermediates This is a good area for intermediates who aren't looking for high mileage or huge challenges. The 'free-ride' routes offer an easy way into off-piste. The blue runs through woods to Obersee are particular pleasures – particularly the 'staggeringly beautiful' one from the Brüggerhorn via Prätschli.
Beginners The Tschuggen nursery slopes are excellent and usually have good snow, but they get a lot of through traffic. Inner-Arosa has a quieter but more limited area usually reserved for children.

Snowboarding There is a specialist school.
Cross-country Arosa's modest 27km/17 miles of loops include some of the best and most varied in the Alps.
Queues Arosa does not suffer from serious queues. There can be waits for the Weisshorn cable-car, though recent reporters have had no problems.
Mountain restaurants The mountain restaurants can get crowded in peak season, but practically all get good reviews. The rustic little Carmennahütte is our favourite; the similarly attractive Tschuggenhütte can involve long waits, despite efficient service. Alpenblick does 'very good food' and Hörnli is a 'welcoming hut in a dramatic position' at the top of the gondola.
Schools and guides Swiss and ABC are the main schools. Class sizes can be large. There's a lot of demand for private lessons.
Facilities for children Arosa seems a good choice for families. Several hotels have kindergartens and the two schools offer children's classes.

STAYING THERE

How to go Arosa is a hotel resort, with a high proportion of 3- and 4-stars.
Hotels The sensitively modernised 4-star Waldhotel National (378 5555) with 'really special food' and direct access to the slopes is 'quite delightful'. The 4-star Sporthotel Valsana (377 0275) is recommended, though it does not have direct access to the slopes.
Eating out Most restaurants are hotel-based, some with a very high reputation. The Kachelofa-Stübli at the Waldhotel National is excellent. Other recommendations include Orchidee Palaste – a 'very good' Chinese – and Pizzeria da Gianni.
Après-ski Après-ski is quite lively. The Carmenna hotel by the ice rink has a popular piano bar. The Sitting Bull is busy and cheerful. Recommended bars include the Grischuna for grown-ups and Mexicalito for kids (both with restaurants attached). The Casino is 'good fun' and its bars are 'lively'.
Off the slopes There are plenty of outdoor alternatives. You can get a pedestrian's lift pass, and many mountain restaurants are reachable via 60km/37 miles of cleared, marked walks (map available). Sleigh rides in the mountains are popular, and there's a busy outdoor ice rink.

Champéry

Picture-postcard village, with access to the Portes du Soleil

433

COSTS

① ② ③ ④ ⑤ ⑥

RATINGS

The slopes
Snow	**
Extent	*****
Expert	***
Intermediate	****
Beginner	**
Convenience	*
Queues	****
Mountain restaurants	***

The rest
Scenery	****
Resort charm	****
Off-slope	***

NEWS

Two six-packs are planned to replace the old double chairs from Grand Paradis and at Planachaux. There are also plans to replace six old lifts in the Morgins-Champoussin area by another two six-packs and to create a new piste in the Foilleuse sector.

However, final permission to build any of these lifts had not been given when we went to press, and they seem unlikely to happen for 2003/04.

- ➕ Charmingly rustic mountain village
- ➕ Cable-car takes you into the very extensive Portes du Soleil slopes
- ➕ Quiet, relaxed – yet plenty to do off the slopes

- ➖ Local slopes suffer from the sun
- ➖ No runs back to the village – and sometimes none back to the valley
- ➖ Not good for beginners
- ➖ Not many tough slopes nearby

With good transport links and sports facilities, Champéry is great for anyone looking for a quiet time in a lovely place, especially if they have a car – but not if they're beginners. Not bad access to the Portes du Soleil: Avoriaz is fairly easy to get to – and there may be fresh powder there when Champéry is suffering.

THE RESORT

Set beneath the dramatic Dents du Midi, Champéry is a village of old wooden chalets. Friendly and relaxed, it would be ideal for families if it wasn't separated from its slopes by a steep, fragmented mountainside.

Down a steepish hill, away from the main street, are the cable-car, sports centre and railway station.

THE MOUNTAINS

Once you get up to them, the local slopes are as friendly and relaxing as the village.

Slopes Champéry's sunny slopes are part of the extensive Portes du Soleil circuit. The village cable-car or a chair-lift from Grand Paradis, a short free bus-ride from Champéry, go to the Planachaux bowl. If snow conditions permit there are a couple of pistes back to Grand Paradis. There are no pistes back to Champéry, though on rare occasions conditions allow off-piste trips. Explore the Portes du Soleil by heading west towards Avoriaz or north-east to Champoussin, Morgins and Châtel. Reporters have praised the system of Discovery Routes around the Portes du Soleil – choose an animal that suits your ability and follow the signs displaying it. For more on the Portes du Soleil, see the Avoriaz, Châtel and Morzine chapters.

Terrain-parks There is a good terrain park at Les Crosets, half of which is natural. The 17 features include a quarter-pipe, gaps and kickers. There's also a half-pipe that's floodlit on Wednesday and Saturday evenings. At Morgins there's a snowskate park in the village. Avoriaz, where the first terrain-park in France was built, and which now has three, is well worth a look too.

Snow reliability The snow on the north-facing French side of the link with Avoriaz is usually better than on the sunnier Swiss side to the south. The local Champéry area would benefit from more snowmaking.

Experts Few local challenges and badly placed for most of the tough Portes du

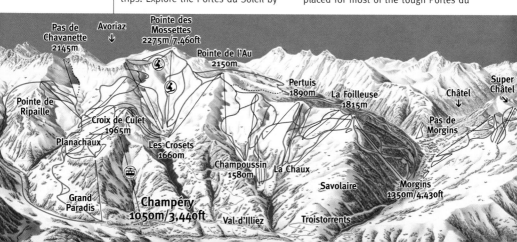

KEY FACTS

Resort	1050m
	3,440ft

For Portes du Soleil

Slopes	975-2275m
	3,200-7,460ft
Lifts	206
Pistes	650km
	400 miles
Green	13%
Blue	38%
Red	39%
Black	10%
Snowmaking	
	252 acres

For Champéry-Les Crosets-Champoussin-Morgins area only

Slopes	1,050-2275m
	3,440-7,460ft
Lifts	36
Pistes	100km
	62 miles

Phone numbers

From elsewhere in Switzerland add the prefix 024.
From abroad use the prefix +41 24.

TOURIST OFFICES

Champéry
t 479 2020
champery-ch@
portes dusoleil.com
www.champery.ch

Les Crosets
t 479 1400
lescrosetstourisme@
bluewin.ch
www.valdilliez.ch

Champoussin
t 477 2727
champoussintourisme
@bluewin.ch
www.valdilliez.ch

Morgins
t 477 2361
touristoffice@morgins.ch
www.morgins.ch

↑ The Planachaux slopes could do with more snowmaking. The Swiss Wall is in the distance
SNOWPIX.COM / CHRIS GILL

Soleil runs. The Swiss Wall, on the Champéry side of Chavanette, is intimidatingly long and steep, but not that terrifying. There's scope for off-piste at Chavanette and on the broad slopes of Les Crosets and Champoussin.

Intermediates Confident intermediates have the whole Portes du Soleil at their disposal. Locally, the runs home to Grand Paradis are good when the snow conditions allow and Les Crosets is a junction of several fine runs. Also worth trying are the slightly tougher pistes down from Mossettes and Pointe de l'Au, Champoussin's leisurely cruising, and runs to Morgins – delightful tree-lined meanders.

Beginners Go elsewhere if you can. The Planachaux runs, where lessons are held, are steepish.

Snowboarding Not ideal for beginners, and access to the Portes du Soleil circuit involves drag-lifts. Good terrain parks for experts though, and some good between-the-pistes powder areas.

Cross-country It's advertised as 10km/ 6 miles with 4km/2 miles floodlit every night, but it's very unreliable snow.

Queues Few local problems. If snow is good, avoid end-of-the-day queues for the cable-car down by taking the Grand Paradis run to the valley floor and getting the free bus back to town.

Mountain restaurants Chez Coquoz at Planachaux and Chez Gaby above Champoussin are recommended. The tiny Lapisa on the way to Grand Paradis is delightfully rustic (they make cheese and smoke their own meats on-site).

Schools and guides The few reports that we've had are free of criticism. The Freeride Company provides competition for the Swiss school.

Facilities for children The tourist office has a list of childminders. The Swiss ski school takes three- to six-year-olds.

How to go Limited packages available. Easy access for independent travellers.

Chalets Tour op Piste Artiste has some.

Hotels Wide choice from 3-star down. Prices low compared with smarter Swiss resorts. The Champéry (479 1071) is the best – a comfy chalet on the main street. Beau Séjour (479 5858) is at the southern end. National (479 1130) has 'friendly staff, lovely breakfast'.

Self-catering Some apartments are available to independent travellers.

Eating out A fair choice. Two of the best for local specialities are just outside the village: Cantines des Rives and Auberge du Grand Paradis. Locally, try the the Farinet for pizza, or the Nord. Mitchell's bar has a good restaurant and the Café du Centre serves Asian food. Two evenings a week, the slopes are floodlit and the restaurant at the top of the cable-car opens.

Après-ski Mitchell's has big sofas and a fireplace. Below the 'rather seedy' Pub, the Crevasse disco is one of the liveliest places. The Café du Centre has its own micro brewery. Try the Bar des Guides in the hotel Suisse, or the Farinet's spacious cellar nightclub.

Off the slopes Walks are pleasant and the railway allows excursions to Montreux, Lausanne and Sion. There's a sports centre, an interesting church, a bell foundry and even a perfumery.

Les Crosets 1660m/5,450ft

A good base for a quiet time and slopes on the doorstep. Not much here, but the Télécabine hotel (479 0300) is homely, with good food in a rustic dining room.

Champoussin 1580m/5,180ft

A good family choice – no through traffic, near the slopes, no noisy late-night revellers and the comfortable Royal Alpage Club hotel (pool, gym, disco, two restaurants – 476 8300).

Morgins 1350m/4,430ft

A fairly scattered, but attractive, quiet resort. The Bellevue (477 8171) and Reine des Alpes (477 1143) are well thought of and Ski Morgins has catered chalets. A reporter enjoyed the Buvette des Sports restaurant for pasta and pizza, the T-bar for drinks, and found the ski school 'very satisfactory'.

Crans-Montana

Sun-soaked slopes, stunning long-distance views and big town base

435

COSTS

① ② ③ ④ ⑤ ⑥

RATINGS

The slopes

Snow	**
Extent	***
Expert	**
Intermediate	****
Beginner	***
Convenience	**
Queues	***
Mountain restaurants	***

The rest

Scenery	****
Resort charm	**
Off-slope	****

NEWS

For 2002/03 a new terrain-park was opened on La Tza in the Aminona sector.

For 2002/03 the Nationale and Barmaz chair-lifts were upgraded and equipped with moving loading carpets.

➕ Large, varied piste area

➕ Splendid wooded setting with magnificent panoramic views

➕ Fair number of woodland slopes – good in bad weather

➕ Modern, well-designed lift system, with few queues

➕ Golf course provides excellent, gentle nursery slopes

➕ Excellent cross-country trails

➕ Very sunny slopes, but ...

➖ Snow badly affected by sun except in early season – often ice in the morning and slush in the afternoon

➖ Large town (rather than village) composed partly of big chalet-style blocks but mainly of dreary cubic blocks – and therefore entirely without Alpine atmosphere

➖ Bus- or car-rides to lifts from much of the accommodation

➖ Few challenges except off-piste

When conditions are right – clear skies above fresh, deep snow – Crans-Montana takes some beating. The mountains you bounce down with the midday sun full on your face are charmingly scenic, the slopes broken up by rock outcrops and forest. The mountains you gaze at – Zermatt's Matterhorn just discernible among them – are mind-blowing. When conditions are right, mountain-lovers may forgive Crans-Montana anything – in particular, its inconvenient, linear layout and the plain, towny style of its twin resort centres.

Sadly, conditions are more often wrong. Except in the depths of winter, the strong midday sun bakes the pistes. For someone booking months ahead, this is enough to keep Crans-Montana off the shortlist. For those who can time a visit according to the weather – and are more interested in impressive distant views than cosy immediate surroundings – the resort is worth serious consideration.

THE RESORT

Crans-Montana celebrates 110 years as a resort in 2003, but is far from being a picturesque Swiss chocolate-box village. Set on a broad shelf facing south to the great mountains across the Rhône valley, it is really two towns, their centres a mile apart and their fringes now merging. Strung along a busy road, the resort's many hotels, villas, apartments and smart shops are mainly dull blocks with little traditional Alpine character.

Fortunately, the resort's many trees help to screen the buildings, and they make some areas positively attractive. And its wonderful setting means you get a lot of sun as well as superb views over the Valais. There are several lakes and two golf courses, one home to the Swiss Open.

The resort is reached by good roads, and by a fast funicular railway up from Sierre to Montana. It depends heavily on summer conference business, which sets the tone even in winter. Hotels tend to be comfortable

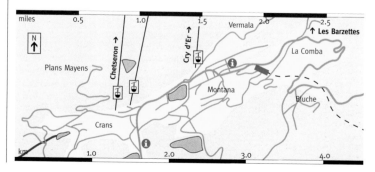

KEY FACTS

Resort	1500m
	4,920ft
Slopes	1500-3000m
	4,920-9,840ft
Lifts	35
Pistes	160km
	99 miles
Blue	38%
Red	50%
Black	12%
Snowmaking	17km
	11 miles

LIFT PASSES

Crans-Montana-Aminona
Covers all lifts in Crans-Montana and Aminona and the ski-bus.

Main pass
1-day pass SF54
6-day pass SF262

Senior citizens
Over 65: 6-day pass SF224

Children
Under 20: 6-day pass SF224
Under 16: 6-day pass SF156
Under 6: free pass

Notes
Half-day passes and passes for 6 non-consecutive days available.

and fairly formal, resort facilities varied but daytime-oriented, and visitors middle-aged and dignified. In the evenings there's little Alpine-village atmosphere.

Gondolas go up to the main slopes from both towns. Crans is the more upmarket, with expensive jewellery shops, a casino, and a high fur-coat count. It is well situated for the pretty golf course area, which has baby lifts for complete beginners, a cross-country trail and lovely walks. Montana has somewhat cheaper restaurants and bars.

Crans-Montana is quite sprawling. A free shuttle-bus links the towns and satellite lift stations during the day but can get very crowded – one reporter recommends taking a car. The main Crans and Montana gondola stations are above the main road and a tiring walk away. Many people store their equipment at lift stations overnight.

There are other gondola base stations and places to stay further east: at Les Barzettes (the lift from here connects directly to the top glacier lift and is the fastest way to the top) and at Aminona.

Anzère is nearby to the west, though the slopes aren't linked. You can make expeditions to Zermatt, Saas-Fee and Verbier by road or rail.

THE MOUNTAINS

Although it has achieved some prominence in ski-racing, Crans-Montana has slopes that suit intermediates well, with few challenges and no nasty surprises. Beginners are well catered for. One of the attractions of the place is that there is a pleasant mix of open and wooded slopes.

THE SLOPES
Interestingly fragmented
Crans-Montana's 160km/99 miles of piste are spread over three well-linked areas, all equally suitable for intermediates of varying abilities and persuasions. Some of the runs down to the valley are narrow woodland paths. Signing of pistes is ridiculously slack; there are lots of intersections where you have to ask for help, or follow your instincts.

Cry d'Er is the largest sector – an open bowl descending into patchy forest, directly above Montana. Cry d'Er itself is the meeting point of many lifts and the starting point of the cable-car up to the sector high point of Bella-Lui. Cry d'Er is served directly by two gondolas – a newish eight-person one from just above Crans, and another from just above central Montana, which has a useful mid-station where beginners can get off and access high-altitude nursery slopes. A third gondola goes from the west side of Crans to Chetseron, with a drag above going on to Cry d'Er.

The next sector, reached by another powerful gondola directly from Les Barzettes, is focused on Les Violettes, starting point of the jumbo gondola up to the Plaine Morte glacier. There are three linking routes from Cry d'Er to the **Violettes-Plaine Morte** sector. The highest, starting at Bella-Lui (or, strictly, at Col du Pochet, a short run and drag beyond) used to be off-piste but is now an official red run. Bella-Lui is also the start of the Men's Downhill course (Piste Nationale) that goes past Cry d'Er to Les Barzettes.

The third, **Petit Bonvin**, sector is served by a gondola up from Aminona at the eastern end of the area. This is linked to Les Violettes by red and blue runs passing the drag and chair-lift at La Toula.

A piste on Cry d'Er is floodlit on Friday evenings for three hours.

TERRAIN-PARKS
Enhanced
Aminona has a new terrain-park, and there's a half-pipe in the more central Cry-d'Er area.

boarding

Despite Crans-Montana's staid, middle-aged image, boarding is very popular. There are plenty of broad, smooth pistes, lots of underexploited off-piste, and good specialist facilities. Aminona is a good area for experienced boarders. There are a number of specialist shops and the Stoked snowboard school. The main lifts are chairs and gondolas, and the drag-lifts are usually avoidable with good planning. It is a good place for beginner and intermediate boarders – and, of course, slush is not such a problem for novice boarders as it is for novice skiers! But avoid the ice first thing in the morning.

SNOW RELIABILITY
The resort's main drawback

Crans-Montana's slopes go up to glacier level at 3000m/9,840ft, but this is misleading; the runs on the Plaine Morte glacier are very limited and, excellent though it is, the solitary run down from there does not make this a snow-sure area as a whole. Few of the other slopes are above 2250m/7,380ft, and practically all get a lot of direct sun. Late in the season, at least, this makes for slush in the afternoons, rock-hard ice in the mornings, and a tendency for snow to disappear. There is now snowmaking on the main runs down from both Violettes and Cry d'Er to Montana, from Cry d'Er to Crans and the bottom part of the run from Chetseron. We applaud these efforts; but it is a losing battle. In numerous visits, we have never found good snow on the runs down to the valley.

FOR EXPERTS
Lacks challenging pistes

There are few steep pistes and the only decent moguls are on the short slopes at La Toula. There's plenty of off-piste in all sectors, but particularly beneath Chetseron and La Tza; guides are usually easy to book. The off-piste tour from Plaine Morte to Aminona is recommended.

The Piste Nationale course is far from daunting taken at 'normal' speed, but has some enormous jumps just above Les Marolires. The direct run from La Tza to Plumachit is fairly challenging in places, especially when icy.

FOR INTERMEDIATES
Lots of attractive, flattering runs

Crans-Montana is very well suited to intermediates. Pistes are mostly wide, and many of the red runs don't justify the grading. They tend to be uniform in difficulty from top to bottom, with few nasty surprises for the nervous. Avid piste-bashers enjoy the length of many runs, plus the fast lifts and good links that allow a lot of varied mileage.

The 11km/7 mile run from Plaine Morte to Les Barzettes starts with top-of-the-world views and powder snow, and finishes among pretty woods. But many people love the top half so much ('my favourite run in Europe') they do it repeatedly, curtailing their descent

Crans-Montana

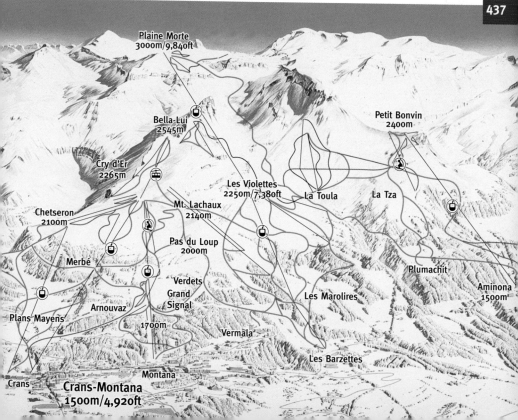

Plaine Morte
3000m/9,840ft

Petit Bonvin
2400m

Bella-Lui
2545m

Cry d'Er
2265m

Les Violettes
2250m/7,380ft

La Toula

La Tza

Chetseron
2100m

Mt. Lachaux
2140m

Pas du Loup
2000m

Plumachit

Merbé

Verdets
Grand
Signal

Les Marolires

Aminona
1500m

Plans Mayens

Arnouvaz

1700m

Vermala

Les Barzettes

Montana

Crans

Crans-Montana
1500m/4,920ft

SCHOOLS

Swiss Crans
t 485 9370
esscrans@bluewin.ch

Swiss Montana
t 481 1480
info@essmontana.ch

Ski & Sky
t 480 4250
info@skiandsky.ch

Stoked Snowboard
t 480 2421
crans-montana@
stoked.ch

Classes (Swiss prices)
6 3hr days SF170

Private lessons
SF60 for 1hr

CRANS-MONTANA TOURISM

It's a marvellous site for a summer resort, but excessively sunny for a winter one ↓

halfway down at either the Barmaz or Cabane de Bois chair-lifts to Les Violettes, for quicker access to the top gondola. Because of the gondola's high capacity the run can get crowded.

The short runs from Bella-Lui to just below Cry d'Er have some of the best snow and quietest slopes in the area, and provide fine views of awesome Montagne de Raul. The Piste Nationale is a good test of technique, with plenty of bumps but also lots of room. The quietest area, and good for groups of varying intermediate standards, is the Petit Bonvin sector.

FOR BEGINNERS
Plenty to offer the first-timer

There are three excellent nursery areas, with slopes of varying difficulty. Complete beginners have very gentle slopes on the golf course next to Crans. Cry d'Er has an area of relatively long, easy runs, with up-the-mountain views and atmosphere as well as better snow. But the runs aren't just for beginners, and you do need a full lift pass. The Verdets-Grand Signal run is steeper, and the drag-lift can get terribly icy. Near-beginners can try the little run up at Plaine Morte.

FOR CROSS-COUNTRY
Excellent high-level trails

There are 40km/25 miles of cross-country trails altogether. There are some pretty, easy trails (skating-style as well as classic) on and around the golf course. But what makes Crans-Montana particularly good for cross-country is its high-level route, in and out of woods, across the whole mountainside from Plans Mayens to beyond Aminona. 10km/6 miles of trails at Plaine Morte are open when the lower trails are closed.

QUEUES
Few problems

The resort's recent investment in gondolas – notably the jumbo 'Funitel' gondola from Les Violettes to the Plaine Morte glacier slopes and the lift out of Crans – has greatly alleviated any queue problems, though bottlenecks can occur at the Nationale drag-lifts. Reporters say you rarely wait longer than five minutes – except occasionally if snow lower down is poor. More of a problem can be bottlenecks on some pistes, including the top run from the glacier. The resort does not get weekend crowds.

CHILDREN

The Montana ski school runs a kindergarten with skiing available up at Signal and the Crans school on the golf course for children aged 3 to 6, from 9.30 to 4.30 (1 day with lunch SF85).

There are several other kindergartens. In Montana, Fleurs des Champs (481 2367) takes children aged 3 months to 7 years; and Zig-Zag (481 2205) takes children from 2 to 6 years.

GETTING THERE

Air Sion 25km/15 miles (30min). Geneva 180km/112 miles (3hr).

Rail Sierre (15km/9 miles), Sion (22km/14 miles); regular buses to resort.

ACTIVITIES

Indoor Hotel swimming pools, tennis, bowling, bridge, chess, golf simulator, squash, snow-shoe walking, concerts, cinemas, casino, curling, ice skating, galleries

Outdoor Toboggan run, ski-bob, horse-riding, ice skating, paragliding, balloon flights

Phone numbers From elsewhere in Switzerland add the prefix 027. From abroad use the prefix +41 27.

TOURIST OFFICE

t 485 0404
info@crans-montana.ch
www.crans-montana.ch

MOUNTAIN RESTAURANTS
A good choice

There are 20 mountain restaurants, many offering table-service. The Merbé, at the Crans-Cry d'Er gondola mid-station, is one of the most attractive, with good food in a pleasant setting just above the tree line. Booking is recommended. Bella-Lui's terrace (with service) offers good views. The Chetseron eatery has fine views.

Petit Bonvin, at the top of the Aminona sector, has self-service and table-service sections inside and out, with a wide-ranging menu and superb views. At Les Violettes, we had a good meal on the table-service terrace. And the self-service Cabane des Violettes, spectacularly set just below, has had rave reviews (be there early for a seat).

SCHOOLS AND GUIDES
Good reports

Both local branches of the Swiss school have attracted mainly favourable comments over the years.

FACILITIES FOR CHILDREN
Adequate, but few reports

The resort facilities for children seem to be adequate, especially in Montana, but we have no recent reports.

STAYING THERE

HOW TO GO
Much more choice on your own

There is a wide choice of hotels and apartments, and some are available through UK tour operators.

Hotels This conference resort has over 50 mainly large, comfortable, expensive hotels. Most have three or more stars though there are more modest places.

(((((5) **Crans-Ambassador** (485 4848) Health spa, with some rooms a bit shabby for its 5-star rating. Excellent treatments, such as plant baths, mud packs. Set just above the Montana gondola.

(((((5) **Pas de l'Ours** (485 9333) Our favourite. Chic, attractive, wood and stone Relais & Chateaux place with nine individually designed suites.

((((4) **Aïda Castel** (485 4111) Beautifully furnished in chic rustic style. Between the two resort centres. Outdoor pool.

(((3) **Beau-Site** (481 3312) Friendly, family-run hotel, a short walk out of Crans.

(((3) **Curling** (481 1242) Comfortable, near the centre of Montana.

(((3) **Forêt** (480 2131) Highly recommended. Almost at Les Barzettes, with minibus to lifts. With pool and good views.

(((3) **Robinson** (481 1353) B&B only; well placed, in central Crans.

Self-catering There are many apartments available.

EATING OUT
Plenty of alternatives

There is a good variety of places, from French to Lebanese. A restaurant guide is given away locally – useful, but not comprehensive.

The best in town is the Bistrot in the Pas de l'Ours hotel. On our next visit we plan to try Le Chalet in Crans, which we found packed when most other places were deserted. The Plaza nearby is better than it looks – big on rösti, but with grills, too. We had a good, simple Italian meal at the Padrino in Crans. The Nouvelle Rotisserie is reputed to be excellent, and the Gréni is a welcoming restaurant on the western fringe of Montana.

APRES-SKI
Can be ritzy, but otherwise quiet

Crans-Montana visitors tend to prefer quiet meals and drinks to raucous nightlife.

Amadeus 2006 and Chez Nanette are tents on Cry d'Er serving close-of-play vin chaud. The George & Dragon in Crans is one of the liveliest, most crowded bars with 'the cheapest beer in town'. Reporters recommend Bar 1900 and the Grange.

The outdoor ice rink in Montana is 'fun'. The cinema has films in English. Bridge is played in the hotels Royal and Aïda.

OFF THE SLOPES
Excellent, but little charm

There are plenty of off-slope activities, including lovely walks. Swimming is available in several hotels.

Sierre is easily reached for shopping, and the larger Sion is only a few minutes further on. Montreux is within reach, too.

Mountain restaurants are mainly at gondola and cable-car stations, so they are accessible to pedestrians.

Davos

A big, grey town surrounded by a glorious Alpine playground

COSTS

①②③④⑤⑥

RATINGS

The slopes

Snow	****
Extent	*****
Expert	****
Intermediate	*****
Beginner	**
Convenience	**
Queues	**
Mountain restaurants	***

The rest

Scenery	****
Resort charm	**
Off-slope	*****

NEWS

The long-awaited replacement of the 70-year-old Parsennbahn railway happened for 2002/03, with a bigger, faster train shifting people from Dorf to the mid-station at 3 times the rate of the old train and eliminating the horrific queues to get up the mountain.

Sadly, the Schatzalp/Strela lift system was closed in 2002/03 and will not reopen for 2003/04. It seems doomed.

Free use of local trains is again included in the lift pass.

A new half-pipe was built in 2002/03 in the terrain-park at the Jatz lift area on the Jakobshorn. And some of the cross-country pistes were modernised and upgraded in 2002/03.

Snowmaking is to be increased in 2003/04.

The Klosters bypass is due for completion in 2005.

440

+ Very extensive slopes

+ Some superb, long, and mostly easy pistes away from the lifts

+ Lots of accessible off-piste terrain, with several marked itineraries

+ Good cross-country trails

+ Plenty to do off the slopes – from sports to shopping

+ Some cute mountain restaurants

+ Klosters is an attractively villagey alternative base

+ New funicular out of Davos for last season was a huge improvement

− Dreary block-style buildings of Davos spoil the views

− Davos is a huge, city-like place, plagued by traffic and lacking Alpine atmosphere and après-ski animation

− The slopes are spread over five separate areas

− Preponderance of T-bars is a problem for some visitors

− Shame that the Strela area of slopes is no longer open

− Only pistes back to Davos are blacks finishing on the outskirts

Davos was one of the original mega-resorts, with slopes on a scale that few resorts can better, even today. But it's a difficult resort to like. It's easy to put up with slopes spread over separate mountains, some queue-prone lifts and lots of T-bars if that's the price of staying in a captivating Alpine village. But Davos is far from that.

Whether you forgive the flaws probably depends on how highly you value three plus-points: the distinctive, super-long runs of the Parsenn area; being able to visit different sectors daily; and the considerable off-piste potential. We value all three, and we always look forward to visiting, especially now the new funicular from town to the main slopes has removed what was the Alps' worst lift-queue.

You don't have to stay in Davos to enjoy its slopes: Klosters offers a much more attractive alternative. Despite royal connections, it is not particularly exclusive. But it is less well placed than Davos for exploring all the mountains.

THE RESORT

Davos is set in a high, broad, flat-bottomed valley, with its lifts and slopes either side. Arguably it was the very first place in the Alps to develop its slopes. The railway up the Parsenn was one of the first built for skiers (in 1931), and the first drag-lift was built on the Bolgen nursery slopes in 1934. But Davos was already a health resort; many of its luxury hotels were built as sanatoriums.

Sadly, that's just what they look like. There are still several specialist clinics and it is for these, along with its conferences and sporting facilities, that Davos has become well known. It is also a popular destination for athletes wanting to train at high altitude.

It has two main centres, Dorf and Platz, about 2km/1 mile apart. Although transport is good, with buses around the town as well as the railway linking Dorf and Platz to Klosters and other villages, location is important. Easiest access to the slopes is from Dorf to the main Parsenn area, via the funicular railway; Platz is better placed for the Jakobshorn area, the big sports facilities, the smarter shopping and evening action.

Davos shares its slopes with the famously royal resort of Klosters, down the valley – an attractive village with good links into the Parsenn area and its own separate sector, the sunny Madrisa. Klosters is described in more detail at the end of this chapter.

Trips are possible by car or rail to St Moritz (the Vereina rail tunnel offers access to the Engadine area without having to negotiate the snowy Flüelapass) and Arosa, and by car to Flims-Laax and Lenzerheide.

LIFT PASSES

Davos/Klosters
Covers all Davos and Klosters, the railway in the whole region and buses between the resorts.

Main pass
1-day pass SF61
6-day pass SF279

Senior citizens
Over 65: 6-day pass SF251

Children
Under 18: 6-day pass SF187
Under 13: 6-day pass SF93
Under 6 (with adult): free pass

Notes
A confusing array of passes are available for individual and combined areas (Parsenn/Gotschna, Jakobshorn, Pischa/Rinerhorn/Madrisa). Several reporters have complained that not all passes are available at each base station.

THE MOUNTAINS

The slopes here have something for everyone, though experts and nervous intermediates need to choose their territory with care.

THE SLOPES
Vast and varied
You could hit a different mountain around Davos nearly every day for a week, but the out-of-town areas tend to be much quieter than the ones directly accessible from the town. Lots of reporters remark on the immaculate grooming of the slopes.

The new Parsennbahn funicular from Davos Dorf ends at a mid-station, where a choice of fast six-pack or old funicular take you on up to the major lift junction of Weissfluhjoch, at one end of the **Parsenn**. The only run back to the valley is a black to the outskirts of Dorf. At the other end of the wide, open Parsenn bowl is Gotschnagrat, reached by cable-car from Klosters. There are excellent intermediate runs down to Klosters, and to other villages (see feature panel). From Davos Platz, a funicular goes up to Schatzalp, but the lifts above here are now closed.

Across the valley, **Jakobshorn** is reached by cable-car or chair-lift from Davos Platz; this is popular with snowboarders but good for skiers too. **Rinerhorn** and **Pischa** are reached by bus or (in the case of Rinerhorn) train.

Beyond the main part of Klosters, a gondola goes up from Klosters Dorf to the sunny, scenic **Madrisa** area.

There are too many T-bars for the comfort of some reporters – Rinerhorn, Pischa and Madrisa have little else.

TERRAIN-PARKS
Lots of choice
The Jakobshorn has traditionally been the main boarder hang-out and now has two half-pipes, one near the bottom in the Bolgen area and another at the top at Jatz – which was added in 2002/03 and is 100m/330ft long. There is also a terrain-park, a boarder-cross course and the funky Jatz Bar nearby. The Rinerhorn and Pischa each have a park and the Parsenn a half-pipe.

SNOW RELIABILITY
Good, but not the best
Davos is high by Swiss standards. Its mountains go respectably high, too – though not to glacial heights. Not many of the slopes face directly south, but not many face directly north either. Snow reliability is generally good higher up but can be poor lower down – you may have to take the lifts down after using the Parsenn slopes. And a 2003 reporter 'nearly killed myself on the red run from Madrisa to Saas; it should have been shut and I ended up walking'. Snow-guns cover a couple of the upper runs on the Parsenn and Jakobshorn and the home runs from the Parsenn to Davos Dorf and Klosters. And piste grooming is excellent, helping to preserve snow.

FOR EXPERTS
Plenty to do, on- and off-piste
A glance at the piste map may give the misleading impression that this is an intermediate's resort – there aren't many black runs. But there are some excellent runs among them – the Meierhofer Tälli run to Wolfgang is a favourite. There are also half a dozen off-piste itineraries (marked but not prepared or patrolled). These are a key feature, adding up to a lot of expert terrain that can be tackled without expensive guidance. Some are on the open upper slopes, some in the woods lower down, some from the peaks right to the valley. Two of the steepest runs go from Gotschnagrat directly towards Klosters – around the infamous Gotschnawang slope. The Wang run is a seriously steep ski route (and often closed on our visits), as is Drostobel.

There is also excellent 'proper' off-piste terrain for which guidance is needed, and some short tours. Arosa

KEY FACTS

Resort	1550m
	5,090ft
Slopes	810-2845m
	2,660-9,330ft
Lifts	54
Pistes	320km
	200 miles
Blue	30%
Red	50%
Black	20%
Snowmaking	18km
	11 miles

boarding

*Intermediate and advanced boarders will get the most out of Davos's vast terrain
and off-piste potential. The established boarder mountain is the Jakobshorn, with
its pipe and park facilities and funky Jatz bar. But there are some lengthy flattish
bits, including on the long runs down the Schifer gondola on the main Parsenn
area. Top Secret is a specialist snowboard shop and school. There are several
cheap hotels specially for boarders, including the 180-bed Bolgenhof near the
Jakobshorn, the Snowboardhotel Bolgenschanze and the Snowboarder's Palace.*

can be reached with a bit of help from
a train or taxi and from there you can
travel on snow to Lenzerheide, but
you'll need a train back. From Madrisa
you can make tours to Gargellen in
Austria. This means an exhausting one-
hour walk on skins on the way back. A
reader also recommends the descent
from Madrisa to St Antönien, north of
Küblis, not least for 'spectacular
views', returning by bus and train.

FOR INTERMEDIATES
A splendid variety of runs
For intermediates of any temperament,
this is a great area. There are good
cruising runs on all five mountains, so
you would never get bored in a week.
This variety of different slopes taken
together with the wonderful long runs
to the valleys makes it a compelling
area with a unique character.

The epic runs to Klosters and other
places (described in the feature panel)
pose few difficulties for a confident
intermediate or even an ambitious
near-beginner (one of your editors did
the run to Klosters on his third day on
skis, and we have heard from reporters
who did the run to Küblis on their
second holiday). And there are one or

two other notable away-from-the-lifts
runs to the valley. In particular, you
can travel from the top of Madrisa
back to Klosters Dorf via the beautiful
Schlappin valley (it's an easy black –
classified red until the mid-1990s).

Pischa is a relatively gentle area
whereas the Jakobshorn has some
genuine challenges. Rinerhorn comes
somewhere between the two.

FOR BEGINNERS
Platz is the more convenient
The Bolgen nursery slope is adequately
spacious and gentle, and a bearable
walk from the centre of Platz. But Dorf-
based beginners face more of a trek
out to Bünda – unless staying out at
the hotel of the same name.

There is no shortage of easy runs to
progress to, spread around all the
sectors. The Parsenn sector probably
has the edge, with long, early
intermediate runs in the main Parsenn
bowl, as well as in the valleys down
from Weissfluhjoch.

FOR CROSS-COUNTRY
Long, scenic valley trails
Davos has a total of 75km/47 miles of
trails – which were modernised and

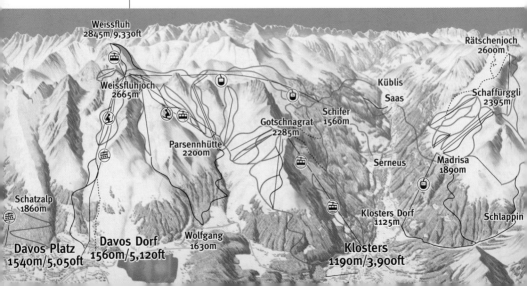

THE PARSENN'S SUPER-RUNS

The runs from Weissfluhjoch that head north, on the back of the mountain, make this area special for many visitors. The pistes that go down to Schifer and then to Küblis, Saas and Serneus, and the one that curls around the mountain to Klosters, are classified red but are not normally difficult – though the latter parts can be challenging if they are not groomed. What marks them out is their sheer length (10-12km/6-7 miles) and the sensation of travel they offer – plus the welcoming huts in the woods towards the end. You can descend the 1100m/ 3,610ft vertical to Schifer as often as you like and take the gondola back. Once past there, the return journey is by train (now included in the lift pass again).

CHILDREN

The Bobo-Club (416 5969) at Bünda takes children aged between 4 and 7 from 10am to noon and from 2pm to 4pm, and offers a 'playful approach to snow and skiing' (SF60 per day). Lunch supervision is possible.

The day nursery Kinderhotel Muchetta at Wiesen takes children from 3 years. There is also a day nursery for babies from 6 months.

The Madrisa Kids' Land offers ski school and childcare for children between the ages of 2 and 6. There are also free facilities for parents with babies, and a children's restaurant, open from noon to 2pm.

upgraded last season – running in both directions along the main valley and reaching well up into Sertigtal, Dischmatal and Flüelatal. There is a cross-country ski centre and special ski school on the outskirts of town.

QUEUES
Worst one now gone

Some of the longest queues in the Alps were ended last season, with the replacement of the first stage of the Parsennbahn. The bigger, faster trains shift the crowds out of Davos Dorf at three times the rate of the old train. One reader found it 'brilliant – the most comfortable and fast ride up a mountain I know'. It seems as if the existing lifts from the mid-station — a six-pack and the existing railway — are coping with the increased loading too. According to one reporter this year, 'everybody piles off at mid-station and on to the six-person, super fast chairlift'. Queues elsewhere can be bad for some cable-cars (including the one out of Klosters) at peak periods — and one high-season visitor found a 45-minute queue for the Madrisa gondola.

MOUNTAIN RESTAURANTS
Stay low down

The main high-altitude restaurants are dreary self-service affairs. The main exception is the highest of all – Bruhin's at Weissflügipfel is a great place for a hang-the-cost blow-out on a snowy day, with table-service of excellent rustic as well as gourmet dishes, and some knockout desserts.

There are other compelling places lower down in the Parsenn sector. A reader describes 'lunching on big portions of chicken and noodles' at the Höhenweg bar outside the mid-station of the Parsennbahn as 'heaven' and another commented on the 'beautifully kept loos'. The old favourites, the rustic 'schwendis' in the woods on the way down to the Klosters valley from the Parsenn, still attract crowds, though a long-standing visitor detects declining standards. Singled out is the 'excellent' Berghaus Schwendi at Schifer with oriental dishes 'freshly cooked in front of our eyes'. These are fun places to end up as darkness falls – Klosters Schwendi, at least, sells wax torches to illuminate your

Davos

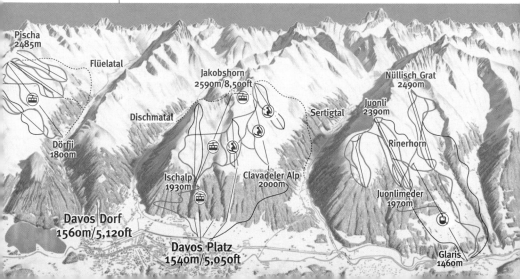

Pischa 2485m

Flüelatal

Jakobshorn 2590m/8,500ft

Nüllisch Grat 2490m

Dischmatal

Sertigtal

Juonli 2390m

Dörfji 1800m

Rinerhorn

Ischalp 1930m

Clavadeler Alp 2000m

Juonlimeder 1970m

Davos Dorf 1560m/5,120ft

Davos Platz 1540m/5,050ft

Glaris 1460m

Swiss Davos
t 416 2454

New Trend
t 413 2040
info@newtrenddavos.ch

Teachers
t 413 1802

Telemark
t 420 1477

Wiesen
t 404 1200

**Top Secret
(snowboard)**
t 413 4043
info@topsecretdavos.ch

Classes
(Swiss prices)
5 4hr days SF240

Private lessons
Half day SF190

GETTING THERE

Air Zürich 144km/89 miles (2hr by car, 3hr by rail or bus).

Rail Stations in Davos Dorf and Platz. 20 minutes from Davos to Klosters.

---

final descent.

On Jakobshorn the Jatzhütte near the boarders' terrain-park is wild – with changing scenery such as mock palm trees, parrots and pirates. This year a reader found the Chalet Güggel on Jakobshorn 'small and cosy with a nice atmosphere but slow service'.

Both restaurants on the Madrisa slopes have been pronounced 'disappointing' in terms of food choice and quality. The Erika at Schlappin below Madrisa is noted for cheese fondue at lunchtime.

At Pischa, the Mäderbeiz at Flüelameder is a friendly and spacious woody hut, cheering on a cold day. On the Rinerhorn, the Hubelhütte was preferred by one reporter to the main restaurant at the top of the gondola.

SCHOOLS AND GUIDES
Decent choice
A reporter last year says that 'nearly all instructors spoke English and were skilled and friendly — both my kids had a terrific time'. There is an alternative ski school called New Trend (maximum of six in a class) and Top Secret is the competing snowboard school.

FACILITIES FOR CHILDREN
Not ideal
Davos is a rather spread-out place in which to handle a family – and indeed the school's nursery is in a rather isolated spot, at Dorf's Bünda nursery slope. A reporter tells us the nursery is 'well organised, but even good instructors forget at times that your child doesn't speak German'.

STAYING THERE

HOW TO GO
Hotels dominate the packages
Although most beds are in apartments, hotels dominate the UK market.

Hotels A dozen 4-star places and about 30 3-stars form the core of the Davos hotel trade, though there are a couple of 5-stars and quite a few cheaper places, including B&Bs. You can book any hotel by calling 415 2121.

⑤ **Flüela** (410 1717) The more atmospheric of the 5-star hotels, in central Dorf. Pool.

④ **Golfhotel Waldhuus** (416 8131) As convenient for langlaufers as for golfers. Quiet, modern, tasteful. Pool.

④ **Davoserhof** (414 9020) Best in town. Small, old, beautifully furnished, with excellent food; well placed in Platz.

④ **Sunstar Park** (413 1414) At far end of Davos Platz. Pool, sauna, games room. Recommended for 'excellent' food.

③ **Parsenn** (416 3232) Right opposite the Parsenn railway in Dorf. An attractive chalet marred by the big McDonald's on the ground floor.

③ **Berghotel Schatzalp** (415 5151) On the tree line 300m/1,000ft above Platz; reached by funicular (free to guests).

② **Alte Post** (414 9020) Traditional and cosy; in central Platz. Popular with boarders.

② **Hubli's Landhaus** (417 1010) 5km/3 miles out at Laret, towards Klosters. Quiet country inn with sophisticated, expensive food.

① **Snowboarder's Palace** (414 9020) Close to Schatzalp funicular, offers good-value dormitory accommodation.

EATING OUT
Wide choice, mostly in hotels
In a town this size, you need to know where to go – if you just walk around hoping to spot a suitable place to eat, you may starve. For a start, get the tourist office's Gastroführer booklet. Most of the more ambitious restaurants are in hotels. There is a choice of two good Chinese restaurants

The train along the valley floor is included in the lift pass and makes getting back from the end of the Parsenn Super-runs easy ↗

KLOSTERS TOURIST OFFICE

ACTIVITIES

Indoor Artificial skating rink, fitness centre, tennis, squash, swimming, sauna, cinema, museums, galleries, libraries, massage, badminton, golf-driving range

Outdoor Over 80km/ 50 miles of cleared paths (mostly at valley level), snow-shoe trekking, full-moon skiing, toboggan run, snow volleyball, natural skating rink, curling, horse-riding, mule-trekking, sleigh rides, hang-gliding, paragliding

Phone numbers
From elsewhere in Switzerland add the prefix 081.
From abroad use the prefix +41 81.

TOURIST OFFICES

Davos
t 415 2121
info@davos.ch
www.davos.ch

Klosters
t 410 2020
info@klosters.ch
www.klosters.ch

– the lavish Zauberberg in the Europe and the Zum Goldener Drachen in the Bahnhof Terminus. Good-value places include the jolly Al Ponte (pizza and steak both approved of), La Carretta (good for home-made pasta), the small and cosy Gentiana (with an upstairs stübli), and a reporter this year found the Pizzeria Palüda and the Hotel Dischma's Röstizerria inexpensive. For local specialities try Heidi's und Haui's Bündnerstübli. An evening excursion for dinner out of town is popular. Schatzalp (reached by a funicular), the Schneider and Landhaus in Frauenkirch have also been recommended.

APRES-SKI
Lots on offer, but quiet clientele
There are plenty of bars, discos and nightclubs, and a large casino in the hotel Europe. But we're not sure how some of them make a living – Davos guests tend to want the quiet life. At tea-time, mega-calories are consumed at the Weber, and Scala has a popular outside terrace. The liveliest place in town is the rustic little Chämi bar (popular with locals); it has 'the best atmosphere later in the evening', according to a reporter. The smart Ex Bar attracts a mixed age group. Nightclubs tend to be sophisticated, expensive and lacking atmosphere during the week. The most popular are the Cabanna and the Cava Grischa (both in the hotel Europe), the Rot Liecht, Paulaner's and Bar Senn.

Bolgenschanze and Bolgen are popular boarder hang-outs.

OFF THE SLOPES
Great apart from the buildings
Provided you're not fussy about building style, Davos can be unreservedly recommended for those not planning to hit the slopes. The towny resort has shops and other diversions, and transport along the

valley and up on to the slopes is good – though the best of the mountain restaurants are well out of range for pedestrians. The sports facilities are excellent; the natural ice rink is said to be Europe's biggest, and is supplemented by artificial rinks, both indoor and outdoor. Spectator events include speed skating as well as hockey. And there are lots of walks up on the slopes as well as around the lake and along the valleys.

Klosters 1190m/3,900ft

In a word association game, Klosters might trigger 'Prince of Wales'. The enlarged cable-car to Gotschna – and the Parsenn – is named after him.

Don't be put off. We don't know why HRH likes to ski in Klosters particularly, but it is certainly not because the place is the exclusive territory of royalty. Most of the really smart socialising goes on behind closed doors, in private chalets.

THE RESORT
Klosters is a comfortable, quiet village with a much more appealing Alpine flavour than Davos. Klosters Platz is the main focus – a collection of upmarket, traditional-style hotels around the railway station, at the foot of the steep, wooded slopes of Gotschna. The Davos road traffic is a problem; a bypass is being built and is due for completion in 2005.

The village spreads along the valley road for quite a way before fading into the countryside; there's then a second concentration of building in the even quieter village of Klosters Dorf.

THE MOUNTAIN
Slopes A cable-car takes you to the Gotschnagrat end of the Parsenn area and a gondola from Klosters Dorf takes you up to the scenic Madrisa area.

Terrain-parks The Madrisa area has a park, and there are more options on the other mountains.

Snow reliability It's usually reliable higher up but can be poor lower down – you may have to take the lifts down after using the Parsenn slopes.

Experts The off-piste possibilities are the main appeal for experts.

Intermediates There are excellent cruising runs in all five ski areas shared with Davos.

Beginners There are some nursery lifts at valley level, but the wide sunny slopes of Madrisa are more appealing.

Snowboarding Local slopes are good, but more boarders stay in Davos.

Cross-country There are 35km/22 miles of trails and a Nordic ski school offers lessons. Further trails are easily accessible at Davos.

Queues Queues for the Gotschna cable-car have been reduced by a doubling of its capacity, but can still be a problem at weekends – a reporter tells of hour-long morning queues.

Mountain restaurants There are a number of atmospheric huts in the woods above the village.

Schools and guides There is a choice of three ski and snowboard schools.

One reader recommends the Saas, with 'excellent English-speaking instructors'.

Facilities for children The ski schools offer classes for children from the age of four and the Madrisa Kids' Club takes children aged two to six.

STAYING THERE

How to go There is a wide choice of packages offered by UK tour operators.

Hotels There are some particularly attractive hotels – all bookable on the central reservations phone number, 410 2020. The central Chesa Grischuna (422 2222) is still a firm favourite, combining traditional atmosphere with modern comfort – and a lively après-ski bar. The Albeina (423 2100) is cheaper than the other 4-stars, runs a mini-bus to the lifts, has a good spa and is 'friendly with good food' says a a fourth-time visitor this year. We get good reports of the 3-star Cresta (422 2525). The very cosy old Wynegg (422 1340) is popular with British visitors. The Bündnerhof (422 1450), next door, is the recommended choice for the 'budget conscious'.

Eating out Good restaurants abound, but a reporter comments that there is a shortage of the cheap and cheerful variety. Top of the range is the Walserhof. Al Berto's serves the best pizza in town and the rösti at the Alpina is recommended. The Chesa Selfranga is 20 minutes' walk from the centre of town, but is noted for fondue, both cheese and Chinoise.

Après-ski In the village, the Chesa Grischuna is a focus from tea-time onwards, with its live music, bowling and restaurant. A reporter enjoyed the music 'at a volume which allowed you to converse'. The hotel Vereina is recommended for its piano bar.

Gaudy's at the foot of the slopes is a popular stop after skiing, as is the lively bar at the four-star Alpina and the warmly panelled Wynegg.

The Casa Antica is a small disco that livens up on Saturday night. The Kir Royal, under the hotel Silvretta Park, is bigger and more brash.

Off the slopes Klosters is an attractive base for walking and cross-country skiing. There is a sport and leisure centre, and some hotels have pools. An excursion by train to the spa at Scuol Tarasp is recommended by one reporter, another suggests a local trip to the spa in the hotel Bad Serneus, and a third took the train to the interesting old town of Chur.

Flims

Splendid slopes that deserve to be better known outside Switzerland

COSTS

① ② ③ ④ ⑤ ⑥

RATINGS

The slopes

Snow	★★★
Extent	★★★★
Expert	★★★
Intermediate	★★★★★
Beginner	★★★★
Convenience	★★★
Queues	★★★
Mountain restaurants	★★★

The rest

Scenery	★★★
Resort charm	★★★
Off-slope	★★★

KEY FACTS

Resort	1100m
	3,610ft
Altitude	1100-3020m
	3,610-9,910ft
Lifts	29
Pistes	220km
	137 miles
Blue	29%
Red	45%
Black	26%
Snowmaking	13km
	8 miles

➕ Extensive, varied slopes ideal for intermediates, shared with Laax

➕ Impressive lift system

➕ Virtually queue-free on weekdays

➕ Just 90 minutes from Zürich airport

➖ Sunny orientation can cause icy or slushy pistes and shut lower runs

➖ Village very spread out, which can mean long walks or bus-rides

➖ Weekend crowds

Flims is virtually unknown outside the Swiss and German market and deserves much more international recognition. It has an impressive 220km/137 miles of mainly intermediate pistes and some good off-piste. The resort is popular with weekenders but can be very quiet during the week. We are delighted that after we complained about their bizarre new piste classification system, they've dropped it and gone back to the usual blue, red and black system for grading pistes.

THE RESORT

Flims is set on a sunny mountain terrace and has two parts: Dorf sprawls along a busy road, while Waldhaus is set in the trees. The slopes spread across to a lift station at Murschetg, an outpost of Laax. There's also a high-speed quad at Falera, 5km/3 miles from Waldhaus. The better hotels in Waldhaus run efficient courtesy buses to and from the slopes.

THE MOUNTAINS

Flims has extensive, varied slopes and some high, exposed peaks, including a small glacier. Because of its sunny aspect, lower runs can deteriorate quickly. In poor visibility there are

plenty of tree-lined runs. Trips are possible to Lenzerheide, Davos-Klosters and Arosa. Flims has at last dropped its own innovative Slope System™ for piste grading because of the confusion that we and many visitors complained about. It now uses a colour system similar to other resorts again, but usefully also marks some flattish connecting runs in orange (coloured green on our map for clarity). Recommended off-piste areas are marked in yellow, and you are told to 'take notice of avalanche bulletins' at various places. The piste map shows the time it takes to ride each lift – useful for meeting others on time.

Slopes The slopes are well planned, and getting around is easy but can mean a lot of traversing. There are

447

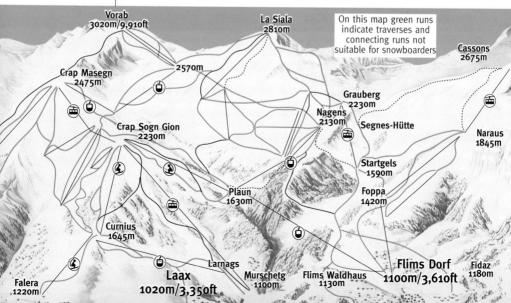

NEWS

The terrain-park on Crap Sogn Gion is due to get a face-lift in 2003/04. And more snowmaking is planned.

A breakthrough took place last season with the abolition of the resort's own Slope System™ for classifying pistes and a return to that used by other resorts.

The children's Dreamland parks in Flims and Laax were developed further in 2002/03 and the Swiss Snow Kids Village programme in the ski school began.

Phone numbers

From elsewhere in Switzerland add the prefix 081.
From abroad use the prefix +41 81.

TOURIST OFFICES

Flims
t 920 9200
tourismus@alpen
arena.ch
www.alpenarena.ch

Laax
t 921 8181
tourismus@alpen
arena.ch
www.alpenarena.ch

Falera
t 921 3030
tourismus@alpen
arena.ch
www.alpenarena.ch

powerful gondolas going into the heart of the slopes from both Flims Dorf and Murschetg (where there's a cable-car too). You can reach the Vorab glacier on piste from La Siala or by a two-way gondola link (sometimes closed by wind) from the Crap Masegn area.

Terrain-parks The resort claims to have Europe's best terrain-park at Crap Sogn Gion, and it is due to get even better for 2003/04. As well as the two half-pipes, walls of which can be built to 6.7m/22ft to create the worldbeating Pipe Monster, there will be drops and jumps, quarter-pipes and rails for all levels. A Pipe & Park day pass is available. There's also boarder-cross and a half-pipe on the Vorab Glacier.

Snow reliability Upper runs are snow-sure, but those back to Flims can suffer from sun. There is snowmaking on the main runs from Crap Sogn Gion, from Segnes-Hütte to Flims and on part of the run to Alp Ruschein.

Experts There is a fair amount to challenge. But most of it is off-piste in areas shown on the map and marked with the US-style black-diamond grades of difficulty. There is also good ski-touring off the back of Cassons, for which a guide is essential. The few official black pistes are not seriously steep except in patches.

Intermediates This is a superb area for all intermediates. There are easy snow-sure blue runs on the Vorab glacier and good blue cruising lower down. For the more adventurous and confident, there are plenty of reds and some blacks worth trying – especially the superb, long Sattel run from the top of the Vorab glacier, and the men's World Cup Downhill piste from Crap Sogn Gion to Larnags, which is often beautifully groomed. Flims is also a good area to learn off-piste.

Beginners There's a nursery area in Dorf, and alternatives at Startgels and Nagens if snow is poor. The Foppa area has good confidence-building runs to move on to. Getting the bus to the easy runs above Falera is possible.

Snowboarding This is a snowboard hot spot. Crap Sogn Gion is a popular meeting point, with loud music from the Rock Bar and the No-Name Café, which overlook half-pipes. Traverses on the piste map are usefully marked as 'not ideal for snowboarders'.

Cross-country There are 56km/35 miles of trails scattered around.

Queues There is little queuing during the week, but at weekends coach loads of day visitors arrive at Murschetg. Lifts closing because of wind has been a common complaint.

Mountain restaurants These are numerous, with a useful short summary of each on the piste map. We prefer the rustic huts lower down (especially the Teglia hut at Larnags).

Schools and guides The school has a good reputation. It offers several innovative programmes such as special free-riding and park and pipe courses.

Facilities for children Children aged three and over can be looked after at one of the Dreamland centres. And there is the new Snow Kids Village in the ski school. Nannies are available.

STAYING THERE

How to go Only a handful of UK tour operators feature Flims.

Hotels The top hotels are in Waldhaus. Reporters recommend the Adula (928 2828) and Cresta (911 3535). The high tech Riders Palace (927 9700) at Murschetg is a trendy place to stay – with dorm as well as normal rooms.

Self-catering The tourist office has a long list of available apartments.

Eating out Most Flims restaurants are in hotels. Reporters recommend the Alpina Garni (Waldhaus) and the Pomodoro – both good for pizzas.

Après-ski Flims is, in general, very quiet. But if you want lots of action, head for Murschetg and the Crap Bar, the Riders Palace bar and its Ministry of Sound-run club. The Iglu and Stenna bars are packed when the slopes close. The Angel is a night club and the Casa Veglia has live bands.

Off the slopes There's an enormous sports centre and 60km/37 miles of marked walks. Historic Chur is a bus-ride away.

Laax 1020m/3,350ft

Laax is a quiet, characterful old farming community, with most of its modern development a bus-ride away at Murschetg at the base of the lifts. Restaurants and bars are hotel-based and nightlife is limited.

Falera 1220m/4,000ft

This tiny village is quiet and traffic-free and has good views over three valleys. Most accommodation is in apartments. Two successive fast quad chairs take you to the heart of the slopes.

Grindelwald

Traditional town in spectacular scenery at the foot of the Eiger

449

COSTS

① ② ③ ④ ⑤ ⑥

RATINGS

The slopes

Snow	**
Extent	***
Expert	**
Intermediate	****
Beginner	***
Convenience	**
Queues	**
Mountain restaurants	***

The rest

Scenery	*****
Resort charm	****
Off-slope	****

NEWS

For 2003/04 the Läger double chair-lift on Männlichen is to be replaced by a fast covered quad, doubling capacity.

On First, the valley runs will have snowmaking.

For 2002/03 a fast quad chair replaced the old Schilt T-bar at the top of First, and improvements were made to the terrain-park.

+ Dramatically set in magnificent scenery, directly beneath the towering north face of the Eiger

+ Lots of long, gentle runs, ideal for intermediates, with links to Wengen

+ Pleasant old village with long mountaineering history, though the tourist trade now sets the tone

+ Fair amount to do off the slopes, including splendid walks and recently expanded toboggan runs

– Village gets very little midwinter sun

– Few challenging pistes for experts

– Inconvenient for visiting Mürren

– Snow-cover unreliable

– Major area accessed by a painfully slow gondola, very queue-prone especially at weekends, and by very slow and infrequent trains – life revolves around timetables

For stunning views from your hotel window and from the pistes, there are few places to rival Grindelwald, and two of them are just over the hill. The village is nowhere near as special as Wengen or Mürren, but staying here does give you direct access to Grindelwald's own First area. But you can spend hours queueing for, waiting for or sitting in the gondola or trains up into the Kleine Scheidegg area shared with Wengen. (The gondola ride takes over half an hour.) Grindelwald regulars accept all this as part of the scene, and some elderly skiers even find it adds to the holiday by enforcing a slow pace.

THE RESORT

Grindelwald is set either side of a road along a narrow valley. Buildings are mainly traditional chalet-style. Towering mountains rise steeply from the valley floor, and the resort and main slopes get very little sun in January.

Grindelwald can feel very jolly at times, such as during the ice-carving festival in January, when huge ice-sculptures are on display along the main street. The village is livelier at night than the other Jungfrau resorts of Wengen and Mürren. There's live music in several bars and hotels, but it isn't a place for bopping until dawn.

The main lifts into the slopes shared with Wengen are at Grund, right at the bottom of the sloping village. Near the opposite end of the village, a gondola goes to the separate First area. Trains run between the centre and Grund, and buses link the lift stations – but these get congested at times and reporters say they are too infrequent.

The most convenient place to stay for the slopes is at Grund. But this is out of the centre and rather charmless. There's a wide range of hotels in the heart of the village, handy enough for everything else, including the First area, at the foot of which are nursery slopes, ski school and kindergarten.

Trips to other resorts are not very easy, but you can drive to Adelboden. Getting to the tougher, higher slopes of Mürren is a lengthy business unless you go to Lauterbrunnen by car.

THE MOUNTAINS

The major area of slopes is shared with Wengen and offers a mix of wooded slopes and open slopes higher up. The smaller First area is mainly open, though there are wooded runs to the village. The Aletsch glacier which can be seen from the Jungfraujoch station (see feature panel later in this chapter) has been declared a UNESCO World Nature Heritage Site.

miles	0.5	1.0	1.5	2.0

↑ First

← Männlichen

Grund 🛈

↓ Kleine Scheidegg

km	1.0	2.0	3.0

KEY FACTS

Resort	1035m
	3,400ft

For Jungfrau region	
Slopes	945-2970m
	3,100-9,740ft
Lifts	44
Pistes	213km
	133 miles
Blue	30%
Red	50%
Black	20%
Snowmaking	34km
	21 miles

For First-Männlichen-Kleine-Scheidegg only	
Slopes	945-2485m
	3,100-8,150ft
Lifts	31
Pistes	160km
	99 miles

boarding

Intermediates will enjoy the area most – the beginners' slopes can be bare, while experts will hanker for Mürren's steep, off-piste slopes. First is the main boarders' mountain, not only because of the terrain-park and big pipe but the open free-ride terrain accessed via the top lifts. There are plenty of drag-lifts to complicate life.

THE SLOPES
Broad and mainly gentle

From Grund, near the western end of town, you can get to **Männlichen** by an appallingly slow two-stage gondola or to **Kleine Scheidegg** by an even slower cog railway. The slopes of the separate south-facing First area are reached by a long, slow three-stage gondola starting a bus-ride east of the centre. From all over the slopes there are superb views, not only of the Eiger but also of the Wetterhorn and other peaks. Piste marking is poor, and one reporter complains that from First it is difficult to determine which run you are on – and therefore easy to end up at the wrong point in the valley.

TERRAIN-PARKS
First things first

There is a terrain-park and a half-pipe at Oberjoch and an enlarged super-pipe at Schrekfeld, both on First.

SNOW RELIABILITY
Poor

Grindelwald's low altitude (the slopes go down to below 1000m/3,280ft and few are above 2000m/6,560ft) and the lack of much snowmaking (though it is increasing) mean this is not a resort to book far in advance. And it's not the place for a late-season holiday. First is sunny, and so even less snow-sure than the main area.

FOR EXPERTS
They are trying

The area is quite limited for experts. The black run on First beneath the gondola back to town is quite tough, especially when the snow has suffered from too much sun. There are now two ungroomed itineraries from the Lauberhorn chair, widening the options slightly.

Heli-trips with mountain guides are organised if there are enough takers.

FOR INTERMEDIATES
Ideal intermediate terrain

In good snow, First makes a splendid intermediate playground, though the general lack of trees makes the area less friendly than the larger Kleine Scheidegg-Männlichen area. The runs to the valley are great fun. Nearly all the runs from Kleine Scheidegg are long blues or gentle reds. On the Männlichen there's a choice of gentle runs down to the mid-station of the gondola up from Grund. In good snow, you can get right down to the bottom

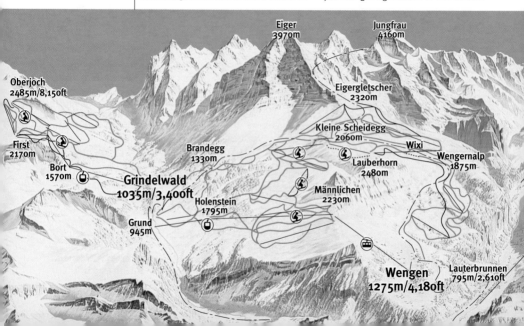

↑ No, it's not the Eiger – that's out of shot on the right. The sunny peak is the Wetterhorn, facing the sunny First slopes
GRINDELWALD TOURISMUS / SWISS-IMAGE.CH

LIFT PASSES

Jungfrau Top Ski Region
Covers Grindelwald, Wengen and Mürren lifts, trains between them and Grindelwald ski-bus.

Beginners
Points card.

Main pass
1-day pass SF55
6-day pass SF282

Senior citizens
Over 62: 6-day pass SF254

Children
Under 20: 6-day pass SF226
Under 16: 6-day pass SF141
Under 6: free pass

Notes
Day pass price is for Grindelwald and Wengen area only.

Alternative passes
Passes available for Grindelwald and Wengen only and for Mürren only. Non-skiers pass available.

CHILDREN

The ski school takes children from age 3 (5 full days SF255), and they can be looked after at lunchtime in the Children's Club kindergarten at the Bodmi nursery slopes. This takes children from age 3, from 9.30 to 4pm. It apparently ceases to function if snow shortage closes the nursery slopes.

The Sunshine nursery on First takes children from 1 month from 8.30-5pm.

on easy red runs – 'barely deserving the grade', says a reporter (and one of these runs used to be marked black).

For tougher pistes, head for the top of the Lauberhorn lift and the runs to Kleine Scheidegg, or to Wixi (following the start of the downhill course). You could also try the north-facing run from Eigergletscher to Salzegg, which often has the best snow late in the season.

FOR BEGINNERS
In good snow, wonderful
The nursery slope is friendly and scenic, just above the village, but in late season it can suffer from the sun and low altitude. There are splendid longer runs served by the railway to Kleine Scheidegg, notably the easy scenic blue Mettlen-Grund run, right from the top to the bottom.

FOR CROSS-COUNTRY
Good but shady
There are over 25km/16 miles of prepared tracks. Almost all of this is on the valley floor at around 1000m/3,280ft, so it's very shady in midwinter and may have poor snow later in the season.

QUEUES
Can be dreadful at peak times
The queues for the gondola and train at Grund can be very bad in high season, especially at weekends. A reporter this year speaks of half-hour waits for the gondola; the mid-station at Holenstein is closed until the queues down in Grindelwald have cleared, producing long queues for

chairs in the Männlichen sector – a problem addressed by the upgrading of the Läger chair for the coming season. You may find long waits for the gondola down from First when the lower runs were closed. Queues for the Oberjoch chair on First have been eased by the new Schilt quad.

MOUNTAIN RESTAURANTS
Wide choice
See the Wengen chapter for restaurants around Kleine Scheidegg and down towards Wengen. Brandegg, on the railway, is recommended for its 'wonderful' apple fritters and sunny terrace. Berghaus Bort does very good rösti, but the 'best rösti anywhere' is at the Jägerstubli, off the Rennstrecke piste.

SCHOOLS AND GUIDES
One of the better Swiss schools
One report declares the Swiss school 'very good'; spoken English is normally excellent. It now has some competition in the form of private lessons from the Buri Sport school.

FACILITIES FOR CHILDREN
Good reputation
A past reporter who put four children through the Grindelwald mill praised caring and effective instructors, and another rates them 'brilliant'. The First mountain restaurant runs a day nursery, which is a neat idea.

SCHOOLS

Swiss
t 854 1280
skischule@
grindelwald.ch

Classes
5 full days SF255
Private lessons
SF70 for 1hr

GETTING THERE

Air Zürich 195km/121
miles (3hr); Bern
70km/43 miles
(1½hr).

Rail Station in resort.

ACTIVITIES

Indoor Sports centre
(swimming pool,
sauna, steam, table
tennis, fitness room,
games room), indoor
skating rink, curling,
bowling, cinema

Outdoor 80km/50
miles of cleared
paths, train rides to
Jungfraujoch,
tobogganing, snow-
shoe excursions,
cross-country skiing,
sleigh rides,
paragliding, heli-
skiing and boarding,
open-air ice skating,
snowrafting, glacier
tours, husky rides

Phone numbers
From elsewhere in
Switzerland add the
prefix 033.
From abroad use the
prefix +41 33.

TOURIST OFFICE

t 854 1212
touristcenter@
grindelwald.ch
www.grindelwald.ch

STAYING THERE

HOW TO GO
Limited range of packages
The hotels UK tour operators offer are
mainly at the upper end of the market.
Hotels One 5-star, a dozen 4-stars, and
plenty of more modest places are
available.
((((⑤ **Regina** (854 8600) The 5-star.
Big and imposing; right next to the
station. Nightly music in the bar. Pool.
(((④ **Belvedere** (854 5454) Family-run,
recently renovated, close to the station
and with a 'wonderful' pool.
(((④ **Schweizerhof** (853 2202)
Beautifully decorated 4-star chalet at
west end of the centre, close to the
station. Pool.
(((④ **Bodmi** (853 1220) Little chalet
right on the village nursery slopes.
(((③ **Hirschen** (854 8484) Family-run 3-
star by nursery slopes. Good food.
(((③ **Fiescherblick** (854 5353)
Hospitable chalet on the eastern fringe,
five minutes from the First gondola.
(((③ **Derby** (854 5461) Popular, modern
3-star next to station, with 'first-class'
service, good food and great views.
((② **Tschuggen** (853 1781) Modest
chalet in a central position below the
nursery slopes.
(① **Hotel Wetterhorn** (853 1218) Cosy,
simple chalet way beyond the village,
with great views of the glacier.
Self-catering A reporter recommends
the apartments of the hotel Hirschen
(854 8484) for comfort and space.
Another rates those in the hotel Eiger
(854 3131) 'excellent, great value'.

EATING OUT
Hotel based
There's a wide choice of good hotel
restaurants, but cheaper pizzeria-style
places are in short supply. The Latino
does home-made Italian cooking.
Among the more attractively traditional
places are: the Swiss Chalet in the

Eiger; Schmitte in the Schweizerhof;
Challi-Stübli in the Kreuz; and the Alte
Post. The Fiescherblick's Swiss Bistro
is repeatedly recommended – 'brilliant
but expensive'. The Kirchbühl and
Oberland are good for vegetarians, the
Bahnhof in the Derby for fondue and
raclette. Hotel Spinne has many
options: Italian, Mexican, Chinese and
the candlelit Rôtisserie for a special
romantic meal. There's even a
Japanese restaurant, the Samurai.

APRES-SKI
Relaxed
There are at least three discos and a
handful of bars that aim to keep going
late. There's also a cinema, plus ice
hockey and curling matches to watch.
There's an excellent sports centre with
pool. Tobogganing and tubing are
organised on First, and some evenings
a 'Sledge Express' train takes people
up to Brandegg/ Alpiglen for fondues
and tobogganing.

OFF THE SLOPES
Plenty to do, easy to get around
There are many cleared paths with
magnificent views, especially around
First – and there's a special (though
expensive) pedestrian bus/lift pass. A
trip to Jungfraujoch is spectacular (see
below), and excursions by train are
easy to Interlaken and possible to
Bern. Tobogganing has undergone a
bit of a renaissance, with runs up
15km/9 miles on First (Europe's
longest) and 70km/43 miles of runs in
total. Helicopter flights from
Männlichen are recommended.

STAYING UP THE MOUNTAIN
Several possibilities
See the Wengen chapter for details of
rooms at Kleine Scheidegg. The
Berghaus Bort (853 1762), at the
gondola station in the middle of the
First area, is an attractive alternative.

THE JOURNEY TO THE TOP OF EUROPE

*From Kleine Scheidegg you can take a train through the Eiger to the highest
railway station in Europe – Jungfraujoch at 3454m/11,332ft. The journey is a bit
tedious – you're in a tunnel except when you stop to look out of a gallery carved
into the sheer north face of the Eiger – magnificent views over to Männlichen and
the villages. At the top is a big restaurant complex. There's an 'ice palace' carved
out of the glacier, with ice sculptures and slippery walkways, an outdoor 'plateau'
to wander around and a viewing tower from which you have fabulous views of
the Aletsch glacier (a UNESCO World Heritage Site).*

*The cost is SF48 with a Jungfrau lift pass for three days plus, SF99.50 without.
At the top the air is thin, and some people have breathing or balance problems.*

Gstaad

Surprisingly unpretentious 'exclusive' resort, with extensive slopes

COSTS

① ② ③ ④ ⑤ ⑥

RATINGS

The slopes

Snow	*
Extent	****
Expert	**
Intermediate	***
Beginner	***
Convenience	*
Queues	***
Mountain restaurants	***

The rest

Scenery	***
Resort charm	****
Off-slope	****

The landscape is not notably dramatic, but it is certainly easy on the eye ↓

- **+** Traditional village, traffic-free in centre, without the towny feel of other fashionable Swiss resorts
- **+** Lift pass covers large area of slopes
- **+** Good long runs for intermediates
- **+** Lively après-ski scene
- **+** Wide range of off-slope diversions, including swanky shops

- **–** Fragmented slopes, none convenient for central hotels – so you are always using buses and trains
- **–** Unreliable snow-cover, except on the limited (and distant) Diablerets glacier slopes
- **–** No budget accommodation
- **–** Few challenges for experts

Gstaad is renowned as a jet-set resort, but for 'ordinary' holidaymakers, too, it has attractions – especially for those with a relaxed outlook, who can happily spend time on trains looking at the landscape without feeling it's precious piste time wasted. It's just a pity most of the slopes are below 2100m/6,900ft.

It's also a pity that the resort authorities can't see their way to giving us permission to modify their piste map to make it suitable for reproduction here.

THE RESORT

Gstaad is a traditional, year-round resort in a spacious, sunny setting surrounded by a horseshoe of wooded mountains. The main street, lined with hotels, smart shops and cafes, has a pleasant and relaxed feel now that it's traffic-free. The Montreux-Oberland-Bernois (MOB) railway station is only yards away, and accesses the numerous surrounding villages. These are smaller (and cheaper), and with their own lifts form good alternative bases to Gstaad itself. Three areas of slopes are accessed via lifts scattered around the fringes of Gstaad and served by a regular shuttle-bus service.

NEWS

The Grand Hotel Bellevue was totally renovated for the 2002/03 season.

KEY FACTS

Resort	1050m
	3,440ft
Slopes	950-3000m
	3,120-9,840ft
Lifts	66
Pistes	250km
	155 miles
Blue	48%
Red	36%
Black	16%
Snowmaking	12km
	7 miles

Phone numbers
From elsewhere in Switzerland add the prefix 033.
From abroad use the prefix +41 33.

TOURIST OFFICE

t 748 8181
gst@gstaad.ch
www.gstaad.ch

THE MOUNTAINS

There are four main areas of slopes, covered by a single, very unclear and confusing map. Most of the slopes are below the tree line, with just the top sections reaching above that.

Slopes Wasserngrat (to the east of the village) and Wispile (to the south) are both small areas with one or two main lifts and runs alongside them. Eggli (to the west) is more complex, and leads via the valley of Chalberhöni to the crags of Videmanette, also accessible by gondola from the rustic village of Rougemont, just over the border into French-speaking Switzerland.

The largest sector is accessed from the lift stations at Saanenmöser and Schönried. The slopes here have for years been linked with those above St Stephan, over the mountain, and more recently have been linked to those above Zweisimmen. Saanenmöser and Schönried are no more inconvenient than Gstaad's local lift stations, given a train timetable. Schönried also has a separate sunny area of slopes on the opposite side of the valley.

The Glacier des Diablerets is also covered by the main area pass but is 15km/9 miles away to the south, with lifts at Reusch and Col du Pillon. There are excellent runs below glacier level – notably the splendid shady red run down the lift-free Combe d'Audon – but the glacier itself is limited.

Slightly further afield, past Rougemont, but included on the map and connected by rail, are Château d'Oex and Les Moulins – both with their own small ski areas, and included on the main pass.

Terrain-parks There's a terrain-park at Eggli, a half-pipe at Zweisimmen and a boarder-cross course at Horneggli.

Snow reliability A lack of altitude means that snow-cover can be unreliable except on the glacier, but most of the slopes are roughly north-facing. A handful of valley runs now have snow-guns.

Experts Few runs challenge experts. Black runs rarely exceed red difficulty, and some should be classified blue. There are off-piste possibilities – steep ones on the wooded flanks of Wispile and Eggli. Heli-skiing is available, though we haven't seen it done.

Intermediates Given good snow, this is a superb area for intermediates, with long, easy descents in the major area to the villages scattered around its edges – that to St Stephan being rather more challenging than most. The run to Rougemont from the top of Eggli is lovely, with no lifts in view.

Beginners The nursery slopes at the bottom of Wispile are adequate, and there are plenty of runs to progress to.

Snowboarding There is good free-riding on Wassengrat.

Cross-country The 60km/37 miles of trails are very pretty, and there are some epic journeys to be done given the stamina. Most loops are low down and can suffer from poor snow; but there are higher loops, notably at the special langlauf centre at Sparenmoos.

Queues Time lost on buses or trains is more of a problem than queues, except at peak times and weekends.

Mountain restaurants Mountain restaurants are plentiful, and most are attractive, although expensive.

Schools and guides We lack recent reports from readers.

Facilities for children There is a ski kindergarten at Schönried, but there are no facilities for non-skiing children.

STAYING THERE

How to go Gstaad is certainly exclusive, with over three-quarters of its accommodation in private chalets and apartments. The remainder of the beds are in 3-star hotels and above.

Hotels The 5-star Palace (748 5000) is extravagantly swish, in secluded grounds. The Bernerhof (748 8844) and the Christiania (744 5121) are recommended 4-stars. The Olden (744 3444) is a charming, central, chalet-style building.

Self-catering There is a wide choice of self-catering accommodation locally.

Eating out Restaurants are mainly hotel-based, and expensive. The Bagatelle in the Grand Chalet and the Chesery are recommended for gourmet meals. Hotel Rössli is reasonably priced and the locals' bar in the central hotel Olden offers filling, value-for-money meals.

Après-ski In season nightlife is lively both at tea-time and later on.

Off the slopes Gstaad's activities are wide-ranging. The tennis centre and swimming pool complex are impressive. There are toboggan runs, ice skating and 50km/30 miles of pretty cleared walks. Getting around is easy, and excursions by rail to Montreux and Interlaken or even further afield are possible.

Mürren

Stupendous views, an epic run, and a chocolate-box village

455

COSTS

①②③④⑤⑥

RATINGS

The slopes

Snow	★★★
Extent	★
Expert	★★★
Intermediate	★★★
Beginner	★★
Convenience	★★★
Queues	★★★
Mountain restaurants	★★

The rest

Scenery	★★★★★
Charm	★★★★★
Off-slope	★★★

NEWS

For 2002/03 extra snowmaking was installed near the Schilthornbahn.

➕ Tiny, charming, traditional 'traffic-free' village, with snowy paths and chocolate-box chalets

➕ Stupendous scenery, best enjoyed on the challenging run from the panoramic Schilthorn

➕ Good sports centre

➕ Good snow high up, even when the rest of the region is suffering

➖ Extent of local pistes very limited no matter what your level of expertise

➖ Lower slopes can be in poor condition

➖ Quiet, limited nightlife

➖ Like other 'traffic-free' Swiss villages, Mürren is gradually admitting more service vehicles

Mürren is one of our favourite resorts. There may be other mountain villages that are equally pretty, but none of them enjoys views like those from Mürren across the deep valley to the rock faces and glaciers of the Eiger, Mönch and Jungfrau: simply breathtaking. Then there's the Schilthorn run – 1300m/4,270ft vertical with an unrivalled combination of varied terrain and glorious views.

Our visits are normally one-day affairs; holidaymakers, we concede, are likely to want to explore the extensive intermediate slopes of Wengen and Grindelwald, across the valley. And you have to accept that getting there takes time.

It was in Mürren that the British more or less invented modern skiing. Sir Arnold Lunn organised the first ever slalom race here in 1922. Some 12 years earlier his father, Sir Henry, had persuaded the locals to open the railway in winter so that he could bring the first winter package tour here. Sir Arnold's son Peter, who first skied here in November 1916, still skis here with his children and grandchildren – or did when we met him in the bar of the hotel Eiger a couple of seasons ago. Mürren's that kind of place.

THE RESORT

Mürren is set on a shelf high above the Lauterbrunnen valley floor, across from Wengen, and can be reached only by cable-car from Stechelberg (via Gimmelwald) or funicular and then railway from Lauterbrunnen. Once you get there you can't fail to be struck by

Mürren's tranquillity and beauty. The tiny village is made up of paths and narrow lanes weaving between tiny wooden chalets and a handful of bigger hotel buildings. The roofs and paths are normally snow-covered.

Two further stages of the cable-car take you up to the high slopes of Birg and the Schilthorn. Nearby lifts go to

miles 0.5
↖ ↑ down to Lauterbrunnen
Allmendhubel
ℹ
Schilthorn ←
N ↑
↓ down to Stechelberg
km 0.5 1.

SNOWPIX.COM / CHRIS GILL

Believe it or not, this is the view from the train window as you approach Mürren ➜

the main lower slopes, and a recently modernised funicular halfway along the village accesses the other slopes.

As noted in our summary above, Mürren's traffic-free status is being eroded: there are a few delivery trucks. But the place still isn't plagued by electric carts and taxis as most other traditional 'traffic-free' resorts now are.

It's not the place to go for lively nightlife, shopping or showing off your latest gear to admiring hordes. It is the place to go if you want tranquillity and stunning views.

The village is so small that location is not a concern. Nothing is more than a few minutes' walk.

THE MOUNTAIN

Mürren's slopes aren't extensive (53km/33 miles in total). But it has something for everyone, including one of our favourite runs, and a vertical of some 1300m/4,270ft. And those happy to take the time to cross the valley to Wengen-Grindelwald will find plenty of options. These resorts are covered by the Jungfrau lift pass.

THE SLOPES
Small but interesting

There are three connected areas around the village, reaching no higher than 2145m/7,040ft. The biggest is **Schiltgrat**, served by a fast quad chair behind the cable-car station. You can also get there from the top of the modernised funicular that goes from the middle of the village to the nursery slope at **Allmendhubel** – from where a run and the new chair take you to the slightly higher **Maulerhubel**. Runs go down from here to the Winteregg stop on the railway, too. These lower slopes take you up to around 2000m/6,600ft.

Much more interesting are the higher slopes reached by cable-car. The first stage takes you to Birg and the **Engetal** area, where an old T-bar serves short, steep, shady slopes. Two chair-lifts below the Engetal serve some snow-sure intermediate slopes. But plans for a third chair, back up to

Birg, have been shelved. To get back to the Birg cable-car station and avoid the tricky black run down to the village, you face an annoying walk up from these chairs to the old T-bar.

The final stage of the cable-car takes you up to the summit of the **Schilthorn** and the Piz Gloria revolving restaurant, made famous by the James Bond film *On Her Majesty's Secret Service*. In good snow you can go all the way from here to Lauterbrunnen – almost 16km/10 miles. The Inferno race (see separate box) takes place over this course, conditions permitting. Below Winteregg it's all boring paths.

The Jungfrau piste map doesn't deal with Mürren's slopes at all well. The one used in the Mürren brochures (on which our own is based) is better.

TERRAIN-PARKS
Affirmative

There is a half-pipe and a terrain-park on the lower slopes of Schiltgrat.

SNOW RELIABILITY
Good on the upper slopes

The Jungfrau region does not have a good snow record – but Mürren always has the best snow in the area. When Wengen-Grindelwald (and Mürren's lower slopes) have problems, the Schilthorn and Engetal often have packed powder snow because of their height and orientation – north-east to east. Piste grooming has improved in recent years.

FOR EXPERTS
One wonderful piste

The run from the top of the Schilthorn starts with a steep but not terrifying slope, in the past generally mogulled but now often groomed. It flattens into a schuss to Engetal, below Birg. Then there's a wonderful, wide run with stunning views over the valley to the Eiger, Mönch and Jungfrau. Since the chair-lifts were built here you can play on these upper runs for as long as you like. Below the lifts you hit the Kanonenrohr (gun barrel). This is a very narrow shelf with solid rock on

boarding

Like other Swiss resorts, Mürren has a traditional image, but it is trying to move with the times and offer a more snowboard-friendly attitude – and the major lifts are cable-cars and chair-lifts. The terrain above Mürren is suitable mainly for good free-riders – it's steep, with a lot of off-piste. Intermediates will find the area tough and limited; nearby Wengen is ideal, and much better for beginners.

SCHOOLS

Swiss
t 8551247

Classes
6 2hr days SF135

Private lessons
SF110 for 2hr

one side and a steep drop on the other – protected by nets. After an open slope and scrappy zig-zag path, you arrive at the 'hog's back' and can descend towards the village on either side of Allmendhubel.

From Schiltgrat a short, serious mogul run – the Kandahar – descends towards the village, but experts are more likely to be interested in the off-piste runs into the Blumental – both from here (the north-facing Blumenlucke run) and from Birg (the sunnier Tschingelchrachen) – or the adventurous runs from the Schilthorn.

FOR INTERMEDIATES
Limited, but Wengen nearby
Keen piste-bashers will want to make a few trips to the long cruising runs of Wengen-Grindelwald. The best easy cruising run in Mürren is the north-facing blue down to Winteregg. The reds on the other low slopes can get mogulled, and snow conditions can be poor. The area below the Engetal normally has good snow, and you can choose your gradient.

FOR BEGINNERS
Not ideal, but adequate
The nursery slopes at Allmendhubel, at the top of the funicular, are on the

steep side. And there are not many easy runs to graduate to – though the blue down the Winteregg chair is easy, and the Schilt-Apollo blue served by the long Gimmeln drag and the less tiring Schiltgrat chair are ideal.

FOR CROSS-COUNTRY
Forget it
There is one small loop above the village in the Blumental, and more extensive loops down at Lauterbrunnen or Stechelberg. But snow is unreliable at valley height.

QUEUES
Generally not a problem
Mürren doesn't get as crowded as Wengen and Grindelwald, except on sunny Sundays. There can be queues for the cable-cars – usually when snow shortages bring in people from lower resorts. The top stage has only one cabin. The new Allmendhubel funicular goes at twice the speed of the old one.

MOUNTAIN RESTAURANTS
Disappointing at altitude
Piz Gloria revolves once an hour, displaying a fabulous 360° panorama of peaks and lakes, but don't expect particularly good food, or a small bill.

Mürren

Schilthorn 2970m/9,740ft

Birg 2675m

Engetal

Schiltgrat 2145m/7,040ft

Blumental

Maulerhubel 1930m

Allmendhubel 1905m

Gimmeln

Grütschalp 1485m

Mürren 1650m/5,410ft

Winteregg

Gimmelwald 1365m

Stechelberg 865m

Lauterbrunnen 795m/2,610ft

CHILDREN

The ski school takes children from age 5 (6 2hr days SF135).

There is non-skiing childcare in the sports centre for children up to 5 years old for SF50 per day.

GETTING THERE

Air Zürich 195km/121 miles (3½hr); Bern 70km/43 miles (1½hr).

Rail Lauterbrunnen; transfer by mountain railway and tram.

ACTIVITIES

Indoor 'Alpine Sports Centre Mürren' swimming pool, whirlpool and children's pool, library, children's playroom, gymnasium, squash, sauna, solarium, steam bath, massage, fitness room

Outdoor Artificial skating rink (curling, skating), toboggan run to Gimmelwald, 15km/9 miles cleared paths

Phone numbers
From elsewhere in Switzerland add the prefix 033. From abroad use the prefix +41 33.

TOURIST OFFICE

t 856 8686
info@muerren.ch
www.wengen-muerren.ch

By the Engetal chair-lifts, the Schilthornhütte is small and rustic.

Lower down, the Suppenalp in the Blumental is rustic and quietly set, does 'excellent food' but gets no sun in January. As you might expect, Sonnenberg is sunnier. Gimmelen is a self-service place with a large terrace, famous for its apple cake. Winteregg does something similar, as well as 'superb rösti' and 'the best burger east of the Rockies'. Both have little playgrounds to amuse kids.

SCHOOLS AND GUIDES
Small, not perfectly formed
Reporters speak of good progress for beginners, but also of one English speaker who had a rather lonely week in a group with six Germans.

FACILITIES FOR CHILDREN
Adequate
There is a baby slope with a rope tow. And there is a children's club at the sports centre. The ski school takes children from five years.

STAYING THERE

HOW TO GO
Mainly hotels, packaged or not
A handful of operators offer packages to Mürren.
Hotels There are fewer than a dozen hotels, ranging widely in style.
(((4 **Anfi Palace** (856 9999) Victorian pile near station – recently renovated.
((((4 **Eiger** (856 5454) Plain-looking 'chalet' blocks next to railway station, widely recommended; good blend of efficiency and charm; good food; pool.
(((3 **Alpenruh** (856 8800) Attractively renovated chalet next to the cable-car.
(((3 **Edelweiss** (856 5600) Block-like but friendly; good food and facilities.
(((3 **Jungfrau** (855 4545) Perfectly placed for families, in front of the baby slope and close to the funicular.

(((2 **Alpenblick** (855 1327) Simple, small, modern chalet near station.
Self-catering There are plenty of chalets and apartments in the village for independent travellers to rent.

EATING OUT
Mainly in hotels
The main alternative to hotels is the rustic Stägerstübli – a bar as well as restaurant. The locals eat in the little diner at the back. The food at the Eiger hotel is good, and the Bellevue and Alpenruh get good reports.

APRES-SKI
Not devoid of life
The Eiger Bar (in the Eiger guest house, not the hotel) is the Brits' meeting place. The tiny Stägerstübli is cosy, and the place to meet locals. Other activities are hotel-based. The Anfi Palace's Balloon bar is an attempt at a trendy cocktail bar; it also has a weekend disco, the Inferno. The Bliemli Chäller disco in the Blumental caters for kids, the nightly Tachi disco in the Eiger for a more mixed crowd.

OFF THE SLOPES
Tranquillity but not much else
There isn't a lot to amuse people who don't want to hit the slopes. But there is a very good sports centre, with an outdoor ice rink. Excursions by car or train to Interlaken and to Bern are easy. It's no problem for friends to return to the village for lunch. The only problem with meeting at the top of the cable-car instead is the expense.

STAYING DOWN THE VALLEY
A cheaper option
Lauterbrunnen is a good budget base. It has a resort atmosphere and access to and from both Wengen and Mürren until late. We've happily stayed at the Schützen (855 3026) and Oberland (855 1241) on several occasions.

THE INFERNO RACE

Every January 1,800 amateurs compete in Mürren's spectacular Inferno race. Conditions permitting, and they usually don't, the race goes from the top of the Schilthorn right down to Lauterbrunnen – a vertical drop of 2175m/7,140ft and a distance of almost 16km/10 miles, incorporating a short climb at Maulerhubel. The racers start individually at 12 second intervals; the fastest finish the course in around 15 minutes, but anything under half an hour is very respectable.

The race was started by Sir Arnold Lunn in 1928 when he and his friends climbed up to spend the night in a mountain hut and then raced down in the morning. For many years the race was organised by the British-run Kandahar Club, and there is still a strong British presence among the competitors.

Saas-Fee

Beautiful, car-free village with slopes on top of the world

➕ Spectacular setting amid peaks and glaciers – slopes open year-round

➕ Traditional, 'traffic-free' village

➕ Good percentage of high-altitude, snow-sure slopes

➕ Powerful lift access to highest slopes for year-round skiing

➕ Good off-slope facilities – even a mountain specially for walking and tobogganing

➖ Disappointingly small area of slopes, with mainly easy runs

➖ Glacier limits off-piste exploration

➖ Much of the area is in shadow in midwinter – cold and dark

➖ Bad weather can shut the slopes

➖ Long village can mean quite a bit of walking to and from the slopes

➖ Some visitors suffer altitude problems at top of mountain

Saas-Fee is one of our favourite places. It oozes Swiss charm, and the setting is stunning – spectacular glaciers and 4000m/13,120ft peaks surround the place. And good snow is guaranteed, even late in the season: the altitude you spend most of your time at – between 2500m and 3500m (8,200ft and 11,480ft) – is unrivalled in the Alps.

But we tend to drop in for a couple of days at a time, so the limited extent of the slopes never becomes a problem; for a week's holiday, it would. Top to bottom there is an impressive 1800m/5,900ft vertical – but there aren't many alternative ways down. Keen, mileage-hungry intermediates should look elsewhere, as should experts (except those prepared to go touring). For the rest, it's a question of priorities and expectations. Over to you.

459

THE RESORT

Like nearby Zermatt, Saas-Fee is a high-altitude mountain village centred on narrow streets lined by attractive old chalets and free of cars (there are car parks at the resort entrance) but not free of electric milk floats posing as taxis. On most other counts, Saas-Fee and its more exalted neighbour are a long way apart in style.

There are some very smart hotels (plus many more modest ones) and plenty of good eating and drinking places. But there's little of the glamour and greed that, for some, spoil Zermatt – and even the electric taxis here are driven at a more considerate pace. Saas-Fee still feels like a village, with its cow sheds more obviously still containing cows. The village may be chilly in January, but when the spring sun is beating down, Saas-Fee is a quite beautiful place in which to just stroll around and relax, admiring the impressive view.

Depending on where you're staying and which way you want to go up the mountain, you may do more marching than strolling. It's a long walk from one end of the spread-out village to the other, though your hotel may run a courtesy bus to and from the lifts. Three major lifts start from the southern end of the village, at the foot of the slopes, and lots of the hotels and apartments are 1km/0.5 miles or more away. The modern Alpin Express starts below the centre, though, quite near the entrance to the resort.

The village centre has the school and guides' office, the church and a

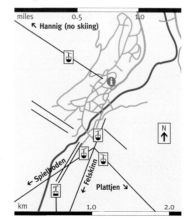

KEY FACTS

Resort	1800m
	5,910ft
Slopes	1800-3500m
	5,910-11,480ft
Lifts	32
Pistes	125km
	78 miles
Blue	25%
Red	50%
Black	25%
Snowmaking	12km
	7 miles

SAAS-FEE TOURISMUS

The close-up views of glaciers are amazing – but the crevasses limit the off-piste potential ↓

few more shops than elsewhere, but it doesn't add up to much. On a sunny day, though, the restaurant terraces fronting the nursery slopes at the far end of the village are a magnet, with breathtaking views up to the ring of 4000m/13,120ft peaks – you can see why the village is called 'The Pearl of the Alps'.

Staying near a main lift makes most sense. If you do end up at the wrong (north) end of the village – and most budget accommodation is there – ease the pain by storing kit near the lifts.

The slopes of Saas-Almagell and Saas-Grund are not far away, and you can buy a lift pass that covers all these resorts and buses between them. Day trips to Zermatt, Grächen and Crans-Montana are also possible options for those itching for a change.

THE MOUNTAIN

The area is a strange mixture of powerful modern lifts (a two-stage 30-person gondola followed by an underground funicular which take you up 1700m/5,580ft vertical) and a lot of old-fashioned T-bars (there's only one chair-lift). Blame the glaciers, which can move downhill by 100m/330ft a year; drag-lift pylons can be moved to cope, but chair-lifts are not practicable.

The upper slopes are largely gentle, while the lower mountain, below the glacier, is steeper and rockier, needing good snow-cover. There is very little shelter here in bad weather: during and after heavy snowfalls you may find yourself limited to the nursery area.

Saas-Fee is one of the leading resorts for mountaineering and ski-touring from valley to valley. Several nearby peaks can be climbed, and the extended Haute Route from Chamonix

via Zermatt ends here.

The top altitude of 3500m/11,480ft means some people suffer faintness there because of the thin air.

THE SLOPES
A glacier runs through it

There are two routes up to the main **Felskinn** area. The efficient 30-person Alpin Express jumbo gondola, starting across the river from the main village, takes you to Felskinn via a mid-station at Morenia (where you have to change cabins). The alternative is a short drag across the nursery slope at the south end of the village, and then the Felskinn cable-car. From Felskinn, the Metro Alpin underground funicular hurtles up to Mittelallalin. From below here, the top two drag-lifts access the high point of 3500m/11,480ft.

Also from the south end of the village, a gondola leaves for Spielboden. This is met by a cable-car which takes you up to **Längfluh**.

Between Felskinn and Längfluh is an off-limits glacier area. A very long drag-lift from Längfluh takes you to a point where you can get down to the Felskinn area. These two sectors are served mainly by drag-lifts, and you can get down to the village from both.

Another gondola from the south end of the village goes up to Saas-Fee's smallest area, **Plattjen**.

TERRAIN-PARKS
Well developed

Saas-Fee was early into the fun-park business, and has well-established facilities in the Felskinn sector including a big half-pipe, a fun-park and a boarder-cross. The nearby Morenia bar is the place for a break.

SNOW RELIABILITY
Good at the highest altitudes

Most of Saas-Fee's slopes face north and many are above 2500m/8,200ft, making this one of the most reliable resorts for snow in the Alps. The glacier is open most of the year. Visitors tell us that the substantial recent investment in snow-guns still doesn't completely ensure good coverage on the rocky lower slopes, though piste grooming is 'excellent'.

FOR EXPERTS
Not a lot to keep your interest

There is not much steep stuff, except on the bottom half of the mountain where the snow tends not to be as

Saas-Fee area
Covers all lifts in
Saas-Fee only.

Beginners
Village area pass
covers 5 beginners'
lifts

Main pass
1-day pass SF60
6-day pass SF290

Children
Under 16: 6-day pass
SF174
Under 6: free pass

Notes
Single and return
tickets on most main
lifts. Afternoon pass
available.

Alternative passes
Separate passes for
each of the other ski
areas in the Saastal
(Saas-Grund, Saas-
Almagell, Saas-Balen).
Pass for all four
villages in the Saastal
also available, and
includes ski-bus
between them. 6-day
pass, SF314.

boarding

Saas-Fee encourages boarding in a big way. In summer, in particular, its glacier slopes are dominated by boarders. While the gentle glacier slopes are ideal for learning, only main access lifts are boarder-friendly (gondolas, cable-cars and a funicular); nearly all the rest are drags. There are a couple of specialist schools. Expert free-riders may be frustrated by the limits imposed on off-piste riding by the glacier. The slopes above Längfluh offer great carving space. The Popcorn board shop and bar is popular.

good. There is a short black run from Felskinn that certainly deserves its grading. The slopes around the top of Längfluh often provide good powder, and there are usually moguls above Spielboden. The blacks and trees on Plattjen are worth exploring. The glacier puts limits on the local off-piste even with a guide – crevasse danger is extreme. But there are extensive touring possibilities, especially late in the season.

FOR INTERMEDIATES
Great for gentle cruising
Saas-Fee is ideal for early intermediates and those not looking for much of a challenge. For long cruises, head for Mittelallalin. The top of the mountain, down as far as Längfluh in one

direction, and as far as Morenia in the other, is ideal, with usually excellent snow. Gradients range from gentle blues to slightly steeper reds which can build up smallish bumps. For more of a challenge, head across to the chair-lift at Längfluh.

The 1800m/5,900ft vertical descents from the top to the village are great tests of stamina – or, if you choose, an enjoyable long cruise with plenty of view stops. The lower runs have steepish, tricky sections and can have poor snow, especially if it isn't cold enough to make snow – timid intermediates might prefer to take a lift down from mid-mountain.

Plattjen has a variety of runs, all of them fine for ambitious intermediates and often underused.

Saas-Fee

461

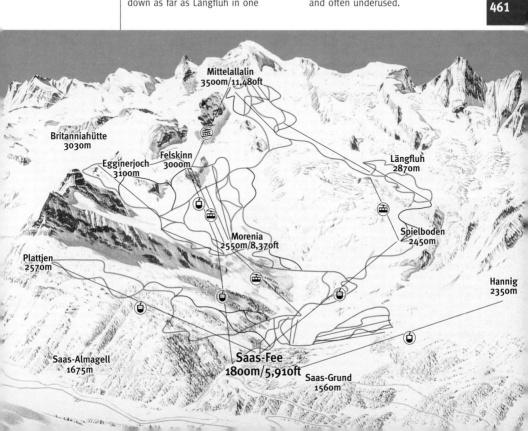

Mittelallalin
3500m/11,480ft

Britanniahütte
3030m

Felskinn
3000m

Egginerjoch
3100m

Längfluh
2870m

Spielboden
2450m

Morenia
2550m/8,370ft

Plattjen
2570m

Hannig
2350m

Saas-Almagell
1675m

Saas-Fee
1800m/5,910ft

Saas-Grund
1560m

FOR BEGINNERS
Usually a nice place to start

There's a good, large, out-of-the-way nursery area at the edge of the village, as snow-sure as any you will find. Those ready to progress can head for the gentle blues on Felskinn just above Morenia – it's best to return by the Alpin Express. There are also gentle blues at the top of the mountain, from where you can head down to Längfluh. Again, use the lifts to return to base.

A useful beginners' pass covers all the short lifts at the village edge, for those not ready to go higher.

FOR CROSS-COUNTRY
Good local trail and lots nearby

There is one short (8km/5 mile) pleasant trail at the edge of the village. It snakes up through the woods, providing about 150m/490ft of climb and nice views. There are more options in the Saas valley.

QUEUES
Only problems at peak times

Lift improvements seem to have done their job and queues are now rare except at peak times. There are few reports of problems except at the 10am morning peak when ski school starts. But things can be different at busy times of the year. One Easter visitor this year found 'a 30-minute wait for the Alpin Express gondola from 9.30 on'. Last year another found 'it could take 75 minutes to reach the upper slopes and then queues for all the drag-lifts were very long'.

MOUNTAIN RESTAURANTS
Fair choice, but it's no Zermatt

The restaurants at the main lift stations are functional; at least Mittelallalin revolves – see separate box. The best places are slightly off the beaten track: the Berghaus Plattjen (just down from Plattjen) and the cosy Gletschergrotte, halfway down from Spielboden (watch for the arrow from the piste). Both have good food in old huts. If you're up for a trek – about 15 minutes each way – the Britanniahütte is special: a real climbing refuge, with atmosphere and views. The restaurant at the top of Plattjen has 'friendly service and the best rösti in the resort'. At Spielboden there's 'good food', a terrace and views of tricky slopes. At Längfluh the large terrace has spectacular views of huge crevasses, and Popcorn Plaza nearby is popular. At mid-mountain the Morenia has 'cheap and very good' pizza. There are also sunny terraces facing the slopes back in the village.

SCHOOLS AND GUIDES
No choice

For skiing, it's the Swiss school or nothing. Last year we had a report of an instructor who was 'very critical and gave little constructive advice'. And a beginner was 'not at all impressed; the instructor left weaker members of the group in a restaurant to make their own way down by lift while he skied down to the village with the bolder members of the group'. On the other hand, we heard from another beginner who had 'excellent tuition'.

FACILITIES FOR CHILDREN
Good reports

The school takes children from four years old, and most of the reports we have had have been positive – 'most classes quite small and English spoken', 'their instructor was strict but they had a fabulous time'. But classes of as many as 15 were spotted. One solution for younger ones is to stay at a hotel with an in-house kindergarten.

GETTING THERE

Air Sion 70km/43 miles (1hr); Geneva 234km/145 miles (3½hr); Zürich 246km/153 miles (4hr); Milan 250km/155 miles (3hr).

Rail Brig (38km/24 miles); regular buses from station.

ACTIVITIES

Indoor Bielen leisure centre (swimming, hot-tub, steam bath, whirlpool, solarium, sauna, massage, tennis, gym), cinema, museum, concerts, badminton

Outdoor 30km/19 miles of cleared paths, natural skating rink (skating, curling, ice hockey), toboggan run, paragliding, dog sledding

Phone numbers
From elsewhere in Switzerland add the prefix 027.
From abroad use the prefix +41 27.

TOURIST OFFICE

t 958 1858
to@saas-fee.ch
www.saas-fee.ch

STAYING THERE

HOW TO GO
Check the location

Quite a few UK tour operators sell holidays to Saas-Fee. But there are surprisingly few chalet holidays.

Hotels There are over 50.

(((((5) **Fletschhorn** (957 2131) Elegant chalet in woods, with original art and individual rooms, a trek from the village and lifts, but fabulous food.

((((4) **Walliserhof** (958 1900) Excellent central 4-star. Friendly welcome and superb service, delicious dinners, champagne breakfast. Wonderful spa.

((((4) **Schweizerhof** (957 5159) Stylish, in quiet position above the centre. 'Fantastic food, friendly staff, excellent kindergarten, wonderful service.' Pool.

(((3) **Beau-Site** (958 1560) 'First-rate' but quiet 4-star in central, but not convenient, position. Good food. Pool.

(((3) **Alphubel** (957 1112) At the wrong end of town, praised by reporters for its own 'brilliant nursery'.

(((3) **Waldesruh** (957 2232) Strongly recommended by a reporter: 'Best situation for the Alpin Express.'

(((3) **Hohnegg** (957 2268) Small rustic alternative to the Fletschhorn, in a similarly remote spot.

((2) **Belmont** (958 1640) The most appealing of the hotels looking directly on to the nursery slopes.

Self-catering Most apartments featured by UK operators are at the north end of the village, but they are generally spacious and well equipped.

EATING OUT
Good variety – but book a table

Gastronomes will want to head for the highly acclaimed Fletschhorn – expensive but excellent. Our favourite is the less formal Bodmen along a path into the woods. It has great food (from rösti to fillet steak) and rustic ambience. We had a delicious Thai meal in one of the Walliserhof's several restaurants. Boccalino is cheap and does pizzas – book or get there early. Alp-Hitta specialises in rustic food and surroundings. The hotel Dom's restaurant specialises in endless varieties of rösti. Arvu-Stuba, Zur Mühle, Gorge, Feeloch, Skihütte and Ferme have all been recommended. Booking is generally necessary.

APRES-SKI
Excellent and varied

Late afternoon, Nesti's Ski-Bar, Zur Mühle and the little snow-bars near the lifts are all pretty lively, especially if the sun's shining. Later on, Nesti's and the Alpenpub keep going till 1am. Popcorn is packed and praised for 'lively atmosphere, brilliant music and catering for all ages'. The Art Club is smarter and more sophisticated, with live music. The Metro Bar is like being in a 19th-century mine shaft; Why-Not the pub is popular; The Metropol has the Crazy Night disco and a couple of other bars.

OFF THE SLOPES
A mountain for pedestrians

The whole of the Hannig mountain is dedicated to walking, tobogganing and paragliding. In the village, the splendid Bielen leisure centre boasts a 25m/80ft pool, indoor tennis courts and a lounging area with sunlamps. There's also the interesting Saas museum and the Bakery Museum, where children can make bread. Don't miss the largest ice pavilion in the world, carved out of the glacier at Mittelallalin.

SNOWPIX.COM / CHRIS GILL

Felskinn, at 3000m/9,840ft, is in the middle of the main area of slopes; for snow reliability, Saas-Fee is difficult to beat →

St Moritz

Luxury living – on and off the flatteringly easy slopes

COSTS

① ② ③ ④ ⑤ ⑥

RATINGS

The slopes

Snow	****
Extent	*****
Expert	****
Intermediate	****
Beginner	**
Convenience	**
Queues	**
Mountain restaurants	****

The rest

Scenery	****
Resort charm	*
Off-slope	*****

NEWS

The 2003 Alpine World Ski Championships were held in St Moritz and the event prompted improvements to road access, lift updating, more snowmaking and refurbishment of all the 5-star hotels.

A new, faster 100-person cable-car from Corviglia to Piz Nair replaced the old queue-prone 40-person one for 2002/03. And a high-speed six-pack replaced the FIS and Pitschen T-bars on Corviglia.

New snowmaking on the Muntanella run beside the Corviglia cable-car and at Furtschellas and Sils Maria was also installed.

- ➕ Beautiful panoramic scenery
- ➕ Off-slope activities second to none
- ➕ Extensive, mainly intermediate slopes
- ➕ Fairly snow-sure
- ➕ Good après-ski, for all tastes
- ➕ Good mountain restaurants, some with magnificent views
- ➕ Painless rail access via Zürich

- ➖ Some hideous block buildings
- ➖ A sizeable town, with little traditional Alpine character
- ➖ Several unlinked mountains, with a bus, train or car needed to most
- ➖ Runs on two main mountains all fairly easy and much the same
- ➖ Expensive

St Moritz is Switzerland's most famous 'exclusive' winter resort: glitzy, expensive, fashionable and, above all, the place to be seen – it's the place for an all-round winter holiday, with an unrivalled array of wacky diversions such as polo, golf and cricket on snow, and gourmet and music festivals. It has long been popular with upper-crust Brits, who stay in the top hotels. The slopes on the two main mountains are almost uniformly easy intermediate – experts must venture off-piste for their fun. But for cross-country, it is superb.

The town of St Moritz doesn't have the chocolate-box image of a Swiss mountain resort, all wooden huts and cows with bells round their necks. Many buildings resemble council flats (extremely neat and clean ones – it is Switzerland, after all).

But you may find, as some readers have, that St Moritz's spectacular setting blinds you to the town's aesthetic faults. This is one of those areas where our progress on the mountain is regularly interrupted by the need to stand and gaze. And the cross-country skiing, walking and other activities on the frozen lake give it a real 'winter wonderland' feel.

THE RESORT

St Moritz has two distinct parts. Dorf is the fashionable main part, on a steep hillside above the lake. It has two main streets lined with boutiques selling Rolex watches, Cartier jewellery and Hermes scarves, a few side lanes and a small main square. A funicular takes you from Dorf to the main slopes of Corviglia, also reached by gondola from down the road at Celerina, and by cable-car from Dorf's other half, the spa resort of St Moritz Bad, spread around one end of the lake.

Everything in Bad is less prestigious. Many of the modern buildings are uncompromisingly rectangular and spoil otherwise superb views. In winter the lake is used for eccentric activities including horse and greyhound racing, show jumping, polo, 'ice golf' and even cricket. It also makes a superb setting for walking and cross-country skiing.

Other downhill slopes, at Corvatsch, are reached via lifts at Surlej and Sils

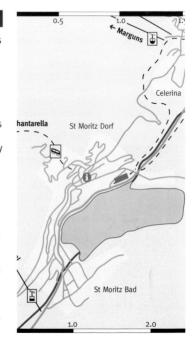

KEY FACTS

Resort	1770m
	5,810ft
Slopes	1730-3305m
	5,680-10,840ft
Lifts	56
Pistes	350km
	217 miles
Blue	16%
Red	71%
Black	13%
Snowmaking	70km
	43 miles

For Corviglia only	
Slopes	1730-3055m
	5,680-10,020ft
Lifts	23
Pistes	61km
	38 miles

Maria. Cross-country skiing is the main activity around the outlying villages of Samedan and Pontresina.

The town's clientele is typified by the results of a Cresta Run race we saw on one of our visits. In the top 29 were three Lords, one Count, one Archduke and a Baronet. But the race was won by a local Swiss guy.

For high society and a better choice of bars and restaurants, stay in Dorf. Bad has the advantage that you can get back to it from Corvatsch and Corviglia. Celerina is another option.

THE MOUNTAINS

Like the resort, most of the slopes are made for posing. There are lots of long, wide, well-groomed runs, with varied terrain. There's an occasional black run, but few are seriously steep. But there is tough off-piste, and it doesn't get tracked out as it does in more macho resorts. Beginners' slopes are few and far between. The piste map is poor, with 'several pistes not even marked' according to one reporter. Trips to other resorts such as Klosters and Davos (around 90 minutes by train or car) and Livigno (around an hour by car) are possible.

THE SLOPES
Big but broken up

The several distinct areas add up to a substantial 350km/217 miles of pistes. The main slopes, shown on our maps, are nearby Corviglia-Marguns and Corvatsch-Furtschellas, a bus-ride away (you can get back to Bad on snow). But some of the more distant slopes are well worth an outing. It helps to have a car, although the free bus service is reported to be fairly efficient.

From St Moritz Dorf a two-stage railway goes up to **Corviglia**, a fair-sized area with slopes facing east and south. The peak of Piz Nair, reached from here by a cable-car, splits the area – sunny runs towards the main valley, and less sunny ones to the north. From Corviglia you can head down (snow permitting) to Dorf and Bad, and via the lower lift junction of Marguns to Celerina.

From Surlej, a few miles from St Moritz, a two-stage cable-car takes you to the north-facing slopes of **Corvatsch**. From the mid-station at Murtèl you have a choice of reds to Margun-Vegl and Alp Margun. From the latter you can work your way to **Furtschellas**, also reached by cable-car from Sils Maria.

Diavolezza (2980m/9,780ft) and Lagalb (2960m/9,710ft), the main additional areas, are on opposite sides of the road to the Bernina pass to Italy, less than half an hour away by bus. **Diavolezza** has excellent north-facing pistes of 900m/2,950ft vertical, down under its big 125-person cable-car, and a very popular and spectacular off-piste route off the back, across a glacier and down a valley beneath Piz Bernina to Morteratsch. **Lagalb** is a smaller area with quite challenging slopes, and an 80-person cable-car serving the west-facing front slope of 850m/2,790ft vertical.

TERRAIN-PARKS
Promises not fulfilled

On Corviglia there is a half-pipe above the Signal area and there are two terrain-parks in the Corvatsch/Furtschellas area (though a reporter last year 'thought the pipe poor and didn't see any prepared terrain-park on Corvatsch'). The piste map also marks, not at all clearly, 'natural freestyle' and 'secret spots' on some mountains.

St Moritz

465

LIFT PASSES

Upper Engadine
Covers all lifts in Corviglia (St Moritz, Celerina, Samedan), Corvatsch (Silvaplana, Sils, Surlej), Diavolezza-Lagalb (Pontresina), and Zuoz, and the swimming pools in St Moritz and Pontresina.

Main pass
1-day pass SF66
6-day pass SF314

Children
Under 21: 6-day pass SF283
Under 16: 6-day pass SF157
Under 6: free pass

Alternative passes
Half-day and day passes available for individual areas within Upper Engadine.

SCHOOLS

St Moritz
t 830 0101
info@skischool.ch

Suvretta
t 836 3600
info@sssc.ch

Classes
(St Moritz prices)
6 4hr days SF250

Private lessons
SF180 for half-day

SNOW RELIABILITY
Improved by good snowmaking
This corner of the Alps has a rather dry climate, but the altitude means that any precipitation is likely to be snowy. There is snowmaking in every sector and piste grooming is excellent.

FOR EXPERTS
Dispersed challenges
If you're looking for challenges, you're liable to find St Moritz disappointing on-piste. Red runs (many of which should really be classified blue) far outnumber black, and mogul fields are scarce. The few serious black runs are scattered about in different sectors and those at Lagalb and Diavolezza are the most challenging. The Minor run down the Lagalb cable-car has 850m/2,800ft vertical of non-stop moguls.

There are plenty of opportunities to venture a little way off-piste in search of challenges – there is an excellent north-facing slope immediately above Marguns, for example. Experts often head for the tough off-piste runs on Piz Nair or the Corvatsch summit. More serious expeditions can be undertaken – such as down the Roseg valley from Corvatsch. To get the most out of the area, you will need to hire a guide.

FOR INTERMEDIATES
Good but flattering
St Moritz is great for intermediates. Most pistes on Corviglia and Corvatsch are very well-groomed, easyish reds that could well have been classified blue. Ideal cruising terrain. As one reporter said: 'as ideal as can be imagined for intermediates'. Another reporter this year enthused, 'has to be one of the best areas in the world'.

One of the finest runs for adventurous intermediates is Hahnensee, from the northern limit of the Corvatsch lift system at Giand'Alva down to St Moritz Bad – a black-classified run that is of red difficulty for most of its 6km/4 mile length and 900m/2,950ft vertical drop. It's a five-minute walk from the end of the run to the cable-car up to Corviglia. (But note

that a reporter found this run 'closed on each of our last three visits'.)

Diavolezza is mostly intermediate. There is an easy open slope at the top, served by a fast quad, and a splendid long intermediate run back down under the lift. The popular off-piste run to Morteratsch requires a bit of energy and nerve. After a gentle climb, you cross the glacier on a narrow ledge, with crevasses waiting to gobble you up on the right. When we last did it, there were ice-picks and shovels at intervals along the path, put there by the enterprising proprietors of the beautifully laid out, welcoming ice bar which greets you at the end of the 30-minute slog. After that, it's downhill through the glacier, with splendid views. Lagalb has more challenging pistes.

FOR BEGINNERS
Not much to offer
St Moritz is not ideal for beginners. It sits in a deep, steep-sided valley, with very little space for nursery slopes at the lower levels. Beginners start up at Salastrains or Corviglia, or slightly out of town, at Suvretta. Celerina has good, broad nursery slopes at village level. Progression from the nursery slopes to intermediate runs is rather awkward – these always include a difficult section.

FOR CROSS-COUNTRY
Excellent
The Engadine is one of the premier regions in the Alps for cross-country, with 150km/90 miles of trails, including floodlit loops, amid splendid scenery and with fairly reliable snow. A 2003 reporter recommends the lessons at the Langlauf Centre near the Hotel Kempinski. The Engadine Ski Marathon is held here every March – over 12,000 racers take part. Pontresina makes a great base for cross-country.

QUEUES
Not much of a problem
St Moritz has invested heavily in new lifts in recent years. Once you get up the mountain, Corviglia has high-speed chairs everywhere. But the area as a

boarding

Despite the high prices and its glitzy image, the terrain in St Moritz is boarder-friendly and there's a special boarders' booklet with lots of good information and profiles of local riders. The Corvatsch area has links that rely on drags – otherwise, most lifts are chairs, gondolas, cable-cars and trains. There are several specialist snowboard shops, including Playground in Paradise.

MOUNTAIN RESTAURANTS
Some special places

Mountain restaurants are plentiful, and include some of the most glamourous in Europe. Prices can be high, and reservations are advisable. But there are plenty of cheaper places too.

On Corviglia, the gourmet highlight is the Marmite; but it is outrageously expensive. And it is housed in the Corviglia lift station, known locally as the highest post office in Switzerland because of its bright yellow paint. Much better for charm is the Paradiso, with glorious panoramic views from the terrace, the inviting terrace of the Chamanna and the Lej de la Pêsch behind Piz Nair. A reader recommends Mathis for 'first-class food and wine'.

On the Corvatsch side, we've heard good reports about the self-service place at the top and the sunny Sternbar, with live music, at the bottom of Rabguisa. Fuorcla Surlej is delightfully secluded, as is Hahnensee, on the lift-free run of the same name down to Bad – a splendid place to pause in the sun on the way home. On stormy days, most captivating is the rustic Alpetta, near Alp Margun (table-service inside).

The hotel-restaurant up at Muottas Muragl, between Celerina and Pontresina, is well worth a visit. It has truly spectacular views overlooking the valley, as well as good food.

Morteratsch restaurant (at the end of the off-piste run from Diavolezza) is splendid – sunny, by the cross-country area and tiny railway station, and with excellent, good-value food.

St Moritz

467

whole has a lot of cable-cars – both for getting up the mountain from the resort and for access to peaks from mid-mountain. Queues can result, though reporters have had good experiences lately – the enlarged cable-car from Surlej to Murtèl is a big improvement, although a 2003 reporter recommends avoiding Surlej and going to Sils Maria instead. The new cable-car to Piz Nair seems to have cut the queues there. The top Corvatsch cable-car can generate queues. Happy reporters comment that many St Moritz visitors are late risers and don't ski after lunch, leaving the slopes quiet at the start and end of the day. 'Peak period is 11 to 12.30, when congestion can be a problem above Marguns on Corviglia and on the run down from Murtèl on Corvatsch,' says a reporter.

CHILDREN

The St Moritz ski school operates a pick-up service for children (ages from 4, 6 full days SF250)

St Moritz and Suvretta schools provide all-day care.

Children aged 3 or more can be looked after in the Schweizerhof hotel nursery, open from 9am to 5.30.

GETTING THERE

Air Zürich 200km/124 miles (3hr); Upper Engadine airport 5km/3 miles.

Rail Mainline station in resort.

Phone numbers
From elsewhere in Switzerland add the prefix 081.
From abroad use the prefix +41 81.

SCHOOLS AND GUIDES
Internal competition

As well as the St Moritz and Suvretta schools, there is The Wave snowboarding school and The St Moritz Experience, for heli-trips. Some hotels have their own instructors for private lessons.

FACILITIES FOR CHILDREN
Choose a hotel with a nursery

Children wanting lessons have a choice of schools, but others must be deposited at a hotel nursery. Club Med has its usual good facilities.

STAYING THERE

HOW TO GO
Several packaged options

Packages are available, but many people make their own arrangements. There is a Club Med – its all-inclusive deal cuts the impact of high prices. The tourist office can provide a list of apartments.

Hotels Over half the hotels are 4-stars and 5-stars – the highest concentration of high-quality hotels in Switzerland. We don't like any of the famous 5-stars or their jacket-and-tie policies. If made to choose we'd prefer the

glossy, secluded Carlton or even more secluded Suvretta House to the staid Kulm or Gothic Badrutt's Palace.

((((**Crystal** (836 2626) Big 4-star in Dorf, as close to the Corviglia lift as any. Recently renovated and now part of the 'Small Luxury Hotels' group.

((((**Schweizerhof** (837 0707) 'Relaxed' 4-star in central Dorf, five minutes from the Corviglia lift, with 'excellent food and very helpful staff'.

((((**Albana** (836 6161) 4-star in Dorf, with walls adorned with big game trophies bagged by proprietor's family.

(((**Monopol** (837 0404) Good value (for St Moritz) 4-star in centre of Dorf. Excellent breakfasts. Jacuzzi, sauna.

(((**Steinbock** (833 6035) 'Friendly, understated, comfortable,' says a 2003 reporter. In Dorf.

(((**Nolda** (833 0575) One of the few chalet-style buildings, close to the cable-car in St Moritz Bad.

((**Bellaval** (833 3245) A two-star between the station and the lake.

EATING OUT
Mostly chic and expensive

It's easy to spend £50 a head eating out in St Moritz – without wine – but you can eat more cheaply. We liked the excellent Italian food at the down-to-earth Cascade in Dorf and the, pricier, three restaurants in the Chesa Veglia (though a 2003 reporter tells of it being 'a rip-off, and the staff were disinterested when we only ordered two pizzas and turned down the wine which started at £35 a bottle'). A reporter last year had a 'week of gourmet eating. The two top restaurants, Jöhri's Talvo at Champfèr and Bumann's Chesa Pirani in La Punt both approach the top restaurants in London or Paris for quality and price – we spent SF200 a head in each. We also liked the rustic Landhotel Meierei, in a bay of the lake opposite Bad.' If you want something less pricey and like fondue, one reporter recommends the new restaurant in the Hotel Schweizerhof.

Try an evening up at Muottas Muragl for the spectacular views, splendid sunset and unpretentious dinner.

APRES-SKI
Caters for all ages

There's a big variety of après-skiing age groups here. The fur coat count is high – people come to St Moritz to be seen.

At tea time, head for Hanselmann's 'fabulous tea and strudels' but 'the place is a bit dull'. Or try Café Hauser.

ACTIVITIES

Indoor Curling, swimming, sauna, solarium, golf driving range, tennis, squash, museum, health spa, cinema (with English films), aerobics, beauty farm, health centre, casino, Rotary International club

Outdoor Ice skating, sleigh rides, ski jumping, toboggan run, snow tubing, hang-gliding, golf on frozen lake, Cresta run, 180km/112 miles cleared paths, greyhound racing, horse-riding and racing, polo tournaments, cricket tournaments, ski-bob run, paragliding, skydiving, kite-sailing on frozen lake, ice-skating, curling

TOURIST OFFICES

St Moritz
t 837 3333
information@stmoritz.ch
www.stmoritz.ch

Celerina
t 830 0011
info@celerina.ch
www.celerina.ch

Pontresina
t 838 8300
info@pontresina.com
www.pontresina.com

The pub-style Bobby's Bar (with Internet access), and the Prince (with a 'disco/lounge') attract a young crowd, as does the loud music of the Stübli, one of three bars in the Schweizerhof: the others are the Muli, with a country and western theme and live music, and the chic Piano Bar. The Cresta, at the Steffani, is popular with the British, while the Cava below it is louder, livelier and younger. The piano bar at the Albana Hotel scored a hit with our readers this year, who found it 'cosy and welcoming'. It is also amusing to put on a jacket and tie and explore bars in Badrutt's Palace and the Kulm.

The two most popular discos are Vivai (expensive) at the Steffani, and King's at Badrutt's Palace (even more expensive; jackets and ties required). And if they don't part you with enough of your cash, try the Casino.

OFF THE SLOPES
Excellent variety of pastimes

Even if you lack the bravado for the Cresta Run, there is lots to do. In midwinter the snow-covered lake provides a playground for bizarre events (see earlier in chapter) but in March the lake starts to thaw. There's an annual 'gourmet festival', with chefs from all over the world.

Some hotels run special activities, such as a curling week. Other options are hang-gliding, indoor tennis and

trips to Italy (Milan is four hours by car). There's a public pool in Bad.

St Moritz gets a lot of sun – 322 sunny days a year, they claim – so lounging on sunny terraces is popular. A reporter this year was bowled over by a train trip on the Bernina Express, with 'amazing bends, gradients and scenery. The high spot of our visit.'

STAYING UP THE MOUNTAIN
Excellent possibilities

Next door to each other at Salastrains are two chalet-style hotels, the 3-star Salastrains (833 3867), with 60 comfy beds, and the slightly simpler and much smaller Chesa Chantarella (833 3355). Great views, and no queues.

Celerina 1730m/5,680ft

At the bottom end of the Cresta Run, Celerina is unpretentious and villagey, if quiet, with good access to Corviglia. It is sizeable, with a lot of second homes, many owned by Italians (the upper part is known as Piccolo Milano). There are some appealing small hotels (reporters suggest Chesa Rosatsch 837 0101) and a couple of bigger 4-stars.

Pontresina 1805m/5,920ft

Pontresina is small and sedate and an excellent base for the extensive cross-country skiing on its doorstep. It's a sheltered, sunny village with one main street, spoiled by the sanatorium-style architecture. Pontresina's own hill, Languard, has a single long piste.

It can be somewhat cheaper to stay here than St Moritz and there is a Club Med (offering its usual all-inclusive deal). Dining is mostly hotel-based and nightlife is quiet. A 2003 reporter found medium-priced eating out here compared favourably with back home and recommends the Kordchendörger, the Locanda at the Bernina Hotel and the Thai restaurant at the Collina Hotel.

St Moritz

469

THE CRESTA RUN

No trip to St Moritz is really complete without a visit to the Cresta Run. It's the last bastion of Britishness (until recently, payment had to be made in sterling) and male chauvinism (women have been banned since 1929 – unless you can secure an invitation from a club member for the last day of their season).

Any adult male can pay around £200 for five rides on the famous run (helmet and lunch at the Kulm hotel included). Watch out for Shuttlecock corner – that's where most people come off and the ambulances ply for trade. You lie on a toboggan (aptly called a 'skeleton') and hurtle head-first down a sheet ice gully from St Moritz to Celerina. David Gower, Sandy Gall are among the many addicts.

Verbier

Paradise for nightlife-loving powder hounds with cash

COSTS

① ② ③ ④ ⑤ ⑥

RATINGS

The slopes

Snow	★★★
Extent	★★★★★
Expert	★★★★★
Intermediate	★★★
Beginner	★★
Convenience	★★
Queues	★★★
Mountain restaurants	★★★

The rest

Scenery	★★★★
Resort charm	★★★
Off-slope	★★★

NEWS

For 2002/03 extra cabins were added to the jumbo Funitel gondola from Les Ruinettes to Les Attelas, increasing capacity by 25%.

Verbier's first six-pack replaced the Saxon chair and Nord drag on the back of the Savoleyres ridge.

➕ Extensive, challenging slopes with a lot of off-piste potential and some good bump runs

➕ Upper slopes offer a real high-mountain feel plus great views

➕ Pleasant, animated village in a sunny, panoramic setting

➕ Lively, varied nightlife

➕ Wide range of chalet holidays

➕ Good advanced-level lessons

➕ Much improved lift system

➕ Much improved piste grooming

➕ Hardly any drag-lifts in the Verbier sector but ...

➖ Still many slow chair-lifts, and drag-lifts in linked resorts

➖ Still some serious queues, particularly on 4 Valleys links

➖ Overcrowded pistes in certain areas

➖ The 4 Valleys network is much less wonderful than it looks on paper

➖ Sunny lower slopes will always be a problem, even with snowmaking

➖ Direction signposting still hopelessly inadequate – and piste map has basic flaws, despite improvements

➖ Busy traffic (and fumes) in centre

➖ Some long walks/rides to lifts

➖ Easily accessed off-piste slopes get tracked out very quickly

➖ Pretty expensive

There is no doubt that Verbier is trying hard to retain its international visitors, improving over the last few years its grooming, snowmaking, ski school and lifts – most notably with the overdue replacement of the Tortin gondola and most recently with more capacity on the central Funitel gondola. But major grouses remain. Some are down to the organisation of the resort: the kind of piste signing shown later in the chapter would be comical if it were not infuriating, and the new clearer piste map introduced last year still fails to identify pistes by name or number. But other problems are down to the lie of the land.

For experts prepared to hire a guide to explore off-piste, Verbier is one of the big names. With its claimed 410km/255 miles of pistes, Verbier also seems at first sight to rank alongside the French mega-resorts that draw keen piste skiers, such as Courchevel and La Plagne. But it doesn't; the 4 Valleys network is an inconveniently sprawling affair, while Verbier's local pistes are surprisingly confined and crowded. Of course, piste skiers who have not been spoilt by the mega-resorts can have a satisfying holiday here – but you can do that in scores of minor resorts from Alpbach to Zell am See. Whether they can match Verbier's sheer style and famously vibrant nightlife is another question.

THE RESORT

Verbier is an amorphous sprawl of chalet-style buildings, without too much concrete in evidence, in an impressive setting on a wide, sunny balcony facing spectacular peaks. It's a fashionable, informal, very lively place that teems with cosmopolitan visitors – a wide range of Scandinavians and Brits among them. Most are younger than visitors to other big Swiss resorts.

Most of the smart shops and hotels (but not chalets) are set around the

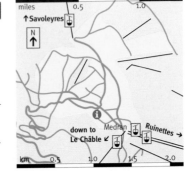

↑ The tiny cable-car to Mont Gelé – seen here from the start of an off-piste route above Lac des Vaux – accesses only off-piste runs, including two itinerary routes

SNOWPIX.COM / CHRIS GILL

KEY FACTS

Resort	1500m
	4,920ft

For 4 Valleys area	
Slopes	1500-3330m
	4,920-10,930ft
Lifts	95
Pistes	410km
	255 miles
Blue	32%
Red	42%
Black	26%
Snowmaking	50km
	31 miles

For Verbier, Bruson and Tzoumas/ Savoleyres sectors only (covered by Verbier pass)

Slopes	1500-3025m
	4,920-9,920ft
Lifts	38
Pistes	150km
	93 miles
Snowmaking	20km
	12 miles

Place Centrale and along the sloping streets stretching down the hill in one direction and up it in the other to the main lift station at Medran 500m/ 1,640ft away. Much of the nightlife is here, too, though bars are rather scattered. These central areas get unpleasantly packed with cars at busy times, especially weekends.

More chalets and apartments are built each year – which means building sites spoil the views in places – with newer properties inconveniently situated along the road to the lift base for the secondary Savoleyres area, about 1.5km/1 mile from Medran.

The Medran lift station is a walkable distance from the Place Centrale, so staying there has attractions. There is accommodation close to the Medran lift station, which is sufficiently distant from nightlife to avoid late-night noise. If nightlife is not a priority, staying somewhere near the upper (north-east) fringes of the village may mean that you can almost ski to your door – and there is a piste linking the upper nursery slopes to the one in the middle of the village.

But in practice most people just get used to using the free buses, which run efficiently on several routes until 7pm. Some areas have quite an infrequent service. We are told that from 7pm to 8.30 there is a special taxi service that will drop you at any of the usual bus stops within the resort for five francs per person.

Verbier is at one end of a long, strung-out series of interconnected slopes, optimistically branded the 4

Valleys and linking Verbier to Nendaz, Veysonnaz, Thyon and other resorts.

These other resorts have their own pros and cons. All are appreciably cheaper places to stay than Verbier, and some are more sensible bases for those who plan to stick to pistes rather than venture off-piste – the Veysonnaz-Thyon sector, in particular, is much more intermediate-friendly than Verbier. As bases for exploration of the whole 4 Valleys, only Siviez is much of an advance on Verbier. They are much less lively in the evening.

You can also stay down in the valley village of Le Châble, which has a gondola up to Verbier and on into the slopes. Across the valley, Bruson is more attractive as a place to visit for a day than to stay in.

These alternatives are all described at the end of the chapter.

Chamonix and Champéry (Portes du Soleil) are within reach by car. But a car can be a bit of a nuisance in Verbier itself. Parking is tightly controlled; your chalet or hotel may not have enough space for all guests' cars, which means a hike from the free parking at the sports centre or paying for garage space.

THE MOUNTAINS

Essentially this is high-mountain terrain. There are wooded slopes directly above the village, but the runs here are either bumpy itinéraires or winding paths. There is more sheltered skiing in other sectors – particularly above Veysonnaz.

LIFT PASSES

4 Valleys/Mont-Fort
Covers all lifts and ski-buses in Verbier, Mont-Fort, Bruson, La Tzoumaz, Nendaz, Veysonnaz and Thyon.

Main pass
1-day pass SF59
6-day pass SF306

Senior citizens
Over 65: 6-day pass SF214

Children
Under 20: 6-day pass SF260
Under 16: 6-day pass SF214
Under 6: free pass

Notes
Afternoon pass available. Reductions for families.

Alternative passes
Verbier pass (covers Verbier, Savoleyres and Bruson sectors); La Tzoumaz/Savoleyres pass (covers Savoleyres and Bruson); and Bruson only pass.

THE SLOPES
Very spread out

Savoleyres is the smaller area, reached by a gondola from the north-west end of the village. This area is underrated and generally underused. It has open, sunny slopes on the front side, and long, pleasantly wooded, shadier runs on the back. When conditions are good runs descend to Verbier, but in sunny weather snow can disappear quickly.

You can take a catwalk across from Savoleyres to the foot of Verbier's main slopes. These are served by lifts from Medran, at the opposite end of the village. Two gondolas rise to **Les Ruinettes** and then on to **Les Attelas**. From Les Attelas a small cable-car goes up to Mont Gelé, for steep off-piste runs only. Heading down instead, you can go back westwards to Les Ruinettes, south to La Chaux or north to Lac des Vaux. From here chairs go back to Les Attelas and on to Chassoure, the top of a wide, steep and shady off-piste mogul field leading down to **Tortin**, with a gondola back.

La Chaux is served by two slow chair-lifts and is the departure point of a jumbo cable-car up to Col des Gentianes and the glacier area. A second, much smaller cable-car then goes up to **Mont-Fort,** the high point of the 4 Valleys. From the glacier is another off-piste route down to Tortin, a north-facing run of almost 1300m/4,270ft vertical. A cable-car returns to

Col des Gentianes.

Below Tortin is the gateway to the rest of the 4 Valleys, **Siviez**, where one chair goes off into the long, thin **Nendaz** sector and another heads for the **Thyon-Veysonnaz** sector, via a couple of lifts and a lot of catwalks.

Allow plenty of time to get to and from these remote corners – the taxi-rides home are expensive.

The slopes of **Bruson** are described briefly at the end of this chapter.

TERRAIN-PARKS
A couple of options

There are two terrain-parks – the Swatch-sponsored boarder-cross course at La Chaux and another one at La Tournelle.

SNOW RELIABILITY
Improved snowmaking

The slopes of the Mont-Fort glacier always have good snow. The runs to Tortin are normally snow-sure too. But nearly all of this is steep, and much of it is formally off-piste. Most of Verbier's main local slopes face south or west and are below 2500m/8,200ft – so they can be in poor condition at times. Snowmaking on the lower slopes has improved a lot in recent years and there are further additions this season. The north-facing slopes of Savoleyres and Lac des Vaux are normally much better.

FOR EXPERTS
The main attraction

Verbier has some superb tough slopes, many of them off-piste and needing a guide. There are few conventional black pistes; most of the runs that might have this designation are now defined as itinéraires – see our special box on finding your way around. The blacks that do exist are mostly indistinguishable from nearby reds.

The very extreme couloirs between Mont Gelé and Les Attelas and below the Attelas gondola are some of the toughest runs. There are safer, less scary off-piste routes from Mont Gelé to Tortin and La Chaux, including two itinéraires. The start of these routes can be very tricky – get local information before committing.

The front face of Mont-Fort is about the only seriously steep piste: a wonderful tough mogul field, all of black steepness (and these days all classified black) but with a choice of gradient from seriously steep to intimidatingly steep. Occasionally you can get from Mont-Fort all the way to Le Châble off-piste. You can also head off-piste down to Siviez via one of two spectacular couloirs off the back of Mont-Fort. The North Face of Mont-Fort is one of the hottest of expert runs.

The two itinéraires to Tortin are both excellent in their different ways. The one from Chassoure is just one wide, steep slope, normally a huge mogul field. The north-facing itinéraire from Gentianes is longer, less steep, but feels much more of an adventure. Those willing to walk up a steep slope near the start (known as the Highway to Heaven) are rewarded by usually good powder in a quiet valley parallel to the main run. Les Attelas is the start of shorter runs towards the village.

A couple of long, but easy, off-piste routes go from Lac des Vaux via Col des Mines. One is a popular route back to Verbier, down a long open slope to Carrefour at the top of the village, the other a very beautiful run through Vallon d'Arbi to La Tzoumaz. They are not opened until a piste-basher has formed a ledge across a steep slope to the Col – without it, the traverse is scary. There is an entertaining itinéraire from Greppon Blanc, at the top of the Veysonnaz-Thyon sector, into the next valley. There are five buses a day from the end of the run to the lifts of Les Collons, below Thyon.

The World Cup run at Veysonnaz is a steepish, often icy, red, ideal for really speeding down.

Helicopters are available; Verbier Lodge offers heli-skiing packages.

FOR INTERMEDIATES
Hit Savoleyres – or Veysonnaz

Many mileage-hungry intermediates find Verbier disappointing. The intermediate slopes in the main area are concentrated between Les Attelas and the village, above and below Les Ruinettes, plus the little bowl at Lac des Vaux and the sunny slopes served by the chairs at La Chaux. This is all excellent and varied intermediate territory, but there isn't much of it – to put it in perspective, this whole area is no bigger than the slopes of tiny Alpbach – and it is used by the bulk of the visitors staying in one of Switzerland's largest resorts. So it is often very crowded, especially the otherwise wonderful sweeping red from Les Attelas to Les Ruinettes served by the big gondola. Even early intermediates should taste the perfect snow on the glacier. The red run from Col des Gentianes to La Chaux is not too difficult, but its high-mountain feel can be unnerving and it's no disgrace to ride the cable-car down instead.

Intermediates should exploit the under-used Savoleyres area. This has good intermediate pistes, usually better snow and far fewer people (especially on Sundays). It is also a good hill for mixed abilities, with variations of many runs.

Verbier

boarding

As with its skiing, Verbier is one of Europe's best off-piste and extreme boarding resorts for those able and willing to pay for a guide or to join a group. The main area is served by gondolas, cable-cars and chairs, with no drag-lifts at all. Less experienced boarders should try Savoleyres, though there are a few drag-lifts. To see some real experts in action, hang around the resort in late March, when the world's best congregate here for the Red Bull Xtreme contest, on the cliff-like north face of the Bec des Rosses. There is a specialist snowboard school and a couple of specialist snowboard shops.

SCHOOLS

Swiss Ski School
t 775 3363
info@maisondusport.
ch

Fantastique
t 771 4141
lafantastique@verbier.
ch

Adrénaline
t 771 7459
info@adrenaline-
verbier.ch

Altitude
t 7716006
info@altitude-verbier.
com

Classes
(Swiss Ski School
prices)
6 2½hr days SF175

Private lessons
SF140 for 2hr for 1 or
2 people

The Verbier slopes as a whole present some difficulties for early intermediates, as editorial daughter Laura can confirm. There is excellent easy blue-run skiing at La Chaux, but there is no easy way back to Les Ruinettes. From Savoleyres there is an easy way to Medran but there may be no easy way down to that link from the top of Savoleyres. In both cases, we had to take quite challenging red runs. Laura managed, but in a properly run resort the difficulties would have been foreseen and sorted out.

A reporter this year reminds us that we don't spell out clearly enough the attractions of the pistes of the Thyon-Veysonnaz and Nendaz sectors – 'Lots of good, long, well-groomed slopes, some of them steep.' Point taken.

FOR BEGINNERS
Progression is the problem
There are sunny nursery slopes close to the middle of the village and at Les Esserts, at the top of it. These are fine provided they have snow (they have a

lot of snowmaking, which helps). The problem is what you do after the nursery slopes. There are easy blues on the back side of Savoleyres, and at La Chaux, but they are not easy to get back from (see above).

FOR CROSS-COUNTRY
Surprisingly little on offer
Verbier is limited for cross-country. There's a 4km/2.5 mile circuit in Verbier, 4km/2.5 miles at Les Ruinettes-La Chaux and 30km/19 miles down at Le Châble/Val de Bagnes.

QUEUES
Not the problem they were
Verbier's queue problems have been greatly eased by recent investment. The jumbo gondola to Les Attelas – its capacity increased last season – has cut queues at Les Ruinettes, but it has increased the overcrowding on the pistes back down. The mega-queues at Tortin for Chassoure are a thing of the past, thanks to the upgraded gondola. The fast chair at Lac des Vaux has greatly eased the bottleneck there. But the cable-car from Tortin to Col des Gentianes can produce queues, and the Mont-Fort cable-car above it can still generate very long ones.

Some queues at the main village lift station at Medran can arise when Sunday visitors fill one of the gondolas by boarding down in the valley at Le Châble. The recent upgrade of this gondola has helped.

There are continuing reports of queues for outdated double chairs and for inadequate drag-lifts in the outlying

FINDING YOUR WAY AROUND THE SLOPES OF VERBIER

It isn't easy. The main area is complicated, and difficult to represent on a single map. Téléverbier's traditional hopeless map has been replaced by one that makes a better job of showing the mountain; but it still fails to show Savoleyres and La Chaux sensibly, and it still fails to identify the pistes. So although the signs on the mountain religiously use numbers to identify pistes, there is no way to connect the signs to the map – insane. The problem is compounded by a strange faith in the kind of 'motorway' signs shown here. We and most of our readers find these impossible to relate to the real choices of route.

Life is further complicated by confusion over which runs it is prudent to tackle. For years now, runs that once were black pistes have been defined as 'itinéraires à ski' (eg both runs down to Tortin) or 'itinéraires de haute-montagne' (eg the Col des Mines run home from Lac des Vaux). We've long campaigned for these runs – especially the former category – to be restored to piste status; but at least their non-piste status needs to be clear. The old piste map did contain an explanation of sorts; astonishingly, the new one does not.

These failures to understand and meet visitors' needs would be surprising in the most backward part of eastern Europe; here, they are simply disgraceful.

VERBIER TOURIST OFFICE /
FRANCOIS PERRAUDIN

Runs down from Les
Ruinettes end up on
the stepped terrain of
the golf course ↓

4 Valleys resorts – notably the
Greppon Blanc drags on the way to
Veysonnaz – and at La Chaux when
crowds descend from the glacier.
Overall, though, recent reporters find
the lift system much improved.

MOUNTAIN RESTAURANTS
Disappointing in main area
There are not enough huts, which
means queues and overcrowding in
high season. Savoleyres is the best
area. The Poste hotel by the Tzoumaz
chair takes some beating for value and
lack of crowds. Also worth trying are
Chez Simon ('simple and cheap'), Au
Mayen (beneath the Combe 1 chair –
'good service, sunny terrace') and the
rustic Marmotte ('wicked, excellent
rösti'). Le Sonalon, on the fringe of the
village, is 'excellent, with great views',
but reached off-piste.

In the main area, the rustic Chez
Dany at Clambin, on the off-piste run
on the southern fringe of the area, is
about the best, and gets packed –
booking needed. Carrefour, with a
large terrace, is popular and
recommended; it is well situated at the
top of the village, above the golf
course. The restaurants at Les

Ruinettes – table-service upstairs –
have big terraces with splendid views.
The Olympique at Les Attelas is a good
table-service restaurant.

Everyone loves the Cabane Mont
Fort – a proper mountain refuge off the
run to La Chaux from Col des
Gentianes; cosy on a bad day, and
great views on a good one, but very
busy – get there early.

SCHOOLS AND GUIDES
Good reports
Verbier is an excellent place for
advanced skiers, in particular, to get
lessons. Several reporters have been
complimentary about the off-piste
lessons with the Swiss ski school.
More than 20 guides are available for
heli-trips, which include trips to
Zermatt and the Aosta valley. The
Vallée Blanche at Chamonix and a trip
to Zinal are cheaper excursions. Verbier
is also quite big on snowboard and
telemark lessons. The consensus is
that the Swiss school's standards have
improved generally, partly thanks to
the retirement of some old-timers. Of
the others, the Adrénaline international
school gets rave reviews, particularly
for its private lessons.

Verbier

CHILDREN

The ski school's Kids Club kindergarten (775 6333), on the slope at Les Moulins, has its own drag-lift and takes children from aged 3 from 8.30 to 5pm (6 days SF415).

The Schtroumpfs non-ski kindergarten (771 6585), close to the middle of the resort, takes children of any age up to 4 years (older ones by arrangement), from 8.30 to 5.30.

Phone numbers
From elsewhere in Switzerland add the prefix 027.
From abroad use the prefix +41 27.

FACILITIES FOR CHILDREN
Wide range of options

The Swiss school's facilities in the resort are good, and the resort attracts quite a lot of families. The playground up at La Chaux has also received favourable reports. Space on the bus back is limited, and priority is given to school groups. The possibility of leaving very young babies at the Schtroumpfs nursery is valuable. British families can travel with family-oriented chalet operators – Esprit Ski and Mark Warner both have nurseries, and Simply Ski has a nanny service you can arrange in advance.

There are considerable reductions on the lift pass price for families on production of your passports.

STAYING THERE

HOW TO GO
Plenty of options

Given the size of the place there are surprisingly few apartments and pensions available, though those on a budget have inexpensive B&B options in Le Châble. Hotels are expensive in relation to their grading. Given a sleeping bag you can bed down at the sports centre for about £10 a night – and that includes the use of the pool.
Chalets Verbier is the chalet-party capital of the Alps. Companies large and small have properties here, including Verbier specialists such as Ski Verbier and Peak Ski. There are chalets of all kinds; small ones, of the kind that you might take over for a family or small group of friends, are particularly common – Ski Activity has several. There are a few luxury options on the UK package market. Flexiski has one property – the deeply comfortable chalet Bouvreuil. Ski Verbier's 10 properties include some impressively luxurious chalets and apartments. Right at the top of the market, Descent

now has two superb chalets in contrasting locations – Goodwood, only yards from the Place Centrale, in addition to Septièrme Ciel, right at the top of the resort under the Savoleyres gondola.
Hotels There is one 5-star hotel, five 4-star, a dozen 3-star and a handful of simpler places.
(((((5) **Chalet d'Adrien** (771 6300) The new best-in-town: a beautifully furnished low-rise 25-room chalet, with top-notch cooking to match. Right next to the Savoleyres lift.
((((4) **Rosalp** (771 6323) The great attraction is the food in Roland Pierroz's Michelin-starred restaurant, which is as good as you'll find in any Swiss resort. Good position midway between centre and Medran.
((((4) **Montpelier** (771 6131) Very comfortable 4-star, but out of town (a courtesy bus is provided).
((((4) **Vanessa** (775 2800) Central 4-star with spacious apartments as well as rooms; 'Great food,' says a reporter.
(((3) **Rotonde** (771 6525) Much cheaper, well positioned 3-star between centre and Medran; some budget rooms.
(((3) **Verbier Lodge** (771 6666) Novel log-built B&B with stylish modern fittings, offering packages with tuition or heli-skiing. On southern fringe, beyond Medran – reachable on skis.
(((3) **Poste** (771 6681) Well placed 3-star midway between centre and Medran; still the only hotel pool. Some rooms rather small.
(((3) **de Verbier** (771 6688) Central 3-star, popular with tour operators and their clientele; renowned for good food; atmospheric and traditional, with helpful owners and staff.
((2) **Farinet** (771 6626) Central 3-star hotel, now British-owned, with a focal après-ski bar on its elevated terrace.
Self-catering Few UK tour operators offer apartments, but they can be booked locally.

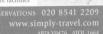

GETTING THERE

Air Geneva 170km/106 miles (2hr).

Rail Le Châble (7km/4 miles); regular buses to resort or gondola.

ACTIVITIES

Indoor Sports centre (swimming, skating, curling, squash, sauna, solarium, steam bath, hot-tub), cinema, ice hockey, indoor golf

Outdoor Ski-bob, 25km/16 miles of cleared walking paths, paragliding, hang-gliding, mountaineering, sledging

EATING OUT
Plenty of choice

There is a very wide range of restaurants; a pocket guide is given away locally which would be much more useful if all its advertisers gave some clues about price.

Hotel Rosalp is clearly the best (and most expensive) in town, and among the best in Switzerland, with an awesome wine cellar to match its excellent Michelin-starred food – splash out on the seven-course Menu Gastronomique if you can afford it. The Pinte bistro in the hotel basement is a less expensive option – worth trying. The 5-star Chale d'Adrien also has two tempting options, with a starred chef at work in the gastronomique Astrance. The Grange is another place serious about its food.

King's is one of our favourites – innovative food in a stylish, clublike setting. We've also had excellent meals in the stylish Millénium, above the Toro Negro steak-house – itself recommended for 'a big spread of good food'.

For Swiss specialities, try the Relais des Neiges, the Robinson, the Caveau ('romantic ambience' says a reporter), Au Vieux-Verbier by the Medran lifts or Esserts by the nursery slopes. The ever-popular Fer à Cheval does reasonably priced pizza and other simple dishes. Arguably the best-value Italian food in town is at Al Capone's out near the Savoleyres gondola. The Hacienda Café is another inexpensive place. Harold's Internet cafe is Verbier's burger joint.

You can be ferried by snowmobile up to Chez Dany or the Marmotte for an evening meal, followed by a torchlit descent.

APRES-SKI
Throbbing but expensive

It starts with a 4pm visit to the Offshore Café at Medran, for people-watching, milk shakes and cakes. The nearby Big Ben pub is 'great and lively on a sunny afternoon'. Au Mignon at the bottom of the golf course has become popular since it was given a large sun deck.

Then if you're young, loud and British it's on to the Pub Mont-Fort – there's a widescreen TV for live sporting events. The Nelson is popular with locals. The Farinet is particularly good in spring, its live band playing to

Verbier

the audience on a huge, sunny terrace – there's now a conservatory-type cover over it when it's cold. Au Fer à Cheval is a fun place full of locals and regular Verbier-ites.

After dinner the Pub Mont-Fort is again popular with Brits and locals alike (the shots bar in the cellar is worth a visit). Crok No Name has good live bands or a DJ and is entertaining for its cosmopolitan crowd. Murphy's Irish bar in the Garbo hotel is popular, with a good resident DJ. The much-loved King's is a quiet candlelit cellar bar with 60s' decor – 'hip crowd, good music'. Bar New Club is a sophisticated piano bar, with comfortable seating and a more discerning clientele. Jacky's is a classy piano bar frequented by big spenders on their way to the seriously expensive Farm Club – on Friday and Saturday packed with rich Swiss paying SF220 for bottles of spirits. You'll find us having a quiet nightcap in the basement Bar'Jo, across the road.

The noisy, glitzy Marshal's Club, in the basement of the Farinet hotel, sometimes has live music. Taratata is a friendly club that seems to be growing in popularity. Scotch is the cheapest disco in town and popular with teenagers and snowboarders. Big Ben is 'lively, crowded and friendly'.

OFF THE SLOPES
No great attraction
Verbier has an excellent sports centre and some nice walks, but otherwise not much to offer if you don't want to hit the slopes. Montreux is an enjoyable train excursion from Le Châble, and Martigny is worth a visit for the Roman remains. Various mountain restaurants are accessible to pedestrians. Both toboggan runs – on the shady side of Savoleyres and from Les Ruinettes – are an impressive 10km/6 miles long. The nursery slope at Les Esserts is floodlit for tubing etc on Saturday and Sunday evenings.

Nendaz 1365m/4,480ft

Nendaz is a big resort with over 17,000 beds, but is little-known in Britain. Although it appears to be centrally set in the 4 Valleys, getting to and from the other sectors – particularly the Verbier slopes – is a slow business unless you drive/take a bus to Siviez. In other respects it has attractions, relatively low prices among them. Airport transfers are quick.

THE RESORT
Nendaz itself is a large place on a shelf above and with great views of the Rhône valley. Most of the resort is modern but built in traditional chalet-style and the original old village of Haute-Nendaz is still there, with its narrow streets, old houses and barns, and baroque chapel dating from 1499.

THE MOUNTAIN
Nendaz has its own area of slopes and a rather tenuous link with rest of the 4 Valleys via Siviez.
Slopes There's a 12-person gondola straight to the top of the local north-facing slopes at Tracouet. Here there are good, snow-sure nursery slopes plus blue and red intermediate runs back to town through the trees.

Intermediate and better skiers and boarders can head off down the back of Tracouet to a cable-car which takes you to Plan du Fou at 2430m/7,970ft. From there you can go down to Siviez and the links to Verbier in one direction and Thyon and Veysonnaz in the other.
Terrain-parks There is a terrain-park.
Snow reliability Nendaz sits on a north-facing shelf so its local slopes don't get the sun that affects Verbier.
Experts Access to the tough stuff is a bit slower from here than from Verbier.
Intermediates The local slopes are quite varied, but not very extensive. For exploration of the 4 Valleys it's quickest to use the shuttle-bus to and from Siviez.
Beginners There are good nursery slopes at Tracouet.
Snowboarding There is a half-pipe.
Cross-country There are 17km/11 miles of cross-country tracks.
Queues There may be queues at Siviez at the end of the day.
Mountain restaurants The most compelling are in the Verbier area.
Schools and guides A reporter tells us that families seemed pleased with the school.
Facilities for children The school has a nursery area at Tracouet.

STAYING THERE
How to go UK tour operators seem to ignore the resort – but Interhome has properties.
Hotels There are a few traditional hotels. Reporters recommend the Sourire: 'Simple, but good food.'
Self-catering There is no shortage of apartments bookable locally.

TOURIST OFFICES

Verbier
t 775 3888
info@verbier.ch
www.verbier.ch

Nendaz
t 289 5589
info@nendaz.ch
www.nendaz.ch

Eating out There are several good restaurants; readers recommend the hotel Sourire and the nearby Mont Rouge restaurant.

Après-ski There are plenty of bars and four discos; a 17-year-old reporter recommends the Cactus Cantina and the Bodega as the liveliest spots.

Off the slopes Nendaz has 70km/43 miles of winter walks, an open-air rink, a fitness centre and squash courts.

Siviez 1730m/5,680ft

Siviez is a small huddle of buildings in an isolated spot in the 'third valley', where the slopes of Verbier, Nendaz and Veysonnaz/Thyon meet. Among them is the 2-star hotel de Siviez (288 1623). Not surprisingly, this is an ideal base from which to explore the whole 4 Valleys lift network. But, being set a little way down the valley from Tortin, at the foot of the steep itinerary runs from Chassoure and Mont-Fort, it is also an excellent base for exploration of the tough skiing of Verbier – you can end the day with a descent of 1600m/5,250ft vertical from Mont-Fort; no noise in the evenings; perfect.

Veysonnaz 1300m/4,270ft

Veysonnaz is a small, quiet resort, sunny in the afternoon, at the foot of an excellent long red slope from the ridge above Thyon. It is an attractive old village complete with church. It has adequate bars, cafes and restaurants, a disco, a 'good' sports centre with swimming pool, and ski school and guides. Accommodation is mainly in apartments. Of the two hotels, the 'very comfortable' Chalet Royal (208 5644) is preferable to the 'tired-looking' Magrappé, which is the focus of noisy après-ski. Taking a car means you can drive to Siviez for quick access to the Verbier or Nendaz slopes – a slow business by lift and piste.

Thyon 2000 2100m/6,890ft

Thyon 2000 (why not Thyon 2100, we wonder?) is a functional, purpose-built collection of plain, medium-rise apartment blocks just above the tree line at the centre of the Thyon-Veysonnaz sector of the 4 Valleys. It has the basics – bakery, supermarket, newsagent, a couple of bar-restaurants. There's a kindergarten as well as a ski school, and an indoor pool.

Les Collons 1800m/5,910ft

At the foot of a broad, east-facing slope down from Thyon 2000, Les Collins could hardly be more different – a couple of strings of chalets along roads following the hillside, mostly apartments but also a couple of modest hotels including the 3-star Cambuse (281 1883). There's a much wider range of bars, restaurants and other diversions than up in Thyon.

Le Châble 820m/2,690ft

Le Châble is a busy roadside village in the valley, at the bottom of the hairpin road up to Verbier. It is linked to Verbier by a queue-free gondola that goes on (without changing cabins) to Les Ruinettes and Les Attelas, which means access to the slopes can be just as quick as from Verbier. Le Châble is on the rail network, and is also convenient for drivers who want to visit other resorts in the Valais or further afield. And it is handy for Bruson, just a short bus-ride up the mountainside facing Verbier. There are several modest hotels, of which the 2-star Gietroz (776 1184) is the pick.

Bruson 1000m/3,280ft

Bruson is a small village on a shelf just above Le Châble, and reached by a short free bus-ride. Its lifts are covered by the Verbier pass. From the village a slow chair goes up over gentle east-facing slopes dotted with chalets to Bruson les Forêts (1600m/5,250ft).

The open slopes above Bruson les Forêts are served by a quad chair up to the ridge, on the far side of which is a short drag-lift serving a tight little bowl. This may not sound much, but in addition to the intermediate pistes served by these lifts there are large amounts of underused off-piste terrain, notably through woods on the front side accessed by the drag on the back side. Off-piste descents down the back towards Orsières are possible, with the return by train. For years there have been great plans to develop Bruson – building a lift from Le Châble to mid-mountain, extending the lift network across the north-east-facing slopes of Six Blanc and on to the shoulder of Mt Rogneux at 2800m/9,190ft, and building a lift up from Orsières. For now, it remains a great place to escape Verbier crowds.

Villars

Traditional old resort with a much-needed but far-flung glacier

COSTS

① ② ③ ④ ⑤ ⑥

RATINGS

The slopes

Snow	**
Extent	***
Expert	**
Intermediate	***
Beginner	****
Convenience	***
Queues	***
Mountain restaurants	***

The rest

Scenery	***
Resort charm	****
Off-slope	****

NEWS

New snowmaking is planned for the lower slopes between Villars and Gryon, and down to the villages – but there may be objections.

- ➕ Pleasant, relaxing year-round resort
- ➕ Fairly extensive intermediate slopes linked to Les Diablerets
- ➕ Good nursery slopes
- ➕ Quite close to Geneva airport
- ➕ Good range of off-slope diversions

- ➖ Unreliable snow-cover
- ➖ Overcrowded mountain restaurants
- ➖ Getting up the mountain means a slow, often crowded train journey or a bus-ride from the town centre to the gondola

With its mountain railway and gentle low-altitude slopes, Villars is the kind of place that has been overshadowed by modern mega-resorts. But for a relaxing and varied family holiday the attractions are clear – and the link with Les Diablerets and its high glacier, now known as Glacier 3000, adds to the appeal.

THE RESORT

Villars sits on a sunny shelf, looking across the Rhône valley to the Portes du Soleil. A busy high street lined with a variety of shops gives it the air of a pleasant small town; all around are chalet-style buildings, with just a few block-like hotels. You can travel to the centre of Villars on a picturesque cog train which goes on up to the slopes. It leaves from Bex in the valley, which is served by direct trains from Geneva airport (as is Aigle, a bus-ride from

Villars). A gondola at one end of town is the main lift; stay nearby if you can, since shuttle-buses get crowded at peak times. You can also stay in Gryon.

The Glacier-Alpes Vaudoises pass covers Villars, the linked slopes of Les Diablerets and Glacier 3000, plus Leysin and Les Mosses, both of which are easy jaunts by rail or road. Other resorts (eg Champéry and Verbier) are within driving distance. Les Diablerets, Leysin and Les Mosses have extended entries in our resort directory, at the back of the book.

KEY FACTS

Resort	1300m
	4,270ft

For Villars, Gryon and Les Diablerets, but excluding Glacier 3000

Slopes	1115-2120m
	3,660-6,960ft
Lifts	35
Pistes	100km
	62 miles
Blue	40%
Red	50%
Black	10%
Snowmaking	4km
	2.5 miles

Phone numbers
From elsewhere in Switzerland add the prefix 024.
From abroad use the prefix +41 24.

TOURIST OFFICE

t 495 3232
information@villars.ch
www.villars.ch

SNOWPIX.COM / CHRIS GILL

If you make it to Glacier 3000, beyond Les Diablerets, don't miss the Combe d'Audon run back to the valley →

THE MOUNTAINS

There's a good mix of open and wooded slopes throughout the area.
Slopes The train goes up to the col of Bretaye, which has intermediate slopes on either side, with a maximum vertical of 300m/1,000ft back to the col and much longer runs back to the village. To the east, open slopes (often spoilt by sun) go to La Rasse and the link to the otherwise separate Les Chaux sector. The gondola from town takes you to Roc d'Orsay, from where you can head for Bretaye or back to Villars. From Bretaye you can head for the slow two-way chair-lift which is the connection to Les Diablerets. The piste map and piste marking are both poor.
Terrain-parks There's a terrain-park at Les Chaux.
Snow reliability Low altitude and sunny orientation mean snow reliability is not good – they badly need the extra snowmaking planned. If local snow is poor, head for Glacier 3000 via Les Diablerets – though it is a long trek.
Experts The main interest for experts is off-piste. There is plenty to enjoy from Chaux Ronde, for example.
Intermediates The local slopes and Les Diablerets offer a good variety and add up to a fair amount of terrain. The lengthy trip to Glacier 3000 for the splendid red run down the Combe d'Audon is worth it if you're adventurous.
Beginners Beginners will enjoy the village nursery slopes and riding the train to Bretaye. There are gentle runs here, too, but it's also very crowded.
Snowboarding Villars is home to a big end-of-season snowboarders' party (visit www.snowbombing.com).
Cross-country The trails up the valley past La Rasse are long and pretty, and there are more in the depression beyond Bretaye (44km/27 miles in all).
Queues Queues appear for the lifts at Bretaye mainly at weekends and peak periods. A recent visitor reported some overcrowding on the buses and train.
Mountain restaurants They are often oversubscribed, especially at Bretaye. The Golf is expensive but good, as is the Col-de-Soud ('best rösti ever'); Lac des Chavonnes (open at peak periods) is worth the walk.
Schools and guides The Villars ski school – aka Ecole Moderne (using the ski évolutif method) – and the Swiss ski school get good reports. A reporter last year gave the Swiss School '10 out

of 10'. Riderschool is a specialist snowboard outfit.
Facilities for children Both ski schools run children's classes. There is also a non-ski nursery for children up to six and a Club Med with good facilities.

STAYING THERE

How to go Several tour operators offer packages here. We continue to receive glowing reports on the Club Med here – 'accommodation, food, instruction first class, equipment very good'.
Hotels The Golf (496 3838) is popular ('great, family tries hard'). The Eurotel Victoria (495 3131) lacks style but is near the gondola. The Bristol (496 3636) is not, but offers 'comfort, good food and service'. All are 4-star.
Eating out Many restaurants are hotel-based. Apart from these, the Sporting is recommended for pizza and the Vieux-Villars for local specialities.
Après-ski Charlie's, the Central, the Sporting and the Mini-Pub are popular bars. The bowling can be a laugh; El Gringo, Live and Fox are the discos.
Off the slopes Tennis, skating, curling, swimming, 'excellent' walks, and trips on the train – to Lausanne for instance.

Villars

481

Wengen

Charming village, stunning views and extensive intermediate terrain

COSTS

① ② ③ ④ ⑤ ⑥

RATINGS

The slopes

Snow	**
Extent	***
Expert	**
Intermediate	****
Beginner	***
Convenience	***
Queues	***
Mountain restaurants	****

The rest

Scenery	*****
Charm	*****
Off-slope	****

NEWS

For 2003/04 the slow Läger double chair on Männlichen is to be replaced by a fast quad. We also hear that the old double Innerwengen chair is to be replaced.

(map)

miles 0.5
Männlichen
down to Lauterbrunnen
Lauterbrunnen
N
Kleine Scheidegg
km 0.5

➕ Some of the most spectacular scenery in the Alps

➕ Traditional, nearly traffic-free Alpine village, reached only by cog railway

➕ Lots of long, gentle runs, ideal for intermediates, leading down to Grindelwald

➕ Rebuilt cable-car now an attractive alternative to slow trains up to the slopes above Grindelwald

➕ Nursery slopes in heart of village

➕ Calm, unhurried atmosphere

➖ Limited terrain for experts

➖ Despite some snowmaking, snow conditions are unreliable – especially on the sunny home run and village nursery slope

➖ Trains to slopes from here and from Grindelwald are slow and infrequent – you have to plan your movements with the aid of timetables

➖ Getting to Grindelwald's First area can take hours

➖ Subdued in the evening, with little variety of nightlife

Given the charm of the village, the friendliness of the locals and the drama of the scenery, it's easy to see why many people – including numbers of middle-aged British people who have been going for decades – love Wengen. But non-devotees should think carefully about the lack of challenge, the unreliable snow and the dependence on cog railways before signing up.

The last of these drawbacks is slightly less serious than it was. The Männlichen cable-car station, destroyed in the devastating avalanches of 1999, was rebuilt in the heart of the village, where it is not only less vulnerable to avalanche but also much more convenient. Of course, the cable-car is now more popular, and gets queues. So those willing to gear their holiday activities to timetables – or to accept half-hour waits for trains – will still mainly rely on the railway. Others will probably conclude that life is too short, and go elsewhere with more reliable snow.

THE RESORT

Wengen is set on a shelf high above the Lauterbrunnen valley, opposite Mürren, and reached only by a cog railway, which carries on up the mountain as the main lift. Wengen was a farming community long before skiing arrived; it is still tiny, but it is dominated by sizeable hotels, mostly of Victorian origin. So it is not exactly pretty, but it is charming and relaxed, and almost traffic-free. The only traffic is electric hotel taxi-trucks, which gather at the station to pick up guests, and a few ordinary engine-driven taxis. (Why, we wonder?)

The short main street is the hub of the village. Lined with chalet-style shops and hotels, it also has the ice rink and village nursery slopes right next to it. The nursery slopes double as the venue for floodlit ski-jumping and parallel slalom races.

The views across the valley are stunning. They get even better higher up, when the famous trio of peaks comes fully into view – the Mönch (Monk) protecting the Jungfrau (Maiden) from the Eiger (Ogre).

The main way up the mountain is the regular, usually punctual, trains from the southern end of the street to Kleine Scheidegg, where the slopes of Wengen meet those of Grindelwald. The cable-car is a much quicker way to the Grindelwald slopes, and now starts conveniently close to the main street.

Wengen is small, so location isn't as crucial as in many other resorts. The main street is ideally placed for the station. There are hotels on the home piste, convenient for the slopes. Those who don't fancy a steepish morning climb should avoid places down the hill below the station.

You can get to Mürren by taking the train down to Lauterbrunnen, and a funicular and connecting train up the other side. The Jungfrau lift pass covers all of this. Outings further afield aren't really worth the effort.

LIFT PASSES

THE MOUNTAINS

Although it is famous for the fearsome Lauberhorn Downhill course – the longest and one of the toughest on the World Cup circuit – Wengen's slopes are best suited to early intermediates. Most of the Downhill course is now open to the public. But the steepest section (the Hundschopf jump) can be avoided by an alternative red route for those who don't fancy it.

Most of Wengen's runs are gentle blues and reds, ideal for cruising.

THE SLOPES
Picturesque playground

Most of the slopes are on the Grindelwald side of the mountain. From the railway station at Kleine Scheidegg you can head straight down to Grindelwald or work your way across the mountain with the help of a couple of lifts to the top of the Männlichen. This area is served by drag- and chair-lifts, and can be reached directly from Wengen by the improved cable-car.

There are a few runs back down towards Wengen from the top of the Lauberhorn, but below Kleine Scheidegg there's really only one.

TERRAIN-PARKS
Not ideal

There's a new terrain-park by the Bumps T-bar, below Wengernalp. Be prepared for slushy conditions.

SNOW RELIABILITY
Why not use the guns?

Most slopes are below 2000m/6,560ft, and at Grindelwald they go down to less than 1000m/3,280ft. Very few slopes face north and Wengen's snowmaking facilities are not up to protecting them. The real shame is that the snowmaking that exists isn't always used when it's needed. As a reporter said last year, 'At least three machines were parked up and decorating the landscape at Kleine Scheidegg and never moved all week while the field below Wengernalp was 500 yards of sheet ice.'

While we've found wonderful snow a couple of times in late March, we've also struggled to find decent snow to ski on in January.

FOR EXPERTS
Few challenges

Wengen is quite limited for experts. The only genuine black runs in the area take you from Eigergletscher towards Wixi and include Oh God (which used to be off-piste but has now been reclassified as a 'free-ride piste'). There are now two 'itinerary' runs from the Lauberhorn chair-lift. Neither of these terms is explained on the piste map, but both are apparently ungroomed. For most of its length, the Lauberhorn Downhill course is merely of intermediate red run gradient.

There are some decent off-piste runs such as White Hare from under

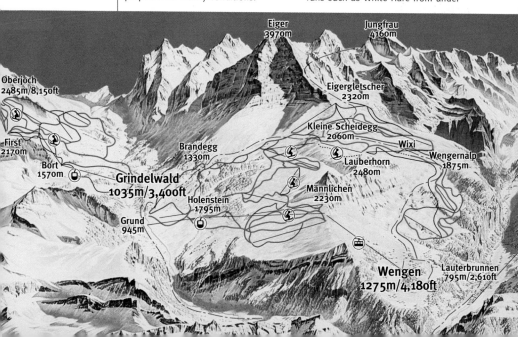

Eiger 3970m
Jungfrau 4160m
Oberjoch 2485m/8,150ft
Eigergletscher 2320m
First 2170m
Brandegg 1330m
Kleine Scheidegg 2060m
Wixi
Wengernalp 1875m
Bort 1570m
Lauberhorn 2480m
Grindelwald 1035m/3,400ft
Holenstein 1795m
Männlichen 2230m
Grund 945m
Wengen 1275m/4,180ft
Lauterbrunnen 795m/2,610ft

↑ The north face of the Eiger dominates the view from much of the ski area
GRINDELWALD TOURISMUS / SWISS-IMAGE.CH

KEY FACTS

Resort	1275m
	4,180ft

For Jungfrau region	
Slopes	945-2970m
	3,100-9,740ft
Lifts	44
Pistes	213km
	133 miles
Blue	30%
Red	50%
Black	20%
Snowmaking	34km
	21 miles

For First-Männlichen-Kleine-Scheidegg only	
Slopes	945-2485m
	3,100-8,150ft
Lifts	31
Pistes	160km
	99 miles

the north face of the Eiger and more adventurous runs from the Jungfraujoch late in the season.

For more serious challenges it's well worth going to nearby Mürren, an hour away by train and funicular. Heli-trips with mountain guides are organised if there are enough takers.

FOR INTERMEDIATES
Wonderful if the snow is good
Wengen and Grindelwald share superb intermediate slopes. Nearly all are long blue or gentle red runs – see Grindelwald chapter. The run back to Wengen is a relaxing end to the day, as long as it's not too crowded.

For tougher pistes, head for the top of the Lauberhorn lift and then the runs to Kleine Scheidegg, or to Wixi (following the start of the Downhill course). You could also try the north-facing run from Eigergletscher to Salzegg, which often has the best snow late in the season.

FOR BEGINNERS
Not ideal
There's a nursery slope in the centre of the village – it's convenient and gentle, but the snow is unreliable. A small part of it is now served by a moving carpet lift, ideal for children. There's a beginners' area at Wengernalp, but to get back to Wengen you either have to climb up to the train or tackle the run down, which can be tricky. There are plenty of good, long, gentle slopes to progress to.

FOR CROSS-COUNTRY
There is none
There's no cross-country skiing in Wengen itself. There are tracks down in the Lauterbrunnen valley, but the snow there is unreliable.

QUEUES
Improving, but a long way to go
The Männlichen cable-car has helped cut the queues for the trains but both

boarding

Wengen is not a bad place for gentle boarding – the nursery area is not ideal, but beginners have plenty of slopes to progress to, with lots of long blue and red runs served by the train and chair-lifts. Getting from Kleine Scheidegg to Männlichen means an unavoidable drag-lift though. For the steepest slopes and best free-riding, experts will want to head for Mürren.

GETTING THERE

Air Zürich 195km/121 miles (3½hr); Bern 70km/43 miles (1½hr).

Rail Station in resort.

SCHOOLS

Swiss
t 855 2022
ski.school@wengen.com

Privat
t 8555005
privat@wengen.com

Classes
(Swiss prices)
6 3hr days SF228

Private lessons
SF138 for 2hr for up to 4 people

CHILDREN

The kindergarten on the first floor of the Sport Pavilion takes children from 18 months from 8.30 to 5pm, Sunday to Friday. Children can be taken to and from lessons with the ski school, which starts at age 4 (6 3hr days SF228).

Sunshine nursery (853 0440) takes children from 1 month upwards. Children can be collected from and returned to your hotel or apartment.

A couple of 4-star hotels have their own kindergartens.

can still suffer from horrific bottlenecks in peak periods, as well as daily scrambles to board the trains that the school uses. Weekend invasions can increase the crowds on the Grindelwald side, especially. Queues up the mountain have been alleviated a lot in the last few years by the installation of fast quad chairs on the Grindelwald side – a process that continues this season with replacement of the Läger chair. But plenty of slow old lifts remain.

MOUNTAIN RESTAURANTS
Plenty of variety

A popular but pricey place for lunch is the Jungfrau hotel at Wengernalp, where the rösti is excellent and the views of the Jungfrau are superb. The highest restaurant is at Eigergletscher. If you get there early on a sunny day, you can grab a table on the narrow outside balcony and enjoy magnificent views of the glacier. The station buffet at Kleine Scheidegg gets repeated rave reviews, so it's not surprising that it also gets packed – the take-away rösti and sausage are a popular option. The Grindelwaldblick is a worthwhile trudge uphill from Kleine Scheidegg, with great food and views of the Eiger.

The newish restaurant Allmend, near the top of the Innerwengen chair and the eponymous train halt, is reportedly 'delightful', with 'friendly service' and wonderful views of the valley from the terrace. For restaurants on the slopes down towards Grindelwald, see that chapter.

SCHOOLS AND GUIDES
Healthy competition

A reporter says, 'The Swiss school is definitely trying harder than a few years ago.' The lessons and the standard of English are usually good. The independent Privat school has been recommended for private lessons.

Snowboarders are well served. And guides are available for heli-trips and powder excursions.

FACILITIES FOR CHILDREN
Apparently satisfactory

Our reports on children's facilities are from observers rather than participants, but are all favourable. It is an attractive and reassuring village for families, with the baby slope in the very heart of the village.

The train gives easy access to higher slopes.

STAYING THERE

HOW TO GO
Wide range of hotels

Most accommodation is in hotels. There is only a handful of catered chalets (and no especially luxurious ones). Self-catering apartments are few, too. There is a Club Med.

Hotels There are about two dozen hotels, mostly 4-star and 3-star, with a handful of simpler places.

(((4 **Beausite Park** (856 5161) Reputedly the best in town. Good pool. But poorly situated at top of nursery slopes – a schlep up from the main street.

(((4 **Wengener Hof** (856 6969) No prizes for style or convenience, but recommended for peace, helpful staff and spacious, spotless rooms with good views.

(((4 **Sunstar** (856 5200) Modern hotel on main street right opposite cable-car. Comfortable rooms (though one reporter thought them 'small and dismally decorated' this year); lounge has a log fire. Live music some nights. Pool with views. Food good. Friendly.

(((4 **Regina** (856 5858) Quite central. Smart, traditional atmosphere. 'Best food in Wengen.' Carousel nightclub.

(((4 **Silberhorn** (856 5131) Comfortable, modern 4-star in central position opposite station, with a choice of restaurants.

(((4 **Caprice** (856 0606) Small, smartly furnished chalet-style hotel across the tracks from the Regina. Kindergarten. 'Comfortable and friendly' according to a reporter.

(((3 **Belvédère** (856 6868) Some way out, but we have good reports of buffet-style meals ('good for families'), spacious rooms and grand art nouveau public rooms.

(((3 **Alpenrose** (855 3216) Long-standing British favourite; eight minutes' climb to the station. Small, simple rooms, but good views; 'first-class' food; friendly staff.

(((3 **Eiger** (856 0505) Very conveniently sited, right next to the station. Focal après-ski bar. Rebuilt with comfy modern rooms.

((2 **Falken** (856 5121) Further up the hill. Another British favourite, known affectionately as 'Fawlty Towers'.

Self-catering The hotel Bernerhof's decent Résidence apartments (855 2721) are well positioned just off the main street, and hotel facilities are available to guests.

ACTIVITIES

Indoor Swimming pool (in Beausite Park and Sunstar hotels), sauna, solarium, whirlpool, massage (in hotels), cinema (with English films), billiards

Outdoor Skating, curling, 50km/ 31 miles of cleared paths, toboggan runs, paragliding, glacier flights, sledging excursions, hang-gliding

Phone numbers
From elsewhere in Switzerland add the prefix 033.
From abroad use the prefix +41 33.

TOURIST OFFICE

t 855 1414
info@wengen.ch
www.wengen-muerren.ch

EATING OUT
Lots of choice

Most restaurants are in hotels. They offer good food and service. The Eiger has a traditional restaurant and a stube with Swiss and French cuisine. The Bernerhof has good-value traditional dishes. The little hotel Hirschen has good steaks. There's no shortage of fondues in the village. Several bars do casual food, including good-value pizza at Sina. Cafe Gruebi has been recommended for 'the most wonderful cakes'. The Jungfrau at Wengernalp has an excellent restaurant – but you have to get back on skis or on a toboggan.

APRES-SKI
It depends on what you want

People's reactions to the après-ski scene in Wengen vary widely, according to their expectations and appetites. If you're used to raving in Kitzbühel or Les Deux-Alpes, you'll rate Wengen dead, especially for young people. If you've heard it's dead, you may be pleasantly surprised to find that there is a handful of bars that do good business both early and late in the evening. But it is only a handful of small places. The Schnee-Bar, at the Bumps section of the home run, is a popular final run stop-off. And the stube at the Eiger hotel and the tiny, 'always welcoming' Eiger Bar are popular at the end of the day. The traditional Tanne and the funky Chili Peppers, almost opposite on the main street, are generally lively. Sina's, a little way out by Club Med, usually has live music. The Caprice bar is also recommended. There are discos and live music in some hotels. The cinema often shows English-language films.

OFF THE SLOPES
Good for a relaxing time

Wengen is a superb resort for those who want a completely relaxing holiday, with its unbeatable scenery and pedestrian-friendly trains and cable-car (there's a special, though expensive, pass for pedestrians). There are some lovely walks, ice skating and a curling club. Several hotels have health spas. Excursions to Interlaken and Bern are possible by train, as is the trip up to the Jungfraujoch (see the Grindelwald chapter). Helicopter flights from Männlichen are recommended.

STAYING UP THE MOUNTAIN
Great views

You can stay at two points up the mountain reached by the railway: the expensive Jungfrau hotel (855 1622) at Wengernalp – with fabulous views of the Eiger – and at Kleine Scheidegg, where there's a choice of rooms in the big Scheidegg-Hotels (855 1212) or dormitory space above the Grindelwaldblick restaurant and the station buffet. The big restaurant at Männlichen also has rooms.

STAYING DOWN THE VALLEY
The budget option

Staying in a 3-star hotel like the Schützen (855 3026) or Oberland (855 1241) down in Lauterbrunnen will cost about half as much as similar accommodation in Wengen. The trains from Wengen run until 11.30pm and are included in your lift pass. Staying in Lauterbrunnen also improves your chances of getting a seat on the morning train to Kleine Scheidegg rather than joining the scramble at Wengen – though of course it also means a much longer journey time. Lauterbrunnen is also much better placed for visits to Mürren.

You can save even more by staying in Interlaken. Choose a hotel near Interlaken Ost station, from which you can catch a train to Lauterbrunnen (22 minutes) or Grindelwald (36 minutes). Driving can take longer at weekends, when the roads get very busy.

THE BRITISH IN WENGEN

There's a very strong British presence at Wengen. Many Brits have been returning for years to the same rooms in the same hotels in the same week, and treat the resort as a sort of second home. There is an English church with weekly services, and a British-run club, the DHO (Downhill Only) – so named when the first Brits persuaded the locals to keep the summer railway running up the mountain in winter so that they would no longer have to climb up in order to ski down again. That greatly amused the locals, who until then had regarded skiing in winter as a necessity rather than a pastime to be done for fun. The DHO is still going strong and organises regular events throughout the season.

Zermatt

Magical in many respects – both on and off the slopes

487

COSTS

① ② ③ ④ ⑤ ⑥

RATINGS

The slopes
Snow	****
Extent	****
Expert	*****
Intermediate	****
Beginner	*
Convenience	*
Queues	***
Mountain restaurants	*****

The rest
Scenery	*****
Charm	*****
Off-slope	****

NEWS

A new Matterhorn Express eight-seater gondola opened for 2002/03, replacing the old Zermatt-Furi gondola and Furi-Schwarzsee cable-car. It takes you from Zermatt via mid-stations at Furi and Aroleid to Schwarzsee in just 10 minutes. It has 50% more capacity than the old gondola and 10 times the capacity of the old cable-car.

Two new fast six-seater chair-lifts are planned for 2003/04. One will go from Trockener Steg to Furggsattel, replacing the queue-prone T-bar here. The other will go from Riffelberg to Gifthittli, below Gornergrat, replacing another T-bar. Two T-bars from Trockener Steg to Theodulpass will be replaced by one, with a mid-station. More snowmaking is also planned.

The new Hörnli chair, originally planned for 2003/04, has been delayed.

- Wonderful, high and extensive slopes and three varied areas
- Spectacular high-mountain scenery, dominated by the Matterhorn
- Charming, if rather sprawling, old mountain village, largely traffic-free
- Reliable snow at altitude
- Fairly new, highly-rated ski school
- World's best mountain restaurants
- Extensive helicopter operation
- Nightlife to suit most tastes
- Smart shops
- Linked to Cervinia in Italy

- Getting to main lift stations may involve a long walk, a crowded (but free) bus or an expensive taxi-ride
- Beginners should go elsewhere
- Europe's most expensive lift pass
- Some restaurants and hotels very expensive – so choose carefully
- One-way link only between Rothorn/Gornergrat and the Klein Matterhorn
- Slow train up to Gornergrat annoys some people, but can be avoided
- Some lift queues at peak periods
- Annoying electric taxis detract from the car-free village ambience

You must try Zermatt before you die. Few places can match its combination of excellent advanced and intermediate slopes, reliable snow, magnificent scenery, Alpine charm and mountain restaurants with superb food and stunning views.

Zermatt has its drawbacks – see the long list above. But for us, and for virtually all our reporters, these pale into insignificance compared to its attractions, which come close to matching perfectly our notion of the ideal winter resort. It's one of our favourites – and one of the editors regularly takes his annual week-long family holiday here.

THE RESORT

Zermatt started life as a traditional mountain village, developed as a mountaineering centre in the 19th century, then became a winter resort. Summer is as important as winter here.

Zermatt is big business and most restaurants and hotels are owned by a handful of families. Many of the workers are brought in from outside Switzerland – but that is probably one of the reasons many reporters have remarked on the increased friendliness and improved service in recent years.

The village sprawls along either side of a river, mountains rising steeply on each side. It is a mixture of chocolate-box chalets and modern buildings, most in traditional style. You arrive by rail or taxi from Täsch, where cars have to be left, for a fee. They can be left for free at more distant Visp, from where you can also get a train. The main street runs past the station, lined with luxury hotels and shops.

Zermatt doesn't have the relaxed, quaint feel of other car-free resorts, such as Wengen and Saas-Fee. That's

partly because the electric vehicles are more intrusive and aggressive, and partly because the clientele is more overtly part of the jet set.

For a resort with such good and extensive slopes, there's a remarkably high age profile. Most visitors seem to be over 40, and there's little of the youthful atmosphere you get in rival resorts with comparable slopes, such as Val-d'Isère, St Anton and Chamonix.

The main street has the station near one end, with the cog railway to

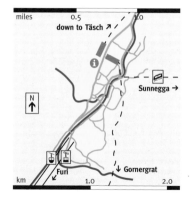

KEY FACTS

Resort	1620m
	5,310ft

For Zermatt only

Slopes	1620-3820m	
	5,310-12,530ft	
Lifts	71	
Pistes	250km	
	155 miles	
Blue	22%	
Red	50%	
Black	28%	
Snowmaking	43km	
	27 miles	

For Zermatt-Cervinia-Valtournenche combined

Slopes	1525-3820m
	5,000-12,530ft
Lifts	101
Pistes	450km
	280 miles
Snowmaking	60km
	38 miles

LIFT PASSES

Zermatt
Covers all lifts on the Swiss side of the border.

Main pass
1-day pass SF64
6-day pass SF320

Senior citizens
Over 65 (male), 63 (female): 6-day pass SF272

Children
Under 20: 6-day pass SF272
Under 16: 6-day pass SF160
Under 9: free pass

Notes
Half-day passes and single-ascent tickets on some lifts also available.

Alternative passes
Combined passes available for Zermatt and Cervinia and for Klein Matterhorn, Schwarzsee and Cervinia.

Gornergrat leaving from the other side of the square. The underground funicular to Sunnegga is a few minutes' walk away and the gondola to the Klein Matterhorn area (and the link to Cervinia) is a 15-minute trek, a (usually very crowded) bus-ride or an expensive taxi-ride ('The best daily SF20 investment of the trip,' says a reader).

The school and guides office, the tourist office and many hotels, shops, restaurants, bars and nightspots are on or near the main street. Another main street runs along the river. To each side are narrow streets and paths; many are hilly and treacherous when icy.

Choosing where to stay is very important in Zermatt. The solar-powered shuttle-buses are small and crowded, but at least they are now free and more frequent than they used to be. Walking from one end of the village to the furthest lifts can take 15 to 20 minutes and can be unpleasant because of treacherous icy paths. If you rent equipment from Flexrent they will transport it free overnight between their shops near the Sunnegga and Klein Matterhorn lifts if you tell them which area you want to use next day.

The best spot to stay is near the Gornergrat and Sunnegga railways, near the end of the main street. Some accommodation is up the steep hill across the river in Winkelmatten – you can ski back to it from all areas and it has its own reliable bus service.

Getting up to the village from Täsch is no problem. The trains run on time and have automatically descending ramps that allow you to wheel luggage trolleys on and off. You are met at the other end by electric and horse-drawn taxis and hotel shuttles.

THE MOUNTAINS

There are slopes to suit all abilities except absolute beginners, for whom we don't recommend the resort. For intermediates and experts Zermatt has few rivals, with marvellously groomed cruising trails, some of the best moguls around, long, beautiful scenic runs out of view of the lift system, exciting heli-trips and off-piste possibilities, as well as the opportunity to get down into Italy for the day and lunch on pasta and chianti. On our 2003 visits we were impressed with the service improvements: the lift staff were more polite, there were useful announcements in several languages (including English)

on the train and some cable-cars and there were free tissues at most lift stations (just as in America). The large 'self-ripping' piste-map was complained of by one reporter (there's another very compact version which shows Cervinia's slopes too).

THE SLOPES
Beautiful and varied

Zermatt consists of three separate areas, two of which are now well linked. The **Sunnegga-Blauherd-Rothorn** area is reached by the underground funicular starting about five minutes' walk from the station. This shifts large numbers rapidly but can lead to queues for the subsequent gondola – you can take a run down to a high-speed quad alternative.

From the top of this area you can make your way – via south-facing slopes served by snowmaking – to Gant in the valley between Sunnegga and the second main area, **Gornergrat–Hohtälli–Stockhorn**. A 125-person cable-car opened a few seasons ago linking Gant to Hohtälli in just seven minutes – a vast improvement on the two gruelling steep T-bars that were the only links before. A gondola makes the link back from Gant to Sunnegga. Gornergrat can be reached direct from Zermatt by cog railway trains which leave every 24 minutes and take 30 or 40 minutes to get to the top – arrive at the station early to get a seat on the right-hand side and enjoy the fabulous views. It can be an uncomfortable journey if you have to stand.

From Gornergrat there's a piste, followed by a short walk, to Furi to link up with the third and highest area, **Klein Matterhorn–Trockener Steg–Schwarzsee**. But you can't yet do the journey in the opposite direction: once on the Klein Matterhorn, moving to a different mountain means heading down and getting from one end of the village to the other to catch a lift up. (A gondola from Furi to Riffelalp is planned for a few years' time). The Klein Matterhorn gives access to Cervinia – you need to buy an 'international pass' or pay a daily supplement to your Zermatt lift pass.

There are pistes back to the village from all three areas – though some of them can be closed or tricky due to poor snow conditions. They can be hazardous at the end of the day due to crowds and speeding skiers.

boarding

Boarders in soft boots have one big advantage over skiers in Zermatt – they have much more comfortable walks to and from the lift stations! Even so, there aren't many snowboarders around. The slopes are best for experienced free-riders, because tough piste and off-piste action is what Zermatt is really about; plus there's the world-class terrain-park near Riffelberg. There is, however, an excellent little beginner area at Blauherd, complete with moving carpet lift, which we've seen many beginner snowboarders having lessons on. The main lifts are boarder-friendly: train, funicular, gondolas and cable-cars. But there are still a few T-bars. Stoked is a specialist snowboard school (that now has a ski section, too).

TERRAIN-PARKS
Two fun winter options
There's a world-class terrain-park and half-pipe near Riffelberg, with table-tops, bumps, rails, a kids' corner, a big igloo and a trendy tepee bar. At Blauherd there's a boarder-cross course and quarter-pipe. In summer, a park is built on the Klein Matterhorn.

SNOW RELIABILITY
Good high up, poor lower down
Zermatt has rocky terrain and a relatively dry climate. But it also has some of the highest slopes in Europe, and quite a lot of snowmaking.

All three areas go up to over 3000m/10,000ft, and the Klein Matterhorn area has summer glacier skiing. There are loads of runs above 2500m/ 8,200ft, many of which are north-facing, so guaranteeing decent snow except in freak years.

Snowmaking machines serve some of the pistes on all three areas, from around 3000m to under 2000m (10,000ft down to 6,500ft). The runs

back to the village can still be patchy, as can the lower part of the south-facing run from Rothorn to Gant (which is getting more snow-guns for 2003/04). Piste grooming is excellent.

FOR EXPERTS
Good – with superb heli-trips
If you've never been, Zermatt has to be on your shortlist. If you have been, we're pretty sure you'll want to return.

If you love long mogul pitches, the slopes at Triftji, below Stockhorn, are the stuff of dreams. 'Fantastic,' says a reader this year. From the top of the Stockhorn cable-car there's a run down to the T-bar that serves another two steep 2km/1 mile runs – one each side of the lift. The whole mountainside here is one vast mogul field – steep, but not extremely so. Being north-facing and lying between 3400m and 2700m (11,150ft and 8,860ft), the snow keeps in good condition long after a new snowfall. But be warned: this whole area does not open until February (the lifts are closed).

You can continue down from here to Gant and catch the gondola up to Blauherd. On that mountain there are a couple of wonderful off-piste 'downhill routes' from Rothorn, which have spectacular views of both the village and the Matterhorn. But they need good snow-cover to be really enjoyable.

On the Klein Matterhorn, the best area for experts is Schwarzsee, from where there are several steep north-facing gullies through the woods. Access to these runs is much improved by the new gondola.

There are marvellous off-piste possibilities from the top lifts in each sector, but they aren't immediately obvious to those without local knowledge. They are also dangerous because of rocky and glacial terrain.

We don't recommend anyone going off-piste without a guide. You can join daily ski touring groups but there aren't standard off-piste groups as there are in resorts such as Val-d'Isère and Méribel; you have to hire a guide privately for a full day. The Ski Club of Great Britain usually hires a guide for off-piste skiing once a week – we joined that group a couple of years ago and had a great day.

Zermatt is the Alps' biggest heli-trip centre; the helipad resembles a bus station at times, with choppers taking off every few minutes. There are only three main drop-off points, so this can mean encountering one or two other groups on the mountain, even though there are multiple ways down. From all three points there are routes that don't require great expertise. The epic is from Monte Rosa, at over 4000m/13,000ft, an easy run down through wonderful glacier scenery to Furi. If there isn't much snow, getting off the end of the glacier can be scary though; in 2003 we needed the help of both our guide and a rope that's fixed to the rocks to navigate a short, almost vertical section.

FOR INTERMEDIATES
Mile after mile of beautiful runs

Zermatt is ideal for adventurous intermediates. Many of the blue and red runs tend to be at the difficult end of their grading. There are very beautiful reds down lift-free valleys from both Gornergrat (Kelle) and Hohtälli (White Hare) to Gant – we love these first thing in the morning, before

anyone else is on them. A variant to Riffelalp (Balmbrunnen) ends up on a narrow wooded path with a sheer cliff and magnificent views to the right.

On Sunnegga, the 5km/3 mile Kumme run, from Rothorn to the bottom of the Patrullarve chair, also gets away from the lift system and has an interesting mix of straight-running and mogul pitches. On Klein Matterhorn, the reds served by the Hörnli drag and the fast quad chair from Furgg are all long and gloriously set at the foot of the Matterhorn. The Matterhornpiste red reached from the new Furggsattel chair has the most stunning views of the mountain it is named after (and is of blue gradient for much of its length).

For less adventurous intermediates, the blues on Sunnegga and above Riffelberg on Gornergrat and the runs between Klein Matterhorn and Trockener Steg are best. Of these, the Riffelberg area often has the best combination of good snow and easy cruising, and is popular with the school. Sunnegga gets a lot of sun, but

the snowmaking means that the problem is more often a foot or more of heavy snow near the bottom than bare patches.

On the Klein Matterhorn, most of the runs, though marked red on the piste map, are very flat and represent the easiest slopes Zermatt has to offer, as well as the best snow. The problem here is the possibility of bad weather because of the height – high winds, extreme cold and poor visibility can make life very unpleasant. To get to Cervinia, you set off from Testa Grigia (confusingly, called Plateau Rosa on the Cervinia piste map) with a choice of two routes – even an early intermediate should find the easier 10km/6 mile route (on the left as you look at the Cervinia piste map) down to the village manageable. The red Ventina run is a delightful cruise for better intermediates.

Beware of the run from Furgg to Furi at the end of the day, when it can be chopped up, mogulled in places and very crowded (the only reason it is graded black that we can see, because

THE WORLD'S BEST MOUNTAIN RESTAURANTS

We once met a man who had been coming here for 20 years simply because of the mountain restaurants. The choice is enormous (the tourist information says 38, but it seems more). Most have table-service, nearly all of those we (and reporters) have tried serve excellent food and many are in spectacular settings. It is impossible to list here all those worth a visit – so don't limit yourself to those we mention. It is best to book; check prices are within your budget when you do! Vegetarian options can be very limited.

Down at Findeln below Sunnegga are several attractive, busy, expensive, rustic restaurants, including Findlerhof (aka Franz & Heidy's) where we had excellent lamb in 2003, Chez Vrony, Paradies and Enzian ('less busy than others'). The hut at Tuftern has great views from the terrace, sells good Heida wine from the highest vineyard in Europe and does simple home made soup, cheese and cold sausage (but a reporter complains of 'watery hot chocolate in a plastic cup').

The restaurants at Fluhalp (which often has live music) and Grünsee have beautiful isolated situations, and the large terraces at Sunnegga and Rothorn have great views. All these are part of the Matterhorn Group and do decent food.

At Furi, the Restaurant Furi, Aroleid above it and Simi's on the road below all have large sun terraces and good food. The hotel at Schwarzsee is right at the foot of the Matterhorn, with staggering views and endless variations of rösti. Round the back from here Stafelalp is simple but charmingly situated. Up above Trockener Steg Gandegghütte has stunning views of the glacier and 'good polenta'. On the way back to the village below Furi, Zum See is a charming old hut serving the best mountain food in Zermatt (which means it is world-class: we had delicious beef, lamb and raspberry tart here). Blatten is good too.

The Kulmhotel, at 3100m/10,170ft at Gornergrat, has both self-service and table-service restaurants, with amazing views of lift-free mountains and glaciers. 'But beware of dive-bombing birds when eating outside!' says a reporter. Wherever you go, don't miss the local alcoholic coffee – in its many varieties.

SCHOOLS

Swiss
t 966 2466
info@
skischulezermatt.ch
Stoked–The SkiSchool
t 967 7020
info@stoked.ch

Classes (Swiss prices)
5 days (10am to 3.30
with lunch break)
SF280
Private lessons
SF160 for 1hr for 1
person

CHILDREN

There are nurseries in
two upmarket hotels.
The one in the
Nicoletta (966 0777)
takes children aged 2
to 8, from 9am to
5pm. The Kinderclub
Pumuckel at the
Ginabelle (966 5000)
takes children from
30 months, from 9am
to 5pm. The
Kinderparadies (967
7252) takes children
from 3 months from
9am to 5pm. The
Snowflakes
kindergarten at
Trockener Steg takes
children from age 4
by the hour (967
7020). Private
babysitters are
available, too.

Ski school lessons
start at age 4 (5 days
SF370 for 4-6 year-
olds at Swiss school).

it isn't very steep). A much more
relaxed way is the beautifully scenic
Weiss Perle run (the Stafelalp variant is
even more scenic but has a short
uphill section).

FOR BEGINNERS
Learn elsewhere
Zermatt is to be avoided by beginners.
The best snow-sure nursery slope area
is at Blauherd. But there are no long
easy runs to progress to except above
Trockener Steg, which can be bitterly
cold and windy.

FOR EVERYONE
A spectacular cable-car ride
The Klein Matterhorn cable-car is an
experience not to miss if the weather
is good. The views down to the glacier
and its crevasses, as the car swings
steeply into its hole blasted out of the
mountain at the top, are stupendous.
When you arrive, you walk through a
long tunnel, to emerge on top of the
world for the highest piste in Europe –
walk slowly, the air is thin here and
some people have altitude problems.
The ice grotto cut into the glacier here
is well worth a visit, with 'incredible
ice carvings'. The top drag-lifts are
open in the summer only.

FOR CROSS-COUNTRY
Fairly limited
There's a 4km/2.5 mile loop at Furi,
3km/2 miles near the bottom of the
gondola to Furi, and 12 to 15km/7 to 9
miles down at Täsch (don't count on
there being snow). There are also
some 'ski walking trails' – best tackled
as part of an organised group.

QUEUES
Main problems being solved
Zermatt has improved its lift system
hugely in recent years, eliminating
major bottlenecks. This year we, and
the readers we heard from,
encountered few problems. The high-
speed quad from Furgg can get busy
now that the new gondola is dumping
people nearby. And the Klein
Matterhorn cable-car has queues much
of the time. The other problem is the
Gornergrat train – you may find there's
only standing room, which can be
tiring and uncomfortable: 'Better to
wait for the next one,' says a reporter.
    One thing we love about Zermatt is
getting the 8am train with the lifties
and restaurant staff. It arrives at the
top just as they are dropping the rope

to open the pistes and you can enjoy
deserted slopes for an hour or two,
before the crowds join you.
    The run down from Furgg is
overcrowded at the end of the day
(see For intermediates for a better way
down) – as are the buses back to town
from the end of the piste home.

SCHOOLS AND GUIDES
Welcome competition at last
The main Swiss school has a poor
reputation: 'Awful – in three days, the
instructor taught our early intermediate
no technique, spoke no English and
used the follow-me method the whole
time,' said a reporter.
    There's a separate Stoked
snowboard school, which we have
good reports of. This has now
combined with The SkiSchool, which
started in 2000/01 and is made up of
talented young instructors, some of
whom are British and all of whom
speak good English. A reporter who
took a private instructor highly
recommends them and another was
impressed by group lessons (with a
British instructor). Their programme
includes freestyle classes (tricks in the
terrain-park).

FACILITIES FOR CHILDREN
Good hotel nurseries
The Nicoletta and Ginabelle hotels
have nurseries. The Kinderparadies,
200m/660ft from the station, takes
children from three months. The
Snowflakes kindergarten, for children
aged at least four years old, is run by
Stoked–The SkiSchool at Trockener
Steg and can be used by the hour
(SF15 for one hour).

STAYING THERE

HOW TO GO
A wide choice, packaged or not
Chalets Several operators have places
here, many of the most comfortable
contained in large apartment blocks.
Scott Dunn Ski, for example, has
several of these. Reporters have
praised Total Ski's operation here. And
Simply Ski has some new Zermatt
chalets for 2003/04.
Hotels There are over 100 hotels,
mostly comfortable and traditional-
style 3-stars and 4-stars, but taking in
the whole range.
《《《⑤ Mont Cervin (966 8888) Biggest in
town. Elegantly traditional, with a good
pool.

↑ Wherever you go on Zermatt's mountains there are fabulous views of the Matterhorn. This photo is taken from the terrace of the Chez Vrony restaurant at Findeln

SNOWPIX.COM / CHRIS GILL

GETTING THERE

Air Geneva 222km/138 miles (4hr by rail); Zürich 245km/152 miles (5hr by rail); Sion 80km/50 miles (1½hr).

Rail Station in resort.

ACTIVITIES

Indoor Sauna, tennis, hotel swimming pools (some open to public), salt water pool, keep-fit centre, squash, billiards, curling, bowling, gallery, excellent Alpine museum, cinema, indoor golf

Outdoor Skating, curling, sleigh rides, 30km cleared paths, helicopter flights, paragliding, cycling, ice-diving

(((((⑤ **Zermatterhof** (966 6600) Traditional 'grand hotel' style with piano bar and pool.

((((⑤ **Riffelalp Resort** (966 0555) Up the mountain, recent smart extension, pool and spa, own evening trains.

((((④ **Alex** (966 7070) Close to station. Reporters love it. 'Wonderful,' says one this year. Pool. Dancing.

((((④ **Ambassador** (966 2611) Peaceful position near Gornergrat station. Large pool; sauna. 'Excellent food and attentive staff,' says one of our reporters this year.

((((④ **Monte Rosa** (966 0333) Well-modernised original Zermatt hotel, near southern end of village – full of climbing pictures and mementos.

((((④ **Ginabelle** (966 5000) Smart pair of chalets not far from Sunnegga lift; great for families – on-the-spot ski nursery as well as day care.

((((④ **Nicoletta** (966 0777) Modern chalet quite close to centre, with nursery.

((((④ **Sonne** (966 2066) Traditionally decorated, in quiet setting away from main street; 'Roman Bath' complex.

(((③ **Julen** (966 7600) Charming, modern-rustic chalet over the river, with Matterhorn views from some rooms.

(((③ **Butterfly** (966 4166) 'Small, friendly, as well furnished as the Alex, but much better food,' says a reporter.

((② **Atlanta** (966 3535) No frills, but 'friendly service'; close to centre, with Matterhorn views from some rooms.

((② **Alpina** (967 1050) Modest but very friendly, and close to centre.

((② **Bahnhof** (967 2406) Right by Gornergrat station. Recently refurbished. Cheapest place to stay in town (SF96 a night in 2003 for double room with shower, SF30 a night for a dormitory bed; with use of communal kitchen).

Self-catering There is a lot of apartment accommodation, but not much finds its way to the UK package market. We have enjoyed staying in the hotel Ambassador apartments, with free use of all its facilities such as a pool and a sauna. The Vanessa complex was recommended by a reporter. The tourist office web site has apartments.

EATING OUT
Huge choice at all price levels
There are over 100 restaurants to choose from, ranging from top-quality haute cuisine, through traditional Swiss food, Chinese, Japanese and Thai to egg and chips and even a McDonald's.

Mood's (see Après-ski) does excellent fish. The Mazot is highly rated and highly priced. At the other end of the scale, Café du Pont has good-value pasta and rösti; Grampi's, Broken and Postli do good pizzas. The Schwyzer Stübli has local specialities and live Swiss music and dancing.

Rua Thai in the basement of the hotel Abana Real has been recommended for excellent food and beautiful decor. Fuji in the same building is a good Japanese.

Chez Heini serves excellent lamb and the owner sings after dinner. Giuseppe's doesn't look much, but has the best Italian food in town – book before your trip, it gets so busy. Avena is recommended by a local for curry.

Da Mario, Casa Rustica, Baku (see Après-ski), the Old Spaghetti Factory (in the hotel Post complex) and the Whymperstube have all been recommended by readers.

APRES-SKI
Lively and varied

There's a good mix of sophisticated and informal fun, though it helps if you have deep pockets. On the way back from the Klein Matterhorn there are lots of restaurants below Furi for a last drink and sunbathe, the final one blasting out loud music in a very un-Zermatt-like fashion but attracting huge crowds – we preferred the delicious fruit tarts at Zum See. Visitors rave about the Baku, on the way back to Winkelmatten. It's got a wigwam outside, so you can't miss it: On the way back from Sunnegga, Othmar's Hutte has great views and organises dinners (followed by tobogganing down) and the Olympia Stübli often has live music. Near the church at Winkelmatten, the Sonnenblick is 'a great place to watch the sun set'.

In town the Papperazi is one of the few popular early places (it's crowded after dinner, too). Elsie's bar is wood-panelled, atmospheric and gets packed with an older crowd both early and late. The North Wall is frequented by seasonal workers. Promenading the main street checking out expensive shoes and watches is popular.

Later on, the hotel Post complex has something for everyone, from a quiet, comfortable bar (Papa Caesar's) to a lively disco (Broken) and live music (Pink) and a selection of restaurants. Grampi's has dancing. Z'Alt Hischi (in an old house, serves huge measures of spirits) and the Little Bar (crowded if there are ten people in) are good for a quiet drink. The Hexenbar is cosy too. The hotel Alex draws a mature clientele for eating, drinking and dancing. The Hotel Pollux has 'lively music in its bar' says a reporter.

The Vernissage is our favourite bar in town for a quiet evening drink. It is an unusual and stylish modern place, with the projection room for the cinema built into the upstairs bar and displays of art elsewhere. Mood's was designed by the same guy and is run by the team that used to run the Post complex. There's a good cocktail bar downstairs, wood-panelled restaurant above and a comfortable bar done out in nautical fashion at the top.

If you like gambling, try the new casino which opened last season.

OFF THE SLOPES
Considerable attractions

Zermatt is an attractive place to spend time. It is easy (but expensive) for pedestrians to get around on the lifts and meet others for lunch and there are some nice walks. The Ice Grotto at Klein Matterhorn and the Alpine museum in town are worth seeing. You can take a helicopter trip around the Matterhorn. There is a cinema, and a reader tells us the free village guided tour is 'well worth doing'.

STAYING UP THE MOUNTAIN
Comfortable seclusion

There are several hotels at altitude, of which the pick is the Riffelalp Resort at the first stop on the Gornergrat railway (see Hotels above) – but you might find its limited evening train service a bit restricting. At the top of the railway, at 3100m/10,170ft, is the Kulmhotel Gornergrat (966 6400) – an austere building with basic rooms.

STAYING DOWN THE VALLEY
Attractive for drivers

In Täsch, where visitors must leave their cars, there are five 3-star hotels, costing less than half the price of the equivalent in Zermatt. The Täscherhof (966 6262) is next to the station; the City (967 3606) is close by. It's a 13-minute ride from Zermatt, with trains every 20 minutes for most of the day; the last train down is 11.10. You can also get taxis to the edge of Zermatt.

Phone numbers
From elsewhere in Switzerland add the prefix 027.
From abroad use the prefix +41 27.

TOURIST OFFICE
t 966 8100
zermatt@wallis.ch
www.zermatt.ch

GET YOUR MONEY BACK
when you book a holiday

You can reclaim the price of Where to Ski and Snowboard when you book a winter sports holiday for the 2003/04 or 2004/05 seasons. All you have to do is book the holiday through the specialist ski travel agency Ski Solutions.

Ski Solutions is Britain's original and leading ski travel agency. You can buy whatever kind of holiday you want through them.

Ski Solutions sells the package holidays offered by all the bonded tour operators in Britain (apart from the very few who are direct-sell only). And if that isn't enough choice, they can tailor-make a holiday, based on any form of travel and any kind of accommodation. No one is better placed to find you what you want than Ski Solutions.

Making a claim
Claiming your refund is easy. At the back of the book are two vouchers. When you make your definite booking, tell Ski Solutions that you want to take up this offer. Cut out the vouchers and send one to Ski Solutions and the other to Where to Ski and Snowboard (the addresses are on the vouchers).

Phone Ski Solutions on
020 7471 7700

In general, people who try American skiing and snowboarding for the first time are captivated by the experience and by the contrasts with European resorts. Nearly everyone is struck by the high standards of service and courtesy, the relatively deserted pistes, the immaculate piste grooming and the quality of accommodation. Depending on the resort, you may also be struck by the cute Wild West ambience and the superb quality of the snow – and for those who like it deep and steep there is the benefit in many resorts of large areas of expert terrain that can be tackled without costly guides.

But don't fall into the trap of lumping all US resorts together – they differ enormously. That's one reason why we have organised our American chapters in five regional sections – California, Colorado, Utah, Rest of the West and New England. US skiing does have some distinct disadvantages, too. Read on.

Most American resorts receive serious amounts of snow (average snowfall is typically in the region of 6m to 12m (20ft to 40ft) in a season). And most have serious snowmaking facilities too. What's more, they use them well – they lay down a base of snow early in the season, rather than patching up shortages later, as in Europe.

There are wide differences in quantity and quality of snowfall, both between individual resorts and between regions – we discuss some of these in our regional introductions.

497

Piste grooming is taken very seriously – most American resorts set standards that the best Alpine resorts are only now attempting to match. Every morning you can expect to step out on to perfect 'corduroy' pistes. But this doesn't mean that there aren't moguls – far from it. It's just that you get moguls where the resort says you can expect moguls, not everywhere. Some resorts even groom only half the width of some runs, leaving the other half mogulled.

The slopes of most American resorts are blissfully free of crowds – a key advantage that becomes more important every year as the pistes of the Alps and Andorra become ever more congested. If you want to let those new skiercross skis travel at the speeds they were designed for, take them to the States. And, because the slopes are mostly below the tree-line, they offer good visibility in bad weather.

Most American resorts offer free guided tours of the area. Lift queues are short, partly because they are highly disciplined, and spare seats on chair-lifts are religiously filled, with the aid of cheerful, conscientious attendants. Piste maps and tissues are freely available at the bottom of most lifts. Mountain 'hosts' are on hand to advise you about the best possible routes to take. School standards are uniformly high, with the added advantage that English is the native language. And facilities for children are impressive too.

Many Europeans have the idea that American resorts don't have off-piste terrain, but this seriously misrepresents the position. It's true that resorts practically always have a boundary, and that venturing beyond into the 'backcountry' may be discouraged or forbidden (though in some resorts it's just limited to certain gates). But within the area there is often very challenging terrain that is very

PETER MCBRIDE /
ASPEN SKIING COMPANY

← US resorts vary in character; they are not all restored mining towns like Aspen (pictured here). But they do mostly have efficient lift systems and quiet slopes

much like off-piste terrain in an Alpine resort – with the important advantage that it is patrolled and avalanche-controlled. Far from being a weakness of American resorts, we rate their expert terrain as one of their great attractions.

There are drawbacks to the US as well, though. One is that many resorts have slopes that are very modest in extent compared with major Alpine areas. But many US resorts are very close to each other – so if you are prepared to travel a bit, you won't get bored. A more serious problem is that the day is ridiculously short. The lifts often shut at 3pm or 3.30. That may explain another drawback for those who like a good lunch on the mountain – the dearth of decent mountain restaurants. Monster self-service cafeterias doing fast food are the norm – so that people can spend as much time on the slopes as possible. Small restaurants with table-service and decent food are rare – but they are now growing in number as resorts try to attract European guests.

It's also true that in many resorts the terrain is slightly monotonous. You don't get the spectacular mountain scenery and the distinctive high-mountain runs of the Alps. Most trails have clearly been cut through the forest; whereas in the Alps the artificial nature of the runs is rarely obvious when they are blanketed by snow, in the Rockies it is inescapable.

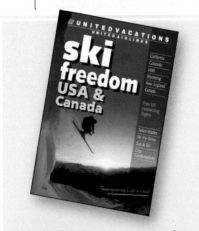
The grading of pistes (or trails, to use the local term) is different from that in Europe. Red runs don't exist. The colours used are combined with shapes. Green circles correspond fairly closely to greens in Europe (that is, in France, where they are mainly found). American blue squares largely correspond to blues in Europe, but also include tougher intermediate runs that would be red in the Alps; these are sometimes labelled as double-blue squares, although in some resorts a hybrid blue-black grading is used instead. Black diamond runs correspond to steeper European reds and easier European blacks. But then there are multiple diamonds. Double-diamond runs are seriously steep – often steeper than the steepest pistes in the Alps – and include high, open bowls. A few resorts have started to class their very steepest runs as triple-diamonds.

US resort towns vary widely in

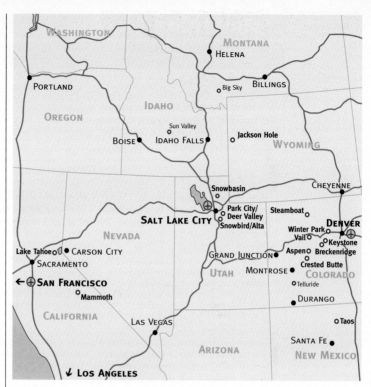

style and convenience. There are old restored mining towns such as Telluride, Crested Butte and Aspen, genuine cowboy towns such as Jackson Hole, purpose-built monstrosities such as Snowbird, and even skyscraping gambling dens such as Heavenly. There is an increasing number of cute car-free, slope-side villages such as Keystone's River Run, Copper Mountain's revamped base and the fledgling village at Squaw Valley. Two important things that they all have in common are good-value, spacious accommodation and good, reasonably priced restaurants. One drawback for young people is that the legal age for buying or consuming alcohol is 21; and the law is rigorously enforced to the extent that anyone under 40 would be well-advised to keep their passport with them as evidence of age.

In the end, your reaction to skiing and snowboarding in America may depend mainly on your reaction to America. If repeated cheerful exhortations to have a nice day wind you up – or if you like to be left in silence on chair-lifts – perhaps you'd better stick to the Alps.

What about the cost? It's never going to be cheap, but the basic cost of getting there is lower than you might think – you can get room-plus-hire-car February packages to California for under £600, eating out is not expensive and it's not difficult to find rooms with kitchenettes where you can economise by doing some of your own catering. But lift passes, tuition and childcare are very expensive by European standards (they can be double the cost). You can often save, especially on lift passes, by buying in advance through tour operators – look out for these deals. When we went to press, the £ had remained pretty stable against the US$ compared with 12 months before, so if things stay the same, at least you won't find local prices higher because of exchange rate changes.

California

California? It means surfing, beaches, wine, Hollywood, Disneyland and San Francisco cable-cars. But it also has the highest mountains in continental USA and some of America's biggest winter resorts, usually reliable for snow from November to May. What's more, winter holidays in California are less expensive than you might expect.

Holidays here are relatively cheap because winter is low season for much of the accommodation and for scheduled flights from Britain into Los Angeles and San Francisco. There is huge capacity available for the massive summer tourist trade, and hotel owners and airlines are happy to offer cut-price deals to keep a contribution coming in towards their overheads.

California's mountains get a lot of snow. In several recent seasons, Californian resorts have recorded the deepest snow-cover in North America. A common allegation is that the snow that falls in California is wet 'Sierra Cement'. Our fat file of reports from visitors has some complaints about that – especially late in the season – but most people have found the snow just fine. So have we: in March 2002 we enjoyed two of the best days of the season skiing powder in the trees of Heavenly and Mammoth.

You might want to start getting to grips with Californian skiing by reading the Lake Tahoe chapter, covering half a dozen resorts dotted around the mountains that ring this spectacular lake. You could visit them all from a single base using a car, and most using buses and boats.

The resorts you might think of spending most time in are Heavenly, Squaw Valley and Mammoth (a long drive south of Tahoe) – all impressive mountains. In the past our main reservation has been the character of the resorts themselves; they don't have the traditional mountain-town ambience that we look for in the States. That's partly because this is California, where walking is regarded as an eccentric way to get around. In compensation, Heavenly, at least, offers uniquely big-time entertainment in its casinos. And the scenery around Lake Tahoe is simply stunning.

But things are changing, with several new pedestrian 'villages' being developed. At Heavenly a gondola now goes from the centre of South Lake Tahoe right into the heart of the slopes – and this season a new car-free 'village' at the gondola base will open. The new village at Squaw Valley continues to develop, making this an increasingly attractive base. A couple of smaller Lake Tahoe resorts – Kirkwood and Northstar – have developed small, attractive slope-side villages. And a new pedestrian village opens this season in Mammoth, too, linked to the slopes by gondola.

One of the attractions of the Tahoe area is the mixture of open and lightly wooded slopes. In this shot from Northstar you can make out the trails of Squaw Valley →

Heavenly

Knockout views over Lake Tahoe, and a unique nightlife scene

COSTS

① ② ③ ④ ⑤ ⑥

RATINGS

The slopes

Snow	****
Extent	***
Expert	***
Intermediate	****
Beginner	****
Convenience	*
Queues	****
Mountain restaurants	*

The rest

Scenery	****
Resort charm	*
Off-slope	**

NEWS

The new 'village' at Heavenly – a pedestrian precinct at the foot of the gondola in South Lake Tahoe – opened in December 2002.

2002/03 also saw the opening of a short new blue trail – Meteor – and extra snowmaking.

A 120m/400ft-long super-pipe is planned for 2003/04.

Future plans of new owner Vail Resorts include two fast quads to replace the Canyon and Ridge chairs, and a new restaurant near the Sky Express chair.

KEY FACTS

Resort	1995m
	6,540ft
Slopes	1995-3060m
	6,540-10,040ft
Lifts	29
Pistes	4,800 acres
Green	20%
Blue	45%
Black	35%
Snowmaking	69 %

+ Spectacular setting, with amazing views of Lake Tahoe and Nevada

+ Fair-sized mountain which offers a sensation of travelling around – common in the Alps, not in the US

+ Large areas of widely spaced trees, largely on intermediate slopes – fabulous in fresh powder

+ Some serious challenges for experts

+ Numerous other worthwhile resorts within an hour's drive

+ A unique nightlife scene

+ Good snow record plus impressive snowmaking facilities

+ Gondola from downtown South Lake Tahoe and pedestrian 'village' under construction are real improvements

− South Lake Tahoe, where you stay, is a bizarre and messy combination of high-rise casino-hotels and shabby low-rise motels, shops and restaurants that spreads for miles along a busy highway

− The new resort 'village' isn't going to transform the whole place

− No trail back to South Lake Tahoe, so it's a gondola ride or bus-ride home if you're based there

− Very little traditional après-ski activity – though the new 'village' should help put that right

− If natural snow is in short supply, most of the challenging terrain is likely to be closed

A resort called Heavenly invites an obvious question: just how close to heaven does it take you? Physically, close enough: with a top height of 3060m/10,040ft and vertical of 1065m/3,500ft, it's the highest and biggest of the resorts clustered around scenic Lake Tahoe (look at the next chapter for more about that). Metaphorically, it's not quite so close. In particular, anyone who (like us) is drawn to Heavenly partly by its exceptionally scenic setting is likely to be dismayed by the appearance and atmosphere of the town of South Lake Tahoe.

The official line is that the place has been transformed into something like a European ski resort by the gondola from downtown up to the mountain, and by the opening of a pedestrian 'village' around its base. We don't buy that. The 'village' will be somewhere for skiers to spend time and money painlessly at the end of the day – the general feel of South Lake Tahoe won't be much affected.

Packages here are not quite as cheap as they were, which may explain why the flow of readers' reports has dried up. Do report if you go this season.

THE RESORT

Heavenly is on California's border with Nevada, at the south end of Lake Tahoe. Other resorts dotted around the lake are described in the next chapter.

Heavenly's base-town – South Lake Tahoe – is primarily a summer resort. In this respect it is unusual, but not unique. What really sets it apart is that its economy is driven by gambling. The Stateline area at its centre is dominated by a handful of monstrous hotel-casinos located just inches on the Nevada side of the line. These brash but comfortable hotels offer good-value accommodation (subsidised by the gambling), swanky restaurants and big-name entertainers, as well as roulette wheels, craps and card games – and endless slot machines into which gambling-starved Americans feed bucketloads of quarters.

The casinos are a conspicuous part of the amazing lake views from the lower slopes (though not from above mid-mountain). They look like a classic American downtown area, which you'd expect to be full of shops and bars. But they are actually just a cluster of high-rise blocks; what's more, the central area is bisected by the seriously busy US Highway 50. The rest of the town spreads for miles along this pedestrian-hostile road – dozens of low-rise hotels and motels (some

LIFT PASSES

Heavenly
Covers all lifts on Heavenly mountain.

Main pass
1-day pass $59
6-day pass $318

Senior citizens
Over 65: 6-day pass $174

Children
Under 19: 6-day pass $258
Under 13: 6-day pass $144
Under 5: free pass

Notes
Half-day passes available

quite smart, but many rather shabby), stores, wedding chapels and so on. The general effect is less dire than it might be, thanks to the camouflage of the tall trees that blanket the area.

The new 'village' built on the California side of the stateline should be a great improvement, providing an après-ski focus that the resort has lacked. If you can afford it, this alpine-themed village is the obvious place to stay – right next to the base of the gondola into the heart of the slopes.

Some of the casino-hotels are also within five minutes' walk of the gondola, making these an attractive choice even for those not keen on the gambling and entertainment, but others are enough of a hike away to justify using the shuttle buses. And much of the cheaper accommodation is literally miles away. If that's where you're staying, you may prefer to access the mountain from the original lift base, the refurbished California Lodge, up a heavily wooded slope 2km/1 mile out of South Lake Tahoe.

Like the town, the slopes spread across the border into Nevada – and there are two other lift bases, which can easily be reached by road, around the mountain in Nevada. There are

'excellent' free shuttle-bus services to the three out-of-town bases. A car is still handy to explore the other resorts around Lake Tahoe and to get to many of the best bars and restaurants.

An amusing way to visit Squaw Valley is to go by boat. The cost in 2002/03 was $87 including lift pass and ground transport. The outward trip can now be done by fast launch; leaving at 7.15, this gets you on to the cable-car by 8.45. The return is more leisurely – an après-ski party with live band 'doing decent cover versions' aboard the stern-wheeler Tahoe Queen. For an extra $20 you can get a 'decent three-course dinner', seated apart from the increasingly 'emotional' throng.

THE MOUNTAIN

Most of Heavenly's slopes suit intermediates down to the ground, but there are also good beginner slopes at the California base, and some splendid easy runs to progress to. Experts can find genuine challenges on the Nevada side – as well as lots of fun in acre upon acre of widely spaced trees. As always in America, this off-piste terrain is avalanche controlled. But it's 'patrolled' only by hollering; since collision with a tree may render you insensible, don't ski the trees alone.

THE SLOPES
Interestingly complex
Heavenly's mountain is quite complicated, and getting from A to B requires more careful navigation than is usual on American mountains. Quite a few of the links between different sectors involve flat tracks.

There is a fairly clear division between the California side of the mountain (the slopes directly above South Lake Tahoe) and the Nevada side (above Stagecoach Lodge and Boulder Lodge). The gondola takes you (almost) to the fast Tamarack six-seater chair, which gives access to either side.

HEAVENLY SKI RESORT /
SCOTT MARKEWITZ

Heavenly pictures that don't include Lake Tahoe do exist, but aren't easy to find ↓

Near the Nevada border you can see beautiful views over Lake Tahoe in one direction and the arid Nevada 'desert' in the other.

On the California side there are four main sectors: blue runs from the Tamarack chair; black and blue runs from the fast Sky quad, supplemented by two slow chairs; everything from black to green runs from the slow Waterfall and Powderhorn chairs; and the lower slopes served by the Tramway and fast Gunbarrel chair – unrelenting steep black runs down the front face, often heavily mogulled, with the alternative of the narrow, blue Roundabout trail snaking its way down the mountain. Right at the California Lodge base is a great beginner area. From here uplift is by a mid-sized cable-car and the recently upgraded Gunbarrel fast quad.

On the Nevada side there are three main bowls. The central one, above East Peak Lodge, is an excellent intermediate area, served by two fast quad chairs, with a downhill extension of the bowl served by the Galaxy chair. On one side of this central bowl is the steeper, open terrain of Milky Way Bowl, leading to the seriously steep Mott and Killebrew canyons, served by the Mott Canyon chair. On the other side is the North Bowl, with lifts up from Nevada's two base lodges.

There are no really easy runs on the Nevada side, apart from limited nursery slopes at the base.

TERRAIN-PARKS
Big improvements
Recent expansion has resulted in three good terrain-parks and half-pipes on both sides of the mountain. With the addition of the country's first tri-level box and planned new super-pipe, Heavenly is set to rival the other West Coast resorts, and to appeal to all levels of skier and boarder.

SNOW RELIABILITY
No worries
Heavenly was one of the first resorts to invest heavily in snowmaking, which proved its value when a severe snow drought hit in the late 80s and early 90s. The system now covers around 70% of the trails and ensures that most sections are open most of the time. In recent years Californian resorts have consistently recorded some of the deepest snow-cover of any North American resorts – and Heavenly is

now able to claim a five-year average of an impressive 360in. Our most recent visits have been blessed by excellent conditions.

FOR EXPERTS
Some specific challenges
There are genuine challenges for the more advanced. The runs under the California base lifts – including The Face and Gunbarrel (often used for mogul competitions) – are of proper black steepness, and very challenging when the snow is hard. Ellie's, at the top of the mountain, may offer continuous moguls too.

The really steep stuff is on the Nevada side. Milky Way Bowl provides a gentle single-diamond introduction to the emphatically double-diamond terrain beyond it. The seriously steep Mott and Killebrew canyons have roped gateways. The less expert are steered to lower gates. The Mott Canyon chair is slow, but you may welcome the rest it affords.

All over the mountain there is excellent off-piste skiing among widely spaced trees – tremendous fun when the conditions are right. Some wooded slopes are identified on the trail map, but you are not confined to those. The trail map gives a good indication of the density of trees in different areas, and the grading of nearby trails gives a good idea of steepness.

FOR INTERMEDIATES
Lots to do
Heavenly is excellent for intermediates, who are made to feel welcome and secure by excellent piste grooming and signposting. The California side offers a progression from the relaxed cruising of the long Ridge Run, starting right at the top of the mountain, to more challenging blues dropping off the ridge towards the Sky Deck restaurant. The confident intermediate may want to spend more time on the Nevada side, where there is more variety of terrain, some longer runs down to the lift bases and more carving space.

FOR BEGINNERS
An excellent place to learn
The California side is more suited to beginners, with gentle green runs served by the Pioneer drag-lift and the Powderbowl chair-lift at the top of the cable-car. There are good nursery slopes at base lodge level.

FOR CROSS-COUNTRY
A separate world
The Spooner Lake Cross Country Area located close to Tahoe is an extensive meadow area of over 100km/60 miles in 21 prepared trails. There are ample facilities for both instruction and rental. Organised moonlit tours are a popular alternative to the noise and bright lights of the casinos.

QUEUES
Some at weekends
Lift lines are generally not a problem, except during some weekends and public holidays when the entire Tahoe area is swamped with weekenders and day-trippers. Thanks to the recent gondola, the key lifts moving people out from the base lodges are now under less pressure on busy days.

MOUNTAIN RESTAURANTS
Even refuelling is problematic
The on-mountain catering is inadequate, at least in bad weather. The only recommendable restaurant is the table-service Monument Peak at the top of the tram from California Lodge – simple food but a calm atmosphere and the famous lake view (reservations necessary). But last time we were there it was closed for a private function. The next-door cafeteria was bursting at the seams, so we had the privilege of sitting on the outdoor Sky Deck eating a burger being rapidly cooled by the blizzard. We were not pleased. In Nevada, East Peak Lodge has a terrace and barbie, but it too gets hideously overcrowded when the weather drives people indoors. There are plans, however, to build a new restaurant at the Sky Deck area.

boarding
Lake Tahoe is quickly becoming known as the snowboarding hub of North America and, as you would expect, boarders are very well catered for at Heavenly. The off-piste in trees and double-black-diamond bowls make a great playground for good free-riders. Beginners and intermediates will enjoy great cruising runs and the easy-to-ride chair-lifts. There are a couple of specialist shops in South Lake Tahoe. Learn some 'hot new moves' in Pipe and Park classes offered by the school.

SCHOOLS

Heavenly
775 586 7000 or
530 542 5143

Classes
Full (5hr) day $99
Private lessons
$149 for 2hr

GETTING THERE

Air San Francisco
275km/171 miles
(3½hr); Reno
89km/55 miles
(1¼hr); South Lake
Tahoe, 15 min.

Phone numbers
Different area codes
are used on the two
sides of the stateline.
For this chapter,
therefore, the area
code is included with
each number.

From distant parts of
the US, add the prefix
1. From abroad, add
the prefix +1.

ACTIVITIES

Indoor 6 casinos, 6
cinemas, cheap
factory shops, ice
skating, bowling,
gyms, spas, Western
museum

Outdoor Boat cruises,
snowmobiling, horse-
drawn sleigh rides,
horse riding, ice
skating, hot springs,
ghost town tours

TOURIST OFFICE

t 775 586 7000
info@skiheavenly.com
www.skiheavenly.com

SCHOOLS AND GUIDES
Good system
The Perfect Turn ski and ride
programmes build on your strengths
rather than focusing on your
weaknesses and are highly regarded.
Several speciality clinics are available.

FACILITIES FOR CHILDREN
Comprehensive
The Perfect Kids learning centre in the
California Base Lodge was recently
expanded by 30%. It attracted
particular praise from one reporter:
'This was an excellent facility – very
convenient and very professionally run.
I would thoroughly recommend it.'

STAYING THERE

HOW TO GO
Hotel or motel?
Accommodation in the South Lake
Tahoe area is abundant and ranges
from the glossy casinos to small, rather
ramshackle motels. Hotel and motel
rooms are easy to find midweek, but
can be sold out at busy weekends.
Chalets UK tour operators run some
good catered chalets, including some
lakeside ones.
Hotels Of the main casino hotels,
Harrah's (775 558 6611) and Harveys
(775 558 2411) are the closest to the
gondola. Rooms booked on the spot
are expensive; packages are cheaper.
((((④ **Embassy Suites** (530 544 5400)
Luxury suites in a modern, traditional-
style building close to the gondola.
((((④ **Marriott's Timber Lodge** (530 542
6600) Part of the new 'village'.
((② **Station House Inn** (530 542 1101)
'Very good, and well located, near the
gondola.'
((② **Tahoe Chalet Inn** (530 544 3311)
Clean, friendly, near casinos. Back
rooms (away from highway) preferable.
((② **Timber Cove Lodge** (530 541 6722)
Bland but well run, with lake views
from some rooms.
Self-catering Plenty of choice. Some
are available from tour operators.
We've had a rave report about The
Ridge Tahoe condos near Stagecoach
Lodge: 'Luxury accommodation. The
bathroom was big enough for
waltzing.' There's an indoor-outdoor
pool, hot-tub and a private gondola to
whisk you to the slopes.

EATING OUT
Good value
The casino hotels' all-you-can-eat
buffets offer fantastic value. They have
some more ambitious 'gourmet'
restaurants too – some high enough to
give superb views (try Harrah's 18th
floor). The sprawling resort area offers
a great choice of international dining,
from cosy little pizza houses to large,
traditional American diners, Mexican
tequila-and-tacos joints, and English
and Irish pubs. Visitors' suggestions
include Fresh Ketch at Tahoe Keys
Marina for 'wonderful fresh fish and
harbour views – though don't expect
snazzy presentation'. The Riva Grill is
also recommended. The new 'village'
also has a selection of dining options.

APRES-SKI
Extraordinary
The casinos on the Nevada side of the
stateline aren't simply opportunities to
throw money away on roulette or slot
machines: top-name entertainers, pop
and jazz stars, circus acts and
Broadway revues are also to be found
in them – designed to give gamblers
another reason to stay. You can dance
and dine your way across the lake
aboard an authentic paddle steamer.

OFF THE SLOPES
Luck be a lady
If gambling is your weakness, you're in
luck. Or then again, perhaps not. If you
want to get away from the bright
lights, try a boat trip on Lake Tahoe,
snowmobiling a short drive from South
Lake Tahoe, or a hot-air balloon ride.
    Pedestrians can use the cable-car or
the gondola to share the lake views
and families might enjoy the Adventure
Park (also at the top of the gondola).

Heavenly

505

Lake Tahoe

A resort a day for a week or even a fortnight – and fine lake views

COSTS

①②③④⑤ ⑥

NEWS

Sierra and Northstar
New on–mountain facilities at West Bowl (Sierra) opened for 2002/03.

2003/04 will see a new Telemark and Backcountry Centre at Sierra.

The terrain-park at Northstar will move to Logger's Loop. There will be guided off-piste skiing/ boarding on offer at both Sierra and Northstar, and various new learning and children's programmes.

Squaw Valley
Phase 2 of the new base village will open for 2003/04. The Olympic Ice Pavilion is being upgraded and there will be further improvements to the terrain-parks.

Mount Rose
Plans include a new six- or eight-person lift to replace the Zephyr quad, and the official opening of some expert terrain in the Fast Bowl – hopefully by 2004/05.

Spectacularly set high in the Sierra Nevada 320km/200 miles east of San Francisco, Lake Tahoe is ringed by skiable mountains containing 14 downhill and 7 cross-country centres – the highest concentration of winter sports resorts in the US. One or two of the resorts may have the extent and variety of slopes to keep you amused for a week, but the real appeal of this area is that from a single base you can easily visit several resorts, spending a day or two at each.

Two resorts stand out from the herd, at least in terms of size. Heavenly (covered in detail in the previous chapter) is the biggest in the area, and has at the foot of its slopes much the biggest development – the bizarre gambling-based town of South Lake Tahoe. It makes an obvious base for visiting a range of resorts both south and north of the lake. Squaw Valley, the biggest north-shore resort, comes a close second to Heavenly in terms of area, but is only now developing a wide choice of accommodation.

In this chapter are brief descriptions of Squaw and four other resorts – all appreciably smaller than Heavenly and Squaw, but all offering a worthwhile 2,000 to 2,500 acres of terrain. At the end of the chapter are very brief pointers to a couple of other resorts worth visiting. Most of the resorts mainly attract weekend visitors from the cities of California's coastal area. Peak weekends apart, the slopes are uncrowded, and queues are rare.

Most of the minor resorts are not fully formed 'destination' resorts of the kind that you find in Colorado or the Alps. A few have no nearby accommodation at all; but there are lots of B&Bs and motels scattered around the lake, and a couple of quite pleasant small towns. The obvious alternative to staying in South Lake Tahoe is the small tourist town of Tahoe City, on the lake's north shore. It has a range of touristy shops and some good restaurants and bars. Our regular Tahoe reporter suggests Incline Village at the north-east corner of the lake (handy for Diamond Peak and Mount Rose) for its 'country charm and ambience, and friendly people'.

The area has a generally impressive snowfall record, particularly in recent years. We enjoyed superb conditions during a recent mid–March visit, despite dodgy February conditions. There is also a lot of snowmaking.

SQUAW VALLEY

The major resort at the north end of the lake, with 4,000 acres of open and lightly wooded bowls on six linked peaks. It's about an hour's drive from South Lake Tahoe. The small base village has undergone major development by Intrawest, with further expansion planned.

There are daily shuttle buses to Squaw from South Lake Tahoe, and you can go by boat (see Heavenly chapter).

The possibilities for experts here are phenomenal, with lots of steep slopes, chutes and big mogul fields – many extreme skiing and boarding movies are made here. But it is also good for

Map

Tahoe Donner

To SACRAMENTO & SAN FRANCISCO

To RENO

TRUCKEE

Truckee River

Mount Rose

Sugar Bowl

Truckee/Tahoe Airport

Northstar at-Tahoe

Diamond Peak

Donner Ski Ranch

INCLINE VILLAGE

Squaw Valley

Tahoe Nordic Centre

TAHOE CITY

STATELINE

Marlette Lake

Alpine Meadows

Tahoe Queen Shuttle

LAKE TAHOE 1890m

Spooner Lake

Granlibakken

CALIFORNIA

NEVADA

Homewood

Daggett Pass 2235m

Emerald Bay

SOUTH LAKE TAHOE

Heavenly

5km / 3 miles

Fallen Leaf Lake

Upper Truckee

Twin Bridges Echo Summit 2250m

Meyers

Luther Pass 2340m

Grover Hot Springs State Park

Sierra-at-Tahoe

To SACRAMENTO Kirkwood

Carson Pass 2615m

Hope Valley

There is some genuinely steep stuff served by Squaw's Silverado chair, with plenty of opportunity to do yourself serious injury ➔

KEY FACTS

Alpine Meadows

Slopes	2085-2630m	
	6,840-8,640ft	
Lifts		12
Pistes	2,000 acres	
Green		25%
Blue		40%
Black		35%
Snowmaking		
		220 acres

Kirkwood

Slopes	2375-2985m	
	7,800-9,800ft	
Lifts		12
Pistes	2,300 acres	
Green		15%
Blue		50%
Black		35%
Snowmaking	55 acres	

Northstar-at-Tahoe

Slopes	1930-2625m	
	6,330-8,610ft	
Lifts		17
Pistes	2,420 acres	
Green		25%
Blue		50%
Black		25%
Snowmaking		
		220 acres

Sierra-at-Tahoe

Slopes	2025-2700m	
	6,640-8,850ft	
Lifts		10
Pistes	2,000 acres	
Green		25%
Blue		50%
Black		25%

Squaw Valley

Slopes	1890-2760m	
	6,200-9,050ft	
Lifts		33
Pistes	4,000 acres	
Green		25%
Blue		45%
Black		30%
Snowmaking		
		360 acres

intermediates, with lovely long groomed runs including a top-to-bottom three-mile cruise. And there's a superb beginner area at altitude.

Until recently, Squaw has had very little accommodation at the base. The main options were Squaw Valley Lodge and the self-contained, luxurious conference-oriented Resort at Squaw Creek, linked into one end of the lift network by its own chair-lift.

But a new resort village is being developed by Intrawest, owners of Whistler and several other pace-setting resorts. Phase 1 of this pedestrian village opened recently, with the next phase scheduled to open for 2003/4.

The peaks and high bowls of the area are treeless, but much of the terrain is lightly wooded – a very attractive compromise between the usual US wooded terrain and the open Alpine style of terrain. The average snowfall is an impressive 450 inches.

Squaw is unusual in having no trails marked on its piste map. Instead it has lifts classified green, blue and black. Like all such wacky ideas, it doesn't actually work as well as a conventional system for a newcomer to the resort. In some sectors, those who are adventurous but not truly expert could find themselves in real difficulty.

There are two impressively powerful lifts out of the village – a twin-cable jumbo Funitel gondola (as in Verbier and Val-Thorens) and a big cable-car (called, unusually for the US, the Cable Car). Both rise 600m/2,000ft to the twin mid-mountain stations of Gold Coast and High Camp. Above these two points (linked by a pulse gondola) is a gentle area of snow-sure beginner slopes, served by several slow chairs.

The peak beyond Gold Coast and High Camp is Emigrant, with fast chairs serving great vertical on both flanks serving great blue cruises and gentle off-piste – an excellent intermediate area. Beyond this is Granite Chief, with a slow triple chair serving a very varied valley with some seriously steep stuff but also easy black slopes. You can get into some of this from the top of Emigrant, too. From the top of the Granite Chief chair people hike up to the steepest slopes on the peak.

From High Camp or the lower peak of Broken Arrow you can descend into a steep-sided valley from which the Silverado chair is the return. For access there is a system of gates – all but two 'For Experts Only'. There are signs

saying that falls in this area can result in long slides and serious injury. What they mean is death; we wouldn't touch these expert slopes without a guide.

The high point of the whole Squaw area is Squaw Peak, served by a slow double chair, the Siberia fast quad and the Headwall six-pack, which lifts you 460m/1,500ft – a modest figure, but one of the biggest verticals on the upper mountain. The high slopes either side of Siberia are broad, not too steep, open off-piste slopes of the kind you so often find in the Alps. The Headwall lift mainly serves the front of the mountain which offers a range of steepness from black to very black.

There are two peaks accessed directly from the village. The fast quad to KT22 gives a quick 550m/1,800ft vertical. Down the front, there are countless steep routes, for which guidance would be prudent at first.

Snow King, at the extreme of the area and reached by the slow Red Dog chair, shouldn't be neglected. Not only are there some excellent cruises – particularly the one down to the Resort at Squaw Creek – but there is also lots of advanced/expert terrain to explore.

You can eat at either of the mid-mountain areas. Avoid Gold Coast's Food Court – a dreary place serving rubbish fast food slowly.

Squaw is a big snowboarding centre and at night a terrain-park and half-pipe are floodlit, along with a run (for skiers too) down from mid-mountain.

Squaw's cable-car runs in the evenings to serve the floodlit slopes and the dining facilities at High Camp. This is an incredible mid-mountain complex, with several restaurants and bars, outdoor pool, ice skating, tennis, bungee jumping and recently improved snowtubing area.

ALPINE MEADOWS
Squaw's next-door neighbour has similar, lightly wooded terrain, with runs of all classifications and an impressive snow record, but a modest total vertical of 550m/1,800ft. There's nothing but a day lodge at the base.
The base is surrounded by excellent beginner slopes with a variety of slow lifts. The major mountain access lifts are a fast quad going half-way up the broad bowl under Ward Peak, and a six-pack to the top of it; this accesses a wide range of black runs (single and double diamond) at the top of the bowl, some of them involving long traverses, but there are also blue runs down to the generally blue terrain lower down the bowl. There is also a double chair on the upper slopes.

Separated from Ward Peak by a low saddle is Scott Peak; a double chair goes up over the steep black slopes on the front, and on the back pleasant blue runs are served by a triple. A second triple serves part of the open slopes on the back of Ward Peak, with steeper areas accessed by the Alpine Bowl chair on the front of the hill.

With an top-notch average snowfall of 495 inches, Alpine Meadows is known for its long season and excellent spring snow – but when it closes depends on ticket sales.

As well as the 'uninspiring' self-service and table-service options at the base, there is a little Chalet on the hill – self-service, but pleasantly woody. There's a terrain-park, a half-pipe and a new super-pipe just above the base.

NORTHSTAR AT TAHOE
Northstar, a few miles from Squaw, is a classic US-style mountain with runs cut through dense forest – mainly blue and single diamond black. With a gondola and five fast chairs, the lift system is slicker than at other minor resorts in the area. It has a tiny car-free 'village' at the base, and is locally regarded as a friendly, well-run resort – a good bet for families.
The whole area is very sheltered and good for bad-weather days. It enjoys long views in various directions.

A short gondola goes up to a mid-mountain lodge at Big Springs, only 160m/525ft above the village. From this point two fast chairs and one slow one radiate to serve a broad bowl with some short steep pitches at the top, with easier blue runs lower down and around the ridges at either extremity – the latter giving excellent runs to the village of almost 700m/2,300ft vertical.

On the back-side of the mountain is a second, steeper bowl with a central fast quad chair rising 575m/1,885ft; on either side of it are three or four runs that are at the easy end of the black spectrum (especially when groomed).

A fast quad serves the most recently opened area – another four black runs with a modest vertical of 390m/1,280ft in a smaller bowl beneath a subsidiary peak called Lookout Mountain, reached by a short tope tow. This is what you see if you approach Northstar by driving south from Truckee; the runs look seriously steep, and the two close to the chair are. The two outer runs are less so (and were groomed when we visited) but are still genuine blacks.

You can eat on the hill. The grand-sounding Summit Grille is a self-service affair in a small woody chalet, with a sun terrace. The several options at Big Springs include a Tex-Mex restaurant.

The small 'village' at the base is a pleasant car-free affair consisting of two stages of development in unrelated styles – one angular and wooden, the other more traditional. Both have apartments and hotel-style rooms (though no recognisable hotel) over shops, a couple of restaurants and a couple of bars. The gondola station is at one end of the village, a short walk from the highly organised drop-off zone and the premium ($15 a day) parking lot – free parking is a bit further away, served by buses. There is also an area of small condo units a little way down the access road.

Phone numbers
From distant parts of the US, add the prefix 1. From abroad, add the prefix +1.

In this chapter area codes are included in the numbers given.

TOURIST OFFICES

Alpine Meadows
t 530 583 4232
info@skialpine.com
www.skialpine.com

Kirkwood
t 877 547 5966
kwd-info@
ski-kirkwood.com
www.kirkwood.com

Northstar-at-Tahoe
t 530 562 1010
northstar@
boothcreek.com
www.skinorthstar.com

Sierra-at-Tahoe
t 530 659 7453
sierra@boothcreek.
com
www.sierratahoe.com

Squaw Valley
t 530 583 6985
squaw@squaw.com
www.squaw.com

SIERRA-AT-TAHOE

Sierra is only a half-hour drive south-west of South Lake Tahoe, off Highway 50. It's a wooded area with a vertical of 675m/2,210ft, and nothing at the base but a day lodge and a car park.
Sierra claims an average of 480in of snow a year – almost a match for better-known Kirkwood. The slopes are spread over two flanks of Huckleberry Mountain, above the base lodge, and West Bowl, off to one side. Both sectors include a fast quad chair among their lifts. The front of the main area and West Bowl both offer good intermediate cruising plus some genuine single-diamond blacks. The back of the main hill has easier slopes.

There are five gates in the area boundary accessing backcountry terrain, and half-day tours guided by ski patrollers. There will shortly be a new Telemark and Backcountry Centre. There are terrain parks for skiers and boarders, and a 'super' half-pipe with huge 17-foot walls The trees provide shelter, so it's a good place to be in bad weather. But bear in mind that the road from SLT passes over the 2250m/7,380 ft Echo Summit, which may require chains. In addition to the day lodge at the base, there's a restaurant at the top of the hill and a BBQ at West Bowl.

KIRKWOOD

Kirkwood is renowned for its powder, and has a lot to offer experts and confident intermediates. It is only a little way south of Sierra, but is twice as far away from South Lake Tahoe. The small base village includes a growing range of condos.
Kirkwood is reached from SLT over the 2360m/ 7,740ft Luther Pass and the 2615m/ 8,575ft Carson Pass. Heavy snowfall often closes the road. There is a daily shuttle bus from SLT, arriving at Kirkwood at 9.30 – reservations needed; the round trip costs only $5.

Kirkwood claims an annual average snowfall of over 500 inches, which puts it right in the first rank, alongside Utah's Alta and Snowbird.

The resort sits at the centre of a semicircle of slopes – lightly wooded at the top, more densely at the bottom. The lift system consists almost entirely of slow chair-lifts radiating from the main base area. One goes up to the top of the main bowl above the base, as does the resort's one fast quad. These two long lifts also give

access to bowls to left and right of the main one. All three bowls have single black slopes at the top, and the main one has a row of seriously steep double diamond chutes. All of these blacks merge with blue runs lower down, served by their own shorter chairs. The two outer bowls also have green runs; the right-hand one is the main beginner area, with the separate Timber Creek day lodge and children's centre at the base.

Over the back of the left-hand bowl is a lightly wooded mountainside of blue/black gradient served by two more chairs, one of them the very long (and slow) Sunrise. This gives access to a range of fairly adventurous ways back to the front of the mountain – mostly double black diamonds but including one splendid easy single diamond.

What all this adds up to is that Kirkwood is an excellent resort for experts and adventurous intermediates, and fine for beginners, but rather limited for less confident intermediates who are not happy to tackle black runs. For them, the Sunrise lift is much the best bet. Deep snow is part of the attraction, but many of the blacks get groomed.

A small 'village' with ski-in, ski-out apartment accommodation is taking shape at the base, with more to open for 2003/4. There are several bars and restaurants. Bub's, Off the Wall and Kirkwood Inn serve 'good, but not great, lunches and dinners'. There is a recreation centre with outdoor heated pool, spa and sun deck. There is an ice rink on the edge of the village plaza, also snowskating and tubing. Après-ski is very limited.

OTHER RESORTS

There are eight other resorts you might visit in the Lake Tahoe region – most are marked on our map. Much the most impressive on paper – and said by a widely experienced local reporter to be a place 'for serious skiers' – is **Sugarbowl** (460m/1,500ft vertical, lifts include four fast quads). But a regular visitor to the region also recommends **Diamond Peak** (vertical 560m/1,840ft, six chairs) for its 'breathtaking views and fab restaurant' and the relatively high **Mount Rose** (440m/1,440ft vertical, seven lifts including a six-pack) for its 'great snow always and carving runs' – and both for its quiet slopes.

COSTS

① ② ③ ④ ⑤ ⑥

RATINGS

The slopes

Snow	★★★★
Extent	★★★
Expert	★★★★
Intermediate	★★★★
Beginner	★★★★
Convenience	★★
Queues	★★★★
Mountain restaurants	★

The rest

Scenery	★★★
Resort charm	★★
Off-slope	★

NEWS

The huge Super-Duper half-pipe, with its 7m/22ft walls, was opened in 2002/03.

Phase 1 of the Village at Mammoth development, including a gondola up to Canyon Lodge, originally planned for completion last season, is now expected to open for the 2003/04 season.

510

➕ One of North America's bigger ski hills, with something for everyone

➕ Good mix of open Alpine-style bowls and classic American wooded slopes

➕ Combination of location and altitude means a good snowfall record

➕ Uncrowded slopes except on peak-season weekends

➕ Mightily impressive terrain parks

➕ Good views, including more Alpine drama than usual in the US

➖ Mammoth Lakes, though not unpleasant, is a rather straggling place with no focus, where life generally revolves around your car

➖ Most accommodation is miles from the slopes – though development is taking place at the lift bases

➖ Weekend crowds in high season

➖ Trail map and signing still poor

➖ Wind can close high lifts, and upper runs can be icy and windblown

Mammoth may not be giant in Alpine terms – from end to end, it is less than one-third of the size of Val-d'Isère/Tignes, in area more like one-sixth – but it is among the bigger resorts in the US, and big enough to amuse many people for a week. It can be a superb mountain for anyone who is happy in deep snow, but is equally suited to families and mixed-ability groups looking for groomed runs. The main thing it lacks is a real village at the base.

Enter Intrawest, owner of Whistler and now of various key plots of land (and the majority of development rights) here. Intrawest is investing heavily, planning to create 10,000 more guest beds over the next decade. It opened the first stage of a new slope-side development, Juniper Springs, a couple of years ago, and the first (quite limited) phase of a new pedestrian 'village' on the edge of the town of Mammoth Lakes is now expected to open for the start of the 2003 season.

For most visitors, though, we don't expect the 'village' to have a huge impact. Mammoth Lakes will essentially remain what it has always been: a resort that expects you to arrive by car, and get around by car.

THE RESORT

The mountain is set above Mammoth Lakes, a small year-round resort town that spreads over a wide area of woodland. The place is entirely geared to driving, with no discernible centre – hotels, restaurants and little shopping centres are scattered along the four-lane highway called Main Street and Old Mammoth Road which crosses it. The buildings are generally timber-clad in traditional style – even McDonald's has been tastefully designed – and are set among trees, so although it may be short on resort ambience, the place has a pleasant enough appearance – particularly when under snow.

The town meets the mountain at two lift bases, both a mile or two from most of the hotels and condos. The major base is Canyon Lodge, with a big day lodge and four chair-lifts; there are hotels, condos and individual

homes in the area below the lodge. Not far from here, Intrawest is building its new pedestrian 'village', which will be linked to Canyon Lodge by a gondola. The minor base, with a single six-pack lift, is Eagle Lodge (previously Little Eagle – also known as Juniper Springs, which strictly is the name of the recently built condos at the base).

A road runs along the north fringe of the mountain past an anonymous chair-lift base to two major base areas: The Mill Cafe, with two fast chairs, and Main Lodge, a mini-resort with three fast access lifts and a big day lodge. You can stay here, in the Mammoth Mountain Inn; but who wants to be based four miles from practically all of the resort's 50 restaurants?

Shuttle-buses run on several colour-coded routes serving the lift bases, but they are limited after 5.30 (and this year a reporter found them erratic in the mornings as well). A car is useful.

KEY FACTS

Resort	2425m
	7,950ft

Mammoth only	
Slopes	2425-3370m
	7,950-11,050ft
Lifts	27
Pistes	3,500 acres
Green	25%
Blue	40%
Black	35%
Snowmaking	
	477 acres

June Mountain only	
Slopes	2300-3090m
	7,550-10,140ft
Lifts	7
Pistes	500 acres
Green	35%
Blue	45%
Black	20%
Snowmaking	none

The Mammoth lift pass also covers June, a small mountain half an hour's drive north, chiefly attractive for its astonishingly people-free slopes. See feature box, later in this chapter.

The drive up from Los Angeles takes six hours (more in poor conditions); but it is not without interest. You pass through the Santa Monica mountains close to Beverly Hills, then the San Gabriel mountains and Mojave Desert (with the world's biggest jet-plane parking lot) before reaching the Sierra Nevada range.

There are plans to extend Mammoth Lakes' small airport to take jet flights.

THE MOUNTAIN

The 27 lifts access an impressive area suitable for all abilities. The highest runs are almost all steep bowls and chutes for experts. In general, the lower down you go, the easier the terrain.

Finding your way around is not easy at first. Many of the chair-lifts now have names, rather than numbers, but the trail map still shows trails by means of isolated symbols, not continuous lines, so it's difficult to see where a run starts and finishes. The signposting of runs on the mountain leaves a lot to be desired, too. On the lower part of the mountain this doesn't matter a lot: head downhill, and you'll come to a lift. But higher up there are real dangers, especially in poor visibility. The map uses a six-point trail difficulty scale, with intermediate green/blue and blue/black categories; rather pointless precision, when the poor signposting means that you often end up on entirely the wrong trail anyway.

THE SLOPES
Interesting variety

From **Main Lodge** the two-stage Panorama gondola goes via McCoy Station right to the top. The views are great, with Nevada to the north-east and the jagged Minarets to the west. From the top, there are essentially three ways down. The first, on which there are countless variations, is down the front of the mountain, which ranges from steep to very steep – or vertical if the wind has created a cornice, as it often does. The second is off the back, down to **Outpost 14**, whence chairs 14 or 13 bring you back to lower points on the ridge. The third is to follow the ridge, which eventually brings you down to the Main Lodge area. This route brings you past an easy area served by chair 12, and a very easy area served by the Discovery fast quad.

McCoy Station can also be reached using the Stump Alley fast chair from **The Mill Cafe**, on the road up from town. The fast Gold Rush quad from here takes you into the more heavily wooded eastern half of the area. This has long, gentle runs served by lifts up from **Canyon Lodge** and **Eagle Lodge** and seriously steep stuff as well as some intermediate terrain on the subsidiary peak known as Lincoln (un-named on the resort trail map) served by lifts 25 and 22.

TERRAIN-PARKS
Among the best

Mammoth initially set out to attract boarders to its sister mountain June, where there's a good terrain-park and half-pipe. But Mammoth itself now has

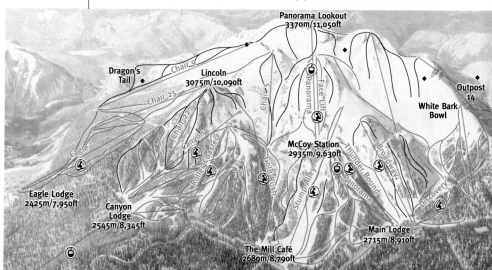

Panorama Lookout
3370m/11,050ft

Dragon's
Tail

Chair 9

Lincoln
3075m/10,090ft

Chair 25

Chair 5

Panorama

Face Lift

Outpost
14

White Bark
Bowl

Chair 22

Canyon

McCoy Station
2935m/9,630ft

Thunder Bound

Broadway

Eagle

Roller Coaster

Gold Rush

Stump Alley

Panorama

Discovery

Eagle Lodge
2425m/7,950ft

Canyon
Lodge
2545m/8,345ft

Main Lodge
2715m/8,910ft

The Mill Café
2680m/8,790ft

three impressive 'Unbound' terrain parks and half-pipes for different abilities – and in 2002/3 opened the astonishing Super-Duper pipe, 183m/600ft long and boasting 7m/22ft walls. With additional rails and boxes last season, 'Unbound' terrain now amounts to more than 60 acres.

SNOW RELIABILITY
A long season
Mammoth has an impressive snow record – an annual average of 385 inches, which puts it in the second rank, ahead of major Colorado resorts and about on a par with Jackson Hole (but a long way behind Alta and Snowbird). Mammoth is appreciably higher than other Californian resorts, and it has an ever-expanding array of snow-guns, so it enjoys a long season – staying open as late as 4 July in many years. But the upper mountain can get icy and windswept. One reporter complains of 'extreme skiing conditions', with lifts remaining open in surprisingly strong winds. The mountain faces roughly north; the relatively low and slightly sunny slopes down to Eagle Lodge are affected by warm weather before those down to the other bases.

FOR EXPERTS
Some very challenging terrain
The steep bowls that run the width of the mountain top provide wonderful opportunities for experts. There are one or two single-diamond slopes, but runs such as Hangman's Hollow and Wipe-Out Chutes are emphatically double-diamond affairs requiring a lot of bottle. The snow up here can suffer from high winds and it can be difficult to find your way – marking is virtually non-existent.

There is lots of challenging terrain lower down, too; Chair 5, Chair 22 and Broadway are often open in bad weather when the top is firmly shut, and their more sheltered slopes may in any case have the best snow. (The top of Chair 22 is higher than the very top of Heavenly, remember.) There are

plenty of good slopes over the back towards Outpost 14, too.

Many of the steeper trails are short by Alpine standards (typically under 400m/1,300ft vertical), but despite this we've enjoyed some great powder days here (with guidance).

FOR INTERMEDIATES
Lots of great cruising
Although there are exceptions, most of the lower mountain, below the tree-line, is intermediate cruising territory. What's more, Mammoth's piste maintenance is generally good, and many slopes that might become intimidatingly mogulled are kept easily skiable. 'Very flattering', says one recent visitor.

As you might hope, the six-point trail difficulty scale – which we haven't tried to replicate on our own small trail map – is a good guide to what you'll find on the mountain.

Some of the mountain's longest runs, blue-blacks served by chairs 9 and 25, are ideal for good intermediates. There are also some excellent, fairly steep, woodland trails down to The Mill Cafe.

Most of the long runs above Eagle Lodge, and some of the shorter ones above Canyon Lodge, are easy cruises. There is a variety of terrain, including lots of gentle stuff, at the western extremity of the slopes, both on the front side and on the back side, down to Outpost 14.

June mountain is great for a leisurely day out. Most of its runs are overclassified. Blues are easy cruisers, single blacks groomed and double blacks advanced rather than expert.

FOR BEGINNERS
Excellent
Chair 7 at Canyon Lodge and Discovery Chair at Main Lodge serve quiet, gentle green runs – so as soon as you're off the nursery slopes you can get an encouraging taste of real skiing. Excellent instruction, top-notch grooming and snow quality usually make progress speedy.

boarding

Mammoth's slopes are ideal for all abilities, with some excellent free-riding in the high bowls and perfect beginner and intermediate runs below. There's only one tiny drag-lift, and none of the flat linking runs that make some American resorts hard work to get around. Competent boarders will revel in the resort's extensive terrain parks (see above).

FOR CROSS-COUNTRY
Very popular
Two specialist centres, Tamarack and
Sierra Meadows (ungroomed), provide
lessons and tours. There are 70km/43
miles of trails in all, including
some through the pretty Lakes Basin area,
and lots of scenic ungroomed tracks.

QUEUES
Normally quiet slopes
During the week the lifts and slopes
are usually very quiet, with no queues;
'empty', 'deserted', say recent
reporters. But even the efficient lift
system can struggle when 15,000
visitors arrive from LA on fine peak-
season weekends. That's the time to
try the wonderfully uncrowded June
Mountain, half an hour away.

MOUNTAIN RESTAURANTS
Not a lot of choice
The only real mountain restaurants are
at mid-mountain McCoy Station. This
was stylishly revamped a couple of
years back and offers 'a good choice'
of roasts, Italian, Asian and other
dishes – but does get 'very busy'. The
Parallax table-service restaurant next
door does satisfying food and offers a
calm atmosphere and a splendid view.
The other on-mountain possibility in
good weather is the primitive outdoor
BBQ at Outpost 14.

Most people eat at the lift bases.
Talons at Eagle Lodge has its
supporters. The Mill Cafe is highly
recommended, as is the Mountain Side
Grill at Mammoth Mountain Inn. The
revamped Canyon Lodge offers
Mexican, Italian, Asian and more.

SCHOOLS AND GUIDES
Excellent reports
Past and recent reporters alike are
favourably impressed by the school,
which apparently contains growing

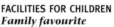

numbers of Scottish instructors. There
is of course the general American
problem that you're likely to get a
different instructor every day. There are
some special 'camps' for experts, and
for seniors and women.

FACILITIES FOR CHILDREN
Family favourite
Mammoth is keen to attract families.
The children's Woollywood school, now
based in the Panorama gondola
station, works closely with the nearby
Small World childcare centre. We've
had glowing reports; one reporter
noted the 'family feel of the resort'.
Another rated the facilities as 'second
to none'.

513

SCHOOLS
Mammoth Mountain
info@mammoth-
mtn.com

Classes
1 3hr morning $58
Private lessons
$120 for 1hr for 1 to
5 people

CHILDREN

Children's classes are
handled by
Woollywood, in the
Panorama gondola
building, and Canyon
Kids, based in Canyon
Lodge (one 6hr day
including lunch
US$90).

Small World Child
Care (934 0646),
based at Mammoth
Mountain Inn, takes
children from
newborn to age 12,
from 8am to 4.30.

JUNE MOUNTAIN: THE WORLD'S QUIETEST SLOPES?

*June Mountain, a scenic half-hour drive from Mammoth, is a small resort in the
same ownership and covered by the Mammoth lift pass. It makes a pleasant day
out, especially if Mammoth is busy. When Mammoth isn't busy, June is quite
incredibly quiet; when we visited on a March weekday morning we rode chair
after chair, skied run after run, without seeing another person.*

*A double chair goes up from the car park at 2290m/7,510ft over black slopes that
are often short of snow to the main lodge, June Meadows Chalet. From here, a
quad chair serves a gentle blue-run hill, and a double chair goes right over very
gentle green runs to the foot of a quad serving short but genuinely black slopes on
June Mountain itself (3100m/10,175ft). June is very sensibly going for the
freestyle market, with two terrain-parks and a super-pipe.*

Unbound Main, directly above Main Lodge, is one of several terrain features that are now an important part of Mammoth's appeal →

MAMMOTH MOUNTAIN

Air Los Angeles 494km/307 miles (5hr); Reno 270km/168 miles (3hr).

Indoor Mammoth museum, art galleries, theatre, mini golf

Outdoor Snowmobiling, ski touring, bob-sleigh, dog-sledding, ice climbing, mountain biking, ice skating, tobogganing, sleigh rides, hot air balloon rides, snow-shoe tour

Phone numbers From distant parts of the US, add the prefix 1 760. From abroad, add the prefix +1 760.

t 934 0745 woolly@mammoth-mtn.com www.mammoth mountain.com

STAYING THERE

HOW TO GO
Good value packages
A good choice of hotels (none very luxurious or expensive) and condos. The condos tend to be out of town, near the lifts or on the road to them.
《《《④ **Mammoth Mountain Inn** (934 2581) Way out of town at Main Lodge. Handy for the gondola, but dreary.
《《③ **Quality Inn** (934 5114) Good main street hotel with a big hot-tub.
《《③ **Alpenhof Lodge** (934 6330) Comfortable and friendly, in central location. Shuttle-bus stop and plenty of restaurants nearby.
《《③ **Austria Hof** (934 2764) Ski-out location near Canyon Lodge, recommended by a reporter despite modest-sized rooms.
《《③ **Sierra Nevada Rodeway Inn** (934 2515) Central, good value, 'great spa'
《《③ **Holiday Inn** (924 1234) Central location, large, comfortable rooms and 'great restaurant'. Pool.
Self-catering The Juniper Springs Lodge is near lifts and town. Close to the Canyon Lodge base-station, the 1849 Condominiums are spacious and well equipped. The Mammoth Ski and Racquet Club, a 10-minute walk from the same lifts, is very comfortable. There is an 'excellent' supermarket in the Minaret Mall, with good discounts.

EATING OUT
Outstanding choice
Reporters continue to be impressed by the wide choice available – over 50 restaurants, scattered over a wide area, catering for most tastes and pockets. Start with a copy of the local menu guide, and book what you fancy. One reporting couple last year dined in 14 different restaurants. Meshing their findings with more recent reports, we offer the following guidance: Slocums Grill – very good meal in wood-panelled room; Angel's – popular, good-value diner; Matterhorn – excellent Swiss-style food, good service; Ocean Harvest – great atmosphere and wonderful fish; Nevados – best in town, excellent modern cooking; Charthouse – excellent seafood, varied meat dishes; Alpenrose – intimate chalet-style place, good food; Matsu – small, simple, with delicious Thai food; Old Mammoth Grill – traditional family diner, 'good bar'. Also recommended are Shogun for Japanese and Gomez's for Mexican. We've had excellent dinners at Skadi and Whiskey Creek, too.

APRES-SKI
Lively at weekends
The liveliest immediate après-ski spot is the Yodler, at the Main Lodge base – a chalet transported from Switzerland (so they say). Later on, things revolve around a handful of bars, which come to life at weekends. The Clocktower cellar is reported to be 'best in town – lively, friendly, good music, great choice of beers'. Whiskey Creek is the liveliest (and stays open latest); it has live bands at weekends, and Wild Wednesday discos. Slocums is popular with locals and 'ideal for an after-dinner drink'. Grumpy's is a sports bar (big-screen TVs). Two nightclubs are reported to be opening in the Village.

OFF THE SLOPES
Mainly sightseeing
The main diversion is sightseeing by car (preferably 4WD). The town of Bishop, 40 minutes' drive south, makes an amusing day out. Factory shopping is recommended for bargains.

Colorado

Colorado was the first US state to market its resorts internationally and is still the most popular American destination for UK visitors. And justifiably so: it has the most alluring combination of attractive resorts, slopes to suit all abilities and excellent, reliable snow – dry enough to justify its 'champagne powder' label. It also has direct flights (by British Airways) from London to Denver.

Colorado has amazingly dry snow. Even when the snow melts and refreezes, the moisture seems to be magically whisked away, leaving it in soft powdery condition. The snow is good even in times of unusual snow shortage; in December a few years ago, when very little snow had fallen so far that season, we had a great week cruising on man-made snow in Breckenridge and Keystone.

Colorado resorts vary enormously, both in the extent and variety of slopes and in the character of the villages. If you want cute, restored buildings from the mining boom days

of the late 1800s, try the dinky old towns of Telluride or Crested Butte (but beware: both these have separate, modern mountain villages too) or the much bigger Aspen (which also has its modern outpost at Snowmass).

Some resorts have easy access to others nearby (eg Breckenridge, Keystone and Copper Mountain). Others, such as Steamboat, Crested Butte and Telluride are rather isolated.

The two biggest Colorado resorts of Vail and Aspen both have substantial amounts of terrain suitable for every ability. And both have been developing their exciting ungroomed terrain in recent years – Vail has opened up Blue Sky Basin, while Aspen has extended its steep bowls at Aspen Highlands.

Colorado is a good area to do a road trip around. As well as linking several of the resorts we give full chapters to, there are entertaining smaller resorts to pop into for a day. These include: snow-sure Loveland, which you can see from the main I70 highway; Monarch, which has snowcat as well as lift-served slopes and is near Crested Butte; and Durango (used to be called Purgatory) and Silverton, both quite near Telluride. Silverton has super-steep, ungroomed runs which were served by a lift for the first time for the 2001/02 season; only 40 people a day in guided groups for $99 each – you need an avalanche transceiver, a probe and a shovel.

Aspen/Snowmass

Don't be put off by its ritzy image – it's America's best resort

COSTS

① ② ③ ④ ⑤ ⑥

RATINGS

The slopes

Snow	★★★★★
Extent	★★★★
Expert	★★★★★
Intermediate	★★★★★
Beginner	★★★★★
Convenience	★★
Queues	★★★★
Mountain restaurants	★★★★

The rest

Scenery	★★★
Resort charm	★★★★
Off-slope	★★★★

NEWS

For 2003/04 the Ajax Express high-speed quad chair to the Sundeck restaurant (where a new table-service dining area is planned) at the top of Aspen Mountain will be replaced with a new state-of-the-art one. Snowmass's Campground two-person chair-lift will be replaced by a faster version.

A new ski patrol HQ on Aspen Highlands at the top of Loge Peak will have a picnic deck overlooking Highland Bowl.

For 2002/03 the steep, ungroomed but avalanche-controlled terrain in Highland Bowl was increased by almost 50%. And a free snowcat service was introduced to save the hike to the start of the Bowl.

The terrain-park at Snowmass – now called the Snowmass Pipeline – doubled in size and is now 2.5km/1.5 miles long.

➕ Endless slopes to suit all abilities, with a vertical drop at Snowmass of 1340m/4,400ft – biggest in the US

➕ Notably uncrowded slopes, even by American standards

➕ Attractive, characterful, old mining town, with lots of smart shops

➕ Lively, varied nightlife

➕ Great range of restaurants, both in the town and on the slopes

➖ Four mountains are widely separated (though there's efficient, free transport between them)

➖ Some accommodation in Aspen town is a long walk or a bus-ride from the local lifts

➖ Expensive

Aspen is our favourite American resort. We reached that view five editions back, and subsequent visits by both editors have simply confirmed it. And readers who have reported on it all love it too. You have to catch (efficient and free) buses to different areas and it is expensive, but those are the only serious drawbacks. The extent and variety of slopes are unparalleled in the USA. The town is authentic modernised Wild West. The restaurants are tremendous. If you're thinking America, put Aspen at the top of your shortlist.

Worried by the film-star image? Forget it. Yes, the resort has many rich and famous guests, with their private jets parked at the local airport, and for connoisseurs of cosmetic surgery it can be a fascinating place. But most celebs are keen to keep a low profile and, like all other 'glamorous' ski resorts, Aspen is actually filled by ordinary holidaymakers.

THE RESORT

In 1892 Aspen was a booming silver-mining town, source of one-sixth of the USA's silver, with 12,000 inhabitants, six newspapers, an opera house and a red-light district. But Aspen's fortunes took a nose-dive when the silver price plummeted in 1893, and by the 1930s the population had shrunk to 700 or so and handsome Victorian buildings – such as the Hotel Jerome – had fallen into disrepair.

Development of the skiing started on a small scale in the late 1930s. The first lift was opened shortly after the Second World War, and Aspen hasn't looked back since. Now, the historic centre – with a typical American grid of streets – has been beautifully renovated to form the core of the most fashionable ski town in the Rockies. There's a huge variety of shops, bars, restaurants and galleries – some amazingly upmarket. Spreading out from this centre, you'll find a mixture of developments, ranging from the homes of the super-rich to the mobile homes for the workers. Though the town is busy with traffic, pedestrians

seem to have priority in much of the central area.

Twelve miles away is Snowmass, with its own mountain and modern accommodation right on the slopes – and set for a big expansion over the next few years. Aspen Highlands now has limited accommodation, too.

Aspen town is the liveliest place to stay, and near the gondola is the most convenient location. Buses for the other areas also leave from nearby. 95% of Snowmass properties offer ski-in/ski-out convenience, and buses from Aspen run until 1am or later.

↓ Aspen Mountain

KEY FACTS

Resort	2425m
	7,950ft
Slopes	2405-3815m
	7,890-12,510ft
Lifts	37
Pistes	4,900 acres
Green	10%
Blue	48%
Black	42%
Snowmaking	
	608 acres

Snowmass	
Slopes	2470-3815m
	8,100-12,510ft
Lifts	21
Pistes	3,010 acres
Green	7%
Blue	55%
Black	38%
Snowmaking	
	180 acres

Aspen Mountain	
Slopes	2425-3415m
	7,950-11,210ft
Lifts	8
Pistes	673 acres
Green	0%
Blue	48%
Black	52%
Snowmaking	
	210 acres

Aspen Highlands	
Slopes	2450-3560m
	8,040-11,680ft
Lifts	4
Pistes	790 acres
Green	18%
Blue	30%
Black	52%
Snowmaking	
	110 acres

Buttermilk	
Slopes	2405-3015m
	7,890-9,900ft
Lifts	7
Pistes	427 acres
Green	35%
Blue	39%
Black	26%
Snowmaking	
	108 acres

ASPEN SKIING COMPANY /
KEN MISSBRENNER

Highland Bowl has wonderful steep, ungroomed runs that are avalanche controlled and patrolled; it's one of our favourite areas in Aspen →

GET THE BEST OF THE SNOW, ON- AND OFF-PISTE

Aspen offers special experiences for small numbers of skiers or riders.

Fresh Tracks *The first eight skiers to sign up each day get to ride the gondola up Aspen Mountain at 8am the next morning, and to get first tracks on perfect corduroy or fresh powder. Free!*

Off-piste Tours *Backcountry guides lead expert skiers and riders around the famous expert terrain of Snowmass (eg Hanging Valley) on Wednesdays and Highlands (eg Steeplechase and Highland Bowl) on Fridays. 10am–3pm, $109.*

Powder Tours *Spend the day exploring the backcountry beyond Aspen Mountain, with a 10-passenger heated snowcat as your personal lift. Away from the lifts and other people, your two guides search out untracked snow – there's 1,500 acres to choose from. You're likely to squeeze in about 10 runs in all. At midday, you break for lunch at an old mountain cabin. Full day, $275.*

THE MOUNTAINS

Aspen has lots for every ability; you just have to pick the right mountain. All of them have regular free guided tours, given by excellent amateur ambassadors, and other guest services on the slopes such as free sunscreen, drinks and biscuits. The ratio of acres to visitor beds is high, and the slopes are usually blissfully uncrowded.

THE SLOPES
Widely dispersed

There are four mountains, only one accessible directly from Aspen town. Each is big enough to keep you amused for a full day or more, but Snowmass is in a league of its own – almost five miles across, with over 60% of Aspen's total skiable acreage and the biggest vertical in the US.

Getting around between the areas by free bus is easy, and for $5 you can have your equipment ferried from one mountain to another overnight.

The Silver Queen gondola takes you from the edge of town to the top of **Aspen Mountain** in 14 minutes. A series of chairs serves the different ridges – Gentleman's Ridge along the eastern edge, the Bell in the centre, and Ruthie's to the west – with gulches in between. In general, there are long cruising blue runs along the valley floors and short steep blacks down from the ridges. There are no greens.

Snowmass is a separate resort some 12 miles west of Aspen town, opened in 1967. Chair-lifts fan out from the purpose-built village at the base towards four linked sectors – Elk Camp, High Alpine, Big Burn and Sam's Knob. You can also access the mountain via the Two Creeks lift base, which is much nearer to Aspen town,

and has free slope-side parking. Many of the Snowmass runs are wide, sweeping cruisers. But it also has some of the toughest terrain.

Buttermilk is the least challenging mountain. The runs fan out from the top in three directions. The West Buttermilk and Main Buttermilk areas are almost all gentle; Tiehack, to the east, is a bit more demanding – ideal for an intermediate keen to progress.

Aspen Highlands was bought by the Aspen Skiing Company 10 years ago and a network of slow lifts has been replaced by three fast quad chairs. Broadly, the mountain consists of a single ridge, with easy and intermediate

Aspen/Snowmass

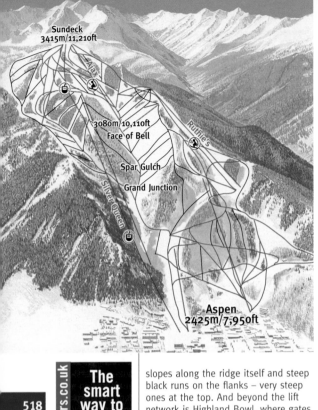

Sundeck
3415m/11,210ft

Ajax

3080m/10,11oft
Face of Bell

Ruthie's

Spar Gulch

Grand Junction

Silver Queen

Aspen
2425m/7,95oft

slopes along the ridge itself and steep black runs on the flanks – very steep ones at the top. And beyond the lift network is Highland Bowl, where gates give access to a splendid open bowl of entirely double-black gradient. The views from the upper part of Highlands are the best that Aspen has to offer – the famous Maroon Bells that appear on countless postcards. There is a base lodge with underground parking and a Ritz-Carlton aparthotel.

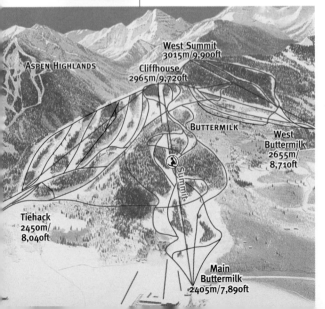

ASPEN HIGHLANDS

West Summit
3015m/9,900ft

Cliffhouse
2965m/9,720ft

BUTTERMILK

West Buttermilk
2655m/8,710ft

Summit

Tiehack
2450m/8,04oft

Main Buttermilk
2405m/7,89oft

TERRAIN-PARKS
Some of the world's best
Buttermilk has a 3km/2 mile long terrain-park with a beginner and intermediate area, 30 rails and 25 jumps, a boarder-cross course and a 100m/330ft long super-pipe. The park was home to the 2002 and 2003 ESPN Winter X games and now incorporates a permanent X Games slope-style course. The newly named Snowmass Pipeline terrain-park doubled in length last season to 2.5km/1.5 miles and incorporates a 90m/300ft long half-pipe. Snowmass also has a terrain-park for beginners and a mini-park for kids.

SNOW RELIABILITY
Rarely a problem
Aspen's mountains get an annual average of 300 inches of snow – not in the front rank, but not far behind. In addition, all areas have substantial snowmaking. Immaculate grooming adds to the quality of the pistes.

FOR EXPERTS
Buttermilk is the only soft stuff
There's plenty to choose from – all the mountains except Buttermilk offer lots of challenges. Consider joining a guided group as an introduction to the best of Snowmass or Highlands.

Aspen Mountain has a formidable array of double-black-diamond runs. From the top of the gondola, Walsh's, Hyrup's and Kristi are on a lightly wooded slope and link up with Gentleman's Ridge and Jackpot to form the longest black run on the mountain. A series of steep glades drops down from Gentleman's Ridge. The central Bell ridge has less extreme single-diamonds on both its flanks. On the opposite side of Spar Gulch is another row of double-blacks collectively called the Dumps, because waste was dumped here in the silver-mining days.

At Snowmass, our favourite area is around the Hanging Valley Wall and Glades – beautiful scenery and wonderful tree-covered slopes, and steep enough everywhere to satisfy the keenest – well worth the short hike. The other seriously steep area is the Cirque. The Cirque drag-lift takes you well above the tree line to Aspen's highest point. From here, the Headwall is not terrifyingly steep, but there are also narrow, often rocky, chutes – Gowdy's is one of the steepest in the whole area. All these runs funnel into a pretty, lightly wooded valley.

LIFT PASSES

Four Mountain Pass
Covers Aspen Mountain, Aspen Highlands, Buttermilk and Snowmass, and shuttle-bus between the areas.

Beginners
Included in price of beginners' lessons.

Main pass
1-day pass $68
6-day pass $384

Senior citizens
Over 65: 6-day pass $366
Over 70: Unlimited period $149

Children
Under 18: 6-day pass $306
Under 13: $246
Under 7: free pass

Notes
Savings on lift passes for 4 days or more if you purchase them more than 7 days in advance or through certain tour operators.

At Highlands there are challenging runs from top to bottom of the mountain. Highland Bowl, beyond the top lift, is superb in the right conditions: a big open bowl with pitches from a serious 38° to a terrifying 48° – facts you can check in the very informative Highlands Extreme Skiing Guide leaflet. There are free snowcat rides from Loge Peak to the first access gate of Highland Bowl but if these are not operating, it's a 20-minute hike. Almost 50% more terrain opened here for 2002/03. Within the lift system, the Steeplechase area consists of a number of parallel natural avalanche chutes, and their elevation means the snow stays light and dry. The Olympic Bowl area on the opposite flank of the mountain has great views of the Maroon Bells peaks and some serious moguls. The Thunderbowl chair from the base serves a nice varied area that's often underused.

FOR INTERMEDIATES
Grooming to die for
Snowmass is the best mountain for intermediates. The Big Burn is a cruising paradise. It's a huge lightly wooded area where the runs merge into each other, though there's a satisfying variety of terrain – including the tempting Powerline Glades for the adventurous. The easiest intermediate slopes are reached from the Elk Camp lift. There's a choice of runs from the top, through spruce trees, and long runs all the way down to Two Creeks. Long Shot is a glorious, ungroomed,

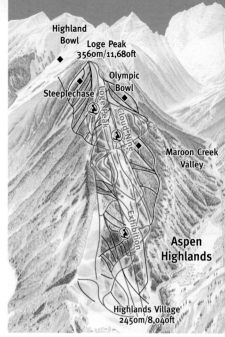

5km/3 mile run, lost in the forest, and well worth the short hike up to get to the start. In the centre of the area, the two chair-lifts below High Alpine serve yet more intermediate slopes – a little trickier and more varied. The Sam's Knob sector offers slightly more advanced challenges, including some regularly groomed single-black runs. Finally, Green Cabin, at the top of the High Alpine lift, is a magical intermediate run cruising from top to bottom of the mountain, with spectacular views.

519

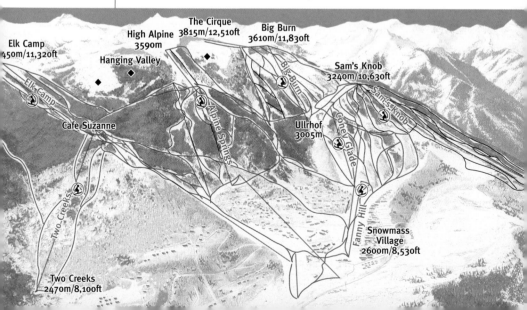

Snowmass has excellent cruising runs and convenient slope-side accommodation – good for families ↗

ASPEN/SNOWMASS PHOTO LIBRARY

COLORADO

SCHOOLS

Aspen Skiing Company
t 923 1227
breakthrough@
aspensnowmass.com

Classes
Full day (5hr) $105
(beginners $115 inc lift pass and equipment hire)

Private lessons
$329 for half day (3hr) for up to 5 people

Most intermediate runs on Highlands are concentrated above the mid-mountain Merry-Go-Round restaurant, many served by the Cloud Nine fast quad chair. But there are good slopes higher up and lower down – don't miss the vast, neglected expanses of Golden Horn, on the eastern limit of the area.

Aspen Mountain has its fair share of intermediate slopes, but they tend to be tougher than on the other mountains. Copper Bowl and Spar Gulch, running between the ridges, are great cruises early in the morning but can get crowded later. Upper Aspen Mountain, at the top of the gondola, has a dense network of well-groomed blues. The unusual Ruthie's chair – a fast double, apparently installed to rekindle the romance that quads have destroyed – serves more cruising runs and the popular Snow Bowl, a wide, open area with moguls on the left but groomed on the right and centre.

The Main Buttermilk runs offer good, easy slopes to practise on. And good intermediates should be able to handle the relatively easy black runs.

FOR BEGINNERS
Can be a great place to learn
Buttermilk is a great mountain for beginners. West Buttermilk has beautifully groomed, gentle runs. The easiest slopes of all, though, are at the base of the Main Buttermilk sector – on Panda Hill. The easiest beginner slope at Snowmass is the wide Assay Hill, at the bottom of the Elk Camp area. Right next to Snowmass Village Mall is the Fanny Hill fast quad and beginners' run. Further up, from Sam's Knob, there are long, gentle cruises.

Despite its macho image, Highlands boasts the highest concentration of green runs in Aspen.

FOR CROSS-COUNTRY
Backcountry bonanza
There are 80km/50 miles of groomed trails between Aspen and Snowmass in the Roaring Fork valley – the most extensive maintained cross-country system in the US. And the Ashcroft Ski Touring Centre maintains around 30km/19 miles of trails around Ashcroft, a mining ghost-town. The Pine Creek Cookhouse – excellent food and accessible by ski, snowshoe or horse-drawn sleigh only – burnt down last spring but is due to re-open for the 2003/04 season. Aspen is at one end of the famous Tenth Mountain Division Trail, heading 370km/230 miles north-east almost to Vail, with 13 huts for overnight stops.

QUEUES
Few problems
There are rarely major queues on any of the mountains. At Aspen Mountain, the gondola can have delays at peak times, but you have alternative lifts to the top. Snowmass has so many alternative lifts and runs that you can normally avoid any problems. But some long, slow chairs can be cold in

boarding

There is great snowboarding for every ability. The ban on snowboarding on Aspen Mountain was lifted from 1 April 2001. It bowed to pressure after becoming one of just five major areas in the world open to skiers only. All four mountains offer excellent boarding, with few flat sections and almost all lifts being chairs or gondolas. There are two world-class terrain-parks, and hosting the Winter X Games in 2002 and 2003 boosted Aspen's image as boarder-friendly.

CHILDREN

Ski school classes for children aged 7 to 12 cost US$340 for 5 days (5¼hr per day, lunch included).

The childcare possibilities for younger children are too numerous to list in detail.

There's a children's 'learning center' at Buttermilk with a special children's shuttle-bus from Aspen. The Powder Pandas classes there take children aged 3 to 6. Snowboarding classes are offered to 5 to 7 year olds. At Snowmass, the Big Burn Bears ski kindergarten takes children from age 3½, and children aged 8 weeks to 3½ have the Snow Cubs playschool. The Nighthawks programme looks after children aged 3 to 10 from 4pm to 11pm. Plus Grizzlies takes kids 5 to 6 years old and there are snowboarding classes for 5 to 7 year olds.

There are several all-day non-skiing nurseries.

mid-winter, and the home slope gets very crowded. Aspen Highlands is almost always queue-free, even at peak times. The two lifts out of Main Buttermilk sometimes get congested.

MOUNTAIN RESTAURANTS
Good by American standards

On Aspen Mountain the Sundeck at the top has quite a stylish self-service section with a good range of food. 'One of the best self-service mountain restaurants I've been to,' says one reporter. A new table-service area is planned for 2003/04. Sadly the swanky lunch club that shares the building is strictly for members. The mid-mountain restaurant Bonnies has a two-tier deck.

At Snowmass, Gordon's High Alpine is an elegant restaurant serving excellent food. The best views are from Sam's Knob, where there are self-service and table-service restaurants.

At Highlands the Cloud Nine 'Alpine bistro' is the nearest thing you will find in the States to a cosy Alpine mountain hut, with great views and excellent food – thanks to an Austrian chef. The Merry-Go-Round has the biggest terrace in the valley.

On Buttermilk the mountaintop Cliffhouse is known for its 'Mongolian Barbecue' stir-fry bar and great views.

SCHOOLS AND GUIDES
Simply the best?

There's a wide variety of specialised instruction – mountain exploration groups, off-piste tours, adrenaline sessions, women's groups, and so on. Reporters rave about the small group lessons ('they say average of three people, but we did five days and my wife had one-to-one the whole time'; 'the best class ever'; 'wonderful instruction'). The Wizard Ski Deck is an indoor ski and snowboard simulator used in combination with some classes or available for a private lesson.

FACILITIES FOR CHILDREN
Choice of nurseries

There is no shortage of advertised childcare arrangements. We have no recent first-hand reports, but reporters' observations were that, as usual in the US, all the kids were having the time of their lives. And past reports have always been first class. Young children based in Aspen town are taken from the gondola building each morning between 8.30 and 8.45 by the Max the Moose bus to Buttermilk's very impressive Fort Frog – a wooden frontier-style fort, with lookout towers, flags, old wagons, a jail, a saloon and a native American teepee village – and delivered back at 4pm. Snowmass has its own facilities. The Kids' Trail Map is a great way to get them used to finding their way around using maps.

STAYING THERE

HOW TO GO
Accommodation for all pockets

There's a mixture of hotels, inns, B&Bs, lodges and condos.

Chalets Several UK tour operators have chalets here – some very luxurious.

Hotels There are places for all budgets. (((((5 **St Regis** (920 3300) Opulent city-type hotel, near gondola. Fitness centre, outdoor pool, hot-tubs, sauna. (((((5 **Little Nell** (920 4600) Stylish, modern hotel right by the gondola with popular bar. Fireplaces in every room, outdoor pool, hot-tub, sauna. (((((5 **Jerome** (920 1000) Step back a century: Victorian authenticity combined with modern-day luxury. Several blocks from the gondola. ((((4 **Sardy House** (920 2525) Elegantly furnished, intimate little hotel 10 minutes from the gondola. Small outdoor pool, hot-tub. ((((4 **Lenado** (925 6246) Smart modern B&B place with open-fire lounge, individually designed rooms.

COLORADO

522

GETTING THERE

Air Aspen 5km/3 miles (a few minutes); Eagle 113km/70 miles (1½hr); Denver 355km/220 miles (4hr).

Rail Glenwood Springs (63km/40 miles).

ACTIVITIES

Indoor The Aspen Club and Spa (racquetball, swimming, free weights, aerobics classes, sauna, steam, hot-tubs), skating, museum

Outdoor Ballooning, paragliding, snowcat tours, snow-shoe tours, sleigh rides, dog sledding, snow tubing, snowmobiles, tours of mines, ice skating

Phone numbers
From distant parts of the US, add the prefix 1 970.
From abroad, add the prefix +1 970.

TOURIST OFFICE

t 925 1220
intlres@skiaspen.com
www.aspensnowmass.com

((((④ **Silvertree** (923 3520) Large slope-side hotel at Snowmass. Pools.

(((③ **Innsbruck Inn** (925 2980) Tirolean-style hotel, 10 minutes from lifts. Consistently liked by reporters.

(((③ **Stonebridge Inn** (923 2420) Good-value hotel close to Snowmass slopes; nice restaurant, pool, hot-tub.

(((③ **Hotel Aspen** (925 3441) Best 'moderate' place in town, 10 minutes from lifts; comfortable, pool, hot-tubs.

Self-catering The standards here are high, even in US terms. Many of the smarter developments have their own free shuttle-buses. The Gant is luxurious and close to the gondola. Chateau Roaring Fork and Eau Claire, four blocks from the gondola, are spacious and well-furnished. The Tamarack Townhouses, Terrace House and Top of the Village have all been highly recommended by reporters. A reader says the two small supermarkets are 'exceptionally well stocked'.

EATING OUT
Dining dilemma
As you'd expect, there are excellent upmarket places, but also plenty of cheaper options.

Piñons serves innovative American food. Syzygy is a suave upstairs place with live jazz from 10pm. Conundrum (modern American food, expensive) and Pacifica Seafood Brasserie are top-notch. L'Hostaria, The Mother Lode and Campo de Fiori are good Italians. Cache Cache does good-value Provençal. Ute City Bar & Grill is in an old bank and good for local game.

Cheaper recommendations include: Bentley's (main courses $8 upwards), Boogie's (a 50s-style diner, great for families), Main Street Bakery & Café, Mezzaluna, Red Onion, Hickory House, Steak Pit, the Skier's Chalet steak house and Woody Creek Tavern – apparently a favourite of gonzo journalist and Aspen resident, Hunter S

Thompson. At Snowmass, the choice is adequate. You can also take snowcat rides for dinner at Cloud Nine on Aspen Highlands some nights and to the Lynn Britt Cabin (with live bluegrass music).

APRES-SKI
Lots of options
As the lifts shut, a few bars at the bases get busy. At Snowmass, the slope-side Cirque has live bands most days. At Highlands the Commonwealth Pub gets packed. In Aspen the Ajax Tavern is popular. The Greenhouse bar at the Little Nell is a great place for gazing at fur coats, face-lifts and celebrities (Steven Spielberg was spotted by a 2003 reporter),

Many of the restaurants are also bars – Jimmy's (spectacular stock of tequila), Mezzaluna, Red Onion, and Ute City, for example. The J-bar of the Jerome hotel still has a traditional feel. Shooters Saloon is a splendid country-and-western dive with pool and line-dancing. For pool in more suave circumstances, there's Aspen Billiards adjoining the fashionable Cigar Bar, with its comfortable sofas (and smoking permitted!). The Double Diamond has live bands most nights (from 11pm). Popcorn Wagon is the place for munchies after the bars close. You can get a week's membership of the famous members-only Caribou club.

OFF THE SLOPES
Silver service
Aspen has lots to offer, especially if you've got a high credit card limit. There are literally dozens of galleries, as well as the predictable clothes and jewellery shops. Just wandering around town is pleasant. It's a shame that all the best mountain restaurants are awkward for pedestrians to get to. Most hotels have excellent spa facilities. There's tubing at Snowmass.

Beaver Creek

The Rolls Royce of resorts: very expensive but smooth and spacious

COSTS

① ② ③ ④ ⑤ ⑥

RATINGS

The slopes

Snow	*****
Extent	**
Expert	****
Intermediate	****
Beginner	*****
Convenience	****
Queues	*****
Mountain restaurants	**

The rest

Scenery	***
Resort charm	***
Off-slope	***

NEWS

For 2003/04 the Westfall double chair from Red Tail Camp to above Spruce Saddle will be replaced by a high-speed quad.

A 237-room Ritz-Carlton hotel opened in November 2002 next to the Bachelor Gulch Express chair.

Made to Measure Holidays

01243 533333

www. mtmhols. co.uk

ATOL 1006 ABTA V6471

KEY FACTS

Resort	2470m
	8,100ft
Slopes	2255-3485m
	7,400-11,440ft
Lifts	13
Pistes	1,625 acres
Green	34%
Blue	39%
Black	27%
Snowmaking	
	605 acres

➕ Blissfully quiet slopes, in sharp contrast to nearby Vail

➕ Mountain has it all, from superb novice runs through fast cruisers to long, daunting mogul-fields

➕ Compact, traffic-free village centre

➖ Rather urban feel to the village core – far from the Wild West atmosphere Europeans might look for

➖ Very expensive

➖ Disappointing mountain restaurants – the best ones are members-only

In contrast to its better-known neighbour, Vail, Beaver Creek is a haven of peace – both on and off the slopes. It gets rather overshadowed by big sister, but we wouldn't dream of making a trip to Vail without spending a day or two in Beaver, and there's a lot to be said for doing it the other way round – if you can live with the prices in this most exclusive of Colorado resorts.

THE RESORT

Beaver Creek, ten miles to the west of Vail, was developed by Vail Resorts in the 1980s. It is unashamedly exclusive, with a choice of top-quality hotels and condos right by the slopes. It centres on a large pedestrian square featuring escalators to the slopes, exclusive shops, exquisite bronze statues and an open-air ice rink. The lift system spreads across the mountains through Bachelor Gulch, with a new Ritz-Carlton, to Arrowhead, which has luxury condos at the base of the mountain. Most of the nightlife, bars and restaurants are in Beaver Creek and the choice is much more limited than in Vail, a 25-minute bus-ride away. There's a free resort shuttle-bus and a taxi service.

THE MOUNTAINS

Beaver Creek, Bachelor Gulch and Arrowhead offer a small-scale version of the linked lift networks of the Alps. Free mountain tours are held four days a week. British guests may get the opportunity to ski the area with Martin Bell, Britain's best-ever downhiller who now lives in Vail and is UK ski ambassador for Vail Resorts.

Slopes The slopes immediately above Beaver Creek divide into two sectors, each accessed by a fast quad chair. The major sector is centred on Spruce Saddle, with lifts above it reaching 3485m/11,440ft. The other is Strawberry Park, which forms the link with Bachelor Gulch and Arrowhead. Between these two sectors, is Grouse Mountain.

Resorts within a two-hour drive include Breckenridge and Keystone

(owned by Vail Resorts and covered by multi-day lift passes), Aspen, Steamboat and Copper Mountain.

Terrain-parks There are two: Moonshine includes a 120m/400ft long super-pipe and the Zoom Room is for intermediates and beginners.

Snow reliability As well as an exceptional natural snow record, Beaver Creek has extensive snowmaking facilities, normally needed only in early season. The Grouse Mountain slopes can suffer from thin snow-cover (some locals call it Gravel Mountain). Grooming is excellent.

Experts There is quite a bit of intimidatingly steep double-diamond terrain. In the Birds of Prey and Grouse Mountain areas most runs are long, steep and mogulled from top to bottom. The Larkspur Bowl area has three short steep mogul runs.

Intermediates There are marvellous long, quiet, cruising blues almost everywhere you look, including top to bottom runs with a vertical of 1000m/3,280ft from the top of the Birds of Prey chair. The Larkspur and Strawberry Park chairs serve further cruising runs – and lead to yet more ideal terrain served by the Bachelor Gulch and Arrowhead fast chairs.

Beginners There are excellent nursery slopes at resort level and at altitude. And there are plenty of easy longer runs to progress to, including runs from top to bottom of the mountains. There's also a beginner's centre at the bottom of the beginners area where you watch a video to learn how to load and unload chair-lifts and other useful tips before you go on the snow.

Snowboarding Good riders will love

A snowcat-drawn sleigh ride to Beano's Cabin and a five-course meal makes a good evening out ↗

VAIL RESORTS / JACK AFFLECK

LIFT PASSES

See Vail chapter.

Central reservations phone number
1 800 427 8308
(toll free from within the US).

Phone numbers
From distant parts of the US, add the prefix 1 970.
From abroad, add the prefix +1 970.

TOURIST OFFICE

t 845 5745
bcinfo@vailresorts.com
www.beavercreek.com

COLORADO

524

the excellent gladed runs and perfect carving slopes. The resort is great for beginners, too, with special teaching methods and equipment that claim to help you learn quicker.

Cross-country There's a splendid, mountain-top network of tracks at McCoy Park (over 32km/20 miles), reached via the Strawberry Park lift.

Queues The slopes are delightfully deserted and virtually queue-free, even at peak times – it is amazing that more skiers don't come here from Vail.

Mountain restaurants There's not much choice. Spruce Saddle at mid-mountain is the main place – a food court in a spectacular log and glass building, where 'greeters' in Old West costumes radio around to find you a table. Red Tail Camp does decent barbecues. The Beaver Creek Tavern (formerly Rendezvous Bar and Grill) at the foot of the main slope is very civilised, with good food. The Broken Arrow at Arrowhead is recommended.

Schools and guides The school has an excellent reputation.

Facilities for children Small World Play School looks after non-skiing kids from 2 months to six years from 8.30-4.30 daily. We've had good reports on the children's school and there are splendid adventure trails and play areas.

STAYING THERE

How to go There's a reasonable choice of packages.

Hotels There are lots of upmarket places, including the new Ritz-Carlton, Inn at Beaver Creek and Hyatt Regency.

Self-catering There's a wide choice of condos available.

Eating out SaddleRidge is luxurious and packed with photos and Wild West artefacts. A sleigh ride to one of the beautiful log cabins that are members-only clubs at lunchtime but open for dinner – Beano's, Allie's or Zach's – makes a good evening out. Toscanini's, the Golden Eagle, Dusty Boot, and Blue Moose have all been recommended.

Après-ski Beaver Creek Tavern and the Coyote Cafe are decent bars. The new Whiskey Elk is said to have a good selection of bourbon, port and wine.

Off the slopes There are smart boutiques and galleries, an impressive ice rink, hot-air balloon rides and some great shows and concerts.

Staying up the mountain Trappers Cabin is a luxurious private enclave up the mountain, which a group can rent (for a small fortune) by the night.

Staying along the valley Avon, a mile away at the foot of the approach road, has budget motels. The Minturn Inn in Minturn is a stylish B&B (827 9647).

Summit Elevation 3485m/11,440ft

Grouse Mountain 3260m/10,690ft

Larkspur Bowl 3160m/10,370ft

The boxed area below is McCoy Park – Beaver Creek Nordic/cross-country and snow-shoe tracks

Spruce Saddle 3110m/10,200ft

Birds of Prey

Westfall

Grouse Mountain

Centennial

Strawberry Park

Red Tail Camp

Arrowhead Mountain 2775m/9,100ft

Bachelor Gulch

Arrow Bahn

Beaver Creek Village 2470m/8,100ft

Bachelor Gulch 2470m/8,100ft

Arrowhead 2255m/7,400ft

Breckenridge

Four linked mountains, reached from a village with Wild West roots

COSTS

① ② ③ ④ ⑤ ⑥

RATINGS

The slopes

Snow	*****
Extent	**
Expert	****
Intermediate	****
Beginner	****
Convenience	***
Queues	****
Mountain restaurants	**

The rest

Scenery	***
Resort charm	***
Off-slope	***

NEWS

For 2002/03 a lift was built on Peak 7 for the first time: a six-pack serving new intermediate runs (increasing the resort's intermediate terrain by 30%).

And a new high-speed quad was introduced, starting above Beaver Run on Peak 9 and running to Peak 8, with a mid-station for boarding higher up.

On Peak 8 a third terrain-park and half-pipe aimed at intermediates and novices was created.

Longer-term plans have been approved to build new villages at the bases of Peaks 7 and 8. They will be linked to parking lots in the valley by a new gondola.

Breckenridge grooms its slopes well and even has some winches so that steep runs can be groomed. But there are plenty of bumps for those who like them →

+ Four varied local mountains, with something for all abilities

+ Good snow record and lots of artificial help

+ Shared lift pass with nearby Keystone and Arapahoe Basin and not-so-nearby Vail and Beaver Creek

+ Efficient lifts mean few queues

+ Lively bars, restaurants and nightlife by US standards

+ Based on restored Victorian mining town, with many new buildings in attractive 19th-century style

+ One of the nearest major resorts to Denver, so relatively short transfer

− Few long runs

− Best advanced slopes can be windy

− At this extreme altitude there is an appreciable risk of sickness for visitors coming straight from lower altitudes (although the lift-accessed terrain does not go super-high, at 2925m/9,600ft the village is one of the highest you will encounter)

− The 19th-century style gets a bit overblown in places, and there are some out-of-place modern buildings that detract from its charm

− Main Street is just that – always busy with traffic

Breckenridge is very popular with first-time visitors to Colorado. It's easy to see why: it is one of the closest resorts to Denver Airport, has slopes for all abilities, usually excellent dry snow, good facilities for families, relatively lively nightlife and good-value slope-side accommodation. Add to that the image of a restored Wild West mining town and a new lift opening up more intermediate runs on a fourth linked mountain last season and you have a very compelling package.

It is true that the slopes do not cover a huge area and most runs are short and that the town is rather spoiled by out-of-style buildings in parts and a rather Disneyesque feel to other parts. But it has skiing and boarding for all abilities, and there are lots of other areas to try on day trips, some covered by a shared lift pass (Vail, Beaver Creek, Keystone and Arapahoe Basin), some not (such as Copper Mountain) – much more than you could cover in a week or 10 days. But take heed of the altitude warnings; drink plenty of water and stay well hydrated.

THE RESORT

Breckenridge was founded in 1859 and became a booming gold-mining town. The old clapboard buildings have been well renovated and form the bottom part of Main Street. New shopping malls and buildings have been added in similar style – though they are obvious modern additions.

The town centre is lively in the evening, with over 100 restaurants and bars. Christmas lights and decorations remain throughout the season, giving the town an air of non-stop winter festivity. This is enhanced by a number of real winter festivals such as Ullr Fest

– a carnival honouring the Norse God of Winter – and Ice Sculpture championships, which leave sculptures for weeks afterwards.

Hotels and condominiums are spread over a wide, wooded area and are linked by regular free shuttle-buses (less frequent in the evening). If you stay in a condo and don't have a car, shopping at the local supermarket can be hard work – it is not in the centre of town. Although there is a lot of slope-side accommodation – Breckenridge boasts more slope-side lodging than any other Colorado resort – there is also a fair amount away from Main Street and the lift base-stations.

THE MOUNTAINS

There are four separate peaks, linked by lift and piste. Boringly, they are named Peaks 7, 8, 9 and 10 – going from right to left as you look at the mountain. Though there's something for all abilities, the keen piste-basher will want to explore other resorts too. Breckenridge and Keystone were bought in 1996 by the owners of Vail and Beaver Creek (around an hour away); a multi-day lift ticket covers these four resorts and Arapahoe Basin, also nearby. Copper Mountain is not covered by the same ticket. All six of these resorts are linked by regular buses (free except for the trips to Vail or Beaver Creek). Steamboat and Winter Park are both less than two hours' drive away.

THE SLOPES
Small but fragmented
Two high-speed chair-lifts go from the top end of town up to **Peak 9**, one accessing mainly green runs on the lower half of the hill, the other mainly blues higher up. From there you can get to **Peak 10**, which has a large

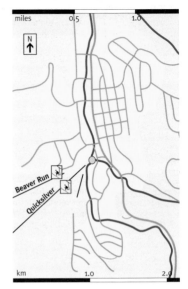

number of blue and black runs served by one high-speed quad.

The **Peak 8** area – tough stuff at the top, easier lower down – can now be reached by the new high-speed quad from Peak 9, which has a mid-station for loading further up the mountain. The base lifts of Peak 8 at the Bergenhof can also be reached by the town shuttle-bus or the Snowflake lift from the edge of town. From the top of the Rocky Mountain Express on Peak 8, you can access the new runs and six-pack on **Peak 7**. Taking a T-bar up from Peak 8 gets you to the resorts' best ski-anywhere bowls.

For the end of the day three trails lead back to town from Peak 8. A regular free shuttle runs around the resort to the Peak 9 and Peak 8 lifts. The grooming is excellent and the signposting very clear.

There are free mountain tours at 9.30 daily. And some weeks British

boarding

Breckenridge is pretty much ideal for all standards of boarder and hosts several major US snowboarding events. Beginners have ideal nursery slopes, easy greens to progress to and – if taking lessons – the opportunity to learn on a boarders-only slope, the Eldorado run, on Peak 9. There is also a boarders-only mini terrain-park and a warming hut. Intermediates have great cruising runs, all served by chairs. The powder bowls at the top of Peaks 7 and 8 make for great riding – unfortunately accessed only by an awkward T-bar, which does not. Boarders of all levels will enjoy the choice of excellent terrain-parks and half-pipes (see Terrain-parks). Nearby Arapahoe Basin is another area for hardcore boarding in steep bowls and chutes. Breckenridge pays homage to the early pioneers of the sport with a history of snowboarding display in the Vista Haus restaurant on Peak 8.

KEY FACTS

Resort	2925m
	9,600ft
Slopes	2925-3965m
	9,600-13,000ft
Lifts	26
Pistes	2,208 acres
Green	13%
Blue	32%
Black	55%
Snowmaking	
	516 acres

guests can ski one day with Martin Bell, Britain's best-ever downhiller and now Vail Resorts' UK ski ambassador.

TERRAIN-PARKS
Something for everyone

There's one of the best terrain-parks in the US on Peak 8, Freeway, with a series of great jumps, obstacles and an enormous championship half-pipe, which one reporter described as 'massive, steep, well kept and awesome'. Less intimidating is the Gold King terrain-park on Peak 9 with jumps and railslides designed for intermediates. Last season Breckenridge introduced a new terrain park for beginners, Swinger, on Peak 8 with gentle jumps and an introductory pipe. There is also a boarders-only mini-terrain-park on Peak 9 (see Boarding).

SNOW RELIABILITY
Excellent

With the village at almost 3000m/ 9,840ft (the highest of the main North American resorts), the slopes going up to almost 4000m/13,125ft and a lot of east and north-east-facing slopes, Breckenridge boasts an excellent natural snow record. That is supplemented by substantial snowmaking (used mainly pre-Christmas to form a good base).

FOR EXPERTS
Quite a few short but tough runs

A remarkable 55% of Breckenridge's runs are classified as 'most difficult'

(single-black-diamond) or 'expert' (double-black-diamond) terrain. That's a higher proportion than the famous 'macho' resorts, such as Jackson Hole, Taos and Snowbird. But remember that Breckenridge is not a big area by European standards, so most experts there for a week or more will want to spend some of their time exploring the other nearby resorts.

The key to reaching Breckenridge's best steep slopes is taking the T-bar at the top of Peak 8. You can then traverse or hike up to great steep runs on Peak 7 with good snow on north-east-facing slopes or to the steepest slopes in Imperial Bowl and Lake Chutes. Without hiking you can reach good open terrain on Peak 8 in Horseshoe and Contest bowls, where the snow normally remains good.

We particularly liked the back bowls of Peak 8. This is basically terrain among a thin covering of trees and bushes accessed from the T-bar or Lift 6 (which starts just below the top of Lift 4). Lots of runs, such as Lobo, Hombre, Amen and Adios, are marked on the trail map. But in practice you can easily skip between them and invent your own way down. It's picturesque and not too steep. Steep black mogul fields lead down under Chair 4 to the junction with Peak 9.

Peak 9 itself has very steep blacks from the top down under Chair E (so steep that we have never seen them retaining good snow) and the double diamond Peak 9 chutes reached by hiking up from the Mercury chair.

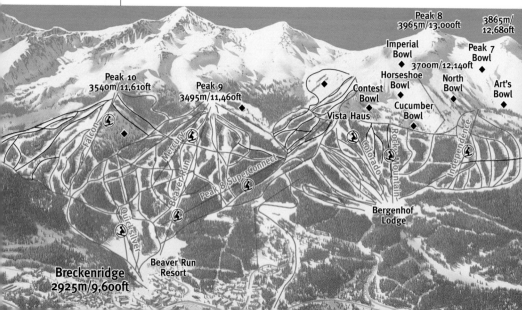

Breckenridge 2925m/9,600ft

COLORADO

528

SCHOOLS

Breckenridge
t 453 3272
lrn2ski@vailresorts.com

Classes
Half day (2¼hr) $65

Private lessons
$140 for 1hr for up to 6 people.

CHILDREN

There are children's ski school/day-care facilities at the bases of Peak 8 and Peak 9. Classes for children aged 3 to 14 cost US$101 per day (9.30 to 3.45) including lunch. There's a complex array of options for all-day care from 8.30 to 4.30 for children from aged 2 months. Prior reservation for day care is essential (453 3528).

On Peak 10, to the right of the chair as you come down the mountain, at the edge of the area, is a network of interlinking black mogul runs by the side of the downhill course – consistently steep and bumpy. To the left of the chair is a lovely, lightly wooded off-piste area called The Burn.

FOR INTERMEDIATES
Nice cruising, limited extent
Breckenridge has some good blue cruising runs for all intermediates. The development of Peak 7 for 2002/03 increased the intermediate terrain by 30%. But dedicated piste-bashers are still likely to find the runs short and limited in extent and will want to visit the other nearby resorts – see 'The mountains' earlier in the chapter.

Peak 9 has the easiest slopes. It is nearly all gentle, wide, blue runs at the top and almost flat, wide, green runs at the bottom. And the ski patrol enforces slow-speed skiing in narrow and crowded areas. Peak 10 has a couple of more challenging runs classified blue-black, such as Crystal and Centennial, which make for good fast cruising. Peaks 7 and 8 both have a choice of blues on trails cut close together in the trees. More adventurous intermediates will also like to try some of the high bowl runs (see For experts).

FOR BEGINNERS
Excellent
The bottom of Peak 9 has a big, virtually flat area and some good gentle nursery slopes. There's then a good choice of green runs to move on to. Beginners can try Peak 8 too, with another selection of green runs and a choice of trails back to town. Reporters praise the good-value beginner package which includes lessons, equipment rental and lift pass.

FOR CROSS-COUNTRY
Specialist centre in woods
Breckenridge's Nordic Center is prettily set in the woods between the town and Peak 8 (served by the shuttle-bus). It has 32km/20 miles of trails and 16km/10 miles of snow-shoeing trails.

QUEUES
Not normally a problem
Breckenridge's eight high-speed chair-lifts make light work of peak-time crowds. Neither we nor our reporters have come across serious queues, except at exceptional times, such as President's Day weekend and on powder days – when the T-bar at Peak 8 can get crowded.

MOUNTAIN RESTAURANTS
Varied but nothing special
Breckenridge is making an effort to improve on the standard US cafeterias.

Tenmile Station, between Peaks 9 and 10, is the newest and best, with a heated deck. Border Burritos ('huge portions') is in the Bergenhof at the base of Peak 8. Spencer's at Beaver Run does all-you-can-eat meals. Vista Haus, at the top of Peak 8, has a couple of restaurants.

SCHOOLS AND GUIDES
Excellent reports
Our reporters are unanimous in their praise for the school: classes of five to eight, doing what the class, not the instructor, wanted. Special clinics include bumps, telemark and powder. 'Excellent,' said a 2003 reporter.

FACILITIES FOR CHILDREN
Excellent facilities
Every report on the children's school and nursery is full of plaudits. Typical comments: 'excellent, combining serious coaching with lots of fun', 'our boys loved it', 'so much more positive than ski schools in Europe'.

↑ Sleigh rides are a popular après-ski activity

VAIL RESORTS, INC / BOB WINSETT

GETTING THERE

Air Denver 166km/104 miles (2½hr).

ACTIVITIES

Indoor Sports clubs, swimming, sauna, massage, hot-tubs, cinema, theatre, art gallery, library, indoor miniature golf course, ice skating, good leisure centre (pool, tubs, gym, climbing wall) on the outskirts of town – accessible by bus

Outdoor Horse- and dog-sleigh rides, fishing, snow-mobiles, toboggans, scooters, mountain biking, snow-shoeing, ice skating, hot-air balloon rides

Phone numbers
From distant parts of the US, add the prefix 1 970.
From abroad, add the prefix +1 970.

TOURIST OFFICE

t 453 5000
international@vail resorts.com
www.breckenridge.com

STAYING THERE

HOW TO GO
Lots of choice
A lot of tour operators feature Breckenridge.

Chalets Several tour operators have very comfortable chalets. A 2003 reporter described Whispering Pines (sold through Ski All America) as, 'an absolutely top notch place to stay'. Ski Independence's two traditional chalets look good – and we have been impressed by their efficiency.

Hotels There's a good choice of style and price range.

((((4) **Great Divide** (453 4500) Owned by Vail Resorts. Prime location, vast rooms. Pool, tubs.

((((4) **Lodge at Breckenridge** (453 9300) Stylish luxury spa resort set out of town among 32 acres, with great views. Private shuttle-bus. Pool, tubs.

((((4) **Little Mountain Lodge** (453 1969) Luxury B&B near ice rink.

(((3) **Beaver Run** (453 6000) Huge, resort complex with 520 spacious rooms. Great location, by one of the main lifts up Peak 9. Pool, hot-tubs.

(((3) **Williams House** (453 2975) Beautifully restored, charmingly furnished four-room B&B on Main St.

(((3) **Village** (547 5725) Central 3-star. 'Good value with spacious rooms,' says a 2003 visitor.

Self-catering There is a huge choice of condominiums, many set conveniently off the aptly named Four O'Clock run. There are lots of houses to rent, too.

EATING OUT
Over 100 restaurants
There's a very wide range of eating places, from typical American food to 'fine-dining'. The Breckenridge Dining Guide lists a full menu of most places.

The Brewery is famous for its enormous portions of appetisers such as Buffalo Wings – as well as its

splendid brewed-on-the-spot beers. We particularly liked the Avalanche beer.

Poirrier's at the Wellington and the sophisticated food at both Café Alpine and Pierre's Riverwalk Café have been recommended. Sushi Breck and Mi Casa (Mexican) have had good reviews. The Hearthstone is said to do 'lovely food in good surroundings', the Blue River Bistro to offer 'a wide selection of food at affordable prices', and Bubba Gump Shrimp Company to have 'good food and exceptional service'. Michael's Italian is recommended for 'extensive menu, large portions and reasonable prices'. Rasta Pasta offers pasta dishes with a Jamaican twist.

APRES-SKI
The best in the area
The Breckenridge Brewery, Tiffany's, Liquid Lounge, the renovated Fatty's and Sherpa & Yetti's are popular. The Gold Pan saloon dates from gold rush days, and is reputedly the oldest bar west of the Mississippi. Cecelia's and the British owned T-Bar serve good cocktails, the Underworld is a disco bar. Mount Java is a relaxed cafe-bookshop with Internet access.

OFF THE SLOPES
Pleasant enough
Breckenridge is a pleasant place to wander around with plenty of souvenir and gift shops. Silverthorne (about 30 minutes away) has excellent bargain factory outlet stores. It is easy to get around and visit other resorts.

STAYING DOWN THE VALLEY
Good for exploring the area
Staying in Frisco makes sense for those touring around or on a tight budget. It's a small town with decent bars and restaurants. There are cheap motels, a couple of small hotels and some B&Bs; Hotel Frisco (668 5009) has been recommended.

Breckenridge

529

Copper Mountain

Great terrain for all ability levels, above a born-again resort

COSTS

① ② ③ ④ ⑤ ⑥

RATINGS

The slopes

Snow	★★★★★
Extent	★★
Expert	★★★★
Intermediate	★★★★
Beginner	★★★★
Convenience	★★★★
Queues	★★★★
Mountain restaurants	★

The rest

Scenery	★★★
Resort charm	★★
Off-slope	★

NEWS

For 2002/03, the first phase of the new seven-building West Lake Market, next to the New Village at Copper, opened, including a Russian-themed vodka bar, restaurants and shops. The development will be completed for 2003/04 and will include more restaurants and bars.

A new Beeline Advantage pass allows you to avoid queues at certain lifts and to go up the mountain 15 minutes before other people to get first tracks. Book it through your tour operator (or direct at least 48 hours in advance, though this may cost extra).

➕ Convenient purpose-built resort undergoing exciting renaissance

➕ Fair-sized mountain, with good runs for all abilities

➕ Excellent snow reliability

➕ Efficient lift system – few queues

➕ Several other good resorts nearby

➖ One fast-food mountain restaurant

➖ Limited vertical on black-diamond bowls at the top

➖ Village still rather limited when compared with established resorts

➖ Can be long lift queues at weekends

➖ Risk of altitude sickness for visitors coming straight from sea level

Copper's slopes are some of Colorado's best, and now there's a fine new village to match the quality of the slopes. As a result, Copper now makes a much more attractive destination. But watch out for that altitude sickness; Copper's village and the top of its slopes are even higher than at Breckenridge.

THE RESORT

Copper Mountain was originally built rather like the French resorts of the 1960s – high on convenience, low on charm. Because of that it never took off on the international market. But it has always had one of Colorado's best ski areas. And the resort has now been transformed by its new owners, Intrawest. 2000/01 saw the opening of 'The New Village at Copper' – four new impressive wood-and-stone-clad buildings with shops, restaurants and car-free walkways and squares, forming the heart of the resort at the foot of the main intermediate area. West Lake Market is now being added on in similar style.

There is also an East Village – with recently built accommodation and base lodge and easy access to the expert and intermediate terrain. A regular free shuttle-bus runs between the two main bases and the family skiing and beginners' area at Union Creek.

Keystone, Breckenridge and Arapahoe Basin are all nearby, and Vail, Steamboat and Winter Park are within an hour or two's drive.

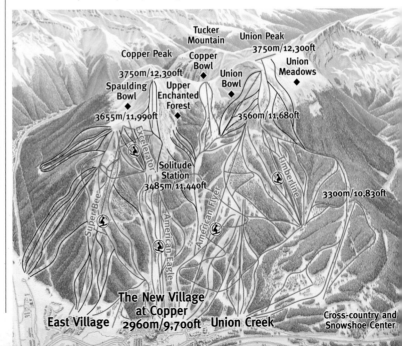

KEY FACTS

Resort	2960m
	9,700ft
Slopes	2925-3765m
	9,170-12,300ft
Lifts	23
Pistes	2,450 acres
Green	21%
Blue	25%
Black	54%
Snowmaking	
	400 acres

Central reservations
Call 968 2882.
Toll-free number
(from within the US)
1 888 263 5302.

Phone numbers
From distant parts of
the US, add the prefix
1 970.
From abroad, add the
prefix +1 970.

TOURIST OFFICE

t 968 2882
copper-marketing@
coppercolorado.com
www.coppercolorado.
com

COPPER MOUNTAIN RESORT /
BEN BLANKENBURG

The Intrawest
influence: the New
Village at Copper
looks a lot better
than the original
soulless buildings ➜

THE MOUNTAIN

The area is quite sizeable by American standards, and has great runs for all ability levels. Mountain tours with a Copper guide are available daily.

Slopes As you look up at the mountain, the easiest runs are on the right-hand side and the forested terrain gradually gets steeper and more challenging the further left you go. Above the forest, a series of steeper open bowls is served by two chairs and a drag on the front and two further chairs on the back side. There is also a free snowcat service to cut out some hiking. And you can access the backcountry through a gate and get a resort bus back.

Terrain-parks There are three. The main park is beside the American Flyer chair and has areas for beginner, intermediate and expert park-users, plus a super-pipe. There's also a special beginners' park and a park for experts, with big jumps, set in full view of the main village at Copper.

Snow reliability Height and an extensive snowmaking operation give Copper an early opening date each season and excellent snow reliability.

Experts There is a lot of good expert terrain, especially in the steep and wild Copper Bowl on the back side of the mountain and the bump runs through the trees below Spaulding Bowl.

Intermediates Good intermediates will find long steep runs in the section on the left of the mountain as you look at it. The slightly less proficient can enjoy gentler runs on the middle section of the mountain, and early intermediates have gentle cruisers below the Union Peak area on the right.

Beginners The nursery slopes are excellent, and there are plenty of very easy green runs to graduate to.

Snowboarding There are great slopes for all abilities, plus three terrain-parks.

Cross-country There are 25km/15 miles of trails through the White River forest.

Queues Weekend visitors pour in from Denver and we have reports of 20-minute queues. The Beeline Advantage pass comes in useful then (see News).

Mountain restaurants Grim. The main place is a fast-food court at Solitude Station. The alternatives are outdoors – a soup shack and a burger bar.

Schools and guides The school offers a wide variety of courses and has a fine reputation, especially for children.

Facilities for children The Belly Button childcare facility takes children from two months old and ski school takes children from age three.

STAYING THERE

How to go A number of tour operators offer packages to Copper.

Hotels and condos There are no hotels but some condos are splendidly luxurious, with outdoor hot-tubs, etc.

Eating out Blue Moose pizza, Endo's and JJ's Rocky Mountain Tavern are popular. Sleigh rides take people out to Western-style dinners in tents.

Après-ski Après-ski is lively as the lifts close. Later on, Endo's Adrenaline cafe and JJ's Rocky Mountain Tavern (with live music) are popular. Pravda is a new Russian-style club and Larkin's Cross a traditional Irish pub.

Off the slopes There's a fine sports club, with a huge pool and indoor tennis, ice skating on the lake and a multi-screen cinema nearby.

Crested Butte

A Jekyll and Hyde resort: one lift takes you from greens to extremes

COSTS

① ② ③ ④ ⑤ ⑥

RATINGS

The slopes

Snow	****
Extent	*
Expert	****
Intermediate	***
Beginner	****
Convenience	***
Queues	*****
Mountain restaurants	*

The rest

Scenery	***
Resort charm	****
Off-slope	**

NEWS

Work is under way on a new out-of-town Prospect ski-in/ski-out accommodation development. For 2003/04 a new fixed-grip quad is planned to take people from here into the slopes. Four new blue trails will also be built in this area.

There are also plans for a new floodlit tubing hill for kids at the base area, open every day after the lifts close.

532

KEY FACTS

Resort	2860m
	9,380ft
Slopes	2775-3620m
	9,100-11,880ft
Lifts	14
Pistes	1,058 acres
Green	14%
Blue	32%
Black	54%
Snowmaking	
	300 acres

➕ Lots of 'extreme' and expert terrain

➕ Excellent for beginners and for near-beginners, with long easy runs

➕ Charming, tiny, restored Victorian mining town with good restaurants

➕ Convenient 'village' at lift base

➕ Attractive scenery, for Colorado

➖ Very limited terrain for confident intermediate piste-bashers

➖ Modern resort village lacks character

➖ Old town is 10 minutes from resort village by shuttle-bus

➖ Out on a limb, away from mainstream Colorado resorts

Among experts who are at home on steep, unprepared runs – and 'extremists' who like their mountains as steep as possible – Crested Butte enjoys cult status. Meanwhile, the commercial success of the place depends on beginners and timid intermediates, who love the long, gentle slopes of the main area. These two groups can safely include Crested Butte on their shortlists. But keen, mileage-hungry intermediates will find there isn't enough suitable terrain.

THE RESORT

Crested Butte is a small resort in a remote corner of Colorado. It takes its name from the local mountain – an isolated peak (a butte, pronounced 'beaut') with a distinctive shape. It started life as a coal-mining town in the late 1800s and is now one of the most attractive resorts in the Rockies – a few narrow streets with beautifully restored wooden buildings and sidewalks and a tiny town jail – straight out of a Western movie.

The town is a couple of miles from the mountain, linked by a regular free shuttle-bus. But at the foot of it is the resort 'village' of Mount Crested Butte – modern and characterless, with a cluster of bars and restaurants at the foot of the slopes, a couple of big hotels and a sprawling area of houses and condos. There is some accommodation in the town, but most is at the resort village. You can stroll to the lifts from some of it; but from many condos you need the bus.

THE MOUNTAIN

It's a small area, but it packs in an astonishing mixture of perfect beginner slopes, easy cruising runs and expert terrain. There are free daily mountain tours for intermediates or better.

Slopes Two fast quad chairs leave the base. The Silver Queen takes experts to black runs and links with lifts to the steepest runs. The Keystone lift takes you to the easiest runs. Intermediates

can access cruising blue runs from either of these two lifts.

Terrain-parks The main Teocalli park is the place for advanced riders, with rails, tables and a half-pipe. Jib World beneath the Keystone lift is aimed more at intermediates. There's also a Kids park with table-tops, rails and a mini-half-pipe.

Snow reliability The resort apparently benefits from snowstorms from several directions, and has a substantial snowmaking installation.

Experts For those who like steep, ungroomed terrain, Crested Butte is idyllic – the 448 acres of the Extreme Limits at the top of the mountain offer seriously steep but prettily wooded and safe terrain. But the area needs a lot of snow-cover – it is not unusual for it to be closed until late January. Guided tours of the North Face are available. Though there are also some 'ordinary' black runs, these are few. Nearby Irwin Lodge did not open its snowcat skiing operation last season and may not do so this season either.

Intermediates Good intermediates are likely to find the area limited. For early intermediates, there are lots of wide, fairly gentle, well-groomed and normally uncrowded cruising runs.

Beginners There are excellent nursery slopes near the village and lots of good long runs to progress to.

Snowboarding There's lots of extreme terrain for good riders. Beginners have a large section of long, wide green runs. Then there are the terrain-parks.

Cross-country There are 30km/20 miles

Lots of easy runs, a few good cruisers and a stack of very steep ungrooming runs through the trees: that's Crested Butte (and the peak on the right is the 'butte' it takes its name from)
→

of cross-country trails near the old town and backcountry tours are available in Elk Mountain and the Gunnison National Forest.

Queues Virtually non-existent.

Mountain restaurants Most people go back to the base for lunch. But the restaurant at the base of the Paradise lift has a big deck, a self-service section and Andiamo's table-service Italian restaurant. A new table-service Ice Bar (literally made from ice) and Restaurant has replaced the former Twister Warming House.

Schools and guides The school has an excellent reputation.

Facilities for children Parents praise the teaching and separate kids' area.

STAYING THERE

How to go Most specialist US tour operators include Crested Butte. Right at the foot of the slopes is a Club Med. **Hotels** There's a wide range. In the resort village, the Sheraton Crested Butte Resort (349 2333) is one of the smartest options, with a pool and outdoor hot-tub and great views. The Nordic Inn B&B (349 5542) is a short

walk from the lifts: 'Full of character, charming hosts', outdoor hot-tub and large rooms. On the outskirts of the old town, the 'Scandinavian-style' Inn at Crested Butte (349 1225) is a non-smoking hotel with an outdoor hot-tub. Elk Mountain Lodge B&B (349 7533) is a renovated miners' hotel.

Self-catering There are thousands of apartments available in the village.

Eating out Top of the pile is Soupçon, a tiny place in an old log cabin just off the main street in the old town, serving refined French food. The Bosquet runs it close, and Bacchanale is a good Italian. The Idle Spur micro-brewery is popular. In the resort village, the WoodStone Grille is recommended. Andiamo's (reached by sleigh) and The Ice Bar & Restaurant (reached by the 4.30pm chair lift; torchlit ski or snowshoe down) open some evenings.

Après-ski At the base area, the Hall of Fame, with live music, was new last season and Casey's is popular. In the old town Kochevar's is an old Wild West saloon. The Wooden Nickel and the Powerhouse are recommended.

Off the slopes There are some galleries, a theatre and a cinema.

Crested Butte

533

Phone numbers
From distant parts of the US, add the prefix 1 970.
From abroad, add the prefix +1 970.

TOURIST OFFICE
t 349 2286
info@cbmr.com
www.crestedbutte
resort.com

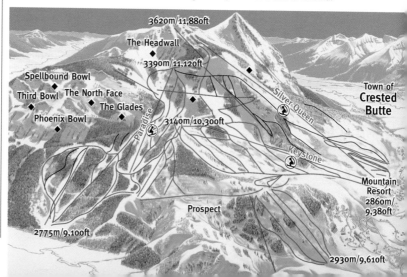

Keystone

For those who want a peaceful, quiet, pampered time

COSTS

① ② ③ ④ ⑤ ⑥

RATINGS

The slopes
Snow	*****
Extent	**
Expert	***
Intermediate	****
Beginner	****
Convenience	**
Queues	****
Mountain restaurants	***

The rest
Scenery	***
Resort charm	**
Off-slope	**

NEWS

For 2002/03, Arapahoe Basin installed snowmaking for the first time – covering 11 runs and 125 acres from top to bottom of the mountain. It also has long-term plans for a mid-mountain restaurant.

A second children's centre has opened in Keystone, offering childcare and activities for kids aged two months to 12 years at River Run.

For 2002/03, Keystone continued to expand its terrain-park.

534

➕ Good mountain for everyone but the double-diamond diehard

➕ Huge night-skiing operation (though no longer daily)

➕ Lots of other nearby resorts

➕ Efficient lift system – few queues

➕ Luxurious condominiums

➖ Very quiet in the evenings

➖ Very high – altitude sickness can be a problem for some visitors

➖ Much of the accommodation is a bus-ride to and from lifts

➖ Resort lacks village atmosphere

➖ Poor shops for self-catering

Keystone's slopes are impressive from many points of view. But there isn't a proper village at the foot of them. Luxurious condos are scattered over a wide area, and there are some excellent restaurants for the odd dinner out, but the nearest thing to a 'village' is the new car-free River Run development near the gondola. This is attractive and convenient for the slopes but you can check out its handful of bars, restaurants and shops in a five-minute stroll. For something more interesting, base yourself elsewhere and visit Keystone's slopes for a day.

THE RESORT

Keystone is a sprawling resort of condominiums spread over wooded countryside at the foot of Keystone Mountain, beside Snake River and the highway to Loveland Pass. It has no clear centre and is divided into seven 'neighborhoods', with regular free buses between them. Some are little more than groups of condos, while others have shops, restaurants and bars (though no supermarkets or liquor stores – they are on the main highway).

River Run, at the base of the main gondola, is the nearest thing to a conventional ski resort village, with condo buildings, a short main street, a square and a few restaurants, bars and shops. A second lift base area half a mile to the west, Mountain House, is much less of a village. Another mile west is Keystone Village, set around a lake – a huge natural ice rink in winter.

THE MOUNTAINS

By US standards Keystone offers extensive intermediate slopes and some challenging steeper stuff. The resort is owned by Vail Resorts, and lift tickets between Vail, Beaver Creek, Breckenridge and Keystone are interchangeable, and also cover Arapahoe Basin a few minutes away by road. Copper Mountain is nearby but not covered by the lift pass.
Slopes Three tree-lined, interlinked mountains form Keystone's local

slopes. The only one directly accessible from the resort is Keystone Mountain, to which lifts depart from Mountain House and River Run. The front face of the mountain has Keystone's biggest network of lifts and runs by far, mainly of easy and intermediate gradient. From the top you can drop over the back down to Keystone Gulch, where there are lifts back up to Keystone Mountain and on to the next hill, North Peak. Or you can ride the Outpost gondola directly to the top of North Peak. From North Peak you can get back to the bases of both Keystone Mountain and the third peak, known as The Outback. Keystone has the biggest floodlit skiing operation in the US, covering Keystone Mountain top to bottom up to 8pm (though it is now open only on certain nights of the week; and it can be bitterly cold).
Terrain-parks The huge Jackwhacker terrain-park with half-pipe is on the front side of Keystone Mountain. It is floodlit on several nights of the week,

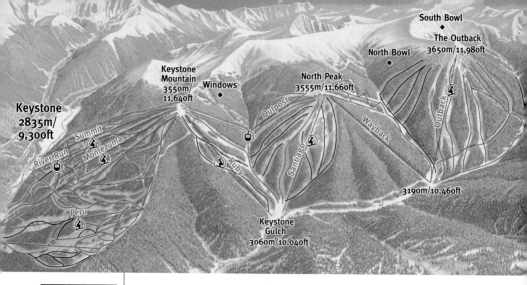

On the map: South Bowl, The Outback 3650m/11,980ft, North Bowl, Keystone Mountain 3550m/11,640ft, Windows, North Peak 3555m/11,660ft, Keystone 2835m/9,300ft, Outpost, Wayback, Outback, River Run, Summit, Montezuma, Ruby, Santiago, 3190m/10,460ft, Peru, Keystone Gulch 3060m/10,040ft

KEY FACTS

Resort	2835m
	9,300ft

For Keystone

Slopes	2835-3650m
	9,300-11,980ft
Lifts	21
Pistes	1,861 acres
Green	12%
Blue	34%
Black	54%
Snowmaking	
	859 acres

For Arapahoe Basin

Slopes	3285-3980m
	10,780-13,050ft
Lifts	5
Pistes	490 acres
Green/Blue	60%
Black	40%
Snowmaking	
	125 acres

Central reservations phone number
1 800 427 8308
(toll free from within the US).

Phone numbers
From distant parts of the US, add the prefix 1 970.
From abroad, add the prefix +1 970.

TOURIST OFFICE

t 496 6772
international@vail
resorts.com
www.keystoneresort.com

making it the biggest night-boarding operation in the US.

Snow reliability Shortage of snow is rarely a problem, and Keystone has one of the world's biggest snowmaking systems. Snow-sure A-Basin installed snowmaking last season, too.

Experts Keystone has a reputation for great groomers, but it also has a lot of steeper, ungroomed terrain. Windows is a 60-acre area of experts-only glade runs on Keystone Mountain's back side. Traversing from the top of the lift on The Outback takes you to open and glade runs in the North Bowl and the South Bowls. A-Basin is a good place for those looking for more of a challenge. The East Wall here has some splendid steep chutes.

Intermediates Keystone is ideal. The front face of Keystone Mountain itself is a network of beautifully groomed blue and green runs through the trees. Enthusiastic piste-bashers will love it. The Outback and North Peak also have easy cruising blues.

Beginners There are good nursery slopes at the top and bottom of Keystone Mountain, and excellent long green runs to progress to.

Snowboarding Keystone is ideal for beginners and intermediates, with mainly chair-lifts and gondolas, good beginner areas and cruising runs. Expert riders will love The Outback and the bowls and chutes of A-Basin.

Cross-country There are 16km/10 miles of groomed trails and 50km/31 miles of unprepared trails.

Queues Except at the morning peak, there are few queues and the trails are usually beautifully quiet, except for

Mozart, the only blue run down from Keystone Mountain to North Peak.

Mountain restaurants Summit House at the top of Keystone Mountain tends to get over-crowded. The table-service Alpenglow Stube (top of North Peak) is excellent and pampering but expensive (the buffet is the best value).

Schools and guides As well as the normal lessons, there are bumps, race and various other advanced classes.

Facilities for children These are excellent, with programmes tailored to specific age groups. Children have their own teaching areas. Kids' nights out are also organised.

STAYING THERE

How to go Regular shuttles operate from Denver airport. Most accommodation is in condominiums.

Hotels There isn't a great choice but they're all of a high standard.

Self-catering All the condominiums are large and luxurious – and we've stayed in some fabulous ones.

Eating out You can eat up the mountain at the Summit House or the Alpenglow Stube. At valley level the restaurants are scattered around and there isn't the range of mid-market restaurants that makes eating out such a pleasure in many American resorts.

Après-ski The Summit House has live music and caters for night skiing customers too. But this is not the resort for late-night revellers.

Off the slopes There are plenty of activities, including skating on the frozen lake, tubing and indoor tennis. It's easy to visit Breckenridge and Vail.

Steamboat

Where they invented the term Champagne Powder™

COSTS

① ② ③ ④ ⑤ ⑥

RATINGS

The slopes

Snow	★★★★
Extent	★★★
Expert	★★★
Intermediate	★★★★
Beginner	★★★★★
Convenience	★★★
Queues	★★★★
Mountain restaurants	★★★

The rest

Scenery	★★★
Resort charm	★★
Off-slope	★★

NEWS

Last season a music system was added to the Bashor terrain-park, which itself opened the season before.

536

KEY FACTS

Resort	2100m
	6,900ft
Slopes	2100-3165m
	6,900-10,380ft
Lifts	20
Pistes	2,939 acres
Green	13%
Blue	56%
Black	31%
Snowmaking	
	438 acres

➕ Excellent beginner and early intermediate runs

➕ Famed for its gladed powder terrain

➕ Good snow record

➕ Good (but not cheap) mountain restaurants – open evenings, too

➕ Plenty of slope-side lodging

➕ Town has some Western character

➖ Old town is a couple of miles from the slopes

➖ Modern 'village' at the foot of the slopes has some eyesore buildings and sprawls over a large area

➖ Not enough runs to amuse keen intermediates for a week

➖ Not a huge amount of double-black terrain – some of it is a hike away

Steamboat's brochures routinely feature cowboys, but after several visits, we've still not seen any. The ski resort has rather swamped the cattle town without developing a village atmosphere. The mountain may not match some of its competitors for extent, but it's one of the best for powder fun among the trees.

THE RESORT

The resort village is a 10-minute bus-ride from the old town of Steamboat Springs. Near the gondola there are a few shop- and restaurant-lined multi-level squares. Some accommodation is up the sides of the piste, but the resort also sprawls across the valley. The old town can be a bit of a disappointment. It may be a working cattle town, but the Wild West isn't much in evidence. The wide main street is lined with bars, hotels and shops in a mixture of styles, from old wooden buildings to concrete plazas.

THE MOUNTAINS

Steamboat's slopes are prettily set among trees, with extensive views over rolling hills and the wide Yampa valley below. But even if a long-awaited expansion goes ahead, it still won't rival places such as Aspen and Vail.

If you have a car, Vail, Beaver Creek, Copper Mountain, Keystone, Breckenridge and Winter Park are all less than a two-hour drive.

Slopes The slopes divide naturally into five sectors. The gondola from the village rises to Thunderhead. From here you can head back to the village or catch a chair to Storm Peak or to the Pony Express chair. From Storm Peak you can drop over the back into the Morningside Park area. If you turn right from Thunderhead you can catch a long, slow chair up to Sunshine Peak which also accesses Morningside Park.

Terrain-parks The Mavericks super-pipe in the Bashor terrain-park is claimed to be the longest in North America.

Snow reliability Steamboat is low for Colorado, but it has an excellent snow record. This is where they invented the term Champagne Powder™. There is also snowmaking from top to bottom.

Experts The main attraction is the challenging terrain in the glades. A great area is on Sunshine Peak below the Sundown Express. Morningside Park and Pioneer Ridge also have excellent gladed runs. Three numbered chutes are easily accessed via the lift back from Morningside, and a short hike gets you to the tree skiing of Christmas Tree Bowl. For bumps, try the series of runs off Four Points.

Intermediates Much of the mountain is ideal, with long cruising blue runs. Morningside Park is a great area for easy black as well as blue slopes. And don't ignore Thunderhead – there are good runs that are easy to miss if you always head straight to the top. The runs on Sunshine are very gentle. For keen intermediates the area is limited.

Beginners There's a big nursery area at the base of the mountain, with a variety of gentle greens to progress to.

Snowboarding There's a special learning area, gentle slopes to progress to and you can get around using chair-lifts and the gondola. For experienced riders, riding the glades in fresh powder is unbeatable. Powder Pursuits shop is highly rated.

Cross-country A free shuttle service takes you to 30km/20 miles of

The ski area is set among rolling hills, is prettily wooded and gets a lot of snow (though we've never been there when it has had its famous Champagne Powder™)
→

Central reservations phone number
1 800 922 2722
(toll free from within the US).

Phone numbers
From distant parts of the US, add the prefix 1 970.
From abroad, add the prefix +1 970.

TOURIST OFFICE

t 879 6111
info@steamboat.com
www.steamboat.com

groomed tracks at the Touring Center.
Queues Queues form for the gondola first thing, but they move quickly; the slow Sunshine lift can be crowded. Noticeboards indicate waiting times.
Mountain restaurants There are two main restaurant complexes on the mountain: Thunderhead and Rendezvous Saddle. There's also a snack bar and sun deck at Four Points.
Schools and guides Reports are very positive. 'Very good indeed ... even by the usual high standards of the USA,' enthused a 2003 couple who had separate lessons and put their three kids in boarding classes.
Facilities for children Arrangements are exceptional, including evening entertainment. Kids under 12 ski free with a parent or grandparent buying a pass for at least five days.

STAYING THERE

How to go A fair number of UK tour operators feature Steamboat.
Chalets There are some catered chalets run by UK tour operators.
Hotels The smarter hotels at the resort have less character than some of the in-town options. The Rabbit Ears Motel (879 1150) and Steamboat Grand (871 5500) have been recommended.

Self-catering There are countless condos, many with good pool/tub facilities, all on a free bus route. Ski Inn Condos at the base of the gondola have been recommended.
Eating out There are over 70 bars and restaurants. Pick up a dining guide booklet to check out the menus. You can dine up the mountain in three restaurants. In downtown Steamboat Springs try the Apogee for French-style food, Old West Steakhouse, or the Cottonwood Grill for its 'fabulously tasty Pacific Rim cuisine'. For a budget meal, head for Double Z.
Après-ski The old town is quiet in the evening – the base lodge area is livelier. At close of play the Slopeside Grill and the Inferno are popular.
Off the slopes Getting to Thunderhead restaurant complex is easy for pedestrians. Visiting town is, too.

Steamboat

The yellow line shows the Pioneer Ridge Expansion area. In the long term 500 acres are due to be developed and another lift installed.

Morningside Park

Christmas Tree Bowl

Storm Peak 3160m/ 10,370ft

Sunshine Peak 3165m/10,380ft

Four points

Pioneer Ridge

Pony Express

Storm Peak

Sundown

Rendezvous Saddle

Thunderhead 2770m/9,080ft

Thunderhead

Silver Bullet

Steamboat
Christie Base   Gondola base 2100m/6,900ft

Telluride

Expansion of slopes has made this cute old town worth considering

538

COSTS

① ② ③ ④ ⑤ ⑥

RATINGS

The slopes

Snow	****
Extent	**
Expert	****
Intermediate	***
Beginner	*****
Convenience	****
Queues	*****
Mountain restaurants	*

The rest

Scenery	****
Resort charm	****
Off-slope	**

NEWS

Two seasons ago three new high-speed chair-lifts opened up Prospect Bowl and another 733 acres of terrain – a 70% increase – and over 20 new runs, creating an entirely different feel to the resort.

For 2002/03, the Sprite Air Garden terrain-park was trebled in size and completely revamped. A new steeper half-pipe was also built.

Also new was Thrill Hill – specially for tubing, snowbiking and snowskating and floodlit till 8pm.

And the Topaten Touring Center opened at the top of the Sunshine Express lift, offering guided snow-shoe tours and 10km/6 miles of groomed cross-country trails.

+ Charming restored Victorian gold- and silver-mining town with a real Wild West atmosphere

+ Slopes for all abilities

+ Dramatic, craggy mountain scenery – unusual for Colorado

– Isolated location

– Despite expansion still a small area

– Mountain Village is still a little quiet but vastly improved on a few years ago

– Limited mountain restaurants

We love the old town of Telluride – it has lots of character, lovely old buildings, good restaurants and shops and dramatic views of the San Juan mountains. The addition of Prospect Bowl two seasons ago has nearly doubled the extent of the slopes. But it is still a small area – only one western US resort in this book has a significantly smaller area of slopes. Keen piste-bashers should rent a car and combine it with another destination for a one-week or 10-day holiday.

THE RESORT

Telluride is an isolated resort in south-west Colorado. The town first boomed when gold was found – and Butch Cassidy robbed his first bank here. The town's old wooden buildings and sidewalks have been well-restored and it has more Wild West charm than any other resort. Shops and restaurants have gone decidedly up-market since its 'hippy' days of a few years ago and a lot of celebrities have plush holiday-homes in the area now. But Telluride is still friendly and small-scale. On the slopes, the Mountain Village is a development of lavish modern condos and hotels. A gondola links the town and village and runs until midnight.

THE MOUNTAINS

There is something for everyone here. **Slopes** Two chair-lifts and a gondola serve the steep wooded slopes above the town, and give access to the bowl beyond which leads down to Mountain Village. This has steep slopes at the top, intermediate terrain in the middle and ideal, wide and gentle beginner slopes beyond the village down to Big Billie's and under the Sunshine Express lift. The Gold Hill lift serves some of the steepest slopes in Colorado. The recently opened terrain in Prospect Bowl is mainly intermediate, with dozens of rolling pitches that meander and weave their way through thickets of trees. A very relaxing and pretty area.

but good for spaghetti and meatballs, pizzas and stunning views. All are getting a facelift for 2003/04.

Schools and guides The resort is proud of its Telluride Teaching System. Bump clinics are a speciality.

Facilities for children The Adventure Club provides indoor and outdoor play before and after children's lessons. The Mountain Village Activity Center has a nursery for toddlers.

STAYING THERE

Telluride is tricky to get to from the UK, involving two or three flights or a long 335 mile drive from Denver.

How to go Packages fly into nearby Montrose or the tiny Telluride airport (prone to closure by the weather).

Hotels Hotel Columbia is luxurious, as is the plush yet friendly Camel's Garden Hotel and Spa. The New Sheridan is one of the town's oldest hotels. The big Wyndham Peaks Resort in the Mountain Village is enormous but has a spectacular lounge area and impressive spa facilities.

Self-catering There are plenty of condos. The Inn At Lost Creek in Mountain Village is the most lavish of the self-catering options.

Eating out The Cosmopolitan in the Hotel Columbia is renowned as the best in town. Other sophisticated options include the Marmotte and Harmon's (in the old station). Allred's at the top of the gondola is a private club for lunch but offers gourmet dining in the evenings.

Après-ski There's a lively bar-based après-ski scene. Leimgruber's is popular in the early evening. The New Sheridan has a lovely old bar. The Last Dollar has been recommended by locals. The Fly Me to the Moon Saloon has live music and stays open late. There's a new swanky candlelit lounge called the Noir Bar attached to the Blue Point Restaurant. There are often concerts at the historic Sheridan Opera House. The Nugget Theatre shows latest cinema releases. Thrill Hill at the Mountain Village has floodlit tubing, sledding and snowbiking.

Off the slopes There's quite a lot to do around town if you are not skiing or boarding, such as dog sledding, horse riding, snow-shoeing, ice skating, and glider rides. The Golden Door Spa in the Wyndham Peaks Resort was voted one of the top 10 spas in the world by *Condé Nast Traveller* readers.

↑ Giuseppe's is a tiny hut, but the views from it are amazing

KEY FACTS

Resort	2665m
	8,750ft
Slopes	2665-3735m
	8,750-12,250ft
Lifts	16
Pistes	1,700 acres
Green	25%
Blue	36%
Black	39%
Snowmaking	
	204 acres

Central reservations
Call 728 7507.
Toll-free number
(from within the US)
1 888 827 8050.

Phone numbers
From distant parts of the US, add the prefix 1 970.
From abroad, add the prefix +1 970.

TOURIST OFFICE

t 728 3041
skitelluride@telski.com
www.telski.com

Terrain-parks The huge, 10-acre Sprite Air Garden terrain-park above the Mountain Village has a big half-pipe and all the features you could dream of. There are also two separate Freestyle Terrain areas to pull tricks in.

Snow reliability With an average of 309 inches of snow a year and a fair amount of snowmaking, snow reliability is average for Colorado, but there have been some slow starts to recent seasons.

Experts The double-black bump runs directly above the town are what has given the area its expert reputation and there are steep gladed runs from all along the ridge between Giuseppe's and Gold Hill – no longer a hike away thanks to the Gold Hill lift. Gold Hill has some truly challenging terrain from wide open steeps to narrow chutes and gnarly wooded trails. There are heli- and snowcat operations.

Intermediates There are ideal blue cruising runs with awesome views right from the top down to Mountain Village (including the aptly-named See Forever) and Prospect Bowl is largely easy cruising. The main easy way back down the front to town is the winding Telluride Trail. But even with the recent expansion, keen piste-bashers could get bored after a couple of days.

Beginners There are ideal runs in the Meadows below Mountain Village, and splendid long greens and blues served by the Sunshine Express chair.

Snowboarding The lift system means it is easy to get about, and the huge terrain-park offers plenty of scope.

Cross-country The beauty of the area makes it splendid for cross-country – both in the valley and at altitude.

Queues These are rarely a problem.

Mountain restaurants Gorrono Ranch is the main on-mountain restaurant, with a big terrace, live music and a BBQ. At the top of the Prospect Bowl lift, you can get sandwiches. Giuseppe's is tiny

Telluride

539

Vail

Luxury living, high prices and the US's biggest single ski area

COSTS

① ② ③ ④ ⑤ ⑥

RATINGS

The slopes

Snow	*****
Extent	****
Expert	****
Intermediate	*****
Beginner	***
Convenience	***
Queues	**
Mountain restaurants	**

The rest

Scenery	***
Resort charm	***
Off-slope	***

KEY FACTS

Resort	2500m
	8,200ft
Slopes	2475-3525m
	8,120-11,570ft
Lifts	34
Pistes	5,289 acres
Green	18%
Blue	29%
Black	53%
Snowmaking	
	380 acres

skiclub.co.uk
0845 45 807 80
100 Years 1903-2003

➕ Biggest area in the US – great for confident intermediates

➕ The Back Bowls are big areas of treeless terrain – unusual in the US

➕ Fabulous area of ungroomed, wooded slopes opened at Blue Sky Basin a few years ago

➕ Largely traffic-free resort village, with great bus service

➖ Slopes can be crowded by American standards, with some lift queues even in low season

➖ The Back Bowls can suffer from the sun and they and Blue Sky Basin may be closed in early season

➖ Inadequate mountain restaurants

➖ Tirolean-style Vail Village doesn't impress many Europeans

➖ Expensive

Blue Sky Basin, an area of shady, wooded, largely ungroomed slopes, has transformed Vail's attraction for good skiers and riders. Not only does it bring a much-needed bit of spice to the resort, but it gets you away from the crowds that are Vail's most serious drawback.

Vail's slopes are now undeniably compelling, especially when you take account of nearby sister-resort Beaver Creek (see separate chapter). What continues to push Vail down our American shortlist are its style and its atmosphere – a curious mixture of pseudo-Tirol and anonymous suburbs. The resort works well, largely thanks to the efficient buses. But if you hope to be captivated, Vail can't compete with the distinctive Rockies resorts based on old mining or cowboy towns. If we're going that far West, we like it to be a bit Wild.

THE RESORT

Standing in the centre of Vail Village, surrounded by chalets and bierkellers, you could be forgiven for thinking you were in the Tirol – which is what Vail's founder, Pete Seibert, intended back in the 1950s. But Vail Village is now just part of an enormous resort, mostly built in anonymous modern style, stretching for miles beside the I-70 freeway – the main route westwards through the Rockies from Denver.

The vast village benefits from a free and efficient bus service, which makes choice of location less than crucial. But there's no denying that the most convenient – and expensive – places to stay are in mock-Tirolean Vail Village, near the Vista Bahn fast chair, or in functional Lionshead, near the gondola. There is a lot of accommodation further out – the cheapest tends to be across the I-70.

Beaver Creek, ten miles away, is covered by the lift pass and is easily reached by bus (see separate chapter). Other resorts within a two-hour drive include Breckenridge and Keystone (both owned by Vail Resorts and covered by the lift pass), Aspen, Steamboat and Copper Mountain.

540

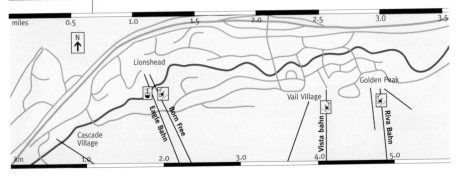

← The heart of the Tirolean part of Vail, with the Vista Bahn chair going up to Mid-Vail

bowls – Mid-Vail in the centre, with Game Creek to the south-west and Northeast Bowl to the, er, north-east. Lifts reach the ridge at three points, all giving access to the **Back Bowls** (mostly ungroomed and treeless) and through them to the **Blue Sky Basin** area (mostly ungroomed and wooded).

The slopes have yellow-jacketed patrollers who stop people speeding recklessly. There's a 'new technology center' where you can test the latest equipment. British guests may get the chance of skiing with Martin Bell, Britain's best-ever downhiller and now UK ski ambassador for Vail Resorts (he lives in Vail).

TERRAIN-PARKS
Head for Golden Peak
There is an excellent terrain-park and a super-pipe (130m/425ft long with 4.5m/15ft walls) at Golden Peak, accessed by the Riva Bahn Express. The park has over 30 rails and lots of jumps and was expanded for last season. There's also a deck where you can chill out.

SNOW RELIABILITY
Excellent, except in the Bowls
As well as an exceptional natural snow record, Vail has extensive snowmaking facilities, normally needed only in early season. Although snow in the Back Bowls is often poor because of its largely south-facing aspect, Blue Sky Basin is largely north-facing and sheltered from sun by trees – so the snow quality can be expected to be excellent, with powder lasting for days after the latest fall.

NEWS

For 2003/04 a new outdoor sundeck is planned at Hawk's Nest overlooking Sun Up Bowl. There will also be a new moving carpet lift in the beginner area at Eagle's Nest. Rock and stump removal continues at Blue Sky Basin and there will be new machines for terrain-park grooming and snowmaking.

New for 2002/03 were free daily guided tours of Blue Sky Basin – a very useful service. The three chair-lifts in Blue Sky Basin had their capacities increased. Also new was a sundeck holding 250 people at Two Elk Lodge.

THE MOUNTAINS

Vail has the biggest area of slopes in the US, with immaculately groomed trails and ungroomed terrain in open bowls and among the trees. There are runs to suit every taste. The main criticism is that some of the runs (especially blacks) are overclassified.

THE SLOPES
Something for everyone
The slopes above **Vail** can be accessed via three main lifts. From right next to Vail Village, the Vista Bahn fast chair goes up to the major mid-mountain focal point, Mid-Vail; from Lionshead, the Eagle Bahn gondola goes up to the Eagle's Nest complex; and from the Golden Peak base area just to the east of Vail Village, the Riva Bahn fast chair goes up towards the Two Elk area.

The front face of the mountain is largely north-facing, with well-groomed trails cut through the trees. At altitude the mountainside divides into three

BLUE SKY BASIN

This is the one of biggest new developments in any Colorado ski area for years – it has added 645 acres of terrain, served by three fast quads. The prospect of it caused outrage among environmental groups, and there were some arson attacks.

When we skied the Basin we loved it. There are some easy blue runs that are frequently groomed, but most of the area is left ungroomed and the runs among the trees – some widely spaced, some very tight – are delightful for strong skiers and boarders. Few of the runs are very steep, but because you are basically finding your own way much of the time, there is a great feeling of adventure. The snow is usually much better than in the Back Bowls because of the shelter given by the trees and the generally north-facing aspect. A 2003 reporter recommends the free daily tours which were new for 2002/03 and start at 10am at the Blue Sky Basin sign at the top of the Mountaintop and Northwoods Express lifts.

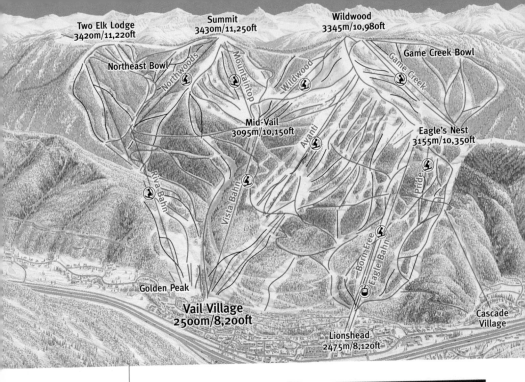

Two Elk Lodge
3420m/11,220ft

Summit
3430m/11,250ft

Wildwood
3345m/10,980ft

Game Creek Bowl

Northeast Bowl

Northwoods

Mountaintop

Wildwood

Game Creek

Mid-Vail
3095m/10,150ft

Eagle's Nest
3155m/10,350ft

Avanti

Riva Bahn

Vista Bahn

Pride

Born Free

Eagle Bahn

Golden Peak

Vail Village
2500m/8,200ft

Lionshead
2475m/8,120ft

Cascade
Village

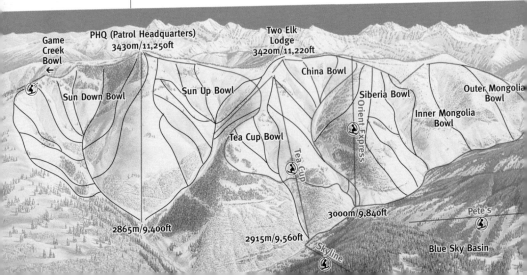

Game
Creek
Bowl
←

PHQ (Patrol Headquarters)
3430m/11,250ft

Two Elk
Lodge
3420m/11,220ft

China Bowl

Sun Down Bowl

Sun Up Bowl

Siberia Bowl

Outer Mongolia
Bowl

Orient Express

Inner Mongolia
Bowl

Tea Cup Bowl

Tea Cup

2865m/9,400ft

3000m/9,840ft

Pete's

2915m/9,560ft

Skyline

Blue Sky Basin

boarding

Vail has been wooing boarders with excellent facilities for years. With beautifully groomed, gentle slopes and lots of high-speed chairs, this is a great area for beginners, and there's plenty for experts too, including some wonderful gladed runs. There are specialist board shops and good instruction. Vail's Burton Learn to Ride programme uses special equipment designed to help you learn. It claims to minimise falls and accelerate the learning curve. There's a Burton test centre at the New Technology Centre at the top of the Mountaintop Express chair.

FOR EXPERTS
Transformed by Blue Sky Basin

Vail's Back Bowls are vast areas, served by three chair-lifts and a couple of short drag-lifts. You can go virtually anywhere you like in the half-dozen identifiable bowls, trying the gradient and terrain of your choice. There are interesting, lightly wooded areas, as well as the open slopes that dominate the area. 87 per cent of the runs in the Back Bowls are classified black but are not particularly steep, and they have disappointed some of our more confident reporters.

Blue Sky Basin has some great adventure runs in the trees – see feature panel.

On the front face there are some genuinely steep double-black-diamond runs which usually have great snow; they are often mogulled but sometimes groomed to make wonderful fast cruising. The Highline lift on the extreme east of the area serves three. And Prima Cornice, served by the Northwoods Express, is one of the steepest runs on the front side.

If the snow is good, try the back-country Minturn Mile – you leave the ski area through a gate in the Game Creek area for an off-piste run starting with a powder bowl and finishing on a path by a river – ending up in the atmospheric Saloon (see Après-ski).

FOR INTERMEDIATES
Ideal territory

The majority of Vail's front face is great intermediate territory, with easy cruising runs. Above Lionshead, especially, there are excellent long, relatively quiet blues – Born Free and Simba both go from top to bottom. Game Creek Bowl, nearby, is excellent, too. Avanti, underneath the chair of the same name, is a nice cruiser.

As well as tackling some of the easier front-face blacks, intermediates will find plenty of interest in the Back Bowls (given good visibility). Some of the runs are groomed and several are classified blue, including Silk Road, which loops around the eastern edge, with wonderful views. Some of the unpisted slopes make the ideal introduction to powder. Confident intermediates will also enjoy Blue Sky Basin – choose the clearly marked blue runs to start with.

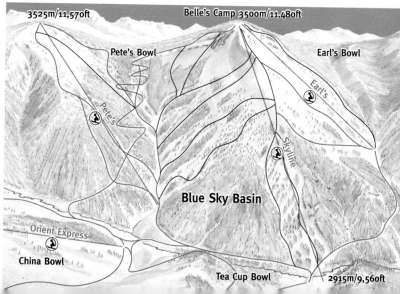

3525m/11,570ft — Belle's Camp 3500m/11,480ft — Pete's Bowl — Earl's Bowl — Pete's — Earl's — Skyline — Blue Sky Basin — Orient Express — China Bowl — Tea Cup Bowl — 2915m/9,560ft

COLORADO

544

SCHOOLS

Vail
t 476 3239

Classes
Full day (9.45-3.30) $100

Private lessons
$135 for 1hr for 1 to 6 people

CHILDREN

School lessons are based at Children's Ski Centers located at Golden Peak and Lionshead (full day for ages 3 to 14 including lift pass and lunch US$104). There are separate programmes to suit children of different ages and ability – Mini-Mice for children aged three, Mogul Mice and Superstars for those aged four to six.

Small World Play School, located at Golden Peak, provides day care for children aged two months to six years, from 8am to 4.30. Reservations are essential – call 479 3285.

SKE-Cology classes let kids learn about mountain wildlife while skiing/ snowboarding.

Kids aged 7-14 can take part in such events as race days and bump and bash sessions through the terrain-parks.

FOR BEGINNERS
Good but can be crowded
There are excellent nursery slopes at resort level and at altitude and easy longer runs to progress to. But they can be rather crowded.

FOR CROSS-COUNTRY
Some of the best
Vail's cross-country areas are at the foot of Golden Peak and at the Nordic Center on the golf course. Cross-country and telemark lessons are available at Golden Peak.

QUEUES
Can be bad
Vail has some of the longest lift queues we've hit in the US, especially at weekends because of the influx from Denver. Most queues move quickly. But at Mid-Vail waits of 15 minutes are common and we have reports of 45-minute waits. The Northwoods Express lift can also be very busy because the alternative Highline lift is so slow.

MOUNTAIN RESTAURANTS
Surprisingly poor (though pricey)
As other major American resorts are gradually improving their mountain restaurants, Vail's are slipping further behind: demand is increasing to the point where the major self-service restaurants can be unpleasantly crowded from 11am to 2pm. They are also expensive (especially Two Elk, where a reporter said 'a hot dog, fries and coke cost £10'). There's table-service (with limited menu) at Eagle's Nest – book ahead.

SCHOOLS AND GUIDES
Among the best in the world
The Vail-Beaver Creek school has an excellent reputation. All the reports we've had of it have again been glowing. Class sizes are usually small – as few as four is not uncommon. A

2003 reporter says the school is 'really excellent – good technical advice without too much standing around'. There are specialist half-day workshops in, for example, bumps and powder. You can sign up on the mountain.

FACILITIES FOR CHILDREN
Excellent
The comprehensive arrangements for young children look excellent, and we've had good reports on the children's school. There are splendid children's areas with adventure trails and themed play areas. There's even a special kids cafe area at Mid Vail. The Night Owl programme gives parents an evening off and includes supervised activities and dinner at Adventure Ridge at the top of the gondola.

STAYING THERE

HOW TO GO
Package or independent
There's a big choice of packages to Vail. It's easy to organise your own visit, with regular airport shuttles.
Chalets Several UK tour operators offer catered chalets. Many are out of the centre at East Vail or West Vail or across the busy freeway.
Hotels Vail has a fair choice of hotels, though most tend to be expensive. Check online for the best deals.
(((((5) Vail Cascade One of the best in town. A resort within a resort – lots of facilities and a chair-lift right outside.
(((((5) Sonnenalp Bavaria Haus Very smart and central. Large spa and splendid piano bar-lounge.
(((((5) Lodge at Vail Owned by Vail Resorts, right by the Vista Bahn in Vail Village. Some standard rooms small. Huge buffet breakfast. Outdoor pool.
(((((5) Marriot Mountain Resort Also owned by Vail Resorts, near the Eagle Bahn gondola. Recently refurbished. Impressive spa facilities

Blue Sky Basin in the foreground has been a great addition to Vail's terrain ↗

VAIL RESORTS, INC / JACK AFFLECK

GETTING THERE

Air Eagle 56km/35 miles (1hr); Denver 177km/110 miles (2½hr).

ACTIVITIES

Indoor Athletic clubs and spas, massage, ski museum, cinema, theatre, tennis courts, artificial skating rink, library, galleries

Outdoor Hot-air ballooning, skating, ice hockey, sleigh rides, fishing, mountaineering, snowmobiles, snow-shoe excursions, snowcat tours, dog-sledding, paragliding, tubing hill, ski biking, thrill sledding, laser tag

Central reservations phone number
Call 1 800 404 3535 (toll-free from within the US).

Phone numbers
From distant parts of the US, add the prefix 1 970.
From abroad, add the prefix +1 970.

TOURIST OFFICE

t 496 9090
international@vail resorts.com
www.vail.com

(((4) **Evergreen Lodge** Cheaper (for Vail!) option. Between village and Lionshead. Outdoor pool. Sports bar.
Self-catering The Racquet Club at East Vail has lots of amenities. Mountain Haus has high-quality condos in the centre of town.

EATING OUT
Endless choice

Whatever kind of food you want, Vail has it – but most of it is not cheap. 'All restaurants require a fat wallet' and 'high standards but at New York prices' are typical comments from reporters. Booking in advance is essential.

Recommended fine-dining options include the Wildflower, in the Lodge, Ludwig's, in the Sonnenalp Bavaria Haus, and the Tour. For a budget option try Bogart's Brewpub, with local ales and filling American food.

Recommendations from readers include May Palace (Chinese) in West Vail, Sapphire (seafood), Blu's (good value), Montauk (seafood), the Bistro at the Racquet Club, Amigos, Russell's, Bottega and Vendetta's. New places are the upmarket Italian Mezzaluna and Billy's Island Grill. For a luxury dining experience try Game Creek Lodge, which is open to the public in the evenings. You are taken there by snowcat from the top of the gondola.

APRES-SKI
Fairly lively

Powderhounds at Lionshead is popular at the end of the day, with live music. Nearby Garfinkel's has a DJ, sundeck and happy hour. The Red Lion in the village centre is popular, with big-screen TVs and huge portions of food. The George tries to be an English-style pub. The Ore House serves 'mean margaritas and hot chicken wings'.

King's Club is the place to go for high-calorie cakes, and becomes a piano bar later; and Los Amigos and Bogart's Brewpub are other lively places at four o'clock.

You can have a good night out at Adventure Ridge at the top of the gondola. As well as bars and restaurants, there's ice skating, tubing, snowmobiling, snow-shoeing, sledding, snowbiking, laser tag and kids' snowmobiling – though a reporter reckons the tubing hill is boring and badly run compared with Keystone's.

Later on, Fubar is a popular disco. 8150 is also good, with a suspended floor that moves with the dancing; the Bully Ranch at the Sonnenalp has great 'mudslide' drinks; The Bridge is a snowboard hangout; Vendetta's does good pizza and beer. The Sanctuary club is above the Tap Room bar.

Out of town in Minturn, the Saloon is worth a trip – genuine old-west style with photos of famous skier patrons.

OFF THE SLOPES
A lot to do

Getting around on the free bus is easy, and there are lots of activities to try. Balloon rides are popular. The factory outlets at Silverthorne are a must for shopaholics who can't resist a bargain.

STAYING UP THE MOUNTAIN
Great if you can afford it

Game Creek chalet above Vail is a luxurious private enclave up the mountain, which a group can rent by the night (for a small fortune). You ski in at the end of the day to a champagne welcome, soak in an outdoor hot-tub and enjoy a gourmet dinner. The cabin-keeper then leaves, returning to prepare your breakfast.

STAYING ALONG THE VALLEY
Cheaper but quiet

Staying out of central Vail is cheaper but not so lively. If you rent a car, staying out of town and visiting nearby resorts makes for an interesting holiday.

Winter Park

Good value, great terrain, huge snowfalls, unpretentious town

COSTS

① ② ③ ④ ⑤ ⑥

RATINGS

The slopes

Snow	*****
Extent	***
Expert	****
Intermediate	****
Beginner	*****
Convenience	***
Queues	****
Mountain restaurants	***

The rest

Scenery	***
Resort charm	**
Off-slope	*

NEWS

Intrawest's agreement to operate and develop Winter Park should mean significant improvements – the company has agreed to invest a minimum of $50m in the resort over the next 10 years. Visitors are unlikely to see any major changes this coming season, however, as the long-term plans are still being finalised.

In 2002/03 Winter Park redesigned and expanded its terrain-parks and half-pipe. It also built a short rope tow to enable people coming down from the Olympia chair to get to the mountain restaurant at Sunspot and to the trails on the front side of Winter Park mountain.

There is a new deli (the Boxcar) and sweet shop (the Candy Cache) at the West Portal base station.

546

➕ The best snowfall record of all Colorado's major resorts

➕ Superb beginner terrain and lots of groomed cruises

➕ Lots for experts, including great tree skiing and countless challenging mogul slopes

➕ Quiet on weekdays, and impressive lift system copes with weekends

➕ Leading resort for teaching people with disabilities to ski and ride

➕ Great snow and expert terrain at Berthoud Pass, accessed by snowcat

➕ Good views by US standards

➕ Largely free of inflated prices and ski-resort glitz, but ...

➖ Also largely lacking the the range of restaurants and shops you expect in a big international resort

➖ Town is a bus-ride from the slopes, and strung-out along the main road

➖ New 'village' at the lift base is very limited, and dead in the evening

➖ Trails tend to be either easy cruises or stiff mogul fields

➖ One or two slow lifts in key spots

➖ The nearest big resort to Denver, so can get crowded at weekends – mainly a problem on runs close to the base, and in rental shops

When we first visited Winter Park – developed for the recreation of the citizens of nearby Denver, and still owned by the city – we were surprised by what we found: a mountain of world class. Now there seems to be the prospect of a world-class resort at the base, too: dynamic Intrawest (developers of famously wonderful Whistler) have signed a 50-year agreement to operate and develop the whole resort. The future looks bright.

For the present, if value for money and snow are more important to you than glamour or variety of shops and restaurants, the place should be high up on your Colorado shortlist. Some of our reporters rate it their favourite Colorado resort, partly because it makes such a refreshing change from the norm.

THE RESORT

Winter Park started life around the turn of the century as a railway town, when Rio Grande railway workers climbed the slopes to ski down. One of the resort's mountains, Mary Jane, is named after a legendary 'lady of pleasure' who is said to have received the land as payment for her favours.

The railway still plays an important part in Winter Park's existence, with a station right at the foot of the slopes where trains deposit Denverites every Saturday and Sunday morning and take them home after the lifts close; it's supposed to be quite a party on the homebound leg.

Most accommodation is down in town, but in the last few years, stylish accommodation has been developed at or near the foot of the slopes, most recently a car-free mini-resort known as The Village at Winter Park Resort. But

most accommodation is a shuttle-bus-ride away in spacious condos scattered around either side of the road through downtown Winter Park – US highway 40, which continues to the nearby town of Fraser. There are also motels, bars and restaurants along the road, and at night Winter Park resembles an established ski resort town – but in the daytime it's clear that the place doesn't amount to much. Reporters complain there's no real 'town centre'. Confusingly, an area between the mountain and the town is known as Old Town. The locals are friendly and helpful – typical small-town America.

Shuttle-buses run regularly between the town and the lift base, and the hotels and condos also provide shuttle services. But a car does simplify day trips to Denver or to other resorts – within a two-hour drive are Steamboat, Breckenridge, Copper Mountain, Keystone and Vail.

Winter Park

KEY FACTS

Resort	2745m
	9,000ft
Slopes	2745-3675m
	9,000-12,060ft
Lifts	22
Pistes	2,886 acres
Green	9%
Blue	34%
Black	57%
Snowmaking	
	294 acres

LIFT PASSES

Winter Park Resort
Covers all lifts in
Winter Park.

Main pass
1-day pass $63
6-day pass $366

Senior citizens
Over 62: 6-day pass
$306
Over 70: free pass

Children
Under 14: 6-day pass
$186
Under 6: free pass

Notes
Half-day passes
available. Special
rates for disabled
skiers.

THE MOUNTAINS

Winter Park has a mountain that's big
by US standards, and an excellent mix
of terrain that suits all abilities.

THE SLOPES
Interestingly divided

There are five distinct, but well-linked,
sectors. From the main base, a fast
quad takes you to the peak of the
original **Winter Park** mountain. From
there, you can descend in all
directions. Runs lead back towards the
main base and over to the **Vasquez
Ridge** area on the far right, served by
the Pioneer fast quad.

You can also descend to the base of
Mary Jane mountain, where four chairs
up the front face serve tough runs;
other chairs serve easier terrain on the
flanks. From the top you can head up to
Parsenn Bowl via the slow Timberline
chair for intermediate terrain above and
in the trees. This chair is exposed at the
top, and can be closed for long periods
in bad weather. From here, conditions
permitting, you can hike for up to half
an hour to access the advanced and
extreme slopes of **Vasquez Cirque**. A
long ski-out takes you to the bottom of
Vasquez Ridge and the Pioneer lift.

TERRAIN-PARKS
Bigger and better...

For 2002/03 Winter Park expanded its
terrain-park and moved the half-pipe
into the same area. The newly named
Rail Yard park, with 12 rails and 15
jumps, runs down much of the front of
Winter Park mountain for over 1100m/
3,650ft. Half way down it breaks for a
trail carrying non-park-users across the
mountain. For the lower half, you can
choose to continue on traditional park
features such as table-tops and spines
or go on the slope-style park designed
for skier- and boarder-cross events.
This runs alongside the 100m/328ft-
long Vertigo half-pipe.

SNOW RELIABILITY
Among Colorado's best

'Copious amounts of beautiful, dry
powder,' enthuses a reporter. 'So much
snow, we were delayed a day getting
to the resort,' says another who visited
in 2003. Winter Park's position, close
to the watershed of the Continental
Divide, gives it an average yearly
snowfall of over 350 inches – the
highest of any major Colorado resort.
As a back-up, snowmaking covers a
high proportion of the runs on Winter
Park mountain.

FOR EXPERTS
Some hair-raising challenges

Mary Jane has some of the steepest mogul fields, chutes and hair-raising challenges in the US ('mogul city USA', in the words of one reporter). The fearsome runs of Mary Jane's back side are accessed by a control gate off a long black run called Derailer. Hole in the Wall, Awe Chute, Baldy's Chute and Jeff's Chute are all steep, narrow and bordered by rocks. More manageable are the wider black mogul fields such as Derailer, Long Haul and Brakeman. There are some good challenges on Winter Park Mountain. Parsenn Bowl has superb blue/black gladed runs and tougher tree skiing on the back side.

When it's open, Vasquez Cirque has excellent ungroomed expert terrain with extensive views. You don't get much vertical before you hit the forest, though. The Improvement Center does a three-hour Cirque Adventure Tour.

FOR INTERMEDIATES
Choose your challenge

From pretty much wherever you are on Winter Park mountain and Vasquez Ridge you can choose a run to suit your ability. Most are well groomed every night, giving you perfect early morning cruising on the famous Colorado 'corduroy' pistes.

For bumps, try Mary Jane's front side. Parsenn Bowl has grand views and some gentle cruising pistes as well as more challenging ungroomed terrain. It's also an ideal place to try ungroomed powder for the first time.

FOR BEGINNERS
The best we've seen

Discovery Park is a 25-acre dedicated area for beginners, reached by a high-speed quad and served by two more chairs. As well as a nursery area and longer green runs, it has an adventure trail through trees and a special terrain park. Once out of the Park, there are easy runs back to base.

FOR CROSS-COUNTRY
Lots of it

There are several different areas, all with generally excellent snow, totalling over 200km/125 miles of groomed trails, as well as backcountry tours.

QUEUES
Rarely a problem

During the week the mountain is generally quiet. 'We had whole runs to ourselves for a couple of miles,' says one delighted reporter. However, there may be a crowd waiting for the opening of the Zephyr Express from the main base and there can be queues on the slow chair up Parsenn Bowl. At weekends the Denver crowds arrive – even then the network of more than 20 lifts (including eight fast quads) makes light work of the people.

MOUNTAIN RESTAURANTS
Some good facilities

The highlight is the Lodge at Sunspot, at the top of Winter Park mountain – 'The nicest I've found in the States,' says one reader. This wood and glass building has a welcoming bar with a

boarding

There is some great advanced and extreme boarding terrain and a high probability of fresh powder to ride. The new Rail Yard park (see Terrain-parks) makes Winter Park even more attractive to advanced riders. The resort is also an ideal beginner and intermediate boarder area, with excellent terrain for learning. A good school provides classes for all levels and special lessons for children aged 7-15.

SCHOOLS

Winter Park
t 726 1551
skischool@skiwinter
park.com

Classes
Half day (2½hr) $40
Private lessons
$140 for 1½hr for 1
or 2 people

**National Sports
Center for the
Disabled**
t 726 1540
Special programme
for disabled skiers
and snowboarders

CHILDREN

The ski school runs
special classes for
children aged 5 to 13
and provides lunch
(US$80 per day
including lunch and
lift ticket).
The Children's Center
has a popular non-
skiing programme for
children aged 2
months to 5 years.
You can rent out
bleepers to keep in
touch. Book early to
ensure a place.
The Children's Center
is open 8am to 4pm.
Lessons are 10am to
3pm.

roaring log fire, a table-service restaurant and very good self-service food – but it gets very busy. Lunch Rock Cafe at the top of Mary Jane does quick snacks and has a deli counter, and there is a self-service at Snoasis, by the beginner area. Mama Mia's Pizzeria is on the lower level of Snoasis – you can order food in advance from a special kiosk on top of Winter Park Mountain so that the food is waiting for you on arrival. Otherwise, it's down to the bases. The Club Car at the base of Mary Jane offers 'a good atmosphere and more varied menu' than the American fast-food norm. The new Boxcar Deli at West Portal Station does sandwiches, pastries and coffees.

SCHOOLS AND GUIDES
A good reputation
'The ski school was a delight and class sizes averaged three!' says a 2003 reporter. As well as standard classes there are ideas such as Family Private, for different abilities together; themed lessons such as Mogul Mania; and Quick Tips, a 'quick fix' based on video analysis (only $5).

FACILITIES FOR CHILDREN
Some of the best
The Children's Center at Winter Park base area houses day-care facilities and is the meeting point for children's classes, which have their own areas, including 'moving carpet' lifts. 'They couldn't do enough for children,' says our most recent reporter.

STAYING THERE

HOW TO GO
Fair choice
Several UK operators offer Winter Park.
Chalets Several operators offer them.
Hotels There are a couple of outstanding hotel/condo complexes.
((((4) **Iron Horse Resort** Slope-side, comfortable, condo-style.
((((4) **Vintage** Near resort entrance; good facilities but some poor past reports of it.
(((3) **Winter Park Mountain Lodge** Across the valley from the lifts; micro-brewery above the bar; lacking character but 'friendly, with large rooms, nice pool, good food'.
Self-catering There are a lot of comfortable condos, including the

NATIONAL SPORTS CENTER FOR THE DISABLED

If you are able-bodied, the most striking and humbling thing you'll notice as you ride your first chair-lift is the number of people with disabilities hurtling down the mountain faster than many of us could ever hope to. There are blind skiers, skiers with one leg, people with paralysis – whatever their problem, they've cracked it.

That's because Winter Park is home to the US National Sports Center for the Disabled (NSCD) – the world's leading centre for teaching skiing and snowboarding to people with disabilities. As well as full-time instructors, there are 1,000 trained volunteers who help in the programme. More than 40 disabilities are specially catered for. If you are disabled and want to learn to ski or snowboard, there's no better place to go. It's important to book ahead so that a suitable instructor is available. The NSCD can help with travel and accommodation arrangements:

NSCD, PO Box 36, Winter Park, CO 80482, USA. Tel: 726 1540.

The Zephyr Mountain Lodge was the first accommodation to be built at the base of Winter Park Resort. Expect more now that Intrawest is involved →

GETTING THERE

Air Denver 108km/67 miles (1½hr).

Rail Leaves Denver Sat and Sun at 7.15am and returns at 4.15pm. Journey time 2hr.

ACTIVITIES

Indoor Cinema, swimming pool, roller skating, amusement arcade, health club, comedy club, aerobics, racquetball

Outdoor Dog-sledding, sight-seeing flights, snow-shoe, sleigh rides, tubing, snowmobiling, ice skating, snowbiking, snowcat tours, ice fishing, hot springs

Central reservations Call 726 5587. Toll-free number (from within the US) 1 800 729 5813.

Phone numbers From distant parts of the US, add the prefix 1 970. From abroad, add the prefix +1 970.

TOURIST OFFICE

t 726 5514 wpinfo@mail.skiwinter park.com www.skiwinterpark. com

slope-side Zephyr Mountain Lodge. 'Large comfortable rooms and couldn't be more convenient,' says a reporter.

EATING OUT
A fair choice
The range of options is gradually improving, but still isn't a match for that in more established 'destination' resorts. Reporters are keen on the long-established Deno's – seafood, steaks etc. Try the Crooked Creek Saloon at Fraser for atmosphere and typical American food. Smokin' Moe's (for sports TV and grills), New Hong Kong (for 'tasty' Chinese) and the Divide Grill (for pasta, seafood and grills): they are all in the Cooper Creek Square area. Readers recommend the Shed ('excellent steak and seafood, reasonably priced'), for Tex-Mex Carlos and Maria's, for pizza/pasta the 'dark but rustic' Hernandos, with open fires. Gasthaus Eichler does German food, at slightly higher prices. One reader reckons Wildcreek is the best in town.

The Lodge at Sunspot, up the mountain, is open some nights, with a 'fantastic' five-course fine-dining option on Saturday. They put gondolas on the chair-lift to get you up there in comfort.

APRES-SKI
If you know where to go ...
At close of play, there's action at the Kickapoo Tavern and Derailer Bar at the main lift base and the Club Car at the base of Mary Jane. Later on, try The Slope (in Old Town) for live music and dancing, or Adolph's, just across the road. The Shed can be lively. The Crooked Creek is popular with locals. Randi's Irish Saloon is usually lively.

OFF THE SLOPES
Mainly the great outdoors
Most diversions involve getting about on snow in different ways. If you like shopping, you'll rapidly exhaust the local possibilities and want to visit Silverthorne's factory outlet stores (90 minutes away on Interstate 70).

DON'T PASS ON BERTHOUD PASS

The drive to Winter Park from Denver – unusually for an American resort – involves a winding climb. It takes you to the summit of Berthoud Pass (3450m/11,320ft), on the Continental Divide, where the average snowfall is somewhere between 400 and 500 inches a year. This puts Berthoud in the Jackson Hole/Alta league. It used to operate with a couple of old chair-lifts and a beaten-up bus to bring you back up to the pass from much lower points on highway 40. Sadly, the chairs have now been removed. But the good news is the area now offers snowcat skiing and boarding, so the excellent terrain here is still accessible, and even less crowded. Like the lifts used to be, the snowcat is supplemented by a bus. There are runs to suit every ability, but in practice this is a mountain for good skiers and riders – the slopes down to the road below the pass are steep, and some are very steep.

A day's snowcat skiing including meals and demo powder skis costs $225 – or a group of 12 can book the whole cat for $2,400, or $200 a person.

For more information go to www.berthoudpass.com.

Utah

Salt Lake City and the resorts just to the east of it got a bit of a boost to their international profile two seasons back, hosting the 2002 Winter Olympics. Now it's back to business as usual, relying on one major ingredient to bring in the customers: The Greatest Snow on Earth.

Until recently Utah's extravagant climatic claim featured on every local car number plate. The state now seems to be targeting broader markets with its number plates, but the claim stands. The Colorado resorts dispute it, and have figures to prove that their famous powder is drier. What they can't dispute is that some Utah resorts do get huge dumps – up to twice the amount, over the season, that falls on some big-name Colorado resorts. In any case, by Alpine standards the snow here is wonderful. If you like the steep and deep, you should at some point make the pilgrimage to Utah.

There are differences in snowfall, though. The biggest dumps have traditionally been reserved for Snowbird and Alta (an average of 500 inches a year), close together in Little Cottonwood Canyon. The snow record of these small resorts has made them

the powder capitals of the world. Their slopes are now linked, making a big area with a shared lift pass.

Park City, the main 'destination' resort of the area, and upmarket Deer Valley next door hosted the lion's share of the Olympic events. These resorts and The Canyons nearby are only a few miles from Alta/Snowbird, but they get 'only' 300 to 350 inches (still more than most Colorado resorts). But it was unknown Snowbasin (400 inches) that got the prestige downhill Olympic events. Separate chapters follow on these six resorts.

There are other Utah resorts that are well worth visiting, too. If you enjoy seeing different resorts you can construct a compelling holiday by staying in Park City (by far the liveliest resort) or Salt Lake City (with a big city rather than a ski resort ambience) and driving to a different resort each day.

One of the fast six-packs that whizz you around the mountain at Park City ⬎

551

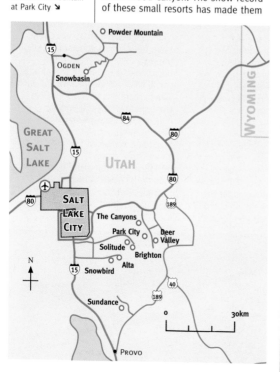

Phone numbers
From distant parts of
the US, add the prefix
1 801.
From abroad, add the
prefix +1 801.

SNOWPIX / CHRIS GILL

The Utah Interconnect
is a not-to-be-missed
off-piste day tour
between Park City
and Snowbird (see
Park City chapter).
This is the Highway to
Heaven traverse from
Solitude to Alta ➔

In recent years, the snow record of Alta and Snowbird has been matched by that of Brighton, at the head of next-door Big Cottonwood Canyon, and almost matched by that of Solitude, just down the canyon from Brighton. In these less well known places the snow gets tracked out less quickly, because the resorts attract far fewer experts. And you can now get a Ski Salt Lake Super Pass that gets you cheap day passes at all four of these resorts, through participating resorts.

In **Brighton** (2670m/8,760ft, vertical 530m/1,750ft, seven lifts, 64 runs, 850 acres), there are a lot of trails packed into quite a small area. Two of the three major lifts – including the area's one fast quad – serve mostly easy-intermediate slopes, but the Great Western slow quad goes over a more testing slope that represents the resort's full vertical of 530m, and the separate Mount Millicent area has some good steep slopes, both in and out of bounds. There are several accommodation options, including a slope-side lodge, cabins and chalets. There is free skiing for children under 10 and the over 70s.

Solitude (2435m/7,990ft, vertical 625m/2,050ft, eight lifts, 63 runs, 1,200 acres) covers a much bigger area, even without counting the excellent out-of-bounds terrain that you can get to from the top lift. Basically, the slopes here get steeper as you go up the

mountain – except that the area's one fast quad, Eagle, serves a slightly separate ridge that is almost entirely blue in gradient; it starts slightly down the valley from the main base. We haven't yet had a chance to explore the entirely black 400 acres of Honeycomb Canyon, on the back of the main mountain; this area was made much more appealing last year by installation of a new quad chair out of the canyon. There are three on–mountain restaurants and a small selection of bars/restaurants in the village. Solitude is home to Utah's original Yurt (Mongolian style tent) restaurant. There is one hotel – the 46-room Inn at Solitude (536 5700) – a few small condo developments (some distinctly luxurious) and some houses. A new ice–rink opened in 2002/3.

The other Utah resort that gets a bit of international attention – not least because it's owned by Robert Redford – is **Sundance** (1860m/6,100ft, 655m/2,150ft vertical, three lifts and a small tow, 41 runs, 450 acres). It gets 'only' 320 inches of snow a year – comfortably more than most resorts in Colorado. It's a small, narrow mountain but the vertical is respectable, the setting beneath Mt Timpanogos is spectacular and there is terrain to suit all abilities. The lower mountain is easy-intermediate, served by a quad chair, the upper part steeper: one triple chair serves purely black slopes, the other blue and black trails. Bearclaw's Cabin, at the top of it, is a small, basic restaurant with spectacular views. There are 17km/10 miles of cross-country trails, of varying difficulty, in a separate area just beyond the downhill slopes. There are beautifully furnished 'cottages' to rent, and grander chalets.

You can ski 'off-piste' with a guide from Park City to Snowbird via Solitude, Brighton and Alta on the Utah Interconnect tour – see Park City chapter.

Alta

Cult powder resort, now sharing one of America's biggest areas

COSTS

① ② ③ ④ ⑤ ⑥

RATINGS

The slopes

Snow	★★★★★
Extent	★★★
Expert	★★★★★
Intermediate	★★★
Beginner	★★★
Convenience	★★★★
Queues	★★★
Mountain restaurants	★★

The rest

Scenery	★★★
Resort charm	★★
Off-slope	★

NEWS

For 2002/03 guided snowcat skiing and boarding (yes, boarding) for advanced/expert levels only were introduced in Grizzly Gulch, next to the main area. Five runs cost from $200 including breakfast.

A 5km/3 mile Nordic skiing track and Centre was also opened.

For 2003/04 a new building is planned to accommodate Alta's children's programme.

Snowmaking facilities at Wildcat will also be improved.

SNOWBIRD / CARL YORK

They said it would never happen, but the link between Alta and Snowbird did happen, and created the fifth-largest ski area in America →

+ Phenomenal snow and steep terrain means cult status among experts

+ New link to Snowbird making one of the largest ski areas in the US

+ Very cheap local lift pass

+ Ski-almost-to-the-door convenience

+ Easy to get to other Utah resorts (so long as access road open)

− 'Resort' is a scattering of lodges – not much après-ski atmosphere and few off-slope diversions

− No snowboarding allowed

− Old-fashioned lift network

− Limited groomed runs for intermediates, though the new link with Snowbird doubles the terrain

Alta is famous for remarkable amounts of powder snow arriving with great regularity, for one of the cheapest lift passes around and for a stubborn refusal to develop or modernise, or do any deals with slick Snowbird a few yards down the canyon. But things seem to be changing: the Sunnyside fast triple chair, installed a few years ago specially for beginners, was then followed by the resort's first fast quad specially to connect Alta to Snowbird. How long, we wonder, before Alta really joins the modern world, and admits snowboarders to its hallowed slopes?

THE RESORT

Alta sits at the craggy head of Little Cottonwood Canyon, 2km/1 mile beyond Snowbird and less than an hour's drive from downtown Salt Lake City. The peaceful location was once the scene of a bustling and bawdy mining town. The 'new' Alta is a strung-out handful of lodges and parking areas, and nothing more; life revolves around the two separate lift base areas – Albion and Wildcat – linked by a bi-directional rope tow along the flat valley floor. All in all, there are about a dozen places to stay – simple hotels and apartments.

THE MOUNTAINS

Alta's slopes are still served by mainly slow double and triple chairs. Check out the Snowbird chapter for information about the slopes there.

Slopes The dominant feature of Alta's terrain is the steep end of a ridge that separates the area's two basins. To the left, above Albion Base, the slopes stretch away over easy green terrain towards the black runs of Point Supreme and Devil's Castle; to the right is a more concentrated bowl with blue runs down the middle and blacks either side. These two sectors are linked at altitude, and by a flat rope tow along the valley floor.

Terrain-parks There aren't any.

Snow reliability The quantity and quality of snow that falls here, and the northerly orientation of the slopes, put Alta in the top rank – 'absolutely amazing', writes a recent visitor.

Experts Even without a link with Snowbird, Alta had cult status among local experts, who flocked to the high ridges after a fresh snowfall. There are dozens of steep slopes and chutes throughout the area. The recent link makes the shared area among the world's best for powder hounds.

Intermediates Adventurous intermediates who are happy to try ungroomed slopes and learn to love powder should like Alta, too. There are good blue bowls in both Alta and Snowbird and not-so-tough blacks to progress too. But if it is miles of perfectly groomed piste you are after, there are plenty of better resorts.

Beginners Timid intermediates and beginners will be happy on the Albion side, where the lower runs are broad, gentle and well groomed. But it's

553

KEY FACTS

Resort	2600m
	8,530ft

For Alta and Snowbird combined area

Slopes	2365-3350m
	7,760-11,000ft
Lifts	26
Pistes	4,700 acres
Green	25%
Blue	37%
Black	38%
Snowmaking	
	150 acres

For Alta only

Slopes	2600-3215m
	8,530-10,550ft
Lifts	13
Pistes	2,200 acres
Green	25%
Blue	40%
Black	35%
Snowmaking	
	50 acres

Phone numbers
From distant parts of the US, add the prefix 1 801.
From abroad, add the prefix +1 801.

TOURIST OFFICE

t 359 1078
info@alta.com
www.alta.com

difficult to recommend such a narrowly focused resort to beginners.

Snowboarding Boarding is banned (but see News for snowcat boarding).

Cross-country Until recently, there was little provision for cross-country skiing, but 2002/3 saw the opening of a new 5km groomed track. The Alta Nordic Centre offers lessons and equipment.

Queues Bottlenecks are not unknown at Alta – the snow record, easy access from Salt Lake City and the slow chair-lifts see to that – especially in spring and on sunny weekends, but they're 'well organised'. The slopes remain uncrowded though.

Mountain restaurants There's a mountain restaurant in each sector of the slopes, offering mainly fast food. Alf's on the Albion side is 'modern, spacious and light' and 'serves very good sandwiches'. Watson's Shelter on the Wildcat side serves 'fantastic burgers', but is in need of a revamp. Upstairs, the small table-service Collins Grill has a limited menu but gets booked up anyway. There are several places at the base open for lunch.

Schools and guides The famous Alf Engen ski school naturally specialises in powder lessons – though regular classes and clinics are also available.

Facilities for children Day care for those over 3 months old is available at the Children's Center at Albion Base.

STAYING THERE

How to go None of the hotels is luxurious in US terms. Most get booked up well in advance by repeat visitors. Unusually for America, most lodges (as they're called) operate half-board deals, with dinner included. One reporter recommends staying more cheaply down in Sandy or South Jordan, within 24km/15 miles of Alta.

Hotels The Alta Lodge (742 3500) is one of Alta's oldest, and feels rather like an over-crowded chalet-hotel in the Alps. Rustler Lodge (742 2200) is more luxurious, with a big outdoor pool, but impersonal. The comfortable, modern Goldminer's Daughter (742 2300) and the basic Peruvian Lodge (742 3000) are cheaper. The Snowpipe Lodge (742 2000) is 'convenient, comfortable and friendly' but is rather 'old-fashioned'.

Eating out It may be possible, but eating in is the routine.

Après-ski This rarely goes beyond a few drinks and possibly the manager's choice of video in the lodges. The Goldminer's Daughter has the main après-ski bar. The cocktail bar in the Rustler Lodge is recommended for a pre-dinner drink.

Off the slopes There are few options other than a sightseeing trip to Salt Lake City.

The Canyons

Potentially the biggest mountain in the US, and already impressive

555

COSTS

① ② ③ ④ ⑤ ⑥

RATINGS

The slopes

Snow	★★★★
Extent	★★★
Experts	★★★
Intermediate	★★★
Beginner	★★★
Convenience	★★★★
Queues	★★★★
Mountain restaurants	★★★

The rest

Scenery	★★★
Resort charm	★★
Off-slope	★★

NEWS

Terrain-park enhancements doubled the number of features available for 2002/03. There are two new half-pipes, including a children's pipe. Additional lighting increased evening opening hours. The parks now cover 18 acres.

Snowmaking was also improved on the Apex Ridge, around the Super Condor Express lift.

➕ Extensive area of slopes for all abilities – and could grow further

➕ Modern lift system with few queues

➕ Convenient new purpose-built resort village taking shape at the base

➕ Park City is nearby – an entertaining alternative base with its own slopes

➕ Easy access to other Utah resorts

➕ Excellent snow in general, but ...

➖ Snow on the many south-facing slopes often not up to the usual Utah standards

➖ Because the area is a series of canyons (valleys) many runs are short and the area is a bit disjointed

➖ Resort village offers limited après-ski and dining possibilities, and few off-slope diversions

This close neighbour of Park City, formerly known as Park West and later as Wolf Mountain, is now approaching its seventh season as The Canyons. The American Skiing Company's ambitious plans to make the slopes the most extensive in the US are gradually being implemented: the area has already more than doubled in size and is sixth-biggest in the US – amazing, considering its low international profile. The lift system is virtually new; the snow, if not out of the top Utah drawer, is great by normal standards; a new slope-side resort village is up and running. What are you waiting for?

THE RESORT

When we visited a few years ago there wasn't a resort – just a muddy car park and building site. A year later the car-free village was really taking shape and there is now a basic selection of shops, bars and restaurants at the main station. Although there is some convenient accommodation at the resort village, staying in Park City will suit many people better at present – regular shuttle-buses run to the resort.

THE MOUNTAINS

The Canyons gets its name from the valleys between the various mountains (now eight of them) that make up the ski area.

Slopes Red Pine Lodge, at the heart of the slopes, is reached by an eight-person gondola from the village. From here you can move in either direction across a series of ridges and valleys. These ridges range from Dreamscape to the south (closest to Park City) to Murdock Peak to the north. Runs come off both sides of each ridge, meaning

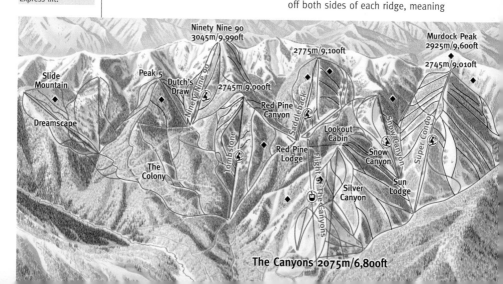

Ninety Nine 90
3045m/9,990ft

2775m/9,100ft

Murdock Peak
2925m/9,600ft

2745m/9,010ft

Slide Mountain

Peak 5

Dutch's Draw

2745m/9,000ft

Red Pine Canyon

2745m/9,000ft

Lookout Cabin

Dreamscape

Ninety Nine 90

Tombstone

Saddleback

Red Pine Lodge

Flight of the Canyons

Snow Canyon

Snow Canyon

Super Condor

The Colony

Silver Canyon

Sun Lodge

The Canyons 2075m/6,800ft

KEY FACTS

Resort	2075m
	6,800ft
Slopes	2075-3045m
	6,800-9,990ft
Lifts	17
Pistes	3,500 acres
Green	14%
Blue	44%
Black	42%
Snowmaking	
	160 acres

Central reservations phone number
Call 1 800 472 6309 (toll-free from within the US).

Phone numbers
From distant parts of the US, add the prefix 1 435.
From abroad, add the prefix +1 435.

TOURIST OFFICE

t 649 5400
info@thecanyons.com
www.thecanyons.com

that they generally face north or south. Most runs finish on the valley floors with some long, relatively flat run-outs. Five of the major lifts are fast quads, all put in – along with the gondola – since 1997. Complimentary mountain tours are offered twice daily.

Terrain-parks There are six natural half-pipes across the mountain. A great terrain-park and half-pipes are located at Red Hawk.

Snow reliability Snow is not the best in Utah. The Canyons gets as much on average as Park City (350in) and more than Deer Valley. But the south-facing slopes suffer in late-season sunshine.

Experts There is steep terrain all over the mountain. We particularly liked the north-facing runs off Ninety Nine 90, with steep double-black-diamond runs plunging down through the trees to a pretty but almost flat run-out trail. There is also lots of double-diamond terrain on Murdock Peak. There are gates for backcountry access – with the right kit and guidance, of course.

Intermediates There are groomed blue runs for intermediates on all the main sectors except Ninety Nine 90. Some are quite short, but you can switch from valley to valley for added interest. A reporter recommends the runs off the Super Condor fast chair.

Beginners There's a recently opened area just for beginners behind Red Pine Lodge. But the run you progress to gets very busy with through-traffic.

Snowboarding It's a great area to snowboard in, with lots of natural hits. Canis Lupis (aka James Bond trail) is a mile-long, tight, winding natural gully with high banked walls and numerous obstacles – like riding a bob-sleigh course. For intermediates there's easy cruising, served by chair-lifts.

Cross-country There are prepared trails on the Park City golf course and the Homestead Resort course. There is also lots of scope for backcountry trips.

Queues We've heard of no problems.

Mountain restaurants The central Red Pine Lodge, a large, attractive log-and-glass building with a busy self-service cafeteria and a table-service restaurant, is recommended. The Lookout Cabin has wonderful views, and we've had excellent table-service food there. A recent reporter found Sun Lodge (with sundecks) 'too noisy'.

Schools and guides The ski school uses the American Skiing Company's Perfect Turn formula, which focuses on an individual's strengths and builds on them (rather than correcting faults). The 'Perfect Kids' clinics are available for children from 4 to 12 years.

Facilities for children There's day care for children from 18 months, located in the Grand Summit Hotel.

STAYING THERE

How to go Accommodation at the resort village is still fairly limited, but you do have the choice of hotel rooms or self-catering.

Hotels The luxurious Grand Summit is right at the base of the gondola.

Self-catering The Sundial Lodge condos are part of the resort village.

Eating out The Cabin restaurant, in the Grand Summit hotel, serves eclectic American cuisine. There is a Viking Yurt for gourmet dining with Norwegian hospitality. And there are many more options in Park City.

Après-ski The Grand Summit contains several bars, and there are many more in Park City.

Off the slopes There's a fair bit going on in Park City – shops, galleries etc – and Salt Lake City has some good concerts, shopping and sights. Balloon rides and snowmobiling are popular activities. Sleigh rides and snow-shoeing are also available.

THE CANYONS / HUGHES MARTIN

It's a big area – sixth biggest in the US – with practically all new lifts →

Deer Valley

The ultimate upmarket ski resort

COSTS

① ② ③ ④ ⑤ ⑥

RATINGS

The slopes

Snow	****
Extent	**
Expert	***
Intermediate	****
Beginner	****
Convenience	****
Queues	****
Mountain restaurants	****

The rest

Scenery	***
Resort charm	***
Off-slope	**

NEWS

The Ruby chair-lift was replaced by a fast quad for 2002/03. Further snowmaking was installed.

2003/04 will see new glade skiing for Empire Canyon, and more snowmaking.

Major expansion is planned for the Snow Park Lodge, to include shops and a children's centre.

DEER VALLEY RESORT

There is lots of accommodation on the mountain, though much of it is private
↓

➕ Highly convenient, upmarket resort with superb skier services

➕ Immaculate piste grooming, good snow record and lots of snow-guns

➕ Good tree skiing

➕ No queues

➕ Easy access to Park City, The Canyons and other Utah resorts

➖ No snowboarding allowed

➖ Relatively expensive

➖ Deer Valley itself is quiet at night – though Park City is right next door

Deer Valley prides itself on pampering its guests, with valets to unload your skis, gourmet dining, immaculately groomed slopes, limited numbers on the mountain, no snowboarding. But there's more to it than that – it has some excellent slopes, with interesting terrain for all abilities, including plenty of ungroomed stuff. It hosted the freestyle and slalom competitions in the 2002 Olympics, and the 2003 Freestyle World Championships.

The slopes of Deer Valley and Park City are separated by nothing more than a fence which, given Deer Valley's ethos, seems likely to be permanent. Any skier visiting the area should try both; for most people, Park City is the obvious base – but there are some seductive hotels here at mid-mountain Silver Lake.

THE RESORT

Just a mile from the end of Park City's Main Street, Deer Valley is unashamedly upmarket – famed for the care and attention lavished on both slopes and guests. It's very obviously aimed at people who are used to being pampered and can pay for it.

The lodgings – luxurious private chalets and swanky hotels – are scattered around the fringes of the slopes, with more concentrated clusters on the valley floor near the main lift base and at Silver Lake Lodge (mid-mountain but accessible by road). There is no village as such. For any real animation you need to head for Park City, and many visitors prefer to stay there. There are free buses.

THE MOUNTAINS

The slopes are varied and interesting. Deer Valley's reputation for immaculate grooming is justified, but there is also a lot of exciting tree skiing (great when snow is falling) – and some steep mogul runs too.

Slopes Two fast quads take you up to Bald Eagle Mountain, just beyond which is the mid-mountain focus of Silver Lake Lodge. You can ski from here to the isolated Little Baldy Peak, served by a gondola and a quad chair-lift, with mainly easy runs to serve property being developed there. But the main skiing is on three linked peaks beyond Silver Lake Lodge, all served by fast quads – Bald Mountain, Flagstaff Mountain and Empire Canyon.

KEY FACTS

Resort	2195m
	7,200ft
Slopes	2000-2915m
	6,570-9,570ft
Lifts	19
Pistes	1,750 acres
Green	15%
Blue	50%
Black	35%
Snowmaking	
	500 acres

Central reservations
phone number
Call 645 6528.

Phone numbers
From distant parts of
the US, add the prefix
1 435.
From abroad, add the
prefix +1 435.

TOURIST OFFICE

t 649 1000
patti@deervalley.com
www.deervalley.com

The top of Empire is just a few metres from the runs of the Park City ski area and could easily be linked.

Terrain-parks There aren't any.

Snow reliability As you'd expect in Utah, snow reliability is excellent, and there's plenty of snowmaking too.

Experts Despite its image of pampered luxury there is excellent expert terrain on all three main mountains, including fabulous glade skiing, bumps, defined chutes and open bowl slopes. And the snow doesn't get skied out quickly.

Intermediates There are lots of immaculately groomed blue runs all over the mountains.

Beginners There are nursery slopes at Silver Lake Lodge as well as the base, and gentle green runs to progress to on all the mountains.

Snowboarding Boarding is banned.

Cross-country There are prepared trails on the Park City golf course and the Homestead Resort course, just out of town. There is also lots of scope for backcountry trips.

Queues Waiting in lift lines is not something that Deer Valley wants its guests to experience, so it limits the number of lift tickets sold.

Mountain restaurants There are attractive wood-and-glass self-service places run by the resort at both Silver Lake and the base lodge, with free valet ski storage. The food is fine (though expensive). The grill restaurant

at the recently opened Empire Canyon Lodge should relieve overcrowding at Silver Lake. For a bit of a treat, we can recommend the restaurants at Stein Eriksen Lodge or the Goldener Hirsch.

Schools and guides The ski school is doubtless excellent.

Facilities for children Deer Valley's Children's Center gives parents complimentary pagers.

STAYING THERE

How to go A car is useful for visiting the other nearby Utah resorts, though Deer Valley, Park City and The Canyons are all linked by regular shuttle-buses.

Hotels Stein Eriksen Lodge and the Goldener Hirsch at Silver Lake are two of the plushest hotels in any ski resort.

Self-catering There are many luxury apartments and houses to rent.

Après-ski The Lounge of the Snow Park Lodge at the base area is the main après-ski venue, with live music. There are lively bars and restaurants around Main Street in Park City.

Eating out Of the gourmet restaurants, the Mariposa is the best. The Seafood Buffet is also recommended. The Royal Street Café is a new restaurant at Silver Lake.

Off the slopes Park City has lots of shops, galleries etc. Salt Lake City has concerts, sights and shopping. Balloon rides and snowmobiling are popular.

UTAH

558

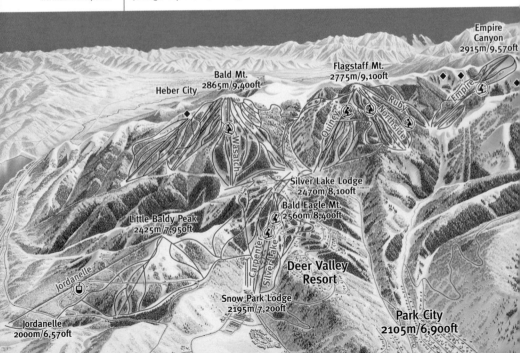

SNOWPIX.COM / CHRIS GILL

Park City

An entertaining base for excursions into Utah's famous powder

① ② ③ ④ ⑤ ⑥

RATINGS

The slopes

Snow	****
Extent	***
Expert	****
Intermediate	****
Beginner	****
Convenience	***
Queues	****
Mountain restaurants	**

The rest

Scenery	***
Resort charm	***
Off-slope	***

NEWS

2002/03 saw the opening of the Eagle Superpipe (featured in the Olympics).

2004 is Park City's 40th Anniversary season. A number of events are planned to mark the occasion.

➕ Increasingly touristy Wild West-style main street, convenient for slopes

➕ Lots of bars and restaurants make nonsense of Utah's Mormon image

➕ Well maintained slopes, good snow record, and lots of snowmaking

➕ Good lift system including four fast six-packs

➕ Good base for visiting other major Utah resorts – Deer Valley and The Canyons are effectively suburbs and other resorts less than an hour away

➖ Rest of town doesn't have same charm as main street – lots of recent building has created an enormous sprawl (and building continues)

➖ The blue and black runs tend to be rather short – most lifts give a vertical of around 400m/1,300ft

➖ Although the snowfall record is impressive by normal standards, it comes nowhere near that of Alta and Snowbird, a few miles away

➖ Lack of spectacular scenery

Park City has clear attractions, particularly if you ignore its sprawling suburbs and stay near the centre to make the most of the lively bars and restaurants in its beautifully restored and developed main street. But the place really comes into its own as a base for touring other resorts as well.

Deer Valley is separated from Park City's slopes by a fence between the tops of two lifts, and by separate ownership with quite different objectives. All that is required to link them is to remove the fence – a small step that is unlikely to be taken, given Deer Valley's exclusive nature. To European eyes, all very strange.

The Canyons is only a little further away, on the outskirts of town, and reached by free buses. And then there are the famously powdery resorts of Snowbird and Alta, less than an hour away by car or bus. Even the Olympic downhill slopes of Snowbasin are within easy reach if you have a car.

LORI ADAMSKI-PEEK

Traffic-free it ain't, but Park City's Main Street gives the resort an entertaining and lively heart ➜

KEY FACTS

Resort	2105m
	6,900ft
Slopes	2105-3050m
	6,900-10,000ft
Lifts	14
Pistes	3,300 acres
Green	18%
Blue	44%
Black	38%
Snowmaking	
	475 acres

THE RESORT

Park City is about 45 minutes by road from Salt Lake City. It was born with the discovery of silver in 1872. By the turn of the century it boasted a population of 10,000, a red-light district, a Chinese quarter and 27 saloons. Careful restoration has left the town with a splendid historic centre-piece in Main Street.

The old wooden sidewalks and clapboard buildings are now filled with a colourful selection of art galleries, shops, boutiques, bars and restaurants – though it is getting rather touristy, with some tacky shops selling T-shirts and souvenirs. New buildings have been tastefully designed to blend in smoothly. But away from the centre the resort lacks charm, sprawls over a wide area and is still expanding.

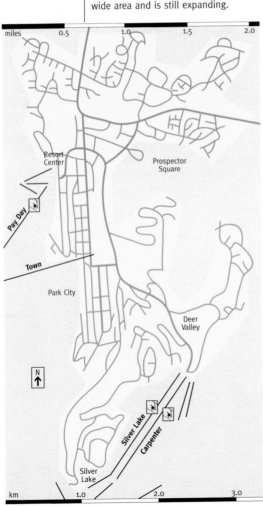

The Town Lift is a triple chair up to the slopes from Lower Main Street, but the main lift base is Resort Center, on the fringes, with modern buildings and its own bars, restaurants and lodgings.

Deer Valley and The Canyons are almost suburbs of Park City, but all three retain quite separate identities. They are linked by free shuttle-buses, which also go around town and run until late. A trolley-bus runs along Main Street. A car is useful for visiting other ski areas on the good roads.

If you're not hiring a car, pick a location that's handy for Main Street and the Town chair or the free bus.

THE MOUNTAIN

Mostly the area consists of blue and black trails cut through the trees on the flanks of rounded mountain ridges, with easier runs running along the ridges and the gullies between. The bite in the system is in the lightly wooded bowls and ridges at the top of the resort's slopes.

THE SLOPES
Bowls above the woods
A fast six-seat chair-lift whisks you up from Resort Center, and another beyond that up to Summit House, the main mountain restaurant.

Most of the easy and intermediate runs lie between the Summit House and the base area, and spread along the sides of a series of interconnecting ridges. Virtually all the steep terrain is above Summit House in a series of ungroomed bowls, and accessed by the McConkey's six-pack and the old Jupiter double chair.

There are free daily tours of the slopes. Twice a week tours of the black-diamond slopes are offered.

A long floodlit run is available until 9pm, together with a floodlit half-pipe.

TERRAIN-PARKS
Good enough for the Olympics ...
The Olympics provided a legacy in the form of the 105m/350ft long Eagle Superpipe, made available to skiers and boarders for the first time in 2002/03. There are three terrain-parks and half-pipes – one floodlit at night.

SNOW RELIABILITY
Not quite the Greatest on Earth
Utah is famous for the quality and quantity of its snow. Park City's record doesn't match those of Alta and

LIFT PASSES

Park City
Covers all lifts in Park City Mountain Resort, with free ski-bus.

Main pass
1-day pass $67
6-day pass $297

Senior citizens
Over 65: 1-day $36
Over 70: free

Children
Under 12: 6-day pass $132
Under 7: free

Notes
Half-day pass available. Multi-day pass prices are advance purchase rates. Reductions for groups but not for students.

Alternative passes
Multi-area passport is available through UK tour operators.

Snowbird, but an annual average of 350 inches is still impressive, and ahead of most Colorado figures. And there's snowmaking on about 15% of the terrain.

FOR EXPERTS
Lots of variety

There is a lot of excellent advanced and expert terrain at the top of the lift system. It is now all marked as double-diamond on the trail map but there are many runs that deserve only a single-diamond rating – so don't be put off. We particularly like the prettily wooded McConkey's Bowl, served by a six-pack and offering a range of open pitches and gladed terrain. The old Jupiter lift accesses the highest bowls, which include some serious terrain – with narrow couloirs, cliffs and cornices – as well as easier wide-open slopes. The Jupiter bowl runs are under the chair, but there is a lot more terrain accessible by traversing and hiking – turn left for West Face, Pioneer Ridge and Puma Bowl, right for Scott's Bowl and the vast expanse of Pinecone Ridge, stretching literally for miles down the side of Thaynes Canyon.

Lower down, the side of Summit House ridge, serviced by the Thaynes and Motherlode chairs, has some little-used black runs, plus a few satisfying trails in the trees. There's a zone of steep runs towards town from further round the ridge. And don't miss Blueslip Bowl near Summit House – so called because in the past, when it was out of bounds, ski company employees caught skiing it were fired, and were given their notice on a blue slip.

Good skiers (no snowboarders, due to some long flat run-outs and hikes) should not miss the Utah Interconnect – see feature panel. For bigger budgets, Park City Powder Guides offers heli-skiing on 20,000 acres of private backcountry land.

FOR INTERMEDIATES
Many better places

There are blue runs served by all the main lifts, apart from Jupiter. The areas around the King Con high-speed quad and Silverlode high-speed six-pack have a dense network of great (but fairly short) cruising runs. There are also more difficult trails close by, for those looking for a challenge.

But the keen intermediate piste-basher who would be happy at Vail or Snowmass won't be so happy here. There are few long, fast cruising runs – most trails are around 1 to 2km/0.5 to 1 mile, and many have long, flat run-outs. The Pioneer and McConkey's chair-lifts are off the main drag and serve some very pleasant, often quiet runs. One reporter complains of too

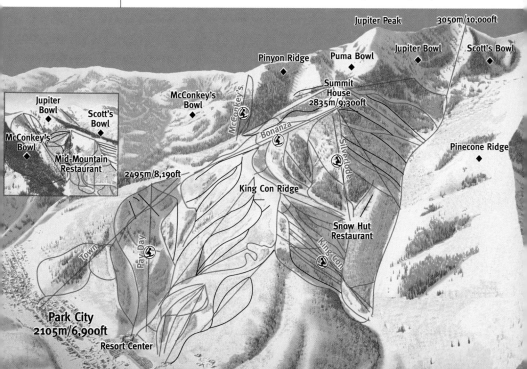

SCHOOLS

Park City
t 1-800-227-2754
pcinfo@pcski.com

Classes
3 3hr days $200

Private lessons
$195 for 2hr

CHILDREN

The ski school's Mountain School takes children aged from 3 to 6, from 8.30 or 9.30 to 4.30, mixing skiing instruction with other indoor and outdoor activities ($135 per day). Classes for children aged 6 to 13 are $118 per day including lunch. There are several nurseries in the town.

boarding

The Olympic boarding events have banished from memory the time when boarding was banned here. The resort has wonderful free-ride terrain, its higher lifts giving access to some great powder bowls. Beginners have their own excellent area, good easy cruising and a lift system which is entirely chair-lifts. Intermediates have to put up with fairly short cruising runs. And now fun can also be had in the Eagle Superpipe (see Terrain-parks).

many ungroomed mogul runs, 'leaving a choice of ultra-easy cruising or bump-running, with little in between'.

Intermediates will certainly want to visit The Canyons and Deer Valley for a day or two (see separate chapters).

FOR BEGINNERS
A good chance for fast progress
Novices get started on short lifts and a dedicated beginners' area near the base lodge. The beginners' classes graduate up the hill quite quickly, and there's a good, very gentle and wide 'easiest way down' – the three-and a half-mile Home Run – clearly marked all the way from Summit House. It's easy enough for most beginners to manage after only a few lessons. The Town chair can be ridden down.

FOR CROSS-COUNTRY
Some trails; lots of backcountry
There are prepared trails on both the Park City golf course, next to the downhill area, and the Homestead Resort course, just out of town. There is lots of scope for backcountry trips.

QUEUES
Peak period problems only
Lift queues aren't normally a problem with so many six-packs. But it can get pretty crowded (on some trails as well as the lifts) on busy weekends.

MOUNTAIN RESTAURANTS
Standard self-service stuff
The Mid-Mountain Lodge is a 19th-century mine building which was heaved up the mountain to its present location near the bottom of Pioneer chair. The food is standard self-service fare but most reporters prefer it to the alternatives. The Summit House is cafe-style – serving chilli, pizza, soup etc. The Snow Hut is a smaller log building and usually has an outdoor grill. Café Amante is a new coffee house located halfway down the Bonanza chair-lift. There's quite a choice of restaurants back at the base area, including the food court at the Legacy Lodge. The Brewhouse is the latest addition to the options here.

SCHOOLS AND GUIDES
Thorough, full of enthusiasm
The school offers performance workshops (Moguls and Beyond, Dealing with the Diamonds) and Power Clinics (for strong intermediates) as well as beginner and private lessons.

FACILITIES FOR CHILDREN
Well organised; ideal terrain
There are a number of licensed carers who operate either at their own premises or at visitors' lodgings. The ski school takes children from the age of three. Book in advance.

THE UTAH INTERCONNECT

Good skiers should not miss this excellent guided backcountry tour that runs four days a week from Park City to Snowbird. (Three days a week it runs from Snowbird, but only as far as Solitude.) When we did it we got fresh tracks in knee-deep powder practically all day. After a warm-up run to weed out weak skiers, you head up to the top of the Jupiter chair, go through a 'closed' gate in the area boundary and ski down a deserted, prettily wooded valley to Solitude. After taking the lifts to the top of Solitude we did a short traverse, then down more virgin powder towards Brighton. After more powder runs and lunch back in Solitude, it was up the lifts and a 30-minute hike up the Highway to Heaven to north-facing, tree-lined slopes and a great little gully down into Alta. How much of Alta and Snowbird you get to ski depends on how much time is left.

The price ($150) includes two guides – one leading, another at the rear – lunch, lift tickets for all five resorts you pass through and transport home.

GETTING THERE

Air Salt Lake City 58km/36 miles (¹/₂hr).

ACTIVITIES

Indoor Park City Racquet Club (4 indoor tennis courts, 2 racquetball courts, heated pool, hot-tub, sauna, gym, aerobics, basketball), Silver Mountain Spa (racquetball courts, weights room, swimming pool, aerobics, spa, massage and physical therapy, whirlpool, sauna), art galleries, concerts, theatre, martial arts studio, bowling

Outdoor Snowmobiles, ballooning, sleigh rides, ski jumping, ice skating, bob-sleigh and luge track, snow tubing, sports and recreation opportunities for disabled children and adults

Phone numbers From distant parts of the US, add the prefix 1 435. From abroad, add the prefix +1 435.

TOURIST OFFICE

t 649 8111
info@pcski.com
www.parkcitymountain.com

STAYING THERE

HOW TO GO
Packaged independence
Park City is the busiest and most atmospheric of the Utah resorts, and a good base for visiting the others.
Hotels There's a wide variety, from typical chains to individual little B&Bs.
((((4) **Silver King** (649 5500) Deluxe hotel/condo complex at base of the slopes, with indoor-outdoor pool.
((((4) **Radisson Inn Park City** (649 5000) Excellent rooms and indoor-outdoor pool, but poorly placed for nightlife (out of town on main road).
((((4) **Yarrow** (649 7000) Recently renovated with big welcoming lobby, outdoor pool and hot-tub. Free shuttle.
((((4) **Washington School Inn** (649 3800) 'Absolutely excellent' historic inn in a great location near Main Street, with free wine and snacks, creating a thriving après-ski social scene.
(((3) **Best Western Landmark Inn** (649 7300) Way out of town near The Canyons and factory outlet mall. Swimming pool. 'Good place to stay with car to visit other resorts.'
(((3) **Old Miners' Lodge** (645 8068) 100-year-old building next to Town lift, restored and furnished with antiques.
((2) **Chateau Apres Lodge** (649 9372) Close to the slopes: comfortable, faded, cheap.
((2) **1904 Imperial Inn** (649 1904) Quaint B&B at the top of Main Street.
Self-catering There's a big range available. The Townlift studios near Main Street and Park Avenue condos are both modern and comfortable and the latter have outdoor pool and hot-tubs. Silver Cliff Village is adjacent to the slopes and has spacious units and access to the facilities of the Silver King Hotel. Blue Church Lodge is a well-converted 19th-century Mormon church with luxury condos and rooms.

EATING OUT
Book in advance
There are over 100 restaurants but they all get busy, so book in advance. Zoom is the old Union Pacific train depot, now a trendy restaurant owned by Robert Redford. The Riverhorse is in a beautiful, high-ceilinged first-floor room with live music. Chimayo has great south-west cuisine. The Juniper at the Snowed Inn has won awards. Chez Betty is small and has perhaps the best food in town – expensive though. Cheaper places include the US Prime

Steakhouse ('best steak ever'), the Grub Steak Restaurant at Prospector Square, Cisero's and Grappa (Italian), Jambalaya (Cajun), Wasatch Brew Pub (good value and an interesting range of beers) and Baja Cantina (Mexican).

APRES-SKI
Better than you might think
Although there are still some arcane liquor laws in Utah, provided you're over 21 and can prove it the laws are never a serious barrier to getting a drink. At the bars and clubs that are more dedicated to drinking (ie don't feature food but do serve spirits) membership of some kind is required. This may involve handing over $5 or more – one member can introduce numerous 'guests' – or else there'll be some old guy at the bar already organised to 'sponsor' you (sign you in) for the price of a beer. But a recent reporter points out that the system can be very expensive if you visit different resorts most days and just want a quick beer before hitting the road.

As the slopes close, the Legacy Lodge is the place to head for at the Resort Centre – Legends and the new Brewhouse are the main spots – or you can make directly for Main Street. The Wasatch Brew Pub makes its own ale. The Claimjumper, JB Mulligans and the scruffy Alamo are lively places and there's usually live music and dancing at weekends. Harry O's and Cisero's nightclub are good too.

OFF THE SLOPES
Should be interesting
There's a factory outlet mall near The Canyons. Scenic balloon flights and excursions to Nevada for gambling are both popular. Snowmobiling is big. In January there's Robert Redford's Sundance Film Festival.

There are lots of shops and galleries. The museum and old jail house are worth a visit. Salt Lake City has some good concerts, shopping and a few points of interest, many connected with its Mormon heritage. The Capitol Building, open until 8pm, gives 'an interesting perspective on the State' and good views of the city.

You might like to learn to ski-jump or try the Olympic bob track at the Winter Sports Park down the road.

Snowbasin

An excellent mountain, worth including in a tour of Utah's finest

COSTS

① ② ③ ④ ⑤ ⑥

RATINGS

The slopes

Snow	✶✶✶✶✶
Extent	✶✶✶
Expert	✶✶✶✶
Intermediate	✶✶✶✶
Beginner	✶✶
Convenience	✶
Queues	✶✶✶✶✶
Mountain restaurants	✶✶

The rest

Scenery	✶✶✶✶
Resort charm	✶✶
Off-slope	✶

NEWS

For 2002/03 a new 7km/4 mile cross-country track, The Maples, was opened. There is also a new ice rink at the top of the Needles gondola.

2003/04 will see a new terrain-park, Porcupine Face.

564

There are amazing views over the Great Salt Lake from the top of the Strawberry gondola →

➕ Fair-sized ski area

➕ Impressive new lift system

➕ Excellent snow record

➕ Smart new mountain restaurants

➖ No resort village as yet

➖ The nearest accommodation is down in nearby Ogden or Huntsville

➖ Bit of a trek from Park City etc

The four Olympic downhill events (men's and women's downhills, plus the downhill elements of the combined) and the two super giant slaloms which were held here in February 2002 have put Snowbasin firmly on the map. It's a great hill, and it gets great snow (usually). All it needs is a great village – and the ski world waits to see what owner Earl Holding (also owner of Sun Valley, Idaho) has got in mind. For now, it makes a great day out from Park City.

THE RESORT

There is no resort, in the European sense of a village with accommodation. But big investment is expected over the next few years. For now you have to stay elsewhere – in the town of Ogden on the Salt Lake plain, or nearer the mountain in the backwater town of Huntsville. Or stay in another Utah resort – the 100km/60-mile trip from Park City takes less than an hour.

THE MOUNTAINS

Snowbasin's slopes cover a lot of pleasantly varied terrain and are served by nine lifts including a fast quad chair and two gondolas, all three installed in 1998. And there are other attractions. Not the least is the amazing view over the ridge at the top of the Strawberry Express gondola across the Great Salt Lake and surrounding plain. Another is the excursion to cutely named Powder Mountain, a few miles away across the other side of the Huntsville basin. This has an extensive snowcat operation.

Slopes A base lodge in the plush style of those at Sun Valley was built for the 2002 Olympics. From this main base, the Needles gondola goes up to the area's central core at Middle Bowl, which has lots of different slopes and gullies presenting different challenges. The John Paul fast quad chair goes up to the right from the base and serves great black slopes, on- and off-piste, with just one blue alternative way down. Above it, a small cable-car goes up to Allen's Peak and the dramatic start of the Olympic men's downhill

course. The Strawberry gondola serves good blue runs at the opposite end.

Terrain-parks A new terrain-park, Porcupine Face, debuts in 2003/04, with features covering about 10 acres.

Snow reliability At 400 inches the average snowfall is in the usual Utah class. And there's lots of snowmaking.

Experts This is a great mountain for experts. All the lifts serve worthwhile terrain – even Strawberry has some severe chutes reached by hiking from the top. The cable-car serves a short black slope that was mogulled when we were there but was glass-smooth

KEY FACTS

Resort	1950m
	6,390ft
Slopes	1785-2850m
	5,860-9,350ft
Lifts	9
Pistes	3,200 acres
Green	13%
Blue	49%
Black	38%
Snowmaking	
	580 acres

Accommodation phone number
For accommodation information call the Ogden Chamber of Commerce on 627 8228

Phone numbers
From distant parts of the US, add the prefix 1 801.
From abroad, add the prefix +1 801.

TOURIST OFFICE

t 620 1000
info@snowbasin.com
www.snowbasin.com

when it served as the start of the Olympic downhill race course. The course, designed by Bernhard Russi drops 883m/2,897ft and is already claimed to be a modern classic. Between the race course and the area boundary is a splendid area of off-piste wooded glades and gullies, served by the fast John Paul chair. This is where most experts will want to spend their time. Less extreme challenges are to be found on the countless blacks in the middle of the mountain.

Intermediates It's a good mountain for intermediates, too. The Strawberry gondola accesses mainly long open blue runs but also leads to a lightly wooded steeper slope at the extremity of the area. Middle Bowl is great terrain for the adventurous, with a complex network of blues and blacks.

Beginners It's hardly an ideal place to start, but there is a nursery slope, and a few green runs to progress to.

Snowboarding There is some excellent free-ride terrain and the new terrain-park should prove popular.

Cross-country The Maples Nordic Loop is a new 7km/4 mile track near the base station, suitable for beginners and intermediates. Nordic Valley is nearby.

Queues Queues are unlikely.

Mountain restaurants There are two, recently built mountain restaurants, both self-service only but otherwise

pleasant. Needles Lodge has a sun terrace with windshields.

Schools and guides The school has special women's clinics as well as the normal offerings.

Facilities for children The services building at the main base includes a day care centre and a ski school.

STAYING THERE

Hotels Ogden has various standard-issue hotels and motels. Huntsville has a small hotel, a couple of small B&Bs and Utah's oldest tavern (opened in 1879), the Shooting Star – a splendid scruffy relic of times past. On the walls are not only stuffed moose and elk but a stuffed St Bernard dog – apparently a beast of record-breaking enormity.

Eating out The Shooting Star, in Huntsville, is famous for its huge Starburgers, which come with sausage, as well as multiple burger patties etc. Gourmet dinners are now served at the Needles restaurant four nights a week. The gondola stays open until 8.30.

Après-ski There are a couple of bars and eating places at the base lodge. Otherwise it's back into town for evening entertainment.

Off the slopes Visits to Ogden, Park City or Salt Lake City are the options. There's a new ice rink at the Needles (top of gondola).

Snowbasin

565

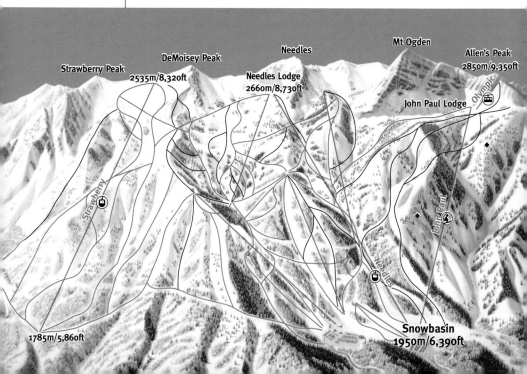

Strawberry Peak

DeMoisey Peak
2535m/8,320ft

Needles

Needles Lodge
2660m/8,730ft

Mt Ogden

Allen's Peak
2850m/9,350ft

John Paul Lodge

Strawberry

John Paul

Needles

1785m/5,860ft

Snowbasin
1950m/6,390ft

Snowbird

One of the best spots for powder hounds, now with access to Alta

COSTS

① ② ③ ④ ⑤ ⑥

RATINGS

The slopes
Snow	*****
Extent	***
Expert	*****
Intermediate	***
Beginner	**
Convenience	*****
Queues	**
Mountain restaurants	*

The rest
Scenery	***
Resort charm	*
Off-slope	*

NEWS

2002/03 saw terrain-park improvements and the introduction of guided snowcat skiing/boarding and snowmobiling. Multi-day passes are now available for the Alta-Snowbird area.

2003/04 will see continued expansion of the terrain-parks.

KEY FACTS

Resort	2470m
	8,100ft

For Snowbird and Alta combined area
Slopes	2365-3350m
	7,760-11,000ft
Lifts	26
Pistes	4,700 acres
Green	25%
Blue	37%
Black	38%
Snowmaking	
	150 acres

Snowbird only
Slopes	2365-3350m
	7,760-11,000ft
Lifts	11
Pistes	2,500 acres
Green	27%
Blue	38%
Black	35%
Snowmaking	
	100 acres

➕ Quantity and quality of powder snow unrivalled except by next-door Alta

➕ New link to Alta makes one of the largest ski areas in the US

➕ Fabulous ungroomed slopes, with steep and not-so-steep options

➕ Luxurious accommodation

➕ Slopes-at-the-door convenience

➕ Easy to get to other Utah resorts

➖ Limited groomed runs for intermediates, though the new link with Alta doubles the terrain

➖ Tiny, claustrophobic resort 'village'

➖ Stark modern architecture

➖ Frequent queues for main cable-car

➖ Avalanche risk can close the road and slopes and keep you indoors

➖ Very quiet at night

There can be few places where nature has combined the steep with the deep better than at Snowbird and neighbouring Alta, and even fewer places where there are also lifts to give you access. The two resorts now have a shared lift pass – and lifts and trails to link the two have been created. The combined area is one of the top powder-pig paradises in the world and one of the US's biggest lift-linked ski areas, so it is a shame that Snowbird's concrete, purpose-built 'base village' is so lacking in charm. Snowboarders are banned from Alta's slopes, so cannot take advantage of the joint lift pass.

THE RESORT

Snowbird lies 40km/25 miles from Salt Lake City in Little Cottonwood Canyon – just before Alta. The setting is rugged and rather Alpine – and both the resort and (particularly) the approach road are prone to avalanches and closure: visitors are sometimes confined indoors for safety. The resort buildings are mainly block-like – but they provide high-quality lodging.

The resort area and the slopes are spread along the road on the south side of the narrow canyon. The focal Snowbird Center (lift base/shops/restaurants) is towards the eastern, up-canyon end. All the lodgings and restaurants are within walking distance. The Tram station is central and the Gad lifts can be reached on snow. The regular shuttle-bus services including a service up to Alta.

THE MOUNTAINS

Snowbird's recent link with Alta forms one of the largest ski areas in the US. The two trail maps don't mesh well (they use different names for one linking lift).

Slopes The north-facing slopes rear up from the edge of the resort. Five access lifts are ranged along the valley floor, the main one being the 125-person cable-car (the Aerial Tram) to Hidden Peak. To the west, in Gad Valley, there are runs ranging from very tough to nice and easy – and six chair-lifts. Mineral Basin, on the back of Hidden Peak, offers 500 acres of terrain for all abilities. A second fast quad there forms the link with Alta.

Terrain-parks There are now two terrain-parks, one of which doubled in size for 2002/03, and a beginner half-pipe. Special classes from Mountain School focus on park skills.

Snow reliability Snowbird and Alta average 500 inches of snowfall a year – twice as much as some Colorado resorts and around 50% more than the nearby Park City area. Snowmaking ensures excellent cover in busy areas.

Experts Snowbird was created for experts; the trail map is liberally sprinkled with double-black-diamonds, and some of the gullies off the Cirque ridge – Silver Fox and Great Scott, for example – are exceptionally steep and frequently neck-deep in powder. Lower down lurk the bump runs, including Mach Schnell – a great run straight down the fall line through trees. There is wonderful ski-anywhere terrain in the bowl beneath the high Little Cloud chair, and the Gad 2 lift opens up attractive tree runs. Mineral Basin has added more expert terrain. Backcountry tours are available, and heli-lifts.

↑ Hidden Peak may
not look much of a
hill by Alpine
standards, but it
offers serious
challenges and great
snow

SNOWBIRD

quad and the slow and exposed Little Cloud chair above it are the only alternative if high winds close it down. **Mountain restaurants** It's the Mid-Gad Lodge self-service cafeteria or else it's back to base. In either case you'll encounter lunchtime crowds.

Schools and guides The ski school offers a progressive range of lessons and speciality clinics – such as women-only clinics, over-50s lessons and experts-only programmes ('A life-altering experience,' said one reporter).

Facilities for children The 'kids ski free' programme allows two children (12 and under) to ski for free ($15 a day extra for use of the Tram) with each adult buying an all-day lift ticket. Camp Snowbird offers day care.

Intermediates The winding Chip's Run on the Cirque ridge provides the only comfortable route down from the top. For adventurous intermediates wanting to try powder skiing, the bowl below the Little Cloud lift is a must. There are some challenging runs through the trees off the Gad 2 lift and some nice long cruises in Mineral Basin. But if you want miles of perfectly groomed piste, there are plenty of better resorts.

Beginners Beginners have the Chickadee lift right down in the resort – and then there's a small network of trails to progress to.

Snowboarding Competent free-riders will have a wild time in Snowbird's legendary powder. There are a couple of good terrain-parks (see above). Alta does not allow boarders.

Cross-country There are no prepared cross-country trails.

Queues For much of the season queues of up to 40 minutes for the Tram are common. The Gadzoom fast

STAYING THERE

How to go If you plan to visit several other resorts, it's worth considering Salt Lake City as a base. A few UK tour operators feature Snowbird.

Hotels There are several lodges, and smaller condominium blocks. The main place is Cliff Lodge, a huge luxury hotel and restaurant complex just up the nursery slopes from Snowbird Center.

Eating out Cliff Lodge and Snowbird Center are the focal points.

Après-ski Après-ski tends to be a bit muted. The Tram Club and the Keyhole Cantina are lively as the slopes close.

Off the slopes Apart from the Cliff Spa there's little else here. The Racquet Club down the valley is owned by Snowbird, and Salt Lake City is easily reached. There is a family tubing hill.

Snowbird

567

TOURIST OFFICE

t 742 2222
info@snowbird.com
www.snowbird.com

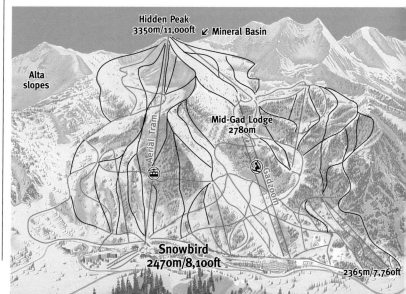

Hidden Peak
3350m/11,000ft   ↙ Mineral Basin

Alta
slopes

Mid-Gad Lodge
2780m

Aerial Tram

Gadzoom

Snowbird
2470m/8,100ft

2365m/7,760ft

Rest of the West

This section covers a varied group of isolated resorts in different parts of the great Rocky Mountain chain that stretches the length of the United States from Montana and Idaho down through Wyoming and Colorado to New Mexico. Each has its own unique character – and each is well worth knowing about.

Sun Valley, Idaho, was America's first purpose-built resort, developed in the 1930s by the president of the Union Pacific Railway. It quickly became popular with the Hollywood jet set and has managed to retain its stylish image and ambience over the years. If you want to indulge yourself a little and be pampered, bear it in mind – it has one of our favourite luxury hotels.

If you don't mind a bit of a cross-state drive, you might combine a visit to Sun Valley with a visit to the famously snowy resorts of Utah or to Jackson Hole in Wyoming – another resort with an impressive snow record. Jackson is the nearest there is to a resort with a genuine Wild West cowboy atmosphere. The mountain is a 15-minute drive away and offers some of America's most extreme terrain, with steeps, jumps and bumps to suit all – a sharp contrast to the tame groomed runs typical of many US resorts. It does have easier runs, but it's the steeps that attract people.

A little way north of both Sun Valley and Jackson, just inside Montana, is Big Sky, not to be confused with Big Mountain at the far northern end of the state, or indeed Big White, over the Canadian border. Big Sky has one of the biggest verticals in the US (1280m/ 4,200ft) thanks to its Lone Peak cable-car.

These three resorts all get their own chapters in this section. There is one other you ought to know about.

Taos, New Mexico, is the most southerly major resort in America, and because of its isolation is relatively unknown on the international market. There's a tiny resort development at the foot of the slopes, which are set high above the traditional adobe town of Taos, 18 miles away in the arid valley. The area was developed in the 1950s by a European and is still family-run, with a friendly feel to it. It is one of the few resorts still to ban snowboarders from its slopes, which have many very challenging runs, including some major mogul fields and terrain you have to hike to.

568

TOURIST OFFICE

Taos
www.skitaos.org

BIG SKY RESORT, MONTANA

Mostly intermediate slopes in the woods, expert terrain above the tree line ➔

Big Sky

Vast, empty slopes for all abilities, plus a fledgling village

NEWS

The north face of Lone Mountain is to be developed for 2003/04, with installation of a long, six-seat chair-lift. The newly developed terrain will form part of a new resort, Moonlight Basin, independent of Big Sky. The two resorts will effectively overlap, with a number of trails and one chair-lift being open to people with either lift pass – but no shared pass, at least for now. The new lift will access two new bowls with 1,400 acres of terrain.

A new gladed run was opened for 2002/03 on Andesite, with another planned for 2003/04.

+ Extensive ski area with runs for all abilities, including great expert runs
+ Excellent snow reliability
+ Big vertical by US standards
+ Few queues, empty slopes

− Only a small resort village as yet, quiet in the evenings
− Some slow, old chair-lifts
− Only one fast-food mountain eatery
− Long journey from the UK – at least three flights

Big Sky is renowned for its powder, steeps and big vertical, and has lots of blissfully empty gentler slopes. At present, there's not much more than three hotels (including a luxury 5-star), with a few shops, restaurants and condos around them. Nightlife is limited, to say the least.

This year, a curious development is taking place next-door to Big Sky. Moonlight Basin Ranch, on the northern fringe of the slopes, is turning itself into the basis of a small new resort, Moonlight Basin, on the north face of Lone Mountain. The two resorts will effectively overlap. But there is no shared lift pass. Mad.

THE RESORT

Big Sky, now over 25 years old, has started to attract a few international visitors who have heard of its huge snowfalls and fabulous, deserted slopes. And as well as locals who live to ski, it is also attracting affluent guests from around the US.

The resort is set amid the wide open spaces of Montana, one hour's drive from airport town Bozeman. And as it's built on private land, it doesn't have to quibble with the US Forest Service for permission to grow. At the foot of the slopes is Mountain Village – with three hotels, some slope-side condominiums and a few shops and restaurants. Despite free buses, condos scattered around more distant locations hold little appeal.

Bridger Bowl is 90 minutes' drive away; after a fresh snowfall, its broad, steep, lightly wooded slopes offer wonderful powder descents.

THE MOUNTAINS

The slopes cover a big area spread over two linked mountains, with long runs for all abilities. Lone Mountain, with steep open upper slopes (very exposed in bad weather) and trees lower down, has fabulous 360° views from the top and 1280m/ 4,200ft vertical. Andesite Mountain is a much more modest wooded hill. Most of the chairs are old triples and doubles. There are daily free mountain tours.

Slopes The wooded lower slopes are laced with runs and lifts. Higher up, the Lone Peak chair leads to the Lone Peak Tram – a tiny 15-person cable-car to the top.

Terrain-parks There is a good terrain-park and a half-pipe on Andesite and a natural half-pipe on Lone Mountain.

Snow reliability Snowfall averages 400+ inches, which puts Big Sky ahead of most Colorado resorts and alongside Jackson Hole. Grooming is good, too.

Central reservations phone number
Call 1 800 548 4486 (toll-free from within the US).

Phone numbers
From distant parts of the US, add the prefix 1 406.
From abroad, add the prefix +1 406.

TOURIST OFFICE

t 995 5000
info@bigskyresort.com
www.bigskyresort.com

Experts The terrain accessed from the Tram is great, and includes the Big Couloir (often limited to two people at a time) and numerous long narrow chutes called by the locals the A to Zs. Castro's Shoulder is the steepest route at 50°. There are good black slopes lower down, around the tree line.

Intermediates There is lots of cruising terrain – the shady runs on Andesite from the Ramcharger chair are splendid, but practically all the lower lifts serve worthwhile blue runs. And recent expansion of the gladed areas has added five new trails here.

Beginners Good nursery area at the base and long greens to progress to.

Snowboarding There's great free-riding and good terrain features.

Cross-country There are 65km/40 miles of trails at Lone Mountain Ranch. There are also trails at West Yellowstone.

Queues The tiny tram attracts serious queues on peak days. Other than that, queues are rare – and the runs are deserted: there are 3,600 skiable acres and typically 2,000 people.

Mountain restaurants The Dug-Out, on Andesite does fast food and BBQs. Or you can head back to base to eat.

School and guides The ski school receives excellent reviews.

Facilities for children Handprints nursery in the slope-side Snowcrest lodge takes children from age six months ('perfection,' says a reporter). Children under 10 years ski for free.

STAYING THERE

Hotels The slope-side Summit with spa baths in the rooms and sculptures in the foyer is 'hugely impressive and up-market' says a recent visitor. Huntley Lodge has also been highly recommended. Mountain Inn is less expensive, as is Buck's T4 Lodge, seven miles away – recommended.

Self-catering The Stillwater condos are much the cheapest and have been recommended by reporters, along with Arrowhead, Beaverhead and Big Horn.

Eating out Huntley Lodge has a smart restaurant; The Peaks (in the Summit) and Dante's Inferno are popular. Shuttle-buses and courtesy cars run to far-flung places.

Après-ski Chet's bar has live music, pool and poker games. The Carabinier lounge in the Summit, Roosters and Black Bear are also popular.

Off the slopes The main things to do are snowmobiling, horse-riding, sleigh rides, visiting Yellowstone national park and shopping in Bozeman.

Moonlight Basin

It's difficult to say what this new resort will have to offer, though the artist's impression of the runs being cut on Lone Mountain looks impressive. Moonlight Lodge, at the base, is recommended by a reporter for luxury accommodation and good food.

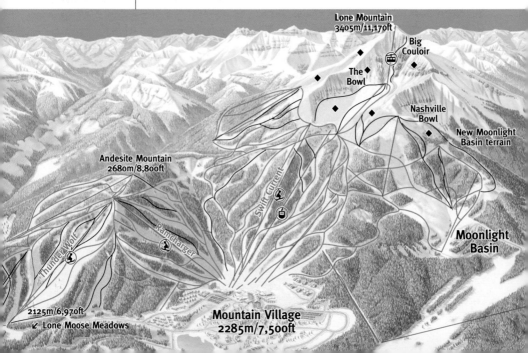

Lone Mountain 3405m/11,170ft
Big Couloir
The Bowl
Nashville Bowl
New Moonlight Basin terrain
Andesite Mountain 2680m/8,800ft
Swift Current
Ramcharger
Thunder Wolf
Moonlight Basin
2125m/6,970ft
Lone Moose Meadows
Mountain Village 2285m/7,500ft

Jackson Hole

Wild West town near exciting slopes and expanding resort village

COSTS

① ② ③ ④ ⑤ ⑥

RATINGS

The slopes

Snow	****
Extent	***
Expert	*****
Intermediate	**
Beginner	***
Convenience	***
Queues	***
Mountain restaurants	*

The rest

Scenery	***
Resort charm	***
Off-slope	***

NEWS

Flying times to the resort should improve, using new services within the US.

New for 2002/03 were the Teton Mountain Lodge condominiums at Teton Village, with indoor and outdoor pools and hot-tubs, spa, service centre and restaurants.

A yurt was opened in a backcountry location at Rock Springs. It offers lunches and overnight stays to guided groups.

The Four Seasons Resort Hotel, with health club, pool, two restaurants, residence house and penthouse suites, is scheduled to open for 2003/04.

JACKSON HOLE / JOHN LAYSHOCK

The town of Jackson really does have wooden sidewalks ➔

➕ Big, steep mountain, with some real expert-only terrain and one of the US's biggest verticals: 1260m/4,140ft

➕ Jackson town has an entertaining Wild West ambience (though not in the Aspen/Telluride league)

➕ Unspoiled, remote location with impressive scenery and wildlife

➕ Excellent snow record

➕ Even more snow (and empty slopes) 90 minutes away at Grand Targhee

➕ Cheap lodgings (winter is off-peak)

➕ Plenty to do off the slopes

➕ Airport is only minutes from town

➖ Intermediates lacking the confidence to tackle ungroomed black runs will find the area very limited

➖ Inadequate mountain restaurants

➖ The cable-car serving the top runs still generates long queues

➖ Low altitude, and slopes face roughly south-east, so snow can deteriorate quickly (and good snow is needed on steep slopes like these)

➖ Town is 15 minutes from the slopes, though the slope-side village has lodgings (and is growing quickly)

➖ Getting there from the UK involves two or (more often) three flights

For those who like the idea of steep slopes smothered in deep powder or plastered with big bumps, Jackson Hole is Mecca. Like many American mountains, Jackson has double-diamond steeps that you can't find in Europe except by going off-piste with a guide. What marks it out from the rest is the sheer quantity of terrain that is classified black, and the scale of the mountain.

Utah devotees will tell you that the snow here isn't as light as at Alta/Snowbird; but it's light enough, and falls in quantities somewhere between those found in Colorado and those famously found in Alta – the average annual total is around 400in, but in recent seasons it has often been around or above the 500in mark.

With its wooden sidewalks, country-music saloons and pool halls, tiny Jackson is a determinedly Western town – great fun, if you like that kind of thing. We do.

THE RESORT

The town of Jackson sits at the south-eastern edge of Jackson Hole – a high, flat valley surrounded by mountain ranges, in north-west Wyoming. Jackson gets many more visitors in summer than winter (thanks to the nearby national parks). This is real 'cowboy' territory, and to entertain summer tourists the town strives to maintain its Wild West flavour, with traditional-style wooden buildings and sidewalks, and a couple of 'cowboy' saloons. It has lots of clothing and souvenir shops as well as upmarket galleries appealing to second-home owners. In winter it's half-empty.

The slopes, a 15-minute drive or $2 bus-ride north-east, rise abruptly from the flat valley floor. At the base is Teton Village, with purpose-built lodgings, shops and restaurants in a pleasantly woody setting, some neo-Alpine but, increasingly, in local style. Teton Village is expanding rapidly; the building sites can be an eyesore, but the place is becoming more attractive as a base as the range of restaurants and bars improves.

KEY FACTS

Resort	1925m
	6,310ft

Jackson Hole

Slopes	1925-3185m
	6,310-10,450ft
Lifts	11
Pistes	2,500 acres
Green	10%
Blue	40%
Black	50%
Snowmaking	
	180 acres

Grand Targhee

Slopes	2310-3050m
	7,600-10,000ft
Lifts	5
Pistes	2,000 acres

(plus 1,000 acres
served by snowcat)

Green	10%
Blue	70%
Black	20%
Snowmaking	none

LIFT PASSES

Jackson Hole
Covers all lifts in
Jackson Hole

Main pass
1-day pass $61
6-day pass $330

Senior citizens
Over 65: 6-day pass
$165

Children
Under 22: 6-day pass
$248
Under 15: 6-day pass
$165
Under 5: free pass

Notes
Afternoon pass
available. Prices may
be cheaper when
booked in advance
through UK tour
operators.

Alternative passes
Grand Targhee (day
pass $49); Snow King
Mountain (day pass
$32)

THE MOUNTAINS

Jackson Hole has long been recognised as one of the world's most compelling resorts for advanced and expert skiers. With recent improvements to the lifts and the new buildings at Teton Village, the resort may seem to have a broader appeal. Don't be fooled: the beginner slopes are fine, but intermediates wanting to build up confidence should look elsewhere. Trail gradings are accurate: our own small map doesn't distinguish black from double-black-diamond runs, but the distinction matters once you are there – 'expert only' tends to mean just that. Some of the double-black runs are simply steep; but there are also cliffs, bumps, jumps and couloirs, including the infamous Corbet's.

THE SLOPES
One big mountain, one small one
One big mountain makes Jackson Hole famous – **Rendezvous**. The summit, accessed by a mid-sized cable-car (the Tram), provides a 1260m/4,130ft vertical – exceptional for the US. Conditions and thighs permitting, you can go from top to almost bottom on black slopes. From the top of the Tram you can also access the backcountry of Cody Bowl. It can be incredibly cold and windy at the top of the Tram even when it's warm and calm below.

To the right looking up is **Apres Vous** mountain, with half the vertical and mostly much gentler runs, accessed by the short Teewinot and the longer Apres Vous fast quads.

Between these two peaks is a broad

mountainside split by gullies, accessed by the Bridger gondola. This gives speedy access to the Thunder and Sublette quad chairs serving some of the steepest terrain on Rendezvous.

To get your bearings, take the Rendezvous Trail from the top of the Tram. This turns into South Pass traverse and goes all the way past the main lifts to the far end of the area on Apres Vous. There are complimentary tours of the mountain daily.

Snow King is a separate area right next to Jackson town. Locals use it in their lunch-hour and in the evening (it's partly floodlit).

TERRAIN-PARKS
They exist
There's a terrain-park and a half-pipe, and Dick's Ditch is a natural pipe, but you really come to Jackson for the steeps and deeps of the free-riding.

SNOW RELIABILITY
Steep lower slopes can suffer
The claimed average of 402 inches of 'mostly dry powder' snow is much more than most Colorado resorts claim – and for a core three-month season conditions are likely to be reasonable. But the base elevation is relatively low for the Rockies, and the slopes are quite sunny – they basically face south-east. If you're unlucky, you may find the steep lower slopes like the Hobacks in poor shape, or even shut. Locals claim that you can expect powder roughly half the time. Snowmaking covers runs from the gondola and on Apres Vous.

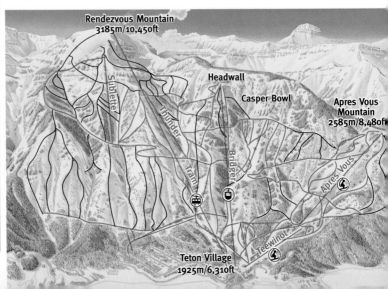

Rendezvous Mountain
3185m/10,450ft

Headwall

Casper Bowl

Apres Vous
Mountain
2585m/8,480ft

Sublette

Thunder

Bridger

Tram

Apres Vous

Teewinot

Teton Village
1925m/6,310ft

↑ Well, what are you waiting for? They say it's only the jump into Corbet's Couloir that is tricky
JACKSON HOLE / TOMAS ANNERBY

to the short but seriously steep Alta chutes, and to the less severe Laramie Bowl beside them. Or you can track over to Tensleep Bowl – pausing to inspect Corbet's from below – and on to the less extreme (and less chute-like) Expert Chutes, and the single black Cirque and Headwall areas). Casper Bowl – accessed through gates only – is recommended for untracked powder. Thunder chair serves further steep, narrow, north-facing chutes.

Again, the lower part of the mountain here offers lightly wooded single-black slopes.

The gondola serves terrain not without interest for experts. In particular, Moran Woods is a splendid, under-utilised area. And even Apres Vous itself has an area of serious single blacks in Saratoga bowl.

The gates into the backcountry access over 3,000 acres of amazing terrain; you should hire a guide to take you there. You can now stay out overnight at the new backcountry yurt. There are some helicopter operations.

FOR EXPERTS
Best for the brave

For the good skier or boarder who wants challenges without the expense of hiring a guide to go off-piste, Jackson is one of the world's best resorts – maybe even the best.

Rendezvous mountain offers virtually nothing but black and very black slopes. The routes down the main Rendezvous Bowl are not particularly fearsome; but some of the alternatives are. Go down the East Ridge at least once to stare over the edge of the notorious Corbet's Couloir. The Tram passes right above it, giving a great view of people leaping off the lip. It's the jump-in that's special; the word is that the slope you land on is a mere 50° to the horizontal.

Below Rendezvous Bowl, the wooded flanks of Cheyenne Bowl offer serious challenges, at the extreme end of the single-black-diamond spectrum. If instead you take the ridge run that skirts this bowl to the right, you get to the Hobacks – a huge area of open and lightly wooded slopes, gentler than those higher up, but still black.

Corbet's aside, most of the seriously steep slopes are more easily reached from the slightly lower quad chairs. From Sublette, you have direct access

FOR INTERMEDIATES
Exciting for some

There are great cruising runs on the front face of Apres Vous, and top-to-bottom quite gentle blues from the gondola. But they don't add up to a great deal of mileage, and you shouldn't consider Jackson unless you want to tackle the blacks. It's then important to get guidance on steepness and snow conditions. The steepest single blacks are steep; intimidating when mogulled and fearsome when hard. The daily grooming map is worth consulting.

FOR BEGINNERS
Fine, up to a point

There are a few broad, gentle runs: fine for getting started. The progression to the blue Werner run off the Apres Vous chair is gradual enough – but what then? Most of the blues are traverses and the exceptions will not help build a novice's confidence.

boarding

Jackson Hole is a cult resort for expert snowboarders, just as it is for expert skiers. The steeps, cliffs and chutes make for a lot of high-adrenalin thrills for competent free-riders. It's not a bad resort for novices either, with the beginner slopes served by a high-speed quad. Intermediates not wishing to venture off the groomed runs will find the resort limited. There are some good snowboard shops, including the Hole-in-the-Wall at Teton Village.

FOR CROSS-COUNTRY
Lots of possibilities

There are three centres, and one at Grand Targhee, offering varied trails. The Spring Creek Nordic Center has some good beginner terrain and moonlight tours. The Nordic Center at Teton has 17km/10 miles of trails and organises trips into the National Parks.

QUEUES
Always queues for the Tram

The Bridger gondola relieved some of the pressure on the Tram, which is now over 30 years old. But the Tram is still the quickest way up, still the only way to the very top and still not able to keep up with demand; there may be queues all day (10 to 30 minutes, at different times of day). You can access all of the mountain except Rendezvous Bowl via the Sublette chair.

MOUNTAIN RESTAURANTS
Head back to base

There's only one real restaurant on the mountain – at the base of the Casper chair-lift; it does a good range of self-service food, but gets very crowded. There are simple snack bars at four other points on the mountain.

SCHOOLS AND GUIDES
Learn to tackle the steeps

As well as the usual lessons, there are also special types – steep and deep, women-only, for example – on certain dates. You can book Early Tram lessons and be first on the slopes. Backcountry guides can be hired.

FACILITIES FOR CHILDREN
Just fine

The area may not seem to be one ideally suited to children, but in fact there are enough easy runs and the 'Kids' Ranch' care facilities are good. There are various classes catering for ages 3 to 17.

SCHOOLS

Jackson Hole
t 739 2663
info@jacksonhole.com

Classes
Full day $70
Private lessons
Half day (3hr) $290

CHILDREN

The Kids' Ranch (739 2691) in the Cody House at Teton Village takes children aged 6 months to 6 years, from 8.30 to 4.30, with indoor and outdoor games and ski lessons from age 3. Kids use the Fort Wyoming snow-garden, with 'magic carpet' lift.

Ski or snowboard classes for ages 7 to 14 cost US$90 for a full day (9am to 3.30).

STAYING THERE

HOW TO GO
In town or by the mountain

Teton Village is convenient and the new Four Seasons Resort Hotel will open there for 2003/4. But stay in Jackson for cowboy atmosphere.

Hotels Because winter is low season, prices are low.

(((((5) **Amangani Resort** (734 7333) Hedonistic (expensive) luxury in isolated position way above the valley.

(((4) **Alpenhof** (733 3242) Our favourite (and our readers') in Teton Village. Tirolean-style, with rooms of varying standard and price. Recently extended and refurbished. Good food. Pool, sauna, hot-tub.

(((4) **Wort** (733 2190) Comfortable, right in the centre of town, above the lively Silver Dollar Bar. Hot-tub.

(((4) **Rusty Parrot Lodge** (733 2000) A stylish place in town, with a rustic feel and handcrafted furniture. Hot-tub.

(((4) **Snake River Lodge & Spa** (732 6000) At Teton Village. Smartly welcoming as well as comfortable and convenient, with fine spa facilities.

(((4) **Spring Creek Ranch** (733 8833) Exclusive retreat between town and slopes; cross-country on hand. Hot-tub.

(((4) **Huff House Inn** (733 4164) Charming old inn – the best of Jackson's many luxury B&B places.

(((4) **Painted Porch** (733 1981) Gorgeous B&B full of antiques.

(((3) **Jackson Hole Lodge** (733 2992) Western-style place on fringe of Jackson town. Comfortable mini-suite rooms, and free breakfast/après-ski munchies. Pool, sauna, hot-tubs.

(((3) **Parkway Inn** (733 3143) Friendly, family-run, central in Jackson town; big rooms, antique furniture, pool, hot-tubs. Recommended by a reporter.

((2) **Hostel x** (733 3415) Basic, good value ($51 a night), at Teton Village. Recommended by a reporter.

((2) **Trapper Inn** (733 2648) Friendly, good value, a block or two from Town Square. Hot-tubs.

Self-catering There is lots of choice around Jackson and at Teton Village; Teton Mountain Lodge was new for 2002/03.

EATING OUT
A reasonable range of options

Teton Village has pizza, Mexican, Japanese, a steakhouse and a number of hotel restaurants. Most people favour the Mangy Moose – good value,

GETTING THERE

Air Jackson 19km/12 miles (½hr).

ACTIVITIES

Indoor Art galleries, ice skating, cinemas, swimming, theatre, concerts, wildlife art museum

Outdoor Snowmobiles, mountaineering, snow-shoe hikes, snowcat tours, floodlit skiing, heli-skiing, sleigh rides, dog-sledding, walks, wildlife safaris and tours of Yellowstone National Park, Grand Teton National Park

Phone numbers From distant parts of the US, add the prefix 1 307. From abroad, add the prefix +1 307.

TOURIST OFFICES

Jackson Hole t 733 7182 info@jacksonhole.com www.jacksonhole.com

Grand Targhee t 353 2300 info@grandtarghee. com www.grandtarghee. com

good fun. In Jackson town there are more places to try – though by US standards the range is modest. The cool art-deco Cadillac Grille does good food. The Blue Lion is small, cosy and casually stylish. The 'saloons' do hearty meals and good steaks. A reporter also recommends Antony's Italian and 'for a treat' the Rusty Parrot Lodge. The cute log cabin Sweetwater is recommended for 'Greek-inspired' food. The Snake River brew-pub is good value – not to be confused with the expensive Snake River Grill.

APRES-SKI
Amusing saloons

For immediate après-ski at Teton Village, the Mangy Moose is a big, happy, noisy place, often with live music. For a quieter time head for Dietrich's bar at the Alpenhof.

In Jackson there are two famous 'saloons'. The Million Dollar Cowboy Bar features saddles as bar stools and a stuffed grizzly bear, and is usually the liveliest place in town, with live music and dancing some nights. The Silver Dollar around the corner is more subdued; there may be ragtime playing as you count the 2032 silver dollars inlaid into the counter. The Rancher is a huge pool-hall. The Shady Lady saloon sometimes has live country and western. The Virginian saloon is quieter.

For a night out of town, join the local ravers at the Stagecoach Inn at Wilson, especially on Sundays.

OFF THE SLOPES
'Great' outdoor diversions

The famous Yellowstone National Park is 100km/60 miles to the north. You can tour the park by snowcat or snowmobile, but you'll be roaring along the snowy roads in the company of several hundred other smelly snowmobiles – 'more like a Grand Prix than a wilderness', as one reporter puts it. We found the trip a great disappointment. There is much more rewarding snowmobiling to be done elsewhere.

The National Elk Refuge, next to Jackson and across the road from the National Museum of Wildlife Art, has the largest elk herd in the US. In town there are some 40 galleries and museums and a number of outlets for Indian and Western arts and crafts. There is, believe it or not, a branch of Ripley's Believe It or Not® – 'a museum unlike any other', as they say.

A DAY OUT IN GRAND TARGHEE 2440m/8,000ft

We'd recommend any adventurous visitor to make the hour-and-a-half trip over the Teton pass to Grand Targhee, especially if there's been a recent big dump. The average snowfall here is over 500 inches – 25% greater than Jackson, and on a par with Utah's best – and the slopes are usually blissfully empty. The slopes are much easier than at Jackson. Locals call it Grand Foggee, because there is often low cloud even when it's not snowing.

On the main Fred's Mountain, the 1,500 acres can all be accessed from a central fast quad. The wide area of open and lightly wooded blue and black runs has a respectable 610m/2,000ft vertical. A long slow double serves a splendid area of tough blues and easy blacks. Lower down, a slow quad serves an excellent area of short green runs. Next-door Peaked Mountain offers a similar area of terrain. One-third of it is accessed by a fast quad. This has a vertical of only 390m/1,280ft and serves four short blue and blue-black trails, as well as some wooded terrain. Two-thirds is accessed by snowcat – over 1,000 acres, mainly great gladed runs in pristine powder.

Daily buses to Targhee pick up from various hotels around town and Teton Village. A combined bus/lift ticket costs $59. The snowcat operation cost $299 a day (including lunch), $225 a half-day. You can also stay at Grand Targhee – there's a small, quiet, modern village right at the base.

Sun Valley

Stylish resort with slopes to flatter its rich and famous guests

COSTS

① ② ③ ④ ⑤ ⑥

RATINGS

The slopes

Snow	✱✱✱
Extent	✱✱✱
Expert	✱✱✱
Intermediate	✱✱✱✱
Beginner	✱✱✱
Convenience	✱✱
Queues	✱✱✱✱
Mountain restaurants	✱✱✱✱

The rest

Scenery	✱✱✱
Resort charm	✱✱✱
Off-slope	✱✱✱

NEWS

The big news for 2003/04 is the planned construction of a half-pipe on the lower Warm Springs run below the Challenger chair.

576

➕ Luxury resort built around the atmospheric old mining town

➕ Ideal intermediate terrain

➕ Wonderful luxurious mountain restaurants and base lodges

➕ Good restaurants and bars in town

➕ Lots of off-slope diversions

➖ Expensive

➖ Erratic snow record though extensive snowmaking back-up

➖ Shuttle-buses between two separate mountains and from most accommodation

Millions of dollars have been pumped into building splendid facilities – high-speed chair-lifts, a huge computerised snowmaking system, beautiful base lodges and mountain restaurants – to maintain Sun Valley's reputation as the US's original luxury purpose-built winter sports resort. For a peaceful, relaxing time, it's hard to beat. For skiing and boarding alone, there are better resorts.

THE RESORT

Sun Valley is based around the old mining village of Ketchum. It was built in the 1930s by Averell Harriman, President of the Union Pacific Railway, and became a favourite with stars such as Clark Gable and Judy Garland. Its current owner has pumped millions of dollars into the mountain to restore it to state-of-the-art luxury and Sun Valley now attracts stars like Clint Eastwood and Arnie Schwarzenegger. The town of Ketchum retains its old-world charm and has atmospheric bars, restaurants and shops. But it's not cheap: 'Expensive. I didn't buy, but I enjoyed looking in the high-quality shops,' says a reporter.

Shuttle-buses from most accommodation makes your choice of location less of an issue.

KEY FACTS

Resort	1755m
	5,750ft

For Bald Mountain

Slopes	1755-2790m
	5,750-9,150ft
Lifts	15
Pistes	2,054 acres
Green	36%
Blue	42%
Black	22%
Snowmaking	
	630 acres

For Dollar Mountain

Slopes	1830-2025m
	6,010ft-6,640ft
Lifts	5
Pistes	10 runs
Green	70%
Blue	30%
Black	0%

Central reservations phone number
Call 1 800 634 3347 (toll-free from within the US).

Phone numbers
From distant parts of the US, add the prefix 1 208.
From abroad, add the prefix +1 208.

TOURIST OFFICE

t 786 8259
ski@sunvalley.com
www.visitsunvalley.com

SUN VALLEY RESORT /
KEVIN SYMS

Ketchum is a spruced-up old mining town with good restaurants and bars to serve its upmarket clientele ↓

THE MOUNTAINS

There are two separate mountains – Bald Mountain, with the main body of runs, and the smaller Dollar Mountain.
Slopes The main slopes of Bald Mountain (known locally as Baldy) are accessed from one of two luxurious base lodge complexes at River Run and Warm Springs, a shuttle-bus-ride from most accommodation. Of the lifts, seven are high-speed quads. The separate Dollar Mountain has good beginner slopes.
Terrain-parks At long last Sun Valley has taken the plunge and plans to build a half-pipe for this season. It is to be 135m/440ft long with 4.5m/15ft walls and snowmaking will be used to keep it in shape. There are no immediate plans for a full terrain-park.
Snow reliability The resort has an erratic natural snow record, so has installed snowmaking which covers over 70% of the groomable runs.
Experts There are a few tough runs and bowls for experts, but nothing beyond single-black-diamond pitch, including the two most famous mogul runs, Exhibition and Limelight. Heli-skiing is available locally.
Intermediates Most of the terrain is ideal, with lots of runs at a consistent pitch. There are good blue bowl runs with great views from the top ridge as well as well-groomed cruisers through the trees, mostly of a good steep pitch, allowing excellent carving.
Beginners Dollar is the place to be, with gentle, long green runs to progress to. Baldy's greens are tougher.
Snowboarding Snowboarding is now allowed and the chair-lifts make getting about easy. But Sun Valley doesn't have a snowboard culture – and is only now getting a half-pipe.
Cross-country 40km/25 miles of prepared trails start at the Nordic Center, with more than 200km/124 miles in the North Valley Trail system. A new free bus will access these trails.
Queues These are rarely a problem, with Sun Valley's network of high-speed quads whisking people around.
Mountain restaurants The mountain restaurants and base lodges have to be seen to be believed. They are way ahead of most US on-slope facilities, with floor-to-ceiling windows, beautiful wooden decor, heated terraces so snow instantly melts, and marble fittings with gold-plated taps in public restrooms. One reporter enjoyed 'the piano and violin players and people-watching at River Run base' at the end of the day.
Schools and guides We have no reason to believe that the lessons are not up to the usual high standards found in most North American resorts.
Facilities for children The ski school takes children from age three, and children 15 and under stay and ski free during certain periods of the year.

STAYING THERE

How to go There are some wonderful hotels and plenty of cheaper options too, including motels and self-catering. Pennays at River Run and Premier (ski-in/ski-out at Warm Springs) condos have been recommended.
Hotels One of our favourite hotels in any resort is the stylish Sun Valley Lodge. As well as magnificent rooms, there is a big outdoor ice rink and a pool, and the corridors are lined with photos of film-star guests. Ernest Hemingway wrote *For Whom the Bell Tolls* here.
Eating out There are over 80 restaurants and Sun Valley was rated number one in the US by readers of *Gourmet* magazine. We had excellent food at the relaxed Evergreen Bistro and a great breakfast at The Knob Hill Inn. A reporter recommends Chandler's, too.
Après-ski Atmospheric places include the Sawtooth Club (popular with locals), Whiskey Jaques for live music and dancing, and the Pioneer Saloon, popular for its prime rib, and Clint Eastwood spotting.
Off the slopes You can have a fine time relaxing off the slopes, including sleigh rides, dog-sledding, walking, snowmobiling, ice skating, swimming, fishing, gliding, paragliding and strolling round the galleries and shops. There's a special snow-shoe trail, too.

New England

You go to Utah for the deepest snow, to Colorado for the lightest powder and swankiest resorts, to California for the mountains and low prices. You go to New England for ... well, for what? Extreme cold? Rock-hard artificial snow? Mountains too limited to be of interest beyond New Jersey? Yes and no: all of these preconceptions have some basis, but they add up to an incomplete and unfair picture.

Yes, it can be cold: one of our reporters recorded –27°C, with wind chill producing a perceived temperature of –73°C. Early in the season, people wear face masks to prevent frostbite. It can also be warm – another reporter had a whole week of rain that washed away the early-season snow. The thing about New England weather is that it varies. Not as much as in Scotland, maybe, but the locals' favourite saying is: 'If you don't like the weather in New England, wait two minutes.' But we got routine winter weather on both of our recent visits – one in January, one in February.

New England doesn't usually get much super-light powder or deep snow to play in. But the resorts have big snowmaking installations, designed to ensure a long season and to help the slopes to 'recover' after a thaw or spell of rain. They were the pioneers of snowmaking technology; and 'farming' snow, as they put it, is an art form and a way of life – provided the weather is cold enough. And they make and groom their snow to produce a superb surface. Many of the resorts get impressive amounts of natural snow too – in some seasons.

The mountains are not huge in terms of trail mileage (the largest, Killington, is smaller than all except one of the resorts we feature in western US). But several have verticals of over 800m/2,620ft (on a par with Colorado resorts such as Keystone) and most have over 600m/1,970ft (matching Breckenridge), and are worth considering for a short stay, or even for a week if you like familiar runs. For more novelty, a two- or three-centre trip is the obvious solution.

You won't lack challenge – most of the double-black-diamond runs are seriously steep. And you won't lack space: most Americans visit over weekends, which means deserted slopes on weekdays – except at peak periods such as New Year and the weekends of Martin Luther King Day in January and President's Day in late February. It also means the resorts are keen to attract long-stay visitors, so UK package prices are low.

But the big weekend and day-trip trade also means that few New England resorts have developed atmospheric resort villages – just a few condos and a hotel, maybe, with places to stay further out geared to car drivers who ski, eat, sleep, ski, go home.

New England is easy to get to from Britain – a flight to Boston, then perhaps a three-or four-hour drive to your resort. And there are some pretty towns to visit, with their clapboard houses and big churches. You might also like to consider spending a day or two in Boston – one of America's most charming cities. And you could save a lot of money on normal UK prices by having a shopping spree at the factory outlet stores that abound in New England.

We cover four of the most popular resorts on the UK market in the separate chapters that follow. But there are many other small areas, too. And if you are going for a week or more, we recommend renting a car and visiting a few resorts. In the rest of this introduction, we outline the attractions of the main possibilities.

From Killington (by far the biggest resort), you can go south to a range of smaller resorts. **Okemo** competes with Smugglers' Notch for the family market. Okemo mountain has southern Vermont's biggest vertical (655m/ 2,150ft) and longest trail (over 7km/4.3 miles). The slopes are largely intermediate or easy – though there are a dozen black runs and a couple of short double-black-diamonds. Last season the area was expanded

SKI arrangements.com

08700 110565
Crich Matlock, DE4 5DE

considerably by construction of a new fast quad on the next-door mountain, Jackson Gore. A new base development naturally follows, and there are more lifts to come, eventually adding 30% to the resort's terrain. There's an extensive terrain-park leading into a half-pipe. There is almost 100% snowmaking cover – and the product is said to be the best in the east. We have reports of serious queues for the main fast quad at peak times.

Mount Snow is a one-peak resort, with a long row of lifts on the front face serving easy and intermediate runs of just over 500m/1,640ft vertical, and a separate area of black runs on the north face – including one short but serious double-black. (The sister resort of **Haystack**, a short drive away, has more steep slopes in its Witches area.) Mount Snow has some of the best terrain-parks in the east, including a super-pipe. There are 2,000 beds at the base, some in hotels.

Stratton offers something like the classic Alpine arrangement of a village at the foot of the lifts. Owned by Intrawest, it's a smart, modern development with a pedestrian shopping street. The slopes – mostly easy and intermediate, with some blacks and some short double-black pitches – is spread widely around the flanks of a single peak, served by modern lifts, including a 12-person gondola (which reportedly produces queues) and four fast six-seat chairs. Stratton calls itself the 'snowboarding

capital of the east', with no fewer than six terrain-parks.

You may find more interest in **Sugarbush**, to the north of Killington, midway between Killington and Stowe, Sugarbush is a fast-developing resort, with one of the larger ski areas. The main sector is an extensive bowl below Lincoln Peak, with lifts up to six points on the rim; a long up-and-over chair-lift links the Mt Ellen area – smaller, but with more altitude and more vertical (810m/2,650ft). The easy runs are confined to the lower slopes; higher up, the direct runs are seriously steep. There are terrain-parks in both areas. Most of the accommodation is in the historic village of Waitsfield, but a village is developing at the base.

Mad River Glen next door is a cult resort with locals, owned for several years now by a co-operative, with some tough ungroomed terrain, a few well-groomed intermediate trails and old-fashioned lifts – it still has a single-person chair-lift. And snowboarding is still banned.

Further north, near the Canadian border, is **Jay Peak**. It gets crowded at weekends (with Canadian as well as American visitors) but is quiet in the week. It has Vermont's only cable-car, which takes you to the summit and to views of four US states plus Canada. It gets a lot of snow (350in on average) and has some good runs for advanced skiers and adventurous intermediates – notably 100+ acres of glades. There is slope-side accommodation.

KILLINGTON RESORT

Typical New England terrain at Killington: modest vertical and entirely wooded ↓

Sugarloaf in Maine already has a much better developed village at the base than most small New England resorts. Sugarloaf is owned by the American Skiing Company, so it includes a Grand Summit hotel. But the mountain is small and a keen piste-basher could ski it out in a day or two. There is something for everybody, with genuine steeps up around and above the tree line and gentle terrain lower down in the woods. On our last visit a few years back we were struck by how safety-conscious the local slope-users were; we estimated well over 50% were wearing helmets.

New Hampshire has several small resorts scattered along the Interstate 93 highway. **Bretton Woods** is one of the smaller areas, 460m/1,510ft vertical on a single mountain face, but it is highly rated, particularly by families, who relish the top-to-bottom easy trails. There is a good mix of terrain, and snowmaking is comprehensive. Snowboarders have a park and a half-pipe. There are a few places to stay near the base, with the grand old Mount Washington hotel five minutes away.

Cannon is a ski area and nothing more – lifts from its two base areas close to I-93 converge on the summit 650m/2,130ft above. This is the state's biggest vertical and the slopes are mainly intermediate level. There are quite a few black runs, but no double-blacks; a new beginners' area has now been created. It's a few minutes' drive to hotels and motels in Franconia in one direction and to Lincoln in the other.

Loon Mountain Resort is a small, smart, modern resort just outside the sprawling town of Lincoln. The mountain (640m/2,100ft vertical) is mostly intermediate, though some fall-line runs merit their black grading. There is a long snowboard park.

Waterville Valley is a compact area with runs dropping either side of a broad, gentle ridge rising 615m/2,020ft above the lift base. There are a couple of short but genuine double-black-diamond mogul fields, but most of the slopes are intermediate. Terrain features include a super-pipe The village is a Disneyesque affair a couple of miles away down on the flat valley bottom.

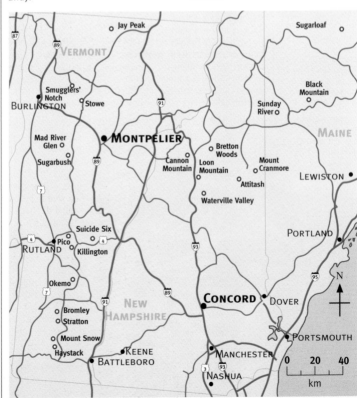

Killington

Good slopes, great après-ski, no village (yet)

KILLINGTON RESORT

Alpine-style blue skies aren't something to rely on in New England ↓

➕ The biggest mountain in the east, matching some Colorado resorts, with terrain to suit everyone

➕ Lively après-ski, with lots of bar-restaurants offering happy hours and late-night action

➕ Excellent nursery slopes

➕ Comprehensive and very effective snowmaking

➕ Good childcare, although it's not a notably child-oriented resort

➖ No resort village: hotels, condos and restaurants are widely spread, mostly along the five-mile access road – a car is almost a necessity

➖ New England weather – highly changeable and can be very cold

➖ The trail network is complex, and there are lots of trail-crossings

➖ Terminally tedious for anyone who is not a skier or boarder

It's difficult to ignore Killington. It claims to have the largest mountain, the largest number of quad chairs, the largest grooming fleet and the longest season in the east and the world's biggest snowmaking installation. (As a result it tries to be the first resort in America to open, in October, but often shuts again shortly after.) It also claims to have America's longest lift and longest trail (a winding 16km/10 miles long) and New England's steepest mogul slope (Outer Limits – 800m/0.5 miles long for a drop of 370m/1,210ft). Impressive by local standards. But it also has weekend and public holiday crowds, and New England's changeable weather.

For those of us used to resorts with villages at the foot of the slopes, Killington is a bit of a shock. It has grown up to suit car drivers arriving for a day or a weekend. Most accommodation is away from the slopes on the long approach road; plans for a slope-side village at the lift base have been put on hold.

Killington is great for New Yorkers, just as Nevis Range is great for Glaswegians. But if you don't live within driving distance, there are more attractive places.

THE RESORT

Killington is an extraordinary resort, especially to European eyes. Most of its hotels and restaurants are spread along a five-mile approach road. The nearest thing you'll find to a focus is the occasional set of traffic lights with a cluster of shops, though there is a concentration of buildings along a two-and-a-half mile stretch of the road. The resort caters mainly for day and weekend visitors who drive in from the east-coast cities (including a lot of New Yorkers). The car is king; provided you have one, getting around isn't that much of a hassle. There's also a good free shuttle-bus service during the day around the base areas and lodgings. Beyond this it costs a dollar.

Plans for a new resort village around the Grand Resort hotel at Snowshed have been put on hold. Practically all the other lodgings are a drive from a lift station – either the one at Snowshed or the Skyeship gondola station on the main highway 100, leading past the resort. Staying near the end of the access road is convenient for this and for outings to Pico, a separate little mountain owned by Killington, perhaps to be linked one day to Killington's Ram's Head mountain.

SKI
arrangements.com

08700 110565
Crich Matlock, DE4 5DE

NEWS

A special snowmobile snow-cross course, for kids aged 6–12 years, opened for 2002/03. Also new was a Winter Adventure Centre. It is the hub for various snow activities – snow-shoeing, tubing and dog-sledding. A new terrain-park was added at Timberline.

For 2003/04 snowmaking will be upgraded.

THE MOUNTAINS

Runs spread over a series of wooded peaks, all quite close together but giving the resort a basis for claiming to cover six mountains – or seven if you count Pico. A huge number of runs and an impressive number of lifts are crammed into a modest area. The result is a very complex network of runs, and signposting isn't always very clear. To some extent the terrain on its six sectors suits different abilities. But there are also areas where a mixed ability group would be quite happy, and there are easy runs from top to bottom of each peak. Some runs of all levels are left to form bumps; there is half-and-half grooming on selected trails; and terrain features – ridges, bumps, quarter-pipes – are created.

Killington has also created areas that are called Fusion Zones – thinned-out forest areas, where you pick your own line. These areas are not groomed or patrolled – and they come in blue and single- and double-black-diamond grades. We found them great fun.

The piste map is one of the largest and most fact-packed we've ever come across. But this makes it unwieldy and awkward to handle.

THE SLOPES
Complicated
The Killington Base area has chairs radiating to three of the six peaks – **Snowdon**, **Killington** (the high-point of the area) and **Skye** – the last also accessible by gondola starting beside US highway 4. Novices and families

head for the other main base area, which has two parts: Snowshed, at the foot of the main beginner slope, served by several parallel chairs; and Rams Head, just across the road up to Killington Base, where there's a Family Center at the foot of the entirely gentle **Rams Head** mountain.

The two remaining peaks are behind Skye Peak; they can be reached by trails from Killington and Skye, but each also has a lift base accessible by road. **Bear Mountain** is the expert's hill, served by two quad chairs from its mid-mountain base area. The sixth 'peak', **Sunrise**, is a slight blip on the mountainside, with a short triple chair up from the Sunrise Village condos area. The area below Sunrise Village is used for snowmobile tours – from the old lift base just off highway 4.

TERRAIN-PARKS
Lots of possibilities
Now with three terrain-parks (plus one at Pico), a super-pipe and a boarder-cross course, Killington has its fair share of excitement. There are various other terrain features scattered around the area.

SNOW RELIABILITY
Good if it's cold
Killington has a good snowfall record and a huge snowmaking system. But even that is no good if temperatures are too high to operate it. Bad weather can ruin a holiday even in mid-season. A reporter who had new powder each night on a March visit a few years ago, went back at the same time the

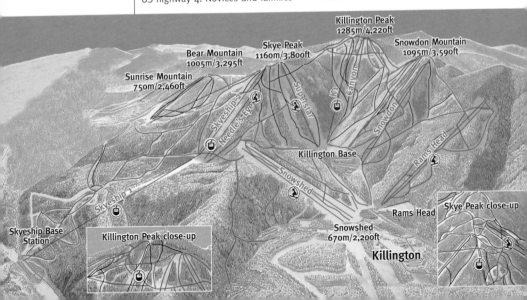

Killington Peak 1285m/4,220ft
Skye Peak 1160m/3,800ft
Bear Mountain 1005m/3,295ft
Snowdon Mountain 1095m/3,590ft
Sunrise Mountain 750m/2,460ft
Skyeship 2
Needle's Eye
Superstar
Ski Canyon
Snowdon
Rams Head
Killington Base
Skyeship 1
Snowshed
Skyeship Base Station
Killington Peak close-up
Rams Head
Snowshed 670m/2,200ft
Skye Peak close-up
Killington

boarding

A cool resort like Killington has to take boarding seriously, and it does. There are terrain features scattered around the area, with lots of interest for all levels, and parts of the mountain have been reshaped to cut out some of the unpleasant flats on green runs. There are excellent beginner slopes, and plenty of friendly high-speed (ie slow-loading) chair-lifts – and the Perfect Turn Discovery Center caters just for beginners. Several big-name board events are held here.

following year to find people skiing in shorts and T-shirts on the few runs that were open. A February visitor told of 'everything from frostbite warnings to pouring rain'.

FOR EXPERTS
Some challenges
The main areas that experts head for are Killington Peak, where there is a handful of genuine double-diamond fall-line runs under the two chair-lifts, and Bear Mountain. Most of the slopes here are single blacks but Outer Limits, under the main quad chair, is a double-diamond, claimed to be 'the steepest mogul slope in the east'. We suspect there are steeper runs at Stowe and Smugglers' Notch. There are two or three worthwhile blacks on Snowdon, too. The Fusion Zones on Skye and Snowdon are well worth seeking out. But one reporter thought many of the black runs overclassified: 'Some would be red in Europe and comfortably skied by an intermediate.'

FOR INTERMEDIATES
Navigation problems?
There are lots of easy cruising blue and green runs all over the slopes, except on Bear Mountain, where the single blacks present a little more of a challenge for intermediates. Snowdon is a splendid area for those who like to vary their diet. There's a blue-classified Fusion Zone on Rams Head. Finding your way around the complicated network of trails may be tricky, though. One reporter liked Pico a lot but complained that the blue run down was more difficult than some blacks.

FOR BEGINNERS
Splendid
The facilities for complete beginners are excellent. The Snowshed slope is one vast nursery slope served by three chair-lifts and a very slow drag-lift. Rams Head also has excellent gentle slopes. The ski school runs a special, purpose-built Discovery Center just for first-time skiers and boarders – they

introduce you to the equipment, show you videos and provide refreshments.

FOR CROSS-COUNTRY
Two main options
Extensive cross-country loops are available at two specialist 'resorts' – Mountain Meadows down on US highway 4, and Mountain Top Ski Touring, just a short drive away at Chittenden.

QUEUES
Weekend crowds
Killington gets a lot of weekend and public holiday business, but at other times the slopes and lifts are likely to be quiet. One New Year reporter told of 'a madhouse with overcrowded slopes, and a 20-minute crawl up the access road', and the gondola to Killington Peak and the Rams Head chair can get oversubscribed. Overcrowded slopes are more of a problem than lift queues.

MOUNTAIN RESTAURANTS
Bearable base lodges
There are only two real mountain restaurants. We have mixed reports on the one at the top of Killington Peak, in what was the top station of the old gondola. Max's Place, on Sunrise, has table-service burgers, pasta, salad etc, and is highly recommended by a reporter for 'escaping the squalor of the other on-mountain eating places'. Each of the lift base stations has an eatery, of which we found the one at Killington Base Lodge the least dreary and crowded.

SCHOOLS AND GUIDES
In search of the Perfect Turn
The philosophy of the Perfect Turn school is to build on your strengths rather than correct your mistakes, and it seems to work for most people. Beginners start and finish their day in a dedicated beginners' building with easy chairs, coffee, videos and help with choosing and fitting your equipment.

Killington has a good
range of terrain
features, including a
super-pipe →
KILLINGTON RESORT

CHILDREN

A Family Center at
Rams Head was built
a few years ago. The
Friendly Penguin
nursery takes kids
from age six weeks to
six years –
reservations required.
Outside the door is
the Snow Play Park,
with magic carpet lift
and handle tow-lift.
There are ski classes
for several age groups
(US$103 for a full day
for a child aged 7-12).

GETTING THERE

Air Boston 251km/156
miles (2½hr).

ACTIVITIES

Indoor Killington
Grand Resort Hotel
has massage, fitness
centre, outdoor pool,
hot-tub, sauna,
aerobics. Cinemas,
bowling at Rutland.
Climbing wall at
Snowshed base.

Outdoor Skating,
snowboarding,
sledding, sleigh rides,
snow-shoe tours.
Tubing, dog-sledding
and snowmobiles.

**Central reservations
phone number**
Call 1 800 621 6867
(toll-free from within
the US).

Phone numbers
From distant parts of
the US, add the prefix
1 802.
From abroad, add the
prefix +1 802.

TOURIST OFFICE

t 422 3333
info@killington.com
www.killington.com

FACILITIES FOR CHILDREN
Fine in practice

There is a Family Center at the Rams
Head base, which takes kids from six
weeks and will introduce them to
skiing from age two years. The
daughter of one of the editors learned
here and approved of it.

STAYING THERE

HOW TO GO
Wide choices

There is a wide choice of places to
stay. As well as hotels and condos,
there are a few chalets.

Hotels There are a few places near the
lifts, but most are a drive or bus-ride
away, down Killington Road or on US4.

(((4) **Cortina Inn** (773 3333) 20
minutes away on US4, near Pico; pool,
'excellent food, poor soundproofing'.

(((4) **Grand Resort** (422 6888) Swanky
resort-owned place at Snowshed, with
outdoor pool and health club.

(((4) **Inn of the Six Mountains** (422
4302) Couple of miles down Killington
Road; 'spacious rooms, good pool'.

(((3) **Red Rob Inn** (422 3303) Short
drive from slopes – 'good restaurant, a
cut above the usual motel style'.

(((3) **North Star Lodge** (422 4040) Well
down Killington Road; 'good budget
accommodation'.

EATING OUT
You name it

There are all sorts of restaurants
spread along the Killington Road, from
simple pizza or pasta through to 'fine
dining' places. They get very crowded
at weekends and many don't take
reservations. Many of the nightspots
mentioned below in the Après-ski
section serve food for at least part of
the evening.

The local menu guide is essential
reading. Claude's Choices, the Grist
Mill, Charity's and the Cortina and Red
Rob Inns have been recommended by
recent reporters.

APRES-SKI
The beast of the east

Killington has a well-deserved
reputation for a vibrant après-ski
scene; many of its short-stay visitors
are clearly intent on making the most
of their few days (or nights) here.

Although there are bars at the base
lodges, keen après-skiers head down
Killington Road to one of the lively
places scattered along its 8km/5 mile
length. From 3pm it's cheap drinks and
free munchies, then in the early
evening it's serious dining time, then
later on the real action starts (and
admission charges kick in). Most of the
places mentioned here would also rate
a mention in Eating out.

The train-themed Casey's Caboose
is said to have the best 'wings' in
town. Charity's is another lively bar,
with an interior apparently lifted from a
turn-of-the-century Parisian brothel.
The Wobbly Barn is a famous live-
music place that rivals Jackson's Mangy
Moose for the position of America's
leading après-ski venue. The Pickle
Barrel caters for a younger crowd, with
theme nights and loud music. The
Outback complex has something for
everyone, from pizzas and free
massages to disco and live bands.

OFF THE SLOPES
Rent a car

If there is a less amusing resort in
which to spend time doing things other
than skiing or boarding, we have yet to
find it. Make sure you have a car, as
well as a book.

Smugglers' Notch

Fine fun for families – but those not saddled with kids should stay away

585

COSTS

① ② ③ ④ ⑤ ⑥

RATINGS

The slopes
Snow	***
Extent	*
Expert	***
Intermediate	***
Beginner	****
Convenience	*****
Queues	****
Mountain restaurants	*

The rest
Scenery	***
Resort charm	**
Off-slope	*

NEWS

A new $1million day care centre, Treasures, (for children aged six weeks to three years), was opened in 2002/03. The centre has a new on-slope location, heated walkways, large playground and ski-in/ski-out access from Morse.

A second teen centre was also opened, and a snowboard camp for four to five year olds.

A new warming hut opened on Stirling Mountain.

+ Excellent children's facilities
+ Lots of slope-side accommodation
+ Varied slopes with runs for all abilities
+ No queues
+ Great for beginners, with excellent ski school

- Family orientation may be too much for some child-free visitors
- New England weather – highly changeable, and can be very cold
- Limited local slopes
- No proper mountain restaurants
- No hotels – condos only
- Little après-ski atmosphere in the village, and few off-slope diversions

Smuggs hits the family target squarely, with a constant round of early-evening activities, sympathetic instructors, comprehensive childcare, a generally child-friendly layout and some long, quiet, easy runs. There are challenging slopes, too, but mileage-hungry intermediates should go elsewhere.

THE RESORT

Smugglers' Notch is about the nearest thing you'll find in the US to a French-style purpose-built family resort – except that it doesn't look so bad. The village isn't genuinely traffic-free but it comes close, and once installed in your condo you can happily do without a car (much of the accommodation is near to or on the slopes).

The resort is energetically managed and produces a constant flow of developments designed to tighten its grip on the family market, on which it is entirely focused. Most years it seems to get voted 'North American family resort of the year' by at least one American skiing publication. Those not afflicted with children would find the family orientation of the resort a bit overpowering – and even those with kids may find the village has little to offer in the evenings.

THE MOUNTAIN

Smuggs has varied and satisfying slopes, spread over three hills – Morse, above the village (with the most recent Morse Highlands area off to the left), and Madonna and Sterling off to the

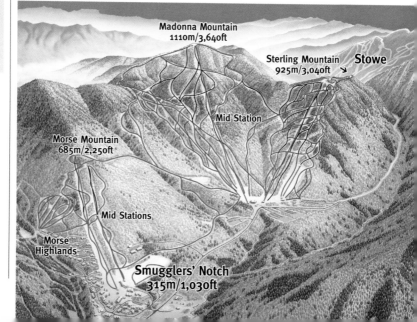

Madonna Mountain 1110m/3,640ft

Sterling Mountain 925m/3,040ft

Stowe

Mid Station

Morse Mountain 685m/2,250ft

Mid Stations

Morse Highlands

Smugglers' Notch 315m/1,030ft

KEY FACTS

Resort	315m
	1,030ft
Altitude	315-1110m
	1,030-3,640ft
Lifts	8
Pistes	1,000 acres
Green	22%
Blue	54%
Black	25%
Snowmaking	
	141 acres

Central reservations phone number
Call 644 8851.
From the UK ring 0800 169 8219.

Phone numbers
From distant parts of the US, add the prefix 1 802.
From abroad, add the prefix +1 802.

TOURIST OFFICE

t 644 8851
smuggs@smuggs.com
www.smuggs.com

SMUGGLERS' NOTCH

There are special trails to encourage kids to explore 'off-piste' ↓

right, reached by green links. From Sterling you can ski to Stowe (see separate chapter), but the on/off lift pass-sharing arrangement with Stowe is currently off, and the run is classified as a backcountry route.

Slopes There are some real challenges as well as easy cruising, and a worthwhile vertical of 800m/2,610ft. But one recent visitor found skiing together as a family and meeting for lunch was very difficult: different levels of ability meant being on different mountains. It's blissfully quiet except at weekends and holidays.

Terrain-parks Smuggs has a couple of impressive terrain-parks and an Olympic-size super-pipe. The beginner's terrain garden will suit children and adults alike.

Snow reliability Snow reliability is good, subject to the inherent variability of New England weather. Snowmaking has been improved.

Experts There are challenges for experts. We were impressed by the two or three double-diamond runs on Madonna – and The Black Hole is the only triple-diamond run in the east, they say. You can go off through the trees – but these areas are not patrolled.

Intermediates There are intermediate runs of every grade; there just aren't many of them.

Beginners It's a great area for beginners. One of the chair-lifts out of the village runs at half speed, and the runs it accesses are of an ideal gradient. Morse Highlands adds another tailor-made novice area. And the higher lifts take you to long easy runs that even 'never-evers' can tackle during their first week.

Snowboarding Smuggs encourages snowboarding. For the little ones, there's a new snowboard camp – specially tailored for 4–5 year olds.

Cross-country The 27km/17 miles of trails may be a bit limited for experts.

Queues We encountered no queues, and away from weekends we'd be surprised if anyone else did.

Mountain restaurants There are no real mountain restaurants, but there are warming huts with snacks at the top of Sterling Mountain and another at the top of the Prohibition terrain-park.

Schools and guides The ski school (or 'Snow Sport University') has often been voted the best in North America. Readers rate it 'outstanding', and 'Our best yet – we all improved a lot'. Among its bright ideas are private lessons for a parent and child, with the idea that the parent learns how to help the child develop while having fun.

Facilities for children The mountain is child-friendly, offering excitement with safety – with a special jolly kids' trail map. There's a terrain-park for kids, and little forest glades where even tinies can be taken 'off-piste'. The Treasures Child Care Centre is a comprehensive nursery. It has taken up a new on-slope location, which now offers parents ski-in/ski-out access. The school arrangements are very good, too, with childcare before and after sessions.

STAYING THERE

How to go There are no hotels in the resort itself – though there are some within driving distance.

Self-catering There are lots of comfortable condos on or near the slopes, none very far from the snow.

Eating out Options are very limited: there are a couple of restaurants in the resort, including the cosy Hearth and Candle, and others a short drive down the road to the outside world – we and the kids enjoyed Banditos. Babysitters can be arranged.

Après-ski The adult après-ski possibilities are about the most limited we have come across. We hear good reports of the teen centre. Camp fires and hot chocolate are popular with the youngsters as the lifts close.

Off the slopes There is very little to do off the slopes. Organised day trips to Vermont or Montreal are possible. A visit to Ben & Jerry's might amuse – the ice-cream factory is nearby.

Stowe

Charming Vermont town some way from its small but serious mountain

COSTS

① ② ③ ④ ⑤ ⑥

RATINGS

The slopes
Snow	★★★
Extent	★
Expert	★★★
Intermediate	★★★★
Beginner	★★★★
Convenience	★
Queues	★★★★
Mountain restaurants	★★

The rest
Scenery	★★★
Resort charm	★★★★
Off-slope	★

KEY FACTS

Resort	475m
	1,560ft
Slopes	390-1110m
	1,280-3,640ft
Lifts	11
Pistes	480 acres
Green	16%
Blue	59%
Black	25%
Snowmaking	
	350 acres

➕ Cute tourist town in classic New England style

➕ Some good slopes for all abilities, including serious challenges

➕ Few queues

➕ Excellent cross-country trails

➕ Great children's facilities

➖ Slope area small and a bus-ride or drive from town

➖ One of the mountains is a short shuttle-bus ride from the other two

➖ New England weather – highly changeable, and can be very cold

➖ Weekend queues

➖ No après-ski atmosphere

Stowe is one of New England's cutest little towns, its main street lined with dinky clapboard shops and restaurants; you could find no sharper contrast to the other New England resorts we feature. Its mountain, six miles away, is another New England classic: something for everyone, but not much of it.

THE RESORT

Stowe is a picture-postcard New England town – and a popular spot for tourists year-round, with bijou shops and more 3- and 4-diamond hotels and restaurants than any other place in New England except Boston. The slopes of Mount Mansfield, Vermont's snow-capped (though mainly wooded) highest peak, are a 15-minute drive away and much of the accommodation is along the road out to it. There's a good day-time shuttle-bus service but a car is recommended for flexibility.

THE MOUNTAIN

There are three different sectors, two linked, the third (Spruce Peak) a short shuttle-bus ride away.
Slopes The main sector, served by a trio of chair-lifts from Mansfield Base Lodge, is dominated by the famous Front Four – a row of seriously steep double-black-diamond runs. But there is plenty of easier stuff, too, including long green runs down to the alternative lift base at Toll House.

An eight-seat gondola serves the next sector: easy-intermediate runs

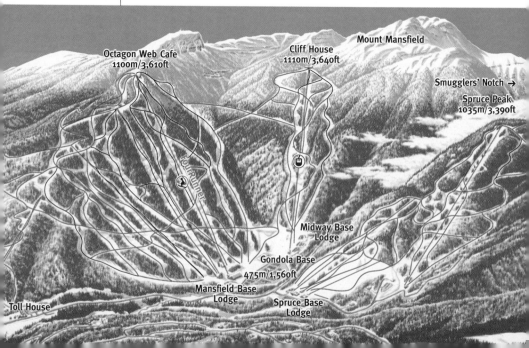

Mount Mansfield

Octagon Web Cafe
1100m/3,610ft

Cliff House
1110m/3,640ft

Smugglers' Notch →

Spruce Peak
1035m/3,390ft

Midway Base Lodge

Gondola Base
475m/1,560ft

Mansfield Base Lodge

Spruce Base Lodge

Toll House

NEWS

The Hayride run down to Mansfield Base was widened and resculpted for 2002/03 to conform to FIS race standards and should be a challenge for racers and experts alike. Also last season, a new moving carpet was built at the beginners' area on Spruce Peak and snowmaking was increased.

Work on a $220m development at the foot of Spruce Peak is due to begin in 2003/04. Projected to take 10 to 15 years, it includes condos, houses, a hotel, new lifts, new pistes, more snowmaking and linking Spruce Peak to the other areas, plus restaurants, shops and a performing arts centre.

Central reservations phone number
Call 1 877 317 8693 (toll-free from within the US).
From within the UK call 0800 731 9279.

Phone numbers
From distant parts of the US, add the prefix 1 802.
From abroad, add the prefix +1 802.

TOURIST OFFICE

t 253 3500
info@stowe.com
www.stowe.com

---

with one black alternative – plus the short but very steep Waterfall, under the gondola at the top.

The third area, Spruce Peak, has the main nursery area at the bottom, with a slow chair-lift to mid-mountain and another beyond that. 'Possibly the slowest chairs in the world,' says a reporter. The old link with Smugglers' Notch, from the top of this sector over the hill, is now a backcountry route. The pass-sharing agreement has also been abandoned. There are free daily mountain tours with a mountain host.

Terrain-parks Stowe has two terrain-parks and a half-pipe. One is for beginner freestylers with a special emphasis on learning to ride snowdecks.

Snow reliability This is helped by snowmaking on practically all the blue (and some black) runs of the main sectors, and on lower Spruce Peak.

Experts The Front Four and their variants on the top half of the main sector present a real challenge – and there are others in this sector. There are various gladed areas, three of them marked on the map.

Intermediates The usual New England reservation applies: the terrain is limited in extent; there's also a severe shortage of ordinary black runs (as opposed to double diamonds).

Beginners The nursery slopes and long green runs are great. 'Spruce Peak is one of the best beginner/early skier areas we've seen,' says a reporter. Progression to longer green runs means moving over to the main sector, where there are splendid long greens down to Toll House.

Snowboarding Stowe attracts many snowboarders. Beginners learn on special customised boards at the Burton Method Center on Spruce Peak. There's a snowboarder-specific resort web site: www.ridestowe.com

Cross-country There are excellent

---

cross-country centres scattered around (including at the musically famous Trapp Family Lodge) – 45km/28 miles of groomed and 100km/62 miles of backcountry trails.

Queues The area is largely queue-free mid-week but we've had reports of 25-minute queues at weekends.

Mountain restaurants Cliff House, at the top of the gondola, is a lofty room with table-service and good food and views. Midway Café near the base of the gondola has a BBQ deck and table-service inside. 'It is the nicest if you do not want to pay for an expensive lunch at the Cliff House,' says a reporter this year. The Octagon Web Café, at the top of the main sector, is a small cafeteria, with 'ugly plastic tables' says a reader.

Schools and guides One reporter was disappointed by the ski school – but this was partly because he had a different instructor every day, which is common in the US.

Facilities for children Facilities are excellent and the nursery takes children from age six months to six years.

STAYING THERE

How to go There are hotels in and around Stowe itself and along the road to the slopes, some with Austrian or Scandinavian names and styles.

Hotels 1066 Ye Olde England Inne is recommended by reporters (despite the appalling name). Stowehof Inn and Green Mountain Inn have also been recommended. The smart Inn at the Mountain, at the Toll House lift base of Mount Mansfield, is the only slope-side accommodation, with chair-lift access to the main sector of slopes.

Self-catering There is a reasonable range of condos available for rent.

Eating out There are restaurants of every kind. The Whip in the Green Mountain Inn, the Shed ('good ribs') and an Italian restaurant Trattoria La Festa have all been recommended.

Après-ski Après-ski is muted – Stowe reportedly goes to bed early. The Matterhorn, Shed and Rusty Nail on the access road are popular. There's a good cinema with new releases.

Off the slopes Stowe is a pleasant town in which to spend time off the slopes – at least if you like shopping. The Vermont Ski Museum is 'interesting and worth a visit,' says a reporter. A trip to the Burlington shopping mall is recommended for more serious retail therapy.

Sunday River

Quiet slopes and the biggest snowmaking system in New England

SUNDAY RIVER SKI RESORT

Sunday River's slopes spread over about 5km/3 miles from east to west and over eight different peaks ↓

➕ Some convenient slope-side accommodation

➕ Some good runs for all abilities

➕ Decent natural snow record with extensive snowmaking back-up

➕ Lots of cross-country in the area

➕ No queues

➖ Scattered slope-side developments mean no village atmosphere

➖ Relatively small area of slopes

➖ No real mountain restaurants

➖ Quiet après-ski scene

➖ Limited off-slope diversions

Sunday River was one of the pioneers of snowmaking, and over 90% of its trails are served by it. So the snow should be as good here as anywhere in the east. The terrain is varied and quite extensive. But it lacks village ambience.

THE RESORT

Sunday River is where the American Skiing Company (which owns several other US resorts) started. Despite this, there isn't really a slope-side village yet – just various developments scattered around the slopes – so there isn't much village ambience.

The plan is for the area around the Jordan Grand hotel to become the focus of the resort, with shops, bars, restaurants, theatre, nightclub and even a village green and pond. For now, Bethel is the nearest small town, a 10-minute drive away; it's a pleasant place with a few shops, restaurants and bars. The resort attracts quite a lot of British school groups, especially at half-term and Easter.

THE MOUNTAINS

The slopes range over about 5km/3 miles from east to west and across eight different peaks and there are numerous base areas, parking lots and accommodation units scattered around. You get a satisfying feeling of travelling around when you use the slopes.

Slopes The White Cap base marks the eastern extremity of the system and is handy for the Grand Summit hotel, the half-pipe and other evening activities. The peaks around the main base areas are fairly packed with lifts and trails. The Jordan Grand hotel is at the western limit of the system, and the western sector (Aurora, Oz and Jordan Bowl) has far fewer lifts and runs and a more remote and backwoods feel.

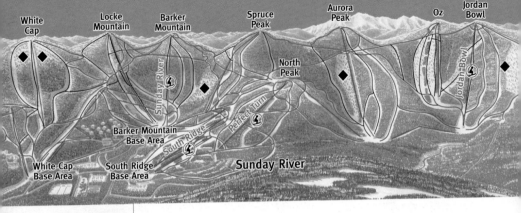

White Cap — Locke Mountain — Barker Mountain — Spruce Peak — Aurora Peak — Oz — Jordan Bowl — North Peak — Sunday River — Perfect Turn — South Ridge — Barker Mountain Base Area — White Cap Base Area — South Ridge Base Area

NEWS

For 2002/03 yet more snowmaking was installed, bringing the total to around 1,700 guns.
The new Enchanted Forest ski adventure trail for families on North Peak was created. A special observation deck was built at the top of Jordan Bowl, pointing out the local peaks. And a nightclub and new restaurant opened in the White Cap Base Lodge.

KEY FACTS

Resort	245m
	800ft
Slopes	245-955m
	800-3,140ft
Lifts	18
Pistes	660 acres
Green	25%
Blue	35%
Black	40%
Snowmaking	
	607 acres

Central reservations phone number
Call 1 800 543 2754 (toll-free from within the US).

Phone numbers
From distant parts of the US, add the prefix 1 207.
From abroad, add the prefix +1 207.

TOURIST OFFICE

t 824 3000
info@sundayriver.com
www.sundayriver.com

Terrain-parks There's something for everyone with a choice of four terrain-parks (Rocking Chair super-park; AMEX and Starlight, both medium-sized; and Who-ville for kids). There are also a super-pipe, quarter-pipe and mini-pipe.
Snow reliability Snow reliability is good because of New England's biggest high-tech system for making and grooming snow.
Experts There are challenging narrow, often mogulled double-blacks on White Cap and Barker Mountain, and there is excellent glade skiing on Aurora, Oz and Jordan Bowl. Indeed, 40% of the trails are classified black.
Intermediates It's generally a good resort for intermediates, who will enjoy cruising around on a series of nice rolling blues (often deserted in mid-week). There are some not too fearsome glades to tempt the bold.
Beginners South Ridge is a well-organised area for beginners, with good, easy runs to progress to.
Snowboarding The quiet après-ski scene might put some boarders off, but there is some good terrain, particularly for experts, and the various terrain-parks and pipes are worthwhile.
Cross-country In and around Bethel there are three cross-country centres with around 140km/90 miles of trails.
Queues Mid-week queues are non-existent – indeed most lifts and slopes are deserted. Even on busy weekends you should be okay if you stick to the four high-speed quads.
Mountain restaurants There are none, but there are civilised table-service places at the two main hotels, as well as the usual self-service places.
Schools and guides A reporter who took a group of 40 schoolchildren said the ski instructors were 'overstretched at half-term but still superb, and one even bought his class baseball caps'.

Facilities for children The Grand Summit and South Ridge Centre house the main children's facilities. The Enchanted Forest adventure trail opened last season and the Who-ville terrain park is for children. There are also family entertainment centres called the White Cap and Big Adventure (see Après-ski).

STAYING THERE

How to go There is slope-side accommodation but some people prefer to stay in Bethel – a 10-minute drive from the ski area (with free buses until 1am) – where there are inns, lodges, motels and B&Bs.
Hotels The main slope-side hotels are the Jordan Grand and the Grand Summit. There's a dorm as well as normal rooms at the Snow Cap Inn.
Self-catering The Brookside condos – with heated outdoor pool and hot tub – have been recommended. There are plenty of others on the slopes too.
Eating out As well as options at the slopes (see Mountain Restaurants) there are several restaurants in Bethel including 'fine-dining', a specialist vegetarian restaurant, a Chinese, a sushi bar and pizza places.
Après-ski Après-ski in Sunday River is quiet. A reporter recommends the Foggy Goggle bar, which also has live music. The White Cap Base Lodge now has a nightclub – Tango Mary's. There's a brew-pub. The White Cap Fun Center has floodlit tubing, sledding and ice skating, while Big Adventure in Bethel has laser tag and rock climbing. There are guided snow-shoe tours two evenings a week. There's also a four-screen cinema and a games arcade.
Off the slopes There's snowmobiling, snow-shoeing, tubing, ice-fishing, swimming; plus a few shops in Bethel.

Get next year's edition **free!**
by reporting on your holiday

There are too many resorts for us to visit them all every year, and too many hotels, bars and mountain restaurants for us to see. So we are very keen to encourage more readers to send in reports on their holiday experiences. As usual, we'll be giving 100 copies of the next edition to the writers of the best reports.

There are five main kinds of feedback we need:
- what you particularly **liked and disliked** about the resort
- what aspects of the resort came as a **surprise** to you
- your other suggestions for **changes to our evaluation** of the resort – changes we should make to the ratings, verdicts, descriptions etc
- your experience of **queues** and other weaknesses in the lift system, and the **ski school** and associated childcare arrangements
- your feedback on **individual facilities** in the resort – the hotels, bars, restaurants (including mountain restaurants), nightspots, equipment shops, sports facilities etc.

You can send your reports to us in three ways. In order of preference, they are:
- by e-mail to: reports@snow-zone.co.uk (don't forget to give us your postal address)
- word-processed and printed on paper
- handwritten on a form that we can provide.

Consistently helpful reporters are invited to become 'resort observers', which means that when possible we'll arrange free lift-passes in your holiday resorts, in exchange for detailed reports on those resorts.

Our postal address is:
Where to Ski and Snowboard, FREEPOST SN815,
The Old Forge, Norton St Philip, Bath BA2 7ZZ

Canada

We were a bit sceptical about Canadian skiing when it first started to find a place on the British market at the start of the 1990s. Canada seemed to offer very few resorts worthy of international attention, and the main one – Whistler – seemed uncomfortably low. But we were soon converted, once we had experienced the friendly welcome, the spectacular scenery, the impressive terrain, the low prices and – last but certainly not least – the frequent and heavy dumps of snow. It is, you'll agree, a compelling combination. Since our conversion, we've enjoyed many of our best days on skis in western Canada – including some, a couple of seasons back, when locals were complaining about snow conditions being the worst in living memory. Basically, people in western Canada don't really know what bad snow conditions are. And when the snow is good it is phenomenal.

A few seasons ago we drove from Whistler to Banff, calling in at lots of smaller resorts on the way. The whole trip took two weeks and for eight consecutive days in the middle it snowed. It snowed and snowed and snowed. It made driving from resort to resort tricky, as we stuck to our normal scheme of driving at night after getting in a full day on the slopes. And we had to drive slowly as elk were likely to leap across the road at any time, mesmerised by the car headlights. But the skiing was spectacular – day after day of dry, light powder. That's a normal winter in western Canada.

In an average year Whistler, for example, gets 360 inches of snow and it snows (or rains, at resort level) for half the days in the season. That makes for superb conditions on the slopes. Inland at Banff-Lake Louise you might not get quite the same frequency of snow, but it stays in great condition because the air is drier and temperatures are lower. You get a better chance of blue skies there – but also a higher chance of a day or two of very low temperatures (–20°C or less).

So you go to western Canada for the skiing or boarding, not the sunbathing. If you prefer long lunches on sun-drenched mountain restaurant terraces, stick to March in the Alps. If you want a good chance of hitting powder, put Canada high on your list of possible destinations.

If you really want untracked powder and are feeling flush, there is nothing to beat Canada's amazing heli- and snowcat skiing operations. The main difference is that the former is faster paced and more expensive than the latter. But with both, you are taken to the middle of nowhere in a deserted mountain wilderness and then let loose with a guide who takes you down untracked slopes to another spot in the middle of nowhere, where you are picked up and taken to the top of another mountain and another untracked run. And so it goes on! You can do it by the day, but the hedonistic option is to book a few days or a week in a luxury lodge run by the heli-skiing or snowcat operation, eating gourmet dinners and stepping out of the door each morning straight into the chopper or snowcat. See our separate chapter near the start of the book on heli-skiing.

If you can't afford the £3,000 plus a week that this would cost, you can always try a day for £200 plus. But if you resist heli-skiing or snowcat heaven, you'll find a holiday in Canada can be very cheap.

SNOWPIX.COM / CHRIS GILL

← Most resorts in western Canada have great high bowls but nowhere has as many as Whistler

Package prices start at under £500 for a week to western Canada (but watch out for low brochure prices that involve sleeping four to a room). These prices are made possible by cheap direct and charter flights to the key airports and the use of accommodation in resorts where winter is low season compared with summer. And once you get there you'll find the cost of meals and drinks very low compared with the Alps. Lift passes fall midway between Alpine and American price levels.

Another difference you'll notice compared with the Alps is the people. Not only do they speak English but they are friendly, and have the American service culture – 'the customer is king'. You'll find mountain hosts to show you around the slopes, immaculately groomed runs, civilised lift queues, lots of fast quad chair-lifts, piste maps available at the bottom of most lifts, and cheerful, helpful staff.

In the west you'll also find spectacular scenery (when the clouds clear) to rival that of the Alps and far superior to anything you'll find in the US. You may also find an amazing variety of wildlife, especially in the Rockies and the interior of British Columbia.

For us, the main attraction of eastern Canada is that the resorts are in the heart of the province of Québec, where the French culture is predominant – it makes for a unique ambience. Québec is now attracting a fair number of British winter visitors, including school groups. It also has the attraction of a shorter flight time – but it does have the disadvantage of extremes of weather.

Both east and west have the disadvantage for young people that laws about buying and consuming alcohol are more strictly enforced than in the UK. The legal age is 18 in Alberta and Québec but 19 in British Columbia; carrying your passport as evidence of age is a good idea even if you are well over the required age. People unable to prove their age may be refused entries to bars and clubs but will usually be allowed in restaurants (though not to drink alcohol). Another disadvantage that many reporters comment on is that, as in the USA, lifts close much earlier than in Europe – as early as 3pm in some cases.

BANFF MT NORQUAY /
LEE SIMMONS

The stylish Cascade Lodge at the base of Norquay, the nearest ski area to Banff town →

Western Canada

For international visitors to Canada, the main draw is the west. It has fabulous scenery, good snow and a wonderful sense of the great outdoors. The big names of Whistler, Banff and Lake Louise capture most of the British market but there are lots of worthwhile smaller resorts that more adventurous travellers are now starting to explore. We recommend renting a car and combining two or more of these resorts, perhaps with a couple of days on virgin powder served by helicopters or snowcats as well. You'll have the holiday of a lifetime.

Five of the smaller resorts you're most likely to want to visit for a while get their own chapters: Big White, BC's highest ski area, and second in size to Whistler; Fernie, with a deserved reputation for great powder and a fast-developing mountain village; Jasper, in the spectacular Jasper National Park, with skiing at nearby Marmot Basin; Panorama, with a big vertical and an attractive new village at the foot of the slopes; and Kicking Horse, the new kid on the block – formerly known as Whitetooth, the mountain has been transformed by the installation of a big gondola and a new chair-lift, and a village at the base of the slopes is in the very early stages of development.

There are quite a few other resorts

that you might want to include in a tour of this area, too.

Kimberley Alpine Resort is the most accessible – about 90 minutes from Fernie and three hours from Banff. Like Fernie, it's under the ownership of Resorts of the Canadian Rockies, owners of Lake Louise.

At the mountain there are in practice two base areas. The original one is not quite at the bottom of the hill; there are two old chairs and a T-bar here (though they are no longer regularly used) and a range of lodgings, including the 'lovely' NorthStar Chalets (condos). On the flat ground below this, a new village is being built, served by a fast quad that is now the resort's staple lift (and it

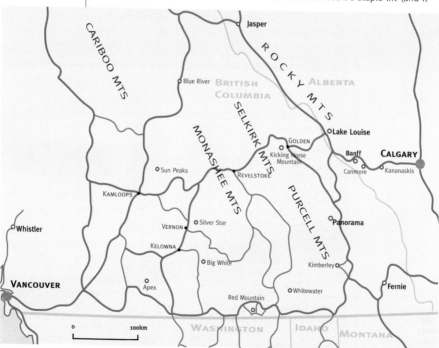

opens for night skiing and riding until 9.30 three nights a week). When we visited a couple of seasons ago, using this chair meant descending a steep, traffic-polished and congested final slope to get back to the lower level. Not ideal.

The new village is at present very limited, but includes the comfortable and very convenient Trickle Creek Residence Inn by Marriott (catchy, eh?), the 'superb' Polaris condos and a couple of restaurants. Trickle Creek Golf Resort is transformed into Trickle Creek Winter Adventure Park each winter (starting last season) – facilities include a skating rink, cross-country skiing, snow-shoeing and campfires.

The town of Kimberley, about five minutes' drive away, is known for its synthetic and indescribably naff 'Bavarian theme'. But it is reported to contain some good restaurants including the Old Bauernhaus (in buildings allegedly brought from Bavaria), midway between the resort and the town.

Kimberley's terrain offers a mix of blue and black runs (plus the occasional green) and a vertical of 750m/2,470ft. In addition to the lifts up the front there are basically two other slow chairs (one is a double discarded from Lake Louise). The runs – all in forest of varying density – are spread over two rather featureless hills. There are only a few short double-diamonds, but grading tends to understate difficulty, and many of the single diamonds are quite challenging. The resort has a reputation for good powder, although it doesn't get huge amounts by the standards of this region. Further expansion is planned.

There are several resorts clustered around the Okanagan valley, of which the aforementioned Big White is one.

Silver Star, above the town of Vernon, is now in the same ownership as Big White. It benefitted from the new ownership for the 2002/03 season by the installation of two new high-speed chairs – one six-pack and one quad. And daily bus and helicopter shuttles are offered between Silver Star and Big White, which makes two-centre holidays and day trips both easy.

Silver Star is a small, recently developed resort built in the style of an 1890s mining town right on the slopes. The centre is a small area of brightly painted Victorian-style buildings with wooden sidewalks and pseudo gas lights. It's rather Disneyesque but works surprisingly well. Some more modern-looking buildings have been built further up the hill. And big chalets are dotted in the trees.

The wooded mountain has two main linked faces. The south face around the village has mainly easy intermediate slopes of 480m/1,570ft vertical served by the new Comet six-pack, which starts below the main village. There's also another slow chair with the half-pipe under it and a couple of T-bars which start at resort level and serve both the terrain-park and slopes that are floodlit Thursday to Saturday until 8pm.

There are a few short black runs on the south side (mostly with a long, flat green section at the end), but the main challenges are on the back, on the north face. This is a splendid bowl, with easy runs along the rim and black and double-black trails dropping into the middle to meet the new 560m/1,840ft-vertical Powder Gulch fast quad. This has some seriously steep double black diamond runs and lots of moguls on offer. But you can stick to a solitary green or a blue alternative, too. Because of the north-facing aspect of most of the runs here the snow normally keeps in good condition.

Reporters have been impressed with the extent of the slopes (at 2,725 acres, it is bigger than better-known names such as Fernie, Big White and Jasper) and with the steep runs on the back side. But they have pointed out that there are lots of flat areas, including the link with the back side which make life difficult for snowboarders.

The Silver Creek hotel is one of three properties managed by the Silver Star Club and has been recommended by a 2003 reporter for its 'central slope-side location, comfortable rooms and roof-top hot-tubs'. We stayed at the Vance Creek hotel, managed by the same group. Another 2003 reporter stayed at the cheap but basic SameSun hostel.

Putnam Station does good steaks in a room decorated with railway memorabilia and with a model train running around the walls. The Italian Garden does good pasta and pizza and the Silver Lode Inn has been recommended for its 'large and interesting menu'.

A fair selection of après-ski

↑ Sun Peaks' cute, car-free main street is supposed to resemble an Austrian village

activities are on offer, including tubing, skating and snowmobiling, and there's a smart new spa.

Sun Peaks, near Kamloops, was known as Tod Mountain. Now major investment has created a cute, car-free, Tirolean-style slope-side village and good intermediate and beginner terrain to go with the steeps that used to dominate. We received several very positive reports from 2003 visitors. They liked the deserted mid-week slopes and the friendly atmosphere.

The 880m/2,900ft vertical is claimed to be the biggest in the BC interior. And the opening of the new Mt Morrissey area for 2002/03, served by a high-speed quad, has taken the skiable terrain up to over 3,400 acres, the second biggest area in BC (Whistler is the biggest).

Mt Morrissey has a network of easy blue runs, several interlinked and with trees left uncut in the trails, making them seem like groomed glade runs. The snow here is kept good by the slopes' northerly orientation and the number of trees. It is a great addition to the terrain for intermediates.

The other two interlinked areas are on the other side of the village. Sundance is directly above the village and served by a fast quad. It has mainly blue cruising runs, a good beginner area and some long green runs. The Sunshine fast quad takes you to mid-mountain on Sun Peaks' original ski hill, Mt Tod. The above-the-tree-line top section of this is served by slow, old chairs. Mt Tod has mainly single and double black diamond runs, mostly left to form bumps. But some are groomed regularly and make great fast cruises. Snow can suffer on the lower part of this mountain because of the southerly orientation, but you can catch the slow Burfield quad at the mid-station to stick to the upper part.

One reporter was very impressed with the multi-day ski school course which included après-ski activities. Another praised the childcare facilities.

We have had positive reports on former Olympic champion Nancy Greene's Cahilty Lodge (complete with her trophy cabinet), the new Delta Sun Peaks Resort and the Sundance Lodge. Powder Hounds was recommended for steaks and Val Sanales and Servus on Creekside for more sophisticated food. The Austrian-style Stube and Masa's are popular bars. The Delta has a night club (open weekends). And reporters commented that Sun Peaks has more choice of bars, shops and restaurants than most of the smaller Canadian resorts.

Probably the least compelling of the Okanagan resorts is **Apex**, a family-oriented place with a modern resort at the foot of its slopes and good views from the top, 610m/2,000ft higher.

Finally, there are a couple of resorts tucked away in the mountains close to the US border.

Red Mountain is up there with Fernie and other cult powder paradises in our estimation. There are green and red runs, but it's the black and double-black stuff that is the real attraction. We loved the terrain here – mostly in trees, and as steep as you can handle. Granite Mountain is a conical peak with more-or-less separate faces of blue, black and double-black steepness, and a total vertical of 880m/2,890ft – all served by a couple of triple chairs. Next-door Red Mountain itself is half the size and has only a double chair, but it is no less interesting. There's accommodation close to the slopes or a couple of miles away in Rossland, a simple little town that has bred countless Canadian ski racers. No wonder.

Whitewater, not far away, is well worth a look in and an absolute must after a storm. Tucked even further into the ranges than Red Mountain, Whitewater's bottomless powder elicits rave responses from those in the know. Accommodation is found in the charming historic town of Nelson.

Banff

A winter wonderland with wildlife

598

COSTS

①②③④⑤⑥

RATINGS

The slopes

Snow	★★★★
Extent	★★★★
Expert	★★★★
Intermediate	★★★★
Beginner	★★★
Convenience	★
Queues	★★★★
Mountain restaurants	★★★

The rest

Scenery	★★★★
Resort charm	★★★
Off-slope	★★★★★

NEWS

In Sunshine Village a new high-speed quad chair is planned for the 2003/04 season, replacing the existing slow chair up to Mount Standish. For 2002/03 the Wawa T-bar on Mount Standish was replaced by a fixed-grip quad chair.

These additions follow the installation for 2001/02 of a new eight-seater gondola from the base car park to Sunshine Village via Goat's Eye. This is the world's fastest and longest single-cable gondola. It has almost double the capacity of the queue-prone old lift and has cut the journey time from the valley to mid-mountain by over 40% to under 13 minutes.

➕ Spectacular high-mountain scenery – quite unlike the Colorado Rockies

➕ Lots of wildlife around the valley

➕ Lots of touristy shops

➕ Good-value lodging because winter is the area's low season

➕ Late season holidays

➕ Extensive slopes with excellent snow record at Sunshine, but ...

➖ Sunshine is a 20-minute drive away

➖ You'll probably want to take in Lake Louise, too – a 45-minute drive

➖ Can be very cold; most lifts have no covers and waiting for shuttle-buses can be unpleasant

➖ Banff lacks ski resort atmosphere – though it's not an unattractive town

➖ Resort can seem over-full of Brits

Huge numbers of British skiers and boarders go to Banff. Price has been a key factor in getting us to make the trip, but that's only half the story: most visitors are delighted with what they find, and keen to go back.

It's not difficult to see why. The landscape is one of glaciers, jagged peaks and magnificent views, and the valleys are full of wildlife that you'll never see in Europe. The slopes have something for everyone, from steep couloirs to gentle cruising. The snow is some of the coldest, driest and most reliable you'll find anywhere in the world, and there's a lot of it (at Sunshine Village, at least). And there are the standard Canadian assets of people who are friendly and welcoming, and low prices for meals and other on-the-spot expenses.

For us, these factors count for more than the drawbacks. But then we, luckily, have never encountered the extremely low temperatures (–35°C is not unknown) that have left some early-season reporters feeling less convinced.

THE RESORT

Banff is a big summer resort that happens to have some nearby ski areas. Norquay is a small area of slopes overlooking the town. Sunshine Village, 20 minutes away, is a bigger mountain; despite the name, it's not a village (it has just one small hotel at mid-mountain) – nor is it notably sunny. Most visitors buy a three-area pass that means they can also spend some time at Lake Louise, 45 minutes away – covered by a separate chapter.

Banff is spectacularly set, with several towering peaks rising up around its outskirts. There is lots of wildlife around; don't be surprised to find a herd of elk or long-horned sheep (though the town is now trying to keep elk away, for visitors' and their own sakes). In spring there may be bears along the highways.

Banff town has grown substantially since 1990, when it became independent of the Banff National Park authority. But it still consists basically of a long main street and a small network of side roads built in grid fashion, lined with clothing and souvenir shops (aimed mainly at summer visitors) and a few ski shops. The buildings are low-rise and some are wood-clad. The town is pleasant enough, but lacks genuine charm; it's a commercial tourist town, not another Aspen or Telluride.

Some of the Banff lodgings (even on the main Banff Avenue) are quite a distance from downtown. A car can be helpful here, especially in cold weather (it's best to splash out on a 4-wheel drive in case you hit heavy snow).

Unless you stay mid-mountain on Sunshine (see Staying up the mountain, at the end of the chapter), getting to the slopes means a drive or a bus-ride. Buses are free to Tri-area lift pass holders, frequent, generally reliable, and 'highly organised' – though, depending on the number of pickups, they can take twice as long as advertised and it can be a cold wait. Buses are also arranged to the more distant major resorts of Panorama and Kicking Horse (see separate chapters) and the smaller (and closer) resorts of Nakiska and Fortress, and day-trip heli-skiing and boarding can be organised.

KEY FACTS

Resort	1380m
	4,530ft

For Norquay, Sunshine and Lake Louise, covered by the Tri-area pass

Slopes	1630-2730m
	5,350-8,950ft
Lifts	29
Pistes	7,558 acres
Green	23%
Blue	38%
Black	39%
Snowmaking	
	1,700 acres

For Norquay only

Slopes	1630-2135m
	5,350-7,000ft
Lifts	5
Pistes	190 acres
Green	20%
Blue	36%
Black	44%
Snowmaking	90%

For Sunshine only

Slopes	1660-2730m
	5,440-8,950ft
Lifts	12
Pistes	3,168 acres
Green	22%
Blue	31%
Black	47%
Snowmaking	none

Norquay's wooded groomed trails are good for finding your ski legs on your first day and for poor-weather days, when Sunshine's upper slopes can be in a white out →

THE MOUNTAINS

The Sunshine Village slopes are set right on the Continental Divide and as a result get a lot of snow. Most of the slopes above the village are above the tree line and can be very cold and bleak during a snowfall or cold snap. Although there is a wooded sector served by the second section of the gondola and a couple of chairs, in bad weather you're better off elsewhere. It is great, however, for late-season skiing, which goes on until May.

Norquay is much smaller. But it's worth a visit, especially in bad weather – it has wooded slopes to suit all abilities and the trails can be delightfully quiet.

THE SLOPES
Lots of variety

The main slopes of **Sunshine Village** are not visible from the base station: you ride a two-stage gondola, first to the base of Goat's Eye Mountain, and then on to Sunshine Village itself. The old slow gondola was replaced by a faster and more capacious one **two** seasons ago.

Goat's Eye is served by one lift, a fast quad chair rising 580m/1,900ft. Although there are some blue runs, this is basically a black mountain, with some genuine double-blacks at the extremities. There has been talk of building an additional fast quad up the middle of the slopes to a point more or less on the tree line; this would make the area more useful in bad weather, but the plan is still awaiting approval.

Lifts fan out in all directions from Sunshine Village, with short runs back from Mount Standish and longer ones from Lookout Mountain. Lookout is where the Continental Divide is, with the melting snow flowing in one direction to the Pacific and in the other to the Atlantic. From the top here experts can pass through a gate (you need an avalanche transceiver to get through) and hike up to the extreme terrain of Delirium Dive.

Many people ride the gondola down at the end of the day. But the 2.5km/1.5 mile green run to the bottom is a pretty cruise. If you go down while the lifts are running you can take the recently installed Jackrabbit chair to cut out a flat section, but the run gets crowded and is much more enjoyable if you delay your descent a bit. The

Canyon Trail provides an alternative for more advanced skiers and riders. Marked black diamond, it was judged by reporters 'no more than a blue and a much more scenic route back' and 'a very narrow cat track'.

The slopes at **Norquay** are served by a row of five parallel lifts. One trail is floodlit at weekends. A reader recommends the Friday night skiing.

TERRAIN-PARKS
Park – and ride...

Both Sunshine and Norquay have good terrain-parks offering half-pipes and a vast array of rails, table-tops and boxes. Norquay built its first super-pipe last season and its park is open on a Friday night for floodlit skiing and boarding. Norquay also offers a lift ticket for those who want to use only the park and pipe.

Banff

599

LIFT PASSES

Tri-area lift pass
Covers all lifts and transport between Banff, Lake Louise, Norquay and Sunshine Village.

Main pass
3-day pass C$186
6-day pass C$372

Senior citizens
Over 65: C$327

Children
Under 13: 6-day pass C$128
Under 6: free pass

Notes
Three-day minimum. Night skiing available on Friday evening at Norquay.

Alternative passes
One-day and half-day passes available for individual areas.

SNOW RELIABILITY
Excellent

Sunshine Village claims '100% natural snow', a neat reversal of the usual snowmaking hype. Certainly, the lack of snowmaking there has never been a problem in our experience other than in the exceptionally poor snow of 2000/01 – when the blues were still fine but the blacks remained rocky during our February visit. 'Three times the snow' is another Sunshine slogan – a cryptic reference to the fact that the average snowfall here is 360 to 400 inches (depending on which figures you believe) – as good as anything in Colorado – compared with a modest 140 inches at Lake Louise and 120 inches on Norquay. But we're told the Sunshine figures relate to Lookout, and that Goat's Eye gets less. There is snowmaking on 90% of pistes at Norquay. So all in all, lack of snow is unlikely to be a problem.

FOR EXPERTS
Pure pleasure

Both areas have satisfying terrain for good skiers and boarders.

Sunshine has plenty of open runs of genuine black steepness above the tree line on Lookout, but Goat's Eye Mountain makes this area much more compelling. It has opened up a great area of expert double-black-diamond trails and chutes, both above and below the tree line – one reporter enjoyed the area so much that he and his party kept 'going back again and again'. But the slopes are rocky and need good cover, and the top can be windswept. There are short, steep runs on Mount Standish, too. One particular novelty is a pitch, near the mid-station, known as the Waterfall run – because you do actually ski down over a snow-covered frozen fall. But a lot of snow is needed to cover the waterfall and prevent it reverting to ice. Also try the Shoulder on Lookout Mountain; it is sheltered and tends to accumulate powder; stay high to make the traverse out easier.

Real experts will want to get to grips with Delirium Dive on Lookout Mountain's north face. You are allowed to hike up to it only if you have a companion, an avalanche transceiver and a shovel – and a guide is recommended. ('Book in advance' and 'rent your transceiver and shovel in Banff – you can't at Sunshine' advise disappointed reporters.) But a local expert says: 'The patrol neurotically carpet-bombs the entire cirque and closes Delirium upon sighting the first tiny fog-bank, making Delirium about the safest off-piste on the planet. The mandatory transceiver routine is pure theatre.' The area was closed on our visit, but we did take a look at it, and it is suitably impressive, with pitches over 40°.

Norquay's two main lifts give only 400m/1,300ft vertical, but both serve black slopes and the North American chair accesses a couple of double-diamond runs that justify their grading.

Heli-skiing is available from bases outside the National Park in British Columbia – roughly two hours' drive.

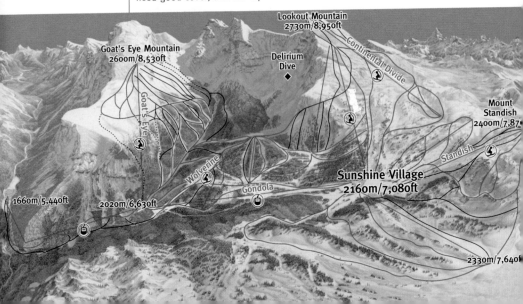

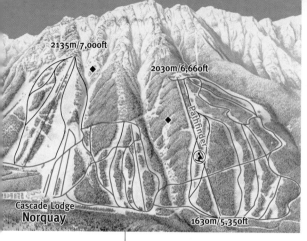

2135m/7,000ft

2030m/6,660ft

Pathfinder

Cascade Lodge
Norquay

1630m/5,350ft

Norquay has a good small nursery area with a moving carpet and gentle greens served by the Cascade chair.

Banff is not the ideal destination for a mixed party of beginners (who may want to stay in one area) and more experienced friends (who are likely to want to visit other places).

FOR CROSS-COUNTRY
High in quality and quantity
It's a good area for cross-country. There are trails near Banff, around the Bow River, and on the Banff Springs golf course. But the best area is around Lake Louise. Altogether, there are around 80km/50 miles of groomed trails within Banff National Park. Beware of the wildlife though: a few seasons ago a cross-country skier was killed by a mountain lion.

QUEUES
No problem most of the time
Half the visitors come for the day from cities such as Calgary – so it's fairly quiet during the week. Lift improvements mean that queues are now rare and short – and we have never encountered anything serious. But one 2003 reporter who was there at UK half-term and a Canadian bank holiday says there was a 45-minute queue for the new gondola one day and 15- to 30-minute queues on the mountain were common.

MOUNTAIN RESTAURANTS
Quite good
Sunshine Village has a choice of eating places at its mid-mountain base. The Day Lodge offers three different styles of food on three floors (table service in the top-floor Lookout Lounge, with great views). Mixed reports of the food but the buffalo stew is recommended. Mad Trapper's Saloon is a jolly western-style place in Old Sunshine Lodge, serving good beer and different food on its two levels (though reporters continue to criticise its disposable plates). The Sunshine Inn hotel has the best food – table-service

SCHOOLS

ClubSki and ClubSnowboard
t 762 4561
info@banffskischool. com

Classes
3 days guided tuition of the three areas (4½hr per day) C$199.

Private lessons
Sunshine (2hr) C$170
Norquay (2½hr) C$125

FOR INTERMEDIATES
Ideal runs
Half the runs on Sunshine are classified as intermediate. Wherever you look there are blues and greens – some of the greens as enjoyable (and pretty much as steep) as the blues.

We particularly like the World Cup Downhill run, from the top of Lookout to the mid-mountain base. Last season the Wawa T-Bar was replaced with a quad chair, which gives access to the Wawa Bowl and Tincan Alley. This is a good area for intermediates and offers treelined protection from bad weather. But the new quad means it is no longer as quiet as it used to be. There's a delightful wooded area under the second stage of the gondola served by Jackrabbit and Wolverine chairs. The blue runs down Goat's Eye are good cruises too.

The Pathfinder fast quad at Norquay serves a handful of quite challenging tree-lined blues and a couple of sometimes-groomed blacks – great for a snowy day or a 'first day of the holiday' warm-up.

FOR BEGINNERS
Pretty good terrain
Sunshine has a good area by the mid-mountain base, served by a moving carpet. The long Meadow Park Green is a great, long, easy run to progress to.

boarding

Boarders will feel at home in Banff and there is some excellent free-riding terrain for experienced riders. 'There are so many natural ledges, jumps and tree gaps to play with that the terrain-park seems almost unnecessary!' says a reporter this year. We have had mainly positive reports about the teaching. Beware green trails, however, as they can be really flat and require some scooting or walking. There are two specialist snowboard shops: Rude Boys and Unlimited Snowboards.

↑ Sunshine's slopes get a lot of snow; two to three times as much as Norquay or Lake Louise

SUNSHINE VILLAGE / BOB ALLEN

CHILDREN

Tiny Tigers Daycare at Sunshine Village and Norquay's The Kid's Place take children aged 19 months to 6 years, from 8.30 to 4.30. Children aged 3 or more can take short ski lessons. Reservation is recommended.

The ski/snowboard school ClubJunior (tel 762 4561) takes children aged 6 to 12 years old. 3 days (including lunch) cost C$186.

ACTIVITIES

Indoor Film theatre, museums, galleries, swimming pools (one with water slides), gym, squash, racquetball, weight training, bowling, hot-tub, sauna, mini-golf, climbing wall

Outdoor Swimming in hot springs, ice skating, heli-skiing, horse-drawn carriage rides, sleigh rides, dog-sled rides, snowmobiles, curling, ice hockey, ice fishing, helicopter tours, night skiing, snow-shoe tours

snacks in the Chimney Corner Lounge or a full lunch in the Eagle's Nest Dining Room. At the bottom of Goat's Eye Mountain there's a tent which we've had mixed reports of (they are hoping to build there but don't have planning permission yet).

At the base of Norquay, the big, stylish, timber-framed Cascade Lodge is excellent – it has great views and a table-service restaurant upstairs as well as a self-service cafeteria.

SCHOOLS AND GUIDES
Some great ideas
Both mountains have their own school. But recognising that visitors wanting lessons won't want to be confined to just one mountain, the resorts have organised an excellent Club Ski and Club Snowboard Program – three-day courses starting on Mondays and Thursdays that take you to Sunshine, Norquay and Lake Louise on different days, offering a mixture of guiding and instruction and including free video analysis, a fun race and a group photo. We'd recommend this to anyone who wants to see the whole area while improving their technique. Reporters rave about it: 'absolutely brilliant', 'improved more in three days than in a week anywhere else'. All abilities are catered for, including beginners. One reporter recommends booking a midweek group lesson: 'Normally only one or two people; I did an excellent Black Diamond class.' We also have a fat file full of praise for the free mountain tours by friendly local volunteer snow hosts.

FACILITIES FOR CHILDREN
Excellent
One reporter who used Sunshine, Norquay and Lake Louise said: 'I'd recommend all three.'

STAYING THERE

HOW TO GO
Superb-value packages
A huge amount of accommodation is on offer – especially hotels and self-catering, but also a few catered chalets.
Hotels Summer is the peak season here. Prices halve for the winter – so you can stay in luxury at bargain rates.
((((4) **Fairmont Banff Springs** (762 2211) A late 19th-century, castle-style property, well outside town. It's virtually a town within itself – it can sleep 2,000 people, has over 40 shops, numerous restaurants and bars, a nightclub and a superb health club and spa (which costs extra).
(((4) **Rimrock** (762 3356) Spectacularly set, out of town, with great views and a smart health club. Luxurious.
(((3) **Inns of Banff** (762 4581) About 20 minutes' walk from town, but good for buses; praised by reporters for large rooms, comfort, room service and fitness facilities; 'very large' hot-tub.
(((3) **Banff Park Lodge** (762 4433) Best-quality central hotel, with hot-tub, steam room and indoor pool.
((2) **Banff Caribou Lodge** (762 5887) On the main street, slightly out of town. A variety of wood-clad, individually designed rooms, sauna and hot-tub and a good restaurant and bar. Repeatedly recommended by reporters.
((2) **Timberline Inn** (762 2281) At foot of Norquay and reachable on skis. Comfortable, good views, hot-tub. Recently renovated and expanded.
((2) **Pension Tannenhof** (762 4636) Central, with comfortable rooms and plusher attic suites. Highly recommended by 2003 reporter. Very friendly. Breakfast included.
((2) **Banff King Edward** (762 2202) Right in the town centre, set above shops; large rooms and surprisingly quiet for its position.
((1) **Banff International Hostel** (762 5521) A bit out of town but cheap ('£60 for the week,' said a reporter).
Self-catering Don't expect the choice or luxury you find in many North American resorts. But there are some decent options. The Banff Rocky Mountain Resort is set in the woods on the edge of town; facilities include indoor pool, squash and hot-tubs. Reporters have also recommended the Douglas Fir resort (762 5591) for families – though 'a bit out of town' – and Woodland Village (762 5521).

GETTING THERE

Air Calgary 122km/76 miles (1½hr).

Phone numbers
From distant parts of Canada, add the prefix 1 403.
From abroad, add the prefix +1 403.

TOURIST OFFICE

Banff
t 762 4561
info@sblls.com
www.skibig3.com

SUNSHINE VILLAGE / GERALD VANDER PYLE

Mad Trappers Saloon is the main après-ski venue at Sunshine Village (reporters love the free peanuts!) ↓

EATING OUT
Lots of choice

Banff boasts over 100 restaurants, from McDonald's to fine dining in the Banff Springs hotel. Many get crowded and don't take bookings. Reader recommendations include the Maple Leaf (Canadian, relatively expensive but 'well worth the money'), Earl's (burgers and ethnic dishes, very popular and lively), Magpie & Stump (Mexican, with Wild West decor), Giorgio's (Italian), Caramba in the Banff Ptarmigan Inn (Mediterranean), the Keg ('quality steaks'), Seoul Country (Korean), Wild Bill's (burgers, grills, Tex-Mex, dancing), Melissa's ('good steaks', 'excellent choice of beers'), Caboose at the train station ('best steak,' 'superb crab'), Bumpers ('big slabs of rib'), Grizzly House ('fondues and fun', 'great selection of meats') and the Old Spaghetti Factory ('great for families'). Tommy's Neighbourhood Pub 'is a must for great food and good beer'. The Banff Park hotel does a Monday curry buffet. Designer-cool Saltlik does good game, steak and fish.

APRES-SKI
Livens up later on

One of the drawbacks of the area is that tea time après-ski is limited because the resort is a drive from the slopes. But Mad Trapper's Saloon at the top of the Sunshine Village gondola is popular during the close of play happy hour (with endless free peanuts). They also do evening parties with tobogganing, a buffet, live music and dancing, followed by a gondola ride down. In town later, Wild Bill's has live country and western music and line dancing. The Rose & Crown has live music and gets crowded. The Barbary Coast nightclub is popular. And Outabounds attracts a young lively crowd, while Aurora is for more serious clubbing. The St James Gate Irish pub has 'great atmosphere, good-value food and a wide range of beers'. Melissa's and Saltlik are popular.

OFF THE SLOPES
Lots to do

For those who do not intend to hit the slopes, Banff is one of the best resorts there is: there are so many other things to do and lots of wildlife to see. There are lovely walks, including ice canyon walks, and you can go snow-shoeing, dog-sledding, skating and snow-mobiling. There are sightseeing tours, several interesting museums to visit and natural hot springs to try. And there are hundreds of shops, aimed at the tourist trade.

STAYING UP THE MOUNTAIN
Worth considering

On the slopes of Sunshine Village, accessible by gondola or snowmobile, the Sunshine Inn (762 6550) is well worth considering. Luggage is transported for you in the gondola while you hit the slopes. Rooms vary in size. Big outdoor hot-pool. Sauna. Good restaurant.

Big White

Big by local standards, white by any standard

COSTS

① ② ③ ④ ⑤ ⑥

RATINGS

The slopes

Snow	*****
Extent	***
Expert	****
Intermediate	****
Beginner	****
Convenience	****
Queues	*****
Mountain restaurants	*

The rest

Scenery	***
Resort charm	**
Off-slope	**

Made to Measure Holidays

01243 533333

www. mtmhols. co.uk

ATOL 1006 ABTA V6471

- ➕ Good snow record
- ➕ Mainly fast lifts, with few queues
- ➕ Extensive, varied slopes, deserted except at weekends and holidays
- ➕ Convenient, purpose-built village
- ➕ Excellent kids' facilities

- ➖ Few off-slope diversions – and isolated without a car
- ➖ Upper mountain is very exposed – and is known for freezing fog
- ➖ No mountain restaurants
- ➖ Limited après-ski

'It's the snow' says the Big White slogan. And as slogans go, it's spot on. If all you want to do is ski or ride, with a fair chance of doing it in deep snow, put Big White high on the shortlist. If other things enter into your holiday equation, the attractions are less clear. That's if you're planning a week-long stay in one place; for anyone planning a tour of BC resorts, Big White should be on your itinerary. And it now owns neighbouring (in Canadian terms) Silver Star, too.

THE RESORT

Big White is a modern, purpose-built resort 45 minutes from Kelowna airport (but a long drive from bigger gateways). The village is rather piecemeal (Intrawest-style urban planning not in evidence) but attractive in wood and stone and built on a sloping hillside, slightly above the main chair-lift bases so that much of the accommodation is ski-in/ski-out. A lot of the resort's business comes from day visitors, who can park near these lift bases, at the more remote Westridge base, or at the Happy Valley area.

THE MOUNTAINS

Much of the terrain is heavily wooded. But the trees thin out towards the summits, leading to almost open slopes in the bowls at the top. There's at least one green option from the top of each lift but a 2003 reporter found some of these 'tricky near the top due to ice and scoured snow'.

Slopes Fast chairs run from points below village level to above mid-mountain, serving the main area of wooded beginner and intermediate runs above and beside the village. Slower lifts – a T-bar and two chairs –

NEWS

Big White has bought Silver Star, and a joint-mountain lift pass and daily bus and helicopter shuttles allow day trips there (and two-centre holidays) – see Western Canada introduction for more on Silver Star.

For 2002/03 a new terrain-park focusing on safe riding features and a super-pipe were built.

Glading around the Black Forest area should open up tree runs in that area for 2003/04.

KEY FACTS

Resort	1755m
	5,760ft
Slopes	1510-2320m
	4,950-7,610ft
Lifts	13
Pistes	2,565 acres
Green	18%
Blue	56%
Black	26%
Snowmaking	none

Central reservations
Call 765 8888.
Toll-free number
(from within Canada)
1 800 663 1772.

Phone numbers
From distant parts of Canada, add the prefix 1 250. From abroad, add +1 250.

TOURIST OFFICE

t 765 8888
bigwhite@bigwhite.com
www.bigwhite.com

serve the higher slopes. Quite some way across the mountainside is the Gem Lake fast chair, serving a range of long top-to-bottom runs to its base at Westridge; with its 710m/2,330ft vertical, this lift is in a different league from the others. There are free daily mountain tours and floodlit skiing.

Terrain-parks In 2002/03 a terrain-park was built with the emphasis on developing solid freestyle techniques without high risk. A super-pipe was also built. Then there's a boarder-cross course and a floodlit half-pipe.

Snow reliability Big White has a reputation for great powder; average snowfall is about 300 inches, which is similar to many Colorado resorts. It gets so much snow that the top trees usually stay white all winter; they are known as snow-ghosts and make visibility tricky in a white out. There is no snowmaking.

Experts There is a fair amount to do, especially if you get good snow. The main bowl off the side of the T-bar (the Cliff area) is of serious double-black pitch. The Sun-Rype bowl at the opposite edge of the ski area is more forgiving. There are some long blacks off the Gem Lake chair and several shorter ones off the Powder chair. There are glades to explore and bump runs to try, too.

Intermediates The resort is excellent for cruisers and families with long blues and greens all over the hill. Good intermediates will enjoy the easier black runs too.

Beginners There's a good dedicated nursery area in the village and lots of long easy runs to progress to.

Snowboarding There's some excellent free-riding terrain. There's also the new terrain-park and the pipes to try. Novices are well catered for with long, chair-lift-served green runs.

Cross-country There are 25km/15 miles of trails in total.

Queues With four fast quads and few visitors still, queues are pretty rare. However, the Alpine T-bar can be a bottleneck on sunny days.

Mountain restaurants The nearest thing to a mountain restaurant is the Westridge base warming hut.

School and guides A 2003 reporter is wildly enthusiastic about the ski school for both adults and children. 'The children's classes are superb and fun – my daughters wanted to stay the full day! As a nervous intermediate I soon gathered confidence and new skills.'

Facilities for children The excellent Kids' Centre takes children from 18 months. And there's a dedicated nursery slope with a moving carpet lift at the Happy Valley area. Evening activities are organised.

STAYING THERE

How to go There's an increasing range of packages to Big White.

Hotels The White Crystal Inn, Inn at Big White and Chateau Big White are recommended by readers.

Self-catering There's a fair choice but grocery shopping is very limited.

Eating out Snowshoe Sam's is good for casual dining. Other options include the de Montreuil restaurant in the White Crystal Inn ('very good venison casserole'), Powder Keg (Greek), Swiss Bear in the Chateau Big White (Swiss!), China White Wok, Kettle Valley Steakhouse and Coltino's in the Hopfbrauhaus (Italian).

Après-ski The atmospheric Snowshoe Sam's has a DJ, live entertainment, dancing and infamous 'gun barrel coffee'. Raakel's in the Hopfbrauhaus has live music and dancing.

Off the slopes The Happy Valley adventure park features tubing hills, ice skating, snowmobiling, snowshoeing and dog-sledding. Helicopter tours and two health spas are popular.

Big White

605

Fernie

Lots of snow and lots of steeps – best with a guide

COSTS

① ② ③ ④ ⑤ ⑥

RATINGS

The slopes

Snow	*****
Extent	***
Expert	*****
Intermediate	**
Beginner	****
Convenience	****
Queues	****
Mountain restaurants	*

The rest

Scenery	***
Resort charm	**
Off-slope	**

NEWS

For 2002/03 Fernie started running two- and four-day Steep and Deep tours for adventurous good intermediate to expert skiers. And Fernie Lodging Company's new Balsam Lodge opened up at the resort.

Downtown, a new Italian restaurant, Ferrelli's, opened for 2002/03.

On-mountain developments for 2003/04 were not confirmed as we went to press, but are likely to include more snowmaking.

Most of Fernie's terrain is ungroomed runs through the trees; and most of them are steeper than this →

- Good snow record, with less chance of rain than at Whistler (and less chance of Arctic temperatures than at resorts up in the Rockies)
- Great terrain for those who like it steep and deep, with lots for confident intermediates too
- Snowcat operations nearby
- More good on-slope accommodation becoming available but …

- Mountain resort is very limited
- Lift system still a weakness, especially for experts
- After a dump it can take time to make the bowls safe
- Little groomed cruising for timid or average intermediates
- Poor trail map and signposts
- No decent mountain restaurants

Fernie has long had cult status among Alberta and BC skiers for its steep gladed slopes and superb natural snow. In the last five years there has been a lot of investment in the development of the village at the foot of the slopes – though it remains small, without many facilities. Some visitors would rather see more investment in the mountain, to cut down the amount of hiking and traversing to the best steep terrain, and to hasten reopening after a serious snowfall. We see their point, but most reports we get are dominated by excitement at Fernie's combination of snow and terrain – 'just like Jackson Hole' and 'the hiking and traversing isn't that bad; Fernie's not for expert wimps', to quote two reporters. You'll enjoy Fernie most if you are a good skier or rider wanting adventure.

THE RESORT

Fernie Alpine Resort is set at the lift base a little way up the mountainside from the flat Elk Valley floor and a couple of miles from the little town of Fernie. It has grown considerably from very little in the last few years, but there's still not much there other than convenient accommodation, a few small shops – the grocery shop is said to be inadequate – and a few bars and places to eat. It is quiet at night.

The town of Fernie is named after William Fernie – a prospector who discovered coal here and triggered a boom at the turn of the century. Much of the town was destroyed by fire in 1908 but some downtown stone and brick buildings survived and are still there. It is primarily a town for locals not tourists. There are some lively bars, decent places to eat and good outdoor shops. It is down to earth rather than charming and reporters' reactions to it vary: 'Like staying in an industrial estate,' said one; 'I liked the way it felt like real Canada and enjoyed staying in a town with some history,' said another.

There are buses between the town and the mountain, which run at half-hourly intervals at peak times and cost C$3 one way (you can buy books of tickets for about C$10 for four).

Outings to Kimberley are possible; a coach does the trip every Thursday – the drive takes about 90 minutes. (there's also a helicopter option).

KEY FACTS

Resort	1065m
	3,500ft
Slopes	1065-1925m
	3,500-6,320ft
Lifts	10
Pistes	2,500 acres
Green	30%
Blue	40%
Black	30%
Snowmaking	
	125 acres

THE MOUNTAINS

Fernie's 2,500 acres pack in a lot of variety, from superb green terrain at the bottom to ungroomed chutes (that will be satisfyingly steep to anyone but the extreme specialist) and huge numbers of steep runs in the trees. A lot of the runs have the rare quality of consistently steep pure fall lines.

THE SLOPES
Bowl after bowl
What you see when you arrive at the lift base is a trio of impressive mogul slopes towering above you. The Deer chair approaches the foot of these slopes, but goes no further. You get to them by traversing and hiking from the main Lizard Bowl, on the right, or you can take a high traverse from Currie Bowl, skirting the boundary. Lizard Bowl is a broad snowfield reached by a series of lifts: the slow Elk quad (which one reporter found stopped 'on average four times per uplift'); the fast Great Bear quad; and finally the short Face Lift, a dreadful rope tow. It often doesn't run, either because of too little or too much snow, and when it does is well-known for shredding gloves. This is also the main way into Cedar Bowl and to Snake Ridge beyond it. The only lift here is the Haul Back T-bar, which brings you out. You can still traverse into the lower parts of both Lizard and Cedar Bowls when the Face Lift isn't working – or if you just can't face it. There is a mini-bowl between them, served by the Boomerang chair.

The Timber Bowl fast quad chair gives access to Siberia Bowl and the lower part of Timber. But for access to the higher slopes and to Currie Bowl you must take the White Pass quad. A long traverse from the top gets you to the steeper slopes on the flanks of Currie (our favourite area), which are otherwise reached by hiking from the main Lizard Bowl. From there you have to go right to the bottom, and it takes quite a while to get back for another go.

There are excellent, free, hosted tours of the area in groups of different abilities for two hours twice a day, but the hosts can only take you on blue and green runs. For the steeper, deeper stuff you need to hire a guide or join the new Steep and Deep tours. Using these services to get your bearings is a good idea. Going with someone who knows the area makes it hugely more enjoyable. We found both signs and trail map dangerously inadequate – see feature panel later in this chapter.

TERRAIN-PARKS
Two to choose from
There's a good half-pipe at the bottom of the mountain, served by the Deer chair, and a terrain-park which was in Siberia Bowl, running next to the upper part of Falling Star, last year. There were berms and boarder-cross features as well as jumps and rails. The park wasn't marked on the trail map, since it was a last-minute decision to move it from near the half-pipe.

SNOW RELIABILITY
A key part of the appeal
Fernie has an excellent snow record – with an average of 350 inches per year, better than practically all of Colorado. But the altitude is modest – rain is not unknown, and in warmer weather the lower slopes can suffer. Snowmaking has increased in recent years, and now covers most of the

Fernie

607

RIDE THE SNOWCATS – HELI-SKIING AT AN AFFORDABLE PRICE

Good skiers who relish off-piste should consider treating themselves to some cat skiing; there are several operations in this area. The best-known is Island Lake Lodge (423 3700), which basically does three or four-day all-inclusive packages. The Lodge is a cosy chalet 10km/6 miles from Fernie, amid 7,000 acres of spectacular bowls and ridges. It has 36 beds, and four snowcats to act as lifts. In a day you might do eight powder runs averaging 500m/1,640ft vertical, taking in all kinds of terrain from gentle open slopes to some very Alpine adventures. We've heard they can be booked solid up to three years in advance. You can do single days without accommodation, but only on a standby basis; we managed this once and loved it, but our second attempt failed. A reader tells us that Fernie Wilderness Adventures (423 6704) offers 'an excellent alternative' to Island Lake Lodge. Others have been less convinced. 'It's billed as intermediate level,' said one, 'but it's not – there's a lot of tree skiing, some steep and tight, and we were always skiing in a big crowd.'

Fernie is a fine place for boarders (and there are a lot of local experts here). Lots of natural gullies, hits and endless off-piste opportunities – including some adrenalin-pumping tree-runs and knee-deep powder bowls – will keep free-riders of all abilities grinning from ear to ear. Snowcat operators can take you to some excellent untouched powder. And, as one reader commented, 'The only flat sections are at the base and coming out of Falling Star.' The main board shops, Board Stiff and Edge of the World, are in downtown Fernie, the latter with an Internet connection and an indoor skate park to use while your board gets tuned.

WESTERN CANADA

608

LIFT PASSES

Fernie

Main pass
1-day pass C$60
6-day pass C$340

Senior citizens
Over 65: 6-day pass
C$276

Children
Under 18: 6-day pass
C$276
Under 13: 6-day pass
C$90
Under 6: free pass

Notes
Half-day pass
available from noon.
Mighty Moose lift
pass available for
beginners.

base area. Reporters found piste maintenance poor in the snow drought season and others said that, while some runs were well groomed after a snowfall, some blue runs were just never groomed at all.

FOR EXPERTS
Wonderful – deep and steep
The combination of heavy snowfalls and abundant steep terrain with the shelter of trees makes this a superb mountain for good skiers. There are about a dozen identifiable faces offering genuine black or double-black slopes, each of them with several alternative ways down. Currie and Timber Bowls both have some serious double-diamonds but mainly are single-diamonds. However, as one of our regular reporters says, 'The majority of the single blacks are tough. Some of them are so steep that I can't work out how you could get anything harder without falling off the mountain ... just like Jackson Hole but without the cliffs.' Even where the trail map shows trees to be sparse, expect them to be close enough together, and where there aren't any, expect alder

bushes unless there's lots of snow. And see our warning in the feature panel below about the poor trail map and signposting.

There are backcountry routes you can take with guidance (some include an overnight camp) and snowcat operations in other nearby mountains – see earlier feature panel.

FOR INTERMEDIATES
Far from ideal
Although there are intermediate runs both low down and high up, they don't add up to a lot of mileage. Most high runs are not groomed, and one reporter said, 'The blues in all bowls except Timber would be black in most resorts.' Adventurous, strong intermediates willing to give the ungroomed terrain a try will enjoy the area. But if you want miles of groomed cruising, go elsewhere.

FOR BEGINNERS
Excellent
There's a good nursery area served by two lifts (a moving carpet and a drag) and the lower mountain served by the Deer and Elk chairs has lots of wide,

THE TRAIL MAP

We have complained about many trail maps over the years. But we have rarely come across one as useless as Fernie's. Combine that with inadequate signposting on the mountain and you get a dangerous combination. When we tried to find the long black Diamond Back run from the top of the White Pass quad, we failed and ended up in tight trees on a slope of triple-diamond steepness – scary. Reporters agree. One said, 'Finding your way to the more expert terrain can be difficult thanks to poor signage and awkward hikes and traverses.' Another said, 'The map is just a rough guide and there are many runs not marked on it.' He went on to point out that the Fernie Guide and the trail map grade some runs differently: single diamond on one, double diamond on the other; green on one, blue on the other. Yet another remarked: 'It's great to go out with someone who knows where they're going, because the difference between what's a trail and what's not a trail is quite often minimal. To make the most of it you've almost got to stop worrying about following what's on the map.'

Fine, as long as you know where you are going and how steep the terrain will be. Others would prefer a more helpful map and on-mountain directions.

SCHOOLS

Fernie
t 423 4655

Classes
Half day C$29
Private lessons
62 for 1hr; each
additional person
C$23.50

CHILDREN

The resort day care
centre (423 2430)
takes children from
newborn to age 6 and
is open daily from
8.30 to 4.30. One-
hour ski lessons are
available for 3 and 4
year olds.

Kids ski/snowboard
school for children
aged 5 to 12 years
costs C$46 per day.

smooth trails to gain confidence on.
But the green runs from the top of the
mountain are usually just cat-tracks,
which nonetheless have tough parts to
them, plus more experienced skiers
and boarders travelling fast.

FOR CROSS-COUNTRY
Some possibilities
There are 14km/9 miles of trails
marked out in the forest adjacent to
the resort, and the Fernie golf and
country club allows enthusiasts on to
their white fairways.

QUEUES
Not usually a problem
Unless there is a weekend invasion
from Calgary, or heavy snow keeps
part of the mountain closed, queues
are rare.

MOUNTAIN RESTAURANTS
What mountain restaurants?
Bear's Den at the top of the Elk chair
is an open-air fast-food kiosk. A
welcome stop for coffee and hot
chocolate say some readers, but it's
back to base for lunch – the ancient
Day Lodge is grim, busy but cheap and
serves good soups and sandwiches to
order, and Lizzard Creek is good for
Sunday brunch. Look at the places
recommended in 'Eating out', too.

SCHOOLS AND GUIDES
Lots of alternatives
Reporters have praised the ski school
and its small classes. One tried
telemarking and described the lessons
as 'outstanding' and 'best ever', with
only two people in the class. Others

loved the beer, snacks and video
session that is part of the deal if you
book a ski week. 'First Tracks' gets you
up the mountain at 8am for two hours,
but when we tried it the instructor
didn't know which lifts were open and
there was a lot of wasted time. Steep
and Deep tours, running for two or
four days, were introduced last season
– you learn the area as well as the
techniques for skiing it (a great idea
given the poor piste map).

FACILITIES FOR CHILDREN
Good day care centre
There's a day care centre in the
Cornerstone Lodge, which a reporter
found 'very well run'. There are also
'Kids' Activity Nights' for children age
six to 12.

STAYING THERE

HOW TO GO
More packages
Fernie is increasingly easy to find in
tour operator brochures. Unless stated,
accommodation listed is at the resort.
Chalets Some UK tour operators run
chalets. Beavertail Lodge
(www.beavertaillodge.com) is run
along chalet lines and received rave
reviews from 2003 reporters. Canadian
Powder Tours has a chalet and
includes in the price guiding by locals
who know the mountain well.
Hotels and condos As the resort
develops, the choice is widening and
shifting upmarket, but self-caterers do
need to go to downtown for groceries.
(((4 **Lizard Creek Lodge** Luxury ski-in,
ski-out condo hotel. Spa, outdoor pool

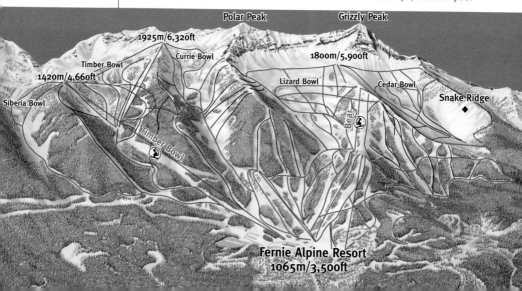

Polar Peak

1925m/6,320ft

Currie Bowl

Timber Bowl

1420m/4,66oft

Siberia Bowl

Timber Bowl

Grizzly Peak

1800m/5,900ft

Lizard Bowl

Cedar Bowl

Snake Ridge

Bear

Fernie Alpine Resort
1065m/3,500ft

ACTIVITIES

Indoor Museum, galleries, aquatic centre, saunas, bowling, fitness centre, ice skating, cinema, curling

Outdoor Sleigh rides, snowmobiling, dog-sledding, snow-shoe excursions, ice fishing

Central reservations phone number
For all resort accommodation call 1 800 258 7669 (toll-free from within Canada).

Phone numbers
From distant parts of Canada, add the prefix 1 250.
From abroad, add the prefix +1 250.

GETTING THERE

Air Calgary 322km/200 miles (3½hr).

TOURIST OFFICE

t 423 4655
info@skifernie.com
www.skifernie.com

FERNIE ALPINE RESORT

Fernie Alpine Resort is convenient for the slopes but still small, and it is quiet at night →

---

and hot-tub. We stayed there and highly recommend it.

((⟨3⟩ **Cornerstone Lodge** Condo hotel in the village core.

((⟨3⟩ **Best Western Fernie Mountain Lodge** Next to golf course near town. Recommended by reporters. Pool, hot-tub, fitness room.

((⟨3⟩ **Griz Inn Sport Hotel** Condo-hotel with good facilities. Pool.

(⟨2⟩ **Wolf's Den Mountain Lodge** 'Simple but comfortable,' say reporters. Indoor hot-tub, games room and small gym. At base of slope.

(⟨2⟩ **Timberline Lodges** Very comfortable condos a shuttle-ride from the lifts.

(⟨2⟩ **Cedar Lodge** Motel on road to town. 'Comfortable and clean, but not very welcoming,' said reporters.

(⟨2⟩ **Alpine Lodge** B&B recommended by a reporter, with a Japanese-inspired restaurant.

EATING OUT
Not a highlight
At the base, the Lizard Creek Lodge is expensive but serves the best gourmet food in the district (in small portions). Kelsey's (part of a chain) is more casual and offers good food and large servings, with Asian dishes as well as

standard burgers, steaks and pasta. The Powder Horn in the Griz Inn does 'good, reasonably priced' food. Gabriella's does cheap and cheerful Italian, and lots of readers have enjoyed it. The Mean Bean coffee shop in the Cornerstone Lodge has been recommended.

In Fernie, there are quite a few options. The Old Elevator is in a converted grain store and does good grills and pasta. Jamochas is a coffee house that does meals. Other reader recommendations include the Curry Bowl (various Asian styles), the Royal hotel, Rip'n Richard's Eatery (south-western food and a lively atmosphere). The current favourite, though, is the Wood bistro and tapas bar – 'Good but expensive. You need to book.'

APRES-SKI
Have a beer
The Grizzly bar in the Day Lodge and the Powder Horn, in the nearby Griz Inn, are quite lively when the lifts close – both with live bands sometimes. During the week, the bars are pretty quiet later on, but one reporter recommends Kelsey's. In town, the bar of the Royal hotel is popular with locals. Other recommendations are the Park Place Lodge Pub, the bar in the Grand Central hotel and the Eldorado Lounge for later on (it's under the Wood). The resort offers barbecue at the Bear's Den two days a week, with a torchlit descent.

OFF THE SLOPES
Get out and about
There is a heritage walking tour of historic Fernie and the old railroad station is now the Art Station. You could take in an ice-hockey game. But the main diversion is the great outdoors.

Jasper

Small area of slopes set amid glorious scenery and wildlife

COSTS

① ② ③ ④ ⑤ ⑥

RATINGS

The slopes

Snow	***
Extent	*
Expert	**
Intermediate	**
Beginner	****
Convenience	*
Queues	****
Mountain restaurants	**

The rest

Scenery	***
Resort charm	***
Off-slope	***

NEWS

The most recent major development was the building of the Eagle Ridge quad chair for the 2001/02 season. This opened up 20 new runs on either side of Eagle Ridge – previously accessible only by taking a long, high traverse from the top of the Knob chair. Since then extensive tree removal has taken place to make the runs through the trees easier and more enjoyable.

For 2002/03 the terrain-park had a facelift with a beginner area and a new sound system. 2003/04 should see a boarder-cross course.

This is the whole ski area. Keen piste bashers will ski all the groomed trails in half a day and the snow has to be better than it was on our two visits to enjoy the top bowls →

- Lots of lovely walks and drives in National Park land
- Extensive cross-country trails
- Spectacular scenery and wildlife

- Slopes of Marmot Basin are a long way from town and limited in size, especially for intermediates
- Town of Jasper is rather spread out and lacks charm

Set in the middle of Jasper National Park, Jasper appeals more to those keen on scenery and wildlife (and perhaps cross-country skiing) than piste mileage. It could be combined with a stay in Whistler, Banff or Lake Louise.

THE RESORT

Jasper is a low-key, low-rise little town that started life as a trapper's staging post and now services visitors to Jasper National Park. It spreads along the trans-continental railway but is only a couple of blocks deep.

Its key attraction is the scenery of the unspoiled National Park land surrounding the town. One of the most beautiful drives in the world is the three-hour trip to Lake Louise on the Columbia Icefields Parkway through the Banff and Jasper National Parks – past glaciers, frozen waterfalls and lakes.

The place is geared to cars: most accommodation is out of town or on the outskirts and the local slopes of Marmot Basin are a 30-minute drive away with convenient slope-side parking (there are shuttle-buses too).

Jasper is a good place to stay for a couple of days as part of a two-centre holiday. You can travel from Whistler to Jasper by overnight train from Vancouver and wake up to spectacular Rocky Mountains scenery. And there's now a daily bus service connecting Jasper and Banff.

THE MOUNTAINS

The slopes are at Marmot Basin, in the heart of the unspoiled National Park.

Slopes A high-speed quad takes you to mid-mountain, with four slow chairs above that including the recently built quad to Eagle Ridge. The highest Knob chair ends way below the 2600m/8,530ft peak that the area includes in its claim of almost 900m/2,950ft vertical.

Terrain-parks There's a terrain-park below Caribou Ridge. Last season it had a new sound system and a beginner park was added. This season a boarder-cross course is planned.

Snow reliability Snowfall is 160 inches on average – a modest figure by North

KEY FACTS

Resort		1065m
		3,500ft
Altitude	1705-2600m	
	5,590-8,530ft	
Lifts		8
Pistes	1,500 acres	
Green		30%
Blue		30%
Black		40%
Snowmaking		
		10 acres

Phone numbers
From distant parts of
Canada, add the
prefix 1 780.
From abroad, add the
prefix +1 780.

TOURIST OFFICE

t 852 3816
f 852 3533
info@skimarmot.com
www.skimarmot.com

American standards. Cover has been sparse on both our visits and there is little snowmaking capacity.

Experts There are some decent mogul runs on the top and bottom halves of the mountain, and some entertaining off-piste on the top half. The Eagle Ridge chair, which was added two seasons ago, has opened up a lot of expert terrain that was difficult to access. In good conditions, there is now lots to do. But slopes like these can be hazardous or unskiable if snow conditions are not good.

Intermediates Keen piste-bashers will cover all the groomed runs in half a day and find the area very small unless they are prepared to brave the ungroomed blacks. Less adventurous intermediates will be happy to cruise the greens and blues for a day or two.

Beginners The area around the base is very gentle, and there are greens to progress to from a T-bar and the quad.

Snowboarding As with skiers, there are plenty of challenges if you are expert and the snow is good, but it's more restricting if you are intermediate. And if you're a beginner, there's a T-bar to contend with.

Cross-country Over 300km/185 miles of trails make this one of the best areas in Canada, with good trails near Jasper.

Queues These are rarely a problem.

Mountain restaurants At mid-mountain the Paradise Chalet has a big self-service cafe and the connected Eagle Chalet is a cosy table-service place. At the base the rebuilt Caribou Chalet is another option.

Schools and guides These are doubtless up to the usual high Canadian standards.

Facilities for children The Little Rascals nursery takes children from 19 months.

STAYING THERE

Hotels The Fairmont Jasper Park Lodge (852 3301) is a beautiful collection of luxurious log cabins set 4km/2 miles out of town around a lake in the middle of 1,000 acres of land rich with wildlife. Room service is delivered on bicycles and you may well have to walk around grazing elk to reach the outdoor pool and other facilities. On the edge of town, the Royal Canadian Lodge (852 5644) has comfortable rooms and an indoor pool.

Eating out There's plenty of choice – from fine dining at the Jasper Park Lodge to Cajun, pizza and Japanese. We had good seafood and steak at the Fiddle River.

Après-ski The bar in the base lodge is crowded at the end of the day. In town, try Astoria, O'Shea's and Nick's.

Off the slopes There's lots to do – beautiful walks, wildlife watching, ice skating, snow-shoeing – as well as an aquatic centre and a sports complex.

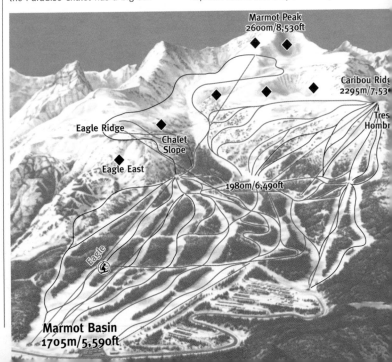

Marmot Peak
2600m/8,530ft

Caribou Ridge
2295m/7,53...

Tres
Hombr...

Eagle Ridge

Chalet
Slope

Eagle East

1980m/6,490ft

Eagle

Marmot Basin
1705m/5,590ft

Kicking Horse

Heli-skiing terrain that now has lifts; a resort village is on the way

COSTS

① ② ③ ④ ⑤ ⑥

RATINGS

The slopes

Snow	*****
Extent	***
Expert	****
Intermediate	***
Beginner	***
Convenience	*
Queues	*****
Mountain restaurants	**

The rest

Scenery	***
Resort charm	*
Off-slope	*

➕ A good bet for powder snow

➕ Some great terrain for experts and adventurous intermediates

➕ Big vertical served by a fast lift

➕ Splendid mountaintop restaurant

➕ Now a couple of places to stay

➖ No resort village yet

➖ Golden, the resort substitute, is neither attractive nor convenient

➖ Single-stage gondola suits summer visitors, not skiers and riders

➖ Few groomed intermediate runs

Four years ago, this was Whitetooth, the local ski hill of the nondescript logging town of Golden: two old lifts, open weekends, serving modest slopes beneath high bowls used for heli-skiing. Enter a Dutch-Canadian consortium, bringing vision, capital and a cute name. Within months, in go a gondola rising 1150m/ 3,770ft to the top of the heli-terrain and a smart base lodge and mountaintop restaurant. Last year in went a new chair-lift. This year a couple of small lodges will open and work is due to start on a mountain village at the lift base, which will make this a real destination resort. Meanwhile, any competent skier or rider staying in Banff or Lake Louise should give Kicking Horse a shot.

THE RESORT

Eight miles from the small logging town of Golden, Kicking Horse is in the very early stages of development. There are a few new houses and condos in the trees, a smart new base lodge and a portacabin housing the rental shop near the base of the gondola. A couple of small lodges will open for 2003/04. Work is due to start on Glacier Lodge, the first phase of a real resort village at the gondola base. Daily round-trip buses run from Banff and Lake Louise to Kicking Horse: C$69 including a lift pass.

Golden is a spread-out place beside the transcontinental highway. It has no real centre – it's the kind of place where you travel from motel to shops to restaurant by car. There's a shuttle-bus from some hotels to the slopes.

THE MOUNTAINS

The lower two-thirds of the hill is wooded, with trails cut in the usual style. The upper third is a mix of open and lightly wooded slopes.

Slopes The only way up to the top part of the mountain is by the eight-seater gondola to Eagle's Eye. Despite the serious vertical of 1150m/3,770ft, this lift goes up in a single stage – to give summer sightseeing visitors a quick ascent. In winter, the lack of a mid-station is a real drawback: unless you ride the chair to the slightly higher peak of Blue Heaven all the time, you have to make the full descent (and the snow conditions on the lower slopes may be poor). As well as the marked runs there are literally hundreds of ways down through the bowls, chutes

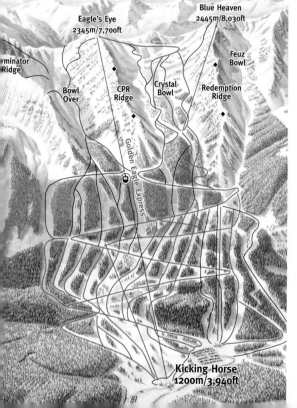

Blue Heaven
2445m/8,030ft

Eagle's Eye
2345m/7,700ft

Terminator Ridge

Feuz Bowl

Bowl Over

CPR Ridge

Crystal Bowl

Redemption Ridge

Golden Eagle Express

Kicking Horse
1200m/3,940ft

NEWS

For 2003/04 the first accommodation at the mountain will open – two 10 to 12 bedroomed lodges.

In 2002/03, a new quad chair from Crystal Bowl to Blue Heaven opened up another 100 acres of terrain. A new snack bar opened near the base of the lift. Extra cabins were added to double the capacity of the Golden Eagle Express gondola.

KEY FACTS

Resort	1200m
	3,940ft
Slopes	1200-2450m
	3,940-8,040ft
Lifts	4
Pistes	2,600 acres
Green	20%
Blue	20%
Black	60%
Snowmaking	None

Central reservations phone number
For resort accommodation call 1 250 439 5400 (toll-free from within Canada).

Phone numbers
From distant parts of Canada, add the prefix 1 250.
From abroad, add the prefix +1 250.

TOURIST OFFICE

t 439 5400
www.kickinghorse resort.com

and trees. The plan is that hardly any of the terrain will be groomed – making the area a paradise for powder pigs. Two chair-lifts from near the base serve the lower runs that formed the original Whitetooth ski area.

Terrain-park There's no terrain-park or half-pipe.

Snow reliability This is excellent: it gets an average of 275 inches of snow a year. Not enough to put the area in the very top flight, but not far off. And the top part of the mountain at least usually has light, dry powder. The lower part, however, may have cruddier snow.

Experts It's advanced skiers and riders who will get the most out of the area. From CPR ridge, drop off to skier's right through trees or to skier's left through chutes – there are endless options. The new Stairway to Heaven quad chair to Blue Heaven opened up easier ski-anywhere terrain down into Crystal Bowl last season. From the top you can also drop down into Feuz Bowl; this was marked as closed on our 2003 visit because Purcell heli-skiing claimed it still had the right to a short essential part of the ski-out, but lots of people were dropping in there. If it's open you can also hike to Terminator Ridge (often closed due to avalanche danger). The lower half of the mountain has fine black runs on cleared trails through the trees, some with serious moguls. Do six or seven laps on the gondola in a day and you'll sleep well that night.

Intermediates Adventurous intermediates will have a fine time at Kicking Horse, learning to play in the powder from Blue Heaven down to Crystal Bowl. Most of it is open but you can head off into trees if you want to. But don't expect many groomed runs. Piste-bashers and timid intermediates should go elsewhere. The only easy, groomed way down the mountain is a 10km/6 mile winding road called It's a Ten.

Beginners There are some excellent nursery slopes and gentle green trails on the lower mountain.

Snowboarding Free-riders will love this powder paradise.

Cross-country There are 12km/7 miles of trails at Dawn Mountain and a 5km/3 mile loop on the golf course.

Queues None of our 2003 reporters experienced any large queues.

Mountain restaurants The Eagle's Eye table-service restaurant at the top of the gondola serves excellent food in stylish log-cabin surroundings and has splendid views. The base lodge is also newly built with logs and beams and has a small self-service restaurant. A yurt (tent) in Crystal Bowl is a yurt (tent) serving simple snacks.

Schools and guides Two 2003 reporters booked group lessons and each was the only pupil. 'Excellent,' they both said. Another joined a free mountain tour and again was the only one: 'A fantastic afternoon in fresh powder with a local guide, all for the price of a hot chocolate.'

Facilities for children The school teaches children from the age of three.

STAYING THERE

How to go Choose between two new lodges at the slopes or stay in Golden. **Hotels** Vagabond Lodge with 10 rooms and Highland Lodge with 12 will open at the mountain for 2003/04. In Golden, the Prestige Inn (344 7990) is a neat, functional hotel with a small pool just off the main highway. Sisters and Beans (344 2443) has some well kept rooms – see below. Moberly Mountain Lodge (344 5544) is a luxury B&B that we've had good reports of.

Eating out In Golden, we enjoyed the cosy Sisters and Beans (pasta, steaks, Asian). The Kicking Horse Grill and the out-of-town Cedar House Cafe are highly rated. Eagle's Eye at the top of the gondola opens some nights.

Après-ski The Mad Trapper is the main drinking spot in Golden – a lively pub.

Off the slopes There is snowmobiling, snow-shoeing, ice-climbing and dog-sledding. But for someone who isn't going to hit the slopes, Golden is a dire place to stay.

SNOWPIX.COM / CHRIS GILL

When this photo was taken you had to hike up to get the best of Blue Heaven; now, all that lovely powder is accessed by chair-lift ↓

Lake Louise

Knockout views from Canada's second-biggest mountain

COSTS

① ② ③ ④ ⑤ ⑥

RATINGS

The slopes

Snow	✱✱✱
Extent	✱✱✱✱
Expert	✱✱✱✱
Intermediate	✱✱✱✱
Beginner	✱✱✱
Convenience	✱
Queues	✱✱✱✱
Mountain restaurants	✱✱

The rest

Scenery	✱✱✱✱✱
Resort charm	✱✱✱
Off-slope	✱✱✱✱

NEWS

For 2002/03 the Top of the World chair at the top of the Front Side was upgraded from a fast quad to a six-pack. This is the first six-person chairlift in the Canadian Rockies.

RESORTS OF THE CANADIAN ROCKIES

The Larch area in the background is served by a solitary fast quad chair ↓

➕ Spectacular high-mountain scenery – the best of any North American resort

➕ Slopes are the largest in the Canadian Rockies

➕ Snowy slopes of Sunshine Village within reach (see Banff chapter)

➕ Lots of wildlife around the valley

➕ Good value for money

➖ Local slopes are a short drive away from the 'village', Banff areas further

➖ Snowfall modest by local standards – though snowmaking is extensive

➖ Can be very cold – and the chair-lifts have no covers

➖ 'Village' is just a few hotels and shops dotted around a road junction

➖ Slopes can seem full of Brits

If you care more for scenery than for après-ski action, Lake Louise is worth considering for a holiday. We've seen a few spectacular mountain views, and the view from the Fairmont Chateau Lake Louise hotel, of the lake and the Victoria Glacier behind it, is as spectacular as they come; it is simply stunning.

Even if you prefer the more animated base of Banff, you'll want to make expeditions to Lake Louise during your holiday. It can't compete with Sunshine Village for quantity of snow, but it's a big and interesting mountain. And from the slopes you get a distant version of that view.

THE RESORT

Although it's a small place, Lake Louise is a resort of parts. First, there's the lake itself, in a spectacular setting beneath the Victoria Glacier. Tom Wilson, who discovered it in 1882, declared, 'As God is my judge, I never in all my exploration have seen such a matchless scene.' Neither have we. And it can be appreciated from many of the rooms of the vast Fairmont Chateau Lake Louise hotel on the shore. Then there's Lake Louise 'village' – a collection of a few hotels, condos, petrol station, liquor store and shops, a couple of miles away on a road junction. Finally, a mile or two across the valley is the lift base station. A car helps, especially in cold weather. Buses to the Lake Louise ski area run every half hour, but a lot less frequently to the Banff areas of Sunshine and Norquay. Bus trips to the more distant resorts of Panorama and Kicking Horse and the small resorts of Nakiska and Fortress are possible. Day-trip heli-skiing can also be arranged.

615

KEY FACTS

Resort	1645m
	5,400ft

For Sunshine, Norquay and Lake Louise, covered by the Tri-area pass

Slopes	1635-2730m
	5,350-8,950ft
Lifts	29
Pistes	7,558 acres
Green	23%
Blue	38%
Black	39%
Snowmaking	
	1,700 acres

For Lake Louise only

Slopes	1645-2635m
	5,400-8,650ft
Lifts	12
Pistes	4,200 acres
Green	25%
Blue	45%
Black	30%
Snowmaking	40%

THE MOUNTAINS

The Lake Louise ski area is big, with an excellent mixture of high open slopes, low trails cut through forest and gladed slopes between the two. Reporters are generally full of praise for the free guided tours given by volunteer 'Ski Friends'. There has been some criticism of inconsistent piste grading 'with some blues being more like blacks' and lots about cold lifts with no covers.

THE SLOPES
A wide variety

One of two fast quads takes you up the **Front Side** (also called the South Face) to mid-mountain; from here, a new six-pack goes to the top. From there, as elsewhere, there's a choice of green, blue or black runs to other lifts. The tree line comes about halfway up the top lift, but there are alternative lifts that stop a bit lower, so you can stay in the trees in bad weather. From mid-mountain, the long Summit drag-lift takes you to the high-point of the area, at the shoulder of Mount Whitehorn – there's a stunning view of peaks and glaciers including Canada's Matterhorn lookalike, Mount Assiniboine.

From either the top chair or the drag you can go over the ridge and into Lake Louise's almost treeless **Back Bowls** – open, predominantly north-facing and mainly steep.

From the bottom of the bowls you can take the Paradise lift back to the top again or continue on to the separate **Larch** area, served by a fast quad chair. With a lift-served vertical of 375m/1,230ft it's not huge, but it has pretty wooded runs of all levels. From the bottom you can return to the top of the main mountain via the Ptarmigan chair or take a long green path back to the main base area.

TERRAIN-PARKS
Huge and varied

The resort redeveloped its terrain-park completely for 2002/03. Now called

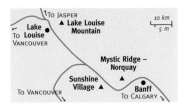

Showtime, and based on the Easy Street run, it's certainly impressive. The park boasts nine varied rails and nine jumps, and there's a quarter-pipe at the bottom. There's also a beginner park next to it, on Sunny Side, with a small half-pipe, rollers and banked turns. There's also an Olympic-sized super-pipe under the Friendly Giant chair, and a boarder-cross course, accessed using the Olympic chair.

SNOW RELIABILITY
Usually OK

Lake Louise gets around 140 inches a year on the Front Side, which by the standards of western Canada is not a lot. But it is usually enough, and there is snowmaking on 40% of the pistes. The north-facing Back Bowls and Larch hold the snow pretty well.

FOR EXPERTS
Widespread pleasure

There are plenty of steep slopes. On the Front Side, as well as a score of marked black-diamond trails in and above the trees, there is the alluring West Bowl, reached from the Summit drag – a wide open expanse of snow outside the area boundary. Because this is National Park territory, you can in theory go anywhere. But outside the boundaries there are no patrols and, of course, no avalanche control. A guide is essential. Inside the boundaries there are also areas permanently closed because of avalanche danger. Going over to the Back Bowls opens up countless black mogul/powder runs. If they are open, try the Whitehorn 2 area directly behind the peak. It gave our Ozzie editor what she called 'some of the most exciting in-bounds skiing

boarding

Lake Louise is a great mountain for free-riders, with all the challenging terrain in the bowls and glades. The Summit drag-lift is a tricky one to ride (very long and with a difficult start and steep pitches), but it's worth it to access the Back Bowls and the views. The long green run that goes from the Larch area back to the base is to be avoided – it's really flat. In Banff, two specialist snowboard shops are Rude Boys and Unlimited Snowboards.

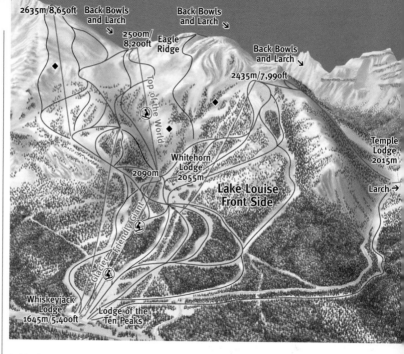

LIFT PASSES

Tri-area lift pass
Covers all lifts and transport between Banff, Lake Louise and Sunshine Village.

Main pass
3-day pass C$186
6-day pass C$372

Senior citizens
Over 65: C$327

Children
Under 13: 6-day pass C$128
Under 6: free pass

Notes
Three days minimum. Night skiing available on Friday evening at Norquay.

Alternative passes
One-day and half-day passes available for individual areas.

in North America' – a row of extreme chutes, almost 1km/0.5 miles long.

The Top of the World six-pack takes you to the very popular Paradise Bowl, served by its own triple chair – there are endless variants here. From the Summit drag you can access wide open Back Bowl slopes that take you right away from all signs of lifts. The seriously steep slope served by the Ptarmigan quad chair provided many of the logs for the newest base lodge, and offers great gladed terrain as a result. It's a good place to beat the crowds and find good snow, suggests one reporter. The Larch area has some steep double-diamond stuff in the trees, and open snowfields at the top for those with the energy to hike up. Heli-skiing is available from bases outside the National Park.

FOR INTERMEDIATES
Some good cruising

Almost half the runs are classified as intermediate. But from the top of the Front Side the blue runs down are little more than paths in places, and there are only two blue and two green routes marked in the Back Bowls. Once you get part way down the Front Side the blues are much more interesting. And when groomed, the Men's and Ladies' Downhill black runs are great fast cruises on the lower half of the mountain. Juniper is a wonderful cruising run in the same area. Meadowlark is a beautiful tree-lined run to the base area – to find it from the Eagle chair, first follow Eagle Meadows. The Larch area has some short but ideal intermediate runs – and recent reporters have enjoyed the

617

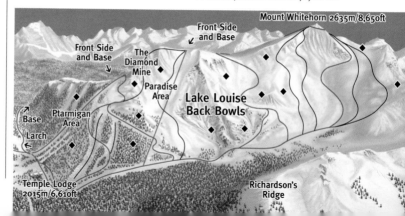

SCHOOLS

**ClubSki and
ClubSnowboard**
t 762 4561
info@banffskischool.
com

Classes
3 days guided tuition
of the three areas
(4½hr per day)
C$199.

Private lessons
Half day (3hr) C$325

RESORTS OF THE CANADIAN
ROCKIES / PERRY THOMPSON

The views across the
valley are stunning –
especially from the
runs down the Front
Side served by the
Summit drag-lift ↓

---

natural lumps and bumps of the aptly
named blue, Rock Garden. The
adventurous should also try the blue-
classified Boomerang, which starts with
a short side-step up from the top of
the Summit drag, and some of the
ungroomed Back Bowls terrain.

FOR BEGINNERS
Excellent terrain
Louise has a good nursery area near
the base, served by a short T-bar; you
progress to the gentle, wide Wiwaxy
(one of several designated slow skiing
zones), Pinecone Way and the slightly
more difficult Deer Run or Eagle
Meadows on the upper mountain.
There are even green slow-skiing zones
round the back bowls and in the Larch
area – worth trying for the views,
though some do contain slightly steep
pitches. A recent reporter lost
confidence on these, and found that
people still skied fast in the slow areas
and that they were quite crowded.

FOR CROSS-COUNTRY
High in quality and quantity
It's a very good area for cross-country,
with around 80km/50 miles of groomed
trails within Banff National Park. There
are excellent trails in the local area
(and on Lake Louise itself). And
Emerald Lake Lodge 40km/25 miles
away has some lovely trails and has
been highly recommended as a place
to stay for a peaceful time.

QUEUES
Not unknown
Half of the area's visitors come for the
day from nearby cities such as Calgary
– so it's fairly quiet during the week,
but can have queues at weekends,
especially for the slow chairs on the
back of the mountain.

MOUNTAIN RESTAURANTS
Good base facilities
There's not much choice up the
mountain. Temple Lodge, near the
bottom of Larch, is built in rustic style
with a big terrace. Sawyer's Nook is its
calm table-service restaurant. 'We were
impressed with both food and prices,'
said a recent reporter. The self-service
cafeteria can get very crowded.
Whitehorn Lodge, at mid-mountain on
the Front Side, is a cafeteria with fine
views from its balcony. At the base,
the Lodge of the Ten Peaks is a hugely
impressive, spacious, airy, modern,
log-built affair with various eating,
drinking and lounging options. The
neighbouring, refurbished Whiskeyjack
building has the good Northface table-
service restaurant and buffet, including
a breakfast menu that 'sets you up for
the whole day'. The Kokanee Kabin has
BBQ food – but a reporter complained
of long queues and poor food.

SCHOOLS AND GUIDES
Generally good reports
'The best teaching we've encountered'
is how a reporter described his

CHILDREN

The nursery at Lake Louise (522 3555) takes children aged 18 days to 6 years, from 8am to 4.30. Children aged 3 or more can take short ski lessons.

The ski/snowboard school (522 1333) takes children aged 5 to 12 years old. 3 days (4½hr per day).

GETTING THERE

Air Calgary 177km/110 miles (1½hr).

ACTIVITIES

Indoor Mainly hotel-based pools, saunas and hot-tubs

Outdoor Ice-skating, walking, cross-country skiing, ice fishing on the lake, swimming in hot springs, heli-skiing, sleigh rides, dog-sled rides, snowmobiles, helicopter tours, snow-shoe tours

Phone numbers
From distant parts of Canada, add the prefix 1 403. From abroad, add the prefix +1 403.

TOURIST OFFICE

t 762 4561
info@sblls.com
www.skibig3.com

'bumps' lesson at Lake Louise. A 2003 reporter enjoyed the lessons, but said she could not get afternoon-only classes. And her five-year-old daughter did not like being put in classes with eight- to ten-year-olds and lost enthusiasm. See the Banff chapter for details on the excellent three-day, three-mountain Club Ski and Club Snowboard Program.

FACILITIES FOR CHILDREN
Varying reports
A reporter who used Lake Louise, Sunshine and Norquay facilities said: 'I'd recommend all three and advise booking in advance at Lake Louise.'

STAYING THERE

HOW TO GO
Good value accommodation
Hotels Summer is the peak season here. Prices halve for the winter – so you can stay in luxury at bargain rates. (((((4) **Fairmont Chateau Lake Louise** (522 3511) Isolated position with stunning views over frozen Lake Louise, 500 rooms, lots of shops, groups of Japanese tourists, pool, hot-tub, steam room. 'Could not be faulted.' (((((4) **Post Hotel** (522 3989) Small, comfortable Relais & Châteaux place in the village with good restaurant (huge wine list) and pool, hot-tub, sauna. ((2) **Lake Louise Inn** (522 3791) Cheaper option in the village, with pool, hot-tub and sauna. 'Comfortable rooms', 'two good restaurants', but 'staff with an attitude problem'. ((2) **Deer Lodge** (522 3747) Charming old hotel next to the Chateau, good restaurant, rooftop hot-tub with amazing views.
Self-catering Some is available but local shopping is limited. The Baker Creek Chalets (522 3761) were highly recommended by 2003 reporters on their honeymoon ('really romantic').

EATING OUT
Limited choice
The Post hotel has a good reputation. The Fairview Dining Room at the Chateau is also top notch. The Outpost (in the Post hotel) does inexpensive pub food. The Station restaurant is in an atmospheric old station building. The small bakery/coffee shop in the village has had praise from reporters and is good for breakfast.

APRES-SKI
Lively at tea time, quiet later
There are several options at the bottom of the slopes. The Sitzmark Lounge in Whiskeyjack Lodge is popular – with an open fire and often a live band. The upstairs part of The Lodge of the Ten Peaks has lovely surroundings, an open fire, a couple of bars and a relaxed atmosphere. The Kokanee Kabin has live music on Spring afternoons. Twice a week there's live music and dancing and a buffet dinner at the mid-mountain Whitehorn Lodge. You ski or ride there as the lifts close and the evening ends with a torchlit descent. It is hugely popular with British visitors, and we loved it. Reporters recommend the Sleigh Ride to Dinner, with BBQ and dancing.

Later on, things are fairly quiet. For most guests, it's a leisurely dinner followed by bed. But the Glacier Saloon, in Chateau Lake Louise, with traditional Wild West decor, often has live music until late. Explorer's Lounge, in the Lake Louise Inn, has nightly entertainment. The Post hotel's Outpost Pub has been recommended.

OFF THE SLOPES
Beautiful scenery
Lake Louise makes a lovely, peaceful place to stay for someone who does not intend to hit the slopes. The lake itself makes a stunning setting for walks, snow-shoeing, cross-country skiing and ice skating. There are plenty of other things to do and lots of wildlife to see. You can go on ice canyon walks, sleigh rides, dog-sledding, tobogganing, sightseeing tours and visit natural hot springs.

For a more lively day or for shopping you can visit Banff.

Lake Louise is near one end of the Columbia Icefields Parkway, a three-hour drive to Jasper through National Parks, amidst stunningly beautiful scenery of high peaks and glaciers – one of the world's most beautiful drives.

Lake Louise

619

Panorama

Great views, some challenging runs, a rapidly developing resort

COSTS

① ② ③ ④ ⑤ ⑥

RATINGS

The slopes

Snow	***
Extent	**
Expert	****
Intermediate	***
Beginner	****
Convenience	****
Queues	****
Mountain restaurants	*

The rest

Scenery	***
Resort charm	**
Off-slope	*

KEY FACTS

Resort	1160m
	3,800ft
Slopes	1160-2380m
	3,800-7,800ft
Lifts	9
Pistes	2,847 acres
Green	20%
Blue	55%
Black	25%
Snowmaking	40%

620

+ Increasing amount of slope-side accommodation, plus a lower village linked by lift till 10pm

+ Fair-sized area with big vertical drop and challenging runs for all abilities

+ Runs are usually deserted

+ Two new lifts for 2003/04 will make getting to the top much quicker

+ Heli-skiing by the day on hand

− May be too challenging for timid intermediates − not many cruisers

− Snowfall record not impressive by high local standards

− Not many lifts serve the upper runs

− No real mountain restaurants

− Village still quiet with no real focus

Panorama has benefited from a huge investment in the last few years. New slope-side accommodation has been built, along with outdoor hot-pools and a skating rink. And this season will see two new quads replacing two T-bars and a slow, queue-prone chair – the source of many complaints by reporters. The mountain's vertical of 1220m/4,000ft is one of the biggest in North America, and it has some excellent terrain for experts and adventurous intermediates. It's good for beginners too. But timid intermediates may find some of the runs intimidating and prefer to stick to the rather limited lower mountain. And the resort is quiet – a better place for families than singles looking for nightlife.

THE RESORT

Panorama is a small, quiet, purpose-built resort above the lakeside town of Invermere in eastern BC, about two hours' scenic drive south-west of Banff. Accommodation is concentrated mainly in two car-free areas. Attractive lodges and a hot-pool complex have recently been built at the foot of the main slopes and, with ski-in, ski-out convenience, this is the best place to stay. But a lot of accommodation is in a 'lower village' which lacks character or life. This is now linked to the 'upper village' and the slopes by a bucket lift which runs until 10pm. There are also houses spread widely around the hillside and the village as a whole lacks a central focus or hub.

Outings by car are possible to Kimberley, less than two hours south, or to Lake Louise or Kicking Horse, slightly further away to the north. And the resort runs day trips to Lake Louise and Kicking Horse.

THE MOUNTAIN

The slopes basically follow three ridges, joined at top and bottom. Almost all of the terrain is wooded. Daily mountain tours are available. And some runs are open for floodlit skiing and riding Thursday to Sunday.
Slopes From the upper village, a fast quad goes over gentle slopes to mid-mountain. Above this the new fast quad for 2003/04 serves both expert and intermediate slopes. Then the new fixed-grip quad takes you to the

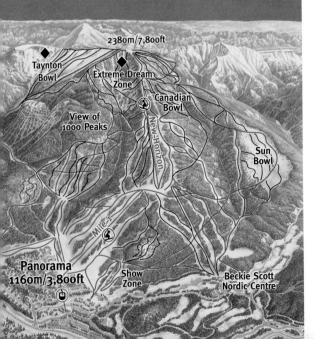

Taynton Bowl

Extreme Dream Zone

Canadian Bowl

View of 1000 Peaks

New Horizon

Sun Bowl

Mile-1

Panorama
1160m/3,800ft

Show Zone

Beckie Scott Nordic Centre

2380m/7,800ft

NEWS

Two new quad chairs planned for 2003/04 will make getting to the top of the mountain much quicker and easier. A high-speed quad will replace the slow, queue-prone, two-person Horizon chair and the Champagne T-bar above it. And the Summit T-bar to the top will be replaced by a fixed-grip quad.

New snowmaking will be installed on the upper sections of the runs served by the new high-speed chair and on the run between it and the new fixed-grip chair.

For 2002/03, a new terrain-park was built, just off the Mile One chair, for freestyle novices and kids, while the experts' Showzone Park had a new C-box and rainbow rail installed. Extensive trail clearing work was also done, particularly the lower Taynton Bowl and Taynton Trail area.

An outdoor skating rink was built in the upper village.

More slope-side hotel and condo accommodation will open for 2003/04.

PANORAMA MOUNTAIN VILLAGE

The lower and upper villages are connected by this lift, which works till 10pm ➜

summit. From the summit there is only one blue run (appropriately named Getmedown). The other runs are all single- or double-black diamonds. There are long runs down the two outer ridges as well as the central one. Those on the right bring you to a triple-chair near the base of the mountain, which also serves its own bunch of runs. Either way, the whole vertical is usable. At the top, between the left and central ridges, is the double-black-diamond Extreme Dream Zone. Off the back is the 'Outback' area in Taynton Bowl – 700 acres of lightly wooded expert terrain which opened in the 2000/01 season (it was previously used for heli-skiing). This funnels down to a long, flattish blue run back to the village.

Terrain-parks In 2002/03 a new intermediate jib park opened for beginner freestylers and kids. The main Showzone terrain-park was improved with the addition of a C-box and a 15m/50ft rainbow rail. There is a half-pipe too. They are floodlit Thursday to Sunday evenings.

Snow reliability Annual snowfall is low by local standards – less than half the Fernie figure. But snowmaking covers 40% of trails and grooming is good.

Experts There are genuine black runs scattered all over the mountain, and some expert-only areas. At the very top of the mountain and accessed through a gate is the Extreme Dream Zone – seriously steep trails with cliffs as well as tight trees, said to contain the best snow on the mountain. Off the back of the summit, is the Taynton Bowl area with challenging but (even though it is marked double-black diamond on the map) less extreme terrain – hiking over to the far runs can be worth it for fresh tracks. There are often good bumps on the blacks at mid-mountain. On the extreme right of the mountain is an area of gentler glades, where you can pick the density of trees and steepness of slope to try. Then there's the local heli-skiing to try – see Intermediates.

Intermediates For adventurous intermediates the terrain is excellent – there are easy blacks all over the mountain, some of them regularly groomed. The black View of 1000 Peaks, which turns into Stumbock's or the blue Messerli's Mile, has fabulous views but can be a bit tricky in parts. Both this and Getmedown from the top which runs into Schober's Dream are beautiful and long for North America (up to 3.5km/2 miles). Sun Bowl is a good introduction to a powder bowl and Millennium (black running into blue) is a great roller-coaster.

But the less confident may find all this uncomfortably challenging. The blues in the centre of the area such as World Cup Way, Skyline and Rollercoaster are gentler but they don't add up to a lot. RK Heli-Skiing operates from a base right next to the village and specialises in one-day sessions for first-time heli-skiers – well worth a go. 'We got in eight runs on the glacier in shin-deep powder. The whole experience was first class with excellent guides and a fine lunch on a ridge with phenomenal alpine views in all directions,' says a 2003 reporter.

Beginners There are a couple of nursery lifts and a moving carpet serving a quiet and gentle nursery area. Then there are good, longer runs to progress to served by the Mile 1 quad.

Snowboarding There is good steep

↑ The Panorama Springs' hot pools are great, but can get packed with families after skiing; the building in the centre is a sauna

PANORAMA MOUNTAIN VILLAGE

Central reservations
1 800 663 2929 (toll-free within Canada).

Phone numbers
From distant parts of Canada, add the prefix 1 250. From abroad, add +1 250.

TOURIST OFFICE

t 342 6941
paninfo@intrawest.com
www.skipanorama.com

terrain and tree runs for expert free-riders. And it's great news that the two top T-bars are being replaced by chairs. The two terrain-parks offer something for all standards. Beginners have several good long green runs to practise on but the main nursery slopes are served by drag-lifts.

Cross-country There are 30 km/19 miles of trails starting from the Nordic Centre, which you can reach on downhill skis and where you can rent cross-country gear.

Queues The two new quads this season should eliminate the only queues on the mountain. And the trails are usually delightfully deserted.

Mountain restaurants There are no real mountain restaurants, just two huts offering basic refreshments. But the Ski Tip day lodge at the base is an excellent modern affair.

Schools and guides We have mainly had glowing reports of the ski school. 'Universally agreed as superb by all who tried it' and 'massive leap in skiing – felt great' are typical comments. But one reporter who joined an all-day free-skiing group thought it 'didn't live up to the publicity and we were disappointed'. Multi-day courses include BBQ lunches at the mid-mountain rustic Elkhorn Cabin.

Facilities for children Wee Wascals is the childcare centre, taking children from 18 months. Snowbirds is for three to five year olds, and the Adventure Club caters for kids from 5 to 14. Kid's Nights for 6 to 13 year olds and a Teen Nightclub for 13 to 18 year olds are arranged some evenings to let parents have a night out. Evening babysitters are also available.

STAYING THERE

How to go The better places are the newer ones in the upper village.
Hotels Panorama Springs is right on the slopes with a big outdoor hot-pool and sauna facility. Next door Tamarack and Ski Tip have been recommended, too. And the slope-side stone and timber-clad Taynton Lodge looks impressive, as no doubt will the new 1000 Peaks Lodge and Summit units due to open for 2003/04. The 1000 Peaks will have its own skating rink, fire pit and hot-tubs. The Pine Inn is a budget option, which has been seen better days say a few reporters this year.
Self-catering There are plenty of condo blocks and town homes. The store is inadequate, so stock up in Invermere.
Eating out Eating out options are mainly in the lodges – the Toby Creek restaurant and the Starbird in the Pine Inn are good. The Heliplex restaurant has great views of the mountain, a shooter bar, sculpted from ice on the outdoor deck and is frequently recommended by reporters. The ski school organises BBQs at Elkhorn Cabin followed by a guided torchlight descent. There's also the Trappers Cabin horsedrawn wagon ride followed by chilli and marshmallows around a campfire. There's a shuttle-bus to the restaurants down in Invermere.
Après-ski Après-ski revolves around the T-bar and Grill in the Pine Inn and the Jackpine pub in the Horsethief Lodge. The Ski Tip Lodge terrace is popular on sunny afternoons. The Heliplex is 'good for a relaxing drink and has friendly staff'.The Glacier is the night club.
Off the slopes The hot-pool facility, with thermal baths, a swimming pool, slides and sauna is excellent, but it gets rather taken over by kids. There are two and three hour snowmobile tours to the peaks, with spectacular views, ice fishing excursions and snow-shoeing.

Panorama

623

Whistler

North America's biggest mountain with terrain to suit every standard

COSTS

① ② ③ ④ ⑤ ⑥

HOW IT RATES

The slopes

Snow	****
Extent	****
Expert	*****
Intermediate	*****
Beginner	***
Convenience	****
Queues	***
Mountain restaurants	**

The rest

Scenery	***
Resort charm	***
Off-slope	**

NEWS

Whistler mountain's terrain-park was improved for last season. Further changes are planned for 2003/04.

Longer term the resort is planning to open more terrain but no dates have been set for this.

Two new upmarket hotels should open in 2004 – the Four Seasons Resort at the base of Blackcomb and, out of town, the London Mountain Lodge, a group of lakeside log cabins.

Whistler Creek continues to be developed. New shops and accommodation make it less of an outpost and more a suitable place to stay in its own right.

Many of the events in the 2010 Winter Olympics will be held in Whistler. The resort says it plans to increase 'visitor volume' in the run-up to the Games, and promises 'infrastructure benefits'.

➕ North America's biggest, both in area and vertical (1610m/5,280ft)

➕ Good slopes for most abilities, with an unrivalled combination of high open bowls and woodland trails

➕ Good snow record

➕ Almost Alpine scenery, unlike the rounded Rockies of Colorado

➕ Attractive modern village at the foot of the slopes, car-free in the centre, with lively après-ski

➕ Good range of restaurants and bars (though not enough of them)

➕ Easy access from the UK – non-stop flights to Vancouver, short transfer

➕ Excellent heli-operation nearby

➖ Proximity to the ocean means a lot of cloudy weather and, with the low altitude, when it's snowing on the mountain it's often raining at resort level

➖ Two separate mountains are linked only at resort level

➖ Some runs get very crowded

➖ Lift queues are often a problem

➖ Mountain restaurants are mostly functional (and overcrowded)

➖ Whistler is in danger of becoming a victim of its own success – attracting more people than the mountain or the village facilities (restaurants in particular) can cope with

Whistler is unlike any other resort in North America. It's bigger, both in terms of vertical drop and skiable area. The town is big too. Combine that with hordes of people pouring in from Vancouver on powder days and weekends and you can get lengthy lift queues and crowded trails – unusual for North America. The facilities in town can get overstretched too, with tables in restaurants difficult to come by. If you want to get away from the crowds, you should go elsewhere.

But a lot of people will put up with the crowds for Whistler's other attractions. There are some fine up-market hotels and a good variety of restaurants. And the mountain is simply the best that North America has to offer. Great open bowls, steeps and deeps, tree-lined intermediate cruising and good beginner slopes. The ski schools are excellent. The lifts are generally fast and efficient. And the snow on the upper half of the mountain is as reliable and powdery as you'll find. But be prepared for rain at resort level and poor snow on the lower slopes.

Whistler will host many events during the 2010 Winter Olympics, and one reader, who 'would not visit in high season because of the pressure on facilities', ponders whether success will mean long-term on-mountain improvements and expansion or more crowding. The former we hope.

THE RESORT

Whistler Village sits at the foot of its two mountains, Whistler and Blackcomb, a scenic 120km/75 mile drive from Vancouver on Canada's west coast. Whistler started as a locals' ski area in 1966 with a few ramshackle buildings in what is now Whistler Creek. Whistler Village was developed in the late 1970s, and a village spread up the lower slopes of Blackcomb Mountain in the 1980s. This village, a 10-minute walk from Whistler, is now known simply as Upper Village.

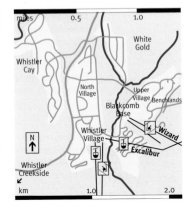

Whistler's high ski-anywhere bowls usually have excellent powder snow →

SNOWPIX.COM / CHRIS GILL

KEY FACTS

Resort	675m
	2,210ft
Altitude	655-2285m
	2,140-7,490ft
Lifts	33
Pistes	7,071 acres
Green	18%
Blue	55%
Black	27%
Snowmaking	
	565 acres

Both centres are traffic-free. The architecture is varied and, for a purpose-built resort, quite tasteful. There are lots of chalet-style apartments on the hillsides. The centres have individually designed wood and concrete buildings, blended together around pedestrian streets and squares. There are no monstrous high-rise blocks – but there are a lot of large five- or six-storey hotel and apartment buildings.

Whistler Village has most of the bars, restaurants and shops, and the two main gondolas (one to each mountain). Whistler North, further from the lifts, is newer and has virtually merged with the original village, making a huge car-free area of streets lined with shops, condos and restaurants. Upper Village is much smaller and quieter. Its huge Fairmont Chateau Whistler hotel dominates the views of the village from the mountain.

Whistler Creek, a 10-minute bus-ride from Whistler Village, is rather out on a limb, with limited bars and restaurants. But it's being developed fast and more readers are staying there now.

There is a free bus between Whistler and Upper Village but, if you're staying near the base of Blackcomb, it's just as quick to walk. Staying further out means paying for buses or taxis – which are not expensive. Some hotels have free shuttle-buses, which you can get to pick you up as well as take you to restaurants and nightlife.

The most convenient place to stay is Whistler Village as you can access either mountain by gondola. Whistler Creek, though convenient for Whistler's slopes, is less so for Blackcomb and is pretty quiet. A lot of accommodation is an inconvenient walk or bus-ride from the villages and slopes.

Whistler is now getting very crowded and some reporters have found the central area around Village Square very noisy in the early hours and complained of rowdy behaviour, especially at peak holiday periods.

boarding

Both mountains are excellent for every level of boarder. All the main lifts are chairs and gondolas and terrain ranges from gentle green runs to wide open bowls and heart-stopping cliff drops and chutes. And snowboarders have one advantage over skiers in Whistler – when the snow gets slushy lower down, it's easier and more fun to ride it on a board! There are T-bars on the glacier, but they're not vicious and any discomfort is worth it for the powder. The resort is popular with snowboarders and known for its summer boarding camps. The school runs a lot of specialist classes, including freestyle lessons and women's camps, and last season Canada's Olympic gold medallist, Ross Rebagliati, joined the team of coaches – he's available on request. The resort regularly hosts big snowboard events so it's not uncommon to see pro riders. Specialist snowboard shops include Showcase and Katmandu Boards.

THE MOUNTAINS

The area has acquired a formidable and well-deserved reputation among experts. But both Whistler and Blackcomb also have loads of well-groomed intermediate terrain. Together they have over 200 marked trails, and form the biggest area of slopes, with the longest runs, in North America.

Many reporters enthuse about the mountain host service and the 'go slow' patrol – some find the latter 'over zealous', but crowded slopes, especially on the runs home ('a human slalom'), mean they're often needed. Reporters also comment on the early closing times for lifts (3pm until end-January, 3.30 in February and 4pm thereafter). Upper lifts may close earlier.

THE SLOPES
The best in North America
Whistler Mountain is accessed from Whistler Village by a two-stage, 10-person gondola that rises over 1100m/3,610ft to Roundhouse Lodge, the main mid-mountain base. There is an alternative of two consecutive fast quads, which take you slightly lower; they make a good alternative when lines for the gondola are long.

Runs back down through the trees fan out from the gondola – cruises to the Emerald and Big Red fast chairs, longer runs to the gondola mid-station.

From Roundhouse you can see the jewel in Whistler's crown – magnificent above-the-tree-line bowls, served by the fast Peak and Harmony quads. The bowls are mostly go-anywhere terrain for experts but there are groomed trails, so anyone can appreciate the views.

A six-person gondola from Whistler Creek also accesses Whistler Mountain.

Access to **Blackcomb** from Whistler Village is by an eight-seater gondola, followed by a fast quad. From the base of Blackcomb you take two consecutive fast quads up to the main Rendezvous restaurant. From the arrival points you can go left for great cruising terrain and the Glacier Express quad up to the Horstman Glacier area, or right for steeper slopes, the terrain-park or the 7th Heaven chair. The 1610m/5,280ft vertical from the top of this chair to the base is the largest in North America (and big even by Alpine standards). Or you can go into the glacier area. A T-bar from the Horstman Glacier brings you (with a very short hike) to the Blackcomb Glacier in the next valley – a beautiful run which takes you away from all lifts.

Fresh Tracks is a deal that allows you to ride up Whistler Mountain (at extra cost) from 7.15, have a buffet breakfast and hit the slopes as soon as they open – very popular with many of our reporters. A good tip is to hit the slopes first and breakfast after – otherwise you may miss the quietest time on the slopes.

Blackcomb has floodlit beginner slopes a couple of nights a week. Free guided tours of each mountain are offered twice a day.

TERRAIN-PARKS
For high-fliers and mere mortals
The resort has an array of different-ability parks. Novices can start in the Big Easy Terrain Garden on Blackcomb, with its unthreatening rails, rollers and hits. Next up in terms of difficulty is the new improved Whistler park, on the Chipmunk run, with lots of rails, plus there's a half-pipe at the top of the Emerald chair. The main park on Blackcomb, next to the Catskinner chair, has slightly bigger hits and rails, fun-boxes, hips, spines and banks, and leads to a monster-sized super-pipe. True experts can head into the Higher Level park, half-way down the main park – to be allowed in you need to wear a helmet and buy a special pass.

LIFT PASSES

Whistler/Blackcomb
Covers all lifts on both Whistler and Blackcomb mountains.

Beginners
Day pass for Magic Chair only.

Main pass
1-day pass C$70
6-day pass C$398

Senior citizens
Over 65: 6-day pass C$338

Children
Under 19: 6-day pass C$338
Under 13: 6-day pass C$199
Under 7: free pass

Notes
Half-day pass available.

SNOW RELIABILITY
Excellent at altitude

Snow conditions at the top are usually excellent – the place gets around 360 inches of snow a year, on average. But because the resort is low and close to the Pacific, the bottom slopes can be wet, icy or unskiable. People may 'download' from the mid-stations due to poor snow, especially in late season.

FOR EXPERTS
Few can rival it

Whistler Mountain's bowls are enough to keep experts happy for weeks. Each has endless variations, with chutes and gullies of varied steepness and width. The biggest challenges are around Glacier, Whistler and West Bowls, with runs such as The Cirque and Doom & Gloom – though you can literally go anywhere in this high, wide area.

Blackcomb has challenging slopes too; not so extensive as Whistler's, but some are more challenging. From the top of the 7th Heaven lift, traverse to Xhiggy's Meadow, for sunny bowl runs.

If you're feeling brave, go in the opposite direction and drop into the extremely steep chutes down towards Glacier Creek, including the infamous 41° Couloir Extreme, which can have moguls the size of elephants at the top. Or try the also serious, but less frequented, steep bowls reached by

hiking up Spanky's Ladder, after taking the Glacier Express lift.

Both mountains have challenging trails through trees. The adventurous can explore the 'Peak to Creek' trails, from below Whistler's West Bowl to Whistler Creek – still outside the area boundary, so rescues are costly. If all this isn't enough, there's also out-of-bounds backcountry guiding available (see Schools and Guides section), and local heli-skiing available by the day.

FOR INTERMEDIATES
Ideal and extensive terrain

Both mountains are an intermediate's paradise. In good weather, good intermediates will enjoy the less extreme variations in the bowls on both mountains.

One of our favourite intermediate runs is down the Blackcomb Glacier, from the top of the mountain to the bottom of the Excelerator chair over 1000m/3,280ft below. This 5km/3 mile run, away from all lifts, starts with a two-minute walk up from the top of the Showcase T-bar. You drop over the ridge into a wide, wide bowl – not too suddenly or you'll get a short, sharp shock in the very steep double-diamond Blowhole. The further you traverse, the shallower the slope.

You are guaranteed good snow on the Horstman Glacier too, and typically

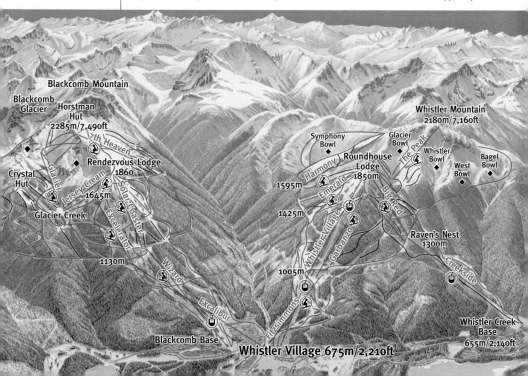

gentle runs. The blue runs served by the 7th Heaven chair are 'heavenly on a sunny day', as a reporter put it. Lower down there are lots of perfect cruising runs through the trees – ideal when the weather is bad.

On Whistler Mountain, there are easy blue pistes in Symphony, Harmony and Glacier bowls. Even early intermediates should try them, since there's always an easy way down. The Saddle run from the top of the Harmony Express lift is a favourite with many of our reporters. The blue Highway 86 path, which skirts West Bowl from the top of the Peak chair, has beautiful views over a steep valley and across to the rather phallic Black Tusk mountain. The green Burnt Stew Trail also has great views.

Lower down the mountain there is a vast choice of groomed blue runs with a series of efficient fast chairs to bring you back up to the top of the gondola. It's a cruiser's paradise – especially the aptly named Ego Bowl. A great long run is the fabulous Dave Murray Downhill all the way from mid-mountain to the finish at Whistler Creek. Although marked black on the map, it's a wonderful fast and varied cruise when it has been groomed.

FOR BEGINNERS
OK if the sun shines

Whistler has excellent nursery slopes by the mid-station of the gondola, as does Blackcomb, down at the base area. Both have facilities higher up too.

The map has a guide to easy runs, and slow zones are marked. On Whistler, after progressing from the nursery slopes, there are some gentle first runs from the top of the gondola. Their downside is other people speeding past. You can return by various chairs or continue to the base area on greens. Check the latter are in good condition first, and maybe avoid them at the end of the day, when they can get very crowded.

On Blackcomb, Green Line runs from the top of the mountain to the bottom. The top part is particularly gentle, with some steeper pitches lower down. As a recent reporter said, 'A tentative beginner in our group found it hard to move around with confidence because of the varying steepness of green runs.'

Another reservation is – you guessed – the weather. Beginners don't get a lot out of heavy snowfalls, and might be put off by rain and unpredictable conditions.

SCHOOLS

**Whistler and
Blackcomb**
t 932 3434

Extremely Canadian
t 938 9656

Classes
(Whistler and
Blackcomb prices)
3 days: C$415

Private lessons
Half day (3hr): C$405

GUIDES

Whistler Guides
t 938 3228

FOR CROSS-COUNTRY
Picturesque but low
There are over 28km/17 miles of cross-country tracks around Lost Lake, starting in the valley by the river, on the path between Whistler and Blackcomb. But it is low altitude here, so conditions can be unreliable. There's a specialist school, Cross-Country Connection (905 0071) offering lessons, tours and rental. Keen cross-country merchants can catch the train to better areas.

QUEUES
An ever-increasing problem
Whistler is becoming a victim of its own success. Even with 15 fast lifts – more than any other resort in North America – the mountains are queue-prone, especially at weekends when people pour in from Vancouver. There are noticeboards displaying waiting times at different lifts, but most people would prefer shorter queues.

Some reporters have signed up with the ski school just to get lift priority. Others have visited Vancouver at the weekend to avoid the crowds.

The routes out of Whistler Village in the morning can be busy. Whistler Creek is less of a problem. Some of the chairs higher up both mountains produce long queues – especially Harmony (where even the singles line seems to take ages). And we had a report of a 45-minute wait for The Peak chair on an early-January 2003 Sunday. Visiting the resort outside peak season may not help – we found some lifts, including the gondola to Blackcomb, were kept closed in an early-December visit and readers have also reported closed lifts in late season. Crowds on the slopes, especially the runs home, can be annoying too.

MOUNTAIN RESTAURANTS
Overcrowded
The main restaurants sell decent, good-value food but are charmless self-service stops with long queues. They're huge, but not huge enough. 'Seat-seekers' are employed to find spaces, but success is not guaranteed.

Past reporters have stressed the need to lunch early. But even that no longer works – 'They're packed by 11.30,' say recent reporters. Late lunches don't work either, because the lifts close early; so the answer may be a big breakfast, ski through the day and snack later.

Blackcomb has the Rendezvous, mainly a big (850-seat) self-service place but also home to Christine's, a table-service restaurant – the best on either mountain. Glacier Creek Lodge, at the bottom of the Glacier Express, is a better self-service place. But even this (1,496 seats) gets incredibly crowded. Whistler has the massive (1,740-seat) Roundhouse Lodge; Steeps Grill is its table-service refuge.

Reporters generally prefer the smaller places – but they're still packed unless you time it right, and may be closed early and late season. On Blackcomb, Crystal Hut at the top of the Crystal Ridge chair and Horstman Hut at the top of the mountain are tiny with great views. On Whistler, Raven's Nest, at the top of the Creekside gondola, is a small and friendly deli/cafe. And the Chic Pea near the top of the Garbanzo chair-lift is 'funky and rustic' for pizza and barbecue. There's also the Harmony Hut, specialising in stews and cider, at the top of the Harmony lift. You can of course descend to the base – the table-service Dusty's at Whistler Creek has good sandwiches and soup and doesn't get too crowded. There's also a Snack-Shack on each mountain, if all you fancy is a quick drink and hot-dog.

Whistler

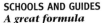

CHILDREN

Whistler Kids (1-800 766 0449) takes non-skiing children aged 3 months to 3 years. It also offers various skiing and snowboarding programmes to children of all ability levels, aged 3 to 17. The Kids' Adventure Camp is a 5-day camp for 3 to 12 year olds. Ride Tribe is a programme for ages 13 to 17.

One 6hr-day including lunch, lift ticket and equipment rental: C$116 for 3 to 4 year-olds.

Après-ski programmes – with a 'Kids' Night Out' – are offered during the season.

GETTING THERE

Air Vancouver 115km/71 miles (2hr).

SCHOOLS AND GUIDES
A great formula

Ski Esprit and Ride Esprit programmes run for three or four days and combine instruction with showing you around the mountains – with the same instructor daily. Many of our reporters have joined these groups (usually small), and all reports are glowing: 'Big improvement in confidence and skill' is typical. There are specialist clinics and snowboard classes, too.

Extremely Canadian specialises in guiding and coaching adventurous advanced intermediates upwards in Whistler's steep and deep terrain. A lot of its coaches compete in free-ride and skier-cross competitions. We have been with them a few times and they really are great! As a reporter said, 'You end up skiing places that other people don't even know about – we were very impressed.' They run two- and four-day clinics and also have their own catered chalet you can stay at.

Backcountry day trips or overnight touring are available with Whistler Guides.

FACILITIES FOR CHILDREN
Impressive

Blackcomb's base area has a special slow-moving Magic Chair to get children part-way up the mountain. Whistler's gondola mid-station has a splendid kids-only area. A reporter found the staff 'friendly and instilled confidence'.

Kids Adventure Zones feature castles and forts, enchanted forests and animals to keep them entertained. A recent reporter was enthusiastic about 'climb and dine', where children can spend a few fun hours at the climbing centre, including a meal, while parents go out to eat.

STAYING THERE

HOW TO GO
High quality packages

A lot of British tour operators go to Whistler and some run catered chalets. A new centralised online booking service run by the resort at www.mywhistler.com started last season.

Hotels There is a very wide range.

((((5 **Fairmont Chateau Whistler** (938 8000) Well run and luxurious at the foot of Blackcomb. Excellent spa with pools and tubs. The Gold floor is expensive and especially cosseting.

((((5 **Westin Resort & Spa** (905 5000) Luxury all-suite hotel at the foot of Whistler mountain next to the lifts.

((((4 **Pan Pacific Lodge** (905 2999) Luxury all-suite place at Whistler Village base. Pool/sauna/tub.

((((4 **Lost Lake Lodge** (932 2882) 'Excellent' place: studios and suites, out by the golf course. Pool/tub.

((((4 **Crystal Lodge** (932 2221) 'Comfortable, friendly, convenient', in Whistler Village. Pool/sauna/tub.

(((3 **Glacier Lodge** (932 2882) In Upper Village. 'Big rooms, quiet area, recommended.' Pool/tub.

Self-catering There are plenty of spacious, comfortable condominiums in both chalet and hotel-style blocks.

EATING OUT
High quality and plenty of choice

Reporters are enthusiastic about the range, quality and value of places to eat, but do book well ahead: there simply aren't enough restaurant seats to meet demand. Some cheaper places won't take bookings for small groups, meaning long waits. One 2003 reporter 'gave up trying to find a table at Easter weekend and ate in the hotel bar'. Bars serve decent food, too. But if you've got kids, as one reporter found, 'Some places don't allow under-19s in, or even to sit outside, and we had to

↑ Mid-mountain on Whistler with the massive Roundhouse Lodge mountain restaurant. Groomed wooded trails lie below and high open bowls above

SNOWPIX.COM / CHRIS GILL

ACTIVITIES

Indoor Ice skating, museum, tennis, hot-tubs

Outdoor Flightseeing, heli-skiing, snow-shoe excursions, snowmobiling, paragliding, fishing, horse-riding, sleigh rides, guided tours

Phone numbers
From distant parts of Canada, add the prefix 1 604.
From abroad, add the prefix +1 604.

TOURIST OFFICE

t 932 3928
www.mywhistler.com
www.whistler-blackcomb.com

wait up to two hours elsewhere.' This depends on the licence – bars that serve food tend not to allow under-19s, but those classed as restaurants do.

At the top of the market, Umberto's in Whistler Village has classy Italian cuisine. The Rimrock Café at Whistler Creek serves 'the best seafood we have ever eaten', says a reporter.

Good mid-market Whistler Village places include Araxi (Italian/Pacific), the Keg (steak and seafood), Teppan Village (Japanese), Mongolie (Asian) and Kipriaki Norte (Greek). Crab Shack has good-value seafood.

Reporters have also suggested La Bocca (Italian: 'excellent home-made pasta, good value') and the Bearfoot Bistro (European: 'the best gourmet restaurant, with a stellar wine list').

In Village North: the good-value Brewhouse has great atmosphere (steaks, burgers), Caramba has 'good Mediterranean food at reasonable prices', and the Tandoori Grill has 'Indian just like at home'. Hy's Steakhouse has the best steaks. Sushi-Ya, and Quattro (Italian) are good.

In Upper Village, Thai One On is 'excellent', and Monk's Grill has 'very good steaks'.

There are plenty of budget places, including the bars mentioned under Après-ski. Uli's Flipside at Whistler Creek and The Old Spaghetti Factory in Whistler Village ('very good value') have been recommended for pasta.

APRES-SKI
Something for most tastes
Whistler is very lively. Most of the après bars seem to compete to see who can serve the biggest dustbin lid of nachos. Popular at Whistler are the Longhorn, with a huge terrace, and the Garibaldi Lift Company. The Dubh Linn Gate Irish pub has 'great live music and Guinness'. Tapley's seems 'the nearest thing to a locals' bar'. Merlin's is the focus at Blackcomb base, though readers also recommend the Monk's Grill, and Dusty's is the place at Whistler Creek – good beer, loud music.

Later on, Buffalo Bill's is lively and loud and the Amsterdam is worth a look. The Cinnamon Bear in the Delta Resort hotel is a sports bar with live music. Tommy Africa's, Maxx Fish, the Savage Beagle, Garfinkel's and Moe Joe's are the main clubs. Try the Mallard bar in Chateau Whistler and the Crystal Lodge piano bar for a quieter time.

Bars and clubs are for over-19s only, and readers have found it's advisable to carry age ID. Smoking is generally not allowed in bars, although most have a smoking area outside, sometimes heated. Garfinkel's and the Mallard have inside smoking areas.

OFF THE SLOPES
Not ideal
Whistler is a long way to go if you don't intend to hit the slopes. Meadow Park Sports Centre has a full range of fitness facilities. There are also several luxurious spas. Reporters have recommended walks around the lake, the Great Wall Underground climbing centre and a shop where you can paint your own pottery. There's an eight-screen cinema in Whistler Village. And Ziptrek Ecotours (935 0001), new for last season, offers three-hour ecological journeys through the forest between Whistler and Blackcomb mountains, using cables and suspension bridges. Excursions to Squamish (famous for its eagles) are easy. A day trip to Vancouver is recommended.

Whistler

631

For us the main attraction of skiing or riding in eastern Canada is the French culture and language that are predominant in the province of Québec. It really feels like a different country from the rest of Canada – as indeed many of its residents want it to become. It is also only a six-hour flight from the UK, compared with ten for Canada's west. Tremblant is the main destination resort and is one of the cutest purpose-built resorts we've seen (though it is now in danger of being spoiled by expansion). The other main base is Québec city, which dates from the 17th century and is full of atmosphere and Canadian history. Slopes of the main resorts are small both in extent and in vertical drop, and the weather can be perishingly cold in early and mid-winter. But at least this means that the extensive snowmaking systems that all the resorts have can be effective for a long season. Be prepared for variable snow conditions and don't go expecting light, dry powder – if that's what you want, head west.

There are lots of ski and snowboard areas in Ontario – Canada's most populated province – but most of them are tiny and cater just for locals. For people heading on holiday for a week or more, eastern Canada really means the province of Québec. Québec and its capital, Québec city, are heavily dominated by the French culture and language. Notices, menus, trail maps and so on are usually printed in both French and English. Many ski area workers are bilingual or just French-speaking. And French cuisine abounds.

The weather is very variable, rather like New England's – but it can get even colder. Hence the snow, though pretty much guaranteed by snowmaking, can vary enormously in quality. When we were there one April we were slush skiing in Tremblant one day and rattling along on a rock-hard surface in Mont-Ste-Anne the next. One

reporter who visited Mont-Ste-Anne, Stoneham and Le Massif in late January experienced mild temperatures and several perfect blue-sky days.

The main destination resort is Tremblant (see separate chapter), about 90 minutes' drive from Montreal. Other areas near here popular with locals include **Mont Blanc** (with only 300m/980ft of vertical, hardly a competitor to the Franco-Italian version) and the **Saint-Sauveur** valley (five areas, each with around 200m/660ft of vertical and with interchangeable lift passes).

The other main place to stay for easy access to several ski resorts is **Québec city**. Old Québec, at the city's heart, is North America's only walled city and is a World Heritage site. Within the city walls are narrow, winding streets and 17th and 18th century houses. It is situated right on

JEAN VAUDREUIL

Stoneham is just 20 minutes from the centre of Québec city and has condos and a smart base lodge right by the mountain
→

TOURIST OFFICES

Mont Blanc
www.ski-mont-blanc.
com
Saint-Sauveur
www.montsaintauveur
.com
Québec city
www.quebecregion.
com
Mont-Ste-Anne
www.mont-sainte-
anne.com
Stoneham
www.ski-stoneham.
com.
Le Massif
www.lemassif.com

CHRISTIAN TREMBLAY

Québec city is a World Heritage site and has three ski areas nearby, all covered on one lift pass ➔

the banks of the St Lawrence river. In January/February there is a famous two-week carnival, with an ice castle, snow sculptures, dog-sled and canoe races, night parades and grand balls. But most of the winter is low season for Québec city, with good-value rooms available in big hotels. Because of this, the area is popular with British school groups, especially in late season. Non-skiers, or those who like the option to do other activities, won't be bored whatever time of year they go.

There are several ski and snowboard areas close to Québec city, and a Carte Blanche pass which covers the three main areas: a total of 106 runs, 26 lifts and Canada's largest night skiing area. A car is handy, but there are buses to some areas.

The biggest and most varied area (though easily skied in a day by a good skier) is **Mont-Ste-Anne**, 30 minutes away and with some accommodation of its own. A gondola takes you to the top, and slopes lead down the front (south) and back (north) sides. The views from the front over the ice-flows of the St Lawrence are spectacular. There are intermediate cruising runs on both sides and some steep blacks (including World Cup runs) through the trees on the front among its 63km/39 miles of trails. There are some easy top-to-bottom runs and good nursery slopes at the base. In spring you can stop by the Sugar Shack and try fresh maple toffee. The resort has two terrain-parks, including a 600m/1,950ft boarder-cross course. Fifteen trails are floodlit until 10pm seven nights a week (five in January). Over 80% of the runs are covered by snowmaking. It also has the largest cross-country centre in Canada, with 223km/139 miles of trails.

Stoneham is the closest resort to Québec city, around 20 minutes away. It also has its own small village with accommodation and an impressive base lodge with bar, restaurant and big wooden deck. Après-ski in the lodge can be lively, and there is often live music. It is a small area, with only around 30km/20 miles of runs spread between three faces and a vertical of 420m/1,380ft. But it is very sheltered in a sunny setting protected from wind. It suits families well, with mainly intermediate and beginner terrain. It has a special learn to ski area equipped with a moving carpet. Snowboarders, freestylers and

freeskiers are attracted to the area by the resort's impressive terrain-park with 15 rails and ten table-tops, its 1000m/3,300ft boarder-cross course, and a super-pipe that meets the requirements for international freestyle competitions. A recent reporter raved about how addictive it was. Stoneham also has the biggest night-skiing operation in Canada, with two of the three faces lit top to bottom. Some 85% of the area has snowmaking.

Le Massif is around an hour away from Québec city and is a cult area with locals. It is in a UNESCO World Biosphere Reserve, and is just metres from the St Lawrence. The views of the ice-flows are stunning, and you feel you are heading straight down into them when you are on the pretty, tree-lined trails.

The area of slopes, though small, has the largest vertical drop in the east. There are a couple of steep double black diamond runs and some good, well-groomed black and blue cruising runs. They have recently added Québec's longest high-speed quad chair and extended their double chair. And 16 new runs have been added to the area, including beginner and intermediate runs and one designed to meet International Ski Federation World Cup standards.

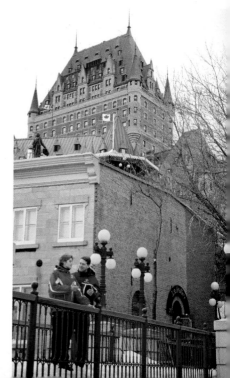

Tremblant

Charming, traffic-free village at the foot of a small area of slopes

RATINGS

The slopes

Snow	****
Extent	*
Expert	**
Intermediate	***
Beginner	****
Convenience	****
Queues	***
Mountain restaurants	**

The rest

Scenery	***
Resort charm	****
Off-slope	***

NEWS

For 2003/04 there will be two new runs on the North Side: a long blue and a black. A second terrain-park is also planned, this time on the South Side. There will also be a new hotel, the 5-star Quintessence.

For 2002/03, the snowmaking was increased again, taking the total up to 76% of trails. A new gladed run was opened at the Edge.

634

➕ Charming purpose-built core village

➕ Slope-side accommodation

➕ Good snow reliability with extensive artificial back-up

➕ Some good runs for all abilities

➕ Good variety of restaurants and bars

➖ Limited area for keen piste-bashers

➖ Can be perishingly cold in midwinter

➖ Weekend queues and overcrowding

➖ New building on edge not in keeping with cute original style – and huge expansion plans

Tremblant is eastern Canada's main destination resort and attracts quite a lot of Brits. But for keen piste-bashers the limited slopes don't really do justice to the cute and lively little core village, which has been built in traditional style.

THE RESORT

Tremblant has been transformed in recent years from a day or weekend ski area for locals to being eastern Canada's leading ski resort. Intrawest (which also owns Whistler and several other North American resorts) developed a charming purpose-built village in the traditional style of old Québec. Buildings in bright, vibrant colours line narrow, cobbled traffic-free streets and squares, and it has a very French feel to it with lots of galleries, boutiques, patisseries and cafes – and French is the first language here. Recent development on the edge of the resort has been of more modern large hotels and condos which contrast sharply with the original development – and there's a 10-year plan to triple the resort's size. Plans include slope-side villages at both North Side and Versant Soleil, where there is currently not even an access road.

THE MOUNTAINS

In its small area, Tremblant has a good variety of pleasantly wooded terrain.
Slopes A heated gondola takes you to the top, from where there are good views over the village and a 14km/9 mile lake on the so-called South Side, and over National Park wilderness on the North Side. The North Side is really north-east facing and gets the morning sun – a high-speed quad brings you back and there are two other chairs to play on. The slow Edge lift accesses another summit, serving mainly expert terrain. Back on the South Side (really south-west facing and so good for the afternoon sun) you can go right back to town on blue or green runs, or use two high-speed quads to explore the top and bottom halves. The Versant Soleil area is more directly south-facing and has one top-to-bottom blue run with all the rest being black runs and tree runs. The Porte du Soleil lift goes

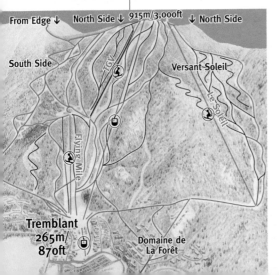

Tremblant
265m/
870ft

From Edge ↓   North Side ↓ 915m/3,000ft   ↓ North Side

South Side

Versant Soleil

TGV

Le Soleil

Flying Mile

Domaine de La Forêt

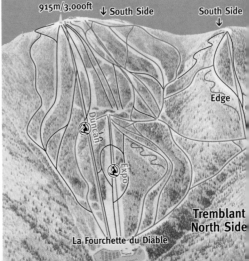

Tremblant
North Side

915m/3,000ft   ↓ South Side   South Side ↓

Edge

Duncan

EXPO

La Fourchette du Diable

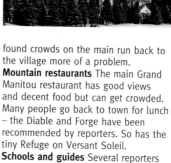

Typical Tremblant: brightly coloured buildings in traditional style and snowmaking going on up the mountain ↗

TREMBLANT RESORT

KEY FACTS

Resort	265m/870ft
Slopes	230-875m
	750-2,870ft
Lifts	13
Pistes	75km
	47 miles
Green	17%
Blue	33%
Black	50%
Snowmaking	76%

Central reservations phone number
Call 425 8681.

Phone numbers
From distant parts of Canada, add the prefix 1 819.
From abroad, add the prefix +1 819.

TOURIST OFFICE

t 681 2000
info_tremblant@intra west.com
www.tremblant.ca

from the Domaine de la Forêt area of town and allows you to access both Versant Soleil and the South Side.
Terrain-parks The excellent 18-acre Gravité terrain-park and half-pipe are on the top half of the North Side. There are some seriously big kickers and berms, and a variety of rails for experts and intermediates. At the bottom is the mini Gravité park – much less intimidating if it's your first time. The resort is planning a third terrain-park for 2003/04, on the South Side.
Snow reliability Usually, Canada's east coast doesn't get as much snow as the west, but over 75% of the trails are covered by snowmaking – claimed to be 'the most powerful in North America'. The grooming is excellent.
Experts Half the runs are classified as suitable for advanced skiers and riders. But we found many of the blacks did not deserve their grading. There are steep top-to-bottom bump runs on the North Side and great gladed tree runs off the Edge lift. The Versant Soleil area has more black runs and some tough runs in the trees. However, the gladed runs really need decent, and preferably fresh, snow to be fun.
Intermediates Both North and South Sides have good cruising and we found the North Side less crowded. There are blue-classified runs in the trees as well as on groomed trails.
Beginners The 2-acre beginner area is excellent and there are long, easy top-to-bottom green runs to progress to on both North and South Sides.
Snowboarding The slopes are good for beginners, but better boarders can't count on fresh natural snow to play in. A specialist shop, Adrénaline, runs a Burton learn-to-ride programme.
Cross-country There are around 100km/62 miles of trails, some at the top of the mountain, with great views.
Queues At weekends there can be lines but they tend to move quickly. We

found crowds on the main run back to the village more of a problem.
Mountain restaurants The main Grand Manitou restaurant has good views and decent food but can get crowded. Many people go back to town for lunch – the Diable and Forge have been recommended by reporters. So has the tiny Refuge on Versant Soleil.
Schools and guides Several reporters have praised the school highly.
Facilities for children Children from age one to 12 can be cared for until 9.30pm.

STAYING THERE

How to go There's no shortage of packages from the UK.
Hotels and condos Many reporters stay at the luxurious Fairmont Tremblant, right by the slopes, and praise it highly. Self-catering readers have recommended the condos in the Place St Bernard, the Tour des Voyagers and the Chouette. Several have warned that the nearest supermarket is in Saint Jovite, a car or bus-ride away.
Eating out There is a good variety of restaurants – recommended are the Forge, the Ya'ooo Pizza Bar and Mexicali Rosa's. The Loup Garou at the Fairmont is excellent.
Après-ski There are several lively bars. Octobar is popular with the Brits, and the Forge is good just after the slopes close. The Shack brews its own beer. There is often live music and a good atmosphere in the main square. There are floodlit slopes some nights.
Off the slopes The Acquaclub La Source pool complex resembles a lake set in a forest, and has been enjoyed by readers with families, though it's 'fairly expensive for the facilities offered'. You can also go ice-climbing, horse-riding, ice skating, snow-shoeing, snowmobiling, dog-sledding and swimming – and visit Montreal (highly recommended by one reader).

Spain

These days it's dangerous to generalise about Spanish resorts – which is why we don't provide the lists of ✚ and ▬ points that we do for other second-division countries. There are now some well equipped Pyrenean resorts with fine, snow-sure slopes that compare favourably with mid-sized places in the Alps. Two resorts are certainly not downmarket – Sierra Nevada and Baqueira-Beret (see next chapter) are both frequented by the King of Spain. Winter sports are becoming more popular with the prosperous Spanish themselves, and as a result many of the smaller resorts are continually improving.

TOURIST OFFICES

Sierra Nevada
www.sierranevadaski.com
Formigal
www.formigal.com
Candanchu
www.candanchu.com
Astún
www.astun.com
La Molina
www.lamolina.com

The general ambience of Spanish resorts is attractive – not unlike that of Italy, with eating, posing and partying taken seriously.

Sierra Nevada (2100m/6,890ft) is in the extreme south of Spain, between Granada and the Costa del Sol, with views from the very top to the Atlas mountains in Morocco.

The hub of the resort is Pradollano, a stylish modern development with shops and a few restaurants and bars set around traffic-free open spaces – likened by one reporter to Whistler. There is a huge but expensive underground car-park here, and parking elsewhere can be difficult.

Most of the accommodation is in older, less smart buildings set along a road winding up the steep hillside. A two-stage chair-lift also goes up the hillside, with red runs back down to the main lift stations at Pradollano. Choose your location with care; the hotel Telecabina is, not surprisingly, ideally placed for the gondolas and is also 'warm, friendly, with good food'.

From Pradollano an old 4-person gondola and a newer 10-person one go up to Borreguiles, at the heart of the slopes. Here there are excellent nursery slopes, and lifts going up to the broad upper slopes beneath the peak of Veleta. There are three identifiable sectors, well linked, with a good range of easy and intermediate runs, some reasonably long. But it is not a big area, and there is not a lot for experts.

Queues develop at Pradollano when buses arrive from lower towns, and higher up there are quite a lot of slow old lifts that cause queues at ski school time and after lunch. The chair up the village slope gets the biggest queues of all. Most chairs have singles lines, though.

Sierra Nevada's weather can be a problem. The resort's natural snow arrives via completely different weather patterns from those supplying the Alps and the Pyrenees; in 1990, when the Alps were disastrously snowless, Sierra Nevada had the best conditions in Europe. But the much-fêted World Championships in the mid-1990s had to be postponed by a year. Although the resort has state-of-the-art snowmaking, high temperatures rendered it useless. The slopes face generally north-west, but some get the full force of the afternoon sun. And when the wind blows, as it does, the slopes close; there are no trees.

An outing to Granada – a 45-minute drive down a winding road – is a must.

There is a group of worthwhile resorts in the western Pyrenees, between Pau and Huesca.

Formigal is working hard to improve its standing. There has been recent expansion and a number of lift improvements but the 57km/35 miles of pistes are windswept. When the wind blows, retreat to nearby Panticosa – a charming old village with sheltered but limited slopes that have recently doubled in size to 34km/21 miles of pistes. **Candanchu** and nearby **Astún**, with almost 100km/62 miles of pistes between them, are popular on the Spanish market. They offer a wide range of lodging set in some of the Pyrenees' most stunning scenery. Candanchu has some tough runs.

The other resorts of international interest are just east of Andorra. The 50km/31 miles of runs at **La Molina** and its purpose-built satellite Supermolina (1700m/5,580ft) are now linked to those of Masella, over the mountain, via a gondola and six-pack. The whole area, called Alp 2500, now extends over 100km/62 miles of mainly intermediate skiing.

Baqueira-Beret

Spain's leading winter resort – fit for their king

COSTS

① ② ③ ④ ⑤ ⑥

RATINGS

The slopes
Snow	***
Extent	**
Expert	***
Intermediate	****
Beginner	**
Convenience	***
Queues	***
Mountain restaurants	**

The rest
Scenery	***
Resort charm	**
Off-slope	*

KEY FACTS

Resort	1500m
	4,920ft
Slopes	1500-2515m
	4,920-8,250ft
Lifts	28
Pistes	88km
	55 miles
Green	8%
Blue	47%
Red	37%
Black	8%
Snowmaking	35km
	22 miles

+ Compact modern resort

+ Efficient lifts with few queues

+ Reasonable snow reliability

+ Some good off-piste potential

+ Lots of good intermediate slopes

+ Friendly, helpful locals

− Drab high-rise blocks dominate the main village, though new developments are more attractive

− Resort is not cleverly laid out, and suffers from traffic around the lift base station

− Few off-slope diversions

Baqueira is in a different league from other resorts in the Spanish Pyrenees – a smart, family-oriented resort with a wide area of north-facing slopes that gives a real feeling of travel. It attracts an almost entirely Spanish clientele (which regularly includes the royal family), so don't count on English being spoken.

THE RESORT

Baqueira was purpose-built in the 1960s and has its fair share of drab, high-rise blocks; these are clustered below the road that runs through to the high pass of Port de la Bonaigua, while the main lift base is just above it. But up the steep hill from the main base are some newer, smaller-scale stone-clad developments. At the very top is an alternative chair-lift into the slopes. The most convenient base is close to the main chair-lift, but the village is small enough for location not to be too much of an issue. There is a lot of accommodation spread down the valley, and a big car park with road-train shuttle up to the lift base.

Baqueira packs a lot of accommodation into the tight valley bottom at the lift base ↓

THE MOUNTAINS

There is an extensive area of long, mainly intermediate, runs, practically all of them on open, treeless slopes and facing roughly west.

Slopes The slopes are split into three distinct but well-connected areas – Baqueira, Beret and Bonaigua. From the base station at Baqueira, a fast quad which you ride without skis (which fit in slots in the back of the chair in front) takes you up to the nursery slopes at 1800m/5,910ft. Fast chairs go on up to Cap de Baqueira. From here there is a wide variety of long runs, served by chairs and drags – including, imminently, a new black down to Orri. From several points you can descend into the Argulls valley and the Bonaigua sector, leading over to the summit of the Bonaigua pass. If all goes to plan, you will now be able to ride a chair from the pass to get to a new slope descending to the east of the pass. From the opposite extremity of the Baqueira sector at Orri a triple chair takes you off to the Beret sector, where a series of more-or-less parallel chairs serve mainly blue and red runs. A fast quad and a drag-lift serve a fourth sector across the valley from the Beret slopes, with three blue and a red piste. Beret, Orri and Bonaigua are accessible by road.

Terrain-parks There's a terrain park with half-pipe in the Beret area.

Snow reliability Most of the slopes are above 1800m/5,910ft and there is extensive snowmaking, but afternoon sun is a problem in spring. Grooming is good – too good for one reporter.

NEWS

For 2003/04 there are plans to expand the slopes beyond Port de la Bonaigua, including new access into the system via a new fast quad on the east side of the pass. The existing Bonaigua double chair will also be replaced by a fast quad.

On Cap de Baqueira the Luis Arias drag is being replaced by a chair, with a new 'spectacular' black piste beneath it.

The beginners' area at Baqueira and the two children's areas are now served by moving carpets.

Phone numbers
From abroad use the prefix +34.

TOURIST OFFICE

t 973 639000
baqueira@baqueira.es
www.baqueira.es

Experts Experts will find few on-piste challenges, but there's plenty of off-piste, some needing guidance. The Escornacrabes itinerary, from the top of Cap de Baqueira, is steep and narrow. Cheap heli-lifts are available.

Intermediates It's excellent, with lots of varied blues and some classic long red runs such as Muntanyo down to Port de la Bonaigua and Mirador above town. Less daring intermediates will enjoy the Beret section and the Argulls valley runs best.

Beginners There are some good nursery runs above Baqueira but some of the blues you move on to can be a bit tough. Beret (reachable by road) has an excellent nursery slope and gentle blues.

Snowboarding The main nursery slopes are served by drags and some blue runs are a bit tricky for novices.

Cross-country There are 7km/4 miles of trails between Orri and Beret.

Queues The network of modern lifts means few queues most of the time. But at weekends some waits can be 10 minutes. Reporters have commented on how orderly queues are compared to many Alpine resorts.

Mountain restaurants Most have decent, good-value food and pleasant terraces. You can get table service at Cap del Port, at the Bonaigua pass, at Baqueira 2200 and at Beret.

Schools and guides The school gets good reports – some spoken English.

Facilities for children The kindergarten takes children from three months but lack of spoken English is a problem. Ski school classes start from age four.

STAYING THERE

How to go There is a reasonable choice of hotels and apartments locally.

Hotels In the main village three have been recommended – the 4-star Montarto (973 639001) with 'pool and wonderful food' and two 3-stars: the 'very satisfactory' Tuc Blanc (973 644350) with pool and Val de Ruda (973 645258). The 5-star Royal Tanau looks good (973 644446). The Parador (973 640801) down the valley in Arties and the 2-star Husa Vielha (973 640275) further down in Vielha have been recommended.

Eating out The more interesting restaurants are down the valley in Salardu, Arties and Vielha. Reporters have enjoyed the local tapas bars.

Après-ski There are lots of pubs and discos in the valley. Tiffany's and Pacha are in the main village. They get going very late (ie 1am or 2am).

Off the slopes Pool and spa facilities are available in several hotels, but not much else. Vielha, 15km/9 miles away, has a good sports centre.

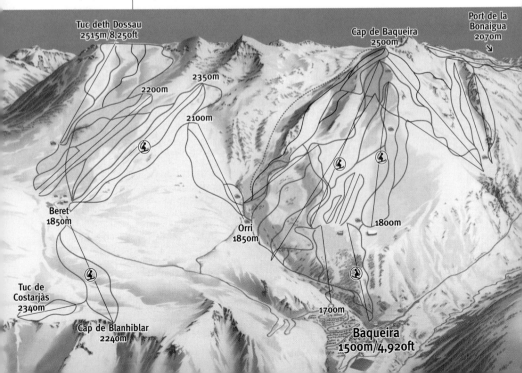

Bulgaria

COSTS

① ② ③ ④ ⑤ ⑥

+ Very cheap
+ A different winter holiday, with the chance to experience a fascinating, although depressed, culture
+ Very friendly, welcoming people
+ Good ski schools

– Poor snow record and not enough snowmaking
– Poor piste and lift maintenance
– Small ski areas
– Borovets hotels and food poor, and tales of beggars and prostitutes

Bulgaria has traditionally attracted beginners and early intermediates on a tight budget: the basic flight-and-hotel-package, equipment rental, school and lift pass are all very cheap. So is alcohol when you get there. Drawbacks include limited slopes, old lifts, and mountain and hotel food that can have you reaching for the Mars bars. There are compensations, mostly listed above. From Borovets an excursion to Sofia is also recommended. But keen piste-bashers, gourmets, posers, and those wanting creature comforts should look elsewhere or be prepared for a shock.

The flow of readers' reports has dried up over the last few seasons, but we have trawled the Internet for holiday reports. Most seem extremely positive for Pamporovo, but much more mixed for Borovets, with tales of no snow, long lift queues, poor rental equipment and problems with beggars and prostitutes.

Bulgaria's two main resorts are some way apart, served by different airports, with similarly short transfer times (less than two hours) – assuming everything runs smoothly (which it might well not). They are similar places, in that both have good ski schools and a poor selection of quality restaurants, but they suit different levels of ability.

Pamporovo 1650m/5,410ft

THE RESORT
Despite the bus-ride to the lifts, visitors praise Pamporovo. The purpose-built village has 'everything to hand'.

THE MOUNTAIN
Pamporovo is Bulgaria's best bet for beginners and early intermediates, with mostly easy runs. Others are likely to find 17.5km/11 miles of mainly short runs too limited.

Slopes The slopes are pretty and sheltered, with pistes starting at a high point of 1925m/6,320ft and cutting through pine forest.

Snow reliability Late-season snow-cover is unreliable.

Experts Experts will find little to challenge them in this limited ski area.

Intermediates The slopes are too limited for most intermediates.

Beginners Book a 'learn to ski'

package through your tour operator, saving up to 80% on local prices.

Snowboarding The Snow Shack is best for snowboard rental and lessons.

Mountain restaurants The best bets are the Lodge and the Spider restaurant.

Schools and guides The ski schools are repeatedly praised by reporters – instructors are patient, enthusiastic and speak good English, and class sizes are usually quite small.

Facilities for children The English-speaking nursery is well regarded.

STAYING THERE
Hotels The main hotels are in the centre of the handy purpose-built village. Hotel Pamporovo offers the best accommodation in the resort. It's close to the village centre, and facilities include an indoor swimming pool, a hot-tub and a gym. More basic are the Perelik (also with a pool) and Mourgavets – both in the centre.

Eating out The food can be poor. You are best off sticking to local Bulgarian stew dishes, which can be delicious. Breakfast buffets offer a fair choice.

Après-ski The nightlife is fairly lively, although limited to a handful of bars and discos – BJ's, White Hart, Dak's and the Havana club are popular.

Off the slopes The organised evening events are recommended by reporters.

Phone numbers
From abroad use the prefix +359.

TOURIST OFFICE

Pamporovo
t 3021 336
info@bulgariaski.com
www.travel-bulgaria.com

Borovets 1307m/4,290ft

THE RESORT
Borovets is a collection of large, modern hotels, with bars, restaurants and shops housed within them. There is a ramshackle selection of quirkier bars, shops and eating places. The beautiful wooded setting provides a degree of Alpine-style charm, and hides some of the worst architectural excesses. In recent years we have had reports of beggars, ski theft, prostitutes and rip-off exchange dealers, which may cloud your holiday.

THE MOUNTAIN
The 40km/25 miles of piste are spread over three sectors – two loosely linked.
Slopes The two largest sectors have fairly steep and awkward slopes. The gondola rises over 1000m/3,300ft to service both the small, high, easy slopes of Markoudjika (up to 2500m/8,200ft), and the mainly long, steepish Yastrebets pistes. A little drag-lift and path connect the two. The third sector – Baraki – is accessed by several lifts. Runs are short, with just 550m/1,800ft of vertical drop.
Snow reliability Reliable cover is by no means guaranteed.
Experts There's little of real challenge.
Intermediates The runs are best suited to good intermediates. Less confident skiers may find the mainly tough red runs a bit intimidating.
Beginners The slopes are not particularly suitable for novices. The nursery slopes are inadequate; Markoudjika is good for near-beginners, but progress beyond that means going on to reds.

Queues These can be bad – especially for the gondola (down as well as up). Grooming is erratic and signing poor.
Mountain restaurants Mostly basic little snack bars with limited seating, serving large portions of very simple fare.
Schools and guides Repeatedly praised by virtually all reporters.
Facilities for children Reports of the ski kindergarten have been complimentary. The non-ski nursery is in the Rila hotel.

STAYING THERE
Hotels Most reporters stayed at the Rila or the Samokov – both huge and impersonal. Our most recent report on the Rila is of 'good, plentiful food and clean, secure rooms'. Late-night noise from the street can be a problem.
Eating out Reporters recommend Katy's Bar for steaks.
Après-ski The nightlife caters well to an 18-30 type crowd. Tour operator reps organise pub crawls, folklore evenings and dinner in a local village. The Black Tiger pub (with karaoke), the Buzz Bar and Titanic are lively.
Off the slopes Excursions to the Rila monastery by coach and to Sofia by coach or helicopter are interesting.

Vitosha 1800m/5,900ft

This is no more than a few widely scattered hotels with very limited, bland runs and a top height of 2290m/7,510ft. The hotels are fairly dour, and most are a bus-ride from the lifts. The resort is just over 20km/12 miles from Sofia, allowing short transfers and easy excursions, but the slopes get overrun at weekends. The slopes are north-facing and have a decent snow record.

TOURIST OFFICES

Borovets
t 7128 450
info@bulgariaski.com
www.travel-bulgaria.
com

Vitosha
info@bulgariaski.com
www.travel-bulgaria.
com

Romania

COSTS

① ② ③ ④ ⑤ ⑥

➕ Extremely cheap

➕ Interesting excursions and friendly local people

➕ Good standard of affordable lessons

➖ Primitive facilities

➖ Uninspiring food

➖ Limited slopes with few real challenges

Like Bulgaria, Romania sells mainly on price. On-the-spot prices, in particular, are very, very low. Provided you have correspondingly low expectations – and provided you go to Poiana Brasov and not Sinaia – you'll probably come back content. If you have any interest in good living, and particularly good lunching, stay away. It's a place for beginners and near-beginners – the slopes are limited in extent and challenge, but lessons are good (and cheap, of course).

There is another possible dimension to a holiday here, which is the experience of visiting (and supporting) an interesting and attractive country with a traumatic recent history. Reporters have commented on the friendliness of the people, and most recommend exploring beyond the confines of the resorts. Bucharest is 'not to be missed'.

It's some years since we visited the country. The abiding impression we brought back then was one of resources stretched to their limits. To judge by the few reports we have since received, post-revolutionary Romania has, sadly, not made much progress.

Romania's two main resorts are in the Carpathian mountains, about 120km/75 miles north-west of the capital and arrival airport, Bucharest. They are very different places, but have one or two things in common apart from low prices: patient instruction, with excellent spoken English, and small classes; and very basic mountain restaurants, with extremely primitive toilets that, according to one reporter, would 'shock the toughest of characters'.

The main resort is **Poiana Brasov** (1030m/3,380ft), near the city of Brasov. It is purpose-built, but not designed for convenience: the hotels are scattered about a pretty, wooded plateau, served by regular buses and cheap taxis. There is nothing resembling a real village – the place has the air of a spacious holiday camp.

The main slopes (approximately 17km/11 miles of pistes in total) consist of decent intermediate tree-lined runs of about 750m/2,460ft vertical, roughly following the line of the main cable-car and gondola, plus an open nursery area at the top. There are also some nursery lifts at village level. A black run takes a less direct route down the mountain, which means that on average it is less steep than the red run under the lifts; it has one steepish pitch towards the end. The more

adventurous would need to seek opportunities to go off-piste. The resort gets weekend business from Brasov and Bucharest, and the main lifts can suffer serious queues then.

The Bradul (0268 262252) and Sport (0268 262252) hotels are handy for the lower nursery slopes and for one of the cable-cars. The Tirol (0268 262460) and the Alpin (0268 262343) get good reports. The Ciucas (0268 262181) is a 'good, basic' place with satellite TV. Après-ski revolves around the hotel bars and discos and can be quite lively at times. The nightclub puts on cheap cabarets. Off-slope facilities are limited; there is a good-sized pool, and bowling. A trip to the Carpathian Stag in Brasov for an evening of tasting in the wine cellars, dinner and a folklore show has been recommended. An excursion to nearby Bran Castle (Count Dracula's home) is also popular.

You may be offered holidays in **Sinaia** – a small town on the busy road from Bucharest to Brasov. When we visited it some years ago the town seemed to us a rather depressing place, and reporters since have been shocked and saddened by the evident poverty. But there are chalets and a 4-star Holiday Inn, which may help to attract your much-needed cash.

Phone numbers
From abroad use the prefix +40 and omit the initial '0' of the phone number.

TOURIST OFFICE

Poiana Brasov
www.poiana-brasov.com

Slovenia

COSTS

① ② ③ ④ ⑤ ⑥

- ➕ Good value for money
- ➕ Beautiful scenery
- ➕ Good beginners' slopes and lessons
- ➕ Good off-slope diversions and excursions

- ➖ Limited, easy slopes on the whole
- ➖ Mainly antiquated lifts
- ➖ Uninspiring food

Slovenia offers good value for money 'on the sunny side of the Alps'. A handful of UK tour operators run packages to some of the better-known resorts. An alternative would be to arrange an independent trip to the mountains, combined with a break in the vibrant city of Ljubljana.

Kranjska Gora and Bohinj are the best-known resorts, popular with economy-minded British and Dutch visitors, and with visitors from neighbouring Italy and Austria, giving quite a cosmopolitan feel to the resorts.

Slovenia is a small country bordering Italy to the west and Austria to the north. It was the first state to break away from former Yugoslavia and has managed to escape the turmoil that engulfed the Balkans. The economy is improving steadily, and there is a positive feel to the resorts – along with a warm and hospitable welcome.

The main resorts are within two and a half hours' bus-ride of the capital, Ljubljana. The ski areas are generally small, with fairly antiquated lifts but few queues. The mountain restaurants are mainly unappealing, while the ski schools are of a high standard and cheap, with reputedly good English. Hotel star ratings tend to be a trifle generous, but standards of service and hygiene are high. Snow reliability is not particularly good, but some resorts have snowmaking.

Kranjska Gora (810m/2,660ft), not far from the Austrian and the Italian borders, is the resort best known on the British market. The pretty village is dominated by the majestic Julian Alps. The Lek, Kompas and Larix hotels – with pools – are the best placed for slope-side convenience.

There are 30km/20 miles of mainly intermediate slopes, rising up to 1625m/5,325ft. The only challenging slopes are a couple of short runs in the Podkoren area and the World Cup slalom run. For those wanting a change of slopes, trips to Arnoldstein in Austria are available. Snow reliability is not good, despite snowmaking and a northerly exposure. The lift system is rather antiquated (most of the 19 lifts

are T-bars), but at least queues are rare. Mountain restaurants are poor and most people choose to lunch in the village. There are 40km/25 miles of cross-country trails. There is a good selection of bars and discos for Austrian-style après-ski.

Vogel (1535m/5,035ft), in the beautiful **Bohinj** basin, has the best slopes and conditions in the area. The 36km/22 miles of slopes are reached by a cable-car up from the valley. There's a collection of small hotels and restaurants at the base. Pistes of varying difficulty run from the high point at 1800m/5,910ft back into a central bowl with a small beginner area. When conditions permit, there is a long run to the bottom cable-car station. For a change of scene, **Kobla**, with 23km/14 miles of wooded runs, is a short bus-ride away.

Bled, with its beautiful lake and fairly lively nightlife, is an attractive base. Its local slopes are very limited indeed, but there are free buses to Vogel (about 20km/12 miles) and Kobla (slightly nearer).

Kanin (2200m/7,220ft), near the village of Bovec, 17km/11 miles from Italy, offers 15km/9 miles of pistes between 980m and 2300m (3,220ft and 7,550ft).

Slovenia's second city, **Maribor** (265m/870ft), in the north-east, is 6km/4 miles from its local slopes – the biggest ski area in the country, with 64km/40 miles of runs and 16 lifts. Accommodation is cheap and there are several atmospheric old inns serving good, Hungarian-influenced food.

TOURIST OFFICES

www.slovenia-tourism.si
Kranjska Gora
info@kranjska-gora.si
www.kranjska-gora.si
Vogel (Bohinj)
tdbohinj@bohinj.si
www.bohinj.si/vogel
Kobla (Bohinj)
tdbohinj@bohinj.si
www.bohinj.si/kobla
Bled
info@dzt.bled.si
www.bled.si
Kanin (Bovec)
www.bovec.si
Maribor
www.maribor.si

Finland

643

COSTS

- ➕ Peace and quiet
- ➕ Ideal terrain for cross-country and gentle downhilling
- ➕ Reliable late snow
- ➕ Jolly outings, often involving huskies or reindeer
- ➕ Lapp charm

- ➖ Cold
- ➖ Small ski areas
- ➖ Quite expensive
- ➖ Uninspiring food

For skiers with no appetite for the hustle and hassle of Alpine resorts in high season – perhaps especially for families – escape to the white silence of Lapland may be an attractive alternative. Finland has the lion's share of Lapland and has successfully marketed it, not only for day-trip visits to Santa in his home environment but also for ski holidays. With limited downhill slopes but limitless cross-country the resorts compete with the established resorts in Norway, the most important difference being that Finnish resorts lie far to the north. Of half a dozen 'main' resorts only Ruka is south of the Arctic Circle (by 80km/50 miles).

The weather, snow and timing of the season are accordingly different, and ski holidays in Finland have an extra ingredient of folklorish charm, plus a good chance of seeing the Northern Lights (three times in the January week when one reporter visited). The main resorts are **Levi** and **Ylläs**, respectively 25km/15 miles north and 50km/31 miles west of Kittilä, which has direct charter flights from Britain.

Ylläs mountain has two gateways, of which the major one is Äkäslompolo – a traditional lakeside Lapp settlement, two miles from the lifts. It has a more relaxing atmosphere and longer runs than Levi, whose great appeal is convenience: it is a purpose-built village of hotels and cabins at the foot of the slopes, with more nightlife and commercial development.

The Arctic landscape of flat and gently rolling forest punctuated by many lakes and the occasional treeless hill is a paradise for cross-country skiing. Weather permitting, it also offers good beginner and intermediate downhilling, albeit on a small scale. In fine weather it is a land of great beauty, but don't expect drama.

The resorts usually open a few runs in late November. For two months in midwinter, the sun does not rise; at least, not at ground level – even at Christmas (a quiet time) the sun may be visible from the slopes for a period of pale daylight between 10am and 2pm. Most of the ski areas have floodlit runs. The mountains do not open fully until mid-February, when a normal skiing day is possible and Finnish schools have holidays that usually coincide with ours – a busy time. Finland comes into its own at the end of the season, with friendlier temperatures and long daylight hours. Understandably, Easter is extremely popular, and the slopes are crowded.

Piste conditions are usually hard-packed powder or fresh snow from the start of the season to the end (usually early May).

The temperature can be extremely variable, yo-yoing between zero and minus 30°C several times in a week. The fine days are the coldest, but usually the best for skiing: it may be 10 to 15 degrees warmer on the slopes than at valley level. 'Mild' days of cloud and wind are much worse on the hill. Face masks are widely sold.

None of the ski areas has significant vertical by alpine standards. Ylläs is the largest in Finland with 463m/1,520ft vertical and, having lifts and pistes on two broad flanks of the mountain, gives plenty of scope for skiers just off the nursery slopes. Second- and third-week skiers will rapidly conquer the benign black runs.

The staple Finnish lift is the T-bar. Ruka has some chairs, and Levi has Finland's only gondola, which must be a godsend in bitter weather. Pistes are wide, uncomplicated and well maintained, with good nursery slopes.

The Finns are great boarders and consider their terrain-parks far superior to those in the Alps.

The runs are so short that there is no great need for mountain restaurants – on a Finnish piste you are never far from the base lodge, with its shops and self-service restaurant. The ski areas also have shelters or 'kotas' – log-built teepees with an open fire and a smoke hole in the roof – where you can eat a snack or grill some food. Ylläs has a welcoming, snow-encrusted, round restaurant – the highest in the country, at 718m/2,355ft – on the flat top of the mountain, with an open fire, reindeer skins on the benches, and alcohol.

Ski school is good, with English widely spoken. All ski areas have indoor playrooms for small children, but they may be closed at weekends.

Cross-country skiing makes sense of a resort such as Äkäslompolo, transforming it from awkward sprawl to doorstep ski resort of limitless scope. People ski alongside the main road, from their cabins to the hotel or supermarket (pulling children on sledges); up to the base of the lifts where trails fan out around the mountain; across the frozen lake and away through the endless forest.

Excursions are common – husky sledding, snowmobile safaris, a reindeer sleigh ride and tea with the Lapp drivers in their tent. 'The whole experience is wonderful,' says a typically enthusiastic participant. A reporter thought the trip to the Ice Hotel in Sweden 'truly memorable,' and worth the four-hour trip each way.

Hotels are self-contained resorts, large and practical rather than stylish, typically with a shop, a cafe, a bar with dance floor, and a pool/sauna with outdoor cooling-off area. Hotel supper is served no later than seven, typically, sometimes followed by a children's disco or cheek-to-cheek dancing to a live band.

Finns usually prefer to stay in cabins, and tour operators offer the compromise of staying in a cabin but taking half-board at a nearby hotel. Cabins vary, but are mostly spacious and well equipped, with a sauna and heated drying cupboard as standard. The Hillankukka log cabins at Äkäslompolo are exceptionally good, but the 10-minute walk to and from meals at the Äkäs hotel (016 553000) is not to be underestimated. A reporter

praises the hotel itself – 'beautiful hotel, excellent hydrotherapy pool'. Levi's biggest hotel, Levitunturi (016 646660), is rated 'great' by a reporter this year, with 'excellent' facilities including a big pool, tennis, children's activity centre and a golf simulator.

Restaurants in Levi recommended by reporters are the Steak House, Myllyn Aija ('good value'), Arran and (for a treat) the White Reindeer. Recommended bars are the Panimo (most popular), Crazy Reindeer (karaoke), Arran ('more sophisticated').

The southernmost of Finland's resorts, **Ruka** lies 80km/50 miles south of the Arctic Circle, 27km/17 miles from Kuusamo airport and only 25km/15 miles from the Russian border, in a region known for abundant and enduring snow. Finns think nothing of driving the 1000km/620 miles from Helsinki, despite the proximity of Kuusamo airport. The ski area, a mixture of open and forest terrain, has 18 lifts (including four chairs), and 28 runs (22 floodlit, 24 with snowmaking, a mogul run and several black runs, none of them steep), and the vertical range is 200m/690ft. The Freestyle World Championships will be held here in 2005 – they are building a super-pipe for 2003/04. The cross-country scope is vast: they advertise 500km/310 miles of trails, of which 40km/25 miles are floodlit.

The atmosphere at the resort and on the slopes is upbeat – with live music in the Wunderbar and sun terraces outside Piste, very popular in spring. Hotels include the Rukahovi (08 85910), only 50m/150ft from the slopes, and the Royal Ruka (08 868 6000), the resort's flagship property; both of these are popular conference venues. The best accommodation is in cabins. Good restaurants include Riipinen Riistaravintola, which has bear, boar and capercaillie on the menu, Vanha Karhu, and Kalakeidas, an intimate little fish restaurant.

Pyhä, 150km/93 miles north-east of Rovaniemi, has seven lifts (including two chairs) and 10 runs on a mountain much of which is a National Park. The vertical is only 280m/920ft and there is no steep terrain, but Pyhä enjoys a reputation among young boarders and skiers for good off-piste. The best powder runs are on both sides of a long T-bar on the north slope. The Hotel Pyhätunturi (016 856111) is at mid-mountain.

Phone numbers
From abroad use the prefix +358 and omit the initial '0' of the phone number.

TOURIST OFFICES

Levi
www.levi.fi

Ylläs
www.yllas.fi

Ruka
www.ruka.fi

Pyhä
www.pyha.fi

Norway

➕ Probably the best terrain and facilities in Europe for serious cross-country skiing

➕ The home of telemark – plenty of opportunities to learn and practise

➕ Complete freedom from the glitziness often associated with downhill resorts, and from the ill-mannered lift queues of the Alps

➕ Quiet atmosphere that suits families and older people

➕ Impressive snowboard parks

➕ Usually reliable snow conditions throughout a long season

➖ Very limited downhill areas – small, and mostly with few challenges

➖ Mountain restaurants that are little more than pit stops

➖ Prohibitively high prices (because of high taxes) for alcoholic drinks

➖ Unremarkable scenery – even 'Alpine' Hemsedal resembles the Pennines more than the Alps

➖ Après-ski that is either deadly dull or irritatingly rowdy

➖ Short daylight hours in midwinter

➖ Highly changeable weather

➖ Limited off-slope activities

Norway and its resorts are very different from the Alps, or indeed the Rockies. Some people find the place very much to their taste. For cross-country there is nowhere like it; and for downhillers who dislike the usual ski-resort trappings, and prefer a simpler approach to winter holidays, it could be just the place. For families with young children, in particular, the drawbacks are less pronounced than for others; you'll have no trouble finding junk food for the kids to eat – the mountain restaurants serve little else.

Speaking for ourselves, any one of the first three ➖ points we've listed above would probably be enough to put us off; when these are combined in a single destination – and when you add in the other non-trivial negative points – you can count us out.

From the 1960s to the 1980s, Norway's popularity with British skiers declined steadily, until the country was attracting only 1,500 or so – about one-tenth of the peak number. So in 1988 the tourist agencies launched an initiative to reverse the trend. Aided by the Alpine snow shortages at the turn of the decade and the award of the 1994 Olympic Winter Games to Lillehammer, the campaign has been a success – bookings from the UK have grown appreciably, with a sizeable number looking to do cross-country skiing.

There is a traditional friendship between Norway and Britain, and we think of Norwegians as welcoming people, well disposed towards British visitors. We have to say that our visits have left us underwhelmed by the warmth of welcome. But at least English is widely spoken – universally spoken, in our experience.

For the Norwegians and Swedes, skiing is a weekend rather than a special holiday activity, and not an occasion for extravagance. So at lunchtime they tend to haul sandwiches out of their backpacks, and in the evening they cook in their apartments. Don't expect a wide choice of restaurants.

The Norwegians have a problem with alcohol. Walk into an après-ski bar at 5pm on a Saturday and you may find young men already inebriated – and by that we mean not merry but incoherent. And this is despite – or, some say, because of – prohibitively high taxes on booze. Restaurant prices for wine are ludicrous, and shop prices may be irrelevant – Hemsedal has no state-controlled liquor store. Our one attempt at self-catering (well, OK, our one takeaway meal) was an unusually sober affair as a result. Crystal, cutely, offers free wine with dinner in some of its hotels. Other prices are generally not high by Alpine standards, and those for ski equipment rental and ski school are relatively low.

Cross-country skiing comes as naturally to Norwegians as walking; and even if you're not that keen, the fact that cross-country is normal, and not a wimp's alternative to 'real' skiing, gives Norway a special appeal. Here, cross-country is both a way of getting about the valleys and a way of exploring the hills. Although you can plod around short valley circuits as you might in an Alpine resort, what distinguishes Norway for the keen cross-country skier is the network of long trails across the gentle uplands, with refuges along the way where backpackers can pause for refreshment or stay overnight. This network of mountain huts offers basic but cheap accommodation which can turn touring into a week-long adventure away from the crowds. Several tour operators now offer ski-touring packages, or they can be arranged on the spot.

More and more Norwegians are taking to telemarking (a bit like cross-country, with a free-heel binding, but with broader skis) for both downhill and backcountry skiing trips.

Snowboarding is very popular, particularly with local youths who swarm on to the slopes and impressive terrain-parks at weekends.

For downhill skiing, the country isn't nearly so attractive. Despite the fact that it is able to hold downhill races, and despite the successes of its Alpine racers during the 1990s, Norway's Alpine areas are of limited appeal.

The most rewarding resort for downhillers is Hemsedal, which we cover in detail in the next chapter.

The site of the 1994 Olympics, the little lakeside town of **Lillehammer** (200m/660ft), is not actually a downhill resort at all. There is plenty of cross-country terrain around, but the nearest downhill runs are 15km/9 miles north at Hafjell (230m/750ft). This is a worthwhile little area, with a vertical of 830m/2,720ft, 11 lifts, and pistes totalling 25km/16 miles. The Olympic slalom events were held here; but the planned women's downhill and super-G races were moved elsewhere after the racers judged the course too easy. They went to Kvitfjell, about 35km/22 miles further north, developed specially for the men's downhill and super-G. It's steeper but a bit smaller – 19km/12 miles of pistes.

Norway's other internationally known resort is **Geilo** (800m/2,620ft). This is a small, quiet, unspoiled community on the railway line that links Bergen, on the coast, to Oslo. It provides all the basics of a resort – a handful of cafes and shops clustered around the railway station, a dozen or so hotels more widely spread around the wide valley, children's facilities and a sports centre.

Geilo is a superb cross-country resort. As the Bergen-Oslo railway runs through the town it is possible to go for long tours and return by train.

Geilo is very limited for downhillers, but it does lay claim to having Scandinavia's only super-pipe. The 28km/17 miles of piste are spread over two small hills – one, Vestlia, a bus-ride away from Geilo, with a good, informal hotel and restaurant at its foot – offering a maximum vertical of 370m/1,215ft and a longest run of 2km/1.25 miles. None of the runs is really difficult.

Clearly the best hotel, and one of the attractions of staying in Geilo, is the Dr Holms Hotel (call central reservations on 320 95940) – smartly white-painted outside, beautifully furnished and spacious inside. This is the centre for après-ski, but prices are steep. All the other hotels we have seen can be recommended. The resort is quiet at the end of the day, but the main hotels provide live entertainment.

A long way north of the other resorts is **Oppdal** (550m/1,800ft), with more downhill runs than any of its rivals (60km/37 miles). The total vertical is 790m/2,590ft, but this is misleading – most runs are short.

There are slightly more extensive slopes at **Trysil** (460m/1,510ft), off to the east, on the border with Sweden, and the runs are longer (up to 4km/2 miles and 685m/2,250ft vertical). The runs here are all around the conical Trysilfjellet, some way from Trysil itself – though there is some accommodation at the hill.

In complete contrast to all of these resorts is **Voss** (50m/160ft), a sizeable lakeside town quite close to the sea. A cable-car links the town to the slopes on Hangur and Slettafjell, with a total of 40km/25 miles of pistes. There are plenty of excursion possibilities, in particular the spectacular Flåm railway, which plunges down the side of a mountain to fjord (sea) level. From there you can take a boat trip to link up with a bus back to Voss. Nearby Bergen is a pleasant city that is worth a visit.

Phone numbers
From abroad use the prefix +47.

TOURIST OFFICES

Lillehammer
www.lillehammerturist.no
Geilo
www.geilo.no
Oppdal
www.oppdal.com
Trysil
www.trysil.com
Voss
www.skiinfo.no/voss/

Hemsedal

The place for Alpine skiing in Norway – though we prefer the Alps

647

COSTS

① ② ③ ④ ⑤ ⑥

RATINGS

The slopes

Snow	****
Extent	*
Expert	**
Intermediate	****
Beginner	***
Convenience	**
Queues	****
Mountain restaurants	*

The rest

Scenery	**
Resort charm	**
Off-slope	*

NEWS

There are plans to expand the children's ski area for 2003/04.

SNOWPIX.COM / CHRIS GILL

Pistes increase neatly in gradient, from green on the right to black on the left ↓

➕ Impressive snow reliability because of northerly location

➕ Increasing amounts of convenient slope-side accommodation

➕ Extensive cross-country trails compared to the Alps

➕ Some quite challenging slopes, and mountains with a slightly Alpine feel

➖ Not much of a village

➖ Infrequent shuttle-buses to slopes

➖ Limited slopes

➖ Exposed upper mountain prone to closure because of bad weather

➖ Weekend queues

➖ One abysmal mountain restaurant

➖ No liquor store for miles (though beer is available in the supermarket)

➖ Après-ski limited during the week and rowdy at weekends

Hemsedal's craggy terrain is reminiscent of a small-but-serious Alpine resort. Most people not resident in Scandinavia would be better advised to go for the real thing, but if you like the sound of Norway, Hemsedal is the place for downhill skiing. Go after the February school holidays, if possible.

THE RESORT

Hemsedal is both an unspoiled valley and a village, also referred to as Trøym and Sentrum ('Centre'), which amounts to very little – a couple of apartment/hotel buildings, a few shops, a bank and a petrol station. Though there has been talk of a lift from Trøym to the slopes, for now the lift base is a mile or two away, across the valley. There are self-catering apartments and houses beside the slopes – with a new development called Skarsnuten linked to the main network by its own lift and red piste – and in a separate cluster a walkable distance down the hill from the lifts. A ski-bus links these points, and others in the valley, but the service is inadequate; really, the place is geared to weekend visitors arriving by car or by coach.

THE MOUNTAINS

Hemsedal's slopes pack a lot of variety into a small space. They are shaded in midwinter, and can be very cold.

Slopes With no fewer than four fast chairs to play on, you can pack a lot of runs into the day. The lift pass also covers smaller Solheisen, a few miles up the valley. A small supplement is required to ski at Geilo, an hour away.

Terrain-parks There's an impressive and 'very well maintained' terrain-park and two half-pipes.

Snow reliability The combination of latitude, altitude and orientation makes for impressive snow reliability – and there's extensive snowmaking. The season runs until early May.

Experts There is quite a bit to amuse experts – several black pistes of 450m/1,480ft vertical served by a fast triple chair from the base (one left as a mogul slope) – and wide areas of gentler off-piste terrain served by drags above the tree line.

Intermediates Mileage-hungry piste-bashers will find Hemsedal's runs very limited. There are quite a few red and blue runs to play on, but the difference in difficulty is slight.

Beginners There's a gentle nursery slope for absolute beginners. And there are splendid long green runs – but they get a lot of traffic, some of it irresponsibly fast. Some long blues and reds also suit near-beginners.

KEY FACTS

Resort	650m
	2,130ft
Slopes	670-1455m
	2,200-4,770ft
Lifts	16
Pistes	42km
	26 miles
Green	32%
Blue	21%
Red	26%
Black	21%
Snowmaking	14km
	8 miles

Phone numbers
From abroad use the prefix +47.

TOURIST OFFICE

t 320 55030
info@hemsedal.net
www.hemsedal.com
www.skistar.com/
hemsedal/

Snowboarding There is plenty of free-riding terrain, and some pistes are suitable for carving. The park is popular.

Cross-country By Alpine standards there is lots to do – 90km/56 miles of prepared trails in the valley and forest and (later in the season) 120km/75 miles at altitude. There is a special trail map. Most of the trails are a few miles down the valley at the Gravset centre, served by one bus a day.

Queues Hemsedal is Norway's premier downhill resort, and it is only a three-hour drive from Oslo, the capital. Good weekend weather fills the car parks, leading to queues for the main access lifts after mid-morning, and possibly for others. But during the week it is quiet. The upper lifts are very exposed, and are easily closed by bad weather, producing crowds lower down the slopes.

Mountain restaurants There is one functional self-service mountain restaurant doing dreary fast food, plus two or three kiosks with benches.

Schools and guides Our most recent reporter was greatly impressed, not only by the standard of English but by the tuition: 'Lots of one-to-one, very encouraging.'

Facilities for children The facilities at the lift base are good, with day care for children over three months, free to parents in ski school. The kids' nursery slope is admirably gentle but not particularly convenient.

STAYING THERE

How to go Most of the accommodation is in apartments, varying widely in convenience. Catered chalets are available through certain UK operators.

Hotels The best hotel is the Skogstad (320 60333) in central Hemsedal – comfortable, but noisy at weekends. Other hotels along the valley are used by UK tour operators. The hotel Skarsnuten, on the mountain, is stylishly modern (with no smoking).

Self-catering The Alpin apartments, a walk from the lift base, are satisfactory if you don't fill all the beds. The adjacent Tinden ones are quite smart.

Eating out There are half-a-dozen restaurants down in the village.

Après-ski It's minimal in the week, rowdy at weekends and holidays.

Off the slopes There are some diversions, including sleighs drawn by horses or dogs. The pool at the hotel Skogstad is open to the public.

Totten
1455m/4,770ft

Hamaren
1350m

Røgjin
1325m

Fjellet
1125m

940m

Skarsnuten

Veslestølen

670m/2,200ft

Hemsedal
Skisenter

Fjellandsby

Hemsedal
650m/2,130ft

Sweden

➕ Snow-sure from December to May

➕ Unspoiled, beautiful landscape

➕ Uncrowded pistes and lifts

➕ Vibrant (but regimented) après-ski

➕ Good range of non-skiing activities

➖ Limited challenging downhill terrain

➖ Small areas by Alpine standards

➖ Lacks the dramatic peaks and vista of the Alps

➖ Short days during the early season

Sweden's landscape of forests and lakes and miles of unspoiled wilderness is entirely different from the Alps' grandeur and traffic-choked roads. Standards of accommodation, food and service are good and the people welcoming, lively and friendly. There are plenty of off-slope activities, but most of its downhill areas are limited in size and challenge. Sweden is likely to appeal most to those who want an all-round winter holiday in a different environment and culture. Don't be put off by the myths that Sweden is expensive, dark and cold – see below.

Holidaying in Sweden is a completely different experience, culturally as well as physically, from a holiday in the Alps. The language is generally incomprehensible to us and, although virtually everyone speaks good English, the menus and signs are often written only in Swedish. The food is delightful, especially if you like fish and venison. And resorts are very family-friendly.

One of the myths about Sweden is that it is expensive. Sweden is significantly cheaper than neighbouring Norway, especially for alcohol, and prices are pretty much on a par with the main Alpine countries.

Another myth is that it is dark. It is true that the days are very short in December and early January. But from early February the lifts generally work from 9am to 4.30 and by March it is light until 8.30. And most resorts have floodlit pistes for night skiing.

On the down side, downhill slopes are generally limited in both challenge and extent and the lift systems tend to be dominated by T-bars. But there is lots of cross-country and backcountry skiing. Snowboarding is also popular, with parks and pipes in most resorts.

Après-ski is taken very seriously – with live bands from mid- to late-afternoon. But it stops suddenly, dinner is served and then the nightlife starts. There is plenty to do off the slopes: snowmobile safaris, ice fishing, dog-sled rides, ice-climbing, and saunas galore. You can also visit a local Sami (Lapp) village.

The main resort is Åre (see separate chapter). **Sälen** is Scandinavia's largest winter sports area – and is made up of four separate sets of slopes totalling 144km/89 miles of piste. Most slopes are very gentle, suiting beginners and early or timid intermediates best. Lindvalen and Högfjället are vaguely linked by a lift and a long cross-country slog. But you need the unreliable bus service to the others.

Vemdalen has two separate areas of slopes 18km/11 miles apart by road. **Björnrike** is great for families, beginners and early intermediates, with eight lifts and 15km/9 miles of mainly gentle pistes. There is a hotel right on the slopes, built in modern style. **Vemdalsskalet** has more advanced intermediate terrain, 10 lifts and 13km/8 miles of pistes. The Högfjällshotell at the base is large, dates from 1936 and prides itself on its lively après-ski.

Riksgränsen, 250km/155 miles north of the Arctic Circle, is an area of jagged mountain peaks and narrow fjords. The season starts in mid-February and ends in June – when you can be on the slopes under the midnight sun. There are only six lifts and 21km/13 miles of piste. But there is some good off-piste and midnight heli-skiing.

Björkliden, also above the Arctic Circle, is famous for its subterranean skiing inside Scandinavia's largest cave system. You need to go with a guide.

Ramundberget is a good, small, quiet family resort with ski-in/ski-out accommodation. It gets large amounts of snow and its 22km/14 miles of pistes are mainly easy or intermediate cruising runs. There is a special children's area with its own lift.

Åre

Sweden's best slopes strung out along a frozen lake

650

COSTS

① ② ③ ④ ⑤ ⑥

RATINGS

The slopes

Snow	★★★
Extent	★★
Expert	★★
Intermediate	★★★★
Beginner	★★★★
Convenience	★★★
Queues	★★★★
Mountain restaurants	★★★

The rest

Scenery	★★★
Resort charm	★★★
Off-slope	★★★

KEY FACTS

Resort	380m
	1,250ft
Slopes	380-1275m
	1,250-4,180ft
Lifts	40
Pistes	93km
	58 miles
Green	12%
Blue	42%
Red	36%
Black	5%
Unpatrolled	5%

NEWS

In 2002/03 a six-pack was installed next to the main cable-car from town, replacing the slow double chair. This feeds a quad chair, also new for 2002/03, itself replacing a T-bar and two double chairs.

The slope-side Sunwing hotel has been renovated and is now called the Tott Hotel & Spa.

Neilson is continuing to offer its charter flights from Gatwick to Ostersund, introduced in 2002/03, which cut the transfer time to 90 minutes.

+ Cute little town centre

+ Good snow reliability

+ Good intermediate and beginner runs

+ Extensive cross-country trails

+ Excellent children's facilities

+ Lively après-ski scene

+ Lots of off-slope diversions

− Lots of T-bars

− Exposed upper mountain prone to closure because of bad weather

− High winds detrimental to snow conditions

− Few expert challenges

− High season and weekend queues

Åre has the biggest area of linked slopes in Sweden and some of its most challenging terrain. But it suits beginners, intermediates and families best. It has a dinky little town centre and a long area of slopes set along a frozen lake.

THE RESORT

Åre is a small town made up of old, pretty, coloured wooden buildings and some larger, modern additions. When we were there the main square had a roaring open fire to warm up by. As well as accommodation in town, there is lots spread out along the valley, with a concentration in the Duved area. All the slopes and accommodation are set on the shore of a huge, long lake, frozen in the winter months.

THE MOUNTAINS

The terrain is mainly green and blue tree-lined slopes, with a couple of windswept bowls above the trees.
Slopes There are two main areas. The largest is accessed by a funicular from the centre of town or by a six-pack or cable-car a short climb above it. This takes you to the hub of a network of runs and (mainly) T-bars that stretches for 10km/6 miles from end to end. The cable-car is often shut because it goes to the top of the above-the-tree-line slopes (known as the 'high zone'), which often suffers from howling gales. A gondola also accesses the high zone from a different point. You can get back on-piste right into the town square. A separate area of slopes is above Duved, the other main bed base, now served by a high-speed chair. There are four floodlit slopes, each open on a different night.
Terrain-parks There's a 1.4km/1 mile long boarder/skier-cross course, a half-pipe and a big terrain-park, plus two smaller parks for beginner freestylers.
Snow reliability Snow reliability is good from November to May. More of a problem is the wind, which can blow fresh snow away. It also means that artificial snow is often deliberately made wet so that it doesn't blow away – it then compacts to a hard, icy surface (and certainly had when we

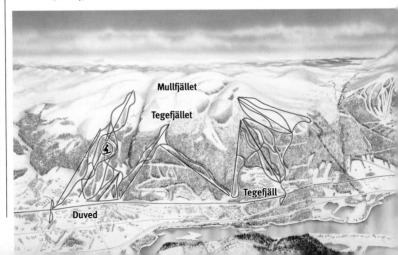

Mullfjället

Tegefjället

Tegefjäll

Duved

Central reservations phone number
For all resort accommodation call 17700.

Phone numbers
From elsewhere in Sweden add the prefix 0647.
From abroad use the prefix +46 647.

TOURIST OFFICE

t 17720
info@areresort.se
www.areresort.se

tried the Olympia night skiing area – the top part was sheet ice).

Experts Experts will find Åre's slopes limited, especially if the 'high zone' is closed. If it is open, there is a lot of off-piste available, including an 8km/5 mile run over the back accessed by a snowcat service in high season. On the main lower area the steepest (and iciest when we were there) pistes are in the Olympia area. There are also steep black and red runs back to town.

Intermediates The slopes are ideal for most intermediates, with pretty blue runs through the trees. Because they tend to be more sheltered, the blue runs also often have the best snow. You can get a real sense of travelling from hill to hill on the main area.

Beginners There are good facilities both on the main area and at Duved.

Snowboarding There's good varied terrain for boarders, plus three terrain parks (see above). But there are a lot of drag-lifts (31 out of a total of 40).

Cross-country There's an amazing 300km/185 miles of cross-country trails, both on prepared tracks and unprepared trails marked with red crosses. Some trails are floodlit.

Queues In high season there can be queues for some lifts, especially in the central area immediately above Åre.

Mountain restaurants There are some good mountain restaurants. Our favourite was the rustic Buustamons, tucked away in the woods near Rödkulleomradret.

Schools and guides The ski school has a good reputation – and this, the easy terrain and excellent childcare facilities make it a good area for families.

Facilities for children There are special children's areas and under 8-year-olds get free lift passes if wearing helmets. There's a kindergarten that takes children from the age of two.

STAYING THERE

How to go Neilson is the only big UK tour operator to offer packages to Åre.

Hotels The main central hotels are the delightful old Åregarden and the simpler Diplomat Ski Lodge. The slope-side Tott Hotel & Spa opened last season with good spa facilities. The Renen in Duved is popular with families.

Self-catering There are plenty of cabins and apartments; reporters have recommended the ones at Åre Fjällby.

Eating out The Bistro is good and there are plenty of other alternatives.

Après-ski Après-ski is amazingly lively. The Diplomat in town is packed from 3pm onwards and has live bands. Later on, the Country Club and Bygget also have live bands and there are plenty of bars for a quiet drink. One reporter recommended going to one of the concerts held in igloos by the Tannforsen frozen waterfall.

Off the slopes Lots to do including dog- and reindeer-sled rides, skating, ice fishing, tobogganing, ice-driving, ice-climbing and snowmobiling.

Åre

651

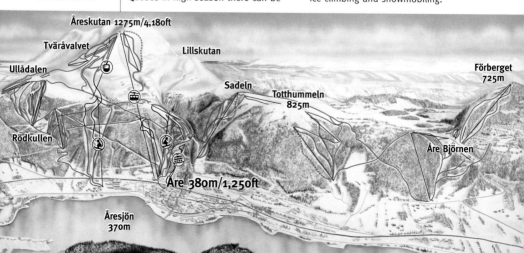

Åreskutan 1275m/4,180ft
Tväråvalvet
Lillskutan
Ulládalen
Sadeln
Totthummeln 825m
Förberget 725m
Rödkullen
Åre Björnen
Åre 380m/1,250ft
Åresjön 370m

Scotland

652

NEWS

The long-awaited funicular railway at Cairngorm opened in 2001/02. The 1960s monstrosity, the Aviemore Centre, is being given a much-needed revamp, due to be finished by June 2004.

At The Lecht, for 2002/03 an additional ski-tow was added to the Eagle run and a new day lodge is expected to be ready for 2004/05.

A limited number of Scotland-wide season tickets are now available. Visit www. ski.visitscotland.com.

FURTHER INFORMATION

The VisitScotland brochure, *Scottish Snow*, has all the information you need to fix up a trip.

t 0131 332 2433
info@visitscotland.com
www.ski.visitscotland.
com

➕ Easy to get to from northern Britain

➕ It is possible to experience perfect snow and stirring skiing

➕ Decent, cheap accommodation and good-value packages are on offer

➕ Mid-week it's rarely crowded

➕ Extensive ski-touring possibilities

➕ Lots to do off the slopes

➖ Weather is extremely changeable and sometimes vicious

➖ Snowfall is erratic, to say the least, and pistes can be closed through lack of snow

➖ Slopes are limited; runs mainly short

➖ Queueing can be a problem

➖ Little ski village ambience and few memorable mountain restaurants

Conditions in Scotland are unpredictable, to say the least. If you are willing to take a chance, or if you live nearby and can go at short notice when things look good, fine. But don't look on it as a replacement for your usual week in the Alps. If you try it, you'll either love it or hate it; but at least you'll know.

For novices who are really keen to learn, Scotland could make sense, especially if you live nearby. You can book instruction via one of the excellent outdoor centres, many of which also provide accommodation and a wide range of other activities. The ski schools at the resorts themselves are also very good.

Most of the slopes in most of the areas fall around the intermediate level. But all apart from The Lecht offer one or two tough or very tough slopes.

Snowboarding is popular and most of the resorts have some special terrain features, but maintaining these facilities in good nick is problematic. The natural terrain is good for free-riding when the conditions are right.

Cairngorm is the best-known resort, with 16 lifts and 37km/23 miles of runs. Aviemore is the main centre (with a shuttle-bus to the slopes), but you can stay in other villages in the Spey valley. The slopes are now accessed by a funicular from the main car park up to Ptarmigan at 1100m/3,610ft.

Nevis Range is the highest and newest Scottish resort – it opened in 1989. It has 12 lifts and 35km/22 miles of runs on the north-facing slopes of Aonach Mor – Britain's eighth highest peak. You get up to the slopes by means of a long six-seater gondola. There are many B&Bs and hotels in and around Fort William, only 10 minutes away by shuttle-bus.

Glenshee now boasts 25 lifts and 40km/25 miles of runs, spread out over three minor parallel valleys. Glenshee remains primarily a venue for day-trippers, though there are hotels, hostels and B&Bs in the area.

Glencoe's more limited slopes (seven lifts, 20km/12 miles of runs) lie just east of moody Glen Coe itself. You have to ride a double chair-lift and a button lift to get to the main slopes, including the nursery area. The isolated Kings House Hotel is 2km/1 mile away.

The Lecht is largely a beginners' area, with 14 lifts and 20km/12 miles of runs on the gentle slopes beside a high road pass with a series of parallel lifts and runs just above the car parks. With a maximum vertical of only 200m/ 66oft, runs are short. The Lecht also has a dry slope. The village of Tomintoul is 10km/6 miles away.

- Offers skiing and boarding during the European summer
- In one holiday you can also take in a visit to tropical northern Australia
- Some of the resorts are year-round destinations offering upmarket slope-side accommodation

- It's a long way from anywhere except New Zealand and south-east Asia
- Mountains are rather low, and lift/trail networks are small by Alpine standards

Even more than New Zealand, Australia offers resorts that are basically of local interest, but which might amuse people with other reasons to travel there – catching up with those long-lost relatives, say. Skiing among snow-laden gum trees is also a unique experience for northern hemisphere skiers, plus there is often the chance to see kangaroos, emus, echidnas and wombats.

The major resorts are concentrated in the populous south-east corner of the country, between Sydney and Melbourne, with the largest in New South Wales (NSW) – in the National Park centred on Australia's highest mountain, Mt Kosciusko (2230m/7,320ft), about six hours' drive from Sydney. Skiing has been going on here since the early 1900s – as in the next-door state of Victoria, where there are several resorts within three or four hours' drive of Melbourne.

The Australian ski season generally runs from early June to mid-October, but may be extended at the end if snow conditions allow. The big snows usually arrive only in late July and the high season of August.

Thredbo, established in 1955, is a relatively upmarket Alpine village in NSW. It hosted the only World Cup race event held in Australia, thanks to a vertical of 670m/2,200ft.

Thredbo is rather like a small and quite smart French purpose-built resort – user-friendly, and mostly made up of modern apartments, many new luxury ski-in/ski-out chalets and lodges run by clubs. But there are many more bars than you would find in the French equivalent, and the party atmosphere thrives. The Austrian flavour brought by Thredbo's founders is now giving way to modern, casual-elegant restaurants and bars. It's a steep little place, with stiff climbs to get around from one part to another. Road access is easy, but it costs A$15 a day just to enter the park.

The slopes, prettily wooded with gum trees, rise up across the valley from the village, served by a regular shuttle-bus through the resort. The runs are many and varied. The dozen lifts include three fast quad chairs, and the trails include Australia's highest (2037m/ 6,680ft) and longest (6km/4

miles). While the blacks are not difficult, they offer variety, and on the higher lifts there are off-piste variants.

Since 1987 well over A$100 million has been poured into Thredbo by its owners. The result is an abundance of luxury architect-designed apartments, an attractive pedestrian mall with good shopping and some high-class restaurants both on and off the mountain. There is also an impressive modern Australian Institute of Sport training complex open to the public. On the hill a 700m/2,300ft bob-sleigh track for the public is popular. You can ride the Crackenback gondola for dinner and there's a spectacular fireworks display every Saturday.

On the other side of the mountain range is the **Perisher Blue** resort complex, with a pass covering 51 lifts – more than anywhere else in Australia – but a vertical of less than 400m/1,310ft. The main area is **Perisher/Smiggins**, where lifts and runs – practically all easy or intermediate – range over three lightly wooded sectors. The resort is reachable by road, or by the Skitube, a rack railway that tunnels up from Bullocks Flat and goes on to the second area, **Blue Cow/Guthega**, where the slopes offer more challenges.

Perisher Blue is doing its best to catch up with Thredbo by upgrading hotels and building more facilities.

Perisher spent A$8 million installing the southern hemisphere's first eight-seater chair-lift in its beginner's area for the 2002/3 season. But the spread-out resort does not have the cosy village atmosphere that attracts so many to Thredbo, although there are plans to put that right. That said, Perisher has no trouble attracting the crowds, and hosts the Australian version of the now world-wide event, the Planet X Winter Games. Perisher also has more ski-in/ski-out accommodation than Thredbo, although it does appeal more to the masses, with its shopping-mall style village centre filled with every manner of shop, bar and fast food restaurant. Its main advantage over Thredbo is its snow, thanks to its position further within the mountain ranges and its altitude: Perisher's lift bases are about as high as Thredbo's mid-station.

Many on a budget choose to stay in the apartments or hotels in the lakeside town of Jindabyne, a half-hour drive from both Thredbo and Perisher, with a lively youth-oriented nightlife scene. There are also some rather upmarket chalets along the Alpine Way, which leads to Thredbo.

From Perisher, a snowcat can take you on an 8km/5 mile ride to the isolated chalets of Australia's highest resort, **Charlotte Pass** (1760m/5,770ft), with five lifts but only 200m/66oft vertical. People visit the Pass more for its charm than for the skiing, although it is a favourite with families. The major hotel is the historic and turreted Kosciusko Chalet, a good spot for romantic weekends.

In Victoria, resorts are not as high as in NSW but many have good snow since they are set well within the ranges. You're better off flying and coaching to these resorts – most Victorian ski fields are approached by tricky winding mountain roads.

Mount Hotham has a reputation for powder snow and some of the steepest runs in Australia. Its popularity has soared since the recent addition of an airport just 20 minutes' drive from the ski field, making it the most accessible resort in Australia, with 10 flights a week from Sydney alone. The 13 lifts serve a complete range of runs with plenty of variety. The longest run is 2.5km/1.5 miles and there is more consistently steep terrain here than at any other area in Australia. Mount Hotham is unique

among the Australian fields in that the village is built along the top of a ridge, with the slopes below it. The place is also distinguished by its Hotham Heights Chalets, a nest of multi-storey buildings atop the slopes, the most upmarket of which is fitted out with a tiny DVD theatre, spa, sauna, bar, and spacious lounge areas. The focus of the village is Mount Hotham Central, comprising apartments, shops and eateries including a few excellent restaurants. You can also stay 15 minutes' drive away at Dinner Plain, a group of architect-designed chalets set prettily among gum trees. There are a few restaurants and bars here, many cross-country trails and horse riding.

There is also a six-minute helicopter link from Mount Hotham to another resort nearby (and covered by the same lift pass), **Falls Creek**, that costs all of A$89. Falls Creek is the most alpine of Australia's resorts, completely snow-bound in winter. Guests not arriving by chopper are taken there by snowcat. There are 18 lifts, though the area is smaller than Mount Hotham's and the runs are mostly intermediate. That said, the big attraction at Falls Creek is being able to access Australia's steepest skiing on the adjacent **Mt McKay** – 365m/1,200ft vertical of true black diamond terrain in anyone's language. Guided snowcat trips from Falls Creek to Mt McKay take place twice a day, three hours costing A$69. It's well worth the trip.

The other Victorian resort of note is the isolated peak of **Mt Buller**. This place is to Melbourne, only a two-hour drive away, what the Hamptons are to Manhattan – a magnet for old money. Big-time entrepreneurs have poured millions into Mt Buller, creating a proper resort village with a luxury hotel, a new pampering spa and even a university campus. Draped around the mountain are 25 lifts – the largest network in Victoria, including 13 chair-lifts. Mt Buller annually hosts the World Aerials. There's also a new A$50,000 family snowplay area.

Mt Buffalo is worth visiting mainly to stay in the historic Mt Buffalo Chalet, with its dramatic views over the craggy Victorian alps. The Chalet is done up in true 1930s style and offers gourmet dining – the local Angus beef a speciality. The slopes, a short drive away, are in an Alpine basin surrounded by boulders, with five lifts almost purely for beginners.

TOURIST OFFICES

Thredbo
www.thredbo.com.au

Perisher Blue
(for Perisher, Smiggins, Blue Cow, Guthega)
www.perisherblue.com.au

Charlotte Pass
www.charlottepass.com.au

Mount Hotham
www.hotham.com.au

Falls Creek
(for Falls Creek and Mt McKay)
www.fallscreek.com.au

Mt Buller
www.mtbuller.com.au

Mt Buffalo
www.mtbuffalochalet.com.au

New Zealand

- For Europeans, good for a combined holiday to the southern hemisphere and more interesting than summer skiing on glaciers
- For Australians, conveniently close, with flights from Sydney
- Huge areas of off-piste terrain accessible by helicopter on the South Island
- Some spectacular scenery, as seen in *The Lord of the Rings* movies

- It's a long way from anywhere except Australia
- Limited on-mountain restaurants – though these are steadily being upgraded
- Half-hour-plus drives from accommodation up to the ski areas (albeit with spectacular views)
- Highly changeable weather
- No trees, so skiing in bad weather is virtually impossible

The number of keen skiers and boarders from New Zealand found kicking around the Alps gives a clue that there must be some decent slopes back home – and indeed there are. The resorts are rather different from those of the Alps or the Rockies – generally, you don't stay near the slopes – and the networks of lifts and runs are rather limited by those exalted standards. If Whakapapa and Turoa on the North Island ever build their link, taken together they will be a match for smaller European resorts. Even so, Alpine glaciers will probably remain a more attractive bet for Europeans – unless of course you've got some other reason to visit New Zealand, as many of us have.

But the heli-skiing around the Mt Cook region on the South Island is definitely worth writing home about. For Europeans already spending a lot to travel to New Zealand, the extra cost of a day or two's heli-drops around the Methven area is well worth while.

Skiing at almost every New Zealand ski resort involves at least a half-hour drive from a nearby town – usually below snowline – to the ski field itself. Coach transfers from the hotels and towns to the ski fields are generally very well organised. The ski fields will have a base lodge, usually with a restaurant and a cafeteria, equipment rental and one or two shops, as well as the main lifts. The only on-snow accommodation is in luxury apartments at Cardrona on the South Island, and some private lodges at the base of Whakapapa on the North Island.

There are resorts on both North Island and South Island. The main concentration on South Island is around the scenic lakeside town (and year-round resort) of Queenstown, covered in detail in the chapter after this one.

In what follows, we describe the most prominent resorts (apart from Queenstown and its two local mountains), but there are a number of other possibilities. The main

commercial ones are described briefly in our directory at the back of the book, but there are also other ski fields run by clubs. Don't expect groomed trails. restaurants or other luxuries: club fields are pretty primitive, involving stiff walks to get to the base and crude rope tows or at best T-bars when you get there. Craigieburn on the South Island, near Mt Hutt, wins the vote for the most impressive terrain out of the selection.

Any of the major resorts is worth a day or two of your time if you're in the area and the conditions are right. But if your credit card is also in good condition, don't miss the heli-skiing; even if you're no expert off-piste, with powder skis it's a doddle, and tremendously satisfying.

We recommend Methven Heliski or Wilderness Heliski. Both operate in the main spine of mountains in the Mt Cook area and offer the longest and most spectacular runs for serious skiers and snowboarders. The cost for about five runs is around NZ$700.

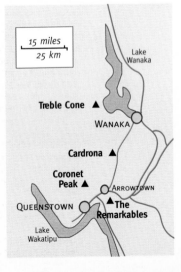

Phone numbers

From abroad use the prefix +64 and omit the initial '0' of the phone number.

KEY FACTS

Whakapapa

Altitude	1625-2300m
	5,330-7,550ft
Lifts	20
Pistes	1,360 acres
	900 hectares
Blue	25%
Red	50%
Black	25%
Snowmaking	some

Mount Hutt

Altitude	1420-2075m
	4,660-6,810ft
Lifts	9
Pistes	900 acres
	365 hectares
Green	25%
Blue	50%
Black	25%
Snowmaking	
	103 acres
	42 hectares

Treble Cone

Altitude	1200-1860m
	3,940-6,100ft
Lifts	5
Pistes	1,360 acres
	165 hectares
Green	15%
Blue	45%
Black	40%
Snowmaking	
	125 acres
	50 hectares

Cardrona

Altitude	1505-1895m
	4,940-6,220ft
Lifts	7
Pistes	790 acres
	320 hectares
Green	25%
Blue	55%
Black	20%
Snowmaking	none

There are several other companies operating on South Island. Harris Mts Heli-Ski, operating out of Queenstown and Wanaka, caters mainly for the large Japanese market, and the three-run days are generally very easy skiing with long waits in between lifts. The other major Queenstown operation, Southern Lakes Heli-Ski, is more amenable to exciting skiing. Try to leave the arrangements loose, to cope with the highly changeable weather.

An alternative adventure is to fly by plane to ski 10km/6 miles down the length of the Tasman Glacier. For a gentle schuss the cost is high – about NZ$800-900 for the day. The main draw is the immense grandeur of the place, along with the ski-plane flights over stunning blue ice-flows and the close proximity of Mt Cook. The Tasman is also one of the few glaciers in the world where it is possible to walk through the eery ice-blue glacial caves – quite a surreal experience.

As in the northern hemisphere, the season doesn't really get under way until midwinter – mid or late June; it runs until some time in October. Mount Hutt aims to open first, in mid-May, and disputes the longest-season title with Whakapapa, which generally stays open until mid-November.

Snowboarding is very popular in New Zealand, and most of the major resorts have special terrain-parks.

Whakapapa (pronounced Fukapapa) is on the slopes of the active volcano Mt Ruapehu, which has occasionally erupted in recent years, leaving the slopes black with volcanic ash. Until the late 1990s the volcano had not caused havoc since the 1950s, when an eruption carried away a bridge.

Mt Ruapehu is in the middle of the North Island and within four hours' drive of both Auckland and Wellington. Whakapapa, New Zealand's largest ski field, is located on the north-facing slopes, with a vertical of 675m/2,210ft served by 20 lifts including one fast quad. Terrain is typified by large, wide open cruisers plus challenging off-piste. Next to the base lodge is an extensive beginners' area, Happy Valley, with half a dozen rope tows, a chair-lift that was new last season and snowmaking that allows this particular section to open early in the season. The resort's lifts and runs range across craggy terrain made especially interesting because of the unpredictable twists, turns and drops of the solidified lava on which it sits. There is a mix of deep gullies, superb natural half-pipes for snowboarders and narrow chutes. There is a handful of mountain restaurants and a new cafe at the nearby Turoa ski field. Views from both resorts are of the surrounding volcanic peaks and wide open fields of tundra – quite surreal.

Accommodation is mostly 6km/4 miles away at Whakapapa village, with the best middle-of-the-road property being a motel named the Skotel. There is on-snow accommodation in ski lodges at the base. A complete anomaly in this area of rustic lodges is the Chateau, a hotel in the grand style of the 1920s, with overly high ceilings, sweeping drapes over picture windows,

TOURIST OFFICES

Whakapapa
t 07 892 3738
f 07 892 3732
snow@whakapapa.
co.nz
www.mtruapehu.com

Mount Hutt
t 03 308 5074
f 03 308 5076
service@nzski.com
www.nzski.com

Treble Cone
t 03 443 7443
f 03 443 8401
tcinfo@treblecone.co.
nz
www.treblecone.co.nz

Cardrona
t 03 443 7411
f 03 443 8818
info@cardrona.com
www.cardrona.com

a marble foyer and formal dining room with grand piano.

Worth knowing about is the hike to Mt Ruapehu's fizzing Crater Lake. Ask a ski patrol for directions or better still talk them into taking you on a guided trip. This involves about a half-hour hike up from the top of the highest T-bar, and then a long traverse across a large flat tundra-like area. A few lefts and rights and you are staring into the mouth of a volcano. Awesome views and neighbouring volcanos give this area an other-worldly feel.

On the south-western slope of Mt Ruapehu is **Turoa** – now under the same ownership as Whakapapa. You can ski both on the same ticket, which cost NZ$62 last season, the cheapest deal in NZ skiing. And there is now a trail that links both – but the snow must be perfect and you must be guided by a ski patroller. Turoa is smaller, but with an impressive 722m/2,36oft vertical – the biggest in Australasia. The longest run is 4km/2.5 miles. There's plenty of off-piste scope away from the gentle intermediate runs, plus the chance to ski on the Mangaehuehu Glacier. Accommodation is 20 minutes away in Ohakune.

The South Island has 15 ski areas, including five club fields. **Mt Hutt**, an hour west of Christchurch in the northern part of the island, has a 670m/2,200ft vertical and some of the country's most impressive, consistently steep, wide-open terrain – all within view of the Pacific Ocean. On a clear day you can even see the sandy beaches in the distance beyond the patchwork Canterbury plains – in fact it often snows on the beaches here. The lift system is half the size of Whakapapa's and a few more fast chair-lifts would not go amiss. The main area is an open bowl with gentle terrain in the centre served by chairs and drags and steeper terrain around the outside, some of which requires a short hike to the top. An impressive big base lodge was built for the 2000 season, including a spacious, welcoming cafe and brasserie with a glorious outdoor terrace, plus a well-stocked rental shop. Mt Hutt Helicopters offers six-run days in the mountains beyond for NZ$600. The helicopter departs from the heli-pad right in the car park – just wander up to the heli hut and book in. There is no accommodation on-mountain – most people stay in the little town of

Methven, where there are several truly comfortable up-market B&Bs as well as motels and apartments. The very British South Island capital of Christchurch, an hour and a half away, is also an option for accommodation.

About six hours' drive south of Christchurch is the quiet lakeside town of Wanaka, which is also 90 minutes from Queenstown, and there are two resorts accessible from here.

Treble Cone, 20km/12 miles from Wanaka, has more advanced slopes than any other NZ ski area, plus the advantage of a better lift system, including the first six-pack in the southern hemisphere. There are two well-maintained intermediate trails, one 3.5km/2 miles, the other 2km/1.2 miles. Both on the main flank and off to the side in Saddle Basin there are long natural half-pipes which are great fun when snow is good, as well as smooth, wide runs for cruising. Treble Cone is reached by a long and winding dirt track that adds to the excitement. The ski field offers stunning views across Lake Wanaka, with snowcapped Alpine-style peaks in the distance. There's a cosmopolitan cafe at the lift base, quite a discovery in such a far flung place. An enormous sundeck sharing that view was added last season. The resort is also adding another chair-lift in 2004 in its advanced Saddle Basin area and a fancy cafe to match. The food at Treble Cone and Cardrona is generally far better than the other resorts.

Cardrona, 34km/21 miles from Wanaka, is famous for its dry snow. The terrain is noted for its well-groomed, flattering cruisers. But there are some serious if short chutes, and the middle basin, Arcadia, hosts the New Zealand Extreme Skiing Championships. The total vertical is a modest 390m/1,280ft. Millions have been poured into the resort by its family owners over the past few years, resulting in a large base area focused around an odd clock tower. There's a bar and brasserie-style restaurant, a new ski-in/ski-out noodle bar with sundeck overlooking the nursery slopes, large rental facility and a licensed childcare centre, plus 10 modern, self-contained apartments at the base (but bring all your own supplies). Six were new last season. There are four half-pipes for boarders. Learners are looked after well, with three magic carpet lifts.

Queenstown

Lively base for sampling a range of South Island resorts

RATINGS

The slopes

Snow	**
Extent	*
Experts	***
Intermediates	***
Beginners	***
Convenience	*
Queues	***
Mountain restaurants	*

The rest

Scenery	****
Resort charm	**
Off-slope	*****

KEY FACTS

Resort	310m
	1,020ft

The Remarkables	
Slopes	1620-1935m
	5,310-6,350ft
Lifts	5
Pistes	545 acres
	220 hectares
Green	30%
Blue	40%
Black	30%
Snowmaking	
	25 acres

Coronet Peak	
Slopes	1210-1650m
	3,970-5,410ft
Lifts	6
Pistes	690 acres
	280 hectares
Green	20%
Blue	45%
Black	35%
Snowmaking	
	200 acres

658

➕ For Europeans, more interesting than summer skiing on glaciers

➕ For Australians, conveniently close, with flights from Sydney

➕ Huge areas of off-piste terrain accessible by helicopters, with excellent snow at the right time

➕ Lots to do off the slopes, especially for adrenalin junkies

➕ Lively town, with lots going on and good restaurants

➕ Grand views locally, and the spectacular 'fjord' country nearby

➖ Slopes (in two separate areas locally) are a drive from town

➖ Limited lift-served slopes in each area

➖ It's a long way from anywhere except Australia

➖ No real mountain restaurants – just pit stops at the lift bases

➖ Highly changeable weather

➖ No trees, so skiing in bad weather is virtually impossible

If you want a single destination in New Zealand – as opposed to visiting a few different mountains on your travels – Queenstown is probably it, especially if you can cope with the cost of a few heli-drops. Although the resorts of North Island are impressive, the Southern Alps are, in the end, more compelling – and their resorts are free of volcanic interruptions. Mount Hutt may be a slightly more impressive area than either of Queenstown's local fields – Coronet Peak and The Remarkables – but it's a rather isolated place. From Queenstown you have a choice of the two local fields plus the option of an outing to Treble Cone and Cardrona, perhaps with a night or two in Wanaka.

THE RESORT

Queenstown is a winter-and-summer resort on the shore of Lake Wakatipu. (There is a map of the area in the introductory chapter.) Although the setting is splendid, with views to the peaks of the aptly named Remarkables range beyond the lake, the town itself

This is the standard arrangement at Treble Cone: snow on the hill, but pastures green or brown in the valley ➔

is no beauty – it has grown up to meet tourists' needs, and has a very commercial feel. Shopping is good, of course. In recent years much effort has been put into smartening up the town, with such additions as the classy new Steamer Wharf complex by the lake and lots of lakeside luxury apartments and hotels. It has a lively, relaxed feel, and makes a satisfactory base, with some good restaurants, plenty of entertaining bars and lots of touristy clothes shops.

THE MOUNTAINS

There are four lift-served mountains – all small by Alpine standards – that you can get to from Queenstown. The two described here – Coronet Peak and The Remarkables – are close by (about a 30-minute drive). The others – Cardrona and Treble Cone – are a more serious drive away (at least 90 minutes), near Wanaka. Most people visiting these two resorts stay at Wanaka. At each base area you'll find a mini-resort – a ski school, a ski rental shop, a functional self-service

Boarding is popular in New Zealand, and although the two mountains close to Queenstown don't seem to have quite such a hold on the boarding market as Cardrona (see New Zealand introduction), they have everything you need, including equipment and tuition. You needn't go anywhere near a drag-lift, and there are no flats to worry about except on the lowest green at The Remarkables.

restaurant, but no accommodation except at Cardrona.

All these areas have something for all abilities of skier or boarder, with off-piste opportunities as well as prepared and patrolled trails. They use the American green/blue/ black convention for run classification, not the European blue/red/black.

THE SLOPES
Not the height of convenience
The Remarkables, true to their name, are a dramatic range of craggy peaks visible across the lake from some parts of Queenstown. The slopes are tucked in a bowl right behind the largest visible peak, a 45-minute drive from town. This resort is fine for families and beginners, (though there is limited extreme skiing for experts), with the emphasis on taking it easy and enjoying entertainment on the restaurant's sundecks during the week.

Two chairs go up from the base. The slow Alta lift has been replaced with a fast quad which serves easy runs and accesses the higher Sugar Bowl chair. This chair accesses mainly long, easy runs plus a couple of black chutes. The Shadow Basin chair leads to steeper terrain, including three hike-accessed, expert-only chutes that drop down to Lake Alta, and the Homeward Run – a broad, fairly gentle, unprepared slope down to the resort access road, where a shuttle-truck takes you back to the base.

Coronet Peak, about 25 minutes' drive from Queenstown, is a far more satisfying resort, especially for intermediates and above. Again, there are three main chair-lifts, one a fast quad that accesses practically all the runs. A new novice trail was added last season to appeal to beginner skiers and boarders. The main mountainside is a pleasantly varied intermediate slope, full of highly enjoyable rolling terrain that snowboarders adore, though it steepens near the bottom. A fourth lift, a T-bar, serves another mainly intermediate area to one side. There are also drags for beginners. Night skiing runs from July to September on Fridays and Saturdays only.

TERRAIN-PARKS
Coronet rules
Coronet Peak has two half-pipes and a terrain-park. The Remarkables has only a kids' adventure terrain-park plus the Ozone Tubing Park.

Queenstown

659

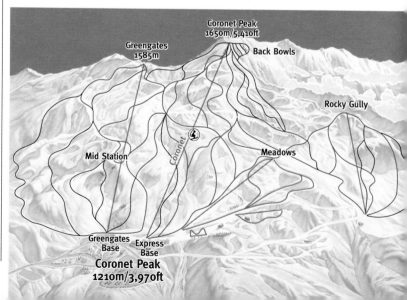

Coronet Peak
1650m/5,410ft

Greengates
1585m

Back Bowls

Rocky Gully

Coronet

Mid Station

Meadows

Greengates Base

Express Base

Coronet Peak
1210m/3,970ft

SNOW RELIABILITY
Good overall, but unpredictable
The New Zealand weather is highly variable, so it's difficult to be confident about snow conditions – though the mountains certainly get oodles of snow. The South Island resorts are at the same sort of latitude as the Alps, but are much more influenced by the ocean; fortunately, their ocean is a lot colder than ours. Coronet tends to receive sleet and/or rain even when it's snowing in The Remarkables. But Coronet Peak has snowmaking on practically all its intermediate terrain, from top to bottom of the mountain.

FOR EXPERTS
Challenges exist
Both areas have quite a choice of genuinely black slopes. Coronet's Back Bowls is an experts-only area, and there are other black slopes scattered around the mountain. The main enjoyment comes from venturing off-piste all over the place. The Remarkables' Shadow Basin chair serves some excellent slopes. And The Remarkables' hike-up expert chutes are truly world-class.

FOR INTERMEDIATES
Fine, within limits
There's some very enjoyable intermediate skiing in both areas –appreciably more at Coronet, where there are also easy blacks to go on to. But remember: these are very small areas by Alpine standards.

FOR BEGINNERS
Excellent
There are gentle slopes at both areas served by rope tows, and longer green runs served by chairs. And many other diversions if you decide it's a drag.

FOR CROSS-COUNTRY
Unremarkable
There is a short loop around a lake in the middle of The Remarkables area, but the only serious cross-country area is the elevated plateau of Waiorau Snow Farm, near Cardrona.

QUEUES
It depends
Coronet and The Remarkables can suffer a little from high-season crowds – there are certainly enough beds locally to lead to queues at peak times. But they aren't normally a major worry.

CHILDREN
At both areas there is a Skiiwiland Club for children aged four to six with morning and afternoon sessions. The Queenstown nursery can take younger children all day. There is a licensed nursery at The Remarkables, taking children from two to four.

MOUNTAIN RESTAURANTS
Er, what mountain restaurants?
Both areas have a simple cafeteria at the base, and Coronet has a brasserie, but nothing up the mountain. The Remarkables cafeteria has a big sunny deck often visited by the large local mountain parrots, called keas, and entertainment most days.

SCHOOLS AND GUIDES
All the usual classes
The schools are well organised, with a wide range of options, including 'guaranteed' beginner classes.

FACILITIES FOR CHILDREN
Look good
Childcare looked okay to us. Free lift passes are available for children under 11 at The Remarkables. There is a nursery at Coronet Peak with mini-call pagers for parents.

STAYING THERE

HOW TO GO
Sheer luxury?
There are lots of big, luxury hotels – all either new or refurbished – built to meet the big summer demand for beds in this popular lakeside resort.
Hotels Some hotels are quite some way from central Queenstown – inconvenient for après-ski unless there's a shuttle-bus. In town they range from the very simple to the glossily pretentious Millennium (03 441 8888). Aim to get a room with a view across Lake Wakatipu and the mountains – the view is worth the extra dollars. Two of the best boutique-style places to stay are the Heritage Hotel (03 442 4988) or the Mercure Grand Hotel St Moritz (03 442 4990).

EATING OUT
Lots of choice
We're told there are now over 160 bars and restaurants – a quite astonishing figure. Restaurants include Chinese, Italian, Malaysian, Japanese – you name it, Queenstown has it. The Boardwalk in the Steamer Wharf complex overlooking the lake is the place to go for seafood, and the upmarket Copper Club nearby is also excellent. A dining experience with a difference is the Bath House, located in a 1911 Victorian bath house right on the lakeshore. Solero Vino has delicious Mediterranean food and a

↑ You don't get views like this from the pistes of The Remarkables – but you do get them from the access road

NZ SKI MARKETING NETWORK

rustic bar, and McNeill's is an excellent brew-pub with a range of tasty beers, housed in a stone cottage. The Bunker does excellent local cuisine such as Bluff oysters and lamb. Gantley's, a little way out of town, is a classic restaurant in an historic home. At the other end of the scale, pizza-lovers crowd into The Cow, a cosy barn-like place where you sit on logs around a fire waiting for tables or takeaways. Lone Star offers big servings of satisfying American-style food.

APRES-SKI
Lively little town
Queenstown has a good range of bars and clubs that stay open late, with disco or live music. A small upmarket casino opened in 1999 in the plush Steamer Wharf, which also holds a classy cigar bar and good duty free shopping.

OFF THE SLOPES
Scare yourself silly
There are lots of scary things to do – see the feature box. Just to the west is the spectacularly scenic 'fjord country', and you can go on independent or guided walks. By all reports, the Milford Sound sightseeing flights by plane or helicopter are to be preferred to the slow bus-ride – but be aware that the weather can ruin your plans. A marvellous thing to do is to take the Skyline gondola 400m above Queenstown for the great view and also a spin down the public go-cart track. Cruise the lake on an historic steamship or go wine tasting. Arrowtown is interesting for a quick visit – a cute, touristy old mining town where you can kit yourself out to go panning for gold. The Winter Festival, held in mid-July, is an annual 'action-packed week of mayhem'.

661

GET THAT ADRENALIN RUSH

The streets of Queenstown are lined by agencies offering various artificial thrills. We've sampled just a few.

AJ Hackett's bungee jump at Kawarau Bridge is where this crazy activity got off the ground – you plunge towards the icy river, but are pulled up short by your bungee cord and lowered into an inflatable boat. You can now also jump off a platform near the sightseeing gondola above town, giving you the illusion of leaping out over the lake and Queenstown.

The Shotover Jet Boat experience is less demanding. You get chauffeured at high speed along the rocky river in a boat that can get along in very shallow water, execute high-speed 360° turns and pass very close to cliffs and trees.

The whitewater rafting is genuinely thrilling – and not as uncomfortable as you'd expect, thanks to the full wet-suit, helmet, boots and gloves, and to the exertion involved. The rivers have some exciting rapids. One route even passes through a tunnel excavated in the gold-mining days, after which comes a small but steep waterfall where your souvenir shots are snapped.

Phone numbers
From abroad use the prefix +64 and omit the initial '0' of the phone number.

TOURIST OFFICE

The Remarkables
t 03 442 4615
service@theremarkables.co.nz
www.nzski.com

Coronet Peak
t 03 442 4620
service@coronetpeak.co.nz
www.nzski.com

Reference section

A classified listing of the names, numbers and addresses you are likely to need.

Tour operators 664

Most people still prefer the convenience of a package holiday, which is what most of the companies listed are set up to provide. But note that we've also included some operators that offer accommodation without travel arrangements.

663

Reference section

664

TOUR OPERATORS

Absolute Ski
Chalet in Méribel
Tel 01788 822100
holiday@absoluteski.com
www.absoluteski.com

Airtours
Mainstream operator
Tel 0800 916 0623
www.airtours.co.uk

Albus Travel
St Anton specialist
Tel 01449 711952
info@albustravel.com
www.albustravel.com

Alpine Action
Chalets in Les Trois Vallées
Tel 01903 761986
sales@alpine-action.co.uk
www.alpine-action.co.uk

Alpine Answers Select
Tailor-made holidays
Tel 020 8871 4656
select@alpineanswers.co.uk
www.alpineanswers.com

Alpine Escapes
Catered chalets in Morzine
Tel 00 33 450 74739 /
020 8859 6327
info@alpine-escapes.com
www.alpine-escapes.com

Alpine Events
Corporate ski specialist
Tel 020 7622 2265
alpine@offsiteevents.com
www.alpineevents.co.uk

Alpine Tours
*Group and schools holidays,
mainly in Austria and Italy*
Tel 01227 738388
sales@alpinetours.co.uk

Alpine Weekends
Weekends in the Alps
Tel 020 8944 9762
info@alpineweekends.com
www.alpineweekends.com

Alps2Go
Holidays in Morzine
Tel 01908 585548
info@alps2go.com
www.alps2go.com

Altitude Holidays
Catered chalets in Courchevel
Tel 0870 870 7669
info@altitudeholidays.com
www.altitudeholidays.com

AmeriCan Ski
*Hotels and apartments in
France and North America*
Tel 01892 511894
ian.porter@via.in2i.net
www.awwt.co.uk

American Ski Classics
*Holidays in major North
American resorts*
Tel 020 8392 6660
sales@holidayworld.ltd.uk
www.americanskiclassics.com

APT Holidays Ltd
*Weekend breaks by coach to
France*
Tel 01268 783878
apt.holidays@virgin.net
www.apt-holidays.co.uk /
www.ski-express.net

Aravis Alpine Retreat
*Chalet in St Jean-de-Sixt (La
Clusaz)*
Tel 020 8878 8760
info@aravis-retreat.com
www.aravis-retreat.com

Avant-ski
Mainly holidays in France
Tel 0191 285 8141
sales@avant-ski.com
www.avant-ski.com

Balkan Holidays
*Holidays in Bulgaria, Slovenia
and Romania*
Tel 0845 130 1114
res@balkanholidays.co.uk
www.balkanholidays.co.uk

Barrelli Ski
*Chalets in Champagny and Les
Houches*
Tel 0870 220 1500
whiplash@barrelliski.co.uk
www.barrelliski.co.uk

Belvedere Chalets
Luxury chalets in Méribel
Tel 01264 738 257
info@belvedereproperties.net
www.belvedereproperties.net

Bigfoot Travel
*Variety of holidays in
Chamonix*
Tel 0870 300 5874
reservation@bigfoot-
travel.co.uk
www.bigfoot-travel.co.uk

Bladon Lines
Chalet arm of Inghams
Tel 020 8780 8800
bladonlines@inghams.co.uk
www.inghams.co.uk

Board and Lodge
*Catered snowboarding
holidays in Chamonix*
Tel 020 7916 2275
info@boardnlodge.com
www.boardnlodge.com

Bonne Neige Ski Holidays
Catered chalets in Méribel
Tel 01270 256966
ukoffice@bonne-neige-ski.com
www.bonne-neige-ski.com

Borderline
Specialist in Barèges
Tel 00 33 562 926895
info@borderlinehols.com
www.borderlinehols.com

**Canadian Powder Tours Chalet
Holidays**
Chalet specialists in Fernie
Tel +1 250 423 3019
cdnpowder@elkvalley.net
www.canadianpowdertours.com
www.skiaccommodation.com

Canterbury Travel
Holidays in Lapland
Tel 01923 822388
reservations@laplandmagic.com
www.laplandmagic.com

The Chalet Company
*Catered chalets in Morzine and
Ardent (Avoriaz)*
Tel 0871 717 4208 /
00 33 450 79 68 40
moran@thechaletco.com
www.thechaletco.com

The Chalet Group
*Chalet holidays in the French
Alps*
Tel 00 33 479 013500
kate@chaletgroup.com
www.chaletgroup.com

Chalet Gueret
Luxury chalet in Morzine
Tel 01884 256542
info@chaletgueret.com
www.chaletgueret.com

Chalet Kiana
Chalet in Les Contamines
Tel 00 33 450 915518 /
01689 838558
chaletkiana@aol.com
www.chaletkiana.com

Chalet Number One
Chalet in Ste-Foy
Tel 01572 717259 /
0033 479069533
info@chaletnumberone.com
www.chaletnumberone.com

Les Chalets de St Martin
Chalets in St-Martin
Tel 01202 473255
les.chalets@virgin.net
www.leschalets.co.uk

Chalet Snowboard
Snowboard holidays in France
Tel 0870 800 4020
info@csbmountainholidays.com
www.csbmountainholidays.com

Chalets 'Unlimited'
Chalets worldwide
Tel 0191 285 8141
sales@avant-ski.com
www.avant-ski.com

Chalet World
Chalets in big-name resorts
Tel 01743 231199 /
020 7373 2096
sales@chaletworld.co.uk
www.chaletworld.co.uk

Challenge Activ
Chalets/apartments in Morzine
Tel 0871 717 4113
info@challenge-activ.com
www.challenge-activ.com

Chamonix Lodge
Chalet in Chamonix
Tel 00 33 674 601167
chamonixlodge@hotmail.com
www.chamonixlodge.com

Chez Jay Ski Chalets
*Chalets in Villaroger (Les Arcs)
and Montchavin (La Plagne)*
Tel 01843 298030
ski@chezjayski.com
www.chezjayski.com

Classic Ski Limited
*Holidays for 'mature'
skiers/beginners*
Tel 01590 623400
info@classicski.co.uk
www.classicski.co.uk

Club Europe Schools Skiing
Schools trips
Tel 0800 496 4996
ski@club-europe.co.uk
www.club-europe.co.uk

Club Med
*All-inclusive holidays in
holiday 'villages'*
Tel 08453 676767 (option 1)
admin.uk@clubmed.com
www.clubmed.co.uk

Club Pavilion
Affordable ski holidays
Tel 0870 241 0427
info@conceptholidays.com
www.conceptholidays.com

Collineige
Chamonix valley specialist
Tel 01276 24262
sales@collineige.com
www.collineige.com

Connick Ski
Chalet in Châtel
Tel 00 33 450 732212
nick@connickski.com
www.connickski.com

Contiki
Coach-travel trips for 18-35s
Tel 020 8290 6422
travel@contiki.co.uk
www.contiki.com

Cooltip Mountain Holidays
Chalets in Méribel
Tel 01964 563563
ski@cooltip.com
www.cooltip.com

The Corporate Ski Company
Corporate specialists
Tel 020 7627 5500
ski@vantagepoint.co.uk
www.thecorporateskicompany.
co.uk

Crystal
Major mainstream operator
Tel 0870 160 6040
skires@crystalholidays.co.uk
www.crystalski.co.uk

Descent International
*Chalets in France and
Switzerland*
Tel 020 7384 3854
ski@descent.co.uk
www.descent.co.uk

Les Deux Chalets
Chalets in Méribel
Tel 01303 246966
anjid@ukonline.co.uk
www.chaletdelauney.co.uk

Directski.com
*Holidays in Austria, France,
Italy and Andorra*
Tel 0800 587 0945
sales@directski.com
www.directski.com

Elegant Resorts
Luxury ski holidays
Tel 01244 897333
enquiries@elegantresorts.co.uk
www.elegantresorts.co.uk

Equity School Ski
School group holidays
Tel 01273 299299
schoolski@equity.co.uk
www.equityschooltravel.co.uk

Equity Ski
All-in holidays
Tel 01273 298298
travel@equity.co.uk
www.equityski.co.uk

Erna Low
*Hotel and self-catering
holidays in Europe*
Tel 0870 750 6820
info@ernalow.co.uk
www.ernalow.co.uk

Esprit Ski
*Families specialist in Europe
and North America*
Tel 01252 618300
travel@esprit-holidays.co.uk
www.esprit-holidays.co.uk

Eurotunnel Motoring Holidays
Self-drive holidays to France
Tel 0870 333 2001
ethols@crestaholidays.co.uk
www.eurotunnel.com

The Family Ski Company
Family holidays in France
Tel 01684 540333
enquiries@familyski.co.uk
www.familyski.co.uk

Fantiski-Ski2k
Self-catering in Val-d'Isère
Tel 01622 861533
admin@fantiski.co.uk
www.fantiski.co.uk

Finlays
Mainly chalets in France
Tel 01573 226611
finlayski@aol.com
www.finlayski.com

First Choice Ski
Major mainstream operator
Tel 0870 754 3477
sales@fcski.co.uk
www.firstchoice.co.uk/ski

FlexiSki
Specialists in flexible breaks
Tel 0870 909 0754
reservations@flexiski.com
www.flexiski.com

Fraser Ralston
*Self-catering accommodation
in Chamonix*
Tel 028 9042 4662
fraser_ralston@hotmail.com
www.chamonix.uk.com

Freedom Holidays
Tailormade holidays to Châtel
Tel 01798 861888
freedomhols@hotmail.com
www.freedomholidays.co.uk

French Freedom Holidays
Holidays in France
Tel 01724 290660
info@french-freedom.co.uk
www.french-freedom.co.uk

Frontier Ski
Holidays in Canada
Tel 020 8776 8709
info@frontier-travel.co.uk
www.frontier-ski.co.uk

**Frosty's Ski and Snowboard
Holidays**
Chalet in St-Jean-de-Sixt
Tel 00 33 450 023728
info@frostys.co.uk
www.frostys.co.uk

Frozenplanet.co.uk
*Chalets and apartments,
mostly in the Alps*
Tel 07947 331606
www.frozenplanet.co.uk

Glacier Dayz
Chalet holidays in Champagny
Tel 01925 485389
info@glacierdayz.com
www.glacierdayz.com

Haig Ski
*Hotels with guiding in Châtel
and Morzine*
Tel 00 33 450 811947
sales@haigski.com
www.haigski.com

Handmade Holidays
Tailor-made specialists
Tel 01285 642555
travel@handmade-holidays.co.uk
www.handmade-holidays.co.uk

Hannibals
Holidays in Serre-Chevalier
Tel 01233 813105
sales@hannibals.co.uk
www.hannibals.co.uk

Headwater Holidays
Cross-country skiing holidays
Tel 01606 720199
info@headwater.com
www.headwater-holidays.co.uk

High Mountain Holidays
Catered chalet in Les Praz
Tel 01993 775540
info@highmountain.co.uk
www.highmountain.co.uk

Huski
Holidays in Chamonix
Tel 020 7938 4844
sales@huski.com
www.huski.com

Independent Ski Links
Tailor-made holidays
Tel 01964 533905
info@ski-links.com
www.ski-links.com

Inghams
Major mainstream operator
Tel 020 8780 4433
reservations@inghams.co.uk
www.inghams.co.uk

Inntravel
Cross-country skiing holidays
Tel 01653 617920
winter@inntravel.co.uk
www.inntravel.co.uk

Interhome
Apartments in Europe
Tel 020 8891 1294
info@interhome.co.uk
www.interhome.co.uk

International Academy
Schools programme
Tel 029 2067 2500
info@international-academy.com
www.international-academy.com

Interski
Group holidays in Italy
Tel 01623 456333
email@interski.co.uk
www.interski.co.uk

Kuoni
Holidays in Switzerland
Tel 01306 747000
switzerland.sales@kuoni.co.uk
www.kuoni.co.uk

Lagrange Holidays
Holidays to France & Andorra
Tel 020 7371 6111
info@lagrange-holidays.co.uk
www.lagrange-holidays.co.uk

The Last Resort
Chalet in St Jean-de-Sixt
Tel 0800 652 3977
thelastresort@cario.fr
www.lastresort.info

Le Ski
Chalets in Courchevel, Val-d'Isère and La Tania
Tel 0870 754 4444
mail@leski.com
www.leski.com

Lotus Supertravel
European and US holidays
Tel 020 7962 9933
ski@lotusgroup.co.uk
www.supertravel.co.uk

Made to Measure Holidays
Tailor-made holidays
Tel 01243 533333
sales@mtmhols.co.uk
www.mtmhols.co.uk

Mark Warner
Chalet-hotel holidays in big-name resorts
Tel 0870 770 4226
sales@markwarner.co.uk
www.markwarner.co.uk

MasterSki
Christian holidays
Tel 020 8942 9442
holidays@mastersun.co.uk
www.mastersun.co.uk

McNab Mountain Sports
Snowboarding holidays based around Argentière
Tel 01546 830243
info@mcnab.co.uk
www.mcnab.co.uk

Meriski
Chalet specialist in Méribel
Tel 01285 648518
sales@meriski.co.uk
www.meriski.co.uk

MGS Ski
Apartments in Val-Cenis
Tel 01799 525984
skimajor@aol.com
www.mgsski.com

Momentum Ski
Tailor-made specialists
Tel 020 7371 9111
sales@momentumski.com
www.momentumski.com

Moswin Tours
Small German programme
Tel 0116 271 9922
germany@moswin.com
www.moswin.com

Mountain Highs
Chalet specialist in Morzine
Tel 0121 550 9321
mhighs@dircon.co.uk
www.mhighs.dircon.co.uk

Mountain Tracks
Ski safaris mainly based on Chamonix and Monterosa Ski
Tel 020 8877 5773
chris@mountaintracks.co.uk
www.mountaintracks.co.uk

Neilson
Major mainstream operator
Tel 0870 333 3347
sales@neilson.com
www.neilson.com

Neilson School Groups
School trips to North America and Europe
Tel 0870 333 3620
info@skiersworld.com
www.skiersworld.com

Optimum Ski
Chalet in Les Arcs
Tel 08702 406198
info@optimumski.com
www.optimumski.com

The Oxford Ski Company
Chalets in the Alps
Tel 01451 810300
info@oxfordski.com
www.oxfordski.com

Panorama Holidays
Budget-oriented holidays
Tel 08707 505060
panoramaski@phg.co.uk
www.panoramaholidays.co.uk

Peak Leisure
Chalet in Ste-Foy
Tel 01256 397010
info@peak-leisure.co.uk
www.peak-leisure.co.uk

Peak Retreats
Holidays to the lesser-known Alpine resorts
Tel 0870 770 0408
bonjour@peakretreats.co.uk
www.peakretreats.co.uk

Peak Ski
Chalets in Verbier
Tel 01442 832629
peakski@which.net
www.peak-ski.co.uk

PGL Ski Europe
Specialist in school group holidays
Tel 01989 768168
ski@pgl.co.uk
www.pgl.co.uk

PGL Teenski
Holidays for teenagers
Tel 01989 767767
holidays@pgl.co.uk
www.pgl.co.uk

Piste Artiste Ltd
Holidays in Champéry
reserve@pisteartiste.com
www.pisteartiste.com

Plus Travel
Specialists in Swiss resorts
Tel 020 7734 0383
sales@plustravel.co.uk
www.plustravel.co.uk

Powder Byrne
Small programme of luxury hotel holidays in Europe
Tel 020 8246 5300
enquiries@powderbyrne.co.uk
www.powderbyrne.com

Powder Skiing in North America Limited
Heli-skiing holidays in Canada
Tel 020 7736 8191
info@psna.co.uk

Premiere Neige
Chalets/apartments in Ste-Foy
Tel 0709 2000 300
ski@premiere-neige.com
www.premiere-neige.com

Ramblers Holidays
Cross-country holidays
Tel 01707 331133
info@ramblersholidays.co.uk
www.ramblersholidays.co.uk

Re-lax Holidays
Hotel holidays in Switzerland
Tel 020 8360 1185
sarah@re-laxholidays.co.uk
www.re-laxholidays.co.uk

Rocketski
All-in holidays online
Tel 01273 262626
info@rocketski.com
www.rocketski.com

Scott Dunn Latin America
Holidays to South America
Tel 020 8682 5030
latin@scottdunn.com
www.scottdunn.com

Scott Dunn Ski
Upmarket holidays
Tel 020 8682 5050
ski@scottdunn.com
www.scottdunn.com

Silver Ski
Chalet holidays in France
Tel 01622 735544
karen@silverski.co.uk
www.silverski.co.uk

Simon Butler Skiing
Holidays in Megève
Tel 0870 873 0001
info@simonbutlerskiing.co.uk
www.simonbutlerskiing.co.uk

Simply Ski
Specialist chalet operator
Tel 020 8541 2209
ski@simply-travel.com
www.simplyski.co.uk

Ski The American Dream
Major N American operator
Tel 0870 350 7547
holidays@skidream.com
www.skidream.com

Ski 'n' Action
Chalet in Le Praz (Courchevel)
Tel 01707 251696
info@ski-n-action.com
www.ski-n-action.com

Ski 2
Monterosa specialists
Tel 01962 713330
info@ski-2.com
www.ski-2.com

Ski Activity
Holidays in big-name resorts
Tel 01738 840888
sales@skiactivity.com
www.skiactivity.com

Ski Addiction
Chalets and hotels in Châtel, St Anton and Gressoney
Tel 01580 819354
sales@skiaddiction.co.uk
www.skiaddiction.co.uk

Ski All America
US and Canadian holidays
Tel 08701 676 676
sales@skiallamerica.com
www.skiallamerica.com

Skialot
Chalet in Chatel
Tel 020 8363 8326
stuey@skialot.com
www.skialot.com

Ski Amis
Chalet holidays in the La Plagne area
Tel 020 7692 0850
info@skiamis.com
www.skiamis.com

Ski Arrangements
Chalets/apartments in Europe and North America
Tel 08700 110565
info@skiarrangements.com
www.skiarrangements.com

SkiAway Holidays
Holidays in the Pyrenees and the French Alps
Tel 01903 824823
skiaway@tourplanholidays.com
www.tourplanholidays.com

Ski Balkantours
Holidays in Eastern Europe
Tel 028 9024 6795
mail@balkan.co.uk
www.balkan.co.uk

Ski Barrett-Boyce
Chalet in Megève with tuition
Tel 01737 831184
info@skibb.com
www.skibb.com

Ski Basics
Chalets in Méribel
Tel 01225 444143
sales@skibasics.co.uk
www.skibasics.co.uk

Ski Beat
Chalets in La Plagne, Les Arcs, Val d'Isere and La Tania
Tel 01243 780405
Ski@skibeat.co.uk
www.skibeat.co.uk

Ski Blanc
Chalet holidays in Méribel
Tel 020 8502 9082
sales@skiblanc.co.uk
www.skiblanc.co.uk

Ski Bon
Chalets in Méribel
Tel 020 8668 8223
infonet@skibon.com
www.skibon.com

SkiBound
Schools division of First Choice
Tel 0870 900 3200
sales@skibound.co.uk
www.skibound.co.uk

Ski Chamois
Holidays in Morzine
Tel 01302 369006
sales@skichamois.co.uk
www.skichamois.co.uk

Ski Club of Great Britain
Holidays for club members
Tel 0845 458 0780
skiers@skiclub.co.uk
www.skiclub.co.uk

The Ski Company
Holidays with tuition
Tel 0870 241 2085
info@theskicompany.co.uk
www.theskicompany.co.uk

Ski Cuisine
Chalets in Méribel
Tel 01702 589543
skicuisine@dial.pipex.com
www.skicuisine.co.uk

Ski Deep
Chalets in La Tania & Le Praz
Tel 00 33 479 081905
info@skideep.com
www.skideep.com

Ski Etoile
Chalets and hotels in Montgenèvre and Argentiere
Tel 01588 640442
ski-etoile@clun25.
freeserve.co.uk
www.skietoile.co.uk

Ski Expectations
Mainly hotels and chalets in Europe
Tel 01799 531888
ski.expectations@virgin.net
www.skiexpectations.com

Ski Famille
Family holidays in Les Gets
Tel 0845 644 3764
info@skifamille.co.uk
www.skifamille.co.uk

Ski France
Chalets and catered apartments in France
Tel 0870 787 3402
ski@skifrance.co.uk
www.skifrance.co.uk

SkiGower
School and group trips, mainly Switzerland
Tel 01527 851411
peter@gowstrav.demon.co.uk
www.skigower.co.uk

Ski Hame
Catered chalets in the Three Valleys
Tel 01875 320157
powderpigs@skihame.co.uk
www.skihame.co.uk

Ski Hillwood
Austrian, French and Canadian family holidays
Tel 01923 290700
sales@hillwood-holidays.co.uk
www.hillwood-holidays.co.uk

Ski Hiver
Chalets in Peisey (Les Arcs)
Tel 023 9242 8586
skihiver@aol.com
www.skihiver.co.uk

Ski Independence
USA, Canada and Europe
Tel 0870 555 0555
ski@ski-i.com
www.ski-i.com

Ski La Cote
Chalet in La Chapelle d'Abondance
Tel 01482 668357
adrian@ski-la-cote.karoo.co.uk
www.ski-la-cote.karoo.net

Ski Leisure Direction
Mainly self-catering in France
Tel 020 8324 4042
sales@leisuredirection.co.uk
www.leisuredirection.co.uk

Ski Life
Self-drive to the French Alps
Tel 0870 429 2180
skilife@frenchlife.co.uk
www.skiinglife.co.uk

Ski Line
Chalet holidays in Europe and North America
Tel 020 8650 5900
angus@skiline.co.uk
www.skiline.co.uk

Ski Link
Holidays in the French Alps
Tel 01983 812883
skilinkuk@aol.com
www.ski-link.co.uk

Ski McNeill
Tailor-made to USA and European weekends
Tel 028 9066 6699
contact@skimcneill.com
www.skimcneill.com

Ski Miquel
Small but eclectic programme
Tel 01457 821200
ski@miquelhols.co.uk
www.miquelhols.co.uk

Ski Morgins Holidays
Chalet holidays in Morgins
Tel 01568 770681
info@skimorgins.com
www.skimorgins.com

Ski Morzine
Holiday accommodation in Morzine
Tel 01372 470104
info@skimorzine.com
www.skimorzine.com

Ski Olympic
Chalet holidays in France
Tel 01302 328820
info@skiolympic.co.uk
www.skiolympic.com

Ski Peak
Specialist in Vaujany
Tel 01428 608070
info@skipeak.com
www.skipeak.com

SkiPlan Travel Service
Schools programme of Tops Travel
Tel 01273 774778
sales@topstravel.co.uk

Ski Rosie
Holidays in Chatel and Morgins
Tel 00 33 450813100
rosie@skirosie.com
www.skirosie.com

Ski Safari
Canadian and US specialist, but also Chile
Tel 01273 223680
info@skisafari.com
www.skisafari.com

Skisafe Travel
Mainly holidays in Scotland
Tel 0141 812 0925
info@osatravel.co.uk
www.osatravel.co.uk

Ski Scott James
Chalets in Argentière
Tel 01845 501139
jamie@skiscottjames.co.uk
www.skiscottjames.co.uk

Ski Solutions
Tailor-made holidays
Tel 020 7471 7777
alc@skisolutions.com
www.skisolutions.com

Ski Success
Group holidays to US/Italy
Tel 01225 764205
info@success-tours.co.uk
www.success-tours.co.uk

Ski Supreme
Coach and self-drive holidays
Tel 01355 260547
info@skisupreme.co.uk
www.skisupreme.co.uk

Ski Total
Chalets in Europe and Canada
Tel 08701 633633
sales@skitotal.com
www.skitotal.com

Ski-Val
Holidays in France and Austria
Tel 0870 746 3030
reservations@skival.co.uk
www.skival.co.uk

Ski Verbier
Specialists in Verbier
Tel 020 7385 8050
info@skiverbier.com
www.skiverbier.com

Ski Weekend
Weekend and ten-day holidays
Tel 0870 060 0615
sales@skiweekend.com
www.skiweekend.com

Ski Weekends & Board Breaks
3- and 6-day holidays to Les Trois Vallées
Tel 01375 396688 / 0870 4423400
sales@harris-travel.com
www.skiweekends.com

Ski Wild
Austria specialist
Tel 0870 746 9668
info@skiwild.co.uk
www.skiwild.co.uk

Ski with Julia
Hotels/chalets in Switzerland
Tel 01386 584478
julia@skijulia.co.uk
www.skijulia.co.uk

Skiworld
European and North American programme
Tel 0870 241 6723
sales@skiworld.ltd.uk
www.skiworld.ltd.uk

Ski Yogi
Italian Dolomites holidays
Tel 01799 531886
ski.expectations@virgin.net
www.skiexpectations.com

Sloping Off
Group holidays by coach
Tel 01725 552833
hilary@slopingoff.fsnet.co.uk
www.equity.co.uk

Slovenija Pursuits
Accommodation in Slovenija and Austria
Tel 0870 220 0201
enquiries@slovenijapursuits.co.uk
www.slovenijapursuits.co.uk

Snowbizz Vacances
Holidays in Puy-St-Vincent
Tel 01778 341455
wendy@snowbizz.co.uk
www.snowbizz.co.uk

Snowcoach
Holidays to Andorra, Austria and France
Tel 01727 866177
info@snowcoach.co.uk
www.snowcoach.co.uk

Snowfocus
Chalet in Châtel
Tel 01392 479555
action@snowfocus.com
www.snowfocus.com

Snowlife
Holidays in La Clusaz
Tel 01534 863630
info@snowlife.co.uk
www.snowlife.co.uk

Snowline
Chalet holidays in France
Tel 020 8870 4807
ski@snowline.co.uk
www.snowline.co.uk

Snowscape
Flexible trips to Austria
Tel 01905 357760
skiandboard@snowscape.co.uk
www.snowscape.co.uk

Solo's
Singles' holidays, ages 25 to 69
Tel 08700 720700
travel@solosholidays.co.uk
www.solosholidays.co.uk

La Source
Luxury chalet in Villard-Reculas
Tel 01707 655988
lasourcefrance@aol.com
www.lasource.org.uk

Stanford Skiing
Megève specialist
Tel 01223 477644
info@stanfordskiing.co.uk
www.stanfordskiing.co.uk

St Anton Ski Company
Hotels and chalets in St Anton
Tel 00 43 676 495 3438
jonathanverney@compuserve.com
www.atlas.co.uk/ski

Susie Ward Alpine Holidays
Flexible holidays to Châtel
Tel 01872 553055
susie@susieward.com
www.susieward.com

Swiss Travel Service
Hotels in Switzerland
Tel 0870 191 7175
swiss@bridge-travel.co.uk
www.swisstravel.co.uk

Thomson Ski & Snowboarding
Major mainstream operator
Tel 0870 606 1470
info@thomson-ski.com
www.thomson-ski.co.uk

Top Deck
Lively, informal holidays
Tel 020 7244 8000
res@topdecktravel.co.uk
www.topdecktravel.co.uk

Tops Ski Chalets and Club Hotels
Chalets hotels in France
Tel 01273 774666
sales@topstravel.co.uk
www.topstravel.co.uk

Trail Alpine
Chalet in Morzine
Tel 0870 750 6560
info@trailalpine.co.uk
www.trailalpine.co.uk

Trailfinders
North American programme
Tel 0845 050 5900
www.trailfinders.com

United Vacations Ski Freedom USA & Canada
US and Canada programme
Tel 0870 606 2222
uvuk@unitedvacations.com
www.unitedvacations.co.uk

Uptoyou.com
Flexible breaks
Tel 0845 070 0203
alison.fox@uptoyou.com
www.uptoyou.com

Val d'Isère A La Carte
Hotels/self-catering holidays
Tel 01481 236800
skialacarte@aol.com
www.skivaldisere.co.uk

Vanilla Ski
Chalet in Seez (La Rosière)
Tel 01932 860696
sam@vanillaski.com
www.vanillaski.com

Vertical Reality at Verbier Ltd
Luxury chalet accommodation
Tel 01268 452337
verticalr@hotmail.com
www.verticalrealityverbier.com

VIP
Specialist in Val d'Isère
Tel 020 8875 1957
ski@valdisere.co.uk
www.valdisere.co.uk

Virgin Ski
Holidays to America
Tel 0870 220 2788
brochure.requests@
virginholidays.co.uk
www.virginholidays.co.uk/snow

Waymark Holidays
Cross-country skiing holidays
Tel 01753 516477
www.waymarkholidays.com

Weekends in Val d'Isère
Weekends not just in Val
Tel 020 8944 9762
info@alpineweekends.com
www.val-disere-ski.com

White Roc
Weekends and tailormade
Tel 020 7792 1188
ski@whiteroc.co.uk
www.whiteroc.co.uk

World Skiers
Tailormade holidays
Tel 0870 757 2288
ski@onlinetravelgroup.co.uk
www.worldskiers.com

YSE
Holidays in Val-d'Isère
Tel 020 8871 5117
sales@yseski.co.uk
www.yseski.co.uk

AIRLINES

Air Canada
Tel 0870 524 7226
www.aircanada.ca

Air France
Tel 0845 082 0162
www.airfrance.com/uk

Air New Zealand
Tel 0800 028 4149
www.airnewzealand.co.uk

Alitalia
Tel 0870 544 8259
www.alitalia.co.uk

American Airlines
Tel 020 7365 0777
www.aa.com

Austrian Airlines
Tel 0845 601 0948
www.austrianairlines.co.uk

Bmibaby
www.bmibaby.com

British Airways
Tel 0845 77 333 77
www.britishairways.com

Continental Airlines
Tel 0800 776464
www.continental.com

Delta Airlines
Tel 0800 414767
www.delta.com

EasyJet
Tel 0870 6 000 000
www.easyjet.com

Flybe
www.flybe.com

KLM
Tel 08705 074074
www.klmuk.co.uk

Lufthansa
Tel 0845 773 7747
www.lufthansa.com

Ryanair
Tel 0871 246 0000
www.ryanair.com

Swiss International Air Lines
Tel 0845 601 0956
www.swiss.com

United Airlines
Tel 0845 844 4777
www.unitedairlines.co.uk

Virgin Atlantic Airways
Tel 01293 450 150
www.virgin-atlantic.com

AIRPORTS

Aberdeen
Tel 01224 722331
www.baa.co.uk

Belfast
Tel 028 9448 4848
www.bial.co.uk

Birmingham
Tel 08707 335511
www.bhx.co.uk

Bournemouth
Tel 01202 364000
www.flybournemouth.com

Bristol
Tel 0870 121 2747
www.bristolairport.co.uk

Cardiff
Tel 01446 711111
www.cial.co.uk

Dublin
Tel +353 1 814 1111
www.dublin-airport.com

East Midlands
Tel 01332 852852
www.eastmidlandsairport.com

Edinburgh
Tel 0131 333 1000
www.baa.co.uk

Exeter
Tel 01392 367433
www.exeter-airport.co.uk

Glasgow
Tel 0141 887 1111
www.baa.co.uk

Leeds-Bradford
Tel 0113 250 9696
www.lbia.co.uk

London Gatwick
Tel 0870 000 2468
www.baa.co.uk

London Heathrow
Tel 0870 0000 123
www.baa.co.uk

London Luton
Tel 01582 405100
www.london-luton.com

London Stansted
Tel 0870 0000 303
www.baa.co.uk

Information correct at time of going to press.

Manchester
Tel 0161 489 3000
www.manchesterairport.co.uk

Newcastle
Tel 0191 286 0966
www.newcastleairport.com

Teesside
Tel 01325 332811
www.teessideairport.com

AIRPORT TRANSFERS

Airport Transfer Service
Tel +33 450 536397
Geneva transfers to Portes du Soleil, Chamonix and Haute Savoie region.

The Alpine Cab Company
Tel 00 33 450 731938
info@alpinecabco.com
www.alpinecabco.com

BREAKDOWN INSURANCE

AA Five Star Europe
Tel 0800 0852840
customer.services@theAA.com
www.theAA.com

Autohome
Tel 0800 371280
www.autohome.co.uk

Direct Line Rescue
Tel 0845 246 8702
www.directline.com/rescue

Europ Assistance
Tel 0870 7375720
www.europ-assistance.co.uk

First Assist Group
Tel 020 8763 3333
assistance.services@firstassist.co.uk
www.firstassist.co.uk

Green Flag Motoring Assistance
Tel 0800 400 638
european-sales@greenflag.com
www.greenflag.com

Leisurecare Insurance Services
Tel 01793 750150

Mondial Assistance UK
Tel 020 8681 2525
enquiries@mondial-assistance.co.uk
www.mondial-assistance.co.uk

RAC Travel Services
Tel 0800 550055
traveladmin@rac.co.uk
www.rac.co.uk

CAR HIRE

Alamo Rent A Car
Tel 0870 599 4000
www.alamo.com

Avis Rent A Car
Tel 08700 100 287
www.avis.co.uk

Budget Car and Van Rental
Tel 08701 565656
www.budget-uk.com

Europcar UK
Tel 0870 607 5000
www.europcar.co.uk

Hertz UK Ltd
Tel 08708 484848
www.hertz.co.uk

Holiday Autos International Ltd
Tel 0870 400 4447
www.holidayautos.com

Suncars
Tel 0870 500 5566
www.suncars.com

CAR WINTER EQUIPMENT

Brindley Chains Ltd
Tel 01925 825555
www.brindley-chains.co.uk
Pewag snowchains

DAP (Cambridge) Ltd
Tel 01223 323488
www.skidrive.co.uk
Thule, Karrite boxes, Skandibox, Konig snowchains

GT Towing Ltd
Tel 01707 262526
www.gttowing.co.uk
Ski boxes and snowchains

Lakeland Roof Box Centre
Tel 08700 766326
www.roofbox.co.uk
Roof boxes, snowchains

Latchmere Motor Spares
Tel 020 7223 5491
Snowchains, roof bars, ski clamps, boxes

Motor Traveller
Tel 01753 833442
www.carbox.co.uk
Thule; Milz snowchains

RUD Chains Ltd
Tel 01227 276611
sales@rudchains.co.uk
Snowchains

Snowchains Ltd
Tel 01732 884408
www.snowchains.co.uk
Thule; Weissenfels snowchains

Spikes Spiders
Tel 01706 819365
www.spikesspider.com

The Roof Box Company
Tel 08700 766326
www.roofbox.co.uk

Thule Ltd
Tel 01275 340404
www.thule.co.uk

CROSS-CHANNEL TRAVEL

Brittany Ferries
Tel 08703 665 333
www.brittanyferries.co.uk
Portsmouth–Caen

Eurotunnel
Tel 08705 35 35 35
www.eurotunnel.com
Folkestone–Calais/Coquelles via the Channel Tunnel

Hoverspeed
Tel 0870 240 8070
www.hoverspeed.com
Dover–Calais; Dover–Ostend; Newhaven–Dieppe

Norfolkline
Tel 0870 870 1020
www.norfolkline.com
Dover–Dunkerque

P&O North Sea Ferries
Tel 08705 202020
www.ponsf.com
Hull–Zeebrugge, Hull–Rotterdam

P&O Portsmouth
Tel 0870 242 4999
www.poportsmouth.com
Portsmouth–Cherbourg; Portsmouth–Le Havre

P&O Stena Line
Tel 08705 20 20 20
www.posl.com
Dover–Calais

SeaFrance
Tel 08705 711 711
www.seafrance.com
Dover–Calais

SpeedFerries
www.speedferries.com
Dover–Boulogne

Stena Line
Tel 08705 707070
www.stenaline.co.uk
Harwich–Hook of Holland

DRY SKI SLOPES

SOUTH-WEST ENGLAND

Christchurch Ski Centre
Matchams Lane, Hurn, Christchurch, Dorset
Tel 01202 499155
www.newforest-online.co.uk/christchurch_ski

Exeter and District Ski Club
Clifton Hill Sports Ground, Belmont Road, Exeter
Tel 01392 211422
exeterclub@ntlworld.com

High Actions' Avon Ski Centre
Lyncombe Lodge, Churchill, North Somerset
Tel 01934 852335
www.highaction.co.uk

John Nike Leisuresport – Plymouth
Plymouth Ski Centre, Alpine Park, Marsh Mills, Plymouth
Tel 01752 600220
www.jnll.co.uk

Torquay Alpine Ski Club
Barton Hall, Kingskerswell Road, Torquay, Devon
Tel 01803 313350
www.skitorquay.co.uk

Warmwell Snow Zone
Warmwell, Dorchester, Dorset
Tel 01305 853245

Wellington Sports Centre
Corams Lane, Wellington, Somerset
Tel 01823 663010

Yeovil Ski Centre
Addlewell Lane, Nine Springs, Yeovil, Somerset
Tel 01935 421702

SOUTH-EAST ENGLAND

Alpine Snowsports Aldershot
Gallwey Road, Aldershot
Tel 01252 325889
www.alpinesnowsports.co.uk

Bishop Reindorp Ski Centre
Larch Avenue, Guildford
Tel 01483 504988
www.brski.co.uk

Bowles Outdoor Centre
Eridge Green, Tunbridge Wells
Tel 01892 665665
www.bowles.ac

Bromley Ski Centre
Sandy Lane, St Paul's Cray,
Orpington, Kent
Tel 01689 876812

Calshot Activities Centre
Calshot Spit, Fawley,
Southampton
Tel 023 8089 2077
www.hants.gov.uk/calshot

Folkestone Sports Centre
Radnor Park Avenue,
Folkestone, Kent
Tel 01303 850333
www.folkestoneski.co.uk

John Nike – Bracknell
Bracknell Ski Centre, Amen
Corner, Bracknell
Tel 01344 789000
www.jnll.co.uk

John Nike – Chatham
Chatham Ski and Snowboard
Centre, Alpine Park, Capstone
Road, Gillingham, Kent
Tel 01634 827979
www.jnll.co.uk

Sandown Ski Centre
More Lane, Esher
Tel 01372 467132
www.sandownsports.co.uk

Southampton Ski Centre
The Sports Centre, Bassett,
Southampton
Tel 023 8079 0970
ski.centre@southampton.gov.uk

Wycombe Summit
Abbey Barn Lane, High
Wycombe, Bucks
Tel 01494 474711
www.wycombesummit.co.uk

MIDDLE ENGLAND

Gloucester Ski/Board Centre
Jarvis Hotel, Robinswood Hill,
Matson Lane, Gloucester
Tel 08702 400375
www.gloucesterski.com

John Nike – Swadlincote
Swadlincote Ski Centre, Hill
Street, Swadlincote
Tel 01283 217200
www.jnll.co.uk

Kidsgrove Ski Centre
Bathpool Park, Kidsgrove,
Stoke-on-Trent
Tel 01782 784908
www.ski-kidsgrove.co.uk

Snozone
Xscape, 602 Marlborough
Gate, Central Milton Keynes
Tel 01908 230260
www.snozonemk.co.uk

Stoke Ski Centre
Festival Park, Stoke-on-Trent
Tel 01782 204159
www.stokeskicentre.co.uk

Tallington Ski/Board Centre
Tallington Lakes, Barholm
Road, Tallington, Stamford
Tel 01778 344990
www.waspdirect.com

Tamworth Snowdome
Leisure Island, River Drive,
Tamworth
Tel 08705 000011
www.snowdome.co.uk

Telford Ski Centre
Court Street, Madeley, Telford
Tel 01952 586862
www.telfordleisure.co.uk

The Ackers
Golden Hillock Road, Small
Heath, Birmingham
Tel 0121 772 5111
www.ackers-adventure.co.uk

EASTERN ENGLAND

Brentwood Park Centre
Warley Gap, Brentwood
Tel 01277 211994
www.brentwoodskicentre.co.uk

Gosling Ski Centre
Stanborough Road, Welwyn
Garden City
Tel 01707 384384
www.goslingsports.co.uk

Hemel Ski Centre
St Albans Hill, Hemel
Hempstead
Tel 01442 241321
www.hemel-ski.co.uk

Norfolk Ski Club
Whitlingham Lane, Trowse,
Norwich
Tel 01603 662781
www.norfolkskiclub.co.uk

Suffolk Ski Centre
Bourne Hill, Wherstead,
Ipswich
Tel 01473 602347
www.suffolkskicentre.co.uk

NORTHERN ENGLAND

Alston Adventure Centre
High Plains Lodge, Alston
Tel 01434 381886
www.alstontraining.co.uk

Halifax Ski/Board Centre
Sportsman Leisure, Bradford
Old Road, Swalesmoor
Ploughcroft, Halifax
Tel 01422 340760
darren@lineone.net

Kendal Ski Club
Canal Head North, Kendal
Tel 01539 732948
sec.kendal@cwcom.net

Pendle Ski Club
Clitheroe Road, Sabden,
Clitheroe
Tel 01200 425222

Runcorn Ski/Board Centre
Town Park, Palace Fields,
Runcorn
Tel 01928 701965
www.runcornskicentre.co.uk

Sheffield Ski Village
Vale Road, Parkwood Springs,
Sheffield
Tel 0114 276 9459
www.sheffieldskivillage.co.uk

Ski Rossendale
Haslingden Old Road,
Rawtenstall, Rossendale
Tel 01706 226457
www.ski-rossendale.co.uk

Whickham Thorns Centre
Market Lane, Dunston
Tel 0191 433 5767
www.gateshead.gov.uk

WALES

**Cardiff Ski & Snowboard
Centre**
Fairwater Park, Fairwater,
Cardiff
Tel 029 2056 1793
www.skicardiff.com

Dan-yr-Ogof Ski Slopes
Abercrave, Upper Swansea
Valley, Powys
Tel 01639 730284

John Nike – Llandudno
Wyddfyd Road, Great Orme,
Llandudno
Tel 01492 874707
www.jnll.co.uk

Plas y Brenin
Capel Curig, Gwynedd
Tel 01690 720214

Pontypool Ski Centre
Pontypool Leisure Park,
Pontypool
Tel 01495 756955

Rhiwgoch Ski Centre
Bronaber, Trawsfynydd
Tel 01766 540578
www.logcabins-skiwales.co.uk

Ski Pembrey
Pembrey Country Park, Burry
Port, Llanelli
Tel 01554 834443

SCOTLAND

Alford Ski Centre
Greystone Road, Alford
Tel 01975 563024
keith.morris@aberdeenshire.
gov.uk

Ancrum Outdoor Centre
10 Ancrum Road, Dundee
Tel 01382 435911
ancrum.centre@dundeecity.
gov.uk

Bearsden Ski & Board
Stockiemuir Road, Bearsden,
Glasgow
Tel 0141 943 1500
www.skibearsden.co.uk

Firpark Ski Centre
Tillicoultry, Clackmannanshire
Tel 01259 751772

Glasgow Ski/Board Centre
Bellahouston Park, 16
Dumbreck Road, Glasgow
Tel 0141 427 4991
www.ski-glasgow.org

Glenmore Lodge
Scottish National Sports
Centre, Aviemore
Tel 01479 861256
www.glenmorelodge.org.uk

**Loch Rannoch Outdoor Activity
Centre**
Kinloch Rannoch, Perthshire
Tel 01882 632201
www.lochrannoch-hotel.co.uk

Midlothian Ski Centre
Hillend, Midlothian
Tel 0131 445 4433
www.midlothian.gov.uk

Newmilns Ski Slope
High Street, Newmilns
Tel 01560 322320

Polmonthill Ski Centre
Polmont, Falkirk
Tel 01324 503835
ski@polmonthill.freeserve.co.uk

NORTHERN IRELAND

Craigavon Golf and Ski Centre
Turmoyra Lane, Silverwood,
Lurgan , Co Armagh
Tel 028 3832 6606
www.craigavon.gov.uk

Mount Ober Ski Centre
24 Ballymaconaghy Road,
Knockbracken, Belfast
Tel 028 9079 5666
mt.ober@ukonline.co.uk

INSURANCE COMPANIES

ABC Holiday Extras
Tel 0870 8444020
www.abctravelinsurance.co.uk

Aon Suretravel
Tel 01883 834003
customer.care@aon.co.uk

Atlas Insurance
Tel 020 7609 5000
www.atlasdirect.net

AUL
Tel 01206 577770
enquiries@aul.co.uk
www.aul.co.uk

Blackwater Travel Indemnity
Tel 01621 855553
www.blackwater-
insurance.co.uk

**British Activity Holiday
Insurance Services**
Tel 020 7251 6821
ansell@easynet.co.uk
www.ansell.co.uk

BUPA Travel Services
Tel 01784 410910
btravint@bupa.com
www.bupa.co.uk/travel

CGNU
Tel 0800 559 3201
www.norwichunion.co.uk

Direct Line Travel Insurance
Tel 0845 246 8704
www.directline.com/travel

Direct Travel Insurance
Tel 01903 812345
info@direct-travel.co.uk
www.direct-travel.co.uk

Douglas Cox Tyrie
Tel 01708 385969

Euclidian Insurance Services
Tel 01784 484601
www.euclidian.co.uk

Europ Assistance
Tel 01444 442442
www.europ-assistance.co.uk

Hamilton Barr
Tel 01483 255666
www.hamiltonbarr.com

Ketteridge Group
Tel 01277 630770

Matthew Gerard Insurance
Tel 01483 730900
sales@mgtis.easynet.co.uk

P J Hayman & Company
Tel 023 9241 9010
www.pjhayman.com

Perry Gamble
Tel 020 8542 1122

Preferential
Tel 01702 423280
www.preferential.co.uk

Primary Insurance Group
Tel 0870 444 3434
www.primaryinsurance.co.uk

Select Travel Insurance
Tel 08707 370870
sxp@inter-group.co.uk

ski-insurance.co.uk
Tel 0870 755 6101
www.ski-insurance.co.uk

Skisure.com
www.skisure-insurance.co.uk

Snowcard Insurance Services
Tel 01327 262805
www.snowcard.co.uk

Sportscover Direct Ltd
Tel 0117 922 6222
www.sportscover.co.uk

Supreme Travel
Tel 01355 260547
www.travelinsurance-uk.com

Travel Insurance Club Limited
Tel 01702 423398
www.ticdirect.co.uk

Travel Protection Group plc
Tel 028 9032 6585
www.thetravelprotectiongroup.
plc.uk

**World Ski and Snowboard
Association**
Tel 0870 757 2288
www.worldski.co.uk

WorldCover Direct
Tel 0800 365 121
www.worldcover.com

**Worldwide Travel Insurance
Services Ltd**
Tel 01892 833338
www.worldwideinsure.com

NATIONAL TOURIST OFFICES

Andorran Embassy
Tel 020 8874 4806

Argentine Embassy
Tel 020 7318 1300
www.turismo.gov.ar

Australian Tourist Commission
Tel 09068 633235
www.australia.com

Austrian National Tourist Office
Tel 020 7629 0461
info@anto.co.uk
www.austria-tourism.at

Canadian Tourism Commission
Tel 0906 871 5000
visitcanada@dial.pipex.com
www.travelcanada.ca

Chile – Consulate General
Tel 020 7580 1023
cglonduk@congechileuk.
demon.co.uk

Czech Tourist Authority
Tel 020 7631 0427
schoppova@visitczechia.org.uk
www.visitczechia.cz

Finnish Tourist Board
Tel 020 7365 2512
finlandinfo.lon@mek.fi
www.finland-tourism.com

French Tourist Office
Tel 09068 244123
info@mdlf.co.uk
www.franceguide.com

German National Tourist Office
Tel 09001 600100
gntolon@d-z-t.com
www.germany-tourism.de

Italian State Tourist Office
Tel 020 7399 3562
italy@italiantouristboard.co.uk
www.enit.it
Brochure line: 09065 508925

Japan Tourist Organisation
Tel 020 7734 9638
info@jnto.co.uk
www.seejapan.co.uk

Norwegian Tourist Board
Tel 0906 302 2003
infouk@ntr.no
www.visitnorway.com

Romanian Tourist Office
Tel 020 7224 3692
uktouroff@romania.freeserve.
co.uk
www.romaniatourism.com

Scottish Tourist Board
Tel 0845 22 55 121
ski.visitscotland.com

Slovenian Tourist Office
Tel 0870 225 5305
info@slovenian-tourism.co.uk
www.slovenia-tourism.si

Spanish Tourist Office
Tel 020 7486 8077
londres@tourspain.es
www.tourspain.co.uk

Swedish Tourism Council
Tel 00800 3080 3080
info@swetourism.org.uk
www.visit-sweden.com

Switzerland Tourism
Tel 00800 100 200 30
info.uk@switzerland.com
www.MySwitzerland.com

Tourism New Zealand
Tel 09069 10 10 10
www.purenz.com

Turkish Tourist Board
Tel 020 7629 7771
info@gototurkey.co.uk
www.gototurkey.com

Visit USA Association
Tel 09069 101020
www.visitusa.org.uk

RAILWAYS

Deutsche Bahn
Tel 0870 243 5363
sales@deutsche-bahn.co.uk
www.dbautozug.de

Eurostar
Tel 0870 518 6186
www.eurostar.com

Rail Europe
Tel 08705 848 848
reservations@raileurope.co.uk
www.raileurope.co.uk

Swiss Federal Railways
Tel 00800 100 200 30
info.uk@switzerland.com
www.rail.ch

- Skiing and Snowboarding
- Servicing and Repair
- Clothing Hire
- Expert Boot Fitting

FORCE
26 Bakers Lane, Lichfield
Tel: 01543 411249 www.skiforce.co.uk

RETAILERS

SOUTH-WEST ENGLAND

Christchurch Leisure Centre
Matchams Lane, Hurn,
Christchurch, Dorset
Tel 01202 499155
www.christchurch-
skicentre.com

Devon Ski Centre
Oak Place, Newton Abbot
Tel 01626 351278
www.devonski.co.uk

Kidski
Suite H3, Romany Centre
Wareham Rd, Poole
Tel 01202 631222

Mission Adventure Ltd
1 Bank Lane, Brixham, Devon
Tel 01803 855796
www.missionadventure.co.uk

Penrose Outdoors
Town Quay, Truro, Cornwall
Tel 01872 272116
www.penroseoutdoors.co.uk

Skate and Ski
104 High Street, Staple Hill,
Bristol
Tel 0117 970 1356

Snow & Rock
1-3 Shield Centre, Gloucester
Road North, Filton, Bristol
Tel 0117 914 3000
www.snowandrock.com

Team Ski
37 High East Street,
Dorchester, Dorset
Tel 01305 268035
www.teamski.co.uk

Two Bare Feet
Fleet Street, Torquay
Tel 01803 296060
www.twobarefeet.co.uk

Westsports
Market House, Marlborough
Rd, Old Town, Swindon
Tel 01793 532588
www.skishops.co.uk

SOUTH-EAST ENGLAND

Activ (Folkestone)
145 Sandgate Road,
Folkestone, Kent
Tel 01303 240110

Alpine Room
71-73 Main Road, Danbury,
Essex
Tel 01245 223563
www.alpineroom.co.uk

Captain's Cabin
93 High Street, Chatham
Tel 01634 819777
www.captainscabin.com

Captain's Cabin
14 St George's Walk, Croydon
Tel 020 8680 6968
www.captainscabin.com

Captain's Cabin
19 Wincheap, Canterbury
Tel 01227 457906
www.captainscabin.com

Edge 2 Edge
Unit 10, Oakwood Industrial
Park, Gatwick Road, Crawley,
West Sussex
Tel 01293 649300
www.edge2edge.co.uk

John Pollock
157 High Road, Loughton,
Essex
Tel 020 8508 6626
www.johnpollock.co.uk

John Pollock
67 High Street, Barnet
Tel 020 8440 3994
www.johnpollock.co.uk

Snow Boats
8-10 The Street, Wrecclesham,
Farnham, Surrey
Tel 01252 715169
www.snowboats.co.uk

Snow & Rock
188 Kensington High Street,
London
Tel 020 7937 0872
www.snowandrock.com

Snow & Rock
4 Mercer Street, Covent
Garden, London WC2
Tel 020 7420 1444
www.snowandrock.com

Snow & Rock
150 Holborn, Corner of Gray's
Inn Road, London EC1
Tel 020 7831 6900
www.snowandrock.com

Snow & Rock
99 Fordwater Road, Chertsey,
Surrey
Tel 01932 566886
www.snowandrock.com

Snow & Rock
The Boardwalk, Port Solent,
Portsmouth, Hampshire
Tel 023 9220 5388
www.snowandrock.com

Snow & Rock
Kings Road, Chelsea, London
(open October 2003)
Tel 0845 100 1000
www.snowandrock.com

Snow Togs
431 Millbrook Road,
Southampton
Tel 023 8077 3925
www.skishops.co.uk

MIDDLE ENGLAND

Active Outdoor & Ski
28 Castle Centre, Banbury
Tel 01295 273700
www.activeoutdoorandski.co.uk

Attwoolls Ski Shop
Bristol Road, Whitminster
Tel 01452 742200
www.attwoolls.co.uk

Beans
86 Sheep Street, Bicester
Tel 01869 246451
www.beansonline.co.uk

BestBuys
Nene Court, 27-31 The
Embankment, Wellingborough
Tel 01933 272699
www.best-buys.co.uk

Force Ltd
26 Bakers Lane, Lichfield
Tel 01543 411249
www.skiforce.co.uk

Fox's
1 London Road, Amersham
Tel 01494 431431
foxsoutdoor.co.uk

High Sports
51-52 Wyle Cop, Shrewsbury
Tel 01743 231649
www.highsports.co.uk

Lockwoods Ski Shop
125-129 Rugby Road,
Leamington Spa, Warwickshire
Tel 01926 339388
www.lockwoodsoutdoor.co.uk

SNOW+ROCK

Manchester	**0845 100 1000**
Chelsea	**0845 100 1000**
Portsmouth Superstore	**023 9220 5388**
Covent Garden	**020 7420 1444**
Kensington	**020 7937 0872**
Holborn	**020 7831 6900**
Surrey Superstore	**01932 566 886**
Hemel Hempstead	**01442 235 305**
Bristol Superstore	**0117 914 3000**
Birmingham	**0121 236 8280**
Sheffield	**0114 275 1700**
Snow+Rock Direct	**0845 100 1000**

Mountain Fever
25 Brunswick Street, Hanley,
Stoke-on-Trent
Tel 01782 266137
www.mountainfever.co.uk

Noahs Ark
London Rd, Chalford, Stroud
Tel 01453 884738
www.noahsark.co.uk

Ski West
9 Draycott Crescent, Dursley
Tel 01453 519084
www.ski-west.co.uk

Snow & Rock
14 Priory Queensway,
Birmingham
Tel 0121 236 8280
www.snowandrock.com

Sporting Triangle
18 West Street, Hereford
Tel 01432 271500
www.sportingtriangle.com

Two Seasons
39 Pelham Street, Nottingham
Te 0115 950 1333
www.twoseasons.co.uk

Two Seasons
229-231 Wellingborough
Road, Northampton
Tel 01604 627377
www.twoseasons.co.uk

Two Seasons
15 Pump Street, Worcester
Tel 01905 731144
www.twoseasons.co.uk

Two Seasons
64 Lower Precinct, Coventry
Tel 024 7663 0020
www.twoseasons.co.uk

Two Seasons
32-34 Mill Lane, Solihull
www.twoseasons.co.uk

EASTERN ENGLAND

Ski Surf
13 Peartree Centre, Peartree
Lane, Stanway, Colchester
Tel 01206 502000
www.skisurf.co.uk

Snow & Rock
Hemel Ski Centre, St Albans
Hill, Hemel Hempstead
Tel 01442 235305

SnowFit
2 Cucumber Lane, Brundall,
Norwich
Tel 01603 716655
www.snowfit.co.uk

Snowsun
Suffolk Ski Centre, Bourne
Hill, Wherstead, Ipswich,
Suffolk
Tel 01473 602601
www.snowsun.com

Two Seasons
34 Chesterton Road,
Cambridge
Tel 01223 356207
www.twoseasons.co.uk

NORTHERN ENGLAND

BAC Outdoor Leisure
Central Hall, Coronation
Street, Elland, Halifax, West
Yorkshire
Tel 01422 371146
www.bac-e.com

Glide & Slide
5/7 Station Road, Otley
Tel 01943 461136
www.glideslide.co.uk

Mayhem Surf Snow Skate
7 Jubbergate, York
Tel 01904 655062
www.mayhemboardstore.com

Mountain & Marine
159 London Road South,
Poynton, Cheshire
Tel 01625 859863
www.mountain-marine.com

Severn Sports / Boardworx
80 Town Street, Armley,
Leeds, West Yorkshire
Tel 0113 279 1618
www.severnsports.co.uk

Snow & Rock
Sheffield Ski Centre, Vale
Road, Parkwood Springs,
Sheffield
Tel 0114 275 1700
www.snowandrock.com

Snow & Rock
Manchester
(opens October 2003)
Tel 0845 100 1000
www.snowandrock.com

WALES

Ski Lodge
Cardiff Road, Barry, Vale of
Glamorgan
Tel 01446 741870

SCOTLAND

Craigdon Mountain Sports
61-65 High Street, Inverurie,
Highland
Tel 01467 625855
www.craigdonmountainsports.
com

Craigdon Mountain Sports
5 St Andrew's Street,
Aberdeen
Tel 01224 624333
www.craigdonmountainsports.
com

Craigdon Mountain Sports
25-29 Kinnoull Street, Perth
Tel 01738 831006
www.craigdonmountainsports.
com

NORTHERN IRELAND

Macski
140 Lisburn Road, Belfast
Tel 028 9066 5525
www.macski.com

REPUBLIC OF IRELAND

The Great Outdoors
Chatham Street, Dublin 2
Tel 00 353 1679 4293
www.greatoutdoors.ie

SKI/BOARDING ORGANISATIONS

**British Association of
Snowsport Instructors (BASI)**
Tel 01479 861717
basi@basi.org.uk
www.basi.org.uk

**British Ski and Snowboard
Federation**
Tel 0131 445 7676
britski@easynet.co.uk
www.bssf.co.uk

**British Ski Club for the
Disabled**
BSCDWeb@hotmail.com
www.bscd.co.uk

British Snowboard Association
Tel 0131 445 2428
info@thebsa.org
www.thebsa.org

English Ski Council
Tel 0121 501 2314
admin@englishski.org
www.englishski.org

Ski Club of Great Britain
Tel 0845 458 0780
skiers@skiclub.co.uk
www.skiclub.co.uk

Snowsport Scotland
Tel 0131 445 4151
info@snowsportscotland.org
www.snsc.demon.co.uk

Snowsport Wales
Tel 029 2056 1904
admin.snowsportwales@virgin.
net
www.snowsportwales.net

The Uphill Ski Club
Tel 01479 861272
info@uphill-skiclub.co.uk
www.uphillskiclub.co.uk
*Ski organisation and ski
school for people with
disabilities*

**World Ski and Snowboard
Association**
Tel 0870 7572288
info@worldski.co.uk
www.worldski.co.uk

Resort index / directory

This is an index to the resort chapters in the book; you'll find page references for about 400 resorts described elsewhere. But you'll also find brief descriptions here of another 700 resorts, most of them much smaller than those we've covered in full, but often still worth a short visit. We also list the companies offering package holidays to each resort. To get in touch with one of these tour operators, look them up in the list starting on page 664.

Key

ⵑ Lifts
ⵐ Pistes
⊠ UK tour operators

49 Degrees North USA
Inland area with best snow in Washington State, including 120-acre bowl reserved for powder weekends.
1195m; slopes 1195–1760m
ⵑ5 ⵐ 780 acres

Abetone Italy
Resort in the exposed Appennines, less than two hours from Florence and Pisa.
1390m; slopes 1390–1900m
ⵑ25 ⵐ 50km
⊠ Alpine Tours

Abtenau Austria
Sizeable village in Dachstein-West region near Salzburg, on large plain ideal for cross-country.
710m; slopes 710–1260m
ⵑ6 ⵐ 10km

Achenkirch Austria
Unspoilt, low-altitude Tirolean village close to Niederau and Alpbach. Beautiful setting overlooking a lake.
930m; slopes 930–1800m
ⵑ7 ⵐ 25km
⊠ Ramblers Holidays

Adelboden 427
⊠ Interhome, Kuoni, Made to Measure Holidays, Swiss Travel Service

Les Aillons France
Traditional village near Chambéry. Sheltered slopes.
1000m; slopes 1000–1900m
ⵑ22 ⵐ 40km

Alagna 402
Small resort on the western fringe of Monterosa Ski area.
⊠ Alpine Answers Select, Ski Club of Great Britain, Ski Weekend

Alba Italy
Picturesque Dolomite village with a small, quiet area; access to the Sella Ronda at nearby Canazei.
1515m; slopes 1515–2440m
ⵑ5 ⵐ 10km

Albiez-Montrond France
Authentic old French village in Maurienne valley with panoramic views. Own easy slopes and close to other ski areas.
1500m; slopes 1500–2200m
ⵑ12 ⵐ 40km
⊠ AmeriCan Ski, Lagrange Holidays

Alleghe Italy
Dolomite village near Cortina in a pretty lakeside setting close to numerous areas.
980m
ⵑ24 ⵐ 80km

Les Allues 282
Rustic village on the road up to Méribel, close to the mid-station of the gondola up from Brides-les-Bains.

Alpbach 112
⊠ Crystal, Equity Ski, Inghams, Interhome, Made to Measure Holidays

Alpe-d'Huez 205
⊠ Airtours, Alpine Answers Select, Avant-ski, Chalet World, Chalets 'Unlimited', Club Med, Crystal, Directski.com, Erna Low, Eurotunnel Motoring Holidays, First Choice Ski, Independent Ski Links, Inghams, Interhome, La Source, Lagrange Holidays, Made to Measure Holidays, Mark Warner, Neilson, Panorama Holidays, Ski Arrangements, Ski Club of Great Britain, Ski Expectations, Ski France, Ski Independence, Ski Leisure Direction, Ski Life, Ski Line, Ski Miquel, Ski Supreme, SkiAway Holidays, Skiworld, Thomson Ski & Snowboarding, Tops Ski Chalets and Club Hotels

Alpe-du-Grand-Serre France
Tiny resort near Alpe-d'Huez and Les Deux-Alpes. Good for bad-weather days.
1400m; slopes 1400–2200m
ⵑ20 ⵐ 55km

Alpendorf Austria
Outpost of St Johann im Pongau, at one end of extensive 3-valley lift network linking via Wagrain to Flachau – all part of the Salzburger Sportwelt ski pass area that our figures relate to.
850m; slopes 800–2185m
ⵑ59 ⵐ 200km

Alpine Meadows 506
⊠ Ski The American Dream

Alps Korea
Korea's most northerly, snow-reliable resort, about five hours from Seoul. ⵑ5

Alta 553
⊠ Ski All America, Ski Independence, Ski The American Dream

Alta Badia 410
Valley area of Colfosco, Corvara, San Cassiano and La Villa – part of the Sella Ronda circuit.

Altenmarkt Austria
Unspoilt village well placed off the Salzburg-Villach autobahn for numerous resorts including snow-sure Obertauern and the Salzburger Sportwelt resorts.
855m
⊠ Made to Measure Holidays, Sloping Off

Alto Campoo Spain
Barren, desolate place with undistinguished slopes, but with magnificent wilderness views.
1650m; slopes 1650–2170m ⵑ11

Alt St Johann Switzerland
Old cross-country village with Alpine slopes connecting into Unterwasser area near Liechtenstein.
900m; slopes 900–2260m
ⵑ21 ⵐ 50km

Alyeska USA
Alaskan area 60km/35 miles from Anchorage, with luxury hotel. Spring best for weather.
75m; slopes 75–1200m
ⵑ9 ⵐ 785 acres
⊠ Inghams, Ski All America

Aminona 435
Purpose-built resort in the Crans-Montana network.
⊠ Lagrange Holidays

Andalo Italy
Atmospheric Dolomite village near Madonna, with low wooded slopes well equipped with snowmakers; best for novices.
1050m; slopes 1035–2125m
ⵑ17 ⵐ 60km
⊠ Equity Ski, Rocketski, Sloping Off

Andermatt 429
⊠ Crystal, Made to Measure Holidays, Ski Club of Great Britain, Ski Weekend

Andorra la Vella 94
⊠ Lagrange Holidays

Angel Fire USA
Intermediate area near Taos, New Mexico. Height usually ensures good snow.
2620m; slopes 2620–3255m
ⵑ6 ⵐ 455 acres

Les Angles France
Attractive resort with one of the best ski areas in the Pyrenees. Pretty, tree-lined, easy skiing.
1650m; slopes 1650–2400m
ⵑ24 ⵐ 40km
⊠ Lagrange Holidays

Annaberg-Lungötz Austria
Peaceful village in a pretty setting, sharing a sizeable area with Gosau. Close to Filzmoos.
775m; slopes 775–1620m
ⵑ33 ⵐ 65km

Anzère Switzerland
Sympathetically designed modern resort on a sunny balcony near Crans-Montana, with slopes suited to leisurely intermediates.
1500m; slopes 1500–2460m
ⵑ13 ⵐ 40km
⊠ Interhome, Lagrange Holidays

Aosta Italy
Historic valley town with gondola up to mountain resort of Pila; it's an 18-minute ride to the slopes. Aosta is a real working town with people in suits rather than skiwear. It has good-value accommodation, a lot more bars and restaurants than Pila, and a lovely traffic-free centre. Other resorts in the Aosta valley are within day-trip distance and are covered by the lift pass.
1800m; slopes 1550–2710m
ⵑ13 ⵐ 70km

Apex 595
⊠ AmeriCan Ski, Frontier Ski, Ski Safari

Aprica Italy
Ugly, straggling village between Lake Como and the Brenta Dolomites, with bland slopes and limited facilities.
1180m; slopes 1180–2310m
ⵑ24 ⵐ 40km
⊠ Interhome, Thomson Ski & Snowboarding

Arabba 410
Tiny village with the Sella Ronda's highest, steepest skiing on its doorstep.
⊠ Independent Ski Links, Inghams, Momentum Ski, Neilson, Ski Yogi

Aragnouet-Piau France
Purpose-built mid-mountain satellite of St-Lary, best suited to families, beginners and early intermediates.
1850m; slopes 1420–2500m
ⵑ32 ⵐ 80km

Arapahoe Basin 534
Small resort with the highest lift-served slopes in the US. Keystone is a few minutes away by road.
⊠ Ski The American Dream

677

Resort index / directory

678

Les Barzettes 435
Smaller base along the road from Crans-Montana, with a gondola up to the main section of slopes.

Bear Mountain USA
Southern California's main area, in the beautiful San Bernardino National Forest region. Full snowmaking.
slopes 2170–2685m
⛷12 ⛷ 195 acres

Bear's Town Korea
Modern resort with runs cut out of thick forest. Biggest resort near Seoul (only an hour's drive), so it can get very crowded. ⛷ 11

Beaulard Italy
Little place just off the road between Sauze d'Oulx and Bardonecchia.
1215m; slopes 1215–2120m
⛷6 ⛷ 20km

Beaver Creek 523
✉ AmeriCan Ski, Crystal, Elegant Resorts, Handmade Holidays, Made to Measure Holidays, Simply Ski, Ski Activity, Ski All America, Ski Independence, Ski Safari, Ski The American Dream, Ski Wild, Trailfinders, United Vacations Ski Freedom USA & Canada

Beaver Mountain USA
Small Utah area north of Salt Lake City, too far from Park City for a day trip.
2195m; slopes 2195–2680m
⛷3 ⛷ 525 acres

Beitostolen Norway
Small family resort in southern Norway (east of Bergen), with lots of cross-country in the region.
900m; ⛷9 ⛷ 25km

Belleayre Mountain USA
State-owned resort near Albany, New York State. Cheap prices but old lifts and short runs.
775m; slopes 775–1015m
⛷7 ⛷ 170 acres

Belle-Plagne 303
High-altitude satellite of La Plagne built in a pleasing neo-Savoyard style.

Ben Lomond Australia
Small intermediate/beginner area in Ben Lomond National Park, Tasmania, 260km/160 miles from Hobart.
1570m ⛷ 8

Berchtesgaden Germany
Pleasant old town close to Salzburg, known for its Nordic skiing but with several little Alpine areas nearby.
550m
✉ Moswin Tours

Bergün Switzerland
Traditional, quiet, unspoiled, virtually traffic-free little family resort on the rail route between Davos and St Moritz. 5km/2.5 mile toboggan run.
1375m; slopes 1400–2550m
⛷5 ⛷ 25km

Berthoud Pass 546
Powder heaven on the drive to Winter Park.

Berwang Austria
Unspoiled village nestling in a spacious valley, close to Lermoos.
1335m; slopes 1335–1740m
⛷12 ⛷ 40km

Bessans France
Old cross-country village near Modane. Well placed for touring Maurienne valley resorts such as Val-Cenis.
1710m; slopes 1740–2200m
⛷4 ⛷ 5km

Besse France
Charming old village built out of lava, with purpose-built slope-side satellite Super-Besse. Beautiful extinct-volcano scenery.
1050m; slopes 1300–1850m
⛷22 ⛷ 45km
✉ Lagrange Holidays

Bethel USA
Pleasant, historic town very close to Sunday River, Maine. Attractive alternative to staying in the slope-side resort.

Le Bettex 274
Small base at the gondola mid-station above St-Gervais, with links to the Megève network.

Bettmeralp Switzerland
Central village of the sizeable Aletsch area near Brig, perched high above the Rhône valley, amid spectacular glacial scenery. Reached by cable-cars from valley.
1955m; slopes 1900–2900m
⛷32 ⛷ 90km

Beuil-les-Launes France
Alpes-Maritimes resort closest to Nice. Shares area with Valberg.
1400m; slopes 1400–2100m
⛷26 ⛷ 90km

Bezau Austria
Virtually no slopes of its own but main village lies in low Bregenzerwald region north-west of Lech.
650m; slopes 1210–1650m ⛷2
✉ Inntravel

Biberwier Austria
Limited little village with a small area of its own. Best as a quiet base from which to access the Zugspitz area.
1000m; slopes 1000–1790m
⛷6 ⛷ 8km

Bichlbach Austria
Smallest of the Zugspitz villages with very limited slopes of its own. Suitable as an unspoiled base for visiting the rest of the area.
1070m; slopes 1070–1620m
⛷3 ⛷ 7km

Bielmonte Italy
Popular with day-trippers from Milan. Worthwhile on a bad-weather day.
1200m; slopes 1200–1620m
⛷13 ⛷ 20km

Big Mountain USA
At least one of our reporters (who now makes an annual pilgrimage) rates this place, close to the Canadian border and even closer to Montana's Glacier National Park, as simply the best. Big is one thing that BM is not, with a modest base altitude, a middling vertical and a mere dozen lifts. But its 3,000 acres embrace a wide range of slopes that are not only impressively snowy but also blissfully devoid of people. There's easy cruising in dense forest around the base area, and steeper stuff higher up on 'gladed' slopes – mainly single diamond but with double-diamond runs dotted around. There is accommodation at the base, and more in the small town of Whitefish, a few miles away. Our principal reporter, a man, reckons Ladies' Night at the Great Northern bar is something not to be missed.
1370m; slopes 1370–2135m
✉10 ⛷ 3000 acres
✉ AmeriCan Ski, Inghams, Ski Activity, Ski All America, Ski Independence

Big Powderhorn USA
Area with the most 'resort' facilities in south Lake Superior region – and the highest lift capacity too. The area suffers from winds.
370m; slopes 370–560m
⛷10 ⛷ 250 acres

Big Sky 569
✉ AmeriCan Ski, American Ski Classics, Ski All America, Ski Independence, Ski The American Dream

Big White 604
✉ AmeriCan Ski, Crystal, Frontier Ski, Made to Measure Holidays, Ski Activity, Ski All America, Ski Club of Great Britain, Ski Independence, Ski Line, Ski Safari, Ski The American Dream

Bischofshofen Austria
Working town and mountain resort near St Johann im Pongau, with very limited local runs and the main slopes starting nearby at Muhlbach.
545m; slopes 545–1000m
⛷1 ⛷ 2km

Bivio Switzerland
Quiet village near St Moritz with easy slopes opened up by a few lifts.
1775m; slopes 1780–2600m
⛷4 ⛷ 40km

Bizau Austria
One of two main areas in the low Bregenzerwald region north-west of Lech.
680m; slopes 680–1700m
⛷6 ⛷ 24km

Björkliden 649

Björnrike 649
✉ Neilson

Blackcomb 624
Smaller and quieter than neighbouring Whistler, conveniently sited at the bottom of its own mountain.
✉ Frontier Ski

Black Mountain USA
New Hampshire area with lodging in nearby Jackson.
⛷4 ⛷ 143 acres

Blatten Switzerland
Mountainside hamlet above Naters, beside the Rhône near Brig. Small but tall area in stunning glacial scenery, with larger Aletsch area nearby.
1320m; slopes 1320–3100m
⛷9 ⛷ 60km

Bled 642
✉ Balkan Holidays, Crystal, Slovenija Pursuits, Thomson Ski & Snowboarding

Blue Cow 653

Blue Mountain Canada
Largest area in Ontario, with glorious views of Lake Huron. High-capacity lift system and 100% snowmaking.
230m; slopes 230–450m
⛷15 ⛷ 275 acres

Blue River Canada
Base of world-famous Mike Wiegele heli-ski operation near Cariboo and Monashee mountains.

Bluewood USA
Particularly remote area even by American north-west standards. Worth a visit if you're in Walla Walla.
1355m; slopes 1355–1725m
⛷3 ⛷ 530 acres

Bogus Basin USA
Sizeable area overlooking Idaho's attractive, interesting capital, Boise.
1760m; slopes 1760–2310m
⛷8 ⛷ 2600 acres

Bohinj 642
✉ Balkan Holidays, Crystal, Slovenija Pursuits, Thomson Ski & Snowboarding

Bois-d'Amont France
One of four resorts that make up Les Rousses area in Jura region.
1050m; slopes 1120–1680m
⛷40 ⛷ 40km
✉ Lagrange Holidays

Bolognola Italy
Tiny area in Macerata region near the Adriatic Riviera.
1070m; slopes 1070–1845m
⛷7 ⛷ 5km

Bolton Valley USA
Resort near Stowe with mostly intermediate slopes.
465m; slopes 465–960m
⛷6 ⛷ 155 acres

Le Bonhomme France
One of several areas with snowmakers near Strasbourg.
830m; slopes 830–1235m
⛷9 ⛷ 12km

Bonneval-sur-Arc France
Unspoiled, remote old village in
the Haute Maurienne valley with
many of its slopes at high
altitude. Pass to neighbouring
Val-d'Isère is closed in winter.
1800m; slopes 1800–3000m
🚡 10 ⛷ 25km

Bons 257
Rustic, unspoiled old hamlet
linked to Les Deux-Alpes' skiing,
conveniently placed down the
valley for day trips to La Grave,
Alpe-d'Huez and Serre-Chevalier.

Boreal USA
Closest area to north Lake
Tahoe town, Truckee. Limited
slopes, best for novices.
2195m; slopes 2195–2375m
🚡 9 ⛷ 380 acres

Bormio 379
✉ *Airtours, Equity Ski,
Inghams, Interhome, Rocketski,
Ski Arrangements, Sloping Off*

Borovets 639
✉ *Airtours, Balkan Holidays,
Crystal, First Choice Ski,
Inghams, Neilson, Ski
Balkantours, Thomson Ski &
Snowboarding*

Bosco Chiesanuova Italy
Weekend day tripper's place
near Verona. A long drive from
any other resort.
1105m; slopes 1105–1805m
🚡 18 ⛷ 20km

Les Bottieres 335
La Bourboule France
Spa and cross-country skiing
with the Alpine slopes of Le
Mont-Dore nearby. Spectacular
extinct-volcano scenery.
85m; slopes 1050–1850m
🚡 41 ⛷ 80km
✉ *Lagrange Holidays*

Bourg-d'Oisans France
Pleasant valley town on main
Grenoble-Briançon road. Cheap
base for visits to Alpe-d'Huez
and Les Deux-Alpes.

Bourg-St-Maurice 213
French valley town, useful as a
base for visiting nearby resorts
and with a funicular to Les Arcs.
✉ *Erna Low, Interhome*

Bovec 642
✉ *Slovenija Pursuits*

Boyne Highlands USA
Impressive, high-capacity lift
system for weekend Detroit
crowds. Fierce winds off Lake
Michigan a major drawback.
225m; slopes 225–390m
🚡 10 ⛷ 240 acres

Boyne Mountain USA
Resort popular with weekend
Detroit crowds. Not as windy as
sister resort Boyne Highlands.
190m; slopes 190–340m
🚡 12 ⛷ 115 acres

Bramans France
Old cross-country village near
Modane. Well placed for touring
numerous nearby resorts such
as Val-Cenis and Valloire.
1230m 🚡 1

Bramberg Austria
Village near Pass Thurn
(Kitzbühel area). Shares odd
area with Neukirchen – the only
valley lift is in Neukirchen.
820m; slopes 820–900m
🚡 2 ⛷ 11km

Brand Austria
Family resort, less popular now,
perhaps because it lacks the
charm to compensate for its
small, low area.
1050m; slopes 1050–1920m
🚡 13 ⛷ 50km
✉ *Inghams, Interhome*

Les Brasses France
Collective name for six
traditional hamlets with some of
the closest slopes to Geneva,
but best known for cross-
country.
900m; slopes 900–1600m
🚡 17 ⛷ 50km

Braunwald Switzerland
Sunny but limited area, a
funicular ride above Linthal.
1300m; slopes 1300–1910m 🚡 8

Breckenridge 525
✉ *AmeriCan Ski, American Ski
Classics, Avant-ski, Chalet
World, Chalets 'Unlimited',
Crystal, First Choice Ski,
Handmade Holidays,
Independent Ski Links,
Inghams, Made to Measure
Holidays, Neilson, Ski Activity,
Ski All America, Ski Club of
Great Britain, Ski Expectations,
Ski Independence, Ski Line, Ski
Safari, Ski The American
Dream, Ski Wild, Skiworld,
Thomson Ski & Snowboarding,
Trailfinders, United Vacations
Ski Freedom USA & Canada,
Virgin Ski*

Brentonico Italy
Little resort just off Verona-
Trento motorway.
1160m; slopes 1160–1520m 🚡 16

La Bresse France
Largest of ski areas near Nancy
and Strasbourg. Snowmaking.
900m; slopes 900–1350m
🚡 21 ⛷ 62km
✉ *Lagrange Holidays*

Bretton Woods 578
✉ *AmeriCan Ski*

Briançon 321
Part of the Grand Serre Chevalier
region, but with own ski area.
✉ *Lagrange Holidays, Ski
Leisure Direction*

Brian Head USA
Utah area south of Salt Lake
City, too far from Park City for a
day trip.
2925m; slopes 2925–3445m
🚡 10 ⛷ 500 acres

Brides-les-Bains 282
Quiet spa town in valley below
Méribel, with a long gondola
connection.
✉ *AmeriCan Ski, Avant-ski,
Directski.com, Erna Low,
Eurotunnel Motoring Holidays,
Lagrange Holidays, Made to
Measure Holidays, Peak
Retreats, Ski Arrangements, Ski
France, Ski Leisure Direction,
Ski Life, Ski Weekends & Board
Breaks, SkiAway Holidays,
Snowcoach*

Bridger Bowl USA
Modest-sized day-trip resort
(just a shop and fast-food
restaurant at the base) –
popular with residents of
Bozeman, half an hour away,
and an interesting excursion
from Big Sky. Easy groomers at
the bottom, but seriously steep
ungroomed stuff at the top,
especially for those who hike up
to the famous Ridge. Good snow
record.
1855m; slopes 1855–2460m
🚡 6 ⛷ 1200 acres

Brighton 551
✉ *AmeriCan Ski, Ski The
American Dream*

Brixen 174
Best equipped of Grossraum
villages, with gondola access to
the slopes, shared with Söll and
Ellmau.

Brodie Mountain USA
Largest Massachusetts area.
100% snowmaking and mostly
easy slopes.
440m; slopes 440–820m
🚡 6 ⛷ 250 acres

Bromley USA
New York City weekend retreat,
reputedly the warmest place to
ski in chilly Vermont.
595m; slopes 595–1000m
🚡 9 ⛷ 300 acres

Bromont Canada
Purpose-built resort an hour
east of Montreal, with one of
the best small areas in eastern
Canada, popular for its night
skiing.
slopes 405–575m
🚡 6 ⛷ 135 acres

Bruck Austria
Low beginners' resort, but could
suit intermediates looking for a
small, quiet base from which to
visit nearby Zell am See.
630m

Brundage Mountain USA
Remote, uncrowded Idaho area
with glorious views across lake
towards Hell's Canyon. Mostly
intermediate slopes. Also has a
snowcat operation.
1760m; slopes 1760–2320m
🚡 5 ⛷ 1300 acres

Bruson 470
Relaxing respite from Verbier's
crowds, on the other side of Le
Châble. Well placed for car trips
to Chamonix and Champéry.

Burke Mountain USA
Uncrowded, isolated family
resort in Vermont with mostly
intermediate slopes. Great views
from the top.
385m; slopes 385–995m
🚡 4 ⛷ 130 acres

Bürserberg Austria
Undistinguished valley town
near Brand.
900m; slopes 1035–1850m
🚡 13 ⛷ 50km

Cairngorm 652
✉ *Skisafe Travel*

Caldirola Italy
Genoese weekend day-tripper
spot in a remote region off the
motorway to Turin.
1010m; slopes 1010–1460m
🚡 3 ⛷ 5km

Camigliatello Italy
Tiny area on the foot of the
Italian 'boot' near Cosenza.
Weekend/day trip spot.
1270m; slopes 1270–1750m
🚡 4 ⛷ 6km

Campitello 410
Linked to the Sella Ronda, with
quick connections to the
interesting Arabba section.
✉ *Airtours, Crystal, Thomson
Ski & Snowboarding*

Campitello Matese Italy
The only slopes near Naples.
Surprisingly large area when
snowcover is complete.
Weekend crowds.
1440m; slopes 1440–2100m
🚡 8 ⛷ 40km

Campo di Giove Italy
Highest slopes in L'Aquila region
east of Rome.
1070m; 🚡 6 ⛷ 23km

Campodolcino Italy
Valley town with new funicular
up to the fringe of Madesimo's
slopes.
1070m; slopes 1545–2880m
🚡 6 ⛷ 8km

Campo Felice Italy
Easiest resort to reach from
Rome, off Aquila motorway. One
of the better lift systems in the
vicinity.
1410m; slopes 1520–2065m
🚡 14 ⛷ 40km

Campo Imperatore Italy
One of the best of many little
areas east of Rome in L'Aquila
region.
1980m; 🚡 8 ⛷ 20km

Canazei 410
Sizeable and lively rustic village
in the Sella Ronda's most
heavily wooded section of
mountain.
✉ *Airtours, Crystal, Equity Ski,
Inghams, Rocketski, Thomson
Ski & Snowboarding*

Candanchu/Astún 636

Canillo 102
Small, quiet town, with good
sports facilities and newly
developed lifts and slopes,
linked to Soldeu.

Canmore Canada
Old frontier town on the way to Nakiska/Fortress, well placed for touring the region and an attractive alternative to staying in Banff.

Cannon 578

The Canyons 555
✉ AmeriCan Ski, Ski All America, Ski Independence, Ski Safari, Ski The American Dream, United Vacations Ski Freedom USA & Canada

Cardrona 655

Les Carroz-d'Arâches 262
An attractive, spacious village on a sunny shelf on the road up to Flaine.
✉ AmeriCan Ski, Eurotunnel Motoring Holidays, Lagrange Holidays, Peak Retreats, Ski Life

Caspoggio Italy
Attractive, unspoiled village north-east of Lake Como, with easy slopes (and more at nearby Chiesa).
1100m; slopes 1100–2155m
⛷8 ⛷ 22km

Castel S Angelo Italy
Tiny area in Macerata region near Adriatic Riviera.
805m ⛷4 ⛷ 2km

Cauterets 371
✉ Lagrange Holidays, SkiAway Holidays

Cavalese Italy
Unspoiled medieval town with its own pretty slopes and close to the Sella Ronda.
1000m; slopes 975–2265m
⛷9 ⛷ 70km
✉ Alpine Tours

Ceillac France
Tight cluster of rustic old buildings near Serre-Chevalier. Not far from the highest village in Europe, St-Veran.
1600m; slopes 1600–2400m

Celerina 464
Quiet, unpretentious village, with links up to St Moritz's Corviglia sector.
✉ Made to Measure Holidays

Cerler Spain
Very limited, purpose-built resort with a compact ski area similar to that of nearby Andorra's Arinsal.
1500m; slopes 1500–2630m
⛷16 ⛷ 45km

Le Cernix France
Hamlet near Megève where Les Saisies' slopes link to those of Crest-Voland. Uncrowded retreat.
1250m; slopes 1150–1950m
⛷41 ⛷ 80km

Cerrato Lago Italy
Very limited area near the coastal town of La Spezia.
1270m; slopes 1270–1890m
⛷5 ⛷ 3km

Cerro Bayo Argentina
Limited area amid stunning scenery 10km/6 miles from Villa la Angostura, and 90km/56 miles from San Carlos de Bariloche.
slopes 1050–1780m
⛷9 ⛷ 20km

Cerro Catedral (Bariloche) Argentina
The most developed ski and boarding resort in South America, to be found 19 km/12 miles) from Bariloche. Lodgings available at the foot of the slopes.
slopes 1040–2050m
⛷32 ⛷ 52km
✉ Scott Dunn Latin America

Cervinia 381
✉ Airtours, Alpine Answers Select, Alpine Events, Club Med, Crystal, Elegant Resorts, First Choice Ski, Independent Ski Links, Inghams, Interhome, Momentum Ski, Rocketski, Ski Arrangements, Ski Solutions, Ski Weekend, Thomson Ski & Snowboarding

Cesana Torinese 292
Little Italian village linking the Sauze d'Oulx, Sestrière and Sansicario side of the Milky Way to the Clavière, Montgenèvre side.

Le Châble 470
Small village below Verbier, linked by gondola.

Chacaltaya Bolivia
Highest lift-served ski area in the world and the only ski area in Bolivia. Reached by four-wheel drive vehicle from La Paz 30km/19 miles away. Only open in summer (too cold in winter).
5190m; slopes 5220–5420m
⛷1 ⛷ 2km
✉ Scott Dunn Latin America

Chaillol France
Cross-country base on the edge of the beautiful Ecrins National Park, near Gap. Small Alpine area, lots of snowmakers.
1600m; slopes 1450–2000m ⛷11

Chamois Italy
A good choice when higher areas are affected by bad weather. Close to Valtournenche and Cervinia.
1815m; slopes 1815–2270m
⛷8 ⛷ 20km

Chamonix 226
✉ Airtours, Alpine Answers Select, Alpine Events, Alpine Weekends, Avant-ski, Bigfoot Travel, Board and Lodge, Chalets 'Unlimited', Chamonix Lodge, Club Med, Club Pavilion, Collineige, Crystal, Erna Low, Esprit Ski, Eurotunnel Motoring Holidays, First Choice Ski, FlexiSki, Fraser Ralston, French Freedom Holidays, Huski, Independent Ski Links, Inghams, Interhome, Lagrange Holidays, Made to Measure Holidays, Momentum Ski, Mountain Tracks, Neilson, Ski Arrangements, Ski Club of

Great Britain, Ski Expectations, Ski France, Ski Independence, Ski Leisure Direction, Ski Life, Ski Line, Ski Solutions, Ski Supreme, Ski Total, Ski Weekend, The Corporate Ski Company, Thomson Ski & Snowboarding, Uptoyou.com, White Roc

Champagny-en-Vanoise 303
Charming village with pretty, south-facing local slopes linking to the La Plagne network.
✉ Barrelli Ski, Erna Low, Glacier Dayz, Handmade Holidays, Independent Ski Links, Lagrange Holidays, Made to Measure Holidays

Champéry 433
✉ Alpine Answers Select, Alpine Events, Made to Measure Holidays, Piste Artiste Ltd, Plus Travel, Ski Weekend, The Corporate Ski Company, White Roc

Champex Switzerland
Lakeside hamlet tucked away in the trees above Orsières. A nice quiet, unspoiled base from which to visit Verbier's area.
1470m; slopes 1470–2220m
⛷4 ⛷ 8km

Champfér 464
Lakeside hamlet between St Moritz and Silvaplana with speedy access to the Corvatsch lifts.

Champoluc 402
Unspoiled, inexpensive village at one end of the Monterosa Ski area.
✉ Alpine Answers Select, Chalets 'Unlimited', Crystal, Esprit Ski, Handmade Holidays, Ski 2

Champoussin 433
Quiet mountainside village with convenient links to the rest of the Champéry slopes.

Chamrousse France
Functional family resort near Grenoble, with good, sheltered slopes.
1650m; slopes 1400–2255m
⛷26 ⛷ 77km
✉ Lagrange Holidays

Chandolin Switzerland
Picturesque, unspoiled village in the Val d'Anniviers off the Valais, with high, easy open slopes (shared with St Luc) served almost entirely by drags. Valley pass also covers Zinal, Grimentz and Vercorin – 200km/125 miles of runs in total.
1935m; slopes 1660–3025m
⛷16 ⛷ 75km

Chantemerle 321
One of the main valley villages with direct access to Serre-Chevalier's slopes.

Chapelco Argentina
Small ski area with full infrastructure of services 19km/12 miles from sizeable town of San Martin de Los Andes. Accommodation in hotels 11km/7 miles from the slopes.
slopes 1250–1980m
⛷7 ⛷ 800 acres

La Chapelle-d'Abondance 234
Unspoiled village 5km/3 miles down the valley from Châtel, with lift access to the Portes du Soleil network.
✉ Ski La Cote

Charlotte Pass 653

Château d'Oex Switzerland
Pleasant little valley town that is the main French-speaking component of the shared lift-pass area around Gstaad. Local slopes are pleasant and undemanding but low (La Braye, at the top, is at only 1650m/5,400ft), and not connected to any of the Gstaad sectors – though the local railway makes moving around to other resorts painless. This is where Alpine hot-air ballooning first took off, and it's still a local speciality.
970m; slopes 890–3000m
⛷67 ⛷ 250km
✉ Alpine Tours, Crystal

Châtel 234
✉ Avant-ski, Chalets 'Unlimited', Connick Ski, First Choice Ski, Freedom Holidays, Haig Ski, Interhome, Lagrange Holidays, Made to Measure Holidays, Peak Retreats, Ski Addiction, Ski Arrangements, Ski Independence, Ski Leisure Direction, Ski Line, Ski Rosie, Skialot, SkiAway Holidays, Snowfocus, Susie Ward Alpine Holidays, Tops Ski Chalets and Club Hotels

Le Chatelard France
Small resort in remote Parc des Bauges between Lake Annecy and Chambéry.

Chiesa Italy
Attractive beginners' resort with a fairly high plateau of easy runs above the resort.
1000m; slopes 1700–2335m
⛷16 ⛷ 50km

Le Chinaillon 239
Modern, chalet-style village at base of lifts above Le Grand-Bornand.

Chiomonte Italy
Tiny resort on the main road east of Bardonecchia and Sauze d'Oulx. A good half-day trip from either.
745m; slopes 745–2210m
⛷6 ⛷ 10km

Chonmasan Korea
Purpose-built resort 30km/20 miles north-east of Seoul. ⛷7

Chsea Algeria
Largest of Algeria's skiable areas, 135km/84 miles south-east of coastal town of Alger in the Djur Djur mountains.
1860m; slopes 1860–2510m ⛷ 2

Churwalden Switzerland
Hamlet on fringe of Lenzerheide-Valbella area.
1230m; slopes 1230–2865m
⛷ 35 ⛷ 155km

Claviere 292
Small Italian village linked to Montgenèvre (in France) and the rest of the Milky Way ski area.
✉ *Crystal, Equity Ski, First Choice Ski, Rocketski*

La Clusaz 239
✉ *Aravis Alpine Retreat, Classic Ski Limited, Crystal, Frosty's Ski and Snowboard Holidays, Interhome, Lagrange Holidays, Made to Measure Holidays, Ski Activity, Ski Arrangements, Ski Leisure Direction, Ski Supreme, Ski Weekend, SkiAway Holidays, Snowlife, The Last Resort*

Les Coches 303
Small, purpose-built village, linked to the La Plagne ski area.
✉ *Erna Low, Eurotunnel Motoring Holidays, Lagrange Holidays, Made to Measure Holidays, Ski Independence, Ski Leisure Direction, Ski Line, The Family Ski Company*

Cogne Italy
One of Aosta valley's larger villages. Ski area worth a short visit from nearby Pila.
1530m; slopes 1530–2245m
⛷ 5 ⛷ 8km
✉ *Inntravel*

Colfosco 410
Small but sprawling village that makes up part of the Sella Ronda circuit.

Colle di Tenda Italy
Dour, modern resort that shares a good area with much nicer Limone. Not far from Nice.
1400m; slopes 1120–2040m
⛷ 33 ⛷ 80km

Colle Isarco Italy
Brenner Pass area – and the bargain-shopping town of Vipiteno is nearby.
1095m; slopes 1095–2720m
⛷ 5 ⛷ 15km

Le Collet-d'Allevard France
Ski area of sizeable summer spa Allevard-les-Bains in remote region east of Chambéry-Grenoble road.
1450m; slopes 1450–2100m
⛷ 13 ⛷ 35km

Collio Italy
Tiny area of short runs in a remote spot between lakes Garda and d'Iseo.
840m; slopes 840–1715m ⛷ 14

Les Collons 470

Combelouvière 364
Quiet hamlet tucked away in the trees at the foot of Valmorel's slopes.
✉ *Lagrange Holidays*

Combloux 274
Quiet, unspoiled alternative to linked Megève.
✉ *Lagrange Holidays*

Les Contamines 245
✉ *Chalet Kiana, Chalets 'Unlimited', Classic Ski Limited, Interhome, Lagrange Holidays, Ski Arrangements, Ski Expectations, Ski Line, Ski Total*

Copper Mountain 530
✉ *AmeriCan Ski, Made to Measure Holidays, Ski All America, Ski Independence, Ski The American Dream, United Vacations Ski Freedom USA & Canada*

Le Corbier 335
✉ *Equity Ski, Erna Low, Interhome, Lagrange Holidays, Rocketski, Ski Life*

Coronet Peak 658
428m/1,400ft vertical. Closest area to Queenstown (20 minutes). Good mix of bowls, chutes, varied piste. Relies on large snowmaking facility for good snowcover. Spectacular views.

Corrençon-en-Vercors France
Charming, rustic village at foot of Villard-de-Lans ski area. Good cross-country, too.
1160m; slopes 1160–2170m
⛷ 25 ⛷ 130km

Cortina d'Ampezzo 386
✉ *Alpine Answers Select, Alpine Events, Chalets 'Unlimited', Crystal, Elegant Resorts, Inghams, Momentum Ski, Ski Arrangements, Ski Club of Great Britain, Ski Solutions, Ski Weekend, Ski Yogi, White Roc*

Corvara 410
The most animated Sella Ronda village, with lots of facilities and good lift links.
✉ *Inghams, Ski Yogi*

Courchevel 247
✉ *Airtours, Alpine Answers Select, Alpine Events, Altitude Holidays, Avant-ski, Bladon Lines, Chalet World, Chalets 'Unlimited', Crystal, Descent International, Elegant Resorts, Erna Low, Esprit Ski, Eurotunnel Motoring Holidays, Finlays, First Choice Ski, FlexiSki, Independent Ski Links, Inghams, Lagrange Holidays, Le Ski, Lotus Supertravel, Made to Measure Holidays, Mark Warner, Momentum Ski, Neilson, Powder Byrne, Scott Dunn Ski, Silver Ski, Simply Ski, Ski Activity, Ski Amis, Ski Arrangements, Ski Club of Great Britain, Ski Expectations, Ski France, Ski Independence, Ski Leisure Direction, Ski Life, Ski*

Line, Ski Link, Ski 'n' Action, Ski Olympic, Ski Solutions, Ski Supreme, Ski Total, Ski Weekend, Ski-Val, Skiworld, The Corporate Ski Company, The Ski Company, Thomson Ski & Snowboarding, Uptoyou.com, White Roc

Courmayeur 391
✉ *Alpine Answers Select, Alpine Events, Alpine Weekends, Chalets 'Unlimited', Crystal, First Choice Ski, Independent Ski Links, Inghams, Interski, Mark Warner, Momentum Ski, Ski Arrangements, Ski Expectations, Ski Line, Ski Solutions, Ski Weekend, Thomson Ski & Snowboarding, White Roc*

Cranmore USA
Area in New Hampshire with attractive town/resort of North Conway. Easy skiing. Good for families.
150m; slopes 150–515m
⛷ 8 ⛷ 190 acres

Crans-Montana 435
✉ *Alpine Answers Select, Alpine Events, Crystal, Erna Low, Independent Ski Links, Inghams, Interhome, Kuoni, Lagrange Holidays, Made to Measure Holidays, Momentum Ski, Plus Travel, Ski Club of Great Britain, Ski Weekend, Swiss Travel Service, The Corporate Ski Company, The Oxford Ski Company*

Crested Butte 532
✉ *AmeriCan Ski, Club Med, Made to Measure Holidays, Ski Activity, Ski Independence, Ski Safari, Ski The American Dream, United Vacations Ski Freedom USA & Canada*

Crest-Voland France
Attractive, unspoiled traditional village near Megève and Le Grand Bornand with wonderfully uncrowded intermediate slopes linked to Les Saisies.
1150m; slopes 1230–1650m
⛷ 17 ⛷ 45km
✉ *AmeriCan Ski, Peak Retreats, SkiAway Holidays*

Crissolo Italy
Small, remote day-tripper area, south-west of Turin. Part of the Monviso ski area.
1320m; slopes 1745–2340m
⛷ 4 ⛷ 20km

La Croix-Fry 239
Couple of hotels on the pass close to La Clusaz.

Les Crosets 433
Isolated and limited mini-resort, in a prime position within the Portes du Soleil circuit, above Champéry.

Crystal Mountain USA
Area in glorious Mt Rainier National Park, near Seattle. Good, varied area given good snow/weather, but both are often wet.
1340m; slopes 1340–2135m
⛷ 10 ⛷ 2300 acres

Cuchara Valley USA
Quiet little family resort in southern Colorado, some way from any other ski area.
2800m; slopes 2800–3285m
⛷ 4 ⛷ 250 acres

Cutigliano Italy
Sizeable village near Abetone in the Appennines. Less than 2 hours from Florence and Pisa.
1125m; slopes 1125–1850m
⛷ 9 ⛷ 13km

Cypress Mountain Canada
Vancouver's most challenging area, 20 minutes from the city and with 40% for experts. Good snowfall record but rain is a problem.
920m; slopes 910–1445m ⛷ 5

Daemyung Korea
One of the less ugly Korean resorts, 75km/47 miles from Seoul. ⛷ 12

La Daille 352
Ugly apartment complex at the entrance to Val-d'Isère.

Daisen Japan
Western Honshu's main area, four hours from Osaka.
800m; slopes 740–1120m ⛷ 8

Damüls Austria
Scattered but attractive village in Bregenzerwald area close to the German and Swiss borders.
1430m; slopes 1430–2010m
⛷ 9 ⛷ 48km

Davos 440
✉ *Alpine Answers Select, Alpine Events, Crystal, FlexiSki, Inghams, Interhome, Kuoni, Made to Measure Holidays, Momentum Ski, Plus Travel, Ski Club of Great Britain, Ski Weekend, SkiGower, Swiss Travel Service, The Corporate Ski Company, White Roc*

Deer Mountain USA
South Dakota area close to 'Old West' town Deadwood and Mount Rushmore.
1825m; slopes 1825–2085m
⛷ 4 ⛷ 370 acres

Deer Valley 557
✉ *AmeriCan Ski, American Ski Classics, Made to Measure Holidays, Ski All America, Ski Independence, Ski Safari, Ski The American Dream, United Vacations Ski Freedom USA & Canada*

Les Deux-Alpes 257
✉ *Airtours, Avant-ski, Chalet World, Chalets 'Unlimited', Club Med, Crystal, Equity Ski, Erna Low, First Choice Ski, Independent Ski Links, Inghams, Interhome, Lagrange Holidays, Made to Measure Holidays, Mark Warner, Neilson, Panorama Holidays, Peak Retreats, Rocketski, Ski Arrangements, Ski Independence, Ski Leisure Direction, Ski Life, Ski Line, Ski Supreme, Skiworld, Thomson Ski & Snowboarding, Tops Ski Chalets and Club Hotels*

Les Diablerets   Switzerland
Unspoiled but spread-out village towered over by the Diablerets massif, with two areas of local slopes, plus Glacier 3000. A high-speed quad followed by a slow chair lead up to the red runs of the Meilleret area and the link to Villars. A gondola in the centre of town takes you to Isenau, a mix of blues and reds served by drag-lifts. From Isenau there's a red run down to Col du Pillon and the cable-car to and from the glacier. You can also reach the glacier cable-cars by bus from town. On Glacier 3000, you'll find blue runs at over 3000m/10,000ft, stunning views and the long, red Combe d'Audon – a wonderful, usually quiet, run away from all the lifts with sheer cliffs rising up on both sides. The splendid Botta 3000 restaurant with stunning views at the top of the glacier is recommended for lunch. There's an evening toboggan run down from Les Mazots; there's also an ice rink and skate park.
1150m; slopes 1150–3000m
⛟ 46 ⛷ 125km
✉ *Crystal, Interhome, Lagrange Holidays, Momentum Ski, SkiGower, Sloping Off, Solo's*

Diamond Peak   USA
Quiet, pleasant alternative to brash South Lake Tahoe.
slopes 2040–2600m
⛟ 7 ⛷ 755 acres
✉ *Ski The American Dream*

Dienten   Austria
Quiet village east of Saalbach at the heart of large, low-altitude Hochkönig area that spreads impressively over four mountains linking Maria Alm to Mühlbach.
1070m; slopes 800–1825m
⛟ 18 ⛷ 150km

Dinner Plain   Australia
Attractive resort best known for cross-country skiing. Shuttle to Mt Hotham for Alpine slopes. 4.5 hours from Melbourne.
1520m

Discovery Ski Area   USA
Pleasant area miles from anywhere except Butte, Montana, with largely intermediate slopes but double-black runs on the back of the mountain – and the chance of seriously good snow. Usually deserted. Fairmont Hot Springs (two huge thermal pools) nearby.
2080m; slopes 2080–2485m
⛟ 4 ⛷ 380 acres

Disentis   Switzerland
Unspoiled old village in a pretty setting on the Glacier Express rail route near Andermatt. Scenic area with long runs.
1135m; slopes 1150–2920m
⛟ 10 ⛷ 60km
✉ *Interhome*

Dobbiaco   Italy
One of several little resorts near the Austrian border; a feasible day out from the Sella Ronda.
1250m; slopes 1250–1610m
⛟ 5 ⛷ 15km
✉ *Ramblers Holidays, Waymark Holidays*

Dodge Ridge   USA
Novice/leisurely intermediate area north of Yosemite. The pass from Reno is closed in winter, preventing crowds.
2010m; slopes 2010–2500m
⛟ 12 ⛷ 815 acres

Dolonne   391
Quiet suburb of Courmayeur – the gondola link is no more, but the off-trail run home is still a classic.

Dorfgastein   114
Quieter, friendlier alternative to Bad Gastein and Bad Hofgastein, with its own intermediate ski area.

Dundret   Sweden
Lapland area with floodlit slopes open through winter when sun barely rises.
slopes 475–825m
⛟ 7 ⛷ 15km

Durango Mountain Resort USA
Mountain formerly known as Purgatory, with good slopes now accessed by a long six-pack (the main base is still known as Purgatory). Durango itself, a half hour away, is a fun western town with an historic main street.
2680m; slopes 2680–3300m
⛟ 11 ⛷ 1200 acres
✉ *AmeriCan Ski, Ski Independence*

Eaglecrest   USA
Close to famous Yukon gold rush town Skagway. Family resort famous for its ski school.
365m; slopes 365–790m
⛟ 3 ⛷ 640 acres

Eaux-Bonnes-Gourette   France
Most snow-sure resort in the French Pyrenees. Very popular with local families, so best avoided at weekends.
1400m; slopes 1400–2400m
⛟ 23 ⛷ 30km

Eben im Pongau   Austria
Part of Salzburger Sportwelt Amadé area that includes nearby St Johann, Wagrain, Flachau and Zauchensee. Village spoilt by the autobahn passing through it.
855m; slopes 855–2185m
⛟ 100 ⛷ 350km

Ehrwald   Austria
Friendly, relaxed, pretty village with several nicely varied areas, notably the Zugspitz glacier. Poor bus services, so a car desirable.
1000m; slopes 1000–3000m
⛟ 11 ⛷ 45km

El Colorado/Farellones   Chile
One of Chile's best ski areas, 40km/25 miles east of Santiago, and connected to Valle Nevado ski area. Crowded at weekends.
slopes 2430–3340m
⛟ 18 ⛷ 2500 acres

Eldora Mountain   USA
Varied terrain close to Boulder City and Denver. Crowded at weekends.
2795m; slopes 2805–3230m
⛟ 12 ⛷ 680 acres

Elk Meadows   USA
Area south of Salt Lake City, more than a day trip from Park City.
2775m; slopes 2745–3170m
⛟ 6 ⛷ 1400 acres

Ellmau   117
✉ *Airtours, Crystal, Inghams, Interhome, Neilson, Ski Wild, Thomson Ski & Snowboarding*

Encamp   94

Enego   391
Limited weekend day-trippers' area near Vicenza and Trento.
1300m; slopes 1300–1445m
⛟ 7 ⛷ 30km

Engelberg   Switzerland
Traditional town resort set amid spectacular mountains and only an hour's drive from Lucerne. The slopes are fragmented: Titlis is snowsure – the glacier is open all year round – but the Brunni sector is less reliable. For experts, the attraction is the famous Laub, which drops 1000m/3,280ft – superb when conditions are right. Generally the pistes suit confident intermediates; there are few easy slopes and the nursery slopes involve lift-rides so it's not ideal for beginners. Cross-country is good with 39km/24 miles of trails. Mountain restaurants are plentiful, friendly and inexpensive by Swiss standards. Package accommodation is in hotels, with chalets and apartments to rent locally. Eating out is mostly in hotels and après-ski is good at weekends. Off the slopes there are good sports facilities, a monastery tour, glassworks and trips to Lucerne and Zürich.
1050m; slopes 1050–3020m
⛟ 23 ⛷ 82km
✉ *Alpine Events, Crystal, Inntravel, Interhome, Kuoni, Made to Measure Holidays, Ski Weekend, Swiss Travel Service, The Corporate Ski Company, White Roc*

Entrèves   391
Unremarkable cluster of hotels at the base of the lift up to Courmayeur's slopes.

Escaldes   Andorra
Central valley town, effectively part of Andorra la Vella.

Etna   Italy
Scenic, uncrowded, short-season area on the volcano's flank, 20 minutes from Nickolossi.
1800m; slopes 1800–2350m
⛷ 5km

Evolène   Switzerland
Charming rustic village in unspoiled, attractive setting south of Sion. Own little area, with Verbier's slopes accessed at nearby Les Masses.
1380m; slopes 1300–3330m
⛟ 100 ⛷ 400km

Faak am See   Austria
Limited area, one of five overlooking town of Villach.
560m; ⛟ 1 ⛷ 2km

Fairmont Hot Springs   Canada
Major luxury spa complex ideal for a relaxing holiday with some gentle skiing thrown in.
⛟ 2 ⛷ 60 acres

Faistenau   Austria
Cross-country area close to Salzburg and St Wolfgang. Limited Alpine slopes.
785m; slopes 785–1000m
⛟ 5 ⛷ 3km

Falcade   Italy
Largest of many little ski areas close to but not part of the Sella Ronda.
1145m; slopes 1145–2170m
⛟ 11 ⛷ 39km
✉ *Alpine Tours*

Falera   447
Small, rustic village, with improved access to big ski area shared by Flims and Laax.

Le Falgoux   France
One of the most beautiful old villages in France, set in the very scenic Volcano National Park. Several ski areas nearby.
930m; slopes 930–1350m

Falkertsee   Austria
Base area rather than a village, with bleak, open slopes in contrast to nearby Badkleinkirchheim.
1690m; slopes 1690–2385m
⛟ 5 ⛷ 15km

Falls Creek   653

La Feclaz   France
One of several little resorts in the remote Parc des Bauges.

Fernie   606
✉ *Alpine Answers Select, AmeriCan Ski, Canadian Powder Tours, Crystal, Frontier Ski, Handmade Holidays, Inghams, Made to Measure Holidays, Ski Activity, Ski All America, Ski Club of Great Britain, Ski Independence, Ski Safari, Ski The American Dream, Skiworld, The Ski Company*

Fieberbrunn   Austria
Atmospheric and friendly
Tirolean village, which sprawls
along the valley road for 2km/1
Mile. Its small but attractive area
of wooded slopes is a bus-ride
away and best suits beginners
and leisurely intermediates. The
nursery slopes are close to the
village centre and graduation to
long, gentle runs is easy. There
are 35km/22 miles of good trails
for cross-country skiers.
Weekday queues are rare, but
Fieberbrunn has a reputation for
snow and can be invaded when
other resorts are lacking. There
are some decent mountain
restaurants. Accommodation in
the village is in hotels, and
there is also accommodation at
the lift station. Restaurants are
mainly hotel-based and après-
ski is liveliest at 4pm. Off the
slopes, there's an adventure
pool, skating, sleigh rides,
cleared walks and a toboggan
run, and train excursions are
possible.
800m; slopes 800–2020m
⛷ 13 ⛷ 35km
✉ Snowscape

Fiesch   Switzerland
Traditional Rhône valley resort
close to Brig, with a lift up to
Fiescheralp (2220m/7,280ft) at
one end of the beautiful Aletsch
area extending across the
mountainside via Bettmeralp to
Riederalp.
1060m; slopes 1900–2900m
⛷ 32 ⛷ 90km
✉ SkiGower

Fiescheralp   Switzerland
Mountain outpost of Fiesch,
down in the Rhône valley. At
one end of the beautiful Aletsch
area extending across the
mountainside via Bettmeralp to
Riederalp.
2220m; slopes 1900–2900m
⛷ 32 ⛷ 90km

Filzmoos   Austria
Charming, unspoiled, friendly
village with leisurely slopes that
are ideal for novices. Good snow
record for its height.
1055m; slopes 1055–1645m
⛷ 12 ⛷ 32km
✉ Inghams

Finkenberg   147
Between Mayrhofen and
Hintertux, with a large area of
mainly intermediate skiing
✉ Crystal, Equity Ski

Fiss   Austria
Nicely compact, quiet, traditional
village with a sunny area well
protected by snowmakers and
linked to Serfaus.
1435m; slopes 1200–2700m
⛷ 42 ⛷ 160km
✉ Alpine Tours, Interhome

Flachau   Austria
Quiet, spacious village in a
pretty setting at one end of
extensive three-valley lift
network linking via Wagrain to
Alpendorf. Flachauwinkl, up the

---

valley, is at the centre of
another similarly extensive lift
system. All these resorts are
covered by the Salzburger
Sportwelt ski pass that our
figures relate to.
925m; slopes 800–2185m
⛷ 59 ⛷ 200km
✉ Interhome

Flachauwinkl   Austria
Tiny ski station beside Tauern
autobahn, at centre of extensive
three-valley lift network linking
Kleinarl to Zauchensee. Flachau,
down the valley, is at one end
of a similarly extensive lift
system. All these resorts are
covered by the Salzburger
Sportwelt ski pass that our
figures relate to.
930m; slopes 800–2185m
⛷ 59 ⛷ 200km

Flaine   262
✉ Avant-ski, Classic Ski
Limited, Club Med, Crystal, Erna
Low, Eurotunnel Motoring
Holidays, French Freedom
Holidays, Independent Ski
Links, Inghams, Made to Measure
Holidays, Neilson, Ski
Arrangements, Ski Club of Great
Britain, Ski Independence, Ski
Leisure Direction, Ski Life, Ski
Supreme, Ski Weekend,
Thomson Ski & Snowboarding

Flims   447
✉ Alpine Answers Select,
Alpine Events, Crystal,
Interhome, Kuoni, Made to
Measure Holidays, Momentum
Ski, Plus Travel, Powder Byrne,
Ski Weekend, Swiss Travel
Service, The Corporate Ski
Company, White Roc

Flumet   France
Surprisingly large traditional
village, the main place from
which to ski the sizable Val
d'Arly ski area. Close to better-
known Megève.
1000m; slopes 1000–1600m
⛷ 10 ⛷ 40km
✉ AmeriCan Ski, Peak Retreats

Flumserberg   Switzerland
Collective name for the villages
sharing a varied area an hour
south-east of Zürich.
1220m; slopes 1220–2220m
⛷ 17

Folgaria   Italy
Largest of several resorts east of
Trento. Old lift system.
1165m; slopes 1185–2005m
⛷ 38 ⛷ 70km
✉ Alpine Tours

Folgarida   400
Pleasant Dolomite village, with
links to Madonna di Campiglio's
extensive area.
✉ Equity Ski, Rocketski,
Sloping Off

Foncine-le-Haut   France
Major cross-country village in
the Jura Mountains with
extensive trails.
✉ Headwater Holidays,
Lagrange Holidays

Fonni Gennaragentu   Italy
Sardinia's only 'ski area' – and
it's tiny.
⛷ 1 ⛷ 5km

Font-Romeu   371
✉ Lagrange Holidays, Solo's

Foppolo   Italy
Relatively unattractive but user-
friendly village, a short transfer
from Bergamo.
1510m; slopes 1610–2160m
⛷ 9 ⛷ 47km
✉ Equity Ski

Forca Canapine   Italy
Limited area near the Adriatic
and Ascoli Piceno. Popular with
weekend day-trippers.
1450m; slopes 1450–1690m
⛷ 11 ⛷ 20km

Formazza   Italy
Cross-country base with some
downhill slopes.
1280m; slopes 1275–1755m
⛷ 8km

Formigal   636
Le Fornet   352
Rustic, old hamlet 3km/2 miles
further down the valley from
Val-d'Isère.

Forstau   Austria
Secluded hamlet above
Radstadt–Schladming road. Very
limited area with old lifts, but
nice and quiet.
930m; slopes 930–1885m
⛷ 7 ⛷ 14km

Fortress Mountain   Canada
Primitive, wild and remote little
mountain between Banff and
Calgary, renowned for powder
snow, dramatic scenery and
uncrowded slopes. Training site
for Canada freestyle teams.
2040m; slopes 2040–2370m
⛷ 6 ⛷ 325 acres
✉ Ski The American Dream

La Foux-d'Allos   France
Purpose-built resort that shares
a good intermediate area with
Pra-Loup.
1800m; slopes 1800–2600m
⛷ 52 ⛷ 167km
✉ Lagrange Holidays

Frabosa Soprana   Italy
One of numerous little areas
south of Turin, well placed for
combining winter sports with
Riviera sightseeing.
850m; slopes 860–1740m
⛷ 7 ⛷ 40km

Frisco   525
Small town based on a Victorian
settlement, down the valley from
Breckenridge.
✉ AmeriCan Ski

Frontignano   Italy
Best lift system in the Macerata
region, near the Adriatic Riviera.
1340m; slopes 1340–2000m
⛷ 8 ⛷ 10km

Fügen   Austria
Unspoiled Zillertal village with
limited area best suited to
beginners.
560m; slopes 560–2400m
⛷ 19 ⛷ 48km

Fulpmes   125
Furano   Japan
Small Hokkaido resort, two
hours from Sapporo. One of the
few Japanese areas to get
reasonable powder.
235m; slopes 235–1065m ⛷ 13

Fusch   Austria
Cheaper, quiet place to stay
when visiting Zell am See.
Across golf course from Kaprun
and Schüttdorf.
805m

Fuschl   Austria
Attractive, unspoiled, lakeside
village close to St Wolfgang and
Salzburg, 30 minutes from its
slopes. Best suited to part-time
skiers who want to sightsee as
well.
670m

Gålå   Norway
Base for downhill and cross-
country skiing, an hour's drive
north of Lillehammer.
930m; slopes 830–1150m
⛷ 7 ⛷ 20km
✉ Inntravel

Gallio   Italy
One of several low resorts near
Vicenza and Trento. Popular
with weekend day-trippers.
1100m; slopes 1100–1550m
⛷ 11 ⛷ 50km

Galtür   129
Charming traditional village near
Ischgl, in the news in 1998/99
due to a tragic avalanche
disaster.
✉ Inghams, Made to Measure
Holidays

Gambarie d'Aspromonte   Italy
Italy's second most southerly ski
area (after Mt Etna). On the 'toe'
of the Italian 'boot' near Reggio
di Calabria.
1310m; slopes 1310–1650m ⛷ 3

Gantschier   Austria
No slopes of its own but
particularly well placed for
visiting all the Montafon areas.
700m

Gargellen   152
Quiet, tiny and secluded village
tucked up a side valley in the
Montafon area, with a small but
varied local area that is blissfully
quiet.
✉ Interhome, Made to Measure
Holidays

Garmisch-Partenkirchen
    Germany
Twin classic old-fashioned winter
sports resorts – unspoiled,
traditional Partenkirchen is much
the prettier. The ski areas are a
bus-ride away, and offer limited
challenge for experts and
adventurous intermediates
(though the long Kandahar black
downhill course is excellent);
there are good beginners areas.
The lift system is rather
antiquated, although the 76-
year-old Kreuzeck cable car was
replaced by a new lift in
2002/03. A recent visitor reports

that piste maintenance and marking is poor. There are no bars or hotels near the slopes so you have to return to town for après-ski. There's plenty for non-skiers to do.
720m; slopes 720–2830m
⛷ 38 🚡 71km
✉ Moswin Tours

Gaschurn 152
Attractive, unspoiled village with the largest of the pretty Montafon areas, well suited to intermediates.

Gaustablikk Norway
Small snow-sure Alpine area on Mt Gausta in southern Norway with plenty of cross-country.
🚡 15km

Geilo 645
✉ Crystal, Headwater Holidays, Inntravel, Neilson, Thomson Ski & Snowboarding

Gérardmer France
Sizeable resort near Strasbourg with plenty of amenities. Night skiing, too.
665m; slopes 750–1150m
⛷ 20 🚡 40km
✉ Lagrange Holidays

Gerlitzen Alpe Austria
A gondola ride above Villach and with good views. A worthwhile excursion from Badkleinkirchheim.
500m; slopes 1003–1911m
⛷ 14 🚡 20km

Gerlos Austria
One of Austria's few inexpensive but fairly snow-sure resorts, now linked to Zell im Zillertal as well as Königsleiten to form a fair-sized intermediate area.
1250m; slopes 1250–2300m
⛷ 44 🚡 115km
✉ Interhome

Les Gets 296
Sprawling chalet resort on low pass near Morzine, on the periphery of the Portes du Soleil area.
✉ Avant-ski, Chalets 'Unlimited', Independent Ski Links, Lagrange Holidays, Made to Measure Holidays, Peak Retreats, Ski Activity, Ski Expectations, Ski Famille, Ski Hillwood, Ski Independence, Ski Total, Ski Weekend, SkiAway Holidays, Skiworld

La Giettaz France
Tiny rural village with small area of its own, but cheap base for skiing La Clusaz, 6km/4 miles away.
slopes 1100–1930m 🚡 20km
✉ Peak Retreats

Gitschtal/Weissbriach Austria
One of many little areas near Hermagor in eastern Austria, close to Italian border.
690m; slopes 690–1400m
⛷ 4 🚡 5km

Glaris Switzerland
Hamlet base station for the uncrowded Rinerhorn section of the Davos slopes.
1455m; slopes 1455–2490m
⛷ 5 🚡 30km

Glencoe 652

Glenshee 652
✉ Skisafe Travel

Going 117
Small local ski area near Ellmau, linked to the huge Ski Welt area.
✉ Inghams, Solo's

Goldegg Austria
Year-round resort famous for its lakeside castle. Limited slopes but Wagrain (Salzburger Sportwelt) and Grossarl (Gastein valley) are nearby.
825m; slopes 825–1250m
⛷ 2 🚡 2km

Golden Canada
Small logging town, the place to stay when visiting Kicking Horse resort 15 minutes away. Also the launch pad for Purcell heli-skiing.

Gore Mountain USA
One of the better areas in New York State. Near Lake Placid, sufficiently far north to avoid worst weekend crowds. Intermediate terrain.
455m; slopes 455–1095m
⛷ 9 🚡 290 acres

Göriach Austria
Hamlet with trail connecting into one of longest, most snow-sure cross-country networks in Europe.
1250m

Gortipohl Austria
Traditional village in pretty Montafontal.
920m; slopes 900–2395m
⛷ 62 🚡 209km

Gosau Austria
Straggling village with plenty of pretty, if low, runs. Snow-sure Obertauern and Schladming are within reach.
765m; slopes 765–1800m
⛷ 37 🚡 65km

Göstling Austria
One of Austria's easternmost resorts, between Salzburg and Vienna. A traditional village in wooded setting.
530m; slopes 530–1800m
⛷ 12 🚡 19km

Götzens Austria
Valley village base for Axamer Lizum slopes.
870m ⛷ 1

Grächen Switzerland
Charming chalet-village reached by tricky access road off the approach to Zermatt. A small area of open slopes, mainly above the trees and of red-run difficulty, reached by two gondolas – one to Hannigalp (2115m/6,940ft), the main focus of activity with a very impressive children's nursery area. The

village has almost a score of hotels, mostly 3-star; most of the accommodation is in chalets and apartments. The sports centre offers tennis and badminton, as well as a natural ice-rink.
1615m; slopes 1615–2890m
⛷ 13 🚡 50km
✉ Interhome

Le Grand-Bornand 239
✉ French Freedom Holidays, Inntravel, Lagrange Holidays

Grand Targhee 571
Powder skiing paradise an hour from Jackson Hole.
✉ AmeriCan Ski, Lotus Supertravel, Ski Safari

Grangesises Italy
Small satellite of Sestriere, with lifts up to the main slopes.

Grau Roig 100
Mini-resort at foot of Pas de la Casa's only woodland runs, with one smart hotel and abundant day-tripper parking.

La Grave 269
✉ Alpine Answers Select, AmeriCan Ski, Interhome, Lagrange Holidays, Peak Retreats, Ski Arrangements, Ski Club of Great Britain, Ski Weekend

Gray Rocks Canada
Very popular family resort, 130km/80 miles north of Montreal; renowned for its ski school.
250m; slopes 250–440m
⛷ 4 🚡 200 acres

Great Divide USA
Area near Helena, Montana, best for experts. Mostly bowls; plus near-extreme Rawhide Gulch.
1765m; slopes 1765–2195m
⛷ 6 🚡 720 acres

Gresse-en-Vercors France
Resort south of Grenoble. Sheltered slopes worth noting for bad-weather days.
1250m; slopes 1600–1800m
⛷ 16 🚡 18km
✉ Interhome, Lagrange Holidays

Gressoney-la-Trinité 402
Smaller and higher of the two villages in the central valley of the Monterosa Ski area.
✉ Alpine Answers Select, Crystal, Mountain Tracks, Ski Addiction, The Ski Company

Gressoney-St-Jean 402
Larger and lower of the two villages in the central valley of the Monterosa Ski area.
✉ Alpine Answers Select

Grimentz Switzerland
Exceptionally cute, unspoiled mountainside village with high, varied runs including genuine reds and blacks, mostly on open slopes above the mid-mountain nursery area of Bendolla (2100m/6,890ft). Mostly served by drag-lifts. In the Val d'Anniviers, a side valley near the Valais town of Sierre; valley

lift pass also covers St Luc/Chandolin, Vercorin and Zinal – 200km/125 miles of runs in total. Zinal is a short bus-ride up the valley, with a splendid itinerary run back to Grimentz. Grimentz has half a dozen small hotels, 2- and 3-star. There's a public pool and a natural ice-rink.
1570m; slopes 1570–2900m
⛷ 12 🚡 50km

Grindelwald 449
✉ Alpine Events, Crystal, Elegant Resorts, Independent Ski Links, Inghams, Kuoni, Made to Measure Holidays, Momentum Ski, Plus Travel, Powder Byrne, Ski Club of Great Britain, SkiGower, Solo's, Swiss Travel Service, Thomson Ski & Snowboarding, White Roc

Grossarl 114
Secluded village linked to Dorfgastein in the Gastein valley.

Grosskirchheim Austria
Very limited area near Heiligenblut.
1025m; slopes 1025–1400m

Grouse Mountain Canada
The Vancouver area with the largest lift capacity. Superb city views from mostly easy slopes; night skiing.
880m; slopes 880–1245m
⛷ 11 🚡 120 acres

Grünau Austria
Spacious riverside village in a lovely lake-filled part of eastern Austria. Nicely varied area, but very low.
525m; slopes 600–1600m
⛷ 14 🚡 40km

Gryon 480
Village below Villars, with which it shares a ski area.

Gstaad 453
✉ Alpine Answers Select, Alpine Events, Elegant Resorts, Headwater Holidays, Interhome, Made to Measure Holidays, Momentum Ski, Ski Weekend, The Corporate Ski Company, White Roc

Gunstock USA
One of the New Hampshire resorts closest to Boston, popular with families. Primarily easy slopes. Gorgeous Lake Winnisquam views. 98% snowmaking.
275m; slopes 275–700m
⛷ 8 🚡 220 acres

Guthega 653

Hakuba Happo One Japan
European-style resort four hours from Tokyo. One of Japan's more challenging areas.
750m; slopes 750–1830m ⛷ 33

Harrachov Czech Republic
Closest resort to Prague, with
enough terrain to justify a day
trip. No beginner area. A new
quad replaced the old chair-lift
in 2002/03.
685m; slopes 650–1020m
⛔4 ⛷ 8km

Hasliberg Switzerland
Four rustic hamlets on a sunny
plateau overlooking Meiringen
and Lake Brienz. Two of them
are the bottom stations of a
varied intermediate area.
1055m; slopes 600–2435m
⛔16 ⛷ 60km

Haus 168
Village next to Schladming, with
good local slopes connected to
the rest of the network.

Haystack 578

Heavenly 501
✉ AmeriCan Ski, American Ski
Classics, Equity Ski,
Independent Ski Links, Made to
Measure Holidays, Neilson,
Rocketski, Ski Activity, Ski All
America, Ski Independence, Ski
Line, Ski Safari, Ski Success,
Ski The American Dream,
Skiworld, Trailfinders, United
Vacations Ski Freedom USA &
Canada

Hebalm Austria
One of many small areas in
Austria's easternmost ski region
near Slovenian border. No major
resorts in vicinity.
1350m; slopes 1350–1400m
⛔6 ⛷ 11km

Heiligenblut Austria
Picturesque village in beautiful
surroundings with mostly high
terrain. Its remote position west
of Bad Gastein ensures that it
remains uncrowded.
1300m; slopes 1300–2910m
⛔14 ⛷ 55km
✉ Solo's

Hemlock Resort Canada
Area 55 miles east of Vancouver
towards Sun Peaks. Mostly
intermediate terrain and with
snowfall of 600 inches a year.
Lodging is available at the base
area.
1000m; slopes 1000–1375m
⛔4 ⛷ 350 acres

Hemsedal 647
✉ Crystal, Neilson, Thomson
Ski & Snowboarding

Heremence Switzerland
Quiet village in unspoiled
attractive setting south of Sion.
Verbier's slopes are accessed a
few minutes' drive away at Les
Masses.
1250m

Hermagor Austria
Carinthian village below the
Sonnenalpe ski area, rated one
of the best areas in Austria by
the famous Franz Klammer.
600m; slopes 600–2000m
⛔30 ⛷ 101km

Hintersee Austria
Easy slopes very close to
Salzburg. Several long top-to-
bottom runs and lifts means the
size of the area is greatly
reduced if the snowline is high.
745m; slopes 750–1470m
⛔9 ⛷ 40km

Hinterstoder Austria
A very quiet valley village – neat
but not overtly charming –
spread along road up the dead-
end Stodertal in Upper Austria.
The local Höss slopes are
pleasantly wooded, less densely
at the top, with splendid views.
It's a small area, but has a
worthwhile vertical of
1250m/4,100ft, and 450m/1,475ft
above mid-mountain. A gondola
from the main street goes up to
the flat-bottomed bowl of
Huttererböden (1400m/4,600ft),
where there are several
restaurants plus the modern 4-
star Berghotel, very gentle but
limited nursery slopes and lifts
up to higher points. Most of the
mountain is of easy red
steepness. The run to the valley
is a pleasant red with one or
two tricky bits where it takes a
quick plunge; it has effective
snowmaking. Queues arise for
the gondola and main chair on
busy weekends. Further up the
valley is the more limited
Bärenalm area. The local pass
also covers the Wurzeralm
slopes near Spital am Pyrn. In
the village there are only half a
dozen hotels and guesthouses,
of which the pick is the fairly
simple Stoderhof.
600m; slopes 600–1860m
⛔12 ⛷ 35km

Hintertux/Tux valley 120
✉ Lagrange Holidays

Hippach 147
Hamlet near a crowd-free lift
into Mayrhofen's main area.

Hochgurgl 155
Quiet mountain-side hotel-
village with a gondola
connection to Obergurgl's
slopes.
✉ First Choice Ski, Inghams,
Ski Expectations

Hochpillberg Austria
Peaceful, virtually traffic-free
hamlet with fabulous views
towards Innsbruck and an
antique chair-lift into varied
terrain above Schwaz with good
vertical of 1000m/3,280ft.
Wonderfully safe for children; all
accommodation within two
minutes' walk of lift. Excellent
restaurant at 1900m/6,230ft.
1000m; slopes 1000–2030m
⛔6 ⛷ 10km

Hochsölden 172
Quieter mountain-side satellite
above lively, sprawling Sölden,
with links to the whole network.

Hoch-Ybrig Switzerland
Purpose-built complex only
64km/40 miles south-east of
Zürich, with facilities for families.
1050m; slopes 1050–2200m
⛔16 ⛷ 50km

Hohuanshan Taiwan
Limited ski area with short
season in high, wild,
inaccessible Miitaku mountains.
3275m ⛔1

Hollersbach Austria
Pass Thurn hamlet near
Mittersill. Uncrowded base from
which to visit Kitzbühel if
snowline is low – or Kaprun,
Gerlos, Matrei and Uttendorf if
high.
805m; slopes 805–1000m
⛔2 ⛷ 5km

Homewood USA
Area with unsurpassed Lake
Tahoe views, near Tahoe City.
Most sheltered slopes in the
vicinity so a good choice in bad
weather.
1895m; slopes 1895–2400m
⛔10 ⛷ 1260 acres

Hoodoo Ski Bowl USA
Typical Oregon area with
sizeable but short runs. Snow
record isn't as good as its
competitors near Portland. Two
new quads installed in 2002/03.
1420m; slopes 1420–1740m
⛔5 ⛷ 800 acres

Hopfgarten 174
Small chalet village with lift link
into extensive Ski Welt area
shared with Söll.
✉ Contiki, First Choice Ski

Horseshoe Resort Canada
Toronto region resort with high-
capacity lift system and 100%
snowmaking. The second
mountain – The Heights – is
open to members only.
310m; slopes 310–405m
⛔7 ⛷ 60 acres

Hospental 429
Small village connected to
Andermatt by road and rail and
with local slopes of its own.

Les Houches 226
Varied, tree-lined area above
spread-out village at the
entrance to the Chamonix valley.
✉ Avant-ski, Barrelli Ski,
Bigfoot Travel, Chalets
'Unlimited', Handmade
Holidays, Lagrange Holidays,
Peak Retreats, Ski
Expectations, Ski Life

Hovden Norway
Big, modern luxury lakeside
hotel in wilderness midway
between Oslo and Bergen.
Cross-country venue with some
Alpine slopes.
820m; slopes 820–1175m
⛔5 ⛷ 14km

La Hoya Argentina
Small uncrowded resort 15km/9
miles from the small town of
Esquel.
slopes 1350–1950m ⛔4

Huez 205
Charming old hamlet on the
road up to Alpe-d'Huez with lift
into ski area.

Hunter Mountain USA
Popular New Yorkers' area so it
gets very crowded at weekends.
485m; slopes 485–975m
⛔14 ⛷ 230 acres

Hüttschlag Austria
Hamlet in dead-end valley with
lifts into Gastein area at nearby
Grossarl.
1020m
⛔24 ⛷ 80km

Hyundai Sungwoo Korea
Modern high-rise resort,
140km/87 miles from Seoul (new
expressway has reduced journey
time). Own English-language
web site at
www.hdsungwoo.co.kr ⛔5

Idre Fjäll Sweden
Collective name for four areas
490km/300 miles north-west of
Stockholm.
slopes 590–890m
⛔30 ⛷ 28km

Igls 125
✉ Inghams, Lagrange
Holidays, Made to Measure
Holidays

Iizuna Japan
Tiny area 2.5 hours from
Tokyo. ⛔6

Incline Village 506
Large village on northern edge
of Lake Tahoe – reasonable
stop-off if touring.

Indianhead USA
South Lake Superior area with
the most snowfall in region.
Winds are a problem.
395m; slopes 395–585m
⛔12 ⛷ 195 acres

Inneralpbach 112
Small satellite of Alpbach, 3km/2
miles up the valley.

Innerarosa 431
The prettiest part of Arosa.

Innsbruck 125
✉ Made to Measure Holidays,
Ramblers Holidays, The
Corporate Ski Company

Interlaken 482
Large lakeside summer resort at
entrance to the valleys leading
to Wengen, Grindelwald and
Mürren.
✉ Kuoni, Swiss Travel Service

Ischgl 129
✉ Alpine Answers Select,
Alpine Events, Inghams, Made
to Measure Holidays,
Momentum Ski, Ski Solutions

**Ishiuchi Maruyama-Gala-
Yuzawa Kogen** Japan
Three resorts with a shared lift
pass 90 minutes from Tokyo by
bullet train and offering the
largest ski area in the central
Honshu region.
255m; slopes 255–920m ⛔52

Isola 2000 France
A small, high, purpose-built family resort, a long way south but easy and cheap to reach since Nice Airport is only 90km/55 miles away. The compact slopes are linked in a horseshoe shape around the resort and most runs are above the tree line. Isola often has snow when other French resorts lack it, but at other times it misses out. However, regular visitors say there is always some snow – and plenty of sun. There are excellent nursery slopes in the heart of the resort. A 2003 reporter comments on the 'poor and crowded' mountain restaurants and recommends returning to the base station for lunch. Accommodation is largely self-catering, much of it slope-side, and there are some hotels; original buildings are now shabby, but there are smarter alternatives. The après-ski scene is muted – though a 2003 reporter tells us 'several new bars have opened and Le Petit Chamois restaurant and Le Cow Club are to be recommended'. Trips to the Riviera and Monte Carlo are easy.
2000m; slopes 1800–2610m
🚡 *24* 🚠 *120km*
✉ *Avant-ski, Club Pavilion, Erna Low, Lagrange Holidays, Made to Measure Holidays, Ski Arrangements*

Isoyöte Finland
The most southern downhill skiing area in Finland. Mostly easy slopes, and the main hotel is at the top of the mountain.
430m; slopes 240–430m
🚡 *11* 🚠 *21km*

Itter 174
Next to Söll, skiing linked to Hopfgarten and Brixen, and to the whole Ski Welt region.
✉ *Directski.com, Panorama Holidays*

Jackson USA
Classic New England village, and a major cross-country base. A lovely place from which to ski New Hampshire's Alpine areas.

Jackson Hole 571
✉ *Alpine Answers Select, AmeriCan Ski, American Ski Classics, Crystal, Inghams, Made to Measure Holidays, Momentum Ski, Neilson, Ski Activity, Ski All America, Ski Club of Great Britain, Ski Independence, Ski Line, Ski Safari, Ski Success, Ski The American Dream, Skiworld, Trailfinders, United Vacations Ski Freedom USA & Canada, Virgin Ski*

Jasná Slovakia
Largest area in the Low Tatras mountains, linked to Chopok, which has an additional 11 lifts covering 11 km/7 miles.
slopes 1240–2005m
🚡 *13* 🚠 *21km*

Jasper 611
✉ *AmeriCan Ski, Crystal, Frontier Ski, Inghams, Made to Measure Holidays, Rocketski, Ski Activity, Ski All America, Ski Club of Great Britain, Ski Independence, Ski Safari, Ski The American Dream, Skiworld*

Jay Peak 578

Jochberg 134
Straggling village, 8km/5 miles from Kitzbühel. Shares its varied, snow-sure ski area with Pass Thurn.

La Joue-du-Loup France
Slightly stylish little purpose-built ski-in/ ski-out family resort a few km north-west of Gap. Shares a fair-sized intermediate area with Superdévoluy.
1500m; slopes 1500–2510m
🚡 *32* 🚠 *100km*
✉ *Lagrange Holidays, Ski France*

Jouvenceaux 405
Less boisterous base from which to ski Sauze d'Oulx's splendid cruising terrain.

Jukkasjärvi Sweden
Centuries-old cross-country resort with unique ice hotel rebuilt every December.

June Mountain USA
Small area a half-hour drive from Mammoth and in same ownership, with empty slopes except on peak weekends.
2300m; slopes 2300–3090m
🚡 *8* 🚠 *500 acres*

Juns 120
Small, spread out village between Lanersbach and Hintertux, with its own tiny beginners' area.

Kals am Grossglockner Austria
Village in remote valley north of Lienz.
1325m; slopes 1325–2305m
🚡 *7* 🚠 *28km*

Kaltenbach Austria
One of the larger, quieter Zillertal areas, with plenty of high-altitude slopes.
560m; slopes 560–2300m
🚡 *18* 🚠 *86km*
✉ *Equity Ski*

Kananaskis Canada
Small area near Calgary, nicely set in woods, with slopes at Nakiska and Fortress Mountain.
slopes 1525–2465m
🚡 *12* 🚠 *605 acres*
✉ *Frontier Ski*

Kandersteg Switzerland
Good cross-country base set amid beautiful scenery near Interlaken.
1175m; slopes 1175–2000m
🚡 *7* 🚠 *13km*
✉ *Headwater Holidays, Inghams, Inntravel, Kuoni, Swiss Travel Service, Waymark Holidays*

Kanin 642

Kaprun 195
Classic Austrian charmer of a village. Extensive sheltered slopes at nearby Zell am See.
✉ *Airtours, Crystal, Directski.com, Esprit Ski, First Choice Ski, Inghams, Made to Measure Holidays, Neilson, Ski Wild*

Les Karellis France
Resort with slopes that are more scenic, challenging and snow-sure than those of better-known Valloire, nearby.
1600m; slopes 1600–2550m
🚡 *19* 🚠 *60km*

Kastelruth Italy
Charming picturesque village in the south Tirolean Italian Dolomites with good cross-country trails. Near the Sella Ronda circuit.
✉ *Inntravel*

Kasurila Finland
Siilinjarvi ski area popular with boarders. 🚡 *5*

Katschberg Austria
Cute hamlet on road pass from Styria to Carinthia, now by-passed by Tauern motorway through Katschberg tunnel. Non-trivial area of intermediate slopes, linked to lower St Margarethen; lifts include several fast chairs, one a six-pack.
1140m; slopes 1075–2220m
🚡 *16* 🚠 *60km*
✉ *Alpine Tours*

Keystone 534
✉ *AmeriCan Ski, American Ski Classics, Crystal, Handmade Holidays, Made to Measure Holidays, Neilson, Ski Activity, Ski All America, Ski Independence, Ski Safari, Ski The American Dream, Trailfinders, United Vacations Ski Freedom USA & Canada*

Kicking Horse 613
✉ *AmeriCan Ski, Crystal, Frontier Ski, Made to Measure Holidays, Ski All America, Ski Independence, Ski Safari, Ski The American Dream*

Killington 581
✉ *American Ski Classics, Chalets 'Unlimited', Crystal, Esprit Ski, Independent Ski Links, Inghams, Made to Measure Holidays, Neilson, Rocketski, Ski Activity, Ski All America, Ski Arrangements, Ski Independence, Ski Line, Ski Safari, Ski Success, Ski The American Dream, Solo's, Thomson Ski & Snowboarding, Trailfinders, United Vacations Ski Freedom USA & Canada, Virgin Ski*

Kimberley 595
✉ *AmeriCan Ski, Crystal, Frontier Ski, Inghams, Made to Measure Holidays, Ski Activity, Ski All America, Ski Safari, Ski The American Dream*

Kirchberg 134
Lively little town close to Kitzbühel, with which it shares its slopes.
✉ *Directski.com, Interhome, Lagrange Holidays, Top Deck, Uptoyou.com*

Kirchdorf 188
Attractive village a bus-ride from St Johann in Tirol, with good local beginner slopes.
✉ *Snowcoach, Thomson Ski & Snowboarding*

Kirkwood 506

Kitzbühel 134
✉ *Airtours, Alpine Events, Avant-ski, Bladon Lines, Chalets 'Unlimited', Crystal, Directski.com, Elegant Resorts, First Choice Ski, Independent Ski Links, Inghams, Interhome, Lagrange Holidays, Made to Measure Holidays, Neilson, Panorama Holidays, Ski Arrangements, Ski Club of Great Britain, Ski Solutions, Ski Wild, Snowscape, The Corporate Ski Company, Thomson Ski & Snowboarding, Uptoyou.com*

Kleinarl Austria
Secluded traditional village up a pretty side valley from Wagrain, at one end of three-valley lift network linking it via Flachauwinkl to Zauchensee – all part of the Salzburger Sportwelt ski pass area that our figures relate to.
1015m; slopes 800–2185m
🚡 *59* 🚠 *200km*

Klippitztörl Austria
One of many little areas in Austria's easternmost ski region near Slovenian border.
1550m; slopes 1460–1820m
🚡 *6* 🚠 *25km*

Klosters 440
Quiet, affluent chalet village with much-improved access to the huge ski area it shares with Davos.
✉ *Alpine Answers Select, Descent International, Elegant Resorts, FlexiSki, Inghams, Kuoni, Made to Measure Holidays, Momentum Ski, Plus Travel, Powder Byrne, Ski Club of Great Britain, Ski Solutions, Ski Weekend, Swiss Travel Service, White Roc*

Kobla 642

Kolsass-Weer Austria
Pair of Inn-side villages with low, inconvenient and limited slopes.
555m; slopes 555–1010m
🚡 *3* 🚠 *14km*

Königsleiten Austria
Quiet, high resort sharing fairly snow-sure area with Gerlos, now also linked to Zell im Zillertal to form a fair-sized ski area.
1600m; slopes 1245–2300m
🚡 *42* 🚠 *115km*

Kopaonik   Serbia
Modern, sympathetically designed family resort in a pretty setting.
1770m; slopes 1110–2015m
🚠 21 🎿 57km

Koralpe   Austria
Largest and steepest of many gentle little areas in Austria's easternmost ski region near the Slovenian border.
1550m; slopes 1550–2050m
🚠 10 🎿 25km

Kössen   Austria
Village near St Johann in Tirol with low, scattered and limited local slopes.
600m; slopes 600–1700m
🚠 9 🎿 25km

Kötschach-Mauthen   Austria
One of many little areas near Hermagor in eastern Austria, close to the Italian border.
710m; slopes 710–1300m
🚠 4 🎿 6km

Kranjska Gora   **642**
✉ *Balkan Holidays, Crystal, Slovenija Pursuits, Solo's, Thomson Ski & Snowboarding*

Krimml   Austria
Sunny area, high enough to have good snow usually. Shares regional pass with Wildkogel resorts (Neukirchen).
1075m; slopes 1640–2040m
🚠 9 🎿 33km

Krispl-Gaissau   Austria
Easy slopes very close to Salzburg. Several long top-to-bottom chairs mean the size of the area is greatly reduced if the snowline is high.
925m; slopes 750–1570m
🚠 11 🎿 40km

Kühtai   Austria
A collection of comfortable hotels beside a high road pass only 25km/16 miles from Innsbruck – higher than equally snow-sure Obergurgl or Obertauern, but cheaper than either. Half a dozen drags and two quad chairs serve red cruisers of about 500m/1,650ft vertical on either side of the road, plus some token black runs; not ideal for novices – no easy blues to graduate to. Very quiet in the week, but liable to weekend crowds if lower resorts around Innsbruck are short of snow. One limited mountain hut. Quiet in the evening, but for its size 'a reasonable selection of bars and restaurants', says a report. 3-star Hotel Elizabeth recommended – 'very friendly, excellent food'.
2020m; slopes 2010–2520m
🚠 11 🎿 40km
✉ *Crystal, Inghams*

Kusatsu Kokusai   Japan
Attractive spa village with hot springs, three hours from Tokyo. 🚠 13

Laax   **447**
Old farming community with a lot of character and some new development nearby – linked to Flims.
✉ *Alpine Answers Select*

Ladis   Austria
Smaller alternative to Serfaus and Fiss, with lifts that connect into the same varied ski area.
1200m; slopes 1200–2540m
🚠 42 🎿 160km
✉ *Alpine Tours*

Le Laisinant   **352**
Tiny hamlet a short bus-ride down the valley from Val-d'Isère.

Lake Louise   **615**
✉ *Airtours, Alpine Answers Select, AmeriCan Ski, Crystal, Equity Ski, First Choice Ski, Frontier Ski, Independent Ski Links, Inghams, Lotus Supertravel, Made to Measure Holidays, Neilson, Rocketski, Ski Activity, Ski All America, Ski Independence, Ski Line, Ski Safari, Ski The American Dream, Thomson Ski & Snowboarding, Trailfinders, United Vacations Ski Freedom USA & Canada, Virgin Ski*

Lake Tahoe   **506**
✉ *AmeriCan Ski, Independent Ski Links, Lotus Supertravel, Ski Activity, Ski Independence, Skiworld, Thomson Ski & Snowboarding, United Vacations Ski Freedom USA & Canada, Virgin Ski*

Lamoura   France
One of four villages that makes up the Les Rousses area in the Jura.
1120m; slopes 1120–1680m
🚠 40 🎿 40km

Lanersbach   **120**
Attractive village with charming little ski area of its own, plus Hintertux glacier nearby.
✉ *Equity Ski*

Lans-en-Vercors   France
Village close to Villard-de-Lans near Grenoble. Highest slopes in region; few snowmakers.
1020m; slopes 1400–1805m
🚠 16 🎿 24km

Lauterbrunnen   **455**
Valley town in the Jungfrau region, with a funicular and rail connection up to Mürren.
✉ *Re-lax Holidays, Ski Miquel*

Le Lavancher   **226**
Quiet village between Chamonix and Argentière, with off-trail runs home for the insane.

Lavarone   Italy
One of several areas east of Trento, good for a weekend day-trip.
1195m; slopes 1075–1555m
🚠 13 🎿 12km

Leadville   USA
Old mining town full of historic buildings. Own easy area (Ski Cooper) plus snowcat operation. Picturesque inexpensive base for visiting Copper Mountain, Vail and Beaver Creek.

Lech   **140**
✉ *Alpine Events, Avant-ski, Chalets 'Unlimited', Crystal, Elegant Resorts, Erna Low, FlexiSki, Inghams, Made to Measure Holidays, Momentum Ski, Ski Expectations, Ski Solutions, Ski Total, Ski Weekend, White Roc*

The Lecht   **652**
✉ *Skisafe Travel*

Lélex   France
Family resort with pretty wooded slopes between Dijon and Geneva.
900m; slopes 900–1680m
🚠 29 🎿 50km

Las Leñas   Argentina
European-style resort, 400km/250 miles south of Mendoza, with varied, beautiful terrain. Lodgings at the foot of the slopes.
2240m; slopes 2260–3430m
🚠 11 🎿 60km
✉ *Scott Dunn Latin America*

Lenk   **427**
Traditional village that shares a sizeable area of easy, pretty terrain with Adelboden.
✉ *Swiss Travel Service*

Lenzerheide   Switzerland
Spacious village, separated by a lake from Valbella and sharing a large intermediate area. 'No queues, excellent value mid-station restaurant,' comments a recent reporter.
1500m; slopes 1230–2865m
🚠 35 🎿 155km
✉ *Crystal, Interhome, Made to Measure Holidays*

Leogang   **162**
Quiet, spread-out village with over-the-mountain link to Saalbach-Hinterglemm.
✉ *Equity Ski, Rocketski*

Lermoos   Austria
Pleasant little village with its own small area of shady intermediate slopes on Grubigstein and a pass giving access to a variety of other areas in the locality, including the towering (and glacial) Zugspitze, on the border with Germany. Lots of cross-country trails along the flat valley.
1005m; slopes 1005–2250m
🚠 9 🎿 30km

Lessach   Austria
Hamlet with trail connecting into one of longest, most snow-sure cross-country networks in Europe.
1210m

Leukerbad   Switzerland
Major spa resort of Roman origin and recently revamped at vast expense. The super-neat towny result is very impressive if you like that kind of thing. It is spectacularly set beneath towering cliffs, which are scaled by a cable-car up to high-altitude cross-country trails. The downhill slopes are on the opposite side of the valley, mainly above the tree line, served by drag-lifts and of red gradient, though there are a couple of blacks including a World Cup downhill course, which descends from the high, open slopes into the woods. There is also a slightly separate wooded sector served by a couple of chair-lifts. The spas have spawned a handful of very swanky 4-star hotels, but there are also over a dozen 3-stars, ranging from cute chalets to the plainly modern. As well as fabulous spa facilities, there are indoor and outdoor ice-rinks, tennis, squash and badminton courts and a golf driving range.
1410m; slopes 1410–2700m
🚠 17 🎿 60km

Leutasch   Austria
Traditional cross-country village with limited slopes but a pleasant day trip from nearby Seefeld or Innsbruck.
1130m; slopes 1130–1605m
🚠 3 🎿 6km
✉ *Headwater Holidays, Inntravel*

Levi   **643**
✉ *Bladon Lines, Inghams*

Leysin   Switzerland
This is a spread-out village, climbing up a wooded hillside. The lifts are to the east of the village and take you to a pretty mix of mainly red and blue runs. A gondola takes you up to La Berneuse, from which you head down to the two-stage Chaux de Mont chair, which takes you to the resort's highest point. There's a choice of black or red back down, both easily sun-damaged. On the lower half of the slope is a terrain-park. Itineraries from the top of Chaux de Mont provide Leysin's best options for experts, along with a heli-operation. From the bottom of Chaux de Mont it's easy to go to the other side of the resort, using a series of chairs and fairly short, mainly blue, runs in and out of trees. There are nursery slopes at village level. The revolving Kuklos restaurant at La Berneuse has stunning views. After hours Leysin has a swimming pool and a tubing park.
1300m; slopes 1300–2205m
🚠 19 🎿 60km
✉ *Crystal, Plus Travel*

Lienz   Austria
Pleasant town in pretty
surroundings.
675m; slopes 730–2290m
⛷17 ⛺ 41km

Lillehammer   **645**
✉ Crystal

Limone   Italy
Pleasant old town not far from
Turin, with a pretty area, but far
from snow-sure.
1010m; slopes 1030–2050m
⛷25 ⛺ 80km

Lincoln   USA
Sprawling New Hampshire town
from which to visit Loon
mountain.
✉ Crystal

Lindvallen-Högfjället   Sweden
Largest ski area (but two
unlinked mountains) in
Scandinavia.
800m; slopes 590–890m
⛷46 ⛺ 85km

Le Lioran   France
Auvergne village with purpose-
built satellite above. Spectacular
volcanic scenery.
1160m; slopes 1160–1850m
⛷24 ⛺ 60km

Livigno   **396**
✉ Airtours, Chalets 'Unlimited',
Crystal, Equity Ski, Inghams,
Interhome, Neilson, Panorama
Holidays, Rocketski, Ski
Arrangements, Thomson Ski &
Snowboarding

Lizzola   Italy
Small base development in
remote region north of Bergamo.
Several other little areas nearby.
1250m; slopes 1250–2070m
⛷9 ⛺ 30km

Llaima   Chile
Exotic area in central Chile,
around and below a mildly
active volcano.
1500m ⛷5

Loch Lomond   Canada
Steep, narrow, challenging
slopes near Thunder Bay on the
shores of Lake Superior. Candy
Mountain is nearby.
215m; slopes 215–440m
⛷3 ⛺ 90 acres

Lofer   Austria
Quiet, traditional village in a
pretty setting north of Saalbach
with a small area of its own, and
Waidring's relatively snow-sure
Steinplatte nearby.
640m; slopes 640–1745m
⛷13 ⛺ 46km
✉ Ski Wild

Longchamp   **364**
Dreary purpose-built resort with
little to commend it over pretty
Valmorel, with which it shares
its ski area.

Loon Mountain   **578**
✉ AmeriCan Ski, Rocketski

Lost Trail   USA
Remote Montana area, open
only Thursday to Sunday and
holidays. Mostly intermediate
slopes.
2005m; slopes 2005–2370m
⛷6 ⛺ 800 acres

Loveland   USA
High, varied slopes, a day trip
from Keystone and renowned for
snow. Long season, good for all
abilities.
3220m; slopes 3220–3730m
⛷11 ⛺ 836 acres

Luchon   France
Sizeable village with plenty of
amenities, with gondola (8
minutes) to its ski area and to
purpose-built Superbagnères.
630m; slopes 1440–2260m
⛷16 ⛺ 35km
✉ Lagrange Holidays

Lurisia   Italy
Sizeable spa resort, a good base
for visits to surrounding little ski
areas and to Nice.
750m; slopes 800–1800m
⛷8 ⛺ 35km

Luz-Ardiden   France
Spa village below its ski area.
Cauterets and Barèges nearby.
710m; slopes 1730–2450m
⛷15 ⛺ 60km

Macugnaga   Italy
Pretty, two-part village set amid
stunning scenery in Piedmont,
not far from the Swiss border.
Novice and intermediate slopes.
1330m; slopes 1330–2970m
⛷12 ⛺ 40km
✉ Interhome, Neilson

Madesimo   Italy
Remote valley village, a mix of
traditional buildings and
piecemeal modern development,
a three-hour drive north from
Bergamo. The mountain is great
for a weekend, but for a week
it's not ideal: beginners will not
find the progression to real runs
easy, and others are likely to
find the terrain limited. Experts
need the upper cable-car to be
open for access to the famous
Canalone, a long, sweeping
itinerary run which keeps its
snow well. The village is quite
spread out, but there is a fair
choice of good-value hotels,
apartments and lively
restaurants. Après-ski is
otherwise fairly quiet and there's
not much to do off the slopes.
1545m; slopes 1545–2880m
⛷12 ⛺ 40km
✉ Equity Ski, Inghams,
Rocketski, Ski Arrangements,
Top Deck

Madonna di Campiglio   **400**
✉ Crystal, Equity Ski, First
Choice Ski, Inghams,
Interhome, Rocketski, Ski
Arrangements, Ski Yogi,
Sloping Off, Solo's

Mad River Glen   **578**

La Magdelaine   Italy
Close to Cervinia, and good on
bad-weather days.
1645m; slopes 1645–1870m
⛷4 ⛺ 4km

Maishofen   Austria
Cheaper place to stay when
visiting equidistant Saalbach
and Zell am See.
765m

Malbun   Liechtenstein
Quaint user-friendly little family
resort, 16km/10 miles from the
capital, Vaduz. Limited slopes
and short easy runs.
1600m; slopes 1595–2100m
⛷6 ⛺ 16km

Malcesine   Italy
Large summer resort on Lake
Garda with a fair area of slopes,
served by a revolving cable-car
from the 2002/03 season.
1430m; slopes 1430–1830m
⛷8 ⛺ 12km

Malga Ciapela   Italy
Resort at the foot of the
Marmolada glacier massif, with a
link into the Sella Ronda.
Cortina is nearby.
1445m; slopes 1445–3270m
⛷8 ⛺ 18km

Mallnitz   Austria
Village in a pretty valley close to
Slovenia, with two varied areas
providing a fine mix of wooded
and open runs.
1200m; slopes 1300–2650m
⛷5 ⛺ 30km

Mammoth Mountain   **510**
✉ AmeriCan Ski, American Ski
Classics, Crystal, Independent
Ski Holidays, Made to Measure
Holidays, Ski Activity, Ski All
America, Ski Independence, Ski
Line, Ski Safari, Ski The
American Dream, United
Vacations Ski Freedom USA &
Canada, Virgin Ski

Manigod   France
Small valley village over the Col
de la Croix-Fry from La Clusaz.

Marble Mountain   Canada
Area near the charming
Newfoundland town Corner
Brook and Gros Morne National
Park. It has one of the east
coast's highest snowfall records.
85m; slopes 85–570m
⛷5 ⛺ 126 acres
✉ Club Pavilion, Frontier Ski

Maria Alm   Austria
Charming unspoiled village east
of Saalbach at one end of varied
Hochkönig area that spreads
impressively over four linked
mountains via Hintertal and
Dienten to Mühlbach.
800m; slopes 800–2000m
⛷36 ⛺ 150km

Mariapfarr   Austria
Village at the heart of one of the
longest, most snow-reliable
cross-country networks in
Europe. Sizeable Mauterndorf-St
Michael Alpine area and
Obertauern area are nearby.
1120m
⛷5 ⛺ 30km

Mariazell   Austria
Traditional Styria village with an
impressive basilica. Limited
slopes.
870m; slopes 870–1265m
⛷5 ⛺ 11km

Maribor   **642**

Marilleva   **400**
Small resort with direct links to
Madonna di Campiglio's
extensive intermediate slopes.
✉ Interhome, Sloping Off

Masella   Spain
Pyrenean village linked with
slopes of La Molina to form the
Alp 2500 area.
1600m; slopes 1600–2535m
⛷20 ⛺ 100km

La Massana   **94**

Le Massif   **632**
✉ Frontier Ski, Ski All America,
Ski Safari, Ski The American
Dream

Matrei in Osttirol   Austria
Large market village south of
Felbertauern tunnel. Mostly high
slopes.
1000m; slopes 1000–2400m
⛷7 ⛺ 33km

Maurienne Valley   **271**

Mauterndorf   Austria
Village near Obertauern with
tremendous snow record.
1120m; slopes 1075–2360m
⛷21 ⛺ 60km
✉ Sloping Off

Maverick Mountain   USA
Montana resort with plenty of
terrain accessed by few lifts.
Cowboy Winter Games venue –
rodeo one day, ski races the
next.
2155m; slopes 2155–2800m
⛷2 ⛺ 500 acres

Mayens de Riddes   **470**
Tiny hamlet next to La Tzoumaz
with its links up to Savoleyres
and the Verbier network.
✉ Interhome

Mayens-de-Sion   **470**
Tranquil hamlet off road up to
Les Collons – part of Verbier
area.

Mayrhofen   **147**
✉ Airtours, Alpine Events,
Crystal, Equity Ski, First Choice
Ski, Inghams, Interhome, Made
to Measure Holidays, Neilson,
Rocketski, Ski Arrangements,
Ski Wild, Snowcoach, Thomson
Ski & Snowboarding

Méaudre   France
Small resort near Grenoble with
good snowmaking to make up
for its low altitude.
1000m; slopes 1000–1600m
⛷10 ⛺ 18km

Megève 274
☒ *Alpine Answers Select, Alpine Events, AmeriCan Ski, Avant-ski, Chalets 'Unlimited', Classic Ski Limited, Equity Ski, Erna Low, Interhome, Lagrange Holidays, Made to Measure Holidays, Momentum Ski, Peak Retreats, Simon Butler Skiing, Ski Arrangements, Ski Barrett-Boyce, Ski Expectations, Ski Independence, Ski Life, Ski Solutions, Ski Supreme, Ski Weekend, SkiAway Holidays, Stanford Skiing, The Corporate Ski Company, White Roc*

Meiringen Switzerland
Varied terrain, a good outing from the nearby Jungfrau resorts or Interlaken. Particularly suitable for beginners. New high-speed gondola planned for 2003/04.
600m; slopes 600–2435m
🚡 16 🚠 60km
☒ *Kuoni*

Les Menuires 280
☒ *Airtours, Club Med, Erna Low, Eurotunnel Motoring Holidays, First Choice Ski, French Freedom Holidays, Independent Ski Links, Interhome, Lagrange Holidays, Neilson, Rocketski, Ski Arrangements, Ski Independence, Ski Leisure Direction, Ski Life, Ski Olympic, Ski Supreme, SkiAway Holidays, The Family Ski Company*

Merano Italy
Purpose-built base on a high plateau near Bolzano.
2000m; slopes 2000–2240m
🚡 18 🚠 28km

Méribel 282
☒ *Absolute Ski, Airtours, Alpine Action, Alpine Answers Select, Alpine Events, Avant-ski, Belvedere Chalets, Bladon Lines, Bonne Neige Ski Holidays, Chalet World, Chalets 'Unlimited', Club Med, Club Pavilion, Cooltip Mountain Holidays, Crystal, Descent International, Directski.com, Elegant Resorts, Erna Low, Eurotunnel Motoring Holidays, First Choice Ski, French Freedom Holidays, Independent Ski Links, Inghams, Interhome, Lagrange Holidays, Les Deux Chalets, Lotus Supertravel, Made to Measure Holidays, Mark Warner, MasterSki, Meriski, Momentum Ski, Neilson, Panorama Holidays, Scott Dunn Ski, Silver Ski, Simply Ski, Ski Activity, Ski Amis, Ski Arrangements, Ski Basics, Ski Blanc, Ski Bon, Ski Club of Great Britain, Ski Cuisine, Ski Expectations, Ski France, Ski Hame, Ski Independence, Ski Leisure Direction, Ski Life, Ski Line, Ski Olympic, Ski Solutions, Ski Supreme, Ski Total, Ski Weekend, SkiAway Holidays, Skiworld, Snowline, The Chalet*

Group, The Corporate Ski Company, The Oxford Ski Company, The Ski Company Ltd, Thomson Ski & Snowboarding, Uptoyou.com, VIP, White Roc

Métabief-Mont-d'Or France
Twin villages in the Jura region, not far from Geneva.
900m; slopes 880–1460m
🚡 22 🚠 42km

Methven 655
Nearest town/accommodation to Mt Hutt, and helicopter base for trips to Arrowsmith range – good for intermediates as well as advanced.

Mijoux France
Pretty wooded slopes between Dijon and Geneva. Lélex nearby.
1000m; slopes 900–1680m
🚡 29 🚠 50km
☒ *Lagrange Holidays*

Mission Ridge USA
Area in dry region that gets higher-quality snow than other Seattle resorts but less of it. Good intermediate slopes.
1390m; slopes 1390–2065m
🚡 6 🚠 300 acres

Misurina Italy
Tiny village near Cortina. A cheap alternative base.
1755m; slopes 1755–1900m
🚡 4 🚠 13km

Mittersill Austria
Valley-junction village near Pass Thurn. A good base from which to visit Kitzbühel if the snowline is low or Kaprun, Gerlos, Matrei and Uttendorf if the snowline is high.
790m; slopes 1265–1895m
🚡 15 🚠 25km

Moena Italy
Large village between Cavalese and Sella Ronda resorts, ideally located for touring the Dolomites area.
1180m; slopes 1180–2515m
🚡 24 🚠 35km

La Molina 636
☒ *Club Pavilion*

Molltall Glacier Austria
Little-known high slopes on the other side of the Tauern tunnel from Bad Gastein. Worthwhile excursion when the snowline is high.
slopes 2570–3122m
🚡 4 🚠 11km

Monarch USA
Wonderfully uncrowded area, a day trip from Crested Butte. Great powder. Good for all but experts.
3290m; slopes 3290–3645m
🚡 5 🚠 670 acres

Monesi Italy
Southernmost of the resorts south of Turin. Close to Monaco and Nice.
1310m; slopes 1310–2180m
🚡 5 🚠 38km

Le Monêtier 321
Quiet little village with a nice rustic feel and direct access to Serre-Chevalier's slopes.
☒ *Equity Ski, Rocketski*

La Mongie 371
☒ *Lagrange Holidays, SkiAway Holidays*

Montafon 152
☒ *Interhome, Made to Measure Holidays*

Montalbert 303
Traditional village with direct access to the La Plagne network and easy, wooded local slopes.
☒ *Interhome, Ski Amis, Ski Arrangements*

Mont Blanc 632

Montchavin 303
Attractively transformed village on fringe of La Plagne ski area.
☒ *French Freedom Holidays, Made to Measure Holidays*

Mont-de-Lans 257
Low village on the way up to Les Deux-Alpes, with lifts to the main resort.

Le Mont-Dore France
Attractive traditional village, the largest resort in the stunningly beautiful volcanic Auvergne region near Clermont-Ferrand.
1050m; slopes 1350–1850m
🚡 20 🚠 42km
☒ *Lagrange Holidays*

Monte Bondone Italy
Essentially a Trento weekenders' area (some lifts are closed on weekdays). New high-speed chair claiming Europe's biggest single vertical ascent opened in 2002/03.
slopes 1300–2100m
🚡 18 🚠 13km
☒ *Solo's*

Monte Campione Italy
Tiny purpose-built resort, spread thinly over four mountainsides. 80% snowmaking helps to offset the low altitude.
1100m; slopes 1200–2010m
🚡 16 🚠 80km

Monte Livata Italy
Closest resort to Rome, popular with weekenders.
1430m; slopes 1430–1750m
🚡 8 🚠 8km

Monte Piselli Italy
Tiny area with the highest slopes of the many little resorts east of Rome.
2100m; slopes 2100–2690m
🚡 3 🚠 5km

Monte Pora Italy
Tiny resort near Lake d'Iseo and Bergamo. Several other little areas nearby.
1350m; slopes 1350–1880m
🚡 11 🚠 30km

Monterosa Ski 402
☒ *Alpine Answers Select, Crystal, Handmade Holidays, Mountain Tracks, Ski 2, Ski Addiction, Ski Arrangements, Ski Weekend, The Ski Company*

Mont Gabriel Canada
Montreal area with runs on four sides of the mountain, though the south-facing sides rarely open. Two short but renowned double-black-diamond bump runs. 🚡 9

Montgenèvre 292
☒ *Airtours, Crystal, Equity Ski, Erna Low, Independent Ski Links, Lagrange Holidays, Neilson, Rocketski, Ski Etoile, Ski France, Ski Life*

Mont Glen Canada
Least crowded of the Montreal areas, so a good weekend choice.
680m; slopes 680–1035m
🚡 4 🚠 110 acres

Mont Grand Fonds Canada
Small area sufficiently far from Québec not to get overrun at weekends.
400m; slopes 400–735m 🚡 4

Mont Habitant Canada
Very limited area in the Montreal region but with a good base lodge. 🚡 3

Mont Olympia Canada
Small, two-mountain area near Montreal, one mostly novice terrain, the other best suited to experts. 🚡 6

Mont Orford Canada
Cold, windswept lone peak (no resort), worth a trip from nearby Montreal on a fine day.
slopes 305–855m
🚡 8 🚠 180 acres

Mont Ste Anne 632
☒ *Frontier Ski, Inghams, Ski Independence, Ski Safari, Ski The American Dream*

Mont St Sauveur 632

Mont Sutton Canada
Varied area with some of the best glade skiing in eastern Canada, including some for novices. Quaint Sutton village nearby.
🚡 9 🚠 175 acres

Morgins 433
Chalet resort on Portes du Soleil, indirectly linked to Champéry.
☒ *Ski Morgins Holidays, Ski Rosie*

Morillon 262
Valley village with a gondola link up to its purpose-built satellite and the Flaine network.
☒ *AmeriCan Ski, Lagrange Holidays, Peak Retreats*

Morin Heights Canada
Area in the Montreal region with 100% snowmaking. Attractive base lodge. 🚡 6

Morzine 296
☒ *Airtours, Alpine Escapes, Alpine Events, Alpine Weekends, Alps2Go, Avant-ski, Chalet Gueret, Chalet Snowboard, Chalets 'Unlimited', Challenge Activ, Crystal, Equity Ski, Esprit Ski, First Choice Ski, Haig Ski, Independent Ski*

Links, Inghams, Lagrange Holidays, Made to Measure Holidays, Momentum Ski, Mountain Highs, Rocketski, Ski Activity, Ski Arrangements, Ski Chamois, Ski Expectations, Ski Life, Ski Line, Ski Link, Ski Morzine, Ski Weekend, SkiAway Holidays, Snowline, Solo's, The Chalet Company, The Corporate Ski Company, Thomson Ski & Snowboarding, Trail Alpine, White Roc

Les Mosses   Switzerland
The resort packs 60km/40 miles of downhill pistes and 35km/20 miles of cross-country trails into a small area. There's also a terrain-park, a few chalet-style hotel-restaurants, shops and a rather fine church. It's easily reached from Villars, Leysin and Les Diablerets and recent Villars visitors have recommended it for its quiet slopes and great views. However, there are only drag-lifts to access the mainly red and blue runs, though a chair is planned to Pic Chaussy. Lunch is mostly at valley level – try Buvette de l'Arsat or the self-service Drosera. There are a number of activities on offer – such as ice-diving, a natural ice rink and an international dog-sled racing course.
1500m; slopes 1500–2200m
⛟13 🚡 25km

Mottaret   282
Purpose-built but reasonably attractive component of Méribel.
✉ *Airtours, First Choice Ski, Panorama Holidays, Ski Leisure Direction, Ski Line, Skiworld, Thomson Ski & Snowboarding*

Mottarone   Italy
Closest slopes to Lake Maggiore. No village – just a base area.
1200m; slopes 1200–1490m
🚡 25km

Les Moulins   Switzerland
Village down the road from Château d'Oex with its own low area of slopes, part of the big Gstaad lift-pass area.
890m; slopes 890–3000m
⛟67 🚡 250km

Mount Abram   USA
Small, pretty, tree-lined area in Maine, renowned for its immaculately groomed easy runs.
295m; slopes 295–610m
⛟5 🚡 170 acres

Mountain High   USA
Best snowfall record and highest lift capacity in Los Angeles vicinity – plus 95% snowmaking. Mostly intermediate cruising.
2010m; slopes 2010–2500m
⛟12 🚡 220 acres

Mount Ashland   USA
Arty town in Oregon renowned for Shakespeare. Mountain includes glaciated bowl rimmed with steeps. Best for experts.
1935m; slopes 1935–2285m
⛟4 🚡 200 acres

Mount Bachelor   USA
Extinct volcano in Oregon offering deserted runs on every side served by many fast chairs. Gets a lot of rain. You have to stay in Bend, 25 miles away.
1740m; slopes 1740–2765m
⛟13 🚡 3680 acres
✉ *AmeriCan Ski*

Mount Baker   USA
Almost on the coast near Seattle, yet one of the top resorts for snow (averages 600 inches a year). Plenty of challenging slopes. Known for spectacular avalanches.
1115m; slopes 1115–1540m
⛟9 🚡 1000 acres

Mount Baldy   Canada
Tiny area, but a worthwhile excursion from Big White. Gets ultra light snow – great glades/powder chutes.
slopes 1705–2150m
⛟2 🚡 150 acres

Mount Baldy   USA
Some of the longest and steepest runs in California. Near Los Angeles, but 20% snowmaking and antiquated lifts are major drawbacks.
1980m; slopes 1980–2620m
⛟4 🚡 400 acres

Mount Baw Baw   Australia
Small but entertaining intermediate area in attractive woodland, with great views. Closest area to Melbourne (150km/93 miles).
1480m; slopes 1340–1565m
⛟8 🚡 61 acres

Mount Buffalo   653

Mount Buller   653

Mount Dobson   New Zealand
Mostly intermediate slopes in a wide, treeless basin near Mt Cook, with good snow-cover. Accommodation in Fairlie, 40 minutes away.
1610m; slopes 1610–2010m
⛟3 🚡 990 acres

Mount Hood Meadows   USA
One of several sizeable areas amid magnificent Oregon scenery. Impressive snowfall record but snow tends to be wet, and weather damp.
1375m; slopes 1375–2535m
⛟12 🚡 2150 acres

Mount Hood Ski Bowl   USA
Sizeable area set amid magnificent Oregon scenery. Weather can be damp.
1095m; slopes 1095–1540m
⛟9 🚡 960 acres

Mount Hotham   653

Mount Hutt   655

Mount Lemmon   USA
Southernmost area in North America, close to famous Old West town Tombstone, Arizona. Reasonable snowfall.
2500m; slopes 2500–2790m
⛟3 🚡 70 acres

Mount McKay   653

Mount Olympos   Greece
Ski mountaineering site with a chain of huts on both faces. Late winter is the best time to visit.
1800m

Mount Pilio   Greece
Pleasant slopes cut out of dense forest, only 15km/10 miles from the holiday resort of Portaria above town of Volos.
1500m 🚡 3

Mount Rose   USA
Only 22 miles from Reno. Relatively high, with good slopes of its own and well placed for trips to other Tahoe resorts.
2515m; slopes 2515–2955m
⛟5 🚡 900 acres

Mount Selwyn   Australia
Popular with beginners and families. 6 hours from Sydney. Good lift system.
1520m; slopes 1490–1610m
⛟12 🚡 111 acres

Mount Snow   578
✉ *Ski Success*

Mount Spokane   USA
Little intermediate area outside Spokane (Washington State).
1160m; slopes 1160–1795m
⛟5 🚡 350 acres

Mount St Louis / Moonstone   Canada
Premier area in Toronto region, spread over three peaks. Very high-capacity lift system and 100% snowmaking.
⛟13 🚡 175 acres

Mount Vermio   Greece
Oldest ski base in Greece. In central Macedonia 60km/35 miles from Thessaloniki. Barren but interesting slopes.
slopes 1420–2000m ⛟4

Mount Washington Resort   Canada
Scenic area on Vancouver Island with lodging in the base village. Impressive snowfall record but rain is a problem. A reporter in 2002 says: 'Great powder, but they shut the lifts too early (3.30pm). There are plans to add more lifts and runs soon.'
1110m; slopes 1110–1590m
⛟6 🚡 970 acres
✉ *Frontier Ski, Ski Safari*

Mount Sunapee   USA
Closest area of any size to Boston; primarily intermediate terrain.
375m; slopes 375–835m
⛟10 🚡 210 acres

Mount Waterman   USA
Small Los Angeles area where children ski free. The lack of much snowmaking is a drawback.
2135m; slopes 2135–2440m
⛟3 🚡 210 acres

Mühlbach   Austria
Village east of Saalbach, a short bus-ride from one end of large but low Hochkönig area that spreads over four mountains via Dienten to Maria Alm.
855m; slopes 800–1825m
⛟23 🚡 80km

Mühltal   192
Small village halfway between Niederau and Auffach in the Wildschönau. No local skiing of its own.

Muhr   Austria
Village by Katschberg tunnel well placed for visiting St Michael, Badkleinkirchheim, Flachau and Obertauern.
1110m

Muju   Korea
Largest area in Korea and with a fair amount of lodging. Though it is the furthest resort from Seoul (some four hours south) it is still overcrowded. ⛟12

Mürren   455
✉ *Alpine Events, Inghams, Kuoni, Made to Measure Holidays, Plus Travel, Ski Club of Great Britain, Ski Solutions, Swiss Travel Service, Top Deck*

Mutters   125

Myoko Suginohara Kokusai   Japan
A series of small resorts 2–3 hours from Tokyo which together make up an area of extensive slopes, with longer, wider runs than normal for Japan. ⛟15

Naeba   Japan
Fashionable resort with lots of accommodation 2 hours north of Tokyo. Crowded slopes.
900m; slopes 900–1800m ⛟28

Nakiska   Canada
Small area of wooded runs between Banff and Calgary, with emphasis on downhill speed. Unreliable snow, but state-of-the-art snowmaking and pancake-flat grooming.
1524m; slopes 1525–2215m
⛟4 🚡 230 acres

Nasserein   180
Quiet suburb of St Anton, a short bus-ride from the lifts.

Nauders   Austria
Spacious, traditionally Tirolean village tucked away only 3km/2 miles from the Swiss border and almost on the Italian one. Its slopes start 2km/1 mile outside the village (free shuttle-bus) and are mainly high and sunny intermediate runs spread over three areas. There is lots of snowmaking. The area is not ideal for experts, though there is a lot of off-piste terrain. It's not ideal for complete beginners either – the village nursery slopes are some way out. There are five cross-country trails amounting to 40km/25 miles in all. Most of the hotels are comfortable 4-stars and many of

the eating out possibilities are hotel-based. The après-ski scene has typically Tirolean jollity and there is quite a bit to do off the slopes, including tobogganing, curling, tennis, squash, bowling, and swimming.
1400m; slopes 1400–2750m
⛷ 30 ⛷ 111km

Nax Switzerland
Quiet, sunny village in a balcony setting overlooking the Rhône valley. Own little area and only a short drive from Veysonnaz.
1300m

Nendaz 470
Enormous apartment development offering quiet alternative to Verbier.
✉ *Interhome*

Neukirchen Austria
Quiet, pretty beginners' resort with a fairly snow-sure plateau at the top of its mountain.
855m; slopes 855–2150m
⛷ 14 ⛷ 35km
✉ *Equity Ski*

Neustift 125
✉ *Alpine Tours, Esprit Ski, Interhome, Made to Measure Holidays*

Nevegal Italy
Weekend place near Belluno, south of Cortina.
1030m; slopes 1030–1650m
⛷ 14 ⛷ 30km

Nevis Range 652
✉ *Skisafe Travel*

Niederau 192
Amorphous chalet-style village in the Wildschönau region.
✉ *Airtours, First Choice Ski, Inghams, Neilson, Panorama Holidays, Thomson Ski & Snowboarding*

Niseko Japan
Town on Hohhaido, three hours from Sopporo and with three ski areas close by. Good snow record and powder. ⛷ 28

Nockberge Innerkrems Austria
Area just south of Katschberg tunnel.
1500m; slopes 1500–2300m
⛷ 10 ⛷ 33km

Nordic Valley USA
Utah cross-country area close to Salt Lake City. Powder Mountain and Snowbasin are nearby Alpine areas.

Nordseter Norway
Cluster of hotels in deep forest north of Lillehammer. Some Alpine facilities but best for cross-country.
850m; slopes 1000–1090m
⛷ 2 ⛷ 2km

Norefjell Norway
Norway's toughest run, a very steep 600m/1,970ft drop. 120km/75 miles north-west of Oslo.
185m; slopes 185–1185m
⛷ 10 ⛷ 23km

La Norma France
Traffic-free, purpose-built resort near Modane and Val-Cenis, with mostly easy terrain.
1350m; slopes 1350–2750m
⛷ 18 ⛷ 65km
✉ *AmeriCan Ski, Erna Low, Interhome, Lagrange Holidays, Peak Retreats, Ski Life*

Norquay 598

North Conway USA
Attractive factory-outlet-shopping town in New Hampshire close to Attitash and Cranmore ski areas.
✉ *AmeriCan Ski, Virgin Ski*

Northstar-at-Tahoe 506
✉ *AmeriCan Ski, Made to Measure Holidays, Ski The American Dream, United Vacations Ski Freedom USA & Canada*

Nôtre-Dame-de-Bellecombe 274
Pleasant village spoiled by the busy Albertville-Megève road. Inexpensive base from which to visit Megève, though it has fair slopes of its own.
✉ *AmeriCan Ski, Peak Retreats*

Nova Levante Italy
Little area used mostly by weekend day-trippers.
1180m; slopes 1180–2200m
⛷ 14 ⛷ 20km

Nozawa Onsen Japan
Spa village with good hot springs 3 hours from Tokyo. The runs are cut out of heavy vegetation.
500m; slopes 500–1650m ⛷ 24

Nub's Nob USA
One of the most sheltered Great Lakes ski areas (many suffer fierce winds). 100% snowmaking; weekend crowds from Detroit. Wooded slopes suitable for all abilities.
275m; slopes 275–405m
⛷ 8 ⛷ 245 acres

Oberau 192
Very pretty village in the Wildschönau region.
✉ *Inghams, Neilson, Thomson Ski & Snowboarding*

Obereggen Italy
Tiny resort used mainly by weekend day-trippers.
1550m; slopes 1550–2200m
⛷ 6 ⛷ 10km

Obergurgl 155
✉ *Airtours, Alpine Events, Crystal, Directski.com, First Choice Ski, Independent Ski Links, Inghams, Made to Measure Holidays, Neilson, Ski Club of Great Britain, Ski Expectations, Ski Solutions, Thomson Ski & Snowboarding*

Oberlech 140
Car- and crowd-free family resort alternative to Lech. Snow-sure due to height, snow-pocket position and snow-guns.

Oberndorf 188
Quiet hamlet with beginners' area and a chair connecting it to St Johann's undemanding ski area.
✉ *Lagrange Holidays*

Oberstdorf Germany
Attractive winter-sports town near the Austrian border with three small areas. Famous ski-jumping hill. The Nordic World Ski Championships will be held here in 2005.
815m; slopes 800–2220m
⛷ 31 ⛷ 30km
✉ *Moswin Tours*

Obertauern 160
✉ *Inghams, Made to Measure Holidays, Thomson Ski & Snowboarding*

Ochapowace Canada
Main area in Saskatchewan, east of Regina. It doesn't get a huge amount of snow but 75% snowmaking helps.
⛷ 4 ⛷ 100 acres

Oetz Austria
Village at the entrance to the Oetz valley with an easy/intermediate ski area of its own and access to the Sölden, Kuhtai and Niederau areas.
820m; slopes 820–2200m
⛷ 10 ⛷ 25km

Ohau New Zealand
Some of NZ's steepest slopes, with great views of Lake Ohau 9km/5 miles away (where you stay). 320km/200 miles south of Christchurch.
1500m; slopes 1425–1825m
⛷ 3 ⛷ 310 acres

Okemo 578

Oppdal 645

Orcières-Merlette France
High, convenient family resort a few km north-east of Gap, Merlette being the only purpose-built ski station above the village of Orcières (1450m). Snow-sure beginner area. Slopes with a good mix of difficulty spread over several mountain flanks, and are currently being expanded – a process due to culminate in 2003/04 with opening of a cable-car up to almost 3000m/9,840ft on Roche Brune. Most accommodation is in apartments, but there are a few simple hotels. There is an impressive Palais des Sports, with pools, ice-rink and other facilities.
1850m; slopes 1850–2725m
⛷ 28 ⛷ 85km
✉ *Lagrange Holidays*

Ordino 94
Valley village near La Massana, on the way up to Andorra's best snow at Arcalis.

Oropa Italy
Little area just off the Aosta-Turin motorway. An easy change of scene from Courmayeur.
1180m; slopes 1200–2390m
⛷ 15km

Les Orres France
Friendly modern resort with great views and varied intermediate terrain, but the snow is unreliable, and it's a long transfer from Lyon.
1550m; slopes 1550–2720m
⛷ 23 ⛷ 62km
✉ *Interhome, Lagrange Holidays*

Orsières Switzerland
Traditional, sizeable winter resort near Martigny. Well-positioned base from which to visit Verbier and the Chamonix valley.
900m

Ortisei 410
Charming, lively, old market town in the Italian Dolomites with indirect links to the Sella Ronda.
✉ *Inghams*

Oslo Norway
Capital city with cross-country ski trails in its parks. Alpine slopes and lifts in Nordmarka region, just north of city boundaries.

Otre il Colle Italy
Smallest of many little resorts near Bergamo.
1100m; slopes 1100–2000m
⛷ 7 ⛷ 7km

Oukaimeden Morocco
Slopes 75km/45 miles from Marrakech with a surprisingly long season.
2600m; slopes 2600–3260m
⛷ 8 ⛷ 15km

Ovindoli Italy
One of the smallest areas in L'Aquila region east of Rome, but it has higher slopes than most and one of the better lift systems.
1375m; slopes 1375–2220m
⛷ 9 ⛷ 10km

Ovronnaz Switzerland
Pretty village set on a sunny shelf above the Rhône valley, with a good pool complex. Limited area but Crans-Montana and Anzère are close.
1350m; slopes 1350–2080m
⛷ 10 ⛷ 25km

Owl's Head Canada
Steep mountain rising out of a lake, in a remote spot bordering Vermont, away from weekend crowds.
⛷ 7 ⛷ 90 acres

Oz-en-Oisans 205
Attractive old village with higher satellite at base of lifts into Alpe d'Huez.
✉ *Independent Ski Links, Lagrange Holidays, Ski Leisure Direction*

Pajarito Mountain   USA
Los Alamos area laid out by
nuclear scientists. Atomic slopes
too – steep, ungroomed. Open
Fridays, weekends and holidays.
Fun day out from Taos.
2685m; slopes 2685–3170m
⛷ *6* ⛷ *220 acres*

Pal   98
Prettily wooded mountain, now
linked with slopes of Arinsal and
soon to be accessible from
valley town of La Massana.
✉ *Panorama Holidays,
Snowcoach*

Palandöken   Turkey
Varied skiing area, transformed
by new lifts and two big hotels,
overlooking the Anatolian city of
Erzurum.
slopes 2125–3125m ⛷ *7*

Pamporovo   639
✉ *Balkan Holidays, Crystal,
First Choice Ski, Inghams, Ski
Balkantours, Thomson Ski &
Snowboarding*

Panarotta   Italy
Smallest of the resorts east of
Trento. It is at a higher altitude
than nearby Andalo, so it is
worth a day out from there.
1500m; slopes 1500–2000m
⛷ *6* ⛷ *7km*

Panorama   620
✉ *AmeriCan Ski, American Ski
Classics, Frontier Ski, Inghams,
Made to Measure Holidays, Ski
Activity, Ski All America, Ski
Independence, Ski Safari, Ski
The American Dream*

Panticosa   Spain
Charming old Pyrenees village
near Formigal with sheltered but
limited slopes.
1200m; slopes 1200–1900m
⛷ *7* ⛷ *34km*

Paradiski   27
Park City   559
✉ *Alpine Answers Select,
AmeriCan Ski, American Ski
Classics, Crystal, Inghams,
Made to Measure Holidays,
Momentum Ski, Ski Activity, Ski
All America, Ski Independence,
Ski Line, Ski Safari, Ski The
American Dream, Thomson Ski
& Snowboarding, Trailfinders,
United Vacations Ski Freedom
USA & Canada, Virgin Ski*

Parnassos   Greece
Biggest and best-organised area
in Greece, 180km/112 miles from
Athens and with surprisingly
good slopes and lifts.
slopes 1600–2300m
⛷ *10* ⛷ *14km*

Parpan   Switzerland
Pretty village linked to the large
intermediate area of
Lenzerheide.
1510m; slopes 1230–2865m
⛷ *35* ⛷ *155km*

Partenen   152
Traditional village in a pretty
setting at the end of
Montafontal. Slopes start at
Gaschurn, and there are lots
more in the vicinity.

La Parva   Chile
One of Chile's best ski areas,
linked with Valle Nevado and El
Colorado ski areas. Only
50km/31 miles east of Santiago
so it gets crowded at weekends.
2660m; slopes 2660–3630m
⛷ *13*
✉ *Scott Dunn Latin America*

Pas de la Casa   100
✉ *Airtours, Chalets 'Unlimited',
Crystal, Directski.com, First
Choice Ski, Independent Ski
Links, Inghams, Lagrange
Holidays, Neilson, Panorama
Holidays, Thomson Ski &
Snowboarding, Top Deck*

Passo Lanciano   Italy
Closest area to Adriatic.
Weekend crowds from nearby
Pescara when the snow is good.
1305m; slopes 1305–2000m
⛷ *13*

Passo Tonale   Italy
Bleak resort set on a high pass
with generally good snow at a
bargain price. Popular with Brits
and school groups as well as
Italian families. Good beginner
and easy slopes, and reporters
praise the ski school – which
has lots of English-speaking
instructors – but complain about
the lack of much après-ski life.
Most runs are on the sunny,
south-facing side of the pass
served largely by chair-lifts. A
cable-car on the other side leads
to a drag-lifts on the
high Presena glacier with
guaranteed good snow and
summer skiing. There is very
little to interest experts and
many of the red runs would be
blue in other resorts. The
Sporthotel Vittoria is popular
with Brits and convenient for the
slopes but is said to have some
very small rooms. One reporter
said that the fast food outlets
and 'English' pubs reminded
them of Tenerife.
1885m; slopes 1885–3025m
⛷ *30* ⛷ *80km*
✉ *Airtours, Alpine Tours,
Crystal, Equity Ski, Inghams,
Neilson, Rocketski, Sloping Off,
Thomson Ski & Snowboarding*

Pass Thurn   134
Road-side lift base for
Kitzbühel's most snow-sure, but
unconnected, ski area.

Pebble Creek   USA
Small area on Utah-Jackson Hole
route. Blend of open and
wooded slopes.
1920m; slopes 1920–2530m
⛷ *3* ⛷ *600 acres*

Pec Pod Snezkou
                  Czech Republic
Collection of hamlets spread
along the valley road leading to
the main lifts and the very
limited ski area.
770m; slopes 710–1190m
⛷ *5* ⛷ *12km*

Peisey   213
Small village (often referred to
as Peisey-Nancroix) linked to Les
Arcs and the Paradiski area.

Peisey-Vallandry   213
Group of small villages linked to
Les Arcs and the Paradiski area.
✉ *Esprit Ski, Independent Ski
Links, MasterSki, Ski Beat, Ski
Hiver, Ski Leisure Direction, Ski
Line, Ski Olympic*

Pejo   Italy
Unspoiled traditional village in a
pretty setting, with a limited
area. A cheap base for nearby
Madonna.
1340m; slopes 1340–2800m
⛷ *6* ⛷ *15km*

Perisher/Smiggins   653
Pescasseroli   Italy
One of numerous areas east of
Rome in L'Aquila region.
1250m; slopes 1250–1945m
⛷ *6* ⛷ *25km*

Pescocostanzo   Italy
One of numerous areas east of
Rome in L'Aquila region.
1395m; slopes 1395–1900m
⛷ *4* ⛷ *25km*

Pettneu   180
Snow-sure specialist beginners'
resort with an irregular bus link
to nearby St Anton.

Petzen   Austria
One of many little areas in
Austria's easternmost ski region
near Slovenian border.
600m; slopes 600–1700m
⛷ *6* ⛷ *13km*

Peyragudes-Peyresourde
                         France
Small Pyrenean resort with its
ski area starting high above.
1000m; slopes 1600–2400m
⛷ *15* ⛷ *37km*
✉ *Lagrange Holidays*

Pfunds   Austria
Picturesque valley village with
no slopes but quick access to
several resorts in Switzerland
and Italy, as well as Austria.
970m; slopes 970–2850m
⛷ *28* ⛷ *110km*

Phoenix Park   Korea
Golf complex with 12 trails in
winter. Two hours (140km/87
miles) from Seoul.
slopes 650–1050m ⛷ *7*

Piancavallo   Italy
Uninspiring yet curiously trendy
purpose-built village, an easy
drive from Venice.
1270m; slopes 1270–1830m
⛷ *17* ⛷ *45km*
✉ *Equity Ski, Sloping Off*

Piani delle Betulle   Italy
One of several little areas near
the east coast of Lake Como.
730m; slopes 730–1850m
⛷ *6* ⛷ *10km*

Piani di Artavaggio   Italy
Small base complex rather than
a village. One of several little
areas near Lake Como.
875m; slopes 875–1875m
⛷ *7* ⛷ *15km*

Piani di Bobbio   Italy
Largest of several tiny resorts
above Lake Como.
770m; slopes 770–1855m
⛷ *10* ⛷ *20km*

Piani di Erna   Italy
Small base development – no
village. One of several little
areas above Lake Como.
600m; slopes 600–1635m
⛷ *5* ⛷ *9km*

Piau-Engaly   France
User-friendly St-Lary satellite in
one of the best areas in the
Pyrenees.
1850m; slopes 1700–2500m
⛷ *20* ⛷ *40km*
✉ *Lagrange Holidays*

Piazzatorre   Italy
One of many little areas in the
Bergamo region.
870m; slopes 870–2000m
⛷ *5* ⛷ *25km*

Pico   581
Low-key little family area (no
resort) close to Killington in
central Vermont.

Piesendorf   Austria
Cheaper, quiet place to stay
when visiting Zell am See.
Tucked behind Kaprun near
Niedernsill.
780m

Pievepelago   Italy
Much the smallest and most
limited of the Appennine ski
resorts. Less than 2 hours from
Florence and Pisa.
1115m; slopes 1115–1410m
⛷ *7* ⛷ *8km*

Pila   Italy
Modern, car-free, purpose-built,
ski-in, ski-out resort, linked by
gondola to old Roman town of
Aosta below. There's an
interesting mix of well-groomed,
snow-sure, mainly intermediate
slopes, with stunning views from
the top. For experts there are
steep pistes and mogul fields at
the top and some good off-
piste, but not huge amounts. It's
a good resort for beginners,
with a good, secluded nursery
area and easy runs to progress
to; the slopes are generally
uncrowded. We have good
reports of the ski school, and
there are several good mountain
restaurants. Most of the hotels
and apartments are right on the
slopes, and there is a choice of

pizza and pasta restaurants. Après-ski is quiet. Other resorts in the Aosta valley are within day-trip distance and are covered by the lift pass.
1800m; slopes 1550–2710m
⛷13 ⛡70km
✉ *Crystal, Interhome, Interski*

Pinzolo Italy
Atmospheric village with slopes well equipped with snowmakers. Cheap base for nearby Madonna.
800m; slopes 780–2100m
⛷8 ⛡29km
✉ *Alpine Tours*

Pitztal Austria
Long valley with good glacier area at its head, accessed by underground funicular.
1250m; slopes 880–3440m
⛷19 ⛡87km

Pla-d'Adet France
Limited purpose-built complex at the foot of the St-Lary ski area (the original village is further down the mountain).
1680m; slopes 1420–2450m
⛷32 ⛡80km
✉ *Lagrange Holidays, Lagrange Holidays*

La Plagne 303
✉ *Airtours, Avant-ski, Chalet World, Chalets 'Unlimited', Chez Jay Ski Chalets, Club Med, Crystal, Directski.com, Equity Ski, Erna Low, Esprit Ski, Eurotunnel Motoring Holidays, Finlays, First Choice Ski, French Freedom Holidays, Independent Ski Links, Inghams, Interhome, Lagrange Holidays, Made to Measure Holidays, Mark Warner, Neilson, Rocketski, Silver Ski, Ski Activity, Ski Amis, Ski Arrangements, Ski Beat, Ski Club of Great Britain, Ski Expectations, Ski France, Ski Independence, Ski Leisure Direction, Ski Life, Ski Line, Ski Olympic, Ski Supreme, SkiAway Holidays, Skiworld, Thomson Ski & Snowboarding, Top Deck*

Plan-Peisey 213
Development above Peisey with cable-car link to Les Arcs and the Paradiski area. For package holidays see Peisey-Vallandry.

Poiana Brasov 641
✉ *Balkan Holidays, Inghams, Neilson, Ski Balkantours, Solo's*

Pomerelle USA
Small area in Idaho on the Utah–Sun Valley route.
2430m; slopes 2430–2735m
⛷3 ⛡300 acres

Pontechianale Italy
Highest, largest area in a remote region south-west of Turin. Day-tripper place.
1600m; slopes 1600–2760m
⛷8 ⛡30km

Ponte di Legno Italy
Attractive sheltered alternative to bleak, ugly neighbour Passo Tonale. Linked by piste and bus.
1255m; slopes 1255–1920m
⛷5 ⛡15km

Pontresina 464
Small, sedate base linked to nearby St Moritz by road, with extensive cross-country trails.
✉ *Club Med, Made to Measure Holidays*

Porter Heights New Zealand
Closest skiing to Christchurch (one hour). Open, sunny bowl offering mostly intermediate skiiing – with back bowls for powder.
1340m; slopes 1340–1950m
⛷5 ⛡200 acres

Portes du Soleil 312

Portillo Chile
Luxury hotel 150km/95 miles north-east of Santiago. Uncrowded snow-sure slopes used for training by US national ski team.
2880m; slopes 2590–3350m
⛷12 ⛡25km
✉ *AmeriCan Ski, Crystal, Momentum Ski, Scott Dunn Latin America, Ski Safari*

Powderhorn USA
Area in west Colorado with plans (in 2002/03) to double its ski area, perched on world's highest flat-top mountain, Grand Mesa. Sensational views. Day trip from Aspen.
2490m; slopes 2490–2975m
⛷4 ⛡300 acres

Powder King Canada
Remote resort in British Columbia, between Prince George and Dawson City. As its name suggests, it has great powder. Plenty of lodging.
880m; slopes 880–1520m
⛷3 ⛡160 acres

Powder Mountain USA
Sizeable Utah area, a feasible day out from Park City. Wonderfully uncrowded locals' secret, renowned for bowls of fluffy virgin powder. Snowcat operation too.
2315m; slopes 2315–2710m
⛷6 ⛡1600 acres

Pozza di Fassa Italy
Pretty Dolomite village with its own slopes, three other small areas close by, and access to the Sella Ronda at nearby Campitello.
1340m; slopes 1340–2155m
⛷6 ⛡20km

Pragelato Italy
Inexpensive base, a short drive east of Sestriere. Its own area is worth a try for half a day.
1535m; slopes 1535–2700m
⛷6 ⛡50km

Prägraten am Grossvenediger Austria
Traditional mountaineering/ski touring village in lovely setting south of Felbertauern tunnel. The Alpine ski slopes of Matrei are nearby.
1310m; slopes 1310–1490m
⛷2 ⛡30km

Prali Italy
Tiny resort east of Sestriere – a worthwhile half-day trip.
1450m; slopes 1450–2500m
⛷7 ⛡25km

Pralognan-la-Vanoise France
Unspoiled traditional village overlooked by spectacular peaks. Champagny (La Plagne) and Courchevel are close by.
1410m; slopes 1410–2355m
⛷14 ⛡30km
✉ *Lagrange Holidays*

Pra-Loup France
Convenient, purpose-built family resort with an extensive, varied intermediate area linked to La Foux-d'Allos.
1500m; slopes 1500–2600m
⛷32 ⛡83km
✉ *Equity Ski, Lagrange Holidays, Rocketski*

Prati di Tivo Italy
Weekend day-trip place east of Rome and near the town of Teramo. A sizeable resort by southern Italy standards.
1450m; slopes 1450–1800m
⛷6 ⛡16km

Prato Nevoso Italy
Purpose-built resort with rather bland slopes. Part of Mondolé ski area with Artesina.
1500m; slopes 1500–1950m
⛷25 ⛡90km
✉ *Equity Ski, Rocketski*

Prato Selva Italy
Tiny base development (no village) east of Rome near Teramo. Weekend day-trip place.
1370m; slopes 1370–1800m
⛷4 ⛡10km

Le Praz 247
The lowest and most attractive of the Courchevel resorts, with direct access to the slopes.
✉ *Ski Deep, Ski 'n' Action*

Les Praz 226
Quiet hamlet 4km/2 miles from Chamonix, with convenient lift link to the varied Flégère area.
✉ *High Mountain Holidays*

Praz-de-Lys France
Little-known snow-pocket area near Lake Geneva that can have good snow when nearby resorts (eg La Clusaz) do not.
1500m; slopes 1200–2000m
⛷23 ⛡60km
✉ *Lagrange Holidays*

Praz-sur-Arly 274
Traditional village in a pretty, wooded setting just down the road from Megève, with its own varied slopes.
✉ *Lagrange Holidays*

Le Pré 213
Charming, rustic hamlet with lifts up to Arc 2000 and excellent runs back down.

Predazzo Italy
Small quiet place between Cavalese and the Sella Ronda resorts. Well positioned for touring the Dolomites area.
1015m; slopes 995–2205m
⛷8 ⛡17km

Premanon France
One of four resorts that make up Les Rousses area in Jura region.
1050m; slopes 1120–1680m ⛷40
✉ *Lagrange Holidays*

La Presolana Italy
Large summer resort near Bergamo. Several other little areas nearby.
1250m; slopes 1250–1650m
⛷6 ⛡15km

Puy-St-Vincent 314
✉ *Equity Ski, Esprit Ski, Interhome, Lagrange Holidays, Snowbizz Vacances*

Pyhä 643
✉ *Canterbury Travel*

Pyrenees, French 371

Pyrenees 2000 France
Tiny resort built in pleasing manner. Shares pretty area of short runs with Font-Romeu. Impressive snowmaking.
2000m; slopes 1750–2250m
⛷32 ⛡52km

Québec 632
✉ *Equity Ski, Inghams, Rocketski*

Queenstown 658

Radium Hot Springs Canada
Summer resort offering an alternative to the purpose-built slope-side resort of Panorama.
slopes 975–2155m
⛷8 ⛡300 acres
✉ *AmeriCan Ski*

Radstadt Austria
Interesting, unspoiled medieval town near Schladming that has its own small area, with the Salzburger Sportwelt slopes accessed from nearby Zauchensee or Flachau.
855m; slopes 855–2185m
⛷100 ⛡350km

Rainbow New Zealand
Northernmost ski area on South Island. Wide, treeless area, best for beginners and intermediates. Accommodation at St Arnaud.
1440m; slopes 1440–1760m
⛷5 ⛡865 acres

Ramsau am Dachstein Austria
Charming village overlooked by the Dachstein glacier. Renowned for cross-country, it also has Alpine slopes locally, on the glacier and at Schladming.
1200m; slopes 1100–2700m
⛷18 ⛡30km

Ramundberget 649

Rauris Austria
Old roadside village close to Kaprun and Zell am See, with a long, narrow area that has snowmakers on the lower slopes.
950m; slopes 950–2200m
⛷9 ⛡30km
✉ *Crystal*

Ravascletto   Italy
Resort in a pretty wooded
setting near Austrian border,
with most of its terrain high
above on open plateau.
920m; slopes 920–1735m
🚠 12 ⛷ 40km
✉ *Sloping Off*

Reallon   France
Traditional-style village, with
splendid views from above Lac
de Serre-Ponçon.
1560m; slopes 1560–2115m
🚠 6 ⛷ 20km
✉ *Lagrange Holidays*

Red Lodge   USA
Picturesque Old West Montana
town. Ideal for combined trip
with Big Sky or Jackson Hole.
1800m; slopes 2155–2860m
🚠 8 ⛷ 1600 acres
✉ *AmeriCan Ski*

Red Mountain   595
✉ *AmeriCan Ski, Frontier Ski,
Ski Safari*

Red River   USA
New Mexico western town –
complete with stetsons and
saloons – with intermediate
slopes above.
2665m; slopes 2665–3155m
🚠 7 ⛷ 270 acres

Reichenfels   Austria
One of many small areas in
Austria's easternmost ski region
near the Slovenian border.
810m; slopes 810–1400m

The Remarkables   658
Three bleak basins with great
views of 'remarkable' jagged
alps 45 minutes from
Queenstown.

Rencurel-les-Coulumes France
One of seven little resorts just
west of Grenoble. Unspoiled,
inexpensive place to tour.
Villard-de-Lans is main resort.

Reutte   Austria
500-year old market town with
many traditional hotels, and rail
links to nearby Lermoos.
855m; slopes 855–1900m
🚠 9 ⛷ 19km

Revelstoke   Canada
Town from which you can heli-
ski in Monashees or cat-ski
locally at a more reasonable
cost than most places.
460m
✉ *Powder Skiing in North
America Limited*

Rhêmes-Notre-Dame   Italy
Unspoiled village in the
beautiful Rhêmes valley, south
of Aosta. Courmayeur and La
Thuile within reach.
🚠 2 ⛷ 5km

Riederalp   Switzerland
Pretty, vehicle-free village
perched high above the Rhône
valley amid the glorious scenery
of the Aletsch area. Access by
cable-car or gondola from valley
village of Mörel near Brig.
1900m; slopes 1900–2900m
🚠 32 ⛷ 90km

Rigi-Kaltbad   Switzerland
Resort on a mountain rising out
of Lake Lucerne, with superb all-
round views, accessed by the
world's first mountain railroad.
1440m; slopes 1195–1795m
🚠 9 ⛷ 30km

Riihivuori   Finland
Finnish area with its 'base' at
the top of the mountain. The
city of Jyvaskyla is nearby. 🚠 5

Riksgränsen   649

Riscone   Italy
Dolomite village sharing a pretty
area with San Vigilio. Good
snowmaking. Short easy runs.
1200m; slopes 1200–2275m
🚠 35 ⛷ 40km

Risoul   316
✉ *Crystal, Erna Low, First
Choice Ski, Erna Low, First
Choice Ski, Erna Low, First
Lagrange Holidays, Made to
Measure Holidays, Neilson, Ski
Arrangements, Ski Life,
Thomson Ski & Snowboarding*

Rivisondoli   Italy
Sizeable mountain retreat east
of Rome, with one of the better
lift systems in the vicinity.
1350m; slopes 1350–2050m
🚠 7 ⛷ 16km

Roccaraso   Italy
Largest of the resorts east of
Rome – at least when snow-
cover is complete.
1280m; slopes 1280–2200m
🚠 12 ⛷ 56km

Rohrmoos   168
Situated below small mountain
in Dachstein-Tauern region, next
to Schladming.

La Rosière   319
✉ *Crystal, Erna Low, Esprit Ski,
Interhome, Lagrange Holidays,
Ski Arrangements, Ski France,
Ski Olympic, Ski Supreme,
Thomson Ski & Snowboarding,
Vanilla Ski*

Rossland   Canada
Remote little town 5km/3 miles
from cult powder paradise Red
Mountain.

Rougemont   453
Cute rustic hamlet just over the
French/German language border
near Gstaad, with worthwhile
local slopes and links to
Gstaad's Eggli sector.

Les Rousses   France
Group of four villages – Les
Rousses, Premanon, Lamoura
and Bois d'Amont in the Jura
mountains.
1120m; slopes 1120–1680m
🚠 40 ⛷ 40km
✉ *Lagrange Holidays*

Ruka   643

Russbach   Austria
Secluded village tucked up a
side valley and linked into the
Gosau-Annaberg-Lungotz area.
The slopes are spread over a
wide area.
815m; slopes 780–1620m
🚠 33 ⛷ 65km

Saalbach-Hinterglemm   162
✉ *Airtours, Crystal,
Directski.com, Equity Ski, First
Choice Ski, Inghams,
Interhome, Made to Measure
Holidays, Neilson, Panorama
Holidays, Rocketski, Thomson
Ski & Snowboarding*

Saalfelden   Austria
Town ideally placed for touring
eastern Tirol. Extensive lift
networks of Maria Alm and
Saalbach are nearby.
745m; slopes 745–1550m
🚠 3 ⛷ 3km

Saanen   Switzerland
Cheaper and more convenient
alternative to staying in Gstaad
– but much less going on.
slopes 950–3000m
🚠 69 ⛷ 250km

Saanenmöser   453
Small village with local slopes
and rail/road links to Gstaad.

Saas-Almagell   Switzerland
Compact village up the valley
from Saas-Grund, with good
cross-country trails and walks,
and a limited Alpine area.
1670m 🚠 4

Saas-Fee   459
✉ *Alpine Events, Avant-ski,
Crystal, Erna Low, Independent
Ski Links, Inghams, Interhome,
Kuoni, Made to Measure
Holidays, Momentum Ski, Plus
Travel, Ski Club of Great
Britain, Ski Independence, Ski
Solutions, SkiGower, Sloping
Off, Swiss Travel Service,
Thomson Ski & Snowboarding*

Saas-Grund   Switzerland
Sprawling valley village below
Saas-Fee, with a separate, small
but high Alpine area.
1560m; slopes 1560–3100m
🚠 7 ⛷ 45km
✉ *SkiGower*

Saddleback   USA
Small area between Maine's
premier resorts. High slopes by
local standards.
695m; slopes 695–1255m
🚠 5 ⛷ 100 acres

Sahoro   Japan
Ugly, purpose-built complex on
Hokkaido island. A limited area,
but one of the most exotic
package destinations.
400m; slopes 400–1100m
🚠 9 ⛷ 15km
✉ *Club Med*

Les Saisies   France
Traditional-style cross-country
venue in a pretty setting,
surrounded by varied four-
mountain Alpine slopes.
1650m; slopes 1150–2000m
🚠 24 ⛷ 40km
✉ *Classic Ski Limited,
Inntravel, Lagrange Holidays,
Peak Retreats, SkiAway
Holidays*

Sälen   649

Salt Lake City   USA
Underrated base from which to
ski Utah. 30 minutes from Park
City, Deer Valley, The Canyons,
Snowbird, Alta, Snowbasin.
Cheaper and livelier than the
resorts.
✉ *AmeriCan Ski*

Salzburg-Stadt   Austria
A single, long challenging run
off the back of Salzburg's local
mountain, accessed by a
spectacular lift-ride from a
suburb of Grodig.
425m

Samedan   Switzerland
Valley town, just down the road
from St Moritz.
1720m; slopes 1740–2570m
🚠 3 ⛷ 7km

Samnaun   129
Shares large ski area with Ischgl.

Samoëns   262
Beautiful rural valley village, a
bus-ride from lifts into Flaine's
skiing.
✉ *AmeriCan Ski, Inntravel,
Interhome, Lagrange Holidays,
Peak Retreats, Ski Life*

San Bernardino   Switzerland
Pretty resort south of the road
tunnel, close to Madesimo.
1625m; slopes 1600–2595m
🚠 8 ⛷ 30km

San Candido   Italy
Austrian border resort on the
road to Lienz.
1175m; slopes 1175–1580m
🚠 4 ⛷ 15km
✉ *Waymark Holidays*

San Carlos de Bariloche
    Argentina
Year-round resort, with five
areas nearby. *790m*
✉ *Scott Dunn Latin America*

San Cassiano   410
Pretty village linked to the Sella
Ronda.

Sandia Peak   USA
World's longest lift-ride ascends
from Albuquerque. Mostly gentle
slopes; children ski free.
slopes 2645–3165m
🚠 7 ⛷ 100 acres

San Grée di Viola   Italy
Easternmost of resorts south of
Turin, surprisingly close to
Italian Riviera.
1100m; slopes 1100–1800m
⛷ 30km

San Martin de los Andes
    Argentina
Sizeable town with
accommodation, 19 km/12 miles
from Chapelco ski area.
✉ *Scott Dunn Latin America*

San Martino di Castrozza Italy
Plain village in the southernmost
Dolomites with varied slopes in
four disjointed areas, none very
extensive.
1465m; slopes 1465–2610m
🚠 20 ⛷ 50km
✉ *Interhome, Rocketski, Solo's*

San Pellegrino Italy
Little ski area close to but not part of the Sella Ronda.

Sansicario 405
Small, stylish, modern resort, well placed in the Milky Way near to Sauze d'Oulx.
⊠ Rocketski

San Simone Italy
Tiny development north of Bergamo, close to unappealing Foppolo area.
2000m; slopes 1105–2300m
🚡9 ↟45km

Santa Caterina Italy
Pretty, user-friendly village near Bormio, with a snow-sure novice and intermediate area.
1740m; slopes 1740–2725m
🚡8 ↟25km
⊠ Airtours, Equity Ski, Rocketski

Santa Cristina 410
Quiet village on the periphery of the Sella Ronda.

Santa Fe USA
One of America's most attractive and interesting towns. Varied slopes – glades, bowls, cruiser pistes, desert views. Great excursion from Taos.
3145m; slopes 3145–3645m
🚡7 ↟600 acres

Santa Maria Maggiore Italy
Resort south of the Simplon Pass from the Rhône valley, and near Lake Maggiore.
820m; slopes 820–1890m
🚡5 ↟10km

San Vigilio Italy
Charming Dolomite village with a delightful, sizeable area well covered by snow-guns.
1200m; slopes 1200–2275m
🚡33 ↟40km

San Vito di Cadore Italy
Sizeable, alternative place to stay to Cortina. Negligible local slopes, though.
1010m; slopes 1010–1380m
🚡9 ↟12km

Sappada Italy
Isolated resort close to the Austrian border below Lienz.
1215m; slopes 1215–2050m
🚡17 ↟21km

Sappee Finland
Resort within easy reach of Helsinki, popular with boarders and telemarkers. Lake views. 🚡7

Sarnano Italy
Main resort in the Macerata region near Adriatic Riviera. Valley village with ski slopes accessed by lift.
540m; 🚡9 ↟11km

Le Sauze France
Fine area near Barcelonnette, sadly remote from airports.
1400m; slopes 1400–2440m
🚡23 ↟65km

Sauze d'Oulx 405
⊠ Airtours, Avant-ski, Chalets 'Unlimited', Crystal, Equity Ski, First Choice Ski, Independent Ski Links, Inghams, Neilson, Panorama Holidays, Rocketski, Ski Arrangements, Thomson Ski & Snowboarding

Savognin Switzerland
Pretty village with a good mid-sized area; a good base for the nearby resorts of St Moritz, Davos/Klosters and Flims.
1200m; slopes 1200–2715m
🚡17 ↟80km

Scheffau 174
Rustic beauty not far from Söll.
⊠ Crystal, Esprit Ski, Ski Wild, Thomson Ski & Snowboarding

Schia Italy
Very limited area of short runs – the only ski area near Parma. No village.
1245m; slopes 1245–1415m
🚡7 ↟15km

Schilpario Italy
One of many little areas near Bergamo.
1125m; slopes 1125–1635m
🚡5 ↟15km

Schladming 168
⊠ Crystal, Equity Ski, Interhome, Made to Measure Holidays, Rocketski, Sloping Off

Schönried 453
A cheaper and quieter resort alternative to staying in Gstaad.
⊠ Interhome

Schoppernau Austria
A scattered farming community, one of two main areas in Bregenzerwald north-west of Lech.
860m; slopes 860–2060m
🚡8 ↟37km

Schröcken Austria
Bregenzerwald area village close to the German border.
1260m; slopes 1260–2050m
🚡14 ↟60km

Schruns 152
Pleasant little town at the heart of the Montafon region, south-west of Lech.
⊠ Interhome

Schüttdorf 195
Ordinary dormitory satellite of Zell am See, with easy access to the shared ski area.
⊠ Airtours

Schwarzach im Pongau Austria
Riverside village with rail links. There are limited slopes at Goldegg; Wagrain (Salzburger Sportwelt) and Grossarl (Gastein valley) are also nearby.
600m

Schwaz Austria
Valley town beside the Inn with a lift into varied terrain shared with village of Pill and its mountain outpost, Hochpillberg.
540m; slopes 540–2030m
🚡6 ↟10km

Schweitzer USA
Excellent small family resort in the Rockies, near Spokane (Washington state), but long journey (from UK) a drawback. Low altitude but snow-sure.
1215m; slopes 1215–1945m
🚡6 ↟2350 acres
⊠ AmeriCan Ski

Scopello Italy
Low area close to the Aosta valley, worth considering for a day trip in bad weather.
slopes 690–1700m
🚡6 ↟35km

Scuol Switzerland
Year-round spa resort close to Austria and Italy, with an impressive range of terrain.
1250m; slopes 1250–2785m
🚡15 ↟80km

Searchmont Resort Canada
Ontario area with modern lift system and 95% snowmaking. Fine Lake Superior views.
275m; slopes 275–485m
🚡4 ↟65 acres

Sedrun Switzerland
Charming, unspoiled old village on the Glacier Express rail route close to Andermatt, with fine terrain amid glorious scenery.
1440m; slopes 1450–2350m
🚡12 ↟50km

Seefeld 125
⊠ Crystal, Inghams, Interhome, Made to Measure Holidays, Thomson Ski & Snowboarding, Waymark Holidays

Le Seignus-d'Allos France
Close to La Foux-d'Allos (which shares large area with Pra-Loup) and has own little area, too.
1400m; slopes 1400–2425m
🚡13 ↟47km

Sella Nevea Italy
Limited but developing resort in a beautiful setting on the Slovenian border. Summer glacier nearby.
1140m; slopes 1190–1800m
🚡11 ↟8km
⊠ Sloping Off

Selva/Sella Ronda 410
⊠ Avant-ski, Bladon Lines, Chalets 'Unlimited', Crystal, Esprit Ski, First Choice Ski, Independent Ski Links, Inghams, Momentum Ski, Ski Arrangements, Ski Total, Thomson Ski & Snowboarding

Selvino Italy
Closest resort to Bergamo.
960m; slopes 960–1400m
🚡9 ↟20km

Semmering Austria
Long-established winter sports resort set in pretty scenery, 100km/62 miles from Vienna, towards Graz. Mostly intermediate terrain.
1000m; slopes 1000–1340m
🚡5 ↟14km
⊠ Slovenija Pursuits

Les Sept-Laux France
Ugly, user-friendly family resort near Grenoble. Pretty slopes for all grades.
1350m; slopes 1350–2400m
🚡25 ↟100km
⊠ Lagrange Holidays

Serfaus Austria
Charming traffic-free village (with underground people-mover to get you to the lifts) at the foot of a long, narrow, relatively snow-sure ski area, linked to Fiss. There are few challenging slopes for experts, but it is a good area for touring. Most of the area is ideal for intermediates and the nursery slopes are good. The 60km/37 miles of cross-country trails include very pretty loops at altitude. Facilities for children are excellent. Most accommodation is in hotels, and restaurants are mainly hotel-based. Après-ski is lively and traditional, but there's not much to do off the slopes, apart from some beautiful walks.
1430m; slopes 1200–2700m
🚡42 ↟160km
⊠ Alpine Tours, Interhome, Made to Measure Holidays

Serrada Italy
Very limited area near Trento.
slopes 1250–1605m 🚡5
⊠ Alpine Tours, Equity Ski

Serre-Chevalier 321
⊠ Airtours, Alpine Answers Select, Avant-ski, Bladon Lines, Chalets 'Unlimited', Club Med, Crystal, Equity Ski, Erna Low, First Choice Ski, Handmade Holidays, Hannibals, Independent Ski Links, Inghams, Interhome, Lagrange Holidays, Made to Measure Holidays, Neilson, Panorama Holidays, Rocketski, Ski Arrangements, Ski Expectations, Ski France, Ski Independence, Ski Leisure Direction, Ski Life, Ski Miquel, Ski Supreme, Skiworld, Sloping Off, Solo's, Thomson Ski & Snowboarding, Tops Ski Chalets and Club Hotels

Sesto Italy
Dolomite village on the road to Cortina, surrounded by pretty little areas.
1310m
🚡31 ↟50km

Sestola Italy
Appennine village a short drive from Pisa and Florence with its pistes, some way above, almost completely equipped with snowmakers.
900m; slopes 1280–1975m
🚡23 ↟50km

Sestriere 418
⊠ Alpine Answers Select, Club Med, Crystal, Equity Ski, Inghams, Interhome, Momentum Ski, Neilson, Rocketski, Ski Arrangements, Ski Weekend, Thomson Ski & Snowboarding

Shames Mountain Canada
Remote spot inland from coastal town of Prince Rupert and with impressive snowfall record. Deep powder.
670m; slopes 670–1195m
3 183 acres

Shawnee Peak USA
Small area near Bethel and Sunday River renowned for its night skiing. Spectacular views. Mostly groomed cruising.
185m; slopes 185–580m
5 225 acres

Shemshak Iran
Most popular of the three mountain resorts within easy reach of Teheran (60km/36 miles). Packed at weekends, though few go to ski.
3600m

Shiga Kogen Japan
Largest area in Japan, the site of Nagano's 1998 Olympic skiing events and including 21 individual resorts.
930m; slopes 1220–2300m
73 130km

Showdown USA
Intermediate area in Montana cut out of forest north of Bozeman. 50km/30 miles to the nearest hotel.
2065m; slopes 2065–2490m
4 640 acres

Sierra-at-Tahoe 506
Made to Measure Holidays, Ski The American Dream

Sierra Nevada 636
Crystal, Independent Ski Links, Thomson Ski & Snowboarding

Sierra Summit USA
Sierra Nevada area accessible only from the west. 100% snowmaking.
2160m; slopes 2160–2645m
8 250 acres

Silbertal 152
Low secluded village in the Montafon area, linked to Schruns. A good base for touring numerous areas.

Sils Maria 464
Pretty lakeside village, linked to the St Moritz Corvatsch slopes via a lift to Furtschellas.
Inntravel

Silvaplana 464
Pretty lakeside village near St Moritz, a short drive from the lift connections.
Inntravel

Silver Creek USA
Child-oriented resort close to Winter Park. Low snowfall record for Colorado.
2490m; slopes 2490–2795m
5 250 acres

Silver Mountain USA
Northern Idaho area near delightful resort town of Coeur d'Alene. Best for experts, but plenty for intermediates too.
1215m; slopes 1215–1915m
6 1500 acres

Silver Star 595
AmeriCan Ski, Crystal, Frontier Ski, Made to Measure Holidays, Ski Activity, Ski All America, Ski Independence, Ski Line, Ski Safari, Ski The American Dream

Silverthorne USA
Factory outlet town on main road close to Keystone and Breckenridge. Good budget base for skiing those resorts plus Vail and Beaver Creek.
AmeriCan Ski

Silverton USA
Expert-only area in southern Colorado that used to be heli-ski country. Served by one lift. Avalanche transceiver, shovel and probe compulsory.
3170m; slopes 3170–3750m 1

Sinaia 641

Sipapu USA
Great little New Mexico area that would be better known if it had more reliable snow-cover. Mostly tree-lined runs. Nice day out from Taos when conditions are good.
slopes 2500–2765m
3 40 acres

Siviez 470
A quieter and cheaper base for skiing Verbier's Four Valleys circuit.
Interhome

Sixt-Fer-a-Cheval 262
Traditional village near Samoëns, at foot of a new run down from the Flaine area. Own little area across the valley, too.
AmeriCan Ski, Lagrange Holidays, Peak Retreats

Sjusjøen Norway
Cluster of hotels in deep forest close to Lillehammer. Some Alpine facilities but better for cross-country.
885m; slopes 1000–1090m
2 2km
Inntravel, Waymark Holidays

Ski Apache USA
Apache-owned area south of Albuquerque noted for groomed steeps. Panoramic views. Nearest lodging in charming Ruidoso.
2925m; slopes 2925–3505m
11 750 acres

Ski Cooper USA
Small area close to historic Old West town of Leadville. Good ski/sightseeing day out from nearby Vail, Beaver Creek and Copper Mountain.
slopes 3200–3565m 4

Ski Windham USA
2 hours from New York City and second only to Hunter for weekend crowds. Decent slopes by eastern standards.
485m; slopes 485–940m
7 230 acres

Smokovec Slovakia
Spa town with small modern centre near Poprad, with three small areas known collectively as High Tatras. Funicular railway and snowmaking facilities.
1480m; slopes 1000–1500m
6 4km

Smugglers' Notch 585
Ski Safari, Ski The American Dream

Snowbasin 564
AmeriCan Ski

Snowbird 566
AmeriCan Ski, Made to Measure Holidays, Ski All America, Ski Independence, Ski The American Dream, United Vacations Ski Freedom USA & Canada

Snowbowl (Arizona) USA
One of America's oldest areas, near Flagstaff, Arizona, atop an extinct volcano and with stunning desert views. Good snowfall record.
2805m; slopes 2805–3505m
5 135 acres

Snowbowl (Montana) USA
Montana area renowned for powder, outside lively town of Missoula. Intermediate pistes plus 700 acres of extreme slopes. Grizzly Chute is the ultimate challenge.
1520m; slopes 1520–2315m
4 1400 acres

Snowmass 516
Purpose-built village with big mountain near Aspen.
Alpine Answers Select, AmeriCan Ski, Made to Measure Holidays, Ski All America, Ski Independence, Ski The American Dream, United Vacations Ski Freedom USA & Canada

Snow Summit USA
San Bernardino National Forest ski area near Palm Springs. Lovely lake views. 100% snowmaking. High-capacity lift system for weekend crowds.
2135m; slopes 2135–2500m
12 230 acres

Snow Valley USA
Area quite near Palm Springs. Fine desert views. High-capacity lift system copes with weekend crowds better than nearby Big Bear.
2040m; slopes 2040–2390m
11 230 acres

Solda Italy
The other side of the Stelvio Pass from Bormio. Very long airport transfers.
1905m; slopes 1905–2625m
19 25km

Sölden 172
Made to Measure Holidays, Neilson, Thomson Ski & Snowboarding

Soldeu 102
Airtours, Chalets 'Unlimited', Club Pavilion, Crystal, Directski.com, First Choice Ski, Independent Ski Links, Inghams, Lagrange Holidays, Neilson, Panorama Holidays, Ski Club of Great Britain, Thomson Ski & Snowboarding, Top Deck

Solitude 551
AmeriCan Ski, Ski Independence, Ski The American Dream

Söll 174
Airtours, Crystal, Directski.com, First Choice Ski, Inghams, Interhome, Neilson, Panorama Holidays, Ski Hillwood, Ski Wild, Thomson Ski & Snowboarding, Uptoyou.com

Sommand France
Purpose-built base that shares area with Praz-de-Lys.
1420m; slopes 1200–1800m
22 50km

Sorenberg Switzerland
Popular weekend retreat between Berne and Lucerne, with a high proportion of steep, low runs.
1165m; slopes 1165–2350m
18 50km

South Lake Tahoe 506
Tacky base for skiing Heavenly, with cheap lodging, traffic and gambling.

Spindleruv Mlyn Czech Republic
Largest Giant Mountains region resort but with few facilities serving several little low areas.
750m; slopes 750–1300m
9 25km

Spital am Pyhrn Austria
Small village near Hinterstoder in Upper Austria, a bus-ride from its limited intermediate slopes at Wurzeralm. From the valley station a 3km/2 mile funicular goes up to a mid-mountain col with several restaurants and nursery slopes. Lifts and runs go off from here in several directions over pleasantly wooded intermediate terrain; the blues are tough, so transition from the nursery slopes is not easy. On the flat Teichlboden (1370m/4,500ft) beyond the col there are cross-country loops. The local lift pass also covers the slopes of Höss and Bärenalm at Hinterstoder, a short drive away.
650m; slopes 810–1870m
8 14km

Spittal/Drau Austria
Historic Carinthian town with a limited area starting a lift-ride above it. A good day trip from Bad Kleinkirchheim or from Slovenia.
555m; slopes 1650–2140m
12 22km

Resort index / directory

697

Sportgastein 114
Mountain village with some of
the more interesting skiing in
the Badgastein valley.

Squaw Valley 506
✉ AmeriCan Ski, American Ski
Classics, Crystal, Made to
Measure Holidays, Ski Activity,
Ski All America, Ski
Independence, Ski Safari, Ski
The American Dream, United
Vacations Ski Freedom USA &
Canada

Stafal 402
Tiny, isolated village, with good
access to the Monterosa Ski
area.

St Andrä im Lungau Austria
Valley-junction village ideally
placed for one of the longest,
most snow-sure cross-country
networks in Europe. Close to the
Tauern pass and to St Michael.
1045m

St Anton 180
✉ Airtours, Albus Travel, Alpine
Answers Select, Alpine Events,
Alpine Tours, Alpine Weekends,
Avant-ski, Bladon Lines, Chalet
World, Chalets 'Unlimited',
Crystal, Directski.com, Elegant
Resorts, First Choice Ski,
FlexiSki, Independent Ski Links,
Inghams, Lotus Supertravel,
Made to Measure Holidays,
Mark Warner, Momentum Ski,
Neilson, Simply Ski, Ski
Activity, Ski Addiction, Ski
Arrangements, Ski Expectations,
Ski Line, Ski Solutions, Ski
Total, Ski Wild, Ski-Val,
Skiworld, St Anton Ski
Company, The Corporate Ski
Company, The Ski Company,
Thomson Ski & Snowboarding,
White Roc

St Cergue Switzerland
Limited resort less than an hour
from Geneva, good for families
with young children.
1045m; slopes 1045–1700m
🚡9 ⛷20km

St Christoph 180
Small village on Arlberg pass
above St Anton.
✉ Elegant Resorts, Inghams,
Made to Measure Holidays,
Powder Byrne, Slovenija
Pursuits

St-Colomban-des-Villards 335
Small resort in next side valley
to La Toussuire, now part of the
Sybelles area.

Steamboat 536
✉ Alpine Answers Select,
American Ski Classics, Chalets
'Unlimited', Crystal, Lotus
Supertravel, Made to Measure
Holidays, Ski Activity, Ski All
America, Ski Independence, Ski
Line, Ski Safari, Ski The
American Dream, Skiworld,
United Vacations Ski Freedom
USA & Canada

Ste-Foy-Tarentaise 329
✉ Alpine Weekends, Chalet
Number One, Independent Ski
Links, Peak Leisure, Premiere
Neige, Ski Arrangements, Ski
Weekend, Weekends in Val
d'Isère

Steinach Austria
Pleasant village in picturesque
surroundings, just off the
autobahn near the Brenner Pass.
An easy outing from Innsbruck.
1050m; slopes 1050–2205m
🚡6 ⛷15km
✉ Alpine Tours

Stevens Pass USA
A day trip from Seattle, and
accommodation 60km/35 miles
away in Bavarian-style town
Leavenworth. Low snowfall and
no snowmakers. Mostly
intermediate slopes.
1235m; slopes 1235–1785m
🚡14 ⛷1125 acres

St-François-Longchamp 364
Sunny, gentle slopes, with a
couple of harder runs. Linked to
Valmorel.
✉ Lagrange Holidays, Peak
Retreats, Ski Independence, Ski
Life

St Gallenkirch 152
Smaller, less attractive village
than Gaschurn, with which it
shares a sizeable intermediate
area in the Montafon valley.

St-Gervais 274
Small town sharing its ski area
with Megève and Chamonix.
✉ APT Holidays Ltd,
Interhome, Lagrange Holidays,
Peak Retreats, Snowcoach

St Jakob in Defereggen Austria
Unspoiled traditional village in a
pretty, sunny valley close to
Lienz and Heiligenblut, and with
a good proportion of high-
altitude slopes.
1400m; slopes 1400–2520m
🚡9 ⛷34km

St Jakob in Haus Austria
Snowy village with its own
slopes. Fieberbrunn, Waidring
and St Johann are nearby.
855m; slopes 855–1500m
🚡8 ⛷16km

St-Jean-d'Arves 335
Small traditional village south of
the Maurienne valley that is now
linked with the slopes of St-
Sorlin-d'Arves, La Toussuire and
Le Corbier, to form Les Sybelles.
✉ Crystal, Lagrange Holidays,
Peak Retreats, Ski France, Ski
Leisure Direction, Ski Life,
Thomson Ski & Snowboarding

St-Jean-de-Sixt 239
Traditional hamlet, a cheap base
for La Clusaz and Le Grand-
Bornand (3km/2 miles to both).

St-Jean-Montclar France
Small village at the foot of
thickly forested slopes. Good
day out from nearby Pra-Loup.
1300m; slopes 1300–2500m
🚡18 ⛷50km
✉ Lagrange Holidays

St Johann im Pongau Austria
Bustling, lively town with a
small area of its own. More
importantly, an extensive three-
valley lift network starts 4km/2
miles away at Alpendorf, linking
via Wagrain to Flachau – all part
of the Salzburger Sportwelt ski
pass area that our figures relate
to.
650m; slopes 800–2285m
🚡59 ⛷200km

St Johann in Tirol 188
✉ Crystal, Directski.com, Ski
Wild, Snowscape, Thomson Ski
& Snowboarding, Top Deck

St Lary Espiaube 371
✉ Crystal

St-Lary-Soulan 371
✉ Lagrange Holidays

St Leonhard in Pitztal
Village beneath a fine glacier in
the Oetz area, accessed by
underground funicular.

St Luc Switzerland
Quiet, unspoiled rustic village in
the Val d'Anniviers on the south
side of the Rhône valley, with
plenty of high, easy slopes
(shared with Chandolin) served
almost entirely by drags. Most
of the slopes are above the
nursery area at Tignousa
(2180m/7,150ft), reached by
funicular – also the site of an
astronomical observatory. Valley
pass also covers Zinal, Grimentz
and Vercorin – 200km/125 miles
of runs in total.
1650m; slopes 1660–3025m
🚡16 ⛷75km
✉ Inntravel

St Margarethen Austria
Valley village near Styria/
Carinthia border, sharing slopes
with higher Katschberg.
1065m; slopes 1075–2210m
🚡14 ⛷50km

St Martin bei Lofer Austria
Traditional cross-country skiing
in a lovely setting beneath the
impressive Loferer Steinberge
massif. Alpine slopes at Lofer.
635m

St-Martin-de-Belleville 332
✉ Equity Ski, Handmade
Holidays, Independent Ski
Links, Les Chalets de St Martin,
Rocketski, Ski Total, Thomson
Ski & Snowboarding,
Uptoyou.com

St Martin in Tennengebirge
Austria
Highest village in the Dachstein-
West region near Salzburg. It
has limited slopes of its own but
nearby Annaberg has an
interesting area.
1000m; slopes 1000–1350m
🚡5 ⛷4km

St-Maurice-sur-Moselle France
One of several areas near
Strasbourg. No snowmakers.
550m; slopes 900–1250m
🚡8 ⛷24km

St Michael im Lungau Austria
Quiet, unspoiled village in the
Tauern pass snowpocket with an
uncrowded but disjointed
intermediate area. Close to
Obertauern and Wagrain.
1075m; slopes 1075–2360m
🚡26 ⛷60km
✉ Alpine Tours, Equity Ski,
Rocketski

St Moritz 464
✉ Alpine Events, Alpine
Weekends, Club Med, Crystal,
Elegant Resorts, FlexiSki,
Headwater Holidays,
Independent Ski Links,
Inghams, Interhome, Kuoni,
Made to Measure Holidays,
Momentum Ski, Plus Travel, Ski
Club of Great Britain, Ski
Solutions, Ski Weekend,
SkiGower, Swiss Travel Service,
The Corporate Ski Company

St-Nicolas-de-Véroce 274
Small hamlet with a handful of
simple hotels on the northern
fringes of the Megève network.

St-Nizier-du-Moucherotte
France
One of seven little resorts just
west of Grenoble. Unspoiled,
inexpensive place to tour.
Villard-de-Lans is main resort.

Stoneham 632
✉ Frontier Ski, Inghams, Ski
All America, Ski Safari, Ski The
American Dream

Stoos Switzerland
Small, unspoiled village an hour
from Zürich. Overcrowded at
weekends. Magnificent views of
Lake Lucerne.
1300m; slopes 570–1920m 🚡7

Storlien Sweden
Small family resort amid
magnificent wilderness scenery.
One hour from Trondheim, 30
minutes from Åre.
600m; slopes 600–790m
🚡7 ⛷15km

Stowe 587
✉ Chalets 'Unlimited', Crystal,
Inghams, Made to Measure
Holidays, Rocketski, Ski All
America, Ski Arrangements, Ski
Independence, Ski Line, Ski
Safari, Ski The American
Dream, Trailfinders, United
Vacations Ski Freedom USA &
Canada, Virgin Ski

St-Pierre-de-Chartreuse
France
Locals' weekend place near
Grenoble. Unreliable snow.
900m; slopes 900–1800m
🚡14 ⛷35km

Stratton 578

Strobl Austria
Close to St Wolfgang in a
beautiful lakeside setting. There
are slopes at nearby St Gilgen
and Postalm.
545m; slopes 545–1510m
🚡9 ⛷12km

St-Sorlin-d'Arves 335
✉ AmeriCan Ski, Crystal, Lagrange Holidays, Peak Retreats, Ski France, Ski Life, Thomson Ski & Snowboarding

St Stephan Switzerland
Unspoiled old farming village at the foot of the largest sector of slopes in the area around Gstaad.
995m; slopes 950–2155m
♨ 69 ⬆ 250km

Stuben 140
Small, unspoiled village linked to St Anton.

St Veit im Pongau Austria
Spa resort with limited slopes at Goldegg; Wagrain (Salzburger Sportwelt) and Grossarl (Gastein valley) are nearby.
765m

St-Veran France
Said to be the highest 'real' village in Europe, and full of charm. Close to Serre-Chevalier and the Milky Way. Snow-reliable cross-country skiing.
2040m; slopes 2040–2800m
♨ 15 ⬆ 30km

St Wolfgang Austria
Charming lakeside resort near Salzburg, some way from any slopes, best for a relaxing winter holiday with one or two days on the slopes.
540m; slopes 665–1350m
♨ 9 ⬆ 17km
✉ Airtours, Crystal, Inghams, Thomson Ski & Snowboarding

Sugar Bowl USA
Exposed area north of Lake Tahoe with highest snowfall in California, best for experts. Lodging in Truckee but Squaw Valley nearby. Weekend crowds.
2095m; slopes 2095–2555m
♨ 8 ⬆ 1500 acres

Sugarbush 578
✉ Ski Arrangements, Ski Success

Sugarloaf 578
✉ American Ski Classics, Ski Success

Summit at Snoqualmie USA
Four areas – Summit East, Summit Central, Summit West and Alpental – with interlinked lifts. Damp weather and wet snow are major drawbacks.
slopes 915–1645m
♨ 24 ⬆ 2000 acres

Sun Alpina Japan
Collective name for three ski areas four hours away from Tokyo. ♨ 20

Sundance 551
✉ AmeriCan Ski, American Ski Classics, Simply Ski, Ski All America, Ski Independence, Ski Safari, Ski The American Dream

Sunday River 589
✉ Crystal, Equity Ski, Rocketski, Ski Independence, Ski Safari, Ski Success, Ski The American Dream, Thomson Ski & Snowboarding

Sunlight Mountain Resort USA
Quiet little area worth the easy trip from Vail to get away from its crowds for a day. Varied terrain. Good snowboard park. $300,000 of capital improvements in 2002/03.
2405m; slopes 2405–3015m
♨ 4 ⬆ 460 acres

Sun Peaks 595
✉ AmeriCan Ski, Frontier Ski, Made to Measure Holidays, Ski Activity, Ski All America, Ski Club of Great Britain, Ski Independence, Ski Line, Ski Safari, Ski The American Dream

Sunrise Park USA
Arizona's largest area, operated by Apaches. Slopes are spread over three mountains; best for novices and leisurely intermediates.
2805m; slopes 2805–3500m
♨ 12 ⬆ 800 acres

Sunshine Village 598
One-hotel mountain station with Banff's second-largest ski area on its doorstep.
✉ Ski The American Dream

Sun Valley 576
✉ AmeriCan Ski, American Ski Classics, Ski Activity, Ski All America, Ski Independence

Suomu Finland
A lodge (no village) right on the Arctic Circle with a few slopes but mostly a ski-touring place.
140m; slopes 140–410m ♨ 3

Superbagnères France
Little more than a particularly French-dominated Club Med; best for a low-cost, low-effort family trip to the Pyrenees.
1880m; slopes 1440–2260m
♨ 16 ⬆ 35km
✉ Lagrange Holidays

Super-Besse France
Purpose-built resort amid spectacular extinct-volcano scenery. Shares area with Mont-Dore. Limited village.
1350m; slopes 1300–1850m
♨ 22 ⬆ 45km
✉ Lagrange Holidays

Superdévoluy France
Purpose-built but friendly family resort, consisting of a few huge apartment blocks, a few km north-west of Gap, with a sizeable intermediate area shared with La Joue-du-Loup.
1500m; slopes 1500–2510m
♨ 32 ⬆ 100km
✉ Lagrange Holidays

Supermolina Spain
Dreary, purpose-built satellite of Pyrenean resort of La Molina, with a reasonable sized area of its own and linked to the slopes of Masella to form area called Alp 2500.
1700m; slopes 1600–2535m
♨ 29 ⬆ 100km

Les Sybelles 335

Tahko Finland
Largest resort in southern Finland. Plenty of intermediate slopes in an attractive, wooded, frozen-lake setting. ♨ 9

Tahoe City 506
Small lakeside accommodation base for visiting nearby Alpine Meadows and Squaw Valley.

Talisman Mountain Resort Canada
One of the best areas in the Toronto region, but with a relatively low lift capacity. 100% snowmaking.
235m; slopes 235–420m ♨ 8

Tamsweg Austria
Large cross-country village with rail links in snowy region close to Tauern Pass and St Michael.
1025m

La Tania 340
✉ Airtours, Alpine Action, Avant-ski, Chalet World, Chalets 'Unlimited', Crystal, Erna Low, Eurotunnel Motoring Holidays, French Freedom Holidays, Independent Ski Links, Lagrange Holidays, Le Ski, Neilson, Silver Ski, Ski Amis, Ski Arrangements, Ski Beat, Ski Deep, Ski France, Ski Hame, Ski Independence, Ski Leisure Direction, Ski Life, Ski Line, Ski Weekends & Board Breaks, Snowline, Thomson Ski & Snowboarding

Taos 568
✉ AmeriCan Ski, American Ski Classics, Made to Measure Holidays, Ski Activity, Ski Independence, Ski The American Dream

Tärnaby-Hemavan Sweden
Twin resorts with own airport. Snow-sure.
slopes 465–1135m
♨ 13 ⬆ 44km

El Tarter 102
Relatively quiet, convenient alternative to Soldeu, with which it shares its slopes.
✉ Airtours, Club Pavilion, First Choice Ski, Panorama Holidays

Tarvisio Italy
Interesting, animated old town bordering Austria and Slovenia. A major cross-country base with fairly limited Alpine slopes.
750m; slopes 750–1860m
♨ 12 ⬆ 15km

Täsch 487
The final base accessible by road on the way to car-free Zermatt – you take the train the rest of the way.
✉ Interhome

Tauplitz Austria
Traditional village at the foot of an interestingly varied area north of Schladming.
900m; slopes 900–2000m
♨ 18 ⬆ 25km

Telluride 538
✉ Alpine Answers Select, AmeriCan Ski, American Ski Classics, Made to Measure Holidays, Ski All America, Ski Independence, Ski Safari, Ski The American Dream, Skiworld, United Vacations Ski Freedom USA & Canada

Temù Italy
Sheltered hamlet near Passo Tonale. Worth a visit in bad weather.
1155m; slopes 1155–1955m
♨ 4 ⬆ 5km

Tengendai Japan
Tiny area three hours by train and bus from Tokyo. One of Japan's best snow records, including occasional powder. ♨ 5

Termas de Chillan Chile
Ski and spa resort 480km/300 miles south of Santiago. Base village has lodgings or you can stay at Las Trancas a few minutes' drive away.
slopes 1600–2700m
♨ 9 ⬆ 35km
✉ Momentum Ski, Scott Dunn Latin America, Ski Safari

Termignon France
Traditional rustic village with good slopes of its own. A good base for touring Maurienne valley resorts such as Valloire and Val-Cenis.
1300m; slopes 1300–2500m
♨ 6 ⬆ 35km
✉ Lagrange Holidays

Terminillo Italy
Purpose-built resort 100km/62 miles from Rome with a worthwhile area when its lower runs have snow cover.
1500m; slopes 1500–2210m
♨ 15 ⬆ 40km

Cedars Lebanon
The largest of Lebanon's ski areas, 130km/80 miles inland from Beirut. Good, open slopes with a surprisingly long season.
1850m; slopes 2100–2700m ♨ 5

Thollon-les-Mémises France
Attractive base for a relaxed holiday. Own little area and close to Portes du Soleil.
1000m; slopes 1600–2000m
♨ 19 ⬆ 50km
✉ Lagrange Holidays

Thredbo 653

La Thuile 420
✉ Avant-ski, Chalets 'Unlimited', Crystal, First Choice Ski, Independent Ski Links, Inghams, Interski, Neilson, Rocketski, Ski Arrangements, Thomson Ski & Snowboarding

Thyon 2000 470
Extremely limited ski-from-the-door mid-mountain resort above Veysonnaz in the Verbier ski area.

Resort index / directory

699

Valmeinier 271
Spread-out resort in the Maurienne valley, with links over a ridge to Valloire.
✉ Crystal, Erna Low, French Freedom Holidays, Lagrange Holidays, Ski Independence, Ski Leisure Direction, Ski Life, Snowcoach, Thomson Ski & Snowboarding

Valmorel 364
✉ Airtours, Chalets 'Unlimited', Crystal, Erna Low, Independent Ski Links, Lagrange Holidays, Made to Measure Holidays, Neilson, Ski Arrangements, Ski Independence, Ski Leisure Direction, Ski Life, Ski Link, Ski Supreme, Thomson Ski & Snowboarding

Val Senales Italy
Top-of-the-mountain hotel, the highest in the Alps, in the Dolomites near Merano.
3250m; slopes 2005–3250m
⛷ 10 ⛷ 24km

Val-Thorens 366
✉ Airtours, Chalet World, Chalets 'Unlimited', Club Med, Crystal, Equity Ski, Erna Low, Eurotunnel Motoring Holidays, First Choice Ski, French Freedom Holidays, Independent Ski Links, Inghams, Interhome, Lagrange Holidays, Made to Measure Holidays, Neilson, Panorama Holidays, Rocketski, Silver Ski, Ski Activity, Ski Arrangements, Ski Club of Great Britain, Ski Expectations, Ski France, Ski Independence, Ski Leisure Direction, Ski Life, Ski Line, Ski Supreme, Ski Total, Ski Weekend, Skiworld, Thomson Ski & Snowboarding, Uptoyou.com

Valtournenche 381
Cheaper alternative to Cervinia, with genuine Italian atmosphere, and access to the extensive area.

Vandans 152
Sizeable working village well placed for visiting all the Montafon areas.

Vars 316
Large, convenient purpose-built resort linked to Risoul.
✉ Interhome, Lagrange Holidays, Ski Supreme, Tops Ski Chalets and Club Hotels

Vaujany 205
Tiny, rustic village with lift accessing the heart of the Alpe-d'Huez ski area.
✉ AmeriCan Ski, Erna Low, Lagrange Holidays, Peak Retreats, Ski Independence, Ski Peak

Vegas Resort USA
Area formerly known as Lee Canyon, cut from forest only 50 minutes' drive from Las Vegas. Height and snowmaking gives fairly reliable snow. Night skiing.
2590m; slopes 2590–2840m
⛷ 3 ⛷ 200 acres

Vemdalen 649
✉ Neilson

Vemdalsskalet 649

Venosc France
Captivating tiny village of cobbled streets, ancient church and craft shops.

Vent Austria
High, remote Oztal village known mainly as a touring base, with just enough lift-served skiing to warrant a day trip from nearby Obergurgl.
1900m; slopes 1900–2680m
⛷ 4 ⛷ 15km

Ventron France
One of several areas near Strasbourg. No snowmakers.
630m; slopes 900–1110m
⛷ 8 ⛷ 15km

Verbier 470
✉ Airtours, Alpine Answers Select, Alpine Events, Alpine Weekends, Avant-ski, Bladon Lines, Chalet World, Chalets 'Unlimited', Crystal, Descent International, Elegant Resorts, Erna Low, First Choice Ski, FlexiSki, Independent Ski Links, Inghams, Interhome, Made to Measure Holidays, Momentum Ski, Peak Ski, Simply Ski, Ski Activity, Ski Club of Great Britain, Ski Expectations, Ski Independence, Ski Line, Ski Solutions, Ski Total, Ski Verbier, Ski Weekend, Ski with Julia, Skiworld, Swiss Travel Service, The Corporate Ski Company, Thomson Ski & Snowboarding, Vertical Reality at Verbier Ltd, White Roc

Vercorin Switzerland
Cluster of picture-postcard chalets on a shelf overlooking the Valais, reached by roundabout road or cable-car from near Chalais. Mix of wooded and open intermediate slopes served by a gondola and drags. Valley pass also covers Zinal, Grimentz and St Luc/Chandolin – 200km/125 miles of runs in total. The village has a natural ice-rink.
1330m; slopes 1330–2400m
⛷ 9 ⛷ 35km

Verditz Austria
One of several small, mostly mountain-top areas overlooking the town of Villach.
675m; slopes 675–2165m
⛷ 5 ⛷ 17km
✉ Sloping Off

Vex Switzerland
Major village in unspoiled, attractive setting south of Sion. Verbier slopes accessed nearby at Mayens-de-l'Ours.
900m

Veysonnaz 470
Little, old village within Verbier's Four Valleys network.

Vic-sur-Mere France
Charming village with fine architecture, beneath Super-Lioran ski area. Beautiful extinct-volcano scenery.
680m; slopes 1250–1850m
⛷ 24 ⛷ 60km

Viehhofen Austria
Cheaper place to stay when visiting Saalbach. It is 3km/2 miles from the Schönleiten gondola, and there is a run back to the village from the Asitz section.
860m

Vigo di Fassa Italy
Best base for the Fassa valley, with Sella Ronda access via nearby Campitello.
1430m; slopes 1465–2060m
⛷ 8 ⛷ 25km

La Villa 410
Quiet Sella Ronda village in pretty setting, surrounded by mostly very easy skiing.

Villacher Alpe-Dobratsch Austria
One of several small, mostly mountain-top areas overlooking the town of Villach.
900m; slopes 980–2165m
⛷ 8 ⛷ 15km

Villar-d'Arêne France
Tiny area on main road between La Grave and Serre-Chevalier. Empty, immaculately groomed, short easy runs, plus a couple of hotels.
1650m

Villard-de-Lans France
Unspoiled, lively, traditional village west of Grenoble. Snow-sure, thanks to snowmaking.
1050m; slopes 1160–2170m
⛷ 29 ⛷ 130km
✉ AmeriCan Ski, Lagrange Holidays, Rocketski

Villard-Reculas 205
Rustic village on periphery of Alpe-d'Huez ski area, with few local amenities.

Villaroger 213
Rustic hamlet with direct links up to Arc 2000 and excellent runs back down.

Villarrica-Pucón Chile
Ski area on side of active volcano in southern Chile, 800km/500 miles south of Santiago. Lodgings are at Pucon village 30 minutes away from the slopes.
1200m; slopes 1200–2080m ⛷ 9

Villars 480
✉ Alpine Events, Club Med, Crystal, Erna Low, Inghams, Interhome, Kuoni, Made to Measure Holidays, Momentum Ski, Plus Travel, Powder Byrne, Ski Independence, Ski Weekend, Swiss Travel Service, The Corporate Ski Company, Thomson Ski & Snowboarding

Vipiteno Italy
Bargain-shopping town close to Brenner Pass.
960m; slopes 960–2100m
⛷ 12 ⛷ 25km

Virgen Austria
Traditional village in a beautiful valley south of the Felbertauern tunnel. Slopes at Matrei.
1200m

Vitosha 639

Vogel 642

Vorderlanersbach 120
Small, satellite village of pretty Lanersbach, with access to Mayrhofen ski area.

Voss 645
✉ Crystal, Inghams

Vuokatti Finland
Small mountain in a remarkable setting, surrounded on three sides by lots of little lakes. Good activity base. ⛷ 8

Wagrain Austria
Traditional village at the heart of the intermediate three-valley lift system linking Flachau and Alpendorf. It's pleasant without being notably charming, mainly off the busy road linking the neighbouring resorts; it's a compact place, but the main lift bases are still a good walk apart. The slopes – wooded at the bottom, open higher up – are practically all easy/intermediate stuff, but cover a huge area almost 15km/9 miles across. Kleinarl, up the valley, is at one end of another similar three-valley system. All these resorts are covered by Salzburger Sportwelt lift-pass that our figures relate to.
900m; slopes 800–2185m
⛷ 100 ⛷ 350km

Waidring 188
Quiet, snowpocket resort near St Johann in Tirol, with good beginner slopes and easy main slopes 4km/2.5 miles away.
✉ Thomson Ski & Snowboarding

Waioru Nordic New Zealand
Specialist cross-country base just over an hour from Queenstown. Spectacular views. Overnight huts.
1600m

Wald im Pinzgau Austria
Cross-country village surrounded by Alpine areas – Gerlos, Krimml and Neukirchen – and with Pass Thurn also nearby.
885m

Wanaka 655
Quiet, diffuse village in beautiful lakeside mountain setting, with two ski areas each half an hour away.

Waterville Valley 578
✉ AmeriCan Ski

Weinebene Austria
One of many gentle little areas in Austria's easternmost ski region near the Slovenian border. No major resorts in the vicinity.
1560m; slopes 1560–1835m
▲5 ☂ 12km

Weissbach bei Lofer Austria
Traditional resort between Lofer and Saalfelden. It has no slopes of its own, but it's well placed for touring the Tirol. Kitzbühel, Saalbach, St Johann and Zell am See are nearby.
665m

Weissensee Naggeralm
Austria
Little area in eastern Austria and the location of Europe's largest frozen lake, which is used for all kinds of ice sports, including ice-golf.
930m; slopes 930–1400m
▲5 ☂ 7km

Weisspriach Austria
Hamlet on snowy pass near Obertauern that shares its area with Mauterndorf and St Michael.
1075m; slopes 1075–2360m
▲21 ☂ 60km

Wengen 482
✉ Alpine Events, Club Med, Crystal, Inghams, Kuoni, Made to Measure Holidays, Plus Travel, Re-lax Holidays, Ski Club of Great Britain, Ski Solutions, SkiGower, Swiss Travel Service, Thomson Ski & Snowboarding

Wentworth Canada
Long-established Nova Scotia area with largest accessible acreage in the Maritime Provinces. Harsh climate ensures good snow-cover despite low altitude.
55m; slopes 55–300m
▲6 ☂ 150 acres

Werfen Austria
Traditional village spoiled by the Tauern autobahn, which runs between it and the slopes. Good touring to the Dachstein West region.
620m

Werfenweng Austria
Hamlet with the advantage over main village Werfen of being away from autobahn and close to the slopes. Best for novices.
1000m; slopes 1000–1835m
▲11 ☂ 40km

Westendorf 190
✉ Inghams, Thomson Ski & Snowboarding

Whakapapa 655

Whistler 624
✉ Alpine Answers Select, AmeriCan Ski, American Ski Classics, Avant-ski, Chalet World, Chalets 'Unlimited', Crystal, Elegant Resorts, Equity Ski, Esprit Ski, First Choice Ski, Frontier Ski, Handmade Holidays, Independent Ski

Links, Inghams, Lotus Supertravel, Made to Measure Holidays, Momentum Ski, Neilson, Rocketski, Ski Activity, Ski All America, Ski Arrangements, Ski Expectations, Ski Hillwood, Ski Independence, Ski Line, Ski Miquel, Ski Safari, Ski The American Dream, Ski Total, Skiworld, Solo's, The Ski Company, Thomson Ski & Snowboarding, Trailfinders, United Vacations Ski Freedom USA & Canada, Virgin Ski

Whitecap Mountains Resort
USA
Largest area in Wisconsin, close enough to Lake Superior and Minneapolis to ensure winds and weekend crowds.
435m; slopes 435–555m
▲7 ☂ 500 acres

Whiteface Mountain USA
Varied area in New York State 15km/10 miles from attractive lakeside resort of Lake Placid. 93% snowmaking ensures good snowcover. Plenty to do off the slopes.
365m; slopes 365–1345m
▲10 ☂ 211 acres

White Pass Village USA
Closest area to Mt St Helens. Remote and uncrowded with a good snowfall record. Mostly intermediate cruising.
1370m; slopes 1370–1825m
▲6 ☂ 635 acres

Whitewater 595
✉ AmeriCan Ski

Wildcat Mountain USA
New Hampshire area infamous for bad weather, but one of the best areas on a nice day. Lodging in nearby Jackson and North Conway.
slopes 600–1250m
▲4 ☂ 225 acres

Wildhaus Switzerland
Undeveloped farming community near Liechtenstein in stunning scenery ; popular with families and serious snowboarders.
1100m; slopes 1100–2075m
▲9 ☂ 50km

Wildschönau 192
✉ Interhome

Wiler Switzerland
Main village in secluded, picturesque dead-end Lötschental, north of Rhône valley, with small but tall slopes reached by cable-car.
1420m; slopes 1420–2700m ▲6

Willamette Pass USA
US speed skiing training base in national forest near beautiful Crater Lake, Oregon. Small but varied slopes popular with weekenders.
1560m; slopes 1560–2035m
▲7 ☂ 550 acres

Williams USA
Tiny area above the main place to stay for the Grand Canyon.
slopes 2010–2270m
▲2 ☂ 50 acres

Windischgarsten Austria
Large working village in Upper Austria with cross-country trails around and downhill slopes at nearby Hinterstoder and Spital am Pyrhn.
600m

Winter Park 546
✉ Alpine Answers Select, AmeriCan Ski, American Ski Classics, Chalets 'Unlimited', Crystal, Equity Ski, First Choice Ski, Lotus Supertravel, Made to Measure Holidays, Neilson, Rocketski, Ski All America, Ski Independence, Ski Safari, Ski The American Dream, Skiworld, Thomson Ski & Snowboarding, United Vacations Ski Freedom USA & Canada, Virgin Ski

Wolf Creek USA
Remote area with highest snowfall record in Colorado. Uncrowded; wonderful powder. Great stop en route between Taos and Telluride.
3155m; slopes 3155–3590m
▲6 ☂ 800 acres
✉ AmeriCan Ski

Xonrupt France
Cross-country venue only 3km/ 2 miles from nearest Alpine slopes at Gérardmer.
715m
✉ Lagrange Holidays

Yangji Pine Korea
Modern resort an hour (60km/37 miles) south of Seoul, with runs cut out of dense forest. Gets very crowded. ▲7

Yllas 643
✉ Bladon Lines, Headwater Holidays, Inghams, Inntravel

Yong Pyeong Korea
Largest resort in Korea, also known as Dragon Valley. 200km/125 miles east of Seoul, with snowmaking on all its runs.
750m; slopes 750–1460m
▲16 ☂ 20km

Zakopane Poland
An interesting old town 100km/ 62 miles south of Kraków on the Slovakian border. Mostly intermediate slopes.
830m; slopes 1000–1960m
▲20 ☂ 10km

Zao Japan
Big area with unpredictable weather, 4 hours from Tokyo by train. Known for 'chouoh' – pines frozen into weird shapes. Hot springs.
780m; slopes 780–1660m ▲42

Zauchensee Austria
Purpose-built resort isolated at the head of its valley, at one end of big three-valley lift network linking it via Flachauwinkl to Kleinarl – all part of the Salzburger Sportwelt ski pass area that our figures relate to.
855m; slopes 800–2185m
▲59 ☂ 200km
✉ Made to Measure Holidays, Ski Hillwood, Sloping Off

Zell am See 195
✉ Airtours, Alpine Events, Crystal, Directski.com, First Choice Ski, Inghams, Interhome, Made to Measure Holidays, Neilson, Panorama Holidays, PGL Teenski, Rocketski, Ski Wild, Thomson Ski & Snowboarding

Zell im Zillertal Austria
Sprawling valley town with slopes on two nearby mountains. Now linked to higher Gerlos and Königsleiten to form a fair-sized area.
580m; slopes 930–2410m
▲40 ☂ 115km
✉ Equity Ski

Zermatt 487
✉ Alpine Answers Select, Alpine Events, Avant-ski, Bladon Lines, Chalet World, Chalets 'Unlimited', Crystal, Elegant Resorts, Erna Low, Independent Ski Links, Inghams, Interhome, Kuoni, Lotus Supertravel, Made to Measure Holidays, Momentum Ski, Plus Travel, Powder Byrne, Scott Dunn Ski, Simply Ski, Ski Club of Great Britain, Ski Expectations, Ski Independence, Ski Solutions, SkiGower, Swiss Travel Service, The Corporate Ski Company, Thomson Ski & Snowboarding, White Roc

Zinal Switzerland
Pretty, rustic village with some modern development, near the head of the Val d'Anniviers off the Valais. Cable-car up to a high area of open, steepish slopes – most runs are justifiably red or black. Excellent views. There are runs to the valley, including one excellent tough red off which an itinerary links to Grimentz, down the valley. The valley pass covers not only these two resorts but also St Luc/Chandolin across the valley, and Vercorin – 200km/125 miles of runs in total.
1680m; slopes 1680–2895m
▲9 ☂ 70km
✉ Interhome

Zug 140
Tiny village in scenic location with Lech's toughest skiing on its doorstep.

Zürs 140
High, smart but soulless village on road to Lech, with which it shares extensive skiing.
✉ Crystal, Elegant Resorts, Inghams, Made to Measure Holidays, Powder Byrne, The Corporate Ski Company

Zweisimmen 453
Limited but inexpensive base for slopes around Gstaad, with its own delightful little easy area too.

MONEY BACK VOUCHER – PART 1

To be sent to
SKI SOLUTIONS, 84 Pembroke Road, London W8 6NX
along with your signed booking form

Name	
Address	
E-mail address	
Daytime phone number	
Tour operator (if applicable)	
Departure date	**Number in party**

I have bought a copy of Where to Ski and Snowboard 2004 and claim a refund of the £15.99 cover price. I understand this amount will be deducted from the cost of the holiday I am booking through Ski Solutions. Offer valid for bookings for 2003/04 and 2004/05 seasons holidays made before 30 April 2004.

Signature	**Date**

MONEY BACK VOUCHER – PART 2

WHERE to SKI
and SnoWboard 2004

To be sent to
WHERE TO SKI AND SNOWBOARD,
The Old Forge, Norton St Philip, Bath BA2 7LW

Name	
Address	
E-mail address	
Daytime phone number	
Resort(s) to be visited	
Departure date	**Number in party**

I have booked a ski holiday through Ski Solutions and claimed a refund of the £15.99 cover price of Where to Ski and Snowboard 2004.

Signature	**Date**

Have you booked any other
holiday through Ski Solutions
in the last two seasons?   Yes   No